Psychology

Contemporary Perspectives

PAUL OKAMI
Widener University

New York   Oxford
Oxford University Press

Oxford University Press is a department of the University of Oxford.
It furthers the University's objective of excellence in research,
scholarship, and education by publishing worldwide.

Oxford   New York
Auckland   Cape Town   Dar es Salaam   Hong Kong   Karachi
Kuala Lumpur   Madrid   Melbourne   Mexico City   Nairobi
New Delhi   Shanghai   Taipei   Toronto

With offices in
Argentina   Austria   Brazil   Chile   Czech Republic   France   Greece
Guatemala   Hungary   Italy   Japan   Poland   Portugal   Singapore
South Korea   Switzerland   Thailand   Turkey   Ukraine   Vietnam

Published by Oxford University Press
198 Madison Avenue, New York, NY 10016
www.oup.com

Library of Congress Cataloging-in-Publication Data

Okami, Paul.
    Psychology : contemporary perspectives / Paul Okami, Widener University. — 1st Edition.
        pages cm
    Includes bibliographical references and index.
    ISBN 978-0-19-985661-9 (alk. paper)
    1. Psychology.   I. Title.
    BF121.O43 2013
    150—dc23
                2013003478

Printing number: 9 8 7 6 5 4 3 2 1

Printed in the United States of America
on acid-free paper

About the Author

Paul Okami (B.A., Hunter College; M.A. and Ph.D., University of California at Los Angeles) is Adjunct Professor of Psychology at Widener University and a member of the Association for Psychological Science. While still a graduate student, Okami published frequently in the areas of sexuality, evolutionary psychology, and child development. Some of this work gained wide recognition by top experts in related fields. A beloved instructor, Dr. Okami's grasp of contemporary perspectives in psychology—and how to teach them—has enabled him to achieve great success teaching introductory students. He has taught at every level of higher education from university to community college, reaching traditional undergraduate and graduate students as well as returning and nontraditional adult students. Dr. Okami is also an amateur jazz musician, dedicated home-schooling parent, and a long-time practitioner and instructor of traditional Japanese and Okinawan martial arts.

PAUL OKAMI

CONTENTS IN BRIEF

CONTENTS

CHAPTER 3

The Nature and Nurture of Behavior 110

CHAPTER 4

Human Lifespan Development 154

CHAPTER 5

Perception and the Senses 214

CHAPTER 6

Varieties of Consciousness 268

CHAPTER 7

Learning 326

CHAPTER 8

Memory 370

CHAPTER 9

Thinking, Language, and Intelligence 414

Motivation 464

CHAPTER 11

Emotion and Health 510

CHAPTER 12

Personality 568

CHAPTER 13

Psychological Disorders 614

CHAPTER 14

Treatment 668

Preface

Teaching the introductory course in psychology is one of my greatest pleasures. But I have often wondered: Given the significant developments in the field of psychology over the past 25 years, why is it so difficult to find introductory psychology textbooks that depict in a compelling and readable manner the science of psychology as it *currently* exists—books that honestly portray *contemporary* psychological science? I wanted a book that depicted modern psychology in all its excitement, complexity, strengths, and fragilities, as well as covering the historical topics central to the traditional introductory psychology curriculum. I have written *Psychology: Contemporary Perspectives* to fulfill these goals.

Hallmark Features

Any instructor currently teaching introductory psychology will immediately feel at home with the chapter sequence and organization of this book. The traditional topics are all included. What distinguishes this book from others is a new balance of contemporary and traditional research that invites the student to develop a modern appraisal of psychology. This approach is exemplified by several key elements of the book.

Current Perspectives—Not Just Current References

A goal of the text is to present contemporary perspectives on psychological science. *Psychology: Contemporary Perspectives* does this not only by strengthening 20th-century perspectives with 21st-century references, but also by including the latest views of psychological science to reinforce understanding of traditional topics. This means rebalancing the space allotted to given topics as well as including material that goes largely unreported in traditional textbooks. Here are a few examples:

- In prior years, the science of morality more or less began and ended with Lawrence Kohlberg and cognitive-developmental theory. Currently, however, Kohlberg's "critics" actually represent the psychological establishment in this area of

research, and so this book presents a balance of traditional and contemporary views of this topic (Chapter 9).

- The fundamental attribution error is a mainstay of social psychology research. However, early in this decade John Sabini and his colleagues seriously challenged the nature and ubiquity of this cognitive error. Therefore, our discussion of FAE gives equal time to Sabini's robust and influential critique, a key to understanding the current state of knowledge in social psychology (Chapter 15).

- The discussion of psychotherapy includes detailed consideration of the difference between efficacy and effectiveness, and explores the circumstances under which psychotherapy can harm as well as heal. This chapter also includes consideration of the important current debate over the possibility that certain disorders (e.g., depression, social phobia) are being overdiagnosed as a result of inadequacies in DSM-IV-TR diagnostic criteria (Chapter 15).

- The discussion of psychopharmacology treatment of disorders includes important recent evidence of undue influence of the pharmaceutical industry on beliefs about the effectiveness of psychiatric medications (Chapter 15).

Nature via Nurture

It has become a cliché to announce that the nature vs. nurture debate is over and both sides have won. As Diane Halpern put it, "biology and environment are as inseparable as conjoined twins who share a common heart" (2004, p. 138). Yet there is a doggedly persistent tendency for people to continue to try to divide psychological processes into categories of "learned" vs. "innate," "biological" vs. "psychological/social," and so forth. To address this tendency, *Psychology: Contemporary Perspectives* repeatedly emphasizes an integrative, biopsychosocial perspective as far as people are concerned, wherein nature exists only via nurture, and nurture via nature (Ridley, 2003). Three examples regarding this nature and nurture interaction include:

- The book examines gene-environment correlation as well as gene-environment interaction, distinguishing the two and providing clear and detailed examples of each (Chapter 3).

- The book discusses research suggesting that East Asians from collectivist cultures are less likely than Westerners from individualist cultures to *self-enhance*—focus on their good qualities as compared with the bad, or as compared with the qualities of other people. However, I simultaneously propose (citing Steven Heine) that Westerners and Far Easterners are equally motivated to be "good selves" as defined in their respective cultures. Thus, human universals are expressed in culturally diverse ways (Chapter 3).
- The concepts of brain development—both critical/sensitive periods *and* plasticity—are illustrated by exploring the experience of Romanian orphans adopted out to Canadian and European homes (Chapter 9).

Bringing Emerging Perspectives to the Forefront

Psychology: Contemporary Perspectives brings to the forefront many vital areas of contemporary research that are often marginalized in other textbooks.

In other textbooks for this course, cross-cultural work is often segregated into optional feature boxes rather than being integrated into the main discussion. Because cross-cultural psychology is a vibrant component of contemporary psychology, I integrate cross-cultural work throughout the text rather than relegate it to side boxes. There is no way to escape the fact that most knowledge of human psychology stems from research studies of middle-class individuals (mostly undergraduates) from Western nations, primarily the United States. However, when competent cross-cultural work attempts to correct this problem, it should be given exposure.

Evolutionary psychology is often similarly isolated (and unfairly misrepresented, adding insult to injury). Currently, not only is evolutionary psychology an important perspective in psychology, but numerous researchers and theorists who do not consider themselves to be evolutionary psychologists incorporate insights of evolutionary psychology into their work—for example, Shelley Taylor, Daniel Schachter, Roy Baumeister, and many others. Evolution-minded insights and research appear throughout the text where they are relevant.

Behavior and molecular genetics deserve to be taken seriously in a book on introductory psychology. But, like evolutionary psychology, behavior genetics was once held suspect by many, its findings and methods often misunderstood or mischaracterized. Currently it is an important component field of psychological science and informs researchers in areas

as disparate as developmental, cognitive, personality, and clinical psychology. This book reflects the importance of genetic research in fields of psychological science.

Finally, the positive psychology movement is producing important research in areas of human experience previously not given serious attention—for example, positive emotions and mental states as explored in Chapter 11 and human strengths and positive motivations as explored in Chapter 10. In addition, positive psychologists are making major contributions to areas of research previously dominated by earlier theories—for example, Jonathan Haidt's important new work on moral intuitions is described in detail in Chapter 9.

Critical Thinking

To my mind, the most important thing I learned as a graduate student in psychology was how to think critically. Because psychology relies so heavily on research design and statistics, it is a jewel among sciences in the teaching of critical thinking. The term *critical thinking* is much overused and over-hyped in textbooks. It often translates into little more than "thinking hard," "thinking well," or "thinking for yourself." While I also foster those attitudes in my students, I use the term *critical thinking* in my book in a more specific way. *Psychology: Contemporary Perspectives* incorporates critical thinking as a set of skills that move the thinker toward the goal of seeing things as they are in actuality without being swayed by bias or error. I encourage critical thinking about claims in psychology throughout the book.

About Pedagogy: Back to Basics

Research demonstrating the superiority of elaborate pedagogical systems employed in many current textbooks is scant (Gurung & Daniel, 2005). I am aware that such systems appeal to many instructors, but my experience and substantial research suggest that students generally do not use aids that are not *directly related to exam performance* (e.g., boldface terms, self-tests, concise chapter summaries; Gurung, 2003; Weiten, Dequara, Rehmke, & Sewell, 2002). Therefore, I have taken a "back to basics" approach to pedagogy for this book that emphasizes ***review, retrieval,*** and ***overlearning***.

- At the end of each major section of every chapter, the "In Summary" feature presents a concise and specific summary of what the student read, fostering ***review***.
- Self-test questions encouraging ***retrieval*** (the "Retrieve!" feature) follow the section summaries. Although some of these questions do rely

upon recognition—the type of test question the student is most likely to encounter (e.g., multiple-choice)—I also *emphasize* questions that rely upon retrieval (e.g., "What are the three components of the triple vulnerability theory of anxiety?"). As students progress through each chapter, they review and retrieve the material and gain a realistic idea of what they can and cannot recall at will.

- Each chapter concludes with a systematic, detailed summary of the contents of the chapter called "Looking Back," a final review for facilitation of overlearning.
- Following this summary, the reader will find a complete list of the important boldface terms first presented in the chapter margins and another, longer group of self-test questions drawn from the chapter (the "Key Terms" and "Test Yourself" features). These features allow for yet more review, retrieval, and overlearning.

Bonus Chapter—Sexuality and Gender

For those instructors who teach gender and sexuality in their introductory psychology course, a comprehensive and distinctive bonus chapter is available at no extra charge. The chapter is called Sex, Gender, and Sexual Behavior. Please ask your sales representative about getting this bonus chapter for your course.

Book + Bonus chapter ISBN: 978-0-19-935068-1

Features Highlighting Important Topics

It is my experience—and many instructors confirm this—that as a general rule, students pay scant attention to textbook boxes set off from the body of text. This book contains three running features, "Living Psychology," "Critical Thinking about Psychology," and "At the Forefront," all of which are integrated into the main body of text rather than set off from the text in side boxes. Thus, the three running features *all contain testable material*—including the introduction of new terms and concepts—and follow the flow of the main discussion. These features represent three important aspects of the study of psychology:

- **Living Psychology**, the application of psychological principals to daily life.
- **Critical Thinking about Psychology**, the importance of critical thinking in understanding human psychology and interpreting research.
- **At the Forefront**, the exposure to new theory and research that promises to add substantially to the body of psychological knowledge.

References

Gurung, R. A. R. (2003). Pedagogical aids and student performance. *Teaching of Psychology, 30,* 92–95.

Gurung, R. A. R., & Daniel, D. (2005). Evidence-based pedagogy: Do text-based pedagogical features enhance student learning? In D. S. Dunn & S. L. Chew (Eds.), *Best practices for teaching introduction to psychology* (pp. 41–55). Mahwah, NJ: Lawrence Erlbaum Associates.

Halpern, D. F. (2004). A cognitive-process taxonomy for sex differences in cognitive abilities. *Current Directions in Psychological Science, 13,* 135–139.

Ridley, M. (2003). *Nature via nurture.* New York: HarperCollins.

Weiten, W., Dequara, D., Rehmke, E., & Sewell, L. (2002). University, community college, and high school students' evaluations of textbook pedagogical aids. In R. A. Griggs (Ed.), *Handbook for teaching introductory psychology* (Vol. 3,. pp. 27–29). Mahwah, NJ: Lawrence Erlbaum Associates.

A Guided Tour of *Psychology, Contemporary Perspectives*

Every chapter of *Psychology, Contemporary Perspectives* uses engaging features to explore the contemporary study of psychology.

Chapter Introductions

CHAPTER OUTLINE

Each chapter of *Psychology, Contemporary Perspectives* begins with *Freeze Frame*, a compelling story about individuals that underscores the theme of the chapter. This snapshot of real life holds clues to the psychological principles that will be discussed in the chapter.

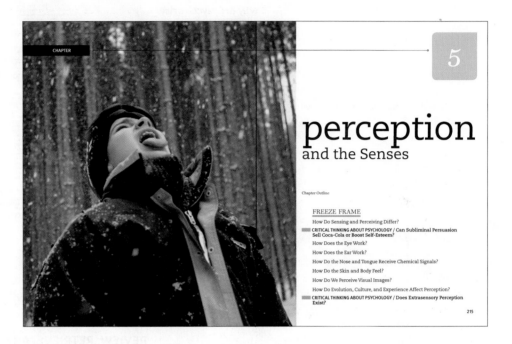

Contemporary Perspectives In Psychology

❶ More than a textbook full of facts and figures, *Psychology, Contemporary Perspectives* provides a balanced view of key topics supported by traditional as well as current scholarship.

❷ Traditional and contemporary points of view on the science of morality.

❸ Changing views of fundamental attribution error, a mainstay of psychological research.

❹ Emphasizes an integrative, biopsychoso-cial perspective on the subject of nature vs. nurture.

❺ Cross-Cultural Research.

❻ Evolutionary Psychology

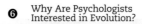

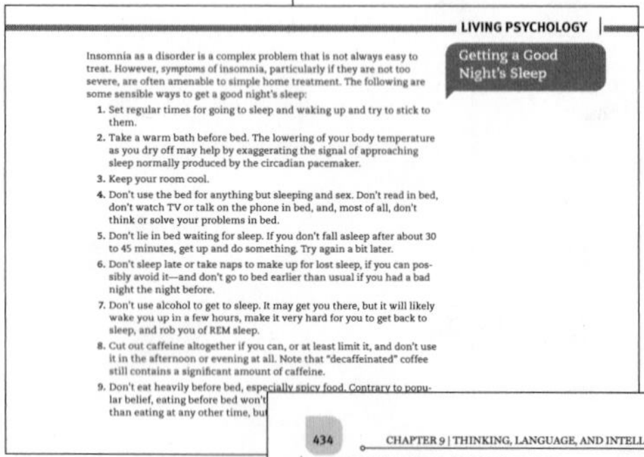

❹ **How Do Genes and Environments Influence Behavior?**

The experimental research methods described in Chapter 1 of this book are based to some degree on methods used by farmers and agricultural scientists to test methods of plant cultivation in the first part of the 20th century (e.g., Fisher, 1925). For example, seeds might be drawn from the same plant (containing the same genetic material) but sown in different plots of land. The plots might then be subjected to carefully controlled environmental variation—for example, the amount of sunlight and water the seeds receive might be varied, the temperature might be controlled in some way, or different types of fertilizer used. Then the results would be compared.

Experiments such as these led to the commonsense conclusion that, regardless of genetic origin, environments to which plants are subjected can have a powerful effect on the way the plant grows. On the other hand, there are limits to the effects of this variation—a green pepper will not grow into a tomato regardless of environmental changes, and a tomato seed taken from a line of generally poorly producing plants will not suddenly blossom into a state fair winner just because the amount of sunlight it receives is increased. Thus, genes and environments interact to determine the way living things develop, and this goes for human psychology as well as for plants in the ground.

Twin and Adoption Studies Disentangle Nature and Nurture

In 1940 identical twin boys who came to be known as Jim Lewis and Jim Springer were separated at birth. Almost four decades later, they were reunited—a highly unusual event. At the time of their reunion, each of the

❻ **Why Are Psychologists Interested in Evolution?**

As we've seen in the preceding section, behavior geneticists are primarily interested in the ways in which individuals differ. Why is one person more likely than another to enjoy risky activities such as riding roller coasters, driving fast, or committing crimes? Why do some people score higher than others on tests of cognitive ability? Why are some people more aggressive than others—or more compassionate? However, these questions suggest other, more basic, questions: Why do people perform risky activities at all? Where is the benefit? Why is *anyone* aggressive—where does aggression come from? Or compassion? Things like risky behavior, aggression, and compassion are present in all known human societies. While individuals and entire cultures may differ in the extent to which these and many other characteristics are exhibited, such characteristics are part of what makes us recognizably human. Despite individual and cultural differences, we are everywhere far more similar than we are different (Brown, 1991; Buss, 2005). The psychological characteristics that make us recognizably human and that we share in common are of greatest interest to psychologists who adhere to evolutionary perspectives.

Evolution Is Both Fact and Theory

Human evolution is a controversial topic in the United States. As of 2009, Only about 39% of Americans accept that humans evolved from earlier forms of life, with the remaining 60% divided between those who reject the idea flat-out and those who are uncertain (Gallup Poll, 2009). However, acceptance or rejection of the idea of human evolution is strongly related to education. Only 21% of those with high-school educations accept human evolution, compared to 74% of those with postgraduate degrees.

The uncertain or negative attitudes among many Americans toward the idea of human evolution contrast with those found in the rest of the industrialized world. In Japan and Europe, for example, approximately twice as many adults accept the idea of human evolution as in the United States. Surveys conducted in 34 nations in 2005 show that only in Turkey do people reject the idea of evolution to an extent greater than in the United States (Miller, Scott, & Okamoto, 2006; see Figure 3.5).

However, the term *controversial* can be misleading as applied to the topic of evolution in the United States, because there is a difference between a *public*

❺ **What Is the Sociocultural Perspective?**

To complete this chapter, we now turn to those theorists whose work highlights the importance of cultural and social influence on human psychology: sociocultural theorists. As I mentioned earlier, the evolutionary and sociocultural perspectives approach questions of nature and nurture in radically different ways. While evolutionary theorists highlight the unity of human psychology, sociocultural theorists highlight its diversity. As we have seen, natural selection elegantly blends nature and nurture by explaining how development and change only occur as a result of the interaction of genes and environments. However, it is undeniably true that evolutionary psychologists and behavior geneticists tend to emphasize the "nature" side of natural selection in their explanations for human behavior. For example, behavior geneticists have identified the nonshared environment as being crucial to cognitive and personality development in human beings, but they have not yet identified with certainty the specific aspects of nonshared environment that exert important effects. Similarly, while evolutionary psychologists have accounted well for *similarities* among humans, they are more tenuous in their accounting for *differences* among individuals and entire cultures. And that is why I now turn your attention to the sociocultural perspective. Sociocultural theorists have expertly developed methods and theories that highlight psychological differences among individuals and entire cultures.

Society and Culture Help Shape Mind and Behavior

Human beings are already social creatures prior to the moment of birth. They learn to differentiate their mother's voice and language from the voices and languages of strangers while still in the womb, and they recognize the sounds of book passages that had been read to them prior to birth (DeCasper & Spence, 1986; Kisilevsky et al 2003; Kisilevsky et al., 2009). Within hours of

IN SUMMARY

1. Scientists and philosophers do not agree on a definition of consciousness.

2. The commonsense definition of consciousness devised by John Searle includes three prominent qualities: qualitativeness, subjectivity, and unity.

3. The "hard problem" of consciousness is explaining how the brain—a material object—creates consciousness, a seemingly immaterial experience.

4. "Altered state of consciousness" could be defined subjectively as a temporary but radical change in the overall pattern of a person's normal subjective experience.

RETRIEVE!

1. Which of the following is NOT among the features of consciousness identified by John Searle?
a) awareness b) qualitativeness c) subjectivity d) unity

2. Why is it difficult to define *altered states of consciousness* objectively in terms of the method by which the state of consciousness was induced (e.g., drugs) or changes in brain activity and physiology?

LIVING PSYCHOLOGY

Getting a Good Night's Sleep

Insomnia as a disorder is a complex problem that is not always easy to treat. However, *symptoms* of insomnia, particularly if they are not too severe, are often amenable to simple home treatment. The following are some sensible ways to get a good night's sleep:

1. Set regular times for going to sleep and waking up and try to stick to them.
2. Take a warm bath before bed. The lowering of your body temperature as you dry off may help by exaggerating the signal of approaching sleep normally produced by the circadian pacemaker.
3. Keep your room cool.
4. Don't use the bed for anything but sleeping and sex. Don't read in bed, don't watch TV or talk on the phone in bed, and, most of all, don't think or solve your problems in bed.
5. Don't lie in bed waiting for sleep. If you don't fall asleep after about 30 to 45 minutes, get up and do something. Try again a bit later.
6. Don't sleep late or take naps to make up for lost sleep, if you can possibly avoid it—and don't go to bed earlier than usual if you had a bad night the night before.
7. Don't use alcohol to get to sleep. It may get you there, but it will likely wake you up in a few hours, make it very hard for you to get back to sleep, and rob you of REM sleep.
8. Cut out caffeine altogether if you can, or at least limit it, and don't use it in the afternoon or evening at all. Note that "decaffeinated" coffee still contains a significant amount of caffeine.
9. Don't eat heavily before bed, especially spicy food. Contrary to popular belief, eating before bed won't
than eating at any other time, but

434 CHAPTER 9 | THINKING, LANGUAGE, AND INTELLIGENCE

CRITICAL THINKING ABOUT PSYCHOLOGY

CONTINUED

small. *Chance does not have a memory*, and the likelihood of a random event occurring (e.g., tails coming up) is not affected by events that have preceded it (e.g., heads coming up five times). The odds for each single new toss are always 50/50.

Probability theory is extremely difficult for the average person to grasp—even highly educated people have trouble with it (Gigerenzer, Gaissmaier, Kurz-Mileke, Schwartz, & Woloshin, 2008; Pinker, 2002). Therefore, the representativeness heuristic creates still more fertile soil for the gambler's fallacy to take hold. Consider the two series of 25 coin tosses depicted here.

A
Heads
Tails
B
Heads
Tails

▲ The Gambler's Fallacy. It might seem that the more times the roulette wheel spins without hitting your number (or color), the more likely the next spin will be to do so. But, in fact, the odds of the table paying off stay exactly the same with each turn of the wheel: They do not "accumulate." The likelihood of a random event is not affected by events that precede it.

Which chart seems more typical of fair coin tosses at a 50/50 level of chance, Chart A or Chart B? Looking at Chart A, if you were to start paying attention on toss number two, there will be a seemingly unlikely streak of eight heads broken only by three tails. However, this is the normal operation of chance (randomness) at odds of 50/50. Ultimately—in the long run—an approximately equal number of heads and tails will be tossed. However, cutting out a small segment of the "long run" can produce remarkable streaks of unlikely events (Gilovich, Vallone, & Tversky, 1985). As statistician Robert P. Abelson (1995) put it, "chance is lumpy." Because Chart B seems more random, the representativeness heuristic prompts us to believe that it is more representative of randomness. In fact, Chart B is not at all typical of a string of random coin tosses. ■

Learning Features

REVIEW, RETRIEVE, AND LEARN

In Summary helps the student **review** the key concepts of each main section of a chapter.

Retrieve! Self-test questions help the student retrieve key concepts from each section, further reinforcing comprehension and preparation for assessment activities.

INTEGRATED FEATURES HIGHLIGHT THREE IMPORTANT ASPECTS OF PSYCHOLOGY

Living Psychology applies psychological principals to daily life.

Critical Thinking about Psychology emphasizes the importances of critical thinking in understanding human psychology.

At the Forefront reveals new, influential research in psychology.

AT THE FOREFRONT: PLACEBO

Treatment or Nontreatment?

One provocative area of research in psychoneuroimmunology is the study of the **placebo**. A placebo is any bogus procedure, or inactive (inert) substance—corn starch or milk sugar, for example—administered to a person who believes the procedure or substance is a genuine treatment. The idea behind this is that the patient's belief in the treatment may trigger actual psychological or biochemical processes which may have a beneficial effect (Price, Finniss, & Benedetti, 2008; Tilburt, Emanuel, Kaptchuk, Curlin, & Miller, 2008).

WHAT PLACEBOS CAN AND CANNOT DO

Are placebos powerful, low-cost treatments, as some enthusiastic promoters suggest (Wampold, Imel, & Minami, 2007; Wampold, Minami, Tierney, Baskin, & Bhati, 2005), or are they relatively useless nontreatments, as skeptics argue (Hróbjartsson & Gøtzsche, 2001, 2004, 2007)? If placebos are useless, doctors are wasting their time. Approximately 50% of physicians surveyed by Jon Tilburt and his colleagues reported either that they did prescribe placebos as classically defined (inert substances such as sugar pills) or, more commonly, they prescribed substances that while not technically inert, had no known use for the ailment in question. These active substances were prescribed in the hopes that they would produce a beneficial placebo effect (Tilburt et al., 2008).

Although there is no evidence that placebos have the sort of pervasive, wondrous effects at no risk to the patient that some believe, there is good evidence that under specific circumstances, placebos can be beneficial—although their effects are usually modest. There are some isolated exceptions, but most reliable evidence suggests that when placebos work at all, they tend to affect *symptoms* rather than signs. **Symptoms** are patient

Placebo ▶ Any bogus procedure or inactive (inert) substance—cornstarch or milk sugar, for example—administered to a patient who believes the substance or procedure is a genuine treatment. Although placebos are sometimes given to patients whose symptoms have no organic cause—to satisfy the patient's desire to be "treated"—research has shown that placebos can sometimes trigger physiological events which actually reduce symptoms.

PHOTOS, TABLES, FIGURES

A compelling visual program brings essential themes to life.

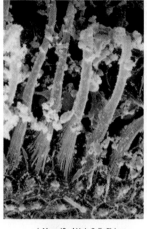

◀ **FIGURE 2.15** The Geography of the Brain. The geographic regions of the brain include the *forebrain, midbrain,* and *hindbrain.*

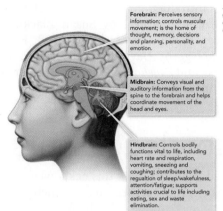

Forebrain: Perceives sensory information; controls muscular movement; is the home of thought, memory, decisions and planning, personality, and emotion.

Midbrain: Conveys visual and auditory information from the spine to the forebrain and helps coordinate movement of the head and eyes.

Hindbrain: Controls bodily functions vital to life, including heart rate and respiration, vomiting, sneezing and coughing; contributes to the regulation of sleep/wakefulness, attention/fatigue; supports activities crucial to life including eating, sex and waste elimination.

▲ Knowing *how* to play the guitar like Jimi Hendrix is an example of procedural knowledge. Knowing *that* Jimi Hendrix was a skilled guitar player who died in 1970 is an example of explicit knowledge.

▲ **Magnified Hair Cells Firing within the Cochlea.** Hair cells are the specialized neurons that act as auditory receptors and initiate transduction of sound.

▶ **FIGURE 5.33** The Incredible Shrinking Girl. The Ames room uses the monocular cue of relative size to create the illusion that a person standing to the right is much larger than a person standing to the left.

KEY TERMS IN CHAPTER MARGINS

A running glossary of key terms appears in chapter context. A complete glossary in the back of the book collects all key terms in one location.

Stress Is a Response to Challenging or Threatening Events

Stress is of great interest to clinicians and researchers in **health psychology**, an interdisciplinary field that examines the ways that health and illness interact with psychology, biology, and society. Biologists often define *stress* as any event that threatens *homeostasis* of an organism—its ordinary physiological and neurobiological state at rest (Gunnar & Quevedo, 2007; Selye, 1936; Ulrich-Lai & Herman, 2009). Any adaptive physiological response that allows an organism to regain homeostasis in the face of changing circumstances is then termed a *stress response* (Cannon, 1929b; Holsboer & Ising, 2010; Segerstrom & Miller, 2004).

However, most psychologists define *stress* in a way that is closer to common understandings of the term: **Stress** is the psychological and physiological consequence of events that challenge a person's ability to *cope* and which threaten well-being or interfere with important goals (Lazarus & Folkman, 1984.) Such life events are known as *stressors,* and they vary from the sorts of day-to-day hassles facing the hapless college student described earlier, to severe life crises such as the death of a loved one, the loss of a job, divorce, or life-threatening illness. Interestingly, even seemingly positive events such as a work promotion, marriage, graduation from college, or winning the lottery may sometimes cause stress if the event entails making a major life change (Holmes & Rahe, 1967; Hobson & Delunas, 2001).

Table 11.3 shows a list of 30 frequently occurring life events in order of their potential stressfulness as rated by a representative national sample of Americans during the 1990s (Hobson et al., 1998). The list, an abbreviated version of the Revised Social Readjustment Rating Scale (SRRS-R), paints a good portrait of the sorts of common events Americans rate as more stressful than others.

Are these events similarly stressful for non-Americans? The answer appears to be "yes," at least as far as college students are concerned. When Francis McAndrew and colleagues surveyed college and university students from Germany, India, South Africa (white and black students), and the United States, they found substantial agreement about the stressfulness of various life

Health psychology ▶ An interdisciplinary field that examines the ways that health and illness interact with psychology, biology, and society. Health psychologists work in clinical settings alongside medical doctors, or in academic settings teaching and conducting research.

Stress ▶ Biologists and psychologists define stress differently. Biologists usually define stress as any event that threatens homeostasis of an organism. Psychologists usually define stress as the psychological and physiological consequence of events which challenge a person's ability to cope and which threaten well-being or interfere with important goals. Each specific stressful event is termed a stressor.

Table 9.1 **Uses and Misuses of Heuristics: Two Mental "Rules of Thumb"**

HEURISTIC	DESCRIPTION	USES	MISUSES
Availability (Tversky & Kahneman 1973)	Things that are cognitively accessible more easily are thought to recur more frequently.	This heuristic can help us make quick decisions about the likelihood of something occurring.	Sometimes things are easily accessible for reasons other than their frequent recurrence (e.g., a fictitious or unrepresentative story or picture is often more easily accessible than factual and statistical information).
Representativeness (Tversky & Kahneman, 1974)	"If it looks like a duck, quacks like a duck and walks like a duck, it probably is a duck." Comparing a new object or person to our idea of a "typical" member of the group to which it belongs	Quickly determining the category or group to which a new object or person belongs	May encourage the failure to take base rates into account; may increase prejudice and inappropriate stereotyping; contributes to failures in reasoning such as the gambler's fallacy.

Chapter Ending Summary and Study Questions

Each chapter concludes with a summary of key points, a list of key terms, and several thought-provoking study questions that reach beyond the facts and figures.

Ensuring Student Success

Oxford University Press offers instructors and students a comprehensive ancillary package for qualified adopters of *Psychology: Contemporary Perspectives.*

- Instructor's Ancillary Resource Center featuring a computerized test bank with 1,400+ questions (available online exclusively to adopters)
- Video clips from YouTube organized by chapter and by topic
- PowerPoint-based lecture slides with chapter outlines and graphics
- Instructor's Companion Website featuring all the teaching tools described above, available for immediate download (www.oup.com/us/okami)
- FREE Online Student Study Guide with chapter outlines, visual concept maps, and multiple-choice questions (www.oup.com/us/okami)
- E-Book on CourseSmart (ISBN 978-0-19-934964-7)
- *Online* Homework (www.oup.com/us/okami). Oxford's Learning Management System delivers quality content and tools to track student progress in an intuitive, nationally hosted learning environment. Assessments are designed to accompany *Psychology: Contemporary Perspectives* and auto-graded so that instructors may check students' understanding without hours of grading. A color-coded gradebook shows instructors at a glance where their students are succeeding and where they need improvement; this allows instructors to adapt their lectures as needed at a moment's notice. For students, this means quality content and instant feedback. Oxford's Learning Management System features a streamlined interface that connects instructors and students with the functions that they perform most often, simplifying the learning experience in order to save instructors time and put students' progress first.

Packaging Options

Adopters of *Psychology: Contemporary Perspectives* can package **ANY** Oxford University Press book with the text for a 20% savings off the total package price. See our many trade and scholarly offerings at **www.oup.com,** then contact your local OUP sales representative to request a package ISBN. In addition, the following items can be packaged with the text for free:

Oxford Pocket World Atlas, Sixth Edition: This full-color atlas is a handy reference for international relations/global politics students.

Very Short Introduction Series: These very brief texts offer succinct introductions to a variety of topics. Titles include *Consciousness* by Susan Blackmore, *Sleep* by Steven W. Lockley and Russell G. Foster, *Forensic Psychology* by David Canter, *The Brain* by Michael O'Shea, and *Psychology* by Gillian Butler and Freda McManus, among others.

Acknowledgments

I have dreaded trying to write this acknowledgment because so many people contributed so much over so many years to the creation of this book, that I fear I cannot thank them all in the space allotted. I will try to start at the beginning. Grateful thanks to my former student and first "editor" Suzy Scherer, who took a very sharp, very heavy axe to my first bloated chapter drafts; equal thanks to Kate Barnes who helped me to develop early drafts into a coherent whole and taught me what textbook writing was really about; thanks to the hundreds of reviewers and colleagues over the years who furthered the development process by reading early drafts and taking the time and expending the effort to critique them thoroughly; and special thanks to Elsa Peterson who completed the developmental arc. Thanks to assistant editor Allison Janice and editorial intern Maredith Sheridan who sweated with me over selection of images. Special thanks to the design and production staff at Oxford University Press, led by Michele Laseau. Grateful, sincere, and very special thanks to the following people at Oxford who literally made this book possible: acquisitions editor Jane Potter, higher education development manager Thom Holmes, and publisher John Challice—all of whom believed in the manuscript enough to publish it. Finally, the following people, in their own way, were even more instrumental than the above in allowing this book to take shape and see the light of day: my beloved wife Laura and loving daughters Naima and Anisa—all of whom unswervingly believed in me and in this book during the times I had my doubts; and the best friend I never met, K.K. (you know who you are!).

Manuscript Reviewers

We have greatly benefited from the perceptive comments and suggestions of the many talented scholars and instructors who reviewed the manuscript of *Psychology, Contemporary Perspectives*. Their insight and suggestions contributed immensely to the published work.

Lori Buuck
Saint Louis University

Larry Barron
Grand Canyon University

Stephen Blessing
University of Tampa

David Campbell
Humboldt State University

Daniel T Cerutti
California State University, East Bay

David Daniel

James Madison University

J.L. Diaz-Granados
Baylor University

Dale V Doty
Monroe Community College

Thomas L. Flagg
Eastern Michigan University

Kelli A. Gardner
Peru State College

Mitchell M. Handelsman
University of Colorado Denver

Jennifer Harriger
Pepperdine University

Brian A. Johnson
The University of Tennessee at Martin

Jonathan Kahane
Springfield College

Christopher Klein
Marietta College

Amanda R. Lipko
State University of New York, Brockport

Thomas E. Malloy
Rhode Island College

Connie Meinholdt
Ferris State University

Juan Salinas
University of Texas at Austin

Steven E. Stern
University of Pittsburgh at Johnstown

John Updegraff
Kent State University

Jeffrey Wagman
Illinois State University

Kathleen L. Whitten
Georgia State University

Alex Michael Babcock
Montana State University

Megan Davies
Northern Virginia Community College

Marlene Groomes
Miami Dade College, Homestead

Darren Iwamoto
Chaminade University of Honolulu

Alisha Janowsky
University of Central Florida

Lavonne Reynolds
Front Range Community College

Danny Benbassat
The George Washington University

Kevin Chun
University of San Francisco

Mark Lynn
Marquette University

Mike Mangan
University of New Hampshire, Durham

Christy Porter
College of William and Mary

Jennifer L. Dyck
State University of New York, Fredonia

Christina Graham
Pacific Lutheran University

Matthew Hayes
Winthrop University

Fred Leavitt
California State University, East Bay

Anne Richards
Highline CC, North Seattle CC, Seattle Central CC

Susan Shapiro
Indiana University East

Kevin Autry
University of Arkansas

Bakhtawar Bhadha
Pasadena City College

Christopher Hayashi
Southwestern College

Susan Haynes
Los Angeles Southwest College

Mark Hicks
Lorain County Community College

James Jordan
Lorain County Community College

Arlene Lacombe
Saint Joseph's University

Heather C. Lum
*Penn State Erie
The Behrend College*

Lisa Newell
Indiana University of Pennsylvania

Vicki Ritts
St. Louis Community College, Meramec

Suzanne Sollars
University of Nebraska at Omaha

Market Development Reviewers

Oxford University Press would also like to acknowledge contributions of the many scholars, instructors, and students of psychology who took part in the latter stages of fine-tuning and testing the book in their courses across the nation.

MARKET REVIEWERS

Denise Lott Arellano
McNeese State University

Micki Atzram
Hunter College

Grace Austin
Sacramento City College

Kevin Autry
University of Arkansas

JP Baird
Amherst College

Lucinda S. Baker
Front Range Community College

Dave Baskind
Delta College

Kristen Begosh
University of Delaware

Danny Benbassat
George Washington University

Bakhtawar Bhadha
Pasadena City College

Susanne Biehle
Kent State University

Tracie Blumentritt
University of Wisconsin La Crosse

Jenn Bonds-Raacke
Fort Hays State University

Julie Blaskewicz Boron
Youngstown State University

Scott Brandhorst
Southeast Missouri State University

Charles Brewer
Tacoma Community College

Wayne Briner
University of Nebraska at Kearney

Eurnestine Brown
Winthrop University

Terry D. Burger
Indiana University Southeast

Ken Callis
Southeast Missouri State University

Jenel T. Cavazos
Cameron University

Steven Christiansen
St. Louis Community College

Matthew Collins
Nova Southeastern University

Cheryl Cohen
University of Illinois at Chicago

Pamela Costa
Tacoma Community College

Brian Kenn Crosby
Penn State

Alexander M. Czopp
Western Washington University

Marice Desrochers
The College at Brockport-SUNY

Robert DuBois
Waukesha County Technical College

Kimberley Duff
Cerritos College

Chris S. Dula
East Tennessee State University

Alison A. Ehlers
Cal State Sacramento

Russell Eisenman
University of Texas-Pan American

Steve L. Ellyson
Youngstown State University

Amber Emanuel
Kent State University

Aldrian Estepa
Chabot College

Jeanne Face
J. Sargeant Reynolds Community College

Stacey A. Feig
Century College

Erica Feuerbacher
University of Florida

Sherecce Fields
Texas A&M University–College Station

Thomas L. Flagg
Central New Mexico Community College

Catherine Forte
Tacoma Community College

Chriss Warren Foster
Merritt College

Jeff Froyd
Community College of Denver

William Rick Fry
Youngstown State University

Suzanne Fust
Century College

Christopher Gade
University of California at Berkeley

Jeanette Gassaway
Ohio University–Chillicothe

Caroline Gee
Saddleback College

Shahram Ghiasinejad
University of Central Florida

Bryan Gibson
Central Michigan University

Miranda Goodman-Wilson
University of the Pacific

Michael S. Gordon
William Paterson University

Donnell Griffin
Davidson County Community College

Julia Hall
Drexel University

Lindsey Harkabus
Colorado State University

Yolanda Harper
Victory University

Shani Harris
Spelman College

Richard W. Hass
University of Delaware-Newark

Christopher Hayashi
Southwestern College

Evan Hill
University of Toledo

Bruce Hinrichs
Century College

Mia Holland
Bridgewater State University

Sandra Holloway
St. Joseph's University

Shareen Holly
Providence College

Joan D. Holmes
William Paterson University

Brian Johnson
The University of Tennessee-Martin

James Jordan
Lorain County Community College

Deana Julka
University of Portland

Yuthika Kim
Oklahoma City Community College

Ken Koenigshofer
Chaffey College

Jason Koerner
Indiana University Southeast

Lee Kooler
Modesto Junior College

Shirley Kuhn
Pitt Community College

Franki Larrabee
Chippewa Valley Technical College

Cynthia Lausberg
University of Pittsburgh

Jennifer Lee
Cabrillo College

Robin Lewis
California Polytechnic State University

Sheryl Leytham
Grand View University

Vicki Lucey
Las Positas College

Mark Lynn
Marquette University

Scott F. Madey
Shippensburg University

Zaareh Manassian
Glendale Community College

Mike Mangan
University of New Hampshire

Laura May
University of South Carolina Aiken

Cindy Matyi
Ohio University-Chillicothe Campus

John Mavromatis
St John Fisher College

Patsy L. McCall
Angelo State

Daniel McConnell
University of Central Florida

Bob McCoy
Skyline College

Maureen McGovern
Southwestern College Chula Vista

David F. McGrevy
University of San Diego

Dani McMay
SUNY Fredonia

Dennis Miller
University of Missouri

Marty Milligan
San Bernardino Valley College

Dan Muhwezi
Butler Community College

Katherine Neidhardt
Cuesta College

Todd Nelson
California State University

Gerald Nissley
East Texas Baptist University

Arthur Olguin
Santa Barbara City College

Lideth Ortega-Villalobos
California State Polytechnic University Pomona

Ann O'Steere
College of DuPage

Eirini Papafratzeskakou
Mercer County Community College

Marion Perlmutter
University of Michigan-Ann Arbor

Anna Kemdal Pho
Skyline College

Gary Popoli
Stevenson University

Christy Porter
College of William & Mary

Shuang Yueh Pui
University of Illinois Springfield

Virginia Pitts
Shippensburg University

Heather Rasinski
University of Toledo

Cynthia K. Shinabarger Reed
Tarrant County College–NE

Elena Reigadas
Los Angeles Harbor College

Kym Richard
Northern Virginia Community College

Tracy Richards
Colorado State University

Hugh Riley
Baylor University

Brandi Rima
Bronx Community College

Carolyn A. Ristau
Columbia University

Kristin Ritchey
Ball State University

Conni Rush
Pittsburg State University

Lawrence J. Ryan
Oregon State University

Andrea Stier Samuels
University of Californai at Berkeley

Kraig L. Schell
Angelo State University

Valerie Bruchon Scott
Indiana University Southeast

Elisa Setmire
Ventura County Community College District

Randi Shane
Bronx Community College

Robert Short
Arizona State University

Alicia Sichan
Los Angeles Harbor College

Jennifer Plunkett Skibins
Suffolk Community College

Ashlea Smith
Phoenix College

Matthew Sopko
Mineral Area College

Susan C. South
Purdue University

Patricia D. Stokes
Columbia University

Ceyhun Sunsay
Indiana University Northwest

Elizabeth Swenson
John Carroll University

Brian Thomas
Baldwin Wallace College

Lisa Thomassen
Indiana University

Kendell Thornton
Dowling College

Ivonne Tjoefat
Rochester Community and Technical College

Adrian Tomer
Shippensburg University

Michael Torello
Capital University

Terry S. Trepper
Purdue University Calumet

Trude Cooke Turner
Community College of Baltimore County, Essex campus

Anton Villado
Rice University

Kay Wallheimer
Front Range Community College

Mark Watman
South Suburban College

Joseph Weeks
Bridgewater State University

Jennifer Wentz
Kutztown University

Diane E. Wille
Indiana University Southeast

Erin Wood
Catawba College

Shelly Wooldridge
University of Arkansas Community College at Batesville

Jim Worthley
University of Massachusetts Lowell

Barry Zwibelman
University of Miami, Coral Gables

CLASS TESTERS—INSTRUCTORS

Kimberly Anderson
Bringham Young University

Orisade Awodola
University of the District of Columbia

Debi Brannan
University of Portland

Eileen Brennan
University of Portland

Charles Brewer
Tacoma Community College

Elizabeth Browning
Central New Mexico Community College

Thomas Capo
University of Maryland University College

Ralph D. Carlini
University of Massachusetts Dartmouth

Julie Carvalho
Northern Virginia Community College

Katrina Cooper
University of Pittsburgh

Pamela Costa
Tacoma Community College

Marlene Crimmen
Erie Community College

Lisa Renee Davidhizar
Ivy Tech Community College

Robert Egbert
Walla Walla University

Roel Evangelista
Community College of Baltimore County

Julio G Farias
El Camino College

Erin Fisher
Rock Valley College

Jerry Green
Tarrant County College

David Grow
US Naval Academy

Susan Haynes-Burton
Los Angeles Southwest College

Ann C. Hennessey
Pierce College

Darren Iwamoto
Chaminade University

Jim Johnson
Illinois State University

Larry Kollman
North Iowa Area Community College

Dana Kuehn
Florida State College at Jacksonville

Fred Leavitt
California State University East Bay

Jose Leon
Yakima Valley Community College

Elizabeth Maloney
San Joaquin Delta College

Robert J. Martinez
University of The Incarnate Word

Kathy McGuire
Western Illinois University

Megan McIlreavy
Costal Carolina University

Margaret Miele
Baruch College Campus High School

Rikki Miller
University of New Hampshire

Anna Kemdal Pho
Skyline College

Christine Selby
Husson University

Jack P. Shilkret
Anne Arundel Community College

Katherine Sliter
Northern Kentucky University

Alexander Soler
Texas A&M International University–Laredo

Matthew Sopko
Mineral Area College

Natalie Stroupe
University of Kansas

William Struthers
Wheaton College

Keith W. Swain
Red Rocks Community College

Kim Taylor
Spokane Falls Community College

Roger Ward
University of Cincinnati, Blue Ash

Stephen Weinert
Cuyamaca College

Joseph Wohkittel
Century College

CLASS TESTERS—STUDENTS

Brigham Young University
Gregory Barker
Taci Beckstrom
Zack Bracha
Levi Nation
Alexis Pearson
Zac Pincock
Teresa Rigby

California State University East Bay
Baldeep Bajwa
Mikaela Burkhart
Hyunah Choi
Alejandra Cornejo
Tanya Cooley
A.J Melisa Fernando
Brian Frank
Leah Guest
Michelle Hall
Karla Ramirez
Diana Duran Robles
Yangxiawa Wang

Central New Mexico Community College
Kiera Rivera

Chaminade University
Ariel Agsalud
Johnny Aldan
Yanita Arnaudova
Ha'Ani Artero
Kevin Barr
Karina Coleman
Eleanor Cordero
Tjaden Cornell
Brittanyann Cowdrey
Cassandra Crawford
Vina Cristobal
Bryant-II R. Dela Cruz
Kevin Fajardo
Anthony Fisher
Jonathan Fukumoto
Britney Marie Galapon
Joshua Horiuchi
Alyssa Jackson

Emmanuel Jimenez
Austin Johnson
Anthony Junker
Siufaga Kaisa
Lousiale Kava
Dana Kojima
Alexia Lawson
Kaipo Leopoldino
Kainoa Makua
Sydney Manansala
Athena Maskarich
Maria Maureene
Justine Erick Miranda
Ernesto Angel Olmos
Ely Pagaduan
Ashley Phelps
Taylor Salas
Aven Santiago
Yurie Tanaka
Kelsie-Ann Valentine
Rhea Dela Vega
Jeff Woodworth

Coastal Carolina University
Nikelle Albright
Allison Astor
Taylor Bartee
Joshua Bernero
Nicole Birkbeck
Marissa Brito
Lauren Colomb
Kathleen Cramer
Neshes Cundiff
Brianne DeFroda
Kathryn D'Onghia
Danielle Dorsaneo
Dana Downey
R. Chris Dutlinger
Jasmine Fitzgerald
Kaylynn Garza
Breonna Gatling
Taylor Genander
Heather Gibson
Dexter Gore
Zac Hallman
Jessica Ham
Emily Haynes
Laura Hordis
Tia Jeffcoat
Essence Jennings
Crystal Johnson
Joshua Jones
Sarah Kandybowicz
Mallory Kohari
Nicole Langer
Michael Lightbourne
Annie MacDonald
Cedrick Malone

Calli Martorana
Julie May
Taylor Miller
Christian Motes
Sara Ouimet
Daniel Parker
Shaleigh Phillips
Bo-Daniel Pinder
Alexis Pittman
Christian Potts
Gabriel L. Pruitt
Laurance Raines
Sarah Rice
Charnice Richardson
Ariana Rivens
Hannah Robidoux
Chelsea Rolinec
Jessica Roos
Alyssa Scarfo
Hannah Sheard
Joscelyn Smalls
Emily Smith
Tiara Smith
Marissa Suggs
Alicia Sullivan
Shota Suzuki
Bethany Tomes
Kimberlee Ward

Cuyamaca College
Haley Abbott
Amanda Ames
Elizabeth Arden
Jennifer Bohensky
Leonel Bovey
Maria Brown
Calvin Cartwright
Olivia Daniel
Hilary Dargavell
Maria de Jerez
Laura Delgado
Liza Farida
Timothy Hebert
Antonette Hicks
Ryan Himaka
Olivia Kiryakos
Nicole Kovacs
Elizabeth Lomas
Lucia Martin
Geriba Mohammad
Marion Mwaura
Amy Nicholson
Veronica Ortiz
Thereza Ramirez
Wendy Richter
Jeremy Rojas
Mario Shamhon
Gabriela Soto

Ryan Stormoen
Brittany Stephens
Darnasia Wright
Jesica Yanez

El Camino College
Francisco Alcala
Maryam Amirteimouri
Eric Ashley
Jeong Busiere
Kimberly David
Rojene Esfahani
Rocio Hernandez
Dipanwita Manna
Anne Marchewka
Antoinette McMillian
Fernando Ramirez
Arnold Ruiz
Yesenia Sanchez
Manuel Serrano
Tenkang Ernest Tiendi
Cynthia Trujillo

Husson University
Danielle Bushey
Abigail Fizell
Sarah Gleeson
Katherine Gray
Nicole Hughes
Brittney Jamieson
Amy Jorgenson
Emily Manchester
Samantha McLaughlin
Kerri Nguyen
Allisha Ouellette
Ashley Rollins
Emily Thorpe
Rachel Wacome
Rebecca Watson
Christin Yi

Illinois State University
Alexis Beauford
Mariah Carpio
Chanel Carter
Lindsey Cheney
Paul Cho
Kaityn Crowther
Javar Cruz
Lily Culver
Paul Doggett
Megan Dowling
Kara Esker
Stephanie Fisher
Kayla Fowler
Danesha Garner
Kerry Garvey
Ashleigh Grindstaff
Jason Gryniewicz

Malia Haanio
Maggie Harju
Kathleen Kroes
Michael Lagger
Alex Laine
Justin Lane
Zack Marshall
Glennah McMahon
Erin Musser
Emily Newcomer
Lindsay Nicholson
Alex Osterbuhr
Kathryn Peacock
Patrick Pendergast
Robyn Piper
Sarah Pozniak
Avery Queen
Hakeem Richmond
Matt Rillie
Brooke Shimon
Rachel Tejada
Katy Tinch
Anna Weltzien
Samantha Yope
Lindsey Yuhas

Los Angeles Southwest College
Omolade Animasaun
Alyssa Burton
Christian Cardenas
Myeisha Clemons
Maria N. Contreras
Yvonne Crowder
Rakeidra Davis
Maria Elizabeth Diaz
Wan'Nisha Efferson
Nnenna Ekejiuba
Michilynn Fitzhugh
Alia Foster-Duette
Steve Gonzalez
Tamera Henderson
Tomeka Jones
Jasmine Lott
Ida McCullam
Reginald O'Guynn
Brandy Ousley
Kimberly Shortridge
Patricia Sterling
Ashley Washington
Amberr Williams

Northern Kentucky University
Raven Barber
Derrick Davis
DeAndre Gross
Elizabeth Herald
Brandon Houston
Isaiah C. Jones

Shanice Lee
Ryan Ogden
Joel Patterson
Myles Roberts
Alaysyah Yahyisrael

Pierce College
Claudia Aceves
Sahira Aguet
Alicia Aguilera
Maricruz Alonso
Luis Alvarez
Michelle Bonsangue
Samson Chua
Ramika Eyvazi
Alex Gellerman
Sanaz Hosseinzadeh
Negin Jahani
Luis Juarez
Saghar Kohan
Cindy Montiel
Anaisabel Saravia
Mohammad S. Shah
Amy Umana
Cecilia Victoria

Rochester Community and Technical College
Dua Al-Manasrah
Brenda Axelson
Odette Bagob
John Crosby
Jesse Donahue
Connor Evans
Logan Gunderson
Collin Johnson
Paul Kramer
Julia Lee
Amanda Nielsen
Sari Pham
Claire Richards
Solida San
Kayla Syring
Max Ulness
Mike Vera
Madison Wurth

Rochester Institute of Technology
Katie Anderson
Marko Andjglkovic
Carol Connors
Zachary DeJager
Solomiya Hiynchuk
Renae Mullenbach
Chloe Richard
Courtney Sciotti
Huong Tran
Samuel Wechter

Rock Valley College
Chrystelle Andrews
Franchesca Appell
Khrystyna Baier
Rebecca Blystone
Aaron Breneman
Audrey Cobb
Ashley Dawson
Devin DiGiovanni
Alex Edgington
Jaclyn Guth
Tammy Jackson
Kari Ligon
Heidi Mackey
Sydney Meris
Anthony Murray
Taylor Neuschwander-Thurow
Patricia Norton
Dustin Novacek
Hannah Pryor
Carolyn Reece
Jeremiah Shearer
Brandy Simpson
Sarah Spillare
Paige Stone
Nicole Sturm
Nadia Umanzor
Amy Wayman

San Joaquin Delta College
Vanessa Martinez Acosta
Dalaitseren Amarjargal
Heather Bayless
Christian Jesus Buenrostro
Norma Byrd
Efrain Cachu III
Reyes Cruz
Sydney Escobar
Sarah Esperson
Augustine Espino
Andrew Estrella
Stephen Fox
Tyler Gonser
Tyler Graham
Chaoping Huang
Huiying Huang
Qi Jiang
Ryan Jones
Alexis Jose
Pamela Kampschmidt
Jennifer Kelly
Abdeen Khalid
Nadeem Khan
Kaolin Jack Leveler
Linda Lopez
Ying Lor
Kellie Mac
Nickole Martinez

Kayla Meeks
Kelsie Monroe
Miguel Ochoa
Flavia Oros
Mario Paredes
Erik Pillsbury
Daniel Ramirez
Helen Rivera
Gary Rudd
Lydia Rudd
Sana Saifuddin
Karin Sanchez
Armand Smith
Huyen Stryker
Cynthia Sullivan
Damon Taylor
Marco Torres
Levi Walls
Michael Zanutto

Skyline College
Marcela Araujo
Michael Blanchard
Ashleigh Cheley
Donna Chiao
Johnson Chuong
Ryan Clark
Chiahui Gao
Mark Anthony Molina
Joel Ramirez
Vanessa Rosas
Gabriela M. Solis
Jasmine Tolentino
Robby Wallace

Spokane Falls Community College
Emily Barber
Honor Bullock
Lin Chang
Orlando Coronado
John Davis
Ricki Dufek
Kevin Edwards
Jennifer Floyd
Tammy Grittner
Cynthia Harper
Daniel Jacobs
Andres Londono
Curtis Lura
Katie Malone
Laura McKee
Julia Meyer
Shelby Pemberton
Nicholas Ramsay
Jamaali Roberts
Mel Serrano
Kayla Tofsrud
Rico Vlastelic
Bryce S. Walden

Rob Whitfield
Xiaomeng Zhao
Zhentao Zhao
Michael Zuidema

St. Louis Community College–Meramac
Kenny Berkholz
Terrance Brown
Mac Callanan
Jon Carey
Alex Egeling
Coortney Flueel
Katrina Hauser
Julie McCabe
Rachel McGuire
Wynna Outland
Bethany Parolin
Elaina Stevenson
Jessica Tipton
Anna Tripolitis
Semsa Zukanovic

Tacoma Community College
Stefanie Ahearn
Julie Barkhoff
Anastasia Bessarabova
Paige Boyer
Margarita (Meg) Buan
Colin Chinn
Michele Crawford
Kris Farrens
Belinda Frederick
Jasmine Garrett
Heather Gerrish
Thalia Calo Gonzalez
Gabriela Gorun
Theresa Greenhalgh
Regina Green
Richelle Hanby
Aimee Huynh
LaMar Hudson
Michaela Jandebeur
Chalice Johnson
Zandra Jones
Nicole Kauer
Ngoc Thai Kien
Sheilena League
Cathy Ly
Peggy Mathias-Simpson
Debora Mayer
Anthony McCane
Hien Nguyen
Zoryana Nichipor
Ran Nuon
Amber O'Donahue
Rachel Peterson
Laury Potter
Evelyn Ramirez

Chris Rasor
Stephanie Richards
Quynh-An Tran
Kyia Tuttle
Maria Woo

University of Maryland University College

Shawntae Berry
Mehdi Boukouss
Malika Glover
Hubert Kong
Thinh Luu
Josephine Oundo
William Powell
Vanessa K Souza
Deborah Squire
Martha Villatoro
Michelle Wimbish

University of Pittsburgh

Brianna Edwards
Jessica Galgiani
Matthew Harvey
Patricia Pesenti
Melissa Reese
Thomas Richards
Nicole Warner
Taryn Welt

University of Portland

Paxton Deuel
Maggie Hoang
Colleen Olinger
Austin Smith

Waukesha County Technical College

Kristin Jerde
Paula Kendziorski

Western Illinois University

Courtney Benge
Megan Bradley
Bianca Brooks
Christian Brown
Yari Bueno
Pierre Celestine
Nolan DeMartino
Taylor Fisher
Carole Fleetwood
Ariel Gillam
Latifah Greer
Steven G. Harris Jr.
Brittney Jefferson
Nina Kuzelka
Rebecca Morton
Sydney Musgrave
Jordan Naranjo
Ashley Peterson
Catherine Rodl
Dionna Sanders
Austin Saunders
John Schneider
Jake Sosin
Makita Stewart
Rodney Stroud-Bryant
Matthew Stuve
Brandon Thomas
Kylee Vilardo
Brittany White
Bria Williams

Western Oregon University

Maria Alba
Nolan Ebert
Sandi Gibbs
Jessica Huston
Kellie Woodward

Yakima Valley Community College

Silvia Arroyo
Amber Avarez
Yessenia Bravo
David Bruton
Andrea Candido
Rubi Chavez
Elizabeth Devlin
Maira Diaz
Allyssa Dunn
Ian Fisk
Bill Foster
Elias Garcia
Brenda Gonsalez
Danielle Hutson
Ryan Leija
Carlos Lopez
Chris Lopez
Sarai Lora
Latifah Lyney
Maria Esther Mendoza
Amanda Montelongo
Meha Naran
Johyda Pulido
Lydia Ramirez
Eric Ri
Tresa Saunders
Jasmine Silva
Erika Vargas
Khadija Zamora

Psychology

Contemporary Perspectives

Psychology as science

Chapter Outline

1

FREEZE FRAME

On December 26, 2004, the single most horrific natural disaster the world had seen in over 40 years occurred in Southeast Asia: a particularly destructive tsunami (the Japanese term to describe the long, high-volume ocean waves that may follow an earthquake). The tsunami claimed the lives of at least one-quarter million citizens of Sri Lanka, Indonesia, Thailand, and India. In addition to the incomprehensible tragedy emerging from news reports of this disaster were reports such as the following:

- An unnamed British man on holiday in Sri Lanka when the tsunami hit spent three days helping to bury the dead, and then emptied his entire bank account to help the survivors. He continued to drive back and forth to the east coast of the island, eight hours in each direction, to ferry water and food to survivors (Hall, 2005).

- An Indonesian bank president, whose family had barely survived the catastrophe, opened the doors to his home to over 230 people, including 60 children. He told them all: "You are my family now. This is your home. Stay as long as you like" ("New heroes, new hope," 2005).

- In Galle, Sri Lanka, Dr. Ruvan Samarasinghe had just delivered new mother Rohini De Silva's baby girl by cesarean section and was preparing to sew up the incision when the first wave hit the lower floors of the hospital, flooding the corridors. The lights went out in the operating room. De Silva, numbed from pain killers but still conscious, begged the doctor to save her baby. Dr. Samarasinghe's own wife and infant son were in the staff quarters situated on a lower floor of the hospital, now threatened with flooding. Dr. Samarasinghe did not flee to be with his own family. For 20 minutes in complete darkness he stitched up the incisions in De Silva's abdomen until both mother and infant could be moved to a nearby temple, from which

they were then taken by ambulance to a hospital outside of Galle. Both mother and infant survived—as did Samarasinghe and his family ("New heroes, new hope," 2005).

Stories such as these are pleasurable to read—they confirm our faith in our own humanity. However, in the same year, 2004, the world was also mesmerized by the story of Abu Ghraib prison, situated 20 miles from Baghdad, Iraq. During the rule of Saddam Hussein, Abu Ghraib was among the most infamous prison complexes in the entire world. Horrendous tortures, executions, and repulsive living conditions greeted tens of thousands of male and female inmates, crammed together into 12' × 12' cells that were little more than pits (Hersh, 2004). Following the fall of Baghdad to U.S. occupying forces, Abu Ghraib was converted to a U.S. military prison where, presumably, the gruesome ghosts of the past would be put to rest.

However, in July 2004, it was found that "sadistic, blatant, and wanton criminal abuses" were taking place at the prison in Tier 1A during the night shift (Taguba, quoted in Hersh, 2004). There were detailed witness accounts. And then there were the photographs. The world looked on in horror as images depicting shocking abuses and their consequences were released and appeared in print and broadcast media everywhere. Prisoners had been kept unclothed and hooded. They had been tortured with glass and liquid from broken chemical lights, tormented by guard dogs, and sexually humiliated and assaulted in a dozen ways. They had been compelled to denounce Allah, had wounds inflicted upon them and then had the wounds stitched up by non-qualified personnel, endured electric shocks to their genitals . . . and more.

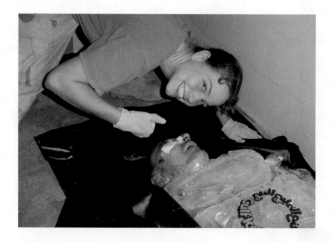

The photograph shown here is that of a smiling American soldier named Sabrina Harman giving the "thumbs up" sign over the dead body of an Iraqi inmate at Abu Ghraib. There were many of these photographs—images of America's best, jauntily smiling over a series of woeful human catastrophes. Looking at this image, a person has to wonder: How did Sabrina Harman arrive at a place where she was capable of posing for such a photograph? The guards at Abu Ghraib appeared to be normal American soldiers in a time of war.

So what happened?

The case of Sabrina Harmon in particular is controversial, as extensive investigation and interviews—even analysis of the infamous smile itself by psychologists—have raised the possibility that the photographs taken by this particular soldier may have been intended to document and expose the wrongdoing at Abu Ghraib rather than revel in them (Gourevitch & Morris, 2008; Morris, 2008). Nonetheless, at the very least Harmon allowed the abuses to occur and failed to take steps to stop them.

Consider now the stories of Southeast Asian tsunami and Abu Ghraib disasters—for although Abu Ghraib is certainly a small-scale disaster, it is a disaster nonetheless. In comparing the stories of tsunami heroes and Abu Ghraib torturers, you might well be tempted to ask, "Are both these groups of people from the same species?" Yet the heroism at Sri Lanka and the cruelty at Abu Ghraib are both typical of human beings.

How cowardice and heroism, cruelty and kindness can coexist within a species—indeed, within a single individual—is a question that may be asked and answered in many ways. For example, innumerable philosophers and spiritual seekers have pondered such questions over the millennia. It was not until the late 19th century, however, that questions such as these came to be considered from a scientific perspective, as the science of psychology was born—and it is the status of psychology as a science with which we are concerned in Chapter 1.

What Is Psychology?

As an incoming undergraduate, I was startled during the first few minutes of my very first introductory psychology class when the professor made an announcement that went something like this:

> *Before you decide whether to take this course, I'm going to warn you that what you probably think the course is about is not what it's about at all. When you think of psychology, you probably think of self-esteem, psychotherapy, emotional problems, addiction, post-traumatic stress, multiple personality, and the like. But I have to tell you that these things have little to do with the science of psychology as I know and teach it. In fact, I am much more at home at conferences of biologists than I would be at conferences of psychotherapists— were I to show up at one for some reason. So if you're expecting self-improvement and insights into your personality, you might as well just leave the room now. It will be a lot less frustrating for both of us.*

In addition to being scared witless, we freshman looked around at each other in genuine puzzlement. In fact, most of us *had* expected to learn about exactly the sorts of things this professor appeared to be dismissing as unworthy of study. For example, I had high hopes of coming to understand some of my self-defeating patterns of behavior, and learning to recognize warning signs that I was in a relationship from which it might be best to ease away. If psychology is not about these things, than what is it about?

This little tale from my personal Annals of Undergraduate Terror reflects a history of conflict within the discipline of psychology itself as to what kinds of questions ought to be studied, how they should be studied, and what one is actually doing when one "does" psychology (Baker, McFall, & Shoham, 2008; Cautin, 2009a, 2009b). Is psychology a science, like chemistry, physics, or biology? Is it a practice, like medicine, or even an art of some sort? A religion? Perhaps it is little more than philosophy wearing a white coat and spouting *jargon*—those incomprehensible terms specific to a discipline which sometimes seem to have been created for the express purpose of mystifying outsiders.

In this book I take the perspective that psychology is indeed a science. However, contrary to the views of my opinionated professor—who almost drove

▲ **"Behavior" Is Not Always Active.** Rather, behavior means all potentially observable or measurable activities of a living organism. All of the individuals in the photos are engaged in behavior.

Psychology ▶ The scientific study of mind and behavior.

me from the study of psychology altogether—we shall see that virtually any human behavior or mental activity can be a topic for scientific study in psychology.

Psychology Is the Scientific Study of Mind and Behavior

A general definition of **psychology** upon which most contemporary psychologists would probably agree might be: *Psychology is the scientific study of mind and behavior*. As we will explore later in the chapter, *scientific* means that specific sorts of methods—grounded in modern scientific knowledge—have been employed to assure accuracy and reduce bias. *Mind* refers to mental processes and events—encompassing consciousness, emotion, motivation, and cognition (thought, memory, language, and so forth). *Behavior* means all potentially observable or measurable activities of a living organism. I say "living organism" because human beings are not the only individuals with a psychology—*any* living thing that has a brain also has a psychology.

Psychological science ▶ The modern scientific study of psychology, originating in the late 19th century.

The word *psychology* is rooted in the Latin terms *psyche* (soul or spirit) and *logia* (study or knowledge); it was used by 18th-century Enlightenment philosophers to describe the study of the human mind. The psychology of the modern era was born in the late 19th century and is often referred to as **psychological science**. It began as a discipline created from the union of philosophy and biology, but has grown to encompass much more. Psychological science examines the rich and complex interplay of biological, sociocultural, and personal factors in the lives of humans and nonhumans (Bandura, 2001). Modern psychologists study questions so varied that one might presume entirely different disciplines were necessary to answer them. For example, here are a few possible questions that have been addressed by psychologists:

- Why do sunsets appear red?
- What is the purpose of sleep?
- Can infants identify their mothers' voices a few hours after birth?
- What is the best treatment for schizophrenia?
- Why are some people more likely than others to harbor negative attitudes toward ethnicities different from their own?
- What happens in the brains of two people falling in love?
- Does a person's genetic inheritance affect his or her tendency to become hostile or violent?
- In what sorts of circumstances will people offer help to strangers in need?
- Why do we forget some things and remember others?
- How does a seemingly ordinary person end up savagely torturing members of an opposing army or civilian population during wartime?

A complete list of such questions, quite apart from their answers, could fill many books many times the size of this one. The topics studied by psychologists, and the points of view taken by psychologists on the topics they choose to study, are extremely diverse. Variable topics and points of view characterize psychology.

Psychology Is Distinct from Psychiatry

Psychology is sometimes confused with **psychiatry**, a medical specialty concerned with the treatment of serious mental health problems known as psychological disorders. (Psychological disorders are discussed in Chapters 13 and 14). Psychiatrists attend medical school, and after obtaining their M.D. degree decide to specialize in the treatment of these problems. Their knowledge of psychology is often restricted to the causes and treatment of psychological disorders, and they are particularly knowledgeable in the use of biologically based treatments such as *pharmacotherapy* (the prescribing of medications which affect psychological states—for example, *antidepressant* medications).

Certain psychologists, known as *clinical and counseling psychologists*, also treat psychological disorders. These psychologists do not have medical degrees, and with very few exceptions they do not have the legal right to prescribe medication (although they often work with psychiatrists who do). Instead, clinical and counseling psychologists tend to emphasize techniques such as psychotherapy in their own practice. As explored in greater detail in Chapter 14, psychotherapy is a unique healing relationship between a person seeking help for psychological distress and another person—usually a mental health professional. The differences between psychologists and psychiatrists are summed up in Table 1.1.

Psychiatry ▶ A branch of medicine concerned with diagnosing and treating mental health problems.

Table 1.1 Comparison of Psychiatrists vs. Clinical and Counseling Psychologists

PSYCHIATRISTS	CLINICAL AND COUNSELING PSYCHOLOGISTS
Are medical doctors (M.D. degree)	Have no medical training (M.A., Ph.D., or Psy.D. degree)[1]
Knowledge of psychology generally limited to mental health problems (psychological disorders)	Usually have a broader knowledge of psychology
Have a thorough knowledge of medications and other biological treatments for psychological disorders and are legally permitted to prescribe them	Have a less thorough knowledge of these treatments and are generally not permitted to prescribe them (although there is a movement among psychologists to change this)
May work in hospital, clinic, or private practice	May work in hospital, clinic, or private practice
Usually do not perform psychotherapy (but occasionally may)	Almost always perform psychotherapy
May or may not conduct research	May or may not conduct research

[1]M.D. stands for Medical Doctor, M.A. stands for Master of Arts (the Master's degree), Ph.D. stands for Doctor of Philosophy, and Psy.D. (a relatively new degree offering) stands for Doctor of Psychology.

Psychology Today Is Distinguished in Three Ways

The world of psychological scientists today is distinguished in three basic ways: by *employment setting* or workplace environment; *field of study*, the particular topics a psychologist is trained to study; and *perspective*, the kinds of questions within an area of study that a psychologist finds interesting and the answers to these questions he or she finds satisfying.

EMPLOYMENT SETTING

There is a general division in the type of setting in which one can be employed as a psychologist. Psychologists may conduct research and teach for the

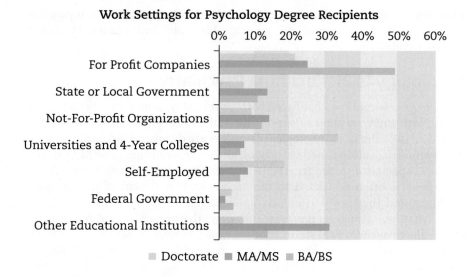

Academic psychology ▶ Basic research and teaching for the purpose of advancing knowledge in psychology.

Applied psychology ▶ Use of psychological principles and methods to address the problems of the individual, society, or industry.

Cognition ▶ Human mental processes concerned with information and knowledge. Cognition includes thinking, memory, language, intelligence, and perception of the world through the senses.

purpose of advancing knowledge (**academic psychology** or *basic research*); or practice psychology in a "hands on" manner to help solve problems of the individual, society, or industry (**applied psychology**). For example, a *psychotherapist* is practicing applied psychology, as is a consultant to an advertising agency hoping to create an effective compaign to sell a product.

The proportion of psychologists employed in various work settings are summarized in Figure 1.1.

The study of psychology also finds a place in careers and settings entirely outside of those pursued by psychologists themselves. For example, undergraduate and graduate training in psychology can be useful in police work, social work, the business world, education, even arts and entertainment.

FIELDS OF STUDY

Psychologists differ in the topics they study. For example, *developmental psychologists* study the various ways human beings change—or remain stable—over the life span. *Cognitive psychologists* study thinking, learning and memory, intelligence, language, sensory perception, and other aspects of human **cognition**—the term used to describe all mental processes concerned in some way with *information*.

Clinical psychologists and *counseling psychologists*, who represent about half of all psychologists currently employed (American Psychological Association, 2003), study and/or treat mental health and other problems in living. Just as undergraduate university students are expected to choose a major, psychology graduate students are expected to choose a field of specialization, such as those listed in Table 1.2.

PERSPECTIVES

Mao Zedong, the leader of the Chinese Revolution, famously quoted an ancient Chinese saying: "Let a hundred flowers bloom, a hundred schools of thought contend" (Nieh, 1981, p.24). Regardless of their political affiliation, psychologists certainly appear to share this sentiment. For any given psychological fact there may be a dozen different interpretations based on competing theories and perspectives. Psychologists working within each field do not necessarily agree on how best to explain the human behavior they study.

For example, as we will explore in depth in Chapter 4, *developmental psychologists* are interested in the ways that people change psychologically over the course of the life span. However, a developmental psychologist working from the *biobehavioral* perspective might emphasize the importance of genetic, hormonal, and nervous system factors in understanding how people

Table 1.2 **Fields of Study in Psychological Science**

FIELD	TOPIC AREAS
I. Academic Psychology (basic research)	
Behavior genetics	How genes and environments contribute to differences among people in attributes, abilities, personality, and behavior
Biopsychology (psychobiology)	Biological origins of behavior, focusing on the endocrine, immune, and nervous systems
Comparative psychology	The study of similarities and differences between human and nonhuman animals
Cognitive psychology	Thinking, learning and memory, intelligence, language, and other aspects of cognition
Cross-cultural and ethnic psychology	Cultural differences (and similarities) within and between societies
Developmental psychology (human development)	Change and continuity across the life span, from birth to death
Educational psychology	How people learn in educational settings; evaluation of educational programs
Experimental psychology	The study of nonhuman animal behavior in controlled laboratory settings
Neuroscience	How the structure and chemistry of the brain affect behavior; includes subspecialties such as *cognitive neuroscience* and *behavioral neuroscience*
Personality psychology	Individual differences among people in characteristic behavior
Social psychology	How situations affect the behavior of individuals, and how the behavior of individuals affects situations; includes the study of the self, group behavior, interpersonal relationships, attitude and belief formation, prejudice, and so forth
II. Applied Psychology	
Clinical and counseling psychology	Causes and treatments of serious mental health problems and ordinary personal, work, and school-related problems
Forensic psychology	The application of psychological methods and knowledge in the legal sphere (for example, in criminal investigations and litigation)
Health psychology	The interaction of psychology and health; includes the study of immune functions, emotion and health, and health problems such as eating disorders and addiction. One subspecialty of health psychology is *sports psychology*.
Industrial and organizational psychology	These psychologists help to train workers, increase productivity and job satisfaction, assist in career choice, and administer tests in organizational settings.
School psychology	School psychologists are trained to conduct testing in school settings, advise administrators, and offer counseling to students and teachers.

develop during infancy and childhood; on the other hand, a developmental theorist working from the *attachment* perspective would emphasize the importance of early parent-infant relationships. These psychologists work in the same field and may study the same topics, but their approaches and understandings will differ radically. We will be comparing perspectives in psychology throughout the chapters of this book. Some of the more important of these current perspectives are the following:

- ***Biobehavioral perspective*** (e.g., Gazzaniga, 2005, 2010; Plomin, DeFries, Craig, & McGuffin, 2003). Psychologists whose work is guided by the biobehavioral perspective believe that the key to understanding human behavior lies in understanding the human brain and body. Almost

▲ **Psychologists Differ in Their Perspectives.** Both Leda Cosmides (top) and Shinobu Kitayama (bottom) study cognition—the way the mind processes information in thought, memory, language, and dreaming. However, as an evolutionary theorist, Cosmides emphasizes the effects of human evolutionary history in shaping human cognition; as a cultural theorist, Kitayama emphasizes the effects of culture.

by definition, those working in the fields of behavioral genetics, neuroscience, and biopsychology are likely to hold to this perspective.

- ***Cognitive Perspective*** (e.g., Fodor, 1983; Pinker, 1997; Tversky & Kahneman, 2005). Those adhering to the cognitive perspective view the human mind as an extraordinarily complex *information-processing* device, in some ways (very loosely) similar to an "organic computer." Again, almost by definition, those working the field of cognitive psychology are likely to hold to this perspective.
- ***Evolutionary perspective*** (e.g., Barkow, 2006; Buss, 2005, 2009; Cosmides & Tooby, 2008; Tooby & Cosmides, 1992). Those taking the evolutionary perspective believe that the human brain and mind evolved in very specific ways to help our ancestors solve the sorts of problems they experienced recurrently over evolutionary time. The evolutionary perspective may be found among psychologists working in virtually any field of psychology.
- ***Positive psychology*** (e.g., Diener, 2009; Gable & Haidt, 2005; Seligman, Steen, Park, & Peterson, 2005). Those working from the positive psychology perspective use psychological science to study human strengths and positive attributes, rather than focusing primarily on human problems as is sometimes the case in branches of psychology such as clinical and counseling psychology. Positive psychologists also work toward developing programs and techniques that promote the expression of these strengths and positive attributes.
- ***Psychodynamic perspective*** (e.g., Westen, 1998; 2005). Psychodynamic theorists believe that human beings are often strongly affected by unconscious conflicts and motivations that may be expressed in their behavior and personality.
- ***Sociocultural perspective*** (e.g., Matsumoto, Yoo, & Nakagawa, 2008; Matsumoto & Yoo, 2006; Miyamoto, Nisbett & Masuda, 2006; Nisbett & Miyamoto, 2005). Sociocultural theorists emphasize the critical role played by society and culture in shaping human psychology. Many of these theorists work in the fields of cultural, cross-cultural, and ethnic psychology.

No one of the schools of thought just described has been demonstrated to be "better" or more productive than another; and in truth, psychologists taking different points of view may sometimes incorporate into their work ideas and concerns from perspectives with which they otherwise might find themselves in vigorous debate. The point is that each of these "hundreds of blossoms" focuses its research energy upon a specific piece of the larger picture of human psychology.

Psychology Did Not Exist in the Ancient World

Modern psychologists are not the first humans interested in questions of mental life and the connection between mental life and behavior. Very ancient peoples undoubtedly shared these concerns. However, *psychology* as a concept did not exist in the ancient world. This is because ancient peoples tended to assume that their thoughts and feelings did not originate in their own minds but were largely spiritual in origin—the work of gods, demons, and other spiritual beings (Hunt, 1993; Jaynes, 1976).

The first comprehensive prescientific system of psychology was probably that created by the Buddha, born Gotama Siddhartha, in India approximately 2,600 years ago. The Buddha believed that human suffering was largely determined by each person's own mental activity. He stressed the important effects of thought both on the thinker and on those with whom the thinker came in contact (Ekman, Davidson, Ricard, & Wallace, 2005; Rahula, 1959). He then set out a concrete "treatment" for mental suffering known as the *noble eightfold path* that offers prescriptions for behavior as well as thought. In this sense, we might consider the Buddha the world's first *cognitive-behavior psychotherapist*. As discussed in Chapter 14, cognitive-behavior therapists who treat psychological problems such as depression and anxiety believe that much emotional distress is caused by a person's own maladaptive patterns of thinking and behaving (e.g., Beck, Rush, Shaw, & Emery, 1979; Beck, 2005). In fact, a recent development in psychotherapeutic treatment of mental illnesses known as *mindfulness-based cognitive therapy* (MBCT) joins techniques of *cognitive therapy* with the very meditation techniques and ideas about the mind first described by the Buddha (e.g., Coelho, Canter, & Ernst, 2007; Kuyken et al., 2010).

During this same time period, the Chinese were also developing new ways of considering the nature of human thought and emotion. Their philosophical systems acknowledged the unique consciousness of the individual. While not denying the importance of the spiritual in human affairs, philosophers such as Confucius and Lao-Tze affirmed that the person played a role in the generation of his or her own internal life.

In the West, the Greek philosopher Aristotle, a pupil of Plato, created a fully comprehensive, systematic psychology, though he did not arrive at his ideas through the methods of science. Aristotle studied theories of learning, memory, perception, motivation, emotion, and social interaction—topics covered extensively in this book. He was the first theorist to stress the importance of objective observation and logical inference, ideas that became exceedingly important in later movements toward scientific psychology (Robinson, 1989).

Indian Buddhism, Chinese philosophies, and Greek philosophers such as Aristotle all addressed what are today called the "big questions of psychology"— questions that continue to be of critical interest to virtually all psychologists, regardless of the field of study. These questions are far less numerous than the ones posed earlier in this chapter, such as why sunsets are red or what is the purpose of sleep. These questions address truly fundamental questions about what it means to be human. Among them are the following:

- Where does the mind reside? Is it in some way separate from the body?
- Are human beings primarily the product of their inherited characteristics or of the environment in which they are reared?
- Does thought arise from experience, or are we born with certain beliefs about the world?
- Is reality "real"—or is it an illusion we all somehow agree to accept?
- What are valid ways of drawing inferences from observations? Why do so many of our beliefs and ideas about the world prove to be false?
- What is the connection between thought and emotion? Do emotions emerge as a result of the content of our thoughts, or do our thoughts arise from our emotions?

▲ **The Buddha, Gotama Siddhartha.** The first comprehensive prescientific system of psychology is attributed to this historical figure.

Prescientific Psychology in the Age of Reason

The first important psychologist of the prescientific modern world was the French philosopher René Descartes (1596–1650), who lived during the Renaissance but whose work greatly influenced philosophical and scientific ideas of the Age of Reason in the next century. The Age of Reason, also called the Enlightenment, emerged at a time when science was on the rise and an attitude of questioning was prevalent throughout Western societies— questioning of customs, beliefs, authorities, and institutions. Rationality became an important value, and Descartes was the founder of the movement known as **rationalism**—the view that beliefs should be formed through close reasoning and logic similar to mathematics, rather than relying on the pronouncements of authorities or personal experiences and biases.

Rationalism ▶ The philosophical movement founded by René Descartes which held that beliefs should be formed through the use of reason, rather than relying upon personal experience or the pronouncements of authorities.

▲ **René Descartes (1596–1650).** The founder of rationalism, Descartes is famous for his observation *"Cogito, ergo sum"*—"I think, therefore I exist."

Dualism ▶ The view that the mind and matter (including the body) belong in separate categories and are constructed of different material.

British empiricism ▶ A 17th-century philosophical movement which held that the mind had no innate content—personal experience was responsible for the development of all thoughts, beliefs, and knowledge.

Empirical ▶ The idea that knowledge should be obtained through personal experience.

Descartes came upon his most famous insight as a young man, while shut up in a small, over-heated room in the dead of winter. After adopting the view that we ought to reject all beliefs that were not obtained by reason and rational thought, Descartes realized there was one thing he could accept as true without hesitation—the fact of his own existence. He reasoned that the very fact that he was thinking about such questions in the first place was all the proof he needed of this fundamental truth: *I think, therefore, I exist.*

From this solidly rational observation, however, Descartes moved to a somewhat less convincing conclusion: He decided that the "I" doing the thinking—the mind or soul—was entirely distinct from the body and might continue to exist without it. As we shall see in Chapter 2, the notion that the body and mind are separate, known as **dualism**, is not supportable by scientific evidence. If it is to be accepted, it must be accepted on faith alone.

Meanwhile, across the English Channel, another philosophical movement was brewing that was to have an effect on the development of modern psychology: **British empiricism**. These English philosophers rejected the rationalist-dualist notion that the contents of the mind are innate, God-ordained, and separate from the body. Instead, they believed that the mind and its contents were unified and that they developed as a result of *experience*. Indeed, the term **empirical** means "knowledge obtained through experience." Thus, the principal division between the rationalists and the empiricists was that the rationalists favored the use of logic and reasoning to acquire knowledge, whereas the empiricists favored personal experience.

THE PHYSIOLOGISTS AND PHYSICIANS

As the preceding discussion indicates, the historical foundations of modern psychology were strongly *philosophical*, rather than *scientific*, in nature. However, in the 18th and early 19th centuries a pioneering group of physiologists, medical practitioners, and researchers became interested in psychological issues. These scholars were unwilling to base their conclusions on either reasoning and logic (rationalism) or the simple evidence of their senses (empiricism). Instead, they set about gathering data ("pieces of information") as evidence through systematic measurement procedures. As we will see in Chapter 2, their theories, measurement techniques, and conclusions cannot be considered *scientific* in the modern sense; nevertheless, they provided the impetus toward the use of scientific procedures that is a hallmark of today's psychological science.

Pioneers of Modern Psychological Science

At about the time the physicalists and physicians interested in psychology were struggling to advance the field, younger men and women more solidly grounded in scientific principles and methods were entering the field, triggering the beginnings of a true science of psychology. I will now briefly describe the contributions of the most important of these early pioneers: Wilhelm Wundt, Edward Tichener, William James and his student Mary Whiton Calkins, Sigmund Freud, James B. Watson, B. F. Skinner, Carl Rogers, and Abraham Maslow. Figure 1.2 summarizes their contributions.

WILHELM WUNDT: THE "FATHER" OF PSYCHOLOGICAL SCIENCE

It is generally agreed that the modern scientific study of psychology, or *psychological science*, originated in 1879 in the laboratory of Wilhelm Wundt (1832–1920) at the University of Leipzig, Germany. At that time, few people believed that psychology *could* be studied scientifically. After all, the objects of study were often invisible—thoughts, feelings, beliefs, motivations, and attitudes. Wundt was the first to take seriously the notion that internal, nonobservable events could be studied using experimental procedures such as those employed in other sciences. He pioneered the use of trained observations and various measurement apparatuses and machines to study psychological phenomena.

One of Wundt's students, Edward Titchener (1867–1927), founded a movement known as **structuralism**, based in part on Wundt's ideas. Titchener revived a technique first introduced by Wundt called *introspection* as a tool to help break down conscious experiences into separate components suitable for research. In a general sense, introspection means "looking within" and examining one's own experience, but in this case introspection is a technique whereby research participants would examine an object—a lamp, for example—and immediately afterward report in great detail the impressions received through each of their senses. Thus, structuralists were interested in studying the *contents* of the mind in a scientific manner.

Although the structuralist movement was an important early attempt to develop a scientific psychology, the movement disappeared entirely upon the death of its founder, Edward Titchener.

WILLIAM JAMES: THE MIND HAS SPECIFIC FUNCTIONS

If Wilhelm Wundt is the father of psychological science, William James (1842–1910) is surely the father of American psychological science. James, a Harvard professor beloved by his students for his informal and irreverent manner, created a body of work that has been described in terms such as "majestic." In 1890 he published the first truly comprehensive textbook of psychology, the 1,400-page *Principles of Psychology* (James, 1890/1981). It quickly became the most important psychology textbook of its time and was highly influential in the development of the new science in the United States.

James argued that the structuralists were misguided in thinking that mental processes could be studied in depth through introspection and experimentation. Moreover, James was more interested in studying the *functions* of the mind than in studying its *contents* like the structuralists. Highly influenced by Charles Darwin (1809–1882), the British naturalist who had developed the theory of *evolution by natural selection* (see Chapter 3), James agreed that human psychology had developed over evolutionary time because it served various functions. In other words, it had *adaptive value* in promoting survival and success in reproduction. Thus, James' psychology is usually termed **functionalism**, because he believed that to understand the mind one had to understand the purposes, or functions, for which it was shaped through evolution. This aspect of James' work foreshadowed by nearly a century the contemporary field of *evolutionary psychology*, which is described in detail in Chapter 3.

Like Wundt, James had many students who went on to contribute to the field in their own right. One of these was Mary Whiton Calkins (1863–1930), whose story is representative of the sorts of difficulties faced by women and people of color who were interested in participating in the new science of psychology. Calkins attended Wellesley College (a women's college), but worked with James as one of her advisors at neighboring Harvard University. She completed her requirements for the Ph.D. degree in 1895, but Harvard refused to grant it to her because women could not be officially admitted to the university. Calkins was never awarded the degree she had earned. In spite of her lack of degree, she became a full professor at Wellesley in 1898, wrote hundreds of papers in philosophy as well as psychology journals, authored four books, and went on to became the first woman president of the **American Psychological Association (APA)**—the largest of the professional organizations advancing the interests of psychology as a profession and science. The APA was founded by G. Stanley Hall (1844–1924), who also created the first psychology laboratory in the United States.

SIGMUND FREUD: PSYCHOANALYSIS AND THE UNCONSCIOUS

Opinions regarding Sigmund Freud (1856–1939) often run to extremes. To some, he was one of the most important scientists of the 20th century; to

▲ **Introspection.** Edward Titchener and the structuralists revived Wundt's technique of *introspection*, or "looking within," to study the contents of the mind. Their goal was to break conscious experience down into separate components. (Painting depicted: *Introspection*, 2006, by Beric Henderson.)

Structuralism ▶ A defunct psychological school founded by Edward Titchener, a student of Wilhelm Wundt. Structuralists believed that experience could be broken down into separate sensory components or "structures." The structuralists used introspection as a tool to investigate the structures of experience.

Functionalism ▶ The psychological school championed by William James which held that the mind could only be understood by referring to the purposes for which it was shaped through evolution.

American Psychological Association ▶ An association founded in 1892 by G. Stanley Hall and others to advance the interests of psychology as a profession and science.

Some of the More Important Names in Early Psychological Science at a Glance

	Name	Date	Psychological School	Important Accomplishment
	Willhelm Wundt	(1832–1920)	No Formal School	Created the first laboratory of psychological science in Germany
	Edward Titchener	(1867–1927)	Structuralism	Founded structuralism
	William James	(1842–1910)	Functionalism	Created the first comprehensive textbook of psychology; applied evolutionary theory to human psychology
	Mary Whiton Calkins	(1863–1930)	Functionalism	First woman president of the American Psychological Association (APA)
	Sigmund Freud	(1856–1939)	Psychoanalysis	Founded psychoanalysis; profoundly influenced Western culture and the treatment of mental health problems
	John B. Watson	(1878–1958)	Behaviorism	Founded behaviorism, applied laws of learning to the study of human behavior
	B. F. Skinner	(1904–1990)	Radical behaviorism	Founded radical behaviorism, applied laws of learning to the study of human behavior
	Carl Rogers	(1902–1987)	Humanistic psychology	A founder of humanistic psychology; created client-centered psychotherapy
	Abraham Maslow	(1908–1970)	Humanistic psychology	A founder of humanistic psychology, developed an important theory of motivation

▲ FIGURE 1.2 Important Names in Early Psychological Science.

others, he was a scoundrel who perpetuated one of the greatest frauds in modern intellectual history. However, all sides in the Freud debate agree on the astonishing breadth of his influence on 20th-century life.

Following a series of experiences with the patient of one of his mentors, Freud and the patient—a young woman named Bertha Pappenheim—came to believe that a person with psychological symptoms could experience relief by talking (according to certain guidelines) with a trained doctor. This "talking cure" became the basis for Freud's psychological theory and practice termed **psychoanalysis**. According to the theoretical aspect of psychoanalysis, the human being is driven by conflicts and desires (usually of a sexual or aggressive nature) that may lie partially or entirely hidden below the level of conscious awareness—a mental "region" Freud described as the *unconscious*. Psychoanalysis as a therapy is designed to bring threatening unconscious material into conscious awareness so that it may be realistically faced and conflicts can be resolved.

As I discuss in greater detail in Chapter 12, Freud's light no longer shines as brightly as it once did within the field of psychology itself, and psychoanalysis has lost adherents to a substantial degree, as both a theory and a treatment (Crews, 2007; Robins, Gosling, & Craik, 1999). In fact, while much of the general public believes that *psychoanalysis* and *psychotherapy* describe pretty much the same thing, only a very small portion of those working in the field of psychotherapy are psychoanalysts. Nevertheless, Freud's influence on Western culture itself is incalculable. Echoes from Freud's consulting room can be heard bouncing off the walls of hospitals, art museums, libraries, advertising agencies, clergy consulting rooms and confession booths, courtrooms, university literature and cultural studies departments, and, of course, therapists' offices. Freud's patients' secrets are told and retold in various forms in popular music, novels, poetry, and jokes. His ghost haunts the theater, movies, television programs, and music videos.

In case you think Freud hasn't influenced you, take the following quiz:

- Do you believe that sometimes people "forget" to do something because they don't really want to do it?
- What if there was a woman in your class named Kate, and one of your friends accidentally said, "I'd love some Kate," instead of "I'd love some cake"—would you wonder if your friend was secretly attracted to Kate?
- Do you think that dreams have symbolic meanings related to a person's inner psychological life?
- Do you believe that talking to a therapist about long-past events sometimes works to help people feel better?
- Do you believe that it is a bad idea to keep your feelings "locked up," and that it is better to get in touch with your feelings and express them?
- Do you believe that people can entirely repress a memory of a traumatic event, so that they do not remember details of it or don't remember its occurrence at all?
- Do you believe that people can be "in denial" about negative aspects of their lives?
- Do you believe that the way parents choose to rear their children has important effects on their children's personalities in adulthood?

If you answered "yes" to any of the preceding questions, you have been influenced by Freud's thinking, at least indirectly. It is truly extraordinary that one Austrian psychologist's ideas should have had such a profound effect on Western thought and life in the 20th century and into the 21st. It is difficult to imagine modern Western culture without Freud. Thus, even if Freud turns out to be the fraud some consider him to have been (e.g., Crews, 2007), the simple fact is this: One can walk the halls of any number of major university psychology and psychiatry departments without finding a single professor

▲ **William James (1842–1910).** Despite James' "majestic" contributions to psychology, he mingled informally with his students who found him unpretentious, unconventional, and "humanly responsive and spiritually sensitive . . . the friend of perhaps every student who came under his tutelage" (Starbuck, 1943, p. 131). James' lectures were always overcrowded and his students described them as "vitalizing."

Psychoanalysis ▶ A theory and psychotherapeutic technique founded by Sigmund Freud and based upon the notion that human beings are driven by unconscious conflicts and desires originating primarily in experiences of early childhood.

who adheres to Freud's views about psychology or teaches his theories; but *outside* of the field of psychology itself—for better or worse—Freud still rules (Cohen, 2007)!

WATSON AND SKINNER: ONLY BEHAVIOR CAN BE STUDIED SCIENTIFICALLY

How were Freud's theories received when he first proposed them? It was a decidedly mixed reaction. The behaviorists were among those who strongly rejected Freudian theories. According to the founder of **behaviorism**, John B. Watson (1878–1958), interior mental states such as Freudian drives and conflicts—even consciousness itself—could not be observed. Therefore, they could only be conjectured upon, not studied in a scientific sense. Only behavior could and should be studied scientifically. For example, Freud asserted that a man might behave in an affectionate manner toward his father, fully believing that he loved the father dearly—while actually seething with anger and hatred below the level of awareness. According to the behaviorists, even if this might be true in some given case, such a thing could never be ascertained scientifically, and it is therefore useless to create scientific theories based on ideas like these.

Watson and the behaviorists who came after him—such as the *radical behaviorist* B. F. Skinner (1904–1990)—wished to discover the laws by which organisms acquired new behaviors, a process they termed *learning* and which I discuss at length in Chapter 7. Like the British empiricists who were their philosophical ancestors, behaviorists denied that human beings come into the world with innate mental content, and they disagreed with the psychoanalysts that human behavior was driven by unconscious conflicts and desires. They believed that most psychological or behavioral facts could be explained by learning. What a person becomes is little more than the result of their experiences in the world and environmental influences. Watson and Skinner differed primarily in their beliefs about which types of learning mechanisms played the most prominent part in acquiring new behaviors.

Behaviorism and radical behaviorism were enormously influential, edging out psychoanalysis as the dominant perspective in psychology for many decades, at least in the United States. It was not until the 1950s and 1960s that new perspectives entered the field and the influence of behaviorism began to wane.

CARL ROGERS AND THE HUMANISTS: FREE WILL AND PERSONAL GROWTH

During the 1950s, a "third force" in psychological theory emerged to join psychoanalysis and behaviorism: **humanistic psychology**, founded in the United States, primarily by Abraham Maslow (1908–1970), whose theory of human motivation is described in Chapter 10, and, perhaps more enduringly, by Carl Rogers (1902–1987), who made major contributions to the development of modern psychotherapy.

Like Freud, Rogers was a clinician who worked with distressed patients. However, unlike Freud, who appeared to view his patients primarily as "cases for study," Rogers emphasized his clients' intrinsic dignity and worth. He dispensed with the term *patient* in favor of *client*—a practice that continues to this day among the large majority of psychotherapists. Humanistic psychologists such as Rogers differed from both the psychoanalysts and the behaviorists in that they did not see human behavior as determined in a predictable manner—either as a result of unconscious conflicts (Freud) or environmental experience (behaviorists). Instead they suggested that human beings have free will and can choose their behavior consciously.

Rogers' therapy, known as *client-centered therapy*, was shaped by these beliefs. The focus in Rogers' therapy was on conscious, not unconscious, experience. Rather than behave in a removed and disinterested manner as psychoanalysts were trained to do, Rogers attempted to counter his clients'

Behaviorism ▶ The early movement in psychology founded by John B. Watson who held that only behavior—not internal mental states—could be studied scientifically. Behaviorists believed that behavior was shaped primarily or entirely by experience.

Humanistic psychology ▶ The movement in psychology founded during the 1950s primarily by Carl Rodgers and Abraham Maslow as a reaction against psychoanalysis and behaviorism. Humanistic psychology held that human behavior was not determined by unconscious drives or by learning, but that people had free will to choose. The humanists emphasized the intrinsic worth and dignity of the human being.

▲ **Surrealism.** The surrealist movement in modern art could not have occurred without the influence of Sigmund Freud in psychology. Freud's influence can also be seen in the surrealistic content of contemporary music videos.

unpleasant experiences of lack of acceptance with corrective experiences of unconditional acceptance and positive regard in therapy.

Like psychoanalysis, the humanistic movement in psychology has waned substantially in popularity and theoretical importance since the 1960s and 1970s. However, the influence of Carl Rogers on the general practice of psychotherapy would be difficult to overestimate. At the time Rogers began his work, those seeking therapy were treated as "sick" individuals seeking help from doctors and experts who were "well," and in a position of implicit (or explicit) superiority. Rogers found this relationship demeaning and counterproductive to recovery. He emphasized his clients' ability to participate in their own healing process. As explored in Chapter 14, this view of the psychotherapeutic relationship is completely integrated into the modern practice of most forms of psychotherapy.

Although there were other important "schools" of psychology in this first era of scientific psychology (for example, the *gestalt* school described in Chapter 5), *structuralism, functionalism, psychoanalysis, behaviorism,* and *humanistic psychology* were likely the most significant from a historical perspective. Much of contemporary psychology is either a development of, or reaction against, the philosophies, methods, and concerns of the men and women who founded early scientific psychology.

▲ **Humanistic Psychology.** With its emphasis on self-expression, genuineness, and self-actualization, the humanist approach greatly influenced—and was influenced by—the counterculture movements of the 1960s and 1970s.

IN SUMMARY

1.	Psychology is the scientific study of mind and behavior. Psychology is distinct from psychiatry, a medical specialty concerned exclusively with mental health problems (psychological disorders).
2.	Psychological science can be distinguished in three basic ways: by employment setting, field of study, and perspective. Field of study refers to the topics a psychologist is trained to study. Perspective refers to the psychologist's beliefs about what sorts of questions are important to ask and which answers to these questions are most satisfying.
3.	In ancient societies and prior to the European Age of Reason, it was generally believed that thoughts and emotions did not originate in people's own minds but were largely spiritual in origin. Modern psychological science was born as a union between philosophy and biology in the laboratory of Wilhelm Wundt in the late 1800s. The most important schools of early psychological science were structuralism, functionalism, psychoanalysis, behaviorism, and humanistic psychology.

RETRIEVE!

1.	List at least three ways in which psychologists and psychiatrists differ in their training, knowledge, or job description.
2.	Which philosopher founded the school of rationalism? **a)** Sigmund Freud **b)** Aristotle **c)** René Descartes **d)** Lao-Tze
3.	Match the statements on the left to the psychological school likely associated with the statement.

Internal, nonobservable events can be studied through introspection.	Behaviorism
To understand the human mind one must understand the functions for which it evolved.	Psychoanalysis
The life of the mind is largely unconscious—comprised of hidden drives, conflicts, and desires.	Structuralism
Unconscious drives and conflicts cannot be studied scientifically.	Humanism
The human being has free will and intrinsic worth.	Functionalism

4.	Differences in topics of study are related to differences in the psychologists' _____. Differences in beliefs about how best to explain human behavior are related to differences in the psychologists' _____. **a)** field of study/perspective **b)** perspective/field of study
5.	Name and briefly describe three different perspectives among contemporary psychologists.

Is Psychological Science Really Scientific?

By now you should have a fairly good idea of the meaning of psychology, its general history, and current structure. However, we have referred to modern psychology as *psychological science*. Is psychology really scientific? Not everyone agrees that it is. Psychology has been characterized variously as an art, an ideology, a philosophy, a fake science (*pseudoscience*), and even a religion. The scientific status of psychology is an important issue to address. To do so, we must first ask: *What is science?*

Science Is an Empirical Way of Knowing

There are two basic types of methods by which we come to know something about the natural world: *empirical* and *nonempirical* methods. As already explained in the discussion of British empiricism, the word *empirical* means "based on experience," so a *non*empirical way of knowing something means that the knowledge is taken on faith rather than experience—for example, accepting the opinion of an expert or the teaching of a religious scripture. Logic is also a nonempirical way of knowing, because it is based on principles of reason rather than experience. Recall that Descartes' philosophy of rationalism is based on the use of reason over experience in the acquiring of knowledge. However, it is important to realize that when we come to know something as a result of logic and reason, we are still taking the knowledge on faith—faith in the principles of reason and the soundness of the assumptions upon which our logical conclusions are based.

Unfortunately, the assumptions are often not at all sound. To illustrate how sound logic can lead to faulty conclusions if the assumptions on which logic is based are false, evolutionary psychologist Donald Symons used to tell a story[1] about a little girl, perhaps 4 years old, whom we'll call Kirsten. Over several months, Kirsten began to notice that her mother's belly was swelling. One day Kirsten asked her mother, "What's in your belly, mama?" Unprepared for this, her mother paused for awhile, and then told her daughter, "Kirsten, there's a baby in there."

Being a curious sort, Kirsten immediately asked, "How did it get there?"

More pauses. "Well, your daddy gave it to me."

That seemed to satisfy Kirsten because she answered "Oh," and left it at that. However, when the girl's father came through the door that night after work, his daughter asked breathlessly, "Daddy, did you give mama a baby?"

Totally unprepared, her father responded, "Well . . . yes I did, Kirsten." Kirsten then spat out, "Well don't do it again, because she's just going to eat it."

As attractive and indispensable as reason and logic are, we still need a way to determine the accuracy of our assumptions. In this case, Kirsten falsely assumed that only through eating could an object (such as a baby) enter a person's abdominal region. Her quite logical conclusion was thus wildly inaccurate.

Intuition Is an Empirical Mixed Blessing

In contrast to nonempirical ways of knowing, empirical knowledge results in some way from direct experience—either the "knower's" own experience or someone else's verified experience. Two empirical ways of knowing that are of particular importance in psychology are intuition and science. **Intuition** refers to obtaining knowledge or understanding without conscious effort or analytical reasoning and often without awareness (Epstein, 2010).

Intuition is generally instantaneous and unexpected (Hodgkinson, Langan-Fox, & Sadler-Smith, 2008; Myers, 2010; Sadler-Smith, 2008). Although intuition is complex and may include nonempirical elements—for example, some innate components of the human mind may contribute to intuition—a person's history of personal experiences plays a critical role in the development of his or her intuitions about any particular subject or event (Cacioppo, 2004; Myers, 2007). In a sense, intuition results from the interaction of a lifetime of personal experiences with mental structures and abilities common to all human beings—including memory, the ability to "read" another person's emotions or intentions, mental "shortcuts" which evolved to allow for rapid decision making, and so forth.

Intuition is a fabulous capacity of the human mind. It allows us to make mental computations and arrive at conclusions that may be stunningly accurate, even as we are completely unaware of the calculations themselves. You may have walked into a new class, taken one look at the professor, and "just known" that it was going to be a rough semester in that room. In other classes, you may immediately have found yourself in an open mood, looking forward to hearing what the professor had to say. Researchers have found that after viewing silent video clips of college instructors standing before their students and teaching—clips lasting only 2 to 5 seconds—strangers could predict with a high level of accuracy how the instructors would be evaluated by their students at the end of the semester (Ambady and Rosenthal, 1993; Ambady, 2010).

In a similar experiment, researchers flashed images of unfamiliar faces to research participants for 100 microseconds (millionths of a second) and asked them to rate the faces for attractiveness, likeability, trustworthiness, competence, and aggressiveness (Willis & Todorov, 2006). These researchers found

Intuition ▶ Literally, "knowledge from within." Obtaining knowledge or understanding without conscious effort or rational thought and often without conscious awareness. Intuition is immediate and unexpected. Although intuition may contain nonempirical aspects, it is an empirical way of knowing because its development depends upon a lifetime of personal experiences.

---

[1] *The story was told to Symons by Margie Profet.*

Perceived Greatest Threats to Health in Women (percent)

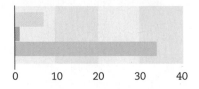

Actual Annual Deaths among Women (in thousands)

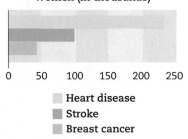

- Heart disease
- Stroke
- Breast cancer

▲ **FIGURE 1.3 Intuition Cannot Be Relied upon to Assess Risk.** While heart disease is responsible for the vast majority of female deaths and breast cancer for a relatively small portion, the perception among women is that the opposite is the case. *(Source: Myers, 2007, p. 31.)*

Science ▶ A unique, systematic, self-correcting empirical method of obtaining knowledge about the natural world. Science incorporates empirical observation and logical inference and is characterized by specific goals and methods. Science is skeptical in outlook.

that the ratings given the faces in these "micro-exposures" were extremely similar to those given when research participants could look at the faces for as long as they liked. In other words, first impressions may form so quickly that we are not even aware of forming them.

How is this possible? When we meet someone for the first time we instantly take in features of the face, then, as we continue to interact with the person, unconsciously note the frequency with which a large number verbal and non-verbal behaviors occur—smiles, frowns, nods and headshakes, yawns, upward or downward gazes, fidgeting, hand gestures, body position, and so forth. To these "data" we apply a complicated mental calculus without being aware that we are doing so. We then come up with a "gut feeling." That's intuition.

But there is a problem with intuition. It is seriously fallible. For example, most of us *intuit* very strongly that air travel is more dangerous than automobile travel. Yet we are vastly safer in a plane. Although exact figures are impossible to arrive at because there are so many factors that can vary, the chance of dying in a motor vehicle accident is somewhere about 1 in 100, while the chance of dying in a plane crash is about 1 in 20,000 (Britt, 2005). Our intuition that air travel is more dangerous is probably based on a number of factors, including the greater certainty of death for those who do find themselves in a plane crash and the substantial amount of publicity surrounding virtually all crashes of commercial jetliners. Moreover, the simple fact that human beings evolved to live on the ground and not fly through the air makes us feel more comfortable traveling close to the ground (Myers, 2002; Pinker, 2002). Our intuitive beliefs about which diseases pose the greatest risks are similarly skewed (see Figure 1.3). Examples of failed intuition are numerous. Clearly, while intuition is a gift, it has serious limitations.

Science Is the Best Method of Gaining Material Knowledge

Science is a unique, systematic application of observation and logic to any question concerning the natural world. It is the best of the empirical methods of obtaining material knowledge of the natural world. Why is science the best of the empirical methods? First, science is self-correcting: It has built-in methods to change errors in thinking, and constantly refines knowledge gained in the past. It recognizes that people are fallible in their thinking and attempts to control for the human errors that often pervade "common sense" and intuition. It was science that caused medical doctors to abandon the practice of bloodletting ("bleeding" the patient) as a cure-all for illnesses, and it was science which later provided evidence that bloodletting, after all, actually *had* uses as a treatment for certain rare conditions (e.g., polycythemia). Although *scientists* may be proud and have difficulty admitting when they are wrong, *science itself* is not proud and readily admits to mistakes. Second, science uses both logic *and* empirical observation—that is, while science is essentially an empirical enterprise, it incorporates the "jewel" of non-empirical methods—logic—in order to make inferences and come to conclusions.

Science is not a perfect way of knowing things—it is not entirely free from cultural biases and the biases inherent in human psychology itself. For example, the general racial and gender biases prevalent in American society during much of the 20th century were often reflected in the way psychological research was conducted. Throughout the first part of the 20th century, research studies of "human behavior" tended to be conducted primarily among white males (Tavris, 1992). However, science is by far less prone to the influences of such biases than are other methods.

The Scientific Method

1. *Make an observation about the world*—Paul Ekman (pictured to the right) observed, "People seem to be able to recognize what others are feeling simply by looking at their facial expressions."
2. *Form a* **hypothesis** *(a precise and testable prediction about what will happen given certain conditions)*—Dr. Ekman considered his original observation and wondered if facial expressions of basic emotions are universal or whether they differ by culture. He decided, "I think members of different cultures can correctly identify emotions from photographs of facial expressions."
3. *Collect data through research*—Dr. Ekman traveled to Papua New Guinea where he showed photos of Westerners to the people of the Fore tribe, knowing that they had never come into contact with Westerners or Western media previously.
4. *Analyze the data*—Dr. Ekman studied the data he collected and found that the majority of the Fore tribespeople correctly identified the emotions depicted in the photos of Westerners.
5. *Draw conclusions*—He concluded from the study, "These facial expressions of basic emotions may or may not be truly universal, but they are definitely not limited to Westerners."

◄ **FIGURE 1.4** Paul Ekman's research on facial expressions accompanying basic emotions is helpful in explaining the five classical steps of the scientific method.

Science Has Goals and Methods

As an enterprise, science has at least four general goals:

1. Science seeks to *describe*. What is the nature of a thing?
2. Science seeks to *classify*. To what category does the thing belong?
3. Science seeks to *explain*. Why does the thing occur?
4. Science seeks to *predict*. Based upon our explanation for the thing, given certain conditions, what will occur?

Science accomplishes these goals through variations on the **scientific method**, a classical succession of five steps which occur in the process of acquiring scientific knowledge; these steps are depicted in Figure 1.4.

In the modern world of science, there is a "sixth step": Publish your findings in a professional journal or book. When you see names and dates in parentheses following or preceding a statement or group of statements in this book, it constitutes a *citation*—pointing the way to sources of published evidence supporting the statements. Consider the following sentence:

> One theory holds that the human mind includes innate mechanisms specifically designed or "set aside" for the task of learning language (Chomsky, 1975; Pinker & Jackendoff, 2005).

The authors' names in parentheses are presented alphabetically in the *References* section at the back of the text along with details about the published work cited (see Figure 1.5).

Science Has a Point of View: Skepticism

The scientific method has a point of view as well as goals and methods, and that point of view is **skepticism**. Often misunderstood, the term *skepticism* means that it is important to see compelling evidence in favor of a claim before you come to believe it—particularly if the claim is new, unusual, or appears to violate known facts. But what exactly is a "fact"? From the scientific (skeptical) perspective, a fact is a claim for which so much evidence exists that it

Scientific method ► A classical sequence of five steps involved in the acquisition of scientific knowledge. In fact, science is often accomplished with variations on this sequence and as such, the scientific method should more accurately be termed scientific *methods*.

Skepticism ► A philosophical approach or point of view based upon the scientific method which proposes that compelling evidence of a claim should be presented before one comes to believe in the claim.

Journal Article:

Author's names. (Date). Title of article. *Journal name, volume number,* page numbers.

Example:

Ambady, N., & Rosenthal, R. (1993). Half a minute: Predicting teacher evaluations from thin slices of nonverbal behavior and physical attractiveness. *Journal of Personality and Social Psychology, 64,* 431–441.

Book Chapter:

Chapter authors' names. (Date). Title of chapter. In [names of book editors] (Eds.), *Title of book* (pages). City of publication: Publisher.

Example:

Lilienfeld, S. O., Lynn, S. J., & Lohr, J. M. (2003). Science and pseudoscience in clinical psychology: Initial thoughts, reflections, and considerations. In S. O. Lilienfeld, S. J. Lynn & J. M. Lohr (Eds.), *Science and pseudoscience in clinical psychology* (pp. 1–14). New York: Guilford.

Examples of use of citations in text:

"Ambady & Rosenthal (1993) used a unique experimental method to provide evidence to support this idea."

Or,

"Unfortunately, the boundaries between science and pseudoscience are not always as clear as one would like (Lilienfeld, Lynn, & Lohr, 2003)."

Note: If an article has more than two authors (a fairly common occurrence), the first mention of the article includes all of the authors names (up to five). However, all subsequent mentions of the article use the Latin abbreviation *et al.* after the first author's name to stand for "and others."

▲ **FIGURE 1.5 Understanding References.** The "References" section at the back of this textbook contains the sources for the citations you will see throughout the text. Most of the entries reference professional journal articles and book chapters. This figure explains how article and book chapter references are constructed.

becomes reasonable to offer agreement on a provisional, or temporary, basis. The term *provisional* is emphasized here because *all* facts are subject to challenge and may eventually be overturned. Therefore, although you may often hear the word *proven* used when some scientific finding is described, in fact *nothing* in science (beyond mathematics) is ever truly "proven." All that we have in science is tentative knowledge that we accept provisionally because there is overwhelming evidence in its favor. Yet, we must always be ready to revise our ideas as necessary if new evidence comes to light. Thus, for science to progress, skepticism must be tempered with openness to new ideas and claims. The trick is to strike the appropriate balance between skepticism and openness—to be open-minded without being "so open-minded that your brains fall out" (James Oberg, cited by Sagan, 1995).

CRITICAL THINKING IS THE KEY

How does one achieve this balance between openness to new ideas and skepticism? It is through *critical thinking*. Critical thinking is perhaps the single most important intellectual skill a person can learn. What does this term actually mean? Critical thinking is not thinking hard, thinking long, or thinking well. It does not mean thinking for yourself or holding your own opinion. (Indeed, critical thinking sometimes means recognizing that you are not qualified to hold an opinion about something!) Critical thinking also does not mean having critical (negative) thoughts about someone or something. **Critical thinking** involves a number of related skills all pointing toward the same goal: seeing things as they actually are, without being swayed by bias or error. Critical thinking is intellectual self-defense against false claims and ideas, propaganda of various sorts, and self-deception.

To some degree, practicing critical thinking is among the most important benefits of studying the field of psychology, because our discipline is noted

Critical thinking ▶ A series of interrelated cognitive skills designed to help one see things as they actually are, free from bias and error.

◄ **FIGURE 1.6 Critical Thinking: Intellectual Self-Defense.** This figure illustrates three of the most important skills in critical thinking. How might other critical thinking skills be depicted?

among the social sciences for its potential for teaching these skills. Here are four of the related but distinct skills involved in critical thinking, as depicted in Figure 1.6 and described by several psychologists, most prominently Diane Halpern (2003, 2007a, 2007b):

1. *Critical thinking is rational.* This means that, when thinking critically, one uses reason in considering claims and facts, rather than relying on emotion. The rational person weighs *all* evidence, not just the evidence that supports his or her favored views, and is more interested in finding the truth than in being right.

2. *The critical thinker is aware of biases—his or her own, as well as others'— and is able to see situations from more than one perspective.* Each person's thinking contains biases, mistaken assumptions, and prejudices. Becoming aware of your own can help you to see others' more clearly and separate fact from error.

3. *The critical thinker is always ready to revise previously held beliefs in light of new evidence.* Critical thinkers are open-minded and willing to "stand corrected."

4. *The critical thinker reflects.* Reflective thinking involves avoiding snap judgments or jumping to conclusions too readily. Critical thinkers do not reduce complex questions to simplistic black/white, either/or dichotomies.

Science Uses Theories to Explain Facts

In Figure 1.4, which depicts the steps of the scientific method, the term **hypothesis** is defined as a *precise, testable prediction* about what will occur given some specific set of circumstances. (This term may be used differently in different contexts.) When Paul Ekman predicted that members of the Fore tribe in Papua New Guinea would be able to interpret emotional facial expressions of Westerners depicted in photographs (as described in Figure 1.4), he was creating a working hypothesis. A hypothesis is not the same as a *theory*, although the two terms are often confused. A **theory** is a set of interconnected

Hypothesis ▶ A specific, testable prediction about what will happen given certain circumstances. Hypotheses are often drawn from *theories*, which are sets of interconnected ideas and statements used to explain facts.

Theory ▶ A set of interconnected ideas and statements used to explain facts.

Table 1.3 **Theories and Hypotheses**

This table shows how more than one specific hypothesis may be drawn from a more general theory.

THEORY	HYPOTHESES
Members of disadvantaged groups "internalize" (i.e., come to believe) negative stereotypes held about them.	**Hypothesis #1:** If research participants are presented with a police-criminal video game scenario where the participant is expected to shoot "armed criminals" but refrain from shooting "fellow officers" or "unarmed civilians," African Americans will make fewer errors (e.g., shooting a civilian or officer) when the criminal is depicted as being black and the police and civilians as white than when the roles are reversed (e.g., Correll, Park, Judd & Wittenbrink, 2002). **Hypothesis #2:** A group of women told that a math test they are about to take is one on which men and women tend to score equally well will score better than a group told that the test is one on which women do not generally score as well as men (e.g., Steele & Aronson, 2004).
Unborn fetuses can learn to distinguish sounds.	**Hypothesis #1:** The heart rate of a fetus will change when a tape recording of its mother's voice is played near the mother's stomach—but not when a recording of a strange woman's voice is played (e.g., Kisilevsky et al., 2003; see Chapter 4). **Hypothesis #2:** Heart rate and body movement in newborn infants will increase when they listen to musical themes their mothers heard regularly while their babies were still fetuses in the womb—but these increases in heart rate and movement will not occur when other music is played (e.g., Hepper, 1991; see Chapter 4).
The human mind did not evolve to solve problems of abstract logical reasoning; it evolved to solve concrete problems critical to survival and reproduction.	**Hypothesis #1:** Abstract problems of logical reasoning that most people find difficult to solve will be made relatively easy when conveyed in a story about a concrete issue that would have been of importance to our evolutionary ancestors (e.g., Cosmides & Tooby, 2005). **Hypothesis #2:** Seemingly foolish errors of reasoning about logical probability committed by people in psychological tests will be committed less often if the problems are framed using concrete numerical language (i.e., "How many . . .") rather than the language of abstract probability ("How probable is it that . . ."; e.g., Hertwig & Gigerenzer, 1999).

ideas and statements used to explain observed facts. The same fact may be explained by two, three, or a half-dozen competing theories.

How does one decide which theory to accept? A good theory is one from which any number of testable hypotheses may be drawn (Popper, 1959). Scientists derive hypotheses from theories and submit them to testing using the scientific method. When the dust settles from a great many such hypothesis tests, the winner will come to be the generally accepted theory. Thus, a successful theory is one that is stated in a form that allows it to be tested and which results in a rich body of fruitful research.

The distinction between theories and hypotheses is explored further in Table 1.3.

THEORY AND LEVELS OF ANALYSIS

Level of analysis ▶ The particular aspect or level of a problem to which a theory is addressed.

Theories differ in the point of view they take when explaining a fact, but they also differ in **level of analysis**: the *aspect* of a particular fact or set of facts they are trying to explain in the first place. Take, for example, the expression "Guns don't kill people, people kill people." This is a comment about level of analysis. Consider the many ways you could explain the following hypothetical fact: Uncle Albert died last night.

1. A bullet shattered his cerebellum and medulla. (*Bullets kill people*)

2. He was shot. (*Guns kill people*)

3. His girlfriend's ex-husband shot him in a fit of jealousy. (*People kill people*)

4. Despair brought on by poverty, inadequate social services, the loss of family, and a street-corner culture of violence triggered the shooting. (*Society kills people*)

5. The shooter's genetic tendency toward aggression inherited from his father's family line interacted with universal male tendencies toward sexual jealousy, cultural factors, and specific prior experiences to cause the shooting. (*Genetic, evolutionary, cultural, and experiential factors interact to kill people*)

None of these statements contradicts any of the other statements—each is addressing a different level, or aspect, of the same question. Throughout fields of psychology, theories differ in their levels of analysis.

CRITICAL THINKING ABOUT PSYCHOLOGY

What Science Is Not: Pseudoscience

On the preceding pages we have differentiated science from other empirical and nonempirical ways of knowing. It is also important to differentiate science from **pseudoscience**—nonscience performed for nonscientific goals, but with the surface appearance of science (Shermer, 1997).

Consider "firewalking." In the 1980s, a number of entrepreneurs were making many thousands of dollars claiming that special psychological "training" would enable an average person to walk on a bed of red-hot coals without injury by learning to put "mind over matter" or to create a "mystical energy field." Firewalking—which dated back many centuries as an Eastern spiritual practice—became a popular activity at corporate retreats and "personal growth" seminars. That people could in fact perform this seemingly miraculous feat after taking the course seemed quite extraordinary and inexplicable until investigators began to look into firewalking seriously.

It turns out that the sort of light and fluffy coals used in these demonstrations do not contain heat very well—the conductivity of heat from the coals to one's feet is poor. As long as a person does not stand on the coals for a period of time, he or she will not get burned at all. Any one of you can get up tomorrow morning and walk across a bed of these hot coals without injury. It has nothing to do with mystical energy fields (Shermer, 1997). It should be emphasized, however, that pseudoscientists are not necessarily liars or scammers. They often believe strongly in their work (Lilienfeld, Lynn, & Lohr, 2003a).

Pseudoscientific claims such as these are everywhere—they not only call to you from tabloids at the checkout stands of supermarkets, but are standard fare on so-called "science" cable channels such as Discovery, where programs about UFOs, ghosts, and other supernatural or otherwise dubious phenomena abound. Pseudoscience is big business.

Pseudoscience ▶ Nonscience performed for nonscientific goals, but with the surface appearance of science.

◀ **"Firewalking" Training Is Pseudoscience.** Anyone can walk on light and fluffy coals because the capacity of these coals to contain heat is very poor. You don't need any special training. Just *don't stand still* on them!

CRITICAL THINKING ABOUT PSYCHOLOGY

CONTINUED

Although the boundaries between science and pseudoscience are not always as clear as one would like (Lilienfeld et al., 2003b), there are a number of indicators that suggest an enterprise is pseudoscientific rather than truly scientific:

1. *Science is self-correcting. Pseudoscience is not.* Pseudoscientists do not correct the errors of their predecessors; instead, they perpetuate them, and pseudoscience cannot advance as can science (Ruscio, 2006; Shermer, 1997). For example, astrology appears to have changed little in the past 2,500 years (Hines, cited by Lilienfeld et al., 2003b, p. 6).

2. *Pseudoscientists rely on testimonials, anecdotes, and bold statements.* Testimonials, anecdotes, rumors, and bold statements are designed to appeal to vulnerable emotions in human beings. Michael Shermer (1997, p. 49) reports a superb example of the bold statement offered by the so-called science of *dianetics* (Scientology): "The creation of Dianetics is a milestone for man comparable to the discovery of fire and superior to the invention of the wheel and the arch." When a statement like that is uttered, it is hard not to believe that at least *something* must be worthwhile about dianetics. Testimonials to the power of dianetics by celebrities such as Tom Cruise and John Travolta foster a climate conducive to the acceptance of such claims.

   Anecdotes (stories about individual cases) can help a researcher formulate theories and hypotheses to test scientifically. However, pseudoscientists rely on anecdotes to convince people of their ideas and *substitute* for evidence (Ruscio, 2006). For example, let us say that your friend Lucinda has a bad cold. She drinks one packet of Super-C Holistic Fizzy Stuff every four hours, and two days later she has recovered from her cold. Although there may be a hundred reasons other than Super-C why Lucinda no longer has a cold, people often look for patterns of cause and effect under these circumstances, and tend to connect the treatment with the effect—even if the treatment in fact had no effect. The story of your friend's miraculous recovery becomes a testimonial and anecdote purportedly showing the effectiveness of Super-C as a treatment for the common cold.

3. *Pseudoscientists reverse the burden of proof from themselves to their critics.* It is a truism in science that extraordinary claims require, if not always extraordinary evidence, at the very least *adequate* evidence before they are accepted. However, pseudoscientists making extraordinary claims tend to place the burden of *disproof* onto others: "Prove that aliens are *not* abducting thousands of people for strange rituals!" However, those who do not believe that aliens are abducting thousands annually do *not* need to prove that such abductions are not taking place. Because the claim of mass abductions is a new, extraordinary claim, *the burden of proof is on the claimant*, not on the rest of us.

4. *Pseudoscientific claims are untestable.* Scientific claims must be testable by independent research in order to be absorbed into the body of scientific knowledge. Pseudoscientific claims are framed in a way that makes them untestable, or, if they are testable, pseudoscientists only accept the findings of their own (confirmatory) research, explaining away negative findings in various *ad hoc* ("after the fact") ways (e.g., "The only reason we couldn't demonstrate thought reading in this test was that your skepticism threw out a negative energy field that blocked transmission"; Ruscio, 2006). ■

Psychological Science Varies Widely in Quality

Now that we have briefly examined the nature of psychology and of science, we can address the question of whether psychological science is really scientific. Psychologists clearly aspire to the goals of science: to describe, classify, explain, and predict—in this case, human behavior and mental activity. Psychologists often employ well-developed theories from which testable hypotheses can be drawn, and they conduct systematic research to test their hypotheses. The body of knowledge in psychology continues to be revised as a result of this research. Thus, psychology is a science, in this sense no different from chemistry or physics.

However, psychologists have difficulties in their work not faced by scientists working in many other fields, and these difficulties may sometimes make rigorous adherence to scientific methods particularly difficult, and research may suffer as a result. Thus, the quality of the science as published by researchers and practiced by applied psychologists may vary greatly (Shea, 2011; Pashler & Wagenmakers, 2012; Simmons, Nelson, & Simonsohn, 2011).

For example, it is a relatively easy matter for a chemist to identify the molecular constituents of a particular compound. Chemical compounds are known entities, and it is likely that all scientists will agree on their make-up and how to measure them. But how does one measure *aggression, self-esteem, happiness,* or *prejudice?* Psychologists often do not even agree on how to define such terms. And how does one examine the thought processes and perceptions of infants who cannot speak, or definitively determine whether the capacity to learn language in childhood is a special, innate faculty of human brains or an ordinary skill that is learned over time like any other?

Questions such as these require extraordinary ingenuity that might turn the hair on some chemists' and physicists' heads white (if their own work has not already done so). The job of psychologists has sometimes been characterized as akin to "measuring the weight of smoke"—creating methods to measure and characterize phenomena that have no material substance and are sometimes difficult to define in a manner upon which all can agree (Pelham & Blanton, 2003).

Moreover, psychologists are human beings. Therefore, at root their work consists of studying themselves—sometimes highly intimate or even disturbing aspects of themselves. Despite rigorous attempts to adhere to scientific principles during research, it is sometimes difficult to avoid the sorts of biases that come into play when conducting research on yourself. Psychology also relies on statistics much more than do sciences such as physics or chemistry. As we shall see later in this chapter, statistics can be a tricky business (Simmons et al., 2011). Finally, psychologists, like many other scientists, "ply their trade" in a world of academic competition and dwindling funds. Such economic realities may cause some psychologists—wittingly or unwittingly—to use "shortcuts" in order to produce research more likely to be funded and published, but less likely to advance the science (Ferguson & Heene, 2012; Giner-Sorolla, 2012).

All of these obstacles are formidable. Nonetheless, as you will see in the next section and throughout the rest of this book, psychology is a vigorous science in spite of such difficulties.

IN SUMMARY

1.	Two primary types of empirical methods for coming to know something about the natural world were discussed in the chapter: intuition and science.
2.	Science has four goals: description, classification, prediction, and explanation.

3.	The term *scientific method* is shorthand for the classical sequence of scientific inquiry: (a) make an observation, (b) form a hypothesis, (c) collect data, (d) analyze data, (e) draw conclusions.
4.	Skepticism is the point of view of the scientific method. Scientific ideas (other than mathematical ideas) can never be proven—they are accepted provisionally because overwhelming evidence exists in their favor.
5.	Pseudoscience is nonscience performed for nonscientific goals, but with the appearance of science.
6.	Hypotheses are specific testable predictions about what will happen under particular circumstances; theories are interconnected ideas and statements used to explain facts. Theories often differ in level of analysis as well as point of view.
7.	Psychology is a true science, although the quality of published research and applied research may vary considerably due to unique difficulties faced by psychological scientists.

RETRIEVE!

1.	Why is science the best of the empirical methods of coming to know something about the natural world?
2.	Name at least three components of critical thinking.
3.	What are the four goals of science and the five steps of the scientific method?
4.	When a discipline relies on bold statements, anecdotes, and testimonials—and reverses the burden of proof from itself to others—it is known as _____.
5.	Name at least one difficulty faced by psychological scientists not encountered by those working in "hard sciences" such as chemistry or physics.

How Do Psychologists Conduct Research?

I am going to make a statement here that might surprise you: The fact that a person has an advanced degree in psychology such as an M.A. or Ph.D. is no indication that he or she can understand you better than you understand yourself, or that he or she is in a position to advise you in how to solve your personal problems (Williams & Ceci, 1998). Nor can persons trained in psychology predict what other people will do in the future, based on interactions with them in a clinical setting or giving psychotherapy to them. For example, by using their "clinical judgment" or "clinical intuition," psychologists are no better than anyone else at predicting whether a mentally ill person is likely to attempt suicide or a convicted felon is likely to commit crimes in the future, even though they sometimes believe themselves able to make such predictions (Dawes, Faust, & Meehl, 1989; Garb, 2005; Sarnoff, 2001). Interestingly, however, psychologists' predictive and diagnostic abilities *are* dramatically increased if they ignore their own judgment and rely instead on statistical information and objective testing (Faust, 2007; Garb, 2005; Swets, Dawes, & Monahan, 2000).

To give you an idea of the limitations of expert opinion, consider the informal study conducted by psychologists Wendy Williams and Stephen Ceci (1998). Williams and Ceci compiled a record of 59 actual problems involving relationships, drawn from their own lives and those of their friends. From a pool of one hundred highly trained and well-known psychologists and psychiatrists, they chose between two and five different experts to address and try to solve each of these problems. Often they found little agreement in the conclusions reached or advice given. In many cases, one expert dispensed advice diametrically opposed to that given by another expert.

As an example: Williams and Ceci reported that a 44-year-old scientist had grown quite fond of a woman 20 years his junior, and that she felt the same toward him. However, the man's friends were perpetually making "midlife crisis" jokes (facetiously suggesting he get a tattoo and motorcycle), and occasionally being openly rude to his new girlfriend. The man wondered if his friends were "seeing something I missed, or [whether] we can make this work despite our differences in age . . . ?" (p. 119). In response, a professor of psychology at University of Wyoming questioned the man's motives in being attracted to so young a woman, a University of North Dakota professor urged the man to consider what a burden the age difference would be, and a clinical psychologist and lecturer at Deakin University claimed that the main problem she sees in the story is how to deal with a bunch of jealous friends. She urged the man to have more faith in his own decisions.

As you can see from this example, expert opinions may differ—just as any other educated opinions may differ. Thus, there is a difference between evidence derived through systematic scientific research and the opinions of experts, which may or may not be based on this research (Dawes, 1994, Hagen, 2003). When expert opinion *is* based solidly on scientific research, however, it ceases to be mere opinion. Psychologists who offer research-based opinions are utilizing the knowledge of their field to the utmost (Dawes, 1994; Faust, 2007; Garb, 2005).

▲ **Motivation Unknowable.** Cho Sueng-Hui massacred 32 innocent persons at Virginia Polytechnic Institute on April 16, 2007. Following this horrific crime, numerous psychologists appeared in the mass media presenting their opinions as to Seung-Hui's motivations for committing the crime. Because Seung-Hui is dead and has only left behind limited data from which any informed view can be drawn, offering these sorts of opinions is a less-than-scientific use of psychology. Regardless of training or degree, psychologists can only speculate on Seung-Hui's motivations and mental state.

There Are Three Categories of Research Methods

Although research is the road to knowledge in psychological science, carrying out a *single* research study is generally not enough to establish the truth status of a claim in psychology. It is critically important that research studies be replicated. **Replication** involves the repetition of a research study by an independent group of researchers who attempt to duplicate the original study's basic procedures and determine whether the results obtained are comparable. Why is replication so important? For any number of reasons (including those described in the next section of this chapter) any given research study may accidentally report results that are false, despite the best efforts of the researchers to adhere to sound scientific methods. Indeed, the majority of scientific research articles published each year turn out to be contradicted by later research (Calhoon, McKeigue, & Davey Smith, 2003; Ioannidis, 2005; Moonesinghe, Khoury, Cecile, & Janssens, 2007). However, the probability that any given article is reporting a false result is reduced when the article is a replication of a previous study (Moonesinghe et al., 2007).

When a psychological researcher wishes to conduct a research study, there are a number of possible **research methods** to choose from. The term *research method* is used differently in different contexts, but I use it here to mean a general strategy that one may choose to address a research problem. These strategies are grouped within three categories: *descriptive, correlational,* and *experimental.* Each type of method has advantages and disadvantages, which we will examine next.

Replication ▶ When a research study is repeated by other researchers working independently. Replications may be exact, following the procedures of the original study to the letter, or they may be *conceptual*—repeating the essence of the study but using somewhat different procedures, variables, or operational definitions.

Research methods ▶ This term is used differently in different contexts, but it is used here to refer to general strategies that may be used for conducting research. There are three basic categories of research method: descriptive, experimental, and correlational.

Descriptive Methods Take "Snapshots" of Individuals or Groups

Descriptive study ▶ A study that characterizes a sample in relation to variables of interest to the researcher. Descriptive studies answer questions of *who, what, when,* and *how,* but cannot determine if one variable influences another. The category "descriptive research" includes surveys, case studies, and naturalistic observations.

A **descriptive study** is one that attempts to *describe* some individual or group in relation to characteristics of interest to the researcher. Descriptive studies answer questions of *who, what, when,* and *how.* The most basic type of descriptive research is the **case study**. Case studies allow the researcher to gain extremely detailed information about a single individual. Psychologists working in the mental health field frequently use the case study to examine a particular client in the hopes of better understanding that client and the symptoms or disorder from which the client suffers.

Descriptive research such as the case study, which examines a single individual (or relatively small group of individuals) in great detail, is considered **qualitative** research because it conveys the *quality* of the psychological state of the research participants in a highly detailed portrait. The problem with qualitative descriptive research, however, is that findings of these studies may not *generalize* to other people—they may be unique to the person or few people being studied. For example, just because it turns out that a particular client began experiencing severe anxiety following a car accident is no indication that most or even many cases of anxiety have resulted from car accidents.

Case study ▶ A descriptive research method in which the researcher gathers detailed, qualitative information about a single individual.

Beyond their ability to allow a psychologist to understand particular individuals in depth, the greatest value of qualitative research methods lies in their ability to generate research hypotheses that may be tested in studies which include a large sample of individuals. Descriptive research conducted among large samples of people is **quantitative** rather than qualitative, because it relies upon statistics to create its descriptive portrait. Properly conducted quantitative research is generalizable to the entire group from which the research sample was drawn.

Qualitative research ▶ Any research study (generally descriptive research) which collects extremely detailed information that conveys the quality of the research participant's experience. Qualitative data are very rich but do not easily lend themselves to quantitative (statistical) analysis.

SURVEYS

The most common type of quantitative descriptive study is the **survey**. A survey will report what some group of people think or feel about something, or whether or not they have ever had some type of experience. "Do you believe that the U.S. was justified in invading Iraq?" "Have you ever been the victim of a crime committed against you because of your gender or ethnicity?" "How much television do you watch per day on average?" Typical survey questions such as these create "snapshots" of groups by characterizing the thoughts or behavior of individuals from those groups. Specifically, surveys are conducted among a sample of individuals drawn from a population of interest to researchers. A **sample** is a relatively small group selected to represent a much larger group, the **population** from which the sample is drawn. As you can undoubtedly see, it would be impossible in most cases to study *every* individual from most populations that might be of interest.

Quantitative research ▶ Any research study which collects data in a form that may be analyzed statistically. Typically, quantitative research is conducted using larger samples than is possible in qualitative research projects.

As an example, national public opinion polls are surveys that use a relatively small sample of people to represent the opinions of the population of an entire nation. The best way to achieve a sample that is truly representative of the population is through a random process known as probability sampling. **Probability sampling** is the category name for any sampling procedure in which the probability of an individual being selected for the sample is known in advance, but each individual is chosen on a random basis.

Survey ▶ A descriptive research method used to obtain self-report data about people's experiences, attitudes, or feelings.

In the most basic type of probability sampling, termed *simple random sampling,* each individual in a population has an *equal* probability of being selected (like choosing names from a hat with a blindfold). If each individual from a population has an equal chance of being selected, the resulting sample should be representative of the population as a whole.

Sample ▶ A relatively small group of individuals selected to represent a larger group—the population from which the sample is drawn.

Probability sampling is important for survey research because a **biased sample**—a sample that in some important respect is *not* representative of the population of interest—can seriously distort research results. As an example, suppose we were interested in the attitudes of college students in the United States toward the invasion of Iraq or Afghanistan. Here the population of interest is "U.S. college students." We would not want to sample only a group of students from San Francisco State University, NYU, and UCLA. These are institutions located in major urban coastal areas of the United States, all of which tend to vote Democratic and probably contain more than the usual number of political liberals. The attitudes of students at such universities might differ considerably from those of students at Dallas County Community College or Coastal Carolina University. Indeed, if we sampled only students at San Francisco State, we might get the impression that most American college students were overwhelmingly opposed to both invasions; whereas if we sampled only at Dallas County or Coastal Carolina, we might get the opposite impression. Numerous published surveys have conveyed misleading information as a result of having used methods of sample selection that resulted in biased samples.

Although probability sampling is necessary to assure an unbiased sample, it is difficult, expensive, and time-consuming. Fortunately, however, not all types of research use or even need to use probability sampling. For example, if you are taking the introductory psychology course in a university setting, you may well be part of a participant pool for research being conducted by professors or graduate students at your school. Use of undergraduate students as participants for research is extremely widespread and constitutes one type of convenience sampling. A *convenience sample* is one that may be drawn in a way that fits the researcher's budget or the logistics of the research setting. Depending on the type of study and the types of inferences being drawn by the researcher, convenience sampling is a perfectly valid way to go about the business of psychological research. If it were not for convenience sampling, for example, it would be impossible to test psychoactive drugs used for treating psychological disorders, evaluate psychotherapy programs, study human cognitive and emotional processes, and innumerable other research enterprises. However, when it comes to descriptive research involving survey methods, probability sampling is the gold standard.

Wording Effects   In addition to issues related to sampling, the way survey questions are composed can have an enormous impact on survey results, a problem known as **wording effects**. For example, consider how a group of people might respond to the question, "Do you agree that women ought to have the right to control their own reproductive activity?" compared to the question, "Do you think a woman ought to have the right to terminate the life of her unborn child?"

NATURALISTIC OBSERVATIONS

Another type of descriptive study is **naturalistic observation**, a technique in which a trained person makes systematic observations in a real-world setting. When you don't know much about a phenomenon, it's sometimes good just to observe it systematically with no particular hypothesis in mind, reporting your observations. This is the sort of research often used by *ethologists*—scientists who study animals (including human animals) in their natural habitats. How frequently do students belonging to different ethnic groups interact in university recreation areas, and which groups are most and least likely to interact? How does the introduction of a daily music program affect the behavior of patients in a psychiatric ward? Are boys actually more aggressive than girls in the schoolyard, and, if so, under what circumstances are girls most aggressive? These sorts of questions are amenable to study using naturalistic observational methods consisting of unobtrusive observations of people's ordinary daily behavior by trained observers using systematic methods.

Population ▶ The larger group of interest to a researcher, from which he or she will draw a smaller sample for the purposes of conducting a research study.

Probability sampling ▶ Any sampling procedure in which the probability of an individual being selected for the sample is known in advance and selection is on a generally random basis (e.g., simple random sampling).

Biased sample ▶ A sample that is not truly representative of the population from which it was drawn.

Wording effects ▶ Potential biases caused by the way survey questions, or questionnaires used in other types of research, are worded.

Naturalistic observation ▶ A descriptive research method used to systematically observe "real life" behavior in a naturalistic setting.

▲ **Naturalistic Observation of Flirting.** Human ethologist Monica M. Moore (e.g., 1995, 2002) has spent much of her career cataloging the nonverbal signals women send to men in dating or public gathering situations which either encourage or reject the men's advances. She found that, while it might seem that men tend to make the "first move" in these settings, the men are usually responding to specific nonverbal signals from individual woman.

Correlational research ▶ A method of study in which the researcher measures two or more variables as they already exist to see if there is an association (correlation) between them.

Variable ▶ Any factor whose magnitude or category can vary.

Correlation ▶ When a change in one variable can predict change in another variable because the variables are associated in some way. However, the association between the variables may not be causal in nature.

Descriptive Research Is Valuable but Limited

Descriptive research such as case studies, surveys, and naturalistic observations can be very informative and has often advanced the science of psychology. Case studies support the creation of research hypotheses. Surveys have the advantage of allowing researchers to study much larger groups of people than would be available for most other types of research. Naturalistic observations allow for precise and open-ended observations of real-life behavior.

Despite the utility of descriptive research, most psychologists want to investigate more complex questions than can be answered using these methods. For example, a survey researcher may want to determine the percentage of the population that has been victimized by violent crime, but after determining this percentage, might then want to know whether victims of violent crime suffer from higher rates of depression than those who were not victims. This question goes beyond computing percentages to ask about the relationship of one *variable* (violent crime) to another variable (depression). In a case like this, the researcher would likely turn to **correlational** research methods.

Correlational Methods Examine Relationships among Variables

In **correlational research**, psychologists are asking whether one variable is associated, or correlated, with another variable. A **variable** is any factor whose magnitude or category can vary. For example, TV watching can vary in magnitude from *no watching at all* to *watching 24/7*. Depression can also vary in magnitude from *not at all depressed* to *extremely depressed*. Ethnicity varies in category—from African American to European American, Native American, Asian American, and so forth. TV watching, depression, and ethnicity are all variables.

In asking whether two variables are correlated, the researcher is asking, if the value of one variable increases or decreases, does the value of the other variable also increase or decrease? Either way—increase or decrease—the variables are correlated if one variable changes when the other changes. A correlational relationship is therefore a predictable relationship, because measuring one of the variables will allow us to *predict* something about the other variable.

As an example, height and weight are highly correlated—taller people tend to weigh more. Of course, this is not the case for every single individual on the planet—if that were true, the correlation would be said to be a *perfect correlation*. Yet the average person of 6 ft. 5 inches does weigh more than the average person of 5 ft. 6 inches, so knowing something about a person's height can help you predict something about their weight in a general way. In this case, as height increases so does weight. When one variable increases as the other variable increases, the correlation is said to be a **positive correlation** (see Figure 1.7).

On the other hand, consider the correlation between the introduction and ultimate widespread use of the smallpox vaccine, and the number of cases of smallpox worldwide (smallpox is now considered eradicated). In this case, as the use of the vaccine increased, the number of cases of smallpox *decreased*. This correlation is every bit as strong as the correlation between height and weight (much stronger, actually). It is, however, in the opposite direction. When one variable (e.g., the smallpox vaccine) increases and the other variable (e.g., smallpox cases) decreases, the correlation is said to be a **negative correlation** (see Figure 1.7). Only when one variable does not predict anything at all about another are the variables said to be *uncorrelated*. For example, weight and musical ability are likely uncorrelated. Correlation is measured with a statistic known as the **correlation coefficient**. This statistic ranges from −1.0 (a perfect negative correlation) to +1.0 (a perfect positive correlation). A coefficient at or close to 0.0 indicates no correlation at all.

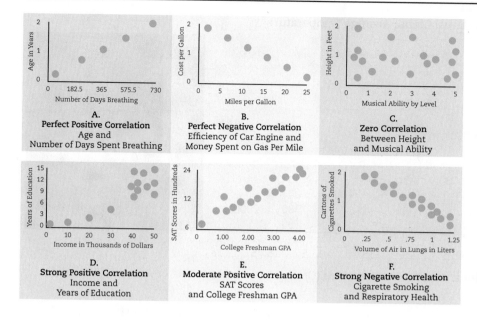

◀FIGURE 1.7 Picturing Correlations Using a Scatterplot. A *scatterplot* is ideally suited to depicting correlations, as it represents the strength of the correlation by how closely together the data points are scattered on the graph. Each data point represents a single score. Depicted here are "ideal" examples of six types of scatterplots. In positive correlations (A, D, and E), the data points cluster in a linear diagonal grouping from lower left to upper right. In negative correlations (B and F), the angle of the slope is reversed, from upper left to lower right. Zero correlations (C) cluster in no discernible pattern at all. Perfect correlations (A and B)— virtually unknown in psychology, and rare elsewhere—form a perfect diagonal line.

Going back to the relationship between violent crime and depression, the correlational researcher is asking whether a person's likelihood of experiencing depression can be *predicted* in part from knowing whether he or she has been the victim of a violent crime. If so, violent crime and depression are variables that are positively correlated. Of course, as I discuss in detail in the next section, even if there were a correlation between being victimized by violent crime and depression, this would say nothing whatever about whether violent crime is a cause of depression. For example, it is always possible that depression is more common in low-income neighborhoods where violent crime may also happen to be more common. In such a case, the variables *depression* and *violent crime* would be associated, and one could still *predict* depression with knowledge of victimhood by violent crime—even if it is poverty, and not violent crime, that is actually the root cause of the higher depression rate.

CORRELATION DOES NOT EQUAL CAUSATION

The possibility that two variables can be correlated without one causing the other is of critical importance. Consider a correlational study published in the medical journal *Pediatrics* in 2004. Dimitri Christakis and his colleagues were interested in discovering whether infants who watched television before the age of 2 were more likely than others to develop attention deficit hyperactivity disorder (ADHD) later in childhood (Christakis, Zimmerman, DiGiuseppe, & McCarty, 2004). The investigators were asking whether these two variables, *TV watching in infancy* and *ADHD in early childhood*, were correlated. These researchers measured the amount of infants' TV watching as reported by the parents, and then observed the rates of ADHD among the children as they reached age 7.

As it turned out, Christakis and his research team found that the more TV an infant had been exposed to prior to age 2, the more likely the child was to develop ADHD by age 7, so the variables were positively correlated. However, this study is a "textbook case" of the problems inherent in interpreting correlational research. Following reports of Christakis and colleagues' findings, health and child care professionals and media outlets catering to parents immediately raised an alarm about the perils of leaving infants in front of the TV for any length of time. However, even though Christakis and his research team reported a positive correlation between TV watching and ADHD, we do not know what conclusion to draw from this information. This is because of

Positive correlation ▶ When an increase in one variable is associated (correlated) with an increase in another variable.

Negative correlation ▶ When an increase in one variable is associated (correlated) with a decrease in another variable.

Correlation coefficient ▶ A statistic which quantifies the strength and direction of correlation (association) between two variables. The correlation coefficient ranges from –1.0 (a perfect negative correlation) to +1.0 (a perfect positive correlation). A correlation coefficient near 0 indicates no association between the variables in question.

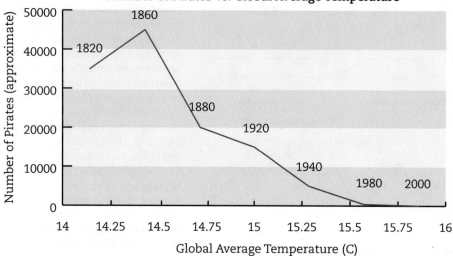

▲ FIGURE 1.8 Correlation Does *Not* Equal Causation. As global temperature has increased, the number of pirates has dramatically decreased. Could global warming be stopped if enough people quit their landlubber jobs and became pirates? (Where is Johnny Depp when we need him?) *(Source: Adapted from www.venganza.org.)*

Directionality ▶ In correlational research, even if two variables are related causally, it may not be clear which variable caused the other to change.

Third variable problem ▶ In a correlational study, when a variable the researcher had not considered is responsible for observed effects in *both* of the variables of interest. The third variable problem is also referred to as an illusory correlation.

the most important law of psychological research: ***correlation does not equal causation***. We cannot conclude that early TV watching is a cause of ADHD merely because it is correlated with ADHD. Why?

First, there is the problem of **directionality**. It may be that watching TV in infancy does cause ADHD. On the other hand, it may be that infants with characteristics that later develop into ADHD are infants who particularly enjoy watching TV or are calmed down by it *because* of those very characteristics, or are infants who are particularly restless and difficult to calm. Either of these factors could result in their parents placing them in front of the tube at every opportunity. Thus, their ADHD characteristics might have *caused their TV watching*, rather than the TV watching causing the ADHD (Miller, Marks, Miller, Berwid et. al., 2007).

In fact, we don't even know if there is *any* causation involved at all between TV and ADHD regardless of direction. Neither may have caused the other to occur. The correlation that Christakis and his team found may have been misleading, because of the **third variable problem**, also known as *illusory correlation*. These terms refer to the possibility that in any given correlation between two variables A and B—where it may appear that one caused the other—there may be a third variable (C) that no one has considered, but which actually caused *both* A and B to occur. In this case, some other variable or variables may have caused *both* more TV watching *and* later ADHD. For example, there is also a strong link between environmental toxins and the development of ADHD (Braun et al., 2006; Faraone, 2004). It turns out that more environmental toxins (such as lead and toxic waste) are present in low income than middle-class communities, and lower-income people also watch more TV (Evans & Kantrowitz, 2002; Kotler, Wright, & Huston, 2001). Therefore, it may be that low-income status is an important cause *both* of ADHD *and* TV viewing. We might think we are studying the relationship between TV viewing and ADHD when, without knowing it, we are actually studying the influence of the third variable of poverty both on TV viewing habits and on ADHD. Although scientists are trained to be aware of the third variable problem, they are not immune to mistaking correlation for causation due to third variables.

If this isn't quite clear yet, consider another example of the very strong negative correlation between global warming and the number of pirates in the world, as graphed in Figure 1.8. As global temperature has increased, the number of pirates has dramatically decreased. What third variable might be responsible for this correlation?

In summary: If a correlation is found between A and B, there are three possible explanations: A caused B, B caused A, or C caused *both* A and B. These possible causal relationships are summarized in Figure 1.9.

Thus, although correlational methods allow researchers to ask questions about important real-world problems—and many branches of psychology could not exist without correlational research—these studies cannot determine *causal effects*. A **causal effect** is what happens when a change in one variable (e.g., increasing consumption of ice cream) *causes* a change in another variable (e.g., percentage of body fat). *Causing* a change in a variable is clearly not the same as merely being *correlated* with a change in that variable. There is only one way to determine causal effects with certainty: a *true experiment*.

Variable A	Causes	Variable B
More TV Watching	►	ADHD Characteristics

Or

Variable B	Causes	Variable A
ADHD Characteristics	►	More TV Watching

Or

Variable C	Causes	Variable A
Low Income Status	►	More TV Watching
	And	
		Variable B
		ADHD Characteristics

Experiments Can Establish Cause and Effect

One often hears the term *experiment* used to describe any type of scientific research study. However, in psychology, the term *experiment* actually applies only to one type of research method: *experimental* research, the purest form of which is the **true experiment**. Most research in many branches of psychology are not experiments at all—they are correlational studies or *quasi-experiments*: studies that fulfill some of the criteria for a true experiment, but not all of them. You can think of a quasi-experiment as a hybrid between experiment and correlational study.

So what then is a true experiment? As just explained, in a correlational study the researcher observes or measures variables as they already exist to see if they are associated. In a sense, the researcher is a passive observer. But in a true experiment, the researcher is asking: "If I do *this*, what will happen to *that*?" More precisely, in an experiment the researcher makes some purposeful change in one variable of interest (rather than simply observing or measuring the variable) and then examines another variable of interest to see if any change has resulted.

As an example, a great deal of research has been conducted on the effects of playing violent video games on aggression in children and teenagers. However, the focus has been on boys and men rather than girls and women, because males spend much more time playing these games and show much higher levels of interest in them; and because males are also responsible for most of the physical violence in the world (Anderson & Murphy, 2003; Archer, 2004). The effect these games may have on female players has largely been ignored. Researchers Craig Anderson and Christine Murphy (2003) wondered the following: If they brought a sample of female introductory psychology students into their lab, and had one group of the women play a nonviolent game such as *Oh No! More Lemmings* while the other group played a violent game such as *Street Fighter II*, would subsequent rates of aggressive behavior differ between the groups? Anderson and Murphy predicted that those playing the violent games would subsequently behave more aggressively.

Here the variable being purposely manipulated is *type of video game*. This variable changes in quality from nonviolent to violent depending on which group of women is playing. *Type of video game* is called the **independent variable (IV)** because it is free (independent) to take on any particular values the researchers decide to give it (*violent* or *nonviolent* in this case). These values are called the **levels of the independent variable**.

The second variable—the one being measured to note any resulting changes—is *aggressive behavior* and it varies by magnitude (i.e., from lower to higher levels of aggression). The variable being measured is known as the **dependent variable (DV)** because changes in this variable are entirely dependent upon the researchers' **manipulation** of the independent variable. *Manipulation* is the technical term to describe the process of making a purposeful change in the IV. In sum: The independent variable (IV) is what we

▲ **FIGURE 1.9 The ABC of Correlation.** There are three possible explanations for the positive correlation found between TV watching in infancy and ADHD at age 7.

Causal effect ► When a change in one variable causes a change in another.

True experiment ► A research study where the experimenter satisfies all criteria necessary for causality to be inferred in the research results. These criteria usually include random assignment to conditions, manipulation of variables, use of control conditions, and control over confounding variables.

Independent variable (IV) ► The variable being manipulated in an experiment to determine possible effects on a dependent variable (DV). The independent variable is "free" to take on any values the investigator decides to give it. These values are known as *levels* of the independent variable.

Levels of the independent variable ► The values assigned by the experimenter to the independent variable.

Dependent variable (DV) ▶ The variable being measured in an experiment to determine if the manipulation of the independent variable has had any effect.

Manipulation (of the independent variable) ▶ The technical term used to describe the process of making a purposeful change in the independent variable (IV) to measure any resultant change in the dependent variable (DV).

Control ▶ In an experiment, making certain that nothing else changes along with changes in the independent variable. More generally, the term *control* may encompass any technique used to avoid the influence of confounding variables.

Conditions (of an experiment) ▶ Groups to which participants may be assigned in an experiment. In an experiment with only one independent variable, each level of the independent variable is also known as a condition of the experiment.

Random assignment to conditions ▶ When each participant has an equal chance of being assigned to any of the conditions of the experiment (i.e., any of the levels of the independent variable).

Control group ▶ Those participants in an experiment who do not receive the level of the independent variable that is of primary interest to the researchers, but are used instead for comparison purposes.

manipulate and the dependent variable (DV) is what we measure to see if our manipulation has had any effect.

True experiments are the only type of research study that can establish un-equivocally whether one thing (e.g., playing violent video games) causes an-other thing (e.g., increased aggression). However, the manipulation of an IV to measure changes in a DV is only part of what constitutes a true experiment. Of equal importance is **control**—making certain that nothing else changes when the level of the IV is changed. In a true experiment, as the level of the IV changes, everything else is held constant.

To clarify this idea, what if Anderson and Murphy had allowed the women in their study to choose which game they preferred to play? Those who were already more aggressive by nature might prefer the violent game. If those who played this game later should demonstrate higher levels of aggression, it might have nothing to do with playing violent video games and everything to do with their already being aggressive people. In this case, Anderson and Murphy would have allowed their research participants' *initial* level of aggressiveness to "change" from less to more aggressive as the type of video game changed from less to more aggressive. This would not be a true experiment.

There are three specific ways to exert control in a true experiment. Without these three basic aspects of control, the study ceases to be a true experiment. These aspects are:

- random assignment to conditions;
- use of control conditions; and
- control over confounding variables.

RANDOM ASSIGNMENT TO CONDITIONS

In an experiment, the groups to which participants may be assigned are known as **conditions** of the experiment, and they represent the levels of the inde-pendent variable. In the video game experiment as described earlier, there are two conditions, *violent game* and *nonviolent game*. Allowing participants to choose the game they preferred to play would have been a nonrandom way of deciding the condition to which each participant would be assigned. The results of such a study could not be relied upon.

In **random assignment to conditions**, on the other hand, each participant has an equal chance of being assigned to either of the conditions of the ex-periment. The purpose of random assignment is to create groups that do not differ in systematic ways prior to exposure to the independent variable. This adds to confidence that any change noted in the dependent variable is due to the manipulation of the IV, and not to any participant characteristics such as initial levels of aggression. If selection is random, it is extremely unlikely that more aggressive participants would end up in one group rather than the other strictly by chance.

USE OF CONTROL CONDITIONS

Anderson and Murphy created two groups of woman volunteers. One group played a violent video game, and the other group played a nonviolent game. However, the researchers were really only interested in the effects of playing violent games. The group playing nonviolent games existed only for the sake of comparison—to control for the possibility that playing any sort of video game might increase aggression. Because the only purpose for the existence of this second group is one of control, it is termed a **control group**. In contrast, the group being administered the level of the IV that is of actual interest to in-vestigators (the "violent" level of video game in this case) is termed the **experi-mental group**. Put another way, any condition of an experiment to which a control group is assigned is known as a *control condition*, and any condition of an experiment to which an experimental group is assigned is known as the *experimental condition*.

An experiment may have one or several control groups. In this case, for example, it may be that *Street Fighter II* is not only more violent than *Oh No! More Lemmings*, but also more exciting and therefore more physically arousing. Physical arousal itself might temporarily increase aggressive responses in laboratory experiments such as this. A second control group could have been added which played a particularly exciting but nonviolent game—for example, a *Wii* interactive tennis game. (See Figure 1.10 for an anatomy of Anderson & Murphy's experiment.)

◀ **The Effects of Playing Violent Video Games.** Researchers such as Craig Anderson have developed a program of correlational and experimental research aimed at identifying possible effects on young people of repeated playing of violent video games.

CONTROL OVER CONFOUNDING VARIABLES

What if, on the days Anderson and Murphy ran their study, the temperature outside was 94 degrees Fahrenheit and the air conditioning was malfunctioning—but only in the room in which the women assigned to *Street Fighter II* were playing their game? Research has shown that extreme temperatures can sometimes increase the risk of aggression (see Chapter 10). If the group playing *Street Fighter II* was then seen to display more aggression than the control group, the investigators might have thought they were witnessing the effects of playing a violent video game when in fact they were seeing the effects of being trapped in a stuffy room at 94+ degrees.

In this case, *room temperature* would constitute a confounding variable. A **confounding variable** is any unknown variable that changes along with changes in the level of the independent variable and exerts a measurable effect on the dependent variable (in this case, aggression) without the experimenter realizing it. (Essentially, this is identical to the *third variable problem* considered in the discussion of correlational research.) Such a variable receives its name because it *confounds* our ability to interpret research findings correctly. In this case, room temperature changes along with changes in the type of video game being played (the level of the IV).

Experimental research can be derailed by confounding variables if the researcher is not careful. These variables must be controlled. Random assignment to conditions and the use of control groups are two essential methods of controlling for certain types of confounding variables, but there are other hazards not addressed by these controls. Although environmental conditions (e.g., broken air conditioners) can become confounding variables, this would be relatively unusual under modern research conditions. However, one type of particularly troublesome confounding variable is known as **demand characteristics**: the tendency for some research subjects to intuit the purpose of a research study and adjust their behavior to match the "demands" of the situation—to behave as they believe they are expected to behave (Orne, 1962). This might not be so bad if not for the **good subject tendency**—the well-known desire of research participants to please the experimenter (Nichols & Maner, 2008; Orne, 1962). Experimenters usually have a certain outcome in mind that they would prefer to find because they usually have a favored hypothesis. Through their attitudes and body language, experimenters can sometimes "push" results in their favor entirely unconsciously, by conveying in

Experimental group ▶ Those participants in an experiment who receive the level of the independent variable whose effects on a dependent variable are of primary interest to the researchers.

Confounding variable ▶ In an experiment, any variable that exerts a measurable effect on the dependent variable without the knowledge of the experimenter. Technically, this means that a confounding variable is one whose values change systematically along with changes in the values of the independent variable.

Demand characteristic: ▶ The tendency for some research participants to intuit the hypotheses or purpose of the research study in which they participate, and to adjust their behavior in response to the "demands" of the situation.

Good subject tendency ▶ The general desire of research participants to please the experimenter or give the experimenter what he or she "wants."

General Research Question:
Do violent video games increase aggression in women?

Hypothesis:
Women who have played a violent video game for a brief period will subsequently behave more aggressively than women who have played a non-violent game.

Independent Variable (IV):
Type of video game (2 levels)

Dependent Variable (DV):
Level of subsequent aggression

Operational Definition of the DV:
In a bogus competitive task, winners blast "losers" with a loud noise. The greater the intensity of the noise they were willing to use, the higher the level of measured aggression.

Level 1 Experimental condition:
Violent game
(*Street Fighter II*)

Level 2 Control condition:
Non-violent game
(*Oh No! More Lemmings*)

Procedure:
A sample of women is randomly assigned to play either *Oh No! More Lemmings* or *Street Fighter II* for a brief period. Subsequently, the women are asked to perform the bogus competitive task.

Results:
Women playing *Street Fighter II* were significantly more likely to "blast" their opponents with higher levels of noise.

Anderson and Murphy's Conclusions:
Playing violent video games is more likely to result in subsequent aggression than playing non-violent games.

▲ **FIGURE 1.10 Anatomy of an Experiment.** Anderson and Murphy's (2003) study of video games and aggression (simplified for illustration purposes).

Blind ▶ In an experiment, when the research participants are unaware of which level of the independent variable they have received and/or are unaware of the nature of the researcher's hypothesis.

Double-blind ▶ In an experiment, when both those running the experiment and the research participants are unaware of which level of the independent variable each participant is receiving and/or are unaware of the nature of the researchers' hypothesis.

subtle ways to participants how they expect and/or want them to behave, and many research subjects are only too happy to oblige.

Because of the always-present possibility of demand characteristics and the good subject tendency, experiments are conducted in a **blind** fashion whenever possible. When studies are conducted "blind" it means that the participants are unaware of which level of the independent variable they have received and/or are unaware of the nature of the researcher's hypothesis. For example, in the Anderson and Murphy experiment, the women were simply seated in front of the game they were assigned to play. They were not told that "some of you will play violent games and others nonviolent games"; if they had been told this, the researcher's hypothesis would have been somewhat obvious.

A **double-blind** study is one in which neither the subject *nor* the persons "running" the study are aware of the exact nature of the hypotheses being tested and/or to which level of the independent variable a participant has been exposed. Thus, in double-blind studies, the researchers designing a study and creating the hypotheses generally do not actually come into contact with research participants. This would be important in a study like the one conducted by Anderson and Murphy because the lead author, Craig Anderson, is an outspoken opponent of violence in media. If Dr. Anderson himself were conducting the study, there would be a significant risk that his personal beliefs could be conveyed to participants inadvertently.

EXTERNAL VALIDITY: THE ACHILLES' HEEL OF THE EXPERIMENTAL METHOD

Although the true experiment is the only method that can definitively establish causes and effects, true experiments are not always desirable or even possible to perform. For example, what if you wished to compare the effects of various parenting practices such as spankings versus time-outs on children's social relationships and adjustment? You cannot very well randomly assign babies to be reared by different parents, or randomly assign some parents to spank their children and others to give time-outs. Few if any parents would agree to participate, and no university would permit such research to be conducted under its authority. It would be entirely unethical.

There is a subtler problem in conducting experiments. Consider again Anderson and Murphy's experimental study of the effects of playing violent video games on aggression in women. Exactly how did these researchers measure "aggression" to determine if playing video games actually does have an effect? *Aggression* is an abstract concept to some extent, and people may disagree about what constitutes aggression. To study the effects of violent video games Anderson and Murphy had to come up with an **operational definition** of aggression—a precise definition fashioned in terms that could be measured in their study. All research studies, experimental or otherwise, use operational definitions of their variables, but in the case of experimental studies such as Anderson and Murphy's there is a problem. The type of aggression about which Anderson and Murphy are actually concerned in regard to violent video games is serious real-world aggression and violence. Shall they follow each participant in their study around for a few weeks, months, or years after the game-playing phase of the study to see if that person commits any armed robberies or axe murders, or gets into any fistfights? Highly unlikely.

Researchers such as Anderson and Murphy who are interested in the topic of real-world aggression, but have chosen to conduct laboratory experiments, must instead create an operational definition that is an *analogue* of aggression—something that will stand in for the type of aggression they are actually interested in. In this case, Anderson and Murphy had each participant compete with a (bogus) other person on a computer purportedly set up in a separate room to see who could respond the quickest when a tone was sounded. The "winner" of each round could blast the "loser" with a loud noise, the intensity of which was under the player's control. Actually, the pattern of wins and loses was preset by computer program, but the participants did not know this. The intensity of the blast used by the player against her "opponent" was the measure of aggression employed by Anderson and Murphy. As they predicted, Anderson and Murphy found that those who played *Street Fighter* were more likely than those who played *Lemmings* to administer stronger noise blasts (see Figure 1.10).

However, critics of these sorts of studies point out that people who administer loud noise blasts are not necessarily also more likely than others to commit murders, muggings, rapes, spousal or child abuse, or even find themselves in more arguments than others. If they are not more likely do these things, experiments such as Anderson's and Murphy's can be said to lack **external validity**—the quality of a study that allows the researcher to apply, or generalize, findings of the research to the world outside the laboratory (Mitchell, 2012). Such experiments have value, certainly, but their value may be limited. In cases such as our proposed study of spankings versus time-outs, where external validity might pose a problem or where true experiments are unethical, impractical, or impossible to perform, investigators have no choice but to adopt correlational (or quasi-experimental) methods.

Table 1.4 summarizes the advantages and disadvantages of the various research methods described in this section.

LEARN TO READ RESEARCH REPORTS

Psychological research is published in professional journals. Learning to read these research reports is not easy. Even trained psychologists may not necessarily be trained in the specific statistical techniques or research methods used in a particular published study, or may not be familiar with jargon and concepts of fields very different from their own. Nonetheless, it is important to practice reading these articles if you want to become an informed consumer of psychological research. This is because research findings can be complex and nuanced, and as a result, can be misinterpreted or even intentionally misrepresented. For these reasons, reading reports of research in news media—or, especially, over the Internet—can be tricky. News media may intentionally exaggerate or distort findings because sensational stories make good copy (even

Operational definition ▶ A precise definition of a variable in terms that can be utilized for a research study.

External validity ▶ The degree to which research results may generalize to the world outside the laboratory.

Table 1.4 **Research Methods at a Glance**

METHOD	DESCRIPTION	ADVANTAGES	DISADVANTAGES
Descriptive	Measures one or more variables as they already exist in a sample of individuals	Can study large numbers of people to create precise estimates (survey); can study a behavior in a "real life" setting when little is known about it (naturalistic observation or case study)	Cannot study the relationships among variables or determine anything about causation
Correlational	Measures two or more variables as they already exist in a sample to determine if the variables are somehow related	Can study problems that cannot be addressed in other ways (e.g., is child abuse related to psychological problems in adulthood?)	Cannot *explain* a relationship between variables even if one is found because "correlation does not equal causation"
Experimental (True experiment)	Manipulate one or more independent variables to determine if this manipulation has an effect on one or more dependent variables	The only method that can determine causation	May sometimes suffer from problems of external validity

if the actual findings of the study are not particularly dramatic). On the other hand, because reporters are not trained to interpret scientific research, even when doing their best to be accurate they may still misrepresent the findings of a study. The Internet is another story entirely. In addition to frequent (if accidental) misinterpretation of research, activists of all sorts, advertisers, and people with multiple axes to grind may willfully misuse and misrepresent psychological research for their own ends. For the researchers involved, watching your work used for these ends can be disturbing, even painful. (This has happened to me, so I know.) So learn to read the research and you will become a more skilled and skeptical consumer. Don't rely on summaries of research in news media or on the Internet.

IN SUMMARY

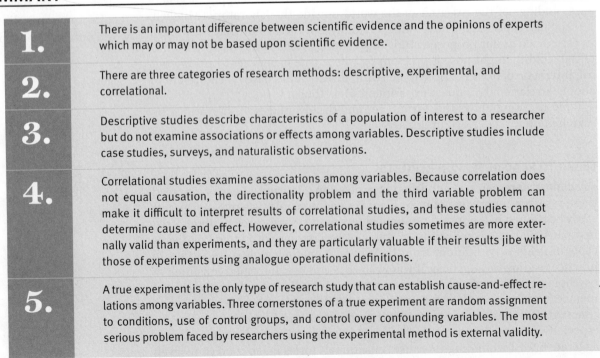

1. There is an important difference between scientific evidence and the opinions of experts which may or may not be based upon scientific evidence.

2. There are three categories of research methods: descriptive, experimental, and correlational.

3. Descriptive studies describe characteristics of a population of interest to a researcher but do not examine associations or effects among variables. Descriptive studies include case studies, surveys, and naturalistic observations.

4. Correlational studies examine associations among variables. Because correlation does not equal causation, the directionality problem and the third variable problem can make it difficult to interpret results of correlational studies, and these studies cannot determine cause and effect. However, correlational studies sometimes are more externally valid than experiments, and they are particularly valuable if their results jibe with those of experiments using analogue operational definitions.

5. A true experiment is the only type of research study that can establish cause-and-effect relations among variables. Three cornerstones of a true experiment are random assignment to conditions, use of control groups, and control over confounding variables. The most serious problem faced by researchers using the experimental method is external validity.

RETRIEVE!

1. Match the study on the left with the research method on the right. You may choose a research method more than once if appropriate.

Researchers study a group of woman who were victims of rape as teenagers to determine whether their experience is associated with relationship problems in adulthood.　　Correlational

A study reports the frequency of bullying acts in a number of middle-school playgrounds at recess.　　Experimental

A study attempts to compare the effects of three types of psychotherapy for depression by randomly assigning depressed patients into one of the three groups. A fourth group is assigned to a placebo (fake) therapy, and a fifth group is put on a waiting list for treatment.　　Descriptive

2. Describe the third variable and directionality problems and give hypothetical examples of each.

3. The variable that the experimenter manipulates is the _____ variable; the variable that the experimenter measures to note any changes that may have resulted from the manipulation is the _____ variable. Different values that may be given to the manipulated variable are known as _____s of the _____ variable.

4. Random assignment to conditions is one cornerstone of a true experiment. Explain why random assignment is important by using a hypothetical example.

5. Control over confounding variables is another cornerstone of a true experiment. What is a confounding variable? Why is it essential to control for these variables? Give an example from the text or a hypothetical example of your own.

6. When the results of a true experiment do not generalize to the world outside the laboratory, that study is said to lack _____.

a) internal validity　　**b)** external reliability
c) reliability　　**d)** control over confounding variables

Why Are Statistics Important in Psychology?

Research will almost always involve collecting data of some sort, whether the data are collected through the use of questionnaires, technology and equipment, or systematic observation. Once a researcher has completed the data collection phase of research, the data need to be analyzed to determine patterns to be expressed in statistics, a process that is usually done by computer. There are two basic types of statistical analysis as described in the next section: *descriptive* and *inferential*.

Both Descriptive and Inferential Statistics Are Important

Descriptive statistics do exactly what you would think—they describe the data and characterize their basic "shape." They tell you how most participants responded, what the range of responses was like, and how participants varied

Descriptive statistics ▶ Basic statistics which provide descriptions of a set of data (e.g., percentage, mean, median, mode).

Mean ▶ A descriptive statistic measuring the numerical average in a set of data.

Median ▶ A descriptive statistic which reports the score above and below which 50% of the sample has scored—that is, the "middle" score.

Mode ▶ A descriptive statistic representing the most frequently occurring score in a set of data.

Inferential statistics ▶ Statistics which help determine the probability that research results reflect actual relationships among variables, or which quantify the magnitude of this relationship.

one from another. Simple percentages are descriptive statistics, as are the *mean, median,* and *mode.* The **mean** is the numerical average, the **median** is the middle score of a data set—the score above which 50% of people scored and below which 50% scored—and the **mode** is the most commonly occurring score in a data set.

Occasionally, descriptive statistics are all you need. The term "occasionally" is appropriate here because in psychology, as compared with many other sciences, another process is usually necessary—**inferential statistics**. Inferential statistics are generally necessary because of a (*really* annoying) factor that makes it difficult for research psychologists to draw conclusions from descriptive statistics alone. That factor is *chance*—the possibility that a study's results are not due to the effects and relationships of variables, but are strictly coincidental. Chance is always lurking behind some research bush, waiting to trip you up, and inferential statistics help to control for the possibility of chance effects.

As a fanciful example, suppose that in a study of violent video games, researchers randomly assigned one group of people to play violent games for a year, and another group to play nonviolent games for a year. The researchers then spent the subsequent year monitoring their research participants' behavior at work, home, or school. They found that those who had played violent games committed an average of 100 aggressive acts over the subsequent year, and those who played the nonviolent games committed an average of two aggressive acts. Leaving aside for a moment the possibility of various confounding variables or problems with the research design, the sheer size of the difference would mean that only descriptive statistics would be necessary to tell the "story" of the research. It is unthinkable for such a large difference to occur strictly by chance.

However, group differences as large as these are quite rare in psychology because most internal psychological states and external behaviors are caused by many variables acting together. Even if violent videos do have any effect on aggressive behavior (a question I address in Chapter 10), they cannot account for the whole story—at best, they only a play a part in a play containing many characters. Yet most psychological studies attempt to isolate single variables that have at least some effect. As a result, in psychology, differences between groups based upon single variables (e.g., whether one habitually plays violent or nonviolent video games) are usually much smaller—small enough that one cannot tell merely by looking at the descriptive statistics whether the effect is a real one or the workings of chance.

Let's suppose that the score were not 100 acts versus 2 acts on average, but 33 versus 24 instead, perhaps a more realistic figure. Depending on several factors (e.g., the size of the sample), a score like this might have resulted if the study inadvertently included a few more than the average number of people prone to being influenced by violent media. Inferential statistics would be an absolute necessity for interpreting these findings because inferential statistics can increase a researcher's confidence that his or her results did not occur merely through the workings of chance.

Statistical Significance and Effect Size: Are Results Real and Meaningful?

Statistical significance ▶ An inferential statistical procedure that allows one to determine the probability that one's research results reflect actual relationships among variables and are not due to chance factors.

The inferential procedure traditionally used to determine the probability of chance factors affecting results is known as **statistical significance**. You may have heard this phrase used in the reporting of research (e.g., "The living individuals in our study were significantly more likely than the dead to report engaging in online gambling during the previous week"). Statistical significance procedures allow researchers to estimate with some accuracy the actual probability of obtaining the results they did obtain if these results had simply been due to chance. If the probability is less than 5 chances in 100 (some investigators use 1-in-100 or even 1-in-1000), the results are termed "statistically significant."

However, a difference found between two groups on some variable is not necessarily large or meaningful merely because it is real and not due to chance. If enough participants are used in a study, real but tiny differences between groups may show up as statistically significant—differences that are so small that they do not have much meaning in the real world. Therefore, statistical significance is only one type of approach used by researchers today for evaluating the meaningfulness of research results. The statistic which measures the *magnitude*, or strength, of a difference found between groups on a variable is known as **effect size**. Effect size is a measure of the magnitude of a result— how meaningful the result is rather than how likely it is to be real and not due to chance. For example, what if it were found that those who eat broccoli have a "statistically significant" reduction in blood pressure compared to those who don't eat broccoli—but this reduction, while real, is not large enough to have any effect whatever on the person's health or likelihood of dying from hypertension? This would probably produce an exceedingly low effect size despite the statistically significant finding. For this reason, effect sizes are now routinely reported along with statistical significance.

Effect size ▶ An inferential statistic that estimates the magnitude of the relationship between variables.

Statistical Literacy Is Urgently Important

Educators and policymakers often talk about the importance of functional literacy—the ability to read and write well enough to do things like read food labels and fill out a driver's license application. Financial literacy—the ability to follow a household budget, stay abreast of credit card payments, assess the pros and cons of taking out a loan, and the like—is another life skill that is hard to get along without. Another important form of literacy is **statistical literacy**—the ability to understand numerical data. Statistical literacy does not require extensive knowledge of formulas or mathematics—indeed, it requires little in the way of advanced education. Instead, it requires only knowledge of basic arithmetic and clear explanations of the meaning of concepts such as "increased risk."

Statistical literacy ▶ A term used by Gerd Gigerenzer and his colleagues to describe a basic arithmetic understanding of the nature of statistical claims, particularly those used in health sciences.

Consider the following, reported by Gerd Gigerenzer and his colleagues (Gigerenzer et al., 2008, p. 54): In October of 1995, the Committee on Safety of Medicines in Great Britain issued a warning that the oral contraceptive pills which were new to the market at the time (known as "third-generation" pills) increased the risk of life-threatening blood clots (thrombosis) by 100%—that is, they doubled the risk. Quite understandably, this news caused a great deal of anxiety among contraceptive pill users and their partners. A great many women stopped using the pills, and a portion of these stopped using pills altogether—resulting in a large increase in unwanted pregnancies and subsequent abortions. At the time, the rates of abortion in Britain had been steadily declining, but it appears that fear over the risk of thrombosis contributed to an additional 13,000 abortions over the next 5 years (see Figure 1.11). Moreover, for every one of these additional abortions there was at least one possibly unwanted birth, particularly among teenagers, at a cost to the British National Health System of approximately 46 million pounds (about $92,000,000 U.S.).

Gigerenzer and colleagues argue that these effects might have been avoided if one important fact had been recognized: A "100% increase in risk" only has real meaning *if the initial risk is already substantial*. As it happened, the risk of thrombosis among users of older ("second-generation") contraceptive pills was quite low—only 1 in 7,000. This meant that among the third-generation pill users, the risk was now 2 in 7,000! Yes, a 100% increase—but from what to what? The end result is a very safe third-generation oral contraceptive, at least as far as thrombosis is concerned (Gigerenzer et al., 2008).

This story points to one important point that needs to be understood as part of general statistical literacy: A statistic that "stands alone"—that is, there is no

▶ **FIGURE 1.11** At the time of the announcement of 100% increased risk of thrombosis among third-generation oral contraceptive users, rates of unwanted pregnancy and abortion had been steadily decreasing in England. In the 5-year period following the announcement, 13,000 additional abortions were performed.

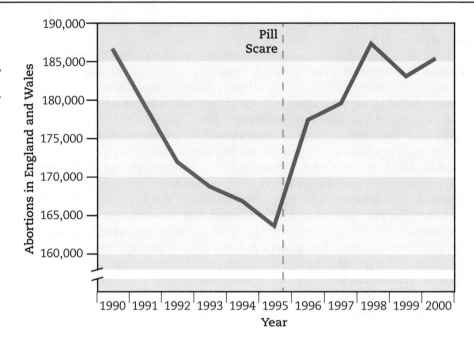

other statistic with which to compare it—is generally meaningless or impossible to interpret. Here are two templates for common statistical claims that require comparison statistics, along with questions that need to be asked to make the stand-alone statistic meaningful:

1. *"Behavior A carries a 100% increased risk of Condition B."* (Ask: "A 100% increase from what to what?") If the original risk is very small, a 100% increase in risk is often unimportant.

2. *"Group A is the fastest growing population of victims of Condition B."* (Ask: "How common is the condition among other groups, and exactly how fast is the condition growing among Group A members?") If the condition is quite rare, "fastest growing" may still mean that the condition is quite rare even among the fastest growing group. This is especially true if Group A is only the "fastest growing" because the other groups *aren't growing at all* (and the condition is actually disappearing)!

IN SUMMARY

1.	Descriptive statistics report the way that most research participants respond, what the range of responses is like, and how people vary in their responses.
2.	Inferential statistics allow the researcher to compute the probability that research results were due to chance or coincidence (statistical significance). They also allow one to compute the magnitude or strength of results (effect size).
3.	A lack of statistical literacy can have important negative consequences for the individual and society. Part of statistical literacy is understanding that "stand-alone statistics" are usually meaningless or uninterpretable.

RETRIEVE!

1.	Why are inferential statistics central to the conduct of psychological research?

2.	What is the problem with relying on statistical significance alone as an inferential statistic?
3.	Consider the following claim: "Children are the fastest growing population of victims of XYZ-disease." Under which conditions might this be good news, not bad news? (Hint: To interpret the "fastest growing sufferers" claim, you need to consider: [a] the *absolute* number of adult and child victims; [b] the *rate* of increase among children [50% per year? 10,000%?]; and [c] whether the rate of adult sufferers is increasing or *decreasing*.)

Why Are Ethics Important in Psychology?

Psychological research is conducted on living beings: human and nonhuman animals. As such, issues of *research ethics* are of paramount concern to psychologists and the general public. **Ethics** are sets of orderly rules for correct behavior, particularly within a specific discipline or workplace. Because of increased concern about ethical treatment of research participants over the past few decades, preparing to perform ordinary research involving human subjects has become a complicated task for researchers.

All research proposals must pass careful scrutiny by a research institution's **Institutional Review Board** (**IRB**)—the institutional ethics committee. Because of recent strengthening of IRB regulations, ethical concerns now strike to the very heart of the research enterprise.

Ethics ▶ A set of orderly rules for correct behavior, particularly within some specific discipline or workplace.

Institutional Review Board (IRB) ▶ An institutional ethics body that must approve and monitor research studies involving human and animal participants.

Ethical Concerns: Scholarship and Treatment of Research Participants

In the discipline of psychology and scientific research generally, concerns about ethics pertain primarily to two domains: *rules of scholarship* and *treatment of research participants*. Yet the focus has often been on treatment of research participants because it is generally assumed that rules of scholarship are well understood by all. While this may or may not have been the case at one time, in the era of the Internet it has become obvious that rules pertaining to scholarship are not always understood as well as they could be, for reasons we shall now consider.

PLAGIARISM AND RULES OF SCHOLARSHIP

Rules of scholarship—primarily those pertaining to the honest reporting of research results and refraining from *plagiarism*—are relatively noncontroversial in that they are agreed upon in principle by all scholars. However, plagiarism concerns have become especially troubling in the context of university education. In the mid-1990s, as many as 30% of students in a sample drawn from major universities admitted to plagiarism (McCabe, Treviño, & Butterfield, 2001). That, of course, was prior to the development of easy-to-use search engines, let alone the advent of social networking. Today, when research papers and essays are routinely bought and sold online and are instantly available through smartphone apps, the scope of the problem appears to be much greater.

What is plagiarism? "Ay, there's the rub," as Shakespeare's Hamlet pronounced. It is relatively easy to recite a definition—most students have had one drummed into them by the time they reach college—but interpreting this definition in actual practice is not always a simple matter (Landau, 2002; Yeo,

2007). As Joshua Landau (2002) reminds us, "plagiarism occurs when people take credit for thoughts, words, images, musical passages, or ideas originally created by someone else." Although many people who plagiarize know exactly what they are doing, a substantial amount of plagiarism also occurs in academic settings because plagiarizers simply do not understand how to interpret the definition just given—a definition whose words they may be able to recite at will (Laundau, Druen, & Arcuri, 2002). For example, most people realize that lifting a word-for-word quotation without credit is plagiarism, but not everyone understands that taking an author's original idea and simply paraphrasing it without citation may also constitute plagiarism—even if little or none of the original wording remains.

Another problem is what Landau (2002) refers to as a *source memory error*. This type of plagiarism is entirely *unintentional*. Those people who do a great deal of research in the context of an academic work—and this includes textbook writers as well as students!—may sometimes find phrases, sentences, or ideas spilling onto the paper that feel self-generated but which actually may have originated elsewhere. This can happen even to writers who studiously attempt to avoid plagiarism. It is therefore important to carefully monitor the sources used to generate ideas when writing academic papers.

TREATMENT OF RESEARCH SUBJECTS

While concerns about plagiarism increasingly bedevil university instructors, it is ethical treatment of research participants that catapulted ethical concerns to the forefront of the research enterprise over the past four decades. Why have these concerns assumed such an important role? First, in the past, ethical concerns regarding the treatment of research participants did not play anywhere near as important a role as they should have. In part then, recent concern is corrective. Neither human nor nonhuman animals should be expected to participate in research without basic protections. Second, we are a highly litigious society, and rules and regulations surrounding the ethical treatment of human research participants are now in place to protect the universities and other institutions and their employees from lawsuits as well as to protect research participants from thoughtless researchers.

Nails in the Coffin of Research Free-for-Alls

A number of controversies involving treatment of human subjects by researchers ultimately led to the major changes in the treatment of research participants in the mid-1970s. We will consider just one of these: the Stanley Milgram studies of obedience.

STANLEY MILGRAM'S STUDIES OF OBEDIENCE

Among the most influential—and controversial—psychological studies in history were Yale professor Stanley Milgram's studies of obedience to authority (Milgram, 1963, 1974). As I describe in detail in Chapter 15, Milgram was interested in studying the conditions under which ordinary people could be convinced to commit acts of cruelty against their own moral standards when instructed to do so by a person in a position of authority.

To summarize the research briefly, Milgram enlisted volunteers for a study in "learning." However, unbeknownst to the volunteers, the study was actually concerned with obedience to authority. Milgram hired an actor to portray a professor whose supposed goal was to study the use of punishment—in the form of electric shock—to enhance learning. The "professor" then instructed the research participants to administer what they believed to be electric shocks of dangerous magnitude to a stranger (also an actor) every time the "learner" responded incorrectly during a learning task. In spite of howls of pain and protest from the "learner," the "professor" would insist that the research participants continue to increase the "voltage" (actually bogus shocks) for each incorrect answer. As explained in Chapter 15, a surprising number of research participants—the majority—continued to administer these shocks past the "danger" level (Milgram, 1963, 1974).

Milgram's research included *deception*. Participants were told that they were volunteering for an experiment in learning, not a study of obedience. They did not know that they would be asked to administer shocks, and they did not know that the shocks were bogus once they were asked to administer them. Although deception is an important feature of many ethical experiments—some important studies could not have been conducted without it—currently, if deception is to be used the investigators must first make the case to the internal review board (IRB) that the results of the study may provide socially important information. The importance of this information must be shown to outweigh the risks involved in deceiving research participants. Participants must also be told what will be expected of them (e.g., administering shocks). Because the participants in Milgram's study knew nothing about the actual purpose of the study or what they were going to be asked to do when they volunteered, they could not have given informed consent to their participation. **Informed consent**—a cornerstone of ethical treatment of research participants—requires that those participating in research have a thorough understanding of the nature of the research including potential risks and possible benefits.

The results of Milgram's experiment caused widespread surprise, and no small measure of dismay. People were upset about the implications of the findings—that ordinary people could easily be led to commit cruel acts—but some were also upset about the experiment itself. Psychologist Diana Baumrind (1964) was one of the first to suggest that research participants in this experiment had not been protected. Instead, Baumrind claimed they had been manipulated without their consent to engage in behaviors that may have caused them psychological anguish during the experiment or its aftermath. Baumrind wondered whether the knowledge gained in this way was worth the psychological risks of the study and the violation of principles of informed consent.

Milgram—who, by all accounts was a researcher of very high skill, integrity, and personal compassion—vigorously defended his procedures. He pointed to data collected from former participants suggesting that only slightly more than 1% regretted having participated, and 74% claimed they had learned something of personal importance (Milgram, 1974). Moreover, Milgram had debriefed his participants fully following their participation. **Debriefing** involves explaining to participants the exact purpose of a study following its completion and addressing any concerns the participants may have had. Debriefing is considered important in upholding the dignity of research participants who may have been deceived, and is an important a part of the ethical conduct of research studies. These assurances did not satisfy critics such as Baumrind, however, and the Milgram experiment was instrumental in fueling the movement to devise more consistent and elaborate ethical principles for researchers.

Nonhuman Animals Also Have Rights

As you will discover while reading this book, psychologists conduct research among nonhuman animals as well as humans; and just as concern has been voiced over treatment of human beings in research, concern has been voiced over treatment of nonhuman animals. Animal rights activists argue that the human attitude toward other types of animals—which leads to their slaughter for food or fun, their housing in cages in zoos, their use as pets, and mistreatment and killing in the context of scientific experiments—is not only immoral, but illogical and philosophically flawed. This argument is clearly laid out in the work of philosopher and animal rights advocate Paola Cavalieri (e.g., Cavalieri, 2004, 2006).

▲ **Informed Consent.** All research participants are given informed consent forms which they must sign prior to the conduct of the research study. The form describes the study and its possible risks and benefits, and assures the participant that he or she may quit the study at any time.

Informed consent ▶ When those participating in a research study have a thorough understanding of the study's potential risks and benefits. Informed consent is a cornerstone of the ethical conduct of research involving human beings.

Debriefing ▶ When the purpose of a study, its procedures, and its potential value are explained to a participant after his or her participation is complete. Debriefing is particularly important in studies which have involved some measure of deception.

According to Cavalieri, the central argument that human beings use to rationalize treating animals in a way that would be considered immoral if we applied it to ourselves is the notion that ethical norms should be addressed only to a particular kind of being—a *moral agent*. Moral agents are those rational beings whose behavior can be subjected to moral/ethical evaluation. Thus, we would not hold a cat ethically responsible for killing a mouse, because cats are not moral agents. Their killing of mice is just something they do—they can't help themselves, and we should not evaluate their behavior in a moral or ethical context.

However, Cavalieri argues that from this idea emerges the unfortunate view that, because animals are not moral agents, they should not themselves be *beneficiaries* of moral or ethical behavior. The problem with this notion from a philosophical perspective, according to Cavalieri, is that infants and the mentally ill are not moral agents either, yet no one suggests we should kill them, eat them, or shut them in cages. To acknowledge that moral agents make morality possible does not mean that moral agents should be the only beneficiaries of moral/ethical behavior.

Therefore, in Cavalieri's view, we treat nonhuman animals as we do—and feel justified in doing it—essentially because we are more powerful than they are and we can get away with it. We must realize the limits of this view in our heart of hearts, however, because we do draw the line somewhere, and we punish people for torture of animals that serves no apparent purpose. However, from the animal rights perspective, this is somewhat similar to the lines drawn by many slave owners in their treatment of slaves.

The arguments brought by animal rights advocates are compelling. However, there is another side to this story, which—unfortunately for those seeking quick and easy solutions—also has merit. This argument is less an argument of logic than a disagreement about the degree of harm caused to animals in research and a plea for recognition of the immense importance of animal research in the relief of suffering. It is an argument that stresses pragmatism (e.g., Miller, 1985; Morrison, 2001; Paul & Paul, 2001).

Those who are in favor of the use of nonhuman animals in research point to statistics suggesting that less than 1% of the killing of animals by humans occurs in the context of research. In fact, 96% of animals killed are killed for food (Nicholl & Russell, cited in McBurney, 2000). Second, animal testing proponents stress that only a very small portion of animal research involves pain to animals, and also point out that anesthesia and painkillers are routinely used in animal research. These critics worry that animal rights activists, in focusing their rhetorical campaigns upon the relatively few animals who actually do experience pain during research, are ignoring the millions of humans who experience pain in diseases like arthritis—diseases that require animal research to create effective treatments (McBurney, 2000). The pro-testing group also reminds us that regulations on the housing of research animals are more stringent than those for human habitation, and that far more pain, abuse, and cruelty are inflicted upon animals by pet owners and farmers than by researchers (Miller, 1985).

Indeed, animal testing advocates believe that there are compelling reasons for the use of animals in research. For example, animal research has led to an improvement in the welfare of animals—from vaccines against feline leukemia, rabies, and distemper, to nonlethal methods of pest control. Research on animals was also instrumental in effecting the startling improvements in health care and human longevity over the past century. According to McBurney (2000), to eliminate the use of animals for research would mean little or no further progress against diseases like AIDS, Alzheimer's, cancer, arthritis, birth defects, traumatic injury, mental illness, and many other conditions that cause pain and suffering to human animals. Clearly, this is a difficult issue to come to grips with, and the controversy is not going away soon.

IN SUMMARY

1.	Ethics are sets of orderly rules for correct behavior within a specific discipline or workplace. In psychology and science generally, concerns about ethics pertain primarily to rules of scholarship and treatment of research participants.
2.	As a consequence of controversies over the treatment of research participants in studies such as the Milgram studies of obedience, explicit principles of ethical conduct in research have been devised. These principles are implemented by Institutional Review Boards (IRBs).
3.	Concern over the treatment of human research participants has increased dramatically over the past several decades due to financial as well as humanitarian considerations.
4.	Animal rights advocates propose that philosophically flawed and immoral rationales are generally given for why it is "okay" to treat nonhuman animals during research in a manner that would be considered abusive were the subjects human. Those advocating the use of animals in research point out that very few animals are actually harmed in research, and the results of animal research are used to eliminate suffering—of nonhuman as well as human animals.

RETRIEVE!

1.	Apart from humanitarian concerns, why are stringent guidelines currently in place for the treatment of human research participants?
2.	Which aspects of the Milgram studies were considered most problematic from an ethical standpoint?
3.	Summarize the arguments for and against the use of nonhuman animals in research studies.

Looking Back

Chapter 1 in Review

WHAT IS PSYCHOLOGY?
- Psychology is the scientific study of mental processes and events (*mind*) and any potentially observable or measureable activity of a living organism (*behavior*). Psychological science uses methods grounded in modern scientific knowledge to conduct research in order to advance psychological knowledge.
- Early attempts to treat psychological questions include the teachings of Buddha, Aristotle, Chinese philosophers such as Confucius and Lao-tze, and Renaissance philosophers such as the rationalists and the British empiricists.

- Scientific psychology was born during the late 19th century as a union between philosophy and biology. Some important early schools of scientific psychology include the work of Wilhelm Wundt *structuralism* (Titchener), *functionalism* (James), *psychoanalysis* (Freud), *behaviorism* (Watson, Skinner), and *humanism* (Rogers, Maslow).
- Psychology today is distinguished by employment setting and focus (basic research or application of research to real-world problems); by the psychologist's field of study (e.g., developmental psychology, clinical psychology, cognitive

psychology); and by the psychologist's perspective, or point of view. Contemporary perspectives include *cognitive, biobehavioral, psychodynamic, evolutionary, sociocultural,* and *positive psychology*.

IS PSYCHOLOGICAL SCIENCE REALLY SCIENTFIC?
- Science is an empirical method of gaining knowledge of the natural world. Compared with other methods of gaining knowledge, science is less prone to bias, has built-in methods to change errors in thinking, and constantly refines knowledge gained in the past.

Looking Back continued

- Science has goals and methods. Goals include *description, classification, explanation,* and *prediction*. Methods are varied, but they are based upon a general model known as the *scientific method* (make an observation, form hypotheses, collect data, analyze data, draw conclusions).
- *Skepticism* is the point of view of science, and *critical thinking* is the key to balancing skepticism with openness to new ideas. Science uses *theories* to explain *facts*, but even if a theory proves to be wrong, the facts it tries to explain do not vanish. Science differs from *pseudoscience*, which is nonscience performed for nonscientific goals with the surface appearance of science.

HOW DO PSYCHOLOGISTS CONDUCT RESEARCH?

- There are three main categories of research methods in psychological science: *descriptive, correlational,* and *experimental*. Only the *true experiment* allows the researcher to determine causal effects with certainty.
- Descriptive research methods such as *surveys, case studies,* and *naturalistic observations* allow the researcher to create "snapshots" at one point in time. These studies answer questions of *who, what, when,* and *how,* but they cannot determine if one variable is associated with another, or if changes in one variable result in changes in another. In the survey, issues of sampling become important because results will not be valid unless the *sample* being used truly represents the *population* of interest.
- Correlational methods allow the researcher to determine if one variable is associated, or correlated, with another variable. Correlations may be *positive* or *negative*. One can never infer causality from correlational studies because *correlation does not equal causation*. Issues of *directionality* and the *third variable problem* must be resolved if causation is to be claimed.
- Experimental methods can establish causal relations with certainty, but only in the case of the *true experiment*. True experiments include at least: *random assignment to conditions, use of control conditions,* and *control over confounding variables*. The "Achilles' heel" of the experimental method is the problem of *external validity*—the application of laboratory research findings to the real world outside the laboratory.

WHY ARE STATISTICS IMPORTANT IN PSYCHOLOGY?

- Statistics enable psychological researchers to interpret and report their data. *Descriptive statistics* describe a set of data and characterize its basic "shape." *Inferential statistics* allow researchers to achieve a level of confidence that their results did not occur by chance and are strong enough to be meaningful in the real world. *Statstical literacy* is important for the average person to be able to interpret the many statistical claims which appear in the media.

WHY ARE ETHICS IMPORTANT IN PSYCHOLOGY?

- *Ethics* in psychology pertain primarily to the *treatment of research participants* and to the adherence to *rules of scholarship*. *Institutional review boards* are ethics committees designed to protect human and nonhuman research participants. Ethical scholarship includes avoiding plagiarism and distortion of research findings.

Key Terms

Key Terms continued

Test Yourself

1. Describe three ways in which psychiatry differs from psychology.
2. Why is it said that psychology did not exist in the ancient world?
3. Name and briefly describe the perspectives of the five schools of psychology which contributed the most during the first 100 years of psychological science. Give one important name associated with each school.
4. What is the difference between a *field* in psychology and a *perspective* in psychology?
5. Name and briefly characterize four contemporary fields and four contemporary perspectives in psychology.
6. What are the four goals of science?
7. What are the five steps of the scientific method?
8. Name at least three ways that science and pseudoscience differ.
9. Name at least three components of critical thinking.
10. Why is it said that intuition is a "mixed blessing"? Give an example.
11. Why is nothing ever "proven" in science?
12. What is the difference between a hypothesis and a theory?
13. What difficulties do psychologists face in conducting research that scientists in fields such as physics or chemistry do not face as often?
14. When are the opinions of psychologists superior to those of the average person in regard to a psychological issue?
15. What is the principal advantage of a true experiment? What is the most frequent problem with the experimental method?
16. What is the greatest advantage of the correlational method? The greatest disadvantage?
17. Name three types of descriptive research studies.
18. What is the term given to any factor or variable which exerts an effect on the dependent variable of an experiment without the knowledge of the researcher?
19. In a research study of the effects of marijuana on memory, researchers divided subjects into three groups: One was given the equivalent of one "joint"; one was given the equivalent of two; and the third was given no marijuana at all. The participants all studied lists of words and later attempted to recall them. In this study, what was the independent variable? The dependent variable? What were the levels of the independent variable? What is the name we give to the group which was given no marijuana at all?
20. Name three important criteria of a true experiment.
21. What is the purpose of random assignment to conditions?
22. What are demand characteristics?
23. Distinguish statistical significance from effect size.
24. How do descriptive statistics differ from inferential statistics?
25. Why do animal rights activists believe that that the rationales for use of nonhuman animals in research are philosophically flawed and immoral? How are these activists answered by those promoting the use of nonhuman animals in research?

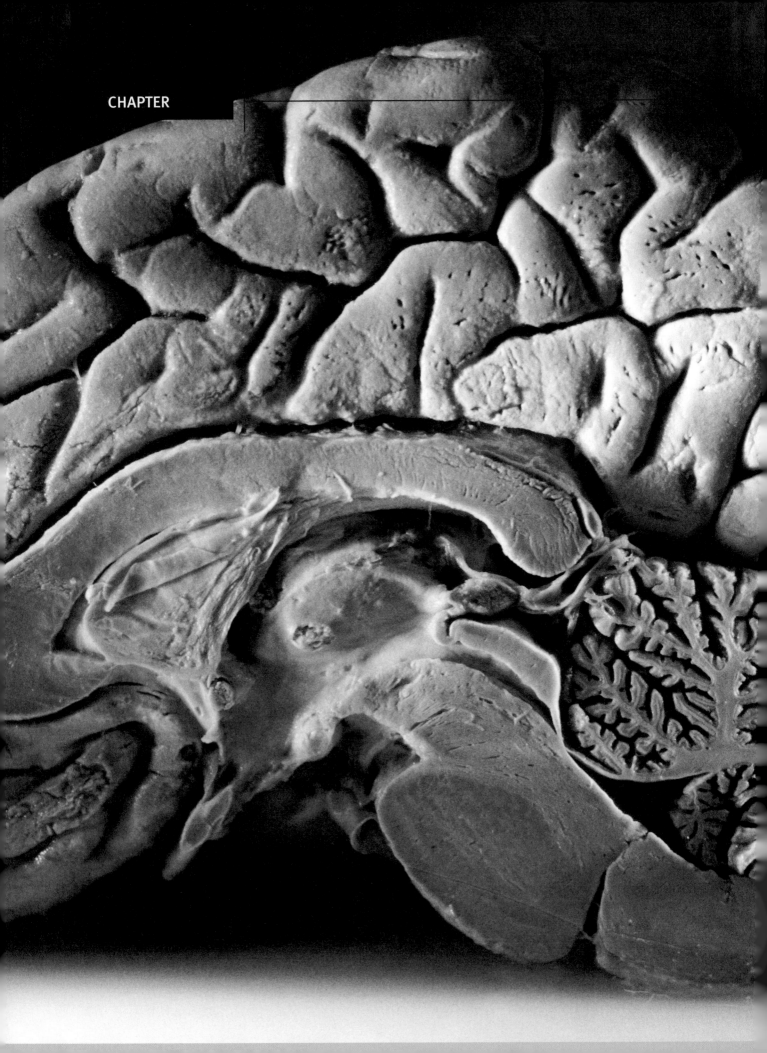

The brain, the Body, and Behavior

Chapter Outline

FREEZE FRAME

João da Silva kissed his 10-year-old daughter Nara—for what he later insisted would be the final time—2 hours and 10 minutes before stepping aboard Delta Flight 89 for Los Angeles on October 14, 1981. He had pulled her down from her treasured place atop his shoulders, turned her upside down, and grasped her by her ankles so she could walk on her hands. He finally let her plop down, giggling, on the carpet. He remembered all this, and numerous other seemingly trivial details, with poignant vividness.

Da Silva spent several weeks in Los Angeles, trying to negotiate a favorable contract to adapt a popular novel for a television mini-series, and then flew back to his home in San Francisco. As he waited for his luggage to appear at the airport baggage carousel, he decided to check his voice mail to see if any messages had arrived that day. What he heard caused his spine to freeze. The first message was from Nara's teacher at school. "I'm just calling to see if there is any news about Nara. If you get the chance, please call me." The next was from João's girlfriend, Reiko. "I just heard about Nara. I'll be at work, but I've arranged to be able to leave as soon as you get here." The next was from his ex-wife. "Call me as soon as you get back."

João slammed the receiver down, picked it up again, and called his ex-wife. "João, please stay calm. . . . Nara was hit by a car—she's hurt pretty badly, but it's going to be all right. They think she will live. I'll meet you at the hospital."

João left without waiting for his luggage, taking a cab straight to Mount Zion Hospital, where he found Nara in intensive care. She was unrecognizable—swollen, bloody, purple with bruises; surrounded by medical people, tubes, wires, oscilloscopes, and an atmosphere of fear. She had suffered head trauma and was unconscious. João lurched out of the room and came face to face with his ex-wife. He burst into tears, and the two parents embraced for the first time in almost 10 years.

Somewhat amazingly, considering the extent of her injuries, Nara not only survived, but completely recovered from her wounds and the emergency surgery she had required. Only a small scar at the edge of one eye and another at her rib cage remained as testimony to the accident. She was released from the hospital within a month. The doctors assured João and his ex-wife that the trauma to her brain had been mild, given a relatively short period of unconsciousness, and that no lasting damage had resulted.

But after eight months, João had to confront a certainty that something was, well, wrong with Nara. The only way that João could describe it was that Nara had "disappeared," leaving another child in her place. What was it exactly? In the past, various teachers and friends had described Nara in terms such as "hilarious and loving," "incredibly talented," "bubbly," "possibly brilliant," "just beautiful—so engaged in life," "almost like a young woman—thoughtful and perceptive."

Who, then, was Nara now? The first adjective that came to João was "flat." Her face had ceased to have much expression, her sense of humor was gone, and no objective observer could now describe her as "bubbly." Perhaps more worrisome, the "possibly brilliant" student had begun to get failing grades at school—and to be unapologetic about it when João came to her with her report card, mystified. She had dropped most of the friends she had once loved. Formerly a voracious reader, she now watched television with her mouth slack and her eyes lidded. She had occasional frightening outbursts of rage.

Had Nara reached the onset of puberty, João might have attributed all these things to "hormones" and "peer pressure." But Nara showed few signs of oncoming puberty.

Finally, João called his ex-wife. Very carefully, he broached the topic of the personality changes he had witnessed in Nara, sending out feelers, not wishing to commit to statements that would put him out on a limb. Surprisingly, Nara's mother began to weep, reciting a story in bits and pieces that matched João's in every detail. Nara had simply disappeared from the face of the earth, leaving someone else in her place.

Nara da Silva has experienced childhood personality change due to traumatic brain injury, a poorly understood event, but one that occurs in a surprising number of cases of head trauma (Chapman et al., 2010; Hawley, Ward, Magnay, & Long, 2004; Max et al., 2006). Often, personality change is temporary, resolving within several months, but sometimes—as with Nara da Silva—it does not resolve for years, if at all. How can a brain with "no lasting damage" produce radical and long-lasting personality change?

This is just one of the thousands of questions addressed by **neuroscience**, the scientific study of the nervous system and its most celebrated portion, the brain. The questions posed by neuroscientists—and answers provided—are highlighted in this chapter.

Neuroscience ▶ The multidisciplinary study of the nervous system.

Where Is the Mind?

"Have you lost your mind?"

People don't usually mean this question in a literal way when they ask it, but let's take it literally for a moment and consider the nature and "placement" of the mind. Where is it, anyway? Is it, or is it not, attached to the brain? All of us—scientists included—conduct our daily lives as though the brain and mind were in fact *dis*connected (Bloom, 2004). "My brain just won't cooperate with me," I complained to my wife last night because I was having difficulty finishing some writing. But where is this "me" with which my brain won't cooperate? How can I talk about "*my* brain" if "I" *am* my brain—or at least am created by my brain?

There Are Two Views about the Location of the Mind

Traditionally, there have been two basic positions on the connection between mind and the brain: *dualism* and *materialism*. Dualism, as developed by René Descartes and his followers during the 17th century and briefly mentioned in Chapter 1, holds that the body consists of matter, which may be objectively measured, while the mind consists of . . . *something else*. This "something else" takes up no space and has no material existence. It is a "ghost" in the "machinery" of the brain (Ryle, 1949).

We all may go about our business as though this were a perfectly reasonable idea. Nevertheless, as a description of reality dualism has been rejected by virtually all scientists and most modern philosophers for a few relatively simple reasons. For one thing, when you take certain substances into the body that affect the brain—drugs and alcohol, for example—these substances also affect the way you think and behave. If the brain and mind were not unified, there should be no reason why changes in brain chemistry should necessarily affect mental states. Moreover, modern neuroscientific evidence presented throughout this book demonstrates fairly conclusively that certain kinds of thoughts and actions are connected to activity in specific regions of the brain.

Finally, even Descartes realized that for a human being to function, the brain and the mind must interact somehow (Dennett, 1991). There must be a way for the "ghost" to talk to the "machine" and the "machine" to talk to the "ghost." But how can something with *no* material existence have a physical effect on something *entirely* material? Philosopher Daniel Dennett uses the cartoon character Casper the Friendly Ghost to demonstrate this idea (Dennett, 1991, p. 36). Casper can float through walls, and falling trees go right through him—yet he can catch wet clothing falling off a clothesline. Casper shouldn't be able to have it both ways—either he is immaterial or he is material. Even small children often catch this contradiction about Casper. The problem, in Dennett's words, is that "anything that can move a physical thing is itself a physical thing" (p. 35). This is why dualism is an unacceptable idea. Spirit may well exist, but if so, it cannot interact physically with matter.

In contrast to dualism, materialism holds that there is only one kind of "stuff" responsible for mind, and that is physical matter. What may seem to be detached from the brain is in some way a material expression of properties of the brain (Harris, 2012). Scientists have provided substantial evidence in favor of the materialist view of the mind. Consider the story of Matthew Nagle.

▲ **Limited "Mind-Reading" via Electrodes.** Electrodes surgically implanted in the right *precentral gyrus* of Matthew Nagle's brain receive signals that are then decoded by computer. This allows Nagle to use robotic limbs to move objects, manipulate a computer cursor, change television channels, and play simple video games—by *thinking* about these activities (Hochberg et al., 2006).

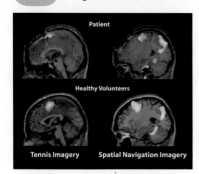

▲ **FIGURE 2.1** **Brain Activation in Supposedly Vegetative Patient.** These fMRI images depict neural activation of the brain of a supposedly vegetative patient in response to requests that she imagine herself playing a game of tennis and walking through the rooms of a house. *(Source: Owen et al., 2007, p. 1100.)*

Matthew was a star linebacker for the Weymouth High School football team in Weymouth, Massachusetts. During a July 4th celebration at Wessagussett Beach in 2001, Matthew came to the aid of a friend who had gotten into a fight with another young man. When Matthew approached his friend's attacker, the man stabbed Matthew with an 8-inch blade through the neck, severing his spinal cord. Matthew is now a tetraplegic. He cannot breathe without a respirator, and he will never regain the use of his arms or legs.

Matthew was undaunted, however. Mind-bogglingly, neuroscientists surgically implanted electrodes into Matthew's brain that allow him to draw on a video monitor, pick up objects with a robotic arm, change television channels, and play video games such as *Pong—merely by thinking about performing these activities* (Hochberg, 2008; Hochberg et al., 2006). The *cyberkenetic* "mind reading" technique used on Matthew Nagle has had only limited results, but it does provide evidence that the mind and brain are in some way unified.

QUESTIONS ABOUT THE PERSISTENT VEGETATIVE STATE

Further evidence of the unity of brain and mind is provided by *functional magnetic resonance imaging* (fMRI) studies of patients in apparent persistent vegetative states (PVS). A person in a PVS has suffered severe brain damage with coma. Although the person has technically awakened from the coma, he or she shows no signs of conscious awareness. However, some people diagnosed with PVS actually do retain some minimal awareness but are unable to communicate this awareness (Coleman et al., 2007; Owen et al., 2006, 2007). At least some type of minimal awareness in an apparently vegetative patient was documented by Adrian Owen and his colleagues. Among other tasks, they asked their (apparently unaware) patient to imagine she was playing tennis and walking through the rooms of her house. The regions of the patient's brain that were activated subsequent to these requests were identical to those activated in the brains of normal patients when asked to perform the same tasks (Owen et al., 2006, 2007; see Figure 2.1). Similar results were found by Martin Coleman and his colleagues, who documented language processing in the brains of several supposedly vegetative patients (Coleman et al., 2007).

DOES OUR BRAIN MAKE DECISIONS BEFORE "WE" DO?

Finally, a number of experiments conducted over the last several decades have shown that the brain begins to initiate the process of performing certain actions, or making certain choices or decisions, before the person becomes aware that he or she intends to perform the action or make the choice or decision (Harris, 2012). For example, researcher John-Dylan Haynes asked volunteers to spontaneously choose to press either of two buttons on a console as they watched letters scroll across a screen. The participants were instructed to record the name of the letter that happened to be visible on the screen at the exact moment they decided which button to press (Haynes, 2011). By using fMRI brain imaging technology (see pp. 104–105), Haynes found that he could predict which button a participant was going to decide to press *several seconds* before the person became aware that he or she was making the decision! Earlier brain imaging studies showed activity in the motor cortex—the area of the brain associated with physical movement—a fraction of a second before the conscious decision was actually made to make a physical motion such as lifting a finger (Libet, 1985).

Like Matthew Nagle's story and fMRI studies of supposedly vegetative patients, evidence of specific brain activity triggered prior to a person's becoming aware that he or she is making a decision leads inescapably to the common-sense idea that understanding the human brain is critical to understanding the human mind. The brain, however, does not perform its tasks alone. It is part of the coordinated effort of the human nervous system, to whose workings we now turn.

IN SUMMARY

1. Dualism, the view developed by René Descartes and his followers, holds that the body is material, but the mind is immaterial and not physically unified with the brain/body. Materialism holds that the mind is a physical, material product of the human brain.

2. Modern science has by and large rejected dualism as a description of mind. Several facts argue against dualism. First, when brain chemistry is altered, mental states are also often altered. Second, neuroscientific evidence suggests that specific kinds of thoughts and actions are connected to activity at specific brain regions, and these brain regions may begin to become active prior to the making of decisions to act. Third, there is a logical problem in proposing that an immaterial structure can affect and communicate with one that is material.

RETRIEVE!

1. How do the results of experimental treatment of tetraplegic Matthew Nagle support a materialist view of the mind? How do some recent fMRI studies of patients in persistent vegetative states also support this view?

How Is the Nervous System Built?

The human *nervous system* is a complex biological system designed for communication—nearly instantaneous communication throughout the human body. Intricate and beautifully integrated communication pathways, which rival astral galaxies in complexity and mystery, coordinate the activity of our muscles, internal organs, and sensory systems. It is through this "interior universe" of intricate networks that we are able to think, feel, respond to the world, and initiate action. The nervous system tells us we are hungry and then allows us to bring lasagna-laden forks to our mouths. The nervous system allows us to distinguish our cat with the injured left ear from his intact sister, and to walk across the room to pet him. The nervous system tells our hearts to race as we watch *Dawn of the Dead*, brings tears to our eyes at the closing of *Pride and Prejudice*, and lets us take both of these films out of the DVD drive if they leave us cold. The nervous system triggers joy at the sight of a loved one and pain on separation. It does all of these things seemingly without effort.

The Nervous System Is Composed of Cells

What are the structures that make up the internal cosmos of the human nervous system? Like all structures of living beings, the nervous system is composed of *cells*, the basic units of all living matter. However, the cells of the nervous system are specialized. The cell type known as the **neuron** plays the principal role in allowing communication to take place throughout the nervous system and the bodily structures with which the nervous system communicates. The neuron receives information and transmits it to other cells. In the past it was thought that the cells of the nervous system were connected, creating a long, unbroken communication pathway. A Spanish physician named Santiago Ramón y Cajal (1852–1934)—an important founder of the field of *neuroscience*—discovered that neurons were independent entities. Although it

Neuron ▶ The cell type that transmits information throughout the nervous system.

is not possible to estimate accurately the number of these entities in the nervous system, the figure usually given for the brain alone is well over 100 billion (Larsen et al., 2006). This exceeds the number of stars in our galaxy! The number of possible ways these 100 billion neurons can communicate runs into the hundreds of trillions.

What is so astonishing about neurons, other than their sheer number, is this: They do not pass on complex pieces of information. If a neuronal message could be translated, it would not read, "This is an important job interview, try to appear relaxed—don't play with your hair and don't cross your arms against your body." The messages neurons pass along to other neurons, if translated, would read only "fire" or "don't fire." Yet the end effect of these communication chains is often massively complex. Like computers, which can generate multicolored video images using binary codes containing only 1s and 0s, the neuron does its work by turning itself on (firing) or off (not firing). Three types of neurons make up the nervous system: *motor neurons, sensory neurons,* and *interneurons.*

MOTOR NEURONS

Motor neuron ▶ A neuron primarily responsible for communication to the muscles and organs.

Motor neurons are the main channel of communication to the muscles and organs of the body. Motor neurons carry commands for actions, actions of which you may or may not be aware. For example, when you chew your food, motor neurons convey orders to your jaw muscles. But after you swallow the chewed food, motor neurons continue—without your awareness—to help the process of digestion along as the food moves through your digestive system and is broken down by that system.

SENSORY NEURONS

Sensory neuron ▶ A neuron that transmits sensory information to the brain.

For each of your senses there are special **sensory neurons** which work to convert physical energy (or chemicals, in the case of the senses of *smell* and *taste*) into information in a form that may be transmitted along chains of neurons to the brain. Your brain is completely isolated from the physical world; sensory neurons bring the world to your brain. Sounds, sights, and sensations are all transformed into electrochemical signals—the only language your brain understands.

INTERNEURONS

Interneuron ▶ Communicates only with adjacent neurons.

Motor neurons communicate with the muscles and organs, and sensory neurons relay sensory information to the brain, but **interneurons** communicate only with *other neurons* that are in a more or less adjacent position. They do not extend long distances, as do motor and sensory neurons. These neurons "pass messages on." Interneurons are vastly more numerous than motor and sensory neurons, however. The majority of those 100 billion total neurons in the brain are interneurons.

Dendrites ▶ The branch-like projections of neurons that receive electrochemical stimulation from other neurons.

Neurons Have an Anatomy

Although neurons come in three types and differ somewhat in appearance, with a few exceptions they share the same components as the motor neuron depicted in Figure 2.2 and described next: *dendrites, cell body, axon,* and *terminal.*

Synaptic receptors ▶ Openings that are embedded in the dendrites of neurons to which neurotransmitters bind during the process of neuronal communication.

DENDRITES

Cell body (*soma*) ▶ The bulb-like end of the neuron containing the cell nucleus. Energy for the neuron is generated here, and waste is eliminated.

Dendrites (literally, "branches") reach out from the neuron *cell body*, as depicted in Figure 2.2. The dendrites are covered with tiny openings called **synaptic receptors** which are embedded in their membranes. Synaptic receptors are designed to receive information in the form of chemical signals released from other neurons.

CELL BODY (SOMA)

The **cell body**, also called the *soma*, contains the *nucleus* of the cell, where most genetic information is stored. It is also here that information from the many surrounding neurons is collected and integrated, to be transmitted by electrical signal across the length of the neuron along the neuron's *axon*.

AXON

The **axon** of a neuron is a narrow extension that transmits information as *neural impulses* from the cell body to other neurons. Enclosed bundles of axons create communication channels extending from the furthest tips of our limbs deep into to the brain and spinal cord. These communication channels are called **tracts** when neural communication occurs *within* the brain or spinal cord (the *central nervous system* as described on pp. 69–70), and **nerves** when communication occurs in points *outside* of the brain or spinal cord (the *peripheral nervous system* as described on pp. 70–73). As an example, the bundle of axons leaving the eye to transmit visual signals to the brain is called the *optic nerve*. Once the axon bundle reaches within the brain, it is called the *optic tract*.

Not all neurons have axons—some interneurons lack them—and axons vary in length from less than an inch to several feet long. However, each neuron has only one axon. The axons of certain neurons may be wrapped in a **myelin sheath**. **Myelin** is a fatty substance that allows neural impulses to travel far more rapidly than they otherwise would. However, the myelin sheath does not cover the entire axon. The sheath has gaps of about 1 micrometer (millionth of a meter), giving the axon a "sausage-like" appearance as in Figure 2.3. The point at which a gap occurs is called the **node of Ranvier**. In the central nervous system disease *multiple sclerosis* (MS), the myelin sheaths are "attacked" by the body's own immune defenses, leading to *demyelenation*. Loss of myelin prevents effective communication between neurons, leading to a very large number of potential debilitating physical and mental symptoms.

TERMINAL

The axon ends in a small, branching, bulb-like structure called the **terminal**. The terminal releases chemical messengers known as *neurotransmitters*, which do the job of transmitting information in chemical form that began as electrical neural impulses. The surface of the terminal faces the dendrites of its neighboring neurons. This point at which one sending, and one receiving, neuron meet is known as the **synapse**. The fluid-filled gap between the terminal of the sending neuron and the dendrite of the receiving neuron is unimaginably small—less than one millionth of an inch. This is the **synaptic gap**, the space over which the neurons pass on their chemical signals. We will look more closely how neurotransmitters pass on their chemical messages a bit later.

Glia Assist Neurons in Their Work

Neurons are not the only type of cell in the nervous system. **Glia** outnumber neurons (including interneurons) by anywhere from 10–1 to 50–1, depending on which part of the nervous system is being considered. Glial cells are smaller than neurons, and they lack axons and dendrites. Although glial cells were discovered over 100 years ago, their actual functions are only beginning to be understood (Angulo, Kozlov, Charpak, & Audinat, 2004; Pfrieger, 2002). In somewhat simplified terms, glial cells assist neurons in their work. First, they build the myelin sheath which surrounds the axon of certain neurons, as just described. They also help supply neurons with nutrients and oxygen, may stimulate repair of damaged neurons, and greatly promote communication between neurons by helping to develop and maintain

Axon ▶ A narrow extension in many neurons that transmits electrical neural impulses from cell body to terminal.

Tract ▶ A bundle of axons (usually enclosed in a myelin sheath) that forms a communication channel within the central nervous system (brain or spine).

Nerve ▶ An enclosed bundle of axons forming a communication channel within the peripheral nervous system (outside of the brain or spine).

Myelin sheath ▶ Fatty substance surrounding the axon of some neurons. Myelin increases the speed of neuronal transmission.

Node of Ranvier ▶ The gap between myelin sheaths of axon segments.

Terminal ▶ The small bulb-like structure at the end of neuron axons that contains the vesicles from which neurotransmitters are released.

Synapse ▶ The juncture of the presynaptic and postsynaptic neuron.

Synaptic gap ▶ The miniscule space over which neurons pass their neurotransmitters, from the terminal of the presynaptic neuron to the dendrites of the postsynaptic neuron.

Glia ▶ Cell type that builds the myelin sheath that surrounds the axon of some neurons, and helps to develop and maintain neuron synapses.

▶ **FIGURE 2.2** Anatomy of a Motor Neuron.

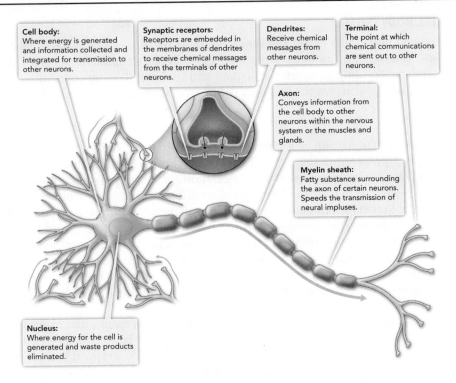

Cell body: Where energy is generated and information collected and integrated for transmission to other neurons.

Synaptic receptors: Receptors are embedded in the membranes of dendrites to receive chemical messages from the terminals of other neurons.

Dendrites: Receive chemical messages from other neurons.

Terminal: The point at which chemical communications are sent out to other neurons.

Axon: Conveys information from the cell body to other neurons within the nervous system or the muscles and glands.

Myelin sheath: Fatty substance surrounding the axon of certain neurons. Speeds the transmission of neural impluses.

Nucleus: Where energy for the cell is generated and waste products eliminated.

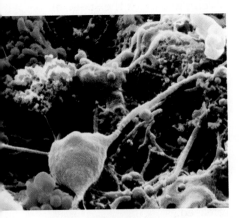

▲ **Magnified Glial Cells.** Glia greatly outnumber neurons in the human body, but they do not carry messages themselves. Instead, they assist neurons in their work by building the myelin sheath, supplying neurons with oxygen and nutrients, stimulating repair of damaged neurons, and maintaining and developing neuronal synapses.

Action potential ▶ The electrical impulse that conveys information from one neuron to another, or from the neuron to bodily muscles and glands.

synapses—the juncture of one neuron sending a signal and another receiving the signal (Pyka, Busse, Seidenbecher, Gundelfinger, & Faissner, 2011; Ullian, Sapperstein, Christopherson, & Barres, 2001). In all, they are likely to play a much larger role in central nervous system functioning than once believed (Pack & Pawson, 2010).

The Action Potential: How Neurons Do Their Work

Neural communication is electrochemical—it has electrical and chemical aspects. The electrical aspect occurs when the neuron generates ("fires") an **action potential**, an electrical impulse that travels from the point where the axon exits the cell body (the axon hillock), to the axon's terminal. This impulse conveys information from the dendrites and cell body—information that will then be transmitted by chemical messengers (neurotransmitters) to other neurons. When we speak of the "firing of a neuron," we are talking about the firing of an action potential, and when we talk of a "neural impulse" it is to a fired action potential that we are referring.

The action potential is an all-or-nothing process, meaning that neurons have only two settings—*on* or *off*. They are either firing or resting. The default setting of a neuron is resting, known as **resting potential**. A minimum level of intensity of stimulation from other neurons is require to successfully "light the fuse" of an action potential—a *threshold of stimulation* that must be met to cause a neuron to fire. At any moment, a neuron may be receiving both *excitatory* (stimulating) and *inhibitory* ("anti-stimulating") messages from surrounding neurons. It sums the information it is getting, and if the "go" signals outweigh the "hold" signals, the neuron will generate an action potential.

POLARIZATION AND DEPOLARIZATION

To understand how the neuron fires an action potential, picture the neuron bathed in fluid from inside and outside of the cell membrane. This fluid contains **ions**—atomic particles that may carry either negative or positive charges. At resting potential, negatively charged ions build up along the inside of the cell membrane. These negatively charged ions attract positively charged ions

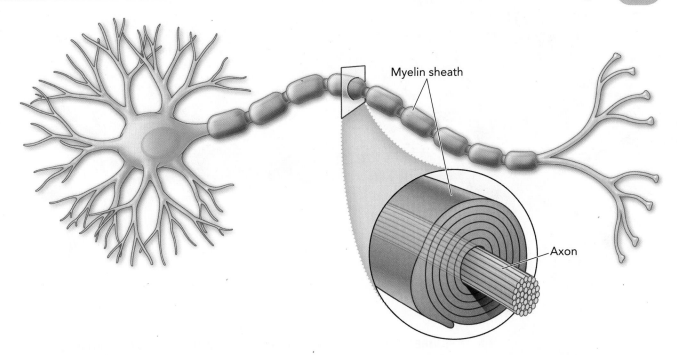

▲ FIGURE 2.3 The Myelin Sheath. The axons of many neurons are wrapped in a fatty substance called *myelin* that greatly speeds transmission of impulses along the axon.

from outside the neuron, causing the positively charged ions to build up in the surrounding fluid. The increase in positively charged ions outside the neuron creates a resting potential balance between a somewhat higher proportion of positive charges outside, and negative charges inside the neuron. This balanced condition, known as **polarization**, is depicted in Figure 2.4.

The most important of the ions contributing to the resting potential are *potassium* (K^+) and *sodium* (Na^+). If both of these positively charged ions could move freely though the membrane of the neuron, they would change the balance of positive and negative within the neuron and disrupt polarization. As it happens, potassium ions (K^+) *do* permeate the cell membrane fairly easily through special segments along the membrane of the neuron known as *ion channels*.

Ion channels are specialized, with one type for potassium (K^+) and another for sodium (Na^+). The potassium channel is highly permeable, allowing potassium (K^+) ions to pass across the neuron membrane. The reason that polarization is not disrupted by the entry of these positively charged ions is that the membrane strongly resists the passage of sodium (Na^+) ions through sodium channels to the inside of the neuron. Instead, most sodium ions that may exist within the cell are pumped *out* through a sodium channel "pump" faster than potassium ions enter. This maintains the balance between negative and positive charges that characterizes polarization (Huxley, 1959; see Figure 2.5).

Polarization comes to a spectacular but extraordinarily brief end when the neuron receives, through its dendrites, an abundance of excitatory signals from other neurons—reaching the threshold of stimulation. At that moment, the sodium ion channels closest to the *axon hillock*—the point where the axon emerges from the cell body—become open to sodium for an infinitesimal fraction of a second, allowing these positively charged ions free entry into the neuron. Sodium ions flood the neuron at the axon hillock, increasing the presence of positively charged ions dramatically. Fittingly, this event is termed **depolarization**. Depolarization begins the firing of the action potential; it is depicted in Figure 2.6.

The action potential now begins to travel down the length of the axon from the hillock. Its electrical charge triggers the opening of the next group of sodium ion channels "down the line," allowing sodium to rush in, depolarizing the axon at this next point, and firing a new axon potential to carry on for the

Resting potential ▶ The "default" resting setting of a neuron—the setting that would be maintained if no action potentials were fired.

Ion ▶ An atomic particle that carries primarily a positive or negative electrical charge.

Polarization ▶ The resting potential balance between primarily negatively charged ions within a neuron and positively charged ions without.

Depolarization ▶ A disruption of the resting potential balance between negatively and positively charged ions within and outside of the neuron. Depolarization begins the process of the firing of an action potential.

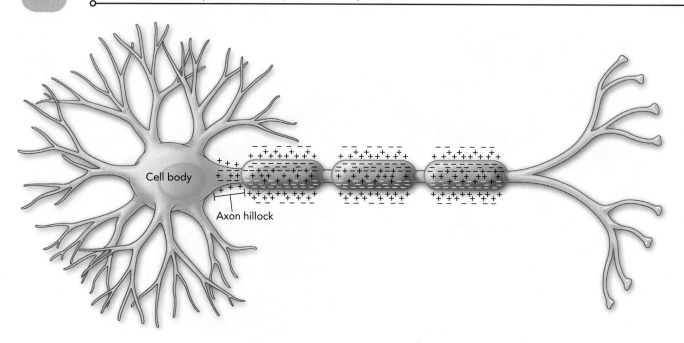

Cell body

Axon hillock

▲ **FIGURE 2.4 The Motor Neuron at Resting Potential.** A neuron at resting potential is said to be *polarized*, meaning that there is a balance between negatively charged ions on the inside of the neuron and positively charged ions on the outside.

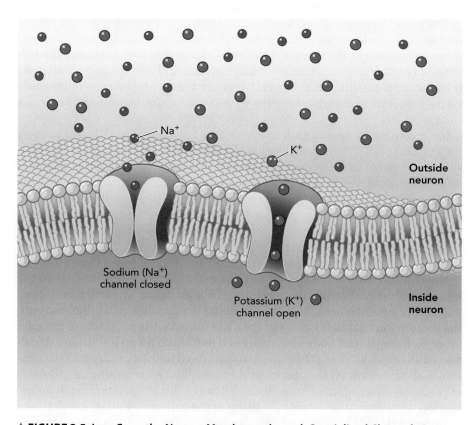

Na$^+$

K$^+$

Outside neuron

Sodium (Na$^+$) channel closed

Potassium (K$^+$) channel open

Inside neuron

▲ **FIGURE 2.5 Ions Cross the Neuron Membrane through Specialized Channels.** Ions enter and exit the neuron through channels specialized for each type of ion. However, the neuron membrane is *selectively permeable*—potassium (K$^+$) ions cross the neuron membrane relatively freely, but sodium (Na$^+$) ions are restricted in their passage until the moment of depolarization.

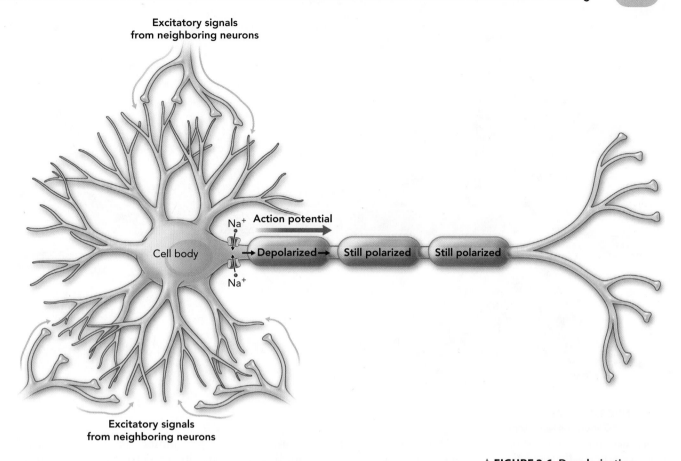

▲ FIGURE 2.6 Depolarization of the Neuron. When the neuron receives an abundance of excitatory signals from other neurons, reaching or exceeding the threshold of stimulation, depolarization occurs, firing an action potential.

previous one. Thus, at each point of depolarization, a new action potential is formed by the activity of the previous one. This allows the neural message to continue rushing toward its terminal in the manner of a relay race or a series of toppling dominoes. Once a new action potential is fired along the neuron, the previous length of neuron immediately reassumes its resting, polarized state—just like a relay runner dropping out of the race once the baton is passed to the next runner. This process is referred to as *repolarization*. Figure 2.7 depicts the triggering of action potentials along the length of the neuron.

Neurotransmitters Send the Signal

We can now look more closely at the work of **neurotransmitters**. Just below the surface of the axon's terminal are a very large number of tiny sacs (called *vesicles*) which contain neurotransmitters—the chemical substances that carry neural signals from one neuron to the next across the synapse (juncture) of two neurons. When the action potential reaches the terminal, depolarization in the action potential signals the terminal's vesicles to open, spilling neurotransmitter molecules into the synapse. Although it was once believed that the vesicles of each neuron release only one type of neurotransmitter, in fact, combinations of neurotransmitters may be released (e.g., Nishimaru, Restrepo, Ryge, Yanagawa, & Kiehn, 2005).

Once they are spilled from the vesicles of the "sending" neuron, known as the **presynaptic neuron**, some of the neurotransmitters will cross the (infinitesimally small) synaptic gap and *bind*, or attach themselves, to synaptic receptors in the dendrites of the "receiving" neuron, known as the **postsynaptic neuron**. These receptors are specialized to receive specific neurotransmitters only. As depicted in Figure 2.8, this is a lock-and-key sort of event. The neurotransmitter will not bind to receptors that do not match its molecular shape.

Neurotransmitter ▶ Chemical substances that carry neural signals from one neuron to another across a neuronal synapse.

Presynaptic neuron ▶ The "sending" neuron in neuronal communication.

Postsynaptic neuron ▶ The "receiving" neuron in neuronal communication.

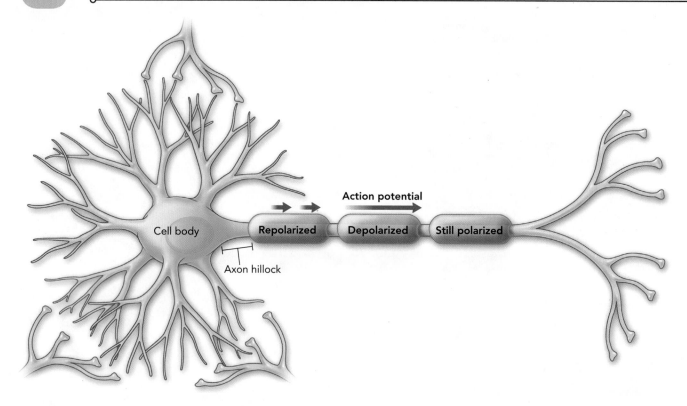

▲ **FIGURE 2.7** **The Action Potential Generates New Action Potentials.** The initial action potential causes new action potentials to be fired along the length of the neuron in the manner of a relay race or a series of falling dominoes. Note that as each new action potential is fired, the previous length of the neuron instantly becomes polarized once again (repolarized).

Reuptake ▶ When the presynaptic neuron reabsorbs some of the neurotransmitter molecules it has released, following binding of the neurotransmitter to receptor sites in the postsynaptic neuron.

Agonist ▶ Any substance that mimics the action of a neurotransmitter and binds to the neurotransmitter receptor.

Antagonist ▶ Any substance that blocks the receptors of a particular neurotransmitter, decreasing the availability and effects of the neurotransmitter.

However, each neurotransmitter may "fit" a number of different "locks," and its effects will differ according to the specific receptor to which it binds. When a neurotransmitter binds to certain types of receptors located at certain sites within the nervous system, the effect on the neuron may be inhibitory—preventing the neuron from firing. But when the same neurotransmitter binds to other receptors, the effect may be excitatory, generating an action potential in the postsynaptic neuron.

What this means is that the same neurotransmitter has different consequences depending on its receptor in the postsynaptic neuron. As an example, the neurotransmitter *serotonin* has *at least* 16 subtypes of receptors located throughout the nervous system (Naughton, Mulrooney, & Leonard, 2000). Consequently, as summarized in Table 2.1, serotonin has various sorts of effects, including influences on sleep, nausea and vomiting, appetite, and sexual desire. It may also be involved in the regulation of anxiety, aggression, and mood.

Once a neurotransmitter exerts an effect on the postsynaptic neuron, it does not hang around to watch the show. Most neurotransmitter molecules are immediately reabsorbed by the presynaptic neuron, a process known as **reuptake**, or converted into inactive chemicals by various enzymes. Certain drugs, such as the antidepressant drugs known as *selective serotonin reuptake inhibitors* (SSRIs), intentionally block this reuptake process to allow the neurotransmitter to keep flooding the receptor site of the postsynaptic neuron.

The entire process of communication between neurons through neurotransmitter activity, from the firing of an action potential to the release and reuptake of neurotransmitters, is summarized in Figure 2.9.

NEUROTRANSMITTERS AND DRUGS

Some drugs alter the effects of neurotransmitters in various ways. When a drug such as the SSRIs just described increases the effects of a neurotransmitter, the drug is known as an **agonist** for that neurotransmitter. Drugs that *decrease* the effects of a neurotransmitter are known as **antagonists**.

Table 2.1 **A Quick Guide to Some Important Neurotransmitters**

This table includes some of the known (and suspected) functions of eight neurotransmitters.

NEUROTRANSMITTER	PRIMARY FUNCTIONS
Acetylcholine	Regulation of muscular activity, learning, and memory
Dopamine	Regulates how we respond to rewarding activities (the "reward system" and experiences of pleasure); affects attention, learning, and memory processes; and helps regulate bodily movement
Endorphins	Opiate-like neurotransmitters that provide analgesia (pain relief) and a sense of well-being
GABA (gamma-aminobutryric acid)	Tends to inhibit the firing of neurons and keeps the overexcitation of neurons in check; GABA-agonist drugs induce relaxation, intoxicating effects, relief from anxiety
Glutamate	Tends to increase the speed and rate of neural transmission throughout the nervous system; increases efficiency of learning and memory
Norepinephrine	Affects attention and impulsivity, learning and memory; helps regulate involuntary responses to stress
Serotonin	Affects mood (possibly including depression), sleep, nausea/vomiting, appetite, sexual behavior; may affect aggression
Substance P	Helps regulate the experience of pain
Oxytocin	Reduces blood pressure and other indicators of stress; may be involved in promoting maternal behavior, bonding between mother and infant, and feelings of love (see pp. 98–100 for more on oxytocin)

(Sources: Hardman, Limbird, & Gilman, 2001; Tobler, Fiorillo, & Schultz 2005; Ordway, Schwartz, & Frazer, 2007; Svenningsson, Chergui, Rachleff, Flajolet et al., 2006.)

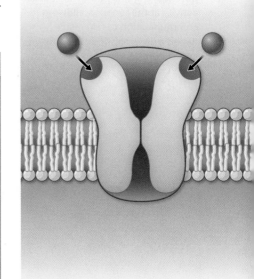

▲ **FIGURE 2.8 Binding of Neurotransmitters to Receptor Sites Is a "Lock-and-Key" Event.** Receptors in the dendrites of the postsynaptic neuron are specialized to receive specific neurotransmitter only. The shape of the neurotransmitter molecule precisely "fits" that of the receptor site.

There are many ways in which a drug may increase or decrease neurotransmitter effects. For example, drug agonists may block the reuptake of a neurotransmitter, as is the case for the SSRI antidepressant drugs, or they may increase synthesis (production) of the neurotransmitter within the vesicles of the presynaptic neuron. This allows more of the neurotransmitter to be spilled out into the synapse. The stimulant *amphetamine*, described in greater detail in Chapter 6, is thought by some researchers to exert its effects in this way, in part by increasing the quantity of the neurotransmitter *dopamine* that is released into the synapse (Rothman & Baumann, 2006).

Quite frequently, an agonist drug mimics the effects of a particular neurotransmitter by binding to postsynaptic neuron receptor sites that the neurotransmitter would ordinarily occupy, directly activating the site. As an example, the *opioid* drugs *morphine* and *heroin*, which provide pain relief and a sense of euphoria, as described in Chapter 6, exert their effects in part by binding to receptor sites (*opioid receptors*). These receptors are ordinarily occupied by a class of neurotransmitters known as **endorphins**, which are associated with pain relief (Pert & Snyder, 1973).

Like the agonists, neurotransmitter *antagonists* may work in a number of ways. They may block the synthesis of the neurotransmitter within the

Endorphin ▶ A neurotransmitter that binds to the same receptor sites as opioid drugs and is associated with relief from pain.

▶ **FIGURE 2.9 Communication Between Two Neurons.** An action potential triggers neurotransmitter activity at the synapse, allowing communication to take place between a presynaptic and a postsynaptic neuron.

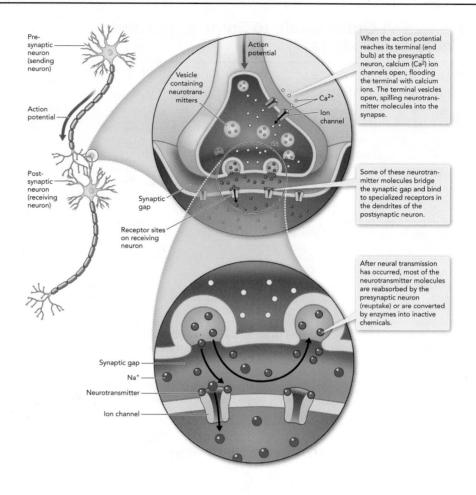

▶ **FIGURE 2.10 Neurotransmitter Agonists and Antagonists.** Drugs that facilitate the effects of neurotransmitters are known as *agonists*. Those that decrease the effects of neurotransmitters are known as *antagonists*.

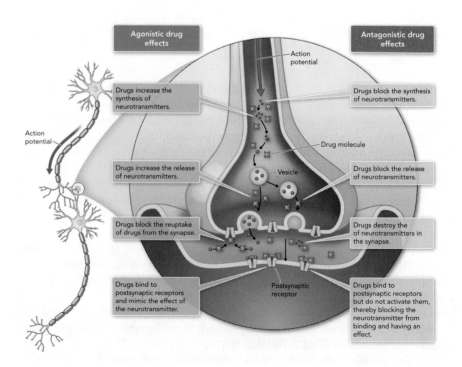

◀**Dopamine and Rewarding Activities.** Among its many functions, the neurotransmitter dopamine is released while engaging in rewarding activities, including eating, psychoactive drug use, romantic behavior, and listening to music.

presynaptic neuron, block its release at the synapse, or destroy it immediately following its release. Most intriguingly, antagonists may prevent a neurotransmitter from binding to receptor sites by "getting there first." Consider the drug *naloxone*, an antagonist for the opioid drugs which bind to endorphin receptor sites. Naloxone occupies these receptor sites by mimicking the structure of these opioid drugs. However, while naloxone does occupy endorphin receptor sites, it does not activate them. Naloxone molecules are like someone sleeping on a park bench, thereby preventing anyone else from sitting there. Thus, naloxone is used in treatment of addiction to drugs such as heroin and morphine. It blocks their effects to discourage their use. Naloxone is also effective as a treatment for overdoses of these drugs (Ashton & Hassan, 2006; Kerr, Kelly, Dietze, Damien, & Barger, 2009). See Figure 2.10 for a depiction of how agonist and antagonist drugs work.

NEUROTRANSMITTERS AND MENTAL LIFE

Neurotransmitters have far-ranging effects on mental life. For example, as already mentioned, the neurotransmitter serotonin has a range of different effects depending on the receptor to which it binds. Another important neurotransmitter, *dopamine*, is involved in learning, memory, attention, and problem solving. Dopamine also helps regulate muscle contraction and movement, and is an important component of our reward systems, the areas of the brain that enable us to experience pleasure. Dopamine is released when we listen to appealing music, gaze at a romantic partner, are presented with delicious food, or use "recreational" psychoactive drugs (Aron et al., 2005; Koob & Le Moal, 2008; Menon & Levitin, 2005). Indeed, dopamine is agonized (promoted) directly or indirectly by almost every pleasurable psychoactive drug, from cocaine to nicotine to ecstasy (MDMA) and LSD, opioids and beyond (e.g., Liechti & Vollenweider, 2000; Koob & Le Moal, 2008).

The neurotransmitter GABA (*gamma-aminobutyric acid*) operates primarily by inhibiting brain neurons from firing (although it serves some excitatory functions as well). In a sense, GABA quiets brain activity. Drugs that tend to produce relaxation or sedation, such as alcohol or *benzodiazepines* (used for the treatment of anxiety and sleeplessness), are GABA agonists and bind to GABA receptor sites. Thus, psychological states such as anxiety and panic may be associated with faulty regulation of GABA neurotransmitter systems. However, this association has not been demonstrated conclusively, and even if true it would not imply that vitamin supplements purportedly containing

GABA are effective treatments for anxiety. They are not (and their safety is questionable). GABA taken orally is unlikely ever to reach the brain because GABA does not cross the *blood-brain barrier* very well. The blood-brain barrier is formed by a group of tightly packed cells that restrict the entry of substances from the blood stream into the brain, and glial cells surrounding brain capillaries which hinder the transport of molecules to and from the brain. The inability of GABA to cross this barrier is one of the reasons that virtually all of it is produced in the brain, unlike many other neurotransmitters.

For a summary guide to the functions of some important neurotransmitters, see Table 2.1.

IN SUMMARY

1.	Neurons and glia are cells that allow communication to occur throughout the nervous system and the rest of the body. Neurons receive and transmit information. Glia assist neurons in their work by building myelin sheaths and developing and maintaining synapses.
2.	Nerves are communication channels made up of chains of neurons. Three types of neurons make up these chains: motor neurons, sensory neurons, and interneurons.
3.	In general, neurons are constructed of the following components: dendrites, cell body, axon, and terminal.
4.	Neural communication is electrochemical. It begins when a neuron fires an action potential. The action potential conveys information in electrical form to the terminal of the presynaptic neuron. This stimulates the release of neurotransmitters from the neuron's vesicles. The neurotransmitters spill into the synapse, some crossing the synaptic gap and binding to receptor sites in the postsynaptic neuron. The "message" received by the postsynaptic neuron may be excitatory or inhibitory, depending on the type of receptor and the placement of the neuron within the nervous system. If the "message" received is excitatory, the postsynaptic neuron will fire an action potential. Otherwise, it will remain at resting potential.
5.	Neurotransmitter agonists increase the effectiveness of neurotransmitters, while antagonists decrease their effectiveness.
6.	Neurotransmitters are important regulators of psychological life.

RETRIEVE!

1.	How do the functions of motor neurons, sensory neurons, and interneurons differ? Which type of neuron is most numerous?
2.	How do the functions of neurons and glia differ? What is the purpose of the myelin sheath?
3.	**a)** The _____ is a narrow extension of the neuron along which the action potential travels. Bundles of these extensions create communication channels called _____. **b)** The surface of a neuron's _____ faces the dendrites of the neighboring neuron.
4.	How is an action potential generated? Include mention of potassium and sodium, polarization, depolarization, and repolarization.

5.	Describe three ways that neurotransmitter agonists and antagonists may exert their effects. (Refer to Figure 2.10.)	
6.	Connect the neurotransmitter with its effect or function. (Refer to Table 2.1.)	
	Norepinephrine	Regulates responses to rewarding activities and pleasurable activities; affects attention, learning, and memory processes.
	Serotonin	Opiate-like neurotransmitters that provide pain relief and sense of well-being.
	Endorphins	Affects mood, sleep, nausea/vomiting, appetite, and sexual behavior. May affect aggression.
	Dopamine	Keeps over-excitation of neurons in check; when agonized by drugs may induce relaxation, intoxication, and relief from anxiety.
	GABA	Affects attention and impulsivity, learning and memory, helps regulate stress response.

How Is the Nervous System Organized?

We have seen how neurons and glia, the building blocks of the nervous system, are constructed to allow communication to occur throughout the body. But these building blocks are organized into interconnected systems and subsystems—the pathways of the nervous system. The organization of these systems and subsystems is depicted in Figure 2.11.

As you can see from Figure 2.11, the whole nervous system has two major divisions: the *central nervous system* and the *peripheral nervous system*. While the central and peripheral nervous systems are anatomically distinct, in actuality they are highly interdependent, and neither could do its work without the other.

The Central Nervous System Is "Command Central"

The **central nervous system** (CNS), consisting of the *brain* and *spinal cord*, is a "command central" of sorts. It receives information from the peripheral nervous system, organizes and interprets the information, and then sends "instructions" back to the peripheral nervous system to take actions or make adjustments to various bodily functions. The brain—to which I devote an entire section later in the chapter—is the source of all thought, emotion, memory, learning, and almost all human action. It controls all voluntary and most involuntary movement and bodily functions, including breathing and the beating of the heart.

The **spinal cord**—which acts primarily as a communication pathway between the brain and the rest of the body—is a thin, tubular bundle of nerve tracts organized in segments. These segments are protected by the *vertebrae* and *discs* of the *spinal column*, the stack of bones which runs from the base of the skull to the lower back just above the pelvis. The spinal cord is composed of two types of tissue mass. As depicted in Figure 2.12, the interior of the spinal cord consists primarily of **gray matter**—cell bodies, unmyelinated axons, dendrites, and glia. The gray matter of the spinal cord is surrounded

Central nervous system (CNS) ▶ The brain and spinal cord. Organizes and interprets the information received from peripheral nervous system (PNS) and sends commands back to the PNS to take actions or make adjustments to bodily functions.

Spinal cord ▶ Thin, tubular bundle of nerve tracts contained in the vertebrae of the spinal column.

Gray matter ▶ Cell bodies, unmyelinated axons, dendrites, and glia.

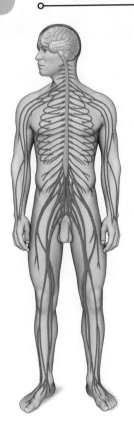

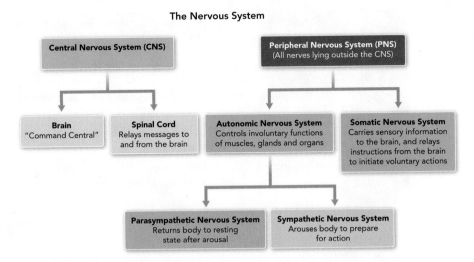

The Nervous System

```
                    Central Nervous System (CNS)          Peripheral Nervous System (PNS)
                                                          (All nerves lying outside the CNS)

        Brain              Spinal Cord        Autonomic Nervous System      Somatic Nervous System
    "Command Central"   Relays messages to    Controls involuntary functions  Carries sensory information
                        and from the brain    of muscles, glands and organs   to the brain, and relays
                                                                              instructions from the brain
                                                                              to initiate voluntary actions

                                    Parasympathetic Nervous System    Sympathetic Nervous System
                                    Returns body to resting            Arouses body to prepare
                                    state after arousal                for action
```

▲ **FIGURE 2.11 The Central and Peripheral Nervous Systems.** An intricate mechanism designed for nearly instantaneous communication throughout the body, the nervous system is organized into two main systems: The central nervous system (shown in yellow) and the peripheral nervous system (shown in purple).

White matter ▶ Axons with myelin sheaths.

Spinal reflexes ▶ Automatic motor actions in response to stimulation. Spinal reflexes bypass the brain entirely.

Central pattern generators ▶ Circuits of neurons that generate routine, rhythmic movements and are controlled entirely by the spine with no input from the brain.

Peripheral nervous system ▶ Cranial and spinal nerves that allow communication to take place between the brain and body. Consists of two divisions: somatic nervous system and autonomic nervous system.

primarily by **white matter**—axons with myelin sheaths allowing for swifter communication. Therefore, gray matter is responsible for collecting and integrating information, while white matter is responsible for transmitting that information.

The principal function of the spinal cord is to send information from the skin, organs, and muscles to the brain, and to convey motor commands back. If the spinal cord is cut at any point, the brain will no longer perceive sensation at that point and below, and the muscles and organs at that point and below will no longer respond to motor commands from the brain.

However, communication to and from the brain is not the only function of the spinal cord. The spinal cord also controls certain **spinal reflexes**—muscle contractions that result in involuntary movement and occur in response to stimulation. These motor actions are automatic and not controlled by the brain. For example, when a doctor strikes your knee with a rubber mallet and your leg kicks, that's the spinal cord, not the brain, working. The spine controls numerous other reflexes—for example, quickly withdrawing the hand from a source of pain. These and similar reflexes evolved to protect our bodies from various threats from the time of infancy.

In addition to spinal reflexes, the spine is responsible for a number of **central pattern generators**—circuits of neurons (or single neurons) that generate routine, common rhythmic movements such as moving the legs while walking (Barrière, Leblond, Provencher, & Rossignol, 2008; Marder & Bucher, 2001). Infants who are not yet able to walk will nonetheless execute walking movements if placed on a treadmill because of central pattern generators in the spine (Lamb & Yang, 2000). The point is that spinal reflexes are responses to stimulation and may result in many types of behaviors, whereas central pattern generators generate repetitive, rhythmic movements only. Figure 2.13 shows the anatomy of the spinal cord and spinal column, and helps clarify the difference between reflexes and central pattern generators.

The Peripheral Nervous System Connects Brain, Body, and the Environment

The communication between brain and body that the spinal cord makes possible is organized by the **peripheral nervous system**. The peripheral nervous

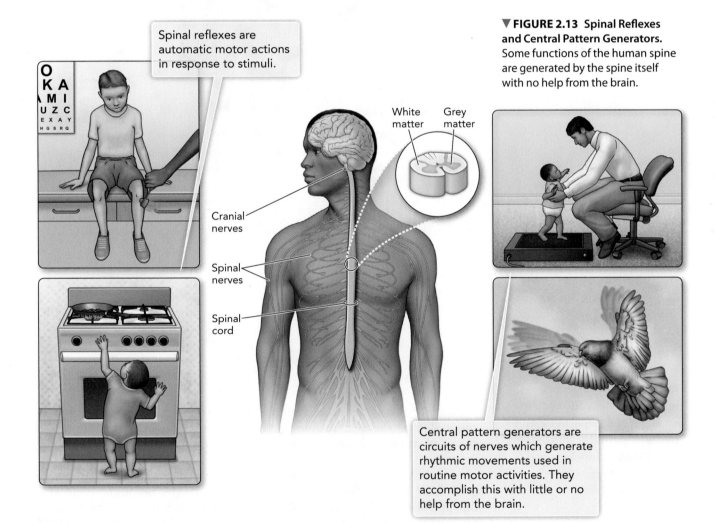

Segment of spinal column showing gray matter, the butterfly shaped area at the interior, surrounded by white matter.

Spinal nerve

◄ FIGURE 2.12 A Segment of the Spinal Cord. The spinal cord is constructed of white and gray matter.

▼ FIGURE 2.13 Spinal Reflexes and Central Pattern Generators. Some functions of the human spine are generated by the spine itself with no help from the brain.

Spinal reflexes are automatic motor actions in response to stimuli.

White matter   Grey matter

Cranial nerves

Spinal nerves

Spinal cord

Central pattern generators are circuits of nerves which generate rhythmic movements used in routine motor activities. They accomplish this with little or no help from the brain.

system consists of *cranial nerves*, which enter and leave the underside of the brain, and *spinal nerves*, which branch out from the sides of the spinal cord, connecting the cord to the rest of the body. The peripheral nervous system has two divisions: The *somatic* and *autonomic* nervous systems.

The **somatic nervous system** is, for the most part, in charge of regulating voluntary motor actions. Voluntary means under conscious control—you decide to catch a ball using your limbs, and these actions are controlled by the

Somatic nervous system
► The nerves that regulate voluntary actions and convey sensory information to the brain.

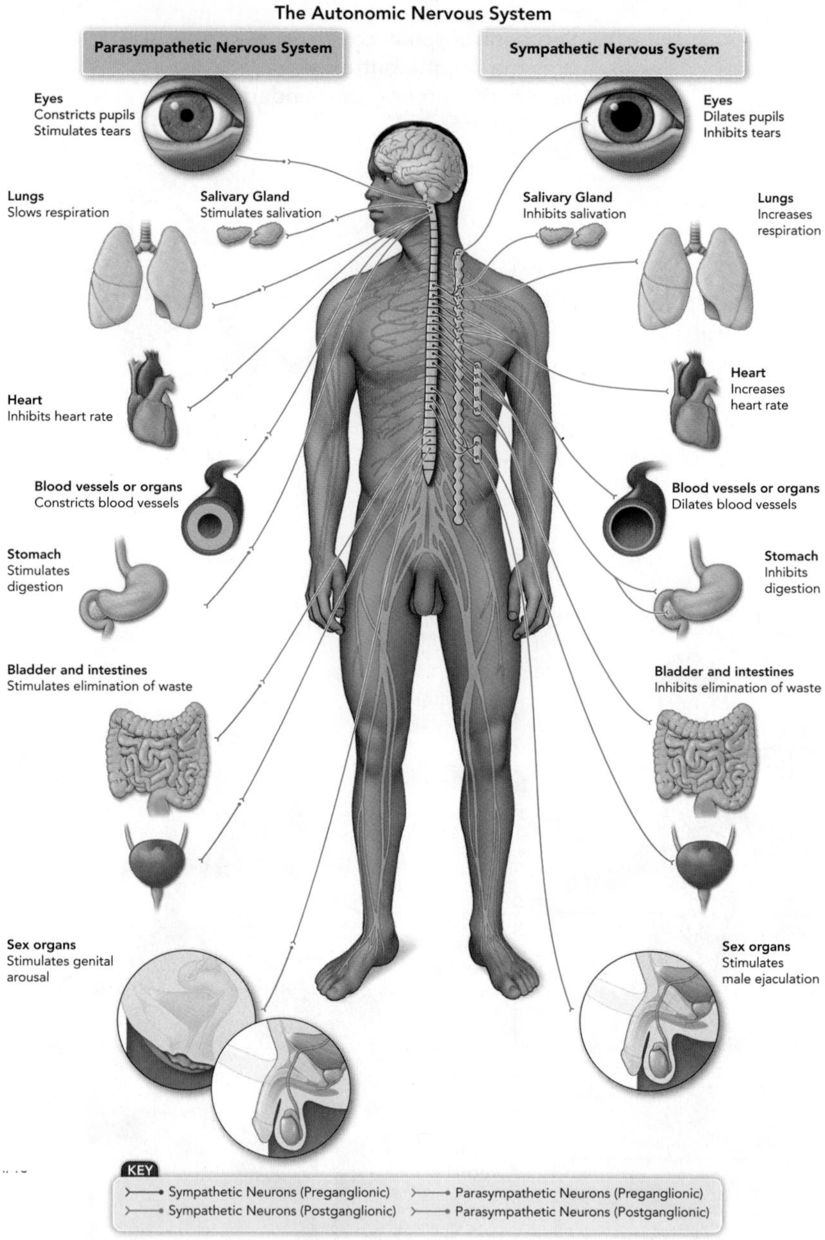

► **FIGURE 2.14 The Autonomic Nervous System.** This diagram depicts the functions of the parasympathetic and sympathetic divisions of the autonomic nervous system.

The Autonomic Nervous System

Parasympathetic Nervous System

Sympathetic Nervous System

Eyes
Constricts pupils
Stimulates tears

Eyes
Dilates pupils
Inhibits tears

Lungs
Slows respiration

Salivary Gland
Stimulates salivation

Salivary Gland
Inhibits salivation

Lungs
Increases respiration

Heart
Inhibits heart rate

Heart
Increases heart rate

Blood vessels or organs
Constricts blood vessels

Blood vessels or organs
Dilates blood vessels

Stomach
Stimulates digestion

Stomach
Inhibits digestion

Bladder and intestines
Stimulates elimination of waste

Bladder and intestines
Inhibits elimination of waste

Sex organs
Stimulates genital arousal

Sex organs
Stimulates male ejaculation

KEY
→● Sympathetic Neurons (Preganglionic)   >—● Parasympathetic Neurons (Preganglionic)
→● Sympathetic Neurons (Postganglionic)   >—● Parasympathetic Neurons (Postganglionic)

Autonomic nervous system
► A part of the peripheral nervous system. The autonomic nervous system consists of sympathetic and parasympathetic subsystems that regulate involuntary activities of muscles, glands, and organs.

Sympathetic nervous system ► Division of the autonomic nervous system that mobilizes the body for arousal, particularly in response to a threat of some sort, but also in response to certain other conditions.

somatic nervous system receiving orders from the brain. The somatic nervous system is also responsible for relaying sensory information about the environment to the brain from your *sense organs*—eyes, ears, nose, tongue, and skin.

In contrast, the **autonomic nervous system** oversees primarily *involuntary* activities of the muscles, glands, and organs—activities not under conscious control. For example, you cannot stop breathing merely by saying to yourself, "I think I'll decline to breathe for the next few hours." If you manage to hold your breath long enough, you will pass out and your autonomic nervous system will insist that you start breathing again.

The Autonomic Nervous System Is Also Subdivided

The autonomic nervous system has its own two distinct subdivisions: the *sympathetic* and *parasympathetic nervous systems*. The **sympathetic nervous system** mobilizes the organs and muscles for arousal, usually to respond to a threat of some sort. Sympathetic arousal triggers a cascade of physiological processes designed to increase the amount of oxygen to the brain and muscles to allow you to meet a threat with flight or aggression. Heart rate increases, the lungs expand to bring in more air, breathing becomes more rapid, perspiration increases, and digestion halts, causing your mouth to become dry. All of these changes are known as the *fight-or-flight* response, because they prepare a person to deal with an oncoming threat with either fists or feet—so to speak (Cannon, 1929; see Chapter 11 for more on the fight-or-flight response). The sympathetic nervous system is also activated by intense physical exercise and strong emotional states.

In contrast, the **parasympathetic nervous system** restores and conserves energy by returning the body to a resting state following arousal and maintaining that state until arousal is once again necessary. Thus, if the sympathetic nervous system supports the fight-or-flight reponse, the parasympathetic nervous system could be said to support "rest and digest" functions. Paradoxically, however, genital arousal is associated with parasympathetic, not sympathetic, activity.

The parasympathetic and sympathetic nervous systems work in a complementary fashion. People who have escaped from life-threatening circumstances often report that the "adrenaline rush" generated from the sympathetic system in response to the threat is followed by a feeling akin to euphoria when the danger is gone (a "whew!" feeling). This euphoria is a sign that the parasympathetic system has taken over to restore the body's resources. Figure 2.14 depicts the complementary functions of the two divisions of the autonomic nervous system.

Parasympathetic nervous system ▶ Division of the autonomic nervous system that returns the body to resting state following arousal and maintains that resting state.

IN SUMMARY

1.	The nervous system is divided into two major systems: the central nervous system (CNS) and the peripheral nervous system (PNS).
2.	The CNS is "command central," receiving, organizing, and interpreting information from the PNS and sending instructions to the PNS to take actions or make adjustments to bodily functions. The PNS transmits information to and from the brain via the spinal cord.
3.	The PNS consists of autonomic and somatic nervous systems. The somatic nervous system controls voluntary motor actions and also conveys information to the brain from the sense organs. The autonomic nervous system controls activities in the muscles, glands, and organs that are primarily involuntary.
4.	The autonomic nervous system has two subsystems: the sympathetic nervous system, which mobilizes the organs and muscles for arousal, and the parasympathetic nervous system, which returns the body to resting state following arousal.

RETRIEVE!

1.	The central nervous system consists of the _____ and _____.
2.	In simple terms, what is the primary function of the peripheral nervous system?
3.	A baby too young to walk will nevertheless exhibit walking movements if he or she is placed, arms held, over a treadmill. What is the mechanism responsible for this motion? **a)** spinal reflex **c)** central pattern generator **b)** parasympathetic activation **d)** fight-or-flight response

4. What is the major function of the somatic nervous system? The autonomic nervous system?

5. What is the major function of the sympathetic nervous system? The parasympathetic system? Which system is associated with the fight-or-flight response?

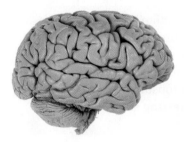

▲ **The Human Brain.**

Magnetic resonance imaging (MRI) ▶ Brain imaging technique that uses radio waves and protons within a magnetic field to produce detailed images of the brain or other neural tissue.

How Is the Brain Organized?

The brain is the center of the nervous system. In the year 1981—when Nara da Silva had the accident that resulted in fundamental changes in her personality as described at the outset of this chapter—the basic anatomy of the brain was known. However, knowledge of how the systems of the brain function and methods of diagnosing damage to the brain were far less sophisticated than those available today. Indeed, when the doctors erroneously told Nara's parents that her brain was undamaged, they could not have been blamed. In 1981, *brain imaging* technologies such as **magnetic resonance imaging** (**MRI**) were still in their infancy and were not being used in hospitals (Mattson & Simon, 1996). These technologies enable neurologists and neuroscientists to create finely detailed images of the brain's structures and activity. Today, brain imaging has begun to provide tentative solutions to mysteries about the human brain previously thought unlikely to be solved. One aspect of the brain these technologies have helped shed light on is its *organization*, which we will explore next.

The Brain Is a Network of Neural Connections

Although the brain is often referred to as an organ, it is more accurate to say that it is a *system* or network of organs made up of clusters of neurons that form intricate neural circuits. However, these circuits/organs are so well integrated, and have evolved over time to work together so smoothly, that they might as well *be* a single organ. That the brain operates as a complex network of neural connections is made vividly clear when brain damage and disorders are considered. These conditions often result in a failure of brain neurons to communicate efficiently with one another. "Failure to communicate" may be involved in psychological disorders as well as brain disorders. For example, there is some evidence that the psychological disorder known as *schizophrenia* may be accompanied by problems with communication to and from the brain's major sensory relay station, the *thalamus*, and many other brain structures (Mitelman, Brickman, et al., 2005; Mitelman, Byne, et al., 2005).

The organization of the brain can be described in a number of ways and depicted according to different conceptual schemes. Consider a map of the world. It could stress political geography by emphasizing borders between nations and state borders within nations, or it could stress natural geography by emphasizing mountain ranges, bodies of water, forestry, and so forth. Moreover, maps can exist at numerous levels of detail, depending on the needs of the reader of the map. At the most basic level, the brain can be divided geographically into three parts: the *forebrain, midbrain,* and *hindbrain.* Figure 2.15 depicts the human brain divided in this way by "geographical" region.

We will consider the divisions of the brain from the bottom up, starting with the parts that are believed to be more evolutionarily ancient (structures that were present in the most primitive animals and that perform the most basic life functions). As we move up into the higher regions of the forebrain, we will

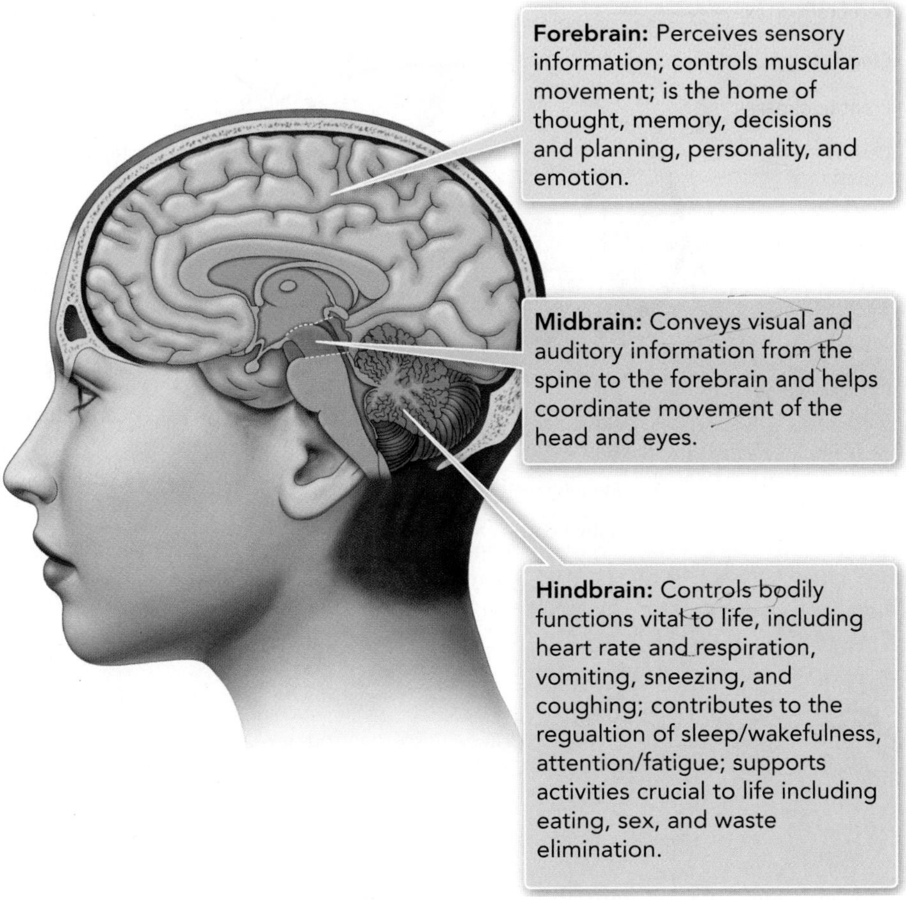

Forebrain: Perceives sensory information; controls muscular movement; is the home of thought, memory, decisions and planning, personality, and emotion.

Midbrain: Conveys visual and auditory information from the spine to the forebrain and helps coordinate movement of the head and eyes.

Hindbrain: Controls bodily functions vital to life, including heart rate and respiration, vomiting, sneezing, and coughing; contributes to the regualtion of sleep/wakefulness, attention/fatigue; supports activities crucial to life including eating, sex, and waste elimination.

◀ **FIGURE 2.15 The Geography of the Brain.** The geographic regions of the brain include the *forebrain, midbrain,* and *hindbrain.*

examine parts that perform tasks you will recognize as being unique to more complex animals such as birds and mammals. Figure 2.16 depicts the "big picture" of the brain, filling in the "contents" of the hindbrain, midbrain, and forebrain, and previewing the major structures we will consider.

The Hindbrain and Midbrain Keep House

Figure 2.17 depicts the major structures of the hindbrain and midbrain. Sometimes these structures—minus the *cerebellum* of the hindbrain, but including the *thalamus* at the lower portion of the forebrain—are considered together and termed the *brain stem.* In this general region of the brain are found most of the vital "housekeeping" functions for survival performed by every brain, such as control over heart rate and breathing. The hindbrain and midbrain are very old regions in evolutionary terms. If you were to crack open the skull of a fish and extract the brain, what you would see would not look radically different from Figure 2.17. The hind- and midbrain regions may be small and quite ancient, but this does not make them less important in the larger scheme of things. Injury to these areas would probably kill you, whereas various kinds of damage to the higher areas of the forebrain would make life difficult but not impossible.

Like most brain areas, one may look at structures of hindbrain and midbrain at varying levels of detail. However, the major structures include: in the **hindbrain,** the *cerebellum, medulla, pons,* and *reticular formation;* and in the **midbrain,** the *inferior* and *superior colliculi.*

CEREBELLUM: THE LITTLE BRAIN

The **cerebellum** (literally "little brain"), located in the hindbrain (see Figure 2.17), is the second largest individual structure in the central nervous system

Hindbrain ▶ A lower geographic area of the brain containing the cerebellum, medulla, pons, and reticular formation.

Midbrain ▶ A small, lower geographic area of the brain containing the inferior and superior colliculi, among other structures.

Cerebellum ("little brain") ▶ The second largest structure in the central nervous system, located in the hindbrain. The cerebellum coordinates sensory inputs and affects balance by assisting visual-spatial perception. It is also involved at least to some degree in attention, learning, and memory, and appropriate expression of emotion.

▶**FIGURE 2.16 The Major Structures of the Brain.** This figure shows major structures of the hindbrain, midbrain, and forebrain in cross-section. Note that no single view of the brain can display *all* the important structures.

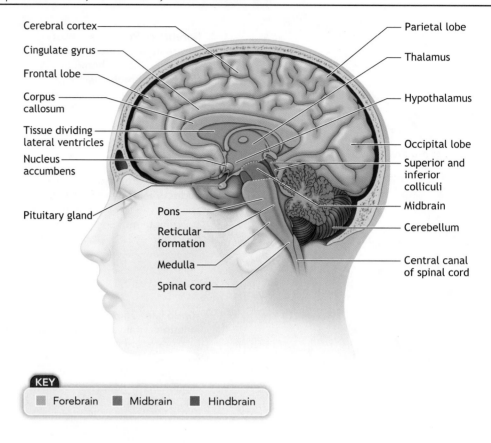

and, although it only contributes 10% of the brain's overall weight, it contains more neurons than the rest of the structures of the brain put together—between 50% and 70% of the total number of brain neurons (Glickstein, 2003; Herculano-Houzel & Lent, 2005).

The cerebellum has been considered something of a mystery since its initial description 50 years ago. It was once thought to be involved only in the control of balance and coordination. Damage to the cerebellum will result in loss of balance, and effects on the cerebellum are responsible for the staggering and clumsiness experienced after drinking too much alcohol, for example. However, the function of the cerebellum is now known to go far beyond regulating balance as we walk or run. It appears instead primarily to coordinate the various sensory inputs we experience during waking consciousness, including visual inputs. The actual source of balance loss in cerebellum damage is problems with visual-spatial perception (Bower & Parsons, 2003). Cerebellum damage also can result in difficulties with processing many functions previously thought to be the exclusive domain of the cortex, including language, attention, and learning and memory—particularly learning and memory of bodily movements. Appropriate expression of emotion may also be affected (Bower & Parsons, 2003; Schmahmann, 2004; Strick, Dum, & Fiez, 2009; Thompson, 2005).

MEDULLA

The medulla, also known as the *medulla oblongata*, is a major structure originating in the hindbrain. Medulla oblongata is sometimes mentioned by those trying to impress others with their knowledge of the anatomy of the brain, especially in the context of describing intellectual function. However, the primary functions of the medulla are to control various autonomic processes, including the regulation of breathing and heartbeat. If the medulla contributes to your intellectual functioning, it is strictly because it keeps you alive so that you may think more clearly! When an individual overdoses on alcohol,

◀ **FIGURE 2.17 Major Structures of the Hindbrain and Midbrain.** The structures of the hindbrain and midbrain—minus the *cerebellum* but including the *thalamus* of the forebrain (not depicted), are collectively known as the *brainstem*.

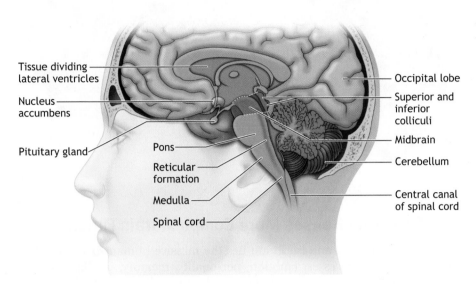

tranquilizers, or opioids, the activity in the medulla can be so badly compromised that the individual stops breathing and dies.

PONS

The pons is a hindbrain structure that plays a vital role in regulating the body during sleep and in relaying information from the hindbrain to the forebrain (hence its name, meaning "bridge" in Latin). Substructures embedded in the pons also project axons into the higher regions of the brain, making them more sensitive and responsive to sensory input under conditions of threat. You could find this extremely useful should you get into a situation where you are running or fighting for your life. These embedded structures also appear to be involved in retrieving memories associated with emotional events (Sterpenich et al., 2006).

RETICULAR FORMATION

The medulla and pons include within them the reticular formation. The reticular formation is a startlingly intricate, net-like web of neurons that begins at the level of the medulla and threads upward through the pons toward the midbrain and downward toward the cerebellum and areas of the spinal cord involved in motor activity. This extensive structure plays a crucial role in variations of consciousness, including sleep/wakefulness, alertness/fatigue, and attention/inattention (Guillery, Feig, & Lozsádi, 1998; Moruzzi & Magoun, 1949). The reticular formation can be put "off-line." When a boxer gets knocked out during a prizefight, chances are the blow temporarily but effectively shut down the operation of the reticular formation. More severe damage typically results in coma (Weisberg, Garcia, & Strub, 1996).

INFERIOR AND SUPERIOR COLLICULI

Whereas the hindbrain is of particular importance because it keeps us alive, the midbrain contributes the inferior colliculus and the superior colliculus. These structures are essential for conveying auditory and visual information from the cranial nerves to the forebrain areas where the information is interpreted as sounds and sights. These structures also help coordinate the movement of the eyeballs and head to allow hearing and vision to occur.

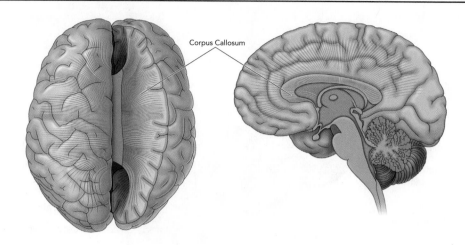

Corpus Callosum

▶ **FIGURE 2.18** Cerebral Hemispheres and Corpus Callosum. This image of the cerebral hemispheres of the forebrain seen from the top and in cross-section depicts the neuronal fibers known as the corpus callosum that allow communication to take place between the hemispheres.

Forebrain ▶ The large, upper geographic area of the brain controlling the "higher" brain functions. Consists of two cerebral hemispheres, each of which contains a limbic system, cerebral cortex, and thalamus.

Cerebral hemispheres ▶ The forebrain is divided nearly symmetrically into left and right hemispheres connected by the bundle of axons known as the corpus collosum. The structures of each hemisphere correspond almost exactly to those in the opposite hemisphere, although there are also subtle, but important, differences left and right.

Corpus callosum ▶ Bundle of axons (white matter) that connects the right and left cerebral hemispheres.

Limbic system ▶ A group of large structures and smaller nuclei that regulate mood, emotion, memory, and basic drives. Includes at least the hypothalamus, hippocampus, amygdala, basal ganglia, and nucleus accumbens.

The Forebrain Houses More Complex Brain Functions

Above the hindbrain and midbrain lies the massive human **forebrain**—the seat of thought processes, emotion, personality, memory, intelligence, language, and consciousness itself. The forebrain is divided into two nearly symmetrical **cerebral hemispheres**, right and left, each with systems and structures that correspond almost exactly. Thus, there are two of each of the forebrain structures, one in each hemisphere. For reasons not yet fully understood, each hemisphere generally receives information from, and conveys commands to, the *opposite* side of the body. Thus, when a sound reaches your left ear, it is conveyed to the right hemisphere for interpretation; when your forebrain issues a command to raise your right arm, the command issues from the left hemisphere.

The hemispheres of the forebrain are connected by a bundle of over 200 million axons called the **corpus callosum**, which allows neurons from the right side of the brain to communicate with neurons on the left. The corpus callosum is the only area of the brain that may be severed, partially or entirely, without damaging critical functions—although such surgery does produce startling effects (see pp. 90–92). Figure 2.18 depicts the hemispheres of the forebrain and the connecting corpus callosum.

The major structures of each hemisphere are: the *limbic system* (composed of its own series of distinct structures and clusters of neurons), the *thalamus*, and the *cerebral cortex*.

THE LIMBIC SYSTEM REGULATES MOOD, EMOTION, MEMORY, AND BASIC DRIVES

The **limbic system** consists of several large structures, and a number of smaller nuclei (clusters of neurons). The limbic system regulates emotions and motivations (particularly "primal" emotions and motivations such as fear and aggression), plays a part in the formation of memory, regulates the sleep/wake cycle, and is the seat of basic drives such as hunger, thirst, and sex. Figure 2.19 depicts the structures of the limbic system.

There are differences of opinion among neuroscientists as to which structures and nuclei should be considered part of the limbic system—and some contemporary researchers deny that a specific "system" exists at all, preferring to describe the structures and their functions as part of the activity of the forebrain. However, among those who accept the limbic system idea, there would be little disagreement that the following structures should be considered among the large structures of that system: the *hypothalamus, hippocampus,* and *amygdala*.

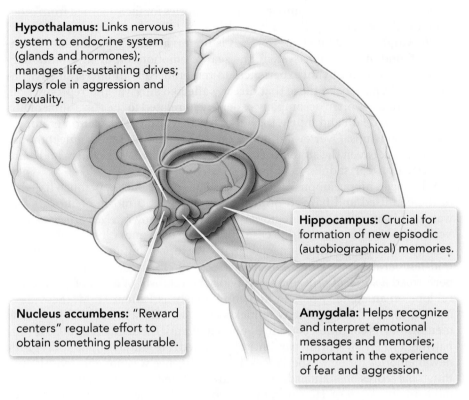

Hypothalamus: Links nervous system to endocrine system (glands and hormones); manages life-sustaining drives; plays role in aggression and sexuality.

Hippocampus: Crucial for formation of new episodic (autobiographical) memories.

Nucleus accumbens: "Reward centers" regulate effort to obtain something pleasurable.

Amygdala: Helps recognize and interpret emotional messages and memories; important in the experience of fear and aggression.

◀ **FIGURE 2.19 The Limbic System.** So called because it forms a border, or *limbus*, around the brain stem, the limbic system regulates emotion and motivation, is involved in formation of memory, regulates the cycle of sleep and wakefulness, and is the seat of drives such as hunger, thirst, and sex. Researchers disagree as to which structures it includes, and even on whether it should be considered a "system."

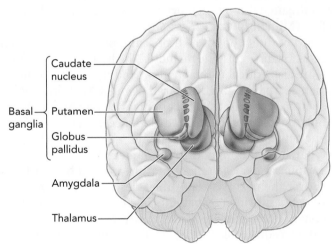

Basal ganglia
- Caudate nucleus
- Putamen
- Globus pallidus

Amygdala

Thalamus

Hypothalamus The hypothalamus (literally "under the thalamus") lives in two worlds. It is part of the brain's limbic system, giving it a home in the nervous system. However, it also helps to control the production of *hormones* by the *endocrine system*—the system of glands and hormones that assists in the work of the nervous system (see pp. 97–100). Thus, it links the nervous system to the system of glands and hormones that support it. The hypothalamus manages our most essential life-sustaining drives—hunger, thirst, and sleep. It also plays a role in regulating sexual impulses and aggression, thus potentially contributing both to the creation and extinguishing of life. A well-known off-color joke in neuroscience makes it easy to remember the basic jobs of the hypothalamus through the "Four F's: Fighting, Fleeing, Feeding, and (politely translated) Fornicating."

Hippocampus The hippocampus is the most crucial structure involved in the process of forming new *episodic* memories—memories associated with personal experiences (as compared with memories for facts learned from other sources; Andersen, Morris, Amaral, Bliss, & O'Keefe, 2007; e.g., Kentros, 2006; Vargha-Khadem et al., 1997). It is not an accident that the hippocampus is found in the limbic system, the seat of emotion. From an evolutionary standpoint, the most vital experiences to remember in our ancestral environment would have been those that directly affected survival and reproduction. Strong emotions often accompany experiences related to the sustaining of life, avoidance of death and injury, the act of mating, and the formation of important relationships. Over evolutionary time, then, an intimate connection has developed between the storage of memories of personal experiences and emotions such as fear, sadness, and joyful satisfaction.

A damaged hippocampus creates a conscious experience very much like that of the confused and harried protagonist of the 2000 movie *Memento*, who was unable to create new memories, a condition known as *anterograde amnesia*. The best-known real-life case of this type of memory loss resulted from a surgical procedure that damaged a patient's hippocampus and surrounding mid-temporal lobe regions. On August 23, 1953, surgeon William Scoville performed a surgical procedure involving the removal of areas of the temporal lobe on an epilepsy patient known famously as Patient H. M. (Scoville & Milner, 1957). The outcome was unexpected: H. M. was unable to form new memories. His condition continued unabated until his death in 2008. The impairment in H. M.' s brain was entirely isolated. He simply could not register new memories for new experiences. His intelligence was not affected—if anything, his scores on standardized measures of intelligence (e.g., IQ) increased following his surgery. However, his life consisted of the constant sensation of waking from a dream, with no memory of anything that had transpired just moments before (Milner, 1988, p. 254, 256).

Another important function of the hippocampus is intimately connected to its importance in forming episodic memory. The hippocampus and surrounding structures are also critical to imagination and the ability to envision future events (Buckner, 2010; Hassabis, Kumaran, Vann, & Maguire, 2007; Maguire, Vargha-Khadem, & Hassabis, 2010). Patients with damage to the hippocampus are not only unable to recall new experiences; they may find it difficult even to *imagine* new experiences. For example, when Demis Hassabis and colleagues asked patients with hippocampus damage to describe the experience of "lying on a white sandy beach in a beautiful tropical bay" or to describe "a possible event over the next weekend" their descriptions dramatically lacked the richness of detail provided by patients in a control group who lacked hippocampal damage. These patients could only report fragmented images and were unable to envision whole scenes "in their mind's eye" (Hassabis et al., 2007, p. 33).

Amygdala The amygdala is an almond-shaped structure (its name means "almond") built of neurons that work together to create an understanding of one's own emotions and those of others (Habel, Windischberger, Derntl, Robinson, & Kryspin-Exner, 2007; LeDoux, 2007). One consequence of damage to the amygdala is the inability to recognize and interpret one's own emotions or respond to situations with appropriate emotion, and failure to pay attention to emotional messages from others (e.g., Adolphs, Tranel, & Buchanan, 2005; Baxter & Murray, 2002; Murray, 2007). Brain imaging studies show that the amygdala may respond differently when an individual is viewing facial expressions expressing different emotions (e.g., Habel et al., 2007; Whalen et al., 2009).

Like the hippocampus, the amygdala is important in the formation of memory—primarily emotionally charged memory (Phelps, 2006; Hamann, 2009). It plays a particularly important role in helping us to remember fear-inducing situations and in generating fearful and aggressive responses for survival and self-defense (Le Doux, 2000, 2007; see discussion of fear in

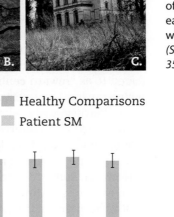

◀FIGURE 2.20 Ho-Hum. Fun, but Not Scary. When researchers Justin Feinstein and his colleagues tried to scare Patient SM out of her wits, they were unsuccessful due to Patient SM's bilateral amygdalae damage. The graph shows the level of fear exhibited by Patient SM to each of the film clips as compared with a sample of healthy controls. *(Source: Feinstein et al., 2011, pp. 35–36.)*

Chapter 11). It is the amygdala that gets the blood pumping and the adrenaline flowing when you are frightened or badly stressed. Rats whose normal amygdala responses have been intentionally destroyed or interfered with by researchers will cozy right up to a cat or climb all over it if the cat is sedated. Monkeys with damage to the amygdala will approach snakes and much larger and more dominant monkeys from whom they ought to steer clear (Adamec, Burton, Shallow, & Budgell, 1999; Blanchard & Blanchard, 1972; Kalin, Shelton, Davidson, & Kelley, 2001; Machado, Kazama, & Bachevalier, 2009).

Human beings suffering from anxiety and exaggerated fears have sometimes been shown to have "hypersensitive" amygdalae, while those whose amygdalae are damaged may tend to be more trusting of others (Adolphs, Tranel, & Damasio, 1998; Stein, Simmons, Feinstein, & Paulus, 2007). In an unusual study, Justin Feinstein and his colleagues intentionally attempted to instill fear in a patient, SM, who had experienced damage to both her left- and right-hemisphere amygdalae. They let Patient SM handle live snakes and spiders (including pythons and tarantulas) and escorted her through a professionally designed "haunted house," the Waverly Hills Sanatorium, a closed-sanitarium now widely publicized as one of the "most haunted" places on earth (see Figure 2.20). Every year at Halloween the sanatorium hosts a very scary tour, complete with scary scenes, noises, monsters, murderers, and ghosts. Finally, Feinstein and colleagues exposed Patient SM to 10 extremely frightening film clips. Although Patient SM found the snakes and spiders fascinating, the haunted house loads of fun, and the film clips "entertaining," she displayed little in the way of fear responses to any of these stimuli (Feinstein, Adolphs, Damasio, & Tranel, 2011).

Nuclei of the Limbic System: Basal Ganglia and Nucleus Accumbens In addition to the three relatively large structures listed previously, the limbic system contains some smaller "workgroups" of nuclei that are considered "minor" in size only—not necessarily in importance. They include *basal ganglia* and *nucleus accumbens*.

The basal ganglia are dopamine- and GABA-producing clusters of neurons surrounding the thalamus. They play a role in the production of voluntary movement and are compromised in *Parkinson's disease*, a degenerative disorder of the central nervous system caused by loss of dopamine within the *substantia nigra* region of the basal ganglia. Like the amygdala, the basal ganglia may also play a role in emotional communication—in understanding facial expressions and nonverbal behavior, and in other forms of social communication (Lieberman, 2000; Satpute & Lieberman, 2006).

The nucleus accumbens are also dopamine-rich nuclei, receiving their dopamine primarily from various other brain structures. The dopamine released in this region accompanies feelings of excitement in the presence of pleasurable stimuli, and deep satisfaction when these stimuli are able to be consumed or enjoyed (Aron et al., 2005). Indeed, the nucleus accumbens are often referred to as "reward centers." If you will recall from our earlier discussion of neurotransmitters, most recreational drugs are agonists (promoters) of dopamine. Because the nucleus accumbens region is so rich in dopamine, it has been argued that suppressing nucleus accumbens activity would be an effective method of treating drug abuse and addiction, by interfering with the rewarding aspects of drug use.

However, some research challenges this view (Salamone, 2002; Salamone, Correa, Farrar, & Mingote, 2007). For example, John Salamone & Mercè Correa (2002) have shown that the release of nucleus accumbens dopamine is not necessarily the "cause" of feelings of wanting to engage in some rewarding behavior such as taking drugs or eating ice cream. Instead, the nucleus accumbens dopamine regulates the amount of *effort* a person is willing to put into attempting to obtain the reward. For example, when nucleus accumbens dopamine is suppressed in caged rats, they are less willing to press bars or engage in tiring work to obtain food. However, their liking for the food and willingness to eat it is in no way diminished. This may have important implications for treatment of drug addiction, because it suggests that merely suppressing dopamine activity may not reduce the desire to take drugs, if the drugs are freely available and the cost does not exceed the perceived benefit (Salamone et al., 2007).

THE THALAMUS REGULATES OUR SENSORY EXPERIENCE OF THE WORLD

Thalamus ▶ A lower forebrain structure that conveys sensory information to the cerebral cortex and receives instructions from the cortex regarding the regulation of sensory and emotional signals.

The **thalamus** is a hard structure to classify. Geographically it sits at the base of the forebrain, but some scientists consider it to be a part of the limbic system because it is located adjacent to the hippocampus and hypothalamus. In terms of function, however, the thalamus is generally thought of as a "gateway" to the higher functions of the forebrain. All types of sensory information (except that related to the sense of smell) must first pass through the thalamus before being relayed to the cerebral cortex to be interpreted and perceived (see Figure 2.21). The thalamus also limits the amount of sensory information that can reach the cerebral cortex during sleep, thus making sleep possible.

The thalamus does not act only as a relay to the cerebral cortex, however. It receives instructions back from the cortex about the type of sensory input that should be given "free passage" and the type that should be slowed or blocked altogether. This determines how much attention one pays to any given sensory stimulus at any particular moment (Komura et al., 2001). For example, imagine yourself ravenously hungry, bringing an aromatic slice of pizza to your mouth, inhaling its aroma, and trying to manage the level of heat on your tongue by blowing on the slice. Simultaneously, someone to whom you are romantically attracted enters the restaurant, a siren from a fire engine or ambulance begins to blare outside, a baby starts to wail, and your favorite song begins to play on the juke box. Which sights, sounds, tastes, and smells receive your attention? The cerebral cortex decides, using the thalamus as its decision tool.

THE CEREBRAL CORTEX ALLOWS US TO PERCEIVE, THINK, AND ACT

When "you" think about "your" brain (don't think about that idea for too long) your image is probably that of the most massive part—the large, wrinkly

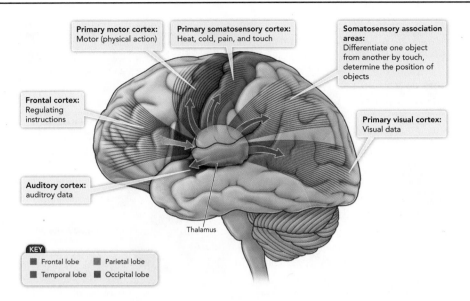

Primary motor cortex:
Motor (physical action)

Primary somatosensory cortex:
Heat, cold, pain, and touch

Somatosensory association areas:
Differentiate one object from another by touch, determine the position of objects

Frontal cortex:
Regulating instructions

Primary visual cortex:
Visual data

Auditory cortex:
auditroy data

Thalamus

KEY
- ■ Frontal lobe
- ■ Parietal lobe
- ■ Temporal lobe
- ■ Occipital lobe

◄ FIGURE 2.21 The Thalamus: Sensory Gateway to the Forebrain. Sensory information passes through the thalamus and is relayed to the cerebral cortex. Information from the prefrontal cortex is also relayed back to the thalamus, regulating the amount of data from each sense that reaches the cortex.

cerebrum that makes up the bulk of the image of the brain in the photo on page 74. The outer layer of the cerebrum is known as the **cerebral cortex**. Most mammals have fairly sizable cortical areas, but in humans these structures are *huge* relative to the rest of the brain. Many animals function with little more than brain stem (mid- and hindbrain) structures, and others who have fairly sizable cortical areas can still function quite well if the cortex is separated from the brain stem. However, we humans *need* our cerebral cortex. It enables us to interpret the raw information we receive from our senses, and it initiates voluntary movement. It is also the home of the higher cognitive processes—the problem solving, planning, learning, memory, and language skills that have given us an enormous edge in the struggle for survival.

Like the spinal cord, the cerebral cortex consists of white and gray matter. However, the location of white and gray matter is exactly reversed in the cortex compared with the spinal cord—the outer layer of the cortex consists of gray matter (cell bodies, dendrites, glia), while the interior consists of white matter (myelinated axons). As with the brain as a whole, "maps" of the cerebral cortex may emphasize one or another aspect of this part of the brain. For example, there are 50 or more identified areas of the cerebral cortex, but they can be grouped (somewhat arbitrarily) into four large regions known as **lobes**. Each lobe contains neurons primarily devoted to specific sorts of tasks, but the lobes are named for the skull bones beneath which they lie. Figure 2.22 depicts the lobes of the cortex and their primary structures.

Occipital Lobe When you look out at the world, the impressions you receive are "translated" into images in the back of your brain, primarily in the primary visual cortex (V1) of the **occipital lobe** (see Figure 2.16). Visual information is so important for survival that well over one-third of our brain tissue is devoted to processing it. In the primary visual cortex, neural messages produced by the light receptors in our eyes arrive after being relayed by the midbrain and thalamus. The primary visual cortex analyzes the information conveyed by these neural signals in very fine detail. It breaks each object down into features: elements of shape, texture, shading, angle, and so on. The specificity is so precise that individual neurons will only fire for one kind of detail—a certain angle or shading, for example.

Humans join predator birds as being perhaps the most gifted of creatures in regard to visual acuity because of our sensitivity to detail on the cortical level. For us, even a small amount of damage in visual processing areas can be highly destructive. Such damage can create devastating forms of "selective" blindness—for example, the inability to see motion or faces (Blanke, Landis,

Cerebral cortex ▶ The outer layers of the hemispheres of the forebrain. Interprets raw sensory information, initiates voluntary movement, and is home to higher cognitive processes.

Lobes of the cerebral cortex ▶ Four large divisions of the cerebral cortex into which specific brain structures are grouped. The lobes are named after for the skull bones beneath which they lie: occipital, parietal, temporal, and frontal.

Occipital lobe ▶ Cerebral cortex lobe containing the primary visual cortex (VI) and visual association areas.

▶ **FIGURE 2.22 The Four Lobes of the Cerebral Cortex.** The hemispheres of the cerebral cortex are divided into four lobes, or regions. The principle structures of the cortex are contained within these lobes.

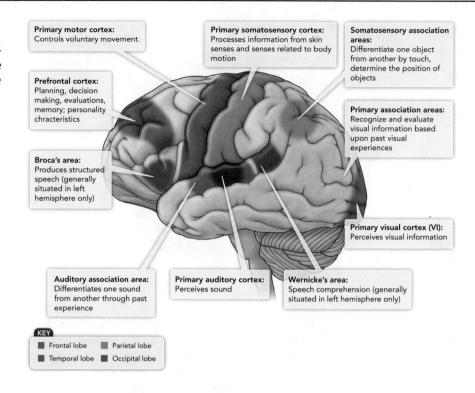

Primary motor cortex: Controls voluntary movement.

Prefrontal cortex: Planning, decision making, evaluations, memory; personality chracteristics

Broca's area: Produces structured speech (generally situated in left hemisphere only)

Primary somatosensory cortex: Processes information from skin senses and senses related to body motion

Somatosensory association areas: Differentiate one object from another by touch, determine the position of objects

Primary association areas: Recognize and evaluate visual information based upon past visual experiences

Primary visual cortex (VI): Perceives visual information

Auditory association area: Differentiates one sound from another through past experience

Primary auditory cortex: Perceives sound

Wernicke's area: Speech comprehension (generally situated in left hemisphere only)

KEY
■ Frontal lobe   ■ Parietal lobe
■ Temporal lobe   ■ Occipital lobe

Mermoud, Spinelli, & Safran, 2003; Busigny, Joubert, Felician, Ceccaldi, & Rossion, 2010; Hubel & Wiesel, 1962). Humans are very talented at working around and adapting to such obstacles, however. Neurologist Oliver Sacks, some of whose case studies are now well known as popular movies (*Awakenings, At First Sight*), writes of "P"—a music teacher afflicted with a degenerative disease that was destroying portions of his visual cortex. Though his deteriorating visual system caused him to misinterpret and misjudge the space around him and to fail to recognize common objects, he compensated by using sound and smell to manage his interactions with the outside world (Sacks, 1985).

Analysis of visual information does not stop with the primary visual cortex. As Figure 2.22 shows, the occipital lobe also contains visual association areas which refine this analysis by comparing the visual information received with past visual information so that whatever is being viewed may be recognized. Visual information is then sent to other areas of the cerebral cortex for further processing.

An important point to remember about the flow of information to the visual cortex and visual association areas is this: As with other forebrain structures receiving sensory signals, visual information is received by each cerebral hemisphere from the *opposite* side—in this case, from the opposite *visual field*. However, this does *not* mean that visual signals sent by each *eye* are conveyed to the opposite hemisphere. Instead, *each* eye has a *right visual field* and a *left visual field*. Therefore, as depicted in Figure 2.23, *both eyes* send signals to both hemispheres, but the signals are divided between right and left.

Parietal Lobe Immediately above and adjacent to the occipital lobe is the **parietal lobe**. The primary functions of the parietal lobe are to process the sensations of heat, cold, pain, and touch, and to inform us about the placement of our limbs and bodies in space. This is all accomplished via a strip of tissue called the somatosensory cortex, which runs the whole diameter of the parietal lobe—from the base on one side, across the top, to the bottom of the other side (see Figure 2.22). The somatosensory cortex of each hemisphere processes information from the opposite side of the body.

Parietal lobe ▶ Lobe of the cerebral cortex containing the somatosensory cortex and somatosensory association areas.

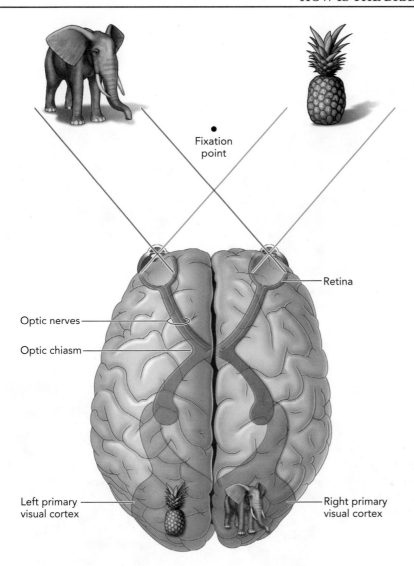

◀ **FIGURE 2.23** Each eye has a left and right visual field. Information from the right visual fields of *both* eyes is sent to the *left* visual cortex; and information from the left visual field of *both* eyes is sent to the *right* visual cortex.

Fixation point

Retina

Optic nerves

Optic chiasm

Left primary visual cortex

Right primary visual cortex

The layout of this area is a kind of topographic "body map" known as a *homunculus*. Sensation in the face, hands, feet, limbs, and torso each corresponds to a particular area of the somatosensory cortex. In addition, each body part is allotted a certain amount of cortical tissue based not on its actual size but on the number of sensory receptors the body part contains. This number corresponds roughly to the importance of the body part in day-to-day-life—and in a larger sense to survival and reproduction. Thus, the face, lips, and fingers (especially the thumb) get far more cortical tissue than the legs, torso, and arms, even though the latter are much larger in absolute size. As you might expect, the genitals get *lots* of brain tissue devoted to them—roughly equivalent to that of the lips. Figure 2.24 is an impressionistic depiction of the relative proportion of cortical tissue allotted to various body parts in the somatosensory homunculus. It also shows the placement of the somatosensory cortex within the parietal lobe.

Like the occipital lobe, the parietal lobe has association areas—in this case, somatosensory association areas, as depicted in Figure 2.22. These association areas allow us to determine the shape of an object or its texture through touch, as well as the placement of objects relative to one another based on memory of past experiences. Damage to these association areas from stroke or other causes can result in *neglect syndrome*, an inability to attend to events on the opposite side of the body or in an area of space opposite to the hemisphere that has sustained damage (usually the right hemisphere). A person with this

▶**FIGURE 2.24** The **Somatosensory Cortex Homunculus and the Primary Motor Cortex Homunculus.** This impressionistic depiction of the homunculus (topographical "map") of the somatosensory cortex shows how various body parts would look if their size were proportionate to the amount of cortical tissue allotted by the somatosensory cortex. Body parts executing more complex or delicate movement receive more cortical tissue in the primary motor cortex homunculus.

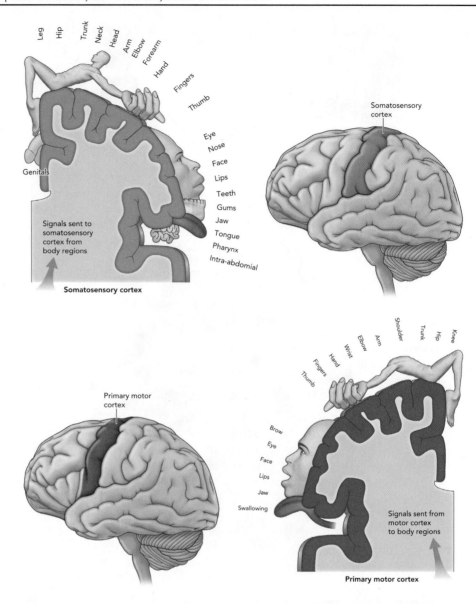

condition may behave as though the opposite side of the body does not exist—shaving or applying makeup on only one side of the face, or dressing only on one side of the body, with no idea that there is anything odd about their behavior (Coulthard, Parton, & Husain, 2007; Husain & Rorden, 2003). Such people truly have "lost" a part of their minds.

Temporal lobe ▶ Lobe of the cerebral cortex containing the auditory cortex, auditory association areas, and Wernicke's area.

Temporal Lobe The **temporal lobe**, adjacent to the occipital lobe and below and adjacent to the parietal and frontal lobes, contains the auditory cortex, which interprets as sound neural messages received from the ears. Like the occipital lobe, the temporal lobe has an auditory association area that allows one to recognize sounds for what they are—music, speech, natural and animal sounds, machine noise, and so forth (see Figure 2.22).

Along the border of the *left* temporal lobe and the frontal lobe, sitting on the temporal lobe side, is Wernicke's area, which bears the name of its discoverer (see Figure 2.22). This area has been recognized from the earliest days of brain research as being critical to speech comprehension. This area may also be involved in the comprehension and processing of music, particularly for trained musicians (Ohnishi et al., 2001).

For most people, Wernicke's areas exist in the left cerebral hemisphere only. This may be surprising given that we have characterized the left and right cerebral hemispheres as essentially symmetrical—including the same structures on each side. The placement of Wernicke's area in the left cerebral hemisphere only is an example of *hemispheric specialization*, the tendency for some differences to exist in the way the two hemispheres function. I have more to say about this a bit later.

Frontal Lobe The most noticeable difference between the brain of *Homo sapiens* and that of our close cousins in the primate family is the size of the frontal lobe. The frontal lobe makes up the bulk of the cerebral cortex and 30%of the entire human brain. The frontal lobe is so large that it is literally curled up behind our eye sockets to fit in the limited space allowed by the skull. Within the frontal lobe is the primary motor cortex, where deliberate body movements are planned and executed by sending neural commands to muscles and joints. As you might expect by now, the motor cortex in one hemisphere primarily controls movement on the opposite side of the body.

As with the somatosensory cortex, a homunculus may be mapped onto the primary motor cortex for the various parts of the body—although specific muscles do not have a specific location in the motor cortex (Graziano, Taylor, & Moore, 2002). More motor cortex tissue is given over to muscles involved in movements that are critical to daily life, or that require greater complexity or delicacy. As with the somatosensory cortex, the extra space allotted to more important muscles is reflected in the motor cortex homunculus. For example, cortical areas devoted to the movement of fingers and hands are larger than those devoted to the movement of toes and feet. Figure 2.24 depicts the primary motor cortex homunculus.

The second major structure of the frontal lobe is the prefrontal cortex, the most complex, mysterious, and elaborate of cortical structures. Just as the frontal lobe makes up the bulk of the cerebral cortex in humans, the prefrontal cortex takes up a disproportionate area of the frontal lobe. The functions of the prefrontal cortex have long been debated. Clearly, the area receives and integrates information from all bodily systems and brain regions. It receives more neural messages than any other area of the brain—up to 23 times as many (Elston, 2003). What, then, are the functions of the prefrontal cortex? It appears primarily to be a grand decision maker, organizer of information, and planner of action. It allows us to weigh competing courses of action and to choose from the bewildering array of possibilities open to us in any given situation (Brass & Haggard, 2007). Consider all the information received by our sensory and motor systems—how can we sort it all out and make wise decisions about how to act? The prefrontal cortex integrates all this information and compares it against our *goals* for any given situation—pointing to appropriate behavior to achieve those goals (Kast, 2001; Kim & Shadlen, 1999; E. K. Miller & Cohen, 2001). Taken together, the functions of the prefrontal cortex are given the name *executive functions* because, like a business manager, they control and manage many types of cognitive and emotional activity (e.g., Ramnani & Owen, 2004).

Finally, a small structure sitting at the border of the frontal and temporal lobes on the frontal lobe side is Broca's area, a kind of "sister" structure to Wernicke's area, which was described earlier (see Figure 2.22). Just as Wernicke's area allows for speech *comprehension*, Broca's area allows a person to *produce* structured (i.e., grammatical) speech. I have more to say about Broca's area a bit later.

Taken together, planning actions, monitoring emotions and behavior, deciding between available alternatives, and communicating in the achieving of goals represent important components of our personalities—who we are as recognizable, unique individuals. It was here, in the prefrontal cortex, that Nara da Silva likely sustained an injury too subtle to have been picked up by diagnostic equipment available in 1981. In a study of 140 children with traumatic brain injury, Jeffrey Max and his colleagues found that almost one-fourth had experienced personality changes in the months following the injury and, further, that only injury in the prefrontal cortex was significantly associated with these personality changes (Max et al., 2005; see also Max et al., 2006).

One of the most controversial treatments ever devised for serious psychological disorders is a *psychosurgical* procedure known as the *prefrontal lobotomy*, which involves destroying the prefrontal cortex entirely or severing it from the rest of the brain. During the early to mid-20th century, this procedure was used to treat a wide range of conditions including *schizophrenia* and *major depression*. It was also promoted at times as a "cure" for those with unpopular beliefs or sexual orientations (e.g., communists and gays), or for those whose behavior was just too rowdy to tolerate (Youngson & Schott, 1998)—although the frequency with which this occurred is probably exaggerated in some accounts (Mashour, Walker, & Martuza, 2005). Tens of thousands of Americans received prefrontal lobotomies during its heyday, yet the procedure rarely produced the benefits purported for it. However, it did often result in radical personality change, characterized by apathy, memory problems, and a general lack of appropriate emotional response, all of which Nara experienced (but to a far lesser degree). Lobotomy was outlawed in the former Soviet Union in the 1950s, and it has fallen into disfavor in the United States over the past decades—for good reason. Although the procedure is rarely if ever practiced in the United States, to date no federal law has been passed banning its use (see Chapter 14 for more about prefrontal lobotomy).

Each Cerebral Hemisphere Is Specialized

As you will recall from our brief discussion of Broca and Wernicke's areas at the border of the temporal and frontal lobes, although each of the cerebral hemispheres contains the same basic structures—*limbic system, thalamus,* and *cerebral cortex*—this symmetry is not absolute. There are some differences between the left and right hemispheres. In fact, each hemisphere is specialized to respond to different kinds of information. The left hemisphere ("left brain") is "detail oriented." It is specialized primarily for tasks involving *sequential* (linear) processing of information. This would include spoken, written, or sign language; logical reasoning; and numerical skills. The right hemisphere ("right brain") is specialized for *integrative processing*, or "taking in the whole picture." Integrative processing is involved in the "reading" of others' nonverbal emotional expressions, facial recognition, musical and other artistic experience, and visual-spatial tasks—such as imagining what an object might look like if it were rotated 90 degrees, determining the location of objects in relation to one another, or recognizing visual patterns (Corballis, Funnell, & Gazzaniga, 2002; Gazzaniga et al., 2009; Narumoto, Okada, Sadato, Fukui, & Yonekura, 2001). This "division of labor" and specialization of each hemisphere of the forebrain is known as **hemispheric specialization**. Table 2.2 summarizes hemispheric specialization in the brain.

Hemispheric specialization ▶ The unique specializations of the two hemispheres of the cerebral cortex.

A study by Manuel Carreiras and his colleagues offers a unique demonstration of hemispheric specialization. Shepherds on the island of La Gomero in the Canary Islands use an unusual language known as *Silbo* that is composed entirely of whistling. This whistling language enables them to communicate over long distances in terrain that is difficult to traverse. Given that whistling is a musical sound, it ought to be perceived primarily by the right hemisphere. However, Silbo is also a language—the province of the left hemisphere. How then is Silbo perceived? Using brain imaging technology, Carreiras and his research team showed that *non-users* of the language perceived Silbo sounds as *music* primarily in their right hemisphere. However, those who used these sounds for communication—that is, as *language*—perceived the sounds primarily in their left hemisphere (Carreiras, Lopez, Rivero, & Corina, 2005). This hemispheric "division of labor" is further explored in Figure 2.25.

Table 2.2 Differences in Function of the Two Cerebral Hemispheres (Brain Lateralization)

Note that both hemispheres participate to some degree in all of these tasks, and that the extent of brain lateralization varies from person to person.

LEFT HEMISPHERE	RIGHT HEMISPHERE
Receives sensory signals from, and controls muscles on, right side of body	Receives sensory signals from, and controls muscles on, left side of body
Logical reasoning	Musical and artistic expression and awareness
Numerical and scientific skills	Visual-spatial skills and pattern recognition
Spoken, written, and sign-language skills	Non-verbal emotional expression recognition

(Adapted from Tortora & Derrickson, 2006, p. 500)

Original picture

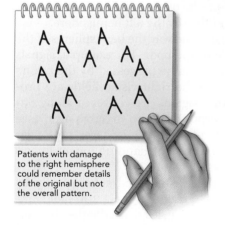

Patients with damage to the right hemisphere could remember details of the original but not the overall pattern.

Patients with damage to the left hemisphere could reproduce the global pattern but not its details.

◀ **FIGURE 2.25 Division of Labor in Brain Hemispheres.** Dean Delis and colleagues asked brain-damaged patients to view an image of the letter "H" composed of smaller letter "A"s, as depicted here, and then redraw it. Those with damage to the right hemisphere—who therefore relied primarily on the left hemisphere for perception—typically drew randomly grouped small letter "A"s. Those with damage to the left hemisphere—who relied primarily on the right hemisphere—drew the letter "H" with no small letter "A"s. *(Source: MacNeilage, Rogers, & Vallortigara, 2009, p. 6.3.)*

WE ARE ALL "RIGHT-BRAINED" AND "LEFT-BRAINED"

One unfortunate misinterpretation of the specialization of the cerebral hemispheres is the idea that some people are logical "left-brained" people and others are creative "right-brained" people—in other words, that people can favor one side of their brains in their daily lives. This idea is simply not true. Despite the reality of hemispheric specialization, for all but the simplest types of real-world tasks, both hemispheres are almost always involved (e.g., Forster & Corballis, 2000). We are dependent on both hemispheres to receive a clear and comprehensive understanding of the world.

Moreover, hemispheric specialization is not absolute. For many individuals there will be a certain amount of language processing occurring the right hemisphere and the processing of tasks typical of the right hemisphere occurring in the left. How extensively each hemisphere is used to process data for which the opposite hemisphere is specialized varies from person to person. The point is that the nonspecialized hemisphere is much less efficient for these tasks, and so is used to a far lesser degree (e.g., Beeman & Chiarello, 1998; Gazzaniga, Ivry, & Mangun, 2008). For examples of the use of the left and right hemispheres for tasks for which the opposite hemisphere is specialized, see the "At the Forefront" feature on sex differences in the brain on pages 92–94.

BEING OF TWO MINDS: WHAT HAPPENS WHEN THE CEREBRAL HEMISPHERES ARE SEPARATED

Nothing demonstrates the reality of hemispheric specialization as dramatically as experiments involving epilepsy patients who have undergone a surgical procedure known as *callosotomy* or **split-brain surgery**. During split-brain surgery, the patient's corpus callosum is severed. As you may recall, the corpus callosum is the bundle of axons that enables communication between the right and left hemispheres to occur. Severing the corpus callosum effectively reduces epileptic seizures when medication and other techniques have failed, because it inhibits neuroelectrical seizure activity from spreading from one side of the brain to the other.

> **Split-brain surgery**
> (*callosotomy*) ▶ A surgical procedure used to treat epilepsy, where the corpus callosum is severed or partially severed.

Although this surgery does not result in any serious disabilities, it does have unusual cognitive effects. Consider that in a normal brain, with the corpus callosum intact, both hemispheres are constantly interacting. They share their respective competencies to process information and produce behavior. In a sense, "the right hand knows what the left hand is doing" in a normal brain. In Nobel-prize-winning research conducted during the 1960s and 1970s, neuroscientist Roger Sperry (e.g., Sperry,1974; 1982) found that severing the corpus callosum resulted in the creation of two independent systems of perception, thought, memory, reasoning, and emotion—in other words, two conscious "minds," one governed by the right and the other by the left hemisphere.

This does not mean that there is a change in the way the hemispheres of the brain control activity on the opposite side of the body. For example, signals from the left visual field of each eye continue to be processed by the brain's right opposite hemisphere, and signals from the right visual fields are processed by the left hemisphere. These neural signals are conveyed along optic nerves that are not dependent on the corpus callosum to "cross over" (see Figure 2.23). However, in split-brain patients, the hemispheres no longer *communicate* with one another. In a sense, the right hand no longer knows what the left is doing. What happens as a result?

In Sperry's early experiments, and in those conducted subsequently by Sperry's collaborator Michael Gazzaniga (see Gazzaniga et al., 2008 for summary), split-brain patients had various sorts of images flashed either in their left or right visual fields. The results were startling. In the first study, depicted in Figure 2.26, a split-brain patient sits in front of a screen. He is asked to stare at the midpoint of the screen and is flashed an image of a horse on the left side of the screen. The image only appears in his left visual field and is therefore sent only to his *right* cerebral hemisphere for processing—the hemisphere that is inadequate for processing language. The picture is flashed too briefly for the patient to move his eyes to the left to perceive the image in his right visual field (left hemisphere).

A researcher then asks the patient to name the object he just saw, but he cannot. "I don't know," he answers. He is then asked to name something that might "go on top" of the object—still, he cannot do so. However, when given the opportunity to *draw* something that could "go on it"—a right brain task— he draws a saddle with no problem. However, he uses his *left* hand to do the drawing, even though he is right-handed! Recall that motor activity of the left hand is controlled by the right hemisphere. This adds to the demonstration that only his right brain has perceived the horse (Gazzaniga et al., 2008).

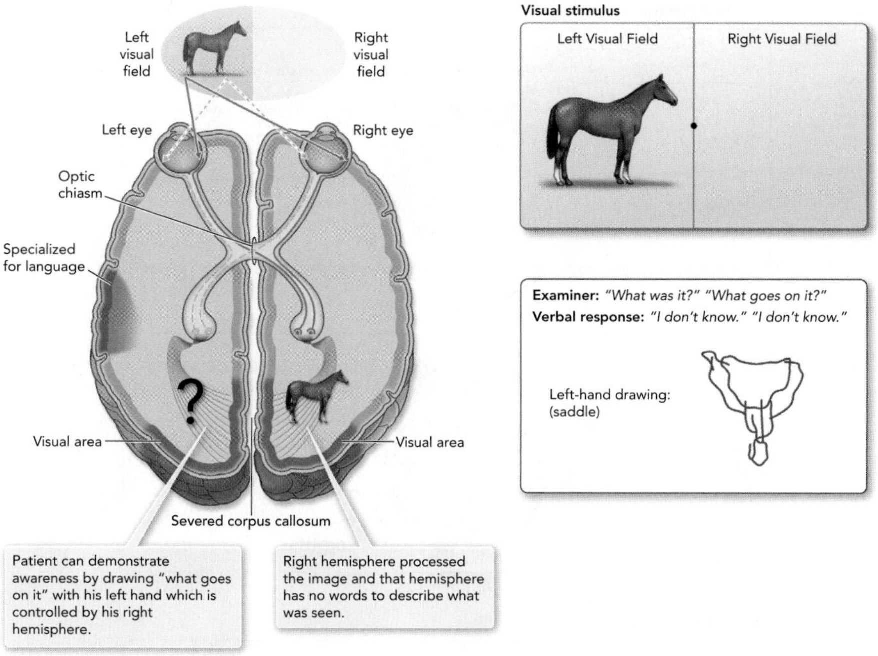

Left visual field

Right visual field

Left eye

Right eye

Optic chiasm

Specialized for language

?

Visual area

Visual area

Severed corpus callosum

Patient can demonstrate awareness by drawing "what goes on it" with his left hand which is controlled by his right hemisphere.

Right hemisphere processed the image and that hemisphere has no words to describe what was seen.

Visual stimulus

Left Visual Field | Right Visual Field

Examiner: *"What was it?" "What goes on it?"*
Verbal response: *"I don't know." "I don't know."*

Left-hand drawing:
(saddle)

◀ **FIGURE 2.26 Split-Brain Study #1.** This split-brain patient has no awareness that a horse was flashed in his left visual field because his right hemisphere processed the image and that hemisphere has no "words" to describe what it saw. But the patient can demonstrate awareness of the object by drawing "what goes on it" with his left hand—the hand controlled by his right hemisphere. (*Source: Gazzaniga, Ivry, & Mangun, 2002, p. 414.*)

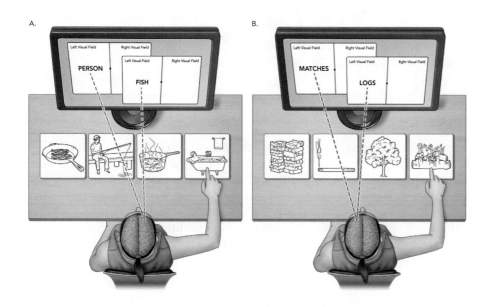

A.

Left Visual Field | Right Visual Field

PERSON

Left Visual Field | Right Visual Field

FISH

B.

Left Visual Field | Right Visual Field

MATCHES

Left Visual Field | Right Visual Field

LOGS

◀ **FIGURE 2.27 Split-Brain Study #2.** When the words *person* and *fish* are presented in the left visual field to be processed in the right hemisphere, the patient cannot successfully choose an image that depicts what might happen if the words occurred together (a person fishing). This is because the left hemisphere, specialized for language, is not involved in the task of deciphering the meanings of the printed words. However, when a similar pairing of words (*matches* and *logs*) is presented in the *right* visual field—and processed in the left hemisphere—the patient finds the task extremely easy. (*Source: Gazzaniga, Ivry, & Mangun, 2002, p. 414.*)

In the second study, depicted in Figure 2.27, a patient is briefly shown two words in sequence: *person* and *fish*. The words appear in her left visual field (right hemisphere) only. She is then shown a series of four pictures and asked to point to the one that depicts what might happen if the two words were "put together." Among the images is a person fishing—that would be the correct choice. However, the patient is unable to interpret the meanings of the words *person* and *fish* in her right hemisphere in a way that would allow her to accomplish the task. She points instead to the picture of a person bathing. Yet when she is later shown a similar *word* pair in her right visual field (left-hemisphere processing) and asked to point with her right hand to the appropriate image, she finds the task trivially easy (Gazzaniga & Smylie, 1984).

Over the years surgeons have developed callosotomy procedures whereby only a portion of the corpus callosum needs to be severed to effectively treat seizures for many patients. What happens to patients' consciousness under these conditions? Some communication between the hemispheres is possible following partial severing of the corpus callosum, but it produces its own

▶ **FIGURE 2.28 When the Corpus Callosum Is Partially Severed.** This diagram demonstrates J. W.'s performance when his corpus callosum was partially severed and again when fully severed. *(Source: Based on data from Sidtis et al., 1981, p. 345.)*

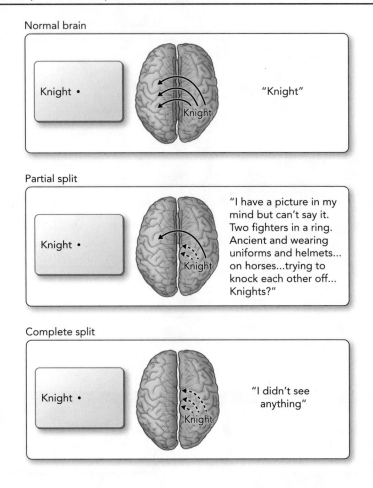

Normal brain

Knight •   "Knight"

Partial split

Knight •   "I have a picture in my mind but can't say it. Two fighters in a ring. Ancient and wearing uniforms and helmets... on horses...trying to knock each other off... Knights?"

Complete split

Knight •   "I didn't see anything"

unusual effects (Sidtis, Volpe, Holtzman, Wilson, & Gazzaniga, 1981). As depicted in Figure 2.28, for example, a patient known as J. W. is shown the word *knight* in his left visual field (right hemisphere) after only a partial severing of the corpus callosum. He struggles to find words to explain what he sees, but he does have some comprehension of the term. After time passes, he manages to think of it. But later, it was necessary to have additional surgery to sever the corpus callosum entirely. Now J. W. *claims to see nothing at all* when a word is flashed in his left visual field!

AT THE FOREFRONT

Male and Female Brains Are Not Identical

When someone proposes that average differences in some characteristic exist between men and women, many people's initial reaction is anger (Eagly, 1995; Pinker, 2002). This is because the early history of characterizations of sex differences in psychology consisted primarily of pseudoscience—*sexist* ideas dressed up in scientific garb, which painted women as generally inferior to men. Such ideas were then used to justify real discrimination against women. However, the past 30 years have seen an explosion of interest among researchers—a great many of them women—in actual sex differences revealed in studies using scientific methods. Real average sex differences have been found in human cognition, emotion, motivation, and sexual behavior—although in some cases the differences are statistically real, but not particularly strong. These differences favor neither men nor women, but suggest that each sex has its own average strengths and weaknesses (Halpern et al., 2007; Kimura, 2004). Most people intuitively share this belief, and, if anything, it is *women*

AT THE FOREFRONT

CONTINUED

who are generally evaluated more favorably than men in most respects by most people—male as well as female (e.g., Eagly, Mladinic, & Otto, 1991).

With the advent of brain imaging technology, it is now possible to examine differences not only between male and female behavior, but between male and female brains as well. It is reasonable to assume that such differences exist in humans if only because average sex differences have been found in the anatomy, biochemistry, and functioning of the brains of all nonhuman mammals yet studied (e.g., Field & Pellis, 2008; Goldstein et al., 2001; Lindenfors, Nunn, & Barton, 2007). There is no reason why humans should be an exception. Given genetic, anatomical, and hormonal differences between men and women, differences in evolutionary pressures historically faced by men and women, and differences in the way the sexes are socialized, it would be quite surprising if brain differences did *not* also exist.

Over the past decade, sex differences have been found within every lobe of the human forebrain—in the size and neuronal density of brain structures (see Figure 2.29), in the way structures function, in brain biochemistry, and in the way the specialization of the right and left hemispheres plays out while men and women perform various tasks (Cahill, 2006; Cosgrove, Mazure, & Staley, 2007; Goldstein et al., 2001; Hofer et al., 2007; Lenroot & Giedd, 2010).

This field is new, and like any new field, findings must be taken as preliminary (Goldstein et al., 2001). For one thing, it is not easy to find large samples of men and women who will lend you their brains for detailed surgical study—even in death (and *far* fewer in life!). In the case of brain imaging studies, conducted in real time on living persons, researchers need to amass a substantial amount of funds and time, as these techniques are costly and labor-intensive.

Another problem, as researcher Cordelia Fine points out, is that some people have taken fanciful leaps from real evidence of sex differences in the brain to questionable assumptions about how these brain differences might affect differences in behavior (Fine, 2010). For example, one writer has assumed that the larger average size of men's hypothalamus (e.g., Swaab, Chung, Kruijver, Hofman, & Ishunina, 2001) explains why men think about sex so much more often than women (Brizendine, 2006)! It is not that men do not think about sex more often on average than women (they do) or that the size of the hypothalamus might somehow be involved—after all, the hypothalamus is important in the regulation of sexual desire. But one cannot automatically assume that a difference in brain structure will translate into a difference in behavior. In fact, it has already been shown that sex differences in brains often do *not* result in sex differences in behavior (Cahill, 2006; Clements et al., 2006; Grabowski, Damasio, Eichorn, & Tranel, 2003).

Take differences in the ways in which men and women use their cerebral hemispheres to perform various tasks. Hemispheric specialization—differences in the specialization of each hemisphere—exist for both sexes, as described earlier. However, the patterns are not identical for men and women. For example, although the left hemisphere is dominant for language tasks in both sexes, it is much more so in men than in women. Women experience at least some language processing using their *right* hemispheres as well as their left, whereas the majority of men use their left hemisphere virtually exclusively. When it comes to visual-spatial

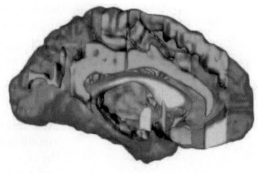

KEY

☐ Structures that are larger in the healthy female brain, relative to cerebrum size

☐ Structures that are larger in the healthy male brain, relative to cerebrum size

▲ **FIGURE 2.29 Sex Differences in the Size and Density of Brain Structures.** The size and neuronal density of brain structures is generally believed to reflect their relative importance to the owner of the brain (Cahill, 2005). As an example, primates rely more on their eyes than their nose to navigate and obtain information about the world, and their visual centers are much larger than those that process olfactory data (sense of smell). The exact opposite is the case for rats and mice, for whom sense of smell is primary. As this figure shows, there are differences in the proportion of men's and women's brains given over to certain critical brain structures (Cahill, 2006; Goldstein et al., 2001).

tasks, the opposite pattern exists: The right hemisphere is dominant for both sexes, but much more so for women than men, who experience at least some visual-spatial processing in the left hemisphere as well (Clements et al., 2006). These differences may give men and women different sorts of cognitive advantages. Women may have the advantage of drawing on right-hemisphere resources when using or comprehending language, while men may have the advantage of drawing on left-hemisphere resources when executing visual-spatial tasks.

It is tempting to conclude that this brain sex difference is one cause (or consequence) of well-established average differences between men and women in their performances of verbal and visual-spatial tasks—differences which favor women in most verbal tasks and men in many visual-spatial tasks (Geary, 2007; Halpern et al., 2007). However, the men and women in the study who showed differences in language and visual-spatial ability were specifically selected for *equal* ability in both of these sorts of tasks—and they performed equally on their tests. Thus, brain differences may exist even where there are *no* differences in ability (see also Bell, Willson, Wilman, Dave, & Silverstone, 2006). ■

Although the Brain Is Specialized, It Is Also Plastic

Plasticity ▶ The brain's ability to change in response to learning, practice, and sensory input; and the ability of specialized regions of the brain to adapt if necessary to perform tasks for which they are not ordinarily used.

Magnetoencephalography (MEG) ▶ A brain imaging technology by which recordings are made of magnetic fields generated by neural activity.

Although neuroscientists have highlighted the specialization of brain regions and the two cerebral hemispheres, these researchers also understand that the human brain has a certain degree of **plasticity**, an important quality that enables it to adapt and be flexible in response to the environment. Brain plasticity means that the brain constantly changes throughout the life span in response to learning, practice, and sensory input (Anderson, 2011; Trachtenberg et al., 2002). Indeed, your brain is changing now, at the synaptic level, through your efforts to learn the information in this book.

Evidence of this type of neural plasticity comes from imaging studies of the brains of people who engage in extensive practice of some skill—professional musicians, athletes, or chess players, for example. In a series of studies of professional musicians using a brain imaging technology known as **magneto-encephalography** (**MEG**), enlargements were found in specific areas of the auditory cortex devoted to processing musical tones as compared with other sounds. Not only were the enlargements correlated with the number of years the musician had been practicing; they also differed in structure depending on the specific quality of sound that each instrument produced (violin vs. trumpet; Pantev et al., 2003).

In a similar study using magnetic resonance imaging (MRI), researchers compared the brains of nonmusicians, amateur musicians, and professional musicians. They found differences in the density of gray matter in regions of the brain controlling motor, auditory, and visual processes correlated with the participants' musical skill and extent of practice (Gaser and Schlaug, 2003; see Figure 2.30).

It is important to keep in mind that these studies were correlational in nature. For example, it may have been that the brains of people who were willing to practice more, who were attracted to one instrument over another, or who were more intrinsically talented in music—and therefore more likely to end up a professional musician—*already* differed structurally from the brains of others.

However, Krista Hyde and her colleagues monitored brain structure and behavioral changes in children with no previous musical training who had been randomly assigned either to study a keyboard instrument seriously for 15 months in weekly lessons, or simply to sit in groups on a weekly basis to sing and play bells and drums over that period of time (Hyde et al., 2009). Using MRI brain imaging technology (see pp. 104–105), Hyde and her colleagues noted structural brain changes in "musically relevant" areas of the brain only in the children who had engaged in serious musical training. These structural changes were correlated with changes in the children's motor skills and auditory experience.

There is another way in which the brain is plastic. Neural tissue generally "assigned" to specific types of processing tasks may sometimes be used for other tasks if the need arises. The fact that some split-brain patients learn over time to produce speech from their right hemisphere is an excellent example of this type of plasticity (Gazzaniga et al., 2008). Another example of this type of plasticity is the neural changes that occur in the brains of blind people learning Braille. Areas of the visual cortex—that should not respond to tactile sensory information—are "co-opted" in the service of reading with the fingers, and the amount of tissue of the somatosensory cortex given over to the reading fingers of Braille readers is much larger than in other individuals. In a certain respect, blind people actually do have "eyes in their fingers" when reading Braille (Hannan, 2006; Melzer & Ebner, 2008; Theoret, Merabet, & Pascual-Leone, 2004).

◄FIGURE 2.30 Gray Matter in Nonmusicians, Amateur Musicians, and Professional Musicians. Green areas are those where gray matter differs only when professional musicians are compared with nonmusicians. Red areas are those that differ when professional musicians are compared with amateurs as well as nonmusicians—thickest in professionals, less so in amateurs, and least in nonmusicians. Yellow areas are those that overlap—they show differences in both types of comparisons. (Source: Gaser & Schlaug, 2003, p. 9243.)

IN SUMMARY

1. The brain is an integrated system of organ-like clusters of neurons that operate as a network of connections. The brain can be divided geographically into the forebrain, midbrain, and hindbrain.

2. Important structures of the hindbrain include the cerebellum, medulla, pons, and reticular formation. Important structures of the midbrain include superior and inferior colliculi. The hindbrain and midbrain control bodily functions vital to maintaining life.

3. The forebrain is the largest region of the brain. It is the seat of cognition, emotion, personality, memory, intelligence, language, and consciousness. It is divided into two symmetrical cerebral hemispheres connected by the corpus callosum. For the most part, each hemisphere contains the same structures.

4. The forebrain includes the limbic system, the thalamus, and the cerebral cortex. The limbic system is a series of substructures (including hypothalamus, amygdala, hippocampus, basal ganglia, and nucleus accumbens) that regulate mood, emotion, memory, and basic drives including hunger, thirst, and sex. The thalamus relays sensory information to the cerebral cortex, and conveys instructions back from the cortex regarding the extent to which certain types of sensory messages should be conveyed. The cerebral cortex, which makes up the bulk of the forebrain, interprets sensory information, controls voluntary movement, and is the home of higher thinking processes.

5. The cerebral cortex can be divided into four regions called lobes. The occipital lobe, which processes visual information, contains the primary visual cortex and visual association areas. The parietal lobe processes sensations of heat, cold, pain, and touch via the somatosensory cortex and somatosensory association areas. The temporal lobe processes auditory information via the auditory cortex and auditory association areas. The frontal lobe includes the primary motor cortex, where deliberate body movements are planned and executed; and the prefrontal cortex—a decision-maker, organizer of information, emotion-monitor, and planner of action in the service of obtaining goals.

6. Although each cerebral hemisphere has structures that "mirror" the other, each is also specialized to accomplish certain tasks. The left hemisphere is specialized primarily for tasks involving sequential processing—language, logical reasoning, and numerical skills. The right hemisphere is specialized for integrative processing—reading nonverbal emotional expressions, facial recognition, music and art, and visual-spatial tasks. Experiments with split-brain people underscore the specialization of each hemisphere.

7. Although the brain is specialized, it is also to some degree plastic.

RETRIEVE!

1. Distinguish the functions of the hindbrain structures: pons, medulla, and cerebellum.

2. Match the following limbic system structures with their primary functions:

hypothalamus	critical to forming new episodic memories
basal ganglia	manages basic drives such as sex, aggression, hunger, thirst, and sleep
hippocampus	allows understanding of one's own and others' emotions
amygdala	dopamine-rich "reward centers"
nucleus accumbens	plays a role in the production of voluntary movement

3. Describe the functions of the thalamus.

4. Match the cerebral cortex lobe with the structures contained within it:

occipital	somatosensory cortex and association areas
temporal	primary motor cortex, prefrontal cortex
parietal	primary visual cortex and visual association areas
frontal	auditory cortex, auditory association area

5. Wernicke's area is critical to _____, whereas Broca's area allows for _____.

a) speech comprehension; speech production
b) speech comprehension; language acquisition
c) speech production; speech comprehension
d) speech production; language acquisition

6. Which of the following are among the probable functions of the prefrontal cortex?

a) processing sensations of heat, cold, pain, and touch
b) planning and executing neural commands to muscles and joints
c) organizing information, making decisions, planning courses of action
d) producing and comprehending speech

7. What is hemispheric specialization? Describe one split-brain experiment that demonstrates hemispheric specialization.

8. There are two general ways in which brain plasticity is apparent. What are they?

What Is the Endocrine System?

The nervous system does not do its vital work alone. There is a second communication system, the **endocrine system**, that partially overlaps the nervous system but is considered separate. The endocrine system is composed of bodily organs known as **glands** and the chemicals they synthesize and release into the bloodstream and tissues. These chemicals, as you may already know, are termed **hormones**. Figure 2.31 shows the major glands of the endocrine system, and Table 2.3 summarizes the activity of the hormones they release.

The Nervous and Endocrine Systems Overlap

What does it mean to say that the nervous and endocrine systems overlap? Consider the **pineal** and **pituitary glands**. These glands are central "players" in the endocrine system. The pineal gland secretes *melatonin*, a hormone critical to establishing the sleep-wake cycle. The pituitary secretes a variety of hormones and triggers other glands to secrete their hormones—helping to regulate blood pressure, body growth, aspects of pregnancy, childbirth, and

Endocrine system ▶ The system of glands and the hormones they produce.

Gland ▶ A bodily organ that synthesizes and/or releases hormones.

Hormone ▶ A chemical synthesized and/or released by a gland.

Pineal gland ▶ Gland situated in the brain that releases the hormone *melatonin*, important in regulating the sleep/wake cycle.

Table 2.3 **Glands at a Glance**

This table is a partial list of some of the major glands and the hormones they release.

GLAND	HORMONES	ACTION
Hypothalamus	Releasing hormones, including TSH-releasing hormone	Regulates hormone synthesis and release in the pituitary gland
Pituitary	Thyroid-stimulating hormone (TSH)	Stimulates thyroid
	Luteinizing hormone Follicle-stimulating hormone Prolactin	Regulates female reproductive cycle and milk production
	Growth hormone	Regulates body growth
	Oxytocin	Facilitates birth, breastfeeding, and mother-infant bonding; associated with sexual activity, possibly with romantic bonding
	Vasopressin	Helps regulate blood pressure
	ACTH	Increases production of steroids
Thyroid	Thyroxine Triiodothyronine	Regulates metabolism and growth
Adrenal glands	Cortisol Epinephrine Norepinephrine	"Stress hormones"—increase blood pressure and blood sugar; work with parasympathetic nervous system to respond to threat or extreme stress
Testes	Androgens (e.g., testosterone)	Regulate production of sperm and male sexual characteristics; associated with sexual desire in both sexes; affect immune function
Ovaries	Progesterone Estrogens	Regulate female sexual characteristics and reproductive cycle, including pregnancy
Pancreas	Insulin Glucagon	Regulate blood sugar levels, fat storage, and conversion of fat to blood sugar

▶ **FIGURE 2.31 Major Glands of the Human Endocrine System.** The endocrine system is composed of glands and the hormones they produce.

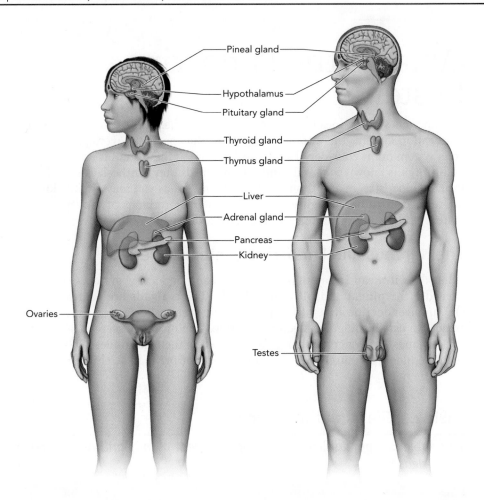

Pineal gland

Hypothalamus

Pituitary gland

Thyroid gland

Thymus gland

Liver

Adrenal gland

Pancreas

Kidney

Ovaries

Testes

Pituitary gland ▶ Gland situated in the brain that secretes a variety of hormones and triggers other glands to secrete their hormones. Helps regulate blood pressure, body growth, aspects of pregnancy, childbirth and lactation, and the functioning of sex and reproductive organs.

lactation, and the functioning of sex and reproductive organs. Yet despite their importance in the *endocrine* system, as you can see in Figure 2.32, they are situated within the brain—the center of the *nervous* system.

Another example of the overlap of the nervous and endocrine systems is the hypothalamus, which, if you recall, is a limbic structure of the forebrain. But the hypothalamus also functions as an important endocrine organ because it synthesizes certain hormones, which are then transmitted to the pituitary gland and released from there. The hypothalamus also secretes *releasing hormones* that stimulate the pituitary to release its own hormones.

A final example of the interconnectedness of the nervous and endocrine systems is the fact that the molecules that make up hormones also may operate as neurotransmitters. If the molecules are synthesized by neurons, they will act as neurotransmitters, exerting their effects directly at specific sites, generally at brain synapses. If the molecules are synthesized by glands, they will function as hormones, and exert their effects less directly at multiple sites in the bloodstream and various body tissues.

A particularly interesting example of a substance that functions both as a hormone and as a neurotransmitter is *oxytocin*. The hormone oxytocin is synthesized by the hypothalamus, but released by the pituitary gland as just described. It has long been known that as a hormone, oxytocin stimulates the muscle contractions of the uterus during labor to facilitate birth, and causes milk to be expelled from the breast during lactation. It also appears to be related to sexual arousal and is released during orgasm in men and women (Hiller, 2005). However, as a neurotransmitter, oxytocin—in addition to reducing blood pressure and other indicators of stress—may be related to the formation of strong bonds between mother and infant, and between romantic

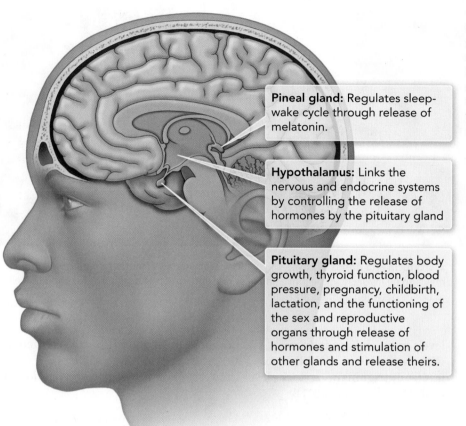

Pineal gland: Regulates sleep-wake cycle through release of melatonin.

Hypothalamus: Links the nervous and endocrine systems by controlling the release of hormones by the pituitary gland

Pituitary gland: Regulates body growth, thyroid function, blood pressure, pregnancy, childbirth, lactation, and the functioning of the sex and reproductive organs through release of hormones and stimulation of other glands and release theirs.

partners as well (Bartels & Zeki, 2004; Feldman, Weller, Zagoory-Sharon, & Levine, 2007; Gonzaga, Turner, Keltner, Campos, & Altemus, 2006). Oxytocin facilitates trust between people and enhances empathic understanding—putting oneself in other person's place (Bartz et al., 2010; Domes, Heinrichs, Michel, Berger, & Herpertz, 2007; Mikolajczak et al., 2010).

Some researchers are tentatively suggesting that the neurotransmitter oxytocin may turn out to be one of the most important chemical components of love itself, if not the most important (Carter, 2004; Diamond, 2004; Kosfeld et al., 2005). In one group of studies of women, researchers found that those women who were in romantic relationships had greater increases in circulating oxytocin when reliving memories of love, and oxytocin levels decreased in general among the women when they relived memories of loss of a loved one (Turner et al., 2002). More recent research has shown that the release of oxytocin is associated with the display of specific nonverbal behaviors associated with feelings of closeness toward one's romantic partner—natural smiling toward the partner, leaning toward him or her, frequent head nodding while the other speaks, and a number of specific hand and arm gestures associated with feelings of wanting to be with another (Gonzaga et al., 2006). Areas of the brain rich in oxytocin receptors are also activated when women gaze at photos of their own children and of romantic partners—but not photos of friends or of unrelated children (Bartels & Zeki, 2004). Finally, Shelly Taylor and her colleagues found that plasma oxytocin levels increase in women whose "pair bonded" romantic relationship is encountering trouble (Taylor, Saphire-Bernstein, & Seeman, 2010).

Research suggesting a possible role for oxytocin in the bonds of romantic love has led some researchers to wonder if other sorts of bonding were also facilitated by the hormone—for example, the bond that forms between human beings and their pets. Indeed, preliminary research suggests that oxytocin

▲ **Oxytocin and Bonds of Love.** Oxytocin is associated with mother-infant bonding, and may also be involved in the formation of sexual and romantic bonds in adulthood as well as bonds between humans and animals.

levels may increase in women, but not men, during affectionate interactions with their dogs (S. C. Miller et al., 2009; Nagasawa, Kikusui, Onaka, & Ohta, 2009). Intriguingly, oxytocin levels may also rise in the pet owners' *dogs* as well (Handlin et al., 2011)!

IN SUMMARY

1.	The endocrine system consists of glands and the hormones they release.
2.	The endocrine system is distinct from the nervous system, but the two also overlap. For example, the pituitary and pineal glands and the hypothalamus are all brain structures critical to the functioning of the endocrine system; and many hormones lead "double lives" as neurotransmitters.

RETRIEVE!

1.	Describe the functions of the pituitary gland and pineal gland. How do the hypothalamus and pituitary interact?
2.	What are the primary functions of oxytocin as a hormone? As a neurotransmitter?

What Is Neuroscience?

I have referred repeatedly during this chapter to the work of neuroscientists, and briefly described neuroscience as the scientific study of the nervous system. Before closing this chapter, it is fitting that I devote more time to the nature and history of neuroscience as a field of study. Neuroscience is multidisciplinary. This means it incorporates a number of different fields, including biochemistry, physiology, anatomy, psychology, genetics, molecular biology, evolutionary biology, and computer science. The bottom line is that all neuroscientists study the central and peripheral nervous systems. However, the methods they use, their perspectives, and the topics that interest them—while sometimes overlapping—may differ radically.

Because of the wide variety of topics included in "neuroscience," the field has been divided into subdisciplines. Neuroscientists usually refer to themselves in terms of these subspecialties—for example, *molecular and cellular neuroscience* is the study of genetic and molecular mechanisms of the central nervous system; *developmental neuroscience* is the study of changes in the brain and nervous system over time during the course of the human life span; *computational systems neuroscience* is the use of computers to model activity of the brain and nervous system; *clinical neuroscience* is the study of diseases of the brain and nervous system (e.g., personality change following traumatic brain injury, as described at the beginning of the chapter). Let us now look at two important subspecialties of neuroscience with the most direct bearing on psychology, *behavioral neuroscience* and *cognitive neuroscience*.

Behavioral Neuroscience Is the Study of the Neural Basis of Behavior

In an important sense, all neuroscience is "behavioral neuroscience," because all neuroscientists seek to understand the brain and nervous system and their relation to behavior in humans and/or nonhuman animals. However, the work of some neuroscientists is more directly concerned with behavior than others, and their work is referred to as **behavioral neuroscience**. Behavioral neuroscientists study the anatomy, physiology, and molecular structure of the entire nervous system and apply knowledge of the nervous system to virtually any question concerning animal (including human) behavior. These researchers conduct experimental studies, frequently using nonhuman animals, to shed light on the neural bases of whatever behavior is of interest.

Behavioral neuroscience ▶ Branch of neuroscience that studies the neural basis of behavior. Behavioral neuroscientists study the entire nervous system, not just the brain, and they may use nonhuman as well as human animals for study.

EARLY HISTORY OF BEHAVIORAL NEUROSCIENCE: PSEUDOSCIENTISTS WITH GOOD IDEAS AND SCIENTISTS WITH BAD IDEAS

Although those believing in dualism as described early on in this chapter and in Chapter 1 (e.g., René Descartes) believed that the mind and brain were made of separate "stuff," they at least suspected that mind and brain were related in some way. This notion is relatively recent as far as history goes, however. For example, the Ancient Greeks believed that the mind lived within the heart. The idea that the mind had an actual physical basis within the brain was not developed to any great extent until the 18th century in the work of Franz Joseph Gall (1758–1828).

According to Gall, the mind was a physical entity residing in the brain and constructed of numerous specific components, each designed to accomplish certain tasks or express certain qualities. This general notion is not necessarily incorrect. Indeed, it is a quite modern perspective, favored by many neuroscientists, cognitive scientists, and evolutionary psychologists.

Unfortunately, Gall and his followers were not scientists in the sense of the term as generally understood today; they were unwilling, or unable, to submit their theories to scientific testing. These early researchers developed a pseudoscientific theory that ultimately came to be known as **phrenology**. Phrenologists believed that the various components of the mind could be attributed to the workings of specific areas of the cerebral cortex—again, a basically sound idea that forms the basis for modern neuroscience. However, they further believed that each of the many characteristics of the mind was expressed in the physical anatomy of the skull, in surface bumps that could

Phrenology ▶ Pseudoscientific theory that proposed that personality characteristics could be determined by skilled examinations of bumps on the top of the skull.

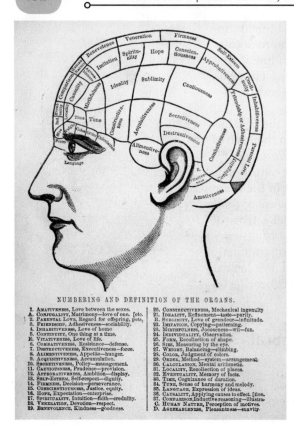

NUMBERING AND DEFINITION OF THE ORGANS.

1. AMATIVENESS, Love between the sexes.
A. CONJUGALITY, Matrimony—love of one. [etc.
2. PARENTAL LOVE, Regard for offspring, pets, &c.
3. FRIENDSHIP, Adhesiveness—sociability.
4. INHABITIVENESS, Love of home.
5. CONTINUITY, One thing at a time.
E. VITATIVENESS, Love of life.
6. COMBATIVENESS, Resistance—defense.
7. DESTRUCTIVENESS, Executiveness—force.
8. ALIMENTIVENESS, Appetite—hunger.
9. ACQUISITIVENESS, Accumulation.
10. SECRETIVENESS, Policy—management.
11. CAUTIOUSNESS, Prudence—provision.
12. APPROBATIVENESS, Ambition—display.
13. SELF-ESTEEM, Self-respect—dignity.
14. FIRMNESS, Decision—perseverance.
15. CONSCIENTIOUSNESS, Justice, equity.
16. HOPE, Expectation—enterprise.
17. SPIRITUALITY, Intuition—faith—credulity.
18. VENERATION, Devotion—respect.
19. BENEVOLENCE, Kindness—goodness.

20. CONSTRUCTIVENESS, Mechanical ingenuity
21. IDEALITY, Refinement—taste—purity.
B. SUBLIMITY, Love of grandeur—infinitude.
22. IMITATION, Copying—patterning.
23. MIRTHFULNESS, Jocoseness—wit—fun.
24. INDIVIDUALITY, Observation.
25. FORM, Recollection of shape.
26. SIZE, Measuring by the eye.
27. WEIGHT, Balancing—climbing.
28. COLOR, Judgment of colors.
29. ORDER, Method—system—arrangement
30. CALCULATION, Mental arithmetic.
31. LOCALITY, Recollection of places.
32. EVENTUALITY, Memory of facts.
33. TIME, Cognizance of duration.
34. TUNE, Sense of harmony and melody.
35. LANGUAGE, Expression of ideas.
36. CAUSALITY, Applying causes to effect. [tion.
37. COMPARISON, Inductive reasoning—illustra
C. HUMAN NATURE, Perception of motives.
D. AGREEABLENESS, Pleasantness—suavity.

▲ **A 19th-Century Phrenology Chart of the Human Brain.**

Data ▶ Literally, "pieces of information." Singular: *datum*.

Equipotentiality ▶ An early neuroscientific theory proposing that all parts of the cortex contributed equally to all aspects of mind.

be perceived by skilled fingers—a notion with no supporting evidence. The reason that phrenologists were barking up the wrong tree is that the skull does not directly follow the shape of the brain, or the size of its various structures. Although phrenology was one of the first psychological disciplines to rely on the systematic gathering of **data** (literally, "pieces of information"), the manner in which Gall and his followers *interpreted* these data deservedly occupies a bottom shelf in the dustiest desk in the Office of the Ministry of Silly Notions.

In reaction against phrenology, the notion of **equipotentiality** emerged. Proponents of this idea agreed with phrenologists that the mind was located within the brain, primarily in the cerebral cortex. However, they insisted that all parts of the cortex had *equal potential* to perform any given mental task, and thus contribute to all aspects of mind. While the methods of the equipotentialists were far more scientific than those of the phrenologists, this conclusion is quite erroneous—as research on brain specialization reported in this chapter has well demonstrated. The phrenologists' view that brain functions are localized and specific in nature is far closer to what is currently accepted as the truth.

Iron Rods and the Word "Tan" Two classic findings best represent the beginnings of modern behavioral neuroscience: the discovery of personality change due to brain injury, and the discovery of Broca's area at the border of the frontal and temporal lobes. The discovery of personality change due to brain injury is among the most dramatic moments in all of psychology. On September 13, 1848, a 25-year-old railway worker named Phineas Gage was working with gunpowder when the powder ignited accidentally, driving a three-foot iron rod through his cheek, up through the left frontal lobe of his brain, and out the top of his head (see Figure 2.33).

Astonishingly, Gage was not killed or even rendered unconscious. He was able to sit up and hold a conversation, and, with a little help, basically walked away from the accident. After the rod was removed and the wound healed, Gage returned to work. However, like Nara da Silva—but to a much more severe degree—the Phineas Gage that everyone had known was no longer. He had "disappeared." By all accounts, prior to the accident Gage had been a modest and well-balanced, calm, hard-working, energetic, and intelligent person—a shrewd businessperson who was a great favorite of the men who worked under him and who was considered the most efficient of foremen by those who employed him (MacMillan, 2000). Following the accident, he became cranky, stubborn, irreverent, and foul-mouthed—problems he had never exhibited prior to the accident. He no longer had patience for those who worked with him, and he became too unstable to hold his foreman job. He was "like a child in his intellectual capacity with the animal passions of a strong man" (MacMillan, 2000, p. 52). Gage spent the remainder of his days drifting—as a circus sideshow exhibit and a carriage driver in Chile, among other things, although it does appear that he eventually learned how to function socially in spite of his injury and mental changes (Macmillan & Lena, 2010). Gage died of epilepsy 12 years after the accident.

The second important finding was the discovery of Broca's area (see p. 87) by physician and surgeon Paul Broca. During an autopsy following the death of a man who had been admitted to his clinic unable to utter anything but the word "tan," Broca found a lesion (abnormality) of substantial size along the border of the left frontal and temporal lobes toward the frontal lobe side, apparently caused by a stroke. As described earlier, this area of the brain became known as *Broca's area*, and it controls important aspects of speech. People

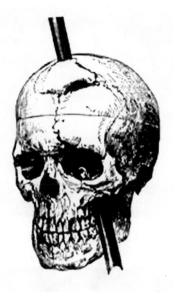
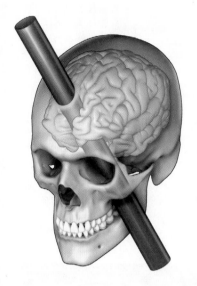

▲ **FIGURE 2.33A The Skull of Phineas Gage.** A computer simulation of the entry and exit points of the iron rod that pierced Phineas Gage's brain and a drawing of Gage's actual skull, with a simulation of entry and exit points of the rod; a daguerreotype of the actual Phineas Gage.

suffering from damage to this area (a condition called *Broca's aphasia*) are unable to create complex sentences, nor to understand spoken language involving complex syntax. Their speech may consist almost entirely of isolated words spoken out of grammatical context. Although Broca was not the first to note the correlation between damage to a specific area of the brain and the development of characteristic behavioral symptoms, he was so highly regarded as a scientist that many were convinced of his findings primarily on the basis of his standing in the scientific community (Finger, 1994).

The second half of the 20th century saw astounding advances in behavioral neuroscience, and some of the most important of these discoveries are summed up briefly in Table 2.4.

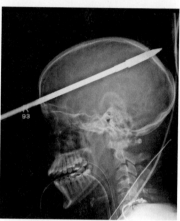

▲ **FIGURE 2.33B Phineas Gage Jr.?** In a freak accident involving a spear gun in 2012, the brain of 16-year-old Yasser Lopez was impaled by an arrow that entered his skull through the right eye, piercing the frontal lobe and exiting through the back of his head. Amazingly, the arrow missed damaging critical brain blood vessels and Lopez survived following surgery to remove the arrow. Whether Lopez will experience behavioral changes similar to that of Phineas Gage is yet to be seen. (*Source: Mestel, 2012.*)

Cognitive Neuroscience: The Neural Basis of Cognition and Emotion

Cognitive neuroscience earned its name in the back seat of a New York City taxicab in the late 1970s. Cognitive psychologist George Miller and neuroscientist Michael Gazzaniga (whose split-brain research was described earlier in the chapter) had just emerged from a conference of scientists who were struggling to decode the ways in which the *brain* creates *mind* (Gazzaniga, Ivry, & Mangun, 2002). Gazzaniga and Miller wished to bring *cognition*—thought, memory, language, and other information-processing aspects of mental life—more clearly to the forefront of neuroscientific research. To do so, they concluded that they needed to focus on the brain itself, rather than the nervous system in its entirety. Although the focus of cognitive neuroscientists is on cognition, over the years many have added *emotion* as an important component of their field of study. Cognitive processes studied by cognitive neuroscientists include language, memory, mental imagery, and problem solving. While cognitive neuroscientists may use nonhuman animals in their research, they are more likely than behavioral neuroscientists to use human subjects and include methodologies such as psychological testing and brain imaging. A number of such brain imaging technologies are available to cognitive neuroscientists, and Figure 2.34 depicts and summarizes several of the most important. However, let us examine one of these technologies in greater depth—*magnetic resonance imaging*, or MRI.

Cognitive neuroscience ▶ Branch of neuroscience that focuses on the human brain to reveal the neural basis of cognition and emotion.

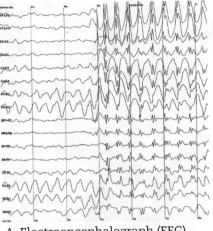

A. Electroencephalograph (EEG)

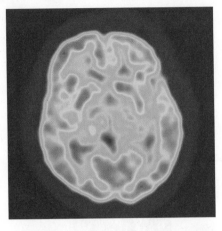

B. Positron Emission Tomography (PET)

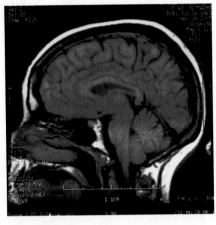

C. Magnetic Resonance Imaging (MRI)

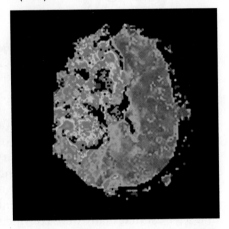

D. functional Magnetic Resonance Imaging (fMRI)

▲ **FIGURE 2.34 Imaging the Brain.** (A) **Electroencephalography (EEG)**, the oldest (and least precise) of available techniques, allows the researcher to note the general area of the brain activated during various tasks, and allows for precise measurement of the *timing* of activation. EEG is particularly useful for predicting and identifying the location of seizures (Schad et al., 2008). (B) **Positron Emission Tomography (PET)** depicts the brain's metabolic activity as a three-dimensional map. First, a benign radioactive substance is injected into the bloodstream of the patient or research subject, who then lies within a scanner that is highly sensitive to radiation. This produces the *tomographic*, or sectioned, map of the brain. As blood flows to various sites in the brain during the performing of a mental task, more radiation is emitted at these sites. The amount of radioactivity produced at a particular site corresponds to the activity of neurons at that site. PET technology has assisted clinical neuroscientists to describe the way the brain functions during clinical depression, anxiety, and post-traumatic stress disorder (e.g., Rauch, Shin, & Wright, 2003) and is particularly good at identifying brain tumors. (C) **Magnetic Resonance Imaging**. (D) **functional Magnetic Resonance Imaging**.

MAGNETIC RESONANCE IMAGING (MRI)

Functional magnetic resonance imaging (fMRI) ▶ The use of MRI whereby continuous images of the brain are generated while a research participant engages in specific tasks.

The human body consists mostly of water, and the MRI takes advantage of this fact. Our cells utilize the equivalent of about eight or nine 8-ounce glasses of water a day—the larger portion of which, however, is normally derived from food, not drink (so you do *not* ordinarily need to drink eight glasses of water per day; Valtin, 2002). The MRI technique uses radio waves and protons of hydrogen atoms to obtain high-resolution photo images of the brain. The patient or research participant lies motionless within a scanner that produces a

Table 2.4 **Neuroscience in the 20th Century: A Brief Sampling**

Moruzzi & Magoun (1949)	These researchers demonstrated that the reticular formation of the brain stem was essential to consciousness.
Scoville & Milner (1957)	Through their study of "Patient H. M." Scoville and Milner showed that damage to the hippocampus could impair or destroy the ability to form new memories—helping to establish that memory has a neural basis.
Penfield & Perot (1963)	By electrically stimulating various cortical regions of the brains of research participants—and noting their reactions—these researchers helped "map" locations of the brain that correspond to specific body parts.
Hounsfield (1972)	In 1972, Godfrey Hounsfield developed *computerized tomography* (CT or "CAT scan"), the forerunner of contemporary brain imaging technologies such as MRI and PET.
Sapolsky (1996)	In 1996, Robert Sapolsky finally demonstrated scientifically what many had suspected was true about the damaging effects of chronic stress on the brain.

benign magnetic field. A pulse of radio waves is generated that momentarily alters the natural alignment of protons in the brain or whatever body part is being examined. As the pulse of radio waves recedes and the protons return to their original positions, the MRI instrument receives the energy that was generated by the realignment activity of the protons. This energy results in a photo image that clearly shows gray matter, white matter, and cerebrospinal fluid (see Figure 2.34*C*). The procedure is safe and noninvasive, although the pulsing radio waves produce rather loud sounds (patients are often advised to wear earplugs or noise-reducing headphones during the procedure).

What do MRI images reveal? The principle use of MRI is by clinical neuroscientists to pinpoint the location of possible brain damage. However, the technology can be used in a slightly different way by cognitive neuroscientists to track blood flow to various portions of the brain while the research participant engages in various tasks and activities. This procedure results in a series of images that reveal ongoing changes in the specific portions of the brain as the person engages in the task. When the technology is used in this manner, it is called **functional magnetic resonance imaging** or **fMRI** (see Figure 2.34*D*).

A compelling use of fMRI technology by cognitive neuroscientists, as reported in the journal *Science*, involved the use of fMRI to test the hypothesis that the neural basis of *social* and *emotional* "pain"—as might be experienced when one is excluded from a social group—is similar to the neural basis for *physical* pain (Eisenberger, Lieberman, & Williams, 2003). Researchers set up a situation in which college students were ultimately excluded from a computerized virtual ball-tossing game. They found that during the experience of exclusion, there was activation of the *anterior cingulate cortex* (ACC), an area of the forebrain which surrounds the corpus callosum and is also activated in response to physical pain (or when a mother hears her baby cry; Eisenberger et al., 2003; see Figure 2.35). One of the study's authors noted, "This doesn't mean a broken arm hurts exactly the same way that a broken heart does, but it shows that the human brain sounds the same alarm system for emotional and physical distress" ("Rejection Really Does Hurt," 2003). Amazingly, in a more recent study, the pain-killer acetaminophen (Tylenol) reduced neural responses in brain regions associated with social rejection—and study participants taking acetaminophen also reported reduced hurt feelings as compared with those taking placebos (DeWall et al., 2010)! Social rejection seems to be associated with "heart*brake*" as well—when study participants were intentionally "rejected" in the laboratory, they experienced an abrupt slowdown of their heart rates (Moor, Crone, & van der Molen, 2010).

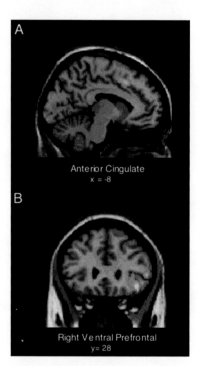

▲ **FIGURE 2.35 Rejection Really Does Hurt.** When research participants in the fMRI study by Naomi Eisenberger and her colleagues (2003) experienced rejection in a social context, areas of the anterior cingulated cortex (ACC) ordinarily associated with the experience of physical pain (particularly emotional aspects of the experience of physical pain) were activated (image *A*). Following activation of the ACC, areas of the right ventral prefrontal cortex (RVPFC) were also activated (image *B*). These areas are associated with *inhibition* of the experience of pain and its emotionally distressing aspects. The RVPFC probably exerts this relieving effect by disrupting ACC activity.

There Are Limits to Neuroscience

Not everyone is impressed with fMRI technology. Some argue that these colorful pictures greatly overstate the degree to which specific areas of the brain control specific aspects of behavior and internal experience (Puldrack, 2010; Vul, Harris, Winkielman, & Pashler, 2009), while others merely point out that, despite the enormous investment of money and time in fMRI studies, there has been little in the way of resulting advancement in psychological theory (Coltheart, 2006, 2013; Page, 2006). Others go so far as to compare the fMRI to phrenology, the pseudoscience initiated by the work of Franz Joseph Gall as described earlier; though they are not in fact comparable (Puldrack, 2010).

Critics worry that psychologists' drive to demonstrate the scientific basis of their discipline incorrectly promotes a view of the brain as a kind of "Swiss army knife"—with different "modules" processing *only* specific types of information and controlling *only* specific aspects of behavior (Shermer, 2008; Uttal, 2001). These critics have a point. In some cases aspects of specific brain functions are carried out by interconnected networks of neurons distributed over numerous areas of the brain. Instead of using a "Swiss army knife" metaphor, critics of fMRI chose the distributed power of the World Wide Web to describe the way the power of the mind is distributed throughout the brain (Shermer, 2008). However, fMRI proponents have countered these criticisms by using this technology to demonstrate the very interconnected distributed networks of neurons hypothesized by critics of the fMRI! (Blumstein & Amso, 2013; Cabeza & Moscovitch, 2013).

The real problem may be that while psychological events are clearly connected to physical events in the brain, they are not the *same* as physical events in the brain. Many researchers are coming to the conclusion that understanding a brain event by itself will not (and perhaps cannot) allow us to fully understand a psychological event (Gazzaniga, 2010; G. A. Miller, 2010).

Subjective states have personal meaning beyond the specific brain changes with which they may be correlated—or even, which may have caused them. This suggests an important limitation of neuroscience data. If psychological states could be entirely reduced to biochemical and structural changes in the brain, the science of psychology would be entirely unnecessary—all that would be needed would be neuroscience. However, although the mind may be a fully physical property of the brain, *the mind is not the same thing* as the brain. As William Uttal (2001) warns, there is a danger of improperly coming to associate brain states and mind states as though they were identical. Neuroscientists *do* make clear that changes in the brain may result from, as well as cause, psychological states, and they acknowledge that the environment and personal experience have important effects on brain chemistry and structure.

To some degree, the argument between neuroscientists and their critics is a variation on a debate regarding human behavior that has existed since antiquity, and is known as the **nature-nurture debate** This is a debate over whether innate biology ("nature") or environmental experience ("nurture") is the more critical factor in the development of human behavioral characteristics. Traditionally, those who take the "nature" side and stress the innate qualities of human characteristics are termed *nativists*. Those who stress "nurture" and emphasize the importance of experience in acquiring characteristics are termed *empiricists*, as I explained briefly in Chapter 1. The advent of new fields informed by biology, such as neuroscience, evolutionary psychology, and behavior genetics, have added fuel to this debate.

Chapter 3 is devoted to exploring the nature-nurture debate, and we will revisit the debate throughout the book. However, contemporary findings in psychology have essentially "solved" the nature-nurture debate by doing away with it. Most psychologists today recognize the importance of both nature and nurture in psychology. Rather than speaking of "nature vs. nurture," more and more scientists are speaking of "nature *via* nurture" (Ridley, 2003).

Nature-nurture debate ▶ A long-standing debate over whether innate biology or environmental experience is the most critical factor in the development of human behavioral characteristics.

IN SUMMARY

1. Behavioral neuroscientists study the anatomy, physiology, and molecular structure of the entire nervous systems of humans and other animals. Cognitive neuroscientists focus on the brain and the neural basis of cognition and emotion in human beings.

2. The early history of behavioral neuroscience includes the pseudoscientific work of phrenologists and the more science-minded but nonetheless equally incorrect views of the equipotentialists.

3. Two classic early neuroscientific findings are the discovery of personality change due to traumatic brain injury (the Phineas Gage case) and the discovery of Broca's area by Paul Broca.

4. Magnetic resonance imaging (MRI) uses radio wave pulses within a magnetic field to momentarily alter the alignment of protons in the brain. When the protons return to their ordinary state, an image is generated. In functional magnetic resonance imaging (fMRI), series of images are produced as a person engages in various tasks and activities.

5. Other brain imaging systems include computerized tomography (CT or "CAT scan") and electroencephalography (EEG).

6. The mind and brain are not identical, even though the mind emerges from the brain. However, there is a danger that in stressing the ways in which the mind and brain differ, one may fall back on dualism.

7. The debate between those who stress innate biology in understanding human psychology and those who stress experience and the environment is known as the nature-nurture dichotomy. Those taking the "nature" side are known as *nativists*, and those taking the "nurture" side are known as *empiricists*.

RETRIEVE!

1. Name two factors that distinguish cognitive from behavioral neuroscience.

2. Franz Joseph Gall was a pseudoscientist with some good ideas. Those who came after Gall and promoted the idea of equipotentiality were far more scientific, but their ideas were incorrect. Explain how this is so.

3. True or False: Phineas Gage ultimately reverted to his preaccident personality characteristics.

4. How have contemporary research findings "solved" the nature-nurture debate?

Looking Back

Chapter 2 in Review

WHERE IS THE MIND?

- The mind remains a somewhat mysterious entity. *Materialism* defines the mind as consisting of physical matter, whereas *dualism* maintains that it consists of something else. Brain imaging and related techniques raise intriguing questions about how the mind can function in the absence of normal brain activity or conscious awareness.

HOW IS THE NERVOUS SYSTEM BUILT?

- The human nervous system is composed of specialized cells—principally, neurons—which allow communication to take place among the various structures of the body. The nervous system also includes glia; cells that assist neurons in their work. Most neurons are composed of dendrites, cell body, axon, and terminal.
- Neurotransmitters such as serotonin, dopamine, and GABA affect many aspects of mental life. Some drugs (agonists) may increase the effects of neurotransmitters, while others (antagonists) may decrease neurotransmitter effects.

HOW IS THE NERVOUS SYSTEM ORGANIZED?

- The nervous system is organized into the central nervous system, consisting of the brain and spinal cord; and the peripheral nervous system.
- The spinal cord is a bundle of nerve tracts organized into segments that act as a communication pathway between the brain and the rest of the body. The spinal cord is composed of gray matter and white matter. The spinal cord also controls spinal reflexes and is responsible for central pattern generators.
- The peripheral nervous system, which is organized into somatic and autonomic nervous systems, makes communication possible between brain and body. The autonomic nervous system is subdivided in turn into the sympathetic and parasympathetic nervous systems.

HOW IS THE BRAIN ORGANIZED?

- The brain is a network of integrated clusters of neurons that form neural circuits. On a basic level, the brain can be divided into three parts: hindbrain, midbrain, and forebrain. The hindbrain consists of the cerebellum, medulla, pons, and reticular formation. The midbrain includes the inferior and superior colliculi.
- The forebrain is the seat of thought, emotion, personality, memory, intelligence, language, and consciousness. The forebrain is divided into two nearly symmetrical cerebral hemispheres, connected by a bundle of over 200 million axons known as the corpus callosum. The major structures of each cerebral hemisphere of the forebrain are the limbic system, the thalamus, and the cerebral cortex. The limbic system is composed of the hypothalamus, the hippocampus, the amygdalae, and clusters of nerves called nuclei—including the basal ganglia and nucleus accumbens. The cerebral cortex is the center of higher cognitive processes, such as problem solving, learning, memory, and language.
- The areas of the cerebral cortex can be grouped into four large regions: the occipital lobe, parietal lobe, temporal lobe, and frontal lobe. The frontal lobe includes the prefrontal cortex, which appears to receive and integrate information from all bodily systems and brain regions to assist in decision making, organizing information, and planning actions.
- Experiments with patients who have undergone split-brain surgery have shown that each cerebral hemisphere is specialized to a certain extent; however, the hemispheres are also at least to some degree plastic.

WHAT IS THE ENDOCRINE SYSTEM?

- The endocrine system consists of glands and the hormones they synthesize. The endocrine system partially overlaps the nervous system.

WHAT IS NEUROSCIENCE?

- Neuroscience is the multidisciplinary study of the central and peripheral nervous systems. Neuroscience can be divided into subdisciplines, including behavioral neuroscience and cognitive neuroscience. Neuroscience has advanced dramatically through the use of contemporary imaging technologies such as MRI and fMRI.

Key Terms

Action potential, 60
Agonist, 64
Antagonist, 64
Autonomic nervous system, 72
Axon, 59
Behavioral neuroscience, 101
Cell body, 58
Central nervous system (CNS), 69
Central pattern generators, 70

Cerebellum, 75
Cerebral cortex, 83
Cerebral hemispheres, 78
Cognitive neuroscience, 103
Corpus callosum, 78
Data, 102
Dendrites, 58
Depolarization, 61
Endocrine system, 97

Endorphin, 65
Equipotentiality, 102
Forebrain, 78
Functional magnetic resonance imaging (fMRI), 105
Gland, 97
Glia, 59
Gray matter, 69
Hemispheric specialization, 88

Key Terms continued

Hindbrain, 75
Hormone, 97
Interneuron, 58
Ion, 60
Limbic system, 78
Lobes of the cerebral cortex, 83
Magnetic resonance imaging (MRI), 74
Magnetoencephalography (MEG), 94
Midbrain, 75
Motor neuron, 58
Myelin sheath, 59
Nature-nurture debate, 106
Nerve, 59
Neuron, 57

Neuroscience, 55
Neurotransmitter, 63
Node of Ranvier, 59
Occipital lobe, 83
Parasympathetic nervous system, 73
Parietal lobe, 84
Peripheral nervous system, 70
Phrenology, 101
Pineal gland, 97
Pituitary gland, 98
Plasticity, 94
Polarization, 61
Postsynaptic neuron, 63
Presynaptic neuron, 63
Resting potential, 60

Reuptake, 64
Sensory neuron, 58
Somatic nervous system, 71
Spinal cord, 69
Spinal reflexes, 70
Split-brain surgery, 90
Sympathetic nervous system, 72
Synapse, 59
Synaptic gap, 59
Synaptic receptors, 58
Temporal lobe, 86
Terminal, 59
Thalamus, 82
Tract, 59
White matter, 70

Test Yourself

1. Name three types of neurons. Which is most numerous in the body? What are glia, and how do they differ from neurons?
2. Name the four major components of the anatomy of a motor neuron.
3. Define the following terms: *nerve, synapse, synaptic gap, synaptic receptor, neurotransmitter, myelin sheath*.
4. Explain how an action potential is fired. Make sure to include the following terms: *resting potential, polarization, depolarization, potassium* and *sodium ions, axon hillock, node of Ranvier*.
5. Describe how neurotransmitters communicate with neighboring neurons. Make sure to include the following terms: *terminal, vesicles, presynaptic* and *postsynaptic neurons, synaptic receptors, synaptic gap*.
6. When a drug mimics the functions of a particular neurotransmitter, it is known as a(n)_____of that neurotransmitter.
7. What is the difference between a spinal reflex and a central pattern generator of the spine?

8. What are the primary functions of the autonomic and somatic systems of the peripheral nervous system? What are the primary functions of the sympathetic and parasympathetic systems of the autonomic nervous system?
9. Name at least two functions of the cerebellum.
10. Name the principal structures of the limbic system. What are the principal functions of each?
11. A type of amnesia where past memories are preserved but no new memories are formed is _____.
12. What are two of the principal functions of the thalamus?
13. The bundle of axons that connects the two cerebral hemispheres of the forebrain is the _____.
14. Which part of the cerebral cortex consists of white matter, and which consists of gray matter?
15. Which lobe of the cortex processes visual information? Auditory information?
16. Where are Broca's and Wernicke's areas, and what are their functions?

17. Where does the somatosensory cortex sit? What is its function?
18. Why are different parts of the body allotted more "space" in the somatosensory cortex?
19. What are the general functions of the prefrontal cortex?
20. Describe the specializations of each cerebral hemisphere. What is the term given to the fact that each hemisphere is specialized?
21. Describe at least one study that has demonstrated hemispheric specialization.
22. Give one example of the ways in which human male and female brains differ on average. Do these average brain differences necessarily result in differences in behavior?
23. Give an example of one way in which the nervous and endocrine systems overlap.
24. What are three of the most important brain imaging technologies?
25. What is one criticism of the way findings in neuroscience have been interpreted?

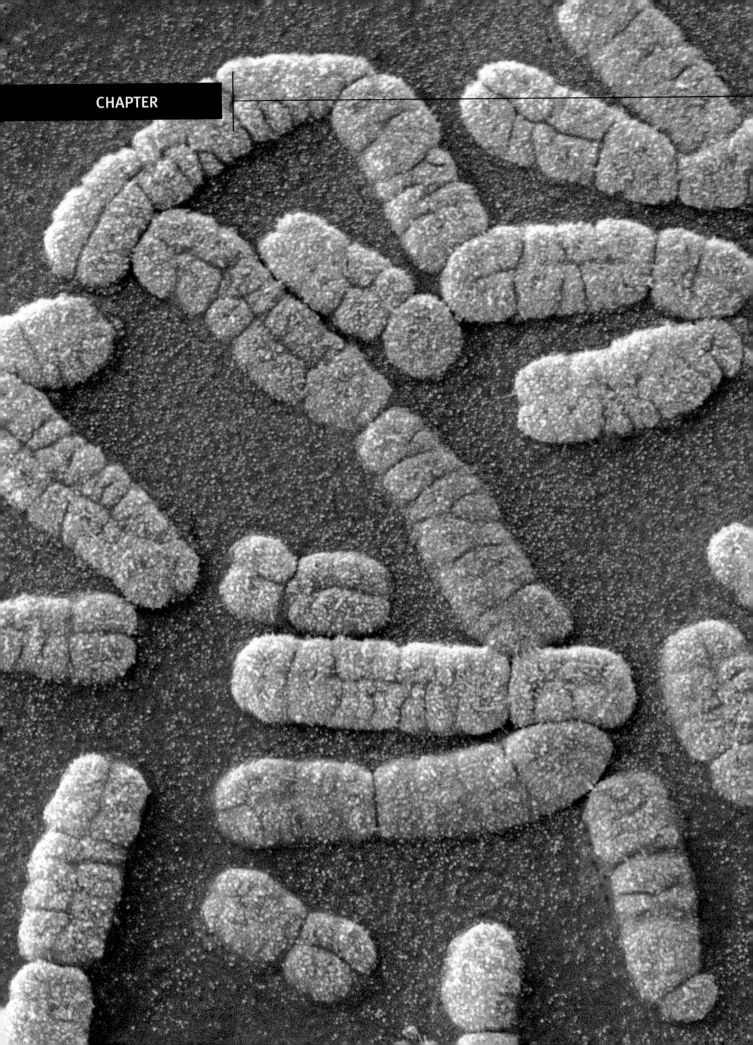

The Nature and Nurture of behavior

Chapter Outline

Freeze Frame

▲ *"What did you just say?"*

Imagine that you are walking around campus or perhaps having coffee at a campus hang-out, and a reasonably attractive member of the other sex approaches you. The person starts up a conversation, mentions that he or she has been noticing you around campus and adds, "I find you very attractive." The stranger then asks you if you would be willing to go out for coffee, to a movie, or something similar over the weekend. What might your response be? Undoubtedly, it would depend to a great extent on your own "chemical" response to the person, your sexual orientation, your moral sense, and numerous other factors—for example, if you are already in a steady relationship.

But what if, instead of asking you out to a movie over the weekend, the person asks if you'd like to go back to his or her dorm to have sex? What might your response be? Do you think your answer would also depend on "numerous factors," or are you fairly certain how you would respond?

If you are young, female, and anything like university research participants in the study conducted by social psychologists Russell Clark and Elaine Hatfield (Clark & Hatfield, 1989), your answer is a virtual certainty—a resounding, unapologetic "No!"—perhaps using even more colorful language to convey the same message. Not a single woman in Clark and Hatfield's study accepted the invitation, nor did any of

the female subjects in two follow-up studies conducted the following year (Clark, 1990). More than a decade later, British professor Robert Lord Winston got identical results when he attempted to duplicate the study in Great Britain, filming the results for a BBC program on human instincts ("Deepest Desires," 2002).

The results for men were just as monotonously similar, but in the opposite direction: Approximately 75% of men in all of these studies immediately agreed to the invitation to have sex, and the comparatively few who declined did so regretfully and apologetically. In fact, men were far more likely to agree to have sex than to agree to have coffee!

The methods used for this research, and the implications of the studies' results, have been debated for 20 years. Some commentators dismiss these studies as little more than stunts with few implications for human psychology, while others claim that the studies are among the best available pieces of evidence of actual sex differences in men's and women's "sexual psychology." What concerns us now, however, is the sheer *size* of the differences between men's and women's responses: 75% vs. 0%. Regardless of the possible flaws in the study, a difference of this size needs to be explained.

These studies, and responses to them by psychologists and other commentators over the years, highlight a scientific debate concerning the origins of human traits and behaviors. This debate is usually termed the "nature-nurture debate," with *nature* standing for supposedly biological, innate characteristics of an individual (or in this case, an entire sex), and *nurture* standing for supposedly nonbiological, learned characteristics—influences from the environment, society, or culture. However, as stressed repeatedly throughout this book, it can be seriously misleading to analyze nature and nurture in psychology as though they are separate entities, opposed to each other. Nature always exists *via* nurture, not *versus* nurture (Champagne & Mashoodh, 2009; Ridley, 2003), and nurture cannot exist without nature. Biology and environment, innate and learned mechanisms, society and the brain all exist in an eternal embrace.

Recall that in Chapter 1, I listed six major perspectives in psychology, each representing different ways of looking at human beings. I emphasized that these perspectives make their appearance in the work of psychologists and researchers from any number of different specific fields. This chapter traces the contours of the relationship between nature and nurture as seen through the lenses of psychologists using three of these perspectives: the biobehavioral perspective, the evolutionary perspective, and the sociocultural perspective.

Let us begin by examining the biobehavioral perspective as it is expressed in one specific field—*behavior genetics*. Then we will examine the *evolutionary* and the *sociocultural* perspectives as they appear in a large number of specific fields of science, including cognitive, developmental, and social psychology; anthropology; computer science; and cultural and cross-cultural psychology. Psychologists favoring these three perspectives approach questions of nature and nurture in radically different ways. We will return to the Clark and Hatfield "I find you very attractive" study later in the chapter, when we examine evolutionary perspectives on behavior. However, evolution is a "big" question, and it's probably best to start small—with the gene.

What Are Genes?

In Chapter 2, I discussed the human nervous system and located the *mind* directly within the *brain*. But where does the brain come from? As psychological scientists we cannot simply say, "Well, we're born with it!" The human nervous system, including the brain, is the result of "programming instructions" from within the **human genome**, the set of hereditary instructions that exists within every cell of every human body. Our human genome "tells" various amino acids and the proteins they construct to build a *human* organism rather than, say, a frog or a fruit fly—both of which actually contain a great many genes in common with human beings (see Figure 3.1). Without the human genome, you might have ended up as a yeast spore. As it is, you share almost 25% of your genes with yeast spores, and between 98% and 99% with the chimpanzee.

Human genome ▶ The entire set of hereditary "instructions," encoded in DNA, for creating a human organism. The human genome exists within every cell of every human body.

The Gene Is the Unit of Heredity

But what exactly is a gene? Most people in the industrialized world have a vague, or intuitive, understanding of the meaning of the word "gene," but the majority of us probably would be hard pressed to provide a precise definition. Briefly, as explained in Chapter 2, the human body is constructed of cells. As depicted in Figure 3.2*A*, the *nucleus*, or inner kernel, of almost every one of these cells contains 23 pairs of **chromosomes**, rod-like bodies made up of proteins and strands of DNA. (The exceptions to the 23-pair rule are the male and female reproductive cells, which have only 23 total chromosomes rather than 23 pairs of chromosomes.) **DNA** (deoxyribonucleic acid) is a complex molecule with a characteristic spiraling shape. DNA contains the unique "code" for creating every living organism, and is therefore the basis for passing on hereditary characteristics in humans (see Figure 3.2*B*).

Heredity is transmitted through an arrangement of functional strands of DNA grouped together along each chromosome (see Figure 3.2*C*). These functional units are called **genes**, and recent estimates suggest that there are about 20,000-25,000 of them in your body, somewhat fewer than was once thought (Human Genome Project Information, 2008). Like chromosomes, genes are laid out in pairs, and each member of a pair occupies a fixed position, or *locus*, along the chromosome.

Genes are important in psychology. As described in several chapters of this book, differences among people in personality traits, cognitive ability and IQ scoring, vulnerability to certain physical and mental disorders, and many other attributes are partially due to genetic differences. So there is no misunderstanding: All humans inherit the same basic collection of genes (the genome), but genes come in two or more different "versions" or **alleles**. For example, the gene that determines hair color is inherited by everyone. But one person might inherit alleles coding for blond hair and another person, alleles coding for black hair.

Thus, when we talk about "different genes" or "genetic differences" among individual people, we are using shorthand to talk about differences in alleles. The unique collection of alleles in an individual that contributes to (or entirely

Chromosomes ▶ Rod-like bodies, present in every human cell, made up of proteins and strands of DNA.

DNA (deoxyribonucleic acid) ▶ A complex molecule with a characteristic spiraling shape. DNA contains the genetic instructions for heredity in all living organisms.

Gene ▶ The unit of heredity in living organisms. Genes are constructed of strands of DNA and grouped together along each chromosome.

Allele ▶ One of two or more forms a particular gene might take. "Genetic differences" among people occur because people inherit unique collections of alleles.

▶ **FIGURE 3.1 25,000 Genes and a Conscience.** A portion of the genes within the human genome are shared with every living organism from bacteria to broccoli to brown bears. These ancient genes likely stem from a common ancestor that lived 3.5 billion years ago. Scientists theorize that through evolution this ancestor's genome became the basis for every species living today. Pictured are estimates of the percentage of genes humans share in common with various species. These genes are so similar that, at least in some instances, the human version can be spliced into the body of an individual of another species, including a plant, worm, or fly, in place of that species' own version of the gene, with no harmful effects (Ridley, 2003). *(Source: Figure and text adapted from material presented on the Canadian Museum of Nature website, http://www.nature.ca/genome/03/c/20/03c_21_e.cfm.)*

	% Common with Humans
Chimpanzee 25,000 genes Just like you, chimpanzees have around 25,000 genes. But then why can't they speak? The difference could be in a single gene, FOXP2, which in the chimpanzee is missing certain sections.	**98%**
Mouse 30,000 genes Thanks to mice, researchers have been able to identify genes linked to skeletal development, obesity and Parkinson's disease, to name but a few.	**90%**
Zebra Fish 30,000 genes 85% of the genes in these little fish are the same as yours. Researchers use them to study the role of genes linked to blood disease, such as anemia falciforme and heart disease.	**85%**
Fruit Fly 13,600 genes For the past 100 years, the fruit fly has been used to study the transmission of hereditary characteristics, the development of organisms, and, more recently, the study of changes in behaviour induced by the consumption of alcohol.	**36%**
Thale cress 25,000 genes This little plant, from the mustard family, is used as a model for the study of all flowering plants. Scientists use its genes to study hepatolenticular degeneration, a disease that causes copper to accumulate in the human liver.	**26%**
Yeast 6,275 genes You have certain genes in common with this organism that is used to make bread, beer and wine. Scientists use yeast to study the metabolism of sugars, the cell division process, and other diseases such as cancer.	**23%**
Roundworm 19,000 genes Just like you, this worm possesses muscles, a nervous system, intestines and sexual organs. That is why the roundworm is used to study genes linked to aging, to neurological diseases such as Alzheimer's, to cancer and to kidney disease.	**21%**
Bacterium, Escherichia coli 4,800 genes The *E. coli* bacterium inhabits your intestines. Researchers study it to learn about basic cell functions, such as transcription and translation.	**7%**

Genotype ▶ The unique collection of alleles that contribute to (or entirely determine) specific traits in living organisms.

Heredity ▶ The transfer of genetic characteristics from parent to offspring.

determines) some trait or characteristic is known as the **genotype** for that characteristic.

Thus, if the *human genome* is the set of genetic instructions necessary to construct human beings, genotypes are sets of unique genetic instructions necessary to create a *specific* human being (or two, in the case of identical twins). Evidence collected by researchers over the past four decades demonstrates that genotypes do play a part in the development of psychological traits just as they do in the development of physiological traits (Bouchard, 1996a, 1996b; Leonardo & Hen, 2006; Plomin, DeFries, McClearn, & McGuffin, 2008; Plomin & Spinath, 2004).

Throughout history the existence of **heredity**—the tendency of offspring to resemble their parents in various ways—has always been taken for granted. However, it was not until the rediscovery during the 20th century of the work of the scientist-monk Gregor Mendel (1822–1884) that scientists came to understand exactly what was being inherited. Mendel realized that heredity

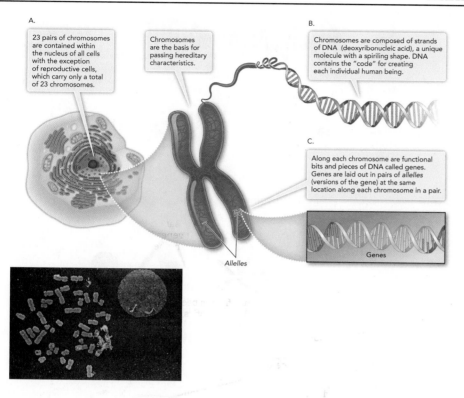

A.
23 pairs of chromosomes are contained within the nucleus of all cells with the exception of reproductive cells, which carry only a total of 23 chromosomes.

Chromosomes are the basis for passing hereditary characteristics.

B.
Chromosomes are composed of strands of DNA (deoxyribonucleic acid), a unique molecule with a spiralling shape. DNA contains the "code" for creating each individual human being.

C.
Along each chromosome are functional bits and pieces of DNA called genes. Genes are laid out in pairs of *allelles* (versions of the gene) at the same location along each chromosome in a pair.

Allelles

Genes

◀ **FIGURE 3.2 The Gene Is the Unit of Heredity.** Genes store the evolutionary information about the specific species (genome) and hereditary information about the specific individual (genotypes).

occurs in separate "packets" that later came to be termed *genes*. Thus, the gene is the unit of heredity.

Phenotypes Are Observable Characteristics

Genes cannot ordinarily be observed. However, the effects of their activity (e.g., blond hair or brown eyes) can be observed. Any potentially observable trait or characteristic of a living organism—be it physiological, anatomical, behavioral, or mental—is known as a **phenotype**. It should not be surprising that genes contribute to the development of mental and behavioral phenotypes. After all, the mind emerges in some way from the physiology and anatomy of the brain. If brains differ due to genetics—as do eyes, legs, and noses—then we might expect minds also to differ as a result of genetic differences, at least to some degree.

Phenotype ▶ Any potentially observable trait or characteristic of a living organism. Phenotypes may be physiological, biochemical, anatomical, behavioral, or mental.

Genes Have at Least Three Functions

If the gene is the unit of heredity, how does it transmit characteristics from one generation to the next? Genes have a number of specific functions. *The first function of the gene is to create proteins*. Proteins synthesize structures in living organisms—creating everything from neurotransmitters to knee joints. Genes create proteins primarily by transmitting genetic information through **RNA (ribonucleic acid)**, a chemical compound found in each cell nucleus and *cytoplasm*—the jelly-like material that fills cells. As depicted in Figure 3.3, RNA does the actual work of constructing proteins by "transcribing" the genetic information into a form that can be used to create proteins. In this way, genes construct an entire organism according to plans laid out in the organism's DNA.

The second function of the gene is to replicate—to make as many copies of itself as it can. In the broadest sense, genes do this by guiding the behavior of their *host organisms* (the organisms in which they reside). Genes guide the behavior of their hosts by doing their protein-construction work in a way that will optimize the chances that the organism will survive and reproduce

RNA (ribonucleic acid) ▶ A chemical compound found in each cell nucleus and cytoplasm. RNA carries out the job of constructing protein from "instructions" contained in genes.

▶ **FIGURE 3.3** **RNA Does the Actual Work of Constructing Proteins.** Genes contained within DNA transmit hereditary information through RNA, which "transcribes" this genetic information into a form that can be used to construct proteins. These proteins build individuals with specific physical and mental characteristics.

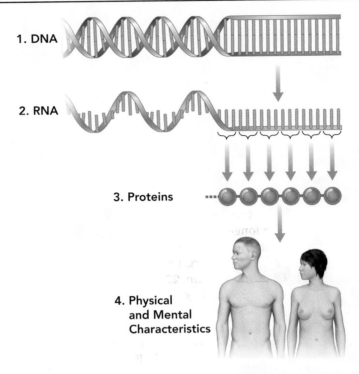

1. DNA

2. RNA

3. Proteins

4. Physical and Mental Characteristics

▲ **The Significance of DNA Evidence.** Michael Morton, wrongly convicted and sent to prison in 1987 for murdering his wife, is a free man 25 years later after DNA evidence pointed toward a different man. With $2 million compensation from the state for his wrongful imprisonment, he is starting a new life.

(Dawkins, 1989). When you jump out of the way of an oncoming car, feel revulsion at the smell of spoiled food, or experience feelings of desire in the presence of your romantic partner or tenderness in the presence of your infant children or younger siblings, you are following the "directives" of the genes to which you are host. These genes have survived through the millennia only because their hosts have behaved in ways that allow genetic reproduction to occur.

Of course, genes can only do their "construction" and "self-copying" work in an environment that is adequate. For example, without proper nutrition, the appropriate chemical and hormonal environment, and protection from toxins of various sorts, a normal brain and nervous system will not develop in a human fetus, in spite of the best efforts of the fetus's 25,000 genes. An infant whose mother drinks excessively during pregnancy may develop *fetal alcohol syndrome* (see p. 159) even if that infant has no particular genetic vulnerability for such a condition. A human being reared in darkness during specific periods of early infancy will never develop normal vision (Hubel & Wiesel, 1970; Maurer, Mondloch, & Lewis, 2007). A genetically normal child deprived of human touch and the chance to play with others may develop profound cognitive and emotional problems as a result (Rutter, O'Connor, and the English and Romanian Adoptees [ERA] Study Team, 2004).

Even relatively ordinary environments can constrain or promote the effects of genes in less extreme ways. Without adequate education and access to educational materials, for example, a person with an inherited aptitude for academic learning cannot be expected to learn much; and a person genetically predisposed to develop a mental illness may never show symptoms if he or she is reared in a particularly supportive environment. Thus, certain effects of genes on behavior may not be apparent in environments that suppress the expression of the genes—or they may be particularly apparent in environments that enhance them (Fox, Hane, & Pine, 2007; Harden, Hill, Turkheimer, & Emery, 2008; Tucker-Drob, Rhemtulla, Harden, Turkheimer, & Fask, 2011).

This idea leads us to a *third* function of genes. *The gene is a "switch" that interacts with other genes* (Ptashne & Gann, 2002; Ridley, 2003). If we share almost 99% of our genes with chimpanzees, why is it that they haven't developed stick shifts, housing projects, and tortilla chips? Why can't they speak Armenian, or rap like NaS? And why don't we spend as much time picking lice off our friends or swinging from trees as chimpanzees do?

The answer is that genes can be switched on and off—they can become active or inactive to varying degrees. If the same gene is switched on for a longer or shorter time, it may have dramatically different effects during the development of an organism and after maturity has been reached. A short period of activity might result in the development of a body with short arms relative to leg size, while a longer period might result in the opposite physique. Similarly, a short period might result in the ability to learn only a few hand signs after years of tutoring, while a longer period might result in the ability to write *The Great Gatsby, Ulysses,* or *The Color Purple.* Genes switched on and off in different patterns and for different lengths of time result in different species and different individuals (Ptashne & Gann, 2002).

What does the switching? Other genes—and the proteins that help regulate them. Changes in genes and their regulating proteins promote or suppress the expression of other genes . . . and these genes may then do the same to still more genes down the line. What we have in essence is a series of genetic switches turning one another on and off—in some ways similar to the way thermostats regulate air conditioning in office buildings by automatically switching cooling or heating units on and off when the temperature drops below or moves above preset temperature points. This also explains why the same gene may have different effects in different parts of the body. As Matt Ridley (2003, p. 236) points out, these facts show why it is highly simplistic to speak of "genes for" specific traits (e.g., a "gene for creativity" or a "gene for homosexuality"). In one context a gene might have a certain effect, and in another context, it might have a radically different, unrelated effect.

▲ **Organisms Do Not Grow by Genes Alone.** These poppy plants were both grown from seeds taken from the same flower. They are genetically virtually identical. However, one plant was watered adequately and the other was not.

IN SUMMARY

1.	Genes are functional units of heredity, made of bits and pieces of DNA grouped together along chromosomes. They do their work by synthesizing proteins via RNA, making copies of themselves, and acting as "switches" to turn other genes on and off. Genes may come in two or more "versions" known as alleles.
2.	The human genome is the set of genetic programming "instructions" for building a human being (as opposed to another life form). A person's genotypes are unique arrangements of alleles that have contributed to, or in certain cases entirely determined, that person's characteristics.
3.	The nuclei of almost all human cells contain 23 pairs of chromosomes, rod-like bodies composed of proteins and strands of DNA. Functional units made of bits and pieces of DNA are grouped together along each chromosome and are known as genes. They transmit hereditary characteristics from parents to their offspring. Genes play an important part in the development of psychological traits.
4.	Genes have three main functions. The first is to create proteins by transmitting genetic information through RNA. The second function is to replicate. The third function is to act as a "switch," turning other genes on and off.
5.	Genes can only do their work in an environment that is adequate.

RETRIEVE!

1. Functional strands of DNA grouped together along each chromosome are called _____.

2. Genes come in two or more "versions." These "versions" are known as _____.

3. True or false: It is likely that one day the gene for homosexuality will be discovered.

4. Portia is a human being rather than a turtle because of her human _____. She has black wavy hair because of her _____. The black wavy hair itself is called a _____.

5. Which of the following is NOT one of the functions of the gene?

a) create DNA   b) create proteins   c) replication   d) interact with other genes

How Do Genes and Environments Influence Behavior?

The experimental research methods described in Chapter 1 of this book are based to some degree on methods used by farmers and agricultural scientists to test methods of plant cultivation in the first part of the 20th century (e.g., Fisher, 1925). For example, seeds might be drawn from the same plant (containing the same genetic material) but sown in different plots of land. The plots might then be subjected to carefully controlled environmental variation—for example, the amount of sunlight and water the seeds receive might be varied, the temperature might be controlled in some way, or different types of fertilizer used. Then the results would be compared.

Experiments such as these led to the commonsense conclusion that, regardless of genetic origin, environments to which plants are subjected can have a powerful effect on the way the plant grows. On the other hand, there are limits to the effects of this variation—a green pepper will not grow into a tomato regardless of environmental changes, and a tomato seed taken from a line of generally poorly producing plants will not suddenly blossom into a state fair winner just because the amount of sunlight it receives is increased. Thus, genes and environments interact to determine the way living things develop, and this goes for human psychology as well as for plants in the ground.

Twin and Adoption Studies Disentangle Nature and Nurture

In 1940 identical twin boys who came to be known as Jim Lewis and Jim Springer were separated at birth. Almost four decades later, they were reunited—a highly unusual event. At the time of their reunion, each of the "Jim twins" was 6 feet tall and weighed 180 pounds. Each had been married twice—first to a woman named Linda, next to a woman named Betty. Jim Lewis's first-born son was named James Alan, while Jim Springer's first born was named James Allen. As children, each had owned a dog named Toy. Jim

◀ **The "Jim Twins."** Jim Lewis and Jim Springer were separated as infants and reunited in adulthood. At the time of their reunion they shared so many attributes in common that they remain "poster children" for the findings of behavior genetics.

Lewis's and Jim Springer's families vacationed on the same beach in Florida, and both Jims had worked as sheriff's deputies in nearby Ohio counties (Wright, 1997).

If the preceding information does not put a strain on your belief systems, consider that both men drank the same brand of beer (Miller Lite) and chain-smoked the same brand of cigarettes (Salem). Both men had woodworking shops in their garages, with Jim Lewis specializing in miniature picnic tables and Jim Springer in miniature rocking chairs. Both men loved NASCAR dearly but hated baseball. Both drove the same model Chevy. Both were described by their wives as romantics who left love notes around the house but who ground their teeth during their sleep and bit their nails to the quick during the day. Their personality and mental ability scores "were all so similar that they could have been the same person" (Wright, 1997, p. 47).

Certainly, some of the similarities just described were due entirely to co-incidence. Lots of people chain-smoked Salems and drank Miller Lite in those days, and plenty of women were named Linda and Betty. Nevertheless, the Jim twins remain "poster children" for the now-well-established findings from the field of **behavior genetics** that most cognitive and personality traits are influenced by a person's genetic inheritance—often substantially so (Johnson, Turkheimer, Gottesman, & Bouchard, 2009; Krueger & Johnson, 2008; Plomin et al., 2008; Plomin & Spinath, 2004). Behavior genetics is the scientific study of the influence of genes and environments on individual differences in traits and behavior.

Psychologists were slow to accept the findings of behavior geneticists, and criticisms of the field still exist (Horwitz, Videon, Schmitz, & Davis, 2003). However, the general notion that genetics accounts for a portion of individual differences in many psychological characteristics is now rarely disputed—even by those who at first strongly criticized such ideas (e.g., Maccoby, 2002).

Behavior geneticists begin with the understanding that for every human trait—intelligence, kindness, religious feeling and social attitudes, hostility, generosity, and so forth—there is *variation* (i.e., differences) from one person to the next. This means that in any given sample, individuals will differ in their scores on measures of such traits. Behavior geneticists attempt to *quantify* (estimate numerically) the portion of these differences that can be accounted for by genetic heredity and that portion resulting from experiences in the world (including experiences in the womb prior to birth). Behavior geneticists accomplish this task by conducting research among groups of people—usually twins or adopted children—whose characteristics make them especially suitable to disentangling genes from the environment.

Behavior genetics ▶ The study of the influence of genes and environments on individual differences in behavior. Behavior geneticists measure the differences in some trait among a sample of people and attempt to quantify the portion of these differences that is due to genes and the portion that is due to environment.

TWIN STUDIES

The Jim twins inaugurated the longest running study of twins reared apart, conducted by Thomas J. Bouchard and colleagues and known as the Minnesota Study of Twins Reared Apart (MISTRA; Bouchard, Lykken, McGue, Segal, & Tellegen, 1990; Bouchard et al., 2004). Studies of twins reared apart or together constitute what is often termed a **natural experiment**. A natural experiment is a situation that occurs naturally, but which an experimenter can utilize to create research that allows conclusions to be drawn about causation (Segal, 2010). In general, as we discussed in Chapter 1, causation can be inferred in a research study only when all the variables are controlled by an experimenter; but in a natural experiment it is nature itself that controls at least some of the variables.[1]

Natural experiment ▶ A situation that occurs naturally, but that creates conditions for drawing conclusions about cause and effect.

In research among twins reared together, nature is controlling the number of genes that pairs of twins and other types of siblings share in common. Identical (**monozygotic**) twins share 100% of their genes in common and develop from a single female egg (*monozygotic* literally means "one egg"). Fraternal (**dizygotic**) twins share only 50% on average—no different from any other pair of siblings—and develop from two eggs (*dizygotic* means "two eggs"). If monozygotic twins are more similar than dizygotic twins and other siblings on some trait, this is evidence of the influence of genes. It is the *logic* of studies of twins reared together. These studies have shown that by the time they reach adulthood, identical twins reared together are about twice as similar in personality and cognitive ability as either pairs of fraternal twins or ordinary siblings (McGue, Bouchard, Iacono, & Lykken, 1993; Plomin & Spinath, 2004). This is predicted from behavior genetics theory because identical twins share twice as many genes in common on average as do ordinary siblings or fraternal twins (Saudino, 2005).

Monozygotic (identical) twins ▶ Twins who emerge from a single ovum (egg) and share 100% of their genes in common.

Dizygotic (fraternal) twins ▶ Twins who emerge from two ova (eggs) and share only 50% of their genes in common, on average.

Yet, if pairs of identical twins reared *apart* like the Jim twins are as similar to one another as identical twins reared *together*, this would present even more powerful evidence that genes play an important role in creating that similarity. Why would this evidence be more powerful? It is because identical twins reared apart share all of their genes in common but have been reared in *different* environments. Therefore, similarities between the twins cannot be accounted for even in part by environmental experiences since the twins have not shared the same environment. This is the logic of studies of twins reared apart. These studies show that identical twins reared apart are often as similar—or nearly as similar—as identical twins reared together for a large number of characteristics.

Taken together, studies of twins reared together and apart have shown the influence of genetics in general cognitive ability such as IQ scoring (see Chapter 9); sexual orientation (gay and straight); personality traits and temperament (see Chapter 12); social attitudes; and tendency toward mental disorders—including *schizophrenia*, depressive and bipolar disorders, and *autism* (Leonardo & Hen, 2006; Haworth et al., 2010; McGuffin, Riley, & Plomin, 2001; Olson, Vernon, Harris, & Jang, 2001; Plomin & Spinath, 2004; Plomin et al., 2008). All of these results point to the importance of genes in the development of differences in human characteristics.

ADOPTION STUDIES

Identical twins reared together or apart are not the only subjects of behavior genetics research. Equally important are natural experiments involving children adopted at birth. Adopted children are raised in environments that do not include their genetic parents in the vast majority of cases. If the children end up

---

[1]*Because no random assignment to conditions is possible in twin studies such as those described here, and for certain other reasons, twin studies would probably better be termed "natural quasi-experiments." (See Chapter 1 for a discussion of quasi-experiments.)*

to be more similar to their *genetic* parents than to their *adoptive* parents—with whom they spend their entire lives—this also would be powerful evidence that genetic differences play an important part in development. Indeed, evidence from adoption studies is even more powerful than that derived from twin studies because the *only* influences on adopted children of their genetic parents are genes (Beer, Arnold, & Loehlin, 1998)!

As it turns out, however, results of adoption studies are mixed. Adopted children—particularly as they grow into adolescence and adulthood—are strikingly closer to their genetic parents than to their adoptive parents in cognitive abilities such as IQ performance and mathematical and reading ability (Petrill et al., 2004; Plomin & Spinath, 2004; Wadsworth, Corley, Hewitt, Plomin, & DeFries, J.C., 2002; see Chapter 9). By the time they enter adolescence, adopted children are no more likely to resemble their adoptive parents or siblings in these abilities than would a person picked randomly off the street. On the other hand, the differences are much less marked in the case of personality characteristics (Beer, Arnold, & Loehlin, 1998; Loehlin, Horn, & Willerman, 1990). In general, adoption research shows a lesser contribution of genes to personality than does the twin research—a discrepancy that behavior geneticists have not yet been able to explain fully (Petrill et al., 2004; Plomin, Corley, Caspi, Fulker, & DeFries, 1998).

The Heritability Statistic Is an Estimate of Genetic Influence

When behavior geneticists conduct studies among twins or adopted children, they compute a statistic known as **heritability**, or h^2. This statistic is based on comparisons of test scores for a particular trait (e.g., intelligence, shyness) among people of varying genetic relatedness (e.g., identical twins, ordinary siblings) and varying environments (i.e., reared together or in different homes). The heritability statistic teases apart the extent of genetic and environmental influence by computing the degree to which genes and environments contribute to the variation on some trait among people in a particular sample.

Values of the heritablity statistic range from 0 to 1.0. The closer the statistic is to 1.0, the greater is the influence of genes and the less the influence of the environment. For example, if heritability is found to be 0.55 in a research study on intelligence, it means that approximately 55% of the variation in intelligence among the specific individuals in the research study is due to variance in genotype for the genes that contribute to intelligence and 45% due to environmental causes (total = 100%).

However, if you were participating in this study, it would *not* mean that 55% of *your* intelligence is "genetic" and 45% is "environmental." Genes and environments are inextricably intertwined in each individual and can never be separated, regardless of scientific technology. It would be like asking, "How much of the flavor of this pizza is due to the heat of the oven, and how much to the mozzarella?" Yet, the relative contributions of genes and environments toward *differences* or variation among a specific sample of people *can* be distinguished using behavior genetics research methods and estimated using the heritability statistic. Figure 3.4 depicts average heritability estimates for a number of traits including adult IQ scoring, personality traits, social attitudes, and a number of psychological disorders.

Note that any given heritability estimate applies only to the specific individuals included in the research study. It cannot be said to apply to all people. As a particularly dramatic example of this, consider Eric Turkheimer and his colleagues' study of the impact of a severely impoverished environment on the genetics of IQ (intelligence) scores (Turkheimer, Haley, Waldron, D'Onofrio, & Gottesman, 2003). Over the past decades, behavior genetics researchers have demonstrated through twin and adoption studies that a substantial

Heritability ▶ A statistic that estimates the extent of genetic influence in the differences among a sample of people on a particular trait.

▶ **FIGURE 3.4 Heritability Estimates Based on Twin Studies.** This bar graph compares recent estimates for heritability and environmental contribution for a number of traits based on twin studies. A trait with zero heritability would be completely determined by the environment. A trait with 1.0 heritability would be completely determined by genetics. *(Sources: Olson et al., 2001; McGuffin, et al., 2001; Rietveld, Hudziak, Bartels, et al., 2004; Skuse, Mandy, & Scourfield, 2005.)*

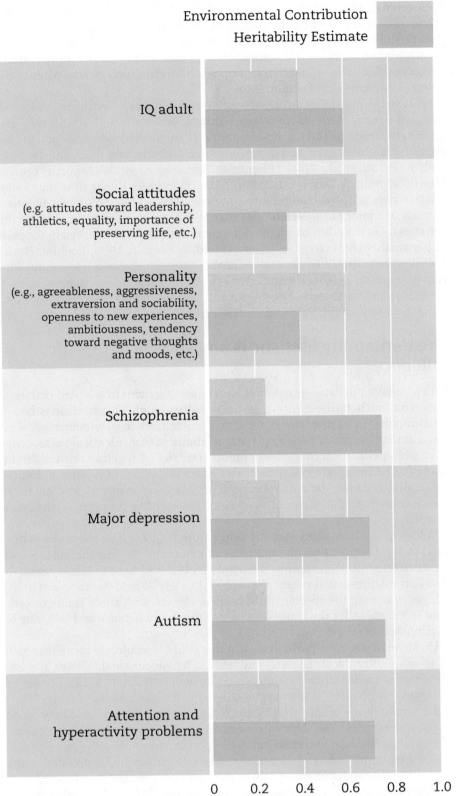

Note: Figures for heritability of personality and social attitudes are averages of heritability estimates for various traits and attitudes. Some traits and attitudes are more heritable than others.

portion of the differences among samples of individuals in IQ scores is due to genetic differences—approximately 50% or perhaps more (Bouchard, 1996a, 1996b). However, most of the participants in these research studies have been of middle-class or lower-middle-class ("working-class") origin. When

Turkheimer and colleagues conducted a twin study using a sample of deeply impoverished and disadvantaged twins and other siblings, they found that less than 10% of the differences in IQ scoring among the individuals in this sample was due to genetic differences.

In a subsequent study comparing very young infants reared in economically advantaged homes with infants reared in disadvantaged homes, researchers found that genes accounted for about 50% of the variation in cognitive abilities, but among the disadvantaged infants the influence of genes was negligible (Tucker-Drob et al., 2011). Taken together, these findings imply that severe disadvantages may "trump" (override) the ordinary expression of genes—underscoring the idea that genetic programs cannot unfold in environments that are inadequate.

Finally, bear in mind that the heritability statistic reports two types of influences on traits and behavior: genetic *and* environmental. Recall that if 50% of variation in a trait can be attributable to genes, then 50% is attributable to the environment. If results of behavior genetics research on cognitive ability, personality traits, and social attitudes are averaged out, for example, genetic heredity usually accounts for between 25% and 50% of the differences among most samples of people—leaving an equal or greater proportion to the environment. This average figure results from the fact that general cognitive ability often shows heritability higher than 50%, while personality characteristics and social attitudes often show heritability estimates that are much lower than 50% (Plomin et al., 1998; Plomin et al., 2008). Because the environment often accounts for greater influence than genetics, primarily in personality and social attitudes, the term *behavior genetics* is a bit misleading. Behavior geneticists are as interested in estimating environmental influences as they are in estimating genetic influences.

"GRANTZ IS CHARTING HIS LIFE BASED ON GENETIC VS. ENVIRONMENTAL FACTORS."

▲ **Behavior Genetics.** It is not possible to identify the amount of genetic and environmental influence on a trait for any single human being. Behavior geneticists study only the *differences* in the trait among *samples* of individuals.

Genes and Environments Interact

Because virtually all researchers consider that the case for at least some heritability of mental characteristics has been made (Maccoby, 2002), many behavior geneticists have moved on to more subtle questions. Some have entered the field of **molecular genetics**, where the hunt goes on for the *specific* genes responsible for various traits (Haworth & Plomin, 2010). Others have stayed within the field of behavior genetics but have turned their attention to the ways in which genes and environments influence one another to produce traits and characteristics. These researchers have demonstrated that genes influence environments, and that environments influence how genes are expressed (Fox et al., 2007; Krueger, South, Johnson, & Iacono, 2008). In other words, they have moved farther from nature *versus* nurture and closer to nature *via* nurture (Ge, Donnellan, & Harper, 2003; Rutter, 2007). Nowhere is this more apparent than in the cases of *gene-environment correlations* and *gene-environment interactions*.

Molecular genetics ▶ Molecular geneticists attempt to identify specific genes responsible for differences among people in particular traits.

GENE-ENVIRONMENT CORRELATIONS

A **gene-environment correlation** occurs when a person's environment is a reflection of, or is somehow associated (correlated) with, that person's genotype—the specific arrangement of genes that contribute to the development of a particular trait. How can this correlation occur? Consider 4-year-old Lucia, who has a relatively high IQ and innate verbal ability, both inherited in part from her parents and grandparents through genetic transmission. These qualities are a reflection of Lucia's genotype. Lucia is extremely curious about

Gene-environment correlation ▶ When a person's environment is correlated with his or her genotype. Example: When a musically gifted child (genotype) lives in a home where music is played frequently and where musical instruments are available.

the world and asks endless questions. She gravitates toward books and spends hours with them each day, looking at the pictures and asking to be read to. At the age of 6, she enters school already highly educated! This is in part because of the environment in which she lives, which consists of substantial time spent with books, receiving ready answers to her many questions from adults around her, being exposed to many opportunities for learning. However, this "bookish" environment exists as it does in part *because of Lucia's genotype*. Lucia makes certain choices (like asking to be read to and asking question after question), and these choices help shape her environment—her parents purchase more books, make them available to her, and respond to Lucia's questions with carefully considered answers. Lucia's genotype has in part determined the types of experiences she has.

Now consider her younger sister, Graciella, who asks fewer questions and is less interested in books and "academic" matters. She enters school with a more restricted knowledge of the world than her sister. On the other hand, from a very early age, Graciella has enjoyed painting and other crafts, in part as a result of *her* genotype (her maternal grandmother and great-grandmother were artists). She asks to be taken to museums more frequently than her sister (who is bored there), and is surrounded with art supplies and people to help her learn to draw well. By the time Graciella enters school her drawing skills are far superior to those of her older sister, in spite of her being much younger. Graciella's genotype has affected the environment in which she developed and is richly correlated with that environment.

Active and Reactive Gene-Environment Correlations There are two types of gene-environment correlations we will consider here, as summarized in Table 3.1: *active* and *reactive* (Plomin, DeFries, & Loehlin, 1977). The active seeking out of certain types of environments through intentional choices—as in the case of Lucia seeking verbal, and Graciella artistic, environments—is known as an **active gene-environment correlation**.

A **reactive gene-environment correlation** occurs when individuals around a child react to the child's genotype in some way, creating a correlated environment. In other words, the child's genotype *evokes* particular kinds of behavior from those around her. For example, some babies love to be cuddled, kissed, and held right from the beginning, while others are more restrained or standoffish. Because parents are human, they respond to these variations—creating a warm, physically affectionate environment in the first case, or one that is perhaps a little less so in the second. These environments in turn affect the developing child. It is a reactive *cycle* of child influencing parent, and parent influencing child in turn (Fox et al., 2007; Ghera, Hane, Malesa, & Fox, 2006).

A particularly interesting demonstration of the importance of reactive gene-environment correlations comes from studies of children adopted at birth. Several of these studies have shown that the degree of harshness and hostility

Active gene-environment correlation ▶ A correlation between environment and genotype that results from active choices made by an organism.

Reactive gene-environment correlation ▶ When an organisms' genotype evokes responses in others, creating an environment that shares characteristics with that genotype.

Table 3.1 Two Types of Gene-Environment Correlations

TYPE	DEFINITION	EXAMPLE
Active	When a person actively seeks out a particular kind of environment as a result of his or her genotype	A temperamentally timid child takes a route to school that will avoid passing by the school bullies' hangout.
Reactive	When a child's genotype-influenced behavior helps to shape his or her environment as a result of other people's responses to the behavior	A disagreeable child elicits annoyance or hostility from those around her. She consequently lives in a rejecting world that further reinforces her disagreeableness.

in the parenting practices of a child's *adoptive* parents can to some degree be predicted by knowing the level of aggressiveness and hostility of the child's *birth parents*—whom the infants have never known! In other words, children who have inherited aggressive tendencies from their *genetic* parents go on to elicit harshness and hostility from their *adoptive* parents in response to those inherited tendencies, through reactive gene-environment correlation (O'Connor, Deater-Deckard, Fulker, Rutter, & Plomin, 1998).

GENE-ENVIRONMENT INTERACTIONS

A *gene-environment interaction* is a concept that is perhaps more intuitive and simpler to grasp than gene-environment correlation. If we consider that each person is different, it stands to reason that two different people may react to the same event in different ways (Fox et al., 2007). Suppose you go to a party with a friend. Your friend comes away glowing, and you come away mumbling. It was the same party, but it elicited radically different responses from different individuals.

Now consider two children, each of whom is mercilessly teased at school because they both have weight problems. The first child, Dylan, is high in *neuroticism*, a tendency toward negative mood states, negative thoughts, and emotionalism. Neuroticism is also highly heritable (Bouchard, 2004; Lake, Eaves, Maes, Heath, & Martin, 2000). Dylan takes the teasing seriously to heart, and its effects border on the traumatic—continuing to affect his personality into adulthood. The second child, Gilberto, is low in neuroticism. He finds the teasing unpleasant but brushes it off as the behavior of "stupid kids" who are jealous of his good grades. It has little effect on his life. Same experience, different genes. When an experience affects people differently as a result of differences in their genotypes, a **gene-environment interaction** has occurred (Dick, 2011).

▲ **Gene-Environment Interaction.** Same experience, different genes.

Gene-environment interaction ▶ When an experience affects people differently as a result of the differences in their genotypes.

IN SUMMARY

1.	Behavior genetics is the study of the influences of genes and environments on individual differences in behavior.
2.	Behavior geneticists use samples of twins and adopted children to compute statistics of heritability (h^2). The heritability statistic is an estimate of the proportion of differences in a sample of individuals that is due to genetic heredity. Subtracting the heritability estimate from 1.0 leaves the proportion of differences due to environmental causes.
3.	Studies of identical (monozygotic) twins reared apart show that these twins are almost as similar as identical twins reared together on a large number of cognitive and personality characteristics. When both twin and adoption studies are averaged out, the heritability of cognitive abilities, personality traits, and social attitudes is about 0.25–0.50, with cognitive ability showing the highest heritability, and personality characteristics and social attitudes showing the lowest.
4.	Gene-environment correlations occur when a person's environment is a reflection of, or is somehow associated with, his or her genotype. Two types of gene-environment correlations were discussed in the chapter: active and reactive. Gene-environment interactions occur when people with different genotypes encounter the same environmental experience but respond differently as a result of their genotypes.

RETRIEVE!

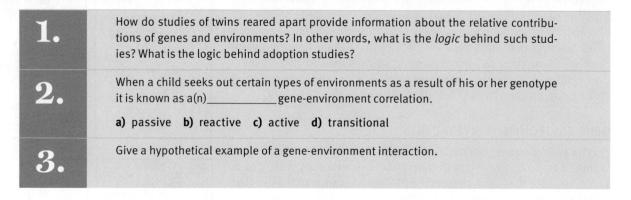

1. How do studies of twins reared apart provide information about the relative contributions of genes and environments? In other words, what is the *logic* behind such studies? What is the logic behind adoption studies?

2. When a child seeks out certain types of environments as a result of his or her genotype it is known as a(n)_____ gene-environment correlation.

a) passive **b)** reactive **c)** active **d)** transitional

3. Give a hypothetical example of a gene-environment interaction.

Why Are Psychologists Interested in Evolution?

As we've seen in the preceding section, behavior geneticists are primarily interested in the ways in which individuals differ. Why is one person more likely than another to enjoy risky activities such as riding roller coasters, driving fast, or committing crimes? Why do some people score higher than others on tests of cognitive ability? Why are some people more aggressive than others—or more compassionate? However, these questions suggest other, more basic, questions: Why do people perform risky activities at all? Where is the benefit? Why is *anyone* aggressive—where does aggression come from? Or compassion? Things like risky behavior, aggression, and compassion are present in all known human societies. While individuals and entire cultures may differ in the extent to which these and many other characteristics are exhibited, such characteristics are part of what makes us recognizably human. Despite individual and cultural differences, we are everywhere far more similar than we are different (Brown, 1991; Buss, 2005). The psychological characteristics that make us recognizably human and that we share in common are of greatest interest to psychologists who adhere to evolutionary perspectives.

Evolution Is Both Fact and Theory

Human evolution is a controversial topic in the United States. As of 2009, Only about 39% of Americans accept the idea that humans evolved from earlier forms of life, with the remaining 60% divided between those who reject the idea flat-out and those who are uncertain (Gallup Poll, 2009). However, acceptance or rejection of the idea of human evolution is strongly related to education. Only 21% of those with high-school educations accept human evolution, compared to 74% of those with postgraduate degrees.

The uncertain or negative attitudes among many Americans toward the idea of human evolution contrast with those found in the rest of the industrialized world. In Japan and Europe, for example, approximately twice as many adults accept the idea of human evolution as in the United States. Surveys conducted in 34 nations in 2005 show that only in Turkey do people reject the idea of evolution to an extent greater than in the United States (Miller, Scott, & Okamoto, 2006; see Figure 3.5).

However, the term *controversial* can be misleading as applied to the topic of evolution in the United States, because there is a difference between a *public*

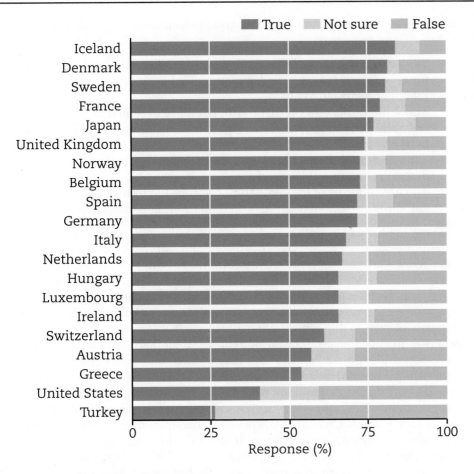

FIGURE 3.5 Public Acceptance of Human Evolution. This graph displays "true / false / not sure" responses from people in 34 countries to the statement: "Humans, as we know them, developed from earlier species of animals." *(Source: Miller, Scott, & Okamoto, 2006, p. 765.)*

controversy and a *scientific controversy.* The controversy over evolution in the United States is a public controversy. There is no controversy about evolution among Americans working in the earth and life sciences—it is accepted as a fact by virtually all of them, including the substantial numbers who also believe in God (Larson & Witham, 1998; Witham, 1997).[2]

If evolution is a "fact," why do we so often hear about the "theory" of evolution? Which is it—a *theory* or a *fact*? In truth, evolution is both theory *and* fact (Gould, 1981; Lenski, 2000). To understand how this is so, let me first define the terms. In general usage, a *fact* is something that exists—an actual happening in time and space. As you may recall from Chapter 1, however, in science a *fact* is an observation about the natural world that has been confirmed so frequently that it would be unreasonable to withhold acceptance, at least on a provisional basis.

Also recall from Chapter 1 that a theory is a set of interconnected ideas or statements used *to explain* (or somehow organize) facts. Theories may be false or true—but if a theory is proved to be wrong, the facts that the theory is attempting to explain do not go away. As popular science writer Stephen Jay Gould (1981) put it, during the 20th century Einstein's theory of gravity replaced Newton's earlier theory of gravity—but this did not change the direction in which apples fell when they left the tree.

How then does evolution qualify as both theory and fact? Here are some basic *facts* of evolution, according to biologist R. C. Lewontin (1981, p. 559),

---

[2]*In the survey reported by Witham, only 95% of scientists polled supported the idea of evolution. However, these scientists included mathematicians, astronomers, and others not educated in the biological and earth sciences. It is likely that the figure for acceptance of the general idea of evolution among biologists, geologists, and others in the life sciences is substantially higher.*

accepted by the vast majority of biologists, paleontologists, physical anthropologists, and geologists:

- The earth is at least 4.5 billions of years old.[3] Cellular life has been around for at least half of that period, and organized multicellular life is at least 1.2 billion years old.[4]
- Major life forms now on earth were not all represented in the past. For example, there were no birds or mammals (including humans) 250 million years ago.
- Some major life forms of the past are no longer living. There used to be dinosaurs, but now there are none.
- All current forms of life come from previous life forms that were different. Birds arose from nonbirds and humans from nonhumans.

These are facts of evolution that are scientifically indisputable. *Theories* of evolution—such as Charles Darwin's *theory of natural selection*, which I discuss below—are another matter. They continue to be debated to some extent.

Psychologists taking an evolutionary perspective propose that without a basic understanding of the facts and theories of evolution, psychological phenomena are very difficult to explain satisfactorily. For example, why do humans behave so differently in some respects from one society to the next, whereas in other respects behavior remains remarkably similar regardless of society and culture? Why do men and women (and males and females of other animal species) differ in certain aspects of their behavior throughout the world? Why do people in all known societies find young people with smooth skin more beautiful than older people with blemishes and wrinkles? Why is pregnancy sickness ("morning sickness") so common throughout the world, and why do women who experience it generally have healthier pregnancies than those who do not (Huxley, 2000; Pepper & Craig Roberts, 2006)? Why do small children learn to fear snakes easily, but have a hard time learning to fear cars or electrical sockets, which pose a far greater danger (LoBue & deLoache, 2008; Öhman & Mineka, 2003)? There are thousands of such questions that could be asked. These are the sorts of questions addressed by *evolutionary psychologists*.

The Theory of Natural Selection Guides Evolutionary Psychology

Theory of natural selection
▶ Charles Darwin's theory of how the most important types of evolutionary events occur.

The most plausible theory of how important evolutionary events occur was offered by Charles Darwin (1859/2003). It is known as the **theory of natural selection**. Because the theory of natural selection is so central to evolutionary views of psychology, it is important that we review this theory briefly before continuing. Darwin made a number of observations about the world that led him to devise the theory of natural selection. The process he eventually described is actually quite simple. Here's how it works:

1. *Darwin first considered that it is theoretically conceivable for a species to grow in numbers without limit.* Take elephants, notoriously slow reproducers. Darwin calculated that in a 60-year period of fertility with an average of six total offspring in a lifetime, the unchecked reproduction of elephants should result in a total of 15 million elephant descendents left alive on earth after only 500 years! If these aren't enough elephants for you, within a few *thousand*

---

[3]At the time Lewontin was writing, the earth was believed to be closer to 3.5 billion years old. I have altered the figure given by Lewontin as additional data have come to light which alter estimation of the age of the earth.

[4]Again, when Lewontin was writing in 1981, estimations of the origin of multicellular life were less precise than they are today. Lewontin wrote that multicellular life was at least "800 million" years old, but since then, the fossils of older multicellular organisms have been discovered, including the 1.2 billion-year-old red algae Bangiomorpha pubescens.

years—a mark that has long passed since elephants first appeared on the scene—there should have been so many elephants left alive that the earth itself ought to be little more than a ball of elephants expanding outward into space at a rate faster than the speed of light!

So where are all the elephants?

2. *In spite of the fact that species can* **conceivably reproduce with unlimited numerical growth, they obviously don't**—or at least not for very long, a fact Darwin also noted. In other words, some elephants just aren't doing their job! But why? Darwin concluded that *although the potential for reproduction among species is nearly infinite, the resources needed to support individuals of any species are always finite.* There just isn't enough air, food, or water to divide among all the elephants—nor are there enough appealing or available partners for them to mate with. The need for resources among all species always outstrips the availability of resources. *And because resources are always finite, there is competition for them.*

3. *Darwin also noted that living organisms of a species varied in their characteristics*—some are taller, some stronger, some more colorful, and so on. During the 20th century, scientists came to understand that this variability in characteristics was due to genetic diversity, but in Darwin's time it was simply acknowledged that diversity existed. Some of these characteristics increased the chances of the individual holding them of winning out in competition for resources. Thus, *those best suited to surviving and reproducing in whatever is the prevailing environment will leave the most offspring.* Some elephants have characteristics that make them better than others at locating food and shelter, avoiding predators, and finding mates.

4. *Darwin added to the fact of diversity the fact of heredity—offspring tend to resemble their parents in various characteristics more than do other members of the population.* Therefore, the offspring of those best suited to surviving and reproducing in the current environment will be more likely than others to have inherited the very advantages in survival and reproduction that produced them. These offspring, in turn, will leave more offspring than others of their generation because they have inherited reproductive advantages. The genetic lines of individuals better adapted to their environment will continue to be represented in new generations in rapidly increasing numbers, while the genetic lines of those who are not so well adapted will die out.

5. *As a result of this natural filtering—or "selection"—process, over many generations, small incremental changes will begin to occur in the characteristics of members of the species.* This is because the genes responsible for reproductively helpful characteristics remain in the gene pool, while genes responsible for less helpful (or overtly harmful) characteristics are filtered out. Over evolutionary time, these small changes result in the accumulation of characteristics in the species as a whole that cause members of the species to be increasingly better adapted to their environments. These accumulated characteristics are known as **adaptations**.

For example, the ability of stick insects to assume the appearance of a stick to fool predators is the result of adaptation, as is the ability of bats to navigate in the dark with *echolocation*. Beginning with only a few individuals with favorable characteristics, over hundreds and thousands of generations these advantages develop into complex adaptations that characterize virtually *all* individuals in the species to a greater or lesser extent ("greater or lesser" because of variation).

Natural selection is not the only evolutionary process. However, it is the only one yet proposed by scientists that can account for the precision with which organisms are adapted to their environments (Williams, 1966), and for the way in which new species come into being over evolutionary time. It is also the ultimate fusion of nature and nurture, because it describes the way that life forms interact with their environments to produce change.

Adaptations ▶ Characteristics of organisms that have evolved over evolutionary time because they confer reproductive or survival advantages. Adaptations arise as a result of small, incremental changes in the genome of organisms over many generations, and they represent solutions to specific challenges and pressures faced recurrently by the organism.

Evolutionary Psychology Is a New Way of Looking at Old Problems

Evolutionary psychology ▶
A multidisciplinary approach to psychology based on evolutionary principles, especially Darwin's theory of natural selection.

Now that we have reviewed the theory of natural selection, we can explore evolutionary psychology itself. Although often described as a field of psychology, **evolutionary psychology** is actually a way of looking at questions of interest to psychologists in any number of fields (Barkow, 2006; Buss, 2005; 2009a; Cosmides & Tooby, 1987; 2008; Tooby & Cosmides, 1992). Evolutionary psychology is a multidisciplinary perspective with roots in evolutionary biology, cognitive science, anthropology, paleontology, computer science, and conventional branches of psychology such as social psychology (Maner & Kenrick, 2010). In addition to its multidisciplinary origins, mainstream evolutionary psychology is characterized by adherence to a number of ideas not found in most other approaches. I will use the following terms as short-hand for two of these ideas: *psychological adaptation* and *environmental mismatch*.

PSYCHOLOGICAL ADAPTATION

Psychological adaptation
▶ A mental characteristic that evolved through natural selection to provide solutions to specific types of problems encountered over evolutionary time by our human ancestors.

Just as the human brain is made up of a large number of complex, evolved biological adaptations that are integrated with one another, according to evolutionary psychologists, the human mind is constructed of a large number of evolved **psychological adaptations** that work together in an integrated fashion (Tooby & Cosmides, 1992). What exactly is a psychological adaptation? Recall that natural selection results in the accumulation over evolutionary time of adaptations—characteristics that allow organisms to be well adapted to their environments. Psychological adaptations are psychological characteristics that have evolved over evolutionary time to allow individuals to be better adapted to their physical and social environments.

These psychological adaptations are somewhat analogous to miniature computer programs, each specialized to solve a specific problem faced recurrently by our ancestors and related to survival or reproduction in the environments in which they evolved. Some of these problems undoubtedly included avoiding animal predators and hostile humans, choosing nutritious food and avoiding poisons, communicating and forming alliances with other humans, selecting and retaining mates, and nurturing and protecting children (Pinker, 2002; Schmitt & Pilcher, 2004). Psychological adaptations are specialized "solutions" to specific problems.

As examples, the emotion of fear and the capacity for aggression evolved as solutions to the problem of how to survive threats from predators and hostile humans (Barrett, 2005; Cosmides & Tooby, 2000). Women's pregnancy sickness in the first trimester is a solution to the problem of unwitting ingestion of substances that would be toxic to the developing embryo (Pepper & Craig Roberts, 2006; Profet, 1992). The universal prohibition against mating with one's parents, children, and siblings is a solution to the problem of how to avoid birth defects and other health problems in infants resulting from a union between close genetic kin (Schmitt & Pilcher, 2004; Lieberman, Pillsworth, & Haselton, 2011).

According to evolutionary psychologists, the reason that we human beings are so flexible in the way we respond to the wide variety of situations in which we find ourselves daily is that our minds possess a vast number of these highly specialized psychological adaptations. As an analogy, consider the flexibility of a carpenter. A carpenter does not have one all-purpose tool that can be used in any situation—the demands of different situations are often unique. Carpenters are flexible and can accomplish many kinds of tasks because they have dozens of different tools, each of which is designed for a specific use. Evolutionary psychologists believe the same is true of the human mind. Psychological adaptations work together in a coordinated fashion, just

◄**Adaptation?** The stick insect's ability to assume to appearance of a stick to elude predators is an often-cited example of adaptation. However, according to evolutionary psychologists, this is no better an example of adaptation than the tendency of men of all ages to be attracted to young women. From the evolutionary perspective, a preference among men for older (nonfertile) women could not have evolved for a simple reason: Men with such preferences would not have reproduced as successfully as those with preferences for young (fertile) women, and eventually the characteristic would have died out. (Pictured are actors Catherine Zeta-Jones at age 31 with husband Michael Douglas, age 56.)

as the carpenter's many tools complement one another, but each evolved for a specific purpose (Tooby & Cosmides, 1992). This view of the mind is known as the **modular** or *domain specific* model because it sees the mind as a large collection of self-contained "modules" or components, each of which evolved to tackle problems that exist only within specific domains of existence. Not all evolutionary psychologists adhere to this view, but it does form the basis of mainstream evolutionary psychology.

Modular model ▶ A model of the mind that sees the mind as a large collection of components (modules), each of which provides solutions only to specific types of problems.

ENVIRONMENTAL MISMATCH

As we've just seen, psychological adaptations evolved to solve problems related to survival and reproduction in the environments in which our ancestors evolved. These environments were vastly different in many respects from those of the modern world. Therefore, according to evolutionary psychologists, we should expect a degree of **environmental mismatch** between some psychological adaptations and life in the modern world.

For example, how is it that KFC, McDonald's, Burger King, and other American fast-food chains do so well all over the world, regardless of traditions of native cuisine? Advertising is powerful, but it is not all-powerful, particularly where food preferences are concerned. It is more likely due to the fact that throughout the world people prefer foods high in fats and sugars (Rozin, 1976). This becomes a puzzle when you consider that a diet high in fats and processed sugars is extremely unhealthy. Why should we apparently have evolved to find an unhealthy diet appealing? It seems to violate the principles of natural selection, where only those characteristics helpful to survival and reproduction survive over evolutionary time.

Evolutionary psychologists answer this question in the following way: In the environments of our ancestors, calories were scarce, and humans worked hard to get them. Those individuals who avoided bitter or lean foods in favor of fatty and sweet foods—which consisted of fruit, not *Froot Loops*—had an advantage because they consumed more calories, which made them better able to survive and reproduce. Therefore, by natural selection, a taste preference for sweet and fatty foods has evolved as part of human psychology throughout the world (Buss, 1994).

Environmental mismatch ▶ When a psychological adaptation is expressed in an environment different from the one in which it evolved and to which it is not suited.

▲ **Environmental Mismatch.** Evolutionary psychiatrist Randolph M. Nesse (2005) suggests that widespread alcoholism is an example of environmental mismatch resulting from the mass production of alcoholic beverages in the modern world. According to this idea, human bodies are adapted only to sporadic alcohol use, as would have been typical in the environments of our ancestors.

However, in current industrial environments, the culture of fast-food outlets and supermarkets makes calories over-plentiful rather than scarce. In our evolutionary past, sweets and fats were primarily available only in ripe fruit and animal flesh, respectively. This is hardly the case today. The modern easy availability of calories interacts in an unfortunate way with a psychological mechanism designed for a low-calorie life in the African savannah (Wadden, Brownell, & Foster, 2002). Thus, we now have genuine epidemics of obesity in many nations throughout the world, partly as a result of the mismatch between our evolved taste preferences and our modern "calorie-dense" environment. In effect, our *adaptation* to prefer sweet and fatty foods is no longer *adaptive* because it is not well suited to survival and reproduction in our current environment. This is a repeating theme in the work of evolutionary psychologists: We are modern humans with Stone-Age minds (Allman, 1995).

Human Sex Differences: A "Test Case" for Evolutionary Psychology

Evolutionary psychologists believe that human beings are a single species with a single human nature. Just as we are all recognizably human in physiology despite differences such as height, skin tone, and eye color, our psychology is essentially unified. This is because the basic environmental and social pressures acting on humans throughout our evolution were much the same, regardless of geography. All of our ancestors needed to find food and shelter, avoid animal predators, find mates, form alliances with friendly humans, avoid attacks from hostile bands, and so forth. The same environmental and social pressures should result in the same basic adaptations, whether in physiology or psychology (Cosmides & Tooby, 1987; Symons, 1995).

One major exception to this generalization is sex differences. In most cases, men and women have faced the same evolutionary pressures—and the psychological adaptations of men and women should be identical in most respects as a result. However, in certain domains of life men and women have faced vastly different sorts of pressures and problems over evolutionary time. Their experiences have been different. For this reason, at least some psychological differences should be expected between men and women. According to evolutionary psychologists, it is primarily in areas related to sexuality, reproduction, and physical aggression that we ought to see sex differences in behavior; and indeed, throughout the world, there are average differences between men and women in just these areas, but not in most other areas (Archer, 2004, 2009; Hyde, 2006; Schmitt, 2003, 2005).

Because sex differences are an exception to the general evolutionary view that human nature is unified, these differences have often been used as a "test case" by evolutionary psychologists to demonstrate the strength of their theories. Some of the most interesting (and controversial) research by evolutionary psychologists pertains to sexual behavior itself. I will discuss findings in one area of sexual behavior: interest in casual sex and partner variety.

SEX DIFFERENCES IN INTEREST IN CASUAL SEX AND PARTNER VARIETY

Most men—particularly as they age—express the desire for a long-term monogamous relationship (Mathes, King, Miller, & Reed, 2002). However, men also frequently are turned on by the idea of sex without long-term commitment (*casual sex* or, technically, **short-term mating**); and by the idea of sex with a variety of partners (Buss, 2005; Schmitt, 2003, 2005; Lippa, 2009; Petersen & Hyde, 2010). On the other hand, while many women also express interest in casual sex under certain circumstances, on average they are choosier about mating—they show less interest than men in casual encounters or in having sex with a variety of partners (Buss, 2005; Geary, 2010; Hyde, 2006; Peplau, 2003; Petersen & Hyde, 2010). Note that women are *not* necessarily

Short-term mating ▶ Sexual behavior that is casual in nature and not part of a committed relationship.

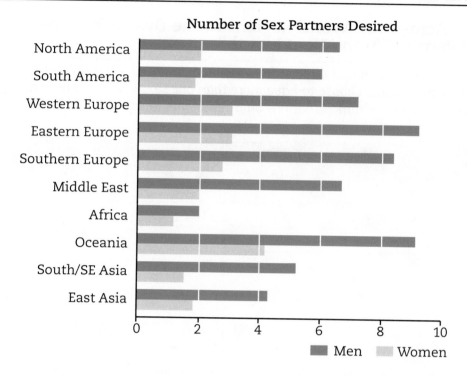

Number of Sex Partners Desired

◄ FIGURE 3.6 Sex Differences in Interest in Partner Variety. In his cross-national study of 52 nations, David Schmitt (2003) found that men tended to express a desire for a greater number of sex partners than women. This graph divides the world by 10 major regions and summarizes the numbers of sexual partners desired by men and women "over the next 30 years." (*Source: Schmitt, 2003, p. 92.*)

less interested in sex itself—they just tend to express this interest differently, in a greater interest in sex as component of an ongoing relationship (termed **long-term mating**).

Men's average greater interest in casual sex and partner variety is evident in decades of behavioral science research (Okami & Shackelford, 2001; Schmitt et al., 2012). As shown in Figure 3.6 and Tables 3.2 and 3.3, this includes research conducted among more than 200,000 individuals in 53 nations, 6 continents, and 13 islands (Schmitt, 2003, 2005; Lippa, 2009). It is also reflected in institutions such as prostitution and pornography, which exist universally and cater primarily to men. Further, it is repeatedly found in folklore, fantasy, literature, art, films, and jokes. The greater tendency of males toward interest in short-term mating and sex with a variety of partners extends to most (but not all) other mammals and to numerous nonmammalian species as well (Bateman, 1948). (In "Critical Thinking about Psychology" we will explore "exceptions that prove the rule.")

Long-term mating ▶ A committed, ongoing sexual relationship (e.g., marriage).

ROBERT TRIVERS'S THEORY OF PARENTAL INVESTMENT AND SEXUAL SELECTION

Evolutionary psychologist Donald Symons (1979) first proposed that men's greater interest in casual sex and partner variety is best explained by Robert Trivers's (1972) **theory of parental investment and sexual selection**. Trivers (1972) noted that parents in all species invest or sacrifice many resources in the conception and rearing of their young—for example, time, energy, nutrients, property, care, and various sorts of safety measures. However, it is virtually always true that one sex must invest more than the other. According to Trivers's theory, this lack of symmetry in the "parental investment" each sex must make as a minimum to reproduce is responsible for a number of average sex differences seen in the animal kingdom. Among these are sex differences in interest in short-term mating and partner variety, choosiness in picking a partner, differences in physical size and aggression, and differences in the tendency to develop physical characteristics that have no use other than attracting mates.

In the cases of humans and much of the rest of animal life, females invest much more in the entire process of reproducing. Consider the reproductive lives of humans throughout evolutionary history. For an ancestral woman to

Theory of parental investment and sexual selection ▶ Robert Trivers's theory which explains various sex differences as resulting from unequal minimal levels of parental investment in reproduction between males and females.

Table 3.2 **Sex Differences Across Ten World Regions in the Desire to Have More Than One Sexual Partner "In the Next Month"**

This table summarizes the percentages of men and women from David Schmitt's (2003) sample of 16,288 to the question of whether they would choose to have more than one sexual partner over the coming month. Schmitt's sample was drawn from 52 nations on 6 continents and 16 islands in 10 major world regions.

WORLD REGION	% OF MEN WANTING MORE THAN ONE SEXUAL PARTNER	% OF WOMEN WANTING MORE THAN ONE SEXUAL PARTNER
North America	23.1	2.9
South America	35.0	6.1
Western Europe	22.6	5.5
Eastern Europe	31.7	7.1
Southern Europe	31.0	6.0
Middle East	33.1	5.9
Africa	18.2	4.2
Oceania	25.3	5.8
South/Southeast Asia	32.4	6.4
East Asia	17.9	2.6

(Source: Schmitt, 2003, p. 93.)

bring a child into the world and help the child survive during its first few years of helplessness, the mother had to invest *at least* the following:

- Nine months of uncomfortable and possibly dangerous pregnancy, during which large quantities of her generally scarce bodily nutrients were shared with her developing fetus.
- A painful and potentially life-threatening experience of labor and childbirth, lasting at least several hours and up to a day or more.
- Several years of breastfeeding following childbirth, during which time the new mother would have continued to share her bodily nutrients as well as her time and energy with her infant.

Consider also that a woman's total opportunities to reproduce are limited not only by this extraordinary effort but also by the fact that in their entire lives women experience only about 350 brief monthly windows of fertility lasting several days, as dictated by the human reproductive cycle.

Now let's look at our ancestral *fathers'* minimal possible parental investment. For these men to have reproduced, they needed only to have invested the following:

- A few highly enjoyable minutes (or even seconds) of their time.
- Barely measurable amounts of protein and amino acids contained in an ejaculation of semen.
- Relatively few of the billions of sperm they produce in their lifetimes.

Moreover, once men reach adolescence, they are potentially fertile every day until they die. Their window of fertility is open as wide as can be.

Obviously, this does not mean that there are no men in the world who invest more than the minimum necessary to reproduce. In the modern world, many men devote their entire lives and most of their earnings to their children. Human beings are unusual in the mammalian world for the extent of fathers'

Table 3.3 Sex Differences in Average Scores on Measures of Interest in Short-Term Mating ("Casual Sex")

In his cross-national study of "sociosexuality"—a concept that includes the idea of interest in short-term mating—Schmitt (2005) noted higher levels of interest among men in all societies studied. A higher mean score indicates stronger interest in short-term mating. "Effect size" refers to the magnitude, or strength, of the sex difference.

	MEAN SCORES		
NATION	**MEN**	**WOMEN**	**EFFECT SIZE**
Argentina	55.52	30.10	Large
Australia	46.52	30.73	Moderate
Austria	55.89	36.75	Moderate
Bangladesh	31.10	11.80	Large
Belgium	39.68	26.80	Moderate
Bolivia	61.47	21.92	Large
Botswana	33.56	23.06	Small
Brazil	53.96	27.13	Large
Canada	44.33	27.30	Moderate
Congo, D.R.	41.16	29.55	Moderate
Croatia	57.35	32.15	Large
Czech Republic	48.96	29.49	Large
Estonia	51.51	31.83	Moderate
Ethiopia	37.88	18.89	Moderate
Fiji	54.30	25.26	Large
Finland	64.03	41.60	Moderate
France	45.88	21.21	Moderate
Germany	46.36	34.34	Small
Greece	43.43	24.32	Large
Hong Kong	29.88	19.21	Moderate
Israel	53.99	21.56	Large
Italy	51.73	21.39	Large
Japan	32.47	20.72	Moderate
Latvia	49.42	41.68	Small
Lebanon	43.90	17.21	Large
Lithuania	60.44	35.25	Large
Malta	40.56	25.17	Moderate
Mexico	49.04	25.99	Large
Morocco	65.58	20.06	Large

(continued)

Table 3.3 Sex Differences in Average Scores on Measures of Interest in Short-Term Mating ("Casual Sex") (continued)

	MEAN SCORES		
NATION	MEN	WOMEN	EFFECT SIZE
Netherlands	50.51	31.56	Moderate
New Zealand	60.42	38.79	Moderate
Peru	51.68	21.23	Strong
Philippines	51.24	17.95	Strong
Poland	44.29	26.90	Moderate
Portugal	41.27	21.32	Large
Romania	48.64	19.48	Large
Serbia	48.99	31.89	Moderate
Slovakia	44.27	28.52	Moderate
Slovenia	59.45	27.01	Large
South Korea	30.53	16.22	Large
Spain	46.08	25.17	Large
Switzerland	45.25	34.26	Small
Taiwan	28.42	14.24	Large
Turkey	54.16	21.71	Large
Ukraine	50.79	17.36	Large
United Kingdom	57.38	29.60	Large
United States	48.03	29.24	Moderate
Zimbabwe	34.80	13.98	Large

(Source: Adapted from: Schmitt, 2005, p. 263.)

typical investment in their offspring. The point stressed by evolutionary psychologists is that men who invest do so *by choice*—they do not need to invest much of anything to reproduce.

According to Trivers, the sex that invests more in reproduction (generally females) is more valuable in reproductive terms. Members of the lesser-investing sex (generally males) compete more fiercely for access to the more "valuable" reproductive resource. This more intense (and often violent) competition among males historically has resulted in males' greater size, upper-body strength, and physical aggressiveness. It is also the reason that, in the animal world, it is usually the male who develops various ornaments or characteristics that appear to have no use other than attracting mates—such as the peacock's tail, the songbird's call, or the bower's nest (Darwin, 1871/1874). Males must distinguish themselves from the rest of the pack so as to be attractive to females.

Females, on the other hand, need do comparatively little to attract a male—they are attractive enough *because they are female*. As the greater-investing sex, the female is thus in the position to be more choosy than the male about which "applicant" she allows sexual access, and under most circumstances it is in her reproductive interest to be highly selective. As was demonstrated in

▲ **Bird Art as Seduction.** Apart from humans, the only animals known to spend substantial time and energy constructing a purely aesthetic display that is separate from their own bodies are male bower birds. The bower expends enormous effort and time securing the most brilliantly colored natural objects, bringing them back to the nest, and arranging them carefully in clusters of uniform color. The purpose? To attract a female. Once mated, the bower's nest is abandoned, and the female moves on to her own nest.

▲ **Robert L. Trivers.** One of the most important modern theorists of evolutionary biology, Trivers proposed a theory of parental investment and sexual selection that has formed the basis of much theorizing about human sexuality by evolutionary psychologists. Trivers is well known for his unconventional personal life and unpredictable intellectual work. Although he has produced relatively few papers, virtually all of them have had a major impact on the field of biology.

a series of experiments with fruit flies (Bateman, 1948), it is virtually never to the female's advantage to mate indiscriminately, because mating with more males than is necessary to become pregnant does not increase her rate of reproduction (and, in fact, may expose her to unnecessary risks such as disease or violence from a jealous partner). In this way, females' rate of reproduction is limited by nature.

On the other hand, the reproductive success of the male is not limited by nature—*it is limited by females' willingness or lack of willingness to mate.* As Roy Baumeister and Dianne Tice (2001) have stated, most acts of sexual intercourse in the mammalian world, including the human world, occur when a female changes her default "no" to a "yes." According to Trivers's theory, unlike our female ancestors, ancestral males *would* have increased their reproductive success by convincing as many females as possible to mate, and to mate with them as often as possible.

We can now see the evolutionary logic behind research findings such as those of the Clark and Hatfield (1989) study described in the "Freeze Frame" feature that opened the chapter. An ancestral woman who was willing to mate with anyone who approached her would have risked wasting one of her relatively few and extremely valuable lifetime opportunities for reproduction by becoming pregnant with a man of low "mate value"—for example, a man who lacked health, skill, strength, status, kindness, intelligence, and access to resources (Buss, 1994; Symons, 1979). On the other hand, an ancestral man would have had relatively little to lose from mating with many women—and potentially much to gain.

According to evolutionary psychologists, these historical behavioral sex differences shaped sex differences in psychological adaptations that persist to the present day—even among people who have no conscious interest in reproducing at all. Indeed, evolutionary psychologists emphasize that people generally have sex for reasons other than the desire to reproduce. The point made by these theorists is that those among our female ancestors who were picky about their mates and those among our male ancestors who were less so, reproduced more successfully and left the most descendents. These descendents would have inherited their ancestors' sexual tastes to some degree and therefore also reproduced more successfully. Over time, then, through the process of natural selection, these aspects of sexual psychology have become widespread among humans.

CRITICAL THINKING ABOUT PSYCHOLOGY

Exceptions May Prove Trivers's Rule

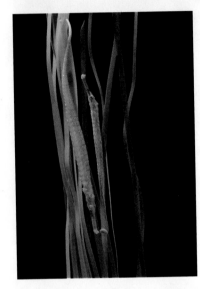

▲ **When the Male Invests More in Reproduction.** In the ophidon pipefish, males invest more in reproduction than females, and the usual gender characteristics in regard to mating are reversed.

Trivers's theory of parental investment and sexual selection is particularly *elegant*—a term used by scientists when a theory explains a great many things with relative simplicity. The Trivers theory is elegant for three reasons: First, it applies to all sexually reproducing species, not just humans or other mammals. Second, it makes no particular predictions about *males and females*—the theory is concerned with differences between the sex that invests the most in reproduction and the one that invests the least. Third, it explains a number of sex differences in sexual and reproductive behavior, not only interest in casual sex and partner variety.

It happens that the female is usually the greater-investing sex, and so Trivers's predictions usually do apply in the same way to males and females regardless of species. However, this is not *always* the case. In some species, these roles are reversed, and the male must invest more in reproduction than the female. What happens under such conditions?

Let's take one of the very best examples of role reversal in reproduction—the *ophidon* species of pipefish, a relative of the sea horse. Among these fish, the female deposits her eggs on male bodies, and the male carries the eggs to term, nursing them all the while—a process that is highly costly in terms of nutrients, energy, and time—and prevents the male from engaging in other reproductive opportunities. It also exposes him to grave danger from predatory fish (Berglund & Rosenqvist, 2003). Thus, the males invest much more in reproduction than the females, and the females can mate with as many males as they can find.

In accord with the Trivers theory, female *ophidon* pipefish are much larger than males due to more intense competition among females for mates. In the animal world, intense competition for mates generally involves physical combat, and in physical combat the larger individual has the advantage. Female ophidons also carry permanent ornamentation to attract males (blue coloring) in contrast to the males' only temporary coloration. Females also are much less choosy when it comes to mating. In short, female ophidons display characteristics generally associated with male animals.

My students frequently point out that among humans, it is women who seem to be more concerned about "ornamentation" (jewelry, clothing, make up, etc.), adding that women do often compete fiercely for the attention of men. Does this contradict Trivers's idea? Humans are another exception proving Trivers's rule. Recall that humans are almost alone in the mammalian world in the extent of care that males provide. Among the vast majority of mammals, males provide *no* parental care at all (Geary, 2010). Therefore,

▶ **Male Ornamentation Is Common in Traditional Societies.** Typical dress for men who hold high status positions in their societies: a chief from the Squamish Nation in North America, an elder from the Kato tribe in Africa, and a modern business executive.

human males are far more reproductively valuable than males of other mammalian species. According to Trivers's theory, we ought to expect (and we do indeed find) lesser sex differences in size and strength among humans than among most mammals, higher levels of competition among women for mates than is normally found among mammalian females, and ornamentation among human females as well as males. (It should also be noted, however, that the relative lack of ornamentation among Western men is not at all typical of traditional societies. For example, African and Native American societies generally favor ornamentation in men.) ■

Questions about the Evolutionary Approach

Like behavior genetics, evolutionary psychology and similar evolution-based theories of human behavior have been quite controversial. Yet, like behavior genetics (if to a lesser extent), aspects of the evolutionary view are now accepted by large numbers of psychologists. Increasingly varied research has been published that incorporates the evolutionary perspective, including research by those who do not consider themselves to be "evolutionary psychologists" at all (e.g., Haidt, 2007; Henrich, Heine, & Norenzayan, 2010; Schacter, 2001; Taylor, 2006).

However, the entire topic of psychological differences between men and women often sizzles with controversy (Eagly, 1995), and it should be expected that when a controversial field tackles a controversial topic, sparks will fly. Among other things, evolutionary psychologists have been accused of the following:

- Telling "just-so stories" of the origin of various human behaviors to try to rationalize sexist views of human sexuality (Rose & Rose, 2000);
- Engaging in "biological determinism"—the tendency to view all behavior as a result of innate biology—and ignoring the importance of the environment (Gould, 1997);
- Wrongly believing that people are motivated to "spread their genes" when engaging in various behaviors, including sex (Rose & Rose, 2000);
- Wrongly attributing stereotypical "masculine" or "feminine" characteristics to all men and women.

Some criticisms of evolutionary psychology and other evolutionary approaches appear to result from a misunderstanding of what it is these theorists are actually saying (Machery & Cohen, 2011; Segersträle, 2000). For example, evolutionary psychologists do not claim that people are motivated to "spread their genes." Instead they claim that the kinds of behaviors that in the past led to increased reproductive success have become part of human nature because more and more people came to be born with these tendencies over evolutionary time, and fewer people born with opposing tendencies. Additionally, contrary to some critics' charges, evolutionary psychologists do not ignore the influence of the environment in psychology; and they take pains to emphasize that sex differences such as those just described are statistical averages only—they do not apply to all men and women (any more than all men are taller and stronger than all women; Buss, 2005; Gangestad & Simpson, 2000; Kenrick, Li, & Butner, 2003; Schmitt, 2003, 2005).

However, many critics of evolutionary approaches make important points. For example:

- Some psychologists who accept the basic notion that evolution has shaped human psychology nonetheless charge that "evolutionary psychologists" have misinterpreted Charles Darwin (Chiappe & MacDonald, 2005; Panksepp & Panksepp, 2000). If these criticisms turn out to have merit, then some of the assumptions of evolutionary psychology may ultimately prove to be wrong.

- Although evolutionary psychology may be useful in understanding the commonalities among people, with few exceptions (Gangestad & Simpson, 2000; Geary, 2005; 2010; Kenrick et al., 2003) evolutionary psychologists have been unable to account very well for individual differences (Buss, 2009b).

- Although increasingly, evolutionary psychology research is cross-cultural, the bulk of it (like the bulk of all psychological research) is conducted among people in highly industrialized Western societies, primarily university students in the United States (Arnett, 2008; Quinones-Vidal, Lopez-Garcia, Penaranda-Ortega, & Tortosa-Gil, 2004). As we shall discover in the next section of the chapter, important truths about human psychology may not emerge from such research (Henrich et al., 2010).

Indeed, it is particularly important that research from the evolutionary perspective include samples from diverse societies and social backgrounds, because evolutionary theorists wish to make claims about the unity of human psychology (Henrich et al., 2010; Norenzayan & Heine, 2005). As you can see from Figure 3.5 and Tables 3.2 and 3.3, entire cultures and world regions may differ in how psychological adaptations are expressed.

IN SUMMARY

1. Evolution is both theory and fact. It is a fact that evolution has occurred, but the mechanisms of evolution—such as natural selection—are theories that are still debated to some extent.

2. Natural selection occurs because the resources needed to sustain life for each species are always limited. There is competition for these resources, and in any given environment, those best suited to surviving and reproducing leave the most descendents. These descendents, at least to some degree, inherit the characteristics that enabled their genetic ancestors to survive and reproduce. Over many generations, these characteristics create small, incremental changes in the species that are beneficial in the struggle to survive and reproduce. The incremental changes that accumulate over evolutionary time are termed *adaptations*.

3. Mainstream evolutionary psychology is characterized in part by adherence to the notions of psychological adaptation and environmental mismatch.

4. Although evolutionary psychologists argue that humans have a single unified human nature, regardless of geography or race, they expect sex differences in psychology, particularly in behavior related to sexuality, reproduction, and aggression.

5. Robert Trivers's theory of parental investment and sexual selection suggests that in any sexually reproducing sex, one sex will have a greater minimal investment in reproduction than will the other sex. This will result in numerous sex differences in behavior related to sexuality, reproduction, and physical aggression. It is also responsible for average sex differences in size and the tendency to develop ornamentation with no apparent function other than attracting mates.

6. Evolutionary psychologists have been criticized for not including enough cross-cultural samples in their research, failing to develop convincing theories to account for individual and cultural differences in behavior, and incorrectly interpreting Darwin's theories.

RETRIEVE!

1. Explain how the theory of natural selection works, using your own words. Include the concepts of success in reproduction, competition for resources, heredity, and adaptation. Why is natural selection a theory and not a fact? Why is evolution a fact and not a theory?

2. Give at least two examples of psychological adaptation proposed by evolutionary psychologists and described in the chapter.

3. When an *adaptation* no longer proves to be *adaptive* because the environment in which it is expressed has changed, it is known as _____.

a) post-adaptation

b) environmental mismatch

c) environmental noise in the system

d) counter-adaptation

4. According to Robert Trivers's theory of parental investment and sexual selection, why are men more interested than women in casual sex and partner variety?

What Is the Sociocultural Perspective?

To complete this chapter, we now turn to those theorists whose work highlights the importance of cultural and social influence on human psychology: sociocultural theorists. As I mentioned earlier, the evolutionary and sociocultural perspectives approach questions of nature and nurture in radically different ways. While evolutionary theorists highlight the unity of human psychology, sociocultural theorists highlight its diversity. As we have seen, natural selection elegantly blends nature and nurture by explaining how development and change only occur as a result of the interaction of genes and environments. However, it is undeniably true that evolutionary psychologists and behavior geneticists tend to emphasize the "nature" side of natural selection in their explanations for human behavior. For example, behavior geneticists have claimed that the unique experiences of each child—rather than overall family environment—are of crucial importance to cognitive development, but these researchers have not yet identified the specific types of unique experiences that exert important effects. Similarly, while evolutionary psychologists have accounted well for *similarities* among humans, they are more tenuous in their accounting for *differences* among individuals and entire cultures. And that is why I now turn your attention to the sociocultural perspective. Sociocultural theorists have expertly developed methods and theories that highlight psychological differences among individuals and entire cultures.

Society and Culture Help Shape Mind and Behavior

Human beings are already social creatures prior to the moment of birth. They learn to differentiate their mother's voice and language from the voices and languages of strangers while still in the womb, and they recognize the sounds of book passages that had been read to them prior to birth (DeCasper & Spence, 1986; Kisilevsky et al., 2003; Kisilevsky et al., 2009). Within hours of birth, they will respond to other people's facial expressions by attempting to imitate them (Field, Woodson, Greenberg, & Cohen, 1982; Meltzoff & Moore, 1983, 1989; see Chapter 7). Even innate reflexes in infants, such as the sucking reflex, will not occur unless they are triggered by physical contact with another person.

Although evolutionary psychologists have a great deal to contribute to our understanding of human psychology, as mentioned in the previous section, they generally lack detailed accounts of how society and culture influence behavior and subjective experience. Those psychologists working from the *sociocultural perspective* focus on these influences.

Society and *culture*—what do these terms mean? Unfortunately, they are often used interchangeably, but they are not exactly the same. The term **society** describes an enduring and cooperating group—anything from the Girl Scouts to the Sioux nation, from ancient Greece to the People's Republic of China—whose members have developed institutions and organized patterns of interacting with one another.

The term **culture**, on the other hand, describes the total pattern of behavior exhibited by citizens of a given society, encompassing all of the products of that society—thought, language, actions, practices, manufactured goods, religion, and artifacts. For example, selling cookies outside of supermarkets is part of Girl Scout culture; the ancient Greek language is part of ancient Greek culture; and a tendency to emphasize the welfare of the group over that of the individual is part of Chinese culture (Matsumoto & Hee Yoo, 2006). In other words, *culture* is what a *society* produces and transmits to new generations. Culture is what makes each society recognizably different from others, even those that may have somewhat similar institutions (Hofstede & McCrae, 2004).

What, then, is the **sociocultural perspective**? It is a general approach that attempts to describe the ways in which society and culture influence brain, mind, and behavior. Like the evolutionary perspective, the sociocultural perspective is not a specific field—it is a perspective that can be found in fields of psychology as diverse as clinical psychology, cognitive psychology, developmental psychology, social psychology, and even neuroscience (Gelfand & Diener, 2010). However, this perspective is strongly associated with the field of **cultural psychology**—the study of psychology as it exists in different cultures (Brouwers, van Hemert, Breugelmans, & van de Vijver, 2004; Markus & Kitayama, 1998; Matsumoto & Hee Yoo, 2006). Cultural psychologists emphasize that different cultures are characterized by different behaviors and subjective experiences—although these psychologists do not deny that numerous similarities among cultures also exist and that certain aspects of psychology may be universal among all cultures (Norenzayan & Heine, 2005; Öngel & Smith, 1994).

In this portion of the chapter I will discuss findings of psychologists working from the sociocultural perspective and then take another look at sex differences in interest in casual sex and partner variety from a very different perspective: *social role theory*.

The Sociocultural Perspective Highlights Differences and Similarities

Human beings are not the only species with culture. For example, bands of chimpanzees living in similar kinds of environments may nonetheless differ in their patterns of behavior and have been shown to learn from one another through observation over the generations (Whiten et al., 1999; Marshall-Pescini & Whiten, 2008; Nishida, Matsusaka, & McGrew, 2009; Whiten et al., 2007). The same is true of herds of dolphins, some of whom have been shown to transmit the use of sponges as tools from mother to daughter (Krützen, Mann, Heithaus, Connor, et al., 2005; Rendell & Whitehead, 2001; Sargeant

---

Society ▶ An enduring and cooperating group whose members have developed institutions and organized patterns of interaction.

Culture ▶ The total pattern of behavior exhibited by citizens of any given society, and the total products of a given society.

Sociocultural perspective ▶ A general approach to psychology that focuses on the ways society and culture mold and influence behavior.

Cultural psychology ▶ The comparative study of psychology as it exists in different cultures.

▲ **Culture Is Not Limited to Humans.** Culture has been shown to exist in chimpanzees and dolphins. When Whiten, Horner, and de Waal (2005) taught rudimentary tool use to a group of chimpanzees, other chimps learned to use the tools through observing those who had the skills. Learning through imitation among herds of dolphins has also been experimentally demonstrated (Krützen et al., 2005; Rendell & Whitehead, 2001).

& Mann, 2009). Because these herds do not differ genetically (they are the same species), their differences in behavior appear to demonstrate cultural differences.

However, human culture is vibrantly unique. It pervades virtually every aspect of human thought and behavior, and proliferates rapidly over generations (Heine & Norenzayan, 2006). Humans cooperate with one another and intentionally teach their young in ways that do not exist among other great apes such as chimpanzees or orangutans (Tomasello & Herrmann, 2010). Although cultural psychologists are interested in cultural similarities as well as differences, it is fair to say that their primary focus has been on cultural differences (Brouwers et al., 2004). Cultural differences are particularly informative with regard to the importance of nurture in shaping human experience and behavior.

How do cultures differ? Naturally, cultures differ in specific ways such as language, rituals, food, and beliefs about what is right and wrong. However, cultural researcher Geert Hofstede (Hofstede, 2001; Hofstede & McCrae, 2004) examined responses of over 115,000 people in 72 countries with questionnaires designed to establish specific *dimensions* of behavior along which entire cultures may typically differ. After statistical analysis, a number of essential dimensions of culture emerged. The most critical of these dimensions are the following:

1. *Individualism vs. collectivism.* Individualist cultures are those, such as the United States, where the welfare and accomplishments of the individual are stressed over those of the group. Collectivist cultures, such as China and Japan and some parts of Latin America, stress the importance of group effort, group membership, and group accomplishment. As will become apparent as you read this book, this dimension has been of greatest interest to cultural psychologists, particularly as relates to differences between East Asian and Western cultures (Matsumoto & Hee Yoo, 2006).

2. *Power distance.* Power distance represents the degree to which the less powerful members of society accept and expect that some individuals will wield power and others will lack power. Europe, Canada, Australia, and Israel are particularly low on this dimension, while most Asian, Arab, and Latin American nations are high on power distance.

3. *Masculinity-femininity.* This dimension measures the degree to which a culture reflects what are considered stereotypical masculine or feminine characteristics. (Note that it does not refer to the presence or absence of patriarchal social relations in the society.) "Masculine" cultural characteristics include competitiveness, assertiveness, ambition, and the accumulation of wealth. "Feminine" cultural characteristics include placing greater value on quality of life, family, and relationships. According to Hofstede, Japan is an example of a strongly "masculine" culture, and Sweden represents a highly "feminine" culture.

▲ **Individualist and Collectivist Tourism.** Typical differences in the way Japanese and American tourists visit other countries may in part reflect general cultural differences in the dimension of individualism-collectivism. Americans typically visit other countries as couples or families, whereas Japanese more often tour in groups.

4. *Uncertainty avoidance.* According to Hofstede, some societies are more likely than others to create conditions that will avoid stress, uncertainty, and risk for their citizens. These cultures have numerous rules that are stringently enforced, and they support highly structured workplaces. Employees typically remain at their jobs for long periods of time in these societies. According to Hofstede, uncertainty-avoidant cultures include Japan, Greece, Israel, and Spain, while cultures low in uncertainty avoidance include the United States, Jamaica, Sweden, and much of East Asia—with Singapore being the least uncertainty-avoidant culture studied.

Three Examples of Cultural Psychology

As you may recall, cultural psychologists have observed that most evolutionary psychology research (and most psychology research generally) is conducted among Western university students. They worry that evidence collected in such research may not always apply to people in other cultures or social circumstances. We will now look at three examples of research by cultural psychologists that illuminate cultural diversity—in one case presenting cultural differences in an aspect of life that most Westerners likely believe is truly universal.

SELF-ENHANCEMENT VS. SELF-IMPROVEMENT: HOW TO BE GOOD

"I am the greatest."

—Muhammad Ali, boxer

Psychologists have long subscribed to the notion that humans are motivated to maintain a positive view of themselves—to *self-enhance* (Allport, 1955; Taylor & Brown, 1994; Sedikides & Gregg, 2008; von Hippel & Trivers, 2011). Self-enhancement exists when people focus on their good qualities while downplaying the bad, when they mentally compare themselves to others and come out smelling sweet, when they underestimate the chances of bad events occurring to themselves relative to others, and so forth. However, some research indicates that self-enhancement may not be universal. Specifically, there may be substantial cultural differences in the desire to self-enhance between Westerners and those from East Asian societies (Markus & Kitayama, 1998; Nisbett & Miyamoto, 2005; Norenzayan & Heine, 2005).

For example, in one study, when asked to choose adjectives to describe themselves, nearly all the European-Americans included the term "special," whereas only about 50% of Japanese students did. On the other hand, 84% of the Japanese students chose the term "ordinary," whereas only 18% of the

European-Americans did (Markus & Kitayama, 1998). Indeed, as a whole, the motivation for self-enhancement, as it appears to exist among Westerners, seems to occur relatively rarely among those who have grown up in East Asia (Norenzayan & Heine, 2005). Instead, East Asians seem more interested in assuring that *others* think well of them (as in "saving face"), and in improving themselves as people. This idea conflicts with arguments from evolutionary psychologists that self-enhancement is a universal psychological adaptation that evolved over evolutionary time (Barkow, 1989; Sedikides & Gregg, 2008; Von Hippel & Trivers, 2011).

However, looking more closely at these cultural differences also highlights how nature and nurture intersect. As cultural psychologist Steven Heine (2005) observes, those who are motivated by self-enhancement and self-esteem, as well as those who are motivated by maintaining "face" and improving themselves, are equally looking to become "good selves"—to be good examples of what is expected of a person in their respective societies. Thus, the motivation to be a "good self" may well be a **human universal**—the result of evolutionary forces at work on human psychology—even as the specific way in which this motivation is expressed differs by culture.

Indeed, there is another way to look at East-West differences in self-enhancement. Constantine Sedikides and his colleagues have provided evidence that both Easterners and Westerners may self-enhance much to the same degree—*if* self-enhancement is understood to refer to promoting attributes that are personally important to the self-enhancer. In the case of Westerners, this would mean promoting one's personal accomplishments and individualism. In the case of Far Easterners, this would mean promoting one's dedication to the group and willingness to conform to group decisions and avoid conflict (Sedikides, Gaertner, & Toguchi, 2003; Sedikides & Gregg, 2008)!

> **Human universal** ▶ A human trait, custom, or sociocultural practice that exists in every known society.

EXPLAINING THE BEHAVIOR OF OTHERS, EAST AND WEST

As I discuss in greater detail in Chapter 15, social psychologists have explored a bias in human thinking known as the **fundamental attribution error**. The fundamental attribution error is the tendency to attribute another person's behavior to that person's inner dispositions and character traits—while downplaying the possibility that situational factors may have played a large role in causing the behavior (Gilbert & Malone, 1995; Ross, 1977). For example, if you are standing in line at the supermarket and witness a woman speaking abusively to the check-out clerk, you might assume that the woman is a mean-spirited, rude, and selfish person. In fact, the woman may rarely behave this way, and her outburst may have largely resulted from a "last straw" experience during a week in which she lost both her job and her husband, and received an audit notice from the Internal Revenue Service. Psychologists have always assumed that the fundamental attribution error is universal (Gilbert & Malone, 1995), but sociocultural theorists have questioned the universality of the fundamental attribution error just as they have done so with the motivation to self-enhance.

> **Fundamental attribution error** ▶ The tendency to attribute another person's behavior to his or her inner dispositions and character traits—while ignoring the possibility that situational factors are at work.

For example, some studies have suggested that East Asians are less likely to commit this error—in other words, they are more likely to take situational variables into account (Choi & Nisbett, 1998). Indeed, sociocultural research has shown that, as a general rule, East Asians may tend to take more information of all sorts into account before coming to final judgments about other people's behavior. This includes social contexts and personal histories (Choi, Dalal, Kim-Prieto, & Park, 2003; Markus, Uchida, Omoregie, Townsend, & Kitayama, 2006).

As another example of this cultural difference, Japanese media coverage of the 2000 and 2002 Olympics differed from that of American media—as did Japanese and American athletes' explanations for their victories and failures. Japanese media and the athletes themselves tended to include the athlete's family backgrounds, social and emotional experiences, team and coach characteristics, and so forth, in addition to the athletes' personal skills and characteristics and the nature of the competition. On the other hand, American media and athletes focused virtually exclusively on the athletes' personal characteristics and skills, and the characteristics of the competition itself. Here are two contrasting quotes from American and Japanese gold medalists from the 2000 Olympics (both quotes cited by Markus et al., 2006, p. 103). American Misty Hyman, winner in the women's 200-m butterfly swim competition noted:

> *I think I just stayed focused. It was time to show the world what I could do. I am just glad I was able to do it. I knew I could beat Suzy O'Neil, deep down in my heart I believed it, and I know this whole week the doubts kept creeping in, they were with me on the blocks, but I just said, "No, this is my night."*

Japanese Takahashi Naoko, winner in the women's marathon, offered this:

> *Here is the best coach in the world, the best manager in the world, and all of the people who support me—all of these things were getting together and became a gold medal. So I think I didn't get it alone, not only by myself.*

LIVING PSYCHOLOGY

Are Friends Good to Have? Friendship in West Africa and North America

Beware of friends.

Some are snakes under grass

Some are lions in sheep's clothing;

Some are jealousies behind their façades of praises

Some are just no good;

Beware of friends. (Ghanaian poem, cited by Adams & Plaut, 2003, p. 333)

Does the preceding poem sound like a description of typical American attitudes toward friendship? It does describe the idea of the *false* friend, the "backstabber" immortalized in a 1970s Motown hit by the O'Jays. But in general, friends are viewed in American and other Western societies as something good to have—the more the better. Being without friends is equivalent to being lonely and having one's belongingness needs unmet. People who are cautious or suspicious about having friends are frequently viewed as people with serious psychological problems. And yet, as researchers Glenn Adams and Victoria Plaut document, the experience of friendship is not the same throughout the world.

As we will explore at length in Chapter 10, researchers have found that people in all cultures feel the need to *belong*—to experience frequent positive interactions with other people in the context of caring relationships (Baumeister & Leary, 1995; Leary & Cox, 2008). However, Adams and Plaut propose that these needs are not always fulfilled in the context of friendship; and being without friends, or having few friends, does not necessarily result in loneliness (Adams & Plaut, 2003).

In their cross-national research, Adams and Plaut compare the world of friendship in West Africa with that in Western societies. In the *individualist* cultures of the West, each person experiences himself or herself as being more or less free to create relationships of spontaneous affection with virtually anyone, because there is an emphasis in Western societies on *independence*. Opportunities for forming friendship are many, and people are expected and encouraged to have many friends. A person's choice of relationships is not "scripted" by obligations or predetermined choices. In North America, people "make friends" with virtually anyone they wish, rather than "choosing friends" from a relatively small pool of appropriate possibilities (e.g., co-workers or neighbors).

However, in collectivist cultures, with their emphasis on *interdependence* rather than independence, relationships are more likely to reflect obligations, and an individual's choices of friends are constrained by custom. According to Adams and Plaut, friendship may be more likely to serve specific purposes, rather than springing spontaneously from affection in these societies. Further, once a friendship is formed, participants may be obligated to support one another in a great many ways. In poor societies such as those of West Africa, this includes the sharing of scarce resources such as food or other material goods. Such costs to friendship in a poor, collectivist society are poignantly described by Barack Obama in his account of his experiences in Kenya, East Africa (Obama, 1995/2007).

Moreover, in poor, collectivist, societies there is less mobility. If a conflict should arise with a friend, one cannot avoid the person as easily as in highly mobile Western societies. Thus, according to Adams and Plaut, in West Africa, people are cautious about creating friendships, understand the potential costs, and form smaller networks of friends.

Another reason North Americans are motivated to form larger networks of friends, according to Adams and Plaut, is that there are fewer opportunities for general companionship in individualist cultures than in collectivist cultures, where people are surrounded by networks of extended family and family-like relationships. Therefore, although North Americans may be more likely to have larger circles of friends, they may also be more likely than West Africans to experience loneliness if they lack friends. People without friends are pitied in North America. In contrast, people without friends are not pitied in West Africa—instead, they are accused of opting out of contributing their fair share to the collective welfare.

Although Adams and Plaut's study is provocative, it bears mentioning that both West Africans and North Americans share the same basic understanding of the difference between friendship and other relationships. In this sense, friendship is the same in West Africa as in North America. Moreover, the portrait Adams and Plaut paint of friendship in the West is not entirely accurate. For example, there are numerous social restrictions on one's choice of friends, as you can see from a quick look at Western literature throughout the centuries or the ethnic composition of groups of friends on your campus. Although North Americans are technically allowed to "make" rather than "choose" friends, this does not always play out in reality. It is possible that Adams and Plaut's portrait of West African friendship is similarly stereotyped. ■

Social Role Theory: The "Social" in Sociocultural

Recall that *society* refers to the institutions and organized patterns of interaction of a cooperating group of individuals. We have looked at the effects of *culture*—the products of society—on psychology, but what of society itself? Like culture, the influence of society pervades human psychology, and we will consider it throughout this book. For the moment, however, let us return to the study by Russell Clark and Elaine Hatfield (1989) that I described in the "Freeze Frame" feature that opened the chapter. As I mentioned earlier, evolutionary psychologists have attributed the greater willingness of men to engage in sex with a stranger as an inevitable consequence of an evolutionary history in which females have a stronger minimal parental investment than males. Regardless of whether you found this a convincing explanation, it is far from

Social role theory ▶ A theory that proposes that people behave in highly variable ways according to differences in the type of social organization in which they live.

Patriarchy ▶ Any social organization where the large majority of the uppermost positions in political and social hierarchies are occupied by men.

the only possible interpretation of the results of this study. One of the most influential alternate accounts is offered by *social role* theorists such as Alice Eagly and Wendy Wood (Eagly & Wood, 1999; Wood & Eagly, 2002; 2007).

Social role theory proposes that people behave in highly variable ways according to differences in the type of *social organization* in which they live. Societies differ in how they organize themselves in response to their prevailing level of technological advancement, physical environment, and social history. Social role theory, in particular, has a lot to say about sex differences—and social role theorists have been influenced by feminist insights regarding the experiences of women throughout history in *patriarchal* society. Although **patriarchy** is defined in different ways depending on the context, in general it describes any social organization where men occupy the very large majority of the uppermost positions in political and social hierarchies (Goldberg, 1993). This is somewhat different from *male dominance*, a related concept, but one less easy to define precisely. Male dominance usually refers to male authority within personal and family relationships. Although patriarchy and male dominance generally go together, this is not always the case.

Social role theorists propose that the behavior of men and women differs according to the ways that their tasks and sex roles have been assigned in patriarchal societies. In particular, the *division of labor* under patriarchy—where women are accorded the roles of child caregiver and homemaker, and men those of warrior and breadwinner—is seen by social role theorists to be the "engine" driving sex differences. This is because the division of labor "summarizes" the social opportunities and constraints under which men and women live (Eagly & Wood, 1999, p. 409). According to social role theorists, the division of labor evolved as it did throughout the world because males are physically larger and stronger—and therefore better suited for hunting and warfare—while females are the sex that bears and nurses children. Men and women thus accommodate themselves to whatever opportunities present themselves and whatever restrictions limit those opportunities under patriarchy.

Let's take two well-established tendencies in human mating preferences: Although both men and women list qualities such as kindness and intelligence as most important in choosing a mate, men and women differ on the importance they place on certain other qualities. Women are more likely than men to prefer a mate a few years older than they are and to emphasize the importance of a prospective mate's status, dependability, and ability to acquire resources (including money). In contrast, men have a general preference for women who are young and attractive: They are usually not as interested in status and resources. This sex difference has been found in every society yet studied (Buss, 1989, 2005; Geary, 2010; Lippa, 2007).

Evolutionary psychologists explain women's interest in status and resources by pointing to women's greater minimal parental investment. Ancestral women who emphasized status and resources over youth and looks in a mate would have been more reproductively successful, because a man with status and resources (who virtually always would have been older than his bride) is better able to support and protect his mate and her offspring during the long (and costly) period of pregnancy and infant care. The genetic line of women who preferred such men would have prospered, and those who did not would have died out.

On the other hand, according to evolutionary psychologists, ancestral men did not need to be protected and supported during the period of reproduction, so status and resources in a mate were not particularly important to them. Instead, men had the problem of detecting which women in the community were most likely to be fertile. Therefore, men evolved to find young, attractive (i.e., healthy) women appealing because *youth* and *health* are the most reliable cues to fertility in human females (Symons, 1995).

A study by Martin Fieder and Susanne Huber, using a sample of 10,000 Swedish men and women, suggests how a man's interest in youthful women, and women's interest in slightly older men, might have evolved (Fieder & Huber, 2007). Fieder and Huber found that significantly more children are born to couples in first marriages where the woman is four to six years younger than the man. Because more children are born to such unions, if the age preferences of the parents had even the slightest genetic component, over evolutionary time these preferences would have spread through the human population through natural selection until most humans shared them.

In contrast to this evolutionary view, social role theorists such as Eagly and Wood (1999) suggest that peoples' mate choices reflect their efforts to make the most of their available options. These options are defined by what an individual's society considers acceptable gender roles. In modern patriarchal society, a woman's preference for a man with status and wealth "can be explained by the simple reality that . . . males monopolize ownership of productive resources" such as real estate, financial institutions, manufacturing plants, and corporate wealth (Hrdy, quoted in Eagly & Wood, 1999, p. 415). From this perspective, sex differences in age preferences and interest in status and resources in a mate reflect a "best fit" to the social roles expected of men and women. Because men have more power, they prefer younger women who, presumably, earn less money and have lower social status, education, and knowledge than same-age peers. Women, on the other hand, prefer slightly older men because older men tend to be more economically and socially successful than younger men.

With social role theory as a backdrop, we can now revisit the findings of Clark and Hatfield (1989), viewing the results of their study through a social role lens. Consider that men are raised with media and other role models who are sexually assertive and are rewarded for being sexually active (Oliver & Hyde 1993). Films such as *The 40-Year-Old Virgin* (Apatow, Robertson, & Townsend, 2005), which depicts a nerdy, sexually naïve man as a hero, are extraordinarily rare in mass media of all sorts. On the other hand, girls have traditionally been raised with female role models at home and in the media who are expected to be sexually unavailable until after marriage. Although women's sexual attitudes in Western societies changed dramatically during the second half of the 20th century—particularly as regards the acceptability of premarital sex—beliefs that women ought to be sexually reserved remain throughout most cultures around the world.

Rewards are given to women for sex-role behavior that is appropriate in the realm of sexuality; and punishments, or the threat of punishments, loom large for violations of those behaviors. These punishments range from simple insults and threats to a woman's reputation (e.g., "She's just a slut") to physical violence, embodied in the stoning to death or hanging of women in certain cultures who have engaged in premarital sex or adultery. Although such punishments are clearly on the way out throughout the world, they continue to be allowed by law in some nations. Even if the laws are not often enforced, the very fact that they exist undoubtedly sends a clear message to girls as they grow up.

Whereas women are pressured to maintain chastity, sexually active men are seen as "players" who are to be envied and admired rather than censured. According to social role theorists, the existence of this continued *double standard* for sexual behavior—one that allows for men what is denied to women—ensures that women will continue to receive negative social messages for engaging in the very behaviors for which men receive positive messages (Aubrey, 2004; Sprecher, McKinney, & Orbuch, 1987).

In sum, according to social role theory, it is perfectly understandable that Clark and Hatfield should have found in their study such a large difference in willingness to have sex with total strangers. It is much easier to judge youth

▲ **Amina Lawal: Sentenced to Death by Stoning.** The sentencing of women to death by stoning or hanging for engaging in premarital sex or adultery is the most extreme expression of the double standard for sexual behavior. Amina Lawal is a Nigerian single mother who, at age 29, was sentenced by court to be stoned to death for conceiving her child, Wasila, out of wedlock. Only after a worldwide public outcry was her sentence overturned by the Islamic Funtua Sharia court of appeals. Lawal was subsequently freed. *(Source: Sengupta, 2003)*

and beauty on first glance, while gauging economic resources may take more time and investigation—more than the few minutes allowed in the Clark and Hatfield study. Social role theorists assert that women may find the idea of casual sex with a stranger just as appealing as men, but need more than the (highly artificial) 5-minute time allotment of the Clark and Hatfield study to make up their minds. Of course, evolutionary psychologists might counter that this is exactly their point—women need time to assess the "value" of their prospective mates, but men do not.

However, as numerous researchers have suggested, there is room for both social role and evolutionary views of human behavior. While these theories often contradict one another, the contradictions are sometimes more apparent than real—resulting because the theories provide answers to different kinds of questions (Kenrick & Li, 2000; Lippa, 2009; van den Berghe, 2009). For example, social role theorists observe that sex differences in size and strength are partially responsible for the division of labor under patriarchy and resultant sex role differences. An evolutionary theorist would probably agree with this observation. However, evolutionary theorists are primarily interested in the question of *why* the size and strength differences exist in the first place—a question not addressed by social role theory.

If you recall from Chapter 1, when theories address different aspects or levels of a problem in this way they differ in *level of analysis*. Social role and evolutionary explanations simply address different levels of analysis. Social role theorists are primarily interested in *how* sex differences shape the lives of individuals, and evolutionary theorists are primarily interested in *why* the differences exist in the first place. But as one research team observed, knowledge of psychology would be advanced if theorists would stop arguing about whether evolved psychological adaptations or social roles cause human behavior, and instead address the more complex question of how social and evolutionary forces interact to produce human behavior (Kenrick & Li, 2000).

IN SUMMARY

1.	The sociocultural perspective focuses on the ways societies and cultures mold human psychology and influence behavior.
2.	Cultural psychologists are interested in cultural similarities as well as differences, but they tend to emphasize cultural differences. The four principal dimensions along which cultures differ are individualism vs. collectivism, power distance, masculinity-femininity, and uncertainty avoidance.
3.	Cultural differences in psychology explored in this chapter include: East-West differences in the tendency to self-enhance, differences in the tendency to commit the fundamental attribution error (FAE), and differences between West African and North American conceptions of friendship.
4.	Social role theory proposes that sex differences may be explained by the opportunities and constraints under which men and women live in patriarchal society. Although social role theory is often presented as an alternative to evolutionary accounts, evolutionary and social role theories sometimes reflect different levels of analysis rather than differences of opinion.

RETRIEVE!

1. Match the cultural practice on the left to the dimension of culture it reflects:

Viewing the interests of your family as more important than your own interests	Power Distance
A plantation owner believing that it is right and proper that he should pay his peasant workers very low wages.	Masculinity-Femininity
A worker ending his work life still working for the same company with which he began his work life	Individualism-Collectivism
Laws guaranteeing child care for all workers, long maternity leaves with pay, and universal healthcare	Uncertainty avoidance

2. East Asians and Westerners apparently differ in their motivation to self-enhance. What is this difference? How do these differences reflect an underlying similarity?

3. True or False: West Africans hold a more conflicted view of the value of friendship than North Americans.

4. What is the social role explanation for the sex differences found in studies such as the Clark and Hatfield study described in the "Freeze Frame" feature at the beginning of the chapter?

Looking Back

Chapter 3 in Review

WHAT ARE GENES?
- Heredity is the tendency of offspring to resemble their parents in various ways. Genes, composed of functional strands of DNA, are units of heredity. DNA contains the unique "code" for creating each living organism.
- Phenotypes are potentially observable traits or characteristics of an organism. The human genome is the set of hereditary instructions that programs amino acids and proteins to build a human organism.
- Genes create proteins by transmitting genetic information through RNA; replicating; and interacting with other genes by "switching them on and off."

HOW DO GENES AND ENVIRONMENTS INFLUENCE BEHAVIOR?
- Behavior genetics is the scientific study of how genes and environments influence individual differences in traits and behavior. Behavior geneticists use studies of twins reared together, twins reared apart, and adopted children to try to estimate the proportion of individual differences on various traits in a given sample of individuals that can be attributable to genetic heredity and the proportion that is due to environmental influences.
- A gene-environment correlation occurs when a person's environment is a reflection of, or is somehow correlated with, that person's genotype. There are two types of gene-environment correlations discussed in the chapter: an active gene-environment correlation and a reactive gene-environment correlation. A gene-environment interaction occurs when different individuals respond differently to the same environmental experience because of differences in their genotypes.

WHY ARE PSYCHOLOGISTS INTERESTED IN EVOLUTION?
- Evolution is both fact and theory. The fact of organic and geological evolution is accepted by virtually all scientists working in the life sciences. However, theories about how evolution occurs are often debated. Evolutionary psychology is less a field in itself than an approach to virtually any field in psychology.
- Adaptations are accumulated characteristics of an organism that have resulted from natural selection as solutions to specific "problems" over evolutionary time, and that allow the organism to be well adapted to its environment. Because these adaptations are shared by virtually all members of our species to varying degrees, evolutionary psychologists believe that humans are a single species with a single human nature.
- Because psychological adaptation occurred among human ancestors over evolutionary time in environments in certain respects very different from modern environments, some adaptations are no longer "adaptive." This is known as environmental mismatch.

Looking Back continued

- Evolutionary psychologists propose that in most respects men and women have faced the same evolutionary pressures over the millennia, and should be expected to have the same psychological adaptations as a result. However, in the areas of sexuality, reproduction, and physical aggression men and women have faced vastly different pressures, and therefore sex differences in adaptations in these areas of life should be expected.

WHAT IS THE SOCIOCULTURAL PERSPECTIVE?

- Psychologists studying the influence of society and culture on psychology take the sociocultural perspective, which is strongly associated with the field of cultural psychology. Cultural psychologists emphasize that different cultures are characterized by different behaviors and subjective experiences.
- Culture pervades virtually every aspect of thought and behavior, and it proliferates over generations. Geert Hofstede has established specific dimensions of behavior along which cultures typically differ, including: individualism vs. collectivism, power distance, masculinity-femininity, and uncertainty avoidance. Although cultures differ in their ideas about morality, morality itself is a human universal.
- Cultural research suggests that some characteristics believed to be universal may actually be primarily characteristics of Western peoples. These include self-enhancement, vulnerability to the fundamental attribution error (FAE), and subscribing to the idea that friendship has no negative consequences.
- Social role theory proposes that people behave in highly variable ways according to differences in the type of social organization in which they live.
- Theories differ in level of analysis when they address different aspects or levels of the same question, without necessarily disagreeing with one another outright. Evolutionary and social role theories of sex differences may be viewed as different levels of analysis.

Key Terms

Active gene-environment correlation, 124
Adaptations, 129
Allele, 113
Behavior genetics, 119
Chromosomes, 113
Cultural psychology, 142
Culture, 142
Dizygotic (fraternal) twins, 120
DNA (deoxyribonucleic acid), 113
Environmental mismatch, 131
Evolutionary psychology, 130
Fundamental attribution error, 145

Gene, 113
Gene-environment correlation, 123
Gene-environment interaction, 125
Genotype, 114
Heredity, 114
Heritability, 121
Human genome, 113
Human universal, 145
Long-term mating, 133
Modular model, 131
Molecular genetics, 123
Monozygotic (identical) twins, 120
Natural experiment, 120

Patriarchy, 148
Phenotype, 115
Psychological adaptation, 130
Reactive gene-environment correlation, 124
RNA (ribonucleic acid), 115
Short-term mating, 132
Social role theory, 148
Society, 142
Sociocultural perspective, 142
Theory of natural selection, 128
Theory of parental investment and sexual selection, 133

Test Yourself

1. Differentiate the following terms: chromosome, gene, DNA, and RNA.
2. Briefly describe three functions of genes.
3. A statistic that teases apart the degree to which genes and environments contribute to variation in a trait among people in a particular sample is known as the _____ statistic.
4. If the results of twin and adoption studies are averaged out, what are the relative contributions of genes and environments to individual differences in cognitive ability, personality, and social attitudes in most groups of humans studied thus far?
5. What is the difference between a gene-environment correlation and a gene-environment interaction? Name two types of gene-environment correlations.
6. How is evolution both a fact and a theory?
7. What is the term used to describe characteristics in a species that have resulted from the accumulation of small incremental changes over time, and that cause members of the species to be better adapted to their environments?
8. Give a few examples of psychological adaptations proposed by evolutionary psychologists.
9. According to evolutionary psychologists, why are humans so flexible in their approaches to solving problems?
10. When an adaptation is no longer adaptive in a current environment, it is known as _____.
11. How does the Trivers theory of parental investment and sexual

Test Yourself continued

selection explain men's greater willingness to engage in casual sex (short-term mating) and greater interest in partner variety?

12. Some criticisms of evolutionary psychology are based on misunderstands of these theories. Name one inaccurate, and one possibly accurate, criticism of evolutionary psychology.

13. Distinguish *culture* from *society*.

14. How do individualist cultures differ from collectivist cultures? Masculine from feminine cultures? What is meant by uncertainty avoidance as a dimension of culture? Power distance?

15. What is one explanation for the greater willingness of Far Easterners to abandon the fundamental attribution error?

16. Why are West Africans more likely than North Americans to believe that there are "costs to friendship?"

17. How does social role theory explain sex differences in willingness to engage in casual sex? Sex differences in interest in status and resources in a mate?

CHAPTER

4

Human Lifespan
development

Chapter Outline

Freeze Frame

The boy in the middle receiving an award is Gregory Robert Smith at age 9-going-on-10. He may look cute, but he's not playing around on the stage. He's preparing to deliver an address to the 1999 senior class at Orange Park High School in Orange Park, Florida, where he is graduating with an A-plus average. Four years after this photo was taken, at age 13, Gregory received a bachelor's degree in mathematics from Randolph-Macon College. He then went on to doctoral studies in mathematics at the University of Virginia. This would be the first of three doctorates he expected to earn over the coming years. If this weren't enough, he has been nominated for a Nobel Peace Prize *three times* for his work on behalf of child victims of war, violence, and poverty. Oh, yes, and he plays football pretty well. Among his plans is to become president of the United States (CBS News, 2009).

As you might suspect, Gregory displayed unusual characteristics from an early age. He spoke his first word at age three months ("dada"), could recite memorized books before the age of 1 year, and began to read to himself shortly thereafter. By the age of 2 he was correcting grammatical errors made by adults in his presence. Greg was equally talented in mathematics. He began solving basic arithmetic problems at the age of 14 months, and by age 6, he was seriously annoying his school teachers and administrators by flagging errors in his math textbooks with Post-It notes. He skipped from second to ninth grade within a year and finished the rest of his high schooling in two years.

Greg's precocity was not limited to academic matters—it also extended to moral issues, a tendency often noted in children with exceptionally high IQs (Winner, 1996). At the age of 9, in response to his increasing distress as he learned about the plight of child victims of violence and poverty, he founded two organizations: the World Children Awards, dedicated to addressing the needs and rights of children throughout the world; and International Youth Advocates, which promotes principles of peace and understanding among young people worldwide.

Greg Smith is an unusually extreme example of what has been termed "profoundly gifted" child development. Exceptional children such as Greg Smith are often "spellbinding" to the rest of us (Ruthsatz & Detterman, 2003, p. 510; Subotnik, Olszewski-Kubilius, & Worrell, 2011). They do not merely fascinate—they may actually elicit awe or even reverence, and it is not unknown for religious practices to be built on their shoulders. On the other hand, the abilities of these children may equally elicit cynicism, envy, or outright hostility.

Greg Smith's abilities seem to stretch the limits of what is normally considered possible for an infant and child to attain. However, research in the field of human lifespan development is providing increasing evidence that the abilities of ordinary infants and children in general have been greatly underestimated in the past. This research is painting a portrait of the human infant as emerging into the world with numerous previously unsuspected competencies already in place, or at least primed to develop in short order.

Why Study Development?

Development means *change* over time. Traditionally—particularly in the United States—developmental psychologists studied the changes that occur throughout human infancy, childhood and, to a lesser extent, adolescence. However, over the past several decades, psychologists studying development have extended their range of inquiry to include the years of adulthood (Baltes, Lindenberger, & Staudinger, 2006; Baltes, Staudinger, & Lindenberger, 1999). This is in recognition of the fact that the patterns of human development do not end as the child evolves into the adult, but continue throughout the life span. Development over the life span includes all the ways we change over time—physiologically, psychologically, and socially—as well as the ways we may retain stable threads and continuities throughout our lives. It is with these patterns of change and stability that this chapter is concerned.

Four Assumptions of the Lifespan Perspective

As mentioned, for most of the 20th century, the primary focus of **developmental psychology** was on the infant, child, and adolescent. It was probably not until the work of developmental theorist Paul Baltes in the 1980s that a true **lifespan perspective** on human development began to emerge—the notion that development continues "from womb to tomb." Although numerous developmental psychologists specialize in one stage of human development or another, the basic assumption of the lifespan perspective—that it is important to study development throughout the stages of human life—has become widely accepted in the field.

Baltes identified a number of key assumptions about human lifespan development with which most developmental psychologists would probably agree, and which frame the material presented in this chapter (Baltes, 1987; Baltes et al., 2006; Baltes et al., 1999). Among these assumptions are the following:

1. *Development is a lifelong process.* Development begins at conception and continues until death.

2. *Development involves constant loss as well as gain.* Development involves both decline and growth. Individuals may gain in wisdom as they age, but may also experience reduced memory functioning; children may increase their verbal and mathematical reasoning ability in later school grades, but simultaneously lose the vivid imagination that characterizes early childhood.

3. *Development is determined by a multiplicity of causes.* Development is rooted in the interaction of genes and other biological factors, environments, cultures, lifespan periods, and historical contexts.

4. *Development is characterized by plasticity throughout the life span.* Although each period of the life span can be characterized by a typical set of abilities and concerns, the course of development can be altered as a result of experience and personal decisions throughout the life span. See Table 4.1 for a summary of the periods of the human life span.

Developmental psychology ▶ The scientific study of changes and continuities in human psychology over time.

Lifespan perspective ▶ The prevailing perspective in developmental psychology that emphasizes the importance of studying human development throughout life, rather than focusing exclusively on infancy and childhood as has often been the case (particularly in the United States).

Table 4.1 **Periods of the Life Span**

PERIOD	AGE RANGE
Prenatal period	Fertilization to birth
Infancy	Birth to age 1
Toddlerhood	1–3 years
Preschool period	3–5 or 6 years
School-age period	6–12 years
Adolescence	12–age when adult roles are assumed (approximately 20)
Early adulthood	20–40 years
Middle adulthood	40–65 years
Late adulthood	Over 65

Conception ▶ The fusion of the nuclei of a sperm and ovum. Also termed *fertilization*.

Secondary oocyte ▶ The mature, unfertilized, female reproductive cell.

Sperm ▶ The male reproductive cell.

Ovum ▶ The female reproductive cell following initial cell division at the point of fertilization.

Fertilization ▶ The fusion of the nuclei of a sperm and ovum. Also termed *conception*.

Zygote ▶ The fused nuclei of a sperm and ovum.

Endometrium ▶ The lining of the uterus.

Uterus ▶ The female womb.

Embryo ▶ The developing human organism at approximately 2 weeks following fertilization, after rapid cell division in the zygote has taken place.

Placenta ▶ The flat organ connected to the uterus on one side and to the embryo on the other. The developing fetus receives nutrition and oxygen from the mother through the placenta, and this organ also provides protection for the fetus from attack by the mother's own immune defenses.

Umbilical cord ▶ The tissue that delivers oxygen and nutrients to the embryo/fetus through the placenta and absorbs waste products. It is the eventual source of the infant's navel.

Fetus ▶ The developing human organism after the embryonic stage has passed, at about 8 to 9 weeks after fertilization.

How Does the Unborn Embryo Become a Newborn Infant?

The processes of **conception**, prenatal growth of the fetus, and childbirth cannot help but engender awe no matter how often they are encountered. The star players in the drama of human reproduction are the woman's **secondary oocyte** (mature female reproductive cell), often somewhat incorrectly termed *ovum*, and the man's reproductive cell, known as **sperm**. Hundreds of millions of *sperm* are released in a male *ejaculation*, but only about 100 of them actually get anywhere close to the woman's secondary oocyte. If one of these hundred sperm manages to pass the oocyte's protective layers of cells and arrive at the interior of the oocyte, a hardened shell forms around the oocyte that will not yield to any other sperm's attempts at penetration.

At this point, the oocyte divides into two cells: the **ovum** (egg), the term now given to the female reproductive cell, and the *second polar body*, which is little more than a collection of discarded chromosomes. The nuclei of the sperm and ovum fuse, producing a single nucleus that contains the genetic contributions of each parent. **Fertilization** (also termed *conception*) has now occurred. This fused nucleus—the first stage of development of the human organism—is known as the **zygote**.

At about 24 hours after fertilization, rapid cell division begins to occur in the zygote, and in about 5 days the zygote attaches itself to the **endometrium**, the lining of the woman's **uterus** (womb), where it will grow over the coming months. After another week of remarkably rapid cell division, the zygote enters the *embryonic stage*, and is thus now referred to as an **embryo**. However, the zygote is extremely vulnerable; a large number do not survive to become embryos, but instead are quietly *miscarried*, usually before the woman knows she was pregnant.

An embryo that survives undergoes major transformations. It is now dependent for nutrition and oxygen on the **placenta**, which provides oxygen and nutrients for the embryo and in turn absorbs waste products from it. The placenta is connected to the uterus on one side and to the embryo on the other by the **umbilical cord** (the eventual source of the baby's navel). The placenta also screens out toxins and transfers the mother's antibodies to the embryo, giving it immunity against diseases. Within 6 to 7 weeks, the embryonic heart begins to beat.

At about 8 to 9 weeks after conception the embryonic stage has passed, and the developing organism comes to be known as a **fetus**. At this point, the fetus is only about 1½ inches long and weighs only about half an ounce, but all human organs have formed and, as you can see in Figure 4.1, it has taken on a distinctly human appearance. Now, if everything goes well, approximately 30 weeks later, the newborn infant will emerge into the glaring light of the world.

The Embryo and Fetus Face Challenges

Although the embryo and fetus are not as vulnerable as the zygote, they also face challenges as they develop. The placenta acts as a screen for toxins, but it is not always successful. Harmful bacteria, viruses, and substances such as drugs or alcohol can be transferred to the developing fetus and result in **congenital malformations**, physical defects or abnormalities present at birth (often termed *birth defects*). These harmful agents are termed **teratogens**. Approximately 15% of infants are born with minor problems resulting from teratogens, and 5% experience severe problems (Sadler, 2004).

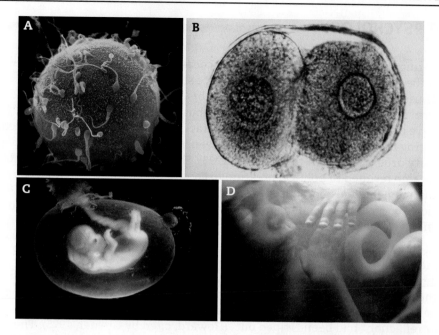

◀**FIGURE 4.1 Prenatal Development from Fertilization to Fetus.** At top left, a single sperm penetrates the secondary oocyte's protective layer. At top right, cell division begins in the zygote. At bottom left, the embryo has formed and by 6 weeks, the developing heart had begun to beat. At bottom right is the fetus at 4 months. (*Source: Nilsson, 1993*)

In terms of the numbers of infants affected, the most damaging of preventable teratogens are cigarettes and alcohol. Maternal prenatal cigarette smoking results in increased rates of miscarriage, premature birth, and low birth weight. The more cigarettes the mother smokes, the worse are the effects (Espy et al., 2011; Law et al., 2003). More than half of infants whose mothers smoked one pack or more per day during pregnancy experience various neurological problems requiring intensive care (Habek, Habek, Ivanisevic, & Djelmis, 2002). Prenatal tobacco exposure also increases the odds of *sudden infant death syndrome* (SIDS; DiFranza, Aligne, & Weitzman, 2004).

As damaging to the fetus as cigarettes may be, alcohol is far more dangerous because alcohol crosses the placental barrier easily. Alcohol remains one of the leading causes of preventable congenital disorders and malformations, intellectual disability, and developmental disorders. The effects of alcohol are particularly pernicious early in pregnancy, often before the mother realizes that she is pregnant—one reason for a woman to eliminate alcohol use if she is attempting to become pregnant.

The most serious outcome of maternal prenatal alcohol use is **fetal alcohol syndrome (FAS)**. Children with FAS have characteristically small heads and weight, and specific types of facial abnormalities. They show signs of damage to the central nervous system and score below normal on IQ tests (Floyd, O'Connor, Sokol, Bertrand, & Cordero, 2005). Currently, *no* amount of alcohol ingestion during pregnancy is considered safe (Ikonomidou et al., 2000), although controversy exists about exactly how much alcohol actually poses a danger. One reason so many health care workers and medical researchers advocate complete abstention from alcohol during pregnancy is the existence of milder forms of FAS known as *fetal alcohol effects* or FAE. Although symptoms of FAE are somewhat less severe than those for FAS, like FAS they are lifelong and irreversible.

Interestingly, the substance that has probably received the most publicity as a teratogen over the past few decades—cocaine—turns out to be far less dangerous to fetuses than previously supposed. (See "Critical Thinking about Psychology" on pp. 160–161.)

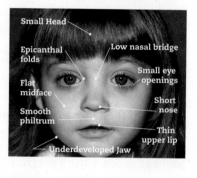

Small Head
Epicanthal folds
Low nasal bridge
Flat midface
Small eye openings
Smooth philtrum
Short nose
Thin upper lip
Underdeveloped Jaw

◀**Typical Facial Features in Fetal Alcohol Syndrome.** Fetal alcohol syndrome (FAS) is likely the single most frequent cause of mental retardation in the United States. FAS infants are lighter in weight and shorter than others, their heads are smaller, and they possess characteristic facial and body features. As they age, they may develop hyperactivity, learning and memory deficits, behavior and attention problems, and mental illness. These effects are not reversible. Pictured here are the characteristic facial features of FAS.

Congenital malformation (birth defect) ▶ Any physical abnormality or defect present at birth. Congenital malformations may result from genetic causes or prenatal events, including exposure to radiation, drugs and alcohol, or maternal illness.

Teratogen ▶ Any harmful substance, bacteria, or virus that can be transferred through the placenta to a developing mammalian organism.

Fetal alcohol syndrome (FAS) ▶ A congenital disorder resulting from prenatal maternal alcohol use.

CRITICAL THINKING ABOUT PSYCHOLOGY

The "Crack Baby": Crackpot Idea?

During the 1980s, a new way to deliver cocaine to the body was discovered in the form of *crack*, a smokable substance similar to cocaine *freebase*. As its use spread rapidly in inner cities and brought with it devastation in the form of increased crime, violence, drug abuse, and child neglect, a tidal wave of public opinion rose up against crack and cocaine in general—which, during the previous decade, had been seen as a rather benign, nonaddictive party drug for the well-to-do (Coles, 1993). This change in the public view of cocaine resulted in political pressure to control use of the drug through law enforcement. It also produced strong pressure on scientists to counteract views of cocaine as benign and to provide research demonstrating harmful effects of the drug (Coles, 1993; Day & Richardson, 1993).

At that time, reports began to surface of babies born to crack-addicted mothers who appeared to have suffered severe birth defects or lasting developmental damage. These findings were seized on by the media, and the idea of the "crack baby" was born. It was said of these infants that the part of their brains that "makes us human beings, capable of discussion or reflection" had been "wiped out" (Howard, cited by Greider, 1995). The babies were reported to shriek, tremble, and be incapable of bonding with anyone. It was stated confidently that their mothers' use of cocaine had marked the infants indelibly for a life of misery and addiction to cocaine. Crack-smoking mothers were viewed with disgust and horror by many, and their children were seen as "damaged goods" (Coles, 1993). Attempts to prosecute such mothers for child abuse or to remove their children from the home ensued.

Although the babies of crack-smoking mothers often *did* show developmental problems, and some showed birth defects, there was a problem with the research that had created the crack baby idea: Women who smoked crack during pregnancy also used alcohol, cigarettes, and other drugs. Moreover, because crack use was characteristic of poor, inner-city communities, pregnant women who smoked crack often lacked access to proper nutrition, prenatal care, and education about pregnancy and health (including information about sexually transmitted infections), and were at increased risk of violence in the home (Rose-Jacobs, Cabral, Posner, Epstein, & Frank, 2002).

Normally, efforts would be made to separate out the effects of all these variables prior to coming to conclusions about the effects of some other factor such as use of a particular drug (e.g., crack). However, in the rush to judgment about cocaine, these other variables were ignored altogether or poorly controlled in research studies (Coles, 1993; Greider, 1995; Mayes, Granger, Bornstein, & Zuckerman, 1992; Neuspiel, 1993). Virtually any symptom in the child was attributed to the mother's use of cocaine. For example, ordinary colic was attributed to "cocaine withdrawal," something that has never actually been demonstrated to exist in newborns (Eyler et al., 2001).

However, as more careful research was conducted over time, it was discovered that while cocaine is clearly a dangerous drug for many reasons, *causing birth defects and developmental disabilities in fetuses does not seem to be one of its dangers* (e.g., Coles, 1993; Eyler et al., 2001; Frank, Augustyn, Knight, Pell, & Zuckerman, 2001; Frank et al., 2005; Messinger et al., 2004). Extensive use of cocaine by pregnant mothers may cause short-lived motor disturbances (jitters) in some newborns, and a few studies do show minor differences between the development of these children and those not exposed. However, in general, researchers were confusing the effects of the many variables that often accompanied crack smoking with the effects of crack itself.

Based on current evidence, at least, the crack baby is mythological. Babies of cocaine-using mothers are *not* born addicted to cocaine, and there is little evidence that they suffer intellectual impairment, developmental disability, permanent motor impairment, or other severe problems when the effects of other variables are controlled (Frank et al., 2001, 2005; Lumeng, Cabral, Gannon, Heeren, & Frank, 2007; Messinger, et al., 2004; Okie, 2009). Experts who claim to be able to tell which children have been born to cocaine-using mothers merely by observing the children in fact cannot do this (Rose-Jacobs et al., 2002; Okie, 2009). Although drug use—including cocaine use—is not healthy for fetuses, there is no evidence that it is any worse for fetuses than smoking during pregnancy (Okie, 2009).

The most important lesson to be learned from this episode for our purposes is this: It is very easy even for sincere and competent researchers to get swept up in popular opinion, media notoriety, and the lure of funds and prestige. It is for this reason that when dealing with highly controversial topics, about which passionate opinions abound, *caveat lector*—"let the reader beware." Consider the source and the evidence. ■

The Newborn Infant Is Already Skilled

Traditionally, the newborn infant was viewed as an utterly helpless organism that perceived the world, in the famous words of William James, as a "blooming, buzzing confusion." At best, the infant was acknowledged to have certain **reflexes**—innate and involuntary responses to stimuli, some of which, known as **survival reflexes**, clearly evolved to assist the infant in survival and growth. Among these are reflexes regulating swallowing and breathing, and those promoting breast feeding behavior.

Despite reflexes, however, infants were not thought to possess much in the way of perceptual capabilities or other psychological competencies geared toward survival and growth. As research methods in developmental psychology have grown more sophisticated, so has the picture of the newborn infant.

Thanks to newly developed methods of research, we now know that infants have perceptual competencies that were never suspected as recently as two or three decades ago. For example, within hours of birth newborn infants prefer to gaze at, and will increase their sucking behavior in response to, images of their mother's face compared with images of other female faces (Pascalis, de Schonen, Morton, Duruelle, & Grenet, 1995; Pascalis & Kelly, 2009; Sai, 2005). Newborns who are breast-fed will be able to recognize and prefer their own mother's scent over that of other women (Mizuno, Mizuno, Shinohara, & Noda, 2004; Nishitani et al., 2009). The hearing of newborns is acute enough to recognize subtle patterns of sound, including the sounds of spoken language; and this acuity develops well before the infant is born. From at least 3 months prior to birth, fetuses respond to changes in sound from the outside world (Fernald, 2004). Indeed, fetuses can distinguish their mother's voice from that of a strange female, and the language spoken by their mother from a foreign language (Kisilevsky et al., 2003; Kisilevsky et al., 2009; Moon, Lagercrantz, & Kuhl, 2013).

You might well ask how researchers could possibly know this. Like much research in infant development, this study took ingenuity. The researchers monitored fetal heart rate as they placed a speaker directly above the mother's stomach and alternately played tape recordings of the infant's mother and a strange female speaking, or their mother's language versus a foreign language. Fetal heart rate consistently increased when the mother's voice or the mother's language was heard and decreased when the stranger's voice (or a foreign

Reflex ▶ An innate, involuntary neuromuscular response to stimuli.

Survival reflex ▶ An innate, involuntary neuromuscular response that serves a functional purpose and likely evolved because it assisted the organism in survival or reproduction.

language) was heard. As another example, when DeCasper and Spence (1986) had mothers recite portions of the Dr. Seuss book *The Cat in the Hat* repeatedly during the last few weeks of their pregnancies, their newborn infants increased their sucking behavior when these passages were read to them, but other passages had no effect.

IN SUMMARY

1. The lifespan perspective in developmental psychology began to emerge in the 1980s, particularly in the work of Paul Baltes. Among the key assumptions in the lifespan perspective Baltes identified are the notions that development is a lifelong process, that it involves loss as well as gain, that it is multiply determined, and that it is plastic.

2. Fertilization occurs when a sperm penetrates the protective layer of cells surrounding a secondary oocyte. The oocyte divides into an ovum and second polar body. The nucleus of the sperm and the nucleus of the ovum fuse, producing a zygote, and conception is complete. If the zygote survives, it attaches itself to the endometrium of the uterus and within 2 weeks becomes an embryo. Within 8 to 9 weeks after conception, the embryonic stage is passed, and the developing organism is a fetus.

3. Teratogens are harmful organisms or substances that can disrupt normal embryonic and fetal development. Cigarettes and alcohol are perhaps the most common serious human teratogens. Cocaine is less harmful to the fetus than once supposed.

4. The newborn comes into the world with reflexes and numerous perceptual skills.

RETRIEVE!

1. Which of the following is NOT one of the assumptions of the lifespan perspective in developmental psychology?

a) The most important development occurs during the first 3 years

b) Development involves constant loss as well as gain

c) Development is determined by a multiplicity of causes

d) Development is characterized by plasticity

2. Beginning about 24 hours after fertilization, rapid _____ begins to occur in the zygote. Approximately 1 week after attaching itself to the endometrium, the zygote enters the _____ stage. Approximately 8 weeks later the embryo comes to be known as a _____.

3. What are the consequences of prenatal maternal cigarette use? What are the consequences of fetal alcohol syndrome?

4. True or false: Prenatal use of cocaine by mothers results in severe, apparently permanent developmental disabilities and birth defects in the fetus.

How Does the Infant Become a Child?

Infancy is said to last from birth to about age 1. During this first year, remarkable and rapid transformation occurs in brain development, motor skills, and social and cognitive capabilities.

Brain Development Is Rapid

Intense brain growth occurs during the first months of life. At the time of your birth your brain equaled 25% of its current size and weight. Within 6 months, that figure was 50%, and by the age of 6 years it had reached 90% of its adult size and weight (Giedd, 2004). During these early years, increasing numbers of neuron axons acquire myelin, the fatty substance that increases the speed with which nerve impulses can travel. Dendrites, the branch-like structures that receive neurotransmitter communications, grow rapidly in number and length. As the number of these dendrites increases, so does the number of synapses that allow communication between neurons to occur.

SYNAPTIC PRUNING AND CRITICAL PERIODS

By the end of the first year, the infant has produced many trillions of synapses, at least twice as many as those in his or her parents' brains. At this point, however, synapses begin to go through a process known as *synaptic pruning* that continues through adolescence. **Synaptic pruning** involves a reduction in the number of seldom-used neurons to allow those that are being used frequently to be maintained efficiently. However, for at least another year or so, more synapses are created than are lost (Webb, Monk, & Nelson, 2001). After that, the ratio is reversed until the onset of puberty (see pp. 181–183).

The infant brain is remarkably plastic. Recall from Chapter 2 that *plasticity* is the property of the brain that enables it to be modified by experience. Nowhere is plasticity more evident than in infancy, where adverse effects of physical trauma, stress, malnutrition, deprivation, and toxins can radically alter brain function in a negative direction. On the other hand, positive events and appropriately stimulating experiences can increase brain efficiency and even correct some of the maladaptive changes caused by negative events (Nelson, 1999; e.g., Maccari et al., 1995; Rutter, O'Conner, and the English and Romanian Adoptees (ERA) Study Team, 2004).

However, brain plasticity is limited in some degree by constraints placed on it by the brain's genetic programming. For example, there are *critical periods*—"windows of opportunity"—for acquiring certain brain functions. **Critical periods** (sometimes referred to as *sensitive periods*) are stages in development where the brain is particularly sensitive to specific types of events or stimulation. Certain skills must be acquired during critical periods if they are to be acquired at all. For example, as depicted in Figure 4.2, if mammals (including humans) are deprived of certain visual experiences during critical periods of infancy, they cannot develop normal vision regardless of subsequent experiences (Hubel & Wiesel, 1970; Maurer, Mondloch, & Lewis, 2007).

A fascinating example of both brain plasticity *and* the importance of critical periods comes from research among severely deprived Romanian orphans. As the Communist government of Romania collapsed during the 1990s, a heartbreakingly large number of impoverished infants and small children were abandoned in orphanages. Conditions in these institutions were often horrific. With no more than one attendant for every 10 to 20 children, the malnourished children were packed into small rooms where they received little in the

Infancy ▶ The developmental stage beginning at birth to about age 1.

Synaptic pruning ▶ A neurological process that "weeds out" the number of seldom-used brain neurons to allow those that are being used frequently to be maintained efficiently. Synaptic pruning begins in infancy and continues through adolescence.

Critical period (*sensitive period*) ▶ A stage in development when the brain displays increased sensitivity to certain types of stimuli, and will develop in specific ways if these stimuli are encountered. Certain skills (e.g., normal vision or language development) may need to be developed during critical periods to develop normally, and social deprivation during critical periods in infancy and toddlerhood results in various types of cognitive impairment.

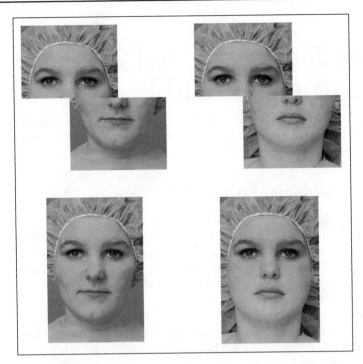

▲ **FIGURE 4.2 A Critical Period for Normal Vision.** Human beings process faces holistically—as a whole—and have difficulty recognizing individual parts of faces as belonging to someone they know. Look at the faces at the top left for less than 1 second, then close your eyes, and ask yourself whether the top halves of the faces (from base of nose to head covering) are identical or different. People whose vision developed normally in infancy cannot accomplish this task easily because of the human tendency to process faces holistically. However, you should have no trouble at all with the task when the faces are split and separated, disrupting the possibility of holistic processing (see images at bottom). But adolescents who were deprived of normal visual development from birth due to congenital cataracts (an opaque covering of the lens of the eye) can accomplish the task just as easily when the image is whole as when split, because they lack the ability to process faces holistically. This is true even if their cataracts are corrected during the first 3 months of life. *(Source: Maurer et al., 2007, p. 42.)*

way of human contact, play, or learning—and often with no access whatever to natural light (Fisher, Ames, Chisholm, & Savoie, 1997; McGeown, 2005).

Many of these children were fortunate enough to have been adopted subsequently into high-functioning homes in the United States, Canada, and Great Britain. Michael Rutter and his colleagues recruited a sample of these adopted orphans, and have followed their development into early adolescence (Kreppner et al., 2007; Rutter et al., 2004). Rutter and his research team found that the majority of the orphans experienced profound and lasting effects on their cognitive development, probably as a result of actual brain damage and/or a lack of exposure to normal stimulation, human contact, and play during critical periods. The longer the period of institutionalization, the greater was the extent of impairment—particularly if institutionalization extended beyond the first 6 months of life. Although there was also remarkable recovery from the initial extremely low level of functioning for some of these children, most of this recovery was complete by the 2-year period following adoption, and the rest by age 6. Between age 6 and 11 little additional recovery was seen, regardless of the quality of the new home life. These findings strongly support the idea that there are critical periods for normal cognitive development in human beings and limits to the corrective effects of beneficial environments.

However, this is not the whole story. The prevailing view of critical periods is that they are fixed and irreversible, as is the case for visual development, and apply across the board to all members of the species. However, for reasons not well

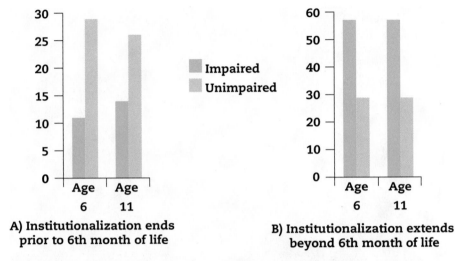

A) Institutionalization ends prior to 6th month of life

B) Institutionalization extends beyond 6th month of life

▲ **FIGURE 4.3 Experiences of Deprivation After the First Six Months Create More Lasting Damage.** Experiences of severely deprived Romanian orphans demonstrate both the importance of critical or sensitive periods of brain development and also the plasticity of brain development. Graph A shows that orphans whose experiences of deprivation ended prior to the sixth month of life were actually more likely to show few ill effects of their experiences. Moreover, although not apparent in the graph, only three of these children who seemed to be unimpaired at age 6 ended up showing impairment at age 11. Graph B shows a very different pattern. The large majority of children whose experiences of deprivation extended beyond the first 6 months of life showed severe impairment. However, while not apparent in the graph, 12 children who were unimpaired at age 6 measured impaired at age 11; and 12 children who were impaired at age 6 tested unimpaired at age 11. *(Source: Kreppner et al., 2007, pp. 939–940.)*

understood, a portion of the orphans showed *no* impairment at all—neither in infancy, nor early childhood, nor early adolescence—in spite of having had the same experiences as many who were severely impaired (Kreppner et al., 2007). Yet, as Figure 4.3 shows, the large majority of children who showed few or no ill effects of their experience ended their institutional life prior to the age of 6 months. Six months appeared to be a "cutoff" threshold for the children, beyond which the likelihood of severe impairment dramatically increased.

Social and Emotional Development Require Nature and Nurture

As every parent of more than one child knows, all babies are different, right from the start. The term **temperament** refers to the initial tendency to act in relatively consistent ways when it comes to certain general qualities and ways of responding to the world (A. H. Buss & Plomin, 1984; Kagan, 2003; Rothbart, 2007; Rothbart, Sheese, & Conradt, 2009). For example, some babies are fussy, while others are calm; some are curious about everything, outgoing, and highly active, while others are shy and less active. Extensive quantitative research conducted by Mary Rothbart and her colleagues has confirmed the idea, first proposed in a somewhat different form by personality psychologist Arnold Buss and behavior geneticist Robert Plomin (1984), that temperament can be summarized along three dimensions of behavior: *effortful control, negative emotionality,* and *extraversion* (e.g., Rothbart & Bates, 2006; Rothbart, Ahadi, Hershey, & Fisher, 2001):

- **Effortful control.** This refers to the extent to which an infant or child is able to focus or shift attention as needed; inhibit behavior that is inappropriate; and plan actions constructively.

Temperament ▶ Each infant's relatively consistent behavioral characteristics, characterized by Mary Rothbart within three dimensions: effortful control, negative emotionality, and extraversion. Temperament emerges as a result of genetic and other biological factors as well as environmental factors, but most theorists stress the importance of biology.

Effortful control ▶ The dimension of temperament that describes the extent to which an infant or child is able to focus or shift attention, inhibit inappropriate behavior, and plan actions constructively. Similar to executive functions in adults.

▶ **Critical Periods and Plasticity Coexist in the Brain.** When Michael Rutter and his colleagues tracked the development of Romanian orphans who had experienced severe deprivation in infancy, they found evidence that some aspects of normal cognitive, emotional, and social development required specific types of experiences during critical periods. At the same time, they found evidence for developmental plasticity, because some orphans did not experience problems to the extent that others did, and/or they recovered from the problems they had to a greater degree than others of their group.

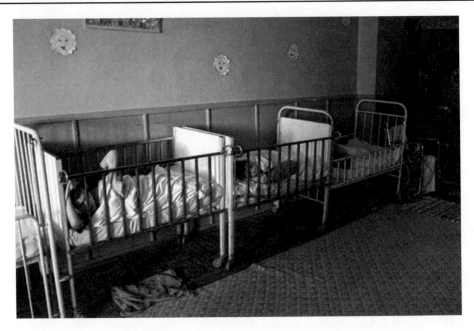

Negative emotionality ▶ The dimension of temperament that describes the degree to which an infant or child is easily frustrated, fearful, uncomfortable, sad, or difficult to soothe.

Extraversion ▶ In temperament theory, the dimension of temperament that describes the degree to which an infant or child lacks shyness, is highly active, anticipates pleasurable activities, laughs and smiles frequently, and desires closeness with others.

- **Negative emotionality**. An infant or child high in this dimension is one easily frustrated, fearful, uncomfortable, sad, or difficult to soothe.
- **Extraversion**. In general usage, an *extraverted* person is outgoing, assertive, self-confident, and enjoys socializing with others. As used by Rothbart and her colleagues to describe temperament, an infant or child high in extraversion lacks shyness, is highly active, experiences anticipation for pleasurable activities, laughs and smiles frequently, and desires closeness with others.

According to Rothbart, aspects of temperament are apparent even in the fetus, and develop rapidly in the newborn (Rothbart 2007; Rothbart & Bates, 2006). Temperament tends to be stable at least through the toddler years (Lemery, Goldsmith, Klinnert, & Mrazek, 1999) and may persist until adolescence (Kagan, 1994). There are sex differences in average temperament as well: Infant girls tend to score higher than boys in measures of effortful control, while boys generally score higher in extraversion (Else-Quest, Hyde, Goldsmith, & Van Hulle, 2006).

Infant temperament may also be apparent in some adult behavior. One longitudinal study tracked a sample of men and women from early childhood into adulthood. The researchers found that those children who lacked sociability at age 3 years were equally shy and unassertive as young adults; those who were impulsive and emotionally undercontrolled at age 3 were impulsive and easily upset as adults—indeed, by age 32, these children were about twice as likely to have compulsive gambling problems. Finally, those who were sociable and emotionally even-tempered as toddlers remained so to adulthood (Caspi, 2000; Slutske, Moffitt, Poulton, & Caspi, 2012; see also McCrae et al., 2000).

WHERE DOES TEMPERAMENT COME FROM?

Although brothers and sisters do tend to resemble one another slightly in temperament, this resemblance is often not a great deal more than what would be found between two strangers picked at random. Indeed, adopted siblings reared in the same home literally do not resemble one another in temperament more than would two strangers. On the other hand, repeated research has demonstrated that identical twins reared together or apart strongly resemble each other in temperament. Thus, even though the identical twin resemblance is far from perfect, it is clear that genes play a substantial role in the development of temperament in infants (Dunn & Plomin, 1990; Plomin,

◀ **Babies are Social Animals.** Babies are social from the moment of their birth. As they grow, they develop characteristic ways of interacting with others. These characteristics are in part a result of temperament—relatively predictable aspects of emotional response, activity level, and sociability displayed by each infant from the earliest months of life.

DeFries, Craig, & McGuffin, 2003; Saudino, 2005). Indeed, specific genes have been tentatively identified as contributing to the development of certain aspects of temperament (Posner, Rothbart, & Sheese, 2007). The prenatal biological environment of the womb (e.g., the presence of toxins, maternal stress, and nutrition) may also play a role in determining aspects of temperament that are present in an infant from birth. Thus, numerous researchers believe that temperament is essentially a biologically based phenomenon.

However, it is not likely that genes and prenatal environments alone account for the entire story of infant temperament. If genes and prenatal environments alone shaped temperament, identical twins would truly be *identical* in temperament because they share 100% of genes and virtually 100% of the prenatal environment. Yet identical twins are not identical in temperament. There must be something else at work that is strictly environmental and that occurs *after* the infant is conceived. Yet, as already mentioned, being reared in the same home does not make children much more similar in temperament. So which "strictly environmental" variables *do* contribute to infant temperament, if not those shared by all siblings in the home—socioeconomic status of the family, ethnic background, parent's child-rearing styles and beliefs, general parental warmth and expressiveness (or their lack), parent education level, and so forth?

It appears to be the *unique experiences of each infant* rather than shared family influences that contribute the most to the environmental portion of temperament (Harris, 1998, 2006; Plomin et al., 2003; Saudino, 2005). Such unique experiences are part of what is termed **nonshared environment**. What might these unique, nonshared experiences be? They could include chance adverse events such as trauma or infection in infancy, differences in the way that important adults treat each sibling (e.g., stricter with one than the other), differences in nutrition (one sibling eats well, the other does not), and any number of chance events, both positive and negative. I will have more to say about this question in Chapter 12, when I discuss the development of adult personality.

ATTACHMENT: THE BOND BETWEEN INFANT AND CAREGIVER

For developmental psychologists, the term **attachment** refers to the unique, intimate bond that develops between infant and caregivers, beginning when

Nonshared environment ▶ The unique environmental factors and experiences encountered by each developing child but not encountered by other children in the home. For example, a childhood illness, a traumatic experience, a different set of friends, and so forth.

Attachment ▶ According to attachment theorists, attachment is the special intimate bond that develops between infant and caregiver, generally the mother, beginning when the infant is about 6 months old.

▲ **Konrad Lorenz and Friends.** Newly hatched goslings become indelibly imprinted with the image of the animal they see first on hatching. They will then prefer that animal—including a human—to their own mother.

Imprinting ▶ Learning that occurs rapidly during a critical period and which the animal is biologically prepared to acquire.

Internal working model ▶ Attachment theorists' notion that the quality of a child's understanding of his or her place in the world, and his or her expectations about the behavior of others, reflects the quality of attachment relations in infancy.

the infant is about 6 months old. Attachment theory, which is probably the most influential of modern theories of early infant social and emotional development, describes the development of this relationship. Attachment theory was initially formulated by psychoanalyst John Bowlby and his colleague Mary Ainsworth as an unusual blending of evolutionary theory of primate development with psychoanalytic theory of child development (Ainsworth, Blehar, Waters, & Wall, 1978; Bowlby, 1988).

According to Bowlby and Ainsworth, the first attachment relationship is formed to the primary caregiver, generally the mother. The infant comes to prefer her and does everything possible to remain in close proximity to her—displaying distress when separated and joy on reunion. It is to this relationship that the infant turns when under stress. After the initial attachment relationship becomes firm, the infant may then develop secondary attachment relationships with others, such as father, grandparents, or siblings.

Bowlby in particular was strongly influenced by the work of Konrad Lorenz, an important early figure in the evolutionary study of animal behavior. Lorenz identified a critical period in the development of the relationship between newly hatched geese (goslings) and their mothers. A gosling becomes indelibly imprinted with the image of whatever animal it sees on hatching. It will subsequently follow this animal and attempt to remain in close proximity to it. That a mother goose hatches the gosling guarantees that the imprinted animal is virtually always the gosling's mother. However, Lorenz (1937) showed that goslings would become imprinted with the image of Lorenz himself if he, and not the mother goose, were present during the critical post-hatching **imprinting** period. Indeed, the Lorenz-imprinted goslings ignored their actual mothers and followed Lorenz on land or water.

Bowlby did not claim that human infants become imprinted with the image of their mothers as do goslings. However, he did suggest that the years of infancy and toddlerhood constitute a critical period in the development of infant attachment relations. He proposed that if such a relationship—with the mother or with another caregiver—did not develop successfully, consequences could be severe and persist throughout the person's life.

The Internal Working Model Why should first attachment relationships be of such critical importance to a person throughout the life span? Attachment theorists have suggested that the infant develops an *internal working model* of the world based largely on these relationships. The **internal working model** is a metaphor for the way the child develops an understanding of his or her place in the world and arrives at expectations about the likely behavior of other people (Dykas & Cassidy, 2011; Johnson, Dweck, & Chen, 2007; Thompson & Raikes, 2003). If an infant has a competent caregiver who provides consistently and predictably kind and responsive treatment, he or she may develop a working model that suggests that the world is a benign place, that other people are to be trusted, and that he or she is a lovable and worthy person. On the other hand, if the early attachment relationship forms with an unkind, unpredictable, and incompetent caregiver, the child may come to view the world as a dangerous place, and its inhabitants untrustworthy. The child may also come to see himself or herself as unlovable and unworthy.

Attachment Styles and the Strange Situation In the example of the working model just given, I referred to an infant becoming attached to an unkind and incompetent caregiver. You might think that an infant is unlikely to become attached to such a person. However, according to attachment theorists, *some* form of attachment will occur for all infants as long as an individual caregiver is consistently present in the infant's life during the critical period.

Mary Ainsworth (Ainsworth et al., 1978) used a research strategy called the *strange situation* to measure individual differences in the quality of infants' attachment relations with their mothers. In the *strange situation*, which

◄ Attachment Objects Hold Special "Essences." Legions of small children have special objects such as blankets or stuffed animals to which they are strongly attached. These objects can hold enormous power for a child, as demonstrated in a recent desperate and massive (but sadly unsuccessful) manhunt in Bristol, England, to locate a knitted mouse belonging to a little girl named Laurel. Research suggests that children believe that their attachment objects hold special "essences" and, like human beings, are simply not duplicable—even by apparent identical copies.

lasts about 20 minutes, the mother and her infant play alone in a room, and a stranger then enters the room. The stranger converses with the mother, and the mother then leaves unobtrusively so that the infant is alone with the stranger. The mother then returns. Next, the mother leaves again so that the infant is alone. The stranger re-enters the room and interacts with the infant. The mother then returns.

Ainsworth originally identified and named three "styles" of response to the strange situation reflecting three styles of attachment relations: *secure, avoidant*, and *insecure-ambivalent*.

1. *Secure attachment.* Securely attached infants are active and curious when placed in a strange room as long as the mother is present. If the mother leaves, the infant may become quite upset, but will react with joy on the mother's return. Securely attached infants show friendliness toward strangers if the mother is present, but wariness if the mother is absent.

2. *Avoidant attachment.* Avoidant attachment is characterized by less interest in exploration and curiosity in the strange situation, even when the mother is present. However, the avoidant infant also shows little distress when the mother leaves, and he or she generally ignores the mother on her return. The assumption among many attachment theorists is that avoidant infants have arrived at this place of "not caring" as a result of having learned that their emotional needs will not be met (Silverman, 2011).

3. *Insecure-Ambivalent attachment.* Unlike avoidant infants, who "shut down," insecure-ambivalent infants are on "high alert." They do not easily venture away from the safety of their mothers to play, may fearfully cling to her, and become even more upset than securely attached infants when she leaves. When the mother returns, the insecure-ambivalent infant may rush back to her, but is equally likely to resist her attempts at soothing, or may even strike her in anger, as though to punish her for having left. Insecure-ambivalent infants are wary of strangers whether or not the mother is present.

Considering Attachment Theory Infants undeniably create important bonds with their caregivers early in life, and the experience of the Romanian orphans (pp. 163–165) show that if no such relationships are formed, consequences can be serious. In addition to the problems in brain and cognitive development described earlier, a large number of the Romanian orphans who remained in the orphanage during the early attachment period displayed maladaptive patterns of social behavior throughout early childhood. Cross-cultural studies of attachment have also provided support for attachment theorists' claims that forming attachment relationships in infancy is a universal human tendency (Reebye, Ross, & Jamieson, 1999), and infants do seem to form expectations of the typical behavior of their caregivers as described in attachment theory (Johnson et al., 2007).

There is less support for certain other assertions by attachment theorists. First, attachment style measured in infancy does not necessarily remain stable throughout life, as attachment theorists claim. Although some studies show at least partial consistency over time (Simpson, Collins, Tran, & Haydon, 2007; Simpson, Rholes, & Winterheld, 2010), many do not, and a child who appears to be securely attached at one age may appear insecure-ambivalent or avoidant a year or 2 years later, or vice versa (NICHD Early Child Care Research Network, 2001; Thompson & Raikes, 2003).

Second, a strong case is made by Judith Rich Harris (2006; 2009) that while infants do form internal working models of their relationships with their mothers or other attachment figures, they do not base their working model of the *world* on this "mother-model." In other words, infants keep these relationships in entirely separate "mental accounts." As Harris points out, a person who assumed that his or her relationships with others would follow a pattern similar to that set by their parental relationships would be at a distinct survival disadvantage compared to a person who had no such expectations. Therefore, a universal tendency to keep "mother" and "the world" in the same mental account would have been unlikely to evolve.

CRITICAL THINKING ABOUT PSYCHOLOGY

Early Child Care Has Benefits—and Costs

Currently, over 80% of U.S. children experience at least some nonparental child care on a regular basis prior to entering school, with the majority of these beginning their day care careers prior to the age of 1, and often prior to the age of 6 months (NICHD Early Child Care Research Network, 2003, 2006). Numerous parents send their children to child care centers voluntarily and not as a result of necessity—believing that their children will benefit socially and/or intellectually from the child care settings. However, a great many parents report great anxiety over leaving their very young children in the care of strangers, and say they would not do so if they could afford to stay home with their children (Cubed, 2002, p. 2; Public Agenda, 2000).

Opinions about the potential benefits or harms of early child care, or day care, can be extreme. Some (Belsky, 2001, 2009) have argued that extensive experience of day care outside the home, particularly in the first few years of life, leads to insecure attachments between parent and child, and increases child aggressiveness and behavior problems. Others counter that high-quality day care may provide cognitive and intellectual development not easily obtainable for infants and toddlers reared in the home (Andersson, 1992). The recent longitudinal study conducted in 10 cities by the National Institute of Child Health and Development (NICHD) Early Child Care Research Network (ECCRN; 2001, 2003, 2006, 2010) provides the best available evidence of the effects of early child care on development. This is because the NICHD study was able to exert important statistical controls on variables such as parenting quality, day care quality, the amount of time spent in day care, and the specific type of day care situation (e.g., center care vs. home care).

The good news is that the NICHD study showed that the relationship between infant and mother *at home* was the best predictor of mother-child attachment and that, in general, parenting quality (and parents' genetic contributions to their children) had a far greater impact on the child than any aspect of the day care experience. Moreover, there was an increase in cognitive and language skills in those children with more hours in day care regardless of their family backgrounds. Children who experienced high-quality day care (but not low-quality care) showed higher levels of academic achievement scores on standardized tests in math, reading, and memory through the third grade.

The news is not all good, however. More hours spent in child care (regardless of its quality) was consistently associated with lower teacher ratings of the child's social skills and work habits through the third grade, higher levels of conflict with parents and other adults, and higher levels of aggressive "acting-out" behavior—although negative effects are much more pronounced in the case of low-quality day care. Thus, high-quality day care appears to be good for very young children's cognitive-intellectual development, but day care as a whole does not appear in such a good light when it comes to social and emotional development (NICHD ECCRN, 2001, 2003, 2006, 2010).

From these findings, some argue that if (high-quality) day care does increase academic achievement in early grades as reported, this may be an important means for increasing economic opportunities and mobility in adulthood not only for the disadvantaged, but for society as a whole. This is because by the third grade, one's academic achievement profile tends to remain relatively stable for the rest of academic life. Widespread use of high-quality day care may therefore increase the general level of academic achievement—and economic progress—of American citizens (see especially Schweinart et al., 2004).

On the other hand, researchers such as Belsky (2001, 2009) warn that introducing increased numbers of children with problem behaviors into school life will have exactly the opposite effect, causing classrooms to swell with children with problem behaviors, poor social skills, and inefficient work habits. Belsky argues that even a few such children in a classroom can cause a catalytic effect by influencing previously well-behaved children to "act out." Clearly, it will take more than a single study to resolve these questions. In any case, people with different agendas and priorities will place greater or lesser weight on the advantages and disadvantages of child care. ■

Cognitive Development: What Infants and Toddlers Know

We have already seen that infants come into the world with their senses in order and a number of perceptual systems already functioning. But newborns apparently also come into the world *knowing things*—or if this is not literally true as some insist, infants learn things in very short order, much more quickly than previously supposed. How do we know what babies know? I must admit to frank admiration for the ingenuity of researchers in infant cognitive development, because they have originated a variety of techniques to discover the dimensions of cognitive development even of newborn infants.

The majority of studies of cognitive development in newborn or very young babies are conducted by tracking eye and head movements. For example, much knowledge of infant cognition has been acquired using the simple insight that people (including infants) tend to become bored viewing the same or similar thing repeatedly or for a long period at a stretch. This is a variation on the form of learning known as *habituation* and described in Chapter 7. By monitoring the length of time a new image holds an infant's attention, researchers can tell

Sequence of events 1+1 = 1 or 2

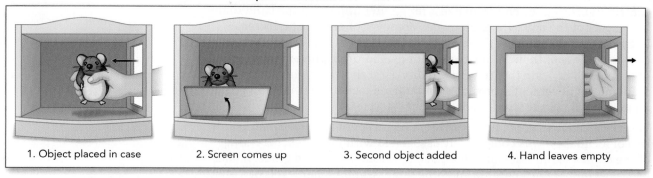

1. Object placed in case   2. Screen comes up   3. Second object added   4. Hand leaves empty

Then either: possible outcome   **Or: impossible outcome**

5. Screen drops...   ...revealing 2 objects   5. Screen drops...   ...revealing 1 object

Sequence of events 2−1 = 1 or 2

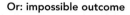

1. Objects placed in case   2. Screen comes up   3. Empty hand enters   4. One object removed

Then either: possible outcome   **Or: impossible outcome**

5. Screen drops...   ...revealing 1 object   5. Screen drops...   ...revealing 2 objects

▲ **FIGURE 4.4 Addition and Subtraction in 5-Month-Old Infants.** Karen Wynn (1992) presented correct and incorrect (impossible) "solutions" to addition and subtraction "problems" to a group of 5-month-old infants. The infants stared longer at the impossible solutions. *(Source: Adapted from Wynn, 1992.)*

whether the baby perceives the image as "something new and different" or as "something old or similar" to a previously viewed image.

Bloom (2004) summarizes evidence gathered in recent studies by Elizabeth Spelke and her colleagues that infants make the same fundamental assumptions about the physical attributes of objects made by adults everywhere. For example, babies, like adults, apparently believe that:

- *Objects are solid.* Babies look longer at set-ups that appear to violate the solidity of objects, such as a screen placed in front of an object tilting all the way back without hitting the object (Baillargeon, Spelke, & Wasserman, 1985). (In such experiments, the object has fallen through a hidden trap door.) Infants also look longer at images of structurally impossible objects, such as a cube where one side is simultaneously in front of, and behind, another (Shuwairi, Albert, & Johnson, 2007). Further, infants expect different behaviors from solids and liquids (Hespos, Ferry, & Rips, 2009).
- *Objects only move through contact.* The example given by Bloom is a ball on a pool table—it will not move unless something touches it. Babies are surprised if objects move without being touched (Spelke, Phillips, & Woodward, 1995).
- *Objects travel through space in a continuous path.* Objects in motion do not suddenly disappear and then reappear somewhere down the line. Babies are surprised at demonstrations where this rule is apparently violated (Spelke et al., 1995).

What else do infants know? Would you believe that they can add and subtract? Developmental psychologist Karen Wynn thought they could, and she provided evidence of the ability of small infants to understand basic addition and subtraction. In the first such demonstration, published in *Nature* in 1992, Wynn presented 5-month-old infants with a shallow, empty case on a small stage-like area (see Figure 4.4). A hand emerges from the side holding a Mickey Mouse doll and places it in the case. A screen slides up obscuring the case from view. The hand emerges once again to place another doll beside the first one, out of sight behind the screen. We would be very surprised if the screen should be lifted and only one doll is left standing—and so were Wynn's 5-month-old infants. They stared longer when the screen fell to display one doll than when two dolls were shown. The same results were found for a subtraction task, also depicted in Figure 4.5. These studies proved quite startling, because it was not believed that infants "should" have a concept of number.

Not everyone was convinced, however (Cohen & Marks, 2002), so cognitive neuroscientists Andrea Berger and her colleagues devised more stringent tests of infants' math perceptions (Berger, Tzur, & Posner, 2006). Berger and her colleagues repeated Wynn's addition and subtraction procedure with a group of 6- to 9-month-old infants while monitoring the infants' brains, using EEG technology (see Figure 4.5). These researchers found that the infants' brain wave activity while viewing impossible solutions was similar to brain-wave activity previously identified in studies of adults as they detected various errors and violations of expectations. This research provides even stronger support for Wynn's views of infant abilities.

Thus, infants can do a great many things they "should not" be able to do. As you might imagine, because some of this evidence goes against our intuitions about what an infant is capable of accomplishing, it has been challenged (Newcombe, 2002; Uller, Carey, Huntley-Fenner, & Klatt, 1999). But there is another reason it has often been challenged, as you might also have surmised: It appears to suggest that humans come into the world with certain knowledge already in place. This raises the specter once again of the *nature-nurture* debate, often referred to in developmental psychology as *nativism vs. empiricism* (Newcombe, 2002; Spelke, 1998). **Nativism** is the view that we come into the world with some number of innate abilities or tendencies, while

Nativism ▶ The view that at least some human abilities and tendencies are innate. Often contrasted with empiricism in "nature-nurture" debates.

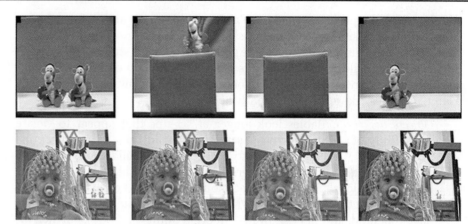

▶ **FIGURE 4.5 2 + 1 equals … 1? Brain Imaging Infant Addition.** Andrea Berger and her colleagues repeated Karen Wynn's "doll arithmetic" procedures with a group of infants whose brains were monitored using EEG technology. They found that the infants looked longer at impossible than correct arithmetic solutions. When viewing impossible solutions, infants simultaneously showed brain activity similar to that in adults whose expectations had been violated or who were in the process of detecting errors. (*Source: Adapted from Berger et al., 2006 p. 12650.*)

Empiricism ▶ The philosophical tradition that emphasizes the importance of experience in acquiring knowledge. In the "nature-nurture" debate in psychology, empiricism is contrasted with nativism, the belief that at least some aspects of human psychology are innate.

Constructivism ▶ The stage theory of child development devised by Jean Piaget. Constructivism holds that each child actively constructs an understanding of the world based on experience and his or her stage of psychological and biological maturation.

Developmental stages ▶ The idea that human beings pass through periods of development with distinct boundaries, and that reflect qualitatively different types of cognitive activity.

Schemas ▶ A mental structure or cognitive model that represents some aspect of the world and how it works.

empiricism, as described in Chapter 1, is the view that most (or all) mental characteristics are acquired through experience.

Finally, evidence of infant competence in cognition such as that provided in the research described previously has also been particularly difficult for many developmental psychologists to accept. These findings appear to contradict much of the work of the most important theorist in the history of developmental psychology of cognition, and one of the greatest of all pioneers in psychology—Jean Piaget (1896–1980).

JEAN PIAGET AND CONSTRUCTIVISM

The Swiss developmental cognitive psychologist Jean Piaget stands out in the history of psychology not only for the extent of his contributions, but for their longevity. Although Piaget was mistaken about many aspects of cognitive development, as we shall see, a surprising number of his insights have remained firmly established in contemporary thinking (Flavell, 1996; T. L. Rose & Fischer, 2009; Morra, Gobbo, Marini, & Sheese, 2008; Siegler & Ellis, 1996).

Piaget (1952, 1954) did not believe that human beings came into the world "pre-equipped" with certain knowledge as the nativists proposed, nor did he believe that the human being was the passive "blank slate" to be "written on" by the environment as portrayed in some empiricist accounts (e.g., behaviorism). Piaget suggested instead that each infant and child actively "constructs" an understanding of the world based on his or her experience, always pushing for an understanding that is more advanced than the one previously held (Siegler & Ellis, 1996). Accordingly, Piaget's theory is known as **constructivism**.

Two important concepts underlie Piaget's theory of cognitive development: *schemas* and **developmental stages**. **Schemas** are cognitive models that people construct of what the world is and how it works—they are a way to make meaningful sense out of experience. While adults as well as children use schemas, Piaget insisted that children possess age-specific schemas. Children's schemas develop and become more realistic over time as a result of biological and psychological maturation, not just experience and learning.

Children use the processes of **assimilation** and **accommodation** to construct increasingly accurate and advanced schemas. Assimilation describes the way a child fits a new experience into a preexisting schema. When my daughter Anisa was about 11 months old, she had just learned the word "ball." It happened that the moon was spectacularly full one night, and we took her outside to see it. She looked up, pointed to the moon and delightedly observed, "Ball!" She was attempting to *assimilate* the new experience of observing a full moon into her schema for round objects ("round objects are 'balls'").

Eventually, however, she began to notice the many differences between the moon and rubber balls, so she began to *alter* her schema for round objects to include, or accommodate, the moon ("round objects can have many names that refer to various things other than balls"). Children's schemas are

▲ **What the Heck Is This Piece of Cardboard?** Schemas are models of the world—ways of organizing one's knowledge and providing a framework by which new experiences may be understood. Without schemas related to eating at a restaurant, you would have no idea what to do with a menu because it would appear to be little more than a random listing of food items with no apparent purpose.

▲ **Children Actively Construct an Understanding of the World.** According to constructivist theory as developed by Jean Piaget, children are neither born "pre-equipped" with cognitive skills, nor are they "blank slates" to be written on by the environment. Their cognitive skills develop due to an interaction between experience and stage of biological and psychological maturity.

constantly being altered according to the push-and-pull of assimilation and accommodation.

Piaget's Developmental Stages Piaget believed that children passed through four distinct stages of development that were invariant—that is, *everyone* passed through them, and they *always* occurred in the same order. However, there is substantial variation in the length of time each individual remains in a given stage. The stages reflect *qualitatively* different ways of thinking and processing information, not just *quantitative* differences in the amount of knowledge acquired. A qualitative difference is a difference *in kind*. For example, when a caterpillar passes into the butterfly stage, it has not simply grown older, larger, and faster moving (quantitative difference). It is a different critter altogether (qualitative difference).

The first stage of development according to Piaget is the **sensorimotor stage** (birth to approximately age 2). Piaget did not believe that small infants possessed the sophisticated skills and understandings of the world reflected in some of the current research described earlier. According to Piaget, small infants learn about the world through basic reflexes such as sucking, senses of hearing and vision, and increasing motor development and the ability to grasp and manipulate objects. Babies in the sensorimotor period lack the capacity to *think*—they merely respond to internal and external events. According to Piaget, only toward the end of the sensorimotor stage, when infants are able to use words and images to *represent* objects, ideas, and experiences, does the capacity for thought develop.

One of the principal cognitive skills Piaget claimed the infant acquires during the sensorimotor period is **object permanence**, which he suggested develops at about the 8th or 9th month of life. As depicted in Figure 4.6, object permanence is the understanding that objects continue to exist when they are no longer in view. For example, Piaget noted that if a blanket is thrown over a toy, an infant who has not yet achieved object permanence will not even attempt to reach for the toy. Piaget concluded that the infant literally believes that the toy no longer exists. However, recent research (including some of the

Assimilation ▶ Piaget's term to describe the process whereby a person processes a new experience by fitting it into a preexisting schema.

Accommodation ▶ Piaget's term for the process whereby a person alters his or her schema to incorporate new information or experiences.

Sensorimotor stage ▶ Piaget's developmental stage lasting from birth to approximately age 2, and characterized by unthinking responses to internal and external stimuli and events.

Object permanence ▶ The child's understanding that objects continue to exist even if they are no longer in view.

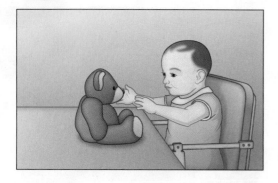

▲ FIGURE 4.6 Object Permanence. Piaget believed that infants younger than 8 or 9 months did not possess an understanding that objects continue to exist when they are no longer in view. However, recent research suggests that infants as young as 2½ months possess a basic understanding of object permanence.

Preoperational stage ▶ Piaget's developmental stage lasting from approximately age 2 to 7, and characterized by development of the symbolic capacity of the child's mind.

Egocentric ▶ When a person lacks the ability to see things from the perspective of another person.

Conservation ▶ The child's understanding that an object may retain its identity even if its appearance has changed.

Theory of mind ▶ The ability to understand that other people have mental states that are different from one's own. Theory of mind usually emerges in a child between ages 3 and 5.

research already described) has shown that infants as young as 2½ months have at least some understanding of object permanence (Baillargeon, 2002; Wang, Baillargeon, & Brueckner, 2004).

The second stage of development is the **preoperational stage** (approximately age 2 to 6 or 7). This is a time of intense development of the symbolic capacity of the child's mind. Imaginative play, intense language development, and the ability to consider the past and possible futures are important new developments that open up a world of possibilities to the preschool age child. Contrary to the concerns of some parents, the creation of imaginary playmates and other seemingly outlandish flights of fancy in children of this age are associated with strong social, imaginative, and cognitive skills, not emotional problems (Taylor, Hulette, & Dishion, 2010; Trionfi & Reese, 2009).

According to Piaget, however, the child is constrained in development during this period by several factors. First, preoperational children are **egocentric**. This term does not mean that babies are "conceited"—it means that they lack the ability to see things from the perspective of another person. When a parent says, "Put yourself in [my, her, his] place—how would *you* feel if someone did that to you?" preoperational children may literally be unable to do so, according to Piaget.

The preoperational child may also have difficulty performing mental operations requiring logic. The classic example of this involves lack of **conservation** in preoperational children. Conservation is the understanding that an object may retain its identity even if its appearance is changed for some reason (see Figure 4.7).

However, as was the case with the sensorimotor period, Piaget appears to have overstated the limitations of preoperational thought and underestimated the abilities of these children—to some degree as a result of the way he constructed tasks for children to perform (Gelman, 1972). Moreover, although very young preoperational children clearly are egocentric in their thinking, focusing on the egocentrism of these children ignores one of the most impressive feats of *surmounting* egocentrism that occurs during these years: the development of a *theory of mind* (Callaghan et al., 2005; Wellman, Cross, & Watson, 2001).

Theory of mind is a rather elegant name for a seemingly simple talent—the ability to understand that other people experience mental states that are different from, and may even conflict with, your own. In other words, other people have *minds*. A person with a theory of mind understands that another person's behavior results from that person's own desires, intentions, and beliefs. A theory of mind allows us to take another person's perspective (Baron-Cohen, Leslie, & Firth, 1985; Premack & Woodruff, 1978). Theory of mind also involves an understanding that another person's beliefs may be false. Indeed, the classic way for measuring the existence of a theory of mind in a child is the *false-belief task* as depicted in Figure 4.8 (Wimmer & Perner, 1983, Baron-Cohen et al., 1985, Leslie, 2000). The false-belief task depicts a situation where children must understand that their own knowledge of the true facts of a situation may conflict with someone else's false beliefs about the situation.

Studies utilizing the false-belief task in cultures around the world suggest that theory of mind develops predictably over time between the ages of 3 and 5 (Callaghan et al., 2005). This is smack in the middle of the preoperational period—far earlier than would be predicted from a strict Piagetian perspective. By the age of 2, Gregory Robert Smith, the prodigy described at the outset of the chapter, had already noticed that humans possessed flat teeth like the Cretaceous-period herbivore dinosaurs he had been reading about. For this reason, and out of apparent compassion for animals, he persuaded his family to become vegetarians (Jones, 2002). Although Smith is quite unusual, such

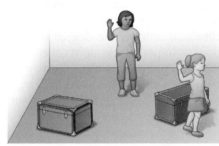

"Do these glasses have the same amount of water, or a different amount?"

"That one has more water."

◀ **FIGURE 4.7** Demonstrating Lack of Conservation in Preoperational Child. Two beakers holding identical amounts of water are shown to a 4- or 5-year-old boy. While the boy watches, one beaker (sealed at the top) is turned upside down. The water level now appears much higher in the upturned beaker. The child is then asked, "Do these glasses have the same amount of water, or a different amount?" In spite of the fact that the boy "should" know that the glasses still hold an identical amount of water, he claims that the beaker on the left holds more.

Ann

Sally puts her marble in the red box.

Sally goes away.

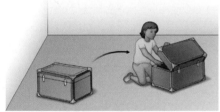

Ann moves the marble.

"Where will Sally look for her marble?"

▲ **FIGURE 4.8 The False-Belief Task Tests for Theory of Mind.** In this false-belief task "Sally" leaves a marble in a red box and walks away. "Ann" then removes the marble and places it in a blue box. Then Ann leaves. Sally returns. Children are then asked: Where will Sally look for her ball? Children who have developed a theory of mind realize that Sally has no idea that her marble has been removed and placed in another box, and so will look in the original (red) box for her marble. Children who have not yet evolved a theory of mind will base their response on *their own* (egocentric) knowledge of where the ball actually is (the blue box), rather than on what they should infer must be Sally's knowledge.

moral compassion and perspective-taking are not possible in a preoperational child, according to constructivist theory.

The third stage of development is the **concrete operations stage** (approximately age 7 to 11 or 12). During this stage, the child begins to master tasks involving the application of logic. Tasks that eluded the preoperational child are performed easily. When I offered the water conservation task to my preoperational daughter Anisa, she failed predictably. When I gave the same task to her concrete operational sister Naima, and asked her if the beakers contained different amounts of water—she looked at me as though I were crazy.

The concrete operational child performs abstract mathematical computations, classifies objects in multiple ways (e.g., human beings are *primates* which are a type of *mammal* which is a type of *animal*), and has a strongly developed theory of mind. As any parent learns, this last development is a mixed

Concrete operations stage ▶ Piaget's developmental stage lasting from approximately age 7 to 11 or 12, and characterized by mastery of tasks involving the application of logic.

Formal operations stage ▶
Piaget's developmental stage beginning at age 11 or 12, and characterized by the ability to apply systematic logic to abstract concepts and to think hypothetically and skeptically.

blessing, because a theory of mind makes the child a far more accomplished liar! Their egocentrism has diminished, and they can now "read minds."

The fourth and final stage of development is the **formal operations stage** (approximately age 11 or 12 and over). According to Piaget, formal operations marks the onset of adolescence. Where the concrete operational child can perform logical operations on *objects* using arithmetic and classification, the formal operational adolescent can perform logical operations on abstract *concepts*. He or she can juggle ideas, think hypothetically and skeptically, and apply logical reasoning in a systematic manner. For example, the formal operational child can understand and explain why the following statement is a fallacy: "All men are fools; Lucinda is a fool; therefore, Lucinda is a man."

The formal operations stage is perhaps the most controversial of Piaget's ideas. Some evidence suggests that many supposedly concrete-operational children can perform characteristically formal operational tasks (Ennis, 1975). On the other hand, consistent research also shows that not only do a great many adolescents *lack* the ability to use formal operations (or, at least, do not use them consistently), but unfortunately, so do a great many adults (Gilovich, Griffin, & Kahneman, 2002; Klaczynski, 2001; Klaczynski & Narasimham, 1998). Moreover, the degree to which a person is capable of formal operations is in part dependent on culture, schooling, and other external variables (Flieller, 1999). As Kuhn (2006, p. 60) forcefully puts it, very few, if any, contemporary researchers endorse the notion of the abrupt emergence in adolescence of a distinct cognitive stage similar to that described by Piaget as formal operations.

Table 4.2 summarizes Piaget's developmental stages.

Table 4.2 Piaget's Developmental Stages

AGES	STAGE	PRINCIPAL CHARACTERISTICS ACCORDING TO PIAGET
Birth–2	*Sensorimotor*	Development proceeds as a result of reflexive, sensory, and motor experiences; object permanence is achieved.
2–6/7	*Preoperational*	Symbolic thought, language, and imaginative play develop; thinking is egocentric; child lacks conservation.
6/7–11/12	*Concrete Operations*	Child learns to apply logic to tasks involving objects and concrete situations; can use arithmetic and multiple classification; diminished egocentrism and developed theory of mind.
11/12–adult	*Formal operations*	Adolescent learns abstract reasoning and systematic application of logic to ideas and concepts; may develop moral and philosophical concerns.

Considering Piaget As we have seen, Piaget often underestimated the abilities of infants and children (and in some cases *over*estimated their abilities). However, this in itself is not a particularly damning criticism of his work. The research technologies and methodologies available in Piaget's time were primitive compared with those accessible to modern researchers. In any case, Piaget's primary concern was not identifying with precision the ages at which certain cognitive changes take place. Rather, his central concern was to establish that children are active participants in their own development, that changes in development proceed in an orderly fashion, and that the order of developmental changes does not vary—that is, children do not develop formal operations in grade school, only to abandon them in favor of concrete operations in adolescence! The case for these assertions has been well made (Flavell, Miller, & Miller, 1993; Lourenço & Machado, 1996).

However, theories undergo revision as a result of research, and more substantial criticisms of Piaget's theory have been made over the past few decades that go beyond observing that he under- or overestimated the capabilities of children at specific ages. Here are a few of these objections:

1. *Piaget overemphasized the notion of stages.* Researchers adhering to information-processing models of development have suggested that cognitive development is often *continuous* rather than occurring in discontinuous stages, and highly dependent on the nature of the specific task at hand (Fischer & Bidell, 1998; S. A. Rose & Feldman, 1995; Siegler & Ellis, 1996). This idea helps to explain why many children who "should" be able to pass certain Piagetian tasks don't, while others who "shouldn't" be able to pass, do.

2. *Piaget did not sufficiently take into account social and cultural influences on development.* While Piaget did not ignore social and cultural influences on the child (Matusov & Hayes, 2000), it is fair to say that he was vague on the subject in comparison to certain other theorists. The most prominent *sociocultural* theorist of Piaget's generation was Lev Vygotsky (1896–1934). Vygotsky (1929) emphasized that cognitive growth in the child is highly variable and dependent on the individual child's social and cultural experiences and the broader sociocultural context as expressed in phenomena such as language. Therefore, development differs not only from child to child but from society to society. Vygotsky's theory readily explains findings that in certain societies formal operational thought seemingly does not exist at all (Neimark, 1975).

3. *Piaget's theory describes development, but does not explain it.* Psychologists working from the evolutionary perspective complain that much of psychology *describes* behavior but does not *explain* it (Barkow, Cosmides & Tooby, 1992, D. M. Buss, 2005). This criticism has been leveled at Piaget. In other words, it is not enough merely to predict that children's cognitive development proceeds in a certain orderly fashion. The question remains, *why* does it do so? *Why* are preschool children unable to understand conservation, and *why* do formal operations develop less predictably than concrete operations?

IN SUMMARY

1.	The infant brain is highly plastic, but it also experiences critical periods for development.
2.	Infant temperament is partly innate and tends to be stable at least through the toddler years, and sometimes into adulthood. Temperament develops primarily due to the action of genes and nonshared environmental experiences.
3.	Mary Ainsworth identified three attachment styles based on research utilizing the Strange Situation: secure, avoidant, and insecure-ambivalent.
4.	Attachment theory has been criticized for failing to account for the fact that attachment styles may change from one strange situation test to another, and for incorrectly proposing that the infant generalizes from experiences with attachment figures to the rest of his or her experiences.
5.	Early child care is associated with increased academic performance in children if the care is of high quality, but it is also associated with more problem behaviors and decreased social and work skills—regardless of its quality.
6.	Very young infants apparently have cognitive skills and competencies much beyond what was previously suspected. Researchers have used research strategies utilizing habituation to measure the cognitive performance of very young infants.

7. Jean Piaget's theory, known as constructivism, suggests that (a) children are active participants in their own development, using assimilation and accommodation to adjust their schemas (models of how the world works); and (b) development proceeds in an orderly and invariant fashion through four developmental stages. These stages are sensorimotor, preoperational, concrete operational, and formal operational.

8. Piaget has been criticized (a) by information-processing theorists for overemphasizing stages and failing to take into consideration continuity in cognitive development; (b) by sociocultural theorists for failing to take social and cultural influences into account; and (c) by evolutionary theorists for describing development without explaining it.

RETRIEVE!

1. Give an example of how the story of the Romanian orphans demonstrates both brain plasticity and critical periods.

2. Match the description on the left with the dimension of temperament on the right.

The extent to which an infant or child is able to focus attention, inhibit behavior and plan constructive actions	Extraversion
The degree to which an infant or child is easily frustrated, fearful, uncomfortable, sad, or difficult to soothe	Effortful control
The degree to which an infant or child is active, anticipates pleasurable activities, laughs and smiles, and desires closeness with others	Negative emotionality

3. Masara is 18 months old. One day, she goes along with her mother for a visit to one of her mother's friends, also the mother of a toddler girl. Masara is left in the friend's daughter's room to play. Two minutes after leaving Masara in the room, the grown-ups hear wails coming from the room. Masara's mother dashes into the room to find out what is wrong. Masara is simply frightened to be in a strange room with a strange child without her mother. As soon as her mother enters the room, Masara stops crying, and runs to her mother with a big smile on her face. Attachment theorists would most likely judge Masara's attachment style as _____.

a) Insecure-Ambivalent　b) Secure　c) Avoidant　d) Anxious-Avoidant

4. True or false: The most important environmental aspect of development of temperament is the unique experiences of each infant, rather than influences of parents and family.

5. Describe research suggesting that small infants have the ability to add and subtract.

6. Define schemas, assimilation, and accommodation as used in Piaget's theory.

7. Which of the following is NOT one of the four Piagetian stages of development?

a) sensorimotor　b) preoperational　c) postoperational　d) concrete operations

8. Explain object permanence, conservation, and theory of mind.

How Does the Child Become Adolescent?

Adolescence—literally, "becoming adult"—has existed throughout all of known history and in all known societies (Schlegel & Barry, 1991; Weisfeld, 1999). However, the nature and length of adolescence differs from culture to culture (see Figure 4.9). In most traditional societies, adolescence ends for women in the early to mid-teens, and for men in their late teens (Frayser, 1985; Schlegel & Barry, 1991). In modern industrial societies adolescence is generally thought to end at about age 20 or even beyond, into the mid-20s (Baumrind, 1987). Clearly, the term *adolescent*, while including a biological dimension (the ability to reproduce), also includes very strong social and cultural components. The end of adolescence relies entirely on the particular society's conception of what it means to be "adult."

Adolescence Is a Process

The transition from childhood to adolescence is momentous—perhaps only at birth does a change as radical as this occur (Weisfeld, 1999). However, adolescence is not something that happens to a child overnight. Even the clearest marker of adolescence, *puberty*, is a process that begins at about age 6 or 7, when the adrenal glands first produce steroid hormones (most prominently testosterone) in both females and males (Remer, Boye, Hartmann, & Wudy, 2005). This hormone production peaks with the full maturation of the adrenal glands at about age 10, an event known as **adrenarche** (Palmert et al., 2001).

Traditionally, the onset of puberty was thought to be marked by **gonadarche**, the maturation of the sexual organs several years later. However, it is adrenarche that is associated with the onset of the romantic and sexual feelings ordinarily associated with puberty and adolescence (Herdt & McClintock, 2000; McClintock & Herdt, 1996). For this reason, and because adrenarche is necessary for many of the physical changes of puberty to occur, most researchers are reframing puberty as a *process* beginning in middle childhood rather than an *event* marking the end of childhood. Coincidentally, the World Health Organization also specifies 10 as the age of onset of adolescence.

Of course, adolescence is not only about puberty—other events of adolescence are equally continuous. Brain development continues unabated from infancy. What began as *temperament* in infancy and the preschool years evolves into *personality* and undergoes further maturation (Klimstra, Hale, Raaijmakers, Branje, & Meeus, 2009). Where once judgments of right or wrong were largely dependent on what parents, teachers, and other authorities said was "bad" or "good," a sense of personal morality often begins to develop that incorporates greater complexity and perspective (Kohlberg, 1963). Relationships with parents change, but the direction these changes take are related to all that has transpired between parent and child since infancy. Relationships with peers take on greater intimacy and urgency.

The Adolescent Brain Is a "Work in Progress"

Until the 1990s it was thought that brain development was essentially complete by adolescence, and that the adolescent was equipped with an adult brain. It was recognized that adolescents were, well, *different* in their behavior. But this was largely ascribed to social factors and hormonal factors—primarily massive increases in the production and availability of the steroidal hormones testosterone and estrogen.

▲ **Age 10: The "Magical Age."** Although it has been thought of as an event that occurs in adolescence, puberty is actually a process that begins in childhood with the onset of steroid hormone production in the adrenal glands. Adrenal maturation culminates at about age 10—the age at which most people recall experiencing their first real feelings of romantic and/or sexual attraction.

Adolescence ▶ Literally, "becoming adult." Adolescence includes cultural as well as biological dimensions. Adolescence begins at age 10, according to the World Health Organization, but the termination of adolescence is highly dependent on sociocultural factors.

Adrenarche ▶ The maturation of the adrenal glands at about age 10.

Gonadarche ▶ The maturation of the sexual organs during puberty.

▲ **FIGURE 4.9 The Length of Adolescence Varies by Culture—Especially for Females.**
When girls of traditional Maasai societies of Kenya begin to experience bodily changes associated with adolescence at about age 10 or 11, they are allowed the freedom to take lovers among the warriors, as long as they do not become pregnant. However, when they reach the ages of 13–15, like the girl pictured on the left, they undergo a ceremony of ritual genital circumcision, after which they are considered to be adult women (*Esiankiki*) and eligible for marriage and the responsibilities of adulthood (Finke, 2003). Thus, their adolescence lasts only a very few years. Although North American girls (such as those on the right) enter adolescence at the same time as the Maasai, they are not permitted to engage in sexual behavior for at least another 5–7 years (although they often do so anyway), and are not expected to assume adult responsibilities for at least another 8–10 years (although they often do *not* do so for considerably longer than that).

The development of brain imaging technologies such as magnetic resonance imaging (MRI) has changed this view. Researchers are now able to chart the development of the human brain through adolescence in detail, and what they have found is "explosive change" throughout the teen years (Dahl & Spear, 2004; Giedd, 2004, p. 83; Giedd, 2008). As one neuroscientist puts it, "The teenage brain is a work in progress" (Sandra Witelson quoted by Brownlee, 2005, p. 15).

Simplifying what is in fact quite a complicated picture, as depicted in Figure 4.10, the quantity of *white matter*—mylenated axons—increases dramatically during adolescence, creating faster and more efficient neuronal transmissions and allowing information from multiple sources to be combined more effectively. At the same time, *gray matter*—the slower, unmylenated axons—generally decreases in density (Giedd, 2008; Markham, Morris, & Juraska, 2007). The development of white matter and loss of gray matter in the *prefrontal cortex*—the brain region associated with planning, weighing consequences, self-control, and judgment—occurs relatively late and is still "under construction" until adulthood (Gogtay et al., 2004). On the other hand, regions in and around the limbic system, associated with social and emotional experiences (particularly those involving reward and gratification), are under rapid mylenization early in adolescence (Giedd, 2004; Steinberg, 2007; Yurgelun-Todd in Brownlee, 2005, p. 17).

Can you see where all this is leading? If brain systems associated with emotion, reward, and gratification are functioning well quite early in adolescence—but systems associated with judgment, weighing consequences, and self-control are still "under construction," certain problems might result. For example, one of the most robust findings of researchers in adolescence (and well known to parents of teenagers) is that adolescents are risk takers and sensation seekers who have a tendency to engage in reckless behavior (Gardner & Steinberg, 2005; Moffitt, 1993; Spear, 2000a, 2000b; Steinberg, 2007). At least 50% of Western adolescents drive drunk, use illegal drugs, have sex without protection, or commit minor crimes. Reckless behavior of all sorts is an ordinary part of normal adolescent development, at least in the

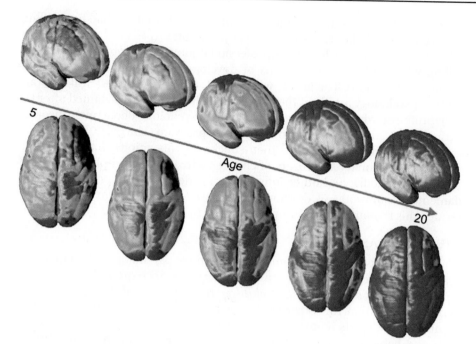

◀**FIGURE 4.10 Loss of Gray Matter from Ages 5 to 20.** A research team from the National Institute of Mental Health, led by Nitin Gogtay, took MRI scans of a group of 13 children on a yearly basis, beginning when the children were 5 and ending at age 20. They were able to produce a "time-lapse" series of images of the thinning of gray matter in the cerebral cortex. This figure shows lateral views of the right cerebral cortex and views of the top of the brain. The thinning of gray matter is represented in the color blue. It proceeds from the back of the cortex to the front, with the prefrontal cortex area maturing last. (*Source: Adapted from Gogtay et al., 2004, p. 8178.*)

West (Arnett, 1992). As Terri Moffitt (1993) observes, it is statistically abnormal to refrain from *all* such behavior.

CRITICAL PERIODS IN ADOLESCENCE

Perhaps of greater concern is evidence that adolescence may represent a second *critical period* in brain development (Kuhn, 2006). Beginning at about age 10 to 12 there is a burst in synaptic production similar to that which occurs in infancy, although not as massive. As in infancy, following this new "over-production" of synapses, there is synaptic pruning. By mid- to late adolescence, then, as the result of pruning and the increased volume of white matter (mylenated axons) described earlier, teenagers have fewer but more selective, faster, and stronger neural connections (Kuhn, 2006).

However, it is the *experiences* of adolescents that *shape* this selectivity of neuronal connections. Experience dictates *which kinds* of synapses remain and become strengthened, and which are lost to pruning (Luna, Garver, Urban, Lazar, & Sweeney, 2004). By engaging in chosen activities, then, adolescents are getting better at what they choose to do—and losing the opportunity to excel at things left unpracticed. *Adolescents shape their own brain development by their behavior.* Therefore, researchers propose that it is important for adolescents to consider carefully how they are spending their time. As neuroscientist Jay Giedd (in Brownlee, 2005) puts it, "You are hard-wiring your brain in adolescence. Do you want to hardwire it for sports and playing music and doing mathematics—or for lying on the couch in front of the television?" (p. 21).

Parents Matter—But How?

In 1998, a grandmother from New Jersey ignited a fiery controversy within the field of developmental psychology that has not died down. Judith Rich Harris was a writer of textbooks in developmental psychology. Earlier in her life, she had been a Ph.D. student in psychology at Harvard. But the department chairman had dismissed her from the program before she received her degree because he thought she lacked the right stuff—particularly in the area of "independence and originality." Because she came to suffer from chronic health problems that kept her housebound, after her children grew up she began writing textbooks in developmental psychology as a way to earn money.

At some point, however, she concluded that most of what she had been telling undergraduates in her textbooks was simply *wrong*.

Harris wrote an article for the professional journal *Psychology Review* detailing why the basic assumptions of developmental psychology were mistaken (Harris, 1995). The article won the prestigious George A. Miller Award for best psychology article of the year. Ironically, this award is named after the very professor who, as chair of the Harvard psychology department decades earlier, had dismissed Harris from the Ph.D. program (Harris, 2006)!

Harris's article advanced the then-shocking propositions that (a) parents were not the primary socializers of children—this was accomplished primarily by peers, media, and other influences outside the home; and (b) the fundamental assumption of developmental psychologists was in error. Harris termed this fundamental assumption the *nurture assumption*.

THE NURTURE ASSUMPTION

The **nurture assumption** is something that most psychologists had taken for granted since the early 20th century: *The way parents treat their children has a profound effect on the way their children turn out as adolescents and adults.* Harris insisted that this error continues to be made because many developmental psychologists ignore the influence of genes on temperament, personality, and behavior; and because they confuse correlation with causation in research about parents and children.

As an example, consider the work of developmental psychologist Diana Baumrind (1967; 1996), who was the first to identify specific *styles* of parenting behavior. According to Baumrind and others (Maccoby & Martin, 1983), parents tend to apply distinct strategies and styles when it comes to setting boundaries and disciplining their children. Baumrind's original three styles (which have been refined somewhat over the years) were labeled *authoritarian, authoritative,* and *permissive* parenting. **Authoritarian parents** (the "shut-up-and-do-what-you're-told" style) impose strict rules, do not explain their rationales for these rules to their children, and expect obedience—sometimes using physical or other severe punishments to ensure their children's compliance.

Authoritative parents, on the other hand, set clear rules and enforce them, but do so in a more flexible manner. They demonstrate love and respect for their children in a warm environment while maintaining firm control on their children's behavior through the use of reason rather than force.

Finally, **permissive parents** do not attempt to control their children's behavior at all, but rather hope for the best. This is distinct from simple neglectful parenting, however, where no attempts at control occur merely because the parents do not care (Maccoby & Martin, 1983).

Two decades of research have shown that the *authoritative* style is associated (correlated) in childhood and adolescence with higher levels of self-esteem, academic achievement, competence, and psychosocial maturity than either the permissive or authoritarian styles (Steinberg & Morris, 2001). While psychologists have used this as evidence of the importance of parenting in determining the way children and adolescents turn out, Harris argues that many other explanations are possible for the correlations found between parenting style and child outcome, including the following:

1. *Parents pass on genes to their children as well as child-rearing style.* If a parent is overly strict or not strict enough, it might be due in part to the parents' personality characteristics (aggressiveness, lack of interpersonal skills or confidence, etc.). As we have seen, research shows that a child's temperament is in part mediated by genes, and the same is true of adult personality (see Chapter 12). Therefore, children of parents with personality problems—problems *expressed* in styles of parenting—may have similar problems themselves in part because they inherit them from their parents, not because of their parents' child-rearing style. The same is true for high-functioning

---

Nurture assumption ▶ The term used by Judith Rich Harris to refer to widespread beliefs that parents are the primary socializers of children and that the behavior of parents has a profound impact on the personalities and behavior of their children as adolescents and adults.

Authoritarian parents ▶ Characterized by imposition of strict rules (the rationales for which are left unexplained to children), expectation of obedience, and severe punishment.

Authoritative parents ▶ Characterized by clear rules, fair enforcement, a warm environment, and the use of reason rather than force.

Permissive parents ▶ Characterized by highly accepting and warm relations between parent and child, but little in the way of setting boundaries, limits, or rules.

children of high-functioning "authoritative" parents. Calm, confident, warm, socially skilled parents—the very type who typically use authoritative styles of parenting—may produce calm, confident, warm, socially skilled children because the children inherit these characteristics, not because they have been exposed to some special parenting style.

2. *The parents' child-rearing style may result from the type of child they have—not vice versa.* As I explained on pp. 124–125 of Chapter 3 in the discussion of reactive gene-environment correlation, the type of child parents have has been shown to affect the way parents treat the child and may also elicit a certain type of parenting style. For example, if a child is "good" she may be treated with flexibility, respect, warmth, and firm but fair discipline. If a child is "bad"—unruly, hostile, deceptive, and so forth—she may be handled with an iron glove (Kerr & Stattin, 2003). Therefore, the research in parenting style might sometimes be mistaking the effects of children on their parents, known as **child-to-parent effects**, for the effects of parents on their children (Hanington, Ramchandani, & Stein, 2010; Kendler, 1996; Kerr & Stattin, 2003). Developmental psychologists may be mistaking correlation for causation by ignoring the directionality problem described in Chapter 1.

Child-to-parent effects ▶ When the behavior of a child alters the way the parent behaves toward the child—including the parent's overall parenting style (e.g., authoritative, authoritarian, or permissive).

Considering Judith Rich Harris How do Harris's criticisms hold up? Harris is on target for faulting most traditional research on the effects of parenting for neglecting to control for the effects of genes and child-to-parent effects. However, even if parents' child-rearing style is in part a response to a child's behavior, this does not necessarily mean that the child-rearing style has no effect. For example, an aggressive and hostile child may elicit an aggressive, authoritarian style of parenting. But the child may then react to his parents' aggressive authoritarianism by even worse behavior and problematic personality development in a spiraling, interactive cycle (Maccoby, 2002; O'Connor, Deater-Deckard, Fulker, Rutter, & Plomin, 1998). Thus, the picture of parent-to-child effects and child-to-parent effects is complex.

Harris is also correct that the importance of peers in the socialization of children has been underestimated in the past. Nevertheless, parents' child-rearing approaches can affect children's choice of peers (Collins, Maccoby, Steinberg, Hetherington, & Bornstein, 2000). If peers are highly influential—and they are (see "Living Psychology" on pp. 186–187)—then parents may have an influence on their children's personality and social development indirectly through their influence on choice of peers.

PARENT-ADOLESCENT CONFLICT

According to a widely held stereotype, the parent-child relationship becomes particularly rife with conflict when the child reaches adolescence. But is this really true? Unfortunately, bickering, squabbling, and day-to-day disagreements do tend to increase substantially beginning in early adolescence, and feelings of closeness and warmth between parents and children tend to decline (Collins & Laursen, 2004; Smetana, Campione-Barr, & Metzger, 2006; Steinberg & Morris, 2001). Adolescents also experience more negative moods throughout early and mid-adolescence (Larson, Moneta, Richards, & Wilson, 2002). While all of this can be unnerving and upsetting to parents, it seems to occur in most families and does not necessarily predict more serious problems. In fact, some research suggests that a modest amount of conflict in early adolescence is associated with *better* adjustment later than no conflict at all (or severe conflict) (Adams & Laursen, 2001).

However, as strong as the evidence of modest increases in conflict in early adolescence is, the evidence is equally strong that the stereotype of adolescence as a time of severe "storm and stress," alienation from parents, rejection of adult values and authority, and rebellion is inaccurate (Smetana et al., 2006). Only between 5% and 15% of adolescents experience such extreme personal problems and conflict with their parents, and of those who do, the origins can often be traced to conditions that existed prior to adolescence (Collins & Laursen, 2004; Smetana et al., 2006).

Peers Matter More than Ever

When I think back on my high school life, with the exception of a relatively few exciting academic experiences, all I remember is my friends. In fact, my friends *were* my life throughout high school. They were the reason I went to school and the reason I didn't go to school. They shared my food, my music, my home some of the time, and my support all of the time. Although I have had deeper and longer-lasting friendships in adulthood, not since the years of adolescence have I experienced peer friendships of such burning *intensity*—relationships that seemed absolutely essential for my continued existence on the planet. The same goes for romantic relationships.

Perhaps because I experienced my adolescent relationships as resolutely beneficial, I often find it puzzling that the overwhelming portion of research on adolescent peer relationships focuses on harmful and negative aspects: negative peer influence, victimization and bullying, sexual harassment, peer rejection and lack of popularity, cliques, "mean girl" behavior, racial prejudice, and so forth (Smetana et al., 2006).

Romantic relationships fare even worse in the psychology literature. These relationships are among the most under-researched topics in all of developmental psychology, and yet they are among the most characteristic aspects of the entire adolescent experience—happening at least once to the majority of adolescents by the time they are in their mid-teens (Steinberg & Morris, 2001). Once again, the large majority of the (very few) psychology articles on adolescent romance focus on the negative aspects of these relationships—for example, risky sexual behavior, rejection, body image problems in females, and physical and sexual aggression. There are, however, a few exceptions to this trend (Crouter & Booth, 2006; Collins, Welsh, & Furman, 2009).

I am not the only one who placed friends first in adolescence. Adolescents in the United States spend more time talking to their friends than performing any activity other than schoolwork (defined as actual classwork and homework), and adolescents report that they are happiest when talking to peers. These relationships are critical to developing important social skills and learning to become adult (Harris, 1995, 2006; Larson & Verma, 1999; Spear, 2000a). As children become adolescent, their friendships become more intimate and supportive, with increased disclosure of personal information between friends (Furman & Buhrmester, 1992; Brown & Klute, 2006).

LIVING PSYCHOLOGY

Our Parents Were Right (Sort of): Choose Your Friends Wisely

When I was in high school, adults around me were prone to reciting the mantra of the time: *Watch out for peer pressure!* Friends were blamed for just about all youthful "bad behavior," be it smoking, drinking, drugs, sex, truancy—whatever. Those of us who found ourselves busted for any of these transgressions tried to explain to parents and counselors that we didn't *need* peer pressure to behave badly—it was *fun*, and we were perfectly able to drive ourselves to the netherworld in a hand-basket with no help whatsoever from our friends.

Social and behavioral science research conducted over the past few decades has, to some extent, exonerated our parents' admonitions. Peers matter—perhaps more than previously suspected. Peers are among the most critical forces of *nurture* in normal human development (Harris, 1998, 2006). For example, as adults of my generation insisted, peers are a critical influence when it comes to behaviors such as adolescent cigarette smoking, drug or alcohol abuse, risky driving, and general antisocial behavior (Chassin et al., 2004; Mahoney, Stattin, & Lord, 2004; Monahan, Steinberg, & Cauffman, 2009). If you are interested in steering clear of these sorts of behaviors, you would probably do well to choose your friends carefully.

However, the relationship between peers and behaviors such as smoking and drinking is not a simple, straightforward one. For example, although adolescents who do not smoke are *much* more likely to begin smoking if their friends smoke, it is not always clear if it is *peer pressure* or *peer selection* that is at work. An adolescent might develop a desire to smoke for any number of non-peer-related reasons, and that adolescent might then *select* friends who already smoke and will therefore be supportive.

Because of this problem, more recent research has attempted to distinguish peer influence from peer selection. Such studies have found that while both influence *and* selection occur, the relationship of peers to the onset of adolescent smoking, for example, is not one of peer selection entirely. Peer influence really is important (J. S. Rose, Chassin, Presson, & Sherman, 1999), and it occurs independently of factors such as personality, genetics, neighborhood, school, and sibling behavior. Something similar is at work in the case of risky sexual behavior. While teenagers do tend to select friends whose attitudes toward sex closely track their own, peer influence is important—for example, in teenagers' willingness to engage in sex and frequency of condom use during sex. However, it must also be said that the effects of peers, through both peer selection and peer influence, are comparatively modest when it comes to sexual behavior. Other outside influences and personal characteristics play more decisive roles (Henry, Schoeny, Deptula, & Slavick, 2007).

A final word about peers: Peer influence is almost always cast in a negative light. However, although peers may help sow the seeds of destruction for some adolescents, they are just as influential in the opposite direction. Peers often effectively *discourage* behaviors such as smoking, drinking, and drugging, and peer influence can serve as an important protective factor against harmful behavior in general (Maxwell, 2002; Padilla-Walker & Bean, 2009). ■

Moral Development in Adolescence Is Complex

Although I will not make the mistake of trying to define *morality* precisely, most people would probably agree in a general way that **morality** includes personal and social *beliefs* about what is right or wrong, *behavior* based on these beliefs, and *feelings* associated with such behavior (e.g., guilt or shame for bad moral choices and pride in good ones). In psychological terms, this means that morality has cognitive, behavioral, and affective (emotional) components (Arnold, 2000). As mentioned in Chapter 3, while moral sentiments are a human universal, and may begin in infancy (Bloom, 2010), the specifics of morality vary by culture (Shweder, Mahapatra, & Miller, 1990). Without doubt, until relatively recently the most influential psychological theory of moral development in childhood and adolescence was that of Piaget's friend Lawrence Kohlberg (1927–1987). It is known as *cognitive developmental theory of moral reasoning*.

Morality ▶ This term is defined differently in different contexts, but generally describes personal or social beliefs, feelings, and behavior regarding what is right or wrong.

LAWRENCE KOHLBERG AND COGNITIVE DEVELOPMENTAL THEORY

Like Piaget's constructivism, Kohlberg's **cognitive developmental theory of moral reasoning** describes moral development as occurring in a series of universal, invariant stages. As in Piaget's theory, each stage of moral development

Cognitive developmental theory of moral reasoning ▶ Lawrence Kohlberg's three-level, six-stage theory of moral reasoning.

builds on the previous one and reflects a child and adolescent's increasingly sophisticated ways of thinking about moral issues and choices. Kohlberg was not so much interested in what people considered to be right or wrong behavior at various stages of development as he was in the *reasons they gave* for having arrived at their judgments. For example, as depicted in Figure 4.11, children of any age might agree that "stealing is wrong," but they may hold this belief for very different reasons.

To clarify this, Kohlberg identified six specific stages of moral development and divided them into three broad levels, with two stages per level. The three broad levels are **preconventional morality**, **conventional morality**, and **postconventional morality**. According to Kohlberg, the *preconventional level*, generally characteristic of preschool and younger school-age children, describes moral judgments based on the prospect of reward or punishment. The *conventional level*, characteristic of older school-age children and young adolescents, is based on respect for law, social norms, and rules set by parents and other authorities. The *postconventional level*, characteristic of older adolescents and adults, involves more complex personal judgments based on abstract principles, such as fairness or justice (see Figure 4. 11). According to Kohlberg, each level is more "adequate" than the level that came before it.

Considering Kohlberg As was the case with Piaget, certain aspects of Kohlberg's theory have stood the test of time. For example, children do seem to move "forward" in a general way on moral reasoning tasks devised by Kohlberg, from preconventional reasoning to conventional reasoning. And some people (only a minority, however) do move in adolescence or adulthood from conventional reasoning to postconventional. As people progress, they do not return to an earlier stage (Dawson, 2002; Krebs, 2005).

However, very strong criticisms of Kohlberg's theory have been offered over the years, and views of moral development have changed considerably, even among those who adhere to many of the basic tenets of the cognitive-developmental approach (Dawson, 2002). The most important of the criticisms leveled at Kohlberg's work is this: *Tests of moral reasoning do not capture actual moral reasoning in children and adolescents and do not predict moral behavior*. As depicted in Figure 4.11, Kohlbergian tests present research participants with short *hypothetical* descriptions of moral dilemmas and record participants' explanations for the moral judgments they give in response. However, there appear to be differences between the way children respond to these stories and how they respond when faced with *real life* moral dilemmas (e.g., seeing one classmate hit another; Nucci, 2001; Smetana, Schlagman, & Adams, 1993). As we shall see in the next section, one problem may be that people often do not make moral decisions based on *reasoning* at all.

POSITIVE PSYCHOLOGY AND THE "MORAL SENSE"

Consider the following scenario:

> You are a passenger on a train whose driver has fainted. On the main track ahead are five people. The main track has a side track leading off to the left, and you could turn the train onto it. There is one person on the left-hand track. You could turn the train to the left, killing the one; or you could refrain from turning the train, letting five die. Is it morally permissible to turn the train to the left, killing one to save five?

After you have made up your mind, now read the following alternative scenario:

> You are on a footbridge over train tracks. You see a train approaching the bridge, out of control. There are five people on

A poor man's wife is dying of a rare disease. Only a special medicine can save her, and in this town only one pharmacy carries the medicine. But the pharmacist is greedy—he knows he can charge what he wants for it, and he is charging many thousands of dollars—much more than the drug is worth. The man goes to the pharmacist and begs him to sell him the medicine for cheaper, but the pharmacist refuses. The man knows his wife will die if he doesn't get the medicine. Late that night, he breaks into the pharmacy and steals the medicine.

Was the man right or wrong in what he did? If he was right, why was he right? If he was wrong, why was he wrong?

Preconventional Morality
(Stages 1 and 2: preschool and younger school age)

"The man was *right* because then his wife would be happy and her parents would thank him and he would be a hero."

Or

"The man would be *wrong* because he would get in trouble with the police."

Conventional Morality
(Stages 3 and 4: older school age, young adolescents)

"The man was *right* because the druggist was overcharging, which is against the law anyway—so the man was just righting a wrong."

Or

"The man was *wrong* because stealing is against the law, and in order for society to function properly, people need to obey the law. The man should have found another way, like taking out a loan or something."

Postconventional Morality
(Stages 5 and 6: older adolescents and adults)

"Whether he was right or wrong may depend on the specific circumstances which aren't really that clear from the story. For example, the druggist was price-gouging—crazy price gouging. But you obviously can't use other people's lawbreaking to excuse your own. On the other hand, human life is more precious than property and justifies property crime. But it could have been the case that the man might have been able to find the drug within a reasonable driving trip or bus ride, and avoided all this. It's just not clear."

◄ **FIGURE 4.11 Kohlberg's Three Levels of Moral Development.** Lawrence Kohlberg divided moral development in children and adolescents into six stages, grouped in three levels, with two stages per level. Children's specific stage and level are determined by the answers to moral problems such as the one depicted here. The important thing is not whether the child believes that something is right or wrong, but rather, the reasons the child gives to explain his or her judgment.

the track. You know that the only way to stop the train is to drop a heavy weight into its path. But the only available, sufficiently heavy weight is a very large man, also watching the train from the bridge. You could shove the man onto the track in the path of the train, killing him; or you can refrain from doing this, letting the five die. Is it morally permissible to shove the man onto the track? (Scenarios adapted from Hauser, Cushman, Young, Jin, & Mikhail, 2007, p. 6).

As depicted in Figure 4.12, if you are like the overwhelming majority of the 5,000 English-speaking men and women of varied income levels, nationalities, ethnicities, education levels, and ages tested by Marc Hauser and his colleagues, you will overwhelmingly approve of killing one person to save five in

Scenario	Image	Description	% "Yes"
1	Denise	Denise is a passenger on a train whose driver has fainted. On the main track ahead are 5 people. The main track has a side track leading off to the left, Denise can turn the train onto it. There is 1 person on the left hand track. Denise can turn the train, killing 1; or she can refrain from turning the train, letting the 5 die.	Is it morally permissible for Denise to turn the train? **85%**
2	Frank	Frank is on a footbridge over the train tracks. He sees a train approaching the bridge out of control. There are 5 people on the track. Frank knows that the only way to stop the train is to drop a heavy weight into its path. But the only available, sufficiently heavy weight is 1 large man, also watching the train from the footbridge. Frank can shove the 1 man onto the tracks in the path of the train, killing him; or he can refrain from doing this, letting the 5 die.	Is it morally permissible for Frank to shove the man? **12%**

▲ **FIGURE 4.12 Moral Dumbfoundedness: When Is It Okay to Kill 1 to Save 5?** When Marc Hauser and his colleagues presented these scenarios to 5,000 men and women of varying ages, ethnicities, nationalities, incomes, and education levels, the overwhelming majority approved of killing 1 to save 5 in Scenario 1, but rejected this choice in Scenario 2. When asked to explain their judgments they could not do so coherently—they were "morally dumbfounded." Hauser and his colleagues hypothesize that moral intuitions differ between dilemmas that invoke social emotions and those that are relatively impersonal.

the first scenario, but reject that action in the second (Hauser et al., 2007). In addition, if you are like the majority of the participants in the study, you will find it difficult to explain your choices: Why is killing one to save five permissible in the first, but not the second scenario? To use positive psychologist Jonathan Haidt's term, you will be *morally dumbfounded*—convinced that something is wrong but unable to explain why in a coherent fashion (Haidt, 2001, 2007, 2008; Haidt & Bjorklund, 2008). Similar results were obtained when research participants were presented with scenarios involving (protected, consensual) sex between adult siblings. They insisted that the behavior was wrong but could not adequately explain why.

According to Haidt (2001), although we often do use reason to arrive at moral judgments, more often than not we arrive at these judgments largely intuitively and often instantaneously in the absence of reasoning. We may *then* engage in a reasoning process—but only to explain to ourselves (and perhaps to others) why we have made the choices we've made. Haidt calls his theory of moral systems **social intuitionism** because it proposes that moral judgments are frequently intuitive and emotional rather than rational.

But where do these moral intuitions come from? Every culture has its own moral system. Moral systems are universal, even though the specifics of what each culture considers moral or immoral behavior may vary (Bloom, 2010; Brown, 1991; Haidt, 2007; Pinker, 2008). Because of the universality of moral systems and their obvious importance to survival and reproduction, positive psychologists and evolutionary psychologists have proposed that the capacity for morality is the result of evolutionary psychological adaptations (Haidt, 2007, 2008; Krebs & Denton, 2005, 2008; Wilson, 1975). These adaptations constitute a kind of *moral sense*, or instinct (Haidt & Bjorklund, 2008; Hauser et al., 2007; Mikhail, 2007; Pinker, 2008). If you recall from Chapter 1, positive psychologists focus on studying human strengths, including moral development and behavior. According to Haidt and several other positive and evolutionary psychologists, the moral sense—like many other psychological adaptations—frequently taps into emotion first and reason second. This is the explanation for moral dumbfoundedness: We make moral decisions based on intuition and emotion, and attempt to explain our decisions with logic after the fact.

There is some neuroscientific evidence to support the view that moral judgments often may be arrived at much too rapidly for deliberate reasoning to take place. When faced with morally objectionable statements, participants in the study by Jos Van Berkum and his colleagues showed instantaneous changes in their brain wave patterns within 200–250 microseconds after the utterance of the first word signaling a morally objectionable idea (Van Berkum, Holleman, Nieuwland, Otten, & Murre, 2009).

Social intuitionism ► Positive psychologist Jonathan Haidt's theory of moral judgment. The theory proposes that moral judgments are more often than not the result of intuition and emotion rather than reasoning. Reasoning tends to occur after the fact to explain to oneself or others why one has arrived at a particular moral judgment.

Five Foundations of Morality Consider now the following acts: Are they morally wrong?

> A family's dog is killed by a car in front of their house. The family has heard that dog meat is delicious, so they cut up the dog's body and cook and eat it for dinner.

> On her deathbed, a mother asks her son to promise to visit her grave each week. The son promises, but even though he loved his mother, after she dies he doesn't visit her grave because he is "too busy."

> A man buys a dead chicken from a supermarket each week and has sex with it. Afterwards, he cooks the chicken and eats it.

The preceding acts share two things in common: Each is upsetting or disgusting to most people, but no apparent harm results to anyone as a result of the acts and no one has been treated unfairly. When scenarios such as these were presented to high-socioeconomic-status (high-SES) college students at elite universities in the United States, judgments tended to reflect the idea that these acts were offensive but not *morally wrong*. The reasons given by these students for their judgments reflected a view that because no one has been treated unfairly, and no real harm has been done to anyone (the dog, chicken, and man's mother were dead and could not suffer), acts such as these boil down to personal decisions.

On the other hand, among those with lesser income and education, particularly those participants who resided in a nation with less industrialization and development (Brazil), these acts were generally seen as both morally wrong *and* personally disturbing. Building on earlier work conducted by anthropologist Richard Shweder, positive psychologist Jonathan Haidt (2007) proposes that there are *five psychological foundations* on which all moral systems are built. However, individuals, social classes, and entire cultures may vary in the importance they place on each of these foundations and the way they are expressed in specific moral codes.

The five foundations are:

- Caring for others and avoiding causing harm
- Fairness and justice
- Loyalty to one's group
- Respect for authority
- Purity and sanctity (see Table 4.3 for examples of each foundation)
- Haidt proposes that educated Westerners are primarily concerned with only the first two of the foundations of moral systems: *caring for others and avoiding harm* and *fairness and justice*. Consequently, most psychological and social science research on morality focuses on these two aspects of moral systems (Haidt & Kesebir, 2010).

However, cross-cultural research and research among various social classes and political ideologies in the West show that there may be more to morality

Table 4.3 **Jonathan Haidt's Five Psychological Foundations of Morality (Haidt, 2007)**

FOUNDATION	EXAMPLES
Care/harm	Stopping to help a person stranded at the side of the road
	Refraining from killing, stealing, or lying
Fairness/justice	Civil rights for minorities
	Overturning wrongful criminal convictions
Loyalty to one's group	Uniting to fight an occupying army
	Ethnic solidarity
	Participating in family feuds
Respect for authority	Speaking respectfully of your leaders even if you disagree with their policies
	Revering teachers and the elderly
	Ancestor worship
Purity and sanctity	Rules about which sexual acts and partners are permissible
	Rules about which foods may be eaten and how they may be prepared
	Rules about menstruation
	Rules about toileting and nudity

than care/harm and fairness/justice. In particular, traditional and tribal cultures and subcultures of lower-SES groups often include the last three foundations in their moral systems to a degree equal—or nearly equal—to the first two (Haidt & Graham, 2007; Graham et al., 2011; Shweder, Much, Mahapatra, & Park, 1997).

The notion that universal moral foundations include more than harm/care and fairness/justice is not universally accepted (Turiel, Killen, & Helwig, 1987). For example, Elliot Turiel and colleagues argued two decades ago that many of the factors that subsequently were incorporated in Haidt's final three foundations (Table 4.4) are actually social conventions—for example, rules about food preparation, sex, nudity, and so forth. Turiel has also proposed that some cultural practices that appear unrelated to harm/care may actually be strongly related to harm/care if the practices are understood from the perspective of a member of the culture in question. As an example, some cultures have strict rules forbidding women to prepare food when they are menstruating. Is this a moral proscription related to purity/sanctity, or is it that members of such cultures truly believe that preparing food during menstruation is harmful to others (harm/care)?

AT THE FOREFRONT

The Neural Basis of Morality

Research in neuroscience may provide a partial framework for understanding the neural basis of moral behavior displayed by very young children in real-life situations. This research shows that when human beings—including children—perceive pain in others, the same brain circuits are activated as when the person himself or herself experiences pain (Decety, Michalska, & Akitsuki, 2008; Jackson, Rainville, & Decety, 2006). This may constitute a "building block" for the important human quality of *empathy*. Empathy is the ability to understand another person's experience or state of mind—to "put yourself in another person's shoes." Empathy in turn is an important component of *compassion*— "feeling another person's pain" and wanting to do something to alleviate it. Empathy at least (and perhaps compassion as well) is thought by many to underlie the ability to develop moral reasoning and behavior. For example, those diagnosed with antisocial personality disorder—characterized in part by expoitiveness toward others and a lack of guilt or remorse over wrongdoing—appear to lack empathy as well as compassion (Decety et al., 2008).

To test the connection between empathy and morality in children from a neuroscience perspective, Jean Decety and his colleagues extended previous fMRI studies of human brain responses to images of pain experienced by others (Decety et al., 2008). First, the researchers found the expected "mirroring" of pain-related brain circuits in the children's brain scans. The perception of other people's pain was associated with increased activity in the children's brain circuits involved in experiencing pain firsthand. However, the researchers took this finding a step further. They showed the children images of people experiencing pain accidentally, and also showed images of people *intentionally* inflicting pain on others—a moral violation. As Figure 4.13 shows, the researchers found that when viewing the images of pain intentionally inflicted by another person, additional areas of the brain "lit up"—those areas that previously have been shown to be engaged when considering social interactions and moral behavior or violations of moral behavior. ■

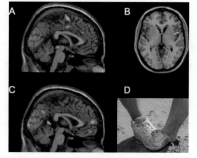

◀ **FIGURE 4.13 Morality in the Children's Brains?** When Jean Decety and his colleagues showed a group of (female) children images of other people accidentally in pain (*A* and *B*), areas of the insula involved in experiencing pain firsthand "lit up." When the images showed pain intentionally inflicted (*D*), additional areas of at the border of the temporal and parietal lobes, the frontal cortex, amygdala, and paracingulate were also "recruited." These areas associated with brain response to social interaction and moral behavior. (*Source: Decety et al., 2008, p. 2611.*)

IN SUMMARY

1.	Adolescence exists in all known societies, but its nature and length are determined by cultural norms.
2.	In the adolescent brain, white matter increases dramatically while gray matter decreases in density. These processes are delayed in the prefrontal cortex relative to other brain regions. Some research suggests that adolescence constitutes a second critical period in brain development.
3.	Judith Rich Harris created controversy when she proposed that peers and other influences outside the family are the primary socializers of children. She also claimed that correlations between parenting style and outcome in childhood and adolescence might result from the transmission of genetic traits as well as from child-to-parent effects.
4.	Minor conflict does increase in early adolescence between parent and child, particularly between adolescents and their mothers. However, this does not necessarily predict serious problems. Only a small minority of adolescents experience extreme personal problems and conflict with their parents.
5.	Peers may influence adolescents' behavior, but people may also select their friends because they exhibit that behavior. Peer influence may have both constructive and destructive consequences.
6.	Kohlberg's cognitive developmental theory of moral reasoning includes three stages: preconventional, conventional, and postconventional morality.

7. The social intuitionist theory of moral judgment proposed by Jonathan Haidt proposes that moral judgments are often the result of intuitive and emotional responses rather than conscious reasoning. The theory states that people may then use reasoning to attempt to explain to themselves or others why they have made these moral judgments and decisions.

8. Jonathan Haidt identifies five universal foundations for morality: harm/care, fairness/justice, group loyalty, respect for authority, and purity/sanctity.

RETRIEVE!

1. During the adolescent years, the development of white matter (mylenization) and loss of gray matter density in the _____ occurs relatively late; this process occurs relatively early in regions in and around the _____.

a) limbic system/cerebral cortex

b) prefrontal cortex/thalamus

c) limbic system/prefrontal cortex

d) prefrontal cortex/limbic system

2. Distinguish authoritarian, authoritative, and permissive child-rearing styles. Why might the authoritative style be associated (correlated) with more positive outcomes, *apart* from actual causal effects on the child of the authoritative style?

3. In Judith Rich Harris's view there are two general alternative explanations for many of the facts used by developmental psychologists to promote the view that parenting style is the most important influence on the way children turn out. What are these two explanations?

4. What is the difference between "peer influence" and "peer selection"?

5. What are the three broad levels of moral reasoning development in childhood, according to Lawrence Kohlberg? Briefly characterize each level.

6. Which of the following is NOT among the five foundations of morality as conceived by Jonathan Haidt?

a) Caring and avoiding harm

b) Fairness and justice

c) Group loyalty

d) Social equality

e) Respect for authority

How Does the Adolescent Become Adult?

Early adulthood ▶ A newly coined term for the developmental stage between adolescence and adulthood.

Unlike societies that practice specific coming-of-age rituals, adolescence in Western societies moves relatively seamlessly into **early adulthood** without a clear point of demarcation. For example, in the United States first-year college students who are 17 to 19 years old are generally considered adolescents. But by the time a student graduates from college, he or she will likely be a *young adult*. However, although 22-year-olds are technically adults for purposes of voting, drinking, marrying, and the like, many college graduates remain under the care and protection of their parents. Therefore, they may lack the respect and resources accorded a "real" adult by the outside world (Arnett, 2010; Furstenberg, Kennedy, McLoyd, Rumbaut, & Settersten, 2004).

What is a "real" adult? In the mid-20th century, most people defined adulthood in terms of five factors: *finishing school, leaving home, becoming financially independent, marrying,* and *parenthood*—all of which tended to occur for most people in their early 20s and often earlier (Furstenberg et al., 2004). These criteria have changed because today many people are postponing marriage and children or opting out of both (Dye, 2008). Further, in the economy of the 21st century, employment does not always result in financial independence, as it once did. Moreover, the amount of schooling and training necessary to find the sort of employment that *does* result in financial independence has increased dramatically (Smeeding & Phillips, 2002). Thus, a vast number of young people are stuck in a netherworld where they are considered neither adolescents nor adults (see Figure 4.14).

In the 1960s, many young couples in their early twenties were already parents and homeowners, supported entirely by the husband's income.

In 2012, fifty years later, young women in their early twenties are often employed at part-time jobs and still dependent on their parents for financial support.

▲ **FIGURE 4.14 Neither Adolescent, nor Adult.** In 1960, 70% of 25-year-old women had achieved all five of the traditional indicators of adulthood, but in 2000, only 25% had done so—and yet their participation in the labor force was equal to that of men. Hence the stage *early adulthood* has been newly identified. For some, this period may last into the early 30s. *(Source: Text and photos adopted from Furstenberg et al., 2004.)*

There are several possible side effects of the emergence of this new stage of life. According to developmental psychologist Jeffrey Arnett, the emergence of early adulthood as a new stage is responsible for a widespread belief that, in comparison to previous generations, those born during the 1970s and after are generally more selfish and self-focused ("narcissistic"), less content with their lives and more likely to be emotionally disturbed, lazier ("slackers"), more materialistic, less concerned with the welfare of others, and less trusting—qualities captured in the epithet "Generation Me" (Arnett, 2010; Trzesniewski & Donnellan, 2010; Twenge, Campbell, & Freeman, 2012). Arnett argues that because aspects of adolescent life have been extended into adulthood, ordinary adolescent experiences such as identity exploration, choosing career paths, developmentally appropriate focus on the self, and youthful optimism have been misinterpreted as suffering, slacking, selfishness, and narcissistic grandiosity.

On the other hand, some researchers worry that the generations of young adults born subsequent to the 1970s really *do* display many of the negative characteristics attributed to them in the label "Generation Me" (Twenge & Campbell, 2010; Twenge et al., 2012). And, according to a 2008 Harris poll, there is at least one group of Americans who believe that the stereotype is accurate—young people themselves (Harris Poll, 2008)!

Development in Adulthood: More Stages and Continuities

I clearly remember when the Beatles' music first became popular in the United States during the mid-1960s. At that time, I was a young teenager who listened primarily to jazz, dressed in what would have been called "beat" style (jeans, black turtleneck, black beret), and hung out in New York City's Greenwich Village. Rock music was the very last thing "someone like me" would have been interested in. And yet, in less than a year, I was listening to Bob Dylan, the Byrds, and the Beatles on a daily basis; had put away my jazz records and

Identity ▶ A sense of oneself as a unique being different from others; an understanding of one's place in the world.

Psychosocial stages ▶ Erik Erikson's notion that there are eight developmental stages from infancy to old age, during which each person experiences a characteristic conflict that must be resolved.

beret (temporarily, as it turns out); altered my circle of friends; and changed my idea of what "someone like me" actually consisted of. Within another year or two, I had grown my hair quite long, was wearing beads and paisley shirts, said things like, "Far out, man, that's really outta sight," and was preoccupied with doing things that never would have occurred to me 2 years earlier. I was unrecognizable from the person I had been.

You may have experienced similar transformations during adolescence, though no doubt in different directions from those I took back in the 1960s. According to psychoanalytic theorist Erik Erikson (1902–1994), the adolescent has to evolve a firm sense of **identity**—a sense of who one is and how one fits into the world—by grappling with the many possible "selves" and possible roles with which a person may be confronted during the teenage years. Erikson (1963, 1968, 1982) proposed that we all go through eight **psychosocial stages** from infancy to old age, roughly corresponding to the eight lifespan periods in Table 4.1 on page 157. For each of Erikson's psychosocial stages, each individual experiences a characteristic conflict that must be resolved to successfully negotiate the stage to follow (see Table 4.4).

Table 4.4 **Erikson's Eight Psychosocial Stages**

LIFESPAN PERIOD	PSYCHOSOCIAL STAGE	PRIMARY ISSUES TO BE RESOLVED
Infancy	Trust vs. Mistrust	Can the world—and its inhabitants—be trusted?
Toddlerhood	Autonomy vs. Doubt	Am I an individual who can make my own decisions and control my own behavior?
Preschool	Initiative vs. Guilt	Can I carry out my plans, accomplish new things, and learn from my mistakes? Will I be punished if I do not succeed?
School Age	Industry vs. Inferiority	Can I work alongside others competently?
Adolescence	Identity vs. Role Confusion	Who am I?
Early Adulthood	Intimacy vs. Isolation	Can I make a lasting commitment to another person in a loving relationship, or will feelings of insecurity isolate me from others?
Middle Adulthood	Generativity vs.Stagnation	Have I accomplished anything of value to pass on to the next generation?
Late Adulthood	Ego Integrity vs. Despair	Have I lived a meaningful life?

Identity vs. role confusion ▶ Erik Erikson's view of the characteristic conflict of adolescence between an integrated sense of personal identity and confusion between possible "selves" and roles.

Intimacy vs. isolation ▶ Erik Erikson's view of the characteristic conflict of early adulthood between social isolation and the formation of a genuinely intimate bond with another person.

For the adolescent, that conflict is **identity vs. role confusion**. Adolescence is a time for "trying on" various possible selves and social roles, and integrating the results into a genuine sense of personal identity. According to Erikson, if this integration does not occur, the adolescent is ill prepared to face the conflict of young adulthood[1] **intimacy vs. isolation**. During young adulthood a person typically initiates for the first time a shared intimate relationship with another person in a committed romantic partnership or marriage. Note that Erikson is not proposing that early adulthood is the time of the first romantic relationship—this occurs for most people in adolescence. However, according to Erikson, no genuine intimacy with another individual is possible without a clear sense of one's own identity. Without a strong sense of self, intimate relationships will be difficult to form and maintain, and the individual will likely remain isolated in adulthood.

---

[1]*Young adulthood is not the same as "early adulthood," which did not exist as a stage of life when Erikson was formulating his theory.*

Erikson and other theorists such as Daniel Levinson (1986) have focused on development in adolescence and adulthood as proceeding in stages. However, much as they did with Piaget's developmental stages, critics argue that development in adulthood is continuous rather than occurring in discrete stages. In other words, people may approach the various tasks and conflicts described by Erikson at different ages; and for any given age there is wide variability in the tasks each person considers most critical (Lachman, 2004; Lawford, Pratt, Hunsberger, & Pancer, 2005). If stage theory is taken too literally, people who have yet to develop concerns about issues appropriate to their lifespan stage might be seen as "maladjusted." Conversely, if they show concerns characteristic of much older people they may be inappropriately considered "remarkably mature."

Nevertheless, some evidence does support Erikson's overall view of the typical conflicts and tasks of various age ranges. In the Harvard Study of Adult Development (e.g., Vaillant, 1977, 2002), which followed three samples of men and women over a period lasting 60 to 80 years, researcher George Vaillant found a tendency for those in their 20s to be concerned primarily with establishing intimate relationships, those in their 30s to focus on work issues, and those in their 40s to become interested in issues of *generativity*—expressing concern for the well-being of future generations and seeking to leave something to the world that "outlives" them (McAdams, 2001; McAdams & Logan, 2004). This corresponds to Erikson's view that the characteristic conflict of middle-adulthood is **generativity vs. stagnation**. One man interviewed for the study expressed this idea succinctly:

> At 20 to 30, I think I learned how to get along with my wife. From 30 to 40, I learned how to be a success in my job. And at 40 to 50, I worried less about myself and more about the children (quoted by Sigelman & Rider, 2006, p. 313).

Research does show that while concerns with identity, intimacy, and generativity may occur at any age, these concerns probably do "cluster" at certain age ranges on average (McAdams, 2001). Successful resolution of developmental conflicts at one stage may also increase the probability of successful resolution of the developmental tasks to follow, as Erikson predicted (Christiansen & Palkovitz, 1998).

Generativity vs. stagnation
▶ Erik Erikson's view of the characteristic conflict of middle-adulthood between productivity and concern for future generations on one hand, and living a self-centered existence on the other.

Work, Marriage, and Parenthood Still Define Adulthood for Most People

Although major changes have occurred over the past half-century in the ages at which people approach various events and tasks traditionally defining adulthood, factors such as work, marriage, and parenthood continue to be important elements defining adult stages of life.

WORK

Currently, the vast majority of Americans have had work experience by the time they reach late adolescence—typically part-time work as a cashier or retail salesperson, in a fast-food store, or as a manual laborer, lifeguard, or babysitter. The extent of adolescent employment in the United States has risen dramatically since the mid-1970s, when only a small minority of U.S. teenagers held jobs (Mortimer, 2003; Staff & Mortimer, 2007).

By late adolescence, most people have made an effort to narrow their available options for adult work and career by weighing their interests, talents, and values against the amount of training necessary for various careers, their probable financial rewards and status, working conditions, likelihood of getting a job, and so forth. However, even by the last year of high school, adolescents do

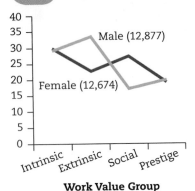

▲ FIGURE 4.15 First-Year College Men and Women Hold Different Values in their Career Decisions. Ryan Duffy and William Sedlacek analyzed responses of 31,000 first-year college men and women over a period of 10 years to questions regarding their career-related values. As this graph shows, men emphasized extrinsic values (i.e., money) and prestige, whereas women emphasized intrinsic interest in the career and social values.

not have a particularly realistic idea of what various careers offer in potential rewards, nor of their various difficulties and downsides (Walls, 2000).

Choosing a career has become an increasingly complex task, and researchers have found changes over time in how college students are making career decisions as well as sex and ethnic group differences in how these decisions are made. For example, as Figure 4.15 shows, men and women differ in their career-related values. A 10-year study of over 30,000 first-year college men and women conducted by Ryan Duffy and William Sedlacek showed that men place higher importance on "extrinsic" rewards, such as high salaries, and are attracted to careers that are high in prestige. Women are more attracted to careers that reflect their intrinsic interests and desire to work with others and be socially useful (Duffy & Sedlacek, 2007).

Duffy and Sedlacek also found ethnic differences: European Americans and Latino/Latinas placed more emphasis on independence and intrinsic interest in the career of their choice, whereas African American and Asian American students were more concerned about extrinsic rewards. There were changes over time as well—between the mid-1990s and mid-2000s, students as a whole become more concerned with intrinsic rather than extrinsic career rewards and less concerned about careers in general.

Why We Work You might think that if you were independently wealthy you would never work again. Perhaps. But consider Walter O'Rourke (pictured here), a train conductor on a New Jersey Transit line.

Mr. O'Rourke claims that there's no place else he'd rather be than calling "All aboard" and punching tickets. Lots of people say things like that about their jobs, and we may take it with a grain of salt. But in Mr. O'Rourke's case, we can have confidence that he's telling the truth, because he actually *could* be elsewhere—for example, on the veranda of one of the two Florida homes he owns, sipping Dom Perignon champagne and watching the sun set. As a lawyer who was part owner of a successful business, Walter O'Rourke became a millionaire decades ago and continues to earn a generous income from his investments. However, being a lifelong train buff, instead of living a life of ease he prefers to walk the aisles of train cars full of commuters for $50,000 per year, punching tickets and asking us to keep our feet off the seats. As he says, "I don't need the money, I need the job" (Mallozzi, 2005).

Although some people are lucky enough to have jobs or careers that are as fulfilling as Walter O'Rourke's, most people work to make ends meet. This doesn't mean that money is all one receives from working, however. Even in jobs consisting of repetitive work with few apparent intrinsic rewards, people form friendships, find spouses, experience feelings of usefulness, and find sources of identity. Even when we work strictly to earn a living we generally derive at least some *meaning* from our work.

MARRIAGE

> *"Marriage is our last, best chance to grow up."*
>
> —Joseph Barth

> *"Marriage is the death of hope."*
>
> —Woody Allen

Is marriage a dying institution in industrialized nations? Without a doubt, the number of households headed by a married couple has declined over the past few decades, and the number of unmarried couples—and parents—has increased dramatically. Looking at the number of adults overall who are married versus those who are unmarried (rather than just heads of households), in 1960, 72% of Americans were married. In 2010, only 52% to 54% of Americans were married (figures vary slightly from different sources; Taylor, 2010; U. S. Bureau of the Census, 2010a; see Figure 4.16). Married couples now head just under 50% of households in the United States, while the number of unmarried couples consisting of a man and woman has increased by almost 100% since the year 2000. In 2000, there were close to 4 million unmarried other-sex couples **cohabiting** in the United States; in 2010 there were close to 8 million (compared with 60 million married couples; U.S. Bureau of the Census, 2010b). Nearly 40% of U.S. births are now to women who are not married (*New York Times*, 2009). In addition, the number of gay and lesbian couples heading households has increased by about 50% since 2000—bringing the number of same-sex couples in the United States close to 1 million (The Williams Institute, 2010). (The sharp increase in the number of same-sex couples reported in census figures, however, is at least in part due to a recent increase in the willingness of gay and lesbian Americans to *report* living as a same-sex couple [Foreman, cited by S. Roberts, 2006]).

Cohabiting ▶ Living together in a romantic relationship without formal marriage.

Interpreting all these statistics can be tricky, however. Do they mean that marriage is dying out? Unlikely. It is far more probable that statistics showing fewer married couples overall reflect the growing trend toward postponing the age of first marriage. Approximately 79% of adult Americans are married by the time they are 35, and 94% marry at least once by the time they turn 50 (U. S. Bureau of the Census, 2005). According to United Nations statistics, the picture is extraordinarily similar throughout the world—the vast majority of people in every nation eventually marry (United Nations Statistics, 2000).

Moreover, although citizens of industrialized nations are postponing the age of first marriage, the majority of the never married still express the desire to marry, list "a happy marriage" as an important life goal, list family life as "extremely important" to them if not the most important thing, expect that one day they will marry, and are "optimistic" about the future of marriage as an institution (Taylor, 2010; Thiessen & Looker, 1999; Thorton & Young-DeMarco, 2001; see Figures 4.17 and 4.18). If those who have been divorced are excluded—this group tends to have a decidedly pessimistic view of marriage—only about 14% of Americans specifically claim they do not want to marry. The rest are either convinced they wish to marry or are "unsure" (Taylor, 2010).

Clearly, not every marrying couple throughout the world is necessarily delighted with the event. People may marry for reasons other than love—for

Current Marital Status, 1960–2008 (%)

■ Never Married ■ Widowed ■ Divorced or Separated ■ Married

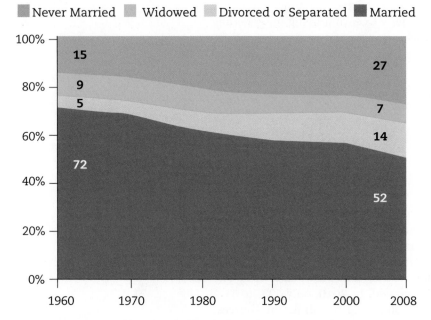

Note: Ages 18 and older. Numbers may not total to 100% due to rounding.

▲ **FIGURE 4.16** Current Marital Status of Americans, 1960–2008. *(Source: Taylor, 2010.)*

The Global Appeal of Family Life

Percent saying family is very important in their life: 2005–2007

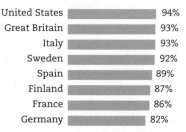

United States	94%
Great Britain	93%
Italy	93%
Sweden	92%
Spain	89%
Finland	87%
France	86%
Germany	82%

▲ **FIGURE 4.17** The Appeal of Family Life: Europe and the U. S., 2005–2007. *(Source: Taylor, 2010.)*

Family Satisfaction, by Marital Status

Percent in each group who say they are . . . with their family life

■ Very satisfied
■ Somewhat satisfied
■ Dissatisfied

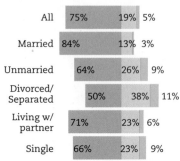

	Very satisfied	Somewhat satisfied	Dissatisfied
All	75%	19%	5%
Married	84%	13%	3%
Unmarried	64%	26%	9%
Divorced/ Separated	50%	38%	11%
Living w/ partner	71%	23%	6%
Single	66%	23%	9%

Note: "Don't know/Refused" responses are not shown.

▲ **FIGURE 4.18** Family Satisfaction According to Marital Status. *(Source: Taylor, 2010.)*

example, out of a sense of familial responsibility, at parental insistence, for financial security, or for other reasons (see Table 4.5). Nonetheless, marriage and the promise of marriage remain important parts of the lives and aspirations of the large majority of adults; and surveys report that marital happiness contributes more to an individual's overall happiness than financial status or satisfaction with work and friendships (Kiecolt-Glaser & Newton, 2001). Moreover, while Western divorce rates did rise throughout most of the 20th century as a result of increasing liberalization of divorce laws, they peaked in the late 1970s and then began to fall. They have been falling slowly but steadily ever since (U.S. National Center for Health Statistics, 1995, 2006, 2010; see Figure 4.19).

Is Marriage Good for You? Why do so many people want to marry? Marriage (and *civil union* for gays and lesbians living in states and nations where these arrangements are legal but marriage is prohibited) promises companionship, intimacy, a committed and supportive relationship, sexual pleasure, children and grandchildren, and increased financial security. Does marriage deliver on these promises? Fortunately, the very large literature on this topic has produced some findings that are by this point indisputable: Virtually all studies, conducted in nations throughout the world, report that, on average, married people of both sexes live longer, are physically healthier, psychologically healthier, more secure financially, and happier than nonmarried people. The children of married people also enjoy some of these advantages (Koball, Moiduddin, Henderson, Goesling, & Besculides, 2010; Graham, Christian, & Kiecolt-Glaser, 2006; Sbarra & Nietert, 2009; Subramanian, Kim, & Kawachi, 2005).

Of course, such studies do not demonstrate that marriage *causes* these beneficial outcomes. At least to some extent it is likely that healthier, more financially secure, and happier people are more appealing as mates and are more likely to marry and less likely to divorce (Koball et al., 2010 ; Stutzer & Frey,

Table 4.5 If a Man (Woman) Had All the Other Qualities You Desired, Would You Marry This Person If You Were Not in Love with Him (Her)?

Love and marriage may—or may not—go together like a horse and carriage. Throughout the world people marry for reasons other than love, although the figures are much higher in some countries than in others.

COUNTRY	RESPONSE		
	YES	UNDECIDED	NO
Australia	4.8%	15.2%	80.0%
Brazil	4.3%	10.0%	85.7%
England	7.3%	9.1%	83.6%
Hong Kong	5.8%	16.7%	77.6%
India	49.0%	26.9%	24.0%
Japan	2.3%	35.7%	62.0%
Mexico	10.2%	9.3%	80.5%
Pakistan	50.4%	10.4%	39.1%
Philippines	11.4%	25.0%	63.6%
Thailand	18.8%	47.5%	33.8%
United States	3.5%	10.6%	85.9%

(Source for table: Hatfield & Rapson, 2005, p. 142; data based on Hatfied & Rapson 1993.)

2006; Umberson, 1992). On the other hand, it would be difficult to argue that people with lower blood pressure are more likely to marry—yet in at least one study, happily married people did show consistently lower blood pressure relative to happy singles with broad networks of social support (Holt-Lunstad, Birmingham, & Jones, 2008). Therefore, there may be something unique to marriage that produces specific beneficial effects. Some of this may be related to the reduced financial strain that often comes with marriage, increased networks of social support, and improvement in health behaviors (particularly among men; Koball et al., 2010).

Whether marriage creates happiness or happiness creates marriage, the association between marriage and positive health and emotional outcomes is substantially lessened—or reversed—in the case of long-term unhappy marriages. Severe long-term marital distress can be as damaging to health and well-being as relative marital harmony can be protective (Hawkins & Booth, 2005; Holt-Lunstad et al., 2008; Kiecolt-Glaser & Newton, 2001).

PARENTHOOD

It is difficult to prepare psychologically for parenthood, because when it arrives it is almost always different from what you expected. The research literature on parenting can be confusing—"costs" and "benefits" of parenting are usually weighed against one another, with some studies stressing costs, and others, benefits. However, whether the transition to parenting is experienced primarily as a joy or a pain, and whether it improves or detracts from the parents' feelings of well-being or relationship with each other, may depend on a great many factors—including the way the study has been conducted (Doss, Rhoades, Stanley, & Markman, 2009; Evenson & Simon, 2005; Nelson, Kushlev, English, Dunn et al., 2013; Nomaguchi & Milkie, 2003; Woo

Marriage Rate	Year	Divorce Rate
9.3%	1900	0.7%
10.3%	1910	0.9%
12.0%	1920	1.6%
9.2%	1930	1.6%
12.1%	1940	2.0%
11.1%	1950	2.6%
8.5%	1960	2.2%
9.3%	1965	2.5%
10.6%	1970	3.5%
10.1%	1975	4.9%
10.6%	1980	5.2%
10.2%	1985	5.0%
9.8%	1990	4.7%
8.9%	1995	4.4%
8.7%	2000	4.1%
7.5%	2005	3.6%
6.8%	2009	3.4%

▲ **FIGURE 4.19 Marriage and Divorce Rates through the 20th Century and Beyond.** *(Source: U. S. National Center for Health Statistics.)*

▶ **New Parents Face Radical Changes in Their Lifestyles.** Sleep deprivation is a common problem, particularly for new mothers, but also for those fathers who share responsibility for feeding and comforting the newborn.

& Raley, 2005). Factors that may (or may not) influence a new parent's experience of parenthood include the following:

- Marital status (married, never-married, cohabiting, separated/divorced)
- Initial level of mental health and expectations for parenthood
- Family history of divorce
- Social status, social support, financial resources and employment status
- Quality of the relationship between the parents
- Gender of the parent (mothers tend to get both the best and the worst of it)
- Gender of the child (New parents with daughters do not fare as well as new parents with sons, perhaps because fathers may tend to be more involved in parenting sons [Doss et al., 2009])
- Temperament of the baby (a "difficult" baby can create a difficult experience for the parents)

One problem in evaluating research on the effects of parenthood on new parents is that the type of sample used, survey questions asked, and statistical analysis chosen can make a very big difference (Lyubomirsky & Boehm, 2010; Nelson et al., 2013).

Three recent studies by Katherine Nelson and her colleagues used elegant methods to test the basic questions of whether a national representative sample of parents 1) were happier overall than nonparents; 2) were happier on a moment-to-moment basis than nonparents; and 3) derived more positive feelings from taking care of their children than from other activities (Nelson et al., 2013). These researchers' results persuasively came down on the "parenthood is positive as a general rule" side: Parents in their studies were happier overall than nonparents, happier moment to moment, and they enjoyed caring for their children on average more than their other daily activities.

However, the effect sizes—the *degree* to which parents were happier than nonparents—were not very large, and the primary beneficiaries in the happiness department were fathers, not mothers, who tend to do the lion's share of the day-to-day hands-on labor of parenthood.

Whether parenting increases or decreases the parent's quality of life, however, only a small number of young people are adamant that they do not want children. In the Pew Research Center poll published in 2010, 95% of 18- to 29-year-olds were either certain they wanted to have children (76%) or were "not sure" (19%; see Figure 4.20). Moreover, consider that the death of a child is considered to be the worst tragedy that can befall an individual in virtually

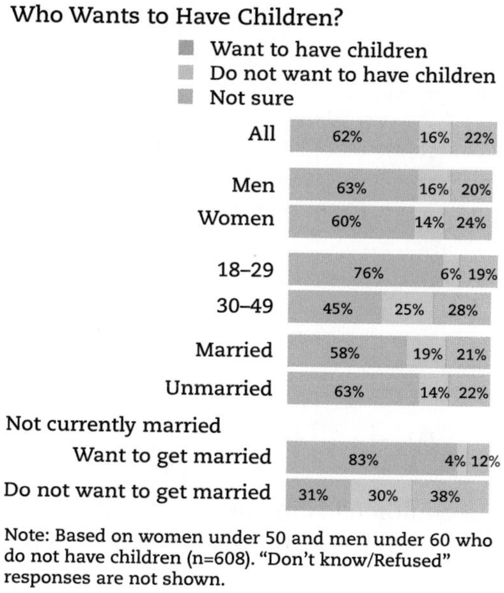

Who Wants to Have Children?

■ Want to have children
■ Do not want to have children
■ Not sure

All	62%	16%	22%
Men	63%	16%	20%
Women	60%	14%	24%
18–29	76%	6%	19%
30–49	45%	25%	28%
Married	58%	19%	21%
Unmarried	63%	14%	22%

Not currently married

Want to get married	83%	4%	12%
Do not want to get married	31%	30%	38%

Note: Based on women under 50 and men under 60 who do not have children (n=608). "Don't know/Refused" responses are not shown.

◀**FIGURE 4.20** **Who Wants to Have Children?** *(Source: Taylor, 2010.)*

all cultures (Lyubomirsky & Boehm, 2010). This suggests at least the possibility that measures of happiness used in studies of parenting may not always be tapping into levels of profound happiness and satisfaction offered by the experience of parenting and may instead be focusing on day-to-day experiences of *pleasure* (Lyubomirsky & Boehm, 2010). Although enduring sleepless nights, repetitive infant crying jags, and the loss of freedom to do as one pleases are obviously unpleasant, one wonders how many parents enduring such discomforts would accept an offer to have their new babies "taken back."

IN SUMMARY

1. Erik Erikson advanced the idea that there are eight psychosocial stages from infancy to old age. For each of these stages a person experiences a characteristic conflict that must be successfully resolved. In adolescence the conflict is identity vs. role confusion, and in early adulthood it is intimacy vs. isolation.

2. The large majority of adolescents have had work experience. Depending on the quality of the work experience, teenage employment can have harmful or beneficial consequences.

3. The vast majority of people desire to marry and do marry. Virtually all studies report that on average, married people of both sexes live longer, are physically healthier, psychologically healthier, more secure financially, and happier than nonmarried people.

4. Parenthood has costs and benefits that differ depending on gender, marital status, quality of marital relationship, initial mental health status and expectations for parenthood, the temperament of the baby, and the type of research study used to measure these variables.

RETRIEVE!

1. For the adolescent, the most important of the conflicts identified by Erik Erikson is _____.

a) generativity vs. stagnation

b) intimacy vs. isolation

c) identity vs. role confusion

d) industry vs. inferiority

2. Married people experience higher levels of happiness and well-being, greater health and financial security, and they live longer than the nonmarried. Does this mean that marriage causes these beneficial effects? Explain your answer.

3. True or false: In the study that compared levels of contentment and happiness among parents as compared with nonparents, it was found that mothers were generally happier than women without children, whereas fathers were less happy than men without children.

How Does the Adult Age?

Exactly how we develop physically in adulthood is in part genetically determined and in part dependent on activity level, nutrition, psychological state, and various socioeconomic factors. However, there comes a point in the life of virtually everyone in their 30s when they realize that changes are beginning to occur that signal the onset of aging. Interesting new lines appear on the face. Somehow, it's a just a bit more difficult to complete that last mile on the morning run. Although overall weight may or may not have changed, that favorite cut of jeans just doesn't fit right anymore because things have *shifted* somehow.

Although there is a general slowing down of nervous system activity as a person ages—and consequent overall slowing down in movement—the degree to which this occurs is in part dependent on personal choices made by the aging individual. To some extent, age is not as good a predictor of vitality and endurance as is *activity level*. The "slowing down" of aging is also represented in positive and negative emotions. Where there was once joyful excitement there is now serenity. Where once there was anxiety and anger there may now be lethargy and depression (Ross & Mirowsky, 2008). It may also be true that a person's own stereotypes and beliefs about what it means to age and what an older person "is like" may influence the degree to which some of the physiological (and psychological) changes of aging actually occur (Levy, 2009).

Physical Changes Are Associated with Aging

Menopause ▶ The cessation of a woman's menstrual cycles—the culminating event of the climacteric.

For most women, the most significant physical change occurring in later adulthood is **menopause**, the cessation of menstrual cycles. Menopause is the culminating event of the *climacteric*—the series of gradual physiological changes lasting about 5 years on average, beginning sometime in the mid-40s. The climacteric represents the woman's natural transition from fertility to infertility. Menopause itself usually occurs somewhere between the late 40s and early 50s, but individuals may vary as a result of genetic, environmental, socioeconomic, and lifestyle factors (for example, earlier menopause is associated with cigarette smoking; Pokoradi, Iversen, & Hannaford, 2011).

Prior to menopause, menstrual periods become shorter or longer, and may become unpredictable in their onset and quality of the menstrual flow. During menopause the woman ceases to menstruate, and the ovaries cease production of the hormones estrogen and progesterone. The cessation of production of these hormones may or may not precipitate various unpleasant symptoms including sweating, "hot flashes," headaches, sleep disturbances, joint pain, mood changes, and skin problems (Cray, Woods, & Mitchell, 2010).

Despite the commonness of the symptoms just described, many women experience menopause and the climacteric as a period of relief from menstrual symptoms, the need to use birth control, and concerns about fertility in general. In fact, cross-cultural research has demonstrated that, while some menopausal symptoms are experienced by women around the globe, the majority of women experience menopause without severe physical or psychological symptoms (Avis et al., 2001).

Cognitive Changes Are Associated with Aging

Cognitive functioning in areas such as memory, reasoning about spatial relations of objects, and perceptual speed begins to decline very gradually in the late 20s or early 30s, and more rapidly beginning at about age 50. However, in areas involving the accumulation of factual knowledge such as vocabulary and verbal memory, cognitive ability actually peaks at age 50 or 60 and then begins to decline (e.g., Lachman, 2001, 2004; Salthouse, 2004, 2006).

Nevertheless, the cognitive changes associated with aging generally occur quite gradually and do not generally lead to actual cognitive impairment in middle age (Willis & Schaie, 1999). While the middle-aged complain bitterly about "senior moments" and other cognitive crises, objective studies show that such declines are not occurring to the extent that many Baby Boomers' subjective experience suggests. The memory of a healthy 60-year-old adult is likely to be closer to that of a 20- or 30-year-old than to that of a 75- or 80-year-old (Cregger & Rogers, 1998).

Moreover, researchers have noted a discrepancy between the cognitive declines of aging adults as measured in laboratory studies and the actual functioning of aging adults in real-world settings, such as employment and family life. As just one fairly obvious example, CEOs of major corporations tend to be in their late 50s or even early 60s, not their 20s or 30s, when most cognitive capabilities as measured in laboratory tests peaks (Salthouse, 2011).

Finally, not all cognitive changes associated with aging are unwelcome. Regardless of declining memory capacity, studies show that as a person ages, her or she pays more attention to positive than to negative stimuli. Indeed, older adults tend to report higher levels of positive mood and well-being, at least until extremely advanced age. They are the happiest of all age groups studied, contrary to stereotypes of "grumpy old men and women" (Ross & Mirowsky, 2008; Stone, Schwartz, Broderick, & Deaton, 2010; Yang, 2008a; 2008b). On the other hand, throughout the world, middle age is associated with the highest levels of *unhappiness*, with the currently middle-aged baby-boom generation being less happy than most previous middle-aged generations (Blanchflower & Oswald, 2008; Yang, 2008b).

WHEN COGNITIVE CHANGES ARE EXTREME: DEMENTIA AND ALZHEIMER'S DISEASE

Although cognitive differences exist between healthy adults in their 80s and those in their 20s, an even greater difference exists between the performance of healthy adults in their 80s and that of a person of any age with *dementia*. **Dementia** involves serious memory loss, confusion, problems with speech and comprehension, and problems negotiating normal activities of daily life. Psychiatric symptoms and apparent personality changes may also appear (Salmon & Bondi, 2009).

Despite stereotypes of the aged, however, dementia does not normally occur with aging. Rates of dementia vary somewhat throughout the world, but even in North America—which has the highest rates of dementia in the world—it is found in no more than about 5% at most of adults by age 79. By age 89, however, the figure rises to about 24%, and about 37% of adults in their 90s and 100s have some form of dementia (Plassman et al., 2007; see also Ferri et al., 2005).

While dementia can result from a number of different diseases and conditions, by far the most common cause is **Alzheimer's disease**, first identified a century ago by neuropathologist Alois Alzheimer and his colleague, psychiatrist Emil Kraepelin. Conducting a postmortem examination following the premature death of a housewife who had shown severe symptoms of dementia

▲ **Menopause May Bring Relief as Well as Symptoms.** Although women throughout the world may experience some degree of symptoms during menopause, for many the relief from concerns over pregnancy and menstrual cycles may outweigh such discomforts.

Dementia (senility) ▶ Age-related severe memory loss, confusion, problems with speech and comprehending others, and difficulty with self-care.

Alzheimer's disease ▶ A neurodegenerative disease characterized by increasingly severe memory loss, confusion, difficulty speaking or comprehending speech, and difficulty with self-care. Alzheimer's disease is the most common type of dementia.

before she died, Alzheimer and Kraepelin found that the woman's brain was covered with clumps of plaque and that brain neurons themselves were infused with unusual tangles of protein. The discoverers agreed to call this pattern of memory loss and brain scarring Alzheimer's disease (Shurkin, 2009). Like other forms of dementia, the likelihood of Alzheimer's disease increases as a person ages. No more than about 2.5% of North Americans under age 79 have Alzheimer's, but as many as 30% of those over 90 have the illness (Plassman et al., 2007), and some estimates are even higher. (See Table 4.6 for a list of common symptoms of Alzheimer's disease.)

Once Alzheimer's begins to progress, the symptoms become more severe. Forgetfulness comes to interfere with daily functions. Alzheimer's patients may forget how to tie their shoes or brush their teeth. Their thinking becomes confused, and they may not recognize members of their own family. They come to have great difficulty speaking or comprehending speech. Eventually, they need 24-hour care (National Institute on Aging, 2006).

However, cognitive problems other than memory loss may predate and possibly contribute to memory problems in early stages of Alzheimer's. In particular, there may be deterioration in *executive functions* (Storandt, 2008). **Executive functions** is a cognitive psychology term used to describe the way the brain manages attention, remains flexible in responding to situations, and plans constructive actions while inhibiting inappropriate actions.

There is no cure for Alzheimer's disease, and its causes are not known with certainty, although it is likely a function of interactions between genes and environmental experience. This interaction may include *epigenetic* effects (the effects of the environment on the way genes are expressed in development, behavior, disease processes, and so forth; Mastroeni et al., 2011; Cacabelos, Fernandez-Novoa, Lombardi, Kubota, & Takeda, 2005). Thus, identical twins share identical DNA, but each co-twin may be more or less vulnerable to the effects of degenerative brain disease over time as a result of environmental experiences. Clearly, then, while aging does not cause Alzheimer's, something about the aging process does involve brain changes that provide "fertile ground" for the development of Alzheimer's, given genetic vulnerability.

Executive functions ▶ Those cognitive functions involved in managing attention, planning constructive action, inhibiting inappropriate action, and remaining flexible in responding to situations.

Table 4.6 Common Symptoms of Alzheimer's Disease

Alzheimer's disease show itself in different ways, depending on the person and the stage of development of the disease. However, here are common symptoms of Alzheimer's disease. As with other psychological disorders, bear in mind that no one of these symptoms—alone or in combination—necessarily means that an individual has the disease. Medical examination is essential for an accurate diagnosis.

- Asking the same questions repeatedly.

- Repeating the same story word for word multiple times.

- Forgetting how to do basic tasks that the person once performed easily, such as cooking, making repairs, and playing cards.

- Problems paying bills or balancing a checkbook (assuming these tasks were not previously difficult).

- Getting lost in familiar places.

- Neglecting personal hygiene habits such as bathing or dressing in clean clothes while insisting on having taken a bath or put on a new outfit.

- Relying on someone else to make decisions—such as what to buy at a supermarket or where to go next—that were easily handled in the past.

(*Source:* Scientific American Mind, *November/December, 2009, p. 60.*)

CAN COGNITIVE DECLINE BE SLOWED?

There is some controversy as to whether the undesirable cognitive effects of aging can be slowed. One difficulty is that much of the research is correlational (epidemiological). Most research does suggest that older adults who maintain an active, intellectually stimulating life suffer less cognitive decline (Hertzog, Kramer, Wilson, & Lindenberger, 2009). Yet, who *are* the adults who lead active, intellectually stimulating lives? Those whose cognitive structures are active and well-functioning! This may have more to do with genes, early environmental experiences, and nutrition than current activity levels. In other words, it may merely be the case that adults who suffer low levels of cognitive impairment . . . suffer low levels of cognitive impairment!

On the other hand, the research is stronger when it comes to the relation of physical exercise to cognitive effects of aging: Evidence derived from research on nonhuman animals as well as humans does strongly suggest that exercise, particularly aerobic exercise, can slow the process of cognitive decline, sometimes substantially (Hertzog et al., 2009). In any case, there is no known harm to attempting to lead a physically active, intellectually stimulating life. It may be difficult to design a study that demonstrates conclusively that this sort of life *causes* a slowing of cognitive decline—but that is not a particularly good reason to refrain from doing so to the best of your ability as you age.

Social and Emotional Changes Involve Loss and Gain

At the outset of this chapter we considered that one key assumption of the lifespan developmental perspective is that development involves gain as well as loss. This is evident in the social and emotional lives of those in the middle and later years. Typical *losses* of middle to late-middle adulthood may (but may not) include the following:

- The exit of grown children from the home
- Reduced health, physical vitality, cognitive ability, and sexual attractiveness
- Loss of employment status and income
- Loss of networks of friendships due to death, geographical relocation, or reduced motivation to attend social events
- The realization that some of the dreams of one's youth are truly unlikely ever to come to pass. (A personal example of this final item: This morning I awoke for the first time with the *certain knowledge* that I would *never* become a film director!)

Gains may (but may not) include the following):

- Increased leisure time
- Increased quality of relationships with one's spouse and children
- Entry of grandchildren into one's life
- Less unpredictability in emotional life, and less frequent negative emotions generally (until extremely advanced age)
- Achievement of long-term career goals with increased income (in some professions this may be more likely than the loss of status and income that tends to occur in other careers)
- A calmer perspective on achievement, success, and matters of romance and sexuality
- Decreased aggression in men and an end to reproductive concerns in women
- Increased feelings of freedom, control, and wisdom.

As Margie Lachman (2004) emphasizes in her review of development in midlife, how all of this plays out is highly dependent on historical and social factors, gender, ethnicity, social class, and personality variables. Researchers

▲ **Alzheimer's Disease Does Not Happen Only to the Aged.** Although symptoms of Alzheimer's disease are relatively unusual prior to the age of 80, those in middle age can acquire early-onset Alzeheimer's. At Northwestern University, an unusual "buddy" program pairs one medical researcher with a specific Alzheimer's patient in a partnership involving friendship as well as research. The experience of Alzheimer's can be made less lonely and distressing through the involvement of family and friends.

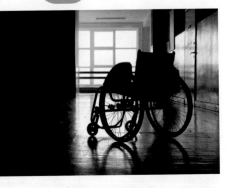

▲ **The Experience of Dying Is a Process.** Although the dying may often experience the emotions described by Kübler-Ross, the notion that these emotions invariably occur, and do so in sequence, has been abandoned.

have isolated three variables that appear to contribute most importantly to the quality of life for older adults, and there are no surprises here: Well-being in older adults is highly dependent on having sufficient financial resources to meet one's basic needs, enjoying good health, and experiencing a sense of meaning and purpose in life (Low & Molzahn, 2007).

Death Is a Process

No one can pinpoint with certainty the moment that life begins. If one believes that life begins at conception, conception is still a process, not a specific moment. No one can specify the instant that it has occurred. And if one believes that life begins at birth, it is still the case that birth is a process, not a specific moment. At some point all reasonable people will agree that a person has been born and is alive, but there will be disagreements as to the precise moment that the person began to exist.

It is the same with death. All reasonable people will agree that a person buried for several months is dead (I should hope so, anyway), but differences of opinion are possible as to the precise moment that death occurred. This is because various bodily systems cease to function at different rates, and whether the cessation in functioning is permanent is sometimes an open question. People are occasionally brought "back to life" after one or more of these systems has apparently "died." Such issues are at the core of contemporary debates and legal cases involving the right to die (Berger, 1993).

The psychological experience of dying is also a process. For those who die in their sleep or who die instantaneously, the dying process is probably not a difficult one. But for those of us who suspect (or know) we are dying of an illness, the process of dying is a challenge. In 1969, Swiss psychiatrist Elisabeth Kübler-Ross contributed substantially to our understanding of the experience of dying in her book *On Death and Dying*. Kübler-Ross outlined a series of stages she believed invariably occur during the process of dying: 1) *denial* ("This can't be happening"); 2) *anger* ("Why is this happening to *me*?"); 3) *bargaining* ("Please God, I'll stop drinking—just give me a few more years"); 4) *depression* ("I don't want to see anyone—I'm losing everything that is important to me"); and 5) *acceptance* that death is an inevitable outcome. At this final stage, the person may achieve a measure of peace prior to dying. However, throughout all the stages, according to Kübler-Ross, runs a thread of *hope*.

Kübler-Ross's model was highly influential, and her work sensitized the medical and mental health professions to the importance of understanding the inner experience of dying. Ultimately, her stage theory was applied to all experiences of grief, for example, the death of a loved one (rather than one's own impending death). However, most theorists no longer accept the idea that grief over one's impending death or that of a loved one occurs in stages (Kastenbaum, 2000). In fact, the first genuinely empirical attempt to validate Kübler-Ross's model failed to do so (Maciejewski, Zhang, Block, & Prigerson, 2007). Indeed, in this longitudinal study, the initial grief response was most typically acceptance rather than denial and anger, and the level of acceptance grew over time. Although the dying may often experience the emotions described by Kübler-Ross, the notion that these emotions invariably occur, and do so in sequence, has been abandoned.

THE DYING PROCESS IS AFFECTED BY CULTURE

As shown in Figure 4.21, social, economic, and cultural factors affect life expectancy around the world. Culture and socioeconomic realities also shape the experience of dying in a great many ways. A cross-cultural look at funerals and wakes makes this abundantly clear. As Metcalf and Huntington (cited by Sigelman & Rider, 2006, p. 487) observe: "funerals are the occasion for avoiding people or holding parties, for fighting or having sexual orgies, for weeping or laughing, in a thousand different combinations."

Scott Murray and his colleagues conducted extensive interviews with patients dying of cancer in Scotland and Kenya (Murray, Grant, Grant, & Kendall, 2003). They found profound differences in the subjective experiences of patients in the two countries. In Scotland, a nation with universal health care and social security benefits, patients and their caregivers were primarily concerned with the prospect of imminent death. As one patient explained, "You're wondering if you're going to see tomorrow. When I first was told, that was the first thing that went through my head, How long?" (p. 369). The Scottish patients, all of whom had access to potent pain medication, found themselves battling worries about their families and feelings of isolation and personal despair rather than personal discomfort. They did not feel that their spiritual needs were being met.

In Kenya, a nation with no universal health care system or social security, few benefits for patients, no affordable pain medication, and a lack of easily available specialist or home care, patients were far more worried about bearing the pain of life than they were about their impending death. The pain was "constant and unbearable" for many (p. 370). As one patient put it, "There are times when the pain is so severe that I feel like hanging myself in the house to die."

Unlike the Scottish, who often experienced anger about their condition, the Kenyans tended to accept their fate ("There is nothing that being angry can achieve" [p. 370]). Also in contrast to the Scottish, the Kenyans felt well supported by their families and communities, and by their religion. These patients did feel that their emotional and spiritual needs were being met. It was their medical needs that were grossly underserved.

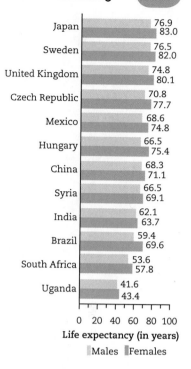

▲ **FIGURE 4.21 Life Expectancy for Men and Women in 12 Nations.** (*Source for data: Kinsella & Gist, 1998, cited in Sigelman & Rider, 2006, p. 488.*)

IN SUMMARY

1. The climacteric is the gradual process of transition for women from fertility to infertility. The climacteric culminates in menopause, the cessation of menstrual cycles.

2. Cognitive functioning in abilities such as memory and processing speed begins to decline very gradually in the late 20s or early 30s, and decreases more rapidly beginning at about age 50. With regard to the accumulation of knowledge, cognitive ability peaks at about age 50 or 60 and then begins to decline.

3. Dementia involves serious memory loss, confusion, and problems with speech and comprehension. Dementia is not a normal part of aging. The most common cause of dementia is Alzheimer's disease.

4. Social and emotional changes in middle and late adulthood involve gain as well as loss.

5. Death is a process. The meaning and experience of dying vary greatly from person to person and culture to culture. Most current theorists do not believe that a person passes through specific psychological stages as part of the dying process, as once believed.

RETRIEVE!

1. What causes the various unpleasant symptoms some women experience during menopause?

a) The cessation of menstruation

b) The ovaries cease to produce estrogen and progesterone

c) The psychological stress of menopause

d) Increase in the production of testosterone

2. True or false: The memory of a healthy 60-year old adult is likely to be closer to that of a 25-year-old than a 75-year-old.

3. True or false: Levels of happiness and well-being tend to decline as a person slips into old age.

4. True or false: Approximately one-third of all adults show symptoms of dementia by the age of 79.

5. Deterioration of which types of cognitive functions may precede symptoms of memory impairment in Alzheimer's disease?

    a) Fluid intelligence   **c)** Numerical fluency

    b) Executive functions   **d)** Emotional intelligence

6. Describe the five stages of dying proposed by Kübler-Ross.

Looking Back

Chapter 4 in Review

WHY STUDY DEVELOPMENT?

- Developmental psychology is the study of change and continuity over the life span. The lifespan perspective views development as a lifelong process, associated with loss as well as gain, determined by many causes, and characterized by plasticity.

HOW DOES THE UNBORN EMBRYO BECOME A NEWBORN INFANT?

- Conception occurs when one of the sperm released by the male pierces the protective covering of the female secondary oocyte. The oocyte divides into two cells, the ovum and the second polar body. The nuclei of the sperm and ovum fuse, producing the zygote. The zygote attaches itself to the lining of the uterus, and after rapid cell division the zygote enters the embryonic stage. At about 8 to 9 weeks after conception the embryo comes to be known as a fetus.
- The fetus faces challenges including exposure to teratogens that may cause congenital disorders such as fetal alcohol syndrome.
- Newborn infants have perceptual competencies not previously recognized. They may recognize their mother's face, voice, and scent; and distinguish language from other sound patterns.

HOW DOES THE INFANT BECOME A CHILD?

- Brain development in the first months of life is intense and rapid. Many trillions of synapses are formed, but then undergo synaptic pruning. Milestones of motor development vary from infant to infant.
- Temperament and attachment are key facets of social and emotional development in infants. Temperament refers to an infant's initial tendency to respond in relatively consistent ways; its dimensions include effortful control, negative emotionality, and extraversion. Infant temperament is largely stable at least through toddlerhood. Temperament is influenced by genetic heredity and environmental experiences.
- Attachment is the intimate bond between infant and caregiver beginning at about age 6 months. Attachment theory was formulated as a blend of psychoanalytic and evolutionary theory. Using the "strange situation," Mary Ainsworth characterized infants as developing either secure, insecure-ambivalent, or avoidant attachment.
- Infants come into the world prepared to develop certain cognitive competencies. Infants understand that objects are solid, that they will only move through contact, and that they travel through space in a continuous path. Infants also appear to understand very basic numerical calculation. Although nativists suggest that such competencies by be already intact at birth, empiricists hold that they are primarily developed through experience.
- Jean Piaget, founder of the constructivist theory of childhood cognitive development, proposed that each child actively "constructs" an understanding of the world based on experience. He believed that these understandings develop in distinct stages through the use of age-specific schemas. The developmental stages identified by Piaget are the sensorimotor stage, the concrete operations stage, and the formal operations stage. Piaget has

Looking Back continued

been criticized for overemphasizing the notion of stages, for underestimating the capabilities of very young children, and for describing development without explaining it.

HOW DOES THE CHILD BECOME ADOLESCENT?

- The length of adolescence differs markedly among societies and cultures. Puberty is a process that begins at about age 6 or 7 when the adrenal glands begin to produce steroid hormones, peaking with adrenarche at about age 10. Gonadarche usually occurs several years later.
- The adolescent brain is a "work in progress." Throughout the teen years, the quantity of white matter increases, while gray matter decreases in density. This process occurs relatively late in the prefrontal cortex, but early on in the limbic system. At least 50 percent of adolescents in Western nations drive drunk, use illegal drugs, have unprotected sex, or commit minor crimes. Because synaptic pruning is extensive in the adolescent brain, adolescents shape their own brain development—and consequently their habits and lifelong skills—by their behavior, which to some degree "hardwires" their brains.
- Judith Rich Harris initiated a major controversy when she proposed that adolescents are primarily socialized by their peers, the media, and other influences outside the home, with parents playing a relatively minor role. Harris uses well-known findings in Diana Baumrind's research on styles of parenting behavior to demonstrate how the nurture assumption produces misleading interpretations of psychological research.
- During early adolescence, day-to-day conflicts with parents tend to increase. However, only 5% to 15% of adolescents experience extreme personal problems and severe conflict with parents. Peer relationships and romantic relationships assume great importance in adolescence. Peers influence one another in positive as well as negative directions, and what appears to be peer influence may sometimes be peer selection.
- Lawrence Kohlberg's cognitive developmental theory of moral reasoning describes stages of development of moral reasoning, much in the manner of Piaget's stages of cognitive development. Positive psychologist Jonathan Haidt's social intuitionist theory of morality proposes that the moral sense is an evolutionary adaptation or instinct, and that there exist five universal foundations of morality: caring and avoiding harm, fairness/justice, group loyalty, respect for authority, and purity/sanctity.

HOW DOES THE ADOLESCENT BECOME ADULT?

- Unlike societies with coming-of-age rituals, modern Western society assumes that adolescents move seamlessly into early adulthood. However, early adulthood is a relatively new stage of life that did not exist for previous generations.
- Erik Erikson proposed eight psychosocial stages of life from infancy to old age, each centered on a characteristic conflict that needs to be resolved in order that the person may pass successfully to the next stage. For Erikson, adolescence deals with identity vs. role confusion, young adulthood with intimacy vs. isolation, and middle adulthood with generativity vs. stagnation.
- Work, marriage, and parenthood continue to be important elements defining adult stages of life. Choosing careers is a much more complex task than it once was. The number of households headed by a married couple has declined, but the vast majority of people worldwide consider marriage as an important life goal. Research suggests that whether parenthood is primarily positive or negative depends on a variety of factors.

HOW DOES THE ADULT AGE?

- A general slowing down of nervous system activity and movement happens with age, but the degree to which this occurs depends partly on the individual. For most women the most significant physical change in late adulthood is menopause.
- Cognitive functions such as memory, spatial reasoning, and perceptual speed begin to decline very gradually in early adulthood and decrease more rapidly beginning around age 50. However, factual knowledge such as vocabulary actually peaks at about age 50 or 60. Nevertheless, cognitive decline in late adulthood can be very rapid and marked.
- Older people report the highest levels of happiness of all groups studied (until extremely advanced age), and aging involves gain as well as loss. Dementia is characterized by serious memory loss, confusion, problems with speech and comprehending others, and problems negotiating normal activities of daily life; it may also involve psychiatric symptoms and apparent personality changes.
- Death is a psychological and physiological process, not a specific moment. Beliefs that dying involves an invariant series of five stages (as proposed by Elisabeth Kübler-Ross) are not supported by research. Dying is also strongly affected by culture and socioeconomic status.

Key Terms

Accommodation, 174
Adolescence, 181
Adrenarche, 181
Alzheimer's disease, 205
Assimilation, 174
Attachment, 167
Authoritarian parents, 184
Authoritative parents, 184
Child-to-parent effects, 185
Cognitive developmental theory of moral reasoning, 187
Cohabiting, 199
Conception, 158
Concrete operations stage, 177
Congenital malformation, 159
Conservation, 176
Constructivism, 174
Conventional morality, 188
Critical period, 163
Dementia, 205
Developmental psychology, 157
Developmental stages, 174
Early adulthood, 194
Effortful control, 165

Egocentric, 176
Embryo, 158
Empiricism, 174
Endometrium, 158
Executive functions, 206
Extraversion, 166
Fertilization, 158
Fetal alcohol syndrome (FAS), 159
Fetus, 158
Formal operations stage, 178
Generativity vs. stagnation, 197
Gonadarche, 181
Identity vs. role confusion, 196
Identity, 196
Imprinting, 168
Infancy, 163
Internal working model, 168
Intimacy vs. isolation, 196
Lifespan perspective, 157
Menopause, 204
Morality, 187
Nativism, 173
Negative emotionality, 166
Nonshared experiences, 167

Nurture assumption, 184
Object permanence, 175
Ovum, 158
Permissive parents, 184
Placenta, 158
Postconventional morality, 188
Preconventional morality, 188
Preoperational stage, 176
Psychosocial stages, 196
Reflex, 161
Schemas, 174
Secondary oocyte, 158
Sensorimotor stage, 175
Social intuitionism, 190
Sperm, 158
Survival reflex, 161
Synaptic pruning, 163
Temperament, 165
Teratogen, 159
Theory of mind, 176
Umbilical cord, 158
Uterus, 158
Zygote, 158

Test Yourself

1. How does the lifespan perspective differ from that of most of developmental psychology throughout the 20th century?
2. What are two of the most serious teratogens threatening the developing embryo and fetus? What specific problems can result when pregnant mothers ingest these substances?
3. Describe at least one previously unsuspected perceptual and one social skill possessed by newborn infants.
4. What is the term used to describe a stage of development during which the brain is particularly sensitive to specific types of events or stimulation, and must experience these events or stimulation to develop normally?
   a) sensitization
   b) critical juncture
   c) critical period
   d) assimilation
5. What are the three dimensions of temperament, according to Mary Rothbart? Characterize each one.
6. Name the three attachment styles identified by Mary Ainsworth. How do infants with each characteristic attachment style respond to the strange situation?
7. What are the possible costs and benefits of early child care?
8. When a child fits a new experience into a preexisting schema, it is known as _____. When a child alters a schema to incorporate new knowledge it is known as _____.
9. Name Piaget's four developmental stages. Describe each one in a general way—give age ranges, and characteristic cognitive limitations and newfound abilities for each stage.
10. Provide at least two criticisms of Piaget's theory.
11. Elizabeth Spelke discovered that small infants make the same three fundamental assumptions of physical attributes of inanimate objects that adults make. What are these assumptions?
12. What is the theory of mind? How does the false-belief test measure development of theory of mind?
13. Why do some psychologists believe that the specific ways in which the adolescent brain develops may partially explain the reckless behavior often seen in adolescence?
14. What is the nurture assumption? According to Judith Rich Harris, developmental psychologists overlook at least two possible alternative explanations for findings that children's behavior is associated with various parental rearing behaviors. What are these two alternative explanations?
15. What is the difference between peer pressure and peer selection? How might each of these affect whether an adolescent decides to smoke or use drugs?
16. Name and characterize the four stages of moral reasoning described by Lawrence Kohlberg.
17. How does Jonathan Haidt's social intuitionist theory of moral judgment differ from previous ideas about morality? What are the five foundations of morality as proposed by Haidt?
18. Name the characteristic conflicts of adolescence, early adulthood, and middle adulthood, according to Erik Erikson.
19. Most studies report similar findings about the association between

marriage and various measures of mental and physical health, financial status, and longevity. What are these findings?

20. True or false: The majority of adults living to their 90s develop dementia.

21. True or false: Rates of mild cognitive impairment in aging adults have declined sharply over the last decade.

22. Describe the events of menopause and some possible symptoms that may result. Why is the notion of andropause controversial?

23. What is the most common cause of dementia?

24. What are some of the gains and losses involved in the process of aging?

25. Why is death a process rather than an event?

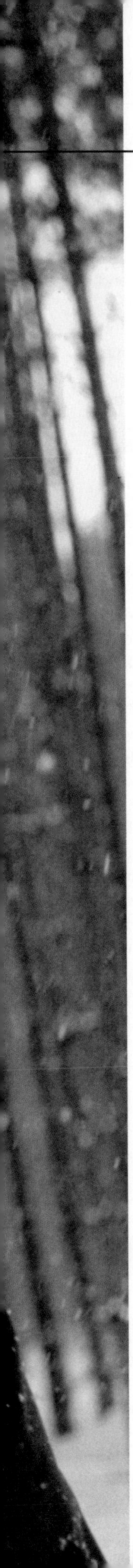

5

perception
and the Senses

Chapter Outline

FREEZE FRAME

Take a good look at the paintings reproduced here. They are exceptionally unusual in the history of the art world. They were all painted by an artist who has been blind from the moment of his birth. Esref Armagan has never seen fruit, windmills, lutes, lamps, candles, or blankets, yet he can paint all of these things vividly. He has never seen light, shading, color, or perspective, but he utilizes all of these in his work. Moreover, Armagan was not trained by a sighted person to produce paintings such as these. Although he gains information about visual imagery by talking to sighted people and asking questions ("Are shadows the same color as the object that creates them?"), Armagan has learned to draw entirely on his own. Born blind and impoverished in Turkey during the 1950s, as

a child Armagan passed the time sketching, first in dirt and then on paper. By age 18 he had taught himself to paint with his fingers using oils and canvas (Motluk, 2005).

Recently, psychologists from the University of Toronto and Harvard University put Armagan through a series of tests to explore the breadth of his ability. For example, they presented him with a series of objects he could feel—a cube, a cone, and so forth—but asked him to draw them as if he were in different locations: hovering above the objects, sitting to the right and then left of them, sitting opposite them. They asked him to draw objects rotated in various directions or stretching out in the distance in rows, difficult tasks for any graphic artist (J. M. Kennedy & Juricevic, 2006). As one of the researchers, John Kennedy of the University of Toronto, exclaimed, "My breath was taken away" (quoted in Motluk, 2005).

The existence of Armagan's work poses intriguing questions for scientists studying perception and the senses. How has the painter developed a "mind's eye" capable of realizing precise visual imagery and color when he has never been able to see and cannot perceive light? Indeed, as Alison Motluk (2005) suggests, the existence of Armagan's work threatens to extend the very meaning of "seeing." For example, researchers using brain imaging techniques with Armagan found that when the artist painted, areas of his visual cortex "lit up" virtually to the same degree as if he were a sighted person viewing something (Amedi et al., 2008; see Figure 5.1). Is Armagan "seeing"?

Sensing is the process by which our sense organs receive information about the world and convert this information into neural signals to be sent to the brain. *Perception* is what our brains make of these signals. The linking of these two processes forms the foundation of our psychological world and is the subject of this chapter.

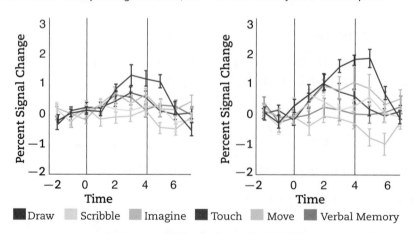

▲ **FIGURE 5.1 Changes in Esref Armagan's Brain as He Draws.** This figure compares changes in the activation of visual processing areas of Esref Armagan's brain as he draws an object (blue line); scribbles on a piece of paper (aqua); imagines an object (brown); touches an object (red); moves an object (brown); and recalls the name of an object (green). There is substantially greater activation of these visual processing areas when Armagan draws the object in comparison to all other conditions. From the perspective of the neuron, something similar to "seeing" occurs when Armagan draws. *(Source: Adapted from Amedi et al., 2008.)*

How Do Sensing and Perceiving Differ?

How do we know what is real and what is not? At age 7, my daughter Naima was for a time preoccupied with this question, wondering if everything that was happening to her was just a dream, and demanding assurance that it was not. I would explain that we don't experience certain types of *sensory* experiences in dreams—we don't feel pain, for example, or smell the pizza about which we may be dreaming (Symons, 1993). I assured her that if she is experiencing a headache or smelling our cat's stinky breath, she cannot be dreaming. Of course, she would usually just turn around and say something like, "Supposing I'm just dreaming you're saying that and it's not really true?" At that point I would realize that I was in for another long afternoon of philosophical discourse with my daughter.

Perhaps we cannot know what is real and what is not in a way that would fully satisfy every philosophical argument, even those thrown out by 7-year-olds. However, it is through the evidence of our senses and perceptions that we come to *believe* we know what is real and what is not. **Sensing** occurs when our sense organs receive raw physical or chemical energy from the natural world—light through the eyes; sound waves (vibrations) through the ears; chemical properties of objects through the nose and taste buds; heat, cold, and pressure through the skin. This received energy is then converted into neural signals, a process known as **transduction**. The signals are then sent to the brain for interpretation. **Perception** occurs when the brain actually does the work of organizing and interpreting transduced sensory signals—when we actually *see* the face, *hear* the sound, *taste* the sweetness, and *feel* the heat (see Figure 5.2).

Thus, to some degree, the often-used term "sensation" can be misleading because it seems to imply an experience of some sort ("When you tickle my back I get a weird sensation," or "I love the sensation of ice cream sliding down my throat on a hot day."). Indeed, what we often call "sensations" in casual speech are actually perceptions. *All conscious experiences derived from physical or chemical information flowing through our sense organs are perceptions.* Without the interpretation of sensory information by the brain there is no experience of "sensation" at all and no ability to engage in activity directed toward any sort of goal—from taking a few steps in a room to earning a Ph.D. So remember: "sensing" is something that happens to your sense organs and neurons; "perception" is something that happens to *you*.

Psychophysicists Study the Relationship between Stimuli and Perception

In the course of ordinary experience, sensing and perception are seamlessly linked. However, it is useful to separate them for scientific purposes. Researchers who study the relationship between physical stimuli and how they are perceived through the senses are known as **psychophysicists**. The distinction between sensing and perception becomes clear when one considers unusual disorders such as *motion blindness*—the inability to perceive movement, a condition which may result from brain damage to the visual cortex or certain other cortical regions (Cooper et al., 2012; Nawrot, 2003; Zeki, 1991). In motion blindness, sensing and perception are no longer seamlessly linked—the visual *sense organs* (eyes) are working perfectly well, performing their task of receiving light and transducing visual images into electrochemical signals. However, visual *perception*—the meaning accorded these signals by the brain—is out of order. Individuals who have acquired motion blindness can see perfectly well—if everything is still. However, when something moves,

Sensation ▶ The receiving of raw physical or chemical energy through the sense organs.

Transduction ▶ The conversion of raw physical or chemical energy into sensory signals.

Perception ▶ Organization and interpretation of sensory signals by the brain.

Psychophysicists ▶ Scientists who study sensation and perception.

▶ **FIGURE 5.2** The Road to Perception.

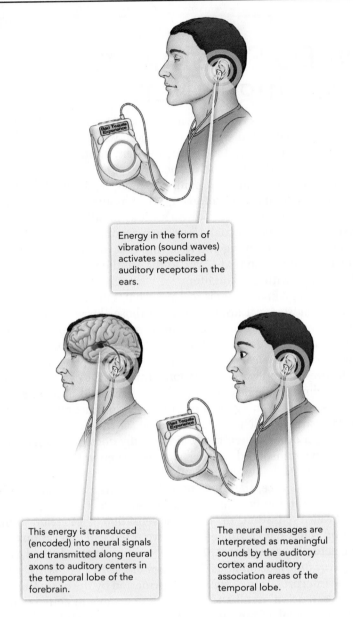

Energy in the form of vibration (sound waves) activates specialized auditory receptors in the ears.

This energy is transduced (encoded) into neural signals and transmitted along neural axons to auditory centers in the temporal lobe of the forebrain.

The neural messages are interpreted as meaningful sounds by the auditory cortex and auditory association areas of the temporal lobe.

it is perceived in a series of "freeze frame" snapshots. For example, watching a single black Porsche glide down the road is watching a series of images of many black Porsches lined up behind one another. As depicted in Figure 5.3, even pouring a cup of coffee can be a daunting task for those with motion blindness.

Even if both your sensory and perceptual systems are in working order, however, there is no guarantee that you will perceive a sensory stimulus. For one thing, a stimulus such as a sound must occur within the normal range our sense organs evolved to detect. Because dog whistles are designed to produce sound waves at *frequencies* too high for human ears to perceive, my neighbor's dog whistle does not disturb me at 7:00 a.m., and would not even if she blew it in my bedroom (although my wife and I might be astonished to see her there). Similarly, I would be unable to use *echolocation* to find my way around a pitch-dark cave or locate my dinner as do bats. They navigate and find prey by sending calls out and detecting the resultant sound waves bouncing off solid objects (Jones, 2005).

Another problem is one of simple *strength* rather than range. Even if a stimulus is within normal human perceptual range, it must be strong enough to

▲ **FIGURE 5.3 In Motion Blindness Perception Is Disordered, but Sensing Is in Order.** In motion blindness, the world is perceived as a sequence of "freeze frames" or snapshots. The fluid from the tip of the coffeepot to the cup appears as a stream of coffee frozen in space. By the time a motion-blindness patient perceives the image of a full cup, the cup is already overflowing.

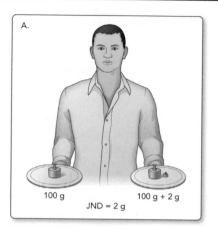

A.

100 g   100 g + 2 g
JND = 2 g

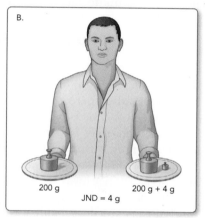

B.

200 g   200 g + 4 g
JND = 4 g

◀**FIGURE 5.4 The Just-Noticeable Difference (JND).** In the top drawing (*A*) the man can detect the difference between a relatively light standard weight (100 g) and another weight just 2 grams heavier. However, in the bottom drawing (*B*), the standard weight is much heavier (200 g), so the comparison weight must also be heavier for a difference to be detected. Notice, however, that the *ratio* of the JND remains constant: The comparison weight in the bottom must be *twice* as heavy as that in the top to be noticed when compared to a standard weight that is also *twice* as heavy.

be detected. In order for you to hear the couple in the apartment next door to you arguing, they have to be going at it loudly enough for your ears to hear. What psychologists call an **absolute threshold** of stimulus intensity must be reached. The absolute threshold is the minimum intensity of a stimulus necessary for it to be detected by a human or nonhuman animal at least 50% of the time. Absolute thresholds for each sense differ from person to person, and may also differ under various sorts of psychological conditions—for example, a person's emotional state, expectations for a situation, or how much attention he or she is directing toward a particular stimulus. Thus, commonly used approximations for the absolute threshold of various senses may be misleading. For example, it is often said that the absolute threshold for vision is equivalent to "a candle flame seen at 30 miles on a dark, clear night." Yet, the absolute threshold for a person walking alone on a clear, dark, but unfamiliar and *scary* road is likely to be different from that for a person walking home on the same clear, dark night after a pleasant meal at a neighbor's house.

There is a different sort of threshold involved in detecting *differences* between two sensory stimuli—for example, in the lengths of two lines, brightness of two lights, or loudness of two sounds. This is known as the **just noticeable difference (JND)**. The JND was first described by an early psychophysicist, Ernst Weber (1795–1878). Weber noticed something interesting about the JND for weights. When people were asked to lift a particular weight (termed the *standard*) and then to lift a comparison weight that differed somewhat in heaviness, their ability to detect a difference between the two weights was highly dependent upon the weight of the standard. If the weight of the standard (the first weight) was light, people were able to detect even slight differences between the standard and a heavier comparison weight. But if the standard was heavy, a much greater difference between the two weights was necessary before a difference could be detected (see Figure 5.4).

Absolute threshold ▶ The minimum intensity necessary for a stimulus to be detected by the appropriate sense organ at least 50% of the time.

Just noticeable difference (JND) ▶ The smallest difference between two stimuli that can be detected by the appropriate sense organ at least 50% of the time.

Weber found that this relationship was true of the JND applied to the other senses. For example, the ability to notice a difference between the magnitudes of two lamp lights is proportionate to the magnitude of the first lamp (termed the *standard*). It would be easy to notice the difference between a 75-watt bulb and a 100-watt bulb, but not between a 300-watt bulb and a 325-watt bulb, even though the difference is 25 watts in both cases. If you think about it, you can see that this principle operates in many aspects of ordinary life unrelated to sensing and perceiving. For example, you might walk a half-mile to avoid paying an extra $3.98 for some blank CDs to make music mixes, but you would probably not even notice a $3.98 difference when buying the computer you intended to use to burn the CDs. Thus, for any given stimulus, the JND is always directly proportionate to the level of the standard. Weber's colleague and the founder of psychophysics, Gustav Fechner (1801–1887), expressed this idea in mathematical terms, calling it **Weber's law**.

Signal Detection Theory Acknowledges the "Human" Factor

The concepts of absolute threshold and JND were important contributions to understanding perception, but they do not fully explain how stimuli come to be detected. This is because Weber and Fechner failed to factor in a most important variable: *human judgment and bias*. A simple example: When I was training intensively in the martial arts in New York City I could detect the sounds of footsteps of strangers walking up behind me while they were still some distance away. This is because my attention was strongly focused on the possibility of physical attack. But nowadays, since I'm no longer practicing martial arts, you'd probably have to clear your throat loudly a quarter-inch from my ear before I would be aware of you on the street. Thus, under certain psychological conditions, weak signals may be detected because the person judges them to be important or is biased in favor of recognizing them. Under other conditions, even strong signals may go undetected. **Signal detection theory** emerged to help understand the interaction between human judgment and bias and the detection of stimuli (Macmillan & Creelman, 2005).

Signal detection theorists have found two specific ways in which human judgment and predisposition interfere in signal detection: *noise* and *response bias*. **Noise** acknowledges that sensory stimuli do not occur in a vacuum—they occur within a specific context consisting of other, competing, sensory stimuli and various psychological states. An expected knock in a quiet dorm room will be much easier to detect than an unexpected knock that occurs while a loud party is going on next door.

Response bias means that for any given stimulus one may be biased in favor of detection or against detection. Bias can result from one's motivations and expectations in a given situation. If you were in your dorm eagerly expecting your romantic partner to knock on the door, you might find yourself mistaking all sorts of irrelevant sounds for a knock, and the chances of your failing to hear the actual knock would approach zero. On the other hand, if you were studying hard, focused upon your work, and hoping no one would come by to bother you, you might be biased against detecting a knock and fail to respond when a knock actually occurred.

Sensory Adaptation Reduces Sensitivity to Stimuli

Another influence on the detection of stimuli is **sensory adaptation**, the tendency for sensitivity to stimuli to be lessened over time during continuous exposure. I once had a friend who used to burn a particular brand of pine-sandalwood incense in her home that I found irresistible. I bought some, hoping my home would smell as fabulous as hers did. However, it seemed that no matter how much I burned, my house never smelled of incense except for a

Weber's law ▶ A mathematical expression of the idea that for any given stimulus, the just noticeable difference (JND) is always proportionate to the level of the standard stimulus.

Signal detection theory ▶ A theory that attempts to explain how stimuli are detected by factoring in the variables of human judgment and bias.

Noise ▶ In signal detection theory, noise acknowledges that detection of sensory stimuli may be affected by the occurrence of other, competing stimuli, or by varying psychological states of the perceiver.

Response bias ▶ In signal detection theory, response bias refers to the fact that a person may be biased in favor of, or against, the detection of a stimulus.

Sensory adaptation ▶ The tendency for one's sensitivity to stimuli to be lessened over time during continuous exposure.

◄ **Sensory Adaptation While Cooking.** If you've ever done any cooking, you might have noticed that after standing over steaming pots or sizzling pans for an hour or two, you are not all that hungry come dinnertime—or that, if you are, the food just doesn't taste quite as good as you thought it would. The problem is that in constantly inhaling the aroma of the food, you are experiencing sensory adaptation. Your sense of smell has adapted to the aroma of the food and has "tired" of it. Because smell and taste are intimately connected, the pleasure of eating is often lessened for the cook.

few minutes first thing in the morning. The answer to this riddle is sensory adaptation. When visiting my friend, I walked in off the street right into the floating aroma of the incense. In my own home, however, I was drenched in the scent all day, so my perception quickly became desensitized to it. You experience sensory adaptation every time you get into a blisteringly hot bath, only to have it seem to turn cool on you within a very short time.

Subliminal Perception Occurs below the Level of Awareness

Finally, it is sometimes possible to perceive a stimulus unconsciously, or *implicitly*, when it is either below the absolute threshold or presented too briefly to reach conscious awareness. This is known as **subliminal perception**. For example, a person may be temporarily affected by messages or images viewed on a screen even if these messages or images are flashed much too briefly to reach conscious awareness. Psychologist Morris Eagle (1959) asked research participants to judge the personality of a boy by looking at his picture. However, half the participants were first subliminally flashed an image of the boy engaged in an aggressive act (throwing a birthday cake) and the other half were flashed an image of the boy smiling and holding the cake. The group that had been flashed the subliminal image of the boy holding the cake gave a much more positive evaluation of the boy's personality.

Subliminal perception was also demonstrated by Robert B. Zajonc (pronounced *Zy*-ounce) and his colleagues as part of their program of research into the *mere exposure effect*—the tendency for people to prefer something they were exposed to repeatedly over something in the same category to which they had no exposure (Monohan, Murphy, & Zajonc, 2000; Murphy, Monohan, & Zajonc, 1995). Zajonc and his colleagues presented one group of non-Chinese research participants with a series of 25 Chinese ideographs (written characters) subliminally flashed only once, too quickly to be consciously perceived (5 microseconds). Another group was presented with only five ideographs, each character subliminally flashed five times. When the participants subsequently viewed all the ideographs, they preferred the characters they had seen repeatedly (but subliminally) over those they had viewed only once.

The mere exposure effect is used to good advantage by advertisers in product placement campaigns, where it is not necessary to provide any information

Subliminal perception ▶ When a stimulus is perceived unconsciously (implicitly), either when it is below the absolute threshold or is presented too briefly to reach conscious awareness.

whatever about a product beyond the fact that it is being used by a character in a film, TV show, music video, or video game. Simple exposure, whether or not it is recalled later, may be enough to turn preferences in the advertiser's favor, particularly if one is already familiar with the product being placed (Auty & Lewis, 2004; Matthes, Schemer, & Wirth, 2007).

CRITICAL THINKING ABOUT PSYCHOLOGY

Can Subliminal Persuasion Sell Coca-Cola or Boost Self-Esteem?

In 1957, newspapers reported a startling claim: Advertiser James Vicary had announced that he had used a device to subliminally subject thousands of moviegoers to the messages "Drink Coke" and "Eat Popcorn" as they watched the featured film. According to Vicary, there was a subsequent 18% increase in Coke sales, and a 58% jump in popcorn sales (Pratkanis, 1992). This was the first public claim that had been made about the effects of subliminal perception.

Quite understandably, the general public was outraged. Liberal political journalist and peace activist Norman Cousins wrote that the best response would be "to take this invention and everything connected to it and attach it to the center of the next nuclear explosive scheduled for testing" (quoted in Pratkanis, 1992). The U.S. government for once agreed with Cousins, and the Federal Communications Commission threatened to revoke the broadcast license of anyone using such a technique on television or radio.

Cousins and the FCC could have saved their outrage for more important matters. When Vicary failed to publish his findings, pressure was put on him to release his data. Finally, he admitted that his claims of having tested "thousands of subjects" in a 6-week long study were largely concocted— a publicity stunt to reverse the fortunes of the advertising agency in which he had a share (Rogers, 1992–1993).

However, the image of subliminal messages persuading unsuspecting people to purchase products or support political candidates took hold of the American imagination and has not let go (Broyels, 2006; Trappey, 1996). Although fMRI brain imaging techniques have shown that subliminal messages may register in the brain (Bahrami, Lavie, & Rees, 2007), and researchers have shown that people's moods can be affected through subliminal techniques (Ruys & Stapel, 2008), no convincing evidence exists that subliminal *persuasion* is even possible. Fifty years of controlled experimental studies have repeatedly shown that the most typical response to

▶ During the 1950s, the public was outraged to hear that images such as this one were being flashed "subliminally" during the screening of movies in order to boost sales of snack foods. However, the initial claims were largely fraudulent, and subsequent research has repeatedly failed to find effects of subliminal advertising strong enough to warrant use of the technique by marketers.

subliminal advertising messages is *no* response at all, or at best very weak, transient, and inconsistent effects (Pratkanis, Eskenazi, & Greenwald, 1994; Smith & Rogers, 1994; Vargas, 2008). If you are fearful that advertisers are using these techniques frequently, consider that weak, transient, and inconsistent effects are *not* what advertisers are after. Who needs subliminal advertising when effective product placement is routinely written into songs, novels, computer games, and television scripts (Chang, Newell, & Salmon, 2009; Taylor, 2009)?

What about the use of subliminal techniques to further one's own personal goals rather than to sell products or political candidates to unsuspecting consumers? Americans spend tens of millions of dollars per year on recordings that claim to use subliminal messages to improve memory or study skills, boost self-esteem, break unwanted habits, or heal psychic traumas (Natale, cited in Pratkanis et al., 1994). But do these tapes work? Controlled research repeatedly indicates that they do not (e.g., Froufe & Schwartz, 2001; Greenwald, Spangenberg, Pratkanis, & Eskenazi, 1991; T. E. Moore, 1995; Russell, Rowe, & Smouse, 1991).

In a particularly clever test of these recordings, Anthony Pratkanis and his colleagues (1994) randomly assigned a group of participants to receive either a memory improvement subliminal tape or one intended to increase self-esteem. However, without their knowledge, a subset of the memory group actually received the self-esteem tape, and a subset of the self-esteem group got the memory tape. In all, those in the self-esteem group reported that they felt better about themselves—regardless of whether they had received the memory or the self-esteem tape—and those in the memory group reported that their memories had improved, again, regardless of which tape they actually had received. However, by objective measures of memory and self-esteem that included a battery of standard tests, there were no significant improvements in any of the groups as a result of the tapes—neither in memory nor self-esteem. ∎

IN SUMMARY

1.	Sensation is the process by which the sense organs receive energy from the natural world and transduce it into neural signals to be sent to the brain. Perception is the process by which the brain organizes and interprets transduced sensory signals.
2.	Psychophysics is the scientific study of the relationship between sensation and perception.
3.	The absolute threshold is the minimum intensity necessary for a stimulus to be detected at least 50% of the time. The just-noticeable difference is the smallest difference between two stimuli that can be detected at least 50% of the time. Weber's law demonstrates that the JND for any given type of stimulus is proportionate to the level of the first (standard) stimulus.
4.	Signal detection theory acknowledges that in addition to thresholds and JNDs, noise and response bias also affect the perception of stimuli. Noise refers to other competing sensory stimuli and varying psychological states of the perceiver. Response bias acknowledges the fact that a person may be intrinsically biased in favor of or against perceiving a stimulus.
5.	Sensory adaptation describes the tendency for sensitivity to stimuli to be lessened over time during exposure.

6. Subliminal perception is the unconscious (implicit) perception of stimuli below the absolute threshold, or of stimuli presented too briefly to reach conscious awareness.

RETRIEVE!

1. Damage to the visual cortex and certain other cortical areas can produce a disorder where a person may perceive moving images as a series of "freeze frame" snapshots. The name for this condition is _____.

2. True or false: The absolute threshold is the point at which one may distinguish the intensity of a stimulus from another stimulus of greater or lesser intensity.

3. Give one possible example of noise and one of response bias in the detection of a stimulus. Use examples not taken from the text.

4. True or false: Advertisers have found that flashing subliminal images of their products so briefly that the viewer is unaware that they have been exposed to the image can nonetheless prompt the viewer to purchase the product.

How Does the Eye Work?

You may take for granted that there are only five human senses—sight, smell, taste, touch, and hearing—but many researchers believe the number is closer to nine or even more. For example, balance is sometimes referred to as a sense, as is pain, temperature, placement of the body in space (the "kinesthetic sense"), and more. One reason why an exact figure for the number of human senses cannot be given is that researchers do not agree on a precise definition of the term *sense*. Regardless of how many senses there may be, however, there are six primary areas of the body that house them: the eyes, nose, tongue, ears, skin, and the non-skeletal interior of the body—including muscles, joints, tendons, and internal organs. These are the sense organs, and in the coming pages we will investigate how they work, beginning with the eye.

The Eye Receives Light

Many of the sense organs perform more than one function for the body. For example, the tongue is essential for spoken language as well as housing the taste buds, and structures within the ear contribute to the sense of balance as well as hearing. But the eye has one function and one function only: *to receive light and process the images that result* so that the person may see. Light is a form of **electromagnetic radiation**—energy that travels around the world in waves that are separated by varying lengths, known as **wavelengths** (see Figure 5.5). All matter is electrically charged and produces radiation, but visible light exists only in a very narrow spectrum of electromagnetic wavelengths. You can see in Figure 5.5 that as the wavelength varies in the spectrum, the color that we see also varies.

In addition to varying by wavelength, light also varies by **amplitude**. Amplitude is a measure of the *intensity* of a light source, expressed as the height of a light wave. In Figure 5.5, the light waves depicted differ by

Electromagnetic radiation ▶ Energy that travels around the world in waves of variable intensity (amplitude) that are separated by varying lengths known as wavelengths.

Wavelength ▶ A measure of the lengths between electromagnetic waves.

Amplitude ▶ The intensity of a sound or light output source expressed in the height of light or sound waves.

Cornea ▶ Transparent membrane comprised of nerve fibers that covers the eye.

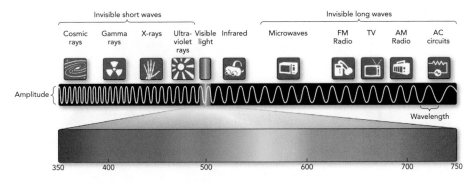

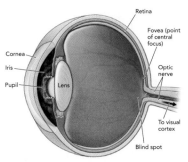

▲ **FIGURE 5.5** **The Electromagnetic Spectrum.** The earth is surrounded by a sea of electromagnetic energy, but only a very small portion is visible. Instruments such as radio, television, and x-ray radiography devices have been designed specifically to detect energy at nonvisible wavelengths.

▲ **FIGURE 5.6** **A Cross-Section of the Human Eye.**

wavelength across the spectrum, but they are all of equal height and therefore of equal amplitude.

Eyes Form Images of the World, but Do Not "See"

How does light turn into visual images in our brain? In order for images to form, light reflected from an object must first pass through the **cornea**, a transparent window membrane which covers the eye and is probably the most important single component in the eye's ability to transmit visual imagery (see Figure 5.6). Light is *refracted* (bent) as it passes through the cornea so that it may be gathered more efficiently and focused.

From the cornea the light passes through the **pupil**, a small opening in the **iris**. The iris is a muscular structure that expands and contracts, altering the size of the pupil to allow more or less light into the eye. If the available light is low, the iris expands (*dilates*) to let more in, and if there is strong light, it contracts.

Light is then conveyed through another transparent structure, the **lens**. Like the iris, the lens alters its shape, but it does so by flattening or thickening to create an even sharper focus of the light upon the **retina**—a light-sensitive membrane spread out across most of the eye's inner surface. It is upon the retina that an image is actually formed. However, before reaching the retina, the light must make the longest leg of its journey, through the gel-like substance known as the **vitreous humor** which fills 80% of the volume of the eye and constitutes much of what is ordinarily thought of as the eyeball.

When light finally reaches the retina, images are formed that are upside down and left/right reversed (see Figure 5.7). However, "seeing" has not yet occurred. It is not until these images are transduced to electrical signals and these signals reach the brain that the process of seeing—that is, visual perception—actually begins and the retinal images are interpreted by the brain in their correct "right side up" orientation.

RODS AND CONES

The retina contains over 125 million **photoreceptors**—neurons dedicated to capturing light. Photoreceptors initiate the process of transduction, which changes light into electrical signals to be sent to the brain. There are two principal types of photoreceptors in the human eye: *rods* and *cones*, which earned their names as a result of their distinctive shapes (see Figure 5.8).

Rods and cones not only have different shapes, but they also perform different functions. **Rods** are specialized to allow us to see at night—they respond in low light, but are not particularly good at capturing fine detail. Moreover, their peak sensitivities for responding to light do not correspond to those necessary

Pupil ▶ A small opening in the iris of the eye.

Iris ▶ A muscular structure of the eye around the pupil that expands and contracts to regulate the amount of light entering the eye.

Lens ▶ A transparent structure of the eye that flattens or thickens to help focus light upon the retina.

Retina ▶ A light-sensitive membrane spread out across most of the inner surface of the rear of the eye. It is upon the retina that images are formed.

Vitreous humor ▶ A gel-like substance through which light must pass before arriving at the retina. The vitreous humor fills 80% of the volume of the eye.

Photoreceptors ▶ Neurons dedicated to capturing light in order to initiate transduction.

Rods ▶ Photoreceptors specialized to allow night vision and vision in low light.

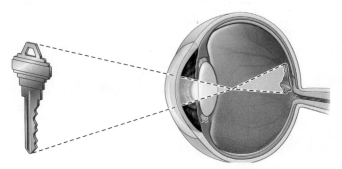

▲ **FIGURE 5.7 Images That Form on the Retina Are Inverted and Reversed.** As a result of the angle at which light hits the eye, images that form on the retina are inverted and left/right reversed. It is not until they are transduced into neural signals and these signals reach the brain that the images are perceived as images in their actual orientation.

▲ **FIGURE 5.8 Rods and Cones Are Photoreceptors.** Rods and cones magnified approximately 14,000 times. Rods are shaped like cylinders; cones have a pear shape at the bottom and a cone shape at the top. Rods are specialized to allow night vision, but are not good at capturing color or detail. Cones are specialized for daylight, detail, and color, but they need more light to function.

Cones ▶ Photoreceptors specialized for day vision, color vision, and capturing fine detail.

Fovea ▶ A small region near the center of the retina that contains the greatest concentration of cones and thus provides the clearest images and sharpest focus.

Optic nerve ▶ The nerve that carries neural signals from the back of the retina to the central nervous system.

for human beings to perceive color particularly well. This is why it is difficult to perceive color at night. However, rods do not perform at their maximum efficiency immediately upon encountering darkness. A period of *dark adaptation* is necessary; it generally takes about 30 minutes for the rods to fully adapt after the lights go out or the person enters a darkened room. That is why, when you enter a darkened movie theater, at first you cannot see your own hand, but within a relatively short time you can count the kernels of your neighbor's popcorn.

Cones are specialized for daylight vision and color vision. They need more light to function than do rods, but they allow for perception of detail, and their peak sensitivities to light include those wavelengths associated with human color vision. Although cones are scattered in various areas of the retina, there is a small region near the center of the retina that contains a particularly large concentration of cones. This area is known as the **fovea** (see Figure 5.6). Because cones are concentrated in the fovea—and these cones are slightly thinner in shape, allowing for this concentration—we perceive images that fall on the fovea especially clearly (Medeiros, 2006).

Images seem less sharply focused the farther from the fovea they get (Levi, Klein, & Aitsebaomo, 1985). You can see this for yourself. Close your left eye and hold up both of your index fingers in front of you about four inches (10cm) apart. Fix your gaze on your right index finger. Your left finger will seem out of focus because its image is to the side of the fovea.

The fovea contains virtually no rods. Instead, rods exist primarily in the peripheral areas of the retina. Because rods are more responsive to dim light than are cones, we actually may have superior vision at night by looking out of the corners of our eyes—a trick used by stargazers to spot dim stars (Wolfe et al., 2009).

Visual Signals Are Interpreted in the Visual Cortex

When rods and cones receive light, they produce chemical changes that initiate transduction of light into neural signals. The signals are modified further by cells whose axons (extensions) are bundled together in a structure known as the **optic nerve**. The optic nerve carries the neural signals out from the back of each retina to the brain. Interestingly, the area where the optic nerve leaves the retina, known as the **optic disc**, has neither rods nor cones and is therefore "blind." Although we do not notice this **blind spot** in the normal course of our lives because the brain "fills in" the missing information for us, based on available information (Ramachandran, 1992), you can demonstrate its existence for yourself fairly easily, as shown in Figure 5.9.

As the optic nerves exit the back of the cornea at the optic disc, each nerve includes information about the right visual field and the left visual field.

(Recall from Chapter 2 that *each* eye contains a right and a left visual field.) This information passes first through the thalamus, a structure of the lower forebrain. From the thalamus, the signals are relayed to the **visual cortex**, a complex, multilayered area dense with hundreds of millions of neurons, located at the back of the brain just above the top of your neck. It is here that much of the information conveyed by the optic nerves is interpreted and perceived as visual images of the world.

It is also in the visual cortex that sensations of touch relayed from the hands and fingers are interpreted as visual images, as in the example of the blind painter, Esref Armagon. This demonstrates that the sensory systems of the human brain possess at least some degree of plasticity.

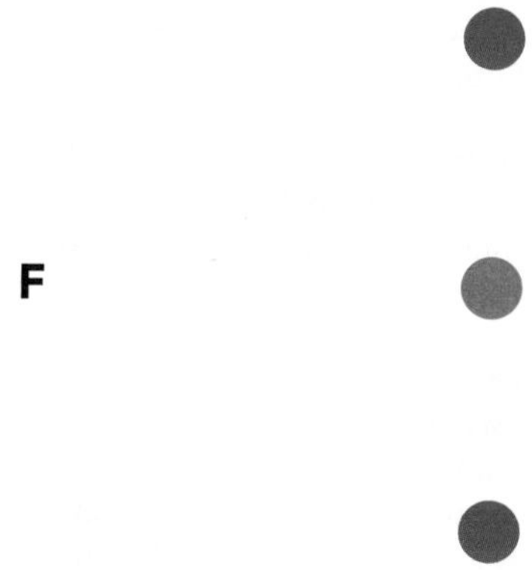

Brains—Not Objects—Have Color

"There is no red in a 700 nm light, just as there is no pain in the hooves of a kicking horse."

—Steven Shevell (cited by Wolfe et al., 2009 p. 105)

As briefly mentioned earlier, the color we see varies according to the wavelength of light reflected from objects. For example, a red rose absorbs all the wavelengths of light the sun or a light bulb can throw its way *except* wavelengths at between approximately 650–750 nanometers. These are the wavelengths associated with the color red, and they are reflected off the surface of the rose to be captured by our vision system. However, *the color red does not exist in these waves of light*. As Isaac Newton pointed out in 1704, "The rays, properly speaking, are not themselves colored." In other words, color is not a physical property of an object; instead, it is created by the brain of the animal perceiving the object. Color results from an interaction between light and brains—just as pain results from an interaction between the hooves of a kicking horse and the brain of the unfortunate recipient of the kick.

The fact that color is a psychological property rather than a physical one becomes even clearer when we consider that in the light of the moon the many colors that were visible just a few hours earlier vanish (Wolfe et al., 2009). Obviously, a mysterious force does not visit the world each night to drain everything of its color. Instead, the dim light of nighttime primarily stimulates the rods of the retina, which do not have the capacity to create color vision alone.

TRICHROMACY: HOW COLORS ARE COMBINED IN THE MIND'S PALETTE

Although most languages have relatively few names for different colors, under good lighting conditions human beings can distinguish at least one million different shades of color and possibly as many as 10 million (Halsey & Chapanis, 1951; Judd & Kelly, 1939; Kaiser & Boynton, 1996). How are all those millions of colors formed?

During the early 19th century, Thomas Young proposed that any color could be created if the light waves typically associated with three primary colors— blue, green, and red—were combined at various intensities and in various combinations—a process known as *additive color mixture*. As Figure 5.10 shows, however, this is entirely different from proposing that any color can be created by mixing red, green, and blue *pigments* or paints, a process known as **subtractive color mixture**.

Young's idea was later elaborated upon by Hermann von Helmholtz and ultimately came to be known as **trichromatic theory of color vision**. This theory has contributed importantly to our understanding of color vision. How does trichromacy work? In the days of Young and Helmholtz, the science of vision was not advanced enough to work this out. But researchers during the mid-20th century identified three types of cones in the vision system.

▲ FIGURE 5.9 See Your Blind Spot. To "see" the blind spot caused by an absence of either rods or cones at the optic disc, close your left eye and fix your gaze on the "F" in this image. Hold the book approximately 6 inches away, and adjust this distance backward or forward until the red dot disappears.

Optic disc ▶ The area where the optic nerve leaves the retina.

Blind spot ▶ An area formed by the optic disc that contains neither rods nor cones.

Visual cortex ▶ The area of the brain that interprets visual neural signals.

Subtractive color mixture ▶ When new colors are formed by mixing pigmented substances such as paints.

Trichromatic theory of color ▶ The theory that describes how all colors are created through the additive mixture of blue, green, and red. Trichromacy results because S-, M-, and L-cones in the retina are particularly sensitive to short, medium, or long wavelengths—which correspond to the perception of blue, green, and red.

▶ **FIGURE 5.10** Additive and Subtractive Color Mixture and Trichromacy. When S-, L-, and M-cones are stimulated by varying wavelengths of light, new colors are formed through an *additive* process of mixing light wavelengths. In contrast, when you mix paints, the colors absorb all light wavelengths *except* those that reflect the new color. Thus, in mixing paint you are *subtracting* all but the relevant wavelengths of light, rather than adding wavelengths.

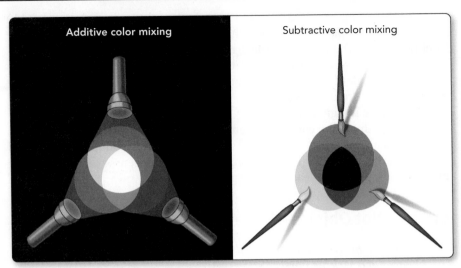

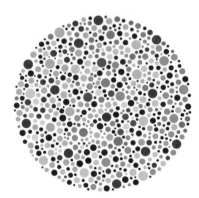

▲ **FIGURE 5.11 Red-Green Color Deficiency.** Red-green color deficiency is a genetic condition that results in a person's M- or L-cones being equally sensitive to red and green. If you are red-green color deficient, you are likely to see a 2 in the circle. If not, you will likely see a 5. (This is *not*, however, a formal test of red-green color deficiency. Such tests are administered under specific lighting conditions.)

Red-green color deficiency
▶ When M- and L-cones (see Trichromatic theory of color) are equally sensitive to red and green, making differentiation of these colors impossible.

Opponent process theory ▶
The theory of color vision that proposes that because certain wavelengths of light cannot be combined in an additive process, colors are created in color vision by mixing in three opposing pairs: blue vs. yellow, red vs. green, and black vs. white.

As we have discussed, it is cones that best allow for the perception of detail and color. Although the three types of cones can be stimulated by all spectrums of light, the peak sensitivity of each type of cone falls within a different spectrum: *short-*, *medium-*, and *long-wavelength*. Thus the cones are known generally known as S-cones, M-cones, and L-cones. It happens that the three primary colors identified by Young and Helmholtz are associated with these spectrums—blue with S-cones, red with M-cones, and green with L-cones. Thus, S-, M-, and L-cones allow us to distinguish between light at different wavelengths, and to perceive different colors as a result of the additive mixture of these wavelengths of light. Figure 5.11 shows what can happen when a person's S-cones are working properly, but the M- or L-cones are not functioning (or are absent entirely—a genetic condition known as **red-green color deficiency** or "color blindness").

OPPONENT PROCESS THEORY

Trichromacy is not the whole story of color vision. As Ewald Hering first observed during the late 19th century, certain additive combinations cannot occur in color vision. For example, you can probably visualize combining blue and green to get a bluish green (aqua), or red and yellow to get to get a reddish yellow (orange), but you cannot create a reddish green or a bluish yellow in color vision (Wolfe et al., 2009). From this observation Hering created a "rival" theory to trichromacy known as the **opponent process theory** of color vision. Herring proposed that, because some colors appeared to be "opposed" to one another, colors actually were mixed in three opposing pairs: blue or yellow, red or green, and black or white. This contrasts with trichromacy, which states that all colors are perceived as a result of the mixture of blue, green, and red.

According to more modern views of opponent process theory emerging during the mid-20th century, specific *opponent neurons* in the retina and the thalamus of the brain will respond with stimulation from one part of the spectrum of light (say, the blue spectrum) while simultaneously inhibiting response to another spectrum (in this case, yellow)—creating an opponent process response pairing blue and yellow. The same occurs for the black/white and red/green pairings (Goldstein, 2010). When a color is a mixture of the basic opponent process colors—for example, orange is a mixture of red and yellow—one of the dimensions of each opponent neurons is firing, and the other suppressed. You can see opponent processes at work in the phenomenon of the *negative afterimage* in Figure 5.12.

Although opponent process theory was at first a "rival" theory to trichromacy, during the 20th century research has established that trichromacy and opponent processes are both part of the color vision system (Hubel, 1995). The

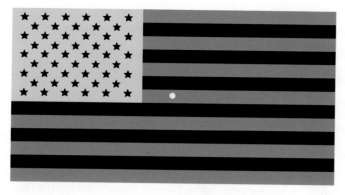

▲ **FIGURE 5.12 Opponent Process Theory Explains the Negative Afterimage.** Take 30 seconds out to stare at the white dot only (don't look around you). After 30 seconds have passed, look to the white space at the right. You should see a much more familiarly colored flag. Why does this afterimage effect occur? Staring for a long time at the image of the flag causes the sensors responding at peak efficiency to black, green, and yellow to "tire" (sensory adaptation). When you suddenly shift to a white surface, they are no longer required to function and they swing back momentarily to their opposing color. Yellow shifts to blue, green to red, and black to white.

retina does contain the three types of cones suggested by trichromatic theory. However, some neurons in the retina (and the brain) react only to blue but are inhibited from responding to yellow, while others respond to yellow but are inhibited from responding to blue. The same holds true for the red-green dimension (Abramov & Gordon, 1994).

IN SUMMARY

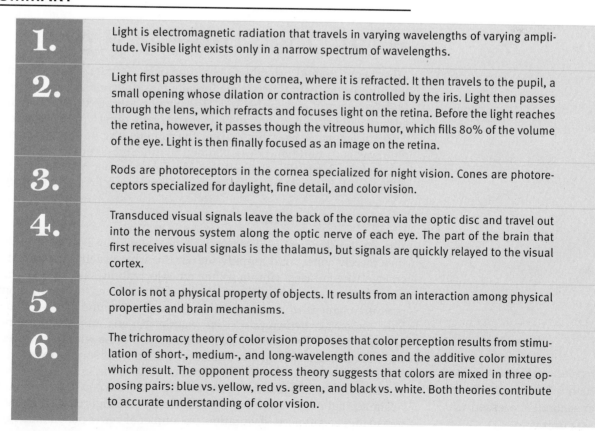

1. Light is electromagnetic radiation that travels in varying wavelengths of varying amplitude. Visible light exists only in a narrow spectrum of wavelengths.

2. Light first passes through the cornea, where it is refracted. It then travels to the pupil, a small opening whose dilation or contraction is controlled by the iris. Light then passes through the lens, which refracts and focuses light on the retina. Before the light reaches the retina, however, it passes though the vitreous humor, which fills 80% of the volume of the eye. Light is then finally focused as an image on the retina.

3. Rods are photoreceptors in the cornea specialized for night vision. Cones are photoreceptors specialized for daylight, fine detail, and color vision.

4. Transduced visual signals leave the back of the cornea via the optic disc and travel out into the nervous system along the optic nerve of each eye. The part of the brain that first receives visual signals is the thalamus, but signals are quickly relayed to the visual cortex.

5. Color is not a physical property of objects. It results from an interaction among physical properties and brain mechanisms.

6. The trichromacy theory of color vision proposes that color perception results from stimulation of short-, medium-, and long-wavelength cones and the additive color mixtures which result. The opponent process theory suggests that colors are mixed in three opposing pairs: blue vs. yellow, red vs. green, and black vs. white. Both theories contribute to accurate understanding of color vision.

RETRIEVE!

1. The two properties by which light varies are _____ and _____.

    a) decibles/wavelength   **c)** wavelength/amplitude

    b) frequency/decibles   **d)** frequency/amplitude.

2. Match the component of the eye on the left with the description on the right:

    Cornea   Small opening in the iris that expands or contracts in response to the amount of available light.

    Pupil   A light-sensitive membrane covering most of the inner surface of the rear of the eye. Images are formed upon this structure.

    Retina   Flattens or thickens to create a sharper focus of light upon the retina.

    Lens   Refracts (bends) light so that it may be gathered and focused more efficiently.

3. True or false: Images that fall on the fovea are especially clearly perceived because this region contains a particularly large concentration of rods.

4. Which structure is responsible for the "blind spot"?

    a) optic nerve   **b)** fovea   **c)** optic disc   **d)** retina

5. The phenomenon of negative afterimage reflects which type of color vision process? _____.

How Does the Ear Work?

Most people would probably agree that vision is the sense that contributes most importantly to functioning in daily life. However, hearing—technically, **audition**—is not very far behind. Hearing not only alerts us to potential dangers or opportunities, but it helps us express ourselves and communicate through language. For this reason, the famous humanitarian Helen Keller, who was both blind and deaf, claimed that deafness, not blindness, was her greatest handicap. She claimed that blindness cut her off from things, while deafness cut her off from people (quoted in du Feu & Fergusson, 2003, p. 95).

Audition ▶ The sense of hearing.

Sound Is Vibration

Just as the eyes do not see but instead collect and focus light, ears do not "hear," they merely collect and amplify sound. But what exactly is sound? Sound is created when objects vibrate. When an object vibrates it causes vibrations in the air (or water) molecules surrounding it. In turn, these vibrations cause pressure changes in the air (or water) known as sound waves. If you recall, light waves vary by two properties, wavelength and amplitude. Sound waves also vary by two properties. The first is *amplitude*. As with light waves, sound wave amplitude refers to the intensity of the output source, expressed in the height of the wave. Amplitude is measured in units known as *decibels* (see Figure 5.13)—the higher the decibels the greater the perception of loudness.

    The second property of sound is **frequency** (see Figure 5.14). Frequency refers to the rate of speed of vibration, or number of waves per second. Frequency

Frequency (of sound wave) ▶ The number of sound waves per second, expressed as hertz units.

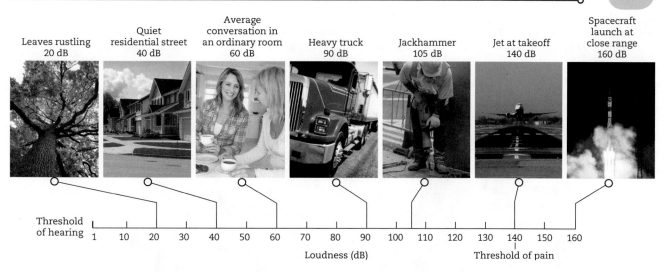

▲ FIGURE 5.13 Amplitude of Common Sounds. Long-term exposure to sound above 85 dB results in hearing loss. Rock bands amplified at close range equal approximately 140 dB, similar to a jet plane take-off. Be forewarned!

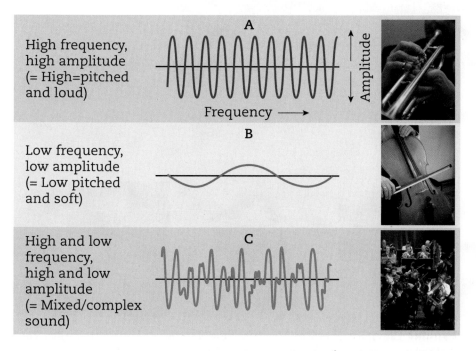

◄FIGURE 5.14 Frequency and Amplitude of Sound Waves. Amplitude refers to the height of the sound wave and determines loudness. Amplitude is measured in decibels. Frequency refers to the number of waves per second and determines pitch. Frequency is measured in hertz units.

is measured in *hertz* units, and it determines the **pitch**, or highness or lowness of the sound (e.g., a flute vs. a bass guitar). The faster the vibration, the greater will be the number of waves per second—and the higher will be the pitch of the sound.

The Ear Collects, Amplifies, and Transforms Sound Waves

The structure of the ear is divided into an *inner, middle,* and *outer ear* (see Figure 5.15). What most people call "the ear" is actually the **pinna** of the **outer ear**. Only mammals have pinnae, and the size and shape of these structures vary considerably among different species. The pinna collects sounds and helps orient us as to the placement of their source (see Figure 5.16).

Pitch ▶ Highness or lowness of a sound.

Pinna ▶ The visible structure of the outer ear that collects sounds and orients us to the placement of their source.

Outer ear ▶ Outer structure of the ear, consisting primarily of the pinna and ear canal.

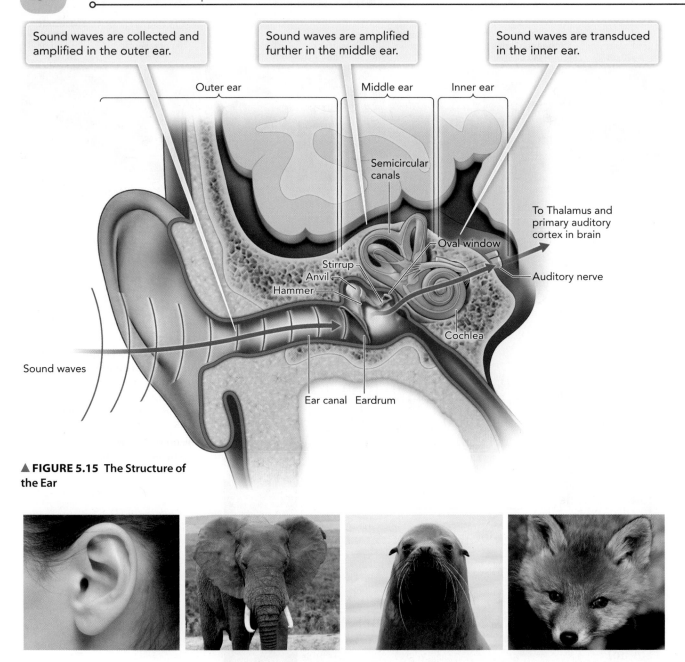

Sound waves are collected and amplified in the outer ear.

Sound waves are amplified further in the middle ear.

Sound waves are transduced in the inner ear.

Outer ear   Middle ear   Inner ear

Semicircular canals

To Thalamus and primary auditory cortex in brain

Oval window

Stirrup

Anvil

Hammer

Auditory nerve

Cochlea

Sound waves

Ear canal   Eardrum

▲ **FIGURE 5.15 The Structure of the Ear**

▲ **FIGURE 5.16 The Pinnae of Mammals Vary Considerably.** The pinna is the "sound collector" of the outer ear and helps orient us as to the source of the sound.

Ear canal ▶ An outer ear structure that funnels sound to the eardrum.

Tympanic membrane (eardrum) ▶ Membrane stretched across the end of the ear canal which vibrates in response to sound waves and marks the border between the outer and middle ear.

After sounds are collected, they are funneled through the **ear canal**, an outer-ear structure whose primary purpose is to protect the membrane tightly stretched across it at the end. This is the **tympanic membrane** or *eardrum*. The eardrum vibrates in response to changes in air pressure (or water pressure if the sound is occurring under water). Your mother may have scared the wits out of you by warning that you'd go deaf if you pressed a cotton swab too far into your ear and broke the ear drum, but in fact, while this might hurt and could potentially cause serious damage through infection, a ruptured eardrum can typically heal without treatment.

The eardrum marks the border to the middle ear, which consists of three tiny bones, or **ossicles**, called the *hammer, anvil,* and *stirrup.* The vibrations of the eardrum are picked up by the ossicles, greatly magnified, and transmitted to a membrane-covered opening known as the *oval window* at the border of the middle and inner ear. From the oval window the sound waves are

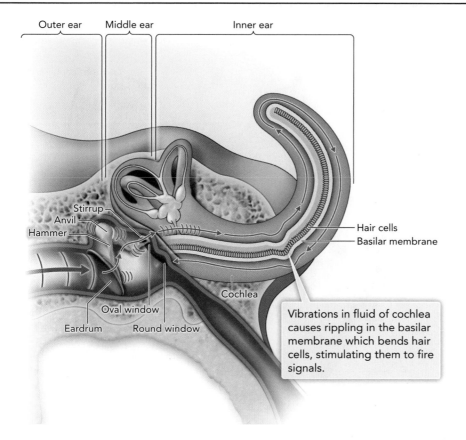

Outer ear   Middle ear   Inner ear

Stirrup
Anvil
Hammer

Hair cells
Basilar membrane

Cochlea

Oval window
Eardrum   Round window

Vibrations in fluid of cochlea causes rippling in the basilar membrane which bends hair cells, stimulating them to fire signals.

◀ **FIGURE 5.17 Magnification of Portions of the Inner and Middle Ear.** This figure places the focus on the cochlea, uncoiling it slightly to demonstrate how it functions. When fluid of the cochlea vibrates in response to sound waves transferred to the oval window, rippling occurs in the basilar membrane. This rippling causes stimulation of hair cells that fire neurons to carry auditory signals to the thalamus and, ultimately, the auditory cortex.

Ossicles ▶ Three tiny bones of the middle ear that amplify sound. The bones are called the hammer, anvil, and stirrup.

transferred to the **cochlea**, a small fluid-filled structure resembling a tube coiled in the shape of a snail. The cochlea is the central auditory component of the inner ear, and by the time sound vibrations reach it, they have been amplified dozens of times.

The fluid of the cochlea vibrates in response to the sound waves transmitted to the oval window, and this vibration causes rippling in the **basilar membrane**—a collection of stiff fibers within the cochlea. Embedded in the surface of these fibers are approximately 16,000 *hair cells*—specialized neurons that act as **auditory receptors**—much as rods and cones function as photoreceptors (see Figure 5.17).

It is in the hair cells that the transduction of sound from vibrations to neural signals begins. When the basilar membrane ripples in response to vibrations from the oval window, the hair cells are bent, resulting in the firing of neural signals. These signals are conveyed toward the cerebral cortex via the **auditory nerve**—collections of axons that emerge from the cochlea. This is similar to the way that visual signals are conveyed toward the brain along the optic nerve. As with visual signals, the auditory signals pass to the thalamus and ultimately reach the cortex. However, rather than reaching the visual cortex in the occipital lobe of the forebrain as with visual signals, auditory signals reach the **auditory cortex** of the temporal lobe. It is here that they are interpreted and perceived as sound (see Figure 5.18).

Both Ears Are Necessary to Locate Sounds

As I close one eye and look at my desk, I am in no danger of thinking that the espresso cup sitting by my right hand actually sits to my left. Although we don't need two eyes to determine the location of an object in the visual field, the same cannot be said for the ears. It may be possible to locate the source of a sound with one ear, but using two ears makes this task immeasurably easier and more accurate. Why? Picture yourself in a coffee shop reading a newspaper that was left on the table by the last customer. You are waiting for a friend

Cochlea ▶ A pea-sized, tube-like structure of the inner ear filled with fluid and curled into the shape of a snail. The cochlea is the central component of the inner ear.

Basilar membrane ▶ A collection of stiff fibers housed within the cochlear of the inner ear. The basilar membrane contains the hair cells that act as auditory receptors.

Auditory receptors ▶ Hair cells of the inner ear that receive auditory signals.

Auditory nerve ▶ A nerve that conducts transduced auditory signals to the thalamus, to be then relayed to the auditory cortex.

Auditory cortex ▶ Portion of the temporal lobe that interprets transduced auditory signals.

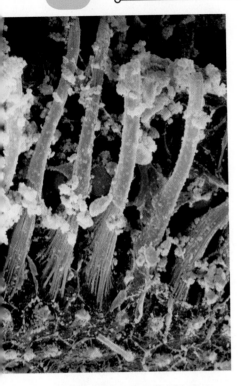

▲ **Magnified Hair Cells Firing within the Cochlea.** Hair cells are the specialized neurons that act as auditory receptors and initiate transduction of sound.

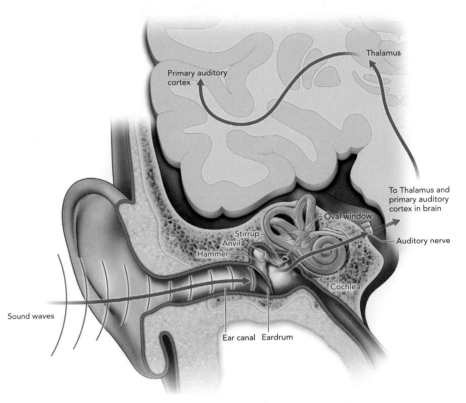

▲ **FIGURE 5.18 Auditory Signals Travel via the Auditory Nerve.** Signals transduced by the hair cells of the cochlea leave the ear via the auditory nerve where they travel to the thalamus, and from there to the auditory cortex of the temporal lobe.

to arrive. Suddenly, you hear your friend calling your name from just behind you as she approaches your table from the left-hand side. You turn to look over your left shoulder. But how do you know to turn to your left instead of right? First, the sound of her voice hits your left ear before it hits your right. The sound of your friend's voice is also louder in your left ear than the right. This is because the waves are partially blocked in their travel to your right ear by your head, which dampens the volume. Your brain factors in both the time of arrival and loudness differences to calculate the source of the sound of your friend's voice (see Figure 5.19).

IN SUMMARY

1. Sound is created when objects vibrate and cause vibrations in surrounding air (or water) molecules. Sound waves vary by amplitude (intensity) and frequency (speed of vibration). Amplitude determines loudness, and frequency determines pitch.

2. The ear consists of an outer ear, middle ear, and inner ear. The pinna is the outer ear structure, which collects sounds. Sounds are conveyed through the ear canal to the tympanic membrane (eardrum) stretched across the end of the canal. Vibrations of the eardrum are transferred to the ossicles of the middle ear, where they are magnified and transmitted to the oval window of the cochlea (the inner ear). The fluid of the cochlea vibrates, causing rippling in the basilar membrane. Hair cells of the basilar membrane are bent by this rippling, and the hair cells fire neurons (transduction) which exit via the auditory nerve to be processed in the auditory cortex of the temporal lobe.

▲ **FIGURE 5.19 How the Brain Locates the Direction of Sound.** Your brain locates the direction of sound by factoring in differences in the time sound waves arrive at each ear (the ITD) and differences in the level of the sound at each ear (the ILD).

3. The brain uses differences in the speed and intensity with which sound hits the ears to detect the location of sound sources.

RETRIEVE!

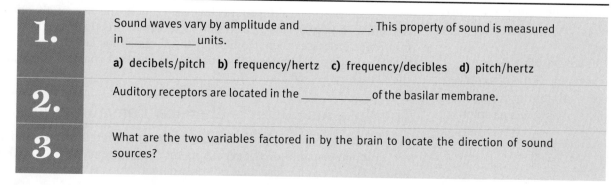

1. Sound waves vary by amplitude and _____. This property of sound is measured in _____ units.

a) decibels/pitch   **b)** frequency/hertz   **c)** frequency/decibels   **d)** pitch/hertz

2. Auditory receptors are located in the _____ of the basilar membrane.

3. What are the two variables factored in by the brain to locate the direction of sound sources?

How Do the Nose and Tongue Receive Chemical Signals?

Olfaction ▶ Sense of smell.

Gustation ▶ Sense of taste.

Olfaction (sense of smell) and **gustation** (sense of taste) are linked in a number of respects. First, both the nose and tongue perform their jobs of smelling and tasting by receiving *chemical* signals—unlike physical signals such as light or sound waves. Aromas in the air and the *tastes* and *flavors* of food are created by chemical compounds. Secondly, unlike the eyes and ears, which are exclusively sensory organs, the nose and tongue serve several purposes other than providing sensory information (e.g., breathing, swallowing). Third, as anyone who has ever had a bad cold knows, little in the way of tasting can occur without a clear sense of smell. Finally, detecting the chemical composition of the environment, as occurs in smelling and tasting, has always been critical for the basic survival of all forms of animal life. This is because knowledge of chemical aspects of the environment as they exist in plants and air allows an organism to take in nutrition and avoid toxins. For this reason it is generally agreed that chemical senses were the first to evolve, although they are not necessarily the "most important" for human survival. (That would be touch, as explained on pp. 241–246.)

The Nose Detects Odors

Every Thursday during the summer months in Westwood, California, a farmer's market is held. In midsummer the air is filled with the scents of ripe nectarines, peaches, grapes, and freshly cut flowers; vendors sell French *crêpes*, Mexican *burritos*, Brazilian *feijoada*, and Korean barbecue . . . it's a miracle anyone ever makes it back to work or school after lunch. In addition, it would not be difficult to close your eyes as you walked and use the aroma to identify fairly confidently which booth you were approaching.

How does the nose know?

Olfactory epithelium ▶ A patch of mucous membrane inside the nasal cavity containing olfactory sensory neurons.

Let's trace the passage of aroma from nectarines, my all-time favorite fruit, to the brain (see Figure 5.20). Molecular particles of aroma-causing chemicals (termed *odorants*) from the fruit pass from the air into the upper portions of the *nasal cavity*, the large, air-filled space behind the nose. Once there, the molecules contact the **olfactory epithelium**, a patch of mucous membrane containing about 20 million sensory neurons. Embedded in these neurons are **olfactory receptors**, much as the retina of the eye is embedded with photoreceptors and the hair cells of the inner ear with auditory receptors. The olfactory receptors convert the chemical signals to neural impulses and relay the information via the *olfactory nerves*, which serve a function similar to the optic and auditory nerves.

Olfactory receptors ▶ Sensory receptors of the olfactory sensory neurons that receive olfactory signals.

Olfactory bulb ▶ A tiny extension of the olfactory cortex that interprets olfactory signals as smell.

Olfactory signals end up at the **olfactory bulb** and other areas of the frontal cortex for processing. It is here that the converted signals are interpreted as the scent of ripe California nectarines. Only in the case of olfaction is the thalamus initially bypassed, and signals received directly in the portion of the brain that processes them (to be sent to the thalamus later, however, for further processing). Therefore, the nose is the quickest route to the brain of all the sense organs (see Figure 5.20).

The Nose Also Detects Chemical Communications

Human beings can detect approximately 10,000 different scents, and aromas are uniquely capable of triggering memories and emotions (von Bothmer, 2006). However, the nose does not only detect odors. It also detects chemical

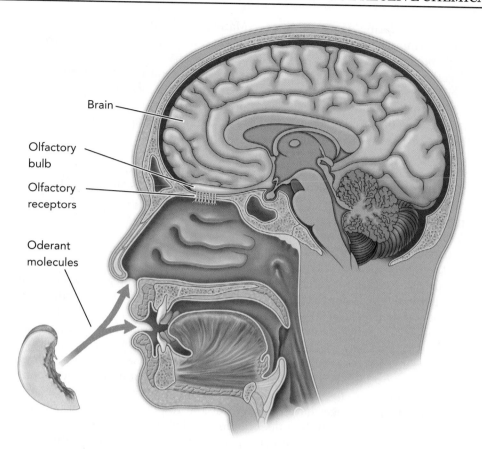

Brain

Olfactory bulb

Olfactory receptors

Oderant molecules

◀ **FIGURE 5.20 How the Nose Knows: The Olfactory System.** Airborne molecular particles from nectarine odorants pass into the upper nasal cavity and contact olfactory receptors. The receptors convert the chemical particles to neural signals and relay them via the olfactory nerves to the olfactory bulb beneath the frontal lobes. After some additional processing in the frontal cortex and thalamus, the signal is interpreted as the aroma of fruit.

communications from other human beings, sometimes referred to as *human pheromones*. What are pheromones? *Pheromones* are hormone-like chemicals excreted in various ways, and picked up by other members of the species—through the nose in mammals. These chemicals act as "communications," often related to mating, aggression, and parenting (Sobel & Brown, 2001).

The existence of pheromones in humans has been a highly controversial proposition. In most mammals, pheromones direct behavior explicitly—and some behaviors, such as mating, will simply not occur in some species without the exchange of pheromonal signals. Thus, the idea of human pheromones recalls the notion of human "instincts," which, as we saw in Chapter 3, has a rocky history in the behavioral sciences. However, it has now been established that humans do excrete, detect, and respond to androgen- and estrogen-like chemical compounds quite similar to the pheromones found in other mammals (Jacob, Kinnunen, Metz, Cooper, & McClintock, 2001; Kohl, Atzmuller, Fink, & Grammer, 2007; Savic, Berglund, & Lindström, 2005; Wyart et al., 2007). Unlike other mammals, who typically detect pheromones through a patch of neurons in the nasal cavity termed the **vomeronasal organ**, in humans these chemicals are most likely detected by specialized receptors in the olfactory epithelium (Liberles & Buck, 2006; Wysocki & Preti, 2004).

We not only detect pheromones, we respond to them in ways that are both unconscious and involuntary. As an example, exposure to an odorless component of male sweat has been shown to maintain higher levels of the stress hormone *cortisol* in women (Wyart et al., 2007), and exposure to the scent of a woman close to the ovulation phase of her reproductive cycle maintains higher levels of available testosterone in men relative to exposure to the scent

Vomeronasal organ (VNO) ▶ A small area inside the nasal cavities of mammals that receives pheromonal signals. Not likely to be the source of pheromonal communication in humans.

▲ **10,000 Taste Buds Can't Be Wrong.** There are about 10,000 taste buds covering the tongue. They are contained within the *papillae,* structures that contribute the rough appearance to the surface of the tongue. Within the buds are taste receptors specialized to sense only specific taste molecules.

of a non-ovulating woman (Miller & Maner, 2010). When a pheromone affects hormonal activity in another person in this way, it is known as a *primer pheromone.*

Perhaps more intriguingly, when male and female research participants were exposed to an odorless substance containing pheromone-like compounds drawn from the sweat glands of members of the other sex, brain imaging scans detected extensive changes in the hypothalamus, an area of the brain associated with emotional and sexual responses (Grosser, Monti-Bloch, Jennings-White, & Berliner, 2000; Jacob et al., 2001; Savic, Berglund, Gulyas, & Roland, 2001). Exposure to odorless components of male sweat were shown to increase levels of positive mood in women as well as subjective feelings of sexual arousal (Wyart et al., 2007). When a pheromonal substance alters mood or other internal psychological states in this way, it is known as a *modulator pheromone* (McClintock, 2000).

If evidence for primer and modulator pheromones in human beings is strongest, evidence for a third type of pheromones, known as *releasing pheromones,* is weakest. Releasing pheromones are those that directly alter the *behavior* of another individual—for example by causing that person to be sexually attracted and act on such feelings (Wysocki & Preti, 2004). Numerous perfume products are marketed—purportedly based on "scientific research" in human releasing pheromones—by manufacturers who claim they will attract members of one's preferred sex. However, all of the promotions for these colognes, sprays, and after-shave lotions seriously misrepresent the state of human pheromone research (Johnston, 1998; Winman, 2004; Wysocki & Preti, 2004). Although brain and mood changes have been recorded in response to exposure human pheromone-like compounds, it does not follow that wearing perfume containing such pheromones will result in an increase in your appeal to your preferred sex. At the very least this is true because brain changes and alterations in mood states are not always associated with behavioral changes (e.g., Cahill, 2006). Table 5.1 summarizes the functions of three categories of pheromones.

The Tongue Tastes, but It Needs the Nose for Flavor

When author Calvin Trillin's 4-year-old daughter finished off a particularly satisfying dish of chocolate ice cream, she commented, "My tongue is smiling" (cited by Wolfe et al., 2009, p. 361). What placed a grin in this most unlikely place? Trillin's daughter was experiencing both *taste* and *flavor.* Although we generally use these words interchangeably, they are not in fact identical.

TASTES

Taste ▶ Gustatory sensations received by the tongue. They are limited to sweet, salty, sour, and bitter, and possibly also umami and fatty.

Taste buds ▶ Clusters of cells covering areas of the tongue and (to a lesser extent) the roof of the mouth which house taste receptors.

Taste receptors ▶ Receptors contained in taste buds, each specialized to sense certain kinds of molecules associated with various tastes.

Tastes are fundamental *gustatory* (eating-related) sensations received by the tongue after food molecules are dissolved in saliva during chewing and passed over the **taste buds.** Taste buds are clusters of cells covering areas of the tongue (and, to a lesser degree, the roof of the mouth). Taste bud cells contain **taste receptors,** sites specialized to sense certain kinds of chemical molecules associated with specific tastes (Mueller et al., 2005; Zhao et al., 2003.) These

Table 5.1 **Categories of Pheromones and Their Functions**

PHEROMONE CATEGORY	FUNCTION
Modulator pheromone	Alters internal psychological state in another individual
Primer pheromone	Alters hormonal activity in another individual
Releaser pheromone	Directly affects the behavior of another individual

receptors transduce taste signals, sending the information to the thalamus along **cranial nerves** (nerves originating in the brain rather than the spine). From the thalamus they are relayed to the *primary* and *secondary taste cortex* of the frontal lobe, where they are interpreted as taste (Rolls, 2006).

There are four basic tastes: *sweet, salty, sour,* and *bitter.* Two additional tastes are accepted by some, but not all, researchers. The first controversial taste, the so-called "fifth taste," is known by the Japanese term *umami* (meaning "yummy," more or less). Umami was initially proposed as a taste by manufacturers of *monosodium glutamate* (MSG) who, concerned about negative press about their seasoning, claimed the existence of taste receptors specialized for detecting it. Umami is described as a savory taste common in seafood and cured meats, some vegetables (such as mushrooms, tomatoes), and fermented foods such as cheeses and soy sauce. In fact, evidence from mice and rats does suggest that there are specialized taste receptors for the components of MSG (R. K. Palmer, 2007; Zhao et al., 2003). However, the jury is still out as to whether umami is a true taste.

The second proposed "new" taste is *fatty.* Researchers have recently identified taste receptors in mice specialized for identifying fatty tastes (Laugerette et al., 2005; Mizushige, Inoue, & Fushiki, 2007). This seems a better candidate than umami for a "fifth taste" because human beings have a universal preference for foods that are relatively fatty, probably because such foods are high in calories—a scarce commodity when our sense of taste was evolving. It makes sense that we should have specialized taste sensors to detect fats. Once again, however, the jury is still out.

FLAVORS

If tastes are either sweet, salty, sour, bitter, and possibly fatty or umami, what then are *flavors?* **Flavors** are what happens when tastes meet *olfaction*—the sense of smell. While taste signals that ice cream is sweet, flavor allows you to distinguish vanilla ice cream from equally sweet chocolate ice cream. As already stated, when food enters the mouth and is chewed, molecules are dissolved by saliva and sensed by taste receptors to provide information about taste. However, other molecules are released into the air inside our mouths. These molecules travel up behind the roof of the mouth through the *retronasal passage,* where they are sensed by receptors in the olfactory epithelium in the same way that ordinary odors are sensed when you inhale. This is why, when one's nose is stuffed and molecules cannot contact the epithelium, we may perceive taste, but have no perception of flavor (see Figure 5.21).

You can test this idea by holding your nose and placing a bite of blueberry pie in your mouth. As you chew, you can taste the sweetness, and you may be able to identify the texture as "pie-like," but that's about all. Now, just before swallowing, release your nose. As molecules from the pie are forced up the nasal cavity, your mouth will be flooded with the flavor of blueberries.

Cranial nerves ▶ Nerves originating in the brain stem.

Flavor ▶ During chewing, molecules are released and travel up behind the roof of the mouth where they are sensed by the olfactory epithelium as retronasal olfactory sensations. When combined with *taste,* these sensations create flavor.

IN SUMMARY

1. The nose detects odors and chemical signals similar to pheromones. Odors are detected when particles of an odor-producing substance pass through the nasal cavity and contact the olfactory epithelium. Olfactory receptors embedded in the olfactory sensory neurons transduce chemical signals and relay the information via the olfactory nerves to the olfactory bulb of the olfactory cortex.

2. Although human pheromones have not been precisely identified, it is highly likely that modulating and priming human pheromones exist. Releasing pheromones may exist in humans, but there is little evidence of it. Pheromones are probably detected by the specialized sensory neurons in the olfactory epithelium.

▶ **FIGURE 5.21** **Anatomy of Flavor.** As you chew and swallow food, molecules released inside your mouth travel upward through the retronasal passage. They are sensed by the olfactory epithelium. Flavor is created when this process is combined with *taste* and the sensation of texture from the mouth and tongue.

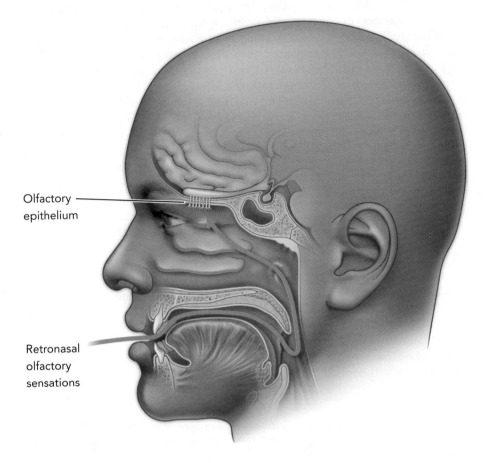

Olfactory epithelium

Retronasal olfactory sensations

3.	Taste is perceived when food molecules are dissolved in saliva during chewing and passed over the taste buds which are embedded with taste receptors. These receptors transduce taste signals, sending the information along cranial nerves to the primary and secondary taste cortexes.
4.	There is a difference between taste and flavor. There are four basic tastes: salty, sweet, sour, and bitter. There may be two additional basic tastes: umami and fatty. Flavor is experienced when taste and olfaction are combined during chewing.

RETRIEVE!

1.	Name three or four ways in which the senses of olfaction and gustation are linked.
2.	A pheromone that alters another individual's internal psychological states is known as a _____ pheromone. A pheromone that alters another individual's hormonal activity is a _____ pheromone. A pheromone that alters another individual's behavior is a _____ pheromone. **a)** primer/releasing/modulator **c)** primer/modulator/releasing **b)** modulator/primer/releasing **d)** releasing/modulator/primer

3. Name the two "new" tastes, accepted by many, but not all, researchers.

4. For flavor to be experienced, food molecules are released into the air inside the mouth and travel up behind the roof of the mouth through the _____, where they are sensed by receptors in the _____.

    a) olfactory epithelium/retronasal passage

    b) olfactory bulb/olfactory epithelium

    c) taste buds/olfactory bulb

    d) retronasal passage/olfactory epithelium

How Do the Skin and Body Feel?

You may never have thought of your skin, muscles, joints, tendons, and internal organs as "sense organs," but they are. **Touch** is the skin's principal sense. The sense of touch can be broken down into three subdivisions: **tactition** (touching), **thermoception** (heat and cold), and **nociception** (pain). The muscles, tendons, and joints primarily contribute to the kinesthetic sense—our awareness of where our limbs are and how we are moving. However, they may also contribute pain sensations and therefore are also part of the nociception subdivision of touch. Our internal organs also contribute to nociception when they are injured or malfunctioning.

Skin: The Agony and the Ecstasy

None of the sense organs can easily trigger the extremes of joy and misery provided by the skin. The sight of a sunset over a Caribbean beach or the flavor of England's finest farmhouse cheddar cheese can provide great pleasure, even joy—but it is doubtful that these experiences can compare to the joy experienced by a child receiving his mother's loving touch after waking from a nightmare, or the sensation of our first embrace and kiss from someone we have secretly loved for a long time. Similarly, viewing an ugly urban landscape or eating burned cafeteria food can provide unpleasant sensations, but these cannot compare to the suffering experienced by a prisoner of war who is being tortured. *Touch* is truly the medium for the expression of love and hatred and the experience of pleasure and pain.

TACTITION: SENSE OF TOUCH

The "touching" subdivision of the sense of touch is known as *tactition*. The possible range of tactile sensations is extraordinary. Just think about all the ways your skin has ever felt (apart from hot, cold, or pained): itchy, tickled, numb, prickly, smooth, bumpy, gooey, slimy, greasy, wet, dry, and on and on. It is through tactition that the blind painter Esref Armagon is able to "see." Touch is of more fundamental importance than the other senses as well, and is the first to emerge in the developing fetus (Ackerman, Nocera, & Bargh, 2010; Field, 2001; Hertenstein, 2002).

Physiologically speaking, how do we *feel* when touching? Touch receptors known as **mechanoreceptors** are embedded in the outer layer of skin (*epidermis*), the layer of skin underneath the epidermis (*dermis*), and the layer of *subcutaneous fat* below the dermis. Tactile sensations are converted into

Touch ▶ The principal sense that obtains sensory information from the skin. It is comprised of three "subsenses" tactition, thermoception, and nociception.

Tactition ▶ The touch component of the sense of touch.

Thermoception ▶ The component of the sense of touch that registers temperature.

Nociception ▶ The component of the sense of touch that registers pain.

Mechanoreceptors ▶ Sensory receptors embedded in the skin that play a role in tactition.

▶ **One of Harry Harlow's Monkeys and His "Mother."** Rhesus monkeys reared by a cloth-covered surrogate "mother" preferred her over a surrogate made of wire cage even when the wire cage mother was the only place where the monkeys could obtain food (Harlow, 1958).

Somatosensory area ▶ Area of the cortex where tactile sensations are perceived.

neural signals by mechanoreceptors and are then carried by trunks of nerves which travel to the spinal column instead of directly to the brain as with other senses. The signals then travel up the spinal column to the thalamus, and from there to the **somatosensory area** of the cortex where they are perceived as touch.

Psychologists came to appreciate the importance of tactition following the experiments of Harry Harlow (1905–1981) and his colleagues during the 1950s and 1960s. In those days, most psychologists subscribed to the notion that infants came to develop strong affectional bonds with their mothers primarily because they depended upon their mothers for nourishment. However, Harlow and his colleagues created two "surrogate mothers" to rear a group of rhesus monkeys that were taken from their mothers (Harlow, 1958; Harlow & Zimmerman, 1959). One of the surrogates was built from comfortable (and comforting) foam and terrycloth. The other was built from uncomfortable wire cage material. Half of the monkeys were fed by the terrycloth surrogate, and half by the wire surrogate. All of the monkeys strongly preferred the terrycloth mother regardless of which provided food. They all spent more time clinging to the cloth surrogate, and in particular were far more likely to run to it when they were frightened or upset. These results strongly imply that primates depend upon touch as a way of developing bonds of affection in infancy.

Touch may possess even more remarkable powers—the communication of specific emotions. Touch has always been known to have the capacity to communicate a *general* emotional tone—a warm and loving touch feels different from the touch of a person feeling pain or anger. However, preliminary research by Matthew Hertenstein and his colleagues has shown that human beings can communicate *specific* emotions through touch—disgust, love, fear, anger, even subtle emotions such as gratitude and sympathy (Hertenstein, Keltner, App, Bulleit, & Jaskolka, 2006).

The touch of a person with whom one has a close relationship also has been shown to substantially lessen brain activation under conditions of stress and fear (Coan, Schaefer, & Davidson, 2006). James Coan and his colleagues enlisted a group of married women and subjected them to a procedure that included the threat of receiving electric shocks. The women underwent the

▲ **Touch Is the Fundamental Sense.** Touch is the medium for the expression of love and hate, pleasure and pain. We could not easily survive without it.

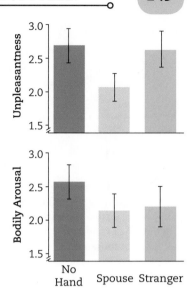

▲ **FIGURE 5.22** Lending a Hand. Women threatened with electric shock by experimenters experienced less unpleasant emotion and physical agitation when they were holding the hand of another person. The effect was greatest when they held their husband's hand. These subjective reports were backed up by functional magnetic resonance imaging (fMRI) data. *(Source: Coan et al., 2006, p. 1036.)*

procedure under three conditions: In one, each woman held her husband's hand during testing, in another the hand of a male stranger, and in a third, no one's hand. Brain imaging techniques (fMRI) were used to monitor the women's brains during testing. As Figure 5.22 shows, the touch of another person reduced the women's reports of agitation and unpleasant emotional responses to the experience, with the touch of the husband having a greater effect than the touch of a stranger. Interestingly, those who reported the happiest marriages showed the greatest effect in this regard (Coan et al., 2006).

Perhaps most astonishing of all, sensations of touch may activate unconscious decision-making processes and behaviors grounded in metaphor. What do I mean by this? A *metaphor* is any kind of figure of speech where some word or phrase that describes one thing is used in place of another word or phrase that describes something else. The purpose of a metaphor is vivid description. For example, to say someone is very *warm* is a metaphor for a person who is kind, open, affectionate, sympathetic, and so forth. After all, the "warm" person's body temperature is no higher than anyone else's.

In a series of experiments, Joshua Ackerman and his colleagues found that various experiences of touch influenced impressions and decisions due to the metaphorical implications of the touch experience (Ackerman et al., 2010). For example, passersby were asked to evaluate a job candidate on the basis of the candidate's resume. Those given the resume attached to a heavy clipboard were more likely to view the candidate as having "more serious interest" in the job opening than those holding a light clipboard (a "heavy" candidate vs. a "lightweight" candidate). In a separate study, negotiators sitting in hard chairs were *harder* and more *rigid* in their negotiations than those sitting in soft chairs. In a third, solving puzzles containing pieces covered with sandpaper (rough) caused puzzle solvers to rate a described social interaction as less friendly, and more adversarial ("rougher") than those solving a puzzle that contained smooth, varnished pieces. And so forth.

THERMOCEPTION: SENSE OF TEMPERATURE

Perception of warm and cold is known as *thermoception*. Like *mechanoreceptors*, **thermoreceptors** are embedded in the skin. There are two types—one for detecting increases in skin temperature, and one for decreases. Thermoreceptors respond when your body temperature rises or lowers in

Thermoreceptors ▶ Sensory receptors embedded in the skin that register temperature.

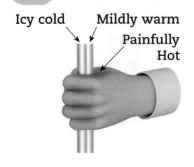

Icy cold   Mildly warm
                    Painfully
                    Hot

▲ **Warm + Cold = Painfully Hot!**
When coils with icy cold water and mildly warm water are grasped together, the experience is of a painfully hot sensation.

response to changes in environmental temperature or when you touch warm and cold objects.

There are a number of odd aspects to our sense of temperature. For example, if you grab a coil of two pipes, one of which contains very cold water and the other mildly warm, you will not perceive both temperatures—instead you will perceive a painfully hot sensation. This is because "hot" is experienced under two conditions: when receptors for rising temperatures are stimulated, or when receptors for rising *and* decreasing temperatures are stimulated simultaneously. On the other hand, cold is experienced only when receptors for decreasing temperatures are stimulated (Craig & Rollman, 1999).

NOCICEPTION: SENSE OF PAIN

Without tactition and thermoception people would be unlikely to reproduce (why bother having sex if you can't feel anything?). Many people live full lives without sight or hearing, and the loss of smell and taste would be miserable, but not necessarily life threatening (as long as we could monitor our food source for toxicity). However, our survival would be seriously threatened without *nociception*, the sense of pain.

Consider children with a rare genetic disorder known as *congenital insensitivity to pain*. Tragically, such children experience burned or severed fingers and hands, multiple fractures, and untreated infections. They often die in childhood because they do not respond to pain as a warning that something is wrong. Thus, the sense of touch is critical to simple survival (Melzack & Casey, 1968; Nagasako, Oaklander, & Dworkin, 2003).

Pain is one of our very best friends—although it certainly is an unwelcome visitor, accounting for the majority of all trips to the doctor (Edwards, Campbell, Jamison, & Wiech, 2009). Pain seems to us the most purely *physical* sensation imaginable. Yet, pain is exquisitely *psychological*. It is not simply the relaying of sensory signals from the site of an injury to the brain. Beliefs, emotions, motivations, prior experiences, and observations of other people's behavior affect the pain experience (Gatchel, Peng, Peters, Fuchs, & Turk, 2007). Consider that a football player might barely notice a broken ankle experienced while playing an important game, while the same broken ankle resulting from a fall after the game might cause excruciating pain. In a similar way, soldiers on the battlefield often report little pain from wounds that, in another context, would be agonizing (Keefe & France, 1999).

The process of perception of pain is quite different from perception of other sensory information. There are no specific receptors designed to receive pain. *Free nerve endings* anywhere in the body can serve as nociceptors—receptors for pain sensations. The way pain messages travel to the brain is also much more complex than that for the other senses.

There are two types of pain experiences that occur when painful stimuli are experienced: *first pain* and *second pain* (Melzack & Wall, 1983). **First pain** is the initial sharp sensation one experiences at the moment of the painful stimulus—when we receive a cut, burn, or splinter, for example. As depicted in Figure 5.23, first pain is conveyed along *A-delta fibers*—myelinated (sheathed) axons that transmit neural signals very quickly. First pain alerts us that "something bad" has happened and tells us *where* it happened and *what type* of injury we have experienced (cut, bruise, burn, etc.).

However, first pain is actually less "painful" than second pain. **Second pain** sensations are conducted along much slower unmyelinated *C-fibers*, and they arrive seconds or even minutes after first pain (see Figure 5.23). Although they may be slower to arrive, they tend to be more unpleasant. Second pain is a throbbing, burning, radiating sensation that is not as localized as first pain. When you receive a splinter in the foot, for example, you may cry out in pain (or utter an impolite expletive) as you sit down and examine your foot. The initial sharp sensation when the splinter entered your foot is quickly followed

First pain ▶ Initial sharp sensations at the moment of a painful stimulus.

Second pain ▶ The generally longer lasting, less localized, and more unpleasant pain sensations, conducted along the slower C-fibers.

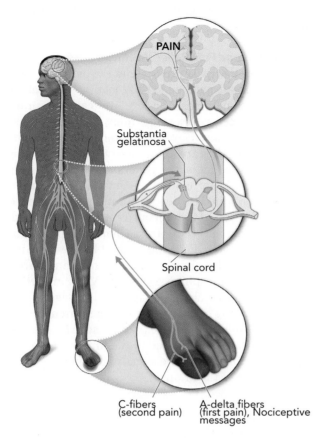

Substantia gelatinosa

Spinal cord

C-fibers (second pain)   A-delta fibers (first pain), Nociceptive messages

▲ **FIGURE 5.23 The Gate Control Theory of Pain.** In Diagram A, the pain gate is open. Nociceptive messages due to a wound travel along A-delta (first pain) and C-fibers (second pain) through the substantia gelatinosa of the spine and are interpreted as pain by the brain. In Diagram B, the pain gate is closed. Anti-nociceptive message can be dispatched from several sources: thoughts, emotions, and endorphin activity originating in the brain; muscle relaxation; or tactile activity such as massaging or bathing the wound in warm water.

by a throbbing ache that spreads out beyond the point of entry of the splinter. This is generally a more unpleasant experience—in other words, *having* a splinter is worse than *getting* a splinter. Second pain sensations tend to be more unpleasant in part because by the time they arrive we have had time to respond *emotionally* and *cognitively* to the pain (Ploner, Gross, Timmermann, & Schnitzler, 2002). Second pain highlights the psychological nature of pain.

There is an evolutionary logic to the experience of first and second pain. First pain sensations provide precise information about threats to the body so that immediate action can be taken (e.g., sit down to examine your foot), whereas second pain, because it is generally more unpleasant, provides longer-lasting motivation to do what is necessary to promote the healing process and take steps to prevent similar injuries in the future (e.g., wear shoes in the house or get the floor refinished; Ploner et al., 2002)!

In 1965, psychologist Ronald Melzack and biologist Patrick Wall wrote a paper for the journal *Science* that revolutionized the way scientists and medical doctors of the time understood pain (Yaksh, 1999). Although their theory, which came to be known as *gate control theory*, does not explain everything important about pain, no other theory has produced as much useful research on pain or stood up as well under scrutiny (Gatchel et al., 2007; Sufka & Price, 2002).

As depicted in Figure 5.23, **gate control theory** proposes that when *nociceptive* (pain) signals travel toward the brain, they pass through a gelatinous mass of small neurons in the outer layers of the spinal column known as the *substantia gelatinosa* ("gelatinous substance"). These neurons act as a

Gate control theory ▶ A theory of pain perception that emphasizes the activity not only of pain signals from the injury site but also of pain blocking signals originating in the brain or elsewhere in the body.

"gate" for pain, because pain signals must pass through them in order to reach the brain.

Anti-Nociceptive Signals and Pain Relief According to gate control theory, only a certain amount of neural activity can occur at the pain gate at any given time. If other neural signals are dispatched to this location, they can "close the gate" for further pain. These signals close the gate by creating neural activity at the pain gate with which nociceptive messages must compete for the gate's limited "entry space" to the brain. Because these neural signals inhibit the transmission of nociceptive signals, they are known as *anti-nociceptive* signals.

How are anti-nociceptive messages generated? They can originate in the brain as a result of cognitive or emotional factors. For example, the soldiers and football players mentioned earlier are emotionally committed to "soldiering on" regardless of injury, and they are also cognitively focused on the game, not on their bodies. As you may recall from Chapter 2, pain-suppressing neurotransmitters known as *endorphins* are created by the body itself, and these also generate anti-nociceptive signals, as do pain-killing narcotic drugs derived from opium, such as morphine, Delaudid, Vicodin (hydrocodone), and Percocet (oxycodone). Pain-blocking signals can also originate at the site of injury. For example, massaging or gently tapping an injured area or bathing it in warm water may sometimes help relieve pain because these sensations stimulate neural activity in the area unrelated to the injury. These anti-nociceptive signals then compete with nociceptive signals at the pain gate, inhibiting the pain signals from passing to the brain.

IN SUMMARY

1. The sense of touch is subdivided into tactition, thermoception, and nociception. Tactition occurs because mechanoreceptors are embedded in the epidermis, dermis, and subcutaneous fat. Tactile sensations are interpreted in the somatosensory area of the cortex.

2. Thermoreceptors sense warm and cold. There are two types: one for detecting increases in skin temperature and one for detecting decreases.

3. Pain is a cognitive, motivational, and emotional experience as well as a physiological experience. Pain is sensed by free nerve endings throughout the body, which act as nociceptors. First pain is conveyed rapidly along A-delta fibers, whereas second pain is conveyed along slower C-fibers.

4. The gate control theory of pain describes the way competing neural messages at the substantia gelatinosa can block pain signals.

RETRIEVE!

1. True or false: Hot sensations are experienced when receptors for rising temperatures are stimulated or when receptors for rising and decreasing temperatures are stimulated simultaneously.

2. What are the differences between first and second pain? What is the likely evolutionary purpose of each type of pain?

3. According to the gate control theory of pain, why might massage help to relieve muscular pain, at least during the time the massage occurs?

How Do We Perceive Visual Images?

As we have seen, sensing is only the beginning of perception. For example, glance briefly at the image in Figure 5.24. If you are like most people, you will probably see bushes or branches in close-up with a series of spider webs covering them. The picture will have little depth.

Now look at the image in Figure 5.25. This image shows a forest view with substantial depth—the scene begins close to the viewer and continues into the distance. However, as you may have surmised already, both images are identical. The first version has been reversed (east to west) and inverted.

Why do we perceive these images so differently? During the course of human evolution, the only available light source was the sun—illumination came from above, and our eyes were primarily adapted to interpret visual imagery based on the "assumption" that light is coming from above (Torralba & Oliva, 2003). When the image is turned upside down, the assumption of lighting from above has been violated because the light is now coming from below. Violation of the "light from above assumption" is the primary reason why human faces look "spooky" when illuminated by a flashlight from underneath the chin in the dark. When you perceive spider webs in Figure 5.24 or a spooky face when you shine a flashlight under someone's chin, your perceptual "machinery" is attempting to impose order on stimuli it did not evolve to interpret.

When the sense organs receive physical or chemical stimuli, these stimuli have no inherent meaning—they merely form the basis for what will happen later in the brain. The signals are sent "up" to the brain for further processing and interpretation. The remainder of this chapter is devoted to exploring the ways in which the machinery of perception does its everyday work, generally succeeding well, but occasionally failing in predictable ways.

Visual Images Are Organized

Consider the following paragraph, which has been floating around the Internet since the early 2000s:

> Aoccdrnig to rseerach at Cmabrigde Uinervtisy, it deosn't mttaer in waht oredr the ltteers in a wrod are, the olny ipmroatnt tihng is taht the frist and lsat ltteer be at the rghit pclae. The rset can be a total mses and you can sitll raed it wouthit porbelm. Tihs is bcuseae the huamn mnid deos not raed ervey lteter by istlef, but the wrod as a wlohe. Amzanig huh?

In fact, no such research exists at Cambridge, and the trick—it is a trick—only works because the misspellings follow certain basic patterns (see if you can figure them out) and small connecting words are correctly spelled. However, if you are a native English speaker you should be able to zip through this paragraph fairly easily. As you read the misspelled paragraph you perceive whole words from what amounts to little more than alphabetic clues. Your brain "fills in" the identity of each word and places it correctly in the context of a thought. In the same way, when you look at a television screen, you do not see a large group of glowing phosphorous dots arranged in patterns (unless you put your eyes right up against the screen). Instead, you see people, places, and things.

At the turn of the 20th century, Max Wertheimer (1880–1943) and his colleagues in Berlin founded a school of early scientific psychology known as the **Gestalt school** to explain how human beings made the necessary decisions to

▲ **FIGURE 5.24 What are you seeing?** When most people view this photo, they see a series of thick spider webs covering some bushes or branches. *(Source: Torralba & Oliva, 2003.)*

▲ **FIGURE 5.25 What are you seeing?** When the image is reversed and inverted, a forest view with depth emerges.

Gestalt school ▶ An early school of psychology that emphasized the mechanisms by which human beings create perceptions of meaningful "wholes" from inherently fragmented and meaningless sensory signals.

▶ **People or Dots?** When we look at a TV screen, we see people, not the cleverly arranged shimmering phosphorous dots that actually appear on the screen. Only when we move right up to the screen are we able to see what is actually there.

A.

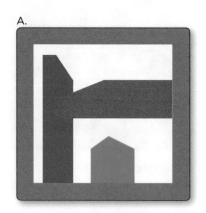

B.

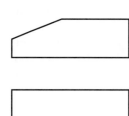

▲ **FIGURE 5.26** Which of the shapes in Image A are reproduced in Image B? *(Source: Adapted from Rubin, 2001.)*

Gestalt ▶ German for "whole form" or "shape."

Figure ▶ Gestalt psychology term for that aspect of a visual image upon which a person focuses, while relegating other aspects of the image to the background (ground).

Ground ▶ Gestalt psychology term for those aspects of a visual image relegated to the background.

organize visual elements in a meaningful way. The term **Gestalt** is German for *whole form* or *shape*. The basic idea behind the Gestalt school is that human beings have an innate tendency to perceive meaningful "wholes" out of inherently meaningless and fragmented sensory impressions. This idea is summed up in the expression *the whole is greater than the sum of its parts*. The most important contributions of Gestalt theory to the study of perception are the notion of *figure-ground relationships* and an explanation for the way human beings group isolated features of objects to form whole perceptions.

FIGURE AND GROUND

The world is a vibrating, teeming mass of sensory signals competing for our attention. Yet we are able to focus our attention on certain pieces of information while filtering out other aspects of the environment. When you and a friend sit at a table in a restaurant, you are surrounded by people speaking, but you probably will be focusing on what your friend is saying. The dozens of dialogues around you are likely little more than background noise. Proud parents watching their daughter on the basketball court may perceive all the other players as background movement as they focus on their child's triumphs and failures. As you read this page, you focus on the words in black—not the white page the words are printed on.

Gestalt theorists proposed that every time we view a scene, we focus on certain elements while others fade into the background. The portion of the image that holds our attention is the **figure**, and the remaining portion of the image is the **ground** (Rubin, 2001). Consider Figure 5.26. Which of the shapes in Figure A is reproduced in Figure B? Most people choose the top shape in Figure B, but the bottom shape is also a part of Figure A. However, the bottom shape exists in white, created by the way the purple and red shapes are placed on the page. Most people perceive the white areas as the *ground* of Figure A, and do not perceive them as shapes at all.

The inherent ambiguity of what constitutes figure and what constitutes ground is most famously presented in the two *reversible images* depicted in

A   B

FIGURE 5.27 Reversible Images. Each image can be seen two different ways, depending upon which aspect of the image you choose as figure and which as ground.

Figure 5.27. In Image A, you may see two human profiles in white, one on the left and one on the right—or you may see a single urn in the middle of the page in black. It all depends on whether you choose white as figure or as ground. In Image B, depending on your choice for figure and ground, you may see a "witch-like" image of an old woman with her chin tucked to her chest, or an elegant young woman in old-fashioned garb, gazing over her right shoulder.

Why does this form of organizing perception occur? It is important to realize that forming perceptions involves an expenditure of energy and mental resources. As Nava Rubin (2001) points out, if we were to take the colored figure shapes from Figure 5.26 and rearrange them on the page, their shape would always remain the same, but the ground shapes would be completely transformed. Thus, ground shapes are "accidental" outcomes of how figures are arranged. As a rule, then, it is a waste of mental resources to pay attention to the shapes of grounds.

FIGURE 5.28 Proximity. People tend to group figures together that are close to one another. This figure could be perceived as six lines on a page, but we tend to perceive them as three sets of two adjacent horizontal lines.

GESTALT PERCEPTUAL GROUPING

Gestalt psychologists also described laws governing the way we *group* specific features of objects once we have discriminated figures from grounds. Aspects of images such as shapes, sizes, colors, and so forth are transformed into meaningful wholes (Wertheimer, 1923/1950). Some of these laws of *perceptual grouping* are apparent in the way infants as young as 3 months attend to various types of visual stimuli, while others develop as the human being gains more experience in the world (Quinn, Bhatt, Brush, Grimes, & Sharpnack, 2002).

Among the more important of the original laws of perceptual grouping described by Gestalt psychologists are:

Proximity: We tend to group figures together that are near one another. For example, in Figure 5.28 you probably see three sets of two horizontal lines, rather than six lines on a page.

Similarity: We tend to group figures together if they are similar to one another. In Figure 5.29 you probably see three vertical rows of similar letters, rather than three horizontal rows of dissimilar letters.

Closure: If there is a gap in the image of a familiar object, we will mentally fill in the missing portion to form a meaningful whole. Consider what happens if you view an automobile behind a pole. The pole dissects the car into two pieces, but you see a whole car, not two disconnected car

Proximity ▶ A Gestalt law of perceptual grouping that states that people tend to group figures together that are near one another.

Similarity ▶ A Gestalt law of perceptual grouping which states that people tend to group figures together if they are similar to one another.

Closure ▶ A Gestalt law of perceptual grouping that states that if there is a gap in the image of a familiar object, people will mentally fill in the missing elements.

▲ FIGURE 5.29 Similarity. If objects are similar, they tend to be grouped together when they are perceived. This figure could be grouped as three horizontal rows of XOZ, but you will almost certainly perceive the figure as three vertical rows of Xs, Os, and Zs.

▲ FIGURE 5.30 Closure. When there is a gap in a familiar object, we tend to mentally fill in the missing portion to form a meaningful whole. You will likely have no trouble recognizing a horse in this incomplete figure.

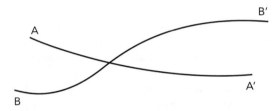

▲ FIGURE 5.31 Good Continuation. When visual elements suggest a line—but may be perceived in other ways as well—the tendency will be to perceive them as a line. You probably have to "struggle" to perceive this image as two V-shapes formed by A–B and A¹–B¹, whereas it is easy to perceive the image as two continuous lines A–A¹ and B–B¹.

Good continuation ▶ A Gestalt law of perceptual grouping that states that any visual elements which suggest a continued line will be grouped together.

Depth perception ▶ The visual perceptual mechanism that allows for the judgment of distance of objects and creates a "3-D" image even though retinal images are "2-D."

halves (S. E. Palmer, 2002). Closure is also illustrated by the drawing in Figure 5.30. Although the drawing consists of disconnected lines, you likely have no trouble recognizing it as a horse.

Good Continuation: According to the law of good continuation, any visual elements that suggest a continued line will be grouped together. For example, the images in Figure 5.31 will be seen as two continuous lines. These lines could just as easily be seen as two V-shapes, but because of the law of good continuation, you have to really work hard to see it that way.

Visual Images Have Depth

When an image forms on your retina, it is two-dimensional, much like the image in a photograph. Yet, we perceive the image in three dimensions, just as we perceive the image contained in a photograph to contain three dimensions even though it is printed on a two-dimensional piece of paper. Moreover, human beings and other animals acquire this talent of **depth perception**— which enables us to judge the distances of objects—extremely early in life. In a classic experiment, Eleanor Gibson and Richard Walk (1960) devised a *visual cliff*—a table with a glass top that extends out over a steep cliff-like drop at one end, and a one-inch drop at the other end (see Figure 5.32). In each trial of the experiment, an infant was placed on the table as the mother stood at one end or the other to try to coax her baby to crawl forward over the apparent steep drop or the one-inch drop. In all, 27 of 36 infants (who ranged in age from 6 to 14 months) moved off the table portion of the device and onto the glass-covered apparent drops. All of these infants crawled toward the mother over the apparent one-inch drop—but only three ventured out over the steep drop. This suggests very early development of depth perception in humans.

DEPTH PERCEPTION RELIES UPON TWO TYPES OF CUES

Depth perception does not only keep infants—or adults—from tumbling over cliffs. Without depth perception we would be unable to find our coffee cups on the table. How do our brains transform two-dimensional retinal images into three-dimensional reality? We use two types of environmental cues—**binocular cues**, which require the use of both eyes, and **monocular cues**, which only require use of only one eye.

Binocular Cues Each of your eyes takes in a very slightly different view of the world because there is a distance of a few inches between the eyes, and therefore a *disparity* between the views of your left and right eyes. This **retinal disparity** in the view of each eye is the first binocular cue to depth. While the views of each eye differ slightly, however, they obviously also overlap, given that our eyes are not on opposite sides of the head (as are rabbits' eyes, for example). The brain makes complex calculations based upon the amount of retinal disparity and overlap to arrive at a judgment of depth. This occurs much the way stereophonic sound creates the illusion of depth by emphasizing one or another instrument in each speaker, yet allowing the instruments also to overlap in both speakers as well. Visual *virtual reality* devices take advantage of retinal disparity as a binocular cue to depth by presenting two slightly different, but overlapping, images on two separate video screens, one for each eye.

A second binocular cue is **convergence**. When you focus on objects that are relatively close to your face, your ocular muscles rotate your eyes inward, allowing them to *converge*. The brain notes the strength of the muscular signal and computes distance accordingly. You can see this by focusing on your fingertip at arm's length, and slowly moving your finger inward toward your nose. Your eyes will increasingly converge until you become "cross-eyed." (This is a great way to amuse small children, by the way—and, no, doing this exercise won't make them cross-eyed.)

Monocular Cues Monocular depth cues are particularly important because binocular cues only operate at short distances. Convergence is irrelevant at long distances because the eyes do not converge at all when viewing distant objects. Neither is there significant retinal disparity when viewing distant objects—each eye sees much the same thing. There are four primary monocular cues.

1. *Relative size.* When objects are closer, their image on the retina is larger than when they are more distant. Thus, closer objects seem larger, and more distant objects smaller. Several wonderful optical illusions have been created that take advantage of our tendency to use relative size as a monocular cue to depth. Undoubtedly the most famous is known as the Ames room (after its creator, Adelbert Ames, Jr.), depicted in Figure 5.33. In the photo on the left, the girl in white is the taller of the two girls. In the photo on the right, she has shrunk, while the girl in the red jacket has become giant-sized—a true Alice in Wonderland situation.

How is the Ames effect achieved? The viewer, who sees the scene only through a peephole (indicated by the red arrow in Figure 5.34), believes that the room is rectangular and therefore assumes that both girls are on the same plane, equally distant from his or her view. If this were true, then the girls really would be different sizes. But in fact, the rear wall is constructed so that it angles forward considerably on the right, making the girl on the right always much closer to the viewer. This plays on our judgments of distance based upon relative size (Sedgwick, 2001). The ceiling is also constructed at an angle so

▲ **FIGURE 5.32 The Visual Cliff.** Very few infants will venture out onto the glass that covers an apparent drop.

Binocular cues ▶ Cues to depth perception that necessitate both eyes—specifically retinal disparity and convergence.

Monocular cues ▶ Cues to depth perception that can operate even when only one eye is available. Specifically: relative size, texture gradient, linear perspective, interposition, atmospheric influence, and position on the horizon.

Retinal disparity ▶ A binocular cue to depth perception based on the fact that each eye takes in a slightly different, but overlapping, view.

Convergence ▶ A binocular cue to depth perception based on the fact that ocular muscles rotate eyes inward when viewing close objects.

▶ **FIGURE 5.33 The Incredible Shrinking Girl.** The Ames room uses the monocular cue of relative size to create the illusion that a person standing to the right is much larger than a person standing to the left.

▲ We have no trouble perceiving the drop into the Grand Canyon (top). Apollo astronauts at first found it disconcerting that they could not accurately judge the depth of moon craters. The crater Daedalus, almost two miles deep, is pictured on bottom.

that it slopes downward, toward the girl on the right, making her head closer to the ceiling.

2. *Linear perspective.* Any parallel lines moving away from an observer—floor boards, railroad tracks, the shoulders of a highway, and so forth—converge as they stretch out into the distance until they eventually meet at a single point, known as the *vanishing point,* as seen in Figure 5.35.

An interesting perceptual illusion that plays upon linear perspective cues to depth is known as the Ponzo illusion, depicted in Figure 5.36. Most people perceive Box A to be larger than Box B. However, both boxes are identical in size, as you can easily ascertain with a ruler. The reason Box A appears larger is because we assume any object seen toward the vanishing point of parallel lines must be farther away than an object seen toward a more parallel point in the lines. And yet, because the boxes actually *are* the same size, they will create retinal images of equal sizes. If an object that is very far away throws an image on the retina that is identical in size to a close object, the farther away object would ordinarily be much larger than the close object. Thus, we misperceive the size of the boxes.

3. *Interposition (object blocking).* When one object blocks the view of another object, we assume that the blocked object is behind the first object and therefore farther away from us, as evident in the photo of two deer in Figure 5.37.

4. *Position on the horizon.* An interesting perceptual reversal occurs depending upon whether we view objects below or above the horizon line. In general, if objects are *below* the horizon line, they are perceived as closer—and the lower in our visual field they appear, the closer they appear.

The opposite happens for objects *above* the horizon line. When objects are *above* the horizon line, the *lower* in your visual field they appear, the farther away they will be perceived to be.

One marvelous natural illusion that may be explainable according to the position on the horizon depth cue is the *moon illusion.* When the moon is at a low point on the horizon (either rising or setting), it always looks much larger than when it is high in the sky, as is evident in Figure 5.38. However, as time-lapse photography of a moon rising over Seattle, Washington, clearly shows in Figure 5.39, the moon is not larger when it is low in the sky. The camera is not fooled—why are we?

Monocular cues to depth depend greatly upon mental "assumptions" (such as the light-from-above assumption) and environmental factors that have remained relatively constant throughout human evolutionary history on earth. Artists spend many years developing the skills necessary to utilize such earthly

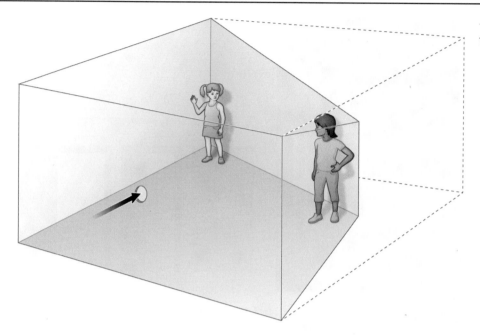

◀ **FIGURE 5.34** The True Shape of the Ames Room.

▲ **FIGURE 5.35** Linear Perspective.

▲ **FIGURE 5.36** The Ponzo Illusion. Which box is larger?

▲ **FIGURE 5.37** Interposition.

▲ **FIGURE 5.38** The Moon Hanging Low on the Horizon.

▲ **FIGURE 5.39** The Moon Illusion—A Genuine Natural Illusion. Time-lapse photography over Seattle, Washington, by Shay Stephans shows that the moon actually remains the same size regardless of its place on the horizon.

▲ FIGURE 5.40 Monocular **Depth Cues on the City Streets.** A particularly astonishing use of monocular depth cues is employed in a type of graphic art known as *trompe l'oeil*, which means literally "fool the eyes." Trompe l'oeil artists such as Julian Beever, whose work is displayed here, create amazing three-dimensional scenes with photographic realism.

▲ FIGURE 5.41 Size Constancy. We perceive that these boys are of approximately the same height even though the image the closer boy casts on the retina is larger.

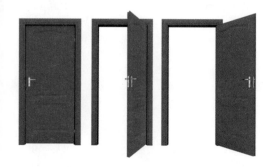

▲ FIGURE 5.42 Shape Constancy. The door remains rectangular in our minds although it changes shape on the retina.

Perceptual constancy ▶ The ability to perceive an object as itself regardless of changes in angle of viewing, distance, or illumination.

Size constancy ▶ The facet of perceptual constancy that allows us to perceive an object as the same size regardless of the size of its image on our retina.

Shape constancy ▶ The facet of perceptual constancy that allows us to perceive an object as the same shape regardless of the angle from which we view it.

constants to fool the eyes into perceiving monocular cues where none exist, as spectacularly depicted in Figure 5.40.

Visual Images Have Constancy

Depth perception allows you to locate objects in your visual field. The only problem is that neither you nor objects are always standing still. If you walk toward, around, or away from an object—or the object itself moves—its image on your retinas may change size or shape, and conditions of illumination may also change. Given these possible changes, how do you continue to recognize an object as being what it is? The human ability to perceive an object as "itself" despite changes in angle of view, distance, illumination, and so forth is known as **perceptual constancy**. There are four primary categories of perceptual constancy: *size constancy, shape constancy, brightness constancy*, and *color constancy*.

Recall that the size of the image an object casts upon the retina changes as we change our distance from the object. **Size constancy** is the ability to perceive that an object remains the same size in the world regardless of changes in the size of its image on our retina. As we watch a friend walk away down the street, we do not scream in horror as she slowly shrinks in size. Our brains factor in both the size of an object on our retina and our *knowledge* of how distant the object is to arrive at a judgment of actual size (see Figure 5.41).

Shape constancy is the way we maintain a constant perception of an object's shape regardless of the angle from which we view it. Consider a door opening from the inside, as depicted in Figure 5.42. When the door is shut it is rectangular in shape. As the door begins to open, it loses its rectangular shape on the retina, but we still perceive it as a rectangle.

Changes in proximity to an object or changes in angle of viewing necessitate size and shape constancy. But changes in environmental conditions such as the extent or type of illumination necessitate *brightness constancy* and *color constancy*. For example, my perception of the brightness of my daughter's gold locket sitting on my desk does not change because it is nighttime and the locket reflects less light. My mind adjusts to less reflected light by perceiving that everything around the locket is also reflecting less light than during the day. Thus, it is the *ratio* of reflected light from the locket to objects around it, rather than the *absolute* level of reflected light from the locket, that accounts for my perception of brightness. This is **brightness constancy**.

Color constancy is trickier to maintain in changing illumination. Our color perceptual system evolved under conditions of natural lighting—sunlight. Some of the qualities of sunlight are mimicked by various types of electric bulbs, but others are not. For example, sunlight contains about equal levels of energy at all wavelengths, but most light bulbs tend to contain more energy at longer wavelengths (Goldstein, 2010). How, then, do I perceive the pink bougainvillea blossoms seen outside my window to be the same color when they drift inside my home at night, illuminated only by artificial indoor lighting? This question is not easily answered—even by scientists studying sensation and perception. It is likely the result of a number of factors. Nevertheless, without color constancy, the color of the bougainvillea blossoms would depend entirely on the light source and its intensity.

Sometimes, however, color constancy breaks down if the conditions of illumination stray too far from those that mimic sunlight. Take the type of mercury vapor lighting often used in outdoor parking lots, for example. Lack of color constancy under such lighting conditions is one reason it can be hard to find your car in outdoor parking lots at night where all cars appear to be of a similar color.

Brightness constancy ▶ The facet of perceptual constancy that allows us to perceive an object as the same brightness regardless of the available illumination.

Color constancy ▶ The facet of perceptual constancy that allows us to perceive an object as the same color regardless of the amount or type of illumination.

IN SUMMARY

1.	Gestalt principles of perceptual organization include the notions of figure and ground and laws of perceptual grouping. When viewing a scene, people choose certain elements on which to focus (figure)and other elements to relegate to the background (ground). Perceptual grouping laws include proximity, similarity, closure, and good continuation.
2.	Depth perception is achieved through binocular and monocular cues. Binocular cues include retinal disparity and convergence. Monocular cues include relative size, linear perspective, interposition, and position on the horizon.
3.	Size constancy is the ability to maintain an awareness of the actual size of an object as we move closer to or farther away from it. Shape constancy involves maintaining a single idea about the shape of an object even if we change our angle of viewing the object. Brightness constancy and color constancy refer to our ability to maintain a consistent perception of the brightness and color of an object regardless of the amount or type of illumination. Of all types of constancy, color constancy is the most likely to fail.

RETRIEVE!

1.	When we mentally fill in the missing portion in an image to form a meaningful whole, we are using the Gestalt perceptual law of _____. When we group figures together that are near one another, we are invoking the law of _____. **a)** good continuation/similarity **c)** closure/proximity **b)** proximity/similarity **d)** similarity/closure
2.	How did experiments with the visual cliff provide evidence of early development of depth perception?

3. When you focus on objects that are relatively close, your ocular muscles rotate your eyes inward. The brain notes the strength of this muscular signal and computes your distance from the object upon which you are focusing. This binocular cue to depth perception is known as _____.

4. Match the description on the left with the monocular cue to depth perception on the right.

When objects are close, their image on the retina is larger than when they are distant.	Position on the horizon
The lower in your visual field an object appears, the closer it is perceived to be.	Linear perspective
Parallel lines converge as they stretch out into the distance.	Relative size
When objects are below the horizon line, they are perceived as closer.	Interposition

5. How is size constancy achieved?

6. Why is it sometimes difficult to locate a car at night in an outdoor parking lot lit by mercury vapor lighting?

How Do Evolution, Culture, and Experience Affect Perception?

Earlier I mentioned how important aspects of visual perception were shaped over evolutionary time by the fact that the sun was the only source of light for our early ancestors. Indeed, all of our sense organs and basic perceptual systems were shaped through evolutionary processes, and evolution has "affected" perception from A to Z. However, the effects of evolution on perception may be more specialized than previously considered. For example, there is evidence that human beings possess specific visual, neural, and cognitive tools "dedicated" to recognizing and distinguishing faces, and those specialized for detecting movement in living creatures—a phenomenon termed *biological motion* (Kanwisher & Yovel, 2006; Moulson, Westerlund, Fox, Zeanah, & Nelson, 2009; Nelson, 2001; Pelphrey & Morris, 2006). Some researchers consider these visual-cognitive tools to result from evolutionary psychological adaptations, as described in Chapter 3 (e.g., Nelson, 2001; Slaughter, Stone, & Reed, 2004). Let us consider the phenomenon of face perception.

Face Recognition: Specialized Tool of Perception?

Face recognition is the ability to distinguish faces from other objects or body parts, and to recognize specific familiar faces. You might think that distinguishing a human face from the back of a human head (or from a bag of *Cheese Doodles*) doesn't take all that much skill, and chalk this talent up to something acquired over time through experience. However, consider the following:

- Infants as young as 3 days prefer to look at faces and patterns depicting faces than at nonface patterns—but this preference does not hold if the images of faces are upside down or the facial features are scrambled

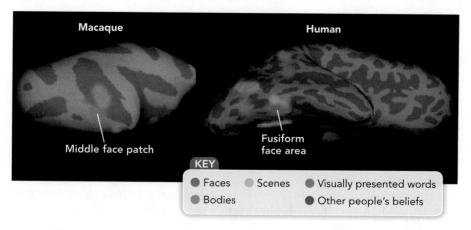

▲ **FIGURE 5.43 The Face Is "Special" to the Brain.** In the image of a human brain on the right, regions that respond to face processing tasks are highlighted in pink, with the fusiform face area (FFA) noted. Other colors represent regions activated in recognizing bodies, visual scenes, words presented visually, and when considering what other people might be thinking. On the left is a macaque monkey brain with the monkey equivalent of the FFA (*middle face patch*) noted. Doris Tsao and colleagues (2006) were able to record the activity of neurons within the middle face patch, demonstrating conclusively that this area is used selectively to respond to faces (but not to bodies or objects). (Both brain images presented here show the back of the brain to the left side.) *(Source: Kanwisher, 2006, p. 617; original credit: D. Tsao, Harvard Medical School; I. Baker & F. Schwarzlose, MIT)*

(Macchi Cassia, Turati, & Simion, 2004; Pascalis & Kelly, 2009; Turati, Bulf, & Simion, 2008). Two- to three-day-old infants are also able to discriminate their mother's face from that of a stranger, and they prefer to gaze at it (Pascalis & Kelly, 2009; Bushnell, 2001).

- People are better able to recognize an image of an upside-down object than an upside-down face (Nelson, 2001).
- Damage to specific brain regions results in an inability to recognize objects or words, but may leave facial recognition processes intact (Moscovitch, Winocur, & Behrmann, 1997); damage to other brain regions does the opposite—it impairs the ability to recognize faces while leaving object and word recognition intact (Kleinschmidt & Cohen, 2006; Kanwisher & Yovel, 2006; Wada & Yamamoto, 2001).

Although certain brain regions that become activated during face perception are also activated during a number of other tasks, neuroscientist Nancy Kanwisher has shown that there is a "blueberry-sized" cortical region of the right hemisphere seemingly set aside exclusively for face perception and recognition. Kanwisher coined the term *fusiform face area* (FFA) to refer to this brain region (e.g., Kanwisher, 2006; Kanwisher & Yovel, 2006; Liu, Harris, & Kanwisher, 2010; see Figure 5.43). Several other brain regions were subsequently identified as "preferential" to face perception (Moulson et al., 2009).

Studies of macaque monkeys strongly support the notion that faces are "special" to the brain. Doris Tsao and her colleagues studied a group of macaques using fMRI technology to detect brain region activity (Tsao, Freiwald, Tootell, & Livingstone, 2006). As with fMRI studies of human beings, these investigators found a specific brain region (in the case of monkeys, the *middle face patch*) that became activated as the monkey viewed images of faces, but not as the animals viewed images of bodies, fruits, and other objects. However, Tsao and her colleagues went a step further and implanted electrodes in the monkeys' brains to record the activity of the neurons of the middle face patch. (This technology cannot be used in human beings for safety reasons.) Tsao and her research team found that 97% of the neurons in this region fired during face recognition tasks, but not during other tasks (see Figure 5.43).

THE IMPORTANCE OF EXPERIENCE IN PERCEPTION

While it certainly is tempting to conclude that specialized visual-cognitive mechanisms such as face perception evolved to assist our ancestors to survive in a world populated with other humans, the story may not be so simple. For example, the evolutionary approach does not account for neuroscientists' discovery that brain regions that appear to respond selectively to the visual presentation of words and strings of letters. Because written language did not exist among our evolutionary ancestors, the mere existence of localized (specialized) brain regions is clearly not sufficient evidence that the regions evolved specifically to serve the functions they apparently now do serve (Kanwisher, 2006).

But let us assume for a moment that evolution did indeed shape face perception mechanisms in the brain through natural selection. Certainly, there is a good case for this being true (Pascalis & Kelly, 2009). However, the evolutionary origin of face perception mechanisms would not necessarily mean that these mechanisms are *innate*—that is, regardless of evolutionary origins, we may or may not come into the world with face perception tools already in place.

Why does "evolutionary origin" not necessarily equal "innate"? Although some researchers do believe that we are born with face perception mechanisms already in place, others argue that *experience* is critical for the development of specialized visual-cognitive mechanisms such as face perception (Nelson, 2001; Turati, Valenza, Leo, & Simion, 2005). These researchers do not deny the importance of evolution. However, they suggest that, rather than being innate, face perception is an experience-expectant process, meaning that neural tissue in the brain is in place at birth that "expects" to receive certain "input"—in this case, visual exposure to faces over time. However, at birth, face perception mechanisms are only a *potential*. Such mechanisms cannot develop without experience. Thus, from the experience-expectant view, natural selection has not shaped face perception—it has shaped the *potential* for face perception. It is experience—repeated visual exposure to faces—that actually forms and "fine-tunes" the mechanisms themselves.

Some evidence supports this view. Daphne Maurer and her colleagues found that specific aspects of normal face recognition ability are profoundly and permanently impaired in children who are born with cataracts that prevent ordinary early experiences of viewing faces—in spite of treatment for these cataracts within months of birth (Maurer, Mondloch, & Lewis, 2007).

Perception Is Influenced by Expectation and Attention

Even if it turns out that face perception mechanisms are innate and not experience-expectant, it is beyond question that experience profoundly influences perception. One aspect of experience that is particularly influential is *expectation*. It is often said that "people see what they want to see," but more frequently it is the case that "people see what they *expect* to see" based on previous experiences.

For example, imagine that a hapless stranger carrying a campus map stops to ask you for directions outside your dorm. As you start to help him, two men carrying a door rudely walk in between the two of you. As they pass through, one of the men carrying the door surreptitiously switches places with the stranger, without skipping a beat. Once the men pass, do you think you would notice that the person now standing before you seeking directions is an entirely different individual—even dressed differently (or of a different sex or ethnicity)? (See Figure 5.44.)

When studies such as this one are conducted, approximately 50% of those stopped for directions do *not* notice the change. This has been shown to occur even when the sex and ethnicity of the person changes! The inability to detect even radical changes in a scene following a very brief distraction is known as **change blindness** (Alva, 2007; Simons & Levin, 1998). It results when our expectations for a scene block out our ability to perceive actual details of the scene.

While expectation may prevent us from noticing radical changes to objects or persons in our environment, *attention*—or, rather *in*attention—can prevent us from seeing the objects and persons at all, even when we are looking straight at them (Mack, 2003; Simons & Chabris, 1999; Chabris & Simons, 2010). A famous example of this (that has ended up in numerous copycat videos on YouTube) is the "Gorillas in Our Midst" experiment by Daniel Simons and Christopher Chabris (1999; see Figure 5.45). These researchers asked volunteers to watch a short video of students playing basketball, with half the students dressed in black t-shirts and the other half dressed in white. The volunteers were asked to count the number of ball passes completed only by one team. (Some volunteers were told to count the black-shirt team's passes, others the white's.)[1]

The volunteers usually were able to count the passes fairly well while watching the tape. However, after the tape was completed, the experimenters asked a number of surprise questions, the most important being, "While you were doing the counting, did you notice anything unusual in the video?" and "Did you see anyone else appear on the video?" Approximately 50% of the volunteers had seen nothing unusual, and had seen no one other than the players. In fact, however, midway through the video a woman in a full-body gorilla suit had walked into the midst of the players, turned to face the camera and thumped her chest—yet half of those watching the video hadn't seen anything unusual! Moreover, when shown the videos again after being told about the gorilla, many refused to believe that this was the same video they had seen, and some even questioned the honesty of the experimenters (Chabris & Simon, 2010). This experiment has been repeated numerous times in different countries and under slightly different conditions, but the result is always the same—about 50% of participants miss what one would think could not be missed.

Inattentional blindness is the term used when a person is *looking* directly at an object without *seeing* the object due to that person's attention being drawn elsewhere. In this case, the viewer's attention is drawn to the task of counting ball passes, and he or she is blind to the chest-thumping gorilla. Inattentional blindness can be funny (just watch the many YouTube videos), but it is not a joke. Plane crashes, car crashes, boating accidents, and mistaken eyewitness testimony in criminal cases all have likely resulted from inattentional blindness (Chabris & Simons, 2010; Mack, 2003, Most, Scholl, Clifford, & Simons, 2005).

Perceptual Set

Although change blindness and inattentional blindness are complex phenomena involving vision, memory, expectation, attention, and other factors, they are also part of a much larger phenomenon known as *perceptual set*. When we view a scene, we bring with us a lifetime of personal experiences, as well as immediate expectations—including expectations for where attention ought to be placed and what ought to be occurring at any given moment—which bias our perceptions. These expectations, biases, and predispositions are our **perceptual set**.

A simple example is displayed in Figure 5.46. If you look at these changing images, beginning with the image to your far right, by the time you reach the

▲ **FIGURE 5.44 "Change Blindness" on Campus.** The bearded man to the right is being asked directions by a young stranger. Two workmen carrying a door interrupt the exchange, and one of the door carriers switches places with the pedestrian. The bearded man is oblivious to the switch. *(Source: Simons & Levin, 1998)*

Change blindness ▶ The inability to detect changes in a scene following a brief distraction.

Inattentional blindness ▶ The inability to see highly visible objects at which one is looking directly when attention is drawn elsewhere.

Perceptual set ▶ The expectations, biases, and preconceptions that we bring to a given perception.

[1]*The actual experiment was considerably more complex than what I have described, but the basic idea remains the same.*

FIGURE 5.45 Gorillas in Our Midst: Inattentional Blindness. Researchers Daniel Simons and Christopher Chabris asked volunteers to count the number of completed passes made by one team in a video of students playing basketball. Approximately 50% failed to notice a woman in full-body gorilla suit who calmly walked out in the middle of the scene, turned to the camera and began to thump her chest. Similar results have been found in numerous studies conducted around the world.

Müller-Lyer illusion ▶ A visual illusion where two lines of identical length appear to be of unequal length.

middle image you will still see an image of a woman's figure. If you begin at the far left, by the time you reach the middle, you will still see a caricatured man's face. This is because you have already acquired a perceptual set by the time you reach the middle image.

The *Rorschach test*, popularly known as the "ink blot test," is a well-known (but highly controversial) psychological instrument for measuring personality and psychopathology that operates on the assumption of perceptual set. In this test, a series of ambiguous ink-blot cards, such as the one in Figure 5.47, are presented to a participant, who is asked to tell the researcher what he or she sees. The expectation is that the participant will "project" aspects of his or her personality or psychopathology on to the ink blot by way of a perceptual set for interpreting the design. However, in general, the most important part of the response is not so much what the person "sees" in the inkblot (I see a bat-like crab), but rather an amalgam of factors including the participant's explanation for *what* it was about the blot that gave it its designated appearance, how similar the blot *actually* looks to the identified object, how the participant organizes his or her responses, and so forth (Hunsley, Lee, & Wood, 2003).

People from Different Cultures May "See Things Differently"

Now take a look at the two lines in Figure 5.48. Which line is longer? You might be surprised to learn that the lines are of identical length (use a ruler to check if you like).

There are several possible explanations for why we see these lines as different in length, a perceptual effect known as the **Müller-Lyer illusion**. Richard Gregory (1973; 1997) proposes that when we view these lines, they are reminiscent of the corners formed by the joining of two walls. The line on the right looks like two walls whose corner points toward us (outside corner), and the line on the left looks like two walls whose corner points away from us (inside corner; see Figure 5.49). In most cases, an outside corner would be closer than an inside corner. If the sizes of the images of two objects on our retinas are identical, but one of the objects is assumed to be farther away, that object will also be perceived to be larger. Therefore, the line to the left in Figure 5.48 will be perceived to be larger because—being an inside corner—we assume that it is farther away. According to Gregory, it is not necessary that we consciously perceive these lines to represent corners. This association is made below the level of awareness.

Some cross-cultural evidence is consistent with this explanation. Throughout the 20th century, researchers in visual perception struggled to explain why some people living in rural, non-Western environments did not seem to be as susceptible to the Müller-Lyer illusion as Westerners. During the 1960s, cross-cultural psychologists suggested that the explanation lay in the fact that Westerners live in a "carpentered world," filled with angular walls and structures. In contrast, many traditional non-Western structures are more often circular, and the forms of nature also tend to lack the angularity of the square and rectangular structures created by Westerners for living and working quarters. These researchers claimed that people living in "noncarpentered worlds" would not see inside or outside corners when viewing the Müller-Lyer lines (Pedersen & Wheeler, 1983; Segall, Campbell, & Herskovits, 1966).

Studies comparing Westerners and East Asians have added evidence for the notion that culture may affect visual perception (Boduroglu, Shah, & Nisbett, 2009; Masuda & Nisbett, 2001). Takahiko Masuda and Richard Nisbett began with the general observation that *context* appeared to be of greater importance in the cognitive processes of East Asians as compared with Westerners. For example, Americans are more likely than native Chinese to explain another person's behavior in terms of stable characteristics and personality, whereas

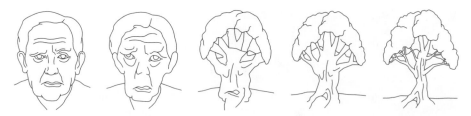

▲ **FIGURE 5.46 Perceptual Set.** If you start at the left and move inward, you will end up viewing the image of a tree. If you begin at the right, you will end up viewing the image of a man's face (Fischer, 1968).

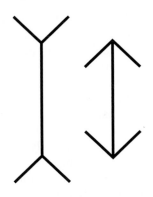

▲ **FIGURE 5.47 A Rorschach Test Card.** What you see in this image may be determined in part by your perceptual set.

▲ **FIGURE 5.48 The Müller-Lyer Illusion.**

◄**FIGURE 5.49 The Gregory (1973) Explanation for the Müller-Lyer Illusion.** We assume that inside corners are farther away than outside corners. If an apparent inside corner throws an image on our retina of identical size to that of an outside corner, we assume that the inside corner is larger.

native Chinese are more likely to take into consideration the context and circumstances in which the behavior occurs as well as the person's characteristics (Norenzayan & Nisbett, 2000).

Masuda and Nisbett then used a unique method to test the hypothesis that these general cultural characteristics would have specific effects on visual perception. They had Japanese and American participants view underwater scenes that included fish prominently moving among other objects such as plants, rocks, and coral. After viewing the scenes, Japanese participants were

▶ **Navajo Hogan** Part of a "noncarpentered" world?

▲ **FIGURE 5.50** When presented with these images, Americans fixed their eyes upon the focal object (the plane and the tiger) sooner and remained there longer than the Chinese. The Chinese engaged in rapid eye movements back and forth between the focal object and the background. Results like these have been used to argue that East Asians perceive objects holistically, taking in the environmental context (Chua et al., 2005).

able to recall many more details about these background objects than Americans, while recalling an equal number of details about the fish. However, when the Japanese were asked to recognize one of the fish they had seen when it was placed in a different background context, they had far more trouble than the Americans, who were uninfluenced by the background context (Masuda & Nisbett, 2001). Thus, the Japanese showed a greater tendency to view objects embedded in their background and context, rather than isolating the object and focusing on its unique properties.

But while these results are provocative, it is not clear exactly why they occurred. Did the Americans and Japanese differ in the way they actually *saw* the scenes, or only in the way they recalled them? Perhaps they merely differed in the way they tended to *report* their perceptions when questioned about them. To more directly test the hypothesis that Far Easterners and Westerners actually *see* things differently, Chua, Boland, and Nisbett (2005) presented European American and Chinese participants with scenes of a focal object (e.g., a tiger) placed in a characteristic background (e.g., jungle). Using devices that precisely track eye movements, these researchers found that Americans fixed their gaze upon the focal object sooner and remained there longer than the Chinese. On the other hand, Chinese participants engaged in more rapid eye movements than the Americans from the object to the background and back again (see Figure 5.50).

According to Nisbett and his colleague Yuri Miyamoto (2005), these results, and a series of others reported by cultural psychologists, suggest specific East-West differences in perception. Far Easterners focus *holistically* on the relationships among objects in context when perceptually organizing the environment, whereas Westerners focus *analytically* on the specific qualities of objects in order to categorize and organize them. This idea has been supported to some extent in subsequent research (Goh & Park, 2009; Goh, Tan, & Park, 2009; Park & Huang, 2010).

From where does this perceptual difference emerge? To some degree, this cultural difference may reflect East-West differences in *social orientation*—with Far Easterners endorsing an *interdependent* orientation that emphasizes harmony, relatedness, and connection with others; and Westerners endorsing an *independent* orientation emphasizing individual achievement (Varnum, Grossmann, Kitayama, & Nisbett, 2010).

IN SUMMARY

1. There is some evidence that a cortical region of the right hemisphere (the fusiform face area) may have been "set aside" as a result of evolutionary forces exclusively for face perception. However, face perception and recognition may necessitate particular types of early experiences in order to develop.

2. Change blindness occurs when a person is unable to detect even radical changes in a scene following a moment of distraction. Inattentional blindness occurs when a person's attention is drawn away from being able to perceive an object at which the person is looking directly. Change blindness and inattentional blindness are complex phenomena involving vision, memory, expectation, and attention, but they are also part of the larger phenomenon of perceptual set—the expectations, biases, and predispositions that we bring to the perception of a scene.

3. Culture has an effect on the way people perceive visual scenes.

RETRIEVE!

1. How have neuroscientific studies of macaque monkeys supported the idea that faces are "special" to the brain?

2. Although some researchers believe that we are born with face perception mechanisms already in place, others argue that *experience* is critical for the development of face perception. These researchers suggest that face perception is an _____ process.

    a) experience-expectant   **c)** experience-exceptioned

    b) experience-contingent   **d)** experience-dependent

3. Failing to notice radical changes in a scene following a very brief distraction is known as _____. Failing to perceive (see) an object at which one is looking because one's attention is drawn elsewhere is known as _____.

4. When shown underwater scenes that included fish moving among objects, Japanese participants excelled at one task in relation to Americans, but Americans excelled at a different task in relation to the Japanese. How did the Japanese and Americans differ?

CRITICAL THINKING ABOUT PSYCHOLOGY

Does Extrasensory Perception Exist?

A colleague of mine had a dream that a long-time friend, who lived 4,000 miles away on another continent, had been killed when a building fell on her. He woke up profoundly disturbed, and vowed to call his friend, as the two hadn't talked in some time. Before he could do so, however, *her* family called *him* . . . to tell him that his friend had been killed the night before in a freak accident involving a gas explosion in a building next to where she had been walking. A portion of the building had exploded outward, killing her instantly.

As you might imagine, he felt chilled to the bone. In addition to the grief he felt about his friend, he found himself questioning all his assumptions about time, reality, psychic phenomena, and so forth. An experience like that could make a believer in the **paranormal**—events that defy ordinary explanation—out of almost anyone. This went on for a while, until he reflected that in his life he had already experienced at least 18,000 dreams about events that had *not* come to pass. Strictly by chance, it should be expected that at least one out of 18,000 would coincide with a real event. Consider this from Susan Blackmore (1990):

> There are about 55 million people in Britain and they live about 70 years each. If each has one such dream [a dream of a person dying that turned out to come true] in a lifetime there should be 2000 every night. Also about 2000 people die in each 24 hours. So there will be 4 million coincidences among 55 million people. In other words such an "amazing" coincidence will be expected about once every two weeks. [*It should happen once a day in the United States.*] No further explanation is required, but try to believe that if it happens to you. As [Christopher] Scott puts it: "You, if you're human at all, you will conclude that there's cause and effect there. You can't regard yourself as just one among 55 million." (p. 63)

Paranormal ▶ Events that defy ordinary explanation.

CRITICAL THINKING ABOUT PSYCHOLOGY

CONTINUED

Apparently a great many people do *not* regard themselves as just one among tens of millions, because experiences that people find difficult to explain are quite common, and these experiences sometimes make believers out of those who previously were skeptical or had no opinion (Alcock, 2003; e.g., Varvoglis, 1997). The more such experiences a person has, the stronger is their belief in the paranormal (Glicksohn, 1990). In a 2005 Gallup survey, approximately 20% to 35% of Americans professed a belief in phenomena such as **telepathy** (communication between minds without speech), **clairvoyance** (psychic ability to predict the future or know about events that have occurred outside of one's own experience), **astrology** (the belief that the position of the stars and planets can affect people's life events and personalities), communication with the dead, and so forth. In all, 73% of Americans profess at least one such belief (D. W. Moore, 2005). Interestingly, some people who find it quite obvious that telepathy exists find the suggestion that some people can predict the future utterly ridiculous; and some who believe in communication with the dead dismiss ghosts and haunted houses as mere superstition.

You may be a believer in the paranormal or you may be a skeptic (or a cynic), but it may interest you to know that a branch of psychology known as **parapsychology** attempts to apply scientific methods to the study of at least certain of these phenomena. Parapsychologists tend to be less concerned with events that most people would term "supernatural," such as ghosts and devil possession, than phenomena that fall under the general category of **extra-sensory perception (ESP)**. ESP is the ability to acquire information by means other than the physical senses, for example by *telepathy* (thought-transference). Some parapsychologists are also interested in *telekinesis*, the ability to move physical objects with mental energy. Taken together, paranormal abilities such as ESP and telekinesis are known in parapsychology as **psi** abilities.

This branch of psychological science is highly controversial, and is considered a pseudoscience by most psychologists. There are a number of reasons for this. First, scientific evidence in support of the existence of psi is scant (many claim it is entirely nonexistent). Most scientists question the utility of continuing to conduct research on abilities that cannot be demonstrated reliably for objective observers and that, because they violate known laws of physics, are extremely unlikely to exist (Hyman, 1989, 2010; Wagenmakers, Wetzels, Bordsboom, & van der Maas, 2011). Secondly, scientific claims of evidence in favor of psi historically are rife with out-and-out fraud (Marwick, 1978) or, more commonly, simple self-delusion and inadequate methodology on the part of experimenters (Blackmore, 2004). Even scientists who are believers in psi often admit that such abilities are, at best, "weak, unreliable, and/or rare" (J. E. Kennedy, 2001, p. 219; J. E. Burns, 2003; Wagenmakers et al., 2011). Finally, studies by the relatively few professional scientists who truly have no particular stake in the existence or nonexistence of paranormal abilities have tended to produce no positive findings (Alcock, 2003; e.g., Jeffers, 2003).

Thus, the bulk of the evidence thus far collected supports the skeptical view of psi and related phenomena (Alcock, 2003). Indeed, numerous open-minded—but science-minded—parapsychologists who initially believed in the existence of psi have abandoned these beliefs after years of investigation (e.g., Blackmore, 2004).

In spite of gloomy prospects for discovering the existence of genuine paranormal phenomena, these possibilities seem to grip the imagination (Bem, 2011). The search will no doubt continue. However, the

---

Telepathy ▶ Thought transference.

Clairvoyance ▶ The ability to predict the future or have knowledge of events that have transpired outside of one's own experience.

Astrology ▶ The belief that the position of the stars and planets can affect people's life events or personalities.

Parapsychology ▶ A branch of psychology that studies paranormal abilities, primarily extrasensory perception and telekinesis.

Extrasensory perception (ESP) ▶ Acquiring information by means other than the senses (e.g., telepathy, clairvoyance).

Psi ▶ The parapsychology term for paranormal abilities such as extrasensory perception and telekinesis.

Meta-analysis ▶ A research study that uses rigorous statistics to summarize data reported in a collection of studies that examine a particular hypothesis or research question. It is a "study of studies."

magician-turned-debunker-of-the-paranormal known as The Amazing Randi (James Randi) has, since 1964, offered substantial prize money (currently $1 million) to anyone who can demonstrate *any* sort of paranormal event or talent under independently monitored scientific test conditions. As of 2013, no one has stepped forward to claim the prize. ■

IN SUMMARY

1. Parapsychologists study psi experiences, particularly extrasensory perception (clairvoyance and telepathy) and telekinesis (movement of objects with mental energy).

2. Very little evidence exists in support of the reality of psi, and decades of attempts to find such evidence have ended in failure.

RETRIEVE!

1. What is the most likely explanation for dreams of events that turn out to be true?

2. Psychic ability to predict the future is called _____. "Thought reading" is called _____. The entire field that studies such phenonmena is known as _____.

Looking Back

Chapter 5 in Review

HOW DO SENSING AND PERCEIVING DIFFER?

- Sensing is the process by which we receive energy from the natural world; perception occurs when our brains organize and interpret sensory signals.
- An absolute threshold of stimulus intensity must be reached in order for a stimulus to be detected. The just-noticeable difference is the smallest difference between two stimuli that the appropriate sense organ can detect. Weber's law is the mathematical expression of the proportion of the standard (the original stimulus) to the JND.
- Signal detection theorists propose that noise interferes with detection of stimuli. Sensory adaptation also influences stimulus detection. Subliminal perception is the unconscious perception of a stimulus.

HOW DOES THE EYE WORK?

- Visible light exists in a narrow spectrum of wavelengths. Eyes allow light to be focused upon the retina where rods and cones begin transducing images into electrical signals to be conveyed to the brain, where they are perceived as visual images. Rods allow us to see at night, while cones are specialized for daylight and color vision.
- Color is not a physical property but rather is created by the brain. Two dominant theories of color are trichromacy theory and opponent process theory.

HOW DOES THE EAR WORK?

- Sound is vibration that causes pressure changes known as sound waves. The ear collects, ampifies, and transduces sound waves into electrical signals, which pass to the brain where they are perceived as sound. Both ears are needed to locate sounds.

HOW DO THE NOSE AND TONGUE RECEIVE CHEMICAL SIGNALS?

- The nose detects odors when molecular particles of odorants pass from the air into the nasal cavity. There, olfactory receptors transduce the chemical signals to electrical impulses and relay the information to the brain where they are perceived as aromas. The nose also detects

Looking Back continued

odorless human pheromones—hormone-like compounds that act as chemical communications.

- Taste sensations are received by the tongue after food molecules are dissolved in saliva and passed over taste buds. There, taste receptors transduce taste signals and send the information to the brain where they are interpreted as taste. There are four established tastes: sweet, salty, sour, and bitter. Two other tastes, fatty and umami, have been proposed. Taste is not the same as flavor, as flavor is perceived through the olfactory epithelium in the nose.

HOW DO THE SKIN AND BODY FEEL?

- Touch includes the subdivisions of tactition, thermoception, and nociception. The muscles, tendons, and joints primarily contribute to the kinesthetic sense. Tactile sensations are converted into neural signals by mechanoreceptors and then carried along trunks of nerves directly to the spinal column. The signals then travel up the spinal column to the brain, where they are perceived as touch.
- Pain is a psychological experience as much as a physiological event; there are no specific pain receptors. First pain is the initial sharp sensation at the moment of painful stimulus, whereas second pain is slower to arrive. Gate control theory has

been highly influential in pain research. Alternative methods for coping with pain without drugs include distraction, relaxation, and counterirritation.

HOW DO WE PERCEIVE VISUAL IMAGES?

- Gestalt theorists propose that human beings have an innate tendency to perceive meaningful visual "wholes" out of inherently meaningless and fragmented sensory impressions. Among the laws of Gestalt perceptual grouping are proximity, similarity, closure, and good continuation.
- Depth perception relies upon binocular and monocular cues. Binocular cues include retinal disparity and convergence. Monocular cues include relative size, linear perspective, interposition, and position on the horizon.
- Perceptual constancy is the ability to perceive an object as "itself" despite changes in angle of view, distance, and illumination. Four primary categories of perceptual constancy are size constancy, shape constancy, brightness constancy, color constancy.

HOW DO EVOLUTION, CULTURE, AND EXPERIENCE AFFECT PERCEPTION?

- Human beings may have evolved specific visual and cognitive tools

and brain regions set aside for the specific task of face recognition—the ability to distinguish faces from other objects and to recognize specific faces. However, this would not rule out the importance of experience in developing and fine-tuning these mechanisms.

- Perception is influenced by experience and expectation. Change blindness and the Rorschach test are two examples of this fact. Expectations, biases, and predispositions that we bring to the viewing of a scene are known as perceptual set. Some researchers suggest that cultural differences exist between Westerners and East Asians in how visual scenes are perceived.

DOES EXTRASENSORY PERCEPTION EXIST?

- Decades of research have failed to find support for telepathy, clairvoyance, astrology, ESP, and other paranormal phenomena. However, a few scientists take these ideas seriously and continue to conduct research.

Key Terms

Key Terms continued

Test Yourself

1. How do sensing and perception differ?
2. How can a behavior or ability be "innate" and "learned" at the same time?
3. Give an example from ordinary life of Weber's law concerning the just noticeable difference (JND).
4. When a nonsmoker enters a smoker's house, the smell can be quite overpowering. However, the smoker may notice no smell at all. What influence on the detection of stimuli explains this fact?
   a) Just noticeable difference
   b) Subliminal perception
   c) Sensory adaptation
   d) Response bias
5. How do rods and cones differ in the way they contribute to the vision system?
6. Describe the journey taken by light from the time it enters the eye until it is interpreted as visual imagery in the brain. Name as many of the relevant anatomical and neural structures as you can.
7. What is meant by the statement that "brains—not objects—have color"?
8. How are we able to determine the location of origin of a sound?

9. Which of the following is NOT one of the ways that perceptual constancy in vision is achieved?
   a) Size constancy
   b) Shape constancy
   c) Color constancy
   d) Darkness constancy
10. Describe the journey of an odorant from the time it enters the nasal cavity to the time it is interpreted as smell in the brain. Name as many of the relevant anatomical and neural structures as you can.
11. The existence of at least three types of pheromone-like chemical signals in humans has been demonstrated. Name these three types of pheromonal signals. Which type of pheromonal signal has *not* been convincingly demonstrated in humans?
12. Why can you perceive taste, but not flavor, when your nose is badly stuffed or you are pinching it closed?
13. Which of the following is NOT one of the subdivisions of the sense of touch?
   a) Nociception
   b) Thermoception
   c) Tactition
   d) Textation

14. How do first and second pain differ? Which is usually "more painful"? What is the "evolutionary logic" behind first and second pain?
15. Name and describe four Gestalt laws of perceptual grouping.
16. Name and describe at least four monocular cues to depth perception.
17. Why is it difficult to maintain color constancy in outdoor parking lots at night?
18. What is a perceptual set? Give an example of a perceptual set.
19. Describe evidence for cultural differences in visual perception gathered from studies of Japanese and American research participants.
20. Name at least two reasons why parapsychology is considered by most psychologists to be a pseudoscience.

CHAPTER

Varieties of **consciousness**

Chapter Outline

FREEZE FRAME

A Long, Strange Trip

▲ **Blotters Once Containing Doses of LSD.** *(Source: www.erowid.org.)*

On April 16, 1943, a chemist named Albert Hoffman was hard at work for the Sandoz pharmaceutical company attempting to synthesize various components of ergot—a fungus that grows on grain and has medicinal (and poisonous) properties. On this particular day, Hoffman was working on his 25th such synthesis; he called it LSD25 (lysergic acid diethylamide). However, as he worked with the chemical he began to experience a stream of intensely vivid and "fantastic" images accompanied by a "kaleidoscope-like play of colors" (Hoffman, 1970).

Hoffman realized that these symptoms must somehow be related to the LSD25, but he was unable to figure out how he could have accidentally ingested enough of the compound to have had any sort of effect at all. He decided to conduct an experiment on himself by ingesting what seemed to him a very small dose of the compound, only .25 mg. His lab notes read:

> 4:20 P.M.: 0.5 cc (0.25 mg LSD) ingested orally. The solution is tasteless.

> 4:50 P.M.: no trace of any effect.

> 5:00 P.M.: slight dizziness, unrest, difficulty in concentration, visual disturbances, marked desire to laugh.... (Hoffman, 1970).

At this point Hoffman's notes ended because he could no longer write. He had discovered LSD.

Sixty years later, people continue to intentionally repeat Hoffman's (now-illegal) experiment. Here are several typical descriptions taken more or less at random from a website devoted to descriptions of LSD trips:

> *My thoughts were powerful, deep and strange.... I looked straight down and focused on the grass. Every single blade was vibrating and pivoting at the root at the same time . . . the individual blades had little purple tinges around the edges of them. . . . Utterly astounded by this, I stood up and watched as they continued their vibrating & pivoting across the whole field. . . . Blink after blink, it didn't cease....*
>
> —Apollo

> *I got the idea that my parents had driven up (an 8-hour drive) and were looking in through the peephole in my apartment door, and that they could see me. I felt an overwhelming feeling of disappointment that they had for me, since I had taken LSD.... I then knew that if I opened the curtains, I would see, literally, all of the people in the world standing on bleachers that extended into infinity, and that all of them would be looking at me, disappointed in me. It made sense that I would be kicked out of my apartment, and would have to go live as a homeless person....*
>
> —Shruman Human

> *I tried to explain to [my husband John] what it was like for me. How reality wasn't reality anymore, and how I didn't know what our purpose was or what we are supposed to do the next day or the day after. I so appreciated his ability to hear what I was saying, and to respond appropriately.... I felt so much love for [him] then, that it swallowed me. No emotion I have felt was ever that strong. All I could say was that I loved him, that I trusted him, that I needed him....*
>
> —Muriel[1]

These experiences constitute *altered states of consciousness*. But what exactly is it that is being altered? Until about two or three decades ago, scientists did not believe that it was possible to study the nature of consciousness, or if they thought it might be possible, they did not consider it an important problem. But now, many psychologists and neuroscientists have come around to philosopher-psychologist John Searle's view that "consciousness is the condition that makes it possible for anything at all to matter to anybody" (Searle, 1997, p. xiv). Thus, *consciousness* has recently come

---

[1]*Source for LSD stories: www.erowid.org. Retrieved on September 9, 2006, from http://www.erowid.org/experiences/subs/exp_LSD.shtml.*

to be considered a very important topic in psychology, and some consider it the most important topic of all. The emerging field of *consciousness studies* seeks to find solutions to what has been called the last surviving mystery of science: *What is consciousness?* In this chapter we begin by considering some proposed answers to this question. We will then review the many varieties of consciousness as they are experienced daily by people all over the world: sleep, dreaming, meditation, hypnosis, and the nonmedical use of *psychoactive* drugs.

What Is Consciousness? No One Knows

"If you think you have found a solution to the problem of consciousness, you haven't understood the problem."

—Susan Blackmore (2004, p. 1)

Although some psychologists may consider *consciousness* the most important topic in all of psychology, researchers in **consciousness studies** can't seem to agree on very much about their topic. Unlike most other areas of psychology, these psychologists, philosophers, and neuroscientists cannot even agree on what they are studying. There is no consensus on how to define consciousness, what consciousness consists of, or how best to study it—or even if it is really possible to study it at all. And there are almost as many ideas about what *causes* consciousness as there are researchers studying it.

Indeed, in one introductory book on the topic, consciousness studies researcher Susan Blackmore begins by warning that the reader is likely to become increasingly perplexed as he or she reads, rather than increasingly enlightened (Blackmore, 2004). Why does Blackmore warn us in this way? It is because we ourselves are so immersed in our own consciousness—"the condition that makes it possible for anything at all to matter"—that we generally give little thought to what consciousness really *is* or where it comes from. Once we begin to ponder such questions, it is easy to get lost in their implications. This is rather like what happens when you contemplate questions such as: "If the universe came into being at some point with a big bang, what existed before the universe?"

However, each person's own subjective experience of himself or herself and the world—that is, *consciousness*—is too important an aspect of psychology to ignore, in spite of the problems inherent in studying it.

Consciousness studies ▶ The study of consciousness—a field created by psychologists, philosophers, and neuroscientists.

A Commonsense Definition of Consciousness

As already stated, there is no consensus on how to define consciousness. But we can map out the general territory with which we are concerned by offering a commonsense definition of consciousness as provided by philosopher-psychologist John Searle: "**Consciousness** consists of inner, qualitative, subjective states and feelings or awareness" (Searle, 2000, p. 559; emphasis added). According to Searle, consciousness defined in this way exists as long as we are alive and not in a state of thoughtless, dreamless sleep or coma. It ends only when we are in such states—or dead. In Searle's words, consciousness "includes everything from feeling a pain, to perceiving objects visually, to states of anxiety and depression, to working out crossword puzzles, playing chess, trying to remember your aunt's phone number, arguing about politics, or to just wishing you were somewhere else" (p. 559).

Consciousness ▶ No definition of consciousness has been agreed upon, but John Searle's "commonsense" definition includes three components: qualitativeness, subjectivity, and unity.

Qualitativeness ▶ The feature of consciousness which suggests that something is conscious only if it "feels like something" to be that thing.

Subjectivity ▶ In consciousness studies this word means that consciousness can only be experienced by an individual being and cannot exist independently.

Unity ▶ In consciousness studies, the idea that consciousness is always a single, unified experience.

Hard problem ▶ The term given to the question of how the human brain is able to produce consciousness.

Of a number of features Searle identifies as associated with consciousness in this commonsense meaning of the term, these three are the most prominent: *qualitativeness, subjectivity,* and *unity.* By **qualitativeness**, Searle means that something is conscious only if it "feels like something" to be that thing—in other words, consciousness has some sort of quality or qualities (Nagel, 1974). Eating a good breakfast *feels* different from learning that you scored 780 on the SAT critical reading section, which *feels* different from finding a rat in your bedroom. As Searle points out, even thinking "2 + 2 = 4" *feels* different from thinking "2 + 2 = 187" (Searle, 2000, p. 560).

Subjectivity means that consciousness can only be experienced by some sort of being and cannot exist independent of its "owner." Even when two people have the same experience—say, listening to the same piece of music—the experience is different because each person has her or his own consciousness (Blackmore, 2005). Subjectivity is the "I" of consciousness.

By **unity** Searle means that consciousness is a single unified experience. As I sit here typing, I do not just *feel* the keyboard keys under my fingertips, *see* the words form on the computer screen, *hear* the sounds of the Horace Silver Quintet coming from the computer speakers, and *think* that it's been raining for far too long. I experience all of these cognitive and sensory experiences together as consciousness (Searle, 2000, p. 561–562). To Searle, consciousness is by definition unified, and individual components such as senses, thoughts, and emotions modify consciousness in an ever-shifting, but always unified, pattern.

The Hard Problem: How Do We Get from Brain to Self?

Now that we have a working, commonsense definition of consciousness (bearing in mind that there is no agreement whatever that it is the best one), what is this definition intended to help us explain? There is a basic problem about consciousness that must somehow be solved—what philosopher David Chalmers (1995) has termed the **hard problem**. It is this: How does our brain—a physical organ composed of neurons, chemicals, and electricity—produce the seemingly disembodied subjective state of consciousness? How is it that we can easily say, "I have a brain" when we can't say for sure whether "I" *is* our brain or is somehow *in* or *caused by* our brain? In other words, how do we get from *there* (our brain) to *here* (our "selves")?

The hard problem of consciousness is a variation of the ancient "mind-body" problem described in Chapter 2. If you recall, *dualism,* the idea that the mind and body are separate and made up of different "substances," has been rejected by all modern scientists and most modern philosophers. Consciousness, like mind, is in some way a property of the brain. Rejecting dualism does not, however, solve the hard problem of consciousness. Even if we grant that consciousness is a property of the brain, we still have no idea how consciousness arises from the brain—despite the efforts of neuroscientists to identify precise neural and biochemical processes and brain sites that take us from "there" to "here" (e.g., Bartels & Zeki, 1998; Crick & Koch, 2007; Damasio, 2010; Hulme, Friston, & Zeki, 2009; Zeki, 2007).

Consciousness Comes in Many Varieties

Whatever consciousness may turn out to be, one thing we know for certain is that it comes in many flavors other than normal waking consciousness. Sleep, dreams, hypnosis, hallucinations, meditation, and drug states are all varieties of consciousness—generally referred to as *altered states of consciousness* (ASC). Just as it is difficult to define consciousness itself, however, it is not easy to define an altered state. As Blackmore (2004) notes, we might decide to define altered states *objectively,* in terms of how the altered state was induced. For example, we could say that an altered state is one that is induced by some unusual activity, such as taking a drug or being hypnotized. Another objective way would be to define an altered state in terms of measurable changes in brain activity and physiology.

There are problems with both of these objective methods, however. In the first method, each person's experience of taking a particular drug or being hypnotized may differ radically. What might be an altered state for one person might not be for another. The second objective method—taking measurements—seems more promising, but with the exceptions of sleep and dreaming, researchers have not been very successful in associating altered states with specific biological measurements.

On the other hand, altered states could be defined *subjectively*—perhaps a more fruitful approach. From this perspective, **altered states of consciousness** are defined as temporary but radical changes in the overall pattern of a person's normal subjective experience (Farthing, 1992; Tart, 1972). For the remainder of this chapter we will consider altered states of consciousness in all their splendor, terror, and ordinariness.

◄ **Chasing Altered Consciousness.** Throughout history and across cultures, human beings have purposely attempted to alter their consciousness in various ways. Pictured here is an attempt to do so through partial sensory deprivation in a soundproof floatation tank. Filled with Epsom salts, the density of the water makes flotation effortless. The tank is completely dark and silent. Some individuals claim to experience altered states of consciousness during such flotation sessions.

Altered state of consciousness ▶ A temporary but radical change in the overall pattern of a person's normal subjective experience.

IN SUMMARY

1.	Scientists and philosophers do not agree on a definition of *consciousness*.
2.	The commonsense definition of consciousness devised by John Searle includes three prominent qualities: qualitativeness, subjectivity, and unity.
3.	The "hard problem" of consciousness is explaining how the brain—a material object—creates consciousness, a seemingly immaterial experience.
4.	"Altered state of consciousness" could be defined subjectively as a temporary but radical change in the overall pattern of a person's normal subjective experience.

RETRIEVE!

1.	Which of the following is NOT among the features of consciousness identified by John Searle? **a)** awareness **b)** qualitativeness **c)** subjectivity **d)** unity
2.	Why is it difficult to define *altered states of consciousness* objectively in terms of the method by which the state of consciousness was induced (e.g., drugs) or changes in brain activity and physiology?

How—and Why—Do We Sleep?

The urge to sleep is profound. After just one night of sleeplessness, human beings may risk their lives for it—falling asleep at the wheel or in wartime at a sentry post. Even if we do not fall completely asleep under such conditions, we may experience **microsleeps**—barely perceptible and involuntary periods of sleep lasting from 3 to 15 seconds (Blavivas, Patel, Hom, Antigua, & Ashtyani, 2007). Human beings love sleep so much that they spend about one-third of their lives doing it—approximately 27 years total. Think of all the things you might accomplish, or the time you could happily waste doing absolutely nothing, if you did not sleep so much! Yet, sleep—ubiquitous, seemingly necessary, and longed-for at least once in every 24-hour cycle—remains in many respects a mystery.

Microsleeps ▶ Barely perceptible and involuntary periods of sleep lasting between 3 and 15 seconds.

How Much Sleep Is Enough?

Total sleep deprivation ▶ Going entirely without sleep for 24 hours or more.

Despite the miseries of sleeplessness, studies have shown that **total sleep deprivation**, even for a period of days, does not necessarily result in the sorts of symptoms one commonly associates with such an experience—for example, bizarre hallucinations or delusions (Gould et al., 2009). However, brief, mild hallucinations are not uncommon, and a person's motor skills and performance on memory and other cognitive tasks will suffer—sometimes severely, depending upon the task (Harrison & Horne, 2000; Lim & Dinges, 2010; Russo et al., 2005; Saxvig et al., 2008). Decision making—including moral decision making—may also be impaired, and without doubt grouchiness rules during total sleep deprivation (Killgore et al., 2007).

But unless you get into a car and try to drive, going without sleep for a period of days will not kill you. On the other hand, sleep deprivation *will* kill a rat in about 2 or 3 weeks (Rechtschaffen, 1998). While no human being (that we know of) has attempted to remain awake that long, it may well be that going without sleep for a *really* extended time actually will kill you. An exceptionally rare genetic condition known as *fatal familial insomnia* does eventually result in death, but only after a period of 7 to 36 *months* of sleeplessness (Schenkein & Montagna, 2006).

In any event, human beings, like all other mammals, birds, reptiles, fish, and insects yet studied, do sleep regularly (Cirelli & Tononi, 2008; Gilestro, Tononi, & Cirelli, 2009). If you are like the average college student in the United States, you probably get less sleep than you'd like—a little less than 7 hours average on most weekday nights (Hicks, Fernandez, & Pellegrini, 2001; National Sleep Foundation, 2005). That's about an hour less per night than students were getting just 30 years ago and more than 2 hours less than most people were getting 100 years ago (Hicks et al., 2001; Webb & Agnew, 1975). Moreover, the pervasive use of cell phones and computers at bedtime among young people (often in bed while "trying to go to sleep") further reduces sleep time and increases daytime sleepiness (National Sleep Foundation, 2011).

Adults in their 40s fare even worse. European-Americans in their 40s average 6.4 hours per night and African Americans, about 5.5 hours. There are sex differences hidden in these figures as well—men get far less sleep on average than women, with African American men in their 40s averaging only 5.1 hours sleep per night (Lauderdaleet al., 2006). When all age groups are averaged together, African Americans get the least amount of sleep of all ethnic groups, averaging 5 to 6 hours per night, compared to European Americans, Asian Americans, and Latinos, who average 6 to 7 hours per night (National Sleep Foundation, 2010; Ram, Seirawan, Kumar, & Clark, 2010).

Although figures such as these have been used to argue that modern people are chronically sleep deprived (Coren, 1998, 2009), the large majority of Americans nevertheless believe they are getting enough sleep (National Sleep Foundation, 2005), and some psychologists agree with them (e.g., Horne, in Buysse, Grunstein, Horne, & Lavie, 2010). But are they? Unfortunately, it is not possible to estimate accurately the number of hours the average person actually does need to sleep, so you should take the advice of experts on this matter with a grain of salt. Different people seem to feel the need for varying amounts of sleep. One thing is clear from research, however: As sleep duration falls below 6 hours per night, the risk of health consequences greatly increases relative to 7 to 8 hours per night (Buysse et al., 2010). Indeed, people who sleep less than 6 hours per night also have much higher mortality rates (Ferrie et al., 2007; Oexman, Knotts, & Koch, 2002).

The obvious conclusion from all of this is that animals, including human beings, *need* to sleep. But why? In other words, what is the *function* of sleep? The answer to this question is not as straightforward as you might think, and we will consider the question of *why* we sleep a bit later. Let's begin with the simpler question of *how* we sleep.

Sleep Patterns Are Regulated by Two Processes

Apart from external demands such as job or school, what determines when a person decides to go to sleep and wake up? Two basic processes interact to regulate normal human sleep: the *circadian pacemaker*, which governs each person's internal "biological clock"; and the *sleep homeostat*, which tracks the amount of sleep you have relative to the number of hours you have been awake (Wright, Gronfier, Duffy, & Czeisler, 2005).

THE CIRCADIAN PACEMAKER

One aspect of the environment has remained constant during the evolution of all forms of life on earth: the 24-hour cycle of the earth's rotation. The sun and moon shine on protozoa, panthers, pythons, and people alike. In a variety of ways, the biology of life forms is synchronized to this 24-hour cycle of light and dark. Bacteria, plants, and animals have internal "biological clocks" they use to regulate important physiological processes such as respiration and reproduction. Any biochemical, physiological, or behavioral cycle that adheres to a near-24 hour schedule is known as a **circadian rhythm** (Conroy & Mills, 1970; Shepherd, 1988).

In human beings, sleep and wakefulness are regulated in part by the numerous circadian rhythm cycles experienced each day (body temperature, hormonal activity, mental alertness, etc.). These rhythms are kept on schedule and synchronized with one another by the **circadian pacemaker**, our "biological clock." The pacemaker consists of a group of neurons forming the **suprachiasmatic nuclei** of the hypothalamus (Weaver, 1998; see Figure 6.1).

How the Circadian Pacemaker Works How does the pacemaker do its work of regulating circadian rhythms? As depicted in Figure 6.1, natural light is conducted from the retina via the optic nerve to the circadian pacemaker, conveying information about the time of day. Light does not merely "set" the biological clock of the pacemaker, however. Once light is conducted to the pacemaker, the light affects the production of hormones. The most important of these to the sleep-wake cycle is **melatonin**, produced by the *pineal gland* deep within the brain. Melatonin production is stimulated during periods of darkness and inhibited by light. The secretion of melatonin during the cycle of darkness is strongly associated with the onset of sleep. This is because melatonin inhibits the brain's mechanisms for promoting wakefulness—allowing various other sleep-related mechanisms to do their work "unopposed" by a drive for wakefulness (Lavie, 2001).

Circadian rhythm ▶ Any biochemical, physiological, or behavioral cycle that adheres to a near-24 hour schedule.

Circadian pacemaker ▶ The "master control" for a person's various circadian cycles, consisting of a group of neurons forming the suprachiasmatic nuclei of the hypothalamus.

Suprachiasmatic nuclei (SCN) ▶ A group of neurons of the hypothalamus that constitute the circadian pacemaker.

Melatonin ▶ A hormone of the pineal gland, stimulated by darkness and inhibited by light, which is associated with the onset of sleep.

▶ **FIGURE 6.1 The Circadian Pacemaker.** The circadian pacemaker helps regulate sleep and wakefulness by keeping circadian rhythms synchronized and on schedule.

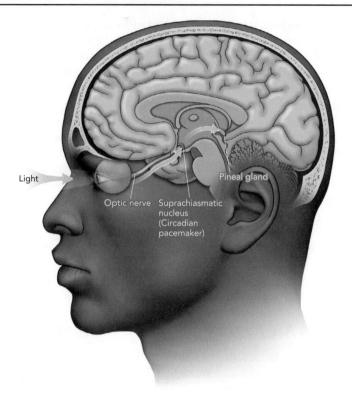

Light

Optic nerve   Suprachiasmatic nucleus (Circadian pacemaker)

Pineal gland

Jet lag ▶ Symptoms caused by travel across multiple time zones by moving west-to-east or east-to-west.

Sleep homeostat ▶ Coordinated biochemical, neural, and psychological functions that "keep track" of the amount of sleep a person has had relative to the number of hours of waking.

Sleep homeostasis ▶ A balance between sleep and waking, governed by the sleep homeostat.

Sleep debt ▶ When the sleep homeostat creates the urge to make up for lost sleep by sleeping longer or more frequently than usual.

The net effect of regulation by the circadian pacemaker is that our best sleep is experienced at night and our most productive periods of wakefulness and activity during the day (Wright et al., 2005). Thus, night-shift workers experience sleep that is less restful and of shorter duration than those on normal schedules, and their levels of alertness and performance on the job also suffer relative to those of day workers (Oexman, et al., 2002). They are fighting their circadian pacemakers. Something similar occurs in **jet lag**, the bane of frequent flyers. Jet lag happens when a flyer crosses multiple time zones in flight while moving from west to east or east to west (it's worse moving from west-to-east). Symptoms include difficulty concentrating, headache, insomnia, fatigue, irritability, and loss of appetite. No jet lag is experienced on flights that do not cross time zones, no matter how long they are and no matter how much *travel fatigue* occurs. Travel fatigue may result from long security lines, uncomfortable seating, inability to sleep on night flights, dehydration, and so forth (Herxheimer & Waterhouse, 2003).

THE SLEEP HOMEOSTAT

While the circadian pacemaker is a critically important determinant of the cycle of sleep and wakefulness, it is not the only determinant. The second important process regulating sleep is the **sleep homeostat**—a kind of internal scorekeeper made up of a number of coordinated biological functions that keep track of how much sleep (particularly deep sleep) you have had the previous night versus how long you have been awake on a given day (Achermann, 2004; Dijk & Archer, 2009). The idea is to maintain a balance between sleep and waking known as **sleep homeostasis**. When the balance tips too far into the "waking" side, the urge to sleep is increased.

What happens if you don't get enough sleep to restore sleep homeostasis? If not enough sleep occurs on a given night relative to the amount you normally require, **sleep debt** is built up, and you will feel pressure to "make up" the lost sleep. Once asleep, you will tend to sleep longer than usual and experience more time in the deepest levels of sleep. When you sleep late on the weekends after a week of insufficient sleep during weekdays, you are experiencing the sleep homeostat's attempt to pay back sleep debt.

Falling Asleep Is a Gradual Process

We all know the difference between being asleep and being awake (well, most of us do, at any rate). But there is no one moment when a person can definitively be said to have passed from waking into sleep. The process of falling asleep is a series of continuous, gradual changes that occur in the brain, body, and subjective experience; and changes in one of these domains (e.g., changes in the brain) do not necessarily coincide with changes in another (e.g., changes in subjective experience). However, eventually, all aspects of physiology, cognition, behavior, and subjective experience are altered during the process of falling asleep (Ogilvie, 2001).

While drifting from relaxed sleepiness toward sleep, many people experience unusual auditory and visual illusions and bodily sensations known as **hypnogogia** or *hypnagogic hallucinations* (Ohayon, Priest, Caulet, & Guilleminault, 1996; D'Agostino & Limosani, 2010). Hypnogogia is a dream-like state during which you may or may not be aware that you are experiencing hallucinations. You may hear voices, see patterns of shape and color, or imagine yourself somewhere else. A sensation of falling is fairly typical, and it may be broken by sudden full awakening with a jerking of the limbs known as *myoclonia*. *Sleep paralysis* may also occur—the sensation of being unable to move during periods of intense and often terrifying hallucination (Cheyne, 2005). If you experience sleep paralysis, it may be possible to emerge from it intentionally by rolling your eyes, fluttering your eyelids, or intentionally wiggling the toes and feet. On the other hand, some people enjoy the experience and learn to induce it on purpose!

Sleep Comes in Two Types and Five Stages

There are two basic types of sleep: **rapid-eye-movement**, or **REM sleep** (sometimes called *active sleep*) and **non-rapid-eye-movement** or **NREM sleep** (sometimes called *slow-wave sleep*). NREM sleep occurs over the greater portion of sleep time, and is characterized by the deepest levels of relaxation and reduced brain activity. REM sleep is characterized by high levels of brain and nervous system activity, rapid movements of the eyes, and intensely vivid dreaming.

REM and NREM sleep are experienced in five **sleep stages**, the first four consisting of NREM and the fifth of REM. Because the stages of sleep are defined in part according to the particular type of **brain wave** that predominates, it will be useful first to describe these brain wave patterns. Brain wave is the term used to describe electrical activity in the brain that occurs in varying frequencies. These waves are measured by a device known as the **electroencephalograph** (**EEG**; see Chapter 2 for details).

There are four principal types of brain waves: *beta, alpha, theta,* and *delta*. During normal wakefulness, brain waves tend to be of the **beta** type—very rapid, relatively narrow oscillations. In some extremely relaxed wakeful states where eyes are closed, however (e.g., meditation), lower-frequency **alpha** waves may predominate. **Theta** waves are produced under conditions of drowsiness and light sleep. **Delta** waves, which are slower and wider, are associated with the deepest levels of NREM sleep. Figure 6.2 depicts EEG patterns of the four brain wave types.

As mentioned, each of the five sleep stages is associated with specific brain wave patterns.

1. *Stage 1 sleep.* Stage 1 represents the transition from relaxed wakefulness to the onset of sleep. In fact, it actually includes both waking and sleep states within its borders, and for this reason, some researchers do not consider Stage 1 an actual stage of sleep at all. These researchers prefer simply to refer to it as *sleep onset* (e.g., Ogilvie, 2001; Yang, Han, Yang, Su, & Lane, 2010). In any

Samples, brain wave patterns

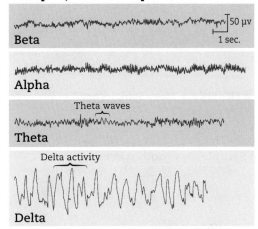

▲ **FIGURE 6.2 The Four Principal Brain Wave Patterns.** Beta, alpha, theta, and delta brain waves are associated with different stages of sleep.

Hypnagogia ▶ A dream-like state at sleep onset during which a person may or may not be aware that he or she is experiencing hallucinations or delusions.

Rapid-eye-movement (REM) ▶ The fifth stage of sleep characterized by high levels of brain and nervous system activity and intensely vivid, hallucinatory dreaming.

Non-rapid-eye-movement (NREM) ▶ Sleep Stages 2–4, characterized by cognitive activity, ordinary dreaming, and reduced brain and nervous system activity relative to REM.

Sleep stages ▶ The five stages of sleep, including a period of sleep onset, three periods of NREM, and one of REM sleep. Each stage is associated with characteristic brain wave activity, and the stages are played out during the night in repeating pattern (the sleep cycle).

Sample sleep spindle and k complex

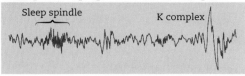

▲ FIGURE 6.3 Sleep Spindles and K Complexes.

Sample saw tooth waves

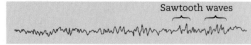

▲ FIGURE 6.4 Sawtooth Wave Patterns.

Brain waves ▶ Characteristic electrical brain activity of various frequencies termed *alpha, beta, theta,* and *delta*.

Electroencephalograph (EEG) ▶ The instrument that measures electrical activity produced by the brain in waves of current termed *brain waves*.

Beta waves ▶ The brain waves that predominate in waking states and are present in REM.

Alpha waves ▶ The brain waves that predominate in relaxed, wakeful states while eyes are closed, and in sleep onset.

Theta waves ▶ The brain waves that predominate at Stage 2 and Stage 3 sleep.

Delta waves ▶ The slow brain waves that predominate at Stage 4 sleep.

Sleep cycle ▶ The repeating pattern of Stages 2–5 sleep that recurs four to six times throughout the night following sleep onset (Sleep Stage 1).

case, as you experience increasing relaxation while lying in bed with your eyes closed preparing to fall asleep, more and more alpha waves are produced. As this process continues and you achieve Stage 1 sleep, theta waves come to predominate, although some alpha is still produced. During Stage 1 sleep you may be vaguely aware of your environment and some of you may experience hypnogogia as just described. If awakened, you may insist that you hadn't actually fallen asleep at all. After a few minutes in Stage 1, however, you will transition to Stage 2 sleep.

2. *Stage 2 sleep.* Stage 2 is light sleep from which you can be easily awakened, but you will be unaware of the environment as you sleep. Although theta waves continue to predominate during Stage 2, there are also characteristic brain wave patterns known as *sleep spindles* and *K complexes* (see Figure 6.3). Sleep spindles are sudden, short bursts in higher voltage brain wave activity. K complexes are much sharper intermittent peaks and drops. Like Stage 1, Stage 2 sleep lasts only a few minutes, perhaps 10 to 20, and then passes into Stage 3.

3. *Stage 3 sleep.* Stage 3 is the first stage of deep or "slow-wave" sleep from which it is difficult to awaken. Although theta waves continue to be produced, they are joined by the much slower delta waves.

4. *Stage 4 sleep.* Sleep deepens further during Stage 4, and delta waves now come to predominate over theta. It is very difficult to awaken from Stage 4 sleep. If someone does manage to wake you up, you may experience disorientation and not know exactly where you are.

5. *Stage 5 sleep: REM.* REM is a somewhat mysterious type of sleep about which there is some controversy, particularly in regard to dreaming (Hobson, Nielson, 2000; Hobson, Pace-Schott, & Stickold, 2000; Solms, 2000). In general, it is agreed that dreaming might occur during any of the sleep stages (Solms, 2000; Squier & Domhoff, 1998). However, it is during REM that the most intense and vivid periods of dreaming seem to occur, and most researchers consider REM and NREM mental activity to arise from different cognitive and brain mechanisms (Hobson, Pace-Schott, & Stickgold, 2000; McCarley, 2007; Solms, 2000; Takeuchi, Miyasita, Inugami, & Yamamoto, 2001).

During REM sleep, the nervous system suddenly revs up: heart rate, blood pressure, and respiration increase; men experience penile erections and women, clitoral erections or vaginal lubrication (this, however, is *not* related to sexual content in dreams—it is purely reflexive). Although the eyelids are shut, the eyeballs dart back and forth frantically, and brain waves suddenly revert to those typical of wakeful states—with beta, alpha, and some theta waves dancing together in helter-skelter, desynchronized patterns. Among these patterns are the unique bursts known as *sawtooth waves* because they resemble the teeth of wood saws (see Figure 6.4).

Perhaps the most intriguing aspect of REM sleep is that at the same time as all this revved-up activity is occurring in the nervous system, muscle tone suddenly decreases dramatically—the sleeper is effectively paralyzed and cannot move. Considering that more intense, vivid, and hallucinatory dreaming tends to occur during this stage, this temporary paralysis may not be such a bad idea. Imagine your body responding to a dream of being chased by demons from beyond the beyond—especially if you are sleeping near a window and live on the 12th floor. (Later in this chapter I describe a sleep disorder where exactly such an event is conceivable.)

The stages of sleep (minus Stage 1, which occurs only once at sleep onset) play out in a cyclical pattern known as the **sleep cycle** throughout the night. The sleep cycle lasts between 90 and 110 minutes and is repeated between 4 and 6 times per night on average. In a normal adult, the time spent in each stage will vary as the night wears on, with REM sleep constituting only a very small amount of one's sleep in the early sleep period, but taking up more and more of the sleep cycle as the sleeper moves toward morning. Finally, the experience of NREM Stages 3 and 4 disappears altogether. When all is said and done, however, NREM still takes up about 80% of the total sleep period, and REM sleep approximately 20% (McCarley, 2007). The sleep cycle is depicted in Figure 6.5, and the five stages of sleep are summarized in Table 6.1.

Table 6.1 **The Five Stages of Sleep**

STAGE	BRAIN WAVE ACTIVITY	CHARACTERISTICS
1 NREM	Alpha Theta	Increasing relaxation, transition from wakefulness to very light sleep . . . You may be partially aware of the environment, and if awoken, you might not be aware that you were asleep at all.
2 NREM	Theta (sleep spindles and K complexes)	Light sleep, unaware of the environment but relatively easily awakened. Preparation to enter deeper levels of sleep
3 NREM	Theta (over 50% of time) Delta (under 50%)	Increasingly deep "slow wave" (delta) sleep. Difficult to awaken.
4 NREM	Delta (over 50% of time) Theta (under 50%)	Profoundly deep sleep; difficult to awaken, and if awoken, you will be disoriented.
5 REM	Beta Alpha Theta ("saw tooth" pattern)	Muscle paralysis; intense dreaming; rapid eye movements; genital arousal, increased heart rate, blood pressure and respiration; extremely difficult to awaken

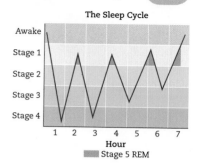

▲ **FIGURE 6.5 The Sleep Cycle.** The five stages of sleep are played out in cycles lasting 90 to 110 minutes, repeated four to six times on average per night.

The Function of Sleep Is Unknown

I noted earlier that it is not possible to determine how much sleep the average person requires. This is not only because different people need differing amounts of sleep—one could still come up with an average figure. The real problem is this: We do not know *why* we sleep (Cirelli & Tononi, 2008). Without understanding what sleep is supposed to accomplish, we cannot confidently address questions to which many of us would like to know the answers: How much sleep does a person really need? Do naps make up for lost nighttime sleep? Do people need less sleep as they grow older? And so forth (Rechtschaffen, 2000).

The most intuitive traditional theory of the function of sleep holds that we sleep because we need to rest and rejuvenate. Sleep is a quiet time, a time when we do rest, and we usually do wake feeling restored or rejuvenated. However, this does not necessarily mean that sleep evolved for this function. We often feel calm and sometimes a little sleepy after a large dinner, but the function of eating is not to make us feel calm and sleepy.

In fact, several facts argue against the "rest and restoration" theory. Most obviously, if you lie awake in bed all day long with your eyes closed in a darkened room listening to recordings of waves lapping, you will *still* need sleep. Sleep must be doing something beyond offering a person rest.

A substantial number of other theories of the general function of sleep exist. All can boast some research to support them, but research can also be found to contradict each one. However, two recent theories show particular promise. The first suggests that the purpose of sleep is to allow the brain to consolidate and retain memories (Rasch & Born, 2008). The second proposes that sleep regulates the strength of brain synapses, allowing unnecessary synapses to die and maintaining those that are important—in effect, to "clean out the junk that's filling up your brain" (Cirelli, quoted in "Sleep: Spring cleaning for the brain?", 2009; Gilestro et al., 2009). We will now briefly explore these ideas.

DO WE SLEEP TO REMEMBER?

Research conducted during the first part of the 21st century has shown that memory processes seem to become profoundly impaired during sleep deprivation, and sleep substantially improves memory for facts and skills one has learned (Rasch & Born, 2008; Payne, Stickgold, Swanberg, & Kensinger, 2008; Rácsmany, Conway, & Demeter, 2010; Walker & Stickgold, 2006). Researchers in sleep and memory believe that this improved recall results in part from a reactivation of memories during sleep—in other words, the memories are "replayed" during sleep and thus recalled better later on, as would be the case following a good study session (Gais, Lucas, & Bom, 2006). Sleep also appears to allow us to draw on different types of personal knowledge "databases" to make connections between newly-learned facts and facts already known (Ellenbogen, Hu, Payne, Titone, & Walker, 2007).

Evidence shows that sleep improves memory for events one has experienced as well as for facts and skills. In particular, sleep improves memories for emotional events over those with more neutral emotional content, and specifically targets the most emotional aspects of these arousing experiences—with background details tending to fade overtime. Thus, a crime victim might recall more details about her assailant's gun than about his or her clothing, with memory for the clothing becoming worse over time, but memory for the gun remaining relatively strong. Sleep enhances this type of effect (Hu, Stylos-Allan, & Walker, 2006; Payne et al., 2008).

Because emotion is often associated with important events or important aspects of events, in this way sleep appears to aid in the recall of particularly valuable memories (Payne et al., 2008). Findings such as these are prompting some researchers to speculate that gathering and replaying memories to allow for their later recall is an important function of sleep—if not its core function (Walker & Stickgold, 2006).

DO WE SLEEP TO FORGET?

The second theory, which remains controversial but is increasingly supported by convincing research, is being advanced principally by researchers Chiara Cirelli and Giulio Tononi (Gilestro et al., 2009; Vyazovsky, Cirelli, Pfister-Genskow, Faraguna, & Tononi, 2008). Cirelli and Tononi recognize that sleep improves memory. But they believe that the specific *ultimate function* of sleep goes beyond replaying and consolidating memories. Instead, these researchers' work with rats, humans, and fruit flies (yes, fruit flies sleep) has led them to conclude that the ultimate purpose of sleep is best understood in terms of brain synapses.

Cirelli and Tononi note that during the waking hours the number of brain synapses and their strength increase. Stronger and more numerous synapses mean better connections between neurons, but they also take up more brain space and require more energy to maintain. Cirelli and Tononi believe that, in the absence of sleep, synapses would continue to become stronger, more numerous, and eventually take up too much brain space and require too much energy to maintain (Gilestro et al., 2009; Vyazovskiy et al., 2008).

Enter sleep. Sleep appears to prune back the strength of synapses and their number, allowing the strongest ones to "scale back" to manageable size and the weaker ones to disappear altogether. Why is this good? It allows relatively unimportant connections to disappear, saving space and energy for more important connections and helping people to perform better following a good night's sleep. This idea could explain findings cited earlier that sleep selectively improves recall of emotional events—that, presumably, have more value on average than emotionally neutral events—while allowing background details (maintained through weaker synaptic connections) to disappear.

Cirelli and Tononi present a strong case in support of their theory, derived from research conducted among members of several animal species. Unfortunately, this evidence, although strong, is essentially correlational. Indeed, theories of the ultimate function of sleep are not easy to test—and some appear virtually impossible to test (Zepelin, Siegel, & Tobler, 2005). Consequently, the function of sleep remains elusive.

IN SUMMARY

1. Sleep is regulated by the circadian pacemaker and the sleep homeostat.

2. Sleep is divided into five stages. Stage 1 is sleep onset, Stages 2 to 4 are NREM, and Stage 5 is REM. The stages of sleep occur in a sleep cycle repeated through the night.

3. NREM is associated with the deepest "slow wave" sleep, whereas REM is associated with the most intense, vivid, and hallucinatory dreaming.

4. The function of sleep is unknown.

RETRIEVE!

1. Circadian rhythm cycles in human beings are kept on schedule and synchronized with one another by the _____, located in the _____ nuclei of the hypothalamus.

2. A number of coordinated biological functions keep track of how much sleep you have had in relation to how much time you have been awake. Collectively these functions are known as the sleep _____.

3. Unusual auditory and visual illusions and bodily sensations experienced by some people during sleep onset are called _____.

4. Describe the two most prominent theories for the function of sleep, and cite at least one fact or piece of evidence in favor of, and opposed to, each one.

5. 5. Match the brain wave with the state of consciousness in which it predominates:

theta	relaxed wakeful states with eyes closed
beta	deepest level of sleep
alpha	normal wakefulness
delta	drowsiness and light sleep

What Are Dreams?

Of the many mysteries of consciousness few are quite as mysterious as the nature of dreams and dreaming. Just as there is no agreement regarding the function of sleep, there is little agreement regarding the important questions of dreaming: What *are* dreams, and what are the brain and mind mechanisms that generate them? Why do we dream at all? What do our dreams mean—if anything?

Sleep Mentation Includes Thinking and Two Levels of Dreaming

Early dream researchers believed that dreams only occurred during REM sleep (Dement & Kleitman, 1957). Indeed, REM sleep was considered virtually synonymous with dreaming. However, these beliefs are now known to be wrong (Foulkes, 1962). REM does not necessarily produce dreaming, and dreamers are not necessarily in REM when they dream (Solms, 2000). Nevertheless, dreaming is without doubt more common in REM than NREM. As many as 95% of awakenings of people in research studies during REM produce reports of dreams, whereas only 12% to 25% of NREM awakenings produce true dream reports (Hobson, 2002; Nielsen, 2000).

However, because it is not always clear exactly what should or should not be considered a "dream," researchers often use the term **sleep mentation** to describe any and all mental activity that occurs during sleep. Sleep mentation exists on a continuum that begins on one side with rational thought characteristic of waking states; and ends on the other side with bizarre, nonrational, hallucinatory experiences typical of the most memorable and intensely vivid dreaming (Fosse, Stickgold, & Hobson, 2004; Hartmann, 2000; Nielsen, 2000). Although sleep mentation exists on a continuum, it can be more easily understood by breaking it up into three categories: *cognitive activity, ordinary dreaming*, and *apex dreaming* (see Nielsen, 2000).

COGNITIVE ACTIVITY ("SLEEP THINKING")

Have you ever become aware during a half-awakening in the middle of the night that you had been thinking during sleep about material on a test scheduled for the following day or making a list of things you needed to take care of over the weekend? Or perhaps you had been repeating certain images or melodies, or reflecting upon some event. This type of mentation is categorized as cognitive activity or "**sleep thinking**." Cognitive activity of this sort differs from dreaming in that it is unemotional, nonhallucinatory, and it lacks a story or dramatic progression. Rational, directed thought of this sort virtually always occurs during NREM sleep (Fosse et al., 2004; Nielson, 2000).

ORDINARY DREAMING

Although dreams are often characterized in the media and literature as irrational, bizarre, and surrealistic, this description does not apply to most dreams. The average dream contains recognizable characters engaged in relatively realistic activities that are based on the dreamer's ordinary concerns and preoccupations (Domhoff, 2003, 2010; Cartwright, Agargun, Kirkby, & Friedman, 2006; Dorus, Dorus, & Rechtschaffen, 1971). One reason why dreams are thought to be "stranger" than they generally are may be that bizarre dreams are more likely recalled the next day (Vogel, 2000). However, when dream research participants are awakened at various points during the night and asked to relate their dreams, they tend to report material that lacks the surrealism and irrationality attributed to dreams in general (Domhoff, 2003, 2010). The majority of dreams that occur during NREM are of the **ordinary dreaming** variety.

APEX DREAMING

Apex dreams are those that are the most intense, vivid, bizarre, hallucinatory, and "dream-like." Nightmares and sexual dreams are good examples of apex dreams, as are dreams that are too "beyond words" to describe, even if you

▲ **Typical Dream?** Although dreams are usually depicted as surrealistic, hallucinatory, and wildly improbable, such as in this image, most dreams are actually relatively realistic and logical. (Painting depicted: *The Nightmare*, 1781, by Henry Fuseli.)

Sleep mentation ▶ Any and all mental activity occurring during sleep, including "sleep thinking" and various levels of dreaming.

Sleep thinking (cognitive activity) ▶ Rational, directed thought occurring during NREM sleep.

Ordinary dreaming ▶ Dreams depicting relatively realistic activities and recognizable characters.

Apex dreams ▶ The most intense, bizarre, nonrational, and hallucinatory dreaming.

recall them. While there is controversy regarding the importance of REM to the entire dream process, evidence very strongly supports the view that apex dreaming occurs primarily during REM sleep (Hobson et al., 2000).

Apex dreams are characterized by the dreamer's acceptance of wildly improbable events as being real (Hobson, 2002). However, one unusual type of apex dream in that this does not occur is known as the **lucid dream** (LaBerge, DeGracia, Kunzendorf, & Wallace, 2000; Voss, Holzmann, Tuin, & Hobson, 2009). Normally, one is unaware that one is dreaming. It is not even common to ask oneself the question, "Am I dreaming?" although this occurs often in movie depictions of dreams. In a lucid dream, however, the dreamer becomes aware that he or she is dreaming. In a lucid dream there is a sense of being one's "real self" in the dream with a consciousness similar to that of waking consciousness. Lucid dreams last about 2 minutes on average, but they may last as long as 50 minutes.

Lucid dream ▶ A type of apex dream where the dreamer becomes aware that he or she is dreaming.

Dreams Have Meaning to the Dreamer

Dream researchers do not agree on what part of the brain is responsible for generating dreams or how the images of dreams are generated. There is even less agreement as to *why* the brain engages in dreaming in the first place.

The founder of psychoanalysis, Sigmund Freud, referred to dreams as the "royal road to the unconscious." He believed that dreams expressed, in disguised and sometimes symbolic form, wishes and desires experienced by the dreamer on an unconscious level—wishes and desires that would be unacceptable or threatening if they were made conscious. Freud's "wish-fulfillment" model of dreams was discarded long ago by scientific psychologists (Fisher & Greenberg, 1996), but it has not been replaced by a model as widely accepted as Freud's once was. Here are a few candidates:

- Dreams are the cerebral cortex's attempt to make sense out of random electrical brain activity while it is operating without the help of neurotransmitters that characterize waking cognition and rational thought. These neurotransmitter systems are lowered during NREM, but "knocked out" during REM, explaining the preponderance of dreams (particularly apex dreams) during REM (Hobson et al., 2000).
- Dreams are the brain's attempt to solve problems during sleep or regulate mood carried over from the previous day (Cartwright, 1996, 2005).
- Dreams (especially negative or threatening dreams) evolved to allow the dreamer to "rehearse" various sorts of responses to threatening situations and thus be better prepared to deal with actual threats (Valli et al., 2005; Valli, Strandholm, Sillanmaiki, & Revonsuo, 2008).

Despite their many differences, each of these theories suggests an important fact: Even if dreams result from nothing more than random brain activation, *dreams have meaning to the dreamer*. They consist of content drawn from the person's life history, circumstances, emotions, and subjective experience.

WHAT DO PEOPLE DREAM ABOUT?

As studies in sleep laboratories show, virtually all people dream, whether they recall their dreams or not (Hobson, 2002). In fact, unless one is awakened during a dream, recall of dreams is actually relatively rare. But what do people dream about? Is dream content as varied as the number of people who dream? While there are substantial individual, cultural, and sex differences in the content of dreams, there are also aspects of dream content that are universal among people regardless of culture, or are universal for a particular sex or age group.

According to William Domhoff (1996, 2002, 2010), the basic findings of studies of the content of dreams can summarized in a few general statements, based on over 50 years of research utilizing systems initially devised by Calvin

▶ **Same Dreams?** Throughout the world, women are more likely than men to dream about people familiar to them and family life, and more likely to dream of being the victim of an aggressive attack and other nightmarish themes. Women are less likely than men to dream *about* men, and less likely to dream about sex (or, at least, less likely to report such dreams to researchers).

Hall and Robert Van de Castle (1966). More details have been added to this picture of dream content by Tore Nielsen and his colleagues (Nielsen, Zadra, Simard, Saucier, & Stenstrom, 2003):

1. *Despite major cultural changes over the second half of the 20th century, the dream life of young adults (college students) has remained essentially unchanged.* The most common types of dreams for both young men and young women are those that contain aggression or fear. Women are somewhat more likely than men to experience nightmarish themes (Nielsen et al., 2003) including themes of social exclusion and rejection. Indeed, one of the most robust findings in the dream research is that unpleasant dreams greatly outnumber pleasant ones, with misfortune occurring in about one-third of all dreams (Domhoff, 2010).

Not all dreams are unpleasant, however. Dreams of friendly interactions are common, as are dreams with sexual content. As one might expect given research suggesting that men think about sex more often than women, sexual dreams are more common for men. In addition to sexuality and friendly interactions, other highly common themes of pleasant dreams are those that depict flying or soaring through the air (Nielsen et al., 2003). Finally, college students dream about school, teachers, and studying extremely frequently.

2. *There are stable cross-cultural similarities and differences in certain aspects of dream content.* In most respects, the general picture for dream content is similar all over the world. However, dream content also varies a great deal from culture to culture, in ways that make sense given major cultural differences. For example, the appearances of animals in dreams occurs with much greater frequency in small-scale societies in which hunting plays an important part in obtaining food. In cultures where the sexes are segregated for most of the day, dreamers have fewer other-sex characters in their dreams.

3. *There is a strong continuity found between the content of people's dreams and their waking thoughts.* There are large individual differences in dream content based upon differences in people's everyday concerns and emotional lives (Domhoff, 2003). If you are concerned about your performance at school or work, or the health of a family member, you may have dreams related to such concerns (Nickles, Brecht, Klinger, & Bursell, 1998). In the years following the September 11, 2001, terrorist attacks, increasing numbers of people incorporated 9/11 imagery into their dreams (Bulkeley & Kahan, 2008).

4. Finally, *sleeping environment can also affect the content of dreams.* Recently, I dreamt that one of my daughters and I had become lost in a frozen wood. I kept struggling to find blankets to cover her but I could not. I suddenly awoke to find that the window had somehow become unlocked and had swung open—letting in blasts of frigid wintry air—and that my wife, in her sleep, had stolen all my covers!

IN SUMMARY

1.	Sleep mentation includes cognitive activity, ordinary dreaming, and apex dreaming.
2.	The function of dreaming is unknown. Researchers theorize that dreams are the cortex's way of making sense of random brain activity in the absence of neurotransmitters associated with rational thought; or that dreams are random activation of memories; or that dreams exist to allow the sleeper to "rehearse" threatening situations.
3.	The content of dreams can be summarized in the following statements: The dream life of young adults has remained unchanged over the last 50 years; there are cultural similarities and differences in dream content; there is a strong continuity between people's waking thought and the content of their dreams; sleeping environment can affect the content of dreams.

RETRIEVE!

1.	Differentiate cognitive activity during sleep ("sleep thinking") from ordinary dreaming, and apex dreaming.
2.	A dream state where the dreamer is aware that he or she is dreaming is known as: **a)** apex dreaming **c)** hypersubjective dreaming **b)** lucid dreaming **d)** participant dreaming
3.	Which of the following is NOT a universal characteristic of dreams of college students? **a)** The dream life of young adults has remained essentially unchanged. **b)** Pleasant dreams outnumber dreams with unpleasant content. **c)** There are stable cross-cultural similarities and also differences in the content of dreams. **d)** There is continuity between the content of people's dreams and their waking thoughts.

What Are Sleep Disorders?

Like romantic relationships and marriages, sleep does not always proceed as we would want or expect. According to the National Sleep Foundation (NSF), an extraordinary number of people have problems connected to their sleep. In 2005, the NSF conducted a poll focusing on adult sleep habits and found that 75% of adult Americans experienced at least one symptom of a sleep problem

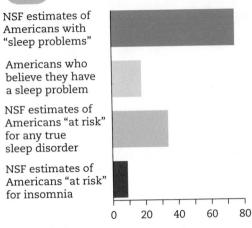

▲ FIGURE 6.6 National Sleep Foundation (NSF) 2005 Report on Sleep Problems in America. Although the National Sleep Foundation estimated that 75% of Americans had "sleep problems," only 43% of Americans believe that they have a sleep problem. According to the NSF, 34% of Americans are at risk for a true sleep disorder, while only 9% are at risk for insomnia.

a few nights a week or more during the past year (National Sleep Foundation, 2005). Results of the NSF poll suggest that problems with sleeping are "normal" among Americans, if we are using the term *normal* in the sense of *average*.

"Sleep Problems" and "Sleep Disorders" Are Not the Same

As alarming as it may seem, the NSF statistic identifying 75% of Americans as having symptoms of sleep problems is easy to misinterpret. First, there is a difference between a "symptom of a sleep problem" as defined by the NSF and a true "sleep disorder," such as *insomnia*, as defined by the medical profession. A parallel example would be the difference between a stuffy nose due to dry heat emanating from an old radiator and a stuffy nose due to a serious cold or flu.

To bring this point home, let's look at another result of the National Sleep Foundation poll mentioned earlier: Of the 75% of Americans defined by the NSF as having at least one symptom of a sleep problem, the large majority—76%—declared that they did *not* believe they had a sleep problem and that the symptoms they experienced had "little or no impact" on their lives (with the majority claiming "no impact"). This means that only 24% of the 75% of adult Americans identified by the NSF as having a sleep problem agree that they do have a sleep problem (this equals 18% of adult Americans in total).

A close look at the NSF poll also shows that only 34% of Americans are "at risk" for any of the major sleep disorders, which means that they *may* (or may not) have a disorder. Yet, the probability even of "at risk" individuals *actually* having a sleep disorder is very slight because the prevalence rate of diagnosable sleep disorders in the United States that are "clinically significant" is likely no greater than 10% (Ram et al., 2010). In other words, "at risk" might just as well read "at extremely low risk" or the equivalent. Figure 6.6 summarizes the findings of the 2005 NSF sleep poll.

Nevertheless, 34% of people being at risk for a sleep disorder is worth paying attention to because under some circumstances sleep disorders can be agonizing, crippling, and even life-threatening. In the United States alone there are more than 100,000 automobile accidents per year due to people falling asleep at the wheel, resulting in over 40,000 injuries and 1,550 deaths annually (Doghramji, 2004). Though not all of these accidents are due to a sleep disorder, without doubt sleep disorders are a major contributing factor. Studies of the potential consequences of inadequate sleep also suggest that sleep disorders might ultimately contribute to the risk of hypertension, hormonal disturbances, heart disease, stroke, obesity, psychological disorders such as depression or anxiety, and metabolic disorders including diabetes (Bagai, 2010; Gottlieb et al., 2005; Leproult & Van Cauter, 2010; Spiegel, Leproult, & Van Cauter, 1999).

Occasional sleep problems probably should be expected for most of us. Genuine sleep disorders are another story. While the American Sleep Disorders Association lists over *eighty* such sleep disorders, the American Psychiatric Association recognizes only 17 (Richert & Baran, 2003). We will consider a few of the most commonly diagnosed of these: *insomnia, obstructive sleep apnea, parasomnias,* and *narcolepsy*.

Insomnia Has a Life of Its Own

Insomnia ▶ A chronic difficulty falling asleep, staying asleep, and/or being unable to obtain restful sleep.

Insomnia is a chronic difficulty falling asleep, staying asleep, and/or being unable to obtain restful sleep (Bootzin & Epstein, 2011; Espie, 2002). Insomnia is not the same as *circadian rhythm disorder*—difficulty going to sleep and waking up at the times one would expect given the local cycle of light and dark. A person who gets into bed at 11:00 p.m., but can't fall asleep until 1:00 a.m.—but who then sleeps a restful 8 hours, waking up at 9:00 a.m.—is much more likely to have *circadian rhythm disorder* than insomnia. On the other hand, it is also true that disruption in circadian rhythms, as might be experienced in jet lag or by night shift workers, can trigger true insomnia.

As many as 30% to 50% of all Americans experience at least symptoms of insomnia at some point, but as indicated earlier it is unlikely that more than about 2% to 10% suffer from chronic, diagnosable insomnia (Becker, 2006; Ohayon, 2002; Ram et al., 2010). As a person ages, his or her likelihood of experiencing this disorder approximately doubles, and at all ages, almost twice as many women as men suffer from insomnia (Buysse, Germain, & Moul, 2005; Espie, 2002).

Insomnia is not something that just happens to a person at night. Exhaustion, irritability, isolation, and hopelessness about the situation ever improving pervade the sufferer's entire day (Kyle, Espie, & Morgan, 2010). As evening approaches, anxiety about what is in store for the night builds, and this anxiety contributes to perpetuating the condition. Sufferers often realize that their anxiety about sleep is working against them, but feel powerless to avoid it. Insomnia takes on a life of its own (Carey, Moul, Pilkonis, Germain, & Buysse, 2005, p. 80).

Insomnia may have long-lasting consequences. Indeed, obtaining adequate, restful sleep is so important to virtually all aspects of functioning that some researchers have proposed that insomnia greatly increases the risk of a large number of physical and psychological problems and disorders (Bootzin & Epstein, 2011; Harvey, 2008). In other words, insomnia is a disorder that also may constitute a partial cause of numerous other disorders.

▲ **Consequences of Insomnia.** Insomnia impacts every aspect of a person's life, contributing to the risk of many physical and psychological disorders.

LIVING PSYCHOLOGY

Getting a Good Night's Sleep

Insomnia as a disorder is a complex problem that is not always easy to treat. However, *symptoms* of insomnia, particularly if they are not too severe, are often amenable to simple home treatment. The following are some sensible ways to get a good night's sleep:

1. Set regular times for going to sleep and waking up and try to stick to them.

2. Take a warm bath before bed. The lowering of your body temperature as you dry off may help by exaggerating the signal of approaching sleep normally produced by the circadian pacemaker.

3. Keep your room cool.

4. Don't use the bed for anything but sleeping and sex. Don't read in bed, don't watch TV or talk on the phone in bed, and, most of all, don't think or solve your problems in bed.

5. Don't lie in bed waiting for sleep. If you don't fall asleep after about 30 to 45 minutes, get up and do something. Try again a bit later.

6. Don't sleep late or take naps to make up for lost sleep, if you can possibly avoid it—and don't go to bed earlier than usual if you had a bad night the night before.

7. Don't use alcohol to get to sleep. It may get you there, but it will likely wake you up in a few hours, make it very hard for you to get back to sleep, and rob you of REM sleep.

8. Cut out caffeine altogether if you can, or at least limit it, and don't use it in the afternoon or evening at all. Note that "decaffeinated" coffee still contains a significant amount of caffeine.

9. Don't eat heavily before bed, especially spicy food. Contrary to popular belief, eating before bed won't cause you to gain weight any more than eating at any other time, but it will keep you awake.

LIVING PSYCHOLOGY

CONTINUED

10. Try to find a way to avoid anxiety about sleep in general. (Admittedly, this is easier said than done.) Interestingly, *chamomile*, taken in a standardized extract capsule (or perhaps also as tea) has been found in at least one study to be superior to placebo in treating anxiety—and it is widely known for its ability to decrease the time needed to fall asleep ("sleep latency"). It makes many people drowsy. If it's anxiety that is keeping you awake, you might try using chamomile extract several times a day and again before bed. Apparently it has few if any side effects (Amsterdam et al., 2009). ■

Obstructive Sleep Apnea (OSA) Can Be Life-Threatening

Obstructive sleep apnea (OSA) ▶ A sleep disorder caused by narrowing at various sites along the upper airway leading to repeated nightly episodes of inability to breathe.

Imagine that you are lying in bed at night, sound asleep, and someone enters the room. The intruder places one hand tightly over your mouth and pinches your nasal passages closed with the other hand so you are unable to breathe. After a few moments, your body fights to awaken, but just at the point of awakening, the intruder removes both hands. You resume sleeping. Now imagine that the intruder repeats this procedure several hundred times during the night. This is the experience of **obstructive sleep apnea** (**OSA**), a sleep disorder that results in repeated narrowing at various sites along the upper airway throughout the night, leading to complete or partial inability to breathe (Aloia, Arnedt, Davis, Riggs, & Byrd, 2004).

OSA is likely the most common of the sleep disorders, much more common than insomnia. The elderly and the obese are at particular risk for OSA, and, unlike insomnia, men are twice as likely as women to suffer from the condition (Pack, 2006; Ram et al., 2010). Younger women are particularly unlikely to have OSA. The central problem in OSA is that repeated episodes of inability to breathe result in insufficient oxygen reaching the brain and the rest of the body. Sufferers from severe OSA who do not obtain treatment are more likely to die of cardiovascular disease than those who have not been treated, and OSA patients have a unique pattern of sudden death due to heart attacks (Gami, Howard, Olson, & Somers, 2005; Marin, Carrizo, Vicente, & Agusti, 2005).

Parasomnias Can Be Nightmarish

Parasomnias ▶ A group of sleep disorders characterized by unusual or bizarre physical behaviors, perceptions, dreams, or emotions during sleep.

Parasomnias are a group of disorders characterized by unusual or even bizarre physical behaviors, perceptions, dreams, or emotions during sleep (Schenck & Mahowald, 2005, 2010). Those who suffer from one or more of the various parasomnias may walk, talk, scream, eat, fight, urinate, grind their teeth, or have sex in their sleep; they may wake in terror or confusion, or experience repeated nightmares. They may find themselves trying to enact their dreams.

There are quite a number of parasomnias, some very rare, and some fairly common. More common parasomnias include talking in one's sleep (*somniloquy*), bedwetting (common in children only), leg cramps during sleep, repeated nightmares, and snoring. Less common parasomnias include REM-sleep behavior disorder, night terrors, and sleepwalking; I will discuss parasomnias next.

REM-sleep behavior disorder (RBD) ▶ A *parasomnia* where the sleeper is missing the muscle paralysis component of REM sleep and "acts out" confrontational and violent dreams.

REM-SLEEP BEHAVIOR DISORDER

Those suffering from **REM-sleep behavior disorder** (**RBD**) are missing an important component of REM sleep: the muscle paralysis that enables one to experience intense dreams without needing to respond in a physical way to the events of the dreams. RBD sufferers may find themselves enacting their dreams, sometimes with dangerous consequences. This is because the dreams RBD sufferers tend to act out are those that are violent and confrontational—dreams where one is attacked by unknown assailants, insects, or animals and is compelled to fight to protect oneself or loved ones (Schenck & Mahowald, 2005, 2010). Bed partners of RBD sufferers may find their partner "punching, kicking, beating, biting, knocking things off the nightstand, sitting on the bed, jumping out of bed, whispering, talking, shouting, swearing, crying, laughing, and singing" (Iranzo, Santamaria, & Tolosa, 2009, p. 386). Bed partners of RBD sufferers need to be careful, for they may suffer cuts, bruises, and even bone fractures as a result of their partner's unusual behavior.

NIGHT TERRORS

Night terrors (also known as *sleep terrors*) are perhaps the most disturbing of the parasomnias. People in the grip of night terrors will suddenly sit up in bed screaming in fear, and may try to run frantically from some perceived threat. Appearing wild-eyed, with dilated pupils—although seemingly unable to see—they will experience increased heart rate and may sweat profusely. Attempts to soothe them may make things worse. The episode may last as long as a half-hour or more. Eventually, the sufferer will calm down and go back to sleep. In the morning he or she likely will not remember anything of the event (Durand, 2006; Manber, 2000).

Unlike episodes of RBD, night terrors do not necessarily result from a nightmare or any sort of dream at all. They tend to occur during those stages of NREM sleep where dreaming is least likely to occur, and may result from sudden arousal from NREM. However, dream-like experiences may sometimes occur (Oudiette et al., 2009). Night terrors are much more common in children and adolescents than in adults, particularly older adults, and they often seem to be triggered by sleep deprivation or fever in vulnerable individuals. Night terrors in children are extraordinarily difficult for parents to cope with because they feel they are unable to do their "job" of soothing their child during a crisis.

One child of my acquaintance described the experience in this way: "It is like having my feet in two different worlds at the same time. I do recognize my parents and I hear the words of comfort that they are saying. But, I am also aware of what seems to me to be actually happening. Those events are terrifying beyond belief and equally (or more) real to me."

SLEEPWALKING

In some respects, night terrors are related to **sleepwalking** (*somnambulism*). Both disturbances are thought to result from sudden arousal from NREM (Szelenberger, Niemcewicz, & Dabrowska, 2005). Sleepwalking, however, is generally more benign. The sleepwalker—again, usually a child—may wander aimlessly, carrying and rearranging objects in the room seemingly for no particular reason. He or she may try to urinate in a closet or wastebasket, or go outside for a walk, or even take an unscheduled swim in a nearby lake. The person's eyes are wide open, but they seem glassy and unfocused. You cannot generally communicate with a person while he or she is sleepwalking, although you can do so if the person is suddenly roused.

Narcolepsy Destroys the Boundaries between Sleep and Wakefulness

From time to time a comic actor will develop a routine involving a character who falls asleep while speaking, in the middle of a sentence. Such an event, however, is not a laughing matter and it is not an uncommon occurrence for someone suffering from **narcolepsy**, a neurological illness whose sufferers not

Night terrors ▶ A *parasomnia* consisting of episodes during which the sleeper may suddenly sit up in bed screaming in fear, flail, or run as though pursued by a terrifying attacker. Night terrors are not caused by nightmares.

Sleepwalking ▶ A *parasomnia* characterized by wandering, often aimlessly, during late-REM sleep.

Narcolepsy ▶ Chronic disruption of the sleep homeostat and sleep cycle. Those suffering from narcolepsy may feel the irresistible urge to sleep at any time, generally falling directly into REM sleep.

only fall asleep while speaking, but may do so while playing baseball, driving a car, or signing loan papers at the bank.

Narcolepsy is a chronic disruption of the sleep homeostat and the sleep cycle. The narcoleptic feels the irresistible urge to sleep at unpredictable times, and during these sleeps the normal progression from NREM to REM does not occur. REM typically begins immediately at sleep onset for narcoleptics rather than following 90 minutes of NREM as would normally be the case. Thus, narcolepsy sufferers may begin to dream vividly the moment they fall asleep. Indeed, narcolepsy can be seen as a disorder where REM intrudes into a person's normal waking experience (Zuberi, 2010).

During the 1990s, researchers established that the unpredictable onset of sleep in narcolepsy was associated with a dysfunction in the ability of the brain to produce *hypocretin*, a hormone that helps to govern the sleep cycle. In 2009, some of these same researchers were able to establish that the dysfunction in production of hypocretin is an autoimmune response linked to a specific gene. In simple terms, the immune system of the narcoleptic interprets hypocretin-producing cells as foreign bodies, and proceeds to kill them off (Hallmayer, Faraco, Lin, Hesselson, & Winkelmann, 2009).

IN SUMMARY

1.	Although the majority of Americans experience sleep problems from time to time, relatively few can actually be diagnosed with a sleep disorder.
2.	Insomnia is a chronic difficulty falling asleep, staying asleep, or obtaining restful sleep.
3.	Obstructive sleep apnea is a disorder caused by narrowing at various sites along the upper airway leading to an inability to breathe.
4.	Parasomnias include talking in one's sleep, bedwetting, leg cramps, REM-sleep behavior disorder, night terrors, and sleepwalking.
5.	Narcolepsy is a neurological disorder characterized by a disruption of the sleep homeostat and sleep cycle. Narcolepsy sufferers fall asleep at unpredictable times.

RETRIEVE!

1.	Why is it said that "insomnia is not something that just happens to a person at night?"
2.	True or false: Approximately 75% of Americans suffer from a sleep disorder.
3.	Connect the symptom to the sleep disorder:

Obstructive sleep apnea (OSA)	Walking during sleep
REM-sleep behavior disorder (RBD)	Suddenly falling asleep at unexpected times
Night terrors	REM sleep without muscle paralysis
Somnambulism	Suddenly waking in fear not as a result of nightmare
Narcolepsy	Repeated difficulty breathing during sleep as a result of the narrowing of various sites along the upper airway

4.   True or false: The unpredictable onset of sleep in narcolepsy is due to an overproduction of the hormone hypocretin.

Is Hypnosis an Altered State of Consciousness?

What could be more *altered* than the state of consciousness known as *hypnosis*? Think of all the movies and television programs you have seen that depict hypnosis: people in trance-like states accurately recalling events that occurred when they were infants, allowing the hypnotist to pierce their skin with needles, displaying outrageous feats of strength, or performing behaviors a year after having being instructed to do so while under hypnosis. While such images of hypnosis are essentially mythological (see "Critical Thinking about Psychology: Hypnotic Myths"), if even a portion of what is commonly believed about hypnosis were true, wouldn't that qualify hypnosis as an altered state of consciousness?

Unfortunately, after 100 years of research, there still is no firm foundation upon which to answer this question, and the question itself can be interpreted in a number of ways. Indeed, there are few debates in psychology as long-lasting and unlikely to be resolved in the near future as the debate over whether the experience of hypnosis represents a special, altered state of consciousness or an interesting variation on ordinary waking states (Wagstaff, 1994). Ten years after Irving Kirsch and Steven Lynn (1995) declared that the debate had ended in the 1990s and was now a "myth," an entire issue of the journal *Contemporary Hypnosis* (Volume 22, number 1, 2005) was given over to articles (including one by Kirsch himself) which demonstrated that the debate was—and is—alive and well and as heated as ever.

Hypnosis Is a Social Event

The term *hypnosis* was drawn from the Greek word *hypnos*, meaning sleep. **Hypnosis** has been newly redefined by the American Psychological Association (2005) in bare-bones terms as a procedure in which a person acting as a "hypnotist" gives a variety of suggestions for "imaginative experiences" to another person, who acts as a "subject" (e.g., "Go ahead, try to open your eyes—you will be unable."). The suggestions given to the subject are generally preceded by an initial hypnotic *induction procedure* that corresponds to what most people would call "being hypnotized" ("You are growing very sleepy . . ." and so forth).

Until about 40 years ago, hypnosis was thought by many psychologists and most of the public to be a special, altered state of consciousness—a *trance state*. This trance state actually defined the term *hypnosis* (Kirsch & Lynn, 1995). However, research has increasingly shown that hypnotic induction procedures are not even necessary to produce hypnotic effects, and there do not seem to be any particular criteria that can clearly distinguish a "hypnotic state" from other states of consciousness (Kirsch, 2005; Sheehan & Perry, 1976; Spanos, 1996). These facts were made clear in a study conducted by Balaganesh Gandhi and David Oakley (2005) when these researchers subjected two groups of people to a hypnotic induction procedure, telling members of one group they would be undergoing "hypnosis" while members of the other group were told they would be undergoing "instructions to help you become relaxed." The induction procedure produced only a very slight increase

Hypnosis ▶ An interaction between "hypnotist" and "subject" involving suggestions for "imaginative experiences."

in suggestibility when it was labeled "relaxation," but a substantial increase in suggestibility when it was labeled "hypnosis."

In fact, the hypnotic induction procedure itself can be done away with entirely as long as subjects believe they are "being hypnotized." It appears to be the suggestions themselves, given to a willing subject in a context that he or she *believes* is hypnosis, that contain whatever power hypnosis possesses (Barber & Calverley, 1965; Kirsch, Mazzoni & Montgomery, 2007; Lynn, Vanderhoff, Shindler, & Stafford, 2002).

If that's all there is to it, what is all the fuss about? The problem is this: While hypnotic induction procedures do not appear to be the cause of hypnotic responses in people, *something* is causing these responses. Although it is likely that a certain amount of fakery is involved in hypnosis (Spanos, 1991), fakery clearly does not account for most hypnotic phenomena. Hypnosis has been shown to be an effective treatment for acute pain (e.g., burns, surgery, childbirth) and a useful adjunct to standard treatments for tobacco and other drug addictions (although it cannot cure these addictions alone). It can also substantially alter people's auditory and visual perceptions and beliefs about their control over their own behavior (Gandhi & Oakley, 2005; Hilgard, 1986; Lynn & Kirsch, 2006; Patterson, 2004).

There is a broad spectrum of views on the question of what is actually happening during hypnosis, and the only points on which everyone seems to agree are these: (1) *imagination* and *suggestion* are somehow involved in hypnosis, and (2) hypnosis is a *social event* involving a "subject" and a "hypnotist." The rest is, to one degree or another, up for grabs.

Special State versus Nonstate Debate

In general, researchers attempt to explain how hypnosis works in one of two ways, a tendency referred to as the *special state* vs. *nonstate* debate. Those in the *special state* camp continue to view the unusual experiences that occur under hypnosis—for example, immersing one's hand in ice water for a prolonged period yet feeling no pain—as altered states of consciousness (Hilgard, 1986; Spiegel, 1994, 2010). However, these researchers also acknowledge that the state a person enters following an induction procedure—"being hypnotized"—is not itself an altered state (i.e., a "trance"; Hilgard, 1986; Kihlstrom, 1998). A person may move into an altered state (e.g., feeling no pain) directly from ordinary consciousness.

On the other hand, those in the *nonstate* camp claim that *nothing* about hypnosis is best explained with the idea of altered states (Kihlstrom, 2005, 2008; Spanos, 1996; Wagstaff, David, Kirsch, & Lynn, 2010). The most influential of the nonstate group are the **sociocognitive** theorists. They take as their starting point a large literature which shows that those who have not undergone hypnotic induction procedures can produce most of the same behaviors and effects seen in hypnosis (e.g., resistance to pain, amnesia, paralysis) through nonhypnotic suggestions, simple instructions designed to increase their motivation, or even through intentional attempts to pretend to be hypnotized (Barber, 1979; Spanos, 1996; Spanos & Chaves, 1989; Wagstaff, 1999).

Moreover, contrary to widespread beliefs, hypnotized individuals do not have improved recall of past events, cannot "regress" to infancy or "past lives," can lie just as easily as at other times, and cannot achieve feats of strength or endure pain beyond their ordinary capabilities. For example, while hypnosis does increase the *number* of memories recalled, it increases the number of false memories just as it increases the number of true memories. When the amount of false information is taken into account, recall under hypnosis turns out no better than recall under normal conditions—indeed, it is worse (Lynn, Loftus, Krackow, & Lilienfeld, 2003; Mazzoni, Heap, & Scoboria, 2010).

However, it is not that sociocognitive theorists are claiming that hypnotic effects are "not real." Instead they are claiming that hypnosis is a bit similar

Sociocognitive theory of hypnosis ▶ A theory that explains hypnotic effects in terms other than "altered states"—generally emphasizing the subject's social role in the hypnotic interaction.

to *placebo* response—where the taking of a phony medication actually brings symptomatic relief as a consequence of a person's belief that the medication is real. In both cases people experience what they *expect* to experience (Kirsch, 2005).

IN SUMMARY

1.	Hypnosis is a social interaction between a "hypnotist" and "subject" involving suggestions for "imaginative experiences." It is not a "trance state."
2.	It is primarily the subjects' belief that they are undergoing hypnosis—not the induction procedure—which causes hypnotic effects to occur.
3.	"State" theorists believe that subjects experience altered states during hypnosis (although they do not generally believe that hypnosis itself is an altered state). "Nonstate" theorists believe that nothing about hypnosis is explained by the idea of altered states.

RETRIEVE!

1.	Explain the statement that "hypnosis is not an altered state, but some of the events experienced under hypnosis may be altered states."
2.	Do sociocognitive theorists believe that hypnosis is not real? Explain your answer.

What Is the Nature of Meditation?

Meditation means many different things to many different people. Closely linked to spiritual practices, in Western religious contexts the word *meditation* usually describes actively thinking about some aspect of scripture—pondering, contemplating, and studying its meaning. Prayer may even be a form of meditation in some of these traditions.

However, in a psychological context it is most often techniques of meditation derived from Buddhist and Hindu or *yogic* practices that are of greatest interest because they may be divorced from their spiritual and religious roots and studied as aspects of consciousness (Blackmore, 2004). Indeed, some of these practices have entered the stream of modern life in secular contexts as aids for relaxation or for preventing (or managing) stress and other mental or physical health problems. We discuss such uses of meditation in Chapter 11, and review an actual technique of meditation that you can use if you wish. For now, we are primarily concerned with the nature of meditation and its relation to consciousness.

Meditation ▶ The term has many definitions, but Eastern meditation generally involves at minimum the qualities of relaxed attention and not-thinking.

Meditation Has at Least Two Basic Characteristics

Most traditional Eastern forms of meditation are based upon two essential characteristics: *relaxed attention* and *not thinking*. "Relaxed attention" means that during meditation a person is awake and aware. He or she is not in a trance, "zoned out," or "on another plane of existence." Although

▲ **Meditation.** While virtually all forms of meditation include relaxed attention and no-thought, traditional Buddhist meditation adds a third characteristic: *insight* into the "true nature of things." Insight is the central practice and purpose of Buddhist meditation, known as *vipassana* meditation.

Vipassana ▶ Traditional Buddhist "insight" meditation that uses either concentrative or open meditation as a starting point only. The object of Vipassana is to see into the "true nature of things" according to the Buddhist worldview.

Zen ▶ A small Buddhist sect emphasizing the use of concentrative and/or open meditation alone to achieve enlightenment. Zen is a Chinese development based upon Chinese Taoism and Mahayana Buddhism.

unintentionally falling asleep or experiencing *microsleeps* (see p. 274) is a rather common experience for many meditators (Austin, 1998), the essential attitude of meditation is that of relaxed attention to the present moment, without strain, expectation, or self-criticism (Gunaratana, 1991; Williams, Teasdale, Segal, & Kabat-Zinn, 2007).

"Not thinking" is not as simple as it may sound. (Try it for just a few seconds!) There are a number of techniques meditators use to avoid thought. One is to focus all one's attention on *something*—noticing the way the breath enters and leaves the body at the point of the nostrils, reciting a *mantra* (a sound or word repeated continuously), placing one's attention on a specific part of one's body, such as the lower abdomen—again noticing the in-and-out movement of the breath—and so forth. Whenever thoughts intrude, the meditator gently brings his or her attention back to the point of focus, whatever it may be, without self-criticism. Examples of this type of meditation popular in the West are *transcendental meditation*, based on Indian *yogic* practices; and *mindfulness meditation* and *insight meditation*, both based upon Buddhist **vipassana** meditation.

A technique that arrives at much the same place using an opposite route is to focus one's attention on *everything* rather than *one* thing, but to respond to *nothing*. In other words, one allows awareness of anything at all to enter consciousness—whatever sensations, sounds, smells, aches and pains, joyful feelings, or negative thoughts may occur, without favoring or disfavoring any of them. One observes their arrival on the scene and then allows them to depart; neither clinging to nor trying to avoid them, and without passing judgment on any of them. All points of awareness are treated with equal indifference. Certain forms of Zen meditation use this technique. **Zen** is a practice that originated in China, based upon Mahayana Buddhism and Taoism; its practitioners in the United States are primarily influenced by Japanese Zen traditions.

Long-time Zen meditator and consciousness researcher Susan Blackmore (2004) uses the term *concentrative meditation* to refer to techniques that focus on a mantra, breathing, or object to attain relaxed attention and no-thought. Techniques that use the opposite strategy of allowing awareness of everything to enter consciousness are referred to as *open meditation*.

Meditation as an Altered State

Many claims for meditation have been made over the centuries. Most recently, claims are being made for the value of meditation as a medical or psychological treatment for various conditions, and as a preventative measure to avoid illness. We will examine some of these claims in Chapter 11. However, meditation is also said to provide an altered state of consciousness, and these claims appear legitimate. If you recall, we defined an altered state as *a temporary but radical change in the overall pattern of a person's normal subjective experience*. Meditators frequently describe radical changes in their normal subjective experience during meditation—including a sense of profound peace, changes in their experience of their place in the universe or within nature, ability to withstand pain and discomfort, reduction in anxiety, and "insight into the true nature of things." Meditation is not necessarily all sweetness and light, however—negative altered states are sometimes reported, including anxiety, panic, a sense of unreality, and a loss of personhood. Meditation may also sometimes result in what can only be described as boredom at a cosmic level.

Brain imaging studies have also suggested that unusual neural activity may occur during meditation, at least for some experienced meditators (Davidson et al., 2003; Kakigi et al., 2005; Manna et al., 2010). As depicted in Figure 6.7, one study showed that a group of people who meditated an average of 40 minutes per day using *insight meditation* (vipassana) techniques had thicker cortical regions associated with attention and perception relative to a control group that did not meditate (Lazar et al., 2005). Other studies have shown similar differences between long-term meditators and controls in regions associated with the regulation of emotion (Luders, Toga, Lepore, & Gaser, 2009).

However, it must be borne in mind that studies such as these have been correlational in nature. They do not show changes over time in the brains of meditators, because participants were not randomly assigned to meditate or not mediate. The study shows only that meditators' brains differ in certain respects from the brains of nonmeditators. Yet, it might be that people who are drawn to meditation, or are capable of sustained meditation for long periods, *already* have brains that differ from those of people not drawn to meditation or who are unable to sustain long periods of stillness and concentration. Moreover, even if meditation does cause changes in activity or structure of the brain, this fact alone would not automatically suggest that there has also been a substantial change in consciousness due to meditation. Nonetheless, when subjective reports and objective measurements are considered together, confidence is increased that meditation can create an altered state.

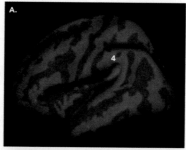

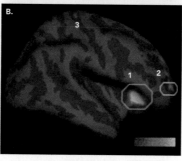

◄ FIGURE 6.7 Cortical Areas Shown to Be Thicker in Vipassana Meditators. New research suggests that meditators have thicker cortical structures within (1) the insula; (2) Broadmann's area; (3) somatosensory cortex; and (4) auditory cortex. *(Source: Lazar, Kerr, Wasserman, Gray et al., 2005.)*

IN SUMMARY

1. Traditional (Eastern) forms of meditation include relaxed attention and not-thinking.

2. One can achieve relaxed attention and not-thinking by concentrative meditation, which involves focusing on a mantra, an object, or one's breathing; or open meditation, in which one allows everything to enter one's consciousness.

RETRIEVE!

1. What is the most basic reason that psychologists are more interested in Eastern than Western meditation techniques?

2. What are the two essential characteristics of most Eastern forms of meditation?

a) correct seated posture and correct understanding

b) relaxed attention and insight

c) not thinking and correct understanding

d) relaxed attention and not thinking

e) correct seated posture and correct understanding

How Do Psychoactive Drugs Affect Consciousness?

A **psychoactive drug** is any substance with properties that affect mental life or consciousness in some way. Although this would include medications used to treat psychological disorders—for example, *antidepressants*—for now we are concerned with drugs that people use without a prescription (and sometimes in violation of the law) specifically to alter their mental state or consciousness. This is termed **nonmedical use of drugs**, or (perhaps unwisely) *recreational* drug use.

Use of Psychoactive Drugs Is an Ordinary Part of Most People's Lives

Nonmedical use of psychoactive drugs is an ordinary part of most people's lives. Try to think of a single person you know who does not use at least one of the following: cigarettes, caffeine (coffee, tea, energy drinks, soft drinks), alcohol (including beer or wine), or illicit drugs (e.g., marijuana or cocaine). Although there are some people who rigorously attempt to resist all such substances for health, religious, or other reasons, the stunning enormity of the alcohol, coffee, tea, cola, tobacco, and illicit drug industries testifies that total abstainers from all mind-altering chemicals are extremely unusual (Phillips & Lawton, 2004; Siegel, 2005; Walton, 2002). As summarized in Figure 6.8, in 2005 the World Health Organization estimated that there were 650 million smokers in the world (World Health Organization, 2005), and although the number is decreasing in the developing world (particularly the United States), it is increasing in much of the rest of the world. Alcohol use is about four times more prevalent even than the rate of tobacco use, and alcohol use is positively dwarfed by use of caffeine.

Illegal drug use is also pervasive. As depicted in Figure 6.9, in 2008, between 155 and 250 million people (3.5% to 5.7% of the world's population aged 15–64) used an illegal substance (mostly marijuana) to alter their consciousness (United Nations Office on Drugs and Crime, 2010). In Western nations approximately one-third of all adults have used illegal drugs (again, mostly marijuana) at least once (United Nations Office on Drugs and Crime, 2004; Phillips & Lawton, 2004). Thus, the total number of individuals using psychoactive drugs (legal and illegal) to alter their consciousness is truly staggering. This is not a recent phenomenon. Every recorded society whose natural environment supports the growing of plants has included use of psychoactive drugs as part of its culture (D. Brown, 1991; Siegel, 2005; Walton, 2002).

However, just because drug use is pervasive does not mean that it is good for you or that it does not pose dangers. In addition to possible medical or psychological consequences of inappropriate or abusive use of illicit drugs, in modern societies the use of these drugs can have extremely serious legal and social consequences, depriving users of their liberty, their possessions, and even their lives.

On the other hand, it is not always easy to obtain accurate information about the effects and dangers of psychoactive drugs. This is because nonmedical use of drugs historically has engaged powerful emotions, moral sentiments, and social, political, legal, and economic interests (Bonnie & Whitebread, 1999; Duster, 1972). Scientists are not immune from the influence of such forces (Cole, Sumnall, & Grob, 2002a, 2002b; Coles, 1993; McCook, 2005).

A good example is the recent history of research on the "club drug" **ecstasy** (**MDMA**). During the late-1980s and early 1990s the public became concerned about "rave" parties that were attracting many teenagers and featured

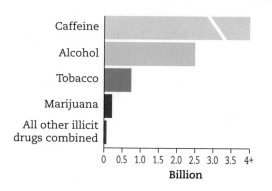

◀ **FIGURE 6.8 Worldwide Use of Psychoactive Drugs.** This chart compares worldwide use of caffeine, alcohol, tobacco, marijuana, and other illicit drugs. *(Sources: Phillips & Lawton, 2004; World Health Organization, 2005.)*

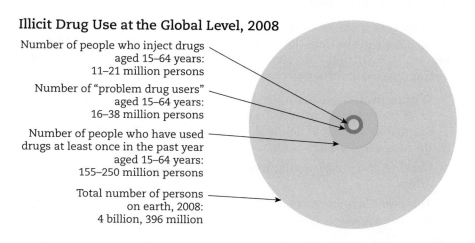

Illicit Drug Use at the Global Level, 2008

Number of people who inject drugs aged 15–64 years: 11–21 million persons

Number of "problem drug users" aged 15–64 years: 16–38 million persons

Number of people who have used drugs at least once in the past year aged 15–64 years: 155–250 million persons

Total number of persons on earth, 2008: 4 billion, 396 million

◀ **FIGURE 6.9** Illicit Drug Use throughout the World, 2008. *(Source: United Nations Office on Drugs and Crime, 2010.)*

all-night dancing and the use of various "club drugs"—in particular, ecstasy (MDMA). As had been the case with cocaine some years earlier (see Chapter 4, pp. 160–161), public, government, law enforcement, and funding-agency pressure was put on scientists to provide evidence of the dangers of ecstasy, and researchers whose work did *not* provide such evidence had a difficult time getting published (Cole et al., 2002a). Extravagant statements that could not be supported by evidence were made in the media about brain damage and other horrors suffered by ecstasy users (Rosenbaum, 2002).

Everyone's worst fears were realized in 2002 when an article reporting research on ecstasy among nonhuman primates appeared in *Science*, the premiere journal of scientific research in the United States. This article indicated that ecstasy had profoundly destructive effects on dopamine-related brain neurons in nonhuman primates, and might predispose human users to develop Parkinson's disease, a degenerative nervous system disorder characterized by severe motor disturbances resulting in difficulty walking, talking, and completing simple tasks.

However, it was later revealed that these researchers had not even been using ecstasy in their research—they had been using *methamphetamine* (popularly known as "crystal meth"). The article had to be retracted by the editors, a very unusual event for *Science*. But episodes of this sort are actually predictable given the sorts of intense pressures and incentives experienced by researchers in the field of nonmedical drug use (Cole et al., 2002a; Coles, 1993).

Yet, people's attitudes toward various psychoactive drugs are in part the result of historical and social forces that change with the times—they are not necessarily inherent in the nature of the drugs themselves. Consider **heroin**, one of the most socially and morally despised of all drugs. But heroin was not always despised. Indeed, it was created for Bayer Pharmaceuticals, the company that produces the world's best-selling aspirin. It was initially cheered by the medical profession for its many uses and sold over the counter as a cough suppressant and as an ingredient in tonics known as "soothing syrups" (see Figure 6.10). At

▲ The "Rave" Scene of the 1980s and 1990s.

Heroin ▶ A powerful, semi-synthetic opioid narcotic derived from morphine.

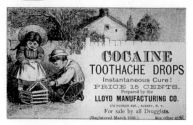

▲ **FIGURE 6.10** When Heroin and Cocaine Were Freely Available.

Addiction ▶ A term frequently used to describe drug dependence. Originally, the term included *withdrawal, tolerance,* and *craving* as necessary components, but currently, *addiction* has no precise definition.

Withdrawal ▶ Unpleasant physiological (and psychological) symptoms experienced when the body is deprived of a drug to which it has become adapted.

Craving ▶ Overpowering feelings of "wanting" and depending upon a drug.

Tolerance ▶ A progressive need for more and more of a drug to achieve the same effect.

the turn of the 20th century the largest numbers of heroin addicts (by a large margin) were middle-class housewives (Acker, 2002; Bonnie & Whitebread, 1999; Duster, 1972). However, these women suffered little moral disapproval and did not necessarily lose the respect of their families or society. Instead, they were more likely pitied for having a medical problem. As the legal status of the drug changed, however, so did the groups of people most likely to use it—and so did the moral and social status of the drug (Duster, 1972).

Therefore, when it comes to the nonmedical use of psychoactive drugs, keep in mind that people feel passionately about this issue, a warning sign that one needs to tread carefully through the mine field of claims and counterclaims.

"Addiction" Has Many Definitions

Drug **addiction** is one of the most destructive consequences of abusive non-medical use of drugs, but the term *addiction* has no accepted definition. Traditionally, *addiction* has referred to dependent and compulsive use of a drug that resulted in three outcomes:

1. **Withdrawal**, unpleasant physiological symptoms or states experienced when the body is deprived of a drug to which it has become biologically adapted as a result of habitual use. In such cases, the body experiences the removal of the drug as a harmful event.

2. **Craving**, the overpowering feeling of "wanting" and depending upon a drug.

3. **Tolerance**, a progressive need for more and more of the drug to achieve the same effect.

This "classical" model of addiction was based on users' physiological responses to *opium* and the various drugs derived from it, such as heroin and morphine. However, this understanding of addiction had to be revised. Consider the drug cocaine. While it does produce a "crash" when its effects dissipate, it does not generally produce withdrawal symptoms in the true sense and does not necessarily result in tolerance. Therefore, cocaine is not "physically addicting" in the sense that the opiates are addicting (Johanson, Roehrs, Schuh, & Warbasse, 1999; Weddington et al., 1990). Yet cocaine can still produce a craving and dependence as powerful as—or in some cases more powerful than—that produced by more "classically" addictive drugs such as heroin.

For this and other reasons, many researchers and clinicians concerned with drug problems have tended to shy away from use of the term "addiction" in recent years (although some still use it). Many prefer to use the term *dependence* while making a point of specifying whether or not symptoms such as withdrawal, craving, or tolerance are present.

Recent estimates suggest that approximately 2.6% of Americans will become dependent upon psychoactive drugs or alcohol at least once in their lifetimes, while an additional 7.7% will abuse these drugs without becoming dependent upon them (Compton, Thomas, Stinson, & Grant, 2007). The term *drug abuse* is generally meant to indicate any pattern of drug use that causes personal distress or impairment in an important aspect of a person's life. However, in practice this term is often applied to *any* illegal use of a drug, and it is sometimes difficult to determine what any particular commentator means by the use of the word *abuse* in connection with illegal drug use.

All Substances Are Potentially Toxic

Although some drugs are considered "safer" and others more "dangerous," or *toxic*, it is important to understand that, in fact, *all substances are potentially toxic*—and this includes water, which, if taken in sufficient amounts, can cause death (Riggs, Dysken, Kim, & Opsahl, 1991). Indeed, on January 15, 2007, Jennifer Lea Strange, a 28-year-old California woman, died of water intoxication after participating in a radio-station-sponsored water-drinking contest. Thus, there is no "nontoxic" drug, which means that there is no "safe" drug. On the other hand, technically speaking, neither is there a "toxic" or "dangerous" drug. Instead, there is a *dose level* for every substance above which it poses danger, and below which it produces no measurable physiological harm (Neubert, 1999).

It is for this reason that researchers use a formula based on studies with laboratory animals and humans to compute a **safety ratio** for psychoactive drugs (Gable, 2004a, 2004b). The *larger* the safety ratio, the *less* toxic the drug given the dosages normally used. For example, if a drug has a safety ratio of 10, it means that 10 times the ordinary "recreational" dose of the drug would probably kill an average person. A safety ratio of 100 means that it would take approximately 100 times the ordinary recreational dose to be lethal (Gable, 2004b).

Table 6.2 lists the safety ratios of a group of drugs often used for nonmedical purposes, along with a ranking of the potential for the drug to create dependence (addiction). Of course, the safety ratios are estimations that cannot be relied on to be precise because there are so many other factors that could come into play—for example, the age and health status of the person, whether a person uses several drugs at once, and so forth. The ratios should be viewed as a general picture of the *relative* toxic potential of various drugs.

In all, at the turn of the 21st century, illegal use of psychoactive drugs resulted in approximately 17,000 deaths per year in the United States—both directly, due to overdose, illness, or drug interaction; and indirectly due to automobile

Safety ratio ▶ A statistic expressing the potential toxicity of a drug in terms of the dose one would need to take to cause death.

Table 6.2 Safety Ratios and Dependence Potential of Some Commonly Abused Drugs

Specific figures for the proportion of users who become dependent are given where known.

SUBSTANCE	SAFETY RATIO	DEPENDENCE POTENTIAL
Narcotics		
Codeine	20	Moderate
Morphine	15	High
Heroin	6	High (23% of users become dependent)
Depressants (Hypnotics)		
Rohypnol ("roofies")	40	Moderate
Alcohol	10	Moderate/high (13%–15% of users become dependent)
GHB	10	Uncertain
Stimulants		
Caffeine	100	Low/moderate
Nicotine	50	Very high (31% of users become dependent)
Cocaine	15	Moderate/high (16% of users become dependent)
Psychedelics ("Hallucinogens")		
Marijuana	>1,000 (no verified case of death)	Low/moderate (9% of users become dependent)
LSD	1000	Very low
Ecstasy (MDMA)	15	Low/moderate

(Source: Adapted from data presented by Anthony, Warner, & Kessler, 1994; Gable, 2004b, 2006; Wagner & Anthony, 2002.)

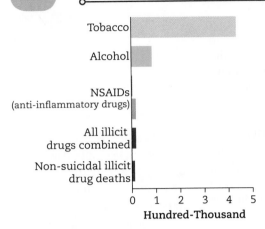

▲ FIGURE 6.11 Comparison of Drug-Use Deaths in the United States. *(Sources: Lee, 2004; Singh, 2000; Tarone, Blot, & McLaughlin, 2004; Wolfe, Lichtenstein, & Singh, 1999.)*

Narcotics ▶ Although this term is often used casually to refer to illicit drugs in general, technically it refers only to those derived from opium (opioid drugs).

Depressants (hypnotics) **▶** Drugs that depress the central nervous system (but are not narcotics).

Stimulants ▶ Drugs that increase alertness and energy.

Psychedelics ▶ Drugs that substantially alter one's perception of reality.

and other accidents (Mokdad, Marks, Stroup, & Gerberding, 2004). However, one-third of these 17,000 deaths were due to suicide (Drug Abuse Warning Network, 2003a), making the actual number of nonintentional drug deaths closer to 11,000.

This figure should be seen in the context of deaths due to *legal* nonmedical and medical drug use: For example, during the same years, approximately 435,000 deaths occurred annually in the United States, directly or indirectly, as a result of cigarette smoking (not including second-hand smoke), and 85,000 resulted from alcohol use (Mokdad et al., 2004; see Figure 6.11). In Great Britain, alcohol and tobacco currently result in approximately 90% of all drug-related deaths (Nutt, King, Saulsbury, & Blakemore, 2007.

Emergency room visits resulting from the misuse and abuse of all psychoactive drugs (including over-the-counter drugs) account for between 1% and 2% of all U.S. emergency room visits (Drug Abuse Warning Network, 2003b, 2004, 2010). If this seems relatively low given the publicity such events receive, looking more closely at data for drug-related emergency room visits adds still more surprises. For example, as Figure 6.12 shows, although teenagers sometimes are viewed as the "champions" of illicit drug abuse, they may be getting a bad rap. It appears to be the age groups of their elder siblings and parents who are responsible for the largest numbers of emergency room visits related to illicit drugs. Indeed, the numbers of high school seniors who have ever used an illicit drug (including marijuana) has decreased over the past three decades, from approximately 66% in 1981, to 50% in 2011. If marijuana is not included, the 2011 figure for high school seniors having ever used an illicit drug is 25% in 2011, down from 43% in 1981 (Johnston, O'Malley, Bachman, & Schulenberg, 2012).

In fact, as Table 6.3 and Figure 6.13 show, in 2008, over-the-counter medications such as aspirin, acetaminophen (*Tylenol*), ibuprofen (*Motrin*), cough syrups, and cold medications accounted for more emergency room visits of 12- to 17-year-olds than cocaine, heroin, amphetamine, methamphetamine, ecstasy, LSD, and PCP combined (34,091 vs.14,719; Drug Abuse Warning Network, 2010). Only marijuana and alcohol were more likely than Tylenol to land teens in this age bracket in the emergency room (but, as the table explains, "marijuana-related" emergency room visits may not always be what they seem).

The 12-to-17 crowd may have gotten a bad rap in regard to illicit drugs, but college-aged teens (18–20) *are* the marijuana abuse "champions," and they trail behind only the 35-to-44 age group in alcohol abuse (Drug Abuse Warning Network, 2010). Looking at all age groups combined, alcohol accounts for many more emergency room visits than any other single drug (see Table 6.4).

In general, psychoactive drugs used for nonmedical purposes are placed in one of four categories: **narcotics**, which are derived from *opium* and have pain-killing and euphoric effects; **depressants** (also termed *hypnotics*), which depress the central nervous system (CNS) and produce relaxation or sleepiness; **stimulants**, which stimulate the CNS and produce alertness and energy; and **psychedelics** (also termed *hallucinogens*), which substantially alter one's perception of reality.

The number of drugs used for nonmedical purposes is vast. I will discuss only a few representative drugs from each of the preceding categories, and devote a special section to a new breed of psychoactive substances—the so-called legal highs.

Narcotics

The term *narcotic* is generally used only in reference *to opioid* drugs—that is, drugs derived from ordinary poppy flower (*popaver somniferum*; e.g., heroin,

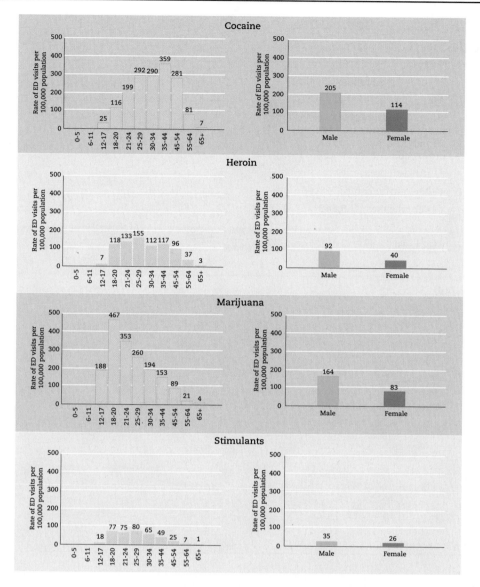

Teenagers often have the reputation of being "druggie wastoids" (Males, 1996). However, it appears that, with the exception of marijuana, this age group relatively rarely ends up in emergency rooms due to illicit drug use—particularly when compared with their older siblings and parents.

morphine, codeine, oxycodone, hydrocodone). **Opium**, the dried nectar of the poppy, is probably the oldest psychoactive substance known to mankind with the exception of alcohol (Booth, 1999). Opium is not a drug itself, but rather a substance containing a number of different **alkaloids** (the technical term for a compound with drug-like effects produced naturally by a plant). The most important of these alkaloids is **morphine**, one of the most powerful pain killers in existence and the drug from which heroin is derived.

Pharmaceutical drugs derived from opium—for example, morphine, codeine, hydrocodone (e.g., *Vicodin*), and oxycodone (e.g., *OxyContin*, *Percocet*)—are known as **opioids**. These drugs are among the most useful ever devised as treatments for pain and certain other conditions, and surprisingly, also among the safest as long as they are used properly for medical purposes (Merskey, 2004; Watson, Watt-Watson, & Chipman, 2004). However, these drugs are extremely dangerous when used for nonmedical purposes, when they can produce a dreamy, cocoon of euphoria and well-being. When used in this way they can, and often do, result in a very serious form of drug addiction or dependence that may take a lifetime of struggle to successfully treat. The most addictive of the opioids is heroin. Approximately 23%—almost one in four—people who use heroin on a regular basis become dependent (but note that this means that over 75% of users do not become dependent; Anthony,

Opium ▶ The dried nectar of the common popaver somniferum (poppy) flower containing a number of alkaloids including morphine.

Alkaloids ▶ Any compound with drug-like effects found naturally in a plant.

Morphine ▶ An alkaloid of opium used as a potent pain killer.

Opioids ▶ Any drug derived from *opium*.

Table 6.3 Drug-Related U.S. Emergency Room Visits for Teens Age 12–17, 2008 (Alcohol Not Included)

Alcohol: 35%
Marijuana: 8%
All major drugs of abuse excepting marijuana (e.g., heroin, methamphetamine, cocaine, etc.): 31%
Anti-depressants: 3%
Over the counter drugs: 23%

Total cases: 156,545

DRUG	TOTAL # OF ER VISITS
Alcohol	55,236 (19,752)[1]
Major Illicit Drugs of Abuse (Total: 29,714)	
Cocaine	6,229
Heroin	1,724
Amphetamines	1,647[2]
Methamphetamines	2,071[3]
Ecstasy	3,188[4]
LSD	551
PCP	1,423
Marijuana	12,881 (34,088)[5]
Over-Counter-Drugs (Total 34,091)	
Ibuprofen (e.g., Motrin)	6,331
Naproxin (Aleve)	794
Aspirin and aspirin combinations	3,971
Acetaminophen (Tylenol)	10,034
Antihistamines (e.g., Benadryl)	908
Cough syrup (dextromethorphan)	6,040[6]
Cough syrups (expectorant type)	1,103
Upper respiratory combination drugs (e.g. Sudafed)	4,910
Anti-Depressants (Total: 5,550)	
SSRI antidepressants (e.g., Zoloft)	5,557
Tricyclic antidepressants (e.g., Elavil)	412[7]
Misc. antidepressants	581

[1]The first figure is for "alcohol alone" admissions; the second is for alcohol in combination with other drugs.
[2]2008 figures were not available—this figure is an estimate for 2009.
[3]2008 figures were not available—this figure is an estimate for 2009.
[4]In fact, at least half or more of tablets sold on the street as "ecstasy" contain no MDMA at all, or only traces of the drug. The actual MDMA content of so-called ecstasy tablets has declined dramatically (e.g., Tanner-Smith, 2006).
[5]Two figures are given here for this reason: A "visit" for a particular illicit drug means that the drug is found in the patient's system, but this does not mean that the drug is the *cause* of the visit. In the case of marijuana, *only 27% of emergency room visits (12,881) are for marijuana alone*—usually alcohol or other potentially dangerous drugs are also present (Drug Abuse Warning Network, 2003c, 2010). Recent national surveys that examine emergency room visits on the part of chronic drug users find that marijuana smokers actually have lower rates of emergency room visits than users of any other illicit drug (Perron et al., 2011). Therefore, it is likely that the large number of "marijuana-related" emergency-room visits actually result from alcohol and other drugs used along with marijuana. When only marijuana is involved, the ER visit is almost always a result of unpleasant psychological responses such as panic or paranoia, or unexpected physical sensations. (The second figure is the total number of cases involving marijuana plus alcohol or other illicit drugs.)
[6]Not available in the 2008 data set—taken from a 2006 publication by the Drug Abuse Warning Network. The figure is for 12- to 20-year-olds. The publication is available at http://dawninfo.samhsa.gov/files/TNDR10DXM.htm.
[7]2008 figures not available—estimates for 2009.

(*Source: Drug Abuse Warning Network, 2010.*)

Table 6.4 Emergency Room Visits for Selected Drugs, 2010 (All Age Groups Combined)

Total U.S. Emergency Room Visits: 118,000,000; Total Visits Due to Drug Misuse/Abuse (includes alcohol) 1,999,861 (1.7%)

DRUG	TOTAL ER VISITS	% OF ALL DRUG MISUSE/ABUSE ER VISITS
Alcohol	656,892	33%
Cocaine	482,188	24%
Marijuana	374,435	18%
Heroin	200,666	10%
Methamphetamine	66,308	3%
PCP	37,266	2%
Amphetamines	31,534	1.5%
Ecstasy (MDMA)	17,865	1/10th of 1%
LSD	3,287	2/100th 1%
Over-the-Counter Drugs (e.g., aspirin, ibuprophen [Motrin], aceteminophan [Tylenol], Naproxin (Aleve), antihistamines, decongestants, cough syrups, laxatives, antacids)		
	139,079	7%
Anti-Depressants	80,881	4%

(Source: Drug Abuse Warning Network, U.S. Department of Health and Human Services, 2010.)

Warner, & Kessler, 1994). Here is how William S. Burroughs, a controversial 20th-century American novelist and infamous narcotics addict, described his life in late-addiction:

> I had not taken a bath in a year or changed my clothes or re-moved them except to stick a needle every hour in the fibrous grey wooden flesh of terminal addiction. I never cleaned or dusted the room. Empty ampule boxes and garbage piled up to the ceiling. Light and water had been long since turned off for non-payment. I did absolutely nothing. I could look at the end of my shoe for eight hours. I was only roused to action when the hourglass of junk [*note: heroin*] ran out. If a friend came to visit—and they rarely did since who or what was left to visit—I sat there not caring that he had entered my field of vision—a grey screen always blanker and fainter—and not caring when he walked out of it. If he had died on the spot I would have sat there looking at my shoe waiting to go through his pockets. (Burroughs, 1959, xxxvi)

Under certain circumstances opioid drugs can cause death, typically due to *respiratory depression,* a severe inhibition of the body's ability to regulate breathing. However, contrary to popular belief, it is not usually a particularly strong dose, or **overdose**, that produces sudden death to regular opioid users—most of whom have developed extreme levels of tolerance to the drug. Rather, it is the use of opioids simultaneously with other central nervous system (CNS) depressants such as alcohol or *benzodiazepine* drugs (e.g., *Valium, Xanax, Klonopin*), which can dramatically increase the risk of "overdose" (Brådvik, Hulenvik, Frank, Medvedeo, & Berglund, 2007; Darke

Overdose ▶ Taking a lethal or nonlethal but toxic dose of a drug.

▲ **Papaver Somniferum—The Opium Poppy.** On the left is an image of the papaver somniferum during its relatively brief flowered state. Soon the petals will fall off, and approximately 2 weeks later, the sap within the pod (head) of the flower will have matured. The pod is then scored with a sharp implement and the resulting milky sap (shown in the image on the right) is collected, thickens, and finally dries into opium.

& Zador, 1996, 2000; Dietz, Jolley, Fry, & Bammer, 2005; Warner-Smith, Darke, Lynskey, & Hall, 2001). Although it is possible for opioid drug users to die from a particularly strong dose (Brådvik et al., 2007; Dietz et al., 2005), this accounts for a small minority of opioid-related deaths. Particularly when heroin is involved, authorities have a tendency to apply the label "overdose" to any sudden death of a known heroin user, even when it is unclear which drug ought to be blamed for the death (Brecher, 1972).

Stimulants

Drugs that are classified as stimulants have the effect of producing feelings of exhilaration, alertness, confidence, and mood elevation—although they can also trigger anxiety, restlessless, sleeplessness, and a number of other undesirable effects. Each stimulant is different and they produce their effects in numerous ways, but frequently stimulant effects are associated with a build-up of the neurotransmitter dopamine in the brain.

COCAINE

Cocaine is a concentrated form of an alkaloid of the *coca* plant, indigenous to South America. For centuries, native peoples have chewed the coca leaves for their pain-killing, appetite-suppressing, and energizing effects. Cocaine is usually inhaled through the nose, but it can also be injected, or the "base" (active ingredient) in cocaine can be isolated and smoked in **freebase**—a much more powerful, habit forming, and potentially toxic way to experience the drug. Cocaine can also be smoked as **crack**, which is similar to freebase but less expensive and easier to produce.

Cocaine users generally experience a rush of energy, elevated mood, euphoria, alertness, and feelings of well-being. However, because these effects are so short lasting (only about 10 or 15 minutes for those who snort the drug, and even less for those who freebase or use crack), users are forced to repeat dosing themselves continuously if they want the high to last. Long term users may experience symptoms of sleeplessness, severe depression, and serious impairment in thought and perception—particularly paranoia. Cocaine-dependent individuals have lost their money, cars, homes, property, jobs, and families as a result of their cocaine habits. Approximately 16% (one in six) cocaine users eventually becomes dependent on the drug, only slightly more than the numbers of alcohol users who become dependent (Anthony et al., 1994).

Cocaine ▶ An alkaloid of the coca plant in concentrated form.

Freebase ▶ A method of using cocaine where the active ingredient of cocaine is isolated and smoked. Unlike cocaine in powder form (cocaine hydrochloride), freebase is not soluble in water and cannot be snorted or administered through injection.

Crack ▶ A solid form of cocaine somewhat similar to freebase, "cooked" from cocaine, water, and baking soda or lye. Street crack often contains other chemical components.

The Faces of Cocaine. Left to right: *coca* leaf, cocaine as powder, cocaine as crack.

AMPHETAMINES

Amphetamines ("speed," "crystal meth," etc.), methamphetamine, *Dexedrine*, and *Adderall* (used to treat ADHD) all belong in this class of drugs.

Unlike cocaine, amphetamines have long-lasting effects, and they are much less expensive. On the other hand, most amphetamines tend to be somewhat "harsher" than cocaine as an experience and are less likely to result in feelings of euphoria and well-being. Those taking "speed" often appear to others to be exhibiting symptoms of *mania* (see Chapter 14)—rapid speech, overconfidence, restless energy, insomnia, and bizarre attention to detailed tasks ("I think I'll clean every inch of this house tonight—and maybe my friend's mother's house too").

Like cocaine, amphetamines can result in severe fatigue, depression, and other unpleasant symptoms when the drug wears off, and symptoms of psychosis similar to those experienced by cocaine users may also be experienced after prolonged use of amphetamines. Some evidence suggests that amphetamines may cause long-lasting changes in brain functioning and structure (Berman, O'Neill, Fears, Bartzokis, & London, 2008; Chang, Alicata, Ernst, & Volkow, 2007). Dependence upon amphetamines (especially methamphetamine) is common, but I could find no data regarding the proportion of users who become dependent.

Amphetamines ▶ A family of stimulant drugs that exert their effects primarily by increasing levels of norepinephrine, serotonin, and dopamine in the brain.

CAFFEINE

Caffeine is an alkaloid found naturally in coffee, tea, and chocolate. It wards off fatigue, produces alertness, and for some people improves performance on a variety of cognitive tasks when taken in moderate doses (Dagan & Doljansky, 2006; van Duinen, Lorist, & Zijdewind, 2005). In larger doses it can produce restlessness, nervousness, insomnia, gastric and heart disturbances, and other problems. Truly excessive doses can result in serious symptoms of mental illness requiring psychiatric treatment (American Psychiatric Association, 2000; Hedges, Woon, & Hoopes, 2009).

The large majority of human beings use caffeine—either as coffee, tea, soft drinks, energy drinks, or chocolate—although some steer clear of it because it can cause insomnia or "jitters." However, at any given time, most people in the world are either under the influence of caffeine in some form, or soon will be (Phillips & Lawton, 2004). As I sit here with my espresso cup filled to the brim, I admit to being an enthusiastic part of this thundering majority.

Whether or not caffeine is "addictive" is controversial, however. Regular caffeine users know that it can produce tolerance, and that suddenly quitting use can cause withdrawal symptoms such as severe headache, fatigue, and irritability (Juliano & Griffiths, 2004). Some caffeine users have attempted to quit or cut down and found it quite difficult, making them technically dependent on the drug. However, caffeine users generally do not display most of the other criteria that would qualify their use as dependence or addiction. These criteria

Caffeine ▶ A stimulant alkaloid of coffee, tea, chocolate, and certain other plants.

would include devoting most of one's time in attempts to locate caffeine, dropping previously important activities so that caffeine can be used, frequent nonfatal overdose, and so forth.

How safe is caffeine? Periodically there are reports of health risks of caffeine, particularly in high doses, but there are also fairly numerous reports of potential benefits. Perhaps the most startling of such reports was the recent large-scale 13-year analysis of mortality data conducted by researchers from the National Institutes of Health. These researchers found that coffee drinkers were less likely to die of all causes combined (or of any specific cause) than non–coffee drinkers, after controlling for various potential confounding variables. More surprising still, it seemed that the more coffee a person drank—up to 4 to 6 cups daily—the stronger was the association with longevity (Freedman, Park, Abnet, Hollenbeck, & Sinha, 2012).

Of course, coffee contains more compounds than caffeine, and these correlational results certainly do not demonstrate that coffee *caused* the increases in longevity. Still, it does make one wonder. In any event, taken as a whole, caffeine seems to be a relatively safe drug that holds strong attraction for most people, but has the potential to produce a mild form of drug dependence. There is at least one exception to this "relatively safe" judgment: so-called energy drinks. The caffeine content of these drinks is generally unregulated, and some may contain many more times the amount of caffeine than in a can of cola or cup of coffee. Consumption of energy drinks has sometimes resulted in fatalities from heart attack or stroke, and more commonly can cause extremely unpleasant symptoms of caffeine intoxication (Reissig, Strain, & Griffiths, 2009). Increasingly, public concern has been raised about the use of these drinks, especially by teenagers.

Look up your favorite caffeine intoxicant in Figure 6.14 to see how much of the drug you are ingesting when you partake. Note that Starbucks Grande brewed coffee is the Queen of Caffeine! Perhaps surprisingly, espresso holds relatively little of the drug because of the small serving size and because some caffeine may be lost during extended roasting times. The mistaken impression that espresso is particularly high in caffeine probably stems in part from the drink's strong flavor, and perhaps also the fact that it is often downed quickly, bringing whatever caffeine it does have rapidly into the body.

NICOTINE

Nicotine is an alkaloid found in the *nightshade* family, which includes tomatoes, green peppers, and a number of other plants including tobacco (although the fruit of these plants contains no nicotine, so there's no need to cut down on your salad intake!). Nicotine produces a slight increase in alertness, and users who are dependent on it may experience a paradoxical sense of relaxation when they use the drug, probably because the experience of "needing" a cigarette is unpleasantly arousing. Nicotine is highly addictive—more users who try a nicotine-containing product ultimately become dependent upon it than any other drug, including heroin and cocaine (Anthony et al., 1994; Heishman, Kozlowski, & Henningfield, 1997). Approximately one-third of all teenagers who smoke a single cigarette become dependent on the drug by the time they are young adults (Centers for Disease Control, 1998). Withdrawal is extremely unpleasant and difficult to endure; it may include headaches, anxiety, irritability, insomnia, and cognitive disturbances. Although it has not yet been demonstrated conclusively that nicotine on its own—that is, apart from its presence in tobacco—is carcinogenic (cancer-causing) in humans, some animal research suggests that it may be (Davis et al., 2009).

Smoking Cigarettes Smoking cigarettes is perhaps the most dangerous and destructive ordinary behavior in which a person may engage. By "ordinary" I mean a behavior that many people perform in the daily course of their lives. Without doubt, jumping off the Brooklyn Bridge, shooting oneself in the head,

Coffees	Serving Size	Caffeine (mg)
Coffee, generic brewed	8 oz.	133 (range: 102-200) (16 oz. = 266)
Starbucks Brewed Coffee (Grande)	16 oz.	320
Einstein Bros. regular coffee	16 oz.	300
Dunkin' Donuts regular coffee	16 oz.	206
Starbucks Vanilla Latte (Grande)	16 oz.	150
Coffee, generic instant	8 oz.	93 (range: 27-173)
Coffee, generic decaffeinated	8 oz.	5 (range: 3-12)
Starbucks Espresso, doppio	2 oz.	150
Starbucks Frappuccino Blended Coffee Beverages, average	9.5 oz.	115
Starbucks Espresso, solo	1 oz.	75
Einstein Bros. Espresso	1 oz.	75
Espresso, generic	1 oz.	40 (range: 30-90)
Starbucks Espresso decaffeinated	1 oz.	4
Teas	**Serving Size**	**Caffeine (mg)**
Tea, brewed	8 oz.	53 (range: 40-120)
Starbucks Tazo Chai Tea Latte (Grande)	16 oz.	100
Snapple, Lemon (and diet version)	16 oz.	42
Snapple, Peach (and diet version)	16 oz.	42
Snapple, Raspberry (and diet version)	16 oz.	42
Arizona Iced Tea, black	16 oz.	32
Nestea	12 oz.	26
Snapple, Just Plain Unsweetened	16 oz.	18
Arizona Iced Tea, green	16 oz.	15
Snapple, Kiwi Teawi	16 oz.	10
Soft Drinks	**Serving Size**	**Caffeine (mg)**
FDA official limit for cola and pepper soft drinks	12 oz.	71
Vault	12 oz.	71 (20 oz. = 118)
Jolt Cola	12 oz.	72
Mountain Dew MDX, regular or diet	12 oz.	71 (20 oz. = 118)
Coke Blak	12 oz.	69 (20 oz. = 115)
Code Red, regular or diet	12 oz.	54 (20 oz. = 90)
Mountain Dew, regular or diet	12 oz.	54 (20 oz. = 90)
Pepsi One	12 oz.	54 (20 oz. = 90)
Mello Yellow	12 oz.	53
Diet Coke	12 oz.	47 (20 oz. = 78)
Diet Coke Lime	12 oz.	47 (20 oz. = 78)
TAB	12 oz.	46.5
Pibb Xtra, Diet Mr. Pibb, Pibb Zero	12 oz.	41 (20 oz. = 68)
Dr. Pepper	12 oz.	42 (20 oz. = 68)
Dr. Pepper diet	12 oz.	44 (20 oz. = 68)
Pepsi	12 oz.	38 (20 oz. = 63)
Pepsi Lime, regular or diet	12 oz.	38 (20 oz. = 63)
Pepsi Vanilla	12 oz.	37
Pepsi Twist	12 oz.	38 (20 oz. = 63)
Pepsi Wild Cherry, regular or diet	12 oz.	38 (20 oz. = 63)
Diet Pepsi	12 oz.	36 (20 oz. = 60)
Pepsi Twist diet	12 oz.	36 (20 oz. = 60)
Coca-Cola Classic	12 oz.	35 (20 oz. = 58)
Coke Black Cherry Vanilla, regular or diet	12 oz.	35 (20 oz. = 58)
Coke C2	12 oz.	35 (20 oz. = 58)
Coke Cherry, regular or diet	12 oz.	35 (20 oz. = 58)
Coke Lime	12 oz.	35 (20 oz. = 58)
Coke Vanilla	12 oz.	35 (20 oz. = 58)
Coke Zero	12 oz.	35 (20 oz. = 58)
Barq's Diet Root Beer	12 oz.	23 (20 oz. = 38)
Barq's Root Beer	12 oz.	23 (20 oz. = 38)
7-Up, regular or diet	12 oz.	0
Fanta, all flavors	12 oz.	0
Fresca, all flavors	12 oz.	0
Mug Root Beer, regular or diet	12 oz.	0
Sierra Mist, regular or Free	12 oz.	0
Sprite, regular or diet	12 oz.	0
Energy Drinks	**Serving Size**	**Caffeine (mg)**
Spike Shooter	8.4 oz.	300
Cocaine	8.4 oz.	280
Monster Energy	16 oz.	160
Full Throttle	16 oz.	144
Rip It, all varieties	8 oz.	100
Enviga	12 oz.	100
Tab Energy	10.5 oz.	95
SoBe No Fear	8 oz.	83
Red Bull	8.3 oz.	80
Red Bull Sugarfree	8.3 oz.	80
Rockstar Energy Drink	8 oz.	80
SoBe Adrenaline Rush	8.3 oz.	79
Amp	8.4 oz.	74
Glaceau Vitamin Water Energy Citrus	20 oz.	50
SoBe Essential Energy, Berry or Orange	8 oz.	48
Product	**Serving Size**	**Caffeine (mg)**
Frozen Desserts	**Serving Size**	**Caffeine (mg)**
Ben & Jerry's Coffee Heath Bar Crunch	8 fl. oz.	84
Ben & Jerry's Coffee Flavored Ice Cream	8 fl. oz.	68
Haagen-Dazs Coffee Ice Cream	8 fl. oz.	58
Haagen-Dazs Coffee Light Ice Cream	8 fl. oz.	58
Haagen-Dazs Coffee Frozen Yogurt	8 fl. oz.	58
Haagen-Dazs Coffee & Almond Crunch Bar	8 fl. oz.	58
Starbucks Coffee Ice Cream	8 fl. oz.	50-60
Chocolates/Candies/Other	**Serving Size**	**Caffeine (mg)**
Jolt Caffeinated Gum	1 stick	33
Hershey's Special Dark Chocolate Bar	1.45 oz.	31
Hershey's Chocolate Bar	1.55 oz.	9
Hershey's Kisses	41 g (9 pieces)	9
Hot Cocoa	8 oz.	9 (range: 3-13)
Over-The-Counter Drugs	**Serving Size**	**Caffeine (mg)**
NoDoz (Maximum Strength)	1 tablet	200
Vivarin	1 tablet	200
Excedrin (Extra Strength)	2 tablets	130
Anacin (Maximum Strength)	2 tablets	64

◀ **FIGURE 6.14 Caffeine Content of Common Caffeine-Containing Beverages.** *(Source: Center for Science in the Public Interest, 2007.)*

September 2007. Most information was obtained from company Web sites or direct inquiries. Serving sizes are based on commonly eaten portions, pharmaceutical instructions, or the amount of the leading-selling container size. For example, beverages sold in 16-ounce or 20-ounce bottles were counted as one serving.

▶ **FIGURE 6.15** Cigarette Smoking Damages Virtually Every Major Organ in the Body. *(Sources: Friedan & Blakeman, 2005; World Health Organization, 2008, p. 8.)*

Tobacco Use Is a Risk Factor for Six of the Eight Leading Causes of Death in the World

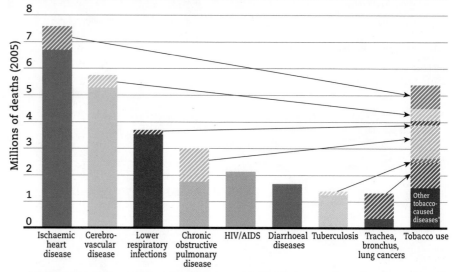

Hatched areas indicate proportions of deaths that are related to tobacco use and are coloured according to the column of the respective cause of death.

*Includes mouth and oropharyngeal cancers, oesophageal cancer, stomach cancer, liver cancer, other cancers, as well as cardiovascular diseases other than ischaemic heart disease and cerebrovascular disease.

Source: Mathers CD, Loncar D. Projections of global mortality and burden of disease from 2002 to 2030. *PLoS Medicine*, 2006, 3(11): e442. Additional information obtained from personal communication with C.D. Mathers.

Source of revised HIV/AIDS figure: AIDS epidemic update. Geneva, Joint United Nations Programme on HIV/AIDS (UNAIDS) and World Health Organization (WHO), 2007.

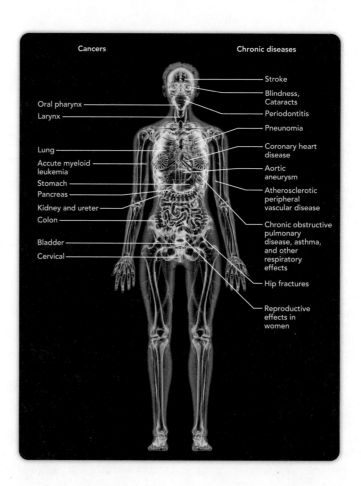

or spitting in Mike Tyson's beer are all more dangerous than smoking cigarettes, but none of these is an ordinary behavior.

Cigarettes are the most deadly recreational drug available. Although heroin and cocaine are far from harmless, they do not compare to cigarettes in destructive physiological effects. Unlike heroin and cocaine, cigarette smoking negatively affects virtually every organ in the body, including the brain. For example, in addition to the many diseases caused by cigarettes, cigarette smoking *increases* stress, it does not decrease it as many smokers believe (Parrott, 1999). The illusion of decrease in stress from smoking arises because cigarette smoking decreases the discomfort of nicotine withdrawal symptoms. However, nicotine dependence/addiction is itself stressful, and those who smoke are more stressed than those who do not. When smokers quit, they report less stress.

According to the World Health Organization (2003), there are 1.3 billion smokers in the world, and 50% of them will die of a disease caused by tobacco before they turn age 70, losing between 16 and 21 years of life on average. As depicted in Figure 6.15, smoking causes disease in almost every organ of the body and is a risk factor for six of the eight leading causes of death in the world (World Health Organization, 2008). In addition to approximately 15 ways that smoking can kill you, there are 15 more ways it can make life miserable through nonfatal but debilitating disease. Smoking is responsible for approximately 5.4 million deaths per year, and if current smoking trends continue, one billion people will die of smoking before the end of the 21st century (World Health Organization, 2008). Smoking is the single most important cause of premature death in the United States and numerous other developed nations, resulting in many times—a *great* many times—more deaths than automobile and other accidents, poisoning and drug overdose, homicide and suicide, AIDS, and alcoholic liver disease combined (Ezzati & Lopez, 2003; Frieden & Blakeman, 2005; Centers for Disease Control, 2005a; Vineis et al., 2004). Did I mention that it wrinkles, dries, and yellows the skin, and causes the breath and entire body to develop an unappealing odor?

Put simply, as suggested in Figure 6.16, there is no single behavior in which you can engage that will increase your life expectancy more than quitting smoking or refraining from taking up the habit in the first place.

Why People Smoke The preceding information is hardly being revealed for the first time in these pages. Anyone who can read and lives in a developed nation has easy access to it. Given that this information is easily available, why does anyone not overtly bent on seriously harming himself or herself and causing distress to loved ones smoke cigarettes?

The answer to this question is not simple. But if a pie chart could be drawn with all probable contributing factors, at least in modern Western societies, the most important of these would probably be *adolescence*. It is well known that if a person has not learned to smoke in adolescence, it is highly unlikely that he or she will ever become a smoker—only about 10% of smokers begin the habit past the age of 18 (Costello, Dierker, Jones, & Rose, 2008; Curry, Mermelstein, & Sporer, 2009). Historically, advertisers have targeted adolescents, or even preadolescents (Curry et al., 2009; Gilpin, White, Messer, & Pierce, 2007; Pierce, 2007). Adolescents receive thesee messages, which include specific product placements in film projects where "cool" actors engage in smoking particular brands or just engage in smoking cigarettes—a benefit to the industry as a whole (Dal Cin, Gibson, Zanna, Shumate, & Fong, 2007; Heatherton & Sargent, 2009; Sargent et al., 2007). Adolescent smokers then infect their friends through peer influence and peer selection (see Chapter 4, p. 187). Because smoking is addictive and extremely difficult to stop, these adolescents will also grow up to be parents who smoke. They will have children who will learn the habit from them as well as from their own peers as they enter adolescence in turn (Chassin, Presson, Rose, Sherman, & Prost, 2002).

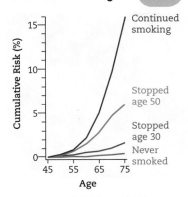

▲ **FIGURE 6.16 Smoking and Lung Cancer.** Smoking causes many more deaths from vascular, respiratory, and other diseases than from cancer. However, looking at just one of the many forms of cancer caused by smoking cigarettes—lung cancer—you can see that quitting smoking markedly reduces risk. This graph shows the way that the cumulative risk of death by lung cancer increases over time for those who do not quit. *(Source: Vineis et al., 2004, p. 104.)*

▲ How Hollywood Promotes Adolescent Smoking. Glamorous portrayals of smoking in Hollywood films have been shown to increase the risk of adolescents acquiring addiction to cigarettes. Moreover, there appears to be a "dose-response curve"—the more film portrayals of smoking an adolescent views, the more likely he or she is to become addicted (e.g., Sargent et al., 2007). Pictured is actress Scarlett Johansson.

Ethanol ▶ The ingestible form of alcohol contained in alcoholic beverages.

Ultimately, advertising becomes less important in the entire process, because the habit is self-perpetuating.

Depressants

In the past, the primary medical use of depressant drugs has been to produce sleep or sleep-like states, either as a treatment for insomnia or in the context of surgical anesthesia. However, today the drugs are just as commonly prescribed as treatments for anxiety, and their nonmedical use is widespread. Alcohol is also considered a (nonmedical) depressant drug, and it is without doubt the most commonly used.

ALCOHOL

If caffeine is the most widely used psychoactive drug in the world, then alcohol (technically, **ethanol**, the type of alcohol that is safe to ingest) is a close second. Although relatively few people drink in the Islamic world, and those following traditional Buddhist precepts also refrain from drinking, over 65% of U.S. adults report that they drink alcohol at least some of the time (Gallop Poll, 2010). In Norway and Sweden the figure is as high as 96% (Phillips & Lawton, 2004). In all, two billion people—about one-third of the Earth's total population—drink alcohol (World Health Organization, 2004). Alcohol is also the oldest psychoactive substance in continuous use by human beings. Evidence of its use dates back at least 12,000 years (Fox, 2011).

Alcohol is a particularly interesting drug in terms of its effects on consciousness and behavior for three reasons. First, effects vary greatly depending upon the person using it. The Aztec name for their alcoholic drink translates as "four hundred rabbits" in recognition of the wide variation in responses different people have while drinking (Fox & MacAvoy, 2011). Responses to drinking alcohol might include tranquility, joviality, sociability, aggression and violence, sexual excess, anger, melancholy, self-pity, tenderness, cheerfulness, relaxation, drowsiness, silliness, and on and on (Social Issues Research Centre, 2006). This is quite a different story from far more predictable behavior of people under the influence of stimulants, narcotics, or even other depressants.

Second, the differing beliefs each society may hold about how alcohol typically affects a person actually affect how the average person from that society *does* respond to alcohol (Heath, 1995; MacAndrew & Edgerton, 1969; Room, 2001). For example, in industrialized societies there is a strong tendency for people, including scientists, to believe that alcohol is a *disinhibitor*—a substance that reduces a person's inhibitions to perform various sorts of behavior. In the case of alcohol, when disinhibition occurs, it is primarily for sexual and aggressive behavior. Scientists have been able to provide explanations for alcohol's disinhibiting effects: Under the influence of alcohol there is a suppression of neuronal activity in centers of the brain connected to judgment and control. However, in some societies, disinhibition of aggression and sexuality are not generally expected to be part of drinking behavior, and they do not typically occur—even though alcohol has the same effect on the neurons of the brains of people everywhere (MacAndrew & Edgerton, 1969; Peele & Grant, 1999).

The third aspect of the effects of alcohol on consciousness that make it so interesting is the importance of dose in determining effect. The effect of one drink consumed in 20 to 30 minutes is dramatically different from the effect of three or four drinks consumed during the same time period. For example, taken in small doses, alcohol tends to produce feelings of relaxation, well-being, interest in conversation and sociability, and other positive benefits recognized for millennia in cultures throughout the world (Peele & Grant, 1999). However, as the dose increases, the drinker's judgment becomes increasingly impaired, as do various psychomotor, cognitive, and reaction processes. As intoxication progresses toward drunkenness, the drinker's behavior may

◄ **FIGURE 6.17 Effects of Alcohol on Behavior.** Although it would be nice to be able to report the number of drinks it takes to produce each of the behavioral changes listed in this figure, the same number of drinks will produce different behavioral changes in different people, depending on many factors. For example, women metabolize alcohol differently from men on average, and so a single drink might produce the same changes in a woman that two drinks will produce in a man. A person's size, how quickly drinks are consumed, how much food the person has taken, and genetic factors will affect the way alcohol enters the bloodstream. Therefore, the total Blood Alcohol Conent (BAC) is used instead of number of drinks to track behavioral changes in response to alcohol.

In general, a single shot of "hard liquor" (e.g. whisky, vodka) equals in alcohol content a 12-ounce bottle of beer or a 5-ounce glass of wine. But watch out—some hard liquor ("150-proof") is almost twice as strong as ordinary liquor, and some ales and sweet wines are considerably stronger than their ordinary counterparts.

- .02% - most people feel relaxed, talkative, and happy
- .03% - still talkative and happy; mild sedation; may have a flushed face
- .05% - most experience giddiness; restraint and judgment are lowered
- .06% - normal ability to make rational decisions about personal capabilities is affected
- .08% - muscle coordination is impaired; reaction time is slower
- .10% - speech is fuzzy; reaction time and muscle control are deteriorating
- .15% - the equivalent of a half pint whiskey in the bloodstream; balance and movement are impaired
- .20% - speech is slurred; double vision and loss of balance are likely
- .40% - usually unconscious; risk of death high even if taken to hospital
- .45% - respiration slows and can stop altogether

Source: Office of Alcohol, Drug, and Health Education, Dennison University.
Available at: http://www.denison.edu/oade/bloodconc.html.

become radically different from his or her norm. The person who had been standing there conversing genially just an hour or two earlier may now be sobbing, fighting, or standing on the table taking off his or her clothes. Figure 6.17 summarizes effects of increasing levels of blood alcohol.

Although many people can use alcohol in moderation for their entire lives without any ill effects, alcohol can also be extremely destructive. According to the World Health Organization, alcohol directly caused 1.8 million deaths in the year 2000—3.2% of the total number of global deaths (World Health Organization, 2004). Approximately 13% to 15% of regular users of alcohol develop alcohol dependence—a condition popularly termed *alcoholism*. Alcohol dependence is at least as difficult to treat as opioid dependence.

Alcohol differs from cigarettes in several important ways, however. First, there is no safe or beneficial way to use cigarettes, but alcohol is safe for most people to use in moderation—up to two drinks per day for men and one drink

▲ "Legal" ≠ "Safe." The legal status of cigarettes and alcohol allow manufacturers to portray their products as contributing greatly to the happiness of the purchaser, whereas illicit drugs are generally portrayed in marketing campaigns designed to decrease their use. Ironically, in terms of sheer numbers of people affected globally, illicit drugs cannot compare to cigarettes and alcohol in terms of death, distress, and disease caused annually.

per day for a woman (women metabolize alcohol differently from men). Alcohol is also *much* less addictive than smoking, with true addiction occurring only at very high doses taken over prolonged periods.

It is much easier to understand why people might start using alcohol than start smoking. Alcohol is a liquid, and drinking any liquid has qualities in common with drinking water—an action necessary for survival. Including alcoholic drinks around meal times has a kind of logic to it. Moreover, at least in moderate doses, the effects of alcohol are experienced by most people as pleasurable right from the beginning. Few people remember their first cigarettes with pleasure. Indeed, many people's first smoked cigarette is followed by nausea, dizziness, and sometimes vomiting.

Alcohol is not only safe and enjoyable for most people in moderate doses, it may actually have certain beneficial physiological and psychological effects. For example, increasingly persuasive research suggests that moderate intake of red or white wine (and possibly even beer) is associated with a lower risk of coronary heart disease and certain forms of cancer (Brügger-Anderson, Pönitz, Snapinn, Dickstein, OPTIMAAL study group, 2008; Kubik et al., 2008; Williams et al., 2004), and many doctors prescribe a glass of wine a day for their heart patients. Indeed, *moderate* alcohol consumption is associated with a lower risk of mortality from a wide variety of causes (Ferreira & Willoughby, 2008). As you may already know from personal experience, alcohol in moderation makes many people simply "feel good," and facilitates socializing by mildly reducing inhibition and relaxing the drinker through the depression of sympathetic nervous system activity (Peele & Grant, 1999).

However—and this is a *big* "however"—when taken at high doses, alcohol is extremely toxic to the body, particularly to the liver—hence the warning signals of nausea, vomiting, and headache. Excessive intake—known as *binge drinking*—over a prolonged period is associated with potentially fatal liver disease, hypertension, heart disease, diabetes, stroke, preventable motor vehicle and other mechanical accidents, loss of brain functioning (particularly memory), depression and anxiety, sexually transmitted disease, and a host of violent and destructive criminal acts. Abuse of alcohol can destroy entire families as well as the lives of individuals.

What constitutes binge drinking? A commonly used definition of a binge drinking episode is the consumption of five drinks for men or four drinks for women in about 2 hours. The lower figure for women is in recognition of women's slower rate of gastric metabolism, which leads to higher blood alcohol levels than men for the same quantity of alcohol (Courtney & Polich, 2009, p. 142). If four or five drinks consumed within 2 hours constitutes binge drinking, what constitutes "a drink"? A 12-oz. bottle of ordinary beer (*not* malt liquor or the new high-alcohol ales), a 5-oz. glass of ordinary wine, or one 1.5-oz. shot of 80-proof spirits (whiskey, vodka, etc.) are all equal to "one drink." Each equals about sixth-tenths of a fluid ounce of ethanol.

Recent figures from the U.S. Centers for Disease Control suggest that binge drinking in America is more widespread and destructive than many people imagine. About 17% of Americans—one in six—report binge drinking four times a month, averaging eight drinks within a few hours. College-age Americans are the worst offenders and also report drinking the most at each binge session, averaging 9.4 drinks within a few hours (see Figure 6.18; Centers for Disease Control, 2012).

ROHYPNOL

Rohypnol (flunitrazapam) ▶ A highly potent benzodiazepine drug often used to treat severe insomnia (street name: "roofies").

Rohypnol (generic name, *flunitrazepam*; street name "roofies") is a drug from the *benzodiazepine* group that has come into favor since the 1980s as one of several "club drugs." Rohypnol has never been legally marketed in the United States, although it is commonly used for psychiatric purposes throughout the rest of the world to treat anxiety and insomnia.

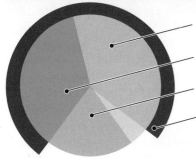

44% of college students report binge drinking at least some of the time.

At least 20% are frequent binge drinkers.

Approximately 36% do not binge drink.

75% of fraternity and sorority students are binge drinkers at least part of the time.

Source: Wechsler, Lee, Kuo, Seibring et al., 2002

◄ **FIGURE 6.18** **Binge Drinking among College Students Is No Joke.** Binge drinking is generally defined as consuming at least four drinks in a row for women and five drinks or more in a row for men. Apart from those in the 35–44 age bracket, no age group ends up in hospital emergency rooms due to binge drinking at a higher rate than those age 18–20 (Drug Abuse Warning Network, 2004). Binge drinking is accompanied by difficulties with schoolwork and low grades, psychological difficulties, social problems, injuries, drug overdoses, lawbreaking and legal problems, risky sexual behavior, and drunk driving. It periodically results in the death of the drinker or others at the drinker's hands.

Small doses of this drug produce pleasant sensations somewhat similar to an alcohol high, but as the dose increases the experience tends to be described by users (at least in research studies) as unpleasant (Roset et al., 2001). Rohypnol is a safer drug than alcohol, most opioids, or cocaine in terms of toxicity and potential for dependence. However, once dependence does result, like addiction to all benzodiazepines, withdrawal can actually be dangerous when attempted without medical supervision and can result in death under some circumstances. Moreover, when mixed with alcohol or opioids, like all benzodiazepines, rohypnol is extremely dangerous.

GHB

GHB (Gamma-hydroxybutyrate) is an unusual central nervous system depressant that initially had been marketed as a food supplement for body builders until it was discovered that it was being abused as a psychoactive drug. It was then taken off the market. The experience of low doses of GHB is similar to alcohol, but at medium doses it may produce both stimulating and relaxing effects simultaneously (Gable, 2004a).

GHB is a particularly dangerous drug because the difference between a "recreational" dose and a potentially fatal dose is not as great as with most psychoactive drugs. Thus, its safety ratio is low (10), identical to the safety ratio of alcohol (Gable, 2004a). Occasional deaths have been reported due to GHB, although most of these have occurred when the drug was used with alcohol (Karch, Stephens, & Nazareno, 2001; Kugelberg, Holmgren, Eklund, & Jones, 2010).

GHB (Gamma-hydroxybutyrate) ▶ A CNS depressant drug initially marketed as a food supplement for bodybuilders.

CRITICAL THINKING ABOUT PSYCHOLOGY

With the increase in use of the newer central nervous system depressant drugs in the club scene, reports of drug-related sexual assaults have increased. Not only do these drugs impair judgment and control, but in high doses they may impair memory for events that transpired during

The Most Common Date Rape Drug Is Alcohol

CRITICAL THINKING ABOUT PSYCHOLOGY

CONTINUED

intoxication, or even cause unconsciousness. In particular, Rohypnol ("roofies") and GHB have been dubbed "date-rape drugs," and concern over the use of these drugs for the purposes of rape has reached past the dormitories and onto the floor of Congress.

Initially, it was reported that men had been "spiking" their dates' drinks—dropping these drugs in alcoholic or nonalcoholic drinks to produce submission for sexual behavior. However, very few such cases could actually be verified, and "drink-spiking" eventually was termed an *urban legend* in the media (Neame, 2003). However, as Alexandra Neame points out, sexual assault occurs whenever there is sexual behavior without genuine consent. If a person is intoxicated—even voluntarily—but is too intoxicated to offer consent, there is a risk that any sexual behavior that might occur can be considered criminal. Therefore, even if the number of drink-spiking events has been greatly exaggerated, sexual behavior in the context of intoxication with drugs such as Rohypnol and GHB is extremely risky and may legally be considered rape under certain conditions.

But are Rohypnol and GHB actually present, even on a voluntary basis, during a substantial number of sexual assaults? Large-scale studies of date rape victims have found exceedingly few instances of the presence either of Rohypnol or GHB in the victim's urine or blood subsequent to the assault. For example, in three large-scale studies—one of 3,303 cases of date rape, one of 2,003 cases and one of 1,000 cases—Rohypnol was found in only approximately one-half of one percent of cases (.06–.05%; ElSohly, 2001; Mullins, 1999; Slaughter, 2000). In a more recent review of forensic evidence from 1,014 blood samples taken over a 3-year period from women reporting date rape in Great Britain, Rohypnol was found in none of the cases and GHB in only two (Scott-Ham & Burton, 2005).

However, while few instances of the presence of Rohypnol and GHB have been found in forensic studies of date rape victims, *all such studies show a high presence of alcohol.* For example, in the aforementioned study by Slaughter (2000) that found evidence of Rohypnol in only .05% of cases, alcohol was present in 63%. In the study by Scott-Ham and Burton that found no cases of Rohypnol and only two of GHB, alcohol was found in 470 cases. Thus, although all depressants such as GHB and Rohypnol have the potential to be used in the context of sexual assault, if there is a "date rape drug," without question it is alcohol. ■

Psychedelics

Unlike the drugs described previously, psychedelic drugs (e.g., *marijuana, hashish, THC, LSD, peyote, mushrooms, ecstasy, love*), frequently referred to as *hallucinogens*, come from a very wide variety of plant- and man-made chemical sources and produce their effects in many different ways. Even more than alcohol, these effects differ dramatically according to the personal characteristics of the user and the characteristics of the setting in which the drugs are used—including the cultural context. For example, psychedelic mushrooms and the cactus peyote have all been used in traditional religious ceremonies in various cultures and subcultures. A person's experience with these drugs in such religious contexts will undoubtedly differ from that of a person using the same drug at an all-night party in Portland, Oregon.

LSD (lysergic acid diethylamide$_{25}$) ▶ A powerful *psychedelic* drug.

Peyote ▶ A psychedelic cactus.

Psychedelic mushrooms ▶ A general term used for various psychedelic fungi.

LSD, PEYOTE, MUSHROOMS

LSD, peyote (and its synthesized version *mescaline*), and **psychedelic mushrooms** (and their synthesized version, *psilocybin*) share in common the ability

◀ **Hallucingens.** Peyote cactus (left); psychedelic mushrooms (right).

to alter perception in a dramatic way, strongly affecting one's senses of sight, hearing, smell, taste, and touch. In addition to sensory distortions and hallucinations, they may effect radical changes in thought and emotion. The LSD stories that opened this chapter could equally have been told about peyote, psilocybin, mescaline, or mushrooms.

The potential for dependence on these drugs is exceptionally low (if not nonexistent), and their safety ratios are very high—it would be quite difficult to take enough of these drugs to cause death. The dangers posed by drugs such as LSD or peyote primarily are psychological in nature. However, because the psychological effects vary so dramatically from one person to the next, it is difficult to predict risk. Depending upon a person's innate psychology and biochemistry, the same LSD event—say, looking into a mirror and seeing a total stranger—might cause one person to react with fascination, another to laugh uproariously, a third to experience a sense of union with the divine, and a forth to endure a terrifying split from his or her sense of self. The fallout from such profoundly negative experiences might last a week, a month, a year, or a lifetime. Therefore, psychedelic drugs should be treated with a very high degree of respect and caution.

Nevertheless, while the fallout from negative experiences can be long lasting, so can the benefit from positive experiences (J. B. Brown, 2007/2008; Griffiths, Richards, McCann, & Jesse, 2006). In a double-blind study using the psychedelic drug psilocybin with placebo controls, Roland Griffiths and his colleagues administered psilocybin to volunteers. These participants frequently reported meaningful, highly positive spiritual experiences whose effects continued to be felt 2 months later (Griffiths et al., 2006). Fourteen months later, interviews with these participants showed that beneficial spiritual and personal aspects of these experiences had persisted (Griffiths, Richards, Johnson, McCann, & Jesse, 2008). Results such as these have rekindled interest in the use of psychedelic drugs as adjuncts to psychotherapy (Brown, 2007/2008).

ECSTASY (MDMA)

First synthesized almost 100 years ago, ecstasy (MDMA) is related to the amphetamine family of drugs. However, its effects are vastly different from amphetamine or any other stimulant. In general, the effects of ecstasy include a sense of "openness," empathy, well-being, energy, and reduced fear. Although all of that might seem a good thing, when such effects are produced by a drug rather than spontaneously, the "genuineness" of such effects is often doubted by ordinary onlookers. The fact that the drug is derived from the amphetamine family—known to cause damage to brain neurons and to produce bizarre psychological symptoms when used in excess—also gives very reasonable cause for wondering about the drug's safety (Morton, 2005).

However, trying to sort out the various claims about the safety of ecstasy is not easy. Very strong claims have been made by some for its dangers (Parrot, 2002), but equally strong claims have been made by others for its safety relative to most other psychoactive drugs (Baggott, Jerome, & Stuart, 2001/2005; Cole et al., 2002b). Several problems facing researchers in their

The Composition of "Ecstasy" Tablets Seized in the United Kingdom, 2006-2009

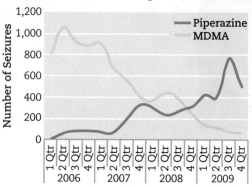

Source: United Kingdom Forensic Science Services

▲ **FIGURE 6.19 Actual Content of Ecstasy Tablets in Great Britain.** Data from the United Nations Office on Drugs and Crime show the recent trend for "ecstasy" tablets to contain more piperazine than MDMA. *(Source: United Nations Office on Drugs and Crime, 2010, p. 11.)*

studies of ecstasy make any statement about its safety tentative at best. Substantial evidence suggests that, at least in certain times and places, a very large portion of "ecstasy" tablets taken by users contain relatively little MDMA (or no MDMA at all), but may contain significant quantities of truly dangerous substances such as 4-MTA ("flatliner"), an amphetamine-related compound with very severe side effects that may include death; or drugs that approximate MDMA in the potential for danger, but which are nonetheless not MDMA—for example, *piperazine (BZP)*, a so-called legal high (see pp. 318–321) initially designed to treat worm infestation (European Monitoring Centre, 2003; Rosenbaum, 2002; United Nations Office on Drugs and Crime, 2010; Wood et al., in press; see Figure 6.19). Therefore, anecdotal reports of negative consequences of ecstasy use in club contexts cannot be taken at face value.

Additionally, because of legal restrictions on the use of ecstasy in research on humans, most prior research has failed to control for the fact that the majority of ecstasy users also use many other drugs. It is not generally clear if effects seemingly found for ecstasy use (including death) are due to ecstasy, other drugs, or the combination of ecstasy with other drugs (Cole et al., 2002a, 2002b; King & Corkery, 2010; Morgan, 2000, 2002).

Without pretending to have the definitive word on the issue of safety of ecstasy, I offer the following summary statements that are supported by research:

1. Ecstasy has *not* been "proven safe." Ecstasy use poses various risks. However, most of these risks appear to result from extremely heavy use, use of ecstasy with multiple other drugs, use of "fake" ecstasy, and/or failure to pay attention to risks posed by the context of use (e.g., failure to drink enough fluid while dancing or, conversely, drinking much too much fluid).

2. Ecstasy has *not* been proven to cause "brain damage" in humans (Morton, 2005; Reneman, 2003). There are tentative data suggesting that *very* heavy, chronic use of MDMA can cause damage to serotonin (but not dopamine) neurons in humans (Reneman, 2003; Gouzoulis-Mayfrank & Daumann, 2006). However, much of this evidence is indirect, some of it derived from poorly designed studies, and its conclusiveness has been strongly contested (Cole et al., 2002a, 2002b; Gouzoulis-Mayfrank & Daumann, 2006).

3. Ecstasy is potentially deadly when taken in excessive doses (Gable, 2004a). Nonetheless, there have been very few deaths reliably attributed to ecstasy taken alone, especially when compared with drugs such as opioids, cocaine, methamphetamine, alcohol, and so forth (Morton, 2005). Researchers at the University of Bristol in Great Britain attempted to devise a matrix exploring the various harms of nonmedical drug use, based as much as possible in scientific evidence of physical and social harm rather than on the legal status of a particular drug or social attitudes toward it (Nutt et al., 2007). These investigators characterized ecstasy among the very least dangerous drugs currently in use. Indeed, of 20 current drugs of misuse, ecstasy ranked third from the bottom.

MARIJUANA

Marijuana ("weed," "pot," "ganga," "dope," "herb," etc.) is the leaf of the **cannabis**, or hemp, plant, formerly cultivated in the United States for making rope. The psychoactive ingredient of cannabis is known as **THC** (tetrahydrocannabinol) and has been synthesized for nonmedical use in pill form. Cannabis is also used in a gummy concentrate known as **hashish**.

As with all psychedelics, effects of cannabis are highly dependent upon the user and the setting, but as a general rule users of cannabis at moderate doses

Marijuana (Cannabis) ▶ A mild psychedelic drug derived from the leaves of cannabis sativa, a flowering plant originally indigenous to Asia.

Cannabis ▶ *Cannabis sativa* is the plant from which marijuana, hashish, and THC are derived.

THC ▶ The active ingredient in cannabis, often taken in pill form.

Hashish ▶ A pasty or gummy concentrated form of cannabis, generally stronger in its effects than marijuana.

experience a dreamy, carefree relaxation and sense of well-being, distortion in perception of time (a minute can seem like an hour), a sharpening of all the senses, a tendency to find hilarity in situations the rest of us find utterly humor-free, and increased hunger—with particular interest in sweets (U.S. National Commission on Marihuana and Drug Abuse, 1972). Stronger doses can produce disruptions in emotion and thought, and as with other psychedelics, some users may experience very negative reactions that include severe anxiety, panic, and nightmarish thoughts or perceptions.

Marijuana has been the focus of decades of intensive research designed to evaluate its potential harms—vastly eclipsing efforts typically applied to safety research on ordinary drugs intended for medical purposes. Given such a massive expenditure of time and resources, it would be truly astonishing if *no* potentially harmful properties of cannabis had been found.

And once again, as with ecstasy and other controversial drugs for which significant funds are available to examine potential harms, it is important to examine media statements about research (and the research itself!) carefully. I was more than a little concerned, for example, to read in the magazine *Science Daily* a headline that read "Cannabis Damages Young Brains More Than Originally Thought, Study Finds" (*Science Daily*, 2009), accompanied by a photo of a young person getting high under which the caption read "Daily consumption of cannabis in teens can cause depression and anxiety, and have an irreversible long-term effect on the brain." However, when I read the actual report of the study itself, published in the journal *Neurobiology of Disease*, I found that the study consisted of exposing young ("adolescent") *rats*—not human teenagers—to cannabis and examining their behavior (Bambico, Nguyen, Katz, & Gobbi, 2010). There is no way to extrapolate from a single study of the brains of young rats to the brains of teenage human beings; and "depression-like behavior" in a rat is not the same as depression in a human being. And *irreversible*? The only way to know this would be to study teenage human beings over a period of many years, if not decades.

So then—is marijuana safe? Are all the warnings mere hype? As I have said, no drug is completely safe. The point, of course, is *what* are the harms of cannabis? And how much does one need to use and how often does one need to use it before experiencing these harms?

It is not possible to make definitive statements about the dangers of using cannabis because virtually any statement might be challenged by *someone*, and the controversy is often bitter (Cohen, 2009). Extreme claims have been made both by researchers who believe that marijuana is uniquely harmless and has the potential for beneficial medical uses (Grinspoon & Bakalar, 1995) and those who warn that marijuana's reputation for harmlessness is entirely unwarranted (Budney & Wiley, 2001). The movement to decriminalize marijuana, successful in 14 of the United States as of February, 2013 (NORML, 2013), and the dramatic recent increase in use of the drug for medical purposes, have greatly fueled the controversy.

However, unlike the case of ecstasy, there is an extensive research database on the effects of cannabis from which to paint a general portrait of its potential for harm:

1. Marijuana use *can* result in dependence. However, dependence is seen only in a small minority of users—approximately 9% to 10%—and this is likely to occur only after very heavy long-term recreational (not medical) use of marijuana (Anthony et al., 1994).

2. Evidence that cannabis use leads to psychological disturbances and "reduced motivation," or that it negatively impacts educational attainment because of effects on cognitive ability, is weak (Degenhardt, Hall, & Lynskey, 2001; Gorman & Derzon, 2002; Macleod et al., 2004). However, some research suggests that marijuana might have an effect on the ability to learn and remember new information and on various sorts

of everyday memory tasks in chronic heavy marijuana users (Cohen, 2009; Grant, Gonzalez, Carey, Natarajan, & Wolfson, 2003; Fisk & Montgomery, 2008). And without doubt, marijuana intoxication impairs the ability to drive (Cohen, 2009)!

3. On the other hand, researchers studying inflammation processes that may underlie the brain degeneration of Alzheimer's disease have produced evidence that chemical components of cannabis, including THC, may reduce this inflammation—thus also reducing memory impairment in elderly patients at risk for Alzheimer's (Marchalant, Brothers, & Wenk, 2008).

4. Marijuana smoke produces at least as many tars hazardous to the lungs as cigarette smoke (Henry, Oldfield, & Kon, 2003). However, no evidence exists to date that marijuana use actually leads to increased mortality from lung disease, or that users are more likely than others to develop cancer or chronic obstructive lung disease (Hashibe et al., 2006; Sidney, 2003; Tan et al., 2009). Indeed, a recent 20-year longitudinal study funded by the U.S. government's National Institutes of Health showed no impairment in lung function even of regular marijuana use, as long as use was not truly excessive or combined with tobacco smoking (Pletcher et al., 2011). The lack of apparent harm to lung function of marijuana smoking may occur because, unlike cigarette smokers, even chronic marijuana users generally do not smoke more than a very small number "joints" a day—and most users quit by the time they are 30 (Iversen, 2003).

5. There is no known fatal dose of cannabis (Cohen, 2009), and—at least to my knowledge—no verified case of a person dying from an overdose of the drug with no other contributing cause (e.g., severe heart disease [Gupta, Jani, & Shah, 2001]). The safety ratio of marijuana has been estimated as somewhere between 1,000 and 40,000, making cannabis the least toxic psychoactive drug in existence (Gable, 2004b; Grinspoon & Bakalar, 1995).

Table 6.5 summarizes the effects of the psychoactive drugs, and what is known of their potential dangers.

"Legal Highs"

Recently, the Internet has exploded with advertisements for "legal highs"—psychoactive drugs that may be purchased legally because they are not on governern ment lists of controlled substances. However, the term "legal high" is a little misleading. As a rule, the only reason the drugs are legal is that the authorities don't yet know about them or haven't yet drafted legislation to control them. Thus, today's legal high is the controlled substance of tomorrow. Indeed, by the time you read this, any number of so-called legal highs discussed in this section may already be controlled or banned outright in areas where they are available legally as I write.

In general, governmental authorities do not recognize "recreation" or "pleasure" as a defensible use for a drug, and the FDA weighs the usefulness of any drug against its potential dangers before approving it for sale. Therefore, if there is even a hint that a "recreational" drug may hold dangers, its nonprescription use is likely to be criminalized or its sale banned outright—in spite of the fact that the drug may actually be far less toxic than any number of legally available prescription or over-the-counter drugs.

Several psychoactive substances have become popular over the past decade and have enjoyed at least some legal protection at various times. These include:

1. Extract of *kratom*. Derived from the leaf of the *mitragyna speciosa* tree as found in Southeast Asia, kratom has the capacity to produce

Table 6.5 **Psychoactive Drugs at a Glance**

DRUG	ORDINARY EFFECTS	SOME POTENTIAL DANGERS
Opioids (e.g., opium, morphine, heroin, *Oxycontin, Vicodin*)	Pain relief, sedation, euphoria, nausea, constipation	Extreme dependence (addiction) when used for nonmedicinal purposes; death may result due to respiratory depression when mixed with other CNS depressants or when taken in an excessive dose
Cocaine	Energy, exhilaration, alertness, confidence, elevated mood, sleeplessness	Extreme dependence (addiction); nervousness, fatigue, depression, psychosis. Death may result due to respiratory failure, cerebral hemorrhage, or stroke in vulnerable individuals taking excessive doses
Amphetamines (e.g., methamphetamine Dexedrine, Adderal)	Energy, alertness, confidence, exhilaration, sleeplessness	Dependence, mania, psychosis, fatigue, depression, possible changes in brain functioning and structure
Caffeine	Energy, alertness, sleeplessness	Dependence, fatigue, nervousness. In rare cases, psychological disorder
Nicotine	Slight increase in alertness	Extreme dependence (addiction); when used in tobacco, death may result due to multiple types of disease processes
Alcohol	Effects vary greatly according to the person and dose	Easily abused drug; dependence (addiction) in those taking large doses over prolonged periods; in large doses: impaired judgment; impaired cognitive, psychomotor, and reaction processes; erratic behavior; potential for violence in some individuals; psychological disturbance; death due to overdose or multiple disease processes in long-term abuse
Benzodiazepines (e.g., Rohypnol, Valium, Xanax, Klonapin)	Relaxation, sedation; effects may vary by dose.	Extreme dependence (addiction); convulsions or psychosis if drugs are discontinued too abruptly; death may result when mixed with alcohol or other CNS depressants
GHB	Simultaneous relaxation and stimulation	Death due to overdose, particularly if used with alcohol
LSD, Peyote, Mushrooms	Hallucinations, extreme alteration of perception and subjective experience	May cause psychotic reactions or other psychological disturbances in vulnerable individuals
Ecstasy (MDMA)	Feelings of well-being, empathy, energy, reduced fear	Potential dangers sharply contested (see pp. 315–316)
Marijuana	Alteration of perception and subjective experience; frequent tendency toward laughter; appetite stimulation; pain relief	Potential dangers sharply contested; mild potential for dependence; the least toxic psychoactive substance known

depressant as well as stimulant effects, depending on the user and how the drug is used. Interestingly, it has sometimes been used to treat addiction to opioids. As of this writing (2011), kratom is considered a controlled substance only in Australia and New Zealand, several Southeast Asian countries, and a few nations of North and East Europe.

2. *BZP* (Benzylpiperazine) is a stimulant with effects somewhat similar to amphetamines (although weaker). It tends to produce elation, energy, and alertness as well as all the negative effects of amphetamines, including insomnia, anxiety, appetite loss, and restlessness (Schep, Slaughter, Vale, Beasley, & Gee, 2011). It is a controlled substance as of 2011 only in the United States, Japan, Denmark, Greece, Poland, Italy, Ireland,

▲ **"Legal Highs."** Still legal at least in some parts of the world (left to right): *kratom, fly agaric* ("shrooms"), *salvia divinorum,* "bath salts" (*mephedrone* and other drugs).

Sweden, Sweden, Malta, and Australia. When BZP is mixed with certain other compounds, the effects may be closer to MDMA (ecstasy) than to amphetamine (Baumann et al., 2005), and at various times and places so-called ecstasy tablets sold on the street have been partly or entirely composed of BZP (see Figure 6.19).

3. The mushroom *fly agaric* (*amanita muscaria*), with hallucinogenic effects somewhat (but not entirely) similar to LSD, psilocybin, or peyote, is still legal to buy and sell almost everywhere as of this writing—but it may not be legal to ingest as a drug (it is not legal to do so in the United States, for example).

4. *Salvia*, derived from the *salvia divinorum* leaf, is a highly potent psychedelic (hallucinogenic drug) with a long history of use for spiritual purposes by native peoples. It has had wide media exposure (including any number of YouTube clips of people using the drug) and has been characterized in various journalistic exposés as uniquely dangerous. On the other hand, it has been characterized by many users as the key to the wisdom of the ages. Neither view appears to be particularly well supported. Salvia is a controlled substance or is banned outright in most (but not all) of the United States, Australia, Italy, Japan, Russia, Spain, Finland, Estonia, Canada, Denmark, and Sweden.

5. "Bath salts" are generally a combination of several drugs, including *mephedrone*. Because bath salts may contain a number of different drugs, it is not so easy to characterize the effects of bath salts in general. However, drugs containing mephedrone, almost always found in bath salts, generally produce effects somewhat similar to ecstasy (MDMA) or stimulants such as cocaine. Users often report elevated mood or euphoria, mental clarity and alertness, feelings of well-being, and decreased hostility. Mephedrone itself is controlled or banned outright in so many nations that "legal high" is truly a misnomer for bath salts. In 2011, the Drug Enforcement Administration (DEA) used its emergency powers to enact a temporary (1-year) ban on the sale of mephedrone and two other drugs often contained in bath salts while it studied the effects and use of these drugs.

SAFETY OF LEGAL HIGHS

The legal-high industry is growing rapidly, and there are a number of reasons why people are attracted to these drugs: (a) they work—unlike previous generations of "legal highs"; (b) there is no legal risk attached to purchasing the drugs; and (c) buyers assume that the drugs must be relatively safe ("Why else would they be legal?"). This last assumption is most unfortunate, and it points out what should be apparent to you by now if you have been reading carefully—the legal status of a drug is not necessarily related to its safety.

There are many factors other than safety which come into play in deciding whether or not a drug should be available for purchase and use, including political, social, and economic factors.

The most obvious examples of this are alcohol, tobacco, and marijuana. Alcohol and tobacco are legal, yet they have proven themselves to hold grave dangers for users. Indeed, reasonable arguments have often been made that they are the most dangerous of all psychoactive substances (Nutt et al., 2007; see Figure 6.8, and Tables 6.3 and 6.4). On the other hand, even if marijuana were even more dangerous, the fact is that marijuana was made illegal long before any evidence had been collected that it was in any way harmful (Bonnie & Whitebread, 1999).

In the case of the new legal highs, there are very few safety data by which to judge them. Therefore, to some degree they should be viewed with even *more* caution than marijuana or prescription drugs such as opiates or amphetamines, because one cannot make an informed decision about using them. Moreover, because the legal highs are not regulated as drugs by the FDA, one has no idea what one is actually buying when one makes a purchase. You may think you are buying *salvia*—but are you? Thus, legal highs are not legal because they are safe. They are legal because they are new.[2]

IN SUMMARY

1.	The large majority of people in the world use some sort of psychoactive drug to alter their mental life or consciousness.
2.	Addiction is one of the most destructive consequences of abusive nonmedical use of drugs, but the term "addiction" has no precise definition. Many researchers prefer the term "dependence," as defined by the American Psychiatric Association.
3.	All substances are potentially toxic, and researchers use a formula based upon studies with laboratory animals and humans to compute a safety ratio for psychoactive drugs.
4.	Psychoactive drugs used for nonmedical purposes can be categorized as narcotics (opioids), depressants (hypnotics such as alcohol and the benzodiazepines), stimulants (such as cocaine, caffeine, and amphetamines), and psychedelics (such as LSD, ecstasy, and marijuana).
5.	Narcotics: Opioids are narcotic drugs derived from the poppy flower. These drugs are highly effective pain killers and may also produce euphoria and feelings of well-being.
6.	Stimulants: Cocaine (including crack) produces euphoria, a rush of energy, and feelings of well-being, but these effects are short-lasting. Although cocaine (including crack) does not produce classical symptoms of addiction, users can experience severe dependence as destructive as addiction to opioids. Amphetamines produce longer-lasting stimulant effects and may produce mania in some cases, and dependence occurs in an unknown number of cases. Dependence on caffeine may occur, but this dependence lacks the destructive qualities of dependence upon other stimulant drugs.
7.	In terms of global deaths, illness, and related destructive effects, no psychoactive drugs can compete with alcohol and tobacco.

---

[2]*Buying a street drug of any sort holds the same unknown dangers as buying a "legal high," because one does not know what one is actually getting.*

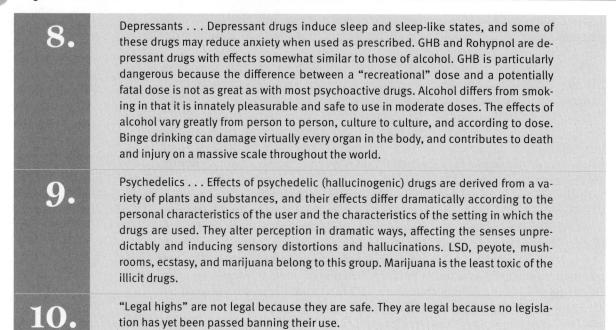

8. Depressants . . . Depressant drugs induce sleep and sleep-like states, and some of these drugs may reduce anxiety when used as prescribed. GHB and Rohypnol are depressant drugs with effects somewhat similar to those of alcohol. GHB is particularly dangerous because the difference between a "recreational" dose and a potentially fatal dose is not as great as with most psychoactive drugs. Alcohol differs from smoking in that it is innately pleasurable and safe to use in moderate doses. The effects of alcohol vary greatly from person to person, culture to culture, and according to dose. Binge drinking can damage virtually every organ in the body, and contributes to death and injury on a massive scale throughout the world.

9. Psychedelics . . . Effects of psychedelic (hallucinogenic) drugs are derived from a variety of plants and substances, and their effects differ dramatically according to the personal characteristics of the user and the characteristics of the setting in which the drugs are used. They alter perception in dramatic ways, affecting the senses unpredictably and inducing sensory distortions and hallucinations. LSD, peyote, mushrooms, ecstasy, and marijuana belong to this group. Marijuana is the least toxic of the illicit drugs.

10. "Legal highs" are not legal because they are safe. They are legal because no legislation has yet been passed banning their use.

RETRIEVE!

1. Which of the following is NOT among the classical (traditional) criteria for defining "addiction"?

a) deterioration   **b)** craving   **c)** withdrawal   **d)** tolerance

2. A numerical estimate of the relative toxicity of a drug is known as the drug's _____.

a) toxicity ratio   **b)** safety index   **c)** safety ratio   **d)** toxicity index

3. Describe the (pleasurable) effects of the following drugs: opioids, cocaine, ecstasy, marijuana. Describe some potential dangers of each.

4. Which are the most toxic of the psychoactive drugs? The least toxic? Which drugs have the highest potential for dependence? The lowest potential?

5. Which drug is most frequently found in the blood stream of victims of date rape?

6. Why are claims of the dangers of ecstasy hard to evaluate?

7. Which of the following is probably NOT TRUE about marijuana, according to research reported in this chapter?

a) Marijuana has almost no potential for dependence.

b) Marijuana use results in reduced motivation and educational attainment.

c) Marijuana users are even more likely than cigarette smokers to develop lung cancer.

d) Marijuana has resulted in numerous deaths, but fewer deaths than drugs such as heroin.

e) None of these statements is true.

Looking Back

Chapter 6 in Review

WHAT IS CONSCIOUSNESS? NO ONE KNOWS

- Consciousness has been defined as consisting of inner, qualitative, subjective states and feelings or awareness. The "hard problem" of consciousness is the question of how a physical organ (the brain) produces the seemingly disembodied subjective state of consciousness. Altered states of consciousness (ASC) include sleep, dreams, hypnosis, hallucinations, meditations, and drug states.

HOW—AND WHY—DO WE SLEEP?

- The urge to sleep is profound, although individuals vary in the amount of sleep they need. Total sleep deprivation results in severe impairments in functioning. Sleep patterns are regulated by the circadian pacemaker and sleep homeostat. There are two types of sleep: REM and NREM. REM is characterized by high levels of nervous system activity and vivid dreaming. NREM, which covers the greater portion of sleep time, is characterized by the deepest levels of relaxation. Sleep is experienced in five sleep stages, which play out in a 90- to 110-minute repeated cycle throughout the night.
- The function of sleep is unknown, but the most often-discussed current theories are the ideas that sleep promotes memory consolidation and that sleep allows for synaptic pruning.

WHAT ARE DREAMS?

- There is little agreement as to the nature and function of sleep mentation, which can be categorized as cognitive activity, ordinary dreaming, and apex dreaming. Cognitive activity during sleep is often called "sleep thinking." Ordinary dreaming involves recognizable characters engaged in relatively realistic activities. Apex dreaming are the most intense, vivid, bizarre, hallucinatory dreams.
- Of the numerous theories advanced regarding the purpose of dreams, none is accepted by all, but it is

clear is that dreams have meaning to the dreamer, consisting of content drawn from each person's life history, circumstances, emotions, and subjective experience.

WHAT ARE SLEEP DISORDERS?

- Many people have problems sleeping, but only a few experience a genuine sleep disorder. Insomnia is a chronic difficulty falling asleep, staying asleep, and/or being unable to obtain restful sleep. Obstructive sleep apnea (OSA) is marked by frequent—and usually unrecognized—moments of awakening throughout the night, caused by the inability to breathe. Parasomnias are characterized by unusual or bizarre physical behaviors, perceptions, dreams, or emotions during sleep. Narcolepsy is characterized by abruptly falling asleep at inappropriate times and places.

IS HYPNOSIS AN ALTERED STATE OF CONSCIOUSNESS?

- The question of whether hypnosis is an actual ASC is known as the "special state" vs. "nonstate" debate. Neodissociation theory proposes that hypnosis is a true ASC, whereas sociocognitive theory proposes that behaviors seen under hypnosis can be produced without any special procedures. Findings suggest that a hypnotic state can be induced merely by giving suggestions when the subject believes he or she is being hypnotized. Hypnotized individuals do not have improved recall of past events, cannot "regress" to infancy or "past lives," can lie just as easily as at other times, and cannot achieve feats of strength or endure pain beyond their ordinary capabilities.

WHAT IS THE NATURE OF MEDITATION?

- Mediation techniques derived from Buddhist, Hindu, or yogic practices are based upon relaxed attention and not thinking. The essential attitude of mediation is relaxed attention to the moment, without strain, expectation, or self-criticism. Unlike hypnosis, evidence strongly

supports the view that meditation is an altered state.

HOW DO PSYCHOACTIVE DRUGS AFFECT CONSCIOUSNESS?

- A psychoactive drug is any substance with properties that affect mental life or consciousness. Nonmedical or "recreational" drug use includes all uses specifically intended to alter consciousness. Most humans worldwide use psychoactive drugs such as alcohol, nicotine, and caffeine. It is difficult to obtain accurate information about nonmedical drug use because powerful moral, social, economic, and political interests are involved.
- Addiction was traditionally defined as dependent and compulsive use of a drug which resulted in withdrawal, craving, and tolerance. However, so-called nonaddictive drugs can produce craving and dependence as powerful as addictive drugs. All substances are potentially toxic if taken in sufficient quantities. Marijuana has the highest safety ratio of all commonly used psychoactive drugs. The most dangerous drugs in terms of potential for death and disease are alcohol and tobacco, although when taken in moderation, alcohol is safe and may even have beneficial properties.
- Psychoactive drugs can be categorized as narcotics, depressants, stimulants, and psychedelics; but some psychoactive drugs do not fit neatly into these categories. Narcotics refer generally to drugs synthesized from the dried nectar of poppy flowers. These drugs are very dangerous when used for nonmedical purposes, especially when combined with other CNS depressants such as alcohol or benzodiazepines.
- Stimulant drugs include cocaine, amphetamines, caffeine, and nicotine. Cocaine produces euphoria, alertness, and feelings of well-being, but long-term users experience sleeplessness, depression, and impairment in thought and perception. Amphetamines produce somewhat similar feelings

Looking Back continued

of exhilaration, alertness, confidence, and mood elevation, but the effects are much longer-lasting and "harsh." Amphetamines may also cause long-lasting changes in brain structure and functioning. Caffeine, found naturally in coffee, tea, and chocolate, wards off fatigue and produces alertness.

- Nicotine produces a slight increase in alertness. It is highly addictive, and withdrawal is difficult to endure. A tobacco-containing cigarette is likely the most dangerous drug because it affects virtually every organ in the body: 50% of smokers will die of a disease caused by smoking by age 70. The percentage of smokers has dropped by at least 50% in the United States and Great Britain since the mid-1960s.

- Depressant drugs include alcohol, rohypnol, and GHB. Alcohol is the oldest and most widely used psychoactive drug, second to caffeine. The effects of alcohol vary according to the user, the setting, beliefs about alcohol, and the dose. Like smoking, binge drinking can damage virtually every bodily organ.

About one-third of the earth's population uses alcohol, and the drug directly causes nearly 2 million deaths per year.

- Rohypnol in low doses produces sensations somewhat similar to alcohol, but high doses are very unpleasant. Rohypnol is safer than alcohol, narcotics, or cocaine, but if dependence does result, withdrawal can be dangerous. GHB in low doses also produces alcohol-like effects, but at medium doses can produce stimulating effects simultaneously. GHB is particularly dangerous because it has a small difference between recreational and fatal doses.

- Psychedelic drugs include LSD, peyote, psychedelic mushrooms, ecstasy (MDMA), and marijuana. These drugs produce effects that vary by individual, setting, dose, and cultural beliefs even more dramatically than is the case with alcohol. LSD, peyote, and psychedelic mushrooms share the ability to alter perception, strongly affecting sensory experiences and effecting radical changes in thought

and emotion. Ecstasy produces a general sense of well-being, openness, empathy, and reduced fear. Its safety is highly controversial. MDMA is deadly if taken in excessive doses, but some evidence suggests that in its pure, "uncut" form it may be among the safest recreational drugs.

- Marijuana is the safest recreational drug commonly in use, but perhaps also the most controversial. Claims that marijuana use results in psychological disturbance, poor cognitive functioning, and reduced educational performance are not well supported. However, there may be small effects on memory, and smoking marijuana produces tars hazardous to the lungs. Marijuana has many recognized medical uses

- "Legal highs" are psychoactive drugs that may be purchased legally because authorities don't yet know about them or haven't yet put them on government lists of controlled substances. There are very few safety data by which to judge "legal high" drugs.

Key Terms

Key Terms continued

Test Yourself

1. Define *consciousness* according to John Searle's commonsense definition, and describe the three most prominent features of consciousness according to Searle.

2. What is the "hard problem" of consciousness?

3. The group of neurons which form the suprachiasmatic nuclei of the hypothalamus and which keep circadian rhythms on schedule is known as:
   a) the sleep homeostat
   b) the circadian homeostat
   c) the circadian pacemaker
   d) the sleep pacemaker

4. When people sleep late on the weekends after a week of obtaining too little sleep, they are said to be making up _____.

5. Distinguish the *sleep homeostat* from the *circadian pacemaker*.

6. Describe the basic experience of each sleep stage.

7. Describe the memory consolidation and synaptic pruning theories of the function of sleep.

8. What is the difference between *ordinary* and *apex* dreaming? Why is it that most people associate dreaming with *apex* dreaming, even though *ordinary* dreaming is more common?

9. Briefly characterize three theories of the function or origin of dreaming.

10. Name one way in which dreams might vary according to culture.

11. What is the important difference between a sleep problem and a sleep disorder?

12. Match the sleep disorder to its description:

Obstructive sleep apnea (OSA)	Walking during sleep
REM-sleep behavior disorder (RBD)	Suddenly falling asleep at unexpected times
Night terrors	REM sleep without muscle paralysis
Somnambulism	Suddenly waking in fear not as a result of nightmare
Narcolepsy	Repeated difficulty breathing during sleep as a result of the narrowing of various sites along the upper airway

13. Describe one study that suggests that it is the subject's *belief* that he or she is being hypnotized that plays a more important role than the specifics of the actual hypnotic induction procedure.

14. Distinguish *open* from *concentrative* meditation. How does each arrive at *relaxed attention* and *not-thinking*?

15. Describe an (infamous) episode in research on the drug *ecstasy (MDMA)* that demonstrates that it is often difficult to obtain accurate information about nonmedical psychoactive drug use.

16. In terms of total number of people who die each year or whose health is seriously compromised, what are the two most dangerous of all psychoactive drugs?

17. Why was it once believed that cocaine was "nonaddictive"? Why is this idea both correct and incorrect?

18. Name the four categories of psychoactive drugs, and give specific examples from each category.

19. What are the three reasons given in the text to support the notion that alcohol is "particularly interesting" in terms of its effects on consciousness and behavior.

20. Answer the following questions based on your reading, and explain why you have answered as you have:
   a) True or False: Ecstasy has been shown to be generally safe, regardless of dose, if it is not used with other drugs.
   b) True or False: Ecstasy has been shown to cause extensive brain damage in human beings.
   c) True or False: Very few deaths have been reliably attributed to use of ecstasy, particularly when other drugs are not involved.

21. Answer the following questions based on your reading, and explain why you have answered as you have:
   a) Can marijuana (cannabis) cause dependence?
   b) Which neurocognitive functions might be affected by chronic use of cannabis? How large is this effect?
   c) Is there strong evidence that marijuana use leads to psychological disturbances and reduced motivation?
   d) What is the relation between marijuana smoking and lung disease?

7

Learning

Chapter Outline

FREEZE FRAME

The last place, the very last place on earth that Shari had expected to be spending her Friday afternoons was at the outpatient substance abuse rehab center she used to pass every day on her way to score cocaine. On reflection, however, there were many places she had ended up on Friday afternoons that had violated her expectations—not to mention those of her parents, siblings, and numerous ex-boyfriends. A short list: crack houses on the Lower East Side, the South Bronx, and Newark, New Jersey; numerous bedrooms and beds of men whose names she had never learned . . . then there was the Women's House of Detention in Greenwich Village and the Edna Mahan Correctional Facility for Women in Clinton, New Jersey. Shari had been around.

And she had spent time in rehab as an inpatient and outpatient. But she had never remained abstinent from cocaine use and eventually had come to believe that she could not stop using cocaine regardless of anyone's best efforts. She had sworn off rehab. But here she was again, donating

urine. There were two interesting differences here from previous clinics: First, she was participating in an experimental program that was part of a research study. Second, the program stipulated that, if Shari remained abstinent, provided evidence of attendance at Cocaine Anonymous meetings—and also provided evidence that she had taken steps to repair her relationship with her parents—she earned cash rewards. In effect, she was being paid to get well. She had already earned $645 over the previous 3 months. She was sober, talking to her mother again, and her CA sponsor had given her a 90-day chip that morning. In spite of herself, Shari was feeling hopeful. And she had a new Bose stereo system.

Shari is participating in a new form of substance abuse treatment known as *contingency management* (CM) (Rash, Alessi, & Petri, 2008). This treatment is based on a simple principle: Any behavior—for example, "just saying no" to cocaine, or giving your long-suffering mother a call—that is followed by desirable consequences or rewards is more likely to be repeated in the future. In psychological terms, Shari is being *reinforced* for her sobriety and efforts to be a good daughter. She is *learning* to associate sobriety and family life with something she wants—in this case, money. Along the way, she may find other, unexpected rewards to her newfound sobriety: health, self-respect, spiritual growth, and at least a taste of the warmth of family life she remembers from her childhood.

Contingency management is one application of *learning theory*—principles discovered by psychological scientists influenced by the *behaviorist* movement that flourished in the wake of disillusionment with psychoanalysis during the mid-20th century. Although the enormous influence of behaviorism has waned to some extent, the principles and research methods these men and women devised have had incalculable influence. This chapter is devoted to an examination of these principles.

Learning ▶ A fundamental way that organisms change. Learning is difficult to define precisely, but it involves relatively enduring change in knowledge and/or behavior resulting from specific experiences.

What Is Learning?

Learning is one of the most fundamental ways that an organism changes. On this, all psychologists agree. A child stops speaking loudly in the presence of her grandmother because the woman glares at her granddaughter malevolently every time the girl's voice is raised; a white rat runs a maze in increasingly shorter times because there is food at the end of the journey; a math major solves a new proof after reviewing solutions to similar proofs by famous mathematicians—all these are examples of learning.

Learning Is Difficult to Define

However, the road gets slippery when we try to pinpoint exactly what is meant by *learning*. You may think you know what the term means, but however you attempt to define it, I guarantee that I can find someone willing to debate you. In fact, my all-time favorite textbook definition of *learning* is the following:

> *"**Learning:** A term devised to embarrass learning psychologists, who tie themselves into knots trying to define it."* (Lieberman, 2000, p. 47)

A more typical definition reads like this:

> *"**Learning:** A relatively enduring change in behavior as a result of specific experiences."*

▲ Knowing *how* to play the guitar like Jimi Hendrix is an example of procedural knowledge. Knowing *that* Jimi Hendrix was a skilled guitar player who died in 1970 is an example of explicit knowledge.

The problem in defining *learning* in this way is that *learning* is bound up with the way it is detected: *behavior.* Psychologists use behavior to measure learning because, although neuroscientists have recently been able to observe changes in brains (and neurons) during learning tasks, it is not yet possible to identify specific changes that reliably signal that learning has taken place. Historically—as pointed out by the *behaviorist* psychologists whose work has profoundly deepened our understanding of how organisms learn—the only way to measure learning is to observe changes in the way a person behaves following certain experiences, and *conclude* that learning has taken place: The normally spirited child uncharacteristically speaks softly and excessively politely—but only in the presence of her crotchety grandmother; the previously clueless rat solves the maze in seconds; proofs that once bewildered the math major are now easily solved—all these behaviors signal that learning has occurred.

However, while learning may not be *detectable* without observing behavior, learning may nonetheless take place without behavior. A perfectly reasonable definition of learning that makes no reference at all to behavior is provided in yet another textbook:

> *"**Learning:** The name we give to the psychological process (or processes) by which knowledge is acquired through experience."* (Frieman, 2002, p. 5)

This definition does acknowledge that learning can occur without behavior—for example, you could bomb on a math test for any number of reasons and yet still have learned the material quite well; or you might learn how to tie a sailor's knot by watching someone else do it, yet never actually tie one yourself. However, definitions that focus upon the acquisition of knowledge are generally useless for research in scientific psychology because, like learning, "knowledge" cannot be measured apart from behavior (i.e., performance). How would you know if a person knows how to tie a knot unless you saw the person tie it?

Because of all these problems (and several more I will spare you), I am going to resist the temptation to offer my own equally inadequate definition of *learning.* Instead, I will enumerate three general statements about learning with which most psychologists would probably agree:

1. *In learning, one acquires some new knowledge or behavior as a result of specific experiences.* The knowledge may be of some new fact, termed **explicit knowledge** ("knowing that") or it may be the acquiring of a new skill or ability, termed **procedural knowledge** ("knowing how").

2. *Learning can only be inferred—it cannot be observed.* Therefore, learning can only be measured scientifically by measuring behavior.

3. *The changes in behavior or knowledge that occur as a result of learning are relatively enduring.* As an example, playing a difficult guitar riff once, but never being able to make the lick again, demonstrates luck, not learning.

Explicit knowledge ▶ Factual knowledge that can be articulated and transmitted to others. Explicit knowledge is "knowing that," as compared with procedural knowledge, which is "knowing how."

Procedural knowledge ▶ Knowledge that is applied to the performance of a task. Procedural knowledge reflects skills and abilities—"knowing how" as compared with "knowing that" (explicit knowledge).

"Learned" Is Not the Opposite of "Innate"

You may have read that behaviors such as sex roles, aggression, competition, altruism, and romantic love are considered "innate" (nature) by some and "learned" (nurture) by others—and that these explanations are in opposition to one another. However, *innate* and *learned* are not in opposition but work together, as do *nature* and *nurture* more generally.

In order for human beings to learn, the neurons of human brains must be arranged in particular ways. Brains contain innate neural circuitry that *allows* them to learn (Tooby & Cosmides, 2005). Thus, *the capacity to learn is itself innate and unlearned*, even if any given result of learning—say, the Mandarin language or California spring-break rituals—may be 100% cultural in origin and therefore acquired through experience. In addition, various forms of purely cultural learning take advantage of specific innate aspects of the human brain. A child learns through experience that touching fire is painful, but will not learn this without innate pain detection brain mechanisms, as described in Chapter 4.

Moreover, while many of the learning mechanisms we will explore in this chapter are universal to all animals, members of different species are born with brains that to some extent "prepare" them to learn certain things, but not other things. Take for example, *specific phobias*—irrational fears that are among the *anxiety disorders* I discuss in Chapter 14. Phobias are without doubt learned over time, yet there are certain phobias that are typical in human beings: fear of heights, the dark, snakes, small animals, spiders, and the sight of blood (LoBue & deLoache, 2008; Öhman & Mineka, 2003; Öhman, Carlsson, Lundqvist, & Ingvar, 2007). Children acquire fear of snakes exceptionally easily, as do at least eleven species of nonhuman primates (LoBue & deLoache, 2008; King, cited by Öhman & Mineka, 2003). Fear responses can be elicited in people even when they are exposed to images of snakes so briefly that they are not aware of having seen the image (Öhman & Mineka, 2003).

The world of nonhuman animals is teeming with examples of such "prepared learning." As described in Chapter 9, for example, newly hatched goslings "learn" to follow whatever moving object they first lay their eyes upon. Although this is virtually always their mother, if the goslings should encounter a human being instead—or a rubber ball for that matter—they will instantly learn to follow him, her, or it (e.g., Lorenz, 1937). Goslings are prepared, via *innate* brain mechanisms, to *learn* to follow their mothers. Thus, "learned" and "innate" are not opposed as explanations for human behavior. All learning takes place as an interaction between our experiences, innate learning mechanisms common to all animals, and mechanisms specific to each species.

Habituation and Sensitization Are the Simplest Forms of Learning

To better understand the meaning of "learning," it may be helpful to consider the simplest and most basic of learning mechanisms. Imagine that you awake one morning at daybreak to the sudden, piercing sound of a jackhammer tearing up the street right outside your first-story window. Someone might need to peel you off the ceiling. And what if, after a pause long enough to lull you into the belief that this insult to your nervous system will not be repeated, the jackhammer suddenly starts up again—you might feel another rush of adrenaline, but perhaps slightly less intense than then the original blast. Eventually, if the work continues all day, you might find yourself hardly noticing the jackhammer at all. When a stimulus at first causes a strong response, but due to repeated exposure over time response is lessened, **habituation** has occurred (see Figure 7.1).

Why does habituation happen? In general, when an organism encounters a stimulus that holds out either potential danger or reward, the organism

Habituation ▶ A simple type of nonassociative learning that occurs when a stimulus comes to elicit decreasing response from an organism as a result of the organism's repeated exposure to the stimulus over time. "I got used to it" expresses the idea of habituation.

Time 1
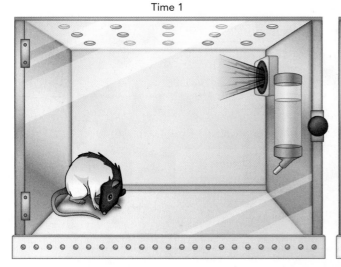

Time 2
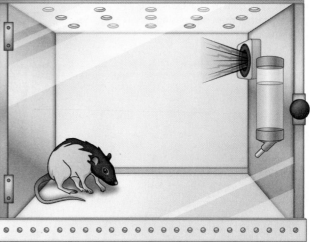

Time 3
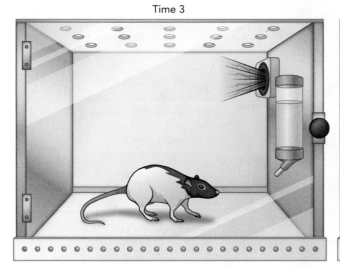

Time 4
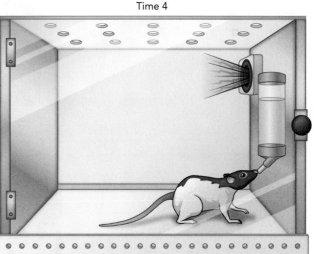

focuses its attention upon the stimulus. If, over time, the stimulus turns out to be neither particularly dangerous nor rewarding, the organism loses interest. It has *learned* that the stimulus does not warrant its attention. When you say, "I got used to it," you are expressing the idea of habituation, the simplest form of learning.

Another form of simple learning, **sensitization**, can be seen as the opposite side of the habituation coin. In sensitization, one responds with *increasing* attention over time to a stimulus that is repeatedly presented—often because the stimulus actually does signal danger (Ji, Kohno, Moore, & Woolf, 2003). For example, your sensitivity to pain generally *increases* the longer the pain continues, both in the affected area of your body and in surrounding areas, rather than decreasing as would be the case in habituation. If you are a city dweller, you may have had the experience of becoming increasingly aware that a noise in the street below, that you at first perceived only vaguely, was in fact a human sound—this awareness then turning quickly to alarm as you realize it was the sound of a person screaming for help. That is *sensitization* as depicted in Figure 7.2

Although sensitization frequently is an adaptive response alerting us to the presence of danger, it can be counterproductive as well. For example, there is some evidence that the more episodes of epilepsy or the mood disorders *depression* and *mania* a person experiences, the more easily subsequent episodes will be triggered. This type of sensitization is known as *kindling* (Morimoto, Fahnestock, & Racine, 2004; Post, 1992).

▲ **FIGURE 7.1 Habituation.** At first the rat reacts with extreme alarm to the sound of a loud tone being sounded. As the tone is sounded on successive occasions, the rat responds with decreasing alarm. Finally, the rat doesn't respond to the tone at all.

Sensitization ▶ A simple type of nonassociative learning that occurs when a stimulus comes to elicit *increased* response from an organism as a result of the organism's repeated exposure to the stimulus over time.

▶ **FIGURE 7.2 Sensitization.**
Sensitivity to pain increases as time goes on, rather than decreasing as in habituation.

Associative Learning Is More Complex

In simple forms of learning such as habituation, there is only a *stimulus* (e.g., the jackhammer) and a *response* (e.g., needing to be peeled off the ceiling). However, most learning involves forming *associations* between two or more stimuli. Organisms have a tendency to *associate* two or more stimuli that occur close together in space and time, particularly if this co-occurrence is frequent and accompanied by significant events. You might see why this would have been highly adaptive for our evolutionary ancestors. If you repeatedly notice that a sharp wind rises and the sky blackens with clouds directly before a storm hits, it would be to your advantage to associate a darkening sky and rising wind with an oncoming storm—and to take refuge accordingly.

The formation of associations between events or stimuli is known as **associative learning**. Although organisms could not survive without associative learning, forming associations between two stimuli can also teach *maladaptive* patterns of behavior. Consider what might happen if a college freshman should come to associate drinking, smoking, or drug abuse with the pleasure

Associative learning ▶
Changes in an organism's knowledge or behavior that result from the association of two or more events or stimuli, or of a stimulus and a response. The most common forms of associative learning are classical conditioning, operant conditioning, and vicarious conditioning (observational learning).

◀ **Habituation and Sensitization in a Marine Mollusk.** Eric Kandel's Nobel-prize-winning research with the marine mollusk *Aplysia californica* has shown that habituation is associated with a decrease in release of the neurotransmitter serotonin, and consequent decrease in the strength of synaptic connections, while sensitization is associated with an increase in neurotransmitter activity and strengthening of synaptic connections (e.g., Kandel, 2000).

of new friendships and feelings of acceptance in the new social environment of her college.

The remainder of the learning portion of this chapter is devoted to exploring three important mechanisms of associative learning through personal experience: Classical conditioning, operant conditioning, and observational learning.

IN SUMMARY

1. Learning is difficult to define precisely, and cannot be directly observed. However, it involves relatively enduring psychological change in knowledge or behavior resulting from specific experiences. "Learned" is *not* the opposite of "innate."

2. Habituation and sensitization are simple forms of learning that involve only a stimulus and a response. Habituation occurs when an organism responds with *decreasing* attention to a stimulus over time. Sensitization occurs when an organism responds with *increasing* attention to the stimulus over time.

3. Associative learning involves forming associations between two or more stimuli.

RETRIEVE!

1. Knowledge of facts ("knowing that") is technically termed _____ knowledge. Knowledge of skills and abilities ("knowing how") is termed _____ knowledge.

2. Why is it said that learning can only be inferred and cannot be observed?

3. Can you think of a hypothetical example (not given in the text) of how associative learning might have been adaptive over evolutionary history?

4. Give an example (from the text or your own observations) of how "learned" and "innate" may coexist.

What Is Classical Conditioning?

Associative learning takes a number of specific forms. The most basic of these is **classical conditioning**. The principles of classical conditioning were discovered accidentally by the Russian physiologist Ivan Pavlov (1849–1936; hence, *classical conditioning* is sometimes referred to as *Pavlovian conditioning*). Pavlov had no particular interest in psychology, but was investigating the digestive systems of mammals, work for which he received a Nobel Prize in 1904. In attempting to gather saliva from dogs by introducing food into their mouths, he noticed an odd occurrence: After undergoing this procedure a number of times, the dogs began to salivate *prior* to eating the food—indeed, they would begin to salivate at the mere sight of the food or its dish—and later, at the sight of the research assistant who placed the food in the dish! Pavlov at first considered these jumping-the-gun salivations—which he termed "psychic secretions"—an impediment to his research. He tried to eliminate them by various means, for example, by sneaking up behind the dogs and popping the food into their mouths.

However, it soon became clear to him that he had stumbled upon an important mechanism of learning: An innate response such as salivation, which should only occur when food is actually in the mouth, could be triggered by a **neutral stimulus**—that is, a stimulus that has no natural relationship to salivation (e.g., the sight of a research assistant or a dish). However, this learning could only occur if the neutral stimulus comes to be *associated* psychologically with a stimulus that normally *would* elicit the innate response—in this case, food in the mouth. In simple terms, this is classical conditioning. You may already have heard about Pavlov's most famous demonstration: Over a period of time, Pavlov and his students trained dogs to salivate at the sound of a bell (or tuning fork tone) by feeding the dogs directly after sounding the bell or tone until the animals began to associate the bell/tone with eating (Anrep, 1920; Pavlov, 1927). Since Pavlov's time, many thousands of organisms have been classically conditioned in this manner—from simple life forms such as the worm to complex life forms such as human beings and other mammals.

Classical Conditioning Prepares an Organism for What Is to Come

In classical conditioning, then, the organism is learning to be *prepared* for what is to come. A forest deer during hunting season may come to associate the sounds of four-wheel drive vehicles (a neutral stimulus) with danger from hunters. The deer will then become more fearful and vigilant upon hearing the sound of a vehicle. However, while a vehicle may be considered a kind of neutral stimulus—there is no intrinsic reason for a deer to fear it unless it happens to be transporting a hunter bent on violence—throughout evolutionary history, animals have been classically conditioned when they learn to associate various naturally occurring sights, sounds, and smells with events that typically follow these stimuli (Domjan, 2005; Hollis, 1997).

For example, the sound of a rattlesnake might condition a rat to experience fear; the smell of rotting or poisonous meat might condition a carnivorous animal to experience nausea; the sensation of the mother's breast at the cheek could condition an infant to begin suckling; and the sight or aroma of an appealing mate may condition a mating response in an animal (Domjan, Cusato, & Krause, 2004; Domjan, 2005).

In other words, as emphasized by learning theorist and researcher Michael Domjan, while classical conditioning to neutral stimuli occurs every day in

---

Classical conditioning (Pavlovian conditioning) ▶ A type of associative learning discovered by Ivan Pavlov. Classical conditioning occurs when an innate (or otherwise reflexive) response known as the unconditioned response (UCR) is triggered by a neutral stimulus as a result of repeated pairings of the neutral stimulus with an unconditioned stimulus (UCS). The UCS is a stimulus that would naturally trigger the reflexive response without a conditioning procedure.

Neutral stimulus ▶ A stimulus that has no natural relationship to an innate response it nonetheless eventually comes to elicit through classical conditioning. For example, a tone has no natural relationship to the human eye-blink response, but a person can be conditioned to blink when hearing a tone if the tone has been repeatedly paired with puffs of air blown at the eye.

psychological laboratories, classical conditioning also occurs naturally in response to naturally occurring stimuli that may not be at all neutral. As Domjan suggests, classical conditioning is *functional*—its purpose is to prepare an organism for likely eventualities (see also Hollis, 1997). According to Domjan, the capacity to be classically conditioned evolved because it conferred survival and reproduction advantages on those who possessed it—for example, by increasing the organism's ability to avoid predators and dangerous environments or take advantage of important opportunities for feeding, mating, and so forth (Matthews, Domjan, Ramsey, & Crews, 2007). I have more to say about "natural" classical conditioning later.

Classical Conditioning Includes Stimulus and Response

Classical conditioning in the laboratory involves a relatively simple association between *stimulus* and *response*. Pavlov divided the stimuli and responses involved in classical conditioning into four categories:

- **Unconditioned Stimulus** (**UCS**) The unconditioned stimulus (UCS) is the stimulus that would naturally trigger an innate response. It is called "unconditioned" because it produces its effect "unconditionally," or without the need for conditioned learning. In Pavlov's bell/salivation demonstration, the unconditioned stimulus is *food placed in the mouth*.
- **Unconditioned Response** (**UCR**) The unconditioned response (UCR) is the reflexive, automatic response to the unconditioned stimulus. In Pavlov's bell demonstration, the unconditioned response is *salivation*.
- **Conditioned Stimulus** (**CS**) The conditioned stimulus (CS) is the stimulus that only begins to have an effect on the unconditioned response (in this case, salivation) *after* it has been repeatedly paired with the unconditioned stimulus (food). In Pavlov's demonstration, the conditioned stimulus is the *tone*. Remember, however, that the conditioned stimulus only earns its name *after* it comes to elicit the unconditioned response by itself following conditioning. Prior to that, it may be referred to as the neutral stimulus.
- **Conditioned Response** (**CR**) The conditioned response (CR) is the reflexive, originally unconditioned response *after* it has come to be elicited by a conditioned stimulus. Thus, both the unconditioned and the conditioned responses in Pavlov's experiment are *salivation* (see Figure 7.3).

Unconditioned stimulus (UCS) ▶ In classical conditioning, the UCS is the stimulus that naturally triggers the innate (or otherwise reflexive) response, known as the unconditioned response (UCR).

Unconditioned Response (UCR) ▶ In classical conditioning, the UCR is the innate or otherwise reflexive response triggered without conditioning by an unconditioned stimulus (UCS).

Conditioned Stimulus (CS) ▶ In classical conditioning, the CS is the originally neutral stimulus that comes to elicit the innate, unconditioned response (UCR) after conditioning.

Conditioned Response (CR) ▶ In classical conditioning, the term conditioned response (CR) is used to describe the innate unconditioned response (UCR) *after* it been has come to be elicited by the a neutral stimulus.

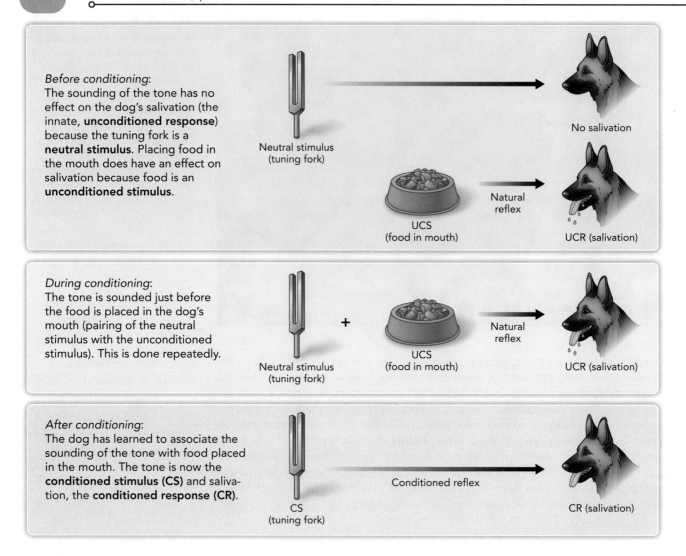

Before conditioning:
The sounding of the tone has no effect on the dog's salivation (the innate, **unconditioned response**) because the tuning fork is a **neutral stimulus**. Placing food in the mouth does have an effect on salivation because food is an **unconditioned stimulus**.

Neutral stimulus (tuning fork)

No salivation

Natural reflex

UCS (food in mouth)

UCR (salivation)

During conditioning:
The tone is sounded just before the food is placed in the dog's mouth (pairing of the neutral stimulus with the unconditioned stimulus). This is done repeatedly.

Neutral stimulus (tuning fork)

+

UCS (food in mouth)

Natural reflex

UCR (salivation)

After conditioning:
The dog has learned to associate the sounding of the tone with food placed in the mouth. The tone is now the **conditioned stimulus (CS)** and salivation, the **conditioned response (CR)**.

CS (tuning fork)

Conditioned reflex

CR (salivation)

▲ **FIGURE 7.3** Pavlov's Demonstration of Classical Conditioning.

Acquisition ▶ In classical conditioning, acquisition is the process of acquiring a conditioned response.

ACQUISITION

Learning a new behavior through conditioning is known as **acquisition**. Because classical conditioning in the laboratory generally involves associating a neutral event (tone) with a non-neutral event to follow (feeding), the order and timing of presentation of the stimuli are of critical importance. For acquisition to occur reliably, two criteria must be met:

1. The conditioning (neutral) stimulus in almost all cases must be presented *before* rather than after the unconditioned stimulus (e.g., the bell must come before the food; Domjan, 2002). In a series of famous demonstrations, Michael Domjan conditioned male Japanese quail to become sexually aroused (and produce more sperm) at the sight of a red light by repeatedly pairing the light with the appearance of a female quail (see Domjan, 2002, for summary). Because the conditioning *prepared* the male quails' bodies for mating, the conditioning would not have worked had the light been flashed *after* the appearance of the female.

2. The unconditioned stimulus must follow *immediately* after the conditioning (neutral) stimulus begins to be presented—no more than a second or two at the very most—or the association between the stimuli will be weakened.

Second-Order Conditioning Once a conditioned stimulus (CS) reliably begins to elicit a conditioned response (CR), that conditioned stimulus becomes powerful enough to be used to create **second-order conditioning**. Second-order conditioning involves a pairing of the CS with a completely new, neutral stimulus—almost as if the CS were an *un*conditioned stimulus! For example, let us say a dog is conditioned to salivate upon hearing a tone. What if a light were now flashed repeatedly moments before the tone is heard? The dog may now become conditioned to salivate to the light, in the complete absence of an unconditioned stimulus (food). However, the strength of the effect of second-order conditioning may be weaker than the original, first-order conditioning.

EXTINCTION, SPONTANEOUS RECOVERY, AND RENEWAL

As already mentioned, in classical conditioning, the organism is learning to be *prepared* for what is to come. We used the example of a forest deer conditioned during hunting season to become more fearful and vigilant upon hearing the sound of a vehicle. But what if, after acquisition of a conditioned response, the conditioned stimulus (e.g., sound of vehicle) continues to be presented *without* the unconditioned stimulus (hunters shooting)? Will the sound of a vehicle forever elicit fear? With repeated presentation of the conditioned stimulus without the unconditioned stimulus, the conditioned response becomes weaker until it disappears entirely, a process known as **extinction**.

However, classically conditioned responses are not "unlearned" or wiped out in extinction. For example, Pavlov found that if he allowed his animals to rest for several hours following the extinction of a behavior, the conditioned response would spontaneously appear again upon *re*-presentation of the conditioned stimulus—although in a somewhat weaker form. This occurred even with no additional pairing of the conditioned stimulus with the conditioned response. This phenomenon is known as **spontaneous recovery**. If new associations are formed for the conditioned stimulus over time, these may produce entirely new conditioned responses. A person conditioned in childhood to associate the taste of broccoli with the unpleasant experience of being forced to sit at the dinner table for hours until all the hated stalks are finished may grow up to be a chef who associates the taste of broccoli with the fabulous 2 years she spent studying Northern Italian cooking in Venice. However, once again, these new associations do not *replace* the old ones, but are instead *superimposed over* them and suppress them. Under certain circumstances the old associations may be *renewed* (Rescorla & Heth, 1975; Chan, Leung, Westbrook, & McNally, 2010).

Renewal is a resurgence of an extinguished behavior if the animal is placed in a different *context* from the one in which extinction originally occurred (Bouton, 1991). An excellent example of *renewal* is relapse in drug addiction. Although addiction is a complex process that cannot be explained entirely with classical conditioning, aspects of addiction may be classically conditioned. For example, addicts may come to associate drug paraphernalia (needles, pipes) or drug-taking environments (bars, certain neighborhoods) or even certain people (stoner friends) either with effects of the drugs or with withdrawal effects and feelings of need for the drug (Childress et al., 1999).

Addicts who recover in the context of a drug treatment facility may experience a resurgence of craving for their drug of choice once they leave the facility and come into contact with people, places, or things associated with the drug. Anna Childress and her colleagues demonstrated how renewal in the context of drug addiction is reflected in brain processes (Childress et al., 1999). Previous research had shown that craving for cocaine is associated with activation of the *amygdala* and *anterior cingulate*, both structures of the limbic system that regulate emotion, motivation, and basic drives. Using positron emission tomography (PET) scans, Childress and her colleagues showed that viewing videos of crack cocaine being prepared and used activated the same areas of the limbic system. On the other hand, these brain areas were not activated in those who had never been cocaine-dependent (see Figure 7.4).

Second-order conditioning
▶ A form of classical conditioning in which an organism is first conditioned to a neutral stimulus; and then that stimulus is used to condition the organism to a new neutral stimulus. For example, a dog conditioned to salivate upon hearing a tone by pairing the tone with food, may then be conditioned to associate the tone with a new neutral stimulus—a bell. The dog will then salivate upon hearing the bell, even if the bell was never actually paired with the unconditioned stimulus of food.

Extinction ▶ When a learned behavior ceases to be performed. In classical conditioning, extinction will occur when the conditioned stimulus occurs repeatedly without being paired with the unconditioned stimulus.

Spontaneous recovery ▶ When an extinguished behavior reemerges (but in a somewhat weaker form) after the organism has rested from exposure to the classically conditioned stimulus. Spontaneous recovery differs from renewal, where an extinguished behavior reemerges specifically because the organism is placed in a context different from the one in which extinction occurred.

Renewal ▶ In classical conditioning, renewal is a resurgence of an extinguished behavior if the animal is placed in a different context from the one in which extinction originally occurred and the original conditioned stimulus (CS) is once again presented.

▶ **FIGURE 7.4 Renewal of Craving in Recovered Cocaine Addicts.** PET scan images show increases in cerebral blood flow to areas of the limbic system associated with craving as former cocaine addicts view drug-related videos. The first image in each row represents the brain area in question prior to viewing the video. The next two images on each row contrast brain activation in the amygdala and anterior cingulate during the viewing of a nature video and viewing of a video depicting use of crack cocaine. Areas of greatest activation are shown in red. *(Source: Childress et al., 1999.)*

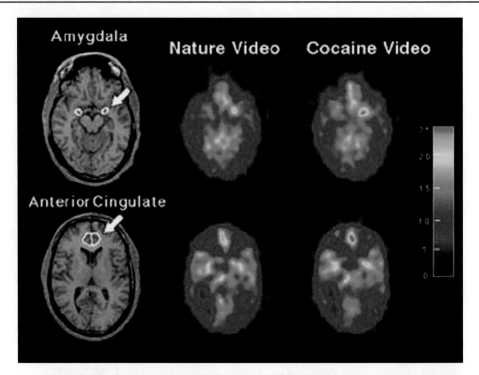

▲ **Generalization and Discrimination.** *Generalization* allows you to extend an association to a new stimulus that, while different in some ways from the original stimulus to which the association was formed, is nevertheless similar in important ways. *Discrimination* prevents you from improperly applying generalization to a new stimulus that, while similar to the original stimulus in some ways, is different in important ways.

GENERALIZATION AND DISCRIMINATION

Pavlov discovered that an animal might display a conditioned response when exposed to a neutral stimulus that is similar but not identical to the original conditioned stimulus. For example, a dog conditioned to salivate on hearing a particular tone generated by a tuning fork will salivate (but to a somewhat lesser extent) to a completely different tone. The closer the second tone is to the original tone, the stronger the response will be. This is known as **generalization**.

The capacity for generalization is one of our greatest cognitive talents. Try to imagine life without it. Let us say you were to cross the path of a snarling pit bull that attacks you viciously (but luckily, the owner subdues the dog before too much damage is done). Now suppose the next week you were to once again cross the path of a snarling dog—but this time it's a snarling Doberman pinscher. Your capacity for generalization tells you, "Hmmm . . . maybe I'd better cross to the other side of the street" instead of, "Oh, well, it's a completely different breed, so, no problem!"

However, just as an organism can be trained to generalize, it can also be trained to *discriminate*. **Discrimination** occurs when one neutral stimulus

Generalization ▶ In classical conditioning, when an animal displays a conditioned response (CR) to a neutral stimulus that is similar, but not identical, to the conditioned stimulus (CS).

Discrimination ▶ In classical conditioning, when one neutral stimulus produces a conditioned response, but another, similar neutral stimulus does not.

(e.g., a tone) produces a conditioned response, but another, similar neutral stimulus (a different tone) does not. For example, animals can be trained to discriminate between tones by repeatedly pairing one tone with an unconditioned stimulus such as food, but also presenting a different tone *without* the food (Anrep, 1920).

Just as generalization is essential to human survival, so is discrimination. Returning to the example of the pit bull, what if, after your first experience, you felt compelled to cross the street not only whenever you saw a snarling dog but whenever you saw *any* dog? Or cat? Or mammal? Or any moving object?

CRITICAL THINKING ABOUT PSYCHOLOGY

Will the Real Little Albert Please Crawl Forward?

Generations of introductory psychology students have read the story of "Little Albert," a 9-month-old infant conditioned to fear small white rats in a demonstration of classical conditioning by the founder of behaviorism, John B. Watson, and his student (and soon-to-be wife) Rosalie Rayner (Watson & Rayner, 1920). Once establishing that Albert showed no fear responses to a wide variety of animals, masks, burning newspapers, and sundry other stimuli, Watson and Rayner proceeded to take a claw hammer and suddenly whack a large steel bar suspended right behind Albert every time he touched a laboratory white rat. Understandably, Albert began to cry. After seven pairings of the rat and the sound over a period of a week, Albert began to show fear when in the presence of the rat alone.

The experimenters then attempted to see if Albert's fear would generalize to other animals or objects. They presented Albert with a rabbit, a dog (who suddenly barked very loudly, seriously frightening the experimenters as well as Albert), a Santa Claus mask, a sealskin coat, and other items. Results were mixed; in some instances it is not clear whether Albert experienced fear or simple ambivalence to these objects (Paul & Blumenthal, 1989). For example, is thumbsucking a fear response?

▲ **Watson and Rayner Frighten Little Albert.**

In any case, Watson and Rayner concluded in their original (1920) article that their research "showed conclusively" (p. 12) that conditioned emotional responses could persist for at least 1 month. As many authors have observed over the years, however, Watson and Rayner's methods and recordings of the events surrounding this experiment are "casual and haphazard" at best (Paul & Blumenthal, 1989, p. 548). Attempts to replicate the research have failed. The Little Albert study simply was not conducted in a way that would normally warrant it being repeatedly presented as an example of an important work of psychological science (Vicente, 2000).

In addition to the apparent lack of ethics involved in purposely attempting to instill potentially long-lasting fear in an infant in order to prove a point, the Little Albert study suffers from enough methodological flaws that textbook authors and others over the years apparently have felt the need to invent details of the study that never occurred in order to paint it in a more positive light (Paul & Blumenthal, 1989; B. Harris, 1979, 2011). For example, some authors have described in great detail the experimenters' attempts to *recondition* Albert away from his fear of rats by pairing presentation of the rat with bowls of ice cream and pieces of chocolate. But in fact, *no* attempts were made to recondition Albert, and evidence suggests that Watson and Rayner had never made plans to do so (Cornwell & Hobbs, 1976; B. Harris, 1979). Other accounts exaggerate the ambiguous findings of the study and claim that Little Albert developed a long-lasting "rat phobia" (Vicente, 2000). The list of items to which Albert (falsely) has been said to have generalized his purported fear of rats is long, and includes a man's beard, a fur belt, his mother's fur coat, and a furry teddy bear.

CRITICAL THINKING ABOUT PSYCHOLOGY

CONTINUED

Several explanations have been offered for the long "shelf life" of the Little Albert study. First, there is a general tendency of those who are strongly invested in a theory to push research results into a mold that supports that theory (Samelson, 1980). This may explain Watson and Rayner's "overplaying" their results, and decades of behaviorists and those sympathetic to their perspective following suit. Secondly, there is a tendency of textbook authors (including this one!) to try to find studies that vividly illustrate principles they are attempting to explain (B. Harris, 1979). What could be more vivid than Little Albert as a demonstration of classical conditioning?

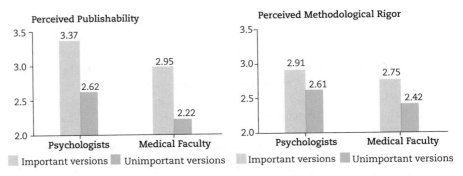

▲ **FIGURE 7.5** Scientists may be more likely to overlook flaws of a study if the study concerns an important topic. In Graph A, two groups of psychologists and medical personnel rated the "publishability" of a study that concerned either a treatment for anorexia (the "important" version) or an intervention to help teenagers stop saying "like," and "you know" (the "unimportant" version). In Graph B, the methodological soundness of the study was rated. As you can see, higher ratings of publishability and methodological rigor were given when the study was described as being about the important topic. (*Source: Wilson et al., 1993, p. 324.*)

Finally, Timothy Wilson and his colleagues (Wilson, DePaulo, Mook, & Klaaren, 1993) have shown that the more important the topic of a piece of research is, the more likely scientists may be to overlook its flaws These researchers presented a different version of the same highly flawed fictitious research study to two groups of scientists. In one version they described the topic of the research as an intervention to help sufferers from anorexia. In the other version the topic was an intervention to help young people stop saying "like" and "you know" countless times a day. As Figure 7.5 shows, scientists were far more lenient in their critique of the "anorexia" study. The same held true for a study topic described for one group of scientists as heart disease and for the other as heartburn, and for four additional such mock study pairs (see also Reich, Green, Brock, & Tetlock, 2007). ■

IN SUMMARY

1. Classical conditioning is the most basic form of associative learning. The principles of classical conditioning were initially discovered by accident by Ivan Pavlov. Classical conditioning does not teach new behaviors to an organism, but elicits typically innate or reflexive behaviors, generally (but not always) using previously neutral stimuli. Classical conditioning prepares an organism for what is to come.

2. Classical conditioning in the laboratory involves forming an association between a neutral stimulus (e.g., the tone of a bell) and an unconditioned stimulus (UCS). The UCS is one that ordinarily elicits a reflexive, unconditioned response (UCR). For example, food placed in a dog's mouth is a UCS that elicits the UCR of salivation. Once the association between the neutral stimulus and the UCR is formed through repeated pairings, that originally neutral stimulus will now elicit the UCR with no UCS necessary. The formerly neutral stimulus is then referred to as the conditioned stimulus (CS). The UCR is then referred to as the conditioned response (CR).

3. Two criteria must usually be met for *acquisition* of a conditioned response to occur in a laboratory: The conditioning stimulus must be presented prior to the UCS, and the UCS must follow rapidly (in most cases within seconds).

4. If a CS is repeatedly presented without the UCS, *extinction* occurs. However, the response is not "unlearned" or "wiped out." *Spontaneous recovery* can occur if the organism is allowed to rest after extinction and the CS is once again presented. Moreover, conditioned responses can be *renewed* after substantial time has passed if the organism is placed in a different context from the one in which extinction occurred.

5. *Generalization* occurs when an organism displays a conditioned response to a stimulus that is similar, but not identical, to the CS. *Discrimination* occurs when an animal only displays a conditioned behavior to the original CS and not to similar stimuli.

6. Classical conditioning may also occur naturally in the wild. In such cases, the stimuli being paired with the UCR are often not neutral at all—for example, the sound of a rattlesnake has a natural connection to fear response in a rodent, because this sound often predicts that the snake is about to strike.

RETRIEVE!

1. Match the term at left with the description at right:

Unconditioned Stimulus (UCS) — An innate or otherwise reflexive behavior that comes to be elicited as a result of repeated pairing with an initially neutral stimulus

Conditioned Stimulus (CS) — An innate or otherwise reflexive behavior as it exists prior to conditioning

Unconditioned Response (UCR) — A stimulus that naturally elicits a particular innate or reflexive behavior

Conditioned Response (CR) — A stimulus that is initially neutral, but eventually comes to elicit an innate or otherwise reflexive behavior after conditioning

2. What is the evolutionary function of the capacity to be classically conditioned?

3. What is the term used to describe conditioning that occurs by the pairing of a CS with a new neutral stimulus?

a) spontaneous recovery   c) backward conditioning

b) second-order conditioning   d) renewal

4. True or false: Classically conditioned responses can be unlearned or wiped out over time, simply by repeatedly presenting the CS without the UCS.

5. What is the term used when one neutral stimulus produces a conditioned response after conditioning, but another, similar, neutral stimulus does not?

a) second-order conditioning   **b)** extinction   **c)** generalization   **d)** discrimination

6. What are the two explanations given in the text to explain the long "shelf life" of the Little Albert study?

What Are the Limits of Classical Conditioning?

Over the past century of research in psychological science, classical conditioning has been demonstrated in a mind-boggling number of animal species and for a similarly astonishing number of stimuli and responses. Classical conditioning has been used to treat psychological disorders such as the irrational fears known as *phobias* and physiological illnesses including hypertension. It also has been used as a powerful tool of advertisers.

Classical conditioning can occur during the normal course of the day without one even being aware of it. Consider those habituated to the use of caffeine. They (all right, *we*) may begin to feel wide awake within moments of taking those first sips of coffee of the day. However, it actually takes the caffeine from coffee about 20–30 minutes to reach the brain. Caffeine users have been classically conditioned to associate the effects of caffeine with the taste and smell of coffee. Consequently, they may often experience at least some of these effects of the drug before the drug actually begins to take effect.

The critical point to remember about classical conditioning, however, is *that it cannot teach new behaviors to an organism;* it can only *elicit* innate or otherwise reflexive behaviors (e.g., fear, physiological arousal, pleasure, salivation, and so forth) with stimuli that ordinarily would not have these effects. Classical conditioning does this by teaching the organism new associations between events.

Classical conditioning has other limitations as well. Early behaviorists such as John B. Watson saw classical conditioning as an automatic process resulting from the simple pairing of a neutral stimulus with an unconditioned stimulus. In their view, conditioning bypassed cognition entirely. Just as the conditioning of a worm can be accomplished without any thinking on the worm's part, so is the conditioning of a human being accomplished with no intervention from the person's higher thought processes. However, substantial changes in these ideas have resulted from research over the past half-century.

Specifically, three important factors have been incorporated into models of classical conditioning: (a) *cognition*; (b) the *evolutionary history* of the organism; and (c) the *ecology* of the organism. Let's examine each of these.

Cognition Plays a Part in Classical Conditioning

In 1968, Robert Rescorla added the element of *cognition* to the equation of classical conditioning (see Figure 7.6). In his experiment, Rescorla conditioned a fear response in a group of rats to a tone by repeatedly presenting the tone just prior to administering a shock to the rats. However, for a second group of rats, Rescorla paired the tone and the shocks the same number of

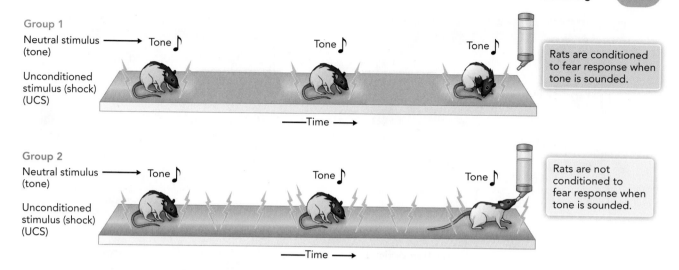

▲ **FIGURE 7.6 Robert Rescorla Introduces Cognition into Classical Conditioning.** In Rescorla's (1968) study, two groups of rats received the same number of shocks paired with a tone, but Group 2 received additional shocks that were not paired with the tone. Only the rats in Group 1, whose shocks were *reliably* paired with the tone, were conditioned with fear reactions to the tone. Rescorla concluded that rats cognitively assess whether a stimulus is a *valid predictor* of a subsequent event. This is cognitive activity—not simply the blind forming of associations.

times, but also shocked the rats an equal number of times *without* the tone. According to the views of early behaviorists, pairing the tone with the shock should have conditioned a fear response regardless of additional shocks minus the tone. Yet, Rescorla found that only when the tone *reliably predicted* the shocks—that is, in the first group of rats—was fear conditioned. Rescorla proposed that the rats were engaging in cognitive activity to determine whether the tone was a valid predictor of a shock to follow. This insight goes a long way toward explaining why conditioning only works if the neutral stimulus is presented before the UCS.

Evolution Prepares Each Animal to Form Certain Associations

As explained previously, the early behaviorists such as Watson and Pavlov saw conditioning as a process that applied equally to all organisms and to any conceivable stimuli. As long as the neutral stimulus was correctly paired with a UCS, conditioning *would* occur. Martin Seligman (1970) termed this idea the *general process view* of classical conditioning. The inadequacy of the general process view was first demonstrated in the 1960s by theorists influenced by the new applications of evolutionary theory to animal behavior. Put simply, some animal species are easier to condition to a particular response than others. In Seligman's (1970) terms, organisms are *biologically prepared* to form certain associations, but not to form other associations.

The most influential demonstration of biological preparedness was offered by John Garcia (Garcia, Brett, & Rusiniak, 1989; Garcia & Koelling, 1966). As depicted in Figure 7.7, Garcia and Robert Koelling showed that rats could easily be conditioned to avoid (fear) the neutral stimulus of sweetened water if tasting the water were paired with a nauseating dose of radiation. But the rats could *not* easily be conditioned to avoid the water if it were paired with shocks. The opposite held true for buzzes and flashes as neutral stimuli: It was much

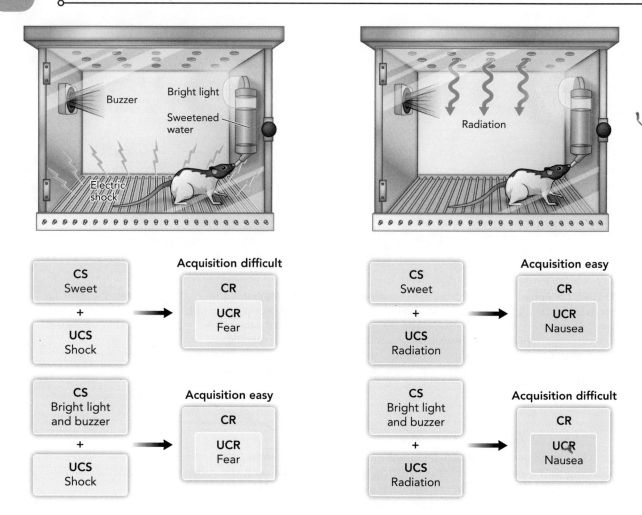

▲ **FIGURE 7.7 Biological Preparedness Affects Classical Conditioning.** In his landmark study, John Garcia exposed one group of rats to sweetened water paired with a nauseating dose of radiation. The rats easily acquired conditioning to avoid the sweetened water. However, when he paired the sweetened water with shock for another group or rats, acquisition of conditioned fear of the taste of the water was very difficult. The situation was reversed when it came to buzzes and flashes. Acquisition of fear was difficult when the buzzes and flashes were paired with radiation, but easy when paired with shock.

easier for rats to learn to fear buzzes and flashes that had been paired with shock than to learn to fear the buzzes and flashes when they were paired with nauseating radiation.

Thus, rats (and most other mammals, including human beings) are biologically prepared to learn to avoid foods that have toxic consequences (nausea), because of the evolutionary value of avoiding poisonous substances (Logue, 1998). Indeed, such conditioning can occur following even a single exposure. Some of you may recall a time you were sickened by eating a particular food that had spoiled, and then found yourself unable to face the prospect of ever eating the food again—even if you knew the food was fresh on subsequent encounters.

On the other hand, foods are rarely associated with physically painful consequences in the real world, making it more difficult to condition mammals to avoid food paired with shocks. The opposite is the case for unusual sights and sounds, which are frequently associated with physical pain and danger in the real world.

These findings appeared to violate the basic assumption of the general process model known as *equipotentiality*, which states that any neutral stimulus can be associated just as easily with one unconditioned stimulus as with any other. Belief in equipotentiality was so strong during the 1960s that Garcia had a very difficult time having his results published, because they were such a direct challenge to conventional learning theory (Garcia, 1981).

The Ecology of the Organism Affects Conditioning

I briefly mentioned earlier that classical conditioning occurs "naturally" in the wild as well as in the laboratory. Theorists taking the **functionalist perspective** on learning propose that classical conditioning in a natural environment differs in important respects from that found in psychology experiments (Domjan, 2005; Hollis, 1997; Matthews et al., 2007). How does classical conditioning in an organism's natural ecology differ from that in the laboratory? There are two principal differences, according to functionalist theorists. The first, most obvious difference is that in the natural ecology (total environment) of an organism, conditioning stimuli are rarely neutral or arbitrary.

Consider salivation as it might occur in a natural environment. Among animals in the wild, the process of obtaining food and chewing it includes a long chain of responses built upon associations—the weather, sounds of prey or sounds associated with the movements of prey, visual contact with prey or with other animals that frequent the same habitats as prey, and so forth (Domjan et al., 2004). If an animal begins to salivate upon hearing such sounds or making visual contact with prey, an unconditioned stimulus has been elicited from a conditioned stimulus. Yet, this conditioned stimulus—the sight of a tasty prey, for example—is hardly neutral! Thus, from the functionalist perspective, definitions of classical conditioning which stipulate that the conditioning stimulus must be neutral or arbitrary are incomplete.

The second way that classical conditioning in an organism's natural ecology may differ is that the process itself is qualitatively different. Classical conditioning to natural stimuli proceeds more rapidly, produces stronger effects, is less dependent upon a very small time interval between the presentation of the conditioning stimulus and the UCS, and is more resistant to various sorts of interference in the conditioning process (Domjan, 2005; Matthews et al., 2007).

At its core, the functionalist perspective is evolutionary. These researchers propose that classical conditioning and other mechanisms of learning evolved because they increased the survival and reproductive success of the individuals who possessed them (Hollis, Pharr, Dumas, Britton, & Field, 1997; Matthews et al., 2007). Given that mechanisms of learning such as classical conditioning are so prevalent throughout the animal world, this is a reasonable position to take (Pappini, 2002). Nevertheless, the simple fact that a trait is universal, or nearly so, is no proof that it evolved through natural selection or is itself an adaptation (Schmitt & Pilcher, 2004). For example, reading and writing is extremely widespread through most large human societies. Yet, there were no books, pens, typewriters, or computers when the human species was evolving. Therefore, written language itself cannot be an adaptation (although various capacities of the brain and mind responsible for modern humans' ability to read and write may be).

Functionalist perspective

▶ Those taking the functionalist perspective on learning believe that learning mechanisms such as classical conditioning evolved because they fulfill *functions*—in this case, preparing the organism for what is to come. Theorists taking this perspective believe that learning mechanisms evolved because they increased the survival and reproductive success of organisms that possessed them.

IN SUMMARY

1. Classical conditioning does not teach new behaviors to an organism, but elicits innate or otherwise reflexive behaviors with previously neutral stimuli.

2. Researchers in cognitive psychology and evolutionary/functional approaches to learning have demonstrated that (a) classical conditioning may involve cognition; (b) the evolutionary history of each organism affects the ease with which specific behaviors may be conditioned to specific stimuli; and (c) the ecological context in which conditioning occurs affects the way conditioning occurs.

3.	Robert Rescorla demonstrated that conditioning rats to fear did not work unless the conditioning stimulus *reliably* predicted the shocks. This implied that the rats were using cognitive processes.
4.	John Garcia overturned the general process behaviorist doctrine of equipotentiality, which proposed that virtually any neutral stimulus could be used to condition virtually any response. Garcia's research showed that the evolutionary history of each organism prepares it to be more or less easily conditioned by various stimuli.
5.	The functionalist perspective proposes that classical conditioning occurs in natural environments as well as in the laboratory. Conditioning stimuli in the natural ecology of an animal are rarely neutral or arbitrary. Conditioning that occurs in nature may be more rapid, robust, and less dependent upon a very small time interval between presentation of the conditioning stimulus and the UCS. It is more resistant to interference in the conditioning process.

RETRIEVE!

1.	According to the Wagner-Rescorla model, the unconditioned stimulus (UCS) must be _____ for conditioning to reliably occur. **a)** intense **b)** predictable **c)** unexpected **d)** presented rapidly
2.	How does the research of John Garcia demonstrate the phenomenon of biological preparedness?
3.	Equipotentiality is the primary assumption of what behaviorist model? **a)** the general process model **c)** the domain neutral model **b)** the computational model **d)** the Rescorla model
4.	Conditioning that occurs in natural ecologies differs in two principal respects from conditioning in the laboratory. What are these two respects?

What Is Operant Conditioning?

As briefly mentioned earlier, classical conditioning has shown practical utility in marketing and in treating disorders of various kinds. However, it remains a relatively limited tool, primarily because it elicits reflexive behaviors only and cannot teach new behaviors. At the turn of the century, however, a graduate student of William James named Edward Thorndike (1874–1949) discovered a principle that would later blossom into a theory of learning with broader applicability.

Thorndike (1898) was impressed with the work of evolutionist Charles Darwin. However, he was highly skeptical of evidence of advanced intelligence in animals—claims that some believed to follow logically from Darwin's theory that all forms of life originated in a single common ancestor. The logic seemed to be, if humans and other animals are related, might not nonhuman animals possess intelligence similar to that of humans?

 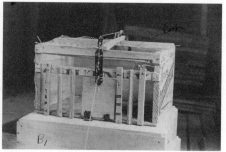

◀ **Two of Thorndike's Original "Puzzle Boxes."**

Thorndike placed a dish with food outside a crate (called the "puzzle box") that held a hungry cat. The food was visible to the cat, but the door on the crate could be opened only by means of a latch. The cat's task was to figure out how to trip the mechanism controlling the latch. Typically, the cat would stumble around, clawing and dashing back and forth until it accidentally stumbled on the correct action to open the latch. It would then be rewarded with the food.

Thorndike reasoned that if the cat truly possessed advanced intelligence, this single successful attempt would be all that was necessary for the cat to be successful on a subsequent trial. However, it was not. When Thorndike again placed the cat in the crate, the animal once more stumbled around until it accidentally tripped the latch. Thorndike found, however, that it took *less time* for this "accident" to occur the second time around—and increasingly less time on the third and fourth attempts. Eventually, the cat had no trouble opening the door immediately.

Thorndike proposed that the cat did not improve as a result of reasoning power. Instead, the presence of *reward* strengthened actions that proved to be successful for the cat while actions that were unsuccessful became increasingly less likely to occur. Thorndike summarized his findings in his **law of effect**, which states that for any organism, those behaviors that lead to a satisfying state of affairs are "stamped in" while those behaviors that lead to an unsatisfying or annoying state of affairs are "stamped out" (Thorndike's words). In other words, the organism learns as a result of the consequences of his or her own actions.

While the *law of effect* remains one of the first valid laws of psychology, Thorndike did not fully envision its implications. This was accomplished by the American psychologist B. F. Skinner (1904–1990), surely one of the most important—and controversial—figures in the history of psychology. Skinner was a solid behaviorist strongly influenced by the work of John B. Watson. Although he appreciated Thorndike's law of effect, he rejected Thorndike's use of concepts such as *satisfying* and *annoying* in his definition. To Skinner, *satisfying* and *annoying* implied mental states that could not be objectively observed. How does one know that an animal feels emotions such as "satisfied" or "annoyed"? Only behavior can be objectively verified (remember our attempts to define the concept *learning*?). Thus, Skinner restated Thorndike's law in terms of what he termed **operant conditioning**. According to Skinner, *operant conditioning is a type of learning in which the consequences of a behavior affect the probability that the behavior will be repeated in the future.* Note that this is simply a restatement of Thorndike's law, minus the emotional component.

In Operant Conditioning, the Organism Teaches Itself

Skinner used the term *operant conditioning* to describe this type of learning because in choosing to behave in a particular manner, the organism is *operating* on his or her environment in a way that results in specific consequences. The organism then comes to associate these consequences with its behavior. Operant conditioning is an active process entirely shaped by the organism's

Law of effect ▶ Edward Thorndike's discovery that behaviors which lead to a satisfying state of affairs are "stamped in," while behaviors that lead to an unsatisfying or annoying state of affairs are "stamped out." The law of effect formed the basis for B. F. Skinner's discoveries of operant conditioning principles.

Operant conditioning (*operant learning, instrumental learning*) ▶ A form of conditioning in which the consequences of a behavior affect the probability that the behavior will be repeated in the future.

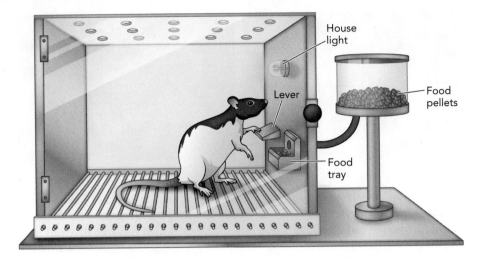

▶ FIGURE 7.8 Skinner's Operant Chamber. Skinner used a temperature-controlled, sound-proofed chamber for his experiments with rats. A house light lit the chamber, and the rat received food by pressing a lever.

Radical behaviorism ▶ B. F. Skinner's version of behaviorism, also referred to as *experimental analysis of behavior*. Radical behaviorists propose that all behavior is lawful—and any given behavior can be analyzed empirically by examining the reinforcements and punishments which follow the behavior. The term "radical" has been applied to this school of psychology because radical behaviorists believe that psychology can only be a science of behavior and never a science of "mind."

Operant chamber ("Skinner box") ▶ The apparatus B. F. Skinner designed to study operant learning in rats. The operant chamber includes a container of food pellets in a container mounted to the outside of the cage, designed so that the pellets will be delivered to the rat when the rat presses down on a lever near its food tray. The cage is placed within a soundproof, temperature controlled, ventilated chamber.

Reinforcement ▶ When the consequence of a behavior increases the likelihood that the behavior will continue or be repeated in the future.

Punishment ▶ When the consequence of a behavior decreases the likelihood that it will continue or be repeated in the future.

own behavior, whereas classical conditioning is a passive process regulated by forces outside the control of the organism. In a sense, in operant conditioning *the organism teaches itself*. Skinner's brand of behaviorism, based in operant conditioning, became known as **radical behaviorism** (although Skinner did not prefer this term) because of Skinner's insistence that psychology could *never* be a science of mind, but *only* a science of behavior.

To study operant conditioning, Skinner modified the box used by Thorndike for his experiments with cats, and chose (hungry) laboratory rats as his animal subjects. Instead of using a box with a latch and placing food outside the box, Skinner placed a supply of food pellets in a container mounted to the outside of a cage. The cage was designed so that the pellets would automatically be delivered to the rat when the rat pressed down on a lever located near the food tray. To make sure that environmental conditions remained identical throughout each experiment, the cage and container were placed inside a soundproofed, ventilated chamber with controlled temperature. Skinner termed this apparatus the **operant chamber**, but it is more popularly known as the *Skinner box* (see Figure 7.8).

Reinforcement and Punishment Are the Conditioning Factors

When the consequence of a behavior increases the likelihood that the behavior will be repeated—for example, when a food pellet rolls down the chute after a rat pushes the correct lever—the behavior is said to have been reinforced, and the food pellet is a *reinforcer*. When a consequence reduces the likelihood that the behavior will be repeated—for example, if a shock follows the pressing of the wrong lever—the behavior has been punished, and the shock is a *punisher*.

Both **reinforcement** and **punishment** can be either *positive* or *negative*. Here the terms "positive" and "negative" **do not** mean "good" and "bad." (What would "good punishment" look like?) Instead, the term *positive* refers to the *addition* or presentation of something following a behavior, and the term *negative* refers to the *removal* of something. Think of positive and negative reinforcement and punishment in terms of addition and subtraction rather than pleasantness and unpleasantness.

Positive reinforcement occurs when the frequency or probability of a behavior is increased as a result of the addition or presentation of something following the performance of the behavior. A bar is pressed and the rat receives food; you smile at a baby and she smiles back; you start going to sleep earlier and your grades improve—all of these consequences are positive reinforcers. They increase the likelihood of the behavior being repeated or continuing by the addition of something—generally something rewarding.

On the other hand, **negative reinforcement** occurs when a behavior is reinforced by the removal or avoidance of something. A bar is pressed and shocks *stop*; you smile and make silly faces at a screaming baby and she *stops* crying; you tell your professor that your dog ate the finished version of your final paper (and your grandmother ate the dog) and you *avoid* the poor grade you might otherwise have received—all of these consequences are negative reinforcers. They also increase the likelihood of the behavior being repeated (or continuing), but do so by removing or allowing one to avoid something—generally something unpleasant or aversive.

Positive punishment occurs when the consequence of a behavior is the addition or presentation of something, generally something aversive. The wrong bar is pressed and the rat is shocked; the baby whines continuously and is spanked for it; you download your final paper from an Internet website and receive an F grade for plagiarism—these are examples of positive punishers. They *decrease* the likelihood of the behavior being repeated (or continuing) through the addition or presentation of something—generally something unpleasant or aversive.

Negative punishment occurs when the consequence of a behavior is the removal of something. The wrong bar is pressed and the rat's food disappears down a trap door; the baby starts to whine and her mother's smile fades; you begin partying too hard on weekends and your previously high grades tumble—all are examples of negative punishers. They also decrease the likelihood of the behavior being repeated (or continuing), but do so through the removal of something—generally something rewarding.

One important point needs to be made about reinforcement and punishment. Although reinforcers tend to be rewarding, and punishments tend to be unpleasant or aversive, this is not always the case. A reinforcer is *anything* that increases the likelihood of a behavior continuing or being repeated; a punisher is *anything* that decreases the likelihood of a behavior continuing or being repeated. Yet, consider the case of a child starving for attention from his or her mother, who generally ignores the child. Such a child might prefer anger, shouting, and even spanking to nothing at all, and may do things that elicit anger. Such a child learns to "push his mother's buttons." In this case, anger and shouting—which most of us would consider a punishment—may actually serve as reinforcement.

Shaping: The Building Blocks of Operant Behavior

Now let us suppose you want to try to teach a rat to press a bar. In this case, bar pressing would be termed the **operant behavior**, or the behavior you are attempting to condition. If operant conditioning is to work, bar pressing must be reinforced. But suppose days go by and the rat never once presses the bar spontaneously? We could all grow old waiting for operant conditioning to occur. For this reason, operant conditioning usually involves **shaping by successive approximation**, or more simply, shaping. Shaping involves successive reinforcement of those behaviors that come increasingly closer to the behavior you ultimately wish to reinforce. It is shaping that is responsible for the astonishing tricks that animal trainers routinely are able to teach their animals.

Suppose you wished to train your dog to play basketball. You might start by reinforcing the dog with praise and biscuits every time he walks close to the ball—the closer he comes, the more praise and biscuits. You might then *fade* or slowly discontinue reinforcement until he starts lapping or gnawing at the ball, at which time reinforcement would begin again, continuing until it seems you had gotten as far as you were going to get rewarding lapping and gnawing behavior.

Luckily, reinforcing a particular response frequently has the effect of also reinforcing similar responses, a phenomenon known as *response generalization*. You might now discontinue reinforcement once more until the dog, as a result

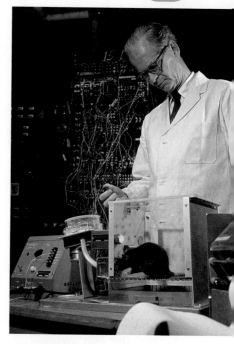

▲ **B. F. Skinner (1904–1990) in His Laboratory.**

Positive reinforcement ▶
When a behavior is reinforced through the addition or presentation of something that increases the likelihood that the behavior will be repeated. Generally it is something pleasant or rewarding that is added or presented.

Negative reinforcement ▶
When a behavior is reinforced through the removal of something that decreases the likelihood of the behavior. Generally it is something aversive or unpleasant that is removed in negative reinforcement.

Positive punishment ▶
When the consequence of a behavior is the addition or presentation of something that decreases the likelihood that the behavior will be repeated. Generally it is something unpleasant or aversive that is added or presented.

Shaping by successive approximation (shaping for short) ▶ Successive reinforcement of those operant behaviors that come increasingly closer to the behavior one ultimately wishes to reinforce.

Negative punishment ▶ When the consequence of a behavior is the removal of something reinforcing, generally something rewarding.

Operant behavior ▶ Any behavior of an organism that produces a consequence that is either reinforcing or punishing. In radical behaviorist experimental research, the *operant behavior* is the behavior the experimenter is attempting to shape or condition.

Primary reinforcer ▶ Any consequence of behavior that is intrinsically reinforcing to virtually any member of the species being conditioned. Primary reinforcers are intrinsically reinforcing because they are essential for the survival or reproduction of the organism (examples: food, water, sex, air, shelter, etc.).

Secondary reinforcer ▶ A reinforcer that has become associated through conditioning with one or more primary reinforcers (Examples: money and status).

of generalization, moves from lapping to picking up the ball in its mouth. At this point, reinforcement begins again. And so forth until you have a champion basket-shooter.

Of course, actual dog training is not this simple, but this is the basic idea of shaping through successive approximation. *Chaining* is a related type of conditioning that is useful when very complex behaviors are being taught (such as doggie basketball). Rather than reinforcing behaviors that come increasingly close to the desired behavior, behaviors are reinforced that form a chain—with each new behavior acting as a cue for the next. In this way, sequences of behaviors are taught by reinforcing each successive element in the chain.

Reinforcers Differ in Strength and Origin

What makes a good reinforcer for an organism? That depends on which organism we're talking about. A goldfish, a rat, and a human being undoubtedly would each find different things reinforcing. This question was addressed by David Premack (1971). Premack found that determining a good reinforcer is a simple matter of noting the length of time the individual engages in a particular behavior when a number of behaviors are freely available. If I spend more time listening to jazz music than going to football games, I suppose I would press more bars (or go to more bars) to hear jazz than to get football tickets.

Premack used this observation as the foundation for what has come to be known as the Premack principle. Simply put, the Premack principle states that high-probability behaviors—those that are freely chosen when other options are available—are good reinforcers for low-probability behaviors—those that are unlikely to be freely chosen. In other words, strong reinforcers can be used to reinforce weak reinforcers.

For example, in the past my kids loved watching classic Japanese films and hated cleaning their room. Cleaning their room was a (way) low-probability behavior, and watching samurai films was a high-probability behavior. Taking advantage of the Premack principle I one day announced: "You can watch *Seven Samurai*, but *only* after you've cleaned your room!" Suddenly, the low-probability behavior becomes a high-probability behavior.

While different individuals find different things reinforcing, certain reinforcers automatically apply to virtually all members of a species, because they are essential for the survival or reproduction of the organism. These are known as **primary reinforcers**. For example, food, water, and sex are primary reinforcers. However, some reinforcers that are not automatically related to survival and reproductive success can nonetheless prove to be just as powerful as primary reinforcers. That is because the organism previously has been *conditioned* to associate them with primary reinforcers. These are termed **secondary reinforcers**. Money and status are excellent examples. Bits of paper and job titles have no intrinsic value as reinforcers for a human being, but many human beings have been conditioned to associate money and status with food and shelter, pleasure, romantic success, and so forth. Under many circumstances, secondary reinforcers can be just as powerful as primary reinforcers.

Reinforcement Schedules Affect Conditioning

Operant conditioning depends on desired behaviors being reinforced or undesirable behaviors punished. But is it essential for the behavior to be reinforced or punished *each time* it occurs? Not at all. Indeed, from the standpoint of conditioning, in most cases it is better that reinforcement *not* occur on a continuous basis, an important finding of operant conditioning research that we now explore.

CONTINUOUS VERSUS PARTIAL REINFORCEMENT

Let us say you were playing a slot machine in Las Vegas and it paid a jackpot every time you inserted a quarter. In other words, your behavior (slipping the coin into the slot) was being continuously reinforced. Now consider what you would do if the machine suddenly *stopped* paying. While the payouts were flowing, you would be highly likely to continue playing. It is hard to stop playing a machine that seems intent on paying you each time it is played. However, after a few tries with no payoff, you would likely conclude that the machine had "gone cold" and move on. The behavior of feeding quarters into that machine, while initially strong, would quickly have been extinguished. The term *extinguish* is used in operant conditioning theory in much the same way *extinction* is used in classical conditioning—to indicate that a learned behavior has ceased to occur.

◄ Shaping. Animals can be taught astonishing tricks through the use of shaping with successive reinforcement and chaining.

Now consider a slot machine that never plays *too* long without a jackpot, but does not pay off *each* time you drop in your quarter. This is the sort of machine that keeps a person glued to it until the player is stone cold broke; and, in fact, all slot machines are programmed to pay off in this way. This is because jackpots, while unpredictable, seem assured *if the person waits long enough.* "It's got to pay off sooner or later." **Partial reinforcement** is the term used to describe situations such as this, where reinforcement occurs only periodically. Although behaviors may be acquired very quickly using **continuous reinforcement** schedules, they are generally much more enduring and difficult to extinguish when they are conditioned with partial reinforcement. This rather counterintuitive fact is known as the **partial reinforcement effect**.

There are reasons why most examples of operant learning—in the laboratory or the "real world"—occur as a result of partial rather than continuous reinforcement, beyond the fact that partial reinforcement generally leads to a stronger, more enduring conditioning. First, continuous reinforcement rarely occurs in the natural world, whereas partial reinforcement is everywhere. One of my favorite websites reports snippets of conversations overheard in public places around New York City. Here is one I found not long ago. A young man is attempting to romantically entice a young woman on the subway:

> *Young man: "My name is TC. You know what that stands for? Too Cool, Too Cute, or Too Crazy. You gotta find out which."*
>
> *The woman says nothing.*
>
> *Young man: "You look depressed."*

If this approach were never to work for this young man, it is unlikely that he would continue to use it. It would have been extinguished and ended up on in the grand dustbin of unsuccessful pickup "lines." But even if the approach did work for him some of the time, it is highly unlikely to work for him *every time.* Thus, if he repeats this line frequently, it surely is a result of partial rather than continuous reinforcement.

PARTIAL REINFORCEMENT SCHEDULES

If continuous reinforcement is difficult to find in the natural world, it is extremely difficult to *maintain* in the laboratory. Rewarding a rat with food

Partial reinforcement
▶ When a behavior is reinforced periodically rather than continuously. Partial reinforcement can be determined by the passage of time (an interval schedule) or the number of times an organism performs a behavior (a ratio schedule).

Continuous reinforcement ▶ When a behavior is reinforced every time it occurs.

Partial reinforcement effect ▶ The name given to research findings which show that conditioned behaviors are more enduring and difficult to extinguish when they are reinforced periodically rather than continuously.

▲ **Trapped by the Partial Reinforcement Effect.** Slot machines are programmed to pay off according to partial reinforcement schedules. This is what makes it so difficult to stop playing a particular machine (and slot machines generally).

Fixed-interval (FI) schedule ▶ A partial reinforcement schedule that provides reinforcement for the first operant behavior after a specific interval of time has passed.

Variable-interval (VI) schedule ▶ A partial reinforcement schedule that provides reinforcement at unpredictable time intervals.

Fixed-ratio (FR) schedule ▶ A partial reinforcement schedule that provides reinforcement after a specific number of operant behavioral responses.

Variable-ratio (VR) schedule ▶ A partial reinforcement schedule that provides reinforcement after an unpredictable number of behavioral responses.

every time it performs a behavior can be costly and time-consuming, as Skinner found out early in his career. In experimenting with partial reinforcement to save time and money, Skinner discovered its advantages in conditioning. Skinner eventually devised four distinct partial reinforcement schedules, highlighted in Figure 7.9 (e.g., Skinner, 1956):

Fixed-interval (FI) schedules (the blue line in Figure 7.9) provide reinforcement for the first response after a *specific interval of time* has passed (e.g., after a minute, hour, or day). The number of responses has no effect on the timing of reinforcement. Therefore, the organism quickly learns exactly when reinforcement will occur, and also realizes that it matters not a whit if it were to press the bar one time or a thousand times unless that time interval has elapsed. Consequently, there is usually a reduction in the number of operant behaviors (bar presses) immediately following reinforcement in a fixed-interval schedule. There is an increase in the behavior (bar presses) just before the time that reinforcement (food pellet) is scheduled to occur once again.

Variable-interval (VI) schedules (the yellow line in Figure 7.9) provide reinforcement at *unpredictable time intervals* (e.g., every 5 minutes *on average*). Here the organism is never sure exactly when reinforcement will occur, although it still realizes that the number of responses is irrelevant. Therefore, variable-interval schedules produce far more consistent and continuous responding than fixed-interval schedules, but responding is still on the slow side given that the number of repetitions does not influence the pattern of reinforcement.

Fixed-ratio (FR) schedules (the red line in Figure 7.9) provide reinforcement after a *specific number of responses*. This is the logic of factory piecework, where workers are paid by the number of items produced rather than the number of hours worked. Under such conditions, the more behaviors that the organism provides, the greater the quantity of reinforcement. Therefore, organisms on fixed-ratio schedules may briefly rest following reinforcement, but then put their noses back to the grindstone and respond at a very high rate.

Variable-ratio (VR) schedules (the green line in Figure 7.9) provide reinforcement after an *unpredictable number of responses*. This is the slot-machine reinforcement schedule. Here the organism is unsure of how many times it must respond for reinforcement to take place. Just as we found with fixed-ratio schedules, variable-ratio schedules are correlated with a very high response rate. However, unlike with fixed-ratio schedules, the organism does not typically pause for rest following reinforcement in variable-ratio schedules—it just continues to respond at high rates to reach the next reinforcement. This is because the organism truly has no idea when reinforcement will occur. Conditioning acquired in this way is the most difficult to extinguish.

Punishment May Be Effective but Can Also Pose Problems

Many misperceptions and outright urban legends surround B. F. Skinner and the theory he developed. One widely repeated story is that Skinner raised his daughter Deborah in a cramped "Skinner box" to "test his theories." Supposedly this so traumatized the poor girl that when she came into adulthood she sued her famous father, and then, at the age of 31, became "frankly psychotic" and committed suicide in a bowling alley in Billings, Montana (Slater, 2004, p. 7). In fact, Deborah Skinner-Buzan is alive and entirely sane—but a little peeved at the stories about herself and her father (Skinner-Buzan, 2004). Another wildly inaccurate myth portrays Skinner as a "mad scientist" who enjoyed shocking rats and using other punishments to "teach" organisms new behaviors.

As it happens, Skinner (1938) believed that punishment for undesirable behavior was in most cases a poor teacher in comparison to reward for desirable behavior (a belief that helped spur him to oppose corporal punishment in the schools). If anything, Skinner *underestimated* the usefulness of punishment. Contrary to Skinner's early beliefs, punishment can be an effective deterrent to behavior—particularly if the punishment is intensely unpleasant, inescapable, consistently applied, and follows the unwanted behavior immediately (Azrin, Holz, & Hake, 1963; Bennett, 1998; Boe & Church, 1967; Matson & Taras, 1989).

However, punishment does pose problems not posed by the use of positive and negative reinforcement. There are two principal problems with the use of punishment in operant conditioning. First, many people simply consider the use of punishment inhumane, a sentiment reflected in the lessening of social tolerance for corporal punishment of children occurring in many parts of the world (Gershoff, 2002).

Second, while punishment may alter an individual's behavior in a desirable direction, it may simultaneously alter his or her behavior in *undesirable* directions (Hiby, Rooney, & Bradshaw, 2004). In other words, punishment can have side effects. For example, it can engender anger and resentment, leading to revenge or retaliation. Bennett (1998) cites the example of workplace shootings by former employees who considered their supervisors to be unjustly punitive. Similarly (but less dramatically), teenagers who are "grounded" for some rule infraction may stop breaking that rule, but begin breaking other rules with a vengeance.

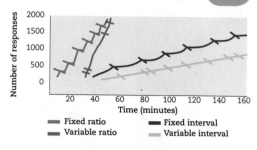

▲ **FIGURE 7.9 Four Reinforcement Schedules for Operant Conditioning.** As you can see, ratio schedules produce the highest rates of responding because under ratio schedules more behavior = more reinforcement. (Note: The slash marks on the graph lines represent instances of reinforcement.) Under interval schedules, reinforcement is limited by the passage of time, and increased numbers of behaviors do not produce greater reward. However, each specific reinforcement schedule produces its own typical pattern.

IN SUMMARY

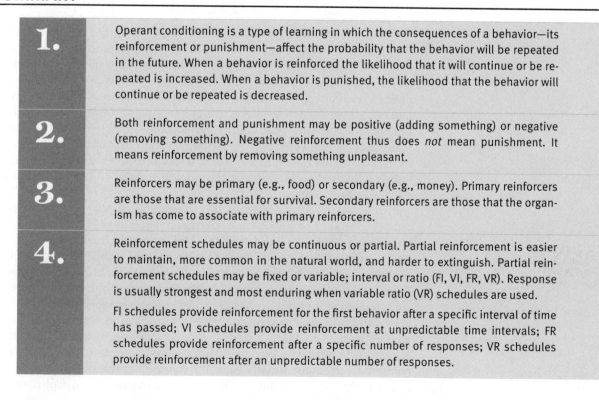

1. Operant conditioning is a type of learning in which the consequences of a behavior—its reinforcement or punishment—affect the probability that the behavior will be repeated in the future. When a behavior is reinforced the likelihood that it will continue or be repeated is increased. When a behavior is punished, the likelihood that the behavior will continue or be repeated is decreased.

2. Both reinforcement and punishment may be positive (adding something) or negative (removing something). Negative reinforcement thus does *not* mean punishment. It means reinforcement by removing something unpleasant.

3. Reinforcers may be primary (e.g., food) or secondary (e.g., money). Primary reinforcers are those that are essential for survival. Secondary reinforcers are those that the organism has come to associate with primary reinforcers.

4. Reinforcement schedules may be continuous or partial. Partial reinforcement is easier to maintain, more common in the natural world, and harder to extinguish. Partial reinforcement schedules may be fixed or variable; interval or ratio (FI, VI, FR, VR). Response is usually strongest and most enduring when variable ratio (VR) schedules are used.

FI schedules provide reinforcement for the first behavior after a specific interval of time has passed; VI schedules provide reinforcement at unpredictable time intervals; FR schedules provide reinforcement after a specific number of responses; VR schedules provide reinforcement after an unpredictable number of responses.

5. Most examples of operant conditioning involve shaping. Shaping involves reinforcement of those behaviors that come increasingly closer to the behavior you actually wish to reinforce. Chaining is similar to shaping, but is primarily used to condition sequences of complex behaviors.

6. Punishment is sometimes effective (particularly if it is severe, inescapable, consistently applied, and immediate), but it may present problems, such as the desire for revenge. Punishment is also considered inhumane by many.

RETRIEVE!

1. What did B. F. Skinner alter about the *law of effect* to describe operant conditioning? Why did he alter it in this way?

2. When a behavior is reinforced by the removal of an unpleasant stimulus it is known as _____. When a behavior is punished by the presentation of an unpleasant stimulus it is known as _____.

3. Distinguish the four principal partial reinforcement schedules from one another: fixed-interval (FI), variable-interval (VI), fixed-ratio (FR), and variable-ratio (VR).

4. What makes a good reinforcer, according to David Premack? What is the Premack principle?

What Are the Limits of Operant Conditioning?

Operant conditioning occurs on a daily basis out in the real world. Consider the small child who throws a tantrum in the middle of the grocery store when his or her parent won't buy that bag of cookies. The child expresses such anguish, at such a loud volume, that the parent—stressed and embarrassed to the limit—eventually gives in and buys the cookies. But not always. Sometimes the parent strives valiantly to stick to his or her guns, and succeeds. Unfortunately, this lack of consistency sets up a variable-ratio (VR) schedule of reinforcement, and the child's behavior is virtually certain to continue because he or she never knows just how much howling it will take to get the reward. The child knows only that, eventually, the reward will come. This is why, in disciplining children, consistency is critical.

Romantic partners are also using operant conditioning on a daily basis in attempts to change or control their partners. If you have ever been involved in a long-term romantic relationship, think of the many times you have attempted to use subtle (or not-so-subtle) reinforcers and punishments to alter your partner's behavior. Much of the time, of course, these attempts are doomed to failure (Christensen & Jacobson, 2000). However, if the behavior in question isn't too deeply ingrained, operant conditioning can work wonders.

I recall that I used to love to listen to a particular musician (John Coltrane), whom my then-girlfriend hated. Whenever she was present in the room and I happened to put on a Coltrane album (it was the years of vinyl), she wouldn't complain—she'd just quietly leave the room (negative punishment). Without consciously realizing what was happening, I began playing Coltrane less and less frequently when she was in the house until I stopped altogether. If she had come right out and said, "I can't stand Coltrane—don't play him while I'm around," I probably would have just tried to argue her into liking the music, a foolish waste of everyone's time.

Like classical conditioning, operant conditioning has been successfully used to treat psychological distress and alter behavior in prisons, hospitals, and other institutions. Whether it is distress or "bad behavior" that is being treated through operant conditioning, the basis is the same: desired behaviors and mental states are shaped using reinforcement and punishment. Consider *contingency management* (CM) as described in the "Freeze Frame" that opened this chapter. These are operant conditioning programs set up in substance abuse treatment facilities, which work by reinforcing desired behaviors with prizes (including cash), chances to win prizes, or tokens that may be redeemed for various privileges (Higgins, Silverman, & Heil, 2007; Kellog et al., 2005; Rash et al., 2008).

Cognition and Evolution Also Affect Operant Conditioning

Just as the movements to incorporate cognition and the evolutionary history of species that began in the 1960s suggested that there were limits to what classical conditioning could accomplish, these movements have had effects just as powerful, or more so, on the way psychologists think about operant conditioning.

COGNITIVE MAPS AND LATENT LEARNING

The first challenge to B. F. Skinner's view that all behavior could be explained by referring to reinforcement and punishment alone arrived in the work of Edward Tolman (1886–1959). Tolman was a dedicated behaviorist. However, unlike Skinner, he believed that it would be possible to use scientific methods to study the impact of *mental activity* on operant conditioning. Most of Tolman's work involved observing rats as they learned to navigate mazes to obtain food (positive reinforcement). According to radical behaviorist views, nonreinforced rats should be expected not to learn to run mazes because they receive no reinforcement for doing so. However, Tolman believed there was a crucial difference between *learning* and *performance*—that is, between the actual learning, and the behavior which demonstrated that learning had taken place.

In a famous experiment, Tolman and Honzik (1930) placed one group of rats in a complicated maze containing a "goal" box. The rats were given no food reinforcement for any movement toward the goal box. As expected, these rats wandered aimlessly through the maze. With no reward of food as a goal, they had no reason to strive to locate the goal box. The researchers gave a second group of rats continuous reinforcement for locating the food box, and after 11 days, these rats learned to navigate the maze. Both of these results are predicted by operant learning theory.

But Tolman and Honzik then placed a *third* group of rats in the maze. At first, the investigators did *not* reinforce these rats, and the rats wandered as aimlessly as had those in the first nonreinforced group. However, on the 11th day, Tolman and Honzik suddenly began to reinforce rats in the third group for finding the box. Within 1 day this group had caught up to the group that had been continuously reinforced in the speed with which they could navigate the maze. Given that Group 3 "learned" in 1 day as much as Group 2 had in 11 days, Tolman concluded that, in fact, Group 3 rats actually had been *learning* the maze all along—they merely had no motivation to *perform* maze-running until they were reinforced for doing so.

Tolman (1948) suggested that during the nonreinforcement period, the rats had been forming a **cognitive map**—a mental representation of how the maze was constructed. As soon as the rats began to be reinforced, they accessed this cognitive map to solve the puzzle of the maze. Tolman used the term **latent**

▲ Reinforcing Tantrums on a Variable Ratio Schedule.

Cognitive map ▶ A mental representation of the structure, location, or attributes of some phenomenon.

Latent learning ▶ Learning that occurs without obvious reinforcement, and that is not apparent in behavior.

Cognitive behaviorism ▶
The psychological school founded by Edward Tolman. Cognitive behaviorists agree with radical behaviorists that behavior is lawful and can be analyzed using concepts of reinforcement and punishment, but they disagree that this analysis must necessarily exclude cognition. Cognitive behaviorists pioneered the concepts of cognitive maps and latent learning.

learning to describe learning that takes place without reinforcement and which is not necessarily apparent in actual behavior. Tolman's brand of behaviorism, which acknowledges the intervention of cognition in learning, came to be known as **cognitive behaviorism**.

EVOLUTIONARY CONSTRAINTS AND OPPORTUNITIES

As explained earlier, evolutionary theorists have demonstrated that the evolutionary history of an organism can have powerful effects on the way classical conditioning occurs—or does not occur. This is also true for operant conditioning, a fact that was brought home to learning psychologists in 1961 by B. F. Skinner's students Keller Breland and Marian Breland. The Brelands had initially subscribed to the equipotentiality notion—the idea that learning mechanisms were equally applicable to all types of behavior and all forms of animal life. According to this idea, barring the physically impossible (e.g., teaching a pig to fly), virtually any animal could be taught to perform virtually any behavior, given the right reinforcement techniques and enough patience.

Breland and Breland found, however, that certain animals *would not* learn specific behaviors in spite of the fact that there appeared to be no reason why they should not. Take the Miserly Raccoon. Breland and Breland attempted to use shaping by successive approximation to teach a raccoon to pick up coins and deposit them in a "piggy bank" box as part of a proposed bank display for promoting thrift. The Brelands had no trouble teaching the raccoon to pick up coins by reinforcing his performance with food. They also had no trouble getting the animal to learn to slip the coins into the box's slot. However, the raccoon would *not* let the coins go, but dipped them in and out of the slot, and rubbed them together in his paws, in the Brelands' words, "in a most miserly fashion" (Breland & Breland, 1961, p. 682). The problem is that raccoons are predisposed to rub food together in their paws to remove dirt or the shells of crayfish. The raccoon had come to associate the coins with receiving food and was treating the coins as food.

Or consider the Profligate Pigs. The Brelands tried to get one pig after another to perform a similar demonstration of thrift by picking up large wooden "dollar" coins and depositing them in a piggy bank, a maneuver for which they would be rewarded by food. At first the pigs were eager and learned the trick easily. But after a few weeks, the pigs began to slow down their efforts, and after picking up the coins they would proceed to drop them on the ground and root the coins (*rooting* is the pigs' instinctive nudging in the dirt with their snouts to discover insects and other treasures). Or these pigs might toss the coins in the air and leave them where they lay. These pigs did *not* understand the value of a dollar.

Instinctive drift ▶ When an instinctive pattern of behavior interferes with the operant conditioning of a behavior.

The Brelends finally realized that when operant conditioning is used to condition a behavior that conflicts with an instinctive behavior, instinct usually wins out—a phenomenon the Brelands labeled **instinctive drift**. They titled their article "The Misbehavior of Organisms" in an ironic tip of the hat to their mentor, B. F. Skinner who first set out the principles of operant conditioning of animals in a book titled *The Behavior of Organisms*.

Thus, by the mid-1960s, operant conditioning theorists also had come to acknowledge that evolutionary biology places constraints on what an animal can learn through operant conditioning. There are some things that individuals of a given species cannot learn, or have great difficulty learning, because these things conflict with innate patterns of behavior (instinct) or psychological adaptations. On the other hand, there are things that each species can learn with particular ease as a result of its evolutionary history.

DOMAIN-SPECIFIC LEARNING

Recall from our discussion of classical conditioning that some innate responses (e.g., nausea) are more easily conditioned through the use of certain neutral stimuli (spoiled food) than others (flashing lights). Something very

▲ **Instinctive Drift Can Ruin an Experimenter's Day.** Keller and Marian Breland (1961) found that if attempts to shape an animal's behavior through operant conditioning conflicted with the animal's instinctive behavior patterns, conditioning would not be successful. Because raccoons instinctively rub food together in their paws and pigs root for food, these animals could not be taught to deposit coins in piggy banks.

similar holds true for operant conditioning as well. Each species differs in the ease or difficulty with which it can be taught specific tasks through the use of specific types of reinforcements.

For example, it would be quite difficult to use operant conditioning to teach a pigeon to peck at computer keyboard keys to avoid electric shock. However, it would be a relatively simple matter to condition the pigeon to flap its wings to avoid shock. This is because wing-flapping, but not pecking, is among the pigeon's innate mechanisms for avoiding danger. On the other hand, a pigeon can easily be taught to peck at a computer keyboard using the positive reinforcement of food, because pecking is one of the pigeon's innate mechanisms for obtaining food (Bolles, 1970; Foree & LoLordo, 1973; Shettleworth, 1975).

Contemporary evolutionary psychologists studying learning generally explain such findings by suggesting that learning mechanisms are *domain specific* rather than *domain general* as behaviorists have always proposed (e.g., Gallistel, 2000). If you recall from Chapter 3, by *domain specific*, evolutionary theorists mean that a mechanism (in this case, a learning mechanism) evolved to help solve a *specific* problem faced recurrently by our evolutionary ancestors. This contrasts with the domain-general views of behaviorists that learning mechanisms such as classical and operant conditioning apply across the board to all species, stimuli, and reinforcements. According to the evolutionary view, the mechanism a pigeon uses when learning to escape from electric shocks is a fundamentally different mechanism from the one a rat might use in a similar situation. Thus, it may be misleading to place both of these mechanisms in the single category "operant learning."

IN SUMMARY

1. Operant conditioning has broad applicability in everyday life, animal training, and treatment of psychological distress and antisocial behavior.

2. Edward Tolman's concepts of the cognitive map and latent learning were the first substantial challenge to the view that all behavior could be explained through contingencies of reinforcement and punishment.

3. The evolutionary history of an organism puts constraints on what it may learn and how easily it may learn specific tasks.

RETRIEVE!

1. Explain what is meant by the terms *cognitive map* and *latent learning*. How did Tolman discover the existence of the cognitive map and latent learning?

2. When an attempt is made to use operant conditioning to shape a behavior that conflicts with an instinctive behavior, instinct usually wins out. This phenomenon is known as _____.

a) instinctive drift

b) domain-specific learning

c) genetic drift

d) counter-conditioning

▲ **Observational Learning.**

Observational learning
▶ Learning through the observation of others. Mechanisms of observational learning include modeling and vicarious reinforcement.

Modeling ▶ Learning through imitation of the behaviors of individuals whom one admires.

What Is Observational Learning?

Early learning theorists such as Watson and Skinner tended to ignore an important fact of learning that seems quite obvious now: At least some animals—particularly but not exclusively humans—learn certain things in the absence of conditioning, merely through observation. In 1941, Neal Miller and John Dollard (1941) first described **observational learning** (sometimes called *social learning*)—the ways in which an organism might learn by observing the experiences of *others*, rather than through his or her own experience (e.g., Bandura, 1977). Theories of observational learning became more important as the influence of behaviorism waned during the 1960s and 1970s.

Modeling Is Learning through Imitation

Observing and imitating the behavior of others is an important part of the way human beings interact, perhaps because imitation facilitates *empathy* among people—understanding and caring about how other people feel (Iacoboni, 2009). An important type of learning through imitation is known as **modeling**. Dollard and Miller claimed that children were especially prone to imitation of the behaviors of adults they admired because of their identification with the adult and desire to be like him or her. In other words, children use favored adults as models for their own behavior. The best-known series of studies based on the work of Dollard and Miller were carried out by social-cognitive learning theorist Albert Bandura and his associates. They are known by the affectionate nickname of the "Bobo doll" experiments (Bandura, 1965; Bandura, Ross, & Ross, 1961, 1963). As depicted in Figure 7.10, in these experiments live adult models (and, in later studies, filmed ones) were used to examine the possible consequences of adult role-modeling of violent behaviors in the presence of children. In the original version, preschoolers were left in the company of an adult model who would either punch and kick an inflatable clown doll ("Bobo")—the kind with a rounded, weighted base that springs back up when knocked down—or, in the control conditions, the adult would do nothing to the doll. When left on their own with "Bobo," children shown the aggressive scenario were much more likely to behave roughly toward the doll than those shown the nonviolent scenario (Bandura et al., 1961).

However, the research team also noted that the boys were much more likely to behave aggressively than the girls and that the male adult models were more likely to elicit a violent imitative response than were the female adult models. The results of the Bobo modeling research suggested that boys in general (and aggressive children of both sexes) may be more vulnerable to the effects of violent role models, at least those in film or TV (Josephson 1987; see Chapter 10 for more on film and TV violence).

These early Bobo doll studies raised concerns about the effects on children of viewing violent television programs and films. However, early theories of

◀ **FIGURE 7.10** The "Bobo Doll" Experiments. In the "Bobo doll" experiments of Albert Bandura and his colleagues, children who observed an admired adult mistreating the inflatable doll were more likely than others to do the same when given the chance. *(Source: Bandura, Ross, & Ross, 1961.)*

modeling did not answer the question of why different children chose widely varying adult models to imitate. One child chooses the local drug dealer, and another, the local police officer. Why? More to the point, recent research (and ordinary experience) suggests that children seem much more likely to imitate other children than adults—particularly older children with higher status in the group (J. R. Harris, 1998, 2006). Think about it—when was the last time you met a child with an interest in 401k plans, health insurance, and local district elections? And, as Judith Rich Harris (1998) points out, when children *do* attempt to imitate adults—staying up late, speaking their minds plainly, interrupting others who are speaking, smoking, drinking, having sex, using swear words, and so forth—they are usually punished for it, not rewarded.

Vicarious Conditioning Is Learning by Observing Consequences

Modeling theory set the stage for the development of more sophisticated theories of observational learning. Following the initial "Bobo" studies, Bandura and his colleagues created a second series of studies where, rather than watching live displays, children watched films of adults kicking and punching the doll, whacking it with a mallet, and generally behaving pretty darn badly toward the doll. The other difference between these and the earlier studies was that in the films, the children were able to watch the adults experience either rewarding or punishing *consequences* for their behavior. There was also a version in which no consequences occurred at all.

As depicted in Figure 7.11, children who witnessed the punishment condition were much less likely to hit "Bobo" than those who witnessed either the reward condition or the no-consequence condition (Bandura 1965; Bandura et al., 1963). Bandura described these results as examples of **vicarious conditioning**, where observation of rewarding or punishing consequences experienced by others serves much the same function as being rewarded or punished oneself.

Interestingly, however, almost all the children could be induced to hit and punch the Bobo doll for a reward of cake and other goodies, regardless of whether they had witnessed reward, punishment, or no consequences. In Bandura's view this result was particularly alarming, demonstrating that *all* the children had acquired aggressive learning at some level, regardless of vicarious rewards or punishments (Bandura, 1965; Bandura, et al., 1963). Moreover, as with the earlier experiments in modeling, boys in Bandura's studies were more vulnerable to the effects of vicarious conditioning of aggression than were girls. As Figure 7.11 shows, boys' aggressive behaviors increased

Vicarious conditioning ▶
Learning through observing the rewarding or punishing consequences of other people's behavior.

Average Number of Agressive Responses

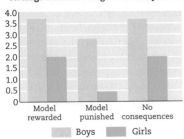

▲ FIGURE 7.11 Vicarious Conditioning of Aggression. In later experiments with the Bobo doll, Bandura and his colleagues demonstrated that observing aggressive behavior being punished may counter the effects of modeling and deter physical aggression in children. However, the deterrent effect of punishment was far more marked for girls than boys. *(Bandura, Ross, & Ross, 1963; Bandura, 1965.)*

Sequence A

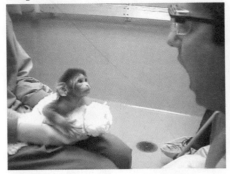
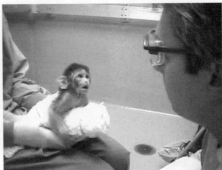

Sequence B

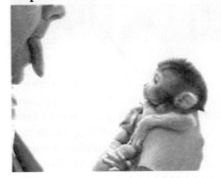
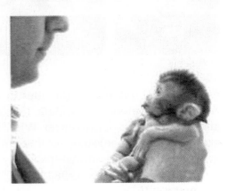

▲ FIGURE 7.12 Monkey See, Monkey Do. Monkeys as young as 1 day old will imitate the facial expressions of human beings. This adds to research demonstrating that the same neurons fire when monkeys use tools as when they observe others using tools. In Photo Sequence A, a 1-day old rhesus monkey imitates the open-mouthed expression of the adult human. In Sequence B, the adult's protruding tongue is returned by a 3-day-old monkey. *(Source: Ferrari et al., 2006.)*

more markedly than girls' in the reward and no consequence conditions, and boys who witnessed punishment were much less likely than girls to be deterred from aggressive behavior.

The "Bobo" studies and Albert Bandura's early work on observational learning were instrumental in sounding an early warning alarm about the presence of violence in the mass media. Could children learn to become aggressive by watching their favorite Saturday morning cartoon show? We will consider this question in detail later in this chapter.

Mirror Neurons May Be the "How" of Observational Learning

Mirror neurons ▶ A neuron that fires both when an animal performs an action and when the animal observes another performing the same action. Mirror neurons are associated with imitation of others' behavior, and comprehension of others' thoughts, intentions, and emotions.

Human beings are not the only ones who engage in observational learning. Researchers have found that pigeons can learn three distinct ways of obtaining food—pecking at a lever, stamping it with their foot, or sliding a door open—by watching other pigeons engaged in one method or the other (Klein & Zentall, 2003). In another series of experiments, capuchin monkeys learned how to open containers containing food by watching other capuchin monkeys fail at the task, but were unable to learn this task reliably by watching the same behavior in humans (the experimenters; Kuroshima, Kuwahata, & Fujita, 2008). And, like human infants, several-hour-old rhesus monkeys will imitate the facial expressions of human beings (Ferrari et al., 2006). It was these experiments with infant rhesus monkeys that set the stage for research into the mechanisms of observational learning—glimmerings of an idea of how observational learning actually operates. The answer may lie in a group of recently discovered neurons known as *mirror neurons*.

In a groundbreaking study, Giacomo Rizzolatti and his colleagues found that in the *premotor cortex* of the monkey brain there is a network of neurons that fire either when a monkey performs a particular action or when the monkey merely *observes* another monkey or a human performing that action (Rizzolatti, Fadiga, Gallese, & Fogassi, 1996). Rizzolatti's research team discovered these neurons by accident. One of the investigators (Fogassi) walked into the room where they had been studying neural activity in the brain of a macaque monkey as the monkey reached for various objects, including raisins from a bowl on the table. Fogassi himself casually reached for a raisin to eat, and the investigators were astonished to see that as the monkey watched Fogassi reach for the raisin, the same neurons fired that had previously fired when the monkey reached for a raisin himself (Dobbs, 2006)! Subsequent research showed that these neurons will fire if the animal *hears the sounds* of a behavior being performed that he or she has previously performed (Kohler et al., 2002). There also appear to be neurons in the monkey brain that are specifically dedicated to firing when the individual monkey uses a tool of some sort (e.g., a stick) or when the animal observes someone else using a tool (Ferrari, Rozzi, & Fogassi, 2005).

Rizzolatti and his colleagues use the term **mirror neuron** to describe a neuron that fires when an animal performs a particular action and also when the animal observes the action performed by someone else. These researchers hypothesize that mirror neurons allow the brain to create mental "representations" of observed behavior, allowing such behavior to be learned (Cataneo & Rizzolatti, 2009; Rizzolatti, Fadiga, Fogassi, & Gallese, 2002; Rizzolatti & Fabbri-Destro, 2010). In other words, at least some of the things we watch others do we mentally rehearse doing ourselves without realizing it. In remarkable research published in 2006, Pier Francesco Ferrari and his colleagues showed that rhesus monkeys possess mechanisms for imitating the facial expressions of adult human beings beginning on the first day of life (see Figure 7.12). This adds to research conducted during the 1980s showing that newborn human infants will also mimic the facial expressions of others.

You may be wondering whether it is premature to assume that human beings possess mirror neurons on the basis of studies of macaque and rhesus monkeys, and films of infants imitating the facial expressions of researchers. However, substantial evidence now exists that human beings possess even *more* of these neurons, and in more locations in the brain, than do monkeys. For example, researchers have found that neurons fire in the brains of human research participants in the same locations of the *anterior insula*—an area of the brain associated with emotional responses to sensory experiences—whether the participants were experiencing disgust themselves after inhaling a foul odor or observing *other people* showing facial expressions of disgust after inhaling the same odor (Wicker et al., 2003; see Figure 7.13). There may also be mirror neurons specific to speech. Some evidence suggests that the same neurons fire when we listen to someone speaking as when we ourselves speak, although this evidence is not without its critics (Gallese, Gernsbacher, Heyes, Hickock, & Iacoboni, 2011; Wilson, Saygin, Sereno, & Iacoboni, 2004).

Mirror neurons are also important in grasping the goals and intentions of others based upon their actions (Fogassi et al., 2005; Gallese, in Gallese et al., 2011; Iacoboni et al., 2005). This skill can be critical in the process of observational learning. Observing a behavior without comprehending the intention or goal behind the act can be a highly ambiguous experience. A person may need to understand the goals and intentions to comprehend the act itself. Without this basic comprehension, initial *attention* to the act—a first step in observational learning as described by Bandura (1977, 1986)—may never occur.

For example, as depicted in Figure 7.14, a mirror neuron in the premotor cortex of monkeys tested by Leonardo Fogassi and his colleagues (Fogassi et al., 2005) fired strongly when the monkeys observed the experimenter's hand moving to grasp an object, but not when the hand moved in similar way but

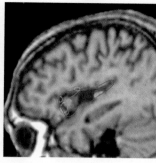

▲ **FIGURE 7.13 Mirrors of Disgust.** Research participants in the study by Wicker et al. (2003) observed film clips of other people smelling a disgusting odor (thumbnail photos at left). When they did so, neurons fired in areas of the insula similar to those that fired when the participants themselves smelled the odor. In this cross-section averaging of the brain responses of participants, neurons activated by experiencing disgust at actually smelling a foul odor are outlined in red; those activated by watching others experience disgust at the odor are circled in yellow. The blue outline highlights the entire insula area under investigation by Wicker et al. *(Source for thumbnail photos: Wicker et al., 2003; averaged brain image: Rizzolatti, Fogassi, & Gallese, 2006, p. 60.)*

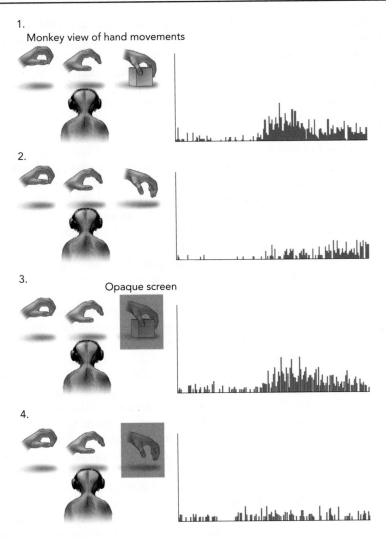

▲ **FIGURE 7.14 Using Mirror Neurons to Grasp Goals and Intentions.** As the graph of neuronal activity beside each image shows, the monkey's mirror neuron fired strongly as the monkey observed the researcher's hand moving to grasp the object (1), but only weakly when there was no apparent goal or intention (2). The neuron fired strongly again when the monkey knew there was an object behind the screen (3), but not when the monkey knew there was no object behind the screen (4). *(Source for diagram: Rizzolatti et al., 2006, p. 57; original source: Fogassi et al., 2005.)*

with no apparent intention or goal (no object to grasp). The neuron also fired strongly when the experimenter moved to grasp an object that was out of the monkeys' sight behind a screen—as long as the monkey knew the object was there—but did not fire when the monkey knew there was no object behind the screen. Similar tests have been carried out on human beings (Iacoboni et al., 2005).

Although the implications of all of this research are not entirely clear as yet, some researchers have proposed that the discovery of mirror neurons is among the most important in the history of neuroscience—on par with the discovery of DNA in the field of biology (Ramachandran, cited by Dobbs, 2006). In part it is because mirror neurons fire when observing the emotional experiences and language expressions of others that there is so much excitement surrounding their discovery. Some researchers believe that mirror neurons may hold the key to the development of *empathy* and language in human beings—as well as explaining mechanisms of observational learning and social interactions in general. At the level of mirror neurons, as we observe someone else experience something, we are experiencing the same thing ourselves (Rizzolatti et al., 2006)! Thus, networks of mirror neurons may represent important brain mechanisms by which human beings forge bonds with one another, communicate, and create human culture (Gallese, 2005).

Effects of Media Violence: An Unsettled, and Unsettling, Question

As briefly mentioned earlier, Albert Bandura's work on observational learning—in particular, the early "Bobo doll" studies—raised new fears about the presence of violence in the mass media. However, worries about violent media did not begin at the time of Bandura's early work. Concerns over violence in media have been voiced by parents and social critics probably ever since the first murder was described in literature. I recall being warned by teachers as a small child during the 1950s that if I continued to read *Batman* and trashy "true-crime" comic books I would inevitably turn into a "juvenile delinquent." Such warnings may seem a bit silly now, considering how wildly the mass media have proliferated in recent decades, with the result that depictions of violence are everywhere—in books, television, films, music, and video games. By the time the average American child has reached the age of 12, he or she will have witnessed more than 100,000 acts of violence on television alone (Signorielli, Gerbner, & Morgan, 1995). Because this estimate comes from research conducted in the 1990s, the true figure is now likely to be much higher. Other forms of media of greatest popularity with children are those that contain substantial amounts of violence (Anderson et al., 2003).

Depictions of violence have also grown more graphic, convincing, and frequently sadistic. There is a long road separating the 1950s *Batman* or *True Crime* from today's *Saw III*. Because there is widespread (but incorrect) perception that real-world violence is also more common or sadistic than in the past (Pinker, 2011), concerns about the effects of all these depictions of brutal violence on people's behavior have taken on a greater urgency, and a substantial body of behavioral science literature now exists exploring this topic, beginning with Bandura's "Bobo" experiments described earlier.

What is the verdict? Does watching media violence cause real-world aggression or violence through modeling or vicarious conditioning? For an increasing number of researchers and medical professionals, the answer is an unequivocal "Yes." For example, aggression researchers Brad Bushman and Craig Anderson assert that the question has been settled, and it is time to move away from asking *if* media violence causes aggression, to the question of *how* it does so (Anderson & Bushman, 2002; Anderson et al., 2010). Indeed, in 2001, the American Academy of Pediatrics issued a formal statement on media violence claiming that "more than 3,500 research studies have examined the association between media violence and violent behavior; all but 18 have shown a positive relationship" (American Academy of Pediatrics, 2001, p. 1223).

When a topic elicits strong opinions and emotions among the general public, strong statements from behavioral scientists and professional organizations usually follow. Sometimes these claims overstate what is actually known about a topic, and this is certainly the case for the question of the effects of media violence. As a quick example, not only is it factually untrue that 3,500 studies have shown a positive relationship between media violence and violent behavior (or even aggressive behavior—and there's a difference), but nothing like 3,500 studies have ever been published on the effects of media violence.[1] Even the lower claim issued in 2000 that "over 1,000 studies" have shown

---

[1]*In 2005 I entered the search terms* media violence, violent media, television violence, *and* violent video games *in the Psychinfo database—that lists virtually all published research*

▶ **Sadistic Media Violence Is Not New.** As these comic book covers from the 1940s and 1950s attest, extreme, sadistic violence is nothing new in mass media. However, with the advent of new movie and video-game technology, this violence has grown far more graphic and realistic.

such an effect (Congressional Public Health Summit, 2000) was a hefty exaggeration, not only of the number of published research studies but also of the consistency of the results of the research that has been conducted.

To some degree, these over-the-top statements are understandable. Human violence causes worldwide suffering on a scale so immense that it literally defies description in words. There is something particularly unsettling in the idea that our forms of entertainment feed upon, and may add to, this devastation and misery. That children are perhaps the most frequent consumers of this material makes it all the more upsetting. Nonetheless, in spite of confident claims made by some researchers, the warnings of professional organizations such as the AAP and the AMA, and the "gut feeling" of many—admittedly, myself among them—that all this media violence *must* have a damaging effect on human psychology and society, this question has by no means been settled (Browne & Hamilton-Giachritsis, 2005; Dahl & DellaVigna, 2008; Ferguson, 2010; Ferguson & Kilburn, 2010; Freedman, 2002; Olson, 2004; Savage & Yancey, 2008).

THE LINK BETWEEN MEDIA VIOLENCE AND AGGRESSION IS REAL, BUT SLIPPERY

It is not easy to sum up the research on the question of media violence and human aggression. There are two contradictory positions on this question, and both sides in the debate often use the same research to buttress their (opposing) positions! One side (sometimes dubbed "media pessimists") is convinced that there is more than adequate evidence to support the view that exposure to television, movie, and video game violence substantially increases the risk of aggressive and violent behavior in the real world (Anderson et al., 2003; Anderson et al., 2010; Huesmann, 2007; Huesmann & Taylor, 2006).

The other side (dubbed "media skeptics") insists that the research is not at all clear-cut—that it contains contradictory findings, inadequate research methods, focuses on trivial aggression while ignoring causes of serious real-world aggression, and has raised more questions than it has answered (Ferguson, 2010; Ferguson & Kilburn, 2010; Freedman, 2002; Olson, 2004; Savage, 2004). What makes this situation particularly difficult for a textbook author is

in psychology—and located fewer than 500 articles, only a portion of which consisted of actual research studies (many were reviews of research or commentaries).

that highly competent, thorough, and insightful articles have been written on both sides of the debate, and many of the issues hinge upon complex questions of scientific methodology and statistics that go far beyond what can be treated in an introductory textbook like this one.

As a relatively simple example of the difficulties in interpreting the research on media violence, look for a moment at Figure 7.15. The chart reproduced there was derived from a recent article written by two researchers from the "media pessimists" camp, L. Rowell Huesmann and Laramie Taylor (2006). The chart (which originally appeared in a slightly different version in the article by Bushman & Anderson, 2001) presents a powerful message: Only the correlation between cigarette smoking and lung cancer is stronger than the correlation between media violence and aggression.

However, there is a big problem in interpreting this chart. Aggression is an abstract concept with widely varying definitions and standards used to measure it. All the other outcomes listed in the chart (e.g., lung cancer, HIV, bone mass, or IQ scores) describe objective conditions with generally agreed-upon measurement standards. "Aggression" can mean anything from spreading a malicious rumor about a person to exploding a nuclear bomb in his living room. As discussed in Chapter 1, "aggression" as measured in laboratory research studies is quite often of the relatively mild variety, occasionally involving thoughts or behaviors that some reasonable people might not define as truly aggressive. Thus, we cannot really know from the chart exactly what it is that is associated with media violence, because research studies differ so radically in how they define and measure "aggression."

Moreover, there has been an unfortunate tendency for some writers to use the terms *aggression* and *violence* interchangeably. To say that media violence is linked to aggression—however you define aggression—is not the same as saying that media violence is linked to real-world *violence* (Savage, 2004).

Additionally, effects of violent media even on relatively trivial types of laboratory aggression are not even always found in research studies, despite what opponents of media violence may claim. As an example, Christopher Ferguson and his colleagues found no effect at all on levels of aggression in a laboratory experiment very similar to the one we discussed in detail in Chapter 1. If you recall, in that study university students exposed to violent video games were more likely to "blast" opponents in a computer game with bursts of punishing noise. However, when Ferguson and his colleagues replicated this experiment, they found no such effect (Ferguson et al., 2008).

Evidence Does Support Two Claims Putting aside the more extreme statements of the "pessimists" and "skeptics," however—and regardless of the true sizes of correlations and effects—enough evidence now exists to be able to make two claims: (a) There *is* a real link between media violence and various forms of aggressive thoughts, emotions, and behavior; but (b) this association is not at all straightforward, and not every person exposed to media violence is affected similarly.

It is likely that media violence has the strongest effect on levels of aggression in people with specific types of vulnerabilities—for example, those who have grown up in violent or abusive homes, who are already aggressive by temperament, are exposed to violent or aggressive peers, or who are particularly attracted to violent media for various reasons (Ferguson et al., 2008; Ferguson, San Miguel, & Hartley, 2009). As might be expected, boys and men seem to be more vulnerable to media effects on direct physical aggression, whereas girls seem more vulnerable to effects on indirect and verbal aggression (Anderson et al., 2003). It is also likely that media violence has no effect whatever on levels of aggression in a great many users.

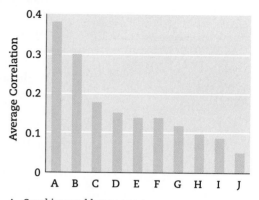

Correlation Between Media Violence and Aggression as Compared with Other Public Health Correlations

A. Smoking and lung cancer
B. Media violence and aggression
C. Condom use and sexually transmitted HIV
D. Passive smoking and lung cancer at work
E. Exposure to lead and IQ scores in children
F. Nicotine patch and smoking cessation
G. Calcium intake and bone mass
H. Homework and academic achievement
I. Exposure to asbestos and laryngeal cancer
J. Self-examination and extent of breast cancer

▲ **FIGURE 7.15 Is This Chart Appropriate?** The implication in the chart is that only the correlation between cigarette smoking and cancer is as strong as the correlation between violent media and aggression. However, all of the other outcomes describe objective conditions with agreed-upon measurement standards (e.g., lung cancer, HIV, IQ scores). Only "aggression" is an abstract concept with widely varying definitions and measurement standards. *(Chart reproduced from an article by L. Rowell Huesmann and Laramie Taylor, 2006, but based on an earlier chart from an article by Brad Bushman and Craig Anderson, 2001.)*

What about Actual Violence? If the link between media violence and aggression has been demonstrated, at least to some degree and for some people, what of the link between media violence and real-world *violence*? Regardless of some claims, the evidence for a connection between media violence and real-world crime and violence is extremely weak (Browne & Hamilton-Giachritsis, 2005; Ferguson et al., 2008; Ferguson & Kilburn, 2010; Olson, 2004; Savage 2004). Although a few studies have found a relationship (Anderson et al., 2003), these studies have not been able to adequately demonstrate a causal relationship between exposure to media and subsequent violent behavior.

For example, when Christopher Ferguson and his colleagues conducted correlational studies of exposure to violent video games and real-life violence as well as aggression, they at first found an apparent connection between a history of violent video game play and a subsequent record of violent criminal offenses. However, when the researchers controlled for their participants' history of exposure to abuse in the home, innate aggressive personality characteristics, and the influence of delinquent peers, they found that the apparent connection between video games and real-life violence disappeared. In other words, it was aggressive personality characteristics and history of abuse and exposure to violent peers that had a strong connection to a record of criminal offences—not the video games themselves (Ferguson et al., 2008; Ferguson et al., 2009). Ferguson and his colleagues speculated that the apparent connection seen between video games and real-world crime is best explained by the fact that innately aggressive people who have been exposed repeatedly to abuse or violence in the home or environment may be particularly attracted to violent video games (Ferguson et al., 2008).

However, the lack of convincing evidence of an effect of violent media on real-world violence is *not* the same as proof that no such causal link exists. It is an unfortunate fact of research life that it would be extraordinarily difficult to design a study that could adequately demonstrate a causal link between violent media and real-world violent behavior. Moreover, even if playing violent video games will not cause an ordinary person to go out and commit a violent crime, if these games in any way increase the probability that a vulnerable person will do so, media pessimists' warnings need to be taken seriously.

IN SUMMARY

1. Observational learning theory describes the ways in which individuals learn by observing others. Important concepts of observational learning include modeling and vicarious conditioning.

2. Recent research suggests that mirror neurons are the neural basis for observational learning, and may also be responsible for qualities such as empathy and the ability to comprehend the intentions of others.

3. Although strong opinions exist regarding the question of effects of violent media on aggression, the question has not been settled to everyone's satisfaction. There is a real link between viewing media violence and aggressive thoughts, emotions, and behavior, but this association is not straightforward, and not every person exposed to media violence is affected similarly. There is also an important difference between possible effects of violent media on *aggression* and effects on *violence*.

RETRIEVE!

1.	In what way does vicarious learning differ from simple modeling?
2.	How did the "Bobo doll" studies demonstrate modeling? Vicarious conditioning?
3.	Specialized neurons that fire when an animal observes an action performed by another individual and also fire when the animal performs that same action are known as _____.
4.	What are two claims about media violence that are well supported by evidence?

Looking Back

Chapter 7 in Review

WHAT IS LEARNING?

- In learning, the organism acquires some new knowledge or behavior as a result of experience. Learning can only be inferred, not observed. The changes in behavior or knowledge that occur in learning are relatively enduring.
- The capacity to learn is innate and unlearned, even if the result of some particular learning is cultural or experiential. Organisms are born "biologically prepared" to learn certain things but not other things.
- Habituation and sensitization are the simplest forms of learning. Habituation occurs when a stimulus at first causes a strong response, but the response is lessened over time due to repeated exposure. Sensitization occurs when the organism responds with increasing attention over time to a repeated stimulus.
- Associative learning occurs when an organism comes to associate two or more stimuli or events that occur close together in space and time.

WHAT IS CLASSICAL CONDITIONING?

- In classical conditioning, a neutral stimulus comes to elicit an unconditioned response (UCR) after it has been repeatedly paired with an unconditioned stimulus (UCS). After conditioning, the neutral stimulus is termed the conditioned stimulus (CS) and the unconditioned response is termed the conditioned response (CR).
- In classical conditioning, the neutral stimulus must be presented before the UCS, and the UCS must follow immediately after the neutral stimulus. Second-order conditioning involves the pairing of a CS with a new neutral stimulus until the UCR is elicited when the new neutral stimulus is presented.
- Extinction occurs when a CS is repeatedly presented over time without the UCS. However, if, after the CS is presented again later (without the UCS), the UCR may once again occur; this is known as spontaneous recovery. Renewal is the resurgence of an extinguished behavior in a different context from the one in which extinction originally occurred. Generalization has occurred when an organism displays a CR when exposed to a neutral stimulus that is similar, but not identical, to the original CS. Discrimination occurs when one neutral stimulus produces a CR, but another similar neutral stimulus does not.

WHAT ARE THE LIMITS OF CLASSICAL CONDITIONING?

- Classical conditioning cannot condition new behaviors; it can only elicit innate or reflexive behaviors. Classical conditioning involves cognition, and various cognitive elements must be in place for strong conditioning to occur. Classical conditioning is also limited by biological preparedness and by the environment in which it occurs.

WHAT IS OPERANT CONDITIONING?

- Thorndike's law of effect provided the basis for B. F. Skinner's development of operant conditioning techniques. In operant conditioning, the organism teaches itself by coming to associate a behavior with its consequences. Reinforcement of a behavior increases the likelihood that the behavior will continue or be repeated, while punishment decreases this likelihood. Reinforcers tend to be rewarding and punishers unpleasant or aversive, but this is not always the case.
- Operant conditioning frequently involves shaping through successive approximation. The Premack principle states that high probability behaviors are good reinforcers for low-probability behaviors. Primary reinforcers are suitable for conditioning with virtually all members of a species because they are essential for survival or reproduction. A secondary reinforcer is not intrinsically associated with survival or reproduction, but has become associated with a primary reinforcer through conditioning.
- Reinforcement schedules affect conditioning. Continuous

Looking Back continued

reinforcement is reinforcement that occurs every time a behavior occurs. Partial reinforcement refers to situations where reinforcement occurs periodically. Partial reinforcement schedules include fixed-interval schedules, variable-interval schedules, fixed-ratio schedules, and variable-ratio schedules.

- Punishment can be effective in operant conditioning if it is severe and consistent. However, it may pose ethical problems, and can result in retaliation or other negative side effects rather than conditioning. Reinforcement is generally superior as a conditioner.

WHAT ARE THE LIMITS OF OPERANT CONDITIONING?

- As with classical conditioning, cognition and the evolutionary history of the organism may set limits on operant conditioning. For example, cognitive activity including latent learning can either interfere with or hasten operant behavior, and conditioning may fail if it runs counter to an animal's instinctual patterns of behavior.

WHAT IS OBSERVATIONAL LEARNING?

- Observational learning describes ways in which an organism might learn by observing the experiences of others. Modeling is a type of observational learning where a child might acquire behaviors he or she observes in an admired adult. Vicarious conditioning involves learning through observing the consequences of others' behavior. Mirror neurons may help explain how observational learning occurs.
- Questions about the effects of media violence on behavior remain unsettled. Evidence does link media violence and aggressive thoughts, emotions, and behavior; but this association is weak and not equally applicable to every person exposed to media violence.

Key Terms

Acquisition, 336
Associative learning, 332
Classical conditioning, 334
Cognitive behaviorism, 356
Cognitive map, 355
Conditioned Response (CR), 335
Conditioned Stimulus (CS), 335
Continuous reinforcement, 351
Discrimination, 338
Explicit knowledge, 329
Extinction, 337
Fixed-interval (FI) schedule, 352
Fixed-ratio (FR) schedule, 352
Functionalist perspective, 345
Generalization, 338
Habituation, 330
Instinctive drift, 356

Latent learning, 355
Law of effect, 347
Learning, 328
Mirror neurons, 360
Modeling, 358
Negative punishment, 349
Negative reinforcement, 349
Neutral stimulus, 334
Observational learning, 358
Operant behavior, 349
Operant chamber, 348
Operant conditioning, 347
Partial reinforcement, 351
Partial reinforcement effect, 351
Positive punishment, 349
Positive reinforcement, 348
Primary reinforcer, 350

Procedural knowledge, 329
Punishment, 348
Radical behaviorism, 348
Reinforcement, 348
Renewal, 337
Secondary reinforcer, 350
Second-order conditioning, 337
Sensitization, 331
Shaping by successive approximation, 349
Spontaneous recovery, 337
Unconditioned Response (UCR), 335
Unconditioned Stimulus (UCS), 335
Variable-interval (VI) schedule, 352
Variable-ratio (VR) schedule, 352
Vicarious conditioning, 359

Test Yourself

1. What is the problem with definitions of learning that rely entirely upon the idea that learning can only be inferred from behavior? What is the problem with definitions that refer to the acquiring of knowledge?

2. When a stimulus at first causes a strong response, but due to repeated exposure over time the response is lessened, what type of learning has occurred? What is the "flip side of the coin" of this type of learning?

3. Describe the meanings of the following terms, and explain how they would be used in a demonstration of classical conditioning: neutral stimulus, unconditioned stimulus, unconditioned response, conditioned stimulus, conditioned response.

4. For acquisition to occur reliably, two criteria must be met. What are they?

5. When conditioning occurs because a new neutral stimulus is paired with a conditioned stimulus rather than an unconditioned stimulus, it is known as:
   a) renewal
   b) second-order conditioning
   c) spontaneous recovery
   d) vicarious conditioning

6. True or false: When a conditioned response has been extinguished, but reappears after a period of rest

Test Yourself continued

if the conditioned stimulus is once again presented, it is known as renewal.

7. What is the term used when an animal displays a conditioned response when exposed to a neutral stimulus that is similar but not identical to the original CS?
   a) spontaneous recovery
   b) discrimination
   c) generalization
   d) renewal

8. What is one explanation for the "long shelf-life" of the Little Albert study?

9. Which model of classical conditioning proposes that for strong conditioning to occur reliably, the unconditioned stimulus must be unexpected?

10. How did the findings of John Garcia and his colleagues violate the assumption of equipotentiality?

11. Name at least one way that classical conditioning in the laboratory and classical conditioning "in the wild" differ, according to functionalist theorists?

12. Operant conditioning through the removal of a (generally) unpleasant or aversive stimulus is known as:
   a) positive reinforcement
   b) negative reinforcement
   c) positive punishment
   d) negative punishment

13. Operant conditioning through the removal of a pleasant or reward stimulus is known as:
   a) positive reinforcement
   b) negative reinforcement
   c) positive punishment
   d) negative punishment

14. What is the major difference between Thorndike's law of effect and Skinner's operant conditioning?

15. Training animals to perform tricks is generally accomplished with the operant conditioning technique or techniques known as:
   a) continuous reinforcement
   b) negative reinforcement
   c) shaping through successive reinforcement or chaining
   d) partial punishment

16. Why do we say that in operant conditioning "the organism teaches itself"?

17. Differentiate the four partial reinforcement schedules.

18. Define the terms *cognitive map* and *latent learning*.

19. If an animal refuses to learn a behavior because it conflicts with an instinctive behavioral pattern, it is known as
   a) equipotentiality
   b) instinctive drift
   c) fixed action pattern
   d) latent learning

20. Researchers have not been able to satisfactorily demonstrate a causal link between violent media and real-world crime and violence. Why is this not the same as demonstrating that no such link exists?

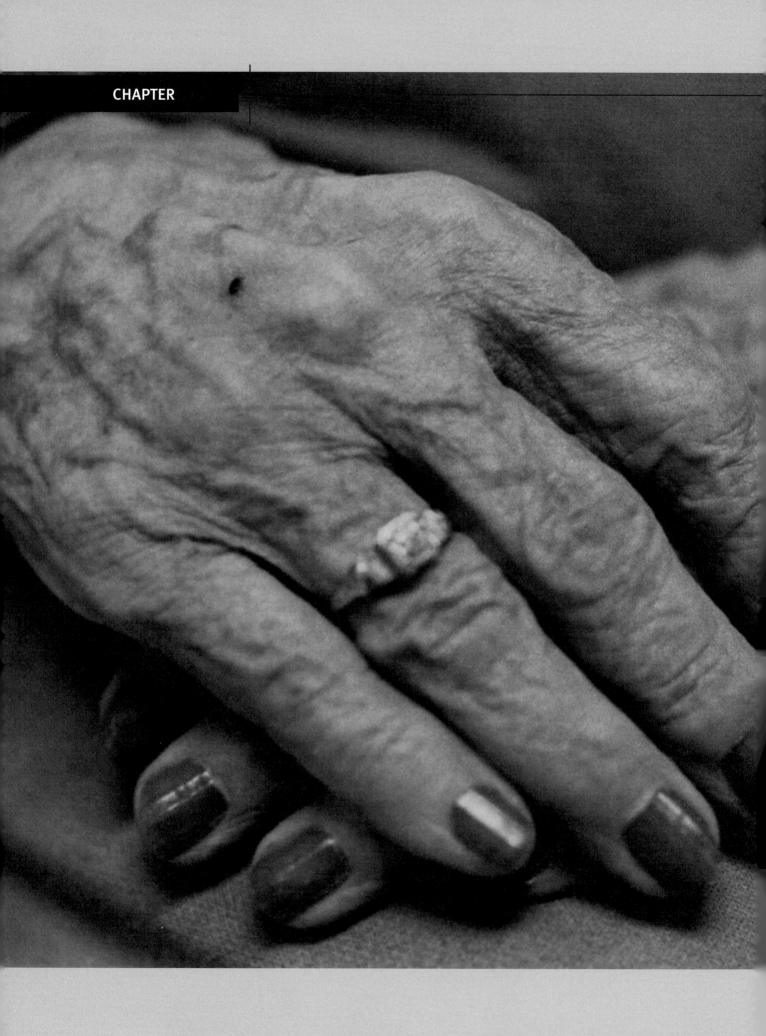

8

Memory

Chapter Outline

FREEZE FRAME

In 1999 the Associated Press (AP) began to investigate allegations that the U.S. 7th Cavalry Regiment had massacred hundreds of South Korean civilians at a village called No Gun Ri in 1950, during the Korean War. The victims included Min-Young-ok and her son, pictured here in a photo provided to the AP by her family. In trying to uncover the truth about these accusations, the AP naturally turned to Edward Daily, who served in the 7th Cavalry in Korea, subsequently wrote three books about the unit, and faithfully attended its veterans' reunions. Daily was well known for his heroism, for having been decorated innumerable times, and for surviving a Korean POW camp.

As Moss (2000) wrote in the *New York Times*, Daily seemed an ideal authority to turn to. When confronted with the accusations against his beloved 7th Cavalry, he broke down and verified them—claiming that ever since the massacre he had been haunted by the sounds of children screaming.

As it turns out, however, Daily fabricated his confession—he had never been at No Gun Ri. Furthermore, virtually every other statement he had ever made about his war experience was fabricated, along with the forged documents

he quickly provided skeptics to back up his tales. While he had spent a few weeks as part of the 7th Cavalry (8 months after the massacre supposedly had taken place), he actually lived out his war career as a clerk and mechanic. He had never been decorated, had committed no heroic acts, had not been promoted to Lieutenant as he claimed, was never taken prisoner of war, and probably did not see a day of combat in his life. Ultimately, he was sentenced to almost 2 years in prison and ordered to repay the U.S. Department of Veterans' Affairs $412,839 which he had collected in war-related disability payments.

The actual details of the events at No Gun Ri are a source of intense debate. While there is no doubt that civilians were massacred, claims that atrocities were committed by direct order from military authorities have been challenged by historians (Bateman, 2002). However, what concerns us here is not the truth or falsehood of the various accounts of the senseless deaths that did in fact occur at No Gun Ri. For now we are concerned with the following indisputable fact: Numerous 7th Cavalry veterans who definitely *were* at No Gun Ri remember Daily participating in the events of that day. At least one veteran recalls Daily pulling him out of a foxhole to safety. "I know that Daily was there," insisted one of these men, "I know that. I know that" (Moss, 2000). Yet Daily was not at No Gun Ri and never pulled anyone to safety. Why are honest men sincerely claiming that things occurred that could not have occurred?

How people can experience memories for events that never happened is an important area of current research in the field of memory. Memory is one of the greatest strengths—and fragilities—of the entire human mental apparatus. It is strongly related to learning. Both learning and memory involve relatively enduring psychological changes that result from experience, and both are associated with many of the same neural mechanisms (Beggs et al., 1999; Frick & Johnston, 2005; Gelbard-Sagiv, Mukamel, Harel, Malach, & Fried, 2008). At the level of the neuron, learning and memory are largely overlapping processes and are both cornerstones of human psychology. As neuroscientist Dan Johnston observes, "Learning and memory, basically, if you think about it, are the essences of who we are" (A. Grant, 2006). If you doubt this, imagine what life would be like if you could not recall any events of your past, nor facts you had learned about the world; nor could you form new memories or learn anything new at all. You would live in a continuous present moment with no sense of yourself as a unique individual or any understanding of the world in which you found yourself. In this chapter we will explore memory—its many triumphs and equally numerous failures.

What Are Memories?

"It is a poor sort of memory that only works backwards."

—Lewis Carroll (in *Through the Looking Glass*)

Cognitive neuroscientist and memory research pioneer Endel Tulving (2002) observed that all happenings in the universe move forward in time. Causes precede effects. Today comes before tomorrow. Plants and creatures as well as stars and galaxies come into being, age, and eventually die. The direction of such happenings never reverses—that is, except once: in the human ability to remember past events. In human memory, says Tulving, "time's arrow is bent in a loop" and the "rememberer" travels back into the past (2002, p. 2). And yet the human "time machine" of memory, while it is designed with powers exquisitely well suited for the purposes for which we use it, has certain properties that can cause time to "warp" in unusual ways. The past we revisit sometimes bears very little resemblance—or *no* resemblance—to the past as it once was.

I found this out in a highly personal way when, at age 7, my daughter Naima was stung simultaneously by a number of wasps whose nest she had inadvertently disturbed. Later she asked me if anything similar had ever happened to me, and I was able to relate in great detail the story of how, at the age of 4, while living briefly in North Carolina, I had stumbled backward into a bush that housed a sea of honey bees. I recalled my uncomprehending pain and terror, my mother's rush to lift me from my tormentors, and my trip to the hospital (my face had swelled horribly). I recalled the kindness of a particular woman doctor with frizzy hair.

One day, in relating the story of her encounter with wasps to her aunt (my older sister), Naima chanced also to mention the story of my having fallen backward into a nest of bees. My sister gave me a very strange look and said, "You didn't fall into a nest of bees in North Carolina—that was me!" "That's ridiculous," I argued, "I remember it in vivid detail." My sister promptly went into her bedroom and emerged with a book of photographs. Flipping to a series of photographs from our childhood time to North Carolina, she pointed with satisfaction to a snapshot showing her at about age 6 with her face swollen with multiple bee stings. She told us how she had stumbled backward, been lifted out by our mother and rushed to the hospital, and how a female doctor with frizzy hair had given her a grape Tootsie Roll pop. I stood open-mouthed as "my" memories came spilling from her mouth—often in language virtually identical to that I used when telling this story to others.

Like the soldiers of the 7th Cavalry described at the opening of this chapter, who recalled the presence of Edward Daily at a scene from which he was entirely absent, I had committed the memory error of *misattribution*—recalling as a personal memory something that actually originated elsewhere, either in the imagination of the rememberer or in someone else's statements about an event (Goff & Roediger, 1998; Schacter, 2001). Apparently, I had listened to the bee story several times as a very small child, and somewhere along the way had forgotten that it had happened to my sister and not to me.

Thus, memory cannot always be taken at face value as an accurate record of past events. And yet, we rely on memory in virtually everything we do. Is our faith in our memory systems misplaced? Are our memories defective? We will consider this question a bit later. First, we will consider what is known about the way memory works.

▲ **FIGURE 8.1 Encode, Store, Retrieve.** Contemporary information-processing models of memory are based on the idea that memory systems encode, store, and retrieve information. Using an (imperfect) computer analogy, in Panel A, information is being encoded as keystrokes = sensory information encoded as perceptions; in Panel B, information is being saved on the hard drive = perceptions stored as memories; in Panel C, the saved file is opened once again = memories are retrieved for recall.

Memory ▶ From the cognitive perspective, memory involves the encoding, storage, and retrieval of information. Neuroscientists are more likely to define memory as learning-induced changes in the activity of neurons.

Encoding ▶ The memory process of "translating" sensory impressions into meaningful perceptions that may then be stored as memory.

Storage ▶ The memory process whereby meaningful perceptions are retained as memory.

Retrieval ▶ Recognizing or recalling something from long-term memory.

Memories Are Encoded, Stored, and Retrieved

There are two basic ways to define **memory**. First, memory can be defined in a general way as the ability to retain information about past personal experiences or facts about the world, and to utilize this information in the present. However, psychologists who study memory generally define it from an *information-processing* perspective. Looked at this way, memory is a group of mechanisms and systems that *encode*, *store*, and *retrieve* information (e.g., Baddeley, 1997; Baddeley, Eysenck, & Anderson, 2009; Tulving & Craik, 2000).

What do we mean when we speak of encoding, storing, and retrieving information? The differences between these terms may quickly be grasped by thinking of a computer: As depicted in Figure 8.1, when you enter data into a computer via your keyboard, the computer *encodes* the keystrokes in the computer's memory in a way that can be processed as information. You may continue to work with the data online or *store* it in files on your hard drive, an action requiring more complex encoding processes. When you wish to access these files later to view or work on them, you are *retrieving* the data.

In a somewhat similar way, when you receive information about the world through your senses, it is encoded as perceptions (e.g., meaningful sights and sounds) and either used immediately in thought ("online") or encoded more deeply as memory and stored for later retrieval (memory access). Put simply, **encoding** means getting the information into your brain, **storage** is keeping it there, and **retrieval** is finding it when you need it.

However, you shouldn't take this computer analogy too seriously. When you open a saved computer file you have retrieved an identical copy of what you have stored. As we shall see later, this is not at all true in the case of memory retrieval.

The Modal Model of Memory Consists of "Stores"

Ideas about the processes of encoding, storage, and retrieval in memory have undergone "near-revolutionary" change over the past 15 years (Jonides et al., 2008, p. 193). However, it makes sense to start with a model of memory known as the **modal model of memory**—*modal* here meaning something like "generally accepted." Although this modal model is no longer quite as "modal" as it was 30 years ago, it is certainly the most widely known model of memory, and many of the newer ways of looking at memory can be fitted into its general structure (Freedman & Martin, 2001).

Devised in 1968 by Richard Atkinson and Richard Shiffrin, the modal model describes three stages in the memory process, with each stage also functioning as a kind of "storage area," or *store*, for memory (Atkinson & Shiffrin, 1968). As depicted in Figure 8.2, these stages/stores are termed *sensory memory*, *short-term memory* (STM), and *long-term memory* (LTM). They differ from one another in their specific function, the amount of information they can store, and the length of time that information can be stored within them:

SENSORY MEMORY IS FLEETING

According to the modal model, new information reaches **sensory memory** first. Sensory memory very briefly stores large amounts of fleeting sensory impressions for further processing by other memory systems. As you walk down a street, drive along the highway, or enter a room and look around, you perceive a great many sights and sounds, but most of what you perceive vanishes from awareness within fractions of a second. It makes sense that most of the sensory impressions to which we are exposed during the day should leave only brief traces on the nervous system. Try to imagine the mental confusion that would result if you were to hold in your awareness every sight that passes before your eyes and every sound that reaches your ears while walking down a busy street.

Sensory memory is divided into two categories. When sensory impressions are visual in nature, they are termed *iconic store*. These traces last less than half a second. When they are auditory, they are termed *echoic store*, and may last as long as a few seconds (hence the term *echoic*; Sperling, 1960; Darwin, Turvey, & Crowder, 1972).

Sensory memory serves two functions. At the most basic level, it "collects" sensory information and briefly holds it for possible further processing in memory. Secondly, it allows us to perceive the world as a continuous stream of events, rather than a disjointed series of visual and auditory "snapshots." For example, consider the arc formed by the gymnast's legs as she does a front walkover in Figure 8.3. In actuality, what is occurring in a walkover is a quickly moving series of disconnected sequential leg and body positions, suggested by the photo. But when we watch the movement, sensory memory retains each position very briefly, so that the position that came before is incorporated in our brain as part of the motion that brings us to the next position.

SHORT-TERM MEMORY (STM) IS BRIEF

When you decide—consciously or unconsciously—to pay attention to a specific piece of information in sensory memory for any particular reason, the information is "transferred" into **short-term memory**, or STM. Of the hundreds of people who pass you while walking down the street, perhaps one is particularly attractive. You may comment on this fact to yourself, holding in mind the image or idea of this person. As you do so, the person leaves sensory memory and enters STM. Or you pass a bar and hear a juke box playing a tune you like. As you walk by you begin to hum the tune to yourself, transferring it

Modal model of memory
▶ The traditional model of memory initially devised by Richard Atkinson and Richard Shiffrin. The modal model views memory as consisting of three stages or stores: sensory memory, short-term memory (STM), and long-term memory (LTM).

Sensory memory ▶
The memory stage that very briefly stores large amounts of fleeting sensory impressions. Sensory memory is comprised of iconic store (visual) and echoic store (auditory).

Short-term memory (STM)
▶ Short-term memory is a memory store used for attending to information in the short term. Short-term memory is limited in the length of time the memory can remain active—no longer than about 20 seconds. It is also limited in the amount of information that can be stored. No more than about four to five items or chunks of information. STM is one component of the modal model of memory.

▶ **FIGURE 8.2 The Modal Model of Memory.** *(Source: Goldstein, 2005, p. 141.)*

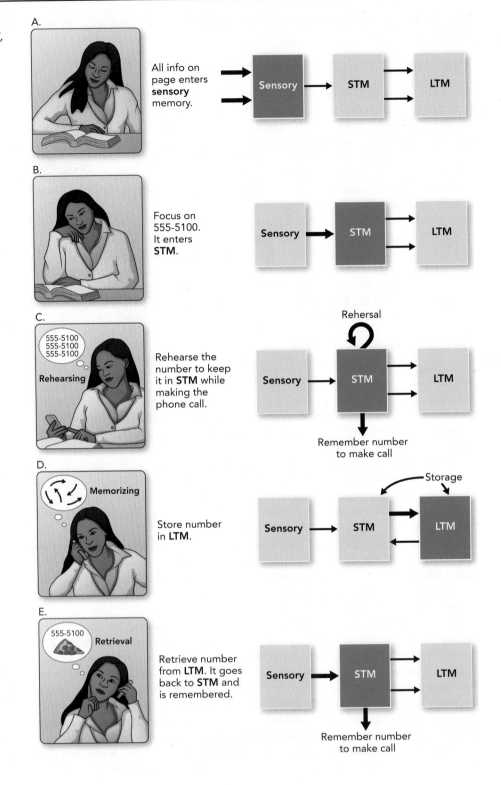

A. All info on page enters **sensory** memory.

B. Focus on 555-5100. It enters **STM**.

C. Rehearse the number to keep it in **STM** while making the phone call.

D. Store number in **LTM**.

E. Retrieve number from **LTM**. It goes back to **STM** and is remembered.

▲ **FIGURE 8.3 Sensory Memory Gives Us Motion.** Sensory memory collects sensory information for processing in memory. It also allows us to perceive the world as a continuous stream of events rather than a series of disjointed snapshots.

▲ **Sensory Memory Stores Brief Impressions.** Sensory memory collects sensory information and briefly stores it for further processing in short- and long-term memory. Sensory memory leaves only brief traces on the nervous system, preventing an overload of sensory information from causing massive confusion.

to STM—while the sounds of the conversations of passers-by slip forever out of sensory memory. Or you visually scan a document trying to find a particular phrase or word—you find what you are looking for and all the rest of the letters and words are gone forever. Only the phrase remains, now part of STM.

The transferring of information from sensory memory to STM is a result of further processing of the information by the brain. Any time you *pay attention* to a sight, sound, feeling, idea, or piece of information—either automatically or as a conscious decision—that information is transferred to STM. *Attention* is the force that singles out information in sensory memory for transference to STM, and it is attention that determines how long the information remains in STM.

However, if sensory memory is fleeting, short-term memory is *brief*. In general, information can remain in STM for no longer than about 20 seconds unless it is actively thought about or repeated—mental effort known as **maintenance rehearsal** (Peterson & Peterson, 1959). The most commonly used example of this is what happens when you ask a friend for their phone number, but you have no pen to write it down. You repeat the number to yourself continuously while looking for a pen. Then someone else calls your name, you answer—and the number is gone!

In addition to its limited duration, STM has a limited *capacity*, which is termed **memory span**. Memory span is the amount of information that can be held in STM at any one time. For almost everyone, memory span averages four single items or pure *chunks* of information (Cowan, 2001, 2010). What is a chunk? Consider the following list of letters:

S B C V T M C B N O B H

Read them once slowly, then look away and try to repeat them back in order. You will almost certainly fail at this task. Now reverse the order of letters:

H B O N B C M T V C B S

If you watch television at all, you should have no trouble remembering the letters in order now after only a single reading. Why? Because they are no longer a series of 12 meaningless, unrelated single items. Instead, they have

Maintenance rehearsal ▶ Actively repeating or thinking about information so that it remains in short-term memory.

Memory span ▶ The amount of information that can be held in a memory store at any one time. The capacity of short-term memory averages four to five items or chunks of information.

Chunk ▶ Individual items that are grouped together in memory because they are meaningfully associated with one another (but only weakly related or unrelated to items in other chunks).

become a series of *four* meaningful and related chunks of information. A **chunk** is any grouping of items that are strongly associated with one another, but only weakly related (or unrelated) to items in other chunks (Gobet, 2005; Gobet et al., 2001).

Chunking involves organizing information into manageable units. Chunking is the reason we can easily remember sentences composed of 20 words, but cannot remember 20 unrelated words in order (unless we use our own highly personal system to create chunks out of otherwise unrelated items). Chunking allows us to remember phone numbers. It is virtually impossible to recall 6107984620 as a string of numbers, but when the digits are characterized in chunks as (610) 798-4620, the task becomes easily manageable. According the modal model, the function of STM is to allow information to be "used online" (i.e., thought about in the present) or held long enough to be transferred to long-term memory (LTM) for more permanent storage.

LONG-TERM MEMORY (LTM) IS LIMITLESS

Long-term memory (LTM) ▶ The deepest level of encoding of information—a theoretically limited memory store that contains memories for facts, autobiographical events, and learned skills. LTM is a component of the modal model of memory.

Encoding in sensory memory is a relatively superficial process involving automatic perception. Encoding in short-term memory is a more active process and will involve maintenance rehearsal if the "shelf life" of information is to be extended—for example, when you continue to repeat a shopping list to yourself as you browse the grocery aisles. But repeating shopping lists or telephone numbers to oneself is not what most people are thinking of when they think of *memory*. Instead, most people are referring to *long-term memory* (LTM)—recalling the time they burned their hand on a hot iron at age 5, correctly remembering how to do prime factorization for a math test, placing the name of that Italian actor they saw eating in a restaurant, or being able to ride a motorcycle competently 10 years after last riding. If STM can be thought of as whatever appears on the screen of your computer at any given moment, then long-term memory represents the data stored in files for later retrieval. Thus, **long-term memory (LTM)** is a relatively permanent store of memory. Unlike STM, LTM has a theoretically limitless capacity (Bahrick, 2000).

Acoustic encoding ▶ Memory encoding according to the sound of the stimulus being encoded.

Visual encoding ▶ Memory encoding according to the visual appearance of the stimulus.

Semantic encoding ▶ Memory encoding according to the meaning of the stimulus.

Long-Term Memory Is a Deeper Level of Processing How does information get from STM to LTM? In other words, how is information *encoded* in LTM? Encoding in LTM generally relies upon the idea of *meaningfulness* of the information being encoded. As depicted in Figure 8.4, memories may be encoded in three ways: through sound, known as **acoustic** encoding; through imagery, known as **visual** encoding; and through meaning, known as **semantic** encoding.

Encoding in *short*-term memory tends to be primarily acoustic, secondarily visual, and much less often semantic (Baddeley, 2007; Zhang & Simon, 1985). For example, when you attempt to keep a string of words or numbers in mind, or when you read words from a page, you are likely to be encoding the information in STM by its sound by mentally "talking to yourself." If you doubt this, try to read this page without reciting the words to yourself and see how far you get! And when abstract shapes, diagrams, and other stimuli that cannot easily be named are being processed in STM, visual encoding may be preferred.

However, *long*-term memories are most effectively encoded when the information being encoded is associated meaningfully with information already known. Therefore, encoding in LTM is primarily semantic and depends upon *meaning*. Because semantic encoding creates longer-lasting memories, it is considered a *deeper level of processing* than acoustic and visual encoding.

Elaborative rehearsal ▶ Mentally encoding information into long-term memory in a way that is personally meaningful and associates the new information with information that already exists in long-term memory.

In general, material is most likely to be recalled at a later date if it has been encoded for LTM during **elaborative rehearsal**, which may or may not occur deliberately. Elaborative rehearsal differs from maintenance rehearsal in that it does not consist of simple repetition. Elaborative rehearsal involves

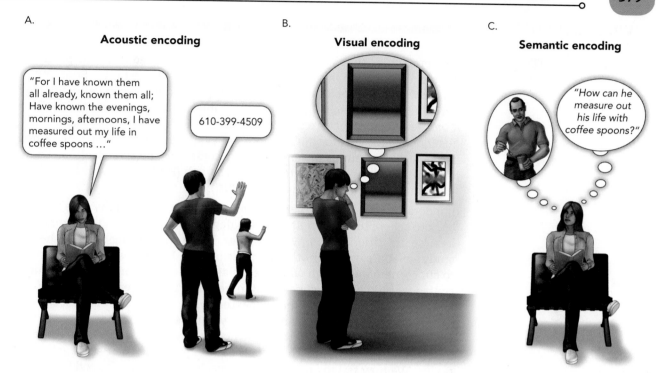

A. **Acoustic encoding**

"For I have known them all already, known them all; Have known the evenings, mornings, afternoons, I have measured out my life in coffee spoons …"

610-399-4509

B. **Visual encoding**

C. **Semantic encoding**

"How can he measure out his life with coffee spoons?"

▲ **FIGURE 8.4** Visual, Acoustic, and Semantic Encoding in Short-Term Memory. Most encoding in short-term memory is acoustic. Visual encoding may happen when abstract shapes or diagrams are being held in STM. Although semantic encoding may occasionally occur in STM, it is characteristic of the elaborative rehearsal used to process long-term memory.

processing new material in a way that is personally meaningful and which associates the new information with other information that already exists in LTM. Repeating a phone number over and over to yourself many times may help you to keep it in mind long enough to locate your cell phone and dial, but it will not guarantee that you will remember the number 10 minutes later, let alone the next year.

On the other hand, I recall my own childhood telephone number as well as that of my best friend and first girlfriend in spite of not having needed to use those numbers in 50 years. These phone numbers are associated in my mind with a host of specific, meaningful events and emotions. You are engaging in elaborative rehearsal when you study for a test successfully by, for example, perceiving the connection between new concepts and concepts already learned, or deliberately creating unique personal systems of associations, mental imagery, and memory tricks. If you recall the time you burned your hand on the hot iron at age 5, it is likely because this event was associated with meaningful sensations and emotions, awareness of the time of day, the identity and responses of people around you, and so forth. This memory may also have been further elaborated upon over the years in discussion with family members or simply by bringing the scene into consciousness and reflecting upon it.

LIVING PSYCHOLOGY

How to Prepare— and Not Prepare—for Exams

You probably have been exposed at some point to "study tips" and methods for improving your exam grades based upon principles derived from research in cognitive psychology. How well do these methods actually work? To some degree it has been assumed that they *must* work if they are based upon genuine principles of learning and memory. However, until relatively recently, evidence in support of the actual effectiveness of these methods in real-life test settings was often contradictory—or in some cases, nonexistent (Gurung, 2005; Hadwin & Winne, 1996).

LIVING PSYCHOLOGY

CONTINUED

The problem is that studying cannot easily be divorced from the particular person doing the studying and the particular test to be taken. Studying exists within a *context* that can include type of course (science/technology, foreign language, etc.), type of test (multiple choice or essay; open or closed book, textbook or lecture based), personal study preferences ("Flash cards just don't work well for me"), amount of available preparation time (When is the test? How many other courses am I taking?), motivation (How badly to I want to do well on this test?), and so forth (Hadwin & Winne, 1996; Hadwin et al., 2001; Hermann et al., 2002).

I understood the student perspective on this better when my wife went back to school to earn an RN nursing degree in preparation to become a nurse practitioner (NP). Watching her desperately trying to juggle her study schedule with her other responsibilities, I saw how she was forced to cut corners and weigh which test was likely to be more difficult, which course was likely to be considered more important in terms of grade if she wanted to go on to obtain the NP degree, what time of day the test would be given (she's better in the morning), what assignments were due that week, and so on. I realized that instructors (myself included) sometimes tend to behave as though their course is the only one their students are taking. We may fail to appreciate that studying is a complicated business that involves more than *studying*.

This insight highlights the frequent confusion between the idea of a study *strategy* and a study *tactic*. A *tactic* is a specific technique—for example, generating a series of test questions to answer or creating flash cards. In contrast, a *strategy* is a way of approaching the entire studying enterprise that is based upon *context*. Prescribing specific study methods for use across the board may be unrealistic, as it does not take context into consideration. To do well studying for exams overall, you need a very wide repertoire of tactics that are adaptable for many contexts. You also need to pay attention to seemingly non-memory-related issues such as physical health and emotional condition (Herrmann et al., 2002).

However, taking the importance of strategy and context into account, recent research by John Dunlosky and his colleagues has separated the wheat from the chaff when it comes to study *tactics* (Dunlosky, Rawson, Marsh, Nathan, & Willingham, 2013). These investigators have taken a very careful look at study tactics over a wide range of contexts to isolate those that really seem to *work* for the largest number of students under the most varied types of conditions. Although Dunlosky and colleagues describe a number of tactics that show "moderate utility," the two techniques showing "high utility" according to these researchers are:

1. *Testing and self-testing.* Testing, as unpleasant as many of us find it, improves learning (Roedigger, Agarwal, McDaniel, & McDermott, 2011). Therefore, in studying for a test, create as many types of self-tests as you can. Have friends quiz you, create flash cards, write your own test questions as you read and answer them later, and so forth. Testing involves *retrieval practice*, long known to improve recall. Moreover, you are going to be taking a test—your practice should reflect as closely as possible the actual task for which you are preparing. The features *Retrieve!* and *Test Yourself* in this textbook attempt to take advantage of the utility of testing to increase later recall.

2. *Distributed practice: short but frequent study sessions over time.* Parents and teachers find it very frustrating trying to compel students to avoid cramming for tests, technically termed *massed practice*. Regardless of what we say, large numbers of students seem to feel that they do not

need to start studying until the night before the test—at which point they pull all-nighters. Overwhelmingly, however, research finds that students who study in relatively short sessions spread out over many days prior to a test recall the material better and receive much higher test scores. The value of distributed over massed practice is now indisputable. Anyone interested in receiving a good test grade should use distributed practice for study (see also Cepeda, Vul, Rohrer, Wixted, & Pashler, 2008; Rohrer & Pashler, 2007). The chapters in this textbook are broken up into chunks in a way that fosters distributed practice when preparing for chapter tests.

At the same time as most students should feel confident that the tactics just described will be helpful for studying for almost any test, research has also identified a number of classroom and study habits known to *reduce* exam performance—in other words, how *not* to prepare for exams!

1. *Sitting toward the back of the classroom.* The tendency of students who sit toward the front of the class to perform better on exams is usually assumed to be the result of student preferences—stronger students prefer to sit up front and weaker students toward the rear, away from the action. However, when researchers randomly assigned students to one of four groups at varying distances from the front of the room, they found that those who sat closest to the front of the room for the first half of the course had better attendance, asked more questions during class, and had better grades on exams (Perkins & Wieman, 2005).

2. *Mistaking reading and re-reading for studying.* Reading and re-reading material is not the same as studying the material. Reading and re-reading alone are generally of little use when trying to remember material for a test. Reading is a fairly passive enterprise, whereas studying is active and involves organization and effort to encode material at a deep level. It also should involve retrieval practice through testing and self-testing, as described earlier (Roedigger, Agarwal, McDaniel, & McDermott, 2011).

3. *Studying with distractions.* Students who study while listening to music, watching TV, using the Internet (for nonresearch purposes), or socializing with nonstudying friends do not do as well as those who avoid these practices (Gurung, 2005; Herrmann et al., 2002).

4. *Cramming* (see earlier discussion of distributed vs. massed practice).

5. *Skipping classes.* Students who attend more classes do better on exams (Gurung, 2005). Duh. ∎

IN SUMMARY

1.	Psychologists define memory as a group of mechanisms and processes that encode, store, and retrieve information.
2.	The modal model of memory describes memory in three stages, or stores: sensory memory, which fleetingly stores sensory perceptions; short-term memory (STM), which is limited in capacity and duration; and long-term memory (LTM), which is a theoretically unlimited long-term store.
3.	STM can hold information for no longer than about 20 seconds unless it is rehearsed. Generally, no more than 4 items or chunks of items can be maintained in STM at one time.

4. There are three types of encoding: Acoustic, visual, and semantic. Acoustic and visual encoding are more typical of STM (particularly acoustic encoding), and semantic encoding is more typical of LTM.

5. Studying for tests involves taking contexts as well as tactics into account. Recent research has identified two study tactics showing high utility for most students under most conditions: testing/self-testing and distributed practice. There are also a number of study habits known to reduce performance on tests.

RETRIEVE!

1. The modal model of memory consists of all of the following EXCEPT

a) sensory memory   c) long-term memory

b) short-term memory   d) elaborative memory

2. Sensory memory is divided into two categories. What are they?

3. True or false? Information can only remain in short-term memory for about 20 seconds at most unless maintenance rehearsal is used.

4. What is the maximum number of individual items that can be maintained in STM at one time? How can one increase the number of items of information that can be held in STM?

5. Is encoding in long-term memory primarily visual, acoustic, or semantic?

6. List at least three classroom or study habits known to decrease performance on tests.

What Is "Remembering"?

How is information in long-term memory accessed when we need it? Retrieval of information from LTM—that is, remembering—may happen either through *recognition* or *recall*. Recognition occurs when you are presented with something and are able to identify it—a fact you have previously learned, a person with whom you have had contact, and so forth. Recall occurs when you produce something from LTM entirely on your own. Thus, multiple choice tests require *recognition*, whereas short-answer and essay questions depend upon *recall*. As you might guess, recognition is much easier than recall, and recall demonstrates a more secure and deeply encoded memory.

Retrieval Cues

Retrieval cue ▶ Any hint or association that helps one retrieve a long-term memory.

Retrieval of long-term memories is greatly enhanced through **retrieval cues**. A retrieval cue is any type of hint or association that helps you sift—consciously or unconsciously—through the immense and complex store of long-term memory to select the appropriate information. These cues may be *external*, originating outside yourself (seeing books stacked on your desk reminds you that you have a paper due); or internal, originating from within (thinking about your best friend reminds you of the time the two of you went hiking and got lost in the woods).

CONTEXT-DEPENDENT MEMORY

An important type of external retrieval cue is *context*. **Context-dependent memory** describes situations in which retrieval of a memory is enhanced in contexts that were similar to the one that existed when the material was encoded. For example, you might be listening to a song and recall another event that occurred when you were listening to the same music. Indeed, Duncan Godden and Alan Baddeley (1975) demonstrated context-dependent memory vividly when they had scuba divers memorize lists of words either under water or on land, and later tested them for recall of these words both on land and under water. As Figure 8.5 shows, words memorized under water are best recalled under water, while words memorized on land are best recalled on land (Godden & Baddeley, 1975).

STATE-DEPENDENT MEMORY

An example of an internal retrieval cue is **state-dependent memory**. Mood and other psychological states, including drug-induced changes in consciousness, can act as retrieval cues. Caffeine is a good example of this. As explained in Chapter 5, caffeine may increase performance on cognitive tasks for some people. However, the probability that it will work, say, to increase your test performance, is increased if you also used caffeine while studying for the test (Kelemen & Creeley, 2003). Indeed, while alcohol and marijuana have been shown to impair memory as a rule, if you happen to learn some new information while high on these drugs, the information is often better recalled when in the same condition than when sober—although this effect is seen primarily in *free-recall tasks* (e.g., a fill-in-the-blank question) as compared with recognition tasks (e.g., a multiple-choice question; Eich, 1989).

FLASHBULB MEMORIES

A unique type of internal retrieval cue that has fascinated researchers and the public alike is the flashbulb memory. A flashbulb memory is a highly vivid and detailed remembrance of one's personal circumstances at the moment of learning of some shocking and unexpected event—the assassination of a public figure, a natural disaster, an attack by a foreign nation (R. Brown & Kulik, 1977; Hirst et al., 2009; van Giezen, Arensman, Spinhoven, & Wolters, 2005). For example, at the moment I first heard about the September 11, 2001, attacks on the World Trade Center and the Pentagon on a radio news report, I vividly recall that I was alone in my car, making a right-hand turn from Normandie Avenue onto Olympic Boulevard in Los Angeles. The time was somewhere between 8:10 and 8:15 a.m., Pacific time. If you asked me what I had been doing at that time on the morning of September 10th or September 12th, I'm quite sure I could not even begin to answer you. In a sense, then, a flashbulb memory is a memory for unremarkable events, cued by memories of remarkable events.

As vivid as flashbulb memories may be, however, they are not necessarily reliable. As I stated, I recall being alone in the car hearing those first news reports of the disaster on September 11, and quickly calling my wife on the cell phone. However, while my wife confirms that right turn onto Olympic Boulevard etched so clearly in my memory, she also assures me that she was sitting right next to me at the time listening to the radio intently!

During the first year after a "flashbulb" event accurate memory deteriorates substantially, as researchers studying the aftermath of the September 11 attacks discovered. Among a sample of Americans drawn from seven cities and surveyed over a period of several years, there was a 20% rate of forgetting for "flashbulb" aspects of memory for 9/11 during the first year and an additional 5% to 10% over the next 2 years. Flashbulb aspects of memory

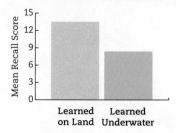
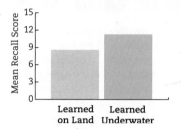

▲ **FIGURE 8.5 Context-Dependent Memory on Land and Under Water.** Scuba divers best remembered words memorized underwater when they were under water (Graph A), whereas words they memorized on land were best recalled on land (Graph B). *(Source: Godden & Baddeley, 1975.)*

Context-dependent memory ▶ When retrieval of a memory is enhanced in contexts that were similar to the one that existed when the memory was encoded.

State-dependent memory ▶ When retrieval of a memory is enhanced by internal states such as mood or drug effects that were present when the memory was encoded.

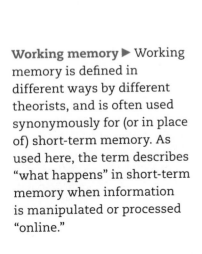

▲ **Depressive Memory: Accentuate the Negative.** A memory is often more accurately recalled when one is in a mood (or drug state) similar to that which existed when the memory was encoded (state-dependent memory). Research has found that those suffering from depression are more apt to recall unhappy memories from their past than happy ones—but this is not the case once their depression passes. On the other hand, mood can also seriously distort memories for the past. In a depressed mood, one may remember an event as primarily negative, but in a good mood, one may focus instead on positive aspects of the same event. Which memory is more realistic (McNally, 2003)?

▲ **Fertile Grounds for Flashbulb Memories.** Indonesia Tsunami, 2004; Columbine High School massacre, 1999; Assassination of Martin Luther King, 1968; Attack on World Trade Center, 2001. Flashbulb memories are intensely vivid, detailed memories for one's personal circumstances at the moment of learning about an unexpected and shocking event ("Do you remember where you were when . . .?"). As vivid as these memories may be, and as confident as their holders may be about their accuracy, in fact they are not always reliable, and they may change over time.

included questions such as, "Where were you at the time?," "What were you doing?," and "How did you feel?" Emotional aspects of the event—how each participant felt at the time—were especially unreliably recalled (Hirst et al., 2009). The unreliability of flashbulb memories suggests an important point about memory: Memory may be fragile, even for events that would seem extremely important.

Working Memory Is Working *With* Memory

A number of influential concepts that move beyond the modal model have recently become part of the accepted picture of human memory. Perhaps the most important of these concepts is **working memory**, most often associated with researcher Alan Baddeley (Baddeley, 1997, 2007, 2012; Baddeley et al., 2009). Although working memory may be defined in a number of different ways by different theorists (e.g., Cowan, 2005), it is probably best to think of working memory as a new way of looking at what happens *in* short-term memory when information is manipulated or processed—for example, during maintenance rehearsal, during the transfer of information from STM to LTM, or during the retrieval of material from LTM back into STM for "online" use. Thus, working memory might better be termed "working *with* memory."

Although working memory does its "work" within the limited-capacity space and duration of short-term memory, as I have implied, it draws from

Working memory ▶ Working memory is defined in different ways by different theorists, and is often used synonymously for (or in place of) short-term memory. As used here, the term describes "what happens" in short-term memory when information is manipulated or processed "online."

STM (maintenance rehearsal)   Working Memory   LTM (recollection)

"Let's see, that was pasta, peppers, butter..."

"The pasta is in this isle, the peppers are down at the other end of the store..."

◀**FIGURE 8.6 Working Memory Is Working *With* Memory.** When shopping for food you are maintaining your shopping list in working memory through short-term memory processes (e.g., maintenance rehearsal), while retrieving memory for the placement of items in the market from long-term memory.

long-term memory as well. For example, when adding or subtracting figures in your head, you keep the figures in mind through maintenance rehearsal, a short-term memory process, while drawing on long-term memories for how to do addition and subtraction in the first place. Because most of the time we actually *are* in some way manipulating and processing information while it is in short-term memory, some psychologists have come to use the term *working memory* in place of *short-term memory*. Figure 8.6 depicts a hypothetical example of working memory.

There Are Two Types (and Two Subtypes) of LTM

Over the years, the notion of long-term memory (LTM) has been greatly expanded and elaborated upon. At present, it is generally accepted that there are two fundamental types of LTM, as depicted in Figure 8.7: *explicit memory* and *implicit memory*.

EXPLICIT MEMORY

Explicit memories are conscious memories for personal experiences or facts about the world. Explicit memories are often termed *declarative memories* because they are memories which we can "declare"—that is, consciously recall. As initially described by Endel Tulving and depicted in Figure 8.8, there are two subtypes of explicit memory: *episodic memory* and *semantic memory* (Tulving, 1972, 2002). **Episodic memories** are those acquired through personal experience—they are our autobiographical memories. **Semantic memories** are memories for facts that we have learned such as numbers, vocabulary words, names of people and places, historical events, scientific information, concepts, and so forth. As an example of the difference between episodic and semantic memory, consider the following memories:

1. I remember that in December, the daytime temperature in Rio de Janeiro rarely falls below 90° Fahrenheit after early morning has passed. (Semantic memory)

2. I remember that during the December *I spent* in Rio de Janeiro, the daytime temperature rarely fell below 90° Fahrenheit. (Episodic memory)

Explicit memory (declarative memory) ▶ Conscious memories for personal experiences (episodic memory) or facts about the world (semantic memory).

Episodic memory ▶ Memories acquired through personal experience. Episodic memories are one subtype of explicit (declarative) memory.

Semantic memory ▶ Memory for facts one has learned, as opposed to personal experiences. Semantic memory is one type of explicit (declarative) memory.

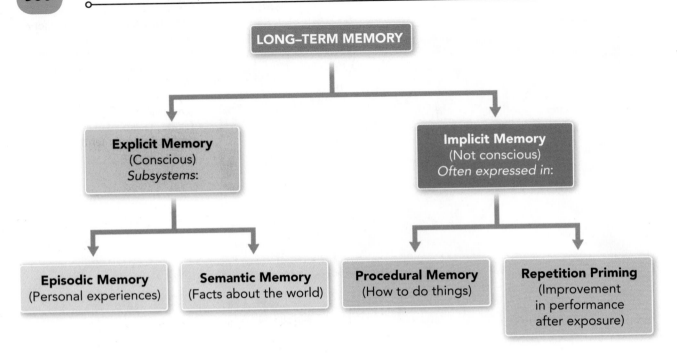

LONG-TERM MEMORY

Explicit Memory
(Conscious)
Subsystems:

Implicit Memory
(Not conscious)
Often expressed in:

Episodic Memory
(Personal experiences)

Semantic Memory
(Facts about the world)

Procedural Memory
(How to do things)

Repetition Priming
(Improvement
in performance
after exposure)

▲ **FIGURE 8.7** The Component
Systems of Long-Term Memory
(LTM).

Memory 1 is semantic, because a fact learned about Rio is being recalled, not an experience of being in Rio. Memory 2 is episodic, because I am recalling a personal experience in Rio. *But:*

3. I recall reading in a *National Geographic* magazine at my sister's house that in December, the daytime temperature in Rio de Janeiro rarely falls below 90°.

Memory 3 is *episodic.* Can you see why? I am not merely recalling a fact—I am recalling a specific personal experience of having learned that fact while reading a magazine. When the personal experience attached to the factual knowledge remains, the memory is episodic. If only the fact remains, the memory is semantic (Squire & Zola-Morgan, 1998). Thus, while *episodic* and *semantic* memory systems are distinct, they are also related because every new piece of semantic (factual) knowledge initially occurs in the context of a personal experience (reading, listening to someone speak, and so forth).

Anterograde Amnesia Evidence for the existence of distinct episodic and semantic memory systems comes from rare cases of *anterograde amnesia,* a condition first described in Chapter 2, and entertainingly depicted in the 2000 film *Memento.* Patients with anterograde amnesia, which generally results from damage to the *hippocampus* and surrounding tissue of the temporal lobe, can form new semantic memories, but cannot form new episodic memories (see Figure 8.8).

Faraneh Vargha-Khadem and her colleagues report the cases of three young adults who had experienced severe hippocampal damage, in one case at birth, in another case by age 4, and in the third at age 9. In childhood, Jon, Beth, and Kate had amnesia for the episodes of daily life. They could not recall where things were located or whether they had made appointments, and they could not make any reliable account of what had happened to them during the day or whom they had seen. They lived in a continuous "present moment" (Vargha-Khadem et al., 1997).

Given the severity of their early memory impairment, it would seem logical that they should be unable to attend school or learn much about their world.

Indeed, according to earlier ideas about LTM—that it was a unitary system regulated by the hippocampus—Jon, Beth, and Kate should have ended up intellectually disabled. Such was not the case, however. These children were able to perform relatively normally in school in reading, writing, and the acquisition of general factual knowledge. They could tell you the major accomplishments of Mahatma Gandhi, identify the nation with the highest population, explain the purpose of the Koran, and define *encumber, sanctuary,* and *boast.* Yet they could not tell you if they had been to school that day and could not remember how they had acquired their factual knowledge. The semantic memories of what they learned remained, but the episodic memories of their *experience* of learning did not. Cases of amnesia that selectively target episodic memory, while leaving semantic memory functional, support the view that these systems are distinct.

However, when performance of one of these children in acquiring new semantic memories was tested against that of ordinary children, the hippocampus-damaged child did not perform as well. Thus, while semantic and episodic memory systems may be distinct, semantic memory is impaired without the support of episodic memory (Gardiner, Brandt, Baddeley, Vargha-Khadem, & Mishkin et al., 2008).

IMPLICIT MEMORY

Implicit memory occurs when we recall something, but have no awareness that we are doing so (Mitchell, 2006). Because people have no recollection of implicit memories, the existence of these memories is generally demonstrated in behavior. For example, when you get into a car and drive to work or school you are demonstrating memory for a complex and varied number of skills that once had to be learned—turning the steering wheel while glancing at the rearview mirror, side-view mirror, and through the front windshield virtually simultaneously and also controlling the rate of acceleration. Yet you perform these actions effortlessly, without the conscious experience of recalling how to do them—and often while talking to a passenger in the car and drinking coffee at the same time!

Although implicit memory is not divided by subtypes, as is explicit memory, it is most frequently expressed in two ways: *procedural memory* and *repetition priming* (see Figure 8.7). **Procedural memory** is implicit memory for skills involving motor coordination, such as driving a car, walking, or flipping a pancake in the pan. These are behaviors that are performed automatically. **Repetition priming** refers to the way that a person's performance of certain tasks can improve without his or her awareness merely as a result of previous exposure to the task—even if the person is unaware of the previous exposure (Goetz, Goetz, & Robinson, 2007; Schacter, 1994).

In a mind-boggling demonstration of the power and long-term stability of implicit memory through repetition priming, David Mitchell (2006) exposed a group of university students in 1982 to a series of black-and-white line drawings. The group only viewed the drawings for between 1 and 3 seconds. Seventeen years later, in 1999, Mitchell contacted the former students and asked them to participate in a follow-up study. He showed these participants small partial fragments of the drawings they had viewed so briefly 17 years earlier, mixed in with fragments of drawings they had never seen.

As depicted in Figure 8.9, when asked to identify the name of the object depicted in the fragment, the students were far more likely to successfully name the object from a fragment of drawing they had seen whole 17 years earlier, as compared with fragments of a second group of drawings they had never seen

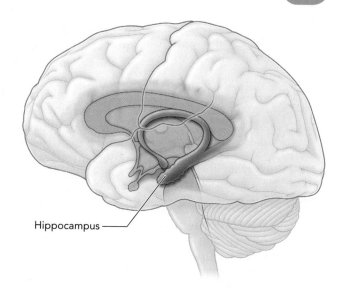

▲ FIGURE 8.8 Amnesia Is Associated with Damage to the Hippocampus. Both anterograde amnesia (inability to form new episodic memories) and retrograde amnesia (inability to access past episodic memories) may result from damage to the hippocampus and surrounding structures of the temporal lobe.

Implicit memory ▶ A memory that affects how we behave without our conscious awareness of the memory itself.

Procedural memory ▶ Implicit memory for skills involving motor coordination.

Repetition priming ▶ When performance on a task improves as a result of previous implicit exposure.

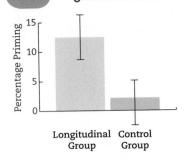

▲ **FIGURE 8.9 Is Implicit Memory Invulnerable?** Participants who had viewed intact drawings for 1 to 3 seconds were better able to identify the objects depicted in these drawings from small fragments viewed 17 years later than from a second group of fragments of drawings they had never seen. A control group of volunteers who had not been part of the original research showed no superior recognition for either group of drawings. *(Source: Mitchell, 2006.)*

Levels of processing framework ▶ The model of memory originated by Fergis Craik and Robert Lockhart which denies the existence of distinct memory stages or stores. Instead, it proposes that the more deeply an item is processed, the more likely it is to be recalled.

whole. This superior recognition ability included four individuals who could not even remember having been brought into the laboratory the first time in 1982! On the other hand, a control group of volunteers who had not been part of the original group showed no difference in ability to identify objects from either group of fragments.

Consider also a group native English-speaking adults under age 40 studied by Jeffrey Bowers and his colleagues. These adults had, in early childhood, been exposed to either Hindi or Zulu languages because their parents had worked in Africa and India. After returning to England, they never heard these languages again. However, as adults in the research lab they were relatively easily able to learn subtle sounds of that childhood language—sounds that do not occur in English. This was in spite of having no explicit memory for any aspect of the language. In contrast, adults who had never been exposed to the language were unable to learn these sounds (Bowers, Mattys, & Gage, 2009). If you recall our discussion of latent learning from Chapter 7—learning that occurs below the level of awareness—you might now see that implicit memory is a record of latent learning, the opposite side of the same coin.

Like explicit memory, implicit memory is associated with specific brain regions, and may become impaired while leaving explicit memory intact (Fleishman, Wilson, Gabrieli, Bienias, & Bennett, 2004; Knowlton, Mangels, & Squire, 1996). However, unlike explicit memories, which deteriorate considerably over time, implicit memories appear to have remarkable longevity.

Levels of Processing Framework: Are Memory Stores Real?

As I mentioned earlier, long-term memory encoded through elaborative rehearsal is often considered a *deeper* level of processing. The idea that information can be encoded at deeper or shallower levels originated in the important work of Fergus Craik and Robert Lockhart (1972, 2009; Craik, 2002) and is known as the **levels of processing framework**. Although the levels of processing framework can be "fit in" to the modal model, Craik and Lockhart did not adhere to the notion that memory consists of separate stores and stages such as STM and LTM. Instead, they simply proposed that the more deeply an item is processed, the more likely it is to be recalled at a later date (Craik & Brown, 2000).

For example, Craik and Lockhart demonstrated that words which had been encoded according to their meanings (semantic encoding) rather than sound or appearance were recalled more readily. These researchers concluded that this was due to a deeper level of processing in semantic encoding. They suggested that it was not necessary to hypothesize the existence of separate memory stages and stores—in understanding levels of processing, one understood the process of memory. They did not deny that short-term and long-term memory existed, but they disputed the idea that they represented distinct mental stores (Craik, 2002).

The levels of processing framework has been enormously influential, not only in memory research, but in cognitive psychology generally (Roediger & Gallo, 2001). However, it has also come under a substantial degree of criticism. Perhaps the most obvious criticism is simply this: How can we know how "deeply" a memory has been processed? We cannot view memories burrowing away into some "deep," secret location in the brain. The only indication we have that the memory had been deeply processed is that it is recalled over time. In other words, to say that an item has been "deeply processed" is not much different from saying that it has been remembered over time. There is a circularity to this definition (Watkins, 2002). If you recall from Chapters 3 and 6, simply giving something a label ("deep level of processing") is not the same as explaining it.

professionals—including Sigmund Freud and the fictional Sherlock Holmes—were regular users of intravenous cocaine.)

One of the premiere British journals of scientific research, *Nature*, recently polled its readers to determine the extent of "brain doping" with cognitive-enhancing drugs among the academic professionals who make up the majority of readers of that journal; 20% of those responding to the poll admitted to having used one or more of these drugs for cognitive enhancement, and over 80% believed people ought to be allowed to do so without regulation (Maher, 2008). Estimates of the use of the drugs by college students vary, but such use is generally thought to be "commonplace" (Smith & Farah, 2011, p. 717).

▲ **Brain Steroids?** New cognitive-enhancing drugs are being used with increasing frequency by healthy individuals to increase alertness, concentration, and overall performance on intellectual tasks and other tasks demanding high cognitive performance.

Like the introduction of any potentially radical technology, the use of these drugs by healthy individuals at their own choice presents a host of debating points, questions, and potential problems. Do the drugs work? Is it ethical to take them? Do they provide the users with an unfair advantage, as do steroid hormones in athletic competition? Should the drugs be legally available without prescription? What will be the ultimate consequences of widespread use?

I cannot address all of these questions here, but let us look at a few. First: Do the drugs work? They do appear to work to some extent—in part by specifically increasing the responsiveness of neurons of the prefrontal cortex (Devilbiss & Berridge, 2008). Recall from Chapter 2 that the prefrontal cortex acts as an executive organizer of information, maker of decisions, and planner of action. It is the king and queen of multitasking. However, the drugs do not work for everyone, they do not work as well as we may have been led to expect by the "neurogossip" on the Internet, and their cognition-boosting effects may attenuate (lessen) over time if use of the drug is continued (Maher, 2008). Some reports suggest that the drugs work best when it comes to recalling facts and strengthening memories as they are encoded (*memory consolidation*) and less reliably when it comes to tasks involving working memory (see pp. 384–385; Smith & Farah, 2011).

More important, when it comes to substances of all kinds—even (or sometimes especially) drugs prescribed for medical reasons—a good rule of thumb is this: *There is no such thing as a free lunch when it comes to drugs*. All drugs have side effects, and cognition-boosting drugs are no exception. In the *Nature* reader survey, 50% of those who responded reported unpleasant side effects including headaches, jitters, anxiety, and sleeplessness. Moreover, as with most new drugs quickly diverted to market, there are no good data on the safety of long-term use for some of the newer cognitive enhancers.

What about the ethics of using these drugs? For example, steroids have been barred from sports competition not only because of obvious health risks, but because they are an ethical violation. Victories gained through factors other than skill, hard work, determination, luck, native ability, and so forth are considered "undeserved" in sports, and because rules forbid the use of steroids, there is the "cheating" factor as well. Sports live or die by the rules, as arbitrary as they might sometimes be, and if people are constantly making up their own rules the sport will die (Mehlman, 2004).

However, sports and games are not the same thing as personal performance on the job or school. Should these drugs be banned from academia simply because they offer an advantage to the user? Forgetting for a

AT THE FOREFRONT

CONTINUED

moment that people use coffee for this purpose all the time and no one complains, some of the ethical problems many seem to have with the use of these drugs run up against logic, as Maxwell Mehlman points out in a critique of ethical objections to cognition-enhancing drugs (Mehlman, 2004). For example, it could be said that achievements that would not have occurred without use of these drugs are unearned and therefore unworthy. However, Mehlman argues that cognitive accomplishments differ from sports, games, and the arts, because it is the benefits they offer that are valued—not the manner in which these benefits are achieved. It is the results that count. As Mehlman suggests, a cure for cancer is a cure for cancer. It is no less an accomplishment if the discoverer was up all night drinking coffee or taking Provigil.

Not everyone will agree with this viewpoint. But we are unlikely to be able to turn back the clock on cognition-enhancing drugs in any case. This particular Pandora's box has been opened, for better or worse. ∎

IN SUMMARY

1. Retrieval cues enhance retrieval of long-term memories. Retrieval cues include context effects, state effects, and flashbulb memories.

2. Working memory is a contemporary way of looking at what happens in short-term memory when information is manipulated or processed.

3. There are two types of long-term memory: explicit memory (conscious memories for personal experiences or facts about the world) and implicit memory (memories that affect our behavior without our conscious awareness).

4. Explicit memory itself has two subtypes: episodic memory, which consists of memory of personal experiences, and semantic memory, which consists of memory for facts learned about the world. Implicit memory is most frequently expressed in procedural memory (implicit memory for skills involving motor coordination) and repetition priming (improvement in performance of a task as a result of previous exposure).

5. Levels of processing theorists deny that separate memory stores and stages exist. Instead, they suggest that the more deeply a memory is encoded, the longer the memory will be retained.

6. Evidence in favor of the existence of separate STM and LTM systems includes the serial position curve and neuroscientific findings showing that items recalled from early positions in lists (primacy effect) primarily activate brain regions associated with LTM. Some studies also show that amnesia patients with damage to the hippocampus and an inability to retrieve long-term memories have no trouble with short-term memory tasks.

7. Evidence against the existence of STM and LTM as distinct systems includes neuroscientific findings showing some overlap in brain areas involved in retrieving short- and long-term memories. In addition, it may not always be the case that that damage to the hippocampus leaves STM intact while only affecting LTM. It may be that only certain types of STM tasks are available to hippocampus-damaged amnesiacs.

RETRIEVE!

1.	Give one possible example each of context-dependent memory and state-dependent memory.
2.	True or false: Flashbulb memories are not only vivid, but they tend to be highly accurate.
3.	Implicit memories for skills involving motor coordination (e.g., driving a car) are known as _____ memories; if a person's task performance can improve as a result of implicit memory of previous exposure to the task, it is known as _____ priming.
4.	Match the description on the left to the component of the multicomponent model of working memory on the right. Episodic buffer Integrates information contained in the phonological loop and visual sketchpad with information coming from LTM through the episodic buffer Phonological loop Holds information pertaining to visual imagery Visual sketchpad Contains verbal and auditory information one is holding in STM or trying to encode in LTM Central executive A temporary "storage area" that encodes information from the loop and sketchpad in a way that can be stored in LTM and retrieves information from LTM for processing in STM
5.	Describe the two "effects" that comprise the serial position curve.
6.	Memories for personal experiences or facts about the world are termed _____ memories; memories acquired with no awareness of having acquired them are called _____ memories.

How Do We Forget Things That Happened (and Remember Things That Never Happened)?

Why did the soldiers of the 7th Cavalry remember vividly Edward Daily's presence at No Gun Ri although he had never been there, as described at the opening of this chapter? And why did I recall being stung by bees in North Carolina when it had actually been my sister's misfortune, not mine? In this portion of the chapter we will explore these and similarly mystifying questions.

Memories Are Constructed, Not Recorded

Much traditional memory research has emphasized questions related to *how much* of various types of memories will "fit" into memory stores and *how long* these memories will remain where we "stick" them (Koriat, Goldsmith, & Pansky, 2001). However, there has recently been a shift among many researchers away from quantitative questions of *how much* and *how long* to the qualitative question of *how accurate?* That is, what is the correspondence between our memories for events and facts about these events as they actually occurred (Brewer & Wells, 2011; Bruck & Ceci, 1997; Frenda, Nichols, & Loftus, 2011; Loftus, 2007; Schacter, 2001)?

This line of research has shown that the popular metaphor for memories as snapshots or videotapes of past events—accurate records that remain in their original condition for access at a later date—has been misguided. Instead, as Steven Lynn and David Payne (1997) propose, memories are *constructed*, not "played back." Rather than resembling a photograph album or VCR library, memory is more like a "theater" of experience where factual events may be interpreted and reinterpreted over time, imbued with dramatic values and subject to distortions that may arise from human bias and our capacity for storytelling.

To some degree the shift from *how long* to *how accurate* has occurred as a result of a series of real-world controversies and startling discoveries in the context of criminal investigations. The first involves the lack of reliability of eyewitness testimony in criminal cases. The second involves controversies over the accuracy of children's testimony in cases of alleged sexual abuse.

Eyewitness Testimony Is Surprisingly Unreliable

Although police departments have long known that eyewitness testimony can be inaccurate, the extent and pervasiveness of this inaccuracy has become painfully apparent with the advent of DNA testing (Eligion, 2009; Gross, 2008). As of 2013, 302 people—who spent a collective total of more than 4,036 years in prison—have been exonerated by DNA testing and had their convictions overturned (The Innocence Project, 2013). At least 80% of these wrongful convictions resulted from erroneous eyewitness testimony (Brewer & Wells, 2011; Gross, 2008).

In one study of 62 cases of exoneration by DNA evidence, 52 convictions had resulted from "confident"—but entirely mistaken—eyewitness accounts (Scheck, Neufeld, & Dwyer, 2000). Another study found that mistaken eyewitness reports result in more wrongful convictions than all other causes combined (Wells & Bradfield, 1998). Because approximately 80,000 criminal cases are decided each year in the United States on the basis of eyewitness testimony, false identifications may have a greater impact on the lives of innocent people than was once presumed (Goldstein, Chance, & Schneller, 1989).

Researchers such as Elizabeth Loftus and Gary Wells have produced numerous laboratory studies that highlight the fragility of eyewitness testimony (Loftus, 1979/1996; 1997; Wells et al., 2000). For example, Gary Wells and Amy Bradfield (1998) had research participants view an 8-second security video of a gunman entering a Target store during a robbery. The participants were asked to focus their attention on the gunman. Later, they were asked to identify the man from a "lineup" photo spread consisting of photos of a number of (entirely innocent) men. The spread was identical to the one used in the actual lineup during the case, except that the real perpetrator's picture had been removed. One hundred percent of the research participants picked someone from the photo spread and expressed confidence that this was the man they had seen on the tape. Moreover, simple feedback comments such as "Good—you identified him" radically altered participants' later reports of how confident they had been when they made the identification, how well they could make out details of his face, how quickly and easily they had recognized him, and how clear their view of the man actually was.

This 100% false identification rate undoubtedly would have been lower had the participants expressly been told that the actual perpetrator might or might not be in the line-up (Brewer & Wells, 2006). However, results of this study are fully supportive of similar experiments showing shocking rates of

Marvin Anderson
Incident Year: 1982
Jurisdiction: VA
Charge: Rape, Abduction, Sodomy, Robbery
Conviction: Rape (2 cts.), Forcible Sodomy, Abduction, Robbery
Sentence: 210 Years

Year of Conviction: 1982
Exoneration Year: 2002
Sentence Served: 15 Years
Real perpetrator found? Yes
Contributing Causes: Eyewitness Misidentification, Government Misconduct, Bad Lawyering
Compensation? Yes

Orlando Boquete
Incident Year: 1982
Jurisdiction: FL
Charge: Att. Sexual Battery, Burglary
Conviction: Att. Sexual Battery, Burglary
Sentence: 50 Years

Year of Conviction: 1983
Exoneration Year: 2006
Sentence Served: 13 Years
Real perpetrator found? Not Yet
Contributing Causes: Eyewitness Misidentification
Compensation? Not Yet

Robert Clark
Incident Year: 1981
Jurisdiction: GA
Charge: Rape, Kidnapping, Armed Robbery
Conviction: Rape, Kidnapping, Armed Robbery
Sentence: Life+

Year of Conviction: 1982
Exoneration Year: 2005
Sentence Served: 23.5 Years
Real perpetrator found? Yes
Contributing Causes: Eyewitness Misidentification
Compensation? Not Yet

Bruce Godschalk
Incident Year: 1986
Jurisdiction: PA
Charge: Rape, Burglary
Conviction: Forcible Rape (2 cts.), Burglary (2cts.)
Sentence: 10-20 Years

Year of Conviction: 1987
Exoneration Year: 2002
Sentence Served: 14.5 Years
Real perpetrator found? Not Yet
Contributing Causes: Eyewitness Misidentification, Unreliable/Limited Science, False Confessions, Government Misconduct, Informants/Snitches
Compensation? Yes

William Gregory
Incident Year: 1992
Jurisdiction: KY
Charge: Attempted Rape, Rape, Burglary
Conviction: Attempted Rape, Rape, Burglary
Sentence: 70 Years

Year of Conviction: 1993
Exoneration Year: 2000
Sentence Served: 7 Years
Realperpetrator found? Not Yet
Contributing Causes: Eyewitness Misidentification, Unreliable/Limited Science
Compensation? Not Yet

Clark McMillan
Incident Year: 1979
Jurisdiction: TN
Charge: Rape, Robbery
Conviction: Aggravated Rape, Robbery With A Deadly Weapon
Sentence: 119 Years

Year of Conviction: 1980
Exoneration Year: 2002
Sentence Served: 22 Years
Real perpetrator found? Yes
Contributing Causes: Eyewitness Misidentification
Compensation? Yes

Calvin Lee Scott
Incident Year: 1982
Jurisdiction: OK
Charge: Rape
Conviction: Rape
Sentence: 25 Years

Year of Conviction: 1983
Exoneration Year: 2003
Sentence Served: 20 Years
Real perpetrator found? Yes
Contributing Causes: Unreliable/Limited Science
Compensation? Not Yet

◀**FIGURE 8.13 Exonerated!** These seven innocent men served a total of 115 total years in jail before being exonerated by DNA evidence. All of them were convicted primarily on the basis of erroneous eyewitness identification. *(Source: Cases selected at random from database maintained by The Innocence Project, www.innocenceproject.org.)*

eyewitness misidentification under a large number of conditions (see Figure 8.13). For example, both blacks and whites are more likely to falsely identify people in lineups if the person is of the other race (Brigham, Bennett, Meissner, & Mitchell, 2007; Wright, Boyd, & Tredoux, 2001).

Children's Memories Can Be Manipulated

In addition to revelations of problems with eyewitness accounts, concern about memory accuracy was heightened by a series of wrongful convictions during the 1980s and early 1990s in cases of alleged sexual abuse of small children in preschools (Bruck & Ceci, 1999; Gross, 2008; Nathan & Snedeker, 1995). Children at these centers were subjected to repeated interrogation, sometimes lasting many months, by well-meaning but misguided social workers, therapists, and police who believed they were "getting at the truth."

Typically, the children at first truthfully denied that any abuse had taken place, but after questioning involving suggestion, threats, brow-beating, and/or bribes, the children ultimately made accusations involving exceedingly bizarre and unlikely forms of sexual abuse, supposedly perpetrated by people (generally women) with no previous records of any sort of misbehavior. Children's denials that abuse had taken place were frequently met by responses such as this from therapists interviewing preschool children in the McMartin case in California during the mid-1980s: "Are you going to be stupid, or are you going to be smart and help us? You must be dumb" (cited by Nathan & Snedeker, 1995, p. 140). Or consider the following, from the Kelly Michaels Wee Care preschool case in New Jersey. The adult interrogator has been repeatedly trying to get the child to admit that Michaels had performed a bizarre sexual act:

Adult:	. . . Did she [touch your "hiney"]?
Child:	I don't know, I forgot.
Adult:	. . . Oh, come on, if you just answer that you can go.
Child:	I hate you.
Adult:	No you don't.
Child:	Yes I do.
Adult:	You love me I can tell. Is that all she did to you [note: the child never said that Michaels did anything to her], what did she do to your hiney?
Adult #2:	What did she do to your hiney? Then you can go.
Child:	I forgot.
Adult #2:	Tell me what Kelly did to your hiney and then you can go. If you tell me what she did to your hiney, we'll let you go.
Child:	No.
Adult:	Please.
Child:	Okay, okay, okay.
Adult:	Tell me now . . . what did Kelly do to your hiney?
Child:	I'll try to remember. . . . (Nathan & Snedeker, 1995, p. 141)

Like the fallibility of eyewitness testimony, the ease with which the memories of small children can be manipulated has been demonstrated in laboratory research. Maggie Bruck and Stephen Ceci created a series of studies showing that even under very gentle, noncoercive forms of repetitious questioning and suggestion, small children could be induced to recall with vivid detail events that never occurred, including having had their genitals penetrated violently with objects by a pediatrician during a routine examination—when the pediatrician in fact had not even gone near the child's genitals (Ceci & Bruck, 1995; Bruck & Ceci, 1999; Bruck, Ceci, Francoeur, & Renick, 1995).

What makes the studies by Bruck and Ceci particularly disturbing is that the children do not merely appear to be pressured to report an event that did not happen primarily to please their questioners—although this undoubtedly does occur in some cases (Cassell, Roebers, & Bjorklund, 1996). In many cases, this pressure seems to have convinced the children to believe that their memories are genuine. That is, their personal "autobiographies" have been rewritten and they have developed **false memories** (Ceci, Loftus, Leichtman, & Bruck, 1994).

False memory ▶ Memory of an event that did not actually occur. In some cases, blatantly inaccurate recollection of details of an event that did occur may also be considered a false memory.

◀ **Memory Distortion in Small Children Leads to False Imprisonment.** Twenty-three-year-old Kelly Michaels, with no record of any wrongdoing or unusual behavior, was accused of bizarre (and in certain cases physically impossible) forms of sexual abuse of children at the Wee Care Day Nursery in Maplewood, New Jersey on the basis of testimony of small children after coercive interviewing by police and therapists. Michaels was convicted of 115 counts of child abuse and sentenced to 47 years in prison. After 5 years in prison her appeal was successful and she was released. (*Sources: Nathan & Snedecker, 1995; Rabinowitz, 2003.*)

Bruck and Ceci and their colleagues have also demonstrated this possibility in studies during which small children are induced to "recall" memories of events that never occurred, such as going on a hot air balloon ride, falling off a tricycle, being taken to the emergency room, and so forth. Many of these children continue to insist that the event actually occurred, even after being informed by parents and others that the events in fact never occurred (Ceci & Bruck, 1995; Bruck & Ceci, 1997, 1999).

The Seven "Sins" of Memory

Cognitive scientist Daniel Schacter has analyzed processes of forgetting, the construction of distorted or false memories, and the unwanted intrusion of unpleasant memories. He characterized these processes in a list of seven memory "sins" along the lines of the "seven deadly sins" described by various religious traditions (Schacter, 2001, 2004; see Table 8.1). Schacter's choice of this metaphor is not meant to be flippant or disrespectful. The seven deadly sins consist of the improper use of human attributes that, when properly used, are not considered sinful at all. For example, *gluttony* is a distortion of the normal appetite for food; *lust* a distortion of normal sexual desire; *pride* a distortion of healthy self-esteem, and so forth. In the same way, according to Schacter, the seven sins of memory are not mistakes in the "design" of memory, but rather, unfortunate "side effects" of memory mechanisms that are in most aspects highly adaptive and without which we could not easily survive. Three of Schacter's sins pertain to forgetting, three to memory distortion, and one to the intrusion of unwanted memories. (Note: The seventh memory sin, related to intrusion of unwanted memories, is examined in "Critical Thinking about Psychology: Memories of Trauma, False and True," later in this chapter.) We begin with Schacter's three sins of forgetting: *transience, absentmindedness*, and *blocking*.

FIRST SIN OF FORGETTING: TRANSIENCE

"I just can't remember—sorry." **Transience** describes the way that retrieval of memories becomes more difficult over time—that is, memories "fade." Transience is responsible for failing to recall how to do long division of fractions expressed as decimal numbers, failing to remember the way to your grandmother's house, failing to recall the story of a book you know you have read, and failing to remember how to play a musical piece you used to play

Transience ▶ The "fading" of memories from long-term memory. Transience describes what most people mean when they say "forgetting."

Table 8.1 **The Seven Sins of Memory**

SIN	DESCRIPTION	EXAMPLE
Transience	Decreasing accessibility of memory over time	Simple forgetting of long-past events
Absentmindedness	Lapses of attention that result in forgetting	Forgetting location of car keys
Blocking	Information is present, but temporarily not accessible	Tip-of-the-tongue phenomenon
Misattribution	Memories are attributed to an incorrect source	Confusing a dream for a memory
Suggestibility	When memory is distorted due to suggestions implanted by others.	Leading questions or misinformation can produce false memories
Bias	Current attitudes, feelings, and beliefs distort memories for the past	Recalling one's past feelings as having been more similar to current feelings than was actually the case; recalling one's past actions as having been more (or less) praiseworthy than was the case
Persistence	Unwanted memories that we cannot forget	Traumatic war memories

(Source: Adapted from Schacter, Chiao, & Mitchell, 2003, p. 328.)

perfectly. When people speak of "forgetting," they are generally referring to memory transience.

Daniel Offer and his colleagues reported results of a 34-year longitudinal study of memory transience for events of adolescence. In 1962, the authors interviewed 73 mentally healthy 14-year-old boys about a wide range of topics. They then re-interviewed them 34 years later, at age 48. The accuracy of study participants' memory of past events was generally no better than would be expected by chance! For example, at age 14, 70% answered that religion was helpful to them, but only 26% of the men remembered having answered in this way. At age 14, 82% claimed that they received physical punishment as discipline, but at age 48, only 33% said they had been physically punished (Offer , Kaiz, Howard, & Bennett, 2000).

If memory for adolescence is transient, memory for childhood events prior to the age of 3 is essentially nonexistent—a fact referred to as **childhood amnesia**. Although fragments of memories and isolated images of events that occur between the ages of 3 and 4 are sometimes available to adults, coherent episodic memories are not usually available for events prior to the fourth birthday—that is, the fifth year of life (Bruce et al., 2005; Davis, Gross, & Hayne, 2008). If you believe you can remember events before then, you are more likely than not remembering photographs, stories, or reveries about the event. In some cases a memory from childhood is mentally rehearsed and repeated throughout childhood, and in such cases you are in effect "remembering remembering" the event—rather than remembering the event as it occurred.

Ebbinghaus and the Forgetting Curve One of the first attempts to study memory transience scientifically was by Hermann Ebbinghaus (1850–1909). Ebbinghaus was interested in determining how much information was lost to awareness after varying lengths of time had passed. He chose himself as his

Childhood amnesia ▶ The term used to describe the fact that adults do not have accurate, coherent memory for events of early childhood. Theorists currently propose that coherent memories are not retained for events prior to the fourth birthday.

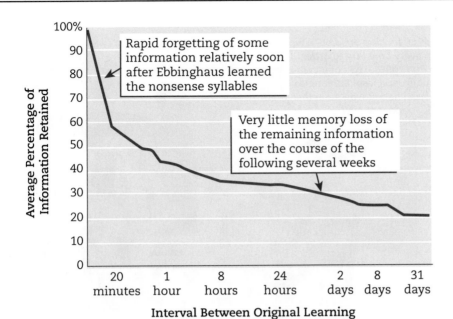

FIGURE 8.14 The Ebbinghaus Forgetting Curve. There is rapid memory loss over the first hour, and within 9 hours 60% of the words are forgotten. After that, the pace of forgetting slows.

research subject and attempted to memorize as many meaningless "nonsense syllables" as he could (Ebbinghaus, 1885/1964). Ebbinghaus tested his memory for such syllables (e.g., TAK, JAV, KOP) at six time periods after having studied the words—from less than 1 hour to 1 month.

As depicted in Figure 8.14, Ebbinghaus noticed that there was a rapid loss of memory within the first hour, and within 9 hours he had forgotten approximately 60% of the words. However, after that the pace of forgetting slowed markedly. One month later he had forgotten only an additional 15% of the words. Thus, most of the "action" in forgetting occurred early on. This discovery came to be known as the **forgetting curve**, and while Ebbinghaus' methods were simple, he had discovered a law of memory transience that has been shown repeatedly to be valid in literally thousands of studies, for ordinary episodic memories as well as lists of words and the like (C. P. Thompson, Skowronski, Larsen, & Betz, 1996).

When One Memory Interferes with Another What causes memory transience? Do long-term memories *decay* or fade away if they are not used, as do short-term memories? Early memory theorists believed that this was the case. However, this theory does not explain why some "unused" memories appear to fade over time while others remain strong for decades or even a lifetime. It also does not explain how the ease or difficulty of retrieving memories is highly dependent upon retrieval cues, regardless of the length of time the memory has remained unused. If memories actually decay over time, then they no longer exist and should not be retrievable regardless of cue.

Instead, most modern researchers speculate that transience is explained in large part by the *interference of one memory in the retrieval of another*. Known as **interference theory** (Anderson, 2003), these theorists have proposed two basic types of interference: *proactive* and *retroactive*. In **proactive interference**, a memory that one has formed in the past interferes with the retrieval of a new memory—particularly if the new information is in some way similar to the old (see Figure 8.15).

For example, as a young man I worked as a cook in a Japanese restaurant, and learned something of the language, with a particular emphasis on matters pertaining to food. Years later, I tried to learn Portuguese. I did alright generally, but when I went to Brazil and tried to order food in a restaurant, Japanese words kept coming to mind and confounding my efforts. I could not recall

Forgetting curve ▶ The discovery made by Hermann Ebbinghaus that forgetting follows a pattern according to the passage of time, with most memory loss occurring rapidly, and the pace then slowing.

Interference theory ▶ The notion, subscribed to by most memory researchers, that problems in retrieving memories results from the interference of one memory with another. There are two types of interference: *proactive* and *retroactive*.

Proactive interference ▶ When an old memory interferes with the retrieval of a new memory.

▶ **FIGURE 8.15** **Proactive and Retroactive Interference.** You experience *proactive interference* when old memories interfere with the retrieval of new memories. *Retroactive interference* occurs when new memories interfere with the retrieval of old ones.

the appropriate Portuguese words due to proactive interference. The effects of proactive interference for a memory tend to *increase* over time (Wixted, 2004).

Retroactive interference is much the same mechanism, but in reverse. In this case, the learning of new information interferes with memory for the old. For example, when you acquire a new cell phone number and learn it, it may soon become virtually impossible to remember the old one due to *retroactive* interference (see Figure 8.19). Retroactive interference may *decrease* over time, and it is less dependent upon the new information being similar to the old (Wixted, 2004).

Retroactive interference
▶ When a new memory interferes with the retrieval of an old memory.

SECOND SIN OF FORGETTING: ABSENTMINDEDNESS

"Did I actually just pay for coffee at Starbucks and walk out without the coffee?" The second memory sin, *absentmindedness*, is usually considered the bane of the middle-aged, but my generation is not the only one afflicted.

Twenty-seven-year-old Tatiana Cooley claims that she is so "incredibly absentminded" that she is forced to "live by Post-Its" (quoted in Levinson, 1999; Schacter, 2001). Without her "to-do lists" she admits she would be lost. This may not seem so remarkable—even young people can be absentminded, after all. However, Tatiana Cooley is a three-time USA Memory Champion. Using methods of elaborative rehearsal and chunking, she can recall strings of 4,000 numbers or 500 words, recite 50-line poems verbatim, and place names to faces with astounding accuracy. So why can't she remember to call her best friend or pick up the dry cleaning?

Absentmindedness describes lapses of attention that result in a failure to recall information. This can happen for two reasons: Either (a) the information was encoded improperly (or not at all); or (b) it was encoded properly and is technically available, but at the moment that its retrieval is necessary it is overlooked for some reason.

An example of the first cause of absentmindedness (improper encoding or non-encoding) is my constant misplacement of my reading glasses. Because I need to put them on and take them off repeatedly during the day, I tend to lay them down in all sorts of odd places. If I am preoccupied when I do so (which I usually am), I do not encode the process of placing them down—it is automatic.

An example of the second cause of absentmindedness, failure to retrieve, is the story of a woman in El Dorado, Arkansas, who, on March 12, 2005, placed her 15-day-old baby on a grocery counter, purchased her food, left the store, and drove off—without the baby. She returned in a panic moments later (but was arrested anyway; "Woman in custody after forgetting baby," 2005). It is unlikely that this woman did not encode where she had placed her baby—she did return to the store, so the knowledge that her baby was there existed in her memory and therefore had been encoded. Instead, when the moment came to retrieve this information, something—*massive* preoccupation, perhaps—interfered with her ability to access this information.

Thus, it is possible to be absentminded and yet have a prize-winning memory, such as that possessed by Tatiana Cooley. Memory feats such as Ms. Cooley's involve retrieval of deeply encoded, elaborated material, under conditions of intense concentration. On the other hand, if Ms. Cooley fails to encode, or is preoccupied at the moment of retrieval, she can be as absentminded as anyone else.

THIRD SIN OF FORGETTING: BLOCKING

"Wait . . . wait, don't tell me!" One day, as I was in the middle of a lecture, I suddenly forgot the word "indicative," which means that one thing is a sign or indication of something else. I was trying to say something like, "But feelings of depression are not necessarily *indicative* of actual clinical depression." I got as far as "are not necessarily . . ." and then I paused and stared at my students blankly for an extremely embarrassing number of seconds that felt like minutes. ". . . depression is not . . . you know . . . what is that word? . . . you know, it means that something implies the existence of something else? . . ." A student (with a pretty good vocabulary) in the back of the room shouted out, "indicative, man!" I had *blocked* the memory of the word.

Blocking differs from transience and absentmindedness. In transience, a memory fades over time, in all likelihood due to interference. In absentmindedness a memory is not encoded properly or a person's attention is diverted when it is time for the memory to be recalled. But in blocking, a memory is encoded properly, is not subject to interference, and is primed by a solid retrieval cue—it *should* be recalled. It just isn't.

While blocking can occur for words like *indicative*, sentences in a speech you have rehearsed, or answers to test questions you knew perfectly well an hour before the test, it occurs most often with names. When you know the face but can't place the name, you are *blocking*. Name blocking is the most

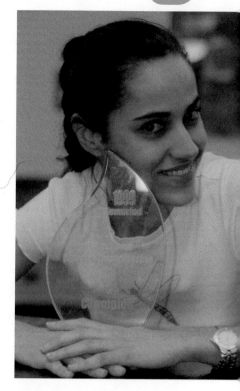

▲ **Three-Time USA Memory Champion Tatiana Cooley.** "I live by Post-Its." Cooley has a fabulous ability to encode and retrieve memory, but she is as absentminded as the next person—perhaps more so!

Absentmindedness ▶ Lapses of attention that result in a failure to recall information. Absentmindedness can result from a failure to encode properly or lapse of attention/preoccupation at the moment of retrieval.

Blocking ▶ When a memory has been encoded properly and primed by a retrieval cue yet cannot be retrieved.

frequent memory complaint of the middle-aged and elderly, particularly when the name seems to be on "the tip of the tongue" but just won't complete the voyage to speech (Cross & Burke, 2004; James, 2006)!

Tip-of-the-Tongue Phenomenon   One may completely block a name while recognizing a face. But what about those times—as just described—when you feel sure you *do* remember the name (or word), but somehow . . . somehow . . . it just won't appear in your mouth to be uttered. It's on the *tip of your tongue.* The **tip-of-the-tongue phenomenon (TOT)** is a specific type of blocking characterized by a powerful sensation that a word or name is remembered, but is somehow just out of reach (R. Brown & McNeil, 1966; Schwartz, 2002). Nearly everyone experiences TOT fairly regularly, generally about once per week—although, as with blocking in general, TOT occurs more frequently as one ages (Schwartz & Frazier, 2005; James, 2006), and more frequently during times of emotional arousal (Schwartz, 2010). About half the time people are successful in resolving the TOT within about a minute (A. S. Brown, 1991), but if you find yourself in a TOT experience, you might do best to stop trying for a few moments and come back to it (Choi & Smith, 2005). In any case, most of those who persevere ultimately succeed.

We now turn to Schacter's three sins of memory distortion: *misattribution, suggestibility,* and *bias.* These are the problems that result not in complete forgetting, but in false and distorted recollection.

MISATTRIBUTION: A CONFUSION OF SOURCE

Misattribution occurs when a person attributes a memory to a source other than its actual origin. My memory of the nest of bees originated with my sister; the 7th Calvary veterans' memories of Edward Daily originated with Daily. These are examples of misattribution. However, while misattribution can result in entirely false beliefs that one has experienced an event when one has not, it may also result in false beliefs about *aspects* of events that one *has* experienced. For example, when you approach a person because you think you have met him or her before, but it turns out the person is an actor whom you've seen numerous times in the movies, you are misattributing your familiarity with the person to an incorrect source.

This latter type of misattribution can have dangerous consequences. Eyewitnesses have been known to identify perpetrators of crimes with confidence, only to find out later that they *had* seen the person—but not at the scene of the crime (Loftus, 1979/1996; Perfect & Harris, 2003). In what is surely the most ironic of such cases, psychologist Donald Thomson, an expert in memory distortion and false recognition, was arrested for rape on the basis of the victim's detailed reconstruction of his face. However, Thomson had an alibi—*he was being interviewed on television about false recognition at the moment the attack occurred.* The victim had been watching the program just prior to the attack and misattributed her memory of Thomson's face to that of the rapist (Schacter, 1996, 2001).

Scripts and Schemas: When Expectations Interfere   Recall the concepts of proactive and retroactive interference, in which one memory can interfere with another, with complete forgetting being the result. In a somewhat similar way, our *expectations,* based on previous experiences of the *type* of situation being recalled—rather than specific memories—can also interfere with the retrieval of accurate memory and result in distorted and false memory as in misattribution. To understand how this works, we need to discuss the workings of *schemas* and *scripts.*

As described in Chapter 4, a schema is an organized mental model or knowledge structure that helps to organize our experience of some type of event or situation, or our understanding of some object or concept. Once a schema is

Tip-of-the-tongue phenomenon (TOT) ▶ A type of *blocking* where there is a powerful sensation that a word or name is remembered but somehow is out of reach.

Misattribution ▶ When a memory is attributed to a source other than its actual origin.

formed, we can then place within the schema new experiences and memories of that, or similar, events, situations, objects, and concepts. For example, suppose you are visiting a dentist for the first time in your life. You take in the events that occur during the visit and end up with a general idea or picture of what dentist visits are about. This becomes your schema for dentist visits. Subsequent visits may alter or refine the schema in various ways, but the schema allows you to anticipate in a general way what is likely to happen on any given visit.

Schemas are useful because they allow us to place new memories into an organizational structure that makes sense. If you were to visit the dentist and find some new piece of equipment, or a new dental hygienist replacing the old one, you would not have to start from scratch in trying to understand the nature of dental visits. You would simply fit this new information into your existing schema for dentists, which now will include the comings and goings of various assistants and pieces of equipment.

Schemas often play out in the form of scripts—structures in long-term memory that represent the typical sequence of events likely to occur in any given situation for which we have a schema—in a sense, the "story" of the situation (Greenberg, Westcott, & Bailey, 1998; Lampinen, Faries, Neuschatz, & Toglia, 2000; Schank & Abelson, 1977). Scripts also include ideas about causes of events within a schema, and roles that different individuals are expected to take. A dental visit script might include being greeted by a polite but insistent person demanding to see your insurance identification, a long wait in an office, being ushered into a room and suited up with aprons by a sympathetic assistant, being forced to wait a seemingly interminable time in an uncomfortable chair until the dentist decides he or she is finished tormenting you with anticipation and arrives to administer a somewhat painful injection to your gum line or inner cheek, and so forth.

As useful as schemas and scripts may be in helping us respond to and interpret new situations, memory researchers have discovered some interesting ways in which they may distort memory or cause outright forgetting:

1. *People often falsely "remember" details or events that do not actually occur because the event is strongly consistent with an existing script or schema* (Kleider, Pezdek, Goldinger, & Kirk, 2008). For example, Heather Kleider and her colleagues presented research participants with slide shows depicting various "male-typical" and "female-typical" actions performed either by men or by women (e.g., sanding down a plumbing pipe, folding baby clothes). When participants were asked to recall information about the slides right after they were shown, they remembered the content fairly well. However, when asked about the slides 2 days later, they often remembered the "male-typical" actions as having been performed by a man even if they had actually been shown a woman performing these actions; and they tended to remember "female-typical" actions as having been performed by a woman even if they actually had been shown a man performing the actions (Kleider et al., 2008; see Figure 8.16)!

2. *People are sometimes more likely to correctly recall details or objects that are* inconsistent *with script or schema expectations for some particular situation or location* (Lampinen et al., 2000; Pezdek, Whetstone, Reynolds, Askari, & Dougherty, 1989). For example, Kathy Pezdek and her colleagues had groups of student volunteers tour either a graduate student's office or a preschool classroom and to take note of the objects in these rooms. Each of the rooms contained objects both consistent and inconsistent with most people's schemas for these locations. Teddy bears, toy trucks, finger paints, and blocks would be consistent with most people's schemas for preschool classrooms, but not graduate students' offices. On the other hand, the reverse might be said for beer bottles, textbooks, calculators, or clock radios.

The groups of volunteers were later tested in various ways for their recall of objects in the rooms. The volunteers were highly accurate in recalling items

▶ **FIGURE 8.16 When Believing Is Seeing.** After a delay of 2 days, research participants who had been shown slide shows depicting men and women engaged in various activities often falsely remembered "female-typical" actions as having been performed by women, and "male-typical" actions as having been performed by men, even when the sex-typical actions were actually performed by a person of the other sex. Studies such as this demonstrate the powerful effects of schemas and scripts upon memory. (Source: Kleider et al., 2008, p. 5.)

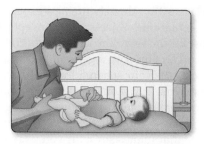

that were *inconsistent* with most people's schemas/scripts for the locations in which they appeared. Beer bottles and textbooks in preschool rooms were recalled quite accurately, as were blocks and toy trucks in graduate student offices.

Can you imagine why people seem to be better at recalling objects or items whose locations or appearances are inconsistent with existing schemas and scripts? It may simply be that things which stand out against their backgrounds are better remembered. Consider the following sequence of words: *apple pear orange banana television plum grapes papaya.* The word *television* is likely to stand out from this list and may therefore be more memorable. Studies such as these demonstrate the importance of the *context in which an event occurs* for subsequent accurate recall (Pezdek et al., 1989).

SUGGESTIBILITY: BEING LED DOWN THE WRONG MEMORY ROAD

I acquired my bee-sting memory by listening to my sister talk about hers, and at some point along the way I forgot where the story came from. No one suggested to me that the memory was mine—I adopted it on my own. However, **suggestibility** is a specific type of misattribution that results from intentional or unintentional suggestions from others. Suggestion is a powerful road to the development of memory distortions, particularly false memory.

Suggestibility ▶ A type of misattribution where a memory originates in suggestions made to a person by someone else.

Elizabeth Loftus has been researching *suggestibility* of memory since the 1970s (Loftus, 1979/1996, 2007; Loftus & Bernstein, 2005; Loftus & Ketcham, 1994). In several series of provocative experiments, Loftus and her colleagues have demonstrated how suggestion may distort existing memories or build entirely new ones from the ground up. Loftus and her colleagues have been interested primarily in two aspects of suggestibility: the *misinformation effect* and the implanting of *rich false memories*.

Much of Loftus' work during the 1980s explored the ways in which people who are exposed to incorrect information about an event they have experienced, later recall the event in a distorted manner by incorporating the false information—a tendency that has come to be termed the **misinformation effect** (Frenda et al., 2011; Loftus, 2005; Loftus & Hoffman, 1989). In a classic demonstration of the misinformation effect, Loftus and her colleagues had university students watch a series of slides depicting an armed robbery in a hardware store in which a screwdriver was taken in addition to money. After viewing the slides the students read narrative reports of the crime with one detail altered—a hammer was described as having been taken instead of a screwdriver. The students were then tested on their memories of the crime. The majority of the students quickly and confidently declared that a hammer had appeared in the depiction of the crime (Loftus, Donders, Hoffman, & Schooler, 1989).

The misinformation effect has been demonstrated in scores of other studies (Ayers & Reder, 1998; Loftus & Bernstein, 2005). People have been fed misinformation that caused them to confuse Minnie for Mickey Mouse, substitute a Yield sign for a Stop sign, change a white car into a blue one, and alter numerous other sorts of details in their reports of witnessed events. People may come to alter their recollection of events if they later speak to other people who have different versions of the event or if they read about the event in the mass media (Loftus, 2003).

However, as Loftus (2003) herself observes, it is one thing to change a hammer into a screwdriver or alter some other detail for an event one has actually witnessed, but quite another for the misinformation effect to create a rich and vivid memory for an event that never occurred at all. Loftus knows that such a thing is possible because she experienced it herself. When Loftus was 14, her mother died in a tragic pool-drowning accident. After that time, vague memories of the event "haunted" her, although they were unfocused and she had no recollection of viewing the death scene itself. Loftus had always thought it had been her aunt Pearl who had discovered the body, but 30 years after the accident, an uncle informed her that it had been Loftus herself who had discovered her mother's lifeless body. Suddenly,

> It all made sense. No wonder I was always haunted by the circumstances of my mother's death. . . . the memory had been there all along, but I just couldn't reach it. . . . Perhaps this new memory, dead and now revived, could explain my obsession with memory distortion, my compulsive workaholism, my unfulfilled yearning for security and unconditional love. (Loftus & Ketcham, 1994, p. 39)

Over the coming days, Loftus was flooded with details of the event—her terror and screams, the police cars, the stretcher with the white blanket tucked around the edges of her mother's body. However, several days afterward, Loftus received a call from her brother. It appeared that the uncle had been mistaken. It *had* been Aunt Pearl who discovered the body, a fact confirmed by numerous other relatives. A casual piece of misinformation—"It was *you* who discovered your mother's body"—triggered the construction of a **rich false memory**, a vivid false memory replete with extensive detail and emotional content.

Misinformation effect ▶ When a person exposed to incorrect information about an event they have experienced later recall the event in a distorted manner by incorporating the false information.

Rich false memory ▶ A vivid false memory replete with rich detail and emotional content.

Loftus and her colleagues began to experiment with the deliberate implanting of rich false memories using the *lost-in-the-mall* technique. In this type of study, relatives of the research participants are enlisted as confederates of the experimenter and asked to provide false information to the participant about a childhood event—such has having been lost in a mall, hospitalized for a serious illness or injury, attacked by an animal, or rescued from drowning by a lifeguard. These events are entirely fabricated by the investigators and the participant's relatives (Heaps & Nash, 2001; Hyman, Husband, & Billings, 1995; Loftus & Pickrell, 1995). Typically, the participant is given descriptions of a number of childhood events, most of them true, but one of them false. The participant is asked if they remember each event and, if so, to provide details.

In most such studies, a substantial minority (approximately 30% on average but as many as 50% or as few as zero) develop rich false memories for the fictitious events. If a doctored photograph is used as supportive "evidence" of the occurrence of the event, the development of false memories may occur in as many as two-thirds or more of participants (Lindsay, Hagen, Read, Wade, & Garry, 2004). After completing these studies, participants are "debriefed"—the purpose of the study is explained, and they are informed that their memories are false. In general, they tend to exhibit great astonishment. As one participant put it: "No way! I remember it! That is so weird!" (Lindsay et al., 2004, p. 153).

Rich false memories have consequences in behavior. Research participants in a study by Elke Geraerts and her colleagues were led to falsely believe they had been sickened as children from eating spoiled egg salad. A substantial minority of these participants subsequently avoided eating egg salad for at least 4 months (Geraerts et al., 2008). Far more serious consequences of rich false memories are described in "Critical Thinking about Psychology: Memories of Trauma, False and True."

CRITICAL THINKING ABOUT PSYCHOLOGY

Memories of Trauma, False and True

We have seen that it is possible for small children to construct detailed false memories of outrageous abuse as a result of suggestive and coercive questioning—memories that the child may come to believe are true. What of reports of the recovery in adulthood of previously "repressed" memories of childhood sexual abuse? Are these memories of real occurrences that have been unconsciously wiped from memory due to their traumatic nature, as some insist, or are they false memories constructed more often than not during psychotherapy sessions with therapists who use dangerously suggestive techniques, as others contend?

Although progress has been made in resolving some of the controversies surrounding this question, it is not likely that all issues will be entirely resolved to everyone's satisfaction, at least not in the near future. The problem is that it is extremely difficult to conduct the sort of research that would unambiguously settle the most important questions. To do so, one would have to be able to determine with certainty that (a) a "remembered" incident of abuse actually took place many years ago as described; and (b) the person actually *had* completely forgotten the abuse for all those years (McNally, 2003).

For example, several people in research studies who sincerely believed they had forgotten their abuse since the time of its occurrence, in fact had discussed it on numerous occasions with their spouses—they had simply forgotten they had remembered (Schooler, Bendiksen, & Ambadar, 1997)! Indeed, in experimental research, recovered memory claimants have been shown to be particularly vulnerable to "forgetting they remembered" in other contexts as well (Geraerts et al., 2006).

However, even if it could be determined that abuse actually occurred and truly had been forgotten for some period of time, it still would not be clear *why* the abuse had been forgotten. For example, the person may simply have not thought about the abuse over a period of years. Many events of childhood, pleasant as well as unpleasant, are not thought about over periods of time (McNally, 2003). On the other hand, as some contend, the memory might truly have been wiped from awareness due to its traumatic nature ("traumatic amnesia" or "repression"). Despite the difficulties in investigating such questions, enough research has been conducted over the years to be able to confidently make at least two statements about the recovered memory controversy:

1. *Most people who experience traumatic events try very hard to forget these memories, but cannot.*

Moreover, the more traumatic the event, the more difficult it is to forget (Alexander et al., 2005; McHugh, 2008; McNally, 2003). Such memories are most likely to display the seventh memory "sin" of **persistence**—the intrusion of unwanted thoughts upon a person's consciousness.

Studies of victims of war, torture, genocide, rape, and other severe traumas show that while these victims may forget specific aspects of a traumatic event, they do not forget the event itself. For example, holocaust survivors may forget a particular incident that occurred while they were interned in a concentration camp as children, but they certainly do not forget having been in the camp, even after a great many decades have passed. In general, their memories for these events are "clear, detailed, orderly, and realistic" (Schelach & Nachson, 2001, p. 129). In long-term studies, memories for traumatic events are more reliable and consistent than memories for pleasant events (Porter & Peace, 2007).

In the specific case of child sexual abuse, Kristen Alexander and her colleagues used documented cases of child sexual abuse to examine victims' memory accuracy 12 to 21 years later for details of the abuse (Alexander et al., 2005). These investigators found that the more traumatic the experience was for the victim, the more likely he or she was to recall details of the event accurately.

2. *Nevertheless, it is has been conclusively demonstrated that a traumatic memory such as sexual abuse or rape can be completely forgotten for many years and later recalled* (Brenneis, 2000; Schooler et al., 1997).

For example, a 41-year-old woman in treatment for her childhood experiences of abuse (which she remembered all too vividly) was driving home from a therapy session during which her therapist had mentioned that child victims sometimes also become adult victims. All of a sudden, she recalled having been raped by a stranger, 13 years previously, at the age of 22. At that time she actually had brought charges against the man, who had been prosecuted and convicted. Astoundingly, she had completely forgotten the entire event, including the trial. The rape, the trial, and her lack of memory for both are well documented.

Cases conclusively documented in this way, however, are quite rare. Most accounts of "recovered memories" of sexual abuse unravel for a wide variety of reasons: The abuse is conclusively shown never to have taken place, the memory's origin in suggestive or coercive psychotherapy sessions is highly probable, the events recalled are wildly implausible (or even physically impossible), and so forth (McHugh, 2008; Ofshe & Watters, 1994; Richardson, Best, & Bromley, 1991).

Is it possible to tell genuine recovered memories from false memories? Although some tentative neuroscientific work has compared brain function

Persistence ▶ When an unpleasant memory intrudes upon a person's thoughts against his or her will.

CRITICAL THINKING ABOUT PSYCHOLOGY

CONTINUED

during false and true memory recall (Sederberg et al., 2007), this science is in its infancy and has yet to provide definite answers. However, conclusively documented cases differ in important respects from the usual account of "recovered memory." In the typical "recovered memory" case, a client (usually a woman) is referred to a therapist for depression or some other complaint. She has no memory of abuse, but is asked by the therapist to recall if "something may have happened" during her childhood that was very upsetting. She is urged to recall dreams and may be placed under hypnosis, given drugs, or asked to engage in "guided imagery"—all highly suggestive techniques that have been shown to produce rich false memories (Loftus & Ketcham, 1994).

Then, what begins as vague imagery is refined over time through intensive dialogue with the therapist (who is typically a strong believer in the reality of recovered memories) into a series of increasingly bizarre and horrifying memories of abuse that the woman sometimes has to be convinced are real by her therapist (Ofshe & Watters, 1994). Rather than healing from this process, as recovered memory therapists insist will occur, the client's mental health generally deteriorates after the "recovery" of the memory (Lynn, Lock, Loftus, Krackow, & Lilienfeld, 2003).

On the other hand, in documented cases of recovered memory, the memory arrives with suddenness "all of one piece," generally triggered by an event or comment of some sort. It is not built from vague imagery over months of suggestive (and in some cases, coercive) psychotherapy. The event recalled is plausible, and the person knows or feels strongly that it is a memory of an actual occurrence. He or she does not need to be convinced (McNally, 2003). Memories recovered this way, like memories that were never forgotten in the first place, are more likely to be corroborated independently than memories recovered over time in the context of psychotherapy (Geraerts et al., 2007; McNally & Geraerts, 2009).

Thus, a traumatic memory can be *forgotten* for a period of time and *recalled* at a later date, although such an event is likely quite rare. Yet, critics of recovered memory point out that it has yet to be demonstrated that a memory can be "repressed"—entirely wiped from memory *because* of its traumatic nature (Rofé, 2008). The controversy will no doubt continue. In an important sense, however, *all memory is false*, at least to some degree (Bernstein & Loftus, 2009). This is because our memories are reconstructions—pieced together narratives and images which constitute our personal autobiographies. ■

BIAS: BEING PREDISPOSED TO SPECIFIC MEMORY DISTORTIONS

I shall never forget the face of my friend Nita's 6-year-old as she watched a videotape of herself at age 2½ walk calmly over to her 6-month-old brother and bop him hard on the head with a book for no particular reason at all, resulting in screams of distress from the baby. Up to that point the girl had been greatly enjoying watching her cute baby brother and her own toddler self on the TV screen, but when that book came down on her brother's innocent head, her own face froze in total disbelief. She shook her head as if to wipe the image from consciousness or deny that she had actually witnessed it. "Why did I do that?" she asked in shamed wonderment.

Her mother explained that the girl had not greeted the appearance of a new baby in the house with total equanimity, as the new arrival had dethroned her from her previous only-child position as reigning queen of the house. Of course she had loved her new brother, but occasionally bopped him on the head unexpectedly.

The point of the story is this: That 6-year-old girl *could not believe what she was witnessing*. Being faced with undeniable evidence of less-than-admirable past behavior violates a general memory *bias* known as the **egocentric bias**—a tendency to recall past events in a way that enhances one's current view of oneself (M. Ross & Wilson, 2003; Taylor, 1989).

The *egocentric bias* is only one of a number of pervasive memory *biases*. A **bias** is any systematic distortion in perception, cognition, or memory that results from some aspect of a person's current psychology. The egocentric bias in memory is particularly interesting, because it does not necessarily cause us to remember ourselves as "better" than we actually were—in fact, it quite often does the exact opposite. Researchers have shown that there is a tendency for people to think of themselves as having "improved" over time (whether or not they actually have), and to exaggerate past failures or unreasonably criticize their former selves as a way of enhancing their views of their selves in the present (Wilson & Ross, 2001, 2003). The further in the past one goes, the more likely one is to distort one's memory for oneself in a negative direction.

In addition to the egocentric bias, memory is distorted through the **consistency bias**, a tendency to recall one's past attitudes, feelings, and beliefs in a way that brings them in line with one's *current* attitudes, feelings, and beliefs (Cameron, Wilson, & Ross, 2004). For example, Elaine Scharfe and Kim Bartholomew (1998) had 77 dating, cohabitating, or married couples fill out extensive questionnaires describing their relationship "style," closeness of the relationship, love for their partner, importance of the relationship, happiness in the relationship, how often their partner "got on their nerves," and so forth. Eight months later the investigators asked the participants to recall how they had answered these questions. Among those participants whose feelings about their partners and their relationships had not changed, memory was highly accurate: 89% of women and 85% of men correctly recalled how they had answered the questions put to them 8 months earlier. However, the picture was dramatically different for those whose feelings *had* changed: only 22% of these women and 13% of the men correctly recalled the answers they had given—with the majority of these incorrect answers bringing former feelings in line with current feelings. Those who no longer felt as loving as they originally had felt claimed that they had always felt less than happy in their relationships; those who no longer felt negatively about the relationship claimed that things had always been blissful!

Egocentric bias ▶ The tendency to recall past events in a way that enhances one's current view of oneself.

Bias ▶ A systematic distortion in perception, cognition, or memory as a result of some aspect of one's current psychology.

Consistency bias ▶ The tendency to recall one's past attitudes, feelings, and beliefs in a way that brings them in line with one's *current* attitudes, feelings, and beliefs.

Are Our Memories Defective?

Why do we forget and distort memory? Are the memory "sins" described earlier evidence of defects in our memory systems? Researchers such as Gary Marcus contend that our memory systems have been constructed over evolutionary history in a more or less haphazard fashion, and have survived not because they are particularly good but because they are "good enough" (Marcus, 2008). Theorists such as Marcus view problems of distortion and forgetting primarily from a "defect" perspective.

However, applying a different type of evolutionary view, Schacter (2001) suggests that mechanisms of forgetting serve specific adaptive functions. For example, *transience* enables us to lose information that is no longer current—where we parked our car last week, as opposed to where we parked it this morning. Memory for last week's parking location no longer needs to be rehearsed, allowing us to place our cognitive resources elsewhere. Something similar is at work in *blocking*, according to Schacter, particularly in tip-of-the-tongue (TOT) experiences. If you recall, names and words that one has not recently used are most frequently subject to TOT. TOT may represent one expression of general mechanisms that inhibit memory for items that are unlikely to be used frequently, freeing up resources for more critical memory tasks.

The principle that fewer memories may make for better memories is even more clearly apparent in *absentmindedness*. Encoding memories at depth requires rich elaboration. Schacter asks, what if *all* events—the unimportant as well as the important—were elaborated and encoded with the same amount of rich detail? The mind would be an "overwhelming clutter of useless details" (2001, p. 190). Thus, in Schacter's view, there is a "trade-off" in forgetting. Although forgetting can prove frustrating, on the whole it maintains the adaptive functioning of memory.

The same applies to memory distortion sins such as *misattribution* and its offspring *suggestibility*. These involve failing to maintain memory for the sources of experience or information. Once again, however, were we to recall *all* the details of context and source for *all* memories, our minds would be excessively cluttered. Source and context details would interfere with the retention of more important information. In general, there is no need to recall many precise details of context and source unless these details are likely to be needed in the future. The important thing is to remember that water does not put out oil fires, not to recall specifically how you learned this fact. Being able to recall the *gist* of events—to benefit from knowledge without necessarily recalling its source—is a memory strength, according to Schacter, not a weakness. The "trade-off" is the unfortunate capacity of the human mind to create distorted memories.

Is there evidence to support Schacter's view of forgetting? Bruce Kuhl and his colleagues used fMRI technology to measure activity in the prefrontal cortex during memory tasks (Kuhl, Dudukovic, Kahn, & Wagner, 2007). These researchers found that better memory for details was associated with increased demands on regions of the cortex, but that these demands were reduced when competing, irrelevant memories were forgotten—just as Schacter's theory would predict.

IN SUMMARY

1.	Memory is more like live theater than a VCR library or photo album. Memories are constructed and interpreted rather than "played back."
2.	Interest in memory accuracy has been heightened by findings that eyewitness accounts are often highly inaccurate and easily manipulated, and that small children subjected to repeated coercive or suggestive questioning can develop false memories for traumatic events.
3.	The "seven sins of memory" is a term coined by Daniel Schacter to describe those memory mechanisms that may result in forgetting, memory distortion, and persistent unwanted memories. The "sins" are transience, absentmindedness, blocking, misattribution, suggestibility, bias, and persistence.
4.	Transience is the "fading" of memory; absentmindedness is the failure to recall due to lapses of attention; blocking is the momentary failure to access a properly encoded memory; misattribution is the attributing of a memory to a source other than its actual origin; suggestibility is a form of misattribution where a memory results from intentional or unintentional suggestions of others; bias is systematic distortion in memory due to some aspect of one's current psychology; persistence is the repeated unwanted intrusion of an unpleasant memory.
5.	Most traumatic memories are difficult to forget. Traumatic events can be forgotten for a period of time and then remembered, but it is not clear whether these events have been "repressed" or merely forgotten temporarily. Documented cases of recovered memories of child abuse are rare, and they usually differ in their character from typical "recovered memory" cases.

6. Schemas are organized mental models or structures that help to organize specific types of experiences. Scripts are mental structures that represent the typical sequence of events likely to occur in any given situation for which we have a schema. Recall is better for items or events that are inconsistent with preexisting schemas and scripts than items or events that are consistent.

RETRIEVE!

1. Describe one study conducted by Stephen Ceci and Maggie Bruck which demonstrated that small children can develop false memories for potentially traumatic events.

2. Failure to recall a newer memory due to interference by an older memory is known as _____. Failure to recall an older memory due to interference by a newer memory is known as _____.

3. What is the term used to describe the fact that people may construct false memories of an event if they are later exposed to misleading information about it?

   a) rich false memory   **c)** retroactive interference

   b) misinformation effect   **d)** proactive interference

4. How do the egocentric bias and the consistency bias affect memory?

5. Why does Daniel Schacter believe that the seven sins of memory are not evidence of defects in our memory systems?

6. True or false: Documented cases of recovered memories of sexual abuse are extremely rare.

Looking Back:

Chapter 8 in Review

WHAT ARE MEMORIES?
- Memory may be defined as a group of mechanisms and systems that encode, store, and retrieve information. The modal model of memory describes three stages and stores in the memory process: sensory memory, short-term memory (STM), and long-term memory (LTM).
- Sensory memory, which very briefly stores fleeing sensory impressions for further processing in STM and LTM, is divided into iconic store and echoic store.
- STM can generally hold information for no longer than 20 seconds unless maintenance rehearsal takes place, and no more than four single items or chunks of information can be held in STM at any time.

- Long-term memory (LTM) is theoretically limitless and relatively permanent. Information moves from STM to LTM through acoustic encoding, visual encoding, or semantic encoding. Although semantic encoding is least often used, it tends to be the most effective form of LTM encoding, because it involves a deeper level of processing. Elaborative rehearsal is generally the best way to encode information in LTM semantically. One way to use elaborative rehearsal is through mnemonic devices such as the acronym, loci, and pegword methods.

WHAT IS "REMEMBERING"?
- Retrieval—"remembering"—can happen either through recognition

or recollection. Recognition is much easier than recall. Retrieval cues are any type of hint or association that helps one to sift through long-term memories to select the appropriate one. Cues may be internal or external. One external cue is context. Examples of internal retrieval cues include state-dependent memory and flashbulb memories.
- Working memory is a way of looking at what happens in short-term memory when information is manipulated or processed. The multicomponent model of working memory suggests that working memory consists of four active components: the phonologic loop, the visuospatial sketchpad, the

Looking Back continued

episodic buffer, and the central executive.

- LTM has two types and two subtypes. Explicit memories are conscious memories for personal experiences or facts about the world. There are two subtypes of explicit memory: episodic memories and semantic memories. Implicit memory occurs when we recall something but have no awareness that we are doing so. Implicit memory is most frequently expressed as either procedural memory or repetition priming.
- The levels-of-processing framework proposes that information can be encoded at deeper or shallower levels. It suggests that so-called "short-term memory" simply represents shallower levels of processing, while LTM results from deeper levels. This idea lacks some of the attributes of a true explanatory theory of memory, and works best as a guide for research. Moreover, there is some evidence to support the existence of separate stages and stores of memory.
- Psychostimulant "smart drugs," derived from amphetamine, can be used to enhance cognitive functioning and improve memory. Although these drugs do appear to work at least to some extent, they often have unpleasant side effects, their long-term safety has not been established, and their use raises ethical concerns.

HOW DO WE FORGET THINGS THAT HAPPENED (AND REMEMBER THINGS THAT NEVER HAPPENED)?

- Memories are constructed, not recorded. Thus, eyewitness testimony can be surprisingly unreliable. Because of revelations of false accusations of abuse arising from improper interview techniques, and the number of eyewitness accounts demonstrated to have been false, many memory researchers have moved away from questions of how much information can be stored in memory (and for how long) to questions of the accuracy of memories.
- The "seven sins of memory" include sins of forgetting and sins of memory distortion. Sins of forgetting include transience, absentmindedness, and blocking. Sins of memory distortion include misattribution, suggestibility, and bias. A seventh sin, persistence, refers to the intrusion of unwanted memories upon consciousness.
- The notion that traumatic memories may be repressed and hidden from later recall has been highly controversial. Research has established that the more traumatic the experience, the more likely it is to be recalled, and the more accurate the recollection. Although some traumatic memories may be completely forgotten for many years and later recalled, it is not clear whether this is simple forgetting or if "repression" is the cause. Although there is no way to tell a false from a true instance of a recovered memory with certainty, conclusively documented cases differ in certain respects from the typical account.
- The fact that human memories are imperfect may reflect evolutionary "trade-offs" which cause fewer problems than we would encounter if forgetting and memory distortions did not exist.

Key Terms

Test Yourself

1. What are the three components of the modal model of memory?

2. When sensory memory impressions are visual in nature they are termed _____ store. When they are auditory they are termed _____ store.

3. What are the two functions of sensory memory?

4. The capacity of short-term memory is _____ items or chunks of information. The duration of STM is generally no more than _____ seconds.

5. Which types of encoding processes are primarily associated with STM? Which type is associated with long-term memory (LTM)?

6. Working memory and short-term memory are often thought to be the same thing. However, they are not exactly the same. Can you distinguish working memory from STM?

7. What is the most effective type of rehearsal to use in order to encode information in long-term memory (LTM)?

8. True or false: Levels-of-processing theorists challenge the view that STM and LTM represent separate stages or stores of memory.

9. True or false: Multiple choice and true/false questions rely on retrieval rather than recollection.

10. Drinking coffee while you study for a test, and then drinking coffee before taking the test, is relying on what sort of retrieval cue?

11. True or false: Flashbulb memories tend to be particularly accurate as well as vivid.

12. Differentiate explicit from implicit memory.

13. Conscious memories for personal experiences or facts about the world are examples of _____ memory. Recalling something without the awareness of having done so is an example of _____ memory.

14. Memories acquired though personal experience are known as _____ memories. Memories for facts about the world are known as _____ memories.

15. Which three memory "sins" are related to forgetting, and which to memory distortion? Define each.

16. The inability to remember your new cell phone number because the old one keeps popping up in your head is known as _____ interference. The inability to remember your old number because it has been mentally replaced by the new one is known as _____ interference.

17. How might the egocentric bias and the consistency bias affect memory?

18. False memory that results when a person is exposed to incorrect information about an event they have witnessed is known as _____.

9

Thinking, Language, and intelligence

Chapter Outline

FREEZE FRAME

His name is Jefferson Pereira, but everyone calls him "Jet" (pronounced "*Jet*chee"). He acquired this nickname for two reasons: his encyclopedic knowledge of the films of martial arts star Jet Li, and his speed in computing sales figures during transactions. Jet is a street vendor in Salvador, Bahía, on the northeast coast of Brazil. Jet's parents and older brother were migrant workers who had been attracted to Bahía from Pernambuco by relatives' stories of money to be made in the tourist sector.

Jet's father and brother sell cheap radios, watches, batteries, and toys imported from Paraguay, but Jet sells fruit—lemons, melons, maracujá (passionfruits), and coconuts (if you like, he'll drill holes in the coconut and you can put straws into them to drink the sweet coconut water). In the course of the day, Jet makes innumerable arithmetic calculations in his head. "How much are the coconuts? Okay, how much for five—no, make it four . . . and throw in three lemons. . . . No, that's too much, take off one lemon, then. How much for everything?" Jet's mental calculations are virtually always accurate and extremely rapid. He never uses a calculator or paper and pencil.

For about a year and a half, Jet's parents were doing well enough to send him to school. His teachers attempted to instruct him in arithmetic. But when Jet tried to "carry over" in addition or subtraction, he got lost. While multiplying, he did not understand when to add zeroes, how many to add, and how to carry out the necessary addition procedures. He could not learn division at all. Because he could not read

and scored very low on mathematics tests, he was thought to have a mild intellectual disability during his brief time at school. When Jet's parents' income dropped, he left school to become a street vendor.

Mild intellectual disability? Hardly.

In 1985, researcher Terrezinha Carraher and her colleagues went into the streets of Recife, another city in northeastern Brazil, to study the mathematical abilities of child street vendors. They were able to enlist a number of these children in their research project. Carraher and her team first created math problems stated in the context of purchase transactions (e.g., "I'll take three coconuts . . ."). After the child computed the answer, the investigators tried to tease out information about the mental processes the children used to solve the problem ("How did you get that so fast?"). The children appeared primarily to be using very rapid series of small, mentally manageable addition and multiplication operations "chained" together. The children's average score for these initial, informal math tests was 98.2% correct. The researchers then created formal arithmetic problems using the identical numbers and operations used in the informal tests, but framing the problems with abstract symbols divorced from context ("What is 6×50?"). The children's average score was 36.8% correct (Carraher, Carraher, & Schliemann, 1985).

Are these children intelligent? They communicate well with language and can perform complex cognitive operations very rapidly. And yet they would undoubtedly score quite low on most tests of cognitive abilities. Results such as those of Terrezinha Carraher and her research team have added fuel to an often ferocious debate over the nature of human cognition—the sheer complexity and power of which separates human beings from all other species.

Although we are not the only animals with cognition, it is beyond question that no other species can compare to human beings in the way cognitive properties develop, the ways they are put to use in aiding survival and controlling important resources, and their many less practically useful—but aesthetically unsurpassed—products. Thus, Einstein's general relativity theory and Darwin's theory of natural selection take their places beside American jazz music, European oil painting, Japanese *Noh* drama, Native American beading, and African drumming and dance. All are the superb products of human cognition. In this chapter, we will look into the most spectacular successes of human cognition: thinking, language, and intelligence.

How Does the Mind Work?

In the late 1960s, philosopher Jerry Fodor (1968, 1983) and several others developed an idea that had been floating around philosophy circles since the 1950s, and in so doing changed the entire direction of many branches of psychology. Fodor and those who had been working along the same lines made the claim that the mind functioned in a manner loosely analogous to a computer—that is, that the mind was designed to process and manipulate *information*. This idea has come to be known as the **computational theory of mind (CTM)**, and it has formed the basis of much of *cognitive science*. **Cognitive science** is the term used to describe those branches of science that study mental activities and attributes that are involved in collecting, processing, storing, retrieving, and manipulating information. In addition to psychologists, cognitive scientists include among their number philosophers, neuroscientists, computer scientists, and linguists.

Of course, Fodor and other early cognitive scientists did not mean that the mind was designed like a PC, MAC, or other commercially available computer, or that people went about their business like robots or androids. Instead, these theorists meant that the mind operates according to sets of largely universal rules and principles for processing and manipulating information—much the way computer programs process and manipulate whatever data are entered into them. In other words, mental activity is *lawful*, and the best way to describe its laws is to invoke the metaphor of computation.

As you might expect, there are many disagreements among cognitive scientists about the nature of the mental computations that make up cognition, and there are those who reject the computational model entirely. Nonetheless, the computer metaphor popularized by Fodor is pervasive throughout cognitive psychology and has been responsible for many of the important insights described in the discussions of *thinking*, *language*, and *intelligence* to follow.

Computational theory of mind (CTM) ▶ The notion that the mind functions as an information processor in a manner loosely analogous to a computer.

Cognitive science ▶ Branches of science that study mental activities and attributes involved in collecting, processing, storing, retrieving, and manipulating information. Cognitive scientists may come from disciplines as varied as psychology, linguistics, philosophy, neuroscience, and computer science.

Thinking and Cognition Are Not the Same

Although people often use the terms *thinking* and *cognition* interchangeably, they are not identical. Cognition encompasses all mental activities and attributes concerned with information. In addition to thinking, cognition includes learning and memory, language, intelligence, and the brain's transformation of pure sensory perceptions (for example, sight and sound) into information—information that one may then *think* about. Thus, we might say that thinking is a subset of cognition.

But what precisely *is* thinking? **Thought** is the active process of mentally manipulating or "working with" information to solve problems, make decisions, increase knowledge, or just fantasize. Thinking is composed of two primary components: *mental images* and *concepts*.

Thought ▶ The active process of mentally manipulating information in order to solve problems, make decisions, increase knowledge, or fantasize. Thought consists of mental images and concepts.

Mental Images Represent Information in Picture Form

How many shelves are in your refrigerator? How many vegetables can you name that are not green? How would you describe your sixth-grade teacher's hairstyle? As Steven Pinker (1997) observes, when asked questions such as these, most people respond by creating mental visualizations for inspection by the "mind's eye," rather than reeling off recalled facts. Such visualizations are known as **mental images**, and they are a type of thought. These pictures—images of people, places, and things that occur to us countless times a day—are *representations* of information in visual form. When you read a story and form mental images of the events about which you are reading, when you hear the front door open and picture your roommate coming through the doorway,

Mental images ▶ A type of thought composed of representations in picture form.

▶ **FIGURE 9.1** The Brain Perceives Faces and Places Differently.
Neuroscientist Nancy Kanwisher has identified a blueberry-size cortical region called the *fusiform face area* (FFA) seemingly set aside virtually exclusively for face perception. Another cortical area, the *parahippocampal place area* (PPA), apparently responds more strongly to indoor or outdoor scenes of places—the layout of local space.

This figure depicts brain-slice fMRI data for four research participants in the study by O'Craven and Kanwisher (2000). The pink arrows in the images on the top two rows show activation in the FFA for these subjects as they viewed images of faces or imagined viewing faces. The top row shows activation while participants actually viewed faces, and the row below that shows activation while participants imagined viewing faces.

Similarly, the bottom two rows show perception and imagination tasks for the viewing of places, with corresponding activation of the PPA as participants actually viewed images of places, or imagined viewing places.

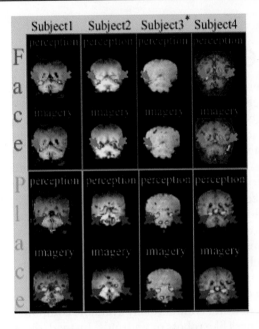

when you feel hungry and imagine a hamburger or an organic sprout salad with avocados, you are representing information in picture form.

The term *mental image* is apt. When research subjects engage in tasks that require the construction of mental images, they utilize areas of the *occipital cortex* normally associated with vision (Ganis, Thompson, & Kosslyn, 2004; Kosslyn, Thompson, & Ganis, 2006). More interestingly, as depicted in Figure 9.1, areas of the brain that are activated during visual perception differ according to the *content* of what is being viewed—whether it is a face or place—and the same differences are found for brain activation during the formation of *mental* imagery of faces and places. Simply by looking at fMRI brain scans, researchers are able to tell whether a person is imagining a face or a place (Liu, Harris, & Kanwisher, 2010; McKone, Kanwisher & Duchaine, 2006; Xu, Liu, & Kanwisher, 2005).

Concepts Are Mental Categories

Pictures may sometimes be worth a thousand words, but not always. What sort of mental image can you conjure up for "ambivalence"? Is it colorful? Does "fatigue" have jagged or smooth edges? Of course, you might be able to conjure up an image of a person you believe to be ambivalent on some issue, or an activity you find particularly fatiguing. But what of the innumerable examples of *ambivalence* and *fatigue* that are not covered in these specific images? To think usefully about such matters, we need more than mental images: We need **concepts**.

Concepts are mental categories or groupings into which we can place people, places, things, events, and ideas that share certain characteristics and qualities in common (even though they may also differ substantially). For example, the concept "food" lets us recognize edible substances. Without this concept it would be meaningless to say, "Let's go get something to eat" or "I have to go buy some things for dinner." We would have to stipulate every single item we intended to purchase, because there would be no obvious relationship between "cucumbers" and "tortilla chips." Thus, concepts provide us with the most information with the least mental effort, and they reduce the need to be endlessly learning new facts. When we utilize concepts in our thinking, the similarities between the things that are contained within the concept are emphasized, while the differences are played down or ignored.

CONCEPTS WITH FUZZY BOUNDARIES

Concepts have features or attributes that define them. Sometimes these features are precise and strictly defined in physical terms. For example, a three-sided shape is a *triangle*, and that's all there is to it. There is no three-sided shape that is *not* a triangle, and no shape that has fewer or greater than three sides that *is* a triangle. Concepts such as *triangle, oxygen,* or *water* have formal rules that cannot be violated—an item is either part of the concept or not. Such concepts have *clear boundaries*.

However, there are relatively few concepts in existence that have clear boundaries. Most concepts have **fuzzy boundaries**—you cannot always say

Concepts ▶ Mental categories into which we can place people, places, things, events, or ideas that share common characteristics. In creating concepts, the similarities between phenomena placed in the mental category are emphasized, and the differences are ignored.

Fuzzy boundaries ▶ When it is not precisely clear where a concept begins and ends, or what does or does not belong in the concept.

▲ **Food Concepts.** Food is a type of concept of which *vegetable* is an example and a concept in its own right. In turn, *broccoli* is an example of the *vegetable* concept and is also a concept on its own. Concepts are often arranged in hierarchies in this way.

exactly where the concept begins and ends or what should or should not be included in it. Take the concepts *life* and *death*. You might think that a person is either alive or dead, and that there would be no argument about it. But the exact moment when a person has died is not always clear, even to scientists and medical professionals. And some patients have been "brought back to life" after they have "died" (i.e., after their heart has stopped, electrical activity has ceased in the brain, and other signs of death have occurred). People also do not agree as to when "life" begins—witness the debate over abortion. Life and death have fuzzy boundaries.

An item thought to be a particularly ideal representative of any given concept is known as a **prototype** of the concept. For example, for people living in the United States, Europe, or Latin America, *trumpet* and *piano* are good prototypes of the concept *musical instrument*, whereas *mbira* and *sitar* are probably not, at least for most of us. On the other hand, in Eastern or Southern Africa, the *mbira* is an excellent prototype of a musical instrument, and throughout Southern India the same could be said for the *sitar*. The more closely some item matches a person's prototype of a concept, the more likely the person is to see the "family resemblance" and include it as part of the concept.

Prototype ▶ An example of a concept or category that is thought to be particularly typical or representative.

Thinking Fast, Thinking Slow: Kahneman's Two-System Theory

Now take a look at this image:

Did you have any trouble immediately grasping that these children were having a good time? Probably not. Now answer the problem 1 + 1 = ? How long did it take? Less than a half-second, I would hope—about the same length of time it should take for you to complete the phrase "bread and _____."

Now consider this problem:

A bat and ball cost $1.10.

The bat costs $1 more than the ball

How much does the ball cost?

An answer likely came to your mind almost as easily and rapidly as the solution to the 1 + 1 problem. Unfortunately, in this case, haste makes waste. If you answered 10¢ you were wrong. Think for a moment: If the bat costs $1 more than the ball, and the ball costs 10 cents, then the bat would cost $1.10 and the bat and ball together would cost $1.20, not $1.10. Give this problem your full attention for just a moment more, and you'll be able to come up with the correct answer.

Where are we going with this? Nobel-prize winner Daniel Kahneman (2011) has proposed a *dual-system theory* of thinking that explains why it is so easy to add 1 + 1 instantly, to automatically come up with "butter" to complete the phrase "bread and butter," and to grasp immediately that the children in the preceding photo are happy—but to drop the ball entirely (along with the bat) on the computational problem.

Building on earlier "dual-process" theories of cognition and many decades of research (his own and others'), Kahneman proposes that there exist two entirely separate, but interacting, *systems* of thought. *System 1* is rapid, intuitive, effortless, and automatic. It is generally not under voluntary control. It allows us to recognize a happy, frightened, or angry face; drive "on automatic pilot" on a familiar route during hours when traffic is light; sense the direction of a sudden loud sound; judge which of two lines is the longer; solve very simple arithmetic (1 + 1) instantly; and understand simple sentences in our native language. Unfortunately, because it is effortless and automatic, we may often employ System 1 thought at times when what we *really* need is System 2.

System 2 is slower, effortful, and demands concentration and attention. It is also lazier than System 1: It would rather not be brought into play at all if it can be avoided. This is why so many of us get the ball-and-bat problem wrong at first. Because of its tricky wording, we sense (wrongly) that the problem can be solved easily with intuitive System 1 thought. If you remember from Chapter 1, intuition is an evolutionary gift—but sometimes it bites us. Attention and effort, if relatively minimal, are needed to solve the ball-and-bat problem, not intuition.

System 2 comes into play when we try to write a term paper or article, judge whether or not a logical argument has merit, solve math problems involving double or triple digits, try to pick a friend's face out of a crowded lecture hall, or decide whom to invite to a party with an eye toward avoiding conflict among the guests. System 2 pays attention, chooses, weighs evidence, and considers. Intense System 2 thinking burns calories (really!) and needs blood glucose to run properly. (*Don't* take important tests on an empty stomach.) System 2 thought also dilates the pupils of the eyes so reliably that by observing changes in pupil dilation researchers can tell when a person has finished working on a difficult mental task.

However, there are limits to what we can do while System 2 is in gear. It demands most of the limited bankroll of attention we have to spend at any given time. As Kahneman states, if you are on a jog or brisk walk with a friend and you turn to her and ask her to solve a double-digit multiplication problem in her head right then and there, the first thing she is likely to do (if she agrees to the task) is to abruptly stop running or walking in order to do the mental work. It is exceedingly difficult to pay attention both to the movements of your body and the cognitive demands of a math problem at the same time.

Similarly, you may find driving on a familiar, relatively deserted freeway an effortless matter. You may be able to do so quite easily while having an intense conversation with a passenger, singing at the top of your lungs if there are no passengers (or very tolerant ones), or following a conversation closely on a talk radio program. But try doing any of this while maneuvering to park in a tight spot on a crowded city street or trying to locate an unfamiliar address on a dark block at night while cars are backed up behind you. There just isn't enough System 2 attention to go around. But don't worry—System 2 will likely prevent you from conversing, singing, or listening closely to the radio. It will focus your attention on the more important task at hand.

When System 2 is fully engaged and attention focused on a task, one may become literally blind to events outside the domain of the task, a phenomenon known as *inattentional blindness*. I described one example of this in Chapter 5 (remember the gorilla in the midst of the group of basketball players?). Consider yet another example: In 1995, a Boston police officer named Kenny Conley was chasing a suspect down the street. An undercover officer arrived at the scene, but was mistaken by Conley's fellow officers for another suspect. The undercover officer was severely beaten by these fellow officers. Conley continued to chase the original suspect over a chain link fence and apprehended him.

During the hearing surrounding the affair, Conley insisted that although he had passed by the place where the undercover officer was being beaten, he had seen no such attack. He was convicted of perjury and sentenced to jail time because it was assumed that he was lying to protect his fellow officers who had executed the beating. However, Christopher Chabris and Daniel Simons, the psychologists responsible for much of the research on inattentional blindness, conducted a study to test the possibility that Conley may have been telling the truth (Chabris, Weinberger, Fontaine, & Simons, 2011). They had student volunteers individually pursue a hired confederate of the experimenters as he jogged a 400-meter route. Each pursuing subject was told to count the number of times the runner touched his head, a command designed to engage System 2. Somewhere along the route, however, three men—also hired by the experimenters—staged a fight in which two of the men pretended to assault the third. The men's fight was clearly visible to the runner and his pursuers for at least 15 seconds as they ran past. At the end of the run, each pursuer was asked whether he or she had seen anything unusual along the route. The pursuers then were asked directly if they had seen anyone fighting. Only 33% of the pursuers reported seeing the fight. The remainder had been blinded by System 2.

Although Kahneman distinguishes System 1 from System 2, he emphasizes that the systems evolved to work together. In general, most of us hum along during the day in System 1 mode, responding relatively automatically and effortlessly, opening and closing doors, eating, brushing teeth, walking up and down stairs, answering the phone, daydreaming, driving familiar routes. System 2 is brought into play only when a question or problem occurs that is beyond the reach of the intuitive System 1: What is the square root of 17? How should I help my brother patch up his fight with dad? Is that an animal in the middle of the road up ahead or just a paper bag? When System 2's work is done, it sits back and relaxes.

System 1, on the other hand, because it is effortless and needs little energy to run, can afford to remain engaged at all times. Indeed, it cannot be turned off at will. Kahneman uses the Müeller-Lyer illusion we discussed in Chapter 5 to demonstrate this idea. Take another look at the image, reproduced here.

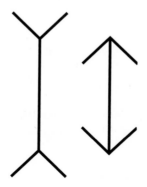

If you studied Chapter 5 you already know that both lines are equal in length. Yet, unless you are very unusual, you will still *see* the line on the left as longer than the line on the right. That's System 1 talking (Kahneman, 2011). System 2 has no problem judging which of two lines is longer—in most cases. But here, due to the unusual construction of the diagram which plays upon biases in perception, System 1 is unable to cope and you are advised not to listen to the messages it is sending. It's time to take out a ruler and allow System 2 to do its work.

ARE THE TWO SYSTEMS REAL?

The notion that two distinct systems of thought exist did not begin with Kahneman (e.g., Stanovich & West, 2000), and there are commentators who do not believe it is productive to "think about thinking" in this way (e.g., Newstead, 2000). Kahneman himself, after introducing the two systems, calls them "fictions"—short-cuts for describing cognitive events that occur automatically versus those that involve effort, are associated with pupil dilation, focused attention, and nervous system arousal. He does not propose that these systems exist in particular brain locations or anywhere else in the material world. Instead, like many such psychological constructions, they are convenient metaphors—relatively simple ways to describe enormously complex processes.

IN SUMMARY

1.	The computational theory of mind suggests that the mind works according to sets of universal rules and principles for processing and manipulating information.
2.	Thinking is composed of forming mental images and concepts.
3.	A particularly good example of a concept is known as a prototype of the concept.
4.	Daniel Kahneman's two-system theory proposes that there exist two systems of thought, which he calls System 1 and System 2. System 1 is rapid, effortless, intuitive, and automatic. It is not under voluntary control. System 2 is slower, effortful, and demands concentration and attention.

RETRIEVE!

1.	How do *thinking* and *cognition* differ as concepts?
2.	Why do we need concepts? What is a mental image?
3.	Which of the following concepts has fuzzy boundaries? **a)** violin **b)** anger **c)** Ph.D degree **d)** summer
4.	True or false: Daniel Kahneman would say that most of our daily activities primarily involve System 2 thinking.

How Do We Use Thinking to Solve Problems?

Problems are obstacles that stand in the way of achieving some goal. *Problem solving* is the process by which people use thought to find a way to remove these obstacles—to move from a situation that *actually* exists now to a situation that is desired but does not yet exist. When confronted with a problem, people generally choose a particular strategy. These choices are not necessarily made consciously—they may be made automatically and below the level of awareness. However, they are often very well suited to the problem at hand. In this section of the chapter we will briefly examine four such strategies: *trial and error, algorithms, heuristics*, and *insight*. We will then consider *creativity*—a unique way to create problems as well as solve them!

Problem ▶ An obstacle that stands in the way of achieving some goal.

Trial and Error Eliminates Solutions One at a Time

Trial and error is the most basic problem-solving strategy. It involves a conscious decision to eliminate one solution at a time until a solution that works is found. When finding a "workaround" to avoid problems caused by a bug in a piece of software, computer users often employ trial and error—trying one method, then another, until they stumble upon a solution that works. If you desperately needed to get your wallet out of a friend's locker and you didn't know the combination for the lock, you might fiddle with it for a while, hoping eventually to hit upon the right numbers.

When a problem has relatively few possible (or available) solutions, slugging it out with trial and error can be effective. However, the greater the number of possible solutions, the less efficient trial and error will be. For example, trying to open your friend's combination lock using trial and error could keep you busy for a bit longer than you probably would want to sit in one place. Nonetheless, sometimes there is no escape from trial and error.

Trial and error ▶ The most basic problem-solving strategy, where solutions are eliminated one at a time.

Algorithms Never Fail, but They Are Not Always Available

An **algorithm** is a step-by-step set of systematic "instructions" that can be used to solve any problem of some given type. The procedure always remains the same, and you can "plug in" whatever variables you like—as long as what you are "inputting" consists of data in the form the algorithm is designed to compute. For example, simple arithmetic, complex mathematical formulas, and methods for converting one type of measurement into another (e.g., inches to millimeters, feet to meters) are all algorithms. They work every time, but the algorithm for converting feet to meters will not work if you "plug in" inches instead of feet; and the algorithm for adding whole numbers will not work if one of the numbers is a fraction.

Computers frequently use algorithms to make computations and to solve problems that are not overly complex. For example, **artificial intelligence (AI)** computers use algorithms to mimic aspects of human thought. AI computers have been designed to play games such as chess; recognize voices; "understand" language well enough to hold basic conversations (but only on highly restricted and specific topics); and make decisions regarding mechanical, diagnostic, and other systems. In general, they are quite good at using algorithms to perform tasks human beings find very difficult, such as the simultaneous computation of large amounts of data. However, they have not yet been able to perform tasks that human beings find simple but which are in fact, highly complex—for example, recognizing faces, seeing in three

Algorithms ▶ A step-by-step set of computational instructions to correctly solve a specific type of problem. Algorithms have a specified beginning and ending and can be applied identically to any problem of the type they were designed to solve.

Artificial intelligence (AI) ▶ Computers or other machines that display intelligent behavior or mimic human thought. The term is also used to refer to the branch of computer science that studies the design of intelligent agents and creates AI computers and machines.

dimensions, or recognizing colors (Tooby & Cosmides, 2005). And, as cognitive scientist Steven Pinker notes, try asking an AI computer questions like, "Which is bigger, Chicago or a breadbox? Do zebras wear underwear? Is the floor likely to rise up and bite you? If Susan goes to the store, does her head go with her?" (1994, p. 193).

Heuristics Are Mental "Rules of Thumb"

When faced with having to make choices or decisions relatively quickly where the number of possible alternatives is uncertain, we sometimes fall back on *heuristics*. A **heuristic** is a problem-solving "rule of thumb"—a mental short-cut designed to help us make judgments and decisions when all the facts are not known. We generally apply heuristics automatically, without consciously deciding to use them. They are a perfect example of Kahneman's System 1 as described earlier, and Kahneman—along with his late colleague Amos Tversky—is, not coincidentally, the most influential researcher and theorist on the topic of heuristics (e.g., Tversky & Kahneman, 1973, 1974; Kahneman, 2011).

THE AVAILABILITY HEURISTIC

A good example of the use of heuristics is the **availability heuristic**, which helps us to judge how often something occurs or how likely it is to occur in the future. This heuristic works by biasing us toward mental information, memories, or images that are more easily "accessible" to our consciousness—that is, those that come to mind easily. The more easily an event comes to mind, the more common and likely to occur in the future we generally believe it to be (Tversky & Kahneman, 1973).

As it happens, things tend to come to mind more easily if they have occurred recently, if they have strong negative emotional content, or both. For example, my neighbor's 3-year-old, Skye, was recently stung multiple times by a yellow-jacket wasp at a particular location in the woods near our house. My wife's and my immediate response was to assume that he probably would not be the last to be attacked in this way. We became hesitant to allow our own children to play in that location, and announced to friends that this particular patch of woods was "full of wasps"—even though, for all we knew, Skye's attacker was the only wasp for miles.

Of course, over the balance of history, a wasp nest is probably more likely to exist near a location where someone has been stung than in some other, random location. So the availability heuristic often serves a purpose. However, it can pose problems. As an example, I have found that students often believe that tens of thousands, or even millions, of children are kidnapped by strangers each year. In actuality the number of people under age 18 kidnapped by strangers each year in the United States ranges from about 50 to 300 at most, according to the FBI and the National Incidence Study on Missing, Abducted, Runaway, and Throwaway Children in America (Best, 1990; Cooper, 2005)—and this includes older teenagers forced to go somewhere against their will for a relatively short period of time (e.g., during a robbery).

Another example, provided by American statistician Nate Silver, concerns airborne terrorism—something that worries many people each time they board a flight. Based upon the number of acts of terrorism on commercial aircraft over an 8-year period, Silver calculates that there has been one terrorist incident per 16,553,385 departures, or one incident per 11,569,297,667 miles flown (that's 1,459,664 trips around the earth). Based upon these statistics (and a few others I won't saddle you with), according to Silver the odds of being on an airplane subject to a terrorist incident would be 1 in 10,408,947 (Silver, 2009). You are undoubtedly far more likely to die as a result of a garden accident, eating spoiled egg salad, or being struck by lightning than at the hand of a terrorist aboard an airplane.

Heuristics ▶ Mental problem-solving short-cuts or "rules of thumb." Heuristics are very fast and often accurate, but they are not always accurate, and relying upon them can result in numerous erroneous assumptions.

Availability heuristic ▶ A heuristic that biases people toward using mental information that is more easily "accessible" or mentally available. The availability heuristic is used when coming to a judgment about how often something occurs or how likely it is to occur in the future.

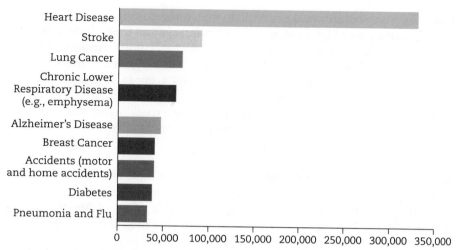

▲ **FIGURE 9.2 The Availability Heuristic and Perceptions of Women's Health Risks.** Because of the publicity surrounding breast cancer, and the high degree of negative emotion generated by thoughts of this disease, actual mortality rates due to breast cancer are often overestimated by the average person. Heart disease, lung cancer, stroke, chronic lower respiratory disease, and Alzheimer's disease all claim many more female lives than breast cancer. Breast cancer mortality is approximately equaled by rates of death due to home and vehicle accidents, and diabetes. *(Sources: U. S. CDC National Vital Statistics Report, 2007, Vol. 56. Retrieved from http://www.cdc.gov/nchs/data/nvsr/nvsr56/ nvsr56_05.pdf on November 17, 2008; American Cancer Society Breast Cancer Facts 2007–2008 retrieved from http://www.cancer.org/downloads/STT/BCFF-Final.pdf on November 17, 2008.)*

Why are so many people's intuitive estimates of the number of child kidnappings and terrorist attacks wildly off the mark? Because these crimes are particularly horrific, and, as such, they linger unpleasantly in our minds. The tendency for people to remember them in detail is also stimulated by the fact that *each* of these events is reported nationally—precisely *because* they are both unusual and horrific. Legislation has even been passed as a result of publicity over a single child kidnapping. Thus, even if only a small number of these dreadful events occur each year, we are presented with one virtually every time we see the news headlines while standing in line at the supermarket! Media coverage and legislative activity increase the cognitive accessibility of child kidnappings and terrorist attacks, and the availability heuristic then inflates our estimates of how frequently they happen (Lichtenstein, Slovic, Fischhoff, Layman, & Combs, 1978; see also Figure 9.2).

THE REPRESENTATIVENESS HEURISTIC

When people are confronted with an example of a person or thing that they do not know how to categorize or explain, they often use the **representativeness heuristic** (Tversky & Kahneman, 1974). This heuristic works in tandem with prototypes; recall that a prototype is a particularly good example of a concept or category. Using the representativeness heuristic involves making instantaneous comparisons of the new person or thing with prototypes of various categories until a "match" is found. As an example, consider the following description (based on Nisbett & Ross, 1980):

> Lawrence Batson is 5′6″ tall, quite slim and not particularly muscular. He likes to read mid-19th-century British poetry and the published correspondence of great authors with their friends and spouses.

Would you say it is more likely that Lawrence is a classics professor at an Ivy League college or a truck driver? If you guessed "classics professor," you were

Representativeness heuristic ▶ When people are confronted with an example of a person or thing that they do not know how to categorize or explain, they may compare the new person or thing with *prototypes* of various categories until a "match" is found.

using the *representativeness* heuristic to match the description of "Lawrence" to your prototypes of Ivy League classics professors and truck drivers, and deciding which made a better match (Nisbett & Ross, 1980). However, by now you might be able to see the problem with heuristics in general. Although they are fast and often accurate, they are not always accurate and can be highly misleading. "Lawrence" might well turn out to be a truck driver after all. In point of fact, Lawrence is *much* more likely to be a truck driver than a classics professor! Why? To understand this, we must consider the important question of *base rates*.

Base rate ▶ The basic probability of something occurring in a population, expressed as a percentage. Can also be understood as an indication of how prevalent something is in a population.

Base Rates and the Representativeness Heuristic

A **base rate** is a probability figure, expressed in percentage, that indicates how prevalent something is in a population or how frequently it occurs. For example, if 5% of Americans suffer from depression, then the base rate of depression in America would be 5%. To estimate the likelihood that Lawrence is a classics professor rather than a truck driver, we have to take into account two important base rates: the base rates of classics professors and that of truck drivers. How many of them are there?

Considering that there are only eight schools in the Ivy League, it should be easy to see that there are no more than a few hundred classics professors at most on Ivy League faculties. Furthermore, it is likely that no more than half of these are male (likely fewer); of these men, fewer still are slim and 5′ 6″ tall. "Slim, relatively short male Ivy League classics professor" is a good example of a category of people with *low base rate* status. On the other hand, there are over 3.5 million truck drivers in the United States (American Trucking Associations, 2013). Even if a large majority of male classics professors—say, 75%—enjoy reading mid-19th-century British poetry (a likely overestimation), and only a tiny percentage of truck drivers fit this description—say, one-half of 1% (a likely underestimation)—that would still amount to at least 170,000 truck drivers who enjoy mid-19th-century British poetry compared with a few hundred male Ivy League classics professors at most.

Perhaps you can now see that in spite of the fact that Lawrence might not sound like a truck driver to you, unless we had specific information about the man such as "he works at Yale University," we would be far better off to guess that he is a truck driver if given the choice between these two occupations. The probability is much higher that Lawrence is a truck driver because it is highly unlikely that virtually *any* specific individual is a classics professor at an Ivy League college, regardless of their personal characteristics (Nisbett & Ross, 1980).

Unfortunately, most people do not take base rate information into account when they make judgments of the likelihood of some event—for example, the likelihood that a person has some disease given that they have particular symptoms, or the likelihood that a person belongs in some category (e.g., truck driver/classics professor) given that they have certain characteristics (e.g., love of English literature; Meehl & Rosen, 1955; Tversky & Kahneman, 1973). In such cases, the representativeness heuristic may lead us astray.

Thus, the moral of the representativeness heuristic and base rate problem is this: If it looks like a duck and walks like a duck—and the base rate of ducks is low—it is probably a goose or a gallinule![1] (See Figure 9.3 for more on base rates and the representativeness heuristic, and Table 9.1 for a summary of the uses and misuses of the heuristics described in this section.)

---

[1] *Gallinules are small, aquatic birds that look remarkably like ducks but are* not *ducks.*

Hypothetical base rate of steroid use among baseball players in a particular state: 3%

Hypothetical base rate of true positive results for the test: 95% (rate of false positives is 5%)

- Suppose we test 600 players. Since only 3% of players overall use steroids, this means that 18 players are true users and 582 players are non-users.

- Of the 18 users, 17 (95%) would be correctly identified as being steroid users.

- Of the 582 non-users, 29 (5%) would be *incorrectly identified* as users.

Therefore, depending upon the base rates for steroid use among baseball players in this state, **a positive test result could be more likely to identify a non-user than a user!**

◀FIGURE 9.3 Base Rates: Don't Leave Home Without Them.
Suppose a hypothetical test for steroid use among baseball players is 95% accurate. In this test there is a 5% rate of *false positive* results for the test (nonusers incorrectly identified as users) and a 95% rate of true positive results. What is the chance that a player who tests positive actually *has* been using steroids? If you guessed 95% you'd be wrong. In fact, simply knowing the rate of true results and false positives for the test tells us practically nothing about the chance that this player actually *has* been using steroids. We are missing a crucial base rate: *the true rate of steroid use among baseball players overall.* As this figure shows, depending upon this base rate, it is entirely possible for a person to receive a test result showing steroid use, and yet be much more likely to be a nonuser than a user. *(Adapted from an example offered by Siegfried, 2010.)*

Table 9.1 Uses and Misuses of Heuristics: Two Mental "Rules of Thumb"

HEURISTIC	DESCRIPTION	USES	MISUSES
Availability (Tversky & Kahneman 1973)	Things that are cognitively accessible more easily are thought to recur more frequently.	This heuristic can help us make quick decisions about the likelihood of something occurring.	Sometimes things are easily accessible for reasons other than their frequent recurrence (e.g., a fictitious or unrepresentative story or picture is often more easily accessible than factual and statistical information).
Representativeness (Tversky & Kahneman, 1974)	"If it looks like a duck, quacks like a duck and walks like a duck, it probably is a duck." Comparing a new object or person to our idea of a "typical" member of the group to which it belongs	Quickly determining the category or group to which a new object or person belongs	May encourage the failure to take base rates into account; may increase prejudice and inappropriate stereotyping; contributes to failures in reasoning such as the gambler's fallacy.

Aha! Insight!

"The problem is not finding [musical ideas], it's—when getting up in the morning and getting out of bed—not stepping on them."

—Johann Sebastian Bach (cited by Myers, 2002, p. 61)

Insight ▶ The term used to describe a situation where the solution to a problem appears suddenly "as if from nowhere" after an impasse had been reached and it seemed that the problem was not solvable.

Impasse ▶ When a person has made repeated unsuccessful attempts to solve a problem yet possesses the mental ability to solve the problem.

Fixation ▶ Being "stuck" in a specific way of mentally representing a problem. Fixation may occur when one applies previously successful problem-solving strategies to new problems that may or may not best be solved with these strategies.

Writing a textbook like this is an extremely lengthy effort. It takes many years, and the problems that must be solved are uncountable. However, I have repeatedly had the experience of struggling all day unsuccessfully attempting to solve one of these problems, falling asleep in a state of general hopelessness about it, and waking the next day with the solution seemingly pouring from my fingertips to the computer keyboard with no assistance at all from "me." This is the process of **insight**. Insight begins when a person is unable to see how a problem can be solved in spite of numerous (sometimes seemingly endless) attempts. He or she is at an **impasse**. Then, suddenly—*"Aha!"* A solution appears with ease as if from nowhere (Jones, 2003; Kaplan & Simon, 1990). It is often accompanied by feelings of pleasure and confidence that one has truly solved the problem (Topolinski & Reber, 2010). Insight occurs in the context of general problem solving, in creative and artistic work, when trying to retrieve an elusive memory, or when trying to understand what a foreign language speaker or toddler is trying to tell you. It also can occur when you are struggling to define some sort of sensory perception that seems mysterious ("What on earth *is* that sound?"; Kounios & Beeman, 2009; Sternberg & Davidson, 1995).

A person who solves a problem through insight is by definition already able to solve that problem. He or she has all the information or experience necessary and the cognitive ability to use this information and experience—otherwise, the problem would not be solved! This is one limitation of insight: It cannot occur if the solution does not already lie somewhere in one's consciousness. But if you are able to solve a problem, why is a point reached where you feel *unable* to solve the problem? That is, why do you reach an impasse? Guenther Knoblich and his colleagues propose that impasses in solving problems often result from the fact that people begin their attempts to solve new problems using approaches that have proved successful in solving previous problems (Knoblich, Ohlsson, Haider, & Ruenius, 1999). In a sense, our successful experiences with old problems *bias* the way we structure and conceptualize new problems by constraining, or limiting, the number of options we can imagine in finding a solution to the new problem (Smith, 2003; Storm & Angello, 2010).

Being "stuck" in a specific way of mentally representing a problem is known as **fixation**. The *nine-dot problem* (Burnham & Davis, 1969) depicted in Figure 9.4 is an excellent example of a problem that typically results in impasse due to fixation. This problem has caused many otherwise stable people to begin to tear their hair out.

How and why does insight occur after impasses are reached? According to Knoblich and his colleagues, insight occurs when we *change the way we mentally represent the problem* (Knoblich et al., 1999). In a sense, we are no longer trying to solve the same problem, but a different one. For example, should you find yourself in a locked room, you may at first assume that you must solve the problem of how to break the door down. After many failed attempts, it may suddenly occur to you that the room is only on the second floor and it might be possible to break the window and shimmy down. The problem is now a completely new one: how to tie enough material together to form a rope that will hold your weight.

This re-representation of the nature of the problem may activate aspects of your memory and knowledge base (the knot-tying class you took at summer camp, for example) not touched by the previous representation—expanding the number of options and possibilities to be considered. The solution can then come quite rapidly if it is "contained" within the new mental spaces that have opened up. The solution to the nine-dot problem is depicted in Figure 9.5.

Neuroscientists have shown that brain wave activity and the sites of brain activation differ in research participants as they solve problems with insight as compared with non-insight strategies (Kounios et al., 2006). For example, using fMRI brain imaging, Mark Jung-Beeman and his colleagues found higher levels of activation in the *anterior superior temporal gyrus* (aSTG) of the right hemisphere around the moment of insight solution of verbal problems—but not while verbal problems were solved with non-insight methods. Among its many functions, aSTG is a brain region associated with making connections between distantly related pieces of information (Jung-Beeman et al., 2004; Kounios & Beeman, 2009).

As depicted in Figure 9.6, using EEG imaging these researchers also found that approximately three-tenths of a second prior to the experience of insight there is a sudden burst of *gamma* band brain-wave activity in the right temporal area, preceded by a spike in *alpha* wave activity at the right parietal-occipital area. These patterns were not found when non-insight solutions were reached. Jung-Beeman and colleagues concluded from these results that insight is characterized first by unconscious glimmerings of a solution—indirectly affecting alpha wave activity—leading to sudden awareness of the solution, reflected in the burst of *gamma* wave activity.

Can a person's method of solving a problem—insight vs. non-insight—be predicted? In other words, can a given mental state *prepare* a person to use insight over a non-insight method? John Kounis and his colleagues studied a group of participants as they prepared to solve, and then solved, a large series of verbal problems. The participants' subjective reports of the way each problem was solved, by insight or non-insight methods, was compared against fMRI and EEG brain imaging scans of brain activity as they *prepared* to solve each problem. As with the earlier study by Jung-Beeman and his colleagues, these researchers found brain-wave patterns and activity of neurons at specific brain regions when problems were solved by insight that differed from that found when problems were solved by other methods (Kounios et al., 2006).

One final word about insight: If some problem has you stumped and you are hoping for insight, you could do worse than "sleeping on it," as I have done so many times while writing this book. Stickgold and Walker (2004) found that a good night's sleep more than doubles the likelihood of discovering an insightful solution.

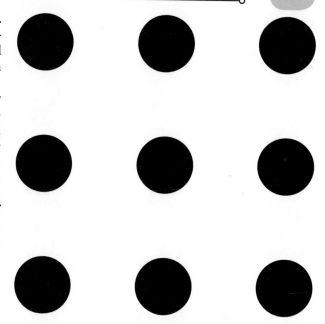

▲ **FIGURE 9.4 The Nine-Dot Problem.** Connect all nine dots with four straight lines *without* lifting your pencil from the paper. (Solution depicted in Figure 9.5).

Creativity: Finding Problems and Solving Them

Creativity has been defined in different and often conflicting ways, but one thing is clear: It is an important engine that drives cultural change and helps society to advance (Hennessey & Amabile, 2010; Runco, 2004). Creativity is more than writing great novels, painting masterpieces, making magnificent music, solving unsolvable equations, or devising unique software applications; it is an important force in human life that encompasses aspects of cognition, skill, personality, motivation, and various environmental variables—including the workings of chance.

▶ **FIGURE 9.6** A Picture of Insight: Brain Wave Activity during Insight Problem-Solving. *(Source: Jung-Beeman et al. 2004.)*

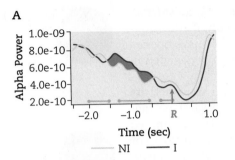

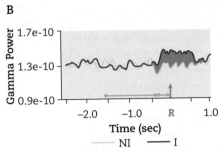

Alpha wave activity just prior to the burst of gamma wave activity. As you can see in the graph above, alpha power increases in insight solutions (purple line) versus non-insight solutions (blue line) beginning about 1.5 seconds before the insight solution (indicated by the green R and arrow). As a solution grows nearer, alpha power decreases.

Gamma wave activity at the moment of solution. The graph above shows that beginning about 3/10ths of a second prior to solution, there is a sudden burst in gamma wave power in insight solutions (purple line), but no such increase in non-insight solutions.

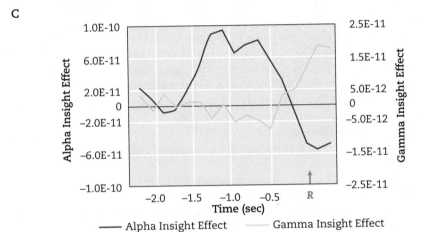

The comparison graph above demonstrates the increase in alpha (purple line) at 1.5 second prior to solution and its decrease as gamma waves shoot up beginning 3/10ths of a second prior to solution.

▲ **FIGURE 9.5** The Nine-Dot Problem Solution: Think Outside the Box! People have a very difficult time solving this puzzle because they are usually fixated on the idea that the lines of the pencil must fall within the boundaries of the outer dots—even though instructions to the puzzle do not limit where lines may be drawn (only that the pencil must not leave the paper). Three of the four lines must extend beyond the boundaries formed by the dots.

Creative individuals solve problems, and problem-solving is perhaps what creativity is best known for. But creativity is much more than problem solving. Indeed, as depicted in Figure 9.7, creative people may spend just as much time *finding* problems to solve as solving them (Csikszentmihályi, 1990).

As stated, there is no established definition of creativity, but we can think of it as a kind of syndrome or complex set of behaviors that include at least the following:

- *Originality*. Creative people are able to think "outside the box." Their thinking and the products of their work diverge in some way from what has come before, and their work represents new ideas or understandings (Mumford & Gustafson, 1988).
- *Utility*. The output or work or creative individuals is considered useful or valuable—particularly by those who are knowledgeable in the area in which the work has been accomplished (Hennessey & Amabile, 2010; Paulus & Nijstad, 2003).

In addition, creativity usually involves flexibility—creative individuals are generally open to new ideas, and are able stay attuned to technological and other changes in the environments in which they work (Runco, 2004).

▲ **FIGURE 9.7 Finding and Solving Musical Problems.** Creative people find problems as well as solving them. The composer Béla Bartók decided that the folk melodies of his native Hungary were beautiful and important enough to be incorporated into serious art ("classical") music. He then masterfully solved the problem of how to do this. The composer-pianist Thelonious Monk decided that the rhythms and "feel" of traditional jazz stride piano could be brought forward and wedded to rigorously modern harmonic and melodic innovation. He set about to do just that in his own thoroughly unique style. The problems of incorporating Hungarian folk melodies into classical music, or creating a modern musical style from the foundation of traditional stride piano, did not exist before Bartók and Monk "found" them—and solved them.

IN SUMMARY

1. Trial and error is the most basic problem-solving strategy; heuristics are "rules of thumb" that produce rapid decisions and judgments; algorithms are step-by-step sets of instructions that are generally infallible; insight is an "Aha!" experience that happens after a person reaches an impasse in his or her attempts to solve a problem.

2. The availability heuristic helps people to judge how often something occurs or how likely it is to occur in the future. The representativeness heuristic involves making instantaneous comparisons of a new person or thing with prototypes of various categories until a "match" is found.

3. A base rate is the prevalence, or relative frequency of occurrence, of something in a population. Knowledge of base rates is essential for making judgments of the likelihood of some event.

4. Insight is a problem-solving process that occurs when a person has reached an impasse—but then a solution suddenly appears as if from nowhere.

5. Creativity cannot easily be defined, but it is likely a syndrome or complex set of behaviors that include originality, utility, and frequently flexibility.

RETRIEVE!

1. Each problem-solving strategy has its own limitations or disadvantages. Name at least one disadvantage of each of the four problem-solving strategies: trial-and-error, heuristics, insight, and algorithms.

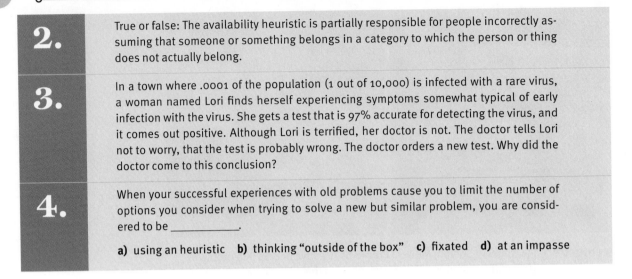

2. True or false: The availability heuristic is partially responsible for people incorrectly assuming that someone or something belongs in a category to which the person or thing does not actually belong.

3. In a town where .0001 of the population (1 out of 10,000) is infected with a rare virus, a woman named Lori finds herself experiencing symptoms somewhat typical of early infection with the virus. She gets a test that is 97% accurate for detecting the virus, and it comes out positive. Although Lori is terrified, her doctor is not. The doctor tells Lori not to worry, that the test is probably wrong. The doctor orders a new test. Why did the doctor come to this conclusion?

4. When your successful experiences with old problems cause you to limit the number of options you consider when trying to solve a new but similar problem, you are considered to be _____.

a) using an heuristic   b) thinking "outside of the box"   c) fixated   d) at an impasse

How Do Biases Affect Decision Making?

Although there is no doubt that human beings can be clear-thinking decision makers, our discussion of heuristics has also shown that human beings are not always rational when making judgments and decisions when some uncertainty is involved (Gilovich, Griffen, & Kahneman, 2002; Tversky & Kahneman, 2005). Of the colleges that are willing to admit me, which offer should I accept? Should I go to the emergency room or just wait until Monday and call the doctor? Is the guy behind me following me, or is it just a coincidence that he's been behind me for five blocks? I've had a few drinks—do I really have to try to find a designated driver, or should I just drive home?

How many questions like these do you suppose you've asked yourself over the course of your life? Seemingly, we do not always consider the risks and benefits of various alternatives open to us in a logical manner, and our perceptions of reality can be biased. In fact, we systematically violate principles of rational decision making in predictable ways in certain types of situations. These tendencies are known as **cognitive biases**—systematic distortions in thinking, memory, and perception. In Chapter 8 I described the consistency bias and the egocentric bias as they apply to memory. I will now discuss one predictable bias as it applies to decision making: the *confirmation bias*.

The Confirmation Bias Tells Us What We Want to Hear

The **confirmation bias** may be the single most prevalent and potentially destructive of all problems with human reasoning (Lilienfeld, Ammirati, & Landfield, 2009). Cognitive psychologist Raymond Nickerson (1998) wonders if this bias, "by itself, might account for a significant fraction of the disputes, altercations, and misunderstandings that occur among individuals, groups, and nations" (p. 175). Although the confirmation bias has many facets, in essence the term refers to the tendency to pay more attention and accord more weight to evidence that *confirms* what we already believe—or even to seek such evidence out—while ignoring evidence that would *disconfirm* our beliefs. Thus, when gathering evidence, people are often simply "building a case" for what they already believe rather than actively attempting to discover the truth.

Cognitive bias ▶ Any tendency toward systematic violation of principles of rational decision-making, judgment, or memory.

Confirmation bias ▶ The tendency to pay more attention and accord more weight to evidence that confirms what we already believe—or even to seek such evidence out—while ignoring evidence that would disconfirm our beliefs.

Belief persistence ▶ Once a belief is formed and confirmed it can be highly resistant to change, even when disconfirming evidence is inescapable.

A good example of the confirmation bias at work is astrology. People who believe in astrology may vividly recall and pay attention to those traits and behaviors that conform to stereotypes of a person's zodiac sign—while ignoring or playing down all the traits and behaviors that flatly contradict characteristics of the sign and are much more typical of other signs.

Prejudice and harmful stereotyping are also strongly reinforced by the confirmation bias. This bias may cause a person to pay attention to and recall only those experiences with members of disliked groups that confirm prior negative beliefs about those groups (e.g., "Hey, that's just been my experience with those people"). Thus, the confirmation bias "tells us what we want to hear" by confirming pet beliefs and theories to which we are emotionally or intellectually attached.

Belief Persistence

What happens when people are faced with disconfirming evidence they cannot ignore? Once a belief is formed, it can be highly resistant to change—a related bias known as **belief persistence** (C. A. Anderson, 2008; M. F. Davies, 1997). When faced with baldly disconfirming evidence, a person may engage in mental gymnastics to play down its relevance or credibility ("Oh, they can do anything they want with statistics!"). If this fails, the person might struggle to find ways to fit the disconfirming evidence into a mental framework that does not threaten the belief—in a sense, to "quarantine" the evidence. For example, when faced with a member of a disliked group who does not display the supposed negative characteristics of that group, someone experiencing belief persistence may say, "Oh, well, he/she is one of the good ones."

Of course, people do change their beliefs and biases. The point is only that, because of confirmation bias and belief persistence, this change may often take more time and more evidence than might be considered "reasonable" by an objective observer.

▲ **What's Your Sign?** The confirmation bias is evident in the popular view of astrology. When reading astrological forecasts, people tend to focus on those few predicted events that actually do come to pass while ignoring the many more that do not. When learning a person's "sun sign" from the zodiac, astrology-minded people generally focus on those characteristics of the person that fit the sign, while ignoring or downplaying those that contradict the sign or that are a better fit to other signs.

CRITICAL THINKING ABOUT PSYCHOLOGY

Chance Is Lumpy: The Gambler's Fallacy

An excellent example of human cognitive biases is the *gambler's fallacy*. Let us say you toss a coin and it comes up heads five times in a row. What would you say the likelihood would be that the next toss would be tails? What if it turned out to be heads yet again? Would the *next* toss be *even more* likely to be tails? The answer is no. Even if a coin were to turn up heads ten times in a row, each and every time you toss it (if the toss is fair) the odds are always exactly the same: 50/50. The odds of tails coming up do not "accumulate" with each toss. As much as it *feels* as though the odds are stronger with each new toss of heads that the next toss will be tails, this is an illusion, known as the **gambler's fallacy**.

The gambler's fallacy keeps slot machine players feeding quarters into the same machine over and over, certain that the odds of a jackpot increase with each play ("This thing is *due* to pay off—I can't leave now!"). Unfortunately, the odds of the machine paying off stay exactly the same with each new button press or handle pull.

Where does the gambler's fallacy come from? The first problem is a simple misunderstanding of the way probability odds work. The chances of tossing heads five times in a row are rather low—1 in 32. However, these odds only exist *prior* to the coin toss. So it would be a good bet when starting out that five straight heads will not show up over the next five tosses. But if you actually *do* manage to flip five heads in a row (which will definitely happen sooner or later if you keep tossing all day), you cannot then presume that the odds of another head coming up on the next toss are very

Gambler's fallacy ▶ A misperception of randomness that causes a person to believe that the likelihood of a random event is affected by events that precede it. For example, people often incorrectly assume that the likelihood of tails occurring in a fair coin toss will increase according to the number of times heads has come up in succession.

CRITICAL THINKING ABOUT PSYCHOLOGY

CONTINUED

small. *Chance does not have a memory*, and the likelihood of a random event occurring (e.g., tails coming up) is not affected by events that have preceded it (e.g., heads coming up five times). The odds for each single new toss are always 50/50.

Probability theory is extremely difficult for the average person to grasp—even highly educated people have trouble with it (Gigerenzer, Gaissmaier, Kurz-Mileke, Schwartz, & Woloshin, 2008; Pinker, 2002). Therefore, the representativeness heuristic creates still more fertile soil for the gambler's fallacy to take hold. Consider the two series of 25 coin tosses depicted here.

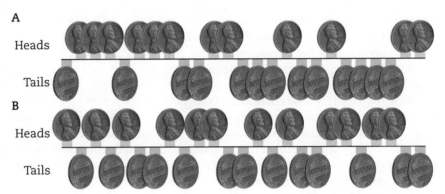

▲ **The Gambler's Fallacy.** It might seem that the more times the roulette wheel spins without hitting your number (or color), the more likely the next spin will be to do so. But, in fact, the odds of the table paying off stay exactly the same with each turn of the wheel: They do *not* "accumulate." The likelihood of a random event is not affected by events that precede it.

Which chart seems more typical of fair coin tosses at a 50/50 level of chance, Chart A or Chart B? Looking at Chart A, if you were to start paying attention on toss number two, there will be a seemingly unlikely streak of eight heads broken only by three tails. However, this is the normal operation of chance (randomness) at odds of 50/50. Ultimately—in the long run—an approximately equal number of heads and tails will be tossed. However, cutting out a small segment of the "long run" can produce remarkable streaks of unlikely events (Gilovich, Vallone, & Tversky, 1985). As statistician Robert P. Abelson (1995) put it, "chance is lumpy." Because Chart B *seems* more random, the representativeness heuristic prompts us to believe that it is more representative of randomness. In fact, Chart B is not at all typical of a string of random coin tosses. ■

IN SUMMARY

1.	The confirmation bias is the tendency to actively seek out, or accord more weight to, information that confirms what we already believe.
2.	Randomness should be expected to produce unlikely seeming streaks over time ("chance is lumpy"). The gambler's fallacy is the false belief that the likelihood of a random event is affected by events that have preceded it.

RETRIEVE!

1.	The _____ causes people to pay more attention and accord more weight to evidence in support of what they already believe.
2.	What is the role played by the representativeness heuristic in the gambler's fallacy?
3.	Once a belief is formed and confirmed through the confirmation bias, it may be highly resistant to change as a result of _____. **a)** confirmation bias **b)** availability heuristic **c)** fixation **d)** belief persistence

Language: What Is It, and How Do We Learn It?

As cognitive scientist Steven Pinker suggested in his influential book *The Language Instinct* (1994, p. 15), each human being has a most extraordinary ability: By marking symbols on a sheet of paper, signing with the hands, or making noises with vocal cords and mouth, each of us, with "exquisite precision," can cause an entirely new idea to form inside the mind of another person. This happens, not through telepathy or any other metaphysical process, but through the use of language.

Take the following description from Raymond Chandler (1940/1992), an American mystery author noted for his descriptive prose:

> He was a big man but not more than six feet five inches tall and not wider than a beer truck. . . . He wore a shaggy borsalino hat, a rough gray sports coat with white golf balls on it for buttons, a brown shirt, a yellow tie, pleated gray flannel slacks and alligator shoes with white explosions on the toes. From his outer breast pocket cascaded a show handkerchief of the same brilliant yellow as his tie. There were a couple of colored feathers tucked into the band of his hat, but he didn't really need them. Even on Central Avenue, not the quietest dressed street in the world, he looked about as inconspicuous as a tarantula on a slice of angel food. (pp. 3–4)

I suspect that a man who stands out like "a tarantula on a slice of angel food" is a man who has never existed in your mind before just now. Chandler's descriptive language causes an entirely new idea (a mental image) to form in the mind of the reader.

Language Is an Open-Ended Code

The term *language* has distinct meanings that differ according to context. In the first, most obvious sense, language is any of the human systems of communication and personal expression (e.g., Chinese, English, Arabic, Swahili) which have been built upon symbols or *representations*. By representations I mean that words (or gestures in the case of sign language) "stand in" for the things they are intended to represent. In other words, languages are *codes*. According to linguistics, the scientific study of language, there are at least

▶ Honeybees have a unique system of "dance language" to communicate distance and location of food sources and nesting sites (Esch et al., 2001). However, this system of communication is closed-ended, and can only convey very limited types of information—unlike human languages.

three important properties that characterize a human language: *generativity*, *recursion*, and *displacement*.

GENERATIVITY

Generativity ▶ The quality of language that allows a speaker to use a relatively small number of words and grammatical structures to compose a theoretically infinite number of sentences and new ideas.

Generativity is the quality of language that allows a person to use the relatively small number of words and grammatical structures of a language to compose a theoretically infinite number of sentences expressing an infinite number of new thoughts and ideas. Moreover, any one of these thoughts and ideas may often be expressed using different words, word orders, and phrases (Chomsky, 1965, 1972). In describing the man who was "no wider than a beer truck" and "as inconspicuous as a tarantula on a slice of angel food," Raymond Chandler took advantage of generativity to create entirely new ideas from a unique arrangement of words. But he might have conveyed much the same idea had he described the man as "no broader than a steamroller" and noted that he was about as inconspicuous as "a cluster of 10-carat diamonds on a slab of black tar."

The generativity of language demonstrates that language is *open-ended*, unlike other animal communication systems. Honeybees have a dance-like system of communication that may be used to alert others to the presence of succulent flowers and direct one another to the flowers' exact location (Esch, Zhang, Srinivasan, & Tautz, 2001; von Frisch, 1967). However, they cannot combine various elements in this dance system to communicate the presence of skunks (who eat them by the handful) or to describe places best avoided for other reasons (Wynne, 2004). Their system of communication is *closed-ended*.

Clive Wynne (2004, p. 107) suggests a mini-experiment for those who may not be convinced that the possibilities for sentence construction are limitless in any language. Take any sentence in this book, even the simplest—say, "The term *language* has distinct meanings that differ according to context." Encase the sentence in quotation marks and Google it (the quotation marks are essential for the engine to search for the exact word order). In spite of the fact that there are billions of pages on the World Wide Web, it is highly unlikely that you will find this sentence anywhere in cyberspace.

RECURSION

Recursion ▶ The quality of language that allows any sentence to be extended indefinitely by embedding clauses or phrases within it or following it.

One way that generativity occurs is through **recursion**. In linguistics, *recursion* means that any sentence can be extended indefinitely by embedding clauses or phrases within or following it. For example, the sentence

Maya was watching a show that featured the Nigerian actor.

can become:

Maya was watching a show that featured the Nigerian actor whom she met last week.

which can become

> *Joel told me this morning that Maya, the woman who just moved next door, was watching a show that featured the Nigerian actor whom she had met last week.*

which can become:

> *Joel, who usually is pretty closed-mouthed, told me this morning that Maya, the woman who just moved next door into the apartment that was vacated last month, was watching a show that featured the Nigerian actor she had met last week—right after she had decided to stop watching the kind of programs that . . .*

You get the idea.

Some linguists believe that the capacity for recursion is the single most important factor separating the evolution of human language from that of other animal communication systems (Hauser, Chomsky, & Fitch, 2002).

DISPLACEMENT

Displacement means that people can converse about things that do not exist at all, things that exist in places other than that where the conversation takes place, or about complete abstractions—feelings, beliefs, opinions, and so on. We can talk about things that occurred in the past, will occur in the future, or that we wish or fear might happen. Imagine for a moment how impoverished your thoughts and conversations would be without displacement!

Displacement ▶ The quality of language that allows one to converse about things that do not exist, exist in other places, or are abstractions.

Language May Also Be a "Mental Organ"

> *"To come to know a human language would be an extraordinary intellectual achievement for a creature not specifically designed to accomplish this task."*
>
> —Noam Chomsky (1975, p. 4)

The term *language* has a second meaning for many cognitive scientists and linguists. It refers to a hypothesized **internal language faculty**. The language faculty includes innate, partly specialized neural circuitry ("hard wiring") in the brain and cognitive structures of the mind designed to acquire language in early childhood and to use language for thought, expression, and communication (Hauser et al., 2002). From this perspective, children acquire language not only because of their human intelligence and powers of observation and learning (which certainly play an important part), but also because they possess brain and mind mechanisms specifically *dedicated* to acquiring and using language (Chomsky, 1975; Jackendoff, 1994; Pinker, 2004; Pinker & Jackendoff, 2005, 2009).

According to this view, all languages possess a **universal grammar**—a basic structure or set of intrinsic "rules" that all languages share in common. Obviously, this does not refer to ordinary rules of grammar that are famously and amazingly diverse among languages. It means that in spite of variance in correct word orders, use of tenses, and so forth, there exist certain commonalities that do not vary. Usually, universal grammar "rules" are expressed by linguists in this way: "If a language has X (e.g., some particular way of placing a verb), it will also have Y (some way of utilizing nouns)." Or "If a language has a word for X (e.g., the color red), it will also have a word for Y (the color purple)." However, proposed rules of universal grammar are actually scientific hypotheses that only hold weight until a language is discovered that violates the rule—something that has been known to occur for numerous proposed universal grammar rules (N. Evans & Levinson, 2009).

Knowledge of universal grammar is considered by its advocates to be innate in human beings, and it is universal grammar that forms the internal language

Internal language faculty ▶ The notion, initially proposed by Noam Chomsky and originally termed the *language acquisition device* (LAD), that human beings possess innate, specialized cognitive structures dedicated to acquiring and using language.

Universal grammar ▶ The concept originated by Noam Chomsky to describe a basic internal structure or set of intrinsic rules that languages share in common.

faculty. It enables children to easily assimilate the language of their parents and community, and second languages if need be, by automatically applying the rules of *universal* grammar to the *specific* grammar they are attempting to learn (Lidz, Gleitman, & Gleitman, 2003; Nowak, Komarova, & Niyogi, 2001; Thomas, 2004).

No one claims that the internal language faculty resides in some specific anatomical location of the brain; instead, numerous areas are no doubt involved. But many cognitive scientists do conceive of this faculty as a kind of mental "organ," much as the heart, kidneys, and lungs are anatomical organs. According to this view, rather than speaking of language as something that one "learns," it may be more accurate to refer to it as something that "grows" (S. R. Anderson & Lightfoot, 1999, p. 698). The optimal "growing period" for this organ—technically known as its *critical period* for development—is in early childhood, when language seems to be acquired effortlessly. Indeed, in those unusual cases where children have not been exposed to any language until puberty, they are generally unable to acquire language at all, or are only able to learn language in a very rudimentary way after rigorous training (Grimshaw, Adelstein, Bryden, & MacKinnon, 1998; Newport, 2002).

"WE KNOW MORE THAN WE LEARN"

The hypothesis that all languages are united by a universal grammar is not new; indeed, it originated several centuries ago. However, the modern scientific version of this idea originated in the work of linguist, cognitive scientist, philosopher, and political activist Noam Chomsky (1972, 1975, 1980), who initially referred to the internal language faculty as a *language acquisition device* or LAD. Chomsky first noted a puzzle about language development in children: When one considers the number of words, word orders, phrases, and sentences that could conceivably be spoken in any language, it is clear that any given child is exposed only to an exceedingly small sample. Moreover, the *actual* speech to which children are exposed is choppy and often lacking in coherence (set up an audio recorder when you and your friends get together and let just let it run for an hour—you'll be amazed at the results). As Chomsky put it, the *stimulus* to which children are exposed for learning language by imitation is *impoverished*. Yet, within a few years of infancy children have developed an extraordinarily rich ability to construct sentences that are theoretically infinite in number—expressing an infinite number of thoughts.

How children are able to do this is a puzzle. Constructing sentences is not a matter of simply stringing words together. The rules governing the construction of grammatically intelligible and meaningful sentences in each language are complex. The number of *incorrect* possibilities for ordering words is limitless. These rules are never taught, and yet children acquire them effortlessly. No English-speaking toddler ever says, "Bottle I my want" instead of "I want my bottle"—not even once as a "test." This is in spite of never receiving instruction in the correct word placement for such sentences. Moreover, when children are corrected for mistakenly saying "badder" instead of "worse" or "taked" instead of "took," they frequently *resist* correction—because in English, *badder* and *taked* are grammatically logical and *ought* to be correct. Children seem to be applying the rules of universal grammar to instances of weird English grammar!

On a more subtle level, consider the word *is*: Contractions of this word are perfectly acceptable when saying something like "Dylan's here" instead of "Dylan *is* here." However, there are some occasions when the word *is* can never be contracted, for example, "I wonder where the book *is* that was on top of the table this morning." No one ever tells a child they are not supposed to say, "I wonder where the book's that was on top of the table." They *just know*—"as if by magic" (Anderson & Lightfoot, 1999, pp. 699–700).

When it comes to language, then, children seem to "know more than they learn," to use Anderson and Lightfoot's (1999) phrase. Children learn language effortlessly—and this is the case whether the language they are exposed to is spoken or signed, as is the case for the Deaf using American Sign Language (ASL). Children learn without effort even if they are rarely spoken to directly at all, except for the occasional command or scolding, as is the case in traditional Samoa (Ochs & Schieffelin, 1984). Thus, Chomsky concluded that a child who speaks or signs cannot have developed this talent only through learning and imitation. Some recent research supports this view: Researchers have shown that infants prefer the sounds of spoken language to other similar sorts of sounds from birth, and can more easily extract abstract rules about patterns of sounds from listening to speech than listening to other types of sounds (e.g., musical sounds; Marcus, Fernandes, & Johnson, 2007; Vouloumanos & Werker, 2007). Additionally, specific genes appear to be involved in the acquisition and use of language (e.g., Enard et al., 2002; van der Lely, Rosen, & McClelland, 1998; Vargha-Khadem, Gadian, Copp, & Mishkin, 2005).

OBJECTIONS

Chomsky met an onslaught of opposition to his ideas at first, but it is probably fair to say that the majority of cognitive scientists and linguists now agree with his basic insight that language acquisition reflects—at least in part—innate cognitive structures and mechanisms. Yet there remain radical disagreements over the precise nature of these structures and mechanisms, whether they evolved by natural selection or some other means, and whether they exist within specific brain sites. As I will discuss in the next section of the chapter, researchers also debate whether or not certain aspects of these mechanisms are shared with nonhuman animals.

Moreover, in spite of the widespread acceptance of the notion of an innate language faculty, some theorists and researchers continue to flatly reject such ideas. One theory that denies the existence of an innate language faculty is known as **connectionism** (Elman, 2001, 2005; McClelland et al., 2010; Westermann, Ruh, & Plunkett, 2009). Connectionists argue that the mechanisms of the mind are "plastic" in the sense of being highly flexible and adaptable, and that many neural structures of the brain as well as mental mechanisms could be adapted for the learning of language. This is a view of the mind that sees mental mechanisms as *domain general* rather than *domain specific* or *modular*, to use terms introduced in Chapter 3.

Connectionism ▶ The belief that the mind is constructed of complex networks of interconnected units similar to the neural networks of the brain. Connectionism is a domain-general theory of how the mind works, in contrast to domain-specific or modular theories.

CRITICAL THINKING ABOUT PSYCHOLOGY

> There Ain't No Such Thing as Bad Grammar, Yo': The Linguistic View

Before she passed away, my wife's grandmother used to remind my then 6-year-old daughter, Naima, on a near-daily basis that "hens *lay* but people *lie*." She did this to try to rid my daughter of the habit of saying things like "I'm going to lay down." She also stressed that "Cakes are *done*, but people are *finished*," to protect Naima from the tragic shame of uttering sentences like "I'm done with these books."

I would usually tell my daughter she was free to ignore most of what great-grandmother told her if she chose. Why? First, language is about communication and expression, and people communicate and express themselves just fine in spite of grammatical errors. Second, from the perspective of *linguistics*—the science of human language—these are not *errors* at all. They are arbitrary conventions of language usage that are constantly changing with the times. In fact, from the linguistics perspective, there really is no such thing as "bad grammar" in English—unless, instead of saying, "The boy went downstairs to find the ball," one were to say, "The downstairs ball went boy the find to," a statement that would be incomprehensible to

CRITICAL THINKING ABOUT PSYCHOLOGY

CONTINUED   an English speaker and which no English speaker would ever make. Now *that's* bad grammar (McWhorter, 1998, 2003; Pinker, 1994)!

There certainly are grammatical practices known as *prescriptive grammar* that are currently considered to reflect standard forms of languages, and one is obviously well advised to learn them in order to sound educated and function well on the job and in society generally. Without doubt, those who do not use standard forms of language are at a very strong disadvantage in the workplace, as writers, at school, and in numerous social settings, some of which may be important to one's personal goals.

However, it might surprise you to learn that in the case of English, most of these rules originated not from learned studies by linguistic scholars, but primarily from two books written in the late 1700s—one by an English bishop and the other by an American lawyer.[2] These books have had an incalculable influence upon what is considered to be correct English grammar for the past 200 years. However, as linguist John McWhorter (1998) recounts, these men were not linguists and knew virtually nothing about the history of the English language. On the other hand, they did know something about the grammars of Latin and ancient Greek. In essence, these authors "decided" that English ought to follow standard rules of Latin and Greek—languages revered by classical scholars, but with roots completely unrelated to those of English!

Consider the "rule" some of us may have learned in school that it is incorrect to end sentences with prepositions ("Which table did you put my book on?" instead of "On which table did you put my book?"). In Latin, ending sentences with prepositions makes no sense. But in English, ending sentences with prepositions takes nothing whatever away from meaning, and may sometimes improve clarity. In fact, if people really followed this rule strictly it would make for some very strange sentences—a problem about which Winston Churchill was famously said to have quipped, "This is the sort of pedantry up with which I shall not put!" (This quote is rendered somewhat differently in different sources.)

John McWhorter (1998, pp. 3–4) lists several insights about language derived from the science of linguistics that helps to put prescriptions for English grammar, pronunciation, and usage into perspective. Among them are the following three (partially paraphrased):

1. *Any language is always on its way to changing into a new one.* Many of the word meanings and pronunciations, and grammatical patterns we now characterize as "sloppy" and "incorrect" are the very things that will be considered "proper" language in the future. McWhorter provides an excellent example of this occurring over the past 125 years. At the end of the 19th century, it was considered sloppy and vulgar to say, "The house is being built across the street" rather than, "The house is building across the street" (sometimes spoken as "The house is a-building"). Anyone who uttered this last sentence today would receive some very strange looks.

2. *Because a language changes in different random directions among different groups, any language is actually a bundle of dialects.* A *dialect* is a unique variety of language specific to a particular group or locale. Typically, the dialect that ends up being considered "standard" is simply the one used by those at the seat of political power. In other words, a standard language is "a dialect with an army and a navy" (Max Weinrich, cited by S. R. Anderson, 2004). There is no reason that dialects which

---

[2]*The authors in question are Robert Lowth and Lindley Murray.*

diverge from the standard one can logically be seen as "degraded" or inferior, because they all arise from the same process of gradual—and unstoppable—change.

3. *No language has ever changed in a way that contradicts basic logic*, and what looks "illogical" in one dialect—for example, the double negative in the English sentence "I don't know nothing"—inevitably turns up as correct in the most elevated standard speech in some other language—as in the Spanish "*Yo no se nada*" or the French "*Je ne sais rien*," which translates literally as "I not know nothing" (Pinker, 1994). ∎

Language May Influence the Way We Think

During the 1930s, a fire prevention engineer and inspector for an insurance company named Benjamin Lee Whorf constructed a linguistic hypothesis that continues to exert influence on the way scientists think about language. Based upon earlier observations by the famed anthropologist Eduard Sapir, with whom he had briefly studied, Whorf proposed that the ways in which each language is grammatically constructed determines the ways in which those who speak the language construct their reality. This idea came to be known as the **Sapir-Whorf hypothesis** or *linguistic determinism*. Whorf and his followers made a number of now-famous claims to support their hypothesis, among them:

- The Hopi are a people with no words indicating past or future, or referring in other ways to time—therefore they have little concern with hours and minutes, the days of the week, calendars, chronology, and so forth.
- Inuit (Eskimo) languages have many more different words to describe various kinds of *snow* than do Western languages such as English, expressing the importance of snow in the Inuit world. Although Whorf himself put the number of words for snow at seven, subsequent accounts incrementally upped this figure until it reached the now commonly repeated "several dozen" or even "several hundred" in some reports.
- Languages differ in the color categories they contain. People whose language contains no word for a given color are unable to differentiate that color, and those whose languages have only words for dark or light color see no specific colors at all.

On the face of it, these claims seem to defy common sense, and for good reason—they are all either factually incorrect or greatly exaggerated. Inuktitut (the Eskimo language of the Inuit) does not have more words for snow than English (Pullum, 1991). In fact, it probably has fewer, although an exact count is impossible due to differences in Inuktitut dialects. Whorf's claims about Hopi conception of time are even more puzzling. In a detailed analysis of Hopi linguistics, Ekkehart Malotki (1983) demonstrated that the Hopi language contains the same time references that are contained in any other language.

What about those cultures with only two color words in their languages? The languages of some cultures do not contain specific words to differentiate colors. However, members of those cultures do differentiate one color from the next by sight—that is, they know how to distinguish colors, they just do not refer to them in speech (I. R. L. Davies, Sowden, Jerrett, Jerrett, & Corbett, 1998; Rosch-Heider, 1972). Moreover, substantial research among Japanese, Chinese, and English speakers provides little or no evidence that language differences result in fundamental differences in the way objects are perceived (Barner, Li, & Snedeker, 2010; Tse & Altarriba, 2008).

As increasing evidence was collected debunking the more excessive claims of Whorf and his followers, by the 1970s the Sapir-Whorf hypothesis began to

Sapir-Whorf hypothesis (linguistic determinism)
▶ The notion that the way we construe reality is determined by the way our particular language is constructed.

▲ **Dozens of Words for "Snow"?** Followers of Benjamin Lee Whorf have made a number of unsubstantiated claims, among them that Inuit (Eskimo) languages contain dozens or hundreds of words for "snow." In fact, English probably contains more words to describe snow than Inuit languages (e.g., Pullum, 1991).

Linguistic relativity hypothesis ▶ The modified "weak form" of the Sapir-Whorf hypothesis (linguistic determinism). Linguistic relativity theory proposes that the way we construct reality is affected, but not necessarily determined, by our language.

lose favor in psychology (I. R. L. Davies et al., 1998). However, while language may not *determine* the way people construe reality, this does not mean that language has no *effect* on the way we think and perceive—and some researchers have continued to explore Whorf's hypothesis in a modified form generally known as the **linguistic relativity hypothesis** (Pilling & Davies, 2004; Roberson, Davies, & Davidoff, 2002). According to this hypothesis, language is one of many factors affecting the way people construe reality.

For example, language does affect the way people notice and categorize aspects of their world (Boroditsky, 2009). In a particularly interesting series of studies demonstrating this idea, Susan Hespos and Elizabeth Spelke (2004) took as their starting point the observation that the Korean language, but not the English language, uses entirely different verbs to describe whether an object fits loosely or tightly inside or on top of another. On the other hand, the English language, but not the Korean language, uses entirely different words to indicate whether an object is *in* or *on* another object.

Hespos and Spelke showed that when native Korean speakers are presented with a series of images of objects placed loosely or tightly inside other objects, or fitted loosely or tightly on top of other objects, the Korean speakers will intuitively rate the images as being similar or dissimilar based only upon the looseness or tightness of the way the objects fit together—not on whether one object is inside or on top of the other. Native English speakers, on the other hand, perform very differently in this task. They intuitively rate images as similar or dissimilar based on whether one object is *in* or *on* the other, but not according to looseness or tightness of fit. This supports the idea that language influences perception.

However, in the same series of experiments, Hespos and Spelke demonstrated that language does not *determine* perception, as Whorf contended. Hespos and Spelke used experimental techniques based upon the tendency of small infants to stare noticeably longer at images that they perceive to be dissimilar to images they have been exposed to previously—a variation on the learning mechanism of *habituation* as described in Chapters 4 and 7 (Aslin, 2007). In Hespos and Spelke's studies, 5-month-old infants stared longer at objects fitting tightly inside other objects after first being exposed to objects fitting loosely—and vice versa. This demonstrates that even very small infants are able to notice the difference between tight and loose fits. According to the Sapir-Whorf hypothesis, perception of the distinction between "tight" and "loose" should not be present at all in very small infants, because infants have not yet learned to distinguish tight from loose in language. Hespos and Spelke's research suggests that at least some categories exist in the human mind prior to language. They may represent innate natural human concepts not dependent upon language for their perception.

IN SUMMARY

1.	Language is an open-ended code-like system of communication and expression built upon symbols and representations. Languages possess the properties of generativity, recursion, and displacement.
2.	The term *language* also refers to a hypothesized internal language faculty made up of universal grammar—a set of intrinsic "rules" common to all languages. Not all linguists and cognitive scientists acknowledge the existence of the innate language faculty or universal grammar.
3.	Language influences the way people perceive their world, but it does not fully determine perception as proposed in the original Sapir-Whorf hypothesis of linguistic determinism. The notion that language has an influence on the way people perceive their world is known as linguistic relativism.

RETRIEVE!

1. Connect the description at the left with the component of human language at the right:

Any sentence can be extended indefinitely by embedding clauses or phrases — Generativity

Small numbers of words and grammatical structures may be used to compose an infinite number of sentences — Displacement

People can converse about things that do not exist, exist in other places, or are complete abstractions — Recursion

2. What do cognitive scientists and linguists mean when they say that children "know more than they learn" about language?

3. Although the sentence "I ain't goin' nowhere, yo'" violates English prescriptive grammar, it does not violate _____ grammar.

4. Which of the following is NOT among the reasons given by linguist John McWhorter for his claim that prescriptive grammar is arbitrary and not set in stone:

a) The grammar books written by experts are virtually never based on accurate knowledge.

b) Any language is always on its way to changing into a new one.

c) Any language is actually a bundle of dialects

d) No language has ever changed in a way that contradicts basic logic.

5. In their studies of infants and adults, how did Hespos and Spelke provide evidence supporting the notion that language does influence perception? How did they provide evidence that language does not *determine* perception?

Do Nonhuman Animals Have Language?

"If a lion could talk we would not understand him."

—Ludwig Wittgenstein

On April 27, 1998, Koko, a gorilla trained in American Sign Language (ASL) for the past quarter-century by developmental psychologist Francine ("Penny") Patterson, became the first nonhuman to conduct a live Internet chat session. Here is my all-time favorite Koko conversational exchange, verbatim from the transcript of the chat session:

Moderator: Storm1004 [e-mail address] asks, "Dear Koko . . . I've watched you for years now . . . your gentle spirit is an inspiration for many. . . . I'd like to know what you'd like for your birthday."

Koko: Birthday. Food and smokes.

Moderator: SMOKES?

Dr. Patterson: You have to understand. . . . Smoke is the name of her kitten.

(Complete transcript available at http://www.geocities.com/RainForest/Vines/4451/KokoLiveChat.html)

▲ **Koko and Lips-Lipstick.**

As a parent, I cannot help but be a Koko fan. Just look at the photo of Koko with her second beloved kitten Lips-Lipstick. Does research indicate that she has learned language?

Without doubt, animals communicate. While some of this communication is extremely minimal and limited to maintaining group solidarity or conveying one's mood or personal identity, some animal communication is *referential* (Wynne, 2004). This means that different signals *refer* to specific things. In addition to the dances of honeybees described earlier—which can refer to distance, direction, and quality of food sources—vervet monkeys can communicate specific information about external events using bark-like calls. For example, they can "say" something like "There's another group of monkeys coming" or "It's a leopard, watch out!" rather than just emitting a general warning signal like "Get out of the way!" (Seyfarth & Cheney, 2003; Wynne, 2004). Wild Campbell and Diana monkeys also produce referential calls (Zuberbüler, 2003), and certain birds—particularly chickens—have this ability (C. S. Evans & Evans, 1999).

However, even these referential forms of communication are *closed-ended*. They may refer to specific situations, but they cannot be recombined to refer to other situations (Nowak, Plotkin, & Jansen, 2000). In contrast, human words can be combined to refer to a potentially infinite number of situations. Human words can also be combined to refer to people, places, and things that do not currently exist, or that only exist elsewhere—a characteristic absent from animal communication systems. Indeed, even 12-month-old infants who do not yet use language will point to locations where a desired object had previously been placed by an experimenter as a way of requesting the object (a toy); however, in the same experimental set-up, chimpanzees will only point to a location to request a desired object (food) if the food is currently there (Liszkowski, Schaëfer, Carpenter, & Tomasello, 2009).

Therefore, animal communication systems do not contain the properties of *generativity, recursion*, and *displacement* described earlier, and they are not languages. Not only are nonhuman communication systems unable to express an infinite number of new thoughts and ideas and refer to nonexistent entities, they are unable to express very many things at all. Interestingly, one species that thus far has *not* been shown to possess referential communication systems is the chimpanzee, whose vocal utterances are quite limited (Wynne, 2004). Yet it is to the chimpanzee that researchers have looked in the hope that nonhuman animals could be taught human language.

Washoe, Nim, and Kanzi: Conversationalists or Trained Chimps?

By 1970, more linguists and cognitive scientists were starting to come around to Noam Chomsky's view that language was unique to humans and required specific brain and cognitive mechanisms to exist. However, certain theorists, notably *behaviorists* such as B. F. Skinner, strongly opposed this idea. Skinner and the behaviorists argued instead that language was a behavior like any other and that it was learned like other behaviors through reinforcement, as described in Chapter 7. From this perspective, even though chimpanzees might not communicate among themselves with natural language, there was no reason to assume that they could not be *taught* to communicate with language. Because chimpanzees are genetically very close to human beings, they were considered to be the best candidates among nonhuman animals for learning language.

Attempts to teach chimpanzees actually to *speak* have always been unsuccessful due to the way the chimpanzee larynx and throat are situated. However, during the late 1960s, Allen and Beatrice Gardner hit upon the idea of teaching a chimpanzee named Washoe to sign, using American Sign Language (ASL). The Gardners successfully taught Washoe to produce more than 130 signs. In a particularly famous utterance, Washoe saw a swan while out in a boat on a lake and signed "water bird." Although it is not clear whether Washoe was giving a name to the swan by combining "water" and "bird," or simply observing a bird on the water, it is a startling achievement nonetheless.

The Washoe project led to other, similar attempts to teach language to nonhuman primates, including Koko the gorilla. One such nonhuman primate was a chimpanzee named Nim Chimpsky (a joking reference to Noam Chomsky), trained by Herbert Terrace (Terrace, 1987). Terrace was a behaviorist, who, like Skinner, rejected Chomsky's views and believed strongly that chimpanzees could learn language given enough time and appropriate methods. Terrace succeeded in teaching Nim about the same number of signs as Washoe had learned. Unfortunately, Terrace's funding ran out, and he had to give Nim away.

Because Terrace was no longer working with Nim, he had a chance to carefully examine the videotapes of his training sessions. What he found startled and disappointed him. Terrace concluded that what Nim had accomplished was not language, but simple operant learning—not much different from that of a rat learning to press a bar to obtain food or a dog learning that the sounds "Do you want to go out?" meant that he or she was about to go for a walk. Terrace claimed that Nim and chimps such as Washoe had learned that when they made certain signs, certain things happened—notably, they obtained things they wanted such as food. This is the method used to train animals to do all sorts of amazing things. Take Wanpen—a Thai elephant trained to paint in Chinese style by the artist Chaowalit (see photo).

Terrace's revelations—in fact, stinging critiques of his own research—caused a storm of controversy. He and other researchers noted a series of problems with the claims of those teaching language to apes. For example, after decades of intense daily training, chimpanzees do not appear to be capable of learning more than a few hundred signs. Even toddlers frequently have vocabularies exceeding those of chimps trained for decades. Thus, critics, including Chomsky, charged that to claim that these chimps use language is equivalent to a claim that people can learn to fly because pole vaulters, divers, and ballet dancers sail through the air.

▲ **BUT IS IT ART?** The Thai Elephant Wanpen creates paintings.

▲ **Training Primates to Use Sign Language.** Pictured from left to right are Washoe, Nim Chimpsky, and Kanzi. Claims and counterclaims have been made regarding the ability of nonhuman primates to learn human language, and research with these chimpanzees has been at the heart of many of the controversies. The primary question is this: Are these chimpanzees learning rudimentary, but genuine, language—or are they simply being trained to do linguistic "tricks"?

In addition, Terrace and other researchers have noted that there is sometimes a discrepancy between what researchers who work with apes claim the ape is "saying" and what videotapes show the chimp is *actually* signing. Wynne (2004, p. 123) provides the following example of a short conversation between a *bonobo* ("pygmy chimp") named Kanzi and his trainer:

> **Kanzi**: Want milk. Milk.
>
> **Human**: You want some milk? I know, you always want some milk when you're planning to be good.
>
> **Kanzi**: Key. Matata. Good.
>
> **Human**: Oh, you want the key to Matata, and you're going to be good. Well, I'm glad to hear that.

Wynne points out that the utterances of Kanzi are abrupt and largely meaningless apart from a demand for milk. He does not say he wants the key to Matata (Kanzi's bonobo companion) and plans to be good—indeed, he says nothing at all about planning to be good. It is the trainer who supplies this meaning.

While these criticisms are important, some evidence suggests that this is not the whole story, and criticisms of ape language research may be overly harsh (Shanker, Savage-Rumbaugh, & Taylor, 1999). First, Zuberbüler (2003) has shown that the meaning of wild Campbell monkeys' referential calls changes according to the order in which they occur. Thus, something similar to *syntax*—the ordering of words in sentences—is at least possible in nonhuman primates.

More dramatically, some evidence collected by Sue Savage-Rumbaugh, the trainer of the bonobo Kanzi "quoted" in the previous dialogue, suggests that not all chimpanzee accomplishments in learning human language are an illusion (Savage-Rumbaugh, Shanker, & Taylor, 1998). For example, Savage-Rumbaugh claims that Kanzi has shown evidence of understanding (but not using) grammar. She tested this ability by giving commands to Kanzi that are grammatically "reversible." For example, if Kanzi had no understanding of grammar, the sentence "put the banana on the plate" could just as easily be understood by him as "put the plate on the banana" because the words *plate, on, banana,* and *put* have radically different meanings depending on how they are ordered. When Savage-Rumbaugh did present Kanzi with a group of such reversible commands, the bonobo scored enough of them correctly to rule out the probability that the results were strictly due to chance (Wynne, 2004).

However, even if the critics are overly harsh and Savage-Rumbaugh's claims are accurate, there is no denying that the linguistic accomplishments of even an extraordinary ape such as Kanzi after decades of training differ dramatically from those of most any healthy 2- or 3-year-old human child—including a child who is not spoken to very often by adults. Therefore, it is worth contemplating the significance of findings that an ape can be trained over decades to learn a few hundred signs and develop rudimentary comprehension of simple syntax.

For example, Povinelli and Bering (2002) argue that in trying to avoid the trap of thinking of human beings as "special" and "higher" than other animals, some scientists are instead struggling to make nonhuman animals fit a human mold—to see them as "watered-down human beings" (p. 170). Instead of looking for signs of humanness in nonhuman animals, Povinelli and Bering argue that we should be listening to these animals tell their own unique stories— radically different from human stories, but no less valuable.

The "stories" animals may have to tell may need to be understood more through gestures than vocalizations, however—at least in the cases of our nearest evolutionary relatives, the bonobo and the chimpanzee. Amy Pollick and Frans de Waal catalogued 31 gestures and 18 facial/vocal signals among groups of bonobos and chimpanzees (Pollick & de Waal, 2007). As depicted in Figure 9.8, Pollick and de Waal found that the facial and vocal signals were highly limited in their "meaning"—they were applied in relatively specific situations, and were used identically in both species. On the other hand, the arm and hand gestures were flexible in their content. Bonobos used them differently from chimpanzees, and the contexts in which the gestures were used also differed among individual bonobos and chimps.

This research provides evidence in favor of one hypothesis about how language developed—that it emerged from hand and arm gestures, not vocalizations. Recall that vocalizations and facial signals were the same for both the bonobos and the chimps—but the hand and arm gestures were not. This suggests that, among apes, gestures may be freer to take on different meanings depending upon context. In comparison, vocalizations and facial signals are "frozen" as to their meanings. As a result, gestures might be more easily adapted to symbolic communication, as in language. Pollick and de Waal also point out that monkeys do not use gestures to communicate—and monkeys are evolutionarily older than bonobos, chimpanzees, or humans. Because vocal language evolved recently with human beings, the evolutionary "youth" of bonobo and chimpanzee communication through gesture adds more weight to the notion that language may have evolved initially through gestures rather than vocalizations.

▲ **FIGURE 9.8** For Bonobos and Chimpanzees, a Gesture May Be Worth a Thousand Words. Among chimpanzees and bonobos, facial expressions and vocalizations are tied to specific and limited contexts. Their "meanings" are frozen. On the other hand, arm and hand gestures are more flexible modes of communication. These findings have been used to support arguments that language may have evolved through gesture, not vocalization.

IN SUMMARY

1.	Animal communication systems are occasionally referential, but they lack generativity, recursion, and displacement.
2.	Claims that apes can be taught human sign language have been challenged. However, some evidence suggests that apes might be able to learn a limited vocabulary of signs and rudimentary understanding of syntax.
3.	Recent evidence suggests that among chimpanzees and bonobos hand and arm gestures are a more flexible method of communication than facial expressions and vocalizations.

RETRIEVE!

1.	Name at least two criticisms of research which claims that apes can be taught human sign language. Give two examples of evidence that apes *can* be taught rudimentary sign language.
2.	Name at least one example of referential communication among animals.

3. Why does chimpanzee and bonobo communication through gesture add weight to the hypothesis that language initially evolved through gesture rather than vocalization?

What Is Intelligence?

"Rocks are smarter than cats because rocks have the sense to go away when you kick them."

—Cognitive scientist Zenon Pylyshyn
(paraphrased by Pinker, 1997, p. 61)

After 100 years of strenuous attempts, experts have not been able to agree on a definition of intelligence (Deary, Weiss, & Batty, 2010; Neisser et al., 1996). Indeed, as intelligence researcher Ian Deary remarked, "Intelligence is rarely discussed for long before the word 'controversial' appears" (Deary, 2012, p. 454). However, most people have a commonsense understanding of what intelligence means, and they often know it when they see it—or, perhaps more accurately, when they *hear* it. A number of studies have shown that people are quite accurate in judging a stranger's intelligence (as measured by formal intelligence tests) after even very brief exposure to the sound of the person reading a few short sentences or speaking for 20 seconds (Borkenau, Mauer, Riemann, Spinath, & Angleitner, 2004; Reynolds & Gifford, 2001).

What are people listening for in making these judgments? Although the researchers conducting these studies attempted to isolate certain factors on which people were basing their decisions (such as the speed and clarity of the target person's speech or the number of words he or she used), such simple cues do not convey what people mean when they call another person "intelligent." For one thing, people sometimes differentiate between *types* of intelligence, captured in the expressions "book smarts" and "street smarts."

There Are Two General Meanings of the Word "Intelligence"

Practical intelligence ▶ A concept hypothesized by Robert J. Sternberg to describe the ability to come up with efficient solutions to everyday problems.

General intelligence (g) ▶ A way of referring to a person's underlying general capacity to process complex information—to perform well on a variety of mental tasks. General intelligence, or *g*, was initially hypothesized by Charles Spearman.

In this sense, the word *intelligence* can be used in two general ways. Intelligence can simply mean rational "humanlike" thought, as in the question "Is there intelligent life in the universe?" (Pinker, 1997). This type of intelligence includes the ability to overcome obstacles, solve problems, and make decisions by means of rational (reality-based) considerations. Such a meaning of intelligence corresponds loosely to "street smarts," or what intelligence researcher Robert J. Sternberg calls **practical intelligence**—the ability to come up with efficient solutions to the problems of everyday life, at home or on the job (Sternberg, 2003c; Grigorenko, Sternberg, & Strauss, 2006). A hunter with no education, but who can devise intricate traps to outwit clever animals, might be thought to possess this type of intelligence—even if he or she cannot read, write, or do arithmetic.

However, it is "book smarts" that probably best captures the average person's idea of the concept "intelligence" (Carroll, 1997; Jensen, 1998). Yet, intelligence researchers themselves are often widely divided as to what "book smarts" actually means and whether it is the most appropriate indication of intelligence.

General Intelligence (*g*) Is One Way of Describing "Book Smarts"

General intelligence, or **g**, is the technical term to describe what is popularly called "book smarts." General intelligence (*g*) describes a person's underlying general capacity to process complex information—to perform well on a wide variety of mental and even manual tasks. In this sense, the term "book smarts" is misleading, because *g* involves much more than book learning. The most frequently administered intelligence tests (e.g., the **Stanford-Binet Intelligence Scale** and the **Wechsler Adult Intelligence Scale [WAIS®-III]**) are thought to measure individual differences in *g*, and reflect the ease and speed with which a person should be expected to be able to learn new information (Carroll, 1997; Johnson, te Nijenhuis, & Bouchard, 2008; Spearman, 1904, 1927). However, test batteries correlated with *g* may include measures of manual dexterity and perceptual speed as well as ability to juggle mental concepts and demonstrate proficiency in math and verbal tasks (Deary, Weiss, & Batty, 2010; Johnson, Bouchard, Krueger, McGue, & Gottesman, 2004; Johnson et al., 2008).

CHARLES SPEARMAN AND PSYCHOMETRICS

It was Charles Spearman (1904, 1927) who first proposed the existence of *g*. In examining groups of tests scores of cognitive ability using a complex statistical procedure known as *factor analysis*, Spearman noted that there were correlations between the way individuals scored on one aspect of cognitive ability—say, numerical ability—and their scoring on other aspects of cognitive ability, such as verbal ability or visual-spatial reasoning. Although it was certainly possible to score exceptionally well on tests of one ability, and less well or even poorly on tests of another, Spearman found that this was the exception rather than the rule. More commonly, Spearman found that he could predict in a general way how a person would score in one type of task just by knowing that person's score on any other type of task. This suggested to Spearman that there was some sort of underlying factor uniting all the abilities. The fact that a person's score on virtually any of the tests he administered could be used to predict that person's score on any of the other tests was termed by Spearman the **theorem of the indifference of the indicator**. This general tendency for those scoring high on tests of one type of cognitive ability also to score relatively high on tests of other abilities is the rationale for hypothesizing the existence of *g*, a general intelligence factor that runs like a current through all mental abilities (Carroll, 1997; Jensen, 1998; Johnson et al., 2008).

Spearman's research initiated the modern **psychometric** tradition, which has long been the dominant one in the field of intelligence research. The psychometric tradition relies upon objective measurement by means of various standardized tests (e.g., *IQ* tests). What is the meaning of "standardized"? You can think of standardization as a kind of "grading on a curve" in test interpretation. The absolute number of correct answers is not at issue. Instead, it is how a person scores in relation to the way large groups of similar individuals have scored in the past. These are groups of people presumably representative of the population for which the test has been designed. The scores produced by these larger groups are known as *norms* for the test, and administering the test to these large groups is called *norming* the test.

IQ Is the Most Commonly Accepted Measure of Intelligence

IQ (intelligence quotient) is the most commonly accepted statistic describing intelligence. It is very highly correlated with *g*, and it is generally considered to be the best test measure of *g*. This statistic was originally developed

g ► (*see* General intelligence)

Stanford-Binet Intelligence Scale ► The first version of the IQ test created by Alfred Binet. The purpose of the test was to predict academic performance so that children of deficient ability could be identified and placed in special remedial programs. The test has been revised four times over its 100-year history.

Wechsler Adult Intelligence Scale (WAIS®-III) ► A standardized test of intelligence designed by David G. Wechsler. This was the first test to extend the IQ to include testing of adults.

Theorem of the indifference of the indicator ► Charles Spearman's idea that you can take a person's score on any test of mental ability and use it in a general way to predict his or her score on a test of any other mental ability.

Psychometric ► Objective measurement of a psychological attribute (such as intelligence or personality) using standardized tests.

IQ (Intelligence Quotient) ► A statistical measure of performance on intelligence tests based upon comparisons of a person's score with the average scores of others of his or her age. IQ was originally conceived as a measure of children's performance. When tests began to be administered to adults, new computational formulas had to be devised.

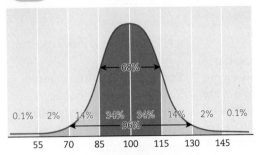

▲ FIGURE 9.9 The Normal Distribution of IQ Scores. This bell-shaped curve charts the normal distribution of IQ scores. Notice that the figures add up to two-tenths of 1% greater than 100%. This is because the figures are approximations, and there is a fraction of 1% of most populations that may score higher than 145 or lower than 55.

Wechsler Intelligence Scale for Children (WISC®-IV)
▶ A standardized test of intelligence for children devised by David G. Wechsler.

Normal distribution ▶
A bell-shaped pattern of scores reflecting predictable individual differences in scoring on standardized tests.

in the first part of the 20th century by intelligence researcher Lewis Terman to interpret student's scores on a mental abilities test known as the *Stanford-Binet Intelligence Scale*. The Stanford-Binet was the most common standardized intelligence test for children prior to the creation of the first version of the **Wechsler Intelligence Scale for Children** (**WISC®-IV**), and it is still in widespread use. Although the IQ is firmly associated with conventional definitions of intelligence, David Wechsler, the creator of the WISC tests, actually defined intelligence in somewhat broader terms than those typically used to define either IQ or *g*. According to Wechsler, intelligence is the "global capacity of the individual to act purposefully, to think rationally and to deal effectively with his environment." Thus, Wechsler's definition includes aspects of "practical intelligence" or "street smarts."

Technically, however, "IQ" no longer exists. The statistic was originally computed by comparing a child's scores against the scores of other children from a similar population but of different ages. Thus, if an 8-year-old scored similarly to the average 10-year-old, it would indicate an elevated IQ. If the score were similar to an average 6-year-old it would indicate low IQ. However, because intelligence tests are now given to adults as well as children, you can see that this method of computing IQ would not work very well for adults, whose mental development does not change year by year as does a child's. It wouldn't be very meaningful to say, "Hey, I'm, like, a genius—I'm only 25 but I read as well as any 30-year-old!" Therefore, intelligence test developers have devised new ways to compute an IQ-like score. These methods work as well for adults as for children. Although the new methods do not really produce an IQ in the technical sense, the term *IQ* is still generally used by researchers and the public alike.

THE BELL CURVE

Scores on standardized IQ tests such the WAIS®-III, WISC®-IV, or the Stanford-Binet Intelligence Scale are designed to reflect a predictable pattern of individual differences with a mean (average) score at the center of the distribution. This pattern is known as the **normal distribution** or, in popular terms, the *bell curve*. As Figure 9.9 shows, the pattern does form a bell shape, with 68% of scores in ordinary populations clustering between 85 and 115. This is considered the normal range of IQ scoring, with 100 being the average IQ score. An additional 28% of scores fall between 115 and 130 at the upper end and between 70 and 85 at the lower end. Scores between 115 and 130 are considered to represent "bright" or "superior" scoring while those between 70 and 85 are termed "borderline" scoring.

In all, then, 96% of people's scores tend to fall between 70 and 130. The remaining 4% of individuals score either lower than 70 or higher than 130. An IQ score between about 50 and 70 (2% of the population) may reflect *intellectual disability*—a psychiatric designation for a person who has difficulty acquiring very basic academic skills, problems in social relationships, and who may need assistance in managing ordinary life tasks (American Psychiatric Association, 2013).

On the other hand, a score above 130 reflects "gifted" or "extremely gifted" scoring, with scores above 150 or thereabouts reflecting "profound giftedness"—a designation that applies only to a very small fraction of 1% of the population.[3]

---

[3]*These IQ scores and labels such as "extremely gifted" and "profoundly gifted" vary sometimes substantially according to who is doing the labeling and which IQ test is being used.*

IQ Measures Something Important, but It May Not Be Intelligence

The IQ is often misunderstood in a number of ways. For example, there is a common perception, sometimes encouraged in the media, that IQ is inherently meaningless and that such tests only measure facts that one has learned in school. In contrast to these characterizations, IQ is actually a highly reliable and meaningful statistic and it does not simply measure facts one has learned at school. Let's explore how and why this is true.

Intelligence tests were initially designed as tools of *prediction*. Their primary job is to *predict* how well a person is likely to do in an academic setting, and they do this job very well. IQ is far from the only factor associated with a person's educational outcome—motivation and engagement with schoolwork, self-discipline and self-control, access to good schooling, personality and socioeconomic factors, and beliefs about one's own ability are also extremely important (Caprara, Vecchione, Alessandri, Gerbino, & Barnaranelli, 2011; Duckworth & Seligman, 2005; Greven, Harlaar, Kovas, Chamorro-Premuzic, & Plomin, 2009; Johnson, McGue, & Iacono, 2006; Winne & Nebit, 2010). Indeed, these factors, if combined, are responsible for the majority of the differences among people in academic achievement, and in some individuals, factors such as self-discipline and self-control can trump IQ in predicting academic success. Yet, IQ scores are still overall the best *single* predictor of grade point average, achievement test scores (e.g., SAT), the number of years a student remains in school, and the academic degree he or she ultimately receives (Deary, Strand, Smith, & Fernandes, 2007; Fergusson, Horwood, & Ridder, 2005; Jensen, 1998; Lubinski, 2004).

A particularly vivid example of the correlation between IQ scores and educational attainment is presented by David Lubinski and his colleagues (Lubinski, Webb, Morelock, & Benbow, 2001). For 10 years, these investigators followed 320 young adolescents whose average IQ scores prior to age 13 put them in the "profoundly gifted" range. By age 23, virtually all had graduated from college, and 56% were already pursuing Ph.D. degrees—a figure 50 times greater than the number of expected Ph.D.s in the general population. Indeed, 12% had already earned a doctorate by age 23. This and quantities of additional evidence collected over decades strongly support the view that educational attainment increases along with increases in IQ (Deary et al., 2007; Jensen, 1998; Lubinsky, 2004).

IQ predicts other things about a person's life as well. For example, these scores are related to health and longevity (Deary, Weiss, & Batty, 2010; Deary, Batty, Pattie, & Gale, 2008; Gottfredson & Deary, 2004; Leon, Lawlor, Clark, Batty, & Macintyre, 2009; Martin & Kubzansky, 2005). Large-scale studies encompassing virtually the entire population of Scotland, as well as long-term studies in Australia and the United States, have shown that higher scores on intelligence tests in childhood are associated with better health throughout adulthood and a longer life (Deary, 2012; Deary et al., 2008; Leon et al., 2009). In one very large-scale study that included approximately 1 million Swedish men, those with lower IQ scores measured at age 18 were more likely to die of all causes (other than cancer) by middle age (Batty et al., 2009).

Although the reasons why IQ should affect health and longevity in this way are not known with certainty, researchers speculate that it may be due primarily to the fact that higher-IQ people are more likely to get regular physical exercise, to eat healthful diets, to drive with care, to comply with medical prescriptions and regimens (e.g., insulin injections for diabetics), and to avoid smoking or excessive use of alcohol. Higher-IQ individuals may also be better at weathering certain types of stressful experiences (Deary, 2012; Gottfredson & Deary, 2004; Martin & Kubzansky, 2005).

Although IQ is far from the most important predictor of how well a person does on the job (Sternberg & Wagner, 1993), IQ and similar tests of cognitive

▲ **Intellectual Disability.** A psychiatric designation for a person who scores lower than 70 on IQ tests and who needs assistance in becoming a self-supporting adult. Erroneous beliefs about intellectual disability (sometimes termed *mental retardation*) are common. With appropriate support systems, the functioning of persons with intellectual disabilities can dramatically improve.

▲ **IQ and Educational Attainment Are Highly Correlated.** Pictured here are a group of exceptionally gifted middle-school students attending at Davidson Institute for Talent Development's THINK Summer Institute in Nevada, where they enroll in two semester-length college courses, but complete them in three weeks. Research has found that students who score in the "profoundly gifted" range on IQ tests are 50 times more likely than others in the population to pursue Ph.D. degrees (e.g., Lubinsky et al., 2001).

ability also predict aspects of job hiring and performance, particularly jobs involving complex tasks (Berry & Sackett, 2009; Gottfredson, 1997; Kuncel & Hezlett, 2010; Schmitt & Hunter, 2004). Not surprisingly, those with higher IQ scores tend to be found more often in higher-status occupations, and their incomes are higher than those with lower IQs. However, researchers have not yet been able to determine if it is IQ itself that predicts higher income and status, or if it is the effect IQ has on the number of years of schooling a person experiences which produces these results (Scullin, Peters, Williams, & Ceci, 2000).

One puzzling, but potentially important fact about IQ: it's on the rise! In most of the developed world, and beginning in portions of the developing world, average IQ scores have risen over the decades. While some of the more developed countries seem to have experienced a "tapping out" of IQ gains, in the United States average IQ scores have continued to rise at the rate of about three points per decade throughout the 20th century and into the 21st (Nisbett et al., 2012). Known as the "Flynn effect," after its discoverer James Flynn, IQ gains over the years have not yet been explained adequately. As Richard Nisbett and his colleagues proclaim, "It is easier to eliminate causes than to provide a convincing causal scenario" (p. 12).

THE QUESTION OF BIAS

As stated earlier, IQ tests were initially designed to predict academic performance. In this sense, IQ tests have repeatedly been shown not to be biased against specific groups such as women or people of color (Carroll, 1997; Neisser et al. 1996). These tests predict the performance of women and minority groups just as well as they do that of men and the white majority population. Thus, as long as a person is representative of the group against which the tests have been normed, the tests are not biased.

On the other hand, if a person is *not* representative of the group against which the test has been normed—for example, if a person does not understand English well and is given an English version of the test—then the test most certainly *is* biased. Moreover, although IQ tests do not "only measure facts one has learned in school," a child's IQ is at least to some degree influenced by schooling. The experience of schooling itself (regardless of the quality of schooling) plays a role in developing the cognitive skills for performing well on IQ tests, as does exposure to learning in the home—for example, exposure to vocabulary words spoken by parents (Bornstein et al., 2006; Carroll, 1997; Ceci & Williams, 1997; Nisbett et al., 2012). Therefore, as John B. Carroll (1997) notes, a child who is not exposed to schooling or to home learning could not be said to be fairly tested by IQ tests in the sense that his or her native ability may not be reflected in scoring—even if the score does predict future academic achievement.

Thus, if one is using IQ as it was originally intended, as a predictor of academic performance and achievement, it is unbiased and highly reliable. However, if one is using IQ as a measure of innate *intelligence*, it may be a biased statistic because some groups have unequal access to experiences and resources that increase both IQ scoring *and* school performance, such as a home life supportive of education (Nisbett et al., 2012; Verney, Granholm, Marshall, Malcame, & Saccuzo, 2005). Some groups may also have greater exposure to experiences that cause both low test scoring and low school performance, such as exposure to environmental toxins, poor nutrition, and the stress of living in a high-crime neighborhood.

In an important sense, then, the IQ may not actually measure *intelligence* per se. IQ is a measure of the degree to which—and the speed at which—people are able to learn the knowledge and skills that are presented to them in modern environments, including the home, school, and the varieties of everyday experience (Carroll, 1997, p. 44). In other words, it is likely a measure of

▲ **FIGURE 9.10 The Heights of Musical, Interpersonal, and Bodily-Kinesthetic Intelligence.** Pictured here are jazz vocalist Billie Holiday (1915–1959), author Fyodor Dostoevsky (1821–1881), and martial artist/actor Bruce Lee (1940–1973). We have no way of knowing their respective IQ scores. However, Holiday was one of the greatest vocalists of the 20th century, prized for her unerring sense of time and the profound emotional impact of her music; Dostoevsky was one of the greatest novelists in history, cherished for his ability to understand human motivations and emotions; and Bruce Lee had truly astonishing athletic control over his body, which, though small, could express enormous power and agility. Intelligence theorist Howard Gardner would likely view Holiday as high in musical intelligence, Dostoevsky as high in interpersonal intelligence, and Lee as high in bodily-kinesthetic intelligence.

g—whatever g may actually turn out to be. "Intelligence" is then *inferred* from a person's IQ score *if* one defines intelligence in terms of g. However, as we will now explore, not all researchers define intelligence as g and IQ.

Multiple Intelligences: An Alternative to g and IQ

Not all researchers accept the idea of a single factor (g) underlying all of intelligence, nor do they define intelligence in terms of scores on standardized IQ tests. Some hypothesize the existence of multiple forms of intelligence not captured in the idea of g and not adequately measured in intelligence tests. For example, during Spearman's time, Louis Thurstone (1938) argued that intelligence actually consisted of a set of seven distinct mental abilities—word fluency, numerical facility, analytical reasoning, and so forth—without any underlying single general factor. He suggested that a person could score very high on one of these dimensions, while quite low on another, and he believed that a person's intelligence was best described by the pattern of these variations in performance, rather than by a single underlying factor. However, research eventually showed that Thurstone's seven specific mental abilities actually *were* united by an underlying factor (Deary, 2012). To score high on some of these abilities but low on others—while possible—was relatively unusual. Thurstone himself ultimately acknowledged this (Thurstone & Thurstone, 1941).

A more modern version of the multiple intelligences idea has been proposed by Howard Gardner (1983, 2006, 2008). In Gardner's view, the entire notion of intelligence needs to be stretched to include talents that are socially valued, such as athletic ability (which he terms *bodily-kinesthetic intelligence*), musical ability (*musical intelligence*), or the ability to understand one's own and others' emotions and motivations (*interpersonal intelligence*). According to Gardner, defining intelligence in terms of IQ or g causes certain human qualities to become greatly overvalued at the expense of other, equally important qualities. On the other hand, critics have charged that some of the abilities cited by Gardner should more properly be termed talents, aptitudes, or skills rather than "intelligences" (See Figure 9.10)

ROBERT STERNBERG'S TRIARCHIC THEORY OF SUCCESSFUL INTELLIGENCE

A more influential challenge to the importance of g as a measure of intelligence comes from researcher Robert J. Sternberg, so I shall treat this theory in greater detail. Sternberg is well known for his skepticism about the ability of IQ tests to measure all aspects of intelligence adequately—and about the usefulness of the notion of *g* as a single factor underlying all types of cognitive abilities. However, it is not that Sternberg denies the existence of *g*. He affirms its existence (Sternberg, 2003b, p. 400). However, he insists that *g* only underlies certain types of mental abilities—specifically, those that involve solving problems through *analytic reasoning*. Such problems (a) are already formulated and clearly defined (e.g., a test question); (b) have a single correct answer; (c) come with all the information necessary to solve them (e.g., a vocabulary question or mathematical problem); (d) are detached from ordinary experience; and (e) have little intrinsic interest—that is, their sole purpose is to test a person's ability (Neisser et al., 1996).

However, life is filled with problems that do not fit this mold. For example, *practical* problems often are not well formulated or defined ("How can I best organize my schedule to balance work, studying, and a social life?"). Such problems usually do not come with all the information necessary to solve them—they require an information-gathering process (e.g., Which classes require the most studying? How much money do I really need to get by?). Practical problems also often have many different possible solutions. Finally, because these problems are embedded in the context of a person's everyday life, they hold intrinsic interest for that person.

Sternberg and his colleagues have used such observations to evolve a theory of intelligence known as the **triarchic theory of successful intelligence** (Sternberg, 2000; 2003b; 2005). Sternberg uses the term *successful*, because he defines intelligence as "one's ability to succeed according to what one values in life, within one's sociocultural context" (2003b, p. 400.) The triarchic theory proposes that there are three distinct forms of intelligence that are independent of one another—that is, a person can be quite high on one and quite low on another.

Triarchic theory of successful intelligence ▶ Robert J. Sternberg's theory that intelligence consists of three distinct types: analytic intelligence, creative intelligence, and practical intelligence.

1. *Analytic intelligence* is a person's ability to solve the sorts of problems one would ordinarily find in an academic setting. This type of intelligence is reflected in the idea of *g* and is measured by intelligence tests.

2. *Creative intelligence* is a person's ability to use insight and his or her existing knowledge base to solve new problems and come up with new ideas—to think "outside the box." According to this idea, a student may have poor IQ and SAT scores yet may excel in creative problem solving and project design.

3. *Practical intelligence* is a person's ability to adapt to his or her environment effectively, solve everyday problems, and achieve personal goals. Jet, the Brazilian street vendor described in the "Freeze Frame" feature that opened this chapter, might be a prime example of this type of intelligence.

Evaluating the Triarchic Theory The triarchic theory is appealing in many ways. Many of us have known people who are exceedingly brilliant academically, but who probably would starve to death if they found themselves stranded in the woods, and they cannot seem to find a way to translate their intellectual brilliance into a salary that can support themselves and their families. Similarly, some people may find academic work extraordinarily difficult, but are brilliant mechanics and can cleverly improvise tools out of common household objects. Moreover, as Sternberg (2000) correctly notes, innumerable highly successful people are not known for their intellectual gifts (he cites former president George W. Bush as one example).

The triarchic theory is also *democratic*. It suggests that there is a place at the "intelligence table" for all. Many people hold a frank distaste for the idea that some individuals are somehow "superior" to others in an attribute (intelligence) on which everyone seems to place so much importance. The triarchic theory is therefore philosophically attractive to those of us with strong egalitarian leanings.

Yet, an important tenet of the skeptical approach to knowledge described in Chapter 1 is that *truth can never be established on philosophical grounds*. This means that we cannot assume something is true because we would like it to be true. So then—how does the triarchic theory hold up to empirical testing? For this theory to be valid, two important criteria would need to be met: First, the three forms of intelligence must be independent of one another. A person's score on one type of intelligence should not predict her score on another type of intelligence. Second, scores on tests of *g* such as IQ tests should only be correlated with scores on tests of *analytic* intelligence—not with scores on tests of practical or creative intelligence. If these criteria are not met, then tests of the triarchic forms of intelligence may differ little from tests of *g*, and "successful intelligence" may be little more than another term for *g* (Gottfredson, 2003).

Unfortunately for all those who find the triarchic theory appealing, tests of its validity conducted over its first 25 years of existence have not been very encouraging. Nathan Brody (2003a, 2003b) found that the scores on tests of the three abilities were correlated, suggesting that the abilities may not be not independent. Specifically, Brody (2003a) found that analytical and creative abilities were correlated .75, analytical and practical abilities were correlated .66, and creative and practical abilities were correlated .62. These are moderate to high correlations. A more serious problem for the theory is the fact that scores on tests of all the triarchic abilities—*including* creative and practical intelligence—are correlated with scores on tests of *g*, also at moderate-to-high levels. Similar results have been found for other theories of multiple intelligences, such as those of Howard Gardner (Deary, Penke, & Johnson, 2010).

Sternberg and his colleagues acknowledge some of these problems, but they suggest that the fault lies not with the theory, but with the tests that have been used to evaluate the theory in the past (Sternberg, 2003c). In fairness, it is undoubtedly true that it is much more difficult to devise effective tests of practical and creative intelligence than to devise tests of analytic intelligence and *g*.

Most Theories of Intelligence Incorporate the Idea of *g*

Despite widespread interest in the idea of multiple intelligences and controversy over *g*, it is probably fair to say that the majority of researchers now believe that the evidence is "overwhelming" (Carroll, 1997, p. 32) that (a) *something* like *g* does exist; (b) it measures important aspects of human cognitive abilities, although it may not measure all important aspects; (c) it predicts a number of important things about how a person will perform in various situations, and (d) people differ in their scores on tests that tap into it (Carroll, 1997; Deary, Weiss, & Batty, 2010; Jensen, 1998; Johnson et al., 2008; Lubinsky, 2004; Meehl, 1990).

THE THREE-STRATUM THEORY OF JOHN B. CARROLL

One compromise between *g* theories and theories of multiple intelligences is the *three-stratum theory* of John B. Carroll, depicted in Figure 9.11. In 1993, Carroll undertook a mammoth reanalysis of 70 years of data involving intelligence testing—encompassing over 460 studies—in an attempt to synthesize a new theory that took into account everything then known about *g* and other aspects of the structure of intelligence. He ended up with a hierarchical model of intelligence with three *strata*, or levels, known as the **three-stratum theory of cognitive abilities**.

According to Carroll, *Stratum I*, at the very bottom, includes 69 highly specific, or *narrow*, abilities—everything from the ability to discriminate musical tones to general science knowledge, perceptual speed, word fluency, reading comprehension, logical reasoning, and so forth.

Stratum II, directly above Stratum I, includes *eight* broad abilities that directly determine one's success in tasks measuring the 69 narrow abilities. Among these eight broad abilities are *fluid intelligence* (Gf) and *crystallized*

Three-stratum theory ▶ An empirically based theory of intelligence devised by John B. Carroll that blends the idea of *g* with Horn and Cattell's Gf-Gc theory and the idea that intelligence includes multiple cognitive abilities.

▶ **FIGURE 9.11** John B. Carroll's Three-Stratum Theory of Cognitive Abilities (1993).

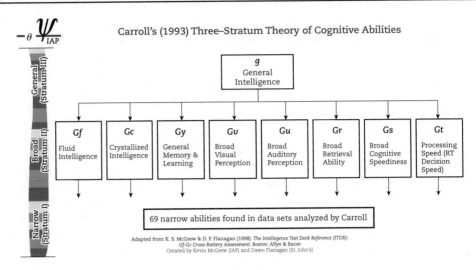

Carroll's (1993) Three–Stratum Theory of Cognitive Abilities

Adapted from K. S. McGrew & D. P. Flanagan (1998). *The Intelligence Test Desk Reference (ITDR):*
Gf-Gc Cross-Battery Assessment. Boston: Allyn & Bacon
Created by Kevin McGrew (IAP) and Dawn Flanagan (St. John's)

Fluid intelligence (Gf) ▶ Cattell and Horn's term used to refer to largely innate analytic skills and abstract reasoning ability.

Crystallized intelligence (Gc) ▶ Cattell and Horn's term used to refer to skills or knowledge one acquires as a result of exposure to education and culture—what one has learned.

intelligence (Gc). These terms were borrowed from earlier, important work by Raymond B. Cattell and John Horn (Horn, 1991; Horn & Cattell, 1966). According to Horn and Cattell, two general factors—not one—constituted general intelligence (*g*) and underlay similarities in the way people scored on various tests of cognitive abilities. **Fluid intelligence** (*Gf*) is a largely innate ability characterized by analytic and abstract reasoning. It is "fluid" because it is adaptable to any situation or task and is not dependent upon previous learning or experience.

In contrast, **crystallized intelligence** (*Gc*) describes skills and knowledge one acquires over time as a result of exposure to education and culture—in other words, what one has been able to *learn*. Doing well on a vocabulary test, a foreign language test, or a test of reading musical notation would all reflect high levels of crystallized intelligence (McArdle, Ferrer-Caja, Hamagami, & Woodcock, 2002).

Finally, *Stratum III* at the very top is *g*—the underlying factor that determines success in tests of both Stratum I and Stratum II abilities.

Evaluating Carroll's Theory: The Fragility of Psychological Science The three-stratum theory has the advantage of being entirely *data-driven*, unlike the triarchic theory. This means that Carroll had few preconceptions of what would happen when he analyzed those 70 years of data sets. His theory emerged entirely from the picture presented in the data. Thus, it is a strongly empirical theory with a base of support in decades of scientific research, and many researchers consider it to be particularly useful as a result (Deary, 2012; Johnson & Bouchard, 2005). On the other hand, because it derives all of its data from standardized tests, possible aspects of intelligence not evaluated in such tests—for example, practical and creative problem solving—do not play a role in his theory.

The three-stratum theory exemplifies the limits of what we can state with confidence about intelligence: In spite of its seeming reasonableness and strong empirical support, many researchers nonetheless oppose it. Instead, they favor various other approaches, including the idea that *g* is all that really matters, theories that focus primarily on crystallized and fluid intelligence, or multiple intelligence theories such as Sternberg's or Gardner's. No consensus regarding the nature of intelligence has been reached in spite of a century of data collected and analyzed. Indeed, the same sets of data are sometimes given opposite interpretations depending upon how the data are analyzed or interpreted.

Thus, nowhere more than in intelligence research is the fragility of psychological science more apparent. Even in this area—where so much research has been conducted—there are few general laws that are accepted without challenge.

IN SUMMARY

1. The term *intelligence* has two general meanings: The first refers to the quality of rational "humanlike" thought—overcoming obstacles, solving problems, and making rational decisions. The second meaning is best summarized in the idea of general intelligence (*g*).

2. IQ began as a statistic that used a specific formula to compare a child's performance on tests of mental abilities with the performance of other children of his or her age.

3. IQ measures not just "book learning" but people's ability to learn the knowledge and skills that are presented to them by their environments.

4. IQ is an unbiased predictor of academic performance. However, it may be biased as a measure of innate ability. Moreover, IQ can only be said to measure "intelligence" if one defines intelligence in terms of *g*.

5. Robert J. Sternberg's triarchic theory of successful intelligence proposes that there are three types of intelligence: analytic (comparable to *g*), creative, and practical.

6. John B. Carroll's three-stratum theory of cognitive abilities is a hierarchal theory which proposes that intelligence consists of three strata, or levels, including 69 narrow (specific abilities), 8 broad mental abilities including fluid and crystallized intelligence, and *g* or general intelligence.

RETRIEVE!

1. Charles Spearman was the first to document the fact that people scoring in a particular way on tests of one aspect of cognitive ability are likely to score the same general way on tests in other aspects of cognitive ability. What is the term used for Spearman's observation?

    a) correlation of the indicator   **c)** bi-correlation of the measures

    b) indifference of the measure   **d)** indifference of the indicator

2. What percentage of IQ test scores among ordinary samples in Western nations will fall between IQ 85 and IQ 115? Between IQ 70 and IQ 130?

3. Why are the statements "IQ tests are unbiased" and "IQ tests are biased" both true?

4. Name and describe the three types of intelligence hypothesized in Sternberg's triarchic theory of intelligence.

5. Describe the three strata of Carroll's three-stratum theory of cognitive abilities.

6. Horn and Cattell termed innate ability in abstract reasoning tasks _____ intelligence. They described accumulated knowledge of facts as _____ intelligence.

    a) fluid/crystallized   **b)** crystallized/fluid   **c)** analytic/practical   **d)** creative/analytic

Where Does Intelligence Come From?

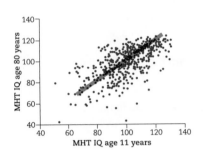

▲ **FIGURE 9.12** This scatterplot shows a strong positive, linear correlation between intelligence test scores at age 11 and scores from tests taken at about age 80. Strong linear positive correlations are shown in scatterplots when the data points group closely together and their direction can be characterized by an upward diagonal line drawn through them.

A person's level of general cognitive ability as measured in standardized tests of intelligence remains much the same throughout his or her adult lifetime. Moreover, measurements of a person's IQ taken at the age of 1 year are generally similar (although not necessarily identical) to measurements taken at age 17 or 18—and this correlation is even stronger beginning at about age 5 (Bornstein et al., 2006; Davis, Haworth, & Plomin, 2009; Deary, Whiteman, Whalley, Fox, & Starr, 2004; Hoekstra, Bartels, & Boomsma, 2007; Lyons et al., 2009).

For example, as shown in Figure 9.12, a 70-year-long study that included virtually the entire population of Scotland found that IQ at age 11 was very highly correlated with IQ at age 80, with positive correlations averaging in the mid-70s (Deary et al., 2004). In another remarkable study, Marc Bornstein and his colleagues found far more modest, but still important, stabilities in measurable mental abilities beginning in the first months of life and continuing through age 4 (Bornstein et al., 2006).

Genes and Environments Determine Cognitive Ability

Findings of long-term stability of IQ scores, combined with observations of similarity in levels of cognitive ability among family members, have led to widespread interest in the genetics of intelligence.

What have researchers found? Behavior genetics research over the course of three decades has demonstrated that both genes *and* environments play their part in the development and expression of cognitive abilities. Averaged out, about 50% of the differences in IQ scores among individuals in most samples are due to genetic differences, and 50% are due to environmental effects (Plomin & Petrill, 1997; Plomin & Spinath, 2004).

However, averages (means) don't really describe the story of heritability of intelligence very well because the contribution of genes to differences in scores on tests of cognitive ability becomes much more pronounced as a child grows older (Deary, 2012; Deary, Weiss, & Batty, 2010; Haworth et al., 2010). In early childhood the contribution may be no greater than 20%, whereas genes may account for as much as 80% of the differences in intelligence test scores found among older adolescents and adults (Davis, Haworth, & Plomin, 2009; Petrill et al., 2004; Plomin & Spinath, 2004).

Why should this be? Logically, it might seem as though as a person grows and has more and more experiences in the world, the effects of *environment* ought to increase and genetic influence decrease. Yet, as Claire Haworth and her colleagues have shown in a study of 11,000 pairs of twins, the opposite is the case (Haworth et al., 2010; Davis et al., 2009). Haworth and her research team suggest that active gene-environment correlations—as described in Chapter 3—are likely responsible. Recall that in an active gene-environment correlation, children to some degree seek out experiences that correspond to their genotype, thus helping to shape their own environments. In doing so they are reinforcing the very characteristics reflected in those genotypes. Young children have relatively little control over their lives, but as they grow older their ability to seek out environments, relationships, and experiences more in keeping with aspects of their genetic heredity increases.

To see how the effects of genetic heredity on cognitive ability increase over time, first take a look at Figure 9.13, which charts average correlations (similarities) between intelligence test scores for various types of siblings—twins and nontwins. These average correlations were taken from studies conducted primarily in childhood and early adolescence.

As you can see, the average correlation for test scores of identical (monozygotic) twins, who share 100% of their genes in common, is substantial when the twins are reared together—approximately .86. This is close to twice the correlation for ordinary siblings (.47), who share only 50% of their genes in common. Thus, identical twins share twice the number of genes in common as ordinary siblings, and have test scores that are about twice as similar. This is strong evidence for genetic influence on intelligence.

However, the correlation of scores for identical twins separated for adoption and reared *apart* (.72) is not quite as high as that for identical twins reared together (.86), demonstrating at least some effect of the environment. A larger effect of the environment is apparent when we compare the scores of fraternal (dizygotic) twins reared together with those of ordinary siblings reared together. Fraternal twins share the same number of genes in common as any ordinary pair of siblings—about 50% on average. Yet the average correlation in their scores (.60) is substantially higher than that for ordinary siblings (.47). Something about the *environment* of fraternal twins causes higher correlations in their test scoring—perhaps their age similarity and the resulting likelihood of exposure to similar school, peer, and home experiences.

Look now at Figure 9.14, which charts *changes* in the correlations of intelligence test scores for identical and fraternal twins as they grow into adulthood. As fraternal twins pass the schooling years, the correlation figure drops from about .60 to less than .40. This is no higher than the correlation for ordinary siblings. This drop in correlations for fraternal twins shows the decreasing influence of the environment as the child grows into adulthood, and increasing importance of genes (McGue, Bouchard, Iacono, & Lykken, 1993; Plomin & Spinath, 2004).

The increasing importance of genes over time is seen even more powerfully in studies of adopted children. Figure 9.15 shows a comparison of correlations in IQ scores between adopted children and their adoptive parents, adopted children and their genetic parents, and control groups of children living *with* their genetic parents.

In very early toddlerhood there is at least some correlation between the IQ scores of adopted children and their adoptive parents. However, by age 4 this correlation drops to 0. In other words, by this age, adopted children resemble their adoptive parents in intelligence to a degree no greater than two strangers selected randomly from the street! On the other hand, the correlation between adoptive children and their *genetic* parents increases steadily over time, so that by age 16 there is no difference at all between the correlations in IQ for children and their genetic parents with whom they were reared and adopted children with their genetic parents whom they have never even met (Plomin, Fulker, Coreley, & DeFries, 1997)!

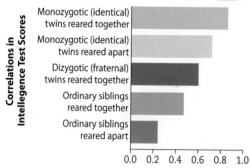

▲ **FIGURE 9.13** Both Heredity and Environment Determine Intelligence Test Scores.

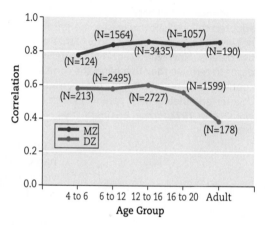

▲ **FIGURE 9.14** The Influence of Genes Becomes More Pronounced as Children Grow into Adulthood. *(Source: Plomin & Spinath, 2004, p. 115.)*

HERITABILITY OF INTELLIGENCE MAY DIFFER AS A RESULT OF ENVIRONMENT

While genes obviously play a major role in intelligence, so does the environment. Bear in mind that if 50% of the differences in cognitive ability among a given sample is due to genetic differences, 50% is due to environmental differences. Indeed, the environmental impact on intelligence is in some ways the more exciting area for research, because the specific environmental factors that influence intelligence are not yet known with certainty.

One interesting area of research concerns the possibility that the environment can influence the extent to which intelligence is heritable. In Chapter

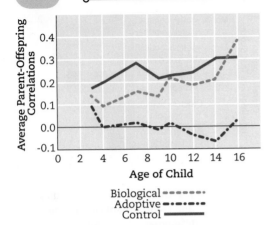

▲ FIGURE 9.15 Over Time, Adopted Children Increasingly Resemble Their Genetic Parents in Intelligence. Tested between the ages of 1 and 3, adopted children show at least some correlation between their IQ scores and those of their adoptive parents. However, by age 4 this correlation drops to zero. On the other hand, the correlations continue to increase over time between adopted children and their genetic parents. *(Sources: Plomin et al. 1997; Plomin & Spinath, 2004.)*

3, we noted that most of the research in heritability of intelligence was carried out on samples that were largely drawn from lower- to upper-middle-class samples. When Eric Turkheimer and his colleagues studied samples of extremely impoverished children, they found that heritability of intelligence dropped dramatically and that the differences in IQ among the poor children was primarily environmental in origin (Turkheimer, Haley, Waldron, D'Onofrio, & Gottesman, 2003). Several other studies have found somewhat similar results, although this effect is not always found, and the opposite effect—*higher* heritability among poorer children—is sometimes found (Nisbett et al., 2012). In any event, effects of social class on the heritability of intelligence are rarely found in adult samples, so even if it is true that social class has an effect on the heritability of intelligence in impoverished children, as the children age, the effects of genes become more pronounced—as is the case among children from wealthier families.

However, as Richard Nisbett and his colleagues note, if cognitive ability can be affected in childhood by environmental factors, this can have an important effect on a person's life—even if the effects of genes become more pronounced as the person grows into adulthood. Therefore, efforts to increase intelligence test scores and school performance among poorer children should not be ignored. Indeed, Eric Turkheimer and his colleagues undertook just such a program. From a sample of parents of lower-SES infant twins, a group was randomly selected to be exposed to a comprehensive program of parent education, mental health counseling and support, and various social services. Between ages 1 and 3, the twins from this intervention group attended free, high-quality day care. At age 8, all of the twins were given a large battery of tests of cognitive ability. It was found that the heritability of cognitive ability among the twins in the intervention group was indeed higher than that among the twins who did not receive the intervention (Nisbett et al., 2012).

IN SUMMARY

1. Both genes and environments contribute to the development of individual differences in scoring on intelligence tests. On average, about 50% of differences between individuals in intelligence scoring are due to genetic differences, and 50% to environmental effects.

2. The contribution of genes to differences in scoring on intelligence tests becomes more pronounced as a child grows older, while the influence of environment becomes less pronounced. This is particularly true once a person reaches adulthood.

RETRIEVE!

1. True or false: As children grow into adulthood, the contribution of genes to differences in cognitive abilities becomes much more pronounced.

2. True or false: Correlations in test scores between identical twins reared together and those reared apart are markedly similar, but not necessarily identical.

Looking Back

Chapter 9 in Review

HOW DOES THE MIND WORK?

- The computational theory of mind holds that the mind functions in a manner loosely analogous to a computer. Cognitive scientists study mental activities involved in collecting, processing, storing, retrieving, and manipulating information.
- Thought is the active process of mentally manipulating or processing information to solve problems, make decisions, increase knowledge, or fantasize. Thinking involves two components: mental images and concepts.

HOW DO WE USE THINKING TO SOLVE PROBLEMS?

- Problems are obstacles that stand in the way of achieving a goal, and we use thought to solve them. Four strategies for problem solving are: trial and error, algorithms, heuristics, and insight. Trial and error works well if the options for possible solutions of a problem are relatively few. Algorithms are step-by-step "recipes" that can solve any problem of a specific type. Heuristics, including the availability heuristic and the representativeness heuristic, are mental shortcuts that are used automatically under conditions of uncertainty. The representativeness heuristic is misleading if base rates are not taken into consideration. A base rate is a percentage probability figure indicating the prevalence of something, or how frequently it occurs.
- Insight occurs when a person has reached an impasse in attempts to solve a problem and then suddenly and effortlessly arrives at a solution. Creativity is a complex set of behaviors generally involving originality, flexibility, and utility; it includes *finding* problems as well as solving them.

HOW DO BIASES AFFECT DECISION MAKING?

- Cognitive biases are systematic distortions in thinking, memory, and perception. The confirmation bias is often considered the most prevalent and destructive of all problems with human reasoning. The confirmation bias is primarily seen in the tendency to pay more attention to evidence that confirms what we already believe. Belief persistence, a related bias, allows a person to resist changing a belief by discounting disconfirming evidence. The gambler's fallacy is a misperception of randomness.

LANGUAGE: WHAT IS IT, AND HOW DO WE LEARN IT?

- At least three principles characterize human language: generativity, recursion, and displacement. The number of human languages is hard to estimate because languages are constantly changing, dying, or emerging from what were previously considered dialects. Languages may influence the way we think, but they do not determine the way we think.
- Many researchers believe that the capacity for language is a special internal faculty comprising innate, specialized neural and cognitive structures and "wiring." From this view, all languages possess a "universal grammar." The internal language faculty allows children to learn language effortlessly, even though they are exposed to only a few of the words and constructions possible in the language.

DO NONHUMAN ANIMALS HAVE LANGUAGE?

- Animals communicate, but they do not have language. Unlike human language, animal communication systems are closed-ended rather than open-ended. Extensive efforts to teach language to chimpanzees have resulted only in the teaching of limited vocabularies and virtually no grammatical structures. Research among primates suggests that language may have evolved from gestures rather than vocal utterances.

WHAT IS INTELLIGENCE?

- There is no accepted definition of *intelligence*, but the word is used to refer to rational, problem-solving, human-like thought; and to general intelligence (*g*), an individual's general capacity to process complex information and perform well on a wide variety of mental and manual tasks. Tests of *g* measure perceptual speed, verbal skills, and the abilities to learn new information and to juggle mental concepts. These tests may also measure math skills and manual dexterity. The psychometric tradition relies upon objective measurement of intelligence using standardized tests, such as IQ tests.
- IQ is the most commonly accepted statistic describing general intelligence, although the true IQ statistic is no longer used. IQ scores are the best single predictor of GPA, achievement test scores, how many years a person remains in school, and the academic degree he or she receives. IQ is also related to job performance and health and longevity. However, IQ is in no way the only factor predicting such things. IQ tests are not biased if they are given to representatives of groups used to "norm" the test, and if the test is used to predict academic achievement. However, IQ may not be an unbiased estimate of innate "intelligence," because some groups have unequal access to experiences and resources that increase both IQ scoring and school performance.
- The idea of multiple intelligences is an alternative to the single factor *g*. Louis Thurstone argued that intelligence consists of seven distinct mental abilities, and that a person could be high on some of the abilities while low on others. This contrasts with Charles Spearman's idea that a person's score on any single mental ability could be used to predict that person's score on any other. Howard Gardner believes that the idea of intelligence should include musical and athletic abilities, as well as the ability to understand emotions and motivations. Robert Sternberg's triarchic theory of successful intelligence states that *g* only underlies analytical reasoning, while creative intelligence and practical intelligence

Looking Back continued

describe equally important mental attributes.

- Most theories of intelligence incorporate the idea of *g*, and the evidence is overwhelming that *g* measures "something" important about intelligence and predicts a number of important things about how a person will perform in various situations. The three-stratum theory of John B. Carroll hypothesizes three levels of intelligence, with *g* as the determining factor for the other two levels.

WHERE DOES INTELLIGENCE COME FROM?

- Cognitive ability is determined by genetic inheritance and environmental experience. Approximately 50% of the differences in IQ scores in most samples are due to genetic differences and 50% to environmental experience. However, this average figure hides the fact that the influence of genetics tends to become more substantial as the person moves out of childhood into adolescence and adulthood.

Key Terms

Algorithms, 423
Artificial intelligence (AI), 423
Availability heuristic, 424
Base rate, 426
Belief persistence, 433
Cognitive bias, 432
Cognitive science, 417
Computational theory of mind (CTM), 417
Concepts, 418
Confirmation bias, 432
Connectionism, 439
Crystallized intelligence (*Gc*), 456
Displacement, 437
Fixation, 428
Fluid intelligence (*Gf*), 456
Fuzzy boundaries, 418
g (*see* General intelligence), 449

Gambler's fallacy, 433
General intelligence (*g*), 449
Generativity, 436
Heuristics, 424
Impasse, 428
Insight, 437
Internal language faculty, 437
IQ (Intelligence Quotient), 449
Linguistic relativity hypothesis, 442
Mental images, 417
Normal distribution, 450
Practical intelligence, 448
Problem, 423
Prototype, 419
Psychometric, 449
Recursion, 436
Representativeness heuristic, 425
Sapir-Whorf hypothesis, 441

Stanford-Binet Intelligence Scale, 449
Theorem of the indifference of the indicator, 449
Thought, 417
Three-stratum theory, 455
Trial and error, 423
Triarchic theory of successful intelligence, 454
Universal grammar, 437
Wechsler Adult Intelligence Scale (WAIS®-III), 449
Wechsler Intelligence Scale for Children (WISC®-IV), 450

Test Yourself

1. The theory that conceives of the mind as loosely analogous to a computer is known as _____.
2. What is the difference between a concept and a mental image?
3. What is a fuzzy boundary? Name a concept with a fuzzy boundary.
4. Explain the differences between trial and error, heuristics, and algorithms as problem-solving strategies. Give an example of a problem most appropriately solved by each method.
5. What is the difference between System 1 and System 2 thinking, according to Daniel Kahneman?
6. Give an example of a situation where the representativeness heuristic could lead one astray.

7. Give an example of a situation where the availability heuristic could lead one astray.
8. What is the confirmation bias? How might it increase the strength of superstitious beliefs?
9. The false belief that the likelihood of a random event occurring is influenced by prior events is known as
   a) the priority fallacy
   b) the gambler's fallacy
   c) the confirmation bias
   d) the representativeness heuristic
10. Why did Herbert Terrace, the trainer of the chimpanzee Nim Chimpsky, ultimately become disillusioned with his own research?
11. Many cognitive scientists believe that human beings possess innate cognitive mechanisms dedicated to learning and using language. These mechanisms are known collectively as the _____. The inner grammatical structure shared by all languages is termed by these theorists _____.

12. Describe the properties of generativity, recursion, and displacement.
13. What is meant by the phrase "children know more than they learn" about language?
14. Distinguish linguistic determinism from linguistic relativity.
15. The notion of a single factor underlying all mental abilities is termed _____. It was initially discovered by _____ using a statistical technique called _____.

Test Yourself continued

16. The IQ was initially designed to predict which aspect of a person's life? What are some other aspects of a person's life that may partially be predicted by IQ?

17. The relative importance of genes and environments to differences in intelligence test scoring changes over time. The importance of _____ increases, while the importance of _____ decreases.

18. What are the three types of intelligence that make up Sternberg's triarchic theory of intelligence? What is the primary criticism that has been voiced against this theory?

19. Name and describe the three hierarchy levels that make up Carroll's three-stratum theory.

20. What is the difference between fluid and crystallized intelligence?

10

Motivation

Chapter Outline

FREEZE FRAME

▲ "The Problem We All Live With" by Norman Rockwell (1966).

In November 1960, a 6-year-old African American girl named Ruby Nell Bridges started school, entering first grade at William Frantz Public School in New Orleans. This may not sound like a particularly remarkable event, but each morning Ruby had to be escorted to school by armed federal marshals who had been ordered to protect her. Mobs of infuriated white people—including mothers with their children—gathered daily outside the school to scream racial epithets and hateful taunts at Ruby, to threaten her life, and to throw cans, tomatoes, and whatever else they could get their hands on. What had this small child done to arouse such hatred? Federal Courts had just ordered New Orleans to desegregate its schools, and Ruby was the first black child to enter the previously all-white William Frantz school.

Each day, for long months, Ruby ran the mob's gauntlet, reportedly without tears or a whimper of fear (Burks, cited in "A class of one," 1997). When she finally entered the school building each day, she found herself not only the only African American student in her class, but the only student in the school. All the other children were kept out by their parents to protest Ruby's presence. All of the white teachers but one also participated in the white boycott of the school.

That one teacher—Ruby's teacher, a white woman from Boston named Barbara Henry—did her best to teach Ruby and to make her feel welcome, but she often found herself amazed and perplexed at the little girl's calm demeanor in her classroom over their many months together. Ruby simply seemed bent on carrying out the business of learning. As Mrs. Henry related to author and child psychiatrist Robert Coles, "Sometimes I'd look at her and wonder how she did it" (Coles & Ford, 1995).

▲ Ruby Bridges with Federal Marshal at the William Frantz Elementary School, 1960.

Ruby's personal trials were not the only consequences of her parents' decision to allow her to attend William Frantz Elementary school. Her grandparents, who made their living as sharecroppers, were evicted from their land. Her father was fired from his job. Even Barbara Henry, the white woman who dedicated herself to teaching Ruby that first year, was not invited back to the school the subsequent year, and returned to Boston. Bridges and Henry, however, had grown close during that first year, and in adulthood rekindled their friendship.

I have read Ruby Bridges' story very often, but, like Mrs. Henry, I am also perplexed. I wonder again and again: What motivates a 6-year-old hero? What did Ruby feel each day as she approached the school? And what motivated Ruby's parents to stand firm in the face of their own personal misfortune and the cruelty directed at their small daughter?

What Are Motivations?

As you will see in this chapter, motivations—the mental states that *energize* us to behave as we do—are evolutionary gifts to the human species from our ancestors. They enable us to survive, avoid danger, thrive, and reproduce. They direct us toward friendship, love, and belonging, and enable us to defend ourselves against aggression—as well as to use aggression to obtain our goals. They are an important part of the fabric of explanation for human behavior.

Motivations Initiate and Direct Behavior

When I was a child, we would ask, "Why did the chicken cross the road?" and answer, "To get to the other side." For some reason, this seemed hilarious to us at the time. Nowadays, children ask, "Why did the turkey cross the road?" and answer, "Because it was the chicken's day off." That doesn't seem a great deal funnier, but I suppose it's an improvement.

In any case, these jokes are essentially statements about *motivation*. **Motivations** are mental states that cause people to engage in *purposive* behavior. Here the term *purposive* means any activity directed toward achieving some goal or satisfying a need or desire—behavior with a purpose. Motivations are psychological forces that initiate actions, direct them toward the desired goal, and encourage us to sustain the effort necessary to attain that goal, whatever it may be: creating a job resume, helping a lost child find her mother, creeping downstairs at midnight to polish off a pint of Ben & Jerry's, or committing a violent crime.

All motivated behavior is purposive. However, not all purposive behavior is motivated. One morning my daughter Anisa threw a ball at me from the side without warning, not realizing that I was not paying attention. My hands flew up to guard my face. Even though my behavior served a purpose (self-protection) and was associated with a specific mental state (extreme alertness due to the effects of an adrenaline rush), the behavior was not intentional. My behavior was reflexive or automatic—like blinking when someone blows air into your eye. Thus, motivated activities have three characteristics:

1. Purpose
2. Causes rooted in specific mental states
3. Intentionality

Purpose and cause are fairly straightforward notions, but *intention* can be tricky because, although it implies that a behavior has been consciously chosen, this is not necessarily the case. Motivations may sometimes be *unconscious*—below a person's level of awareness (Forgas, Williams, & Laham, 2005; Latham, Stajkovic, & Locke, 2010). However, because it may be difficult or impossible to demonstrate the existence of any specific unconscious motivation, some argue that the entire concept of unconscious motivation is more or less useless in explaining behavior. Still, most of us can look back on our lives and identify at least some instances when we were motivated by internal forces of which we were unaware at the time, or occasions when a behavior that seemed to be unintentional was in fact intended.

One possible example of this was provided by a student following a class discussion of unconscious motivation. This student privately confided to me that she once had been having great difficulty generating the courage to tell her boyfriend that she wanted to end their relationship. She wrote about this problem one day in her journal—describing in very forceful language her negative feelings toward the man and her wish to be free of the relationship. The prose was so forceful, in fact, that it would be difficult to see how anyone could stick around after reading it. And this is exactly what happened. On a night when the man was scheduled to have dinner with her at her home, the student "accidentally" left the journal open on the dining room table to the very page on which she had described her feelings about the man and the relationship. Yet, she had no conscious intention of wanting him to read the journal—quite the opposite. Indeed, she was horrified and felt deeply ashamed when it happened. Yet, she never saw the man again after that night, which was what she had wanted all along.

Motivation ▶ Mental states which cause people to engage in behavior directed toward achieving some goal or satisfying a need or desire (purposive behavior). Motivations initiate actions, direct them toward the desired goal, and help the person sustain the necessary effort to attain the goal.

▲ **Ambivalence.** In this cover of her comic book depiction of her own ambivalence toward the idea of quitting smoking, Emily Flake humorously captures the smoker's dilemma.

Ambivalence ▶ When a person experiences conflicting emotions or motivations—being "of two minds" about something.

Instinct ▶ An innate, automatic behavior tendency that will occur reliably in all normally developed members of a species in response to a releasing stimulus, or cue, from the environment. Because of past difficulties in identifying instincts, more often than not the term *fixed-action pattern* is used instead of the term *instinct*.

There is no empirical way to demonstrate that my friend leaving her journal open to the explosive page was a motivated action. It may merely have been an unfortunate coincidental blunder. Yet this and similar events familiar to most of us—such as "forgetting" to keep appointments one does not wish to keep, or to perform a chore one does not wish to perform—suggest the existence of unconscious motivation.

HIGHLY MOTIVATED BEHAVIOR IS INTENSE AND PERSISTENT

Motivations cannot be observed directly, and for this reason behaviorists have long argued that they are not an appropriate topic for scientific study (Skinner, 1965). However, motivations can be measured to a certain extent by looking at the *intensity* and *persistence* of a behavior (L. V. Brown, 2007). An action has *high intensity* if it is engaged in with great physical or mental effort, or with strong application of will. Actions high in intensity tend to be highly motivated actions. For example, pulling an all-night study session when you'd rather be out partying or in bed asleep is an example of intense activity in the service of a motivation (to avoid failing a test).

Persistent behaviors are those that continue over a long period of time, even in the face of adversity. The intensity of such behavior may or may not be great, but its persistence implies the existence of strong motivation. Staying in college over the long haul, even if one does not work very hard at it and does not do particularly well, is an example of persistent (but not intense) behavior. Behavior that is both intense and persistent is likely to be the most highly motivated type of behavior. Obtaining a Ph.D. in a rigorous field of study generally requires both intense and persistent behavior and is thus highly motivated.

Motivation, then, involves specific mental states which initiate or "energize" intentional behavior directed toward specific goals. Motivation cannot be observed, but it may be measured by changes in the intensity and persistence of behavior.

MOTIVATIONS ARE VARIED, AND THEY SOMETIMES CONFLICT

Motives can be extremely varied and complex. Consider the act of eating. The most obvious motive for doing so is hunger. But people may also eat when they are not particularly hungry—for the pure pleasure of taste, to be sociable at a dinner party, as a result of psychological distress or disorder, to foster a political alliance between families or tribes, and so forth.

Motives may also conflict with one another, a state known as **ambivalence**. The attempt to quit smoking is a good example. A person may wish to increase her health, life span, and attractiveness and therefore be motivated to quit smoking. Yet the same person might also want to avoid the extreme discomfort brought on by tobacco withdrawal and therefore be motivated *not* to quit smoking. Conflicting goals produce ambivalent motivation.

Motivations Include Instincts and Adaptations

Over the past 100 years, a number of theories about the nature of motivation have emerged. But motivation is a slippery concept, and no one of these theories has been able to account for human motivation in full. However, each has made important contributions. The first coherent psychological theory of motivation was proposed by the important early psychological scientist William James (1890/1981). Heavily influenced by Darwin's theory of evolution by natural selection, James proposed that most human behavior is motivated by *instincts*. **Instincts** are innate, automatic behavioral tendencies that will occur reliably in all (normally developed) members of a species in response to some sort of cue from the environment. These cues are known as *releasing stimuli* because they "release" the instinctive behavior.

James believed that characteristics such as aggression, sympathy, playfulness, modesty, parental love, curiosity, fear, and jealousy were all instincts that are evoked by releasing stimuli. A releasing stimulus for jealousy might consist of telephone calls received by one's spouse secretively late at night. A releasing stimulus for parental love might consist of a hearing one's small child uttering a particularly charming statement. Sympathy could be released by the sight of a homeless person on the street.

James and others, such as the English psychologist William McDougall (1912/2005), who further developed ideas about instinctive motivations, hypothesized that human beings had a great many highly specific instincts that served as motivators—far more than those possessed by other animal species. James did not believe, however, that human instincts were rigid and unchangeable. He saw them instead as behavioral *tendencies* that were relatively consistent but still subject to change over time through experience or as a result of differences among types of releasing stimuli.

Since James's time, scientists have come to define the concept of instinct more narrowly to include only patterns of behavior that are entirely predictable and that will occur virtually invariably unless they are somehow blocked. Because instincts are now considered to be truly "fixed" sequences of behavior initiated by some releasing stimulus, the term *fixed-action pattern* was coined to replace use of the term *instinct* among most scientists. Examples of fixed-action patterns in human beings include the consequences of stroking the cheeks of newborn infants—they will respond by opening their mouths and turning their heads in the direction of the stroke. In this case, stroking is the releasing stimulus that elicits the fixed-action pattern.

Fixed-action patterns are so strongly "encoded" in the nervous system that an animal may sometimes engage in instinctive behaviors when faced with inappropriate stimuli. Tinbergen (1974) showed that cardinals who have lost their nests and offspring may end up feeding worms to minnows when the fish come to the surface of a pond looking for food. The birds are responding with a fixed-action pattern to the releasing stimulus of the opening and closing of hungry mouths in search of food.

▲ **Fixed-Action Pattern in the Black-Backed Kelp Gull.** When a black-backed kelp gull chick views the red spot on its mother's beak, it pecks at it. This causes the mother to regurgitate food into the chick's mouth. Here the red dot is the releasing stimulus, and pecking is the fixed-action pattern.

A LABEL IS NOT AN EXPLANATION

Although theorizing about instinctive motivations was extremely popular for a few decades, this approach eventually hit a brick wall for a simple reason: Rather than providing true *explanations* for motivations and behavior, theorists were for the most part merely *describing* motivations by *labeling* them with the names of hypothetical instincts (Tolman, 1923). For example, a person who goes along with the group does so out of a "conformity instinct," but should she oppose the group, it is out of her "individuation instinct." When an explanation consists merely of a label or a description, it cannot be said to be an explanation at all, and is of limited value. Such "explanations" are *circular*, because they attempt to define a thing in terms of itself. "He is constantly starting fights because he is very aggressive" is a circular explanation, because "very aggressive" is little more than another way of saying "constantly starts fights."

It also became clear that there were no standards for distinguishing what did or did not constitute a human instinct. Various lists of instincts produced by psychologists appeared to consist primarily of guesses and opinions.

ADAPTATION: THE EVOLUTIONARY VIEW OF INSTINCT

Interestingly, over the past few decades the notion of human instincts has been revived and "rehabilitated" by evolutionary psychologists, who have reframed human instincts as *psychological adaptations* (see Chapter 3). Evolutionary psychologists propose that these adaptations evolved through natural selection to allow human beings to respond "instinctively" to cues from the environment in ways that helped our ancestors to solve important problems they encountered repeatedly over evolutionary time (Barkow, 2006; Buss, 2005; Tooby & Cosmides, 1992).

▶ **Why Are These People Having Fun?** Evolutionary theories of motivation propose that over evolutionary time, activities that increased an individual's chances of survival and successful reproduction became associated with pleasure. Working alongside peers toward a common goal is one such pleasurable activity. Here, young people work together to load donated books into boxes to be delivered to Ghana.

To evolutionary psychologists, motivations are part of the psychological "architecture" of adaptations in humans. An example of a motivational adaptation is *pleasure-seeking*. Good food and drink, sex and love, friendship, meaningful work, spending time with one's children—such things are intrinsically pleasurable in most cases, and people are motivated to pursue them. They give us pleasure because, on average, finding them pleasurable promoted the survival and reproduction of our distant ancestors. They then passed on their preferences for such activities to us through psychological adaptation as part of our human genetic inheritance.

Modern evolutionary theorizing about instinct and motivation is a substantial advance over the descriptive labeling engaged in by early instinct theorists. This is because evolutionary psychologists offer *explanations*—not just labels—for how various motivations may have evolved, and they are sometimes able to test these explanations using empirical methods (Alcock, 2001).

Motivations Also Include Drives, Incentives, and Needs

Following the demise of instinct theories of motivation in the 1920s and 1930s, psychologists interested in motivation began to look toward aspects of human life that held greater power of explanation. Over the years, three variables have been most frequently studied: human *drives, incentives,* and *needs*.

DRIVES

During the 1930s, psychologists began to wonder if motivations were mostly automatic attempts to achieve certain physiological states. The earliest of these ideas was known as **drive theory** of motivation (Hull, 1943). Drive theorists proposed that behavior is motivated primarily by the desire to *reduce* unpleasant conditions of arousal that result from basic physiological needs. For example, a thirsty person experiences unpleasant arousal (thirst) as a result of his or her need for water. This drive state motivates behavior—drinking—intended to reduce the drive. Desires to reduce unpleasant arousal states are known as **drives**. Thus, drive theory is sometimes referred to as *drive-reduction theory*.

Drive theory is based on the notion that organisms seek to maintain a steady, consistent, and balanced physiological state. This means maintaining appropriate levels of oxygen and water intake, blood sugar, body temperature, and so forth. This steady, regulated state is known as **homeostasis**, which literally

Drive theory ▶ A theory initially proposed by Clark Hull in 1943 which proposed that behavior is motivated primarily by the desire to reduce unpleasant conditions of arousal which have resulted from basic physiological needs.

Drive ▶ The desire to reduce unpleasant arousal states resulting from basic psychological needs.

Homeostasis ▶ Literally meaning "to stay the same," the term *homeostasis* is used to describe a steady, regulated state where various physiological processes (e.g., water intake, blood sugar, body temperature) are maintained at appropriate levels.

means "to stay the same." Motivational systems such as hunger and thirst are triggered when any of our basic physiological systems is out of balance and needs attention—as when we are cold, hungry, tired, or thirsty.

Although drive theory made sense for certain motivational behaviors, particularly those related to basic drives such as hunger or thirst, it soon became clear that maintaining homeostasis was not necessarily the goal of all motivations. Human beings are sometimes motivated to *increase* arousal rather than reduce it. For example, it is difficult to imagine the biological need for which bungee-jumping produces homeostasis, yet some people will go to great lengths (i.e., are highly motivated) to bungee jump. Curiosity, the enjoyment of pure sensation and stimulation, and simple boredom are all motivating forces which cause individuals to increase their levels of arousal. Thus, many theorists turned from drive theory to **optimal arousal theory**. According to this idea, people seek to maintain an optimal level of physiological arousal (Hebb, 1955; Korman, 1974). If arousal levels are too high, as when drives are activated, the organism seeks to reduce arousal (drive reduction). But if they are too low, as during periods of boredom or excessive rest, arousal is actively sought.

INCENTIVES

Researchers eventually also demonstrated that human beings are frequently motivated by the idea of rewards or **incentives**, rather than internal drives or arousal needs. Incentive theory suggests that while drives and needs for optimal arousal may *push* us in certain behavioral directions, incentives *pull* us. What does this push-pull distinction mean? As a result of learning over time, people come to associate certain experiences with pleasurable sensations and mental states. We are then "pulled" (motivated) toward such states and sensations, even if no specific drive or arousal system has been activated to "push" us there. Getting high on recreational drugs or alcohol is a good example of behavior that is often incentive motivated—although it may also result from arousal needs (to alleviate boredom), or, in the case of addiction, from drive reduction motivation. Consider that an addict is motivated to reduce the unpleasant arousal created by the emergence of withdrawal symptoms.

Intrinsic and Extrinsic Motivations The idea that incentives, in addition to needs and drives, often motivate behavior led psychologists to differentiate two general categories of motivation: **intrinsic** and **extrinsic** (e.g., Deci, 1975; Niemiec, Ryan, & Deci, 2009). An intrinsic motivation compels us to engage in some behavior because it is rewarding for its own sake. For example, studying hard for an exam and doing well can be intrinsically rewarding in that it brings a sense of personal accomplishment and satisfaction—regardless of any external, tangible reward. If you are motivated to study for such reasons, you are *intrinsically* motivated.

On the other hand, studying hard and doing well may also bring higher grades, the approval of your parents or teachers, chances of scholarships, and so forth. Studying hard for purposes such as these is *extrinsically* motivated behavior because you are working toward some sort of *external* reward. Most behavior probably occurs as a result of a combination of intrinsic and extrinsic motivations. However, educators have been particularly interested in understanding how intrinsic motivation arises, because research has shown that when students work from intrinsic motivation they learn more efficiently, are more engaged and enthusiastic, and use more effective study strategies (Ryan & Deci, 2000; Schunk, 1996).

The distinction between extrinsic and intrinsic motivations was first acknowledged in the context of animal studies, where it was noted that animals may engage in some behaviors apparently out of simple curiosity, playfulness, and sense of exploration, even in the absence of any obvious payoff or reward (Harlow, 1953; Harlow, Harlow, & Meyer, 1950; White, 1959). These early

Optimal arousal theory
▶ A theory proposed in reaction to problems with drive theory, optimal arousal theory states that people seek to maintain an optimal level of arousal. This could mean reducing levels of arousal from unpleasantly high levels, as described in drive theory, but it could also mean *increasing* levels of arousal from unpleasantly low levels, as in states of boredom or excessive rest.

Incentives ▶ Any rewarding condition that provides a motive for some behavior.

Intrinsic motivation ▶ A category of motivation which compels a person to engage in a behavior because the behavior is rewarding for its own sake, rather than providing some sort of additional external incentive or reward.

Extrinsic motivation ▶ A category of motivation which compels a person to engage in a behavior for an external reward that the behavior might bring.

▲ **"Because It Was There."** Mammals are intrinsically motivated to play, explore, and satisfy their curiosity. When asked why he decided to climb Mt. Everest, George Mallory famously responded, "Because it's there." At left, rhesus monkeys studied by Harry Harlow and his colleagues spent over 10 days playing with a series of clasps and hooks, with the only reward being discovery of how the mechanisms worked. When they subsequently were rewarded for their activity with food, they became less interested in the locks and clasps. At right, the children are engrossed in a puzzle.

researchers discovered some surprising properties of intrinsic as compared with extrinsic motivations.

For example, it makes sense that doing work which is intrinsically interesting and satisfying in its own right might produce a higher-level learning experience. But you might equally expect that if the prospect of *external rewards* were added to the mix, motivation to learn might be strengthened even further. However, in studies among rhesus monkeys, Harry Harlow and his colleagues (Harlow et al., 1950) found that the monkeys' natural inclination to learn through exploration and play *diminished* when rewards were offered for performing the same activity. These findings led researchers to hypothesize that extrinsic motivation might actually undermine rather than support the learning experience in human beings, particularly if the learning experience is intrinsically interesting (Lepper, Greene, & Nisbett, 1973; Covington, 2000). As researcher Martin Covington phrased it, "If someone has to pay me to do this, then it must not be worth doing for its own sake" (Covington, 2000, p. 23). The end result is that if the reward is no longer available, the person loses motivation to continue performing the task. This effect is also known as the *overjustification effect*, but tests of the idea have been mixed. Some research suggests that if extrinsic rewards such as grades are viewed as feedback to help improve one's performance, or if the reward is well-earned for intrinsically interesting work successfully performed, intrinsic motivation may be increased (Covington, 2000). Specific rewards that stimulate intrinsic aspects of a learning experience—such as rewards of books for reading tasks accomplished—may also increase performance (Marinak & Gambrell, 2008).

Interestingly, pursuing extrinsic life goals such as financial rewards, fame, and beauty may lead to more than disappointment if these goals are not achieved; they may lead to reduced feelings of well-being when they *are* achieved! In research on individuals during their second year after graduating from college, Christopher Niemiec and his colleagues found that students who had set out to fulfill intrinsic goals such as "deep, enduring relationships" or helping others to "improve their lives," and who had fulfilled these goals in part, experienced increased feelings of contentment, well-being, connection with others, and satisfaction with life. However, those who has set out to fulfill extrinsic goals such as wealth, fame, or beauty—*and who had fulfilled their goals* at least in part—reported *reduced* feelings of well-being, increased physical symptoms of anxiety (headaches, stomach aches, fatigue), and more negative emotions such as shame and anger (Niemiec et al., 2009).

NEEDS

Needs are internal states of tension that motivate a person toward some action (Kanfer, 1990). Experiencing a need for food, we are motivated to eat. A need for the company of others can get us out of bed, into our clothes, and out into the street. Experiencing a need for security, we may be motivated to seek a career with a good salary and secure employment in the hopes that this will help resolve the inner tension produced by our security needs.

Maslow's Hierarchy of Needs   Humanist psychologist Abraham Maslow (1970) proposed that human motivations form a hierarchy based on the urgency of the motivating need. For example, perhaps you are an ambitious person, highly motivated by a need for achievement in the career of your choice. Now imagine that you are a climber rappelling down a vertical cliff and you suddenly notice that the rope which anchors you to the mountain and is your only life line is being damaged as it passes over a sharp rock edge. The rope is in danger of snapping and you are still about 50 feet off the ground. Now—how concerned do you think you would be about your career at this moment?

As depicted in Figure 10.1, Maslow proposed five categories of needs which form a hierarchical pyramid.[1] The importance of each category of needs at any given time is determined by the order in which they are fulfilled. The first (bottom) category must be satisfied before the second category of need will become important; the first and second must be satisfied before the third category becomes important, and so forth.

In the first category at the very bottom of the pyramid are immediate physiological survival needs such as food, water, and oxygen (and keeping your eye on that rope!). At the top of the hierarchy is *self-actualization*—the fullest flowering of a person's creative potential—which Maslow believed represented a fundamental human need. In between these two extremes are needs including safety and security, love, belonging, prestige and achievement, and so forth.

It certainly makes intuitive sense that motivations to fulfill life-sustaining needs, sometimes termed *primary motivations*, generally take precedence over *secondary motivations*—motivations to fulfill less basic needs such as the need for belonging with others or the need for achievement (see pp. 491–493, 505–506). Despite the commonsense nature of this basic idea, however, early research found relatively little evidence that Maslow's needs existed universally, particularly self-actualization needs (Wahba & Bridwell, 1976). It was also often pointed out that primary and secondary motivations cannot always be neatly separated into categories. In some cases, so-called secondary motivations may be stronger than primary motivations. Consider the lives of saints, martyrs, soldiers, artists, and others who sacrifice their comfort and their very lives in the service of causes, religions, or ideas in which they believe. Ruby Bridges and her family, whose story opened this chapter, clearly placed love, esteem, and self-actualization needs before needs for safety. In spite of threats of bodily harm, loss of employment and resources, they persisted.

Consequently, the notion of a hierarchy of needs fell into general disfavor for a time. However, beginning in the 1990s, research studies were conducted with superior methods to those of earlier research which had cast doubt on the hierarchy of needs. These newer studies began to corroborate parts of

▲ **FIGURE 10.1 Maslow's Hierarchy of Needs.** Humanistic psychologist Abraham Maslow proposed that human needs form a hierarchy, with higher level needs becoming activated only when lower level needs are satisfied. Maslow's levels of needs are: *physiological needs, safety needs, needs for love and belonging, needs for self-esteem and the esteem of others,* and *self-actualization needs.*

Need ▶ An internal state of tension that motivates a person to perform some action.

---

[1]*Maslow later proposed that there were six categories of needs, with the sixth being "self-transcendence." However, the vast majority of research and writing on Maslow's ideas adheres to the five-category model.*

▲ Secondary Motivations May Trump Primary Motivations: The Case of Thich Quang Duc. In 1963, Mahayana Buddhist monk Thich Quang Duc immolated himself in a busy street in Saigon, South Vietnam to protest the oppressive policies of then President Ngo Dinh Diem. This photograph starkly demonstrates that basic physiological and safety needs are not always primary in human motivation.

Maslow's basic commonsense theory of motivation (Kluger & Tikochinsky, 2001). For example, researchers provided ample evidence that throughout the world, people in most cases do turn toward satisfaction of higher level needs only after their basic physiological and safety needs are fulfilled (Hagerty, 1999; Oishi, Diener, Lucas, & Suh, 1999; Ronen, 1994).

Fundamental Motivations: Maslow's Hierarchy "Renovated" In spite of research confirming some of the intuitive aspects of Maslow's theory, Maslow's pyramid of needs itself is often considered by psychological scientists to be a "quaint" idea without much contemporary relevance (Kenrick, Neuberg, Griskevicius, Becker, & Schaller, 2010, p. 292). However, recently, Douglas Kenrick and his colleagues have attempted to "renovate" Maslow's pyramid by bringing it in line with contemporary thinking in anthropology, psychology, and evolutionary science. Their goal was to preserve what is most useful in Maslow's model, while expanding its accuracy and contemporary relevance (Kenrick, Neuberg, et al., 2010; Kenrick, Griskevicius, Neuberg, & Schaller, 2010).

As depicted in Figure 10.2, according to Kenrick and his colleagues, certain needs/motivations are *fundamental* in an evolutionary sense. They have arisen in human beings everywhere because they reflect the evolutionary history of our species. Kenrick and colleagues' updated pyramid of fundamental needs includes some of Maslow's original needs, specifically: *immediate physiological needs, safety needs* (termed *self-protection*) and *esteem/respect* (termed *status/esteem*). However, Kenrick and colleagues contained Maslow's needs for love and self-actualization within their categories of *affiliation/belongingness, mate acquisition, mate retention,* and *parenting.*

More than simply adding some new needs and shuffling the placement of others, however, Kenrick and his research team view the pyramid not as a series of needs stacked on top of one another—each one brought into play only when the one below has been satisfied—but as overlapping motivational systems that must be understood according to different *levels of analysis*. If you recall from our brief discussion in Chapter 3, different levels of analysis address different aspects of the same question. Consider the question "Why did my roommate bite my head off when I turned on the radio this morning?" You might answer it like this: "She woke up feeling irritable." Or you could say, "She just split up with her boyfriend last night." Both of these answers may be correct, but they address different aspects of the question. The first answer explains the immediate reason why your roommate reacted as she did even though you had done nothing wrong (she woke up feeling irritable). The second answer explains her irritability itself—that is, it addresses a fundamental cause but ignores the immediate cause.

Kenrick and his colleagues use three levels of analysis to create their revised pyramid of needs: the *evolutionary* level, the *developmental* level, and the *cognitive* level. The evolutionary level examines how the various needs evolved through natural selection to help solve specific survival- or reproduction-related problems faced recurrently by our ancestors. Immediate needs for food, water, shelter, and self-protection have obvious relevance to survival and reproduction, but also important are needs to associate with other people (affiliation), enter close relationships (belongingness), obtain status or esteem in one's group, acquire and maintain mating relationships, and parent children.

The developmental level views the pyramid of needs as they play out across the life cycle in a *life history*. Different organisms mature at different rates and engage in different kinds of activities related to survival and reproduction at different points in their life cycle and for shorter or longer lengths of time. As a result, different needs may become more or less prominent, not only because more basic needs have or have not been satisfied but also due to the organism's developmental stage and the genetic "program" common to its species (the genome).

The cognitive level of analysis explores which of the motivational systems is operating to motivate a behavior at any given time. This level looks at immediate or *proximate* causes of motivated behavior (see Chapter 15). An example given by Kenrick and his colleagues is this: If you are having lunch with your boss, and you discover a scorpion crawling up your leg, self-protection goals are likely to supersede goals for satisfying hunger as well as goals for status and esteem. But if it is an ant instead of a scorpion, and your boss has just offered a promotion, esteem goals are likely at the forefront (Kenrick, Griskevicius, et al., 2010, p. 302).

Kenrick and colleagues' "renovation" of Maslow's hierarchy of needs is new and will undoubtedly undergo scrutiny from other researchers. However, various early commentaries on their work, while taking issue with certain details, have generally applauded their basic notion: that Maslow's hierarchy contains truths about human nature that should be preserved, but that the original model needs to be brought into line with contemporary thinking based upon empirical research and theory (Schaller, Neuberg, Griskevicius, & Kenrick, 2010).

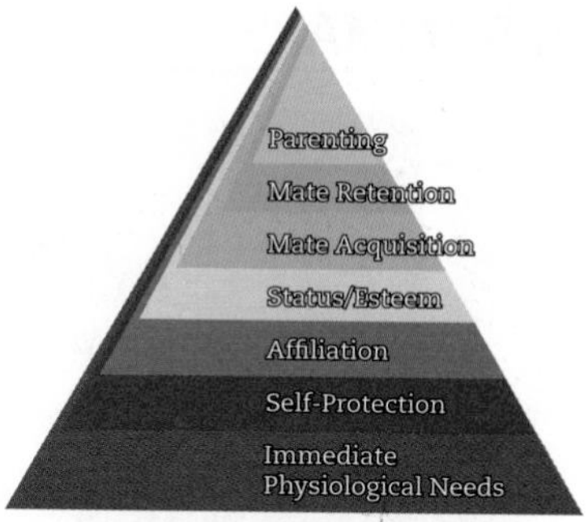

▲ **FIGURE 10.2** **Maslow's Hierarchy "Renovated."** In Kenrick and colleagues' model, needs form an overlapping pyramid according to levels of analysis: evolutionary, developmental, and cognitive.

Some Motivations Are Universal or "Nearly Universal"

Douglas Kenrick and colleagues' "renovation" of Maslow's hierarchy of needs raises the issue of *universality* of certain human motivations. From time to time in this chapter, one motivation or another may be referred to as *universal* or *nearly universal*. This does not mean that every individual or nearly every individual experiences a particular motivation every day, as is typically (but not always) the case with hunger. Instead, these terms refer to motivations that are *species-typical*—common to our species regardless of culture or historical era, and reflecting fundamental evolutionary forces that have operated on the history of the human species (D. E. Brown, 1991; Kenrick, Griskevicius, et al., 2010; Kenrick, Neuberg, et al., 2010). Universal and nearly universal motivations may take different behavioral forms and be interpreted quite differently in different societies and time periods. Their strength may also vary from person to person, and they may need different types of cues or situations to become apparent. Yet, they are typically human. Such motivations are likely to be experienced by virtually everyone at some time in his or her life, or repeatedly throughout our lives.

Certain motivations are clearly universal because they sustain and reproduce human life itself—motivations to breathe, eat, drink, and engage in sexual behavior, for example. However, the story is less clear for the motivations often termed *secondary*, such as belonging and achievement. Nonetheless, both empirical evidence and theory suggest that many such secondary motivations are experienced by people all over the world and deserve the term *universal* or *fundamental* (Barkow, Cosmides, & Tooby, 1992; Baumeister & Leary, 1995; D. E. Brown, 1991; Kenrick, Neuberg, et al., 2010).

Take *aggression*, for example, which I discuss in detail later in the chapter. The typical forms that aggressive acts took in the American frontier town of Deadwood, South Dakota, during the 19th century undoubtedly differed from typical forms of aggression one might see today in an average day in a corporate office on the 40th floor of a skyscraper in New York City. But aggression is in no way absent from the corporate world, although it is undoubtedly less often manifested by saloon gunfights. Moreover, some people are motivated to aggress under a great many conditions, whereas others experience such motivations only under extremely unusual circumstances. But regardless of these differences, aggression is seen in all societies and at all times throughout history.

IN SUMMARY

1. Motivations are mental states that initiate and direct purposive behavior and encourage individuals to engage in sustained effort to achieve goals. Motivations have purpose, causes rooted in specific mental states, and intentionality.

2. Why did theorizing about human instincts lose favor?

3. Motivation can be measured by observing the intensity and persistence of behavior.

4. In explaining motivations, various theorists have invoked human instinct and psychological adaptation; needs to reduce drive states to maintain homeostasis; needs for optimal arousal; incentives; and a hierarchy of needs.

5. Motivations may be intrinsic or extrinsic. Under certain conditions, extrinsic rewards may undermine intrinsic motivation.

6. Maslow's pyramid of needs contains important truths about human nature, although it lacks sufficient research support. Kenrick and colleagues have attempted to renovate Maslow's idea by using somewhat different needs, and by using three levels of analysis to allow for a pyramid design in which needs overlap. The three levels of analysis are evolutionary, developmental, and cognitive.

7. Some motivations are universal or nearly universal among human beings regardless of culture.

RETRIEVE!

1. Why are some motivations referred to as primary and others as secondary? What are some potential problems with this idea?

2. Beginning about 24 hours after fertilization, rapid _____ begins to occur in the zygote. Approximately 1 week after attaching itself to the endometrium, the zygote enters the _____ stage. Approximately 8 weeks later the embryo comes to be known as a _____.

3. Losing interest in an intrinsically interesting activity if offered a reward for the activity is known as the _____ effect.

a) overjustification   b) underjustification   c) extrinsic reward   d) instrinsic reward

4. What theory proposes that behavior is motivated primarily by the desire to reduce unpleasant conditions of arousal resulting from basic physiological needs?

a) drive theory   b) optimal arousal theory   c) evolutionary theory   d) incentive theory

5. What are the five needs that form Abraham Maslow's hierarchy, and in which order did Maslow predict they would occur?

6. The "renovated" pyramid designed by Kenrick and colleagues contains which categories of needs?

a) survival, belongingness, and self-actualization

b) evolutionary, developmental, and cognitive

c) intrinsic, extrinsic, and intuitive

d) conscious, subconscious, and intuitive

How Is Work a Window onto Motivation?

Regardless of the causes of motivation, a variety of factors affect the direction and strength of motivated behavior. This can be seen clearly in research on **work motivation**—the mental forces which determine the form, direction, intensity, and persistence of each person's work-related activities (Locke & Latham, 2002; Pinder, 1998). Differences in work motivation prompt one person to seek a job and another to quit; one to train for a career and another to change careers. Work motivation helps determine whether a person works conscientiously or sloppily, resentfully or gratefully. Examining work motivation is useful because the world of work illuminates factors that affect motivation in general.

As discussed in Chapter 4, work is a central part of human life, and it affords people more than just the means to support themselves financially. Indeed, the motivation to work is generally strong even for those whose basic physiological and safety needs are already fulfilled. Throughout the world, the unemployed consistently report less overall satisfaction with life. In fact, as shown in Figure 10.3, a period of unemployment can reduce a person's ordinary level of well-being to such a degree that full recovery may not occur following re-employment (Lucas, Clark, Georgellis, & Diener, 2004). The reduced quality of life is not only a question of having less money to spend. You may believe that you would never work another day if you had enough money to live on (I certainly feel that way on occasion), but there is no evidence that people actually would be happier with no work to do. Yet, each person's motivation *to* work and motivation *at* work obviously varies, sometimes quite substantially.

Psychologists in the field of **industrial and organizational psychology (I/O psychology)** study human psychology in the context of work. These psychologists have placed great emphasis on the study of work motivation. Among the large number of factors identified by I/O psychologists to explain individual differences in work motivation are *traits, perceived self-efficacy,* and *goal-setting* (Latham & Pinder, 2005).

Traits Influence Work Performance

As I will discuss in greater detail in Chapter 12, **traits** are relatively stable, enduring personal characteristics, attributes, and motives for behavior. Traits can generally be described using adjectives of various sorts. For example, *conscientious, honest, lazy, aggressive, sociable, shy, short-tempered,* and *kind* are all adjectives that could be used to describe traits.

The influence of traits on motivation is complex, however, because (as discussed in Chapter 12) people may behave differently in different situations regardless of their overall traits. This is true of work situations as much as any other (Tett & Burnett, 2003). For example, in jobs with high levels of autonomy, performed without substantial reliance on others (e.g., textbook author, house cleaner, repair person, CEO, traveling sales representative), people high in the trait *conscientiousness* tend to outperform those who are less conscientious. On the other hand, in jobs involving working with other people, conscientiousness seems to have little positive effect on performance, and might even reduce job performance if the conscientious worker in question generally lacks "people skills" and has difficulty in social situations (Witt & Ferris, 2003; Witt et al., 2002).

Perceived Self-Efficacy

Think back over your own life for a moment. How often have you wanted to learn to do something—drawing, ballet, auto repair, martial arts, fiction

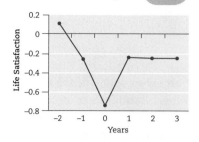

▲ **FIGURE 10.3 Life Satisfaction after a Period of Unemployment.** Richard Lucas and his colleagues studied 24,000 German citizens over a period of 15 years. As depicted in the graph, life satisfaction dropped radically during the time of unemployment (Year 0 on the graph). Although life satisfaction increased following re-employment (beginning in Year 1), it did not rebound to its pre-unemployment levels.

Work motivation ▶ Mental forces which determine the form, direction, intensity, and persistence of each person's work-related activities.

Industrial and organizational psychology (I/O psychology) ▶ The study of psychology in the context of work.

Traits ▶ Relatively stable, enduring personal characteristics, attributes, and motives for behavior.

writing, computer programming, carpentry—but did not even try to learn because "I'm not good at that sort of thing"? On the other hand, how often have you attempted something difficult because "I know I can do that"? Your core belief about your ability to produce change or accomplish a specific task through your own efforts is known as **perceived self-efficacy** (Bandura, 2000, 2007). First described by social-cognitive theorist Albert Bandura, whose work in observational learning we explored in Chapter 7, perceived self-efficacy is an important influence on human motivation that is particularly relevant to the workplace.

According to Bandura, human beings first and foremost work to exercise *control* over the nature and quality of their lives. These efforts are channeled in part through the mechanism of perceived self-efficacy. If we do not believe that we can actualize a goal or produce a desired effect by our actions—that is, if we are low in self-efficacy for that goal or effect—we may not be motivated to forge ahead when faced with difficulties. From Bandura's perspective, all other motivating factors, emotional or cognitive, have at their roots a core belief that we can produce change by our own actions.

Perceived self-efficacy first influences your choice of goals—whether you enroll in that class, apply for the job, buy the art supplies or the book on computer programming in the first place. Next, it influences how much effort you put into accomplishing your chosen goals. Finally, it affects the length of time you are willing to persevere in the face of difficulties. In other words, self-efficacy affects the direction, intensity, and duration of motivated behavior.

LOCUS OF CONTROL

Self-efficacy is sometimes confused with a related idea—the *locus of control*, a concept pioneered in the work of Julian Rotter (Rotter, 1966). Locus of control refers to a person's beliefs about the causes of events in their lives. Those who are high in *internal* locus of control generally attribute their successes and failures to their own efforts and behaviors, while those low in internal locus but high in *external* locus of control tend to attribute life events to factors beyond their control—the workings of fate, circumstance, or the actions of other people.

However, self-efficacy refers to a person's specific evaluation of the extent to which he or she can have an effect in a given situation through his or her own efforts and skill. Locus of control is a more general orientation to explaining events in one's life in terms of internal or external factors. Yet the constructs are clearly related, and those who are high in internal locus of control have a tendency toward high perceived self-efficacy in many situations.

Goal Setting

Recall from the beginning of the chapter that motivated behavior is *purposive* behavior—defined in part as any activity directed toward achieving a goal. But how we set goals for ourselves and others has a profound impact on motivation and the performance of tasks. This is the essence of *goal-setting theory*, devised over the past several decades by Edwin Locke and Gary Latham (Locke & Latham, 2002, 2006). It is among the most influential theories in all of I/O psychology (Mitchell & Daniels, 2003).

What is **goal-setting theory**? As Locke and Latham observed, "When people are asked to do their best, they do not do so" (2002, p. 706). Locke and Latham do not mean that people are contrary by nature. They mean that motivation is increased and performance enhanced in the workplace when *specific* rather than general goals are set. "Do your best" does not work as well as "Please finish eight of these boxes before 3:00 p.m." This applies to goals one sets for oneself as well: "I'm going to finish as many of these stupid boxes as I can" does not work as well as "I'm going to finish eight of these stupid boxes before 3:00 p.m."

Perceived self-efficacy ▶ Albert Bandura's term to describe one's core beliefs about ability to produce change or accomplish a specific task through one's own effort. Although some people may be higher than others in perceived self-efficacy across many domains, perceived self-efficacy is not a trait in which a person can be globally high or low. It always refers to specific tasks, and a person high in perceived self-efficacy on one task can be quite low on another.

Goal-setting theory ▶ An important theory of work motivation devised by Edwin Locke and Gary Latham. According to goal-setting theory, work motivation and performance are enhanced when *specific* and *difficult* (but not impossible) goals are set. Setting specific and difficult goals directs attention toward appropriate activities to reach goals, increases effort to achieve goals, and increases persistence in working toward goals.

However, goals must not only be specific, they must be *difficult*. Contrary to what you might think, the more difficult the goal, the higher the level of motivation and performance. Although easy goals are by definition easier to attain, people do not work as hard or as well to attain them as they do when the stated goal is difficult. Only when the goal is *impossible* are motivation and performance reduced.

Setting specific and difficult goals for yourself or others (e.g., employees) increases motivation and performance in three basic ways:

- First, it directs *attention* toward activity that will help accomplish the job and away from activity that is not relevant to the job.
- Second, setting specific and difficult goals increases *effort*.
- Third, it increases *persistence*. People are more willing to work harder and longer to attain specific and difficult—but possible—goals.

LIVING PSYCHOLOGY

"Do What You Are": Using Positive Psychology to Help Choose a Career

"What do you want to be when you grow up?"

In past decades and centuries, most people had a fairly good idea of how to answer this question by the time they reached age 18 or 19. However, as mentioned in Chapter 4, this may no longer be the case for many people (Walls, 2000). Opportunities are vastly more varied than they once were (particularly for women and minorities, who in past generations were excluded from many career paths), training often involves substantial investments of time and money, and economic shifts may without warning make once-desirable careers no longer quite so desirable.

Thus, factors involved in choosing a career are highly complex and numerous. However, regardless of the factors that seem of greatest importance to you—money, intrinsic interest, ease of obtaining employment, prestige, social responsibility, fun—it is probably not a good idea to choose a job you will not be highly motivated to perform! How can you predict this? Research from the field of positive psychology can help.

The basic teaching of positive psychology in relation to career choice is this: *Do what you are.* In other words, choose an occupation that reflects what Martin Seligman, one of the founders of positive psychology, calls *signature strengths*. According to Seligman, **strengths** are those enduring qualities that result from consistently having made constructive life choices in specific areas. These are choices that lead to universally valued virtues including wisdom and knowledge, courage, humanity, and justice. According to Seligman, there are 24 principal and universal (or nearly universal) strengths each associated with six specific virtues (Peterson & Seligman, 2004; Seligman, 2002; see Table 10.1).

However, in Seligman's view, each of us has a few strengths in particular—perhaps four or five—with which we particularly identify. These qualities define who we are in the best sense. They are our *signature strengths*. Seligman urges you first to identify your signature strengths (his website www.authentichappiness.org has several online tests to help us in this task) and then choose an occupation *that allows you to use these strengths daily*. If you already have a job (or a career), Seligman urges you to try to alter the way you are performing your job, or alter conditions on the job, so that you can use your signature strengths.

Thus, according to positive psychologists, it is generally best to avoid choosing careers that involve the types of skills you have difficulty learning or for which you know from long experience you are not very well suited. They advocate working toward sharpening the skills and strengths

Strengths ▶ Martin Seligman describes strengths as those enduring qualities which result from a person having consistently made constructive life choices in specific areas. Strengths are the choices one makes which lead to the development of universally valued virtues such as wisdom, courage, humanity, and justice. According to Seligman there are 24 principal human strengths.

LIVING PSYCHOLOGY

CONTINUED

Table 10.1 The Strengths and Virtues of Positive Psychology

Positive psychologists such as Martin Seligman have advanced the view that human nature includes at least 24 strengths, each associated with one of six specific universal (or nearly universal) virtues.

VIRTUE: Wisdom and knowledge—Mental strengths that entail the acquisition and use of knowledge
• **Creativity:** Thinking of novel and productive ways to do things
• **Curiosity:** Taking an interest in all of ongoing experience
• **Open-mindedness:** Thinking things through and examining them from all sides
• **Love of learning:** Mastering new skills, topics, and bodies of knowledge
• **Perspective:** Being able to provide wise counsel to others
VIRTUE: Courage—Emotional strengths that involve the exercise of will to accomplish goals in the face of internal or external opposition
• **Authenticity:** Speaking the truth and presenting oneself in a genuine way
• **Bravery:** Not shrinking from threat, challenge, difficulty, or pain
• **Persistence:** Finishing what one starts
• **Zest:** Approaching life with excitement and energy
VIRTUE: Humanity—Interpersonal strengths that involve "tending and befriending" others
• **Kindness:** Doing favors and good deeds for others
• **Love:** Valuing close relations with others
• **Social intelligence:** Being aware of the motives and feelings of self and others
VIRTUE: Justice—Civic strengths that underlie healthy community life
• **Fairness:** Treating all people the same according to notions of fairness and justice
• **Leadership:** Organizing group activities and seeing that they happen
• **Teamwork:** Working well as member of a group or team
VIRTUE: Temperance—Strengths that protect against excess
• **Forgiveness:** Forgiving those who have done wrong
• **Modesty:** Letting one's accomplishments speak for themselves
• **Prudence:** Being careful about one's choices; not saying or doing things that might later be regretted
• **Self-regulation:** Regulating what one feels and does
VIRTUE: Transcendence—Strengths that forge connections to the larger universe and provide meaning to one's life
• **Appreciation of beauty and excellence:** Noticing and appreciating beauty, excellence, and/or skilled performance in all domains of life
• **Gratitude:** Being aware of and thankful for the good things that happen
• **Hope:** Expecting the best and working to achieve it
• **Humor:** Liking to laugh and tease; bringing smiles to other people
• **Religiousness:** Having coherent beliefs about the higher purpose and meaning of life

(Source: Adapted from Peterson & Seligman, 2004.)

you already have rather than strengthening the areas in which you believe you are weak (Rath, 2007).

Of course, this advice does not hold in every case. Some people become highly skilled in activities for which few would have predicted success based on early indicators, and most of us take delight in hearing stories of Nobel Prize–winning mathematicians who had failed high school geometry and algebra classes. However, these are "exceptions that prove the rule." Most Nobel Prize–winning mathematicians received A+ grades in math, and many were already far beyond their teacher's level while still in high school!

Finally, discover those sorts of activities you look forward to doing rather than those you do your best to avoid. Consider in particular activities during which you are fully immersed in what you are doing—where you may lose track of time, experience little fatigue, and from which you are not easily distracted. Positive psychologist Mihaly Csikszentmihalyi has a word for these sorts of experiences of timeless, effortless focus on an activity: **flow** (Csikszentmihalyi, Abuhamdeh, & Nakamura, 2005; Nakamura & Csikszentmihalyi, 2009). Any career in which you are likely to experience flow for substantial portions of the day is a career well worth considering. ■

◀ **Flow.** Artists are often privileged to experience *flow* as they work.

Flow ▶ Mihaly Csikszentmihalyi's term to describe experiences when one is fully immersed in what one is doing—where there is a timeless, effortless focus on an activity from which one is not easily distracted. During flow a person may lose track of time and experience little fatigue.

IN SUMMARY

1.	Work motivations determine the form, direction, intensity, and persistence of each person's work-related activity.
2.	I/O psychology is concerned with human psychology in the context of work. Among the factors I/O psychologists have identified which influence work motivation are traits, perceived self-efficacy, and goal-setting.
3.	Although traits can influence work motivation in a straightforward way, this is not always the case because traits may be expressed very differently in different work settings.
4.	Perceived self-efficacy describes a person's core belief about his or her ability to produce change or accomplish a specific task. Locus of control refers to a person's beliefs about the causes of events in their lives.
5.	Research conducted by goal-setting theorists has found that work motivation and performance are enhanced when specific and difficult (but not impossible) goals are set.
6.	Positive psychologists advise people to determine their signature strengths and use them in choosing a career or improving conditions on the job.

RETRIEVE!

1.	Under which conditions would a conscientious person experience the highest level of work motivation and perform best?

2.	People's core beliefs about their ability to produce change or accomplish a specific task through their own efforts are known as _____.
3.	Why do Locke and Latham assert that "When people are asked to do their best, they do not do so"?
4.	There are three basic ways in which setting specific and difficult goals increases motivation and performance. What are these three ways?
5.	Experiences of effortless focus on an activity, when you may lose track of time and are not easily distracted, are called _____ by positive psychologists such as Mihaly Csikszenthihalyi.

Why Do We Eat?

"Please sir—I want some more."

—Oliver Twist

In his novel *Oliver Twist*, Charles Dickens (1838) described the life of abused orphan boys who were fed nothing but small portions of bland cereal day in and day out: "At last they got so voracious and wild with hunger, that one boy . . . hinted darkly to his companions, that unless he had another basin of gruel *per diem*, he was afraid he might some night happen to eat the boy who slept next him . . ." (p. 28).

The hunger of prolonged semistarvation is indeed a powerfully unpleasant experience. This was demonstrated experimentally by researchers who induced semistarvation in a group of 36 male volunteer subjects by controlling their food intake over the period of a year (Keys, Brozek, Henschel, Mickelsen, & Taylor, 1950). During the first 3 months the men ate normally. Their food rations were then cut in half as their physical activity levels were increased. Eventually their body weights fell to approximately 25% below their starting levels. Finally, the men were slowly brought back to their normal weights.

How did the men respond psychologically to their experience? As their weight dropped during the "starvation" period, they began to have increasingly incessant thoughts of food, and found concentration on any of their usual activities difficult as a result. When they talked among themselves, the most common topic was food. They read about food, traded recipes, collected cooking utensils, fantasized about eating, and gazed at images of food. They would obtain pleasure by watching one another eat. They lost interest in sex. At mealtime some of the men would gulp their food down in a quick moment, while others would draw out the mealtime literally for hours. Following the end of the experiment almost 40% of the men, few of whom had expressed any interest in cooking or food industries prior to the study, announced their intention to learn to cook. In fact, several changed careers and became chefs, and at least one entered the field of agriculture!

Hunger and Appetite Are Not the Same

The experience of the subjects in the semistarvation experiment by Keys and colleagues is a good example of a situation where Maslow's (1970) notion of a hierarchy of needs makes good sense. These men's hunger took precedence over almost everything in their lives. Drive-reduction theory may also be

Hunger ▶ A primarily homeostatic drive state turned on and off by physiological changes in the body and intended to satisfy needs for immediate energy and/or overall nutrition. Hunger naturally leads to eating.

appropriate in this case. As the men's physiological needs for energy and nourishment became urgent, an unpleasant drive state—hunger—was initiated. It demanded attention so that the men's bodies could return to a state of homeostasis, or stable internal environment.

However, hunger is not the only motivator to eat food, nor is homeostasis always the object of eating. To understand why, we first need to distinguish two terms: *hunger* and *appetite*. It is important to separate these concepts, because increasing evidence suggests that much food intake is probably initiated in the modern world (at least the industrialized world) *not* as a result of hunger but as a result of appetite.

Hunger is a largely homeostatic drive state turned on and off by various physiological changes in the body. It is intended to satisfy needs for immediate energy and/or overall nutrition. Hunger naturally leads to eating.

On the other hand, **appetite** is a desire to eat. Imagine how you might feel, for example, after a long, delicious, and filling meal in a very elegant restaurant if, instead of bringing your check, the server brings a cart loaded with the most magnificent assortment of French pastries you had ever seen. You might experience a return of your appetite—but not of hunger.

Therefore, although appetite is often driven by hunger, it can also be influenced by a number of other events, such as the appearance or disappearance of appealing foods (known as *high-incentive foods* because they promise a pleasurable reward). Appetite also may be increased by being in a place where eating is expected or desirable, or if one is forced to take advantage of a limited time during the day in which one is able to eat, such as a lunch break at work (Melanson, 2004).

Thus, *hunger* is a fairly straightforward homeostatic mechanism best understood in terms of physiology and biochemistry, whereas *appetite*, while equally "biological" in nature, is nonetheless highly influenced and sometimes entirely controlled by psychological, social-environmental, or cultural factors.

People Tend to Maintain an Energy Balance

Hunger and appetite regulate eating behavior, but what is the purpose of eating in the first place? Food represents fuel that is first broken down by *enzymes*, absorbed into the intestines and converted into *proteins*, *fatty acids*, and *sugars*, all of which provide *energy* to the body. Energy is necessary even if you are asleep, because without it your brain could not control your vital functions, including breathing and heart rate.

People have a general tendency to maintain an **energy balance** by taking in only as many *calories* (a measurement of energy units) as are expended overall in activity and the maintenance of bodily functions. Maintaining an energy balance leads to a tendency toward maintaining a fairly consistent body weight over time, known as **baseline body weight** (Keesey & Hirvonen, 1997). This has sometimes been referred to as weight *set point*, the implication being that one's "optimal" weight is relatively fixed. The general tendency to maintain baseline weight is probably one reason that dieters have difficulty keeping pounds off after successfully losing them.

However, people also tend to gain weight slowly over time as they age (Brownell & Rodin, 1994). Why does one's set point often seem to get "reset" to a higher baseline in this way? This is a complicated question that involves, first, a general slowdown in **metabolic rate** that begins to occur during the 30s or 40s. Metabolic rate is the speed with which food is transformed into energy. When this process slows, more food is stored as fat than is utilized as energy. Most people's activity levels also slow down with age. Because we are in the habit of eating enough to sustain previously higher levels of energy expenditure, the energy balance may be tipped in the direction of greater caloric intake than is required. There is also a reduction in the sensitivity of taste and smell over time, which may create appetites for more heavily salted or

▲ **Appetite ≠ Hunger.** You may have eaten at 3:00 p.m., but coming home at 5:00 p.m. to the aroma and warmth of a home-cooked meal may increase your *appetite*—even if you are no longer *hungry*.

Appetite ▶ A desire to eat. Unlike hunger, which always results from a need for energy or overall nutrition, appetite can result from any number of causes including, but not limited to, hunger. Appetite is highly influenced or even controlled by psychological, social-environmental, or cultural factors.

Energy balance ▶ Energy balance is maintained by taking in only as many calories as are expended overall in activity and the maintenance of bodily functions.

Baseline body weight ▶ Sometimes referred to as weight set point, the baseline body weight is the fairly consistent body weight achieved over time by maintaining an energy balance.

Metabolic rate ▶ The speed with which food is transformed into energy.

sweetened food, further increasing the tendency to gain weight. This adjustment in weight set point over time suggests that the set point is not truly "set" at all, but rather responsive to changes in physiology, environment, activity level, and so forth (Pinel, Assanand, & Lehman, 2000).

Eating Disorders Have Become More Common

Beginning in the late 1960s and early 1970s, Western nations began to see a dramatic upsurge in the number of cases of what seemed to be mostly young, relatively affluent women of European ancestry either starving themselves intentionally or alternating self-starvation with *binge eating* (consuming abnormally large amounts of food) and *purging* (self-induced vomiting or overuse of laxatives in an effort to rid the body of the calories just consumed). Reported rates of *eating disorders* which include symptoms such as these have continued to rise over the years, although not as dramatically as during the 1970s.

Some of this rise in reported rates is undoubtedly due to increased awareness of the disorders and willingness to report them (Wakeling, 1996). However, it is also beyond dispute that actual rates of eating disorders worldwide have increased over the past 60 years, particularly among women aged 15 to 24, although these disorders are not limited to only this group (Hoek & van Hoeken, 2003; Hudson, Hiripi, Pope, & Kessler, 2007). Despite the rise in the number of cases, however, the overall prevalence of eating disorders still remains extremely low, particularly among people of color and men (Alegria et al., 2007; Hudson et al., 2007; Nicdao, Hong, & Takeuchi, 2007; Taylor, Caldwell, Baser, Faison, & Jackson, 2007).

An **eating disorder** is any of a number of complex conditions involving unhealthful patterns of eating or not eating. The most frequently diagnosed of medically recognized eating disorders are **anorexia nervosa** (AN) and **bulimia nervosa** (BN). Overall, in the United States .9% (nine-tenths of 1%) of women have suffered from anorexia nervosa at some time in their lives, and 1.5% of women have suffered from bulimia nervosa. Although it has long been recognized that men also suffer from these disorders, the rate among men is so low that no truly dependable estimate exists (Hudson et al., 2007). It is generally thought that somewhere between three and ten times more women than men suffer from eating disorders (Hoak & van Hoeken, 2003; Hudson et al., 2007).

Binge-eating disorder (BED) is a newly coined disorder that is just beginning to gain some acceptance by the medical profession due to its inclusion in the recent fifth revision of the American Psychiatric Association's compendium of mental disorders, *The Diagnostic and Statistical Manual* (DSM-5) (American Psychiatric Association, 2013). Because BED is defined as overeating with a "sense of lack of control" at least once per week during a three-month period, it can no longer be said that eating disorders are rare, because the prevalence of BED is much greater than that of anorexia and bulimia nervosa combined (Hudson et al., 2007). Indeed, millions of people who were not considered to have a psychological disorder prior to the publication of the DSM-5 in May 2013 may now be diagnosed with an eating disorder. Table 10.2 describes diagnostic criteria for anorexia nervosa and bulimia nervosa.

Thinking about eating disorders is in flux among researchers and clinicians, and there are many debates in the field over the precise number of such disorders, or even whether they each deserve separate labels (Keel, Brown, Holland, & Bodell, 2012; Wonderlich, Joiner, Keel, & Williamson, 2007). For example, although most researchers probably consider each eating disorder a separate entity, some have proposed that disordered eating behavior ought to be thought of along a continuum of severity, from mild to severe, with a variety of possible symptoms, rather than as a group of distinct disorders that a person either has or doesn't have (Williamson, Gleaves, & Stewart, 2005).

Eating disorder ▶ Any of a number of complex conditions involving unhealthful patterns of eating or not eating. The most commonly diagnosed of medically recognized eating disorders are *bulimia nervosa* and *anorexia nervosa*. However, *binge-eating disorder*, which has not yet been accepted by the medical profession (but is likely to be in the future), is more common than anorexia and bulimia combined.

Anorexia nervosa ▶ An eating disorder usually characterized by a refusal to maintain normal body weight for one's age and height; intense fear of gaining weight or becoming fat; and a disturbed perception of one's body weight or shape, exaggerated emphasis on body weight or shape when making self-evaluations, or a denial of the seriousness of one's current low body weight. Sometimes one or more of these symptoms is not present, however.

Bulimia nervosa ▶ An eating disorder usually characterized by recurrent episodes of binge-eating, where there is a sense of lack of control over the quantity of food eaten; behavior designed to compensate for binging, such as purging (forced vomiting), abuse of laxatives, excessive exercise, or fasting; and self-evaluation that is unduly influenced by body shape and weight concerns.

Table 10.2 Diagnostic Criteria for Anorexia Nervosa and Bulimia Nervosa

Anorexia Nervosa: According to proposed changes to the DSM in its fifth revision (DSM-5), for a diagnosis of anorexia nervosa to be made, a person must display the following:
1. Refusal to maintain body weight at or above a minimally normal weight for age and height or failure to make expected weight gain during period of growth.
2. Intense fear of gaining weight or becoming fat or persistent behavior that interferes with weight gain, even though at a significantly low weight.
3. Disturbance in the way in which one's body weight or shape is experienced; undue influence of body weight or shape on self-evaluation; or denial of the seriousness of current low body weight.
Bulimia Nervosa: The following criteria must be met for a diagnosis of bulimia nervosa:
1. Recurrent episodes of binge eating (eating much more food during a given episode that most people would eat; or a sense of lack of control during an eating episode).
2. Recurrent inappropriate behavior designed to prevent weight gain, such as self-induced vomiting; misuse of laxatives, diuretics, enemas, or other medications; fasting; or excessive exercise.
3. The binge eating and inappropriate behavior each occur on average at least once a week for 3 months.
4. Self-evaluation is unduly influenced by body shape and weight.

RISK FACTORS FOR ANOREXIA AND BULIMIA ARE COMPLEX

As with most psychological disorders, it has not been possible to identify the causes of eating disorders with any certainty, although literally thousands of attempts have been made (Polivy & Herman, 2002). Nevertheless, several factors have repeatedly emerged as psychological, biological, and sociocultural risk factors for developing these disorders.

Sex and Age Without doubt the most glaring risk factor for the development of eating disorders is being young and female (Striegel-Moore & Bulik, 2007). Depending on the study, between three and ten or more times as many women as men suffer from eating disorders, with the majority of these between the high-risk ages of adolescence and early adulthood (Hoek & van Hoeken, 2003; Hudson et al., 2007). Why women are overwhelmingly affected has not been successfully explained (Striegel-Moore & Bulik, 2007).

Psychology A number of psychological risk factors for eating disorders have repeatedly been emphasized by researchers, although the evidence supporting these factors is not always very strong (Jacobi, Haward, de Zwaan, Kraemer, & Agras, 2004). First, generally negative mood states and negative emotionality as a personality characteristic—leading to habitually negative self-evaluations—have been thought to result in attempts to elevate mood and increase self-esteem through weight and body shape control (Cassin & von Ranson, 2005; Polivy & Herman, 2002).

Second, *cognitive factors* may contribute to the development of the disorders as well as to their persistence over time (Williamson, Gleaves, & Stewart, 2005). For example, some researchers claim that those with eating disorders tend to have distorted ideas about the importance of striving for perfection, and they often engage in "all or nothing," thinking. Others propose that eating disordered individuals have low levels of cognitive flexibility in general—that is, the ability to shift attention from one thing to another, or to consider a number of things at the same time (Roberts, Tchanturia, & Treasure, 2010). Perfectionism and lack of cognitive flexibility are characteristics that could lead to negative self-evaluations when a person falls short of her perfectionist ideals or inflexible beliefs, making her vulnerable to eating disorders. However, again, the evidence supporting these notions is not very strong (Jacobi et al., 2004).

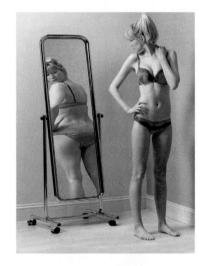

▲ **Anorexia Nervosa Often Includes Distortions in Body Perception.** In some cases, individuals suffering from anorexia may think of themselves as much heavier than they actually are. When viewing their image in the mirror, they may perceive a body shaped quite differently from that which others see. However, the effect is less like the hallucinatory distortions depicted in images such as this, and more like a subtle perceptual shift that cannot easily be displayed as a photographic image.

Genes Research has repeatedly documented that eating disorders run in families. If you have a genetic relative with an eating disorder, you are approximately ten times more likely to develop one during your lifetime than if no one in your family is affected (Bulik, 2005). Twin studies conducted throughout the world have also demonstrated that that if one monozygotic (identical) twin has an eating disorder, the other twin is much more likely also to have one than would be the case for dyzygotic (fraternal) twins or ordinary siblings (Bulik et al., 2010; Klump, Burt, McGue, & Iacono, 2007; Thornton, Mazzeo, & Bulik, 2011).

Culture More than most other groups of psychological disorders, eating disorders are powerfully shaped by cultural and social forces (Pike & Borovy, 2004). Indeed, for several decades eating disorders were defined primarily in cultural terms. For example, many theorists during the 1970s and 1980s considered eating disorders to be virtually entirely the result of Western societal obsessions with thinness and female physical attractiveness as tirelessly depicted in the mass media—interacting with specific psychological factors in vulnerable women.

Beginning in the 1990s, however, evidence began to be collected which contradicted aspects of these simple cultural models. For example, historical evidence shows that eating disorders, particularly anorexia nervosa, have existed throughout history, centuries before Western standards of beauty emphasized thinness (Bemporad, 1996; Russell, 1995). Studies of eating disorders in non-Western nations demonstrate that anorexia nervosa and bulimia are not necessarily accompanied by "fear of fat," internalization of ideals of beauty dependent upon thinness, or concerns about appearance at all—factors which have been considered defining features of these disorders and which do in fact pervade the experience of eating disorders in the West (Bhattacharya, Unadkat, & Connan, 2010; Lee, 2001; Littlewood, 1995; Russell, 1995). Studies of eating disorders among non-Western peoples with virtually no prior exposure to Western ideals show that anorexia nervosa, at least, does exist in such places (Keel, et al., 2012).

And yet, eating disorders are increasingly being seen in those non-Western and developing nations that are experiencing rapid social transition due to globalization and exposure to Western culture (Anderson-Fye & Becker, 2003). The conclusion is inescapable that causes of anorexia and bulimia include powerful cultural components, and that these components are somehow related to the influence of the industrialized Western nations. But what is the nature of this influence?

A number of current theorists insist that it is more important to understand the **culture of modernization** as a contributor to the global spread of these illnesses, rather than focusing on more simplistic models of "Westernization" (Katzman, Hermans, van Hoeken, & Hoek, 2004; Lee, 1995). What is meant by the "culture of modernization"? Developing nations are undergoing vast transformations in their economies, social structures, levels of food abundance and variety, technology, birth and death rates, gender relations, urbanization, and so forth. Eating disorders may be a symptom of ways in which mostly adolescent and young adult women adapt to these rapid sociocultural and economic transformations. Mervat Nassar and her colleagues state this idea succinctly when they refer to eating disorders as a "global marker of change" (Nassar, Katzman, & Gordon, 2001, xv; see also Katzman et al., 2004; Lee, 1995).

Consider the enormous changes in the availability, variety, abundance, palatability, portion sizes, calorie content, and marketing of food as packaged products which occurred in the United States as part of modernization during the mid-20th century. Such changes likely played important roles in the rise in ideals about slimness in the West, because they radically altered traditional ways of relating to food and made weight gain a virtually inevitable result of

Culture of modernization

▶ A term sometimes used to describe the vast transformations being experienced by developing nations in response to globalization. These transformations occur in economy, social structure, food abundance and variety, technology, birth and death rates, relations between the sexes, urbanization, and so forth.

participating in the ordinary culture of eating in our society (Critser, 2003; Finkelstein & Zuckerman, 2008; Rolls, 2003). Just as plumpness may sometimes appear as a badge of health in nations afflicted with food shortage, slimness may be seen as a badge of immunity against unhealthful overconsumption in a culture where high-calorie foods in "supersize" portions are freely available and marketed ferociously. Ideals of slimness can be seen as almost inevitable consequences of the "modernization of food"—a modernization that is now also occurring in many developing nations (Littlewood, 2004).

The importance of exposure to Western media imagery glorifying slender physiques should not be minimized, for these images do contribute to the problem of eating disorders in women who are already vulnerable (Grabe, Ward, & Hyde, 2008; Striegel-Moore & Bulik, 2007). However, according to modernization theorists it is the effect of the West on global modernization, rather than the simple spread of Western media images, that promotes ideals of thinness.

Overweight and Obesity Are Epidemic

Ideals of thinness exist against a backdrop of increasing weight gain. Approximately two-thirds of Americans are currently overweight or obese, with about half of this number being technically **obese**—excessively overweight with body mass index (BMI) at 30 or higher. This is an increase of approximately 32% from the 1960s. Judging by current figures and rates of increase, by the year 2015, 75% of Americans will be overweight, and 41% will be obese (Wang & Beydoun, 2007).

Although obesity is highly unlikely ever to overtake tobacco as the number one preventable health hazard (barring a major reduction in tobacco use), it is now somewhere between the seventh and second most serious preventable cause of death in the United States (estimates differ) and accounts for higher health care costs than either smoking or alcohol abuse (Finkelstein, Fielbekorn, & Wang, 2003). Many other nations are not far behind (Lustig, 2006a, 2006b; Wadden, Brownell, & Foster, 2002; World Health Organization, 2008).

Obese ▶ Refers to a pathological level of fatness. Obesity is not the same as *overweight*, a lesser degree of heaviness that may or may not cause health problems. Obesity and overweight are defined in practice somewhat differently in different contexts.

WHY ARE PEOPLE GAINING WEIGHT?

The history of the modern epidemic of overweight and obesity is truly astonishing. To some degree, the tendency to overweight and obesity is heritable, as genetics play an important role in how fat is metabolized, how insulin and glucose are regulated, and how appetite and hunger are experienced. Behavior geneticists and molecular geneticists have demonstrated the connection between genes and obesity (Livshits, Kato, Wilson, & Spector, 2007; Mutch & Clément, 2006; Willer et al., 2008).

However, genetics alone cannot account for the dramatic increase in weight problems in just a single generation. To a large extent it is a problem of behavior. Although the behaviors resulting in weight gain in the modern world are at least theoretically preventable, as depicted in Figure 10.5, overweight and obesity may actually be reasonable and predictable responses to a series of recent historical events (Crister, 2003; Finkelstein & Zuckerman, 2008; Rolls, 2003). What are these events?

Corn Surplus and the Invention of High-Fructose Corn Syrup (HFCP) During the 1970s, government policies began to encourage overproduction of food, particularly corn (Critser, 2003). Growers were faced with a perplexing problem—how to get rid of the surplus of food. At the same time, Japanese scientists had invented *high fructose corn syrup* (HFCS), a sweetener six times sweeter than sugar and much less expensive. Food manufacturers began using HFCS in increasing numbers of products in place of sugar to lower costs. They even began to use it in products that did not traditionally use sweeteners of any kind, to increase their taste appeal and shelf life.

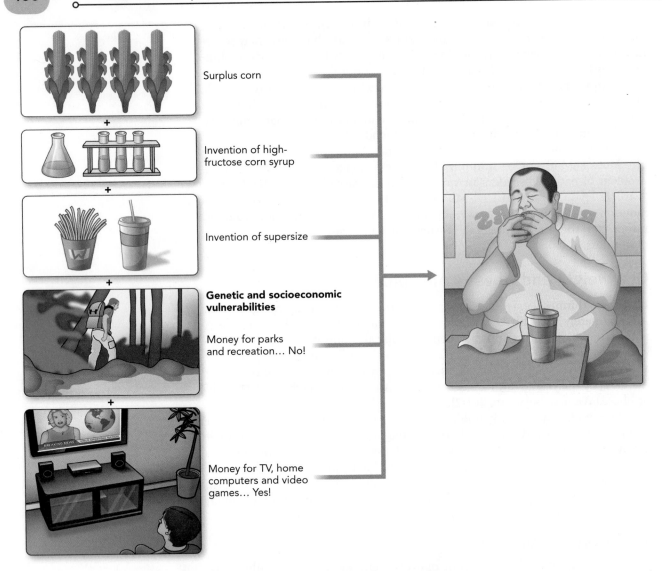

Surplus corn

Invention of high-fructose corn syrup

Invention of supersize

Genetic and socioeconomic vulnerabilities

Money for parks and recreation… No!

Money for TV, home computers and video games… Yes!

▲ **FIGURE 10.4 Recipe for Epidemic of Obesity.** Historical factors may have combined with socioeconomic and genetic factors to create the current epidemic of overweight and obesity. Historical factors create an environment of easy availability of calories, greatly increased caloric intake, and low levels of physical activity. These factors will result in increased weight in the average person. However, some people have genetic or socio-economic vulnerabilities which put them at particular risk of obesity, and such people not only gain weight but become obese. Deregulation of insulin and leptin systems make weight loss for obese people extremely difficult.

Unfortunately, in addition to adding a large amount of unnecessary calories to American meals, high concentrations of fructose in HFCS appear to contribute to the disregulation of insulin and leptin, the hormones which govern hunger. This seems to be a particular problem for the obese, who experience sensations of starvation when they actually have overly plentiful reserves of fat and energy (Lustig, 2006a, 2006b).

Thus, HFCS helps to make us obese, and once we are there, it keeps us there. If you read food labels you will find HFCS as an ingredient in all sorts of foods, from ketchup and spaghetti sauce to bacon and alcoholic drinks.

Invention of the Supersize At the same time that HFCS was being added to seemingly everything, researchers at McDonald's, who were trying to come up with ways to get Americans to eat more of their food, noted that customers had what seemed like a strong internal prohibition against buying two servings of soda, shakes, hamburgers, or fries. They did not want to be seen to commit the fifth deadly sin of gluttony. However, McDonald's researchers found that Americans would gladly pay for and eat two servings *if the two servings were packaged as one.* Thus, the *supersize* was born.

In support of the economic wisdom of McDonald's move to the supersize, Rolls (2003) reports that:

- Adults eat about twice as many M&Ms when eating from a jumbo bag as from a small one—63 M&Ms from a small bag of 114 but 122 from a jumbo bag of 342.
- Moviegoers eat 61% more popcorn when eating from jumbo buckets.

Similar results were reported by Nicole Diliberti and her colleagues (Diliberti, Bordi, Conklin, Roe, & Rolls, 2004). In their study, the size of restaurant portions was varied, with some customers getting standard portions and others getting supersize. Diliberti and colleagues found that customers essentially ate whatever was given to them, with no differences in subsequent ratings of the appropriateness of the portions or their satisfaction with the meal. In other words, they would have been perfectly happy with the standard size, but were more than willing to eat (and pay for) the supersize if it was given to them. Those eating the supersize increased their calorie intake by 43% over those eating the standard portion. In a later study, investigators found that typical portions of food chosen by research participants were much larger than typical portions chosen by participants in a similar study from the 1980s (Schwartz & Byrd-Bredbenner, 2006).

Decreased Access to Physical Activity At the same time as the preceding factors caused Americans and some others in the Western world to greatly increase their calorie intake, money allotted to physical education in the schools, and to parks and recreation outside of schools, was sharply declining due to socioeconomic factors (Critser, 2003). The decades of the 1970s were also the years of increasing proliferation of television screens throughout the world and increases in the amount of time people spent watching TV. The final nail was driven home with the invention of the home computer and video games in the next decade. Americans now took in many more calories, and burned up many fewer calories.

Considering this history, a case can be made that overweight and obesity are the expected outcomes of growing up in the United States post-1970s—and, increasingly, in other developed nations as well (Lustig, 2006a, 2006b). In the past, one had to go out of one's way to become overweight or obese; now it seems that one must truly go out of one's way to *avoid* these problems.

IN SUMMARY

1.	*Hunger* is a largely homeostatic drive state intended to satisfy needs for immediate energy and/or overall nutrition. *Appetite* is the term which refers to a desire to eat. Appetite may be triggered by psychological, social, cultural, and environmental factors as well as by hunger.
2.	The most commonly diagnosed of recognized eating disorders are anorexia nervosa (AN) and bulimia nervosa (BN). Symptoms of AN include refusal to maintain normal weight, fear of gaining weight, and a distorted body image. Symptoms of BN include binge eating, behavior such as purging or fasting designed to compensate for binge eating, and undue emphasis on body shape and weight in self-evaluation.
3.	Risk factors for eating disorders include being young and female; exposure to modernization and Western culture; various psychological characteristics including habitual negative moods, negative self-evaluations and perfectionism; and genetic vulnerability.

| **4.** | Overweight and obesity are epidemic. Factors responsible for the epidemic include genetics, socioeconomics, historical events, and eating behavior. |

RETRIEVE!

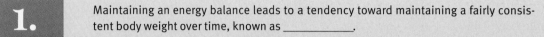

1.	Maintaining an energy balance leads to a tendency toward maintaining a fairly consistent body weight over time, known as _____.
2.	Many theorists studying eating disorders in developing nations claim that exposure to Western images glorifying thinness is only one part of general cultural changes responsible for the spread of eating disorders. What is the term used to describe these cultural changes?
3.	Which of the following is NOT one of the historical factors likely responsible for the current epidemics of overweight and obesity? **a)** food surplus and the invention of high-fructose corn syrup **b)** invention of the supersize **c)** a series of genetic changes in the population **d)** decrease in financial investment in parks and recreation

The Social Motivations: Why Do We Turn Toward One Another?

Human beings are social creatures from birth. Newborn infants display apparently innate interest in the faces and voices of humans, but not those of other species (Quinn & Slater, 2003; Sai, 2005). In childhood and adulthood, virtually all people require a certain amount and quality of contact with others to maintain feelings of well-being (Baumeister & Leary, 1995). We do not thrive in isolation; the use of solitary confinement as a severe punishment for prisoners reflects this. Lack of social contact is a significant risk factor for the development of heart disease, depression, and premature death (Seeman, 2001; Uchino, Uno, & Holt-Lunstad, 1999; see Chapter 11). As described in Chapter 2, social rejection activates neural responses associated with physical pain (DeWall et al., 2010; Eisenberger, 2012).

People form bonds with others quickly and easily, even when there is no particular reason for bonds to form, such as shared interests, history, or mutual dependence. Sitting in a room with others waiting for something to happen, participating in an experiment where participants are arbitrarily divided into groups, or living next door to someone may be enough for people to want to form bonds with one another (Festinger, Schachter, & Back, 1950; Schachter, 1959; Sherif, Harvey, White, Hood, & Sherif, 1954/1961; Tajfel & Billig, 1974). We may even form bonds with people we used to hate or against whom we once held strong prejudices (Dovidio & Gaertner, 1996; Pettigrew, 1998; Wilder & Thompson, 1980). On the morning of the day I am writing this, one of my daughters brought home her new best friend—the girl she wanted to beat over the head with a sledge hammer just 4 months ago.

Put simply, human beings are motivated to turn toward one another, a general tendency known as **social motivation**. It is not difficult to imagine why we are innately social—as infants we need assistance from other people, and as we grow up other people continue to play important roles throughout our lives. Psychologists have identified two specific types of social needs that motivate us to turn toward one another: **need to affiliate** and **need to belong**.

Affiliation Means Being Near, but Not Necessarily Close

In 1959, a group of female college students volunteered for a psychology experiment conducted by Stanley Schachter. Schachter was a leading researcher in social motivation, particularly affiliation—the motivation to be with other people in the same space. In his 1959 experiment, the students were divided into two groups. One group met a severe, forbidding "professor" named "Dr. Gregor Zilstein" (actually an actor hired by Schachter) who informed them that the experiment would involve their receiving highly painful shocks from a Frankenstein-esque apparatus they were allowed to view. The other group met a friendly and mild-mannered "professor" (in reality, the same actor) who told them that they would be receiving shocks, but that the shocks would be quite mild and feel no worse than a tickling sensation.

This introduction produced very different levels of anxiety in the two groups. The "Frankenstein" group became quite anxious (as measured by self-ratings of anxiety), while the other group became much less so. The research participants were then asked to wait for the experiment to begin, and they were given the choice of waiting alone or in groups. Schachter found that about two-thirds of the high-anxiety group chose to wait in groups, whereas only one third of the low-anxiety group chose to do so.

This research triggered great interest among social psychologists in determining the conditions under which people are most motivated to affiliate. Affiliation is the process of "flocking together" and does not necessarily imply that strong relationships will form (although they may). Schachter's work and the research that followed seems to suggest that under conditions of anxiety, stress, danger, disappointment, illness, and disaster, people have a particularly increased need to be with one another and find comfort from affiliation—particularly if those with whom they are affiliating are sharing (or have shared) a similar experience (Elder & Clipp, 1988; Gump & Kulik, 1997; McAdams & Vaillant, 1982).

However, there are important sex differences in the tendency to affiliate under stressful conditions that are sometimes overlooked when this research is discussed. As Shelly Taylor and her colleagues document, it is primarily women, not men, who tend to seek out the company of other people when under stress and express greater liking for those around them (Taylor, 2006; Taylor et al., 2000). In fact, the opposite effect often occurs for men. Although men sometimes have been shown to affiliate under conditions of extreme stress—for example, in wartime (Elder & Clipp, 1988)—they more often react to stress by becoming less social, expressing greater dislike of the people around them, and keeping a greater physical distance between themselves and others. The effect of women's tendency to affiliate with others under stress and men's tendency to withdraw is so strong that some researchers in affiliation, including Stanley Schachter himself, gave up using men in their studies of affiliation and focused entirely on women. (I discuss some possible reasons for this sex difference in Chapter 11.)

Belonging Means Caring Relationships that Endure

Human beings need more than merely to "hang out" with one another—they need to *belong*. In a thoughtful and comprehensive review of the psychological literature, Roy Baumeister and Mark Leary (1995) make a strong case that the need to belong is a fundamental human need and motivator.

Social motivation ▶ The innate human motivation to interact with other humans.

Need to affiliate ▶ The need to mingle with other people in the same space. Affiliation does not necessarily imply that strong relationships form (although they may), only that one is near other people.

Need to belong ▶ An innate need hypothesized by Roy Baumeister and Mark Leary. According to Baumeister and Leary, for belonging needs to be met, a person must experience frequent, primarily positive interactions with at least a few other people. These interactions must take place in the context of stable, enduring relationships where there is concern for one another's welfare.

▲ **Affiliation and Belonging.**
People need more than merely to affiliate (left) . . . they need to belong (right).

Although Abraham Maslow (1970) also hypothesized that human beings had *belongingness* needs, Baumeister and Leary's view of the concept of belonging is somewhat different. According to these researchers, satisfying the need to belong involves two criteria: First, there must be *frequent, primarily positive interactions* with at least a few other people. Second, these interactions must take place in the context of *stable, enduring relationships* where there is concern for one another's welfare. Unlike the need to affiliate, the need to belong cannot be satisfied by casual interactions with relative strangers or by interactions even with people one knows well and cares about, if such interactions are infrequent.

According to Baumeister and Leary, three predictions logically flow from the idea that belonging is a fundamental human need:

1. Relationships with frequently shifting partners, or relationships that are enduring and caring—but where contact is not frequent—will be equally unsatisfying.

2. A lack of belonging will be experienced extremely negatively and will have various kinds of psychological and/or physiological ill effects.

3. A substantial amount of human behavior, emotion, and thought will be motivated by the need to belong.

An impressive array of evidence supports Baumeister and Leary's case (Leary & Cox, 2008). Throughout the world, people form close bonds with one another and try hard to avoid dissolving these bonds even when actual contact becomes rare or the relationship turns sour (Hazan & Shaver, 1994). Human thought is characterized by concern for, and interest in, intimate relationships. If groups of people are intentionally denied brief experiences of belonging and acceptance in laboratory studies, their thoughts turn to social matters in the same way that those denied food become obsessed with thoughts of eating (Gardner, Pickett, & Brewer, 2000).

Maintaining close personal relationships is probably the single most important determinant of human happiness, life satisfaction, and sense of well-being (Diener, 2000; Diener & Seligman, 2002; Haller & Hadler, 2006). Those who experience belonging have higher levels of self-esteem, are better able to cope with stress, and are less likely to die from strokes or heart disease if they do develop these illnesses (Gailliot & Baumeister, 2007; Seeman, 2001; Taylor et al., 2004). In fact, an early study suggests that a lack of close personal relationships is as likely to lead to premature death as smoking and high levels of cholesterol (House, Landis, & Umberson, 1988).

On the other hand, if caring and concern for another person is not returned, distress is the usual result, and it can be quite severe. Consider unrequited love, a miserable experience which surely makes most of our lists of things we'd rather not have happen to us today (Baumeister & Dhavale, 2001;

Khatwani, 2003). Being rejected by an individual or ostracized from a group can be so unpleasant that it may cause emotional turmoil even when the rejecting or ostracizing entity is a computer! When people are ignored by unknown Internet partners in virtual computer games their mood may worsen substantially and they experience anger and a loss of enjoyment. They are also likely to make adjustments to their behavior to ensure that they are not rejected again—even if these adjustments entail agreeing with obviously false information (Williams, Cheung, & Choi, 2000; Zadro, Williams, & Richardson, 2004). Amazingly, these results hold even if research participants are told that they are playing against *computer-generated opponents*—that is, the rejecting partners are computers themselves, not other humans! These findings suggest that we have psychological adaptations exquisitely attuned to rejection and ostracism—experiences that may well have spelled serious loss of resources or even death in our evolutionary past (Fiske & Yamamoto, 2005; Williams, 2001). In sum, belonging is associated with a host of highly positive outcomes and lack of belonging appears to have a many negative consequences.

LONELINESS

Baumeister and Leary (1995) also discuss conditions under which the criteria for belonging are partially, but not fully, met—for example, where relationships are caring and enduring, but contact is infrequent; or where contact is frequent, but a bond of caring is absent.

When looking at relationships that are caring and enduring, but where contact is infrequent, Baumeister and Leary focus on the distress experienced by parents separated from their children through imprisonment or divorce. These parents will often go to great lengths to increase the amount of actual time they are able to spend with their loved ones. Merely knowing their children exist in the world and that they are loved does not seem to be enough.

What about the case of relationships where contact is frequent, but enduring bonds of caring are absent? Most of us have had the experience of feeling "alone in a crowd" at least once, and this sums up a frequent outcome of such relationships: *loneliness*. What exactly is loneliness? **Loneliness** is a universal experience—the large majority of all people experience it at some time, particularly during adolescence and older adulthood (Heinrich & Gullone, 2006; Hawkley & Cacioppo, 2010). However, until relatively recently it has been treated by psychologists primarily as a symptom of other states such as depression, anxiety, or simple social isolation (McWhirter, 1990). Loneliness is an overwhelmingly unpleasant feeling that results when there is some type of discrepancy between our perception of the interpersonal relationships we have, and the relationships we wish to have (Heinrich & Gullone, 2006).

The important word here is *perception*. Loneliness does not necessarily result from any particular situation, such as being separated from a loved one or losing an important relationship. Loneliness does not mean being alone, which can be a very pleasant experience. Instead, loneliness results from a person's perception and interpretation of the *meaning* of being alone or isolated from specific others—or of the *quality* of the relationships he or she does have (Hawkley & Cacioppo, 2010). For example, you may have spent periods of your life actively involved in learning or developing a skill, leaving little time for social interaction, and yet you did not experience loneliness. In contrast, there may be periods when you have many social contacts and acquaintances and yet feel paralyzingly lonely. This sense of loneliness is likely to occur if the contacts are not enduring, caring, and relatively frequent.

Of the many subjective experiences resulting from lack of belonging, loneliness is one of the most severe. Not only can it cause acute subjective suffering, but it can have serious implications for mental and physical health (particularly among the elderly). Loneliness has been found to be associated with reduced life expectancy as well as increased levels of stress, substance abuse,

Loneliness ▶ An overwhelmingly unpleasant feeling which results when there is a discrepancy between one's perceptions of the interpersonal relationships one has and the relationships one wishes to have. Loneliness does not arise from any particular situation, and one may be alone and never feel lonely. Loneliness results from a person's interpretation of the *meaning* of being alone or isolated from specific others.

▲ **Intimate?** According to psychologists studying intimacy, an intimate relationship requires self-disclosure and a supportive response from the partner—a response which frequently includes the partner's own self-disclosures. However, many would argue that relationships involving children and adults or animals and humans are genuinely intimate relationships even though they contain little or no self-disclosure / partner responsiveness / partner disclosure.

antisocial behavior, heart disease, and suicide rates (Cacioppo, Hawkley, & Berntson, 2003; Caspi, Harrington, Moffitt, Milne et al., 2006; Hawkley & Cacioppo, 2007; 2010; Seeman, 2001; Shiovitz-Ezra, & Ayalon, 2010).

INTIMACY

There are many types of interpersonal relationships that satisfy needs for belonging. Such relationships often—perhaps usually—include **intimacy**, a quality that some have characterized as a need and motivator by itself (McAdams, 1992). Although the term *intimacy* is used differently by different theorists, it is usually understood to describe interpersonal relationships, or moments within relationships, that are characterized by warmth, closeness, and mutual support and communication (McAdams, 1989).

How is intimacy achieved? According to intimacy theorists, interpersonal intimacy contains two key elements: *self-disclosure* and *partner responsiveness* (Belcher et al., 2011; Laurenceau & Kleinman, 2006). *Self-disclosure* is the sharing of revealing personal information, thoughts, and feelings to another person. The partner then *responds* in a way that demonstrates understanding, support, and caring, often by offering his or her own self-disclosures. Over time, such experiences increase the general level of warmth and closeness in the relationship. This is particularly true if the self-disclosures refer to one's emotional life, rather than simply revealing factual information about one's life, or reveal aspects of the self that are close to one's "core" (Laurenceau, Feldman Barrett, & Pietromonaco, 1998). In general, the higher the levels of self-disclosure and the more appropriate the partner's response, the more intimate people consider their relationship and the more liking they express for one another (Collins & Miller, 1994).

Intimacy ▶ Interpersonal relationships, or moments within relationships, characterized by warmth, closeness, and mutual support and communication. Intimacy is frequently present in relationships of belonging, and some researchers characterize intimacy as a need and motivator in itself.

IN SUMMARY

1. Human beings have a basic social motivation composed primarily of the need to affiliate and the need to belong.

2. To affiliate means to be with other people in the same space, without the implication that strong relationships are formed. Women's affiliation needs tend to increase under conditions of stress, anxiety, and danger, whereas men's generally do not.

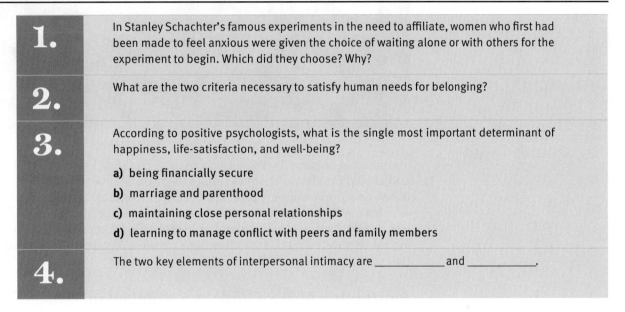

3. Motivation to belong involves a need for frequent, primarily positive interactions with at least a few people in the context of stable, enduring relationships where there is concern for one another's welfare. Relationships of belonging often include intimacy.

4. Among the many subjective experiences resulting from lack of belonging, loneliness is one of the most severe.

RETRIEVE!

1. In Stanley Schachter's famous experiments in the need to affiliate, women who first had been made to feel anxious were given the choice of waiting alone or with others for the experiment to begin. Which did they choose? Why?

2. What are the two criteria necessary to satisfy human needs for belonging?

3. According to positive psychologists, what is the single most important determinant of happiness, life-satisfaction, and well-being?

   a) being financially secure

   b) marriage and parenthood

   c) maintaining close personal relationships

   d) learning to manage conflict with peers and family members

4. The two key elements of interpersonal intimacy are _____ and _____.

Aggression: Why Do We Turn Against One Another?

The history of the world attests to the fact that, just as human beings are motivated to turn toward one another, they are also frequently motivated to turn *against* one another. **Human aggression** is the general term used when an individual or group carries out an act that is intended to harm another individual or group in some way. This definition has two important qualifiers:

1. For an act to constitute aggression, the aggressor must *believe* that the act is truly harmful.

2. The target of the aggression must be *motivated to avoid* the behavior. (Anderson & Bushman, 2002)

To be considered aggression, the harm must be intentional, not accidental, and the victim must experience it as harmful, or at least potentially harmful.

Like the social motivations, motivation to aggress has strong evolutionary roots throughout the animal world and in human history. Although it has clearly been the cause of some of the greatest tragedies in human existence, it also results in small daily miseries that may escape notice. Human aggression results in human wounds—from the death, destruction, and despair of world war and genocide to tears streaming down the face of a small child who has been ostracized from her playgroup out of cruelty.

Human aggression ▶ The general term used when a person carries out an act intended to harm another in some way. However, for an act to constitute aggression, the aggressor must believe that the act is harmful, and the target of aggression must be motivated to avoid the behavior.

▶ **Hostile or Instrumental Aggression?** One aspect of wartime aggression is clearly instrumental—soldiers typically have no particular grudge against individual soldiers of an opposing army. Yet, wartime aggression is often accompanied by hostile emotions, particularly as a soldier's tour of duty continues and he or she experiences repeated violence from the other side.

Human aggression is also an enormously complex topic, one that cannot, and should not, be understood simply in psychological terms. It includes political, economic, military, philosophical, sociocultural, and historical aspects which would take many volumes many times the size of this one to consider adequately. However, aggression has been studied intensively from a psychological perspective, and researchers have clarified certain important aspects of the psychology of aggression.

Aggression May Be Violent or Nonviolent

Violence is an aggressive act whose goal is to inflict serious physical injury or even death (Anderson & Bushman, 2002). All violent acts constitute aggression, because they are by definition intended to cause harm. However, not all aggressive acts are violent. For example, aggression can be *verbal* in the form of taunts, insults, cruel criticism, ostracism, or gossip. If verbal behavior is intended to harm or denigrate a person, it can be said to constitute a form of aggression (Archer, 2004; Moore & Pepler, 2006).

On the other hand, some aggressive acts may be physical in nature, but intended to cause only minor harm, as when one child shoves another on the playground. In these cases "violence" is too strong a term, because there is a difference not only in the *quantity* of harm intended in a shove—as compared with, say, the cluster bombing of a village—but also in the *quality* of harm intended.

Aggression May Be Hostile or Instrumental

Consider two murders. In the first, an organized crime contract hit man pursues a target he knows only by name and photograph. When the target individual is in the hit man's gun sight, he pulls the trigger and quickly leaves the scene—soon afterward depositing "twenty large" or thereabouts in his secret bank account. In the second killing, a usually mild-mannered man comes home from work early to find his wife in bed with the superintendent of the building. In a rage, he grabs his handgun from the closet and fatally shoots the superintendent.

Both unfortunate victims were shot to death in violation of homicide laws. But most of us intuitively understand a difference between these two forms of violent aggression. The hit man was motivated by an ultimate purpose—the acquisition of money—that had nothing to do with any specific desire to kill his victim, whom he did not even know. In all likelihood, had the killer been

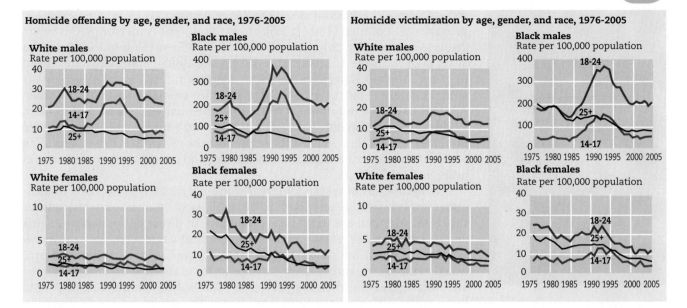

▲ **FIGURE 10.5** Homicide Is the Domain of Young Men. *(Source: U. S. Justice Department Statistics. Retrieved from http://www.ojp.usdoj .gov/bjs/homicide/homtrnd.htm on January 13, 2008.)*

given a chance to collect the money without doing the killing, he would have jumped at the opportunity. When aggression occurs to *serve an ultimate purpose other than causing harm to a victim*, it is termed **instrumental aggression** (Berkowitz, 1993). Instrumental aggression is usually planned rather than impulsive, although this may not always be the case. Instrumental aggression is also not necessarily accompanied by an emotion such as anger (although it may be).

On the other hand, when the ultimate purpose for aggression is harming the victim, it is termed **hostile aggression**. These actions tend to be in reaction to some sort of provocation, accompanied by emotion such as anger, and are often (but not always) impulsive (Anderson & Bushman, 2002). The betrayed husband just described was committing an act of hostile aggression.

Although the categories of *hostile* and *instrumental* aggression are useful in a general way, they are not always easy to distinguish in behavior. These categories do not take into account the fact that motivations for aggression are often mixed, containing both instrumental and hostile elements (Bushman & Anderson, 2001a). For example, some years ago, a childhood friend of mine was robbed at gunpoint by two men at an ATM on a relatively deserted street. My friend was perfectly willing to give up his money (eager, actually, as he stared down the barrel of a 9mm automatic), but the man who held the gun proceeded to beat him so severely that he spent a number of weeks hospitalized and ended up with possibly permanent facial nerve damage. The important point for purposes of this example is that the gunman beat my friend *after* he had already given up his money without argument. In staying at the scene of the crime longer than was necessary to complete the robbery, the muggers increased the likelihood that they would be caught, and the assault added additional, unnecessary, criminal charges to their crime. No one would claim that these men had no instrumental motive for the robbery (profit). However, at least one of them may have had hostile motives as well.

There Are Sex Differences in Aggression

Although both men and women are capable of the most extreme forms of aggressive behavior, direct physical aggression is much more characteristic of boys and men. This is particularly true when it comes to risky and deadly physical violence.

As a glaring example, throughout the world the vast majority of murders are committed by men (generally against other men), and there is no known

Instrumental aggression ▶ A type of aggression which has an ultimate purpose other than causing harm to the victim. Ultimate aggression is often (but not always) planned, and is not necessarily accompanied by an emotion such as anger, although it may be. Instrumental aggression is in contrast to *hostile aggression*, where the ultimate purpose is harming the victim.

Hostile aggression ▶ A type of aggression where the ultimate purpose is harming the victim. Hostile aggression is generally accompanied by emotion, such as anger, and is often (but not always) impulsive. This is in contrast to *instrumental aggression*, where the aggressor has an ultimate purpose other than harming the victim.

▲ **Girls Are More Practiced at Indirect Aggression.** John Archer's 2004 meta-analysis of sex differences in real-world aggression suggests that girls are more practiced than boys in indirect aggression, including "bad-mouthing" others and ostracizing others from the group.

society where the level of deadly violence committed by women even approaches that of men (Daly & Wilson, 1988, p. 146; Anderson & Bushman, 2002; Archer, 2004, 2009; see Figure 10.5). When the homicide rate was at its highest in the United States during the 1990s, approximately 64 out of every 100,000 European American men committed murder, while only approximately 5 out of every 100,000 white women committed murder. Approximately 36 out of every 100,000 white men were victims of murder, while only approximately 9 out of every 100,000 white women were victims. Similarly, although a much higher proportion of African Americans than white Americans were victimized by murder and committed murder, the sex difference is identical.

A meta-analysis of research on real-world aggression (as opposed to laboratory experiments), conducted in 10 nations on four continents, affirms that boys and men are more likely to engage in direct aggression than girls and women (Archer, 2004), particularly physical aggression. Laboratory research tells much the same story: Although women can sometimes be provoked to the same degree of aggressive behavior in the laboratory as men, men are more aggressive when *not* provoked—that is, they are more aggressive to begin with (Bettencourt & Kernahan, 1997). The size of the sex difference in real-world aggression is also much greater than that found in laboratory research (Archer, 2004).

In certain forms of aggression, however, sex differences are slight or nonexistent. For example, differences between men and women in verbal aggression or *indirect aggression*—deliberately excluding or ostracizing others from a group, or speaking maliciously about another person—are very small, if they exist at all (Archer, 2004; Card, Stucky, Sawalani, & Little, 2008).

WHY ARE MEN MORE DIRECTLY AGGRESSIVE?

Why should men be more directly aggressive and violent than women? This question once again raises the issue of *levels of analysis*, discussed earlier. Different researchers will have different ways of interpreting the "why" in "why are men more directly aggressive?" For example, neuroscientists and biopsychologists may interpret this question as "Which sex differences in hormones, brain structures, brain chemistry, and body build are responsible for the sex differences in aggression?" An answer rooted in hormones, brains, and bodies is an answer which addresses the most immediate or *proximate* mechanisms which cause the differences in aggression. In a sense, answers rooted in proximate mechanisms tell the "how" side of the story, explaining *how* sex differences in aggression are triggered and play out.

However, other researchers are interested in those factors which might have caused men and women to differ in their hormones, brains, and bodies in the first place—the *ultimate* causes of the sex difference in aggression (Archer, 2009). Such answers are rooted in the evolutionary history of human males and females and they tell the "why" side of the story. It is important to realize that ultimate and proximate explanations do not contradict one another. Instead, they are both needed to fully understand important questions such as the origin of sex differences in aggression (Alcock, 2009; Scott-Phillips, Dickens, & West, 2011).

Is Testosterone Responsible? One of the most frequently suggested immediate, direct (proximate) causes of the sex difference in aggression is the sex difference in levels of the steroid (sex) hormone *testosterone* (Book, Starzyk, & Quinsey, 2001). Men secrete, on average, 8 to 10 times the amount of testosterone produced by women, the exact amount primarily being dependent upon genetic factors (Dabbs, 2000; Harris, 1999). Some researchers hypothesize that testosterone assists men in accomplishing those things necessary to attract a mate (e.g., charm, resourcefulness, bravery, sexuality, dominance over other men), but simultaneously hinders those qualities necessary for parenting and long-term bonds by increasing restlessness, interest in multiple sex partners, competitiveness, anger, and aggression (Storey, Walsh, Quinton, & Wynn-Edwards, 2000).

Of all the "crimes" attributed to testosterone, aggression is clearly the worst. But does testosterone actually increase aggression in men? The bulk of the research does suggest that some sort of link between testosterone and aggression exists (Archer, 2004, 2006; van Bokhoven et al., 2006). However, the nature of this link is not straightforward. For example, there is no increase in aggression in boys at the onset of puberty when testosterone levels sharply rise; in fact, there may be a decrease in aggression (Archer, 2004, 2006; van Bokhoven et al., 2006). Moreover, injecting volunteers with doses of testosterone does not increase their aggression (O'Connor, Archer, & Wu, 2004). And yet, the connection between aggression and testosterone in nonhuman animals is well established. Moreover, when studies of humans are considered together, the majority of them do find at least some sort of link—particularly in men—even if this link is inconsistent and difficult to predict.

The Challenge Hypothesis John Archer (2004, 2006), who has carefully examined the available research as well as conducting his own studies, has advanced a hypothesis regarding the connection between testosterone and aggression in humans that would account for the inconsistency in findings. Archer's idea, known as the *challenge hypothesis*, is based on research on aggression and testosterone in birds. Simply stated, the hypothesis holds that the association between testosterone and aggression in men is highly dependent on age and context.

For example, the initial rise in testosterone at puberty is associated with increased interest in sexuality and mating, not aggression. However, beginning in later adolescence and early adulthood, increases in testosterone levels are associated with contests and challenges of various sorts. Levels of testosterone rise in young men when they win contests and competitions and drop when they lose; these changes are not found in women (Bateup, Booth, Shirtcliff, Granger et al. 2002; Mazur & Booth, 1998; Schultheiss et al., 2005). Testosterone even rises and drops in male spectators watching sports competitions as their team wins or loses, and, as Figure 10.6 shows, it drops in male voters when their candidate loses (Bernhardt, Dabbs, Fielden, & Lutter, 1998; Stanton, Beehner, Saini, Kuhn, & LaBar, 2009)!

In the animal world, contests and challenges among males are frequently experienced in the context of mate competition, and they usually involve aggression. Thus, testosterone becomes associated with aggression in men when they move into later adolescence and adulthood, a time of establishing serious mating relationships. However, rather than "causing" aggression, testosterone may simply facilitate it—that is, rising in response to aggression or situations calling for aggression (Sapolsky, 1997).

Although the challenge hypothesis does *fit* the available research on testosterone and aggression in men fairly well—and there is much evidence in its favor in nonhuman species, particularly birds—the hypothesis has not specifically been *tested* in humans using adequate experimental designs. Before the hypothesis is accepted, such studies will need to be conducted.

Aggression Is Triggered by Specific Factors

Psychologists have been attempting to isolate the psychological causes of aggression ever since the time of Freud. An important early theory, known as the *frustration-aggression hypothesis* (Dollard, Doob, Miller, Mowrer, & Sears, 1939), stated that aggression occurs primarily (or even exclusively) when a person is frustrated in attaining an important goal. According to this idea,

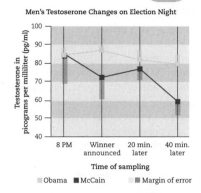

▲ **FIGURE 10.6 McCain Voters' Testosterone Levels Drop on Election Night.** Testosterone was measured in the saliva of samples of male and female voters on election night in the United States, November 4, 2008, when Barack Obama was elected over John McCain. In male voters supporting John McCain, a drop in testosterone was noted immediately upon announcement of President Obama's victory, and a more dramatic drop was noted 40 minutes later. No such effect was found for women. *(Source: Data from Stanton et al., 2009.)*

▶ **Testosterone Levels Change in Men According to Circumstances.** Testosterone levels are highest in young, unmarried men (*A*). They drop when the men marry and drop further when they become fathers (*B*). Testosterone levels also rise or fall in male sports fans, depending upon whether their team comes out on top or loses (*C*), and testosterone drops in men when they lose competitions (*D*).

Reformulated frustration-aggression hypothesis ▶ Leonard Berkowitz's revision of an earlier theory which stated that all aggression is in response to the frustration of a goal. According to the reformulated theory, frustration is only one of many types of unpleasant events that could lead to aggression. The theory holds that aggression occurs when an unpleasant event (e.g., provocation by another person, extreme noise) may trigger feelings, images, and memories associated with the physiological changes that ordinarily accompany threat and danger.

General aggression model (GAM) ▶ Craig Anderson and Brad Bushman's theory of aggression which holds that whether aggression does or does not occur in any interaction is dependent upon a complex interaction between four factors: personal characteristics; characteristics of the situation; emotions, thoughts, and biological arousal levels; and decision-making processes.

frustration leads to anger which leads to aggression. If you've ever studied a musical instrument, been repeatedly unable to master a passage, and felt ready to smash the instrument to the ground, you were providing support for the frustration-aggression hypothesis.

However, it soon became apparent to researchers that many acts of aggression are not preceded by frustration of a goal, and the theory was then revised by Leonard Berkowitz in 1989. According to this **reformulated frustration-aggression hypothesis**, anger and consequent aggression can arise from virtually any form of unpleasant event—including frustration but also including various forms of provocation by other people or even unpleasant environmental stimuli such as loud noises and extreme temperatures. According to the theory, aggression will occur when the unpleasant event triggers feelings, images, or memories associated with the physiological changes that normally occur during conditions of threat and danger, including increased heart rate and respiration.

Because Berkowitz's reformulated theory stresses the power of cognitive associations to produce anger and subsequent aggression, it is often referred to as the *cognitive neoassociation model* of aggression (Berkowitz, 1993). Although Berkowitz's theory was an advance over the original frustration-aggression hypothesis, it failed to explain instrumental aggression and other forms of aggression apparently not accompanied by strong emotions such as anger.

Other attempts to explain how aggression occurs have focused on how aggression may be *learned* through exposure to social models that promote aggression, such as violent media or aggressive individuals present in one's environment (Bandura, 1983; see also Chapter 7, this volume). Like the reformulated frustration-aggression hypothesis, however, this *social learning* model only provides part of the story and cannot account for all psychological aspects of aggression. If social learning were entirely responsible for aggression, all people exposed to aggressive models would themselves become aggressive, and this is clearly not the case.

Recognizing the many contributions of various theories of the psychological causes aggression—but also acknowledging their limitations—Craig Anderson has integrated various perspectives into a single model he hoped would offer a more powerful explanation (Anderson & Bushman, 2002; DeWall & Anderson, 2011). This model is known as the **general aggression model**, or

◀ **Freedom Fighters or Terrorists?** Victims of aggressive acts will generally consider the acts to be senseless or evil. However, those committing the acts may be motivated by deeply felt moral concerns.

GAM. According to this model, aggression will (or will not) occur in any given situation as a result of a complex interaction among four factors:

1. *Personal characteristics* (e.g., a person's traits, sex, beliefs, and attitudes).

2. *Characteristics of the specific situation* (e.g., provocation, incentives to aggression, frustration of a goal).

3. *Emotions, thoughts, and biological arousal levels* which result from the interaction of items 1 and 2.

4. *Decision-making processes* (how the person sizes up the situation and decides to act).

As an example, people who come to the table with already heightened levels of aggressive tendencies often have a cognitive bias toward interpreting other people's actions as having some sort of hostile motive, even when no such motive exists ("That @#$%! brushed up against me *on purpose!*"; Bushman & Anderson, 2002). This is a *personal characteristic* (#1 in the preceding list) that might be brought to a situation. Consider such a person on an extremely hot day in a bar with no air conditioning. He tries to make a call on his mobile phone, but cannot get a connection because he is unlucky enough to subscribe to a cell carrier with poor coverage in the area (#2 in the list, *characteristics of the specific situation*). Someone then accidentally brushes up against him as he is trying to get the phone to work. He is already physiologically aroused with frustration and feeling a fair amount of anger at the phone. He is also uncomfortable from the heat and has a bias toward interpreting ambiguous interactions as being hostile (#3 in the list, *emotions, thoughts, and arousal levels*). He then may decide to act impulsively and aggress against the offender by shoving him—or he may give thought and refrain from aggression (#4, *decision-making processes*).

Theories such as the reformulated frustration-aggression hypothesis or GAM were designed primarily to help explain aggression in the individual. But what about aggression committed against groups or entire nations? We will consider this question in Chapter 15.

Aggressors Believe They Are in the Right

One final observation needs to be made about aggression, whether committed against individuals or entire peoples: Aggressors almost always believe

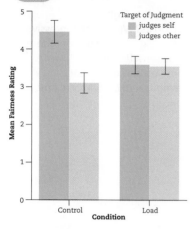

▲ FIGURE 10.7 Moral Hypocrites May Know "Deep Down" That They Are Wrong. When researchers manipulated participants into making self-serving, blatantly unfair decisions, most insisted nevertheless that they had been just. But when these same individuals observed others behaving in the same self-serving manner, they sharply condemned the others' actions as unfair. This "moral hypocrisy" is depicted in the graph on the left, labeled "control." Yet when a second group made evaluations of their own and others' behavior under conditions with a heavy "cognitive load" consisting of a distracting memory task, the moral hypocrisy was not evident, and people judged themselves as severely as they judged others. At some level, moral hypocrites might realize that they are wrong and engage in various cognitive strategies to avoid confronting the truth.

that they are in the right, and they do not apply the same moral judgments to themselves in regard to aggression and other destructive acts (such as betrayals) that they apply to others (Baumeister, 1997; Pinker, 2011; Tavris & Aronson, 2007). This human tendency to let oneself off the moral hook makes aggression a particularly dangerous motivated behavior. It means that aggression can be difficult to inhibit once it begins to build up steam.

The notion that certain people—like over-the-top villains in movie thrillers—are simply evil, know they are evil, and commit aggressive and other destructive acts with full knowledge that they are morally wrong is likely misguided (Baumeister, 1997; Trivers, 2010, 2011; Valdesolo & DeSteno, 2008). As Steven Pinker (2011) points out, many of the greatest villains of history—not to mention perpetrators of ordinary day-to-day violence and aggression—are "deeply moral" in the sense that they believe what they are doing in some way rights previous wrongs done to them or to their loved ones, their nation, their neighborhood, their religion, or to mankind in general. In other words, aggressive and violent people may *truly* believe—at least consciously—that their actions are just; they are not merely hypocritically claiming justification, all the while knowing that they are really in the wrong (Pinker, 2011).

Consider the differences in perspective between members of two sides in a violent conflict, each of whom may use similar tactics, but each of whom claims that the other side is composed of "terrorists" whereas their own side is composed of "freedom fighters." Steven Pinker (2011) fleshes this idea out by describing two ways each for viewing a series of well-known armed conflicts. For example, take the Crusades and the American Civil War:

- The Crusades were an explosion of religious idealism that may have had a few excesses, but left the world better off for its promotion of cultural exchange.

or:

- The Crusades were yet another vicious attack on Jewish communities and a brutal invasion of Muslim lands and subjugation of Muslims by Christian extremists.

- The American Civil War was unfortunate but necessary to rid the nation of the evil institution of slavery.

or:

- The American Civil War was a self-serving "power grab" of a bloated centralized Northern government intent on destroying the way of life of Southern states.

Yet, some researchers have suggested that despite aggressors' conscious certainty that they are on the moral high road, there may be a lower level of consciousness at which they may be aware of their own hypocrisy (Trivers, 2011; Valdesolo & DeSteno, 2008). For example, Piercarlo Valdesolo and David DeSteno had research participants help plan a study in which half of the group would get a simple task involving a brief survey and viewing of photographs, while the other half would engage in a grueling 45 minutes of solving logic and math problems. When given the opportunity to assign themselves to one task or the other, participants were highly inclined to assign themselves to the easy task. This may not be particularly unexpected, but when questioned in detail about the fairness of the procedures they used, those who assigned themselves to the easy task were adamant that their procedures had been fair (Valdesolo & DeSteno, 2008). Of course, those receiving the short end of the stick disagreed!

Yet, when these participants, who had been so kind in their own self-evaluations, were asked to evaluate the behavior of *others*, what do you suppose happened? When these others were described as having chosen the easy road for themselves, they were condemned in harsh terms. Obviously, participants in this research had different standards for judging their own actions as compared with that of other people.

However, Valdesolo and DeSteno wanted to discover whether these "moral hypocrites," who seemed oblivious to the blatant unfairness of their procedures, really did understand at some level that they had been in the wrong. Therefore, they repeated the entire study with a second group of participants who, following their self-serving assignments of themselves to the easier task (or observing other participants doing the same) were asked to evaluate their procedures and those of others, as the first group had done. However, these participants were asked to make their evaluations under conditions of heavy "cognitive load"—a distracting task requiring them to keep seven digits in memory while answering questions about the experience flashed on a computer.

As Figure 10.7 shows, the result was that participants who had assigned themselves to the easy task evaluated their own behavior equally harshly to that of others who also had chosen the easy task. Keeping these digits in memory had the effect of "tying up" cognitive resources they would otherwise have been able to apply to convincing themselves and everyone else they had been justified. The moral "blinders" had been removed, suggesting that those who behave in an aggressive or hurtful manner and seem to believe in the rightness of their actions may have a hidden level of self-awareness that might somehow be reachable. As Steven Pinker states: "It may take ridicule, it may take argument, it may take time, it may take being distracted, but people have the means to recognize that they are not always in the right" (2011, p. 492). This may be encouraging news.

IN SUMMARY

1.	*Aggression* is the general term used when an individual carries out an act intended to harm another. To constitute aggression, the perpetrator must believe the act is harmful, and the victim must be motivated to avoid the act.
2.	Aggression may be violent or nonviolent. It may be hostile or instrumental.
3.	There are sex differences in aggression, with boys and men being more likely than girls and women to show direct aggression. However, girls and women may show more indirect aggression than men.
4.	The general aggression model (GAM) proposes that aggression is a result of a complex interaction among a person's characteristics; characteristics of the situation; emotions, thoughts, and biological arousal levels; and decision-making processes.
5.	Those who commit violent aggression generally believe that they are in the right on a conscious level, but many may know they are in the wrong at an unconscious level.

RETRIEVE!

1.	Aggression which primarily serves an ultimate purpose other than harming the victim is termed _____ aggression. Aggression that has no purpose other than harming the victim is termed _____ aggression.
2.	The theory which states that virtually any unpleasant event can lead to aggression—including frustration, provocation from others, or noxious environmental stimuli—is known as the _____ theory of aggression.

3. Explain the four factors that make up the general aggression model (GAM). What is the advantage of the GAM over previous models of the psychological causes of aggression?

4. True or false: It has been demonstrated conclusively that testosterone is a major cause of the sex difference in aggression.

Competence: Why Do People Seek to Do Well?

Darby is 13 years old. It is 3:30, school is over for the day, and Darby's friends are going to the mall. She'd like to go with them, but there's something she wants more than that: She wants to play college basketball 5 years down the line. So she's out on the court, practicing driving and faking.

At that moment, her 9-month-old brother, Murphy, is putting all his concentration and effort into trying to remain upright without having to hold on to the leg of the black leather easy chair in the living room. He's been struggling with this task for almost 25 minutes.

Darby's mother is at Starbucks instead of her office at this moment because she knows that her boss is on the floor looking for her to ask her to prepare a report. Normally, preparing a report would not be a problem, but in this particular case she fears she will not be able to finish the report in the time she will be allotted, even though someone in her position should be expected to be able to do so. She is hoping someone else will be chosen for the task.

As Darby's mother sips her drink, her husband is standing in their kitchen. He has finally gathered up the courage to call the manager of the local Little League team and beg off coaching this year. He can see that it's going to cut too deeply into his time parenting Murphy. He had not "been there" for Darby when she was an infant, and he had promised himself things would be different with Murphy.

There is a thread running through all of the activities of Darby and her family, and that is **competence motivation** (Deci & Ryan, 2000; Elliot & Dweck, 2005; White, 1959). Competence means *effectiveness*—the ability to perform some action or task successfully. A number of theorists, beginning with Robert White in 1959, have hypothesized an innate human need for competence—one that begins at birth and doesn't end until death. According to these researchers, the competence motivation guides a great deal of our behavior throughout the day, and strongly affects our emotional life; it also exists across cultures, although it may be experienced and expressed somewhat differently from one culture to the next (Chang, Wong, & Teo, 2000; Elliot & Dweck, 2005).

Competence motivation
▶ The need to be effective in one's life—to be able to perform some action or task successfully.

Approach and Avoidance Are Two Strategies for Competence

According to Andrew Elliot and Carol Dweck (2005), competence motivation may be expressed in either of two ways. First, we may seek out—or *approach*—possibilities to increase or demonstrate competence. This is the case both for Darby in her basketball practice and her baby brother Murphy in his attempts to stand upright. But, secondly, we also attempt to *avoid* negative possibilities associated with incompetence and failure. Darby's mother and father are choosing this avoidance strategy. The distinction between motivations to seek positive experiences and motivations and to avoid negative ones is called the

▲ Competence Motivation Includes Achievement Motivation. If you are practicing martial arts forms in a garden primarily to perfect your technique, you are tapping competence motivation. If you are performing a martial arts form in a tournament to win a competition, you are tapping achievement motivation.

approach-avoidance distinction. Having your child skip a grade at school is an application of approach strategy for competence; enrolling a child in kindergarten a year late to increase her competitive edge is avoidance strategy.

However, differences have been noted in a person's emotional responses depending upon whether an experience has resulted from approach or avoidance. Logically, we might feel either positively or negatively about either type of situation. For example, pride and joyful feelings typically occur when we seek competence and attain it (*approach/positive feeling*). Darby's little brother feels this when he finally manages to stand up with no help. On the other hand, *relief*—also a positive feeling—may occur when we avoid an impossible situation that would undoubtedly have resulted in failure (*avoidance/positive feeling*). Darby's father experiences this sort of relief when he withdraws his offer to coach Little League, avoiding feelings of failure as a father.

Both approach and avoidance can also have negative emotional consequences. We feel a sense of sadness and disappointment when we attempt something but fail (*approach/negative feeling*). Darby feels this way every time she tries to shoot from the dribble, because she usually misses. On the other hand, we feel a sense of shame and upset when we avoid trying something that might have worked out had we given it our best shot (*avoidance/ negative feeling*). This was Darby's mother's reaction on her way home from work as she reflected on her on-the-job behavior and labeled it "cowardice."

Approach-avoidance ▶
The distinction between motivations to seek positive experiences and motivations to avoid negative experiences.

Achievement Is a Part of Competence Motivation

A number of motivations have been proposed over the years that represent specific aspects of competence motivation. The most important of these is **achievement motivation** (McClelland, Atkinson, Clark, & Lowell, 1953; Murray, 1938). Indeed, there has been a great deal more research and writing on achievement motivation than on competence motivation itself. This is probably because achievement—which measures a person's attainments and accomplishments primarily in relation to those of others—is a particularly important aspect of competence in Western societies, where most psychology research originates (Elliot & Dweck, 2005; Markus & Kitayama, 1998; Murray, 1938). Thus, when a person desires to increase her gardening skills to grow a tastier tomato, or her conversational ability so she will feel more socially at ease, she is expressing competence motivation, but not necessarily achievement motivation (Elliot & Dweck, 2005). On the other hand, if she plans to enter her tomatoes at the State Fair, or try out for her college debating

Achievement motivation
▶ An aspect of competence motivation which describes the motivation to attain and to accomplish. A person generally measures his or her attainments and accomplishments in relation to those of others, so the achievement motivation involves comparing oneself to others.

team, she may be expressing achievement motivation as well as competence motivation.

Individuals differ strongly in their achievement motivation. Those high in achievement motivation have high levels of self-control and are able to delay gratification. They tend to succeed in business enterprises, hold elected offices, and be leaders in organizations (Woike & McAdams, 2001). The greatest innovator in the history of modern dance, Martha Graham, declared that it took 10 years of hard work and delayed gratification to master any complex art or craft. Those who do so are very high in achievement motivation.

However, those with high achievement needs also seem to know better than to bite off more than they can chew. They tend to set goals that are realistic rather than overly lofty, thus reducing the chances of failure. Yet, they are also less fearful of failure than others (Elliot & Church, 1997; McClelland & Koestner, 1992). High achievers also tend to explain their successes in terms of *internal* rather than *external* factors, meaning that they take credit for their accomplishments rather than attributing them to luck or to the intervention of others (Weiner, 1989).

There may be cultural differences in achievement motivation, particularly as regards the way that *failure* and *success* are interpreted. Steven Heine and his colleagues compared the way a sample of North Americans and Japanese dealt with failure and success on tasks presented to them by researchers (Heine et al., 2001). The Japanese used failure as a kind of feedback for self-improvement, and if they failed they subsequently *increased* their efforts to succeed. In contrast, the North Americans tended to increase their efforts at tasks for which they had already shown some success, while *decreasing* their efforts subsequent to failure. This suggests that, in comparison with Japanese, North Americans interpret failure either as a threat to feelings of competence or as information suggesting that one ought to cut their losses and move on to a different endeavor.

IN SUMMARY

1.	Competence is an innate motivation to perform a task successfully.
2.	One may express competence needs through either approach or avoidance behaviors. Approach behaviors can result in joy at success or disappointment and sadness at failure. Avoidant behaviors can result in relief or in shame and distress.
3.	Achievement motivation is part of competence motivation. It is the motive to accomplish and excel, particularly in relation to others.

RETRIEVE!

1.	Give examples other than those from the textbook of how avoidance and approach strategies can produce either positive or negative emotional experiences.
2.	How does achievement motivation differ from competence motivation?
3.	True or False: The detrimental consequences of avoidance strategies may not always apply to individuals from collectivist cultures.

Looking Back

Chapter 10 in Review

WHAT ARE MOTIVATIONS?

- Motivations are mental states that cause people to engage in behavior that is purposive—that is, it has a purpose, causes rooted in specific mental states, and intentionality. Highly motivated behavior is intense and persistent. Motivations are varied and may sometimes conflict.
- Instincts are innate, automatic behavioral tendencies that occur in response to an environmental cue. Labeling a motivation *instinct* has been seen as merely a way of describing the motivation, not explaining it. However, evolutionary psychologists have used the Darwinian notion of adaptation to explain instinct-like motivations and behavior.
- Motivations include drives and incentives. Early drive theorists proposed that behavior is primarily motivated by the desire to reduce unpleasant conditions. Drive-reduction theory proposes that organisms seek to maintain homeostasis, while optimal arousal theory is concerned with achieving an optimal level of arousal. Humans are also motivated by incentives, which may be intrinsic or extrinsic.
- Motivations include needs—internal states of tension that motivate a person toward some action. Abraham Maslow proposed that human motivations form a hierarchy comprising five categories of need. At the bottom of Maslow's pyramid are basic survival needs; at the top are self-actualization needs. In between these extremes are needs including safety and security, love, belonging, prestige, and achievement. Douglas Kenrick and colleagues proposed a model in which needs form an overlapping pyramid based upon three levels of analysis: evolutionary, developmental, and cognitive.

HOW IS WORK A WINDOW ONTO MOTIVATION?

- Many factors influence work motivation, including traits, perceived self-efficacy, and goal setting. Positive psychologists advise choosing a career that reflects one's signature strengths. The term *flow* is used to describe experiences of effortless, timeless focus on a desired activity.
- Some motivations are universal or nearly universal; however, they take different behavioral forms and are interpreted differently in different cultures and historical periods.

WHY DO WE EAT?

- Hunger and appetite are not the same. Hunger is a physiologically based, homeostatic drive state intended to satisfy needs for energy and nutrition. Appetite is the desire to eat, and it can be driven by many types of events and motivations.
- People tend to maintain a baseline body weight, but they also tend to gain weight as they age. Eating disorders (EDs), which are characterized by unhealthful patterns of eating or not eating, have become more common over the past 60 years. The most frequently diagnosed of the medically recognized EDs is binge eating disorder. Risk factors for EDs include being young and female, having a family history of EDs, and possible psychological factors such as negative mood states and self-evaluations or perfectionism. Some researchers suggest that the culture of modernization has been a contributor to the global spread of EDs. It is possible, but rare, for a person to die from complications of an eating disorder.
- Today's epidemic of overweight and obesity cannot be fully explained by genetics. Some research suggests that overweight and obesity may be responses to societal changes in diet and daily activity.

THE SOCIAL MOTIVATIONS: WHY DO WE TURN TOWARD ONE ANOTHER?

- Human beings are motivated to turn toward one another, a general tendency known as social motivation. The principal social needs are the need to affiliate and the need to belong. Affiliation means being with others in the same space, not necessarily in strong relationships. Belonging needs are met by frequent positive interactions in the context of stable, enduring relationships of caring. Loneliness results from lack of belonging; it involves a discrepancy between our perception of the interpersonal relationships we have and those we wish to have. Relationships of belonging usually include intimacy, which is achieved through self-disclosure and partner responsiveness.

AGGRESSION: WHY DO WE TURN AGAINST ONE ANOTHER?

- Human aggression occurs when an individual or group carries out an act intended to harm another in which the aggressor believes that the act is harmful, and the target of aggression is motivated to avoid the act. Aggression may or may not be violent, and it may be hostile or instrumental. Physical aggression is much more characteristic of boys and men, but there are few or no sex differences in verbal aggression and indirect aggression. The question of why men are more physically aggressive may be answered in different ways depending on the level of analysis.
- Specific factors may trigger acts of aggression. An important early theory suggested that aggression occurs when a person is frustrated in attaining an important goal, but the reformulated frustration-aggression hypothesis suggested that virtually any form of unpleasant event could lead to aggression. The general aggression model (GAM) proposes that aggression will (or will not) occur in any given situation as a result of an interaction among four factors: personal characteristics; characteristics of the situation; emotions, thoughts, and arousal levels; and the decision-making process.

COMPETENCE: WHY DO PEOPLE SEEK TO DO WELL?

- Competence motivation is the need to perform actions effectively or

Looking Back continued

successfully. Approach and avoidance are two strategies to achieve competence in a given task or situation. Achievement motivation, a component of the competence motivation, refers to aspiring to attainments and accomplishments primarily in relation to those of other people. Individuals high in achievement motivation have high levels of self-control, are able to delay gratification, and set realistic goals.

Key Terms

Achievement motivation, 505
Ambivalence, 468
Anorexia nervosa, 484
Appetite, 483
Approach-avoidance, 505
Baseline body weight, 483
Bulimia nervosa, 484
Competence motivation, 504
Culture of modernization, 486
Drive, 470
Drive theory, 470
Eating disorder, 484
Energy balance, 483
Extrinsic motivation, 471
Flow, 481

General aggression model (GAM), 500
Goal-setting theory, 478
Homeostasis, 470
Hostile aggression, 497
Human aggression, 495
Hunger, 482
Incentives, 471
Industrial and organizational psychology (I/O psychology), 477
Instinct, 468
Instrumental aggression, 497
Intimacy, 494
Intrinsic motivation, 491
Loneliness, 493
Metabolic rate, 483

Motivation, 467
Need, 473
Need to affiliate, 491
Need to belong, 491
Obese, 487
Optimal arousal theory, 471
Perceived self-efficacy, 478
Reformulated frustration-aggression hypothesis, 500
Social motivation, 491
Strengths, 479
Traits, 477
Work motivation, 477

Test Yourself

1. Which of the following is NOT a characteristic of a highly motivated activity?
   a) intensity
   b) intentionality
   c) persistence
   d) time-limitation
   e) purpose
2. William James proposed that most human behavior was motivated by _____.
3. Desires to reduce unpleasant states of arousal which have resulted from physiological needs are known as:
   a) drives
   b) needs
   c) incentives
   d) homeostasis
4. The idea that human motivations form a hierarchy based on the urgency of the motivating need was first proposed by humanistic psychologist _____.
5. Distinguish intrinsic from extrinsic motivations.

6. Core beliefs about one's ability to produce change or accomplish a specific task through own effort are known as:
   a) perceived efficiency
   b) perceived effectiveness
   c) perceived self-competence
   d) perceived self-efficacy
7. Distinguish *hunger* from *appetite*. Describe a situation where appetite might be increased in the absence of hunger.
8. True or false: Some evidence suggests that those perpetrating aggressive violence may at a deep level understand that they are in the wrong.
9. Name at least two symptoms of anorexia nervosa and two symptoms of bulimia nervosa.
10. How does the need to affiliate differ from the need to belong? What are the two defining criteria for satisfying the need to belong?
11. According to positive psychologists, the single most important

determinant of human happiness, life satisfaction, and well-being is:
   a) safety and personal security
   b) close personal relationships
   c) health
   d) financial security
12. Why is it that loneliness may not necessarily result from any particular event, such as being separated from a loved one or losing an important relationship?
13. Interpersonal relationships—or moments within relationships—characterized by warmth, closeness, and mutual support and communication are said to contain _____.
14. Human aggression is the general term used when a person carries out an act intended to harm another. However, there are two important qualifiers to this definition. What are they?
15. How does "aggression" differ from "violence"?

Test Yourself continued

16. Aggression with an ultimate purpose other than harming the victim is known as _____ aggression.

17. Which form of aggression is more typical of girls and women than of boys and men?

18. Which of the following is NOT among the four factors which must interact for aggression to occur, according to the general aggression model (GAM)?
    a) personal characteristics
    b) frustration of a goal
    c) characteristics of the situation
    d) decision-making processes

19. What is the difference between the competition motivation and the achievement motivation?

20. The motivation to seek positive experiences is known as _____. The motivation to avoid negative experiences is known as _____.

CHAPTER

11

emotion
and Health

Chapter Outline

FREEZE FRAME

Decades ago, when I lived in on the Upper West Side of New York City, my neighbor and friend Miguel was separated from his wife, Adriana, whom he desperately loved. Unfortunately, Miguel had a very serious drinking problem, and Adriana had left him 4 months earlier, taking their infant son with her. When Miguel learned through the grapevine that his estranged wife now had a boyfriend, he was overcome with rage and grief. Late one night, he dressed in black from head to toe, like a ninja. He painted Adriana's name across his wall in blood-red paint and, shrouded by night shadows, stole up to her boyfriend's apartment house. He leaped to the fire escape and climbed to the third floor.

With repetitive images of his wife and her lover blotting out all other thoughts, and brandishing a short sword, Miguel broke through the second-story window and jumped on the bed in a violent frame of mind. Fortunately for everyone, the couple was out for the evening, and it was Adriana's German shepherd who lay asleep on the bed. The dog easily repelled the attack. Nonetheless, Miguel, bitten firmly on the leg and arm, left numerous clues to his identity behind. Adriana immediately grabbed her son and disappeared. Miguel searched for her, but she had covered her tracks.

This event was a turning point in Miguel's life. He began going to meetings of Alcoholics Anonymous and stopped drinking. Over the course of a year he grew profoundly regretful of his actions, and felt as though he had been a victim of his own emotions and the thoughts and behaviors that accompanied them. He renewed his attempts to contact Adriana to apologize and ask for permission to see their son, who by then was 2½ years old. Word finally got back to Adriana that Miguel was not only genuinely remorseful, but had also been sober for some time.

One day, Miguel received a phone call. It was Adriana. She had decided to allow him to meet with her in a public park so that he might spend an hour with their son. Because things went relatively well during the visit, and the boy was delighted to be with his father, Adriana told Miguel that he could see his son in this manner every 2 weeks for an hour. But as time went on, 1 hour led to 2, which soon led to Adriana allowing Miguel to take the boy overnight . . . which soon led to weekends. Within 5 months, the former husband and wife were talking on the phone frequently, Adriana asking Miguel for fatherly advice about the boy. One year after the first meeting in the park, Adriana asked Miguel to come to live with her once again. However, by this time, Miguel was a changed person and had fallen in love with another woman. He was no longer interested in Adriana.

Like motivations, which we discussed in Chapter 10, emotions are evolutionary gifts (Izard, 2007, 2009; Panskepp, 2007a, 2007b; Toronchuk & Ellis, 2007). They are, in part, the *feeling* aspect of motivation. They provide us with information that the goals we are motivated to achieve are being either thwarted or advanced (Lazarus, 1991b; Lyubomirsky & Boehm, 2010), or that our present courses of action are producing positive or negative results. Positive emotions provide feedback that all is going well—we feel happy when we get a phone call from someone with whom we are infatuated. Negative emotions signal that something has gone wrong—we feel sad (or fearful) if we lose a job that has been paying our rent (Nesse, 1991). Emotional feedback alters our course of action (Baumeister, Vohs, DeWall, & Zhang, 2007).

But, as Miguel's story suggests, emotions can also miscarry, and to some extent they are mysterious. How can a person experience an emotion so strong that he is willing to kill or die for it, and a scant 18 months later be utterly indifferent to the person who had triggered that emotion, and with whom he had fathered a child? In this chapter we will first explore such mysteries and then consider connections between the emotions we experience, stress, and our physical health.

What Is Emotion?

My friend Miguel felt in the powerful grip of his emotions—a grip that blinded him to the consequences of his actions. Although it is unlikely that you have scaled the walls of a New York City brownstone to enact a turbulent melodrama as did Miguel, it is highly likely that you have at some time allowed your emotions to "get the better" of you and thrust you toward some decision or action you later regretted. (I certainly do so with astonishing regularity.)

The view of *emotion* as a kind of human flaw—an obstacle to intelligent action—has a long history in philosophy going back to the ancient Greeks, and for much of the 20th century psychologists tended also to adhere to this notion (Evans, 2001). It is not difficult to see why: All they had to do was look at their own lives. But would a person *without* emotion really behave more intelligently and live a more successful life? What are emotions, anyway? If they are more hindrance than help, why do we have them in the first place?

How Are Your Feelings?

New York City disc jockey and jazz historian Phil Schapp begins his daily early-morning program devoted to the music of saxophonist Charlie Parker in exactly the same way: "This is Phil Schapp—how are your feelings?" From a psychological science perspective you could answer this question in any or all of three ways: You could report your *emotion, mood,* or *affect*. Before we tackle the question of why we have emotions and what they do for us, we need to differentiate these terms.

Like most important questions in psychology, there is disagreement about specifics of definitions of the term *emotion*, and no definition has gained wide acceptance (Izard, 2009). However, most behavioral scientists agree in a general way when it comes to certain basic facts about the characteristics of emotion: An **emotion** is a psychological state consisting of five essential components:

1. *Neural systems* dedicated to processing or producing emotion.
2. *A subjective experience* or *feeling*.
3. *Physiological changes*.
4. *Cognitive changes* associated with the emotion.
5. *Behavioral responses* which express the emotion. (Izard, 2007, 2009; Panskepp, 2007b)

As an example, *fear* is characterized by:

1. Neural pathways from the thalamus and cerebral cortex to the amygdala, insula, and other brain regions.
2. A distinct subjective feeling of alarm and the presence of danger.
3. An increase in activity of the sympathetic nervous system.
4. Fear-related changes in thinking.
5. Any number of behavioral responses, such as the appearance of characteristic facial expressions, changes in tone of voice, actions, or postures designed to protect the body from harm, and so forth.

Emotions are relatively intense but short-lived experiences. Consider *anger*. You may recall being angry with someone "for days," but if you think more carefully about it, you'll probably note that you slipped in and out of a genuinely angry state, perhaps reigniting angry feelings periodically with thoughts about the offender or the triggering event. Thus, emotions can be distinguished from **moods**, which are typically less intense states, but which

Emotion ▶ A psychological state consisting of subjective experience or feeling, physiological changes, and behavioral responses. Emotions tend to be intense, attributable to a potentially identifiable cause, and relatively short-lived.

Mood ▶ A feeling state that is typically less intense than an emotion, but which may last for a much longer time. Moods may or may not be attributable to specific causes.

▶**FIGURE 11.1 The Two Dimensions of Affect.** Affect exists along two dimensions which interact: valence (negative-positive) and activation (low-high). For example, two equally pleasant states— *exhilarated* and *peaceful*—differ markedly in their levels of activation. Exhilaration is associated with an excited, high-activated state, whereas peacefulness is associated with calm and low levels of activation. Similarly, lethargy and fear are both unpleasant, but lethargy is low in activation and fear high in activation. *(Source: Adapted from Russell, 2003, p. 148.)*

Affect ▶ A general feeling state which provides the "raw material" from which emotions and moods are created. Affect differs along two dimensions: valence (positive-negative) and activation or arousal (high-low).

may pervade a person's life for days, weeks, months, or possibly even years at a time. A person may be *depressed* (mood) more or less continuously on an ongoing basis, but he or she is not likely to remain in a state of acute *sadness* (emotion) 24 hours per day for very long. Moods and emotions differ in one other respect. The origin of a particular mood is often difficult to trace to specific events, and it might be hard to pinpoint the reasons underlying its presence. Emotions are more likely to have identifiable causes (Lazarus, 1991a, 1991b; Morris, 1999).

Affect describes the general quality of your feelings. Affect does not refer to any specific emotion or mood, and it does not differentiate between moods and emotions in general. Instead, it is the raw material from which emotions and moods are created (J. A. Russell, 2003). For example, there are many ways of feeling "good" in affect. You could be joyous, serene, peaceful, buoyant, content, excited, and so forth—all specific emotions or moods.

As depicted in Figure 11.1, affect differs along two dimensions. The first is *valence*, the positive-negative dimension of affect. Positive affect is experienced under conditions that are pleasant, helpful, or rewarding. Negative affect is experienced under conditions that are unpleasant, hurtful, or threatening (Barett, Mesquita, Ochsner, & Gross, 2007).

As Figure 11.1 depicts, affect also differs by *level of activation*, or strength of arousal. Affect can be highly activated (in either good or bad ways) or low in activation (also in good or bad ways; Feldman, 1995; J. A. Russell, 2003). Understanding the way affect differs from emotion or mood is important to understanding some of the ongoing debates about emotion we will attend to later.

Unpleasant Emotions Outnumber Pleasant Ones

Although most of us prefer to experience pleasant emotions, unfortunately, the number of possible unpleasant emotional states greatly outnumbers the number of pleasant ones. This unappealing fact is reflected in the statistic that in most languages there are at least twice as many words to describe negative as positive emotions. As depicted in Figure 11.2, the ratio is even greater if we consider only the emotions *fear, anger, joy/happiness, disgust, interest/*

Anger   Sadness   Happiness   Fear

Disgust   Surprise   Contempt

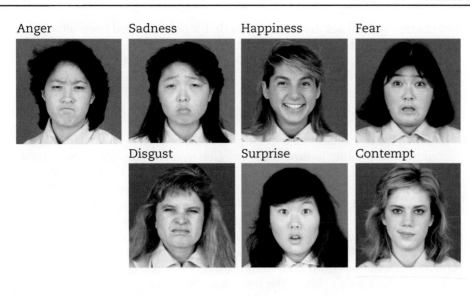

◄FIGURE 11.2 **Negative Basic Emotions Outnumber Positive Emotions.** Depicted here are expressions of seven of the most commonly identified basic emotions. Of these, only one is unequivocally positive. *(Source: Original material from David Matsumoto; figure from Levay & Valente, 2002, p. 172.)*

surprise, contempt, and *sadness.* These are often termed *basic emotions,* in part because they are universal and thought to form the basis for other emotions when they are blended—much like the primary colors form the basis for other colors when they are blended (Ekman & Cordaro, 2011; Izard, 2007; Schrauf & Sanchez, 2004; see pp. 518–520 for a complete discussion of basic emotions). When we consider how prevalent unpleasant emotions are, it is clear that the notion frequently advanced on talk shows and in self-help books that emotional pain is somehow "not normal" (and therefore needs to be treated) is not well grounded in human history and experience (Horwitz & Wakefield, 2007; Nesse & Williams, 1994).

Why do we experience so many different negative emotions in comparison to positive ones? There is no definitive answer to this question. However, if we consider that our emotions, like our motivations, are the products of human evolutionary history, it may be that the consequences of ignoring potentially harmful situations (e.g., danger and death, loss of mate or family) were greater on average during most of our evolutionary history than were the consequences of ignoring potentially helpful ones (e.g., the chance to form a beneficial love relationship or friendship; Baumeister, Bratslavsky, Finkenauer, & Vohs, 2001; Nesse & Williams, 1994). Harmful situations may have commanded our attention to a greater degree than situations that were benign or helpful, and caused us to evolve more subtle distinctions in our feelings about negative events (Baumeister et al., 2001; Schrauf & Sanchez, 2004). This would have resulted in more varied types of negative emotions and the words to describe them. Some research also suggests that people have a tendency to assume that someone is expressing a negative emotion when the person's facial expression might be interpreted as either positive or negative—as in the emotion of surprise (Neta & Whalen, 2010).

This theory explains two other facts: People try harder and have more varied techniques to escape bad moods than they have to induce good moods; and they remember experiences of bad emotions better than they recall experiences of good emotions. As one group of researchers put it, "bad is stronger than good" (Baumeister et al., 2001, p. 323).

Emotions Serve Important Functions

As these ideas suggest, emotions, like motivations, were likely to have fulfilled numerous functions over human evolutionary history. These functions might have included enabling communication and social interaction with friends, family, potential mating partners, co-workers, and strangers; motivating people to avoid harmful situations or relationships and seek out beneficial ones;

and providing feedback on behavior so that a person could have altered his or her course of action if it had proved counterproductive (Baumeister et al., 2007; Ekman, 2003a; Izard, 2009; Nesse, 1990). While there is little doubt that emotions can deceive us and lead us into ill-chosen actions, it is equally clear that their benefits greatly outweigh their risks, and if they really hindered intelligent action they would have disappeared long ago (Baumeister et al., 2007; Evans, 2001).

Research has demonstrated that rational decision-making is disastrously disrupted when the ability to experience emotion is lost. Antonio Damasio (1994) describes a person known as "Elliot." Elliot suffered damage to a circuit between the prefrontal cortex and the amygdala (a brain structure associated with emotional life—see Chapter 2). Following the damage, Elliot continued to score in the normal or above-normal range on intelligence tests. However, his emotional experience was blocked. Rather than increasing the rationality of his decision-making processes, however, his condition utterly disrupted his ability to make intelligent decisions—from what would be a good menu choice when dining out to which restaurant to visit in the first place. He could not make decisions as simple as whether to use a pen with black or blue ink. Why? Because he had no particular *emotional* preference for any of the many options available to him in any given situation. He could not fathom the connection that exists between bad feelings and bad choices. Consequently, he soon lost his job, his wife, and his ability to earn a living. Elliot's lack of emotional response extended to the disastrous consequences of his injury, which he seemed to accept with icy calm. Elliot's case suggests that emotion and reasoning processes must be balanced to produce intelligent and productive action. Without emotion, we cannot truly learn from our mistakes because these mistakes would not produce punishing consequences (Bechara, Damasio, Tranel, & Damasio, 1997; Loewenstein, Weber, Hsee, & Welch, 2001).

The ability to identify, manage, and express one's emotions constructively and to empathize with the emotions of others has been termed **emotional intelligence** by the writer Daniel Goleman (Goleman, 1995; Mayer, Salovey, & Caruso, 2004). As Goleman puts it, emotional intelligence is a set of abilities "such as being able to motivate oneself and persist in the face of frustrations; to control impulse and delay gratification; to regulate one's moods and keep distress from swamping the ability to think; to empathize and to hope" (Goleman, 1995, p. xii). Although psychologists continue to debate whether such talents are akin to a form of intelligence or are simply a set of skills or personality traits (Locke, 2005; Schulte, Ree, & Carretta, 2004), the qualities that are included under the label "emotional intelligence" are associated with a host of positive outcomes in areas such as academic performance, personal relationships, social behavior, and organizational leadership (Mayer et al., 2004).

Emotional intelligence ▶ The ability to identify, manage, and express one's emotions constructively and to empathize with the emotions of others.

Everyone Wants to Feel Good—But What Is "Feeling Good"?

One drug user is attracted to heroin, a "low fly" drug; another is drawn to cocaine, a "high fly." One person's idea of a *really* good time is surfing the big waves off Oahu's north shore, while another experiences bliss sitting in a deck chair at the Cape Cod seashore watching the gentlest of waves roll in as he knits a beret for his wife. As researcher in culture and emotion Jeanne Tsai points out, although most people report that they want to feel good, what people mean by "feeling good" and what they do to achieve this affective state may differ from individual to individual and from culture to culture (Tsai, 2007). For example, Tsai and her colleagues have found that personality traits and innate temperament are probably far more important than culture in determining a person's *actual* affect (Tsai, 2007)—that is, how we feel *now*. However, culture is an important force in determining the type of affect each individual

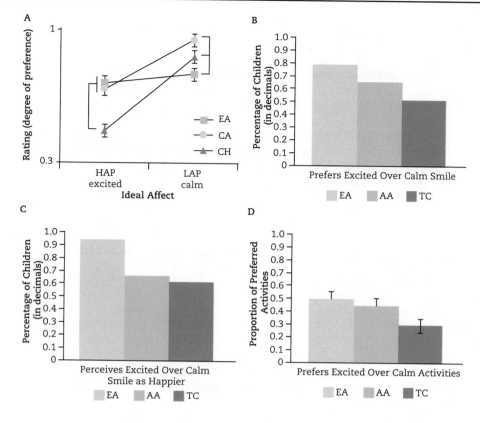

◀FIGURE 11.3 Chasing Affect: Culture Affects the Way We Want to Feel. In studies among European American (EA), Chinese American (CA), and Hong Kong Chinese (CH) adults (see Graph A), Tsai and her colleagues found that European Americans valued highly activated positive states (HAP) more than did both Chinese groups, whereas the Chinese groups valued low-activated positive states (LAP) more than the European Americans (Tsai et al., 2006). In studies among European American, Asian American, and Taiwan Chinese pre-schoolers (Graphs B, C, and D) these researchers found that European American children (EA) were more likely than either Asian Americans (AA) or Taiwanese Chinese (TC) to prefer an excited smile over a calm smile, to believe those with excited smiles to be happier, and to prefer activities that were both pleasant and exciting over those which were pleasant and calm (Tsai et al., 2007). *(Sources: Adapted from figures in Tsai, 2007, p. 244; Tsai et al., 2007, p. 21.)*

considers *ideal*—the affective states people value, prefer, and ideally wish to feel. Culture influences the type of affect we "chase."

Members of all nationalities, all cultures, and both sexes agree on the *valence* dimension of ideal affect—we all want to "feel good" rather than "feel bad." But there appear to be important cultural differences in the level of *activation* or arousal we prefer. As an example, Tsai and her colleagues compared ideal affect in a sample of European Americans, Chinese Americans, and Chinese from Hong Kong (Tsai, Knutson, & Fung, 2006). In addition to taking various objective measurements of how the research participants rated various affects, Tsai came right out and asked each person, "What is your ideal state?" A typical European American response: "I just want to be happy. Normally for me that means I would be doing something exciting. I just want to be entertained . . . I just like excitement." A typical Chinese Hong Kong response: "My ideal state is to be quiet, serene, happy, and positive" (Tsai, 2007, p. 244). Both the American and Chinese participants wanted to be "happy" but, as Figure 11.3 depicts, their idea of what "happy" looks like was somewhat different.

Because it was not clear when during human development preferences for ideal affect appear, Tsai and her colleagues also conducted studies among pre-schoolers in the United States and Taiwan (Tsai, Louie, Chen, & Uchida, 2007). The results they found were markedly similar: European American preschoolers wanted to be excited, while Asian children preferred the calmer variety of happiness (see Figure 11.3). Regardless of the cause of development of such standards for ideal affect, they seem to occur early in life.

IN SUMMARY

1. Emotions are short-lived, relatively intense psychological states consisting of distinct subjective experience or feeling, physiological changes, and behavioral responses. Moods are longer lasting, less intense emotional states whose origin may be difficult to pinpoint. *Affect* is an umbrella term for the "raw material" from which emotions and moods are drawn. Affect exists along two dimensions: valence and activation.

2.	The number of unpleasant emotions greatly exceeds that of pleasant emotions.
3.	Although emotion can sometimes overwhelm rational action, emotions are also necessary for rational decisions and behavior to take place. It is unlikely that human beings could have survived as a species without emotions.
4.	Ideal affect is the sort of affect each person values, prefers, and wishes to experience. This may differ from the person's actual affect. Some evidence shows that Far Eastern peoples may be more attracted to low-activated positive affect, while Americans (and perhaps other Westerners) prefer high-activated positive affect.

RETRIEVE!

1.	The term *angry* describes _____; *irritable* describes _____; *very upbeat* describes _____. (Choose from *affect*, *emotion*, and *mood*)
2.	True or false: The positive and negative aspects of affect are captured in the dimension *activation*.
3.	What is one explanation for the facts that negative emotions outnumber positive emotions, and people are more concerned about avoiding negative emotions than they are about attaining positive ones?
4.	Why are emotions necessary for rational decision making?
5.	Turn back to Figure 11.3 on page 517. Which group of participants rated LAP the highest? Which group rated it the lowest? Which group rated HAP lowest? Highest?

Are Some Emotions "Basic"?

Researcher Dylan Evans (2001) recalls the time when, at age 15, he was asked by members of a punk rock band to replace their lead singer who suffered from stage fright. Evans was delighted enough to join the band, but when one of its members told Evans that he was personally very happy Evans had joined the band, Evans reports that he experienced an intense reaction:

> A warm wave spread outwards and upwards from my stomach, rapidly enveloping the whole of my upper chest: It was a kind of joy, but unlike any moment of joy I had felt before. It was a feeling of acceptance, of belonging, of being valued by a group of people whom I was proud to call my friends. I was momentarily lost for words, shocked by the novelty of the sensation. In the years since then, the feeling has never repeated itself exactly, and I have never forgotten it. (pp. 1–2)

Evans acknowledges that he is not the only person to have experienced such a response, but he laments that there is no word in English to describe the "oceanic feeling" he experienced that day. It was not until he heard the Japanese word *amae*, which translates loosely as "feeling secure and comforted in the complete acceptance and benevolence of another person" that Evans believed he had found the right word. But while Japanese-speakers have a single word for this emotional experience and English-speakers do not, it is clear that many English-speakers have experienced a similar emotion (Hupka, Lenton, & Hutchison, 1999).

Numerous emotion theorists have come to the conclusion that certain emotions are experienced at some time by virtually *all* human beings, whether or not we have words for them in our language. They may be part of our evolutionary heritage—and perhaps the heritage of at least some other mammals as well (Panksepp, 2005a, 2005b). These emotions are termed **basic emotions** (Ekman, 2003; Ekman & Cordaro, 2011; Izard, 2007; Panksepp, 2007a; Levenson, 2011; Plutchik, 2003).

Basic Emotions Are Primary

As mentioned earlier, according to basic emotion theorists, basic emotions are universal, entirely distinct, "hard-wired" into the human nervous system, and *primary*. Just as a vast number of colors may be derived from primary colors, a vast number of emotions may be derived from basic emotions. For example, the emotion described earlier which the Japanese refer to as *amae* is one of an uncountable number of emotions derived from the basic emotion of enjoyment/happiness. *Annoyance* and *rage* are among the emotions derived from anger; *anxiety, worry*, and *terror* from fear; *anguish, melancholy*, and *loneliness* from sadness. Emotion researcher Carroll Izard refers to emotions which are derived from basic emotions as emotion schemas (Izard, 2007, 2009, 2011), while other theorists merely refer to each basic emotion as having a large "family" of more complex or subtle emotions (Ekman & Cordaro, 2011; Matsumoto & Ekman, 2004).

Exactly which emotions are basic, and how would one know such a thing? Not only have psychologists been unable to come to a consensus on this issue, but the problems in coming to agreement have led some investigators to doubt that it would ever be possible to devise a definitive list. Others claim that the very concept of basic emotion is misleading and results from misinterpretation of the evidence (Barrett, 2006; Russell, 2003). Nevertheless, it is probably fair to say that the majority of psychologists affirm the existence of basic emotions—even as there are differences of opinion as to how exactly to define and identify a basic emotion, and which specific emotions are basic (Prinz, 2004; Izard, 2007, 2009).

In this book I use a relatively short list of basic emotions including only those upon which there is fairly wide (although not unanimous) agreement: *fear, anger, sadness, enjoyment/happiness, disgust, contempt*, and *surprise*. Each of these emotions is entirely distinct—a person simply cannot confuse enjoyment/happiness with fear, sadness with disgust, or contempt with surprise (see Figure 11.4). Each is readily identified and comprehended by others and, as Paul Ekman has shown in 40 years of research (see Chapter 1, p. 21), each is associated with specific facial expressions and frequently with specific body language as well (Ekman, 1994, 1999a, 2003a; see Figures 11.2 and 11.4).

While basic emotions are distinct, it is relatively rare to experience a pure basic emotion for very long. Emotions play off one another and are often experienced in sequence. For example, we may initially feel fear, then immediately become angry because we have been made to feel afraid. We may then feel frightened by our own anger, followed by contempt at ourselves for having experienced this entire sequence. The whole thing may then make us miserably sad (Ekman, 2003).

Basic emotions may also sometimes blend. Consider the emotion described by Brazilians and Portuguese as *saudade*. Saudade is a dreamy, wistful, and fatalistic longing for a beloved person or place that currently is absent from one's

▲ **Blending Basic Emotion: Enjoyment/Happiness + Contempt = Smugness.** Basic emotions may sometimes blend to form an emotion schema, as in the case of *smugness*—an enjoyable and pleasant form of contempt. *(Source: Ekman, 2003a, p. 212.)*

Basic emotion ▶ Universal, innate, distinct emotions from which a vast number of other emotions may be derived. Characteristic facial expressions and/or body language are generally associated with basic emotions. Psychologists are not in agreement as to the number of basic emotions, which specific emotions are basic, or even if the concept itself is valid.

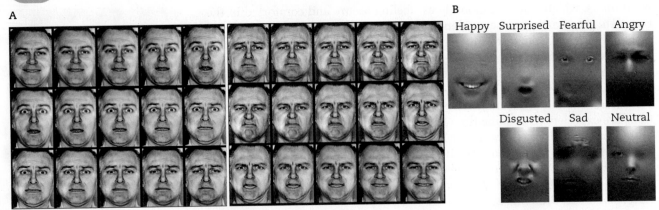

▲ **FIGURE 11.4** How Much Visual Information Do We Need to Identify Basic Emotions?
In Figure A, each face depicts a "pure" basic emotion at the far left of each row. The face is then morphed through various stages by blending it with another emotion as it moves to the right. By the time the image reaches the far right it has become a different "pure" basic emotion. The researchers found that only the 50%-50% blended image (the middle image of each row) was not reliably identified as whichever was the predominating emotion. In Figure B, researchers presented research participants with small portions of faces randomly sampled by computer. The images here represent the amount of visual information that was necessary for the participants to correctly distinguish each emotion at 75% accuracy. *(Sources: [A] Calder, Lawrence, & Young, 2001, p. 355; [B] M. L. Smith, Cottrell, Gosselin, & Schyns, 2005, p. 187)*

Facial action coding system
▶ Paul Ekman's coding scheme of the facial muscle configurations which create expressions of basic emotion.

Duchenne smile ▶ A smile of genuine enjoyment or pleasure, characterized by contraction of the orbicularis oculi muscle surrounding the eye. This muscle is extremely difficult to contract at will.

life, but for which there is at least a possibility of reunion in the future (slim as the chance may be). This subtle and complex emotion schema is derived from a blending of sadness in the present with happiness in memories of the past and hopes for the future.

Paul Ekman eventually discovered that specific facial muscles were involved in creating the expressions of basic emotion, and he has catalogued these muscular configurations into a coding scheme known as the **facial action coding system** (FACS; Ekman & Friesen, 1978; Ekman & Rosenberg, 2005). For example, a smile of genuine enjoyment, known as a **Duchenne smile**, can easily be distinguished from a forced or a polite smile, but not by looking at the smile itself. The key is the eyes. A true smile includes a contraction of the *orbicularis oculi* muscle which surrounds each eye. A portion of this muscle is difficult for most untrained people to contract at will, and only 10% of those studied by Ekman over the past 40 years have been able to do it. According to Ekman, actors who convincingly appear to be enjoying themselves are among those few who can voluntarily display a Duchenne smile (Ekman, 2003a; see Figure 11.5).

Basic Emotions Are Affected by Culture

Human beings are particularly good at "decoding" each other's facial expressions of basic emotion, and it is likely that this skill evolved along with the evolution of the emotions themselves (Schyns, Petro, & Smith, 2009). However, members of some cultures do better than others at this task, and members of all cultures studied do better at assessing the facial expressions of individuals from their own society (Elfenbein & Ambady, 2002, 2003; Matsumoto et al., 2002). This effect is largely *cultural* in nature, not racial or ethnic. As Figure 11.6 shows, Hilary Elfenbein and Nalini Ambady (2003) demonstrated that Chinese Americans, and even Chinese students who had only been living in America for several years, were more accurate in judging basic emotional expressions of *non*-Asian Americans than they were in judging the expressions of Chinese people residing in China. Moreover, with each successive generation of Chinese Americans, the ability to accurately judge the emotional expressions of

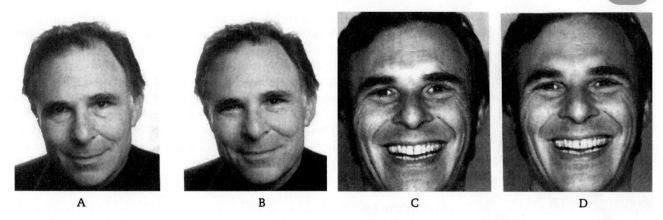

▲ **FIGURE 11.5 Unmasking the Fake Smile.** Photos A and B depict the "closed" smile, with no teeth showing. Photos C and D depict "open" smiles, with teeth visible. However, the smiles in Photos A and C are forced. Photos B and D show the real thing—the Duchenne smile involving contraction of the *orbicularis oculi* muscle. Incidentally, Photos A and B depict Ekman himself. *(Source: Ekman, 2003a.)*

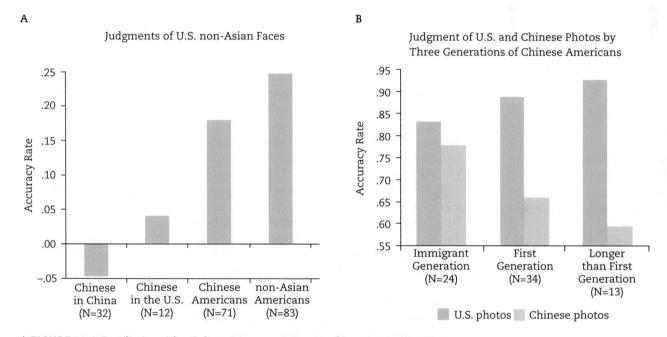

▲ **FIGURE 11.6 Familiarity with a Culture Increases Accuracy of Emotion Recognition.** As Graph A shows, for those of Chinese ancestry, the further one is removed from U.S. culture, the less accurate is recognition of emotion in non-Asian U.S. faces. Graph B demonstrates this by showing increasing accuracy in judging U.S. faces—and decreasing accuracy in judging Chinese faces—with each successive generation of Chinese Americans. *(Adapted from Elfenbein & Ambady, 2003, p. 283.)*

non-Asian Americans grew better, while the ability to judge the expressions of Chinese living in China grew worse.

There may even be cultural differences in the parts of the face used to recognize emotions. Masaki Yuki and his colleagues hypothesized that, when recognizing emotion, people in a culture such as Japan—where emotional expression is subdued and controlled—will focus on parts of the face that are difficult to control intentionally (Yuki, Maddux, & Masuda, 2007). On the other hand, in a culture such as the United States, where emotional expression is encouraged, people may focus on the part of the face that is easiest to control. As depicted in Figure 11.7, when Yuki and his colleagues presented Japanese and American participants with images of faces which had been morphed to reflect

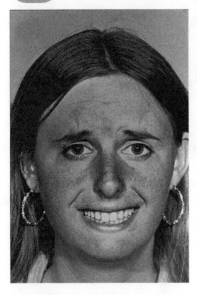

▲ **FIGURE 11.7 Happy or Sad?** In this photograph, a smiling mouth has been joined to a face expressing sadness in the area surrounding the eyes. Japanese observers were more likely to characterize this as a sad face, while American observers were more likely to call it happy. *(Source: Yuki et al., 2007.)*

Display rules ▶ Implicit cultural standards and expectations which regulate the way emotion is displayed.

happiness around the eyes and sadness at the mouth—or sadness around the eyes and happiness at the mouth—the American participants used the mouth to diagnose the emotion, whereas the Japanese participants tended to use the eyes (which are more difficult to control in genuine smiles and frowns).

This cultural difference is evident in differences in the computer *emoticons* used to suggest pleasure or displeasure in emails and such. In the United States the emoticon :-) suggests pleasure or happiness and :-(suggests displeasure or sadness. These emoticons focus on the up- or down-turned mouth to characterize the emotion. Japanese generally use the symbols (^_^) for happiness and (;_;) for sadness (crying), both of which focus upon on the eyes (Yuki et al., 2007).

DISPLAY RULES

Recognizing emotion and expressing emotion may be related, but they are not identical. In addition to cultural differences in emotion recognition, the specific manner in which emotions are expressed varies across cultures as well as among individuals and between the sexes in any given society (Barrett, Gross, Christensen, & Benvenuto, 2001; Costa, Terracciano, & McCrae, 2001; Ekman & Friesen, 1975; Matsumoto, Willingham, & Olide, 2009).

Display rules are implicit standards and expectations that regulate the way emotion is displayed in a given culture. Consider the expression of bereavement at funerals: In certain cultures or subcultures one is expected to express grief at funerals of loved ones by wailing, weeping, pounding the coffin, and so forth. In other cultures, one is expected to keep one's grief tightly contained. The emotion of grief in each case is equally profound, but the unspoken rules governing its expression differ.

The existence of display rules was discovered by Paul Ekman and his colleagues when they compared the reactions of American and Japanese participants as they watched stressful or disgusting films. The investigators observed the participants as they watched the films while sitting alone and also while in the presence of others (Ekman, 1972; Ekman & Friesen, 1975). In Ekman's original study, American subjects rarely varied their reactions to the film whether they were watching alone or in the presence of others. However, Japanese subjects were much more likely to keep their reactions to a minimal smile in the presence of the experimenter—perhaps because the experimenter was perceived to be in a position of authority or it was deemed unseemly to display negative feelings too openly. On the other hand, when alone, the Japanese participants reacted with disgust and displeasure, just as the Americans had.

Display rules are complex and vary according to the emotion, the situation, the sex, and the status of those expressing and those observing emotion, as well as the general cultural setting. Ekman identified four ways in which display rules might vary:

- *Intensifying,* as at a funeral where one is expected to show a great deal of vivid grief.
- *De-intensifying,* as after a tennis match when the victor is usually expected to tone down expressions of joy while the defeated opponent is present (Friedman & Miller-Herringer, 1991).
- *Masking,* as when one pretends to feel a certain emotion while actually feeling a different (probably unacceptable) one. Consider your response as you accept a disappointing gift in the presence of the gift-giver.
- *Neutralizing,* the complete hiding of emotions—as while attempting to be convincing during a lie.

Deception Is Linked to Emotion and Cognition

Have you lied yet today?

Before you vigorously deny that you lie at all, consider this: Unless you are unlike the majority of college students studied in the United States, you will have told an average one or two lies before the sun goes down (DePaulo, 2004; DePaulo, Kashy, Kirkendol, Wyer, & Epstein, 1996). The average rate for the rest of us is somewhat lower, and, interestingly, almost half of all lies told are accounted for by a very small number of people—the deception champions among us (Serota, Levine, & Boster, 2010).

Some researchers have wondered if rates of lying might differ according to the communication mode—face-to-face, telephone, or in computer-mediated communication such as email, texting, or instant messaging. In one study, substantial differences in rates of lying emerged: Phone conversations elicited the highest rate of lies, while email elicited the lowest rate (Hancock, Thom-Santelli, & Ritchie, 2004).

Lying may be destructive and immoral, and it may get you into various degrees of trouble, but being deceptive and spotting deception in others is part of the way human beings—and any number of other animals—go about the business of their daily lives (Dawkins, 1976; Trivers, 2010; von Hippel & Trivers, 2011). Evolutionary theorists such as Robert Trivers and Richard Dawkins propose that deception evolved as one tool in the struggle for survival and reproductive success.

So then: To whom might you lie today? If you are like Bella DePaulo's research participants, you will tell fewest lies to those to whom you feel closest—and you will feel more distressed at having told these lies. The exceptions to the *feel closer → tell fewer lies* rule are romantic partners (one lie in every three interactions) and mothers (one lie in every *two* interactions!) (De Paulo & Kashy, 1998; DePaulo et al., 1996). But cheer up: Many of the lies you tell those to whom you feel close (including Mom) will be lies designed to spare the other person's feelings in some way, known as *altruistic lies*. Most of the lies you tell others will be entirely self-serving.

Without doubt, then, lying is a part of most people's lives, although some of us lie quite a bit more often than others. And, while we try hard not to be discovered in a lie, we would all very much like to be able to tell when *others* are lying. Unfortunately, research has shown that most people are unable to tell a lie from the truth when it comes to the lies of relative strangers intent on deception. On average, people can tell a truth from a lie no better than 54% of the time in research studies, which is only slightly better than chance guessing (Bond & DePaulo, 2006, 2008; Hartwig & Bond, 2011; Vrij, Granhag, Mann, & Leal, 2011). If you think you can "just tell" when a person is lying, you are probably wrong.

On the other hand, human beings evolved under conditions where attempts at deception must have been common (as they continue to be). People lie outright or withhold the truth to gain advantages of various sorts. It stands to reason that at least a modest ability to *detect* lies also ought to have evolved, in a co-evolutionary process as the talent for deception evolved (Trivers, 2010). As liars got better, it stands to reason that we should have gotten better at ferreting them out. Then why does research paint us all as terrible lie detectors?

Part of the problem may lie in the research itself (von Hippel & Trivers, 2011). Most research in human lie detection involves relatively trivial lies told by strangers under laboratory conditions. However, this is not how the vast majority of lies are told. Lies are told in real life, often by people known to one another, and these lies may have important consequences—such as during police investigations. When researchers had participants keep "lie diaries," the journal keepers reported that their lies were detected by those close to them a substantial portion of the time (DePaulo et al., 1996); and in a study of police officers evaluating statements made on video tape by actual suspects in high-stakes cases, the officers' average accuracy in detecting lies was 72%—substantially above chance and better than they themselves predicted they would perform (Vrij, Mann, Robbins, & Robinson, 2006).

When people do detect the lies of others, face to face, how do they do so? There is no foolproof method of human lie detection, because cues that a person is telling a lie can be faint, and some of them appear when a person is telling the truth as well (DePaulo et al., 2003; von Hippel & Trivers, 2011). For example, although liars are often nervous in telling their lies because they are afraid of being discovered, truth tellers may be just as nervous if they are afraid of not being believed! Emotions linked to lying may be linked to truth-telling as well.

However, researchers using cognitive psychology to increase the effectiveness of face-to-face lie detection have made a simple but powerful observation about lying: Telling a lie is more *demanding* on a person's cognitive resources than telling the truth—that is, lying increases *cognitive load* (Vrij, 2008; Vrij et al., 2011). As Aldert Vrij and his colleagues point out, liars need, first, to make up a good, plausible story. They need to remember the details of the story to keep it consistent. They need to keep from providing inadvertent leads to the truth. They need to strictly monitor their behavior so they appear to be honest and credible people—and they need to monitor the behavior of the person to whom they are lying to make sure they are getting away with their lie. Liars may be preoccupied with reminding themselves to remain in the role they have created for themselves. All of this can require extreme mental effort (Vrij et al., 2011).

Vrij and colleagues note that since liars have fewer cognitive resources remaining than truth-tellers, this deficit can be exploited by those seeking to ferret out the truth. For example, the next time you believe you are being lied to, ask the suspected liar to tell his or her story *in reverse order* of its occurrence. This may increase the person's cognitive load to the point that the whole enterprise may fall apart. Another technique is to ask the person to maintain eye contact with you as he or she speaks. When people need to concentrate to tell a story—for example, when trying to remember forgotten details of a true event, or when lying—they often look away from their conversation partner to a fixed point, because maintaining eye contact can be distracting. Unfortunately, such techniques are very far from foolproof, and the holy grail of lie detection is still beyond our grasp.

IN SUMMARY

1.	Certain emotions may warrant the term *basic* because they are innate, distinct, and form the basis for "families" of emotions derived from them. Most researchers include at least *fear, sadness, enjoyment/happiness, anger, disgust, contempt,* and *surprise* in their lists of basic emotions.
2.	Emotion researcher Paul Ekman has charted the specific muscular configurations which form facial expressions of basic emotion in his *facial action coding system*.
3.	In research studies people do poorly at detecting lies, but when people keep journals of the lies they tell, they report that their lying is frequently detected. Police officers viewing video tapes of suspect interrogations are often able to detect lying quite well. Lying increases cognitive load, so that techniques which increase cognitive load further may be helpful in ferreting out liars.
4.	Basic emotions are universal, but they are affected by culture. People are better at decoding emotional expressions of others from their own culture, and those in Western societies may use different parts of the face from those in Far Eastern societies when coming to judgments about others' facial expressions of emotions.
5.	Display rules are unspoken standards and expectations which regulate the way emotion is displayed in a given culture.

RETRIEVE!

1.	A smile that is genuine involves a contraction of the orbicularis oculi muscle. This type of smile is called the _____ smile.
2.	True or false? An African American who grows up in Hong Kong will still be more accurate in judging the emotional expressions of African Americans living in America than he or she would be in judging the emotional expressions of Chinese living in Hong Kong.
3.	Paul Ekman identified four ways in which display rules might vary. Which of the following is NOT one of these four ways? **a)** intensifying **b)** de-intensifying **c)** solidifying **d)** masking **e)** neutralizing

How Do Psychologists Explain Emotion?

Most of us subjectively experience the onset of an emotion in a sequence that runs something like this:

1. *There is some sort of event, or perhaps a thought or image enters your mind.* For example, while at the supermarket, you see a mother angrily spank her child because the little boy complains of being hungry and asks for food.

2. *You feel an appropriate emotion or series of emotions.* In this case, perhaps shock at first, then anger.

3. *The emotion is expressed in physiological changes and behavior.* In this case, your heart rate, respiration, and blood pressure may increase as a result of autonomic nervous system arousal, your fists may clench and your face may assume the characteristic expressions of shock, anger, and/or contempt.

Early Theories: Which Comes First, *Feeling* or *Emotion*?

William James, whose view that human beings possessed extremely numerous instincts we briefly described in Chapter 1, believed that the preceding sequence was an illusion. Instead, he argued that emotion exists first and foremost in a person's physiology. That is, *emotion is feeling*. He concluded that it is the physiological response which triggers the emotion, not the other way around. For James, the proper sequence is 1, 3, 2: There is a thought or event; it creates physiological changes such as an increase in autonomic nervous system activity; awareness of these physiological changes reaches the cerebral cortex; and only *then* do we feel the appropriate emotion. Thus, we are happy because we are smiling, sad because we are crying, and frightened because our hearts are racing and our palms are sweating (James, 1890/1981).

Because this theory was also proposed by Danish psychologist Carl Lange, it has become known as the **James-Lange theory of emotion**. Does it seem unlikely to you? It did to physiologists Walter Cannon and Phillip Bard during later decades. Cannon and Bard argued that any number of emotions, including anger, love, and fear, could be responsible for identical

James-Lange theory of emotion ▶ The theory proposed by Carl Lange and William James which states that thoughts or the perception of events trigger directly autonomic nervous system changes; awareness of these changes reaches the cerebral cortex; and only then is there an experience of emotion.

Cannon-Bard theory of emotion ▶ The theory proposed by Walter Cannon and Phillip Bard which states that during the perception of an event, sensory impulses are first relayed to the thalamus. From there the impulses are relayed to the autonomic nervous system and the cerebral cortex at about the same time, rather than to the autonomic nervous system first and secondly to the cerebral cortex, as proposed in the James-Lange theory.

physiological symptoms of arousal such as racing heart, sweaty palms, and elevated blood pressure. How would a person know which emotion to feel (Cannon, 1929a)? Cannon and Bard advanced a competing theory which has come to be known as the **Cannon-Bard theory of emotion**. According to Cannon and Bard, when some sort of emotion-laden event is perceived, the sensory impulses are relayed to the thalamus first. The thalamus in turn stimulates *both* the autonomic nervous system *and* the cerebral cortex at about the same time. The autonomic nervous system alters levels of physiological arousal (increasing or decreasing them through activation of the sympathetic or parasympathetic nervous systems, as the case may be) and the cerebral cortex does the work of allowing the person to feel the emotion. In contrast to James and Lange, who insisted that our levels of arousal are altered first and that we experience the emotion subsequently, Cannon and Bard argued that changes in arousal and the experience of emotion occur at the same time (Cannon, 1929b).

Although Cannon and Bard's idea may make more intuitive sense than the James-Lange theory—and the thalamus does receive most sensory signals first—a number of research findings challenge Cannon and Bard's theory. For example, as we shall discover a bit later in the chapter, although activating the nervous system by injecting adrenaline does not necessarily produce a specific emotion, assuming the facial expression associated with a given emotion may produce—at least to some extent—aspects of the emotion in question (Izard, 1990; Mori & Mori, 2009; Soussignan, 2002). Thus, changes in physiology may well create emotional changes, as James and Lange insisted.

However, even if it turned out to be the case, as James and Lange argued, that emotions such as fear originate in feelings of arousal, exactly how does the body know to produce arousal? Wouldn't we somehow need to evaluate the implications or *meaning* of a mother spanking her child when the child asked for something to eat? That is, wouldn't we need to have a sense of the injustice of the mother's actions prior to experiencing physiological arousal and emotion? Questions such as this have been of major concern to modern researchers in the *cognitive* aspects of emotion.

Cognitive Theories Stress Interpretation of Events

Each of us has been in situations in which we felt afraid for what turned out to be no good reason. From my own memories: While staying at a relatively secluded cabin in the Vermont woods as a very young man, I heard a noise in the house in the middle of the night that sounded to me like someone breaking glass. I had a vision of someone breaking a window pane to enter the cabin. My heart began to pound, my limbs started trembling and my mouth became dry. I tried to remember my martial arts training and plan what I would do, but my mind had gone blank. I grabbed a hatchet that I had been using to chop kindling wood, tiptoed slowly into the kitchen and found . . . a raccoon rooting around in the kitchen garbage pail. I had been seriously *afraid*—but suddenly I was not. Yet all that had really changed was the way I *thought* about the situation—my interpretation of the noises. The raccoon was still making noise in the kitchen, but the noise was no longer frightening.

Moreover, as I had been sitting up in bed experiencing a racing heart and the other symptoms of an aroused autonomic nervous system, how did I know I was *afraid*? As Cannon and Bard complained, symptoms such as sweaty palms and thumping heart could have occurred if I were angry or even when asking someone out with whom I was seriously infatuated. But I certainly knew I was afraid, not in love. Why?

Most modern theorists of emotion acknowledge the importance of *cognition* in the experience of emotion—even those researchers primarily concerned with the neuroscience and biochemistry of emotion. Although both the James-Lange and the Cannon-Bard theories *implicitly* recognize that cognitive activity must take place in the experience of emotion, they did not *explicitly* address the nature of this activity.

THE SCHACHTER-SINGER TWO-FACTOR THEORY

The first important cognitive theory was devised by Stanley Schachter and Jerome Singer (1962) and is known as the **two-factor theory of emotion**. Schachter and Singer agreed with James and Lange that autonomic nervous system activity preceded emotion. However, they believed that the changes in arousal produced by this activity were general and not specific to any particular emotion. How then did specific emotions emerge? Schachter and Singer claimed that *only when a cognitive label is attached to arousal in order to explain it does the person experience emotion*. According to this idea, the brain needs to interpret or *appraise* the source of the physiological effects it is experiencing to "choose" the correct emotion to feel.

From this perspective, the stimuli of the noise in the kitchen set my heart racing that night, but it was only when I interpreted the noise as having been caused by a human intruder that I experienced actual fear. As soon as my interpretation changed, my fear instantly disappeared—even though the arousal took some time to subside completely. The two-factor theory differs from the James-Lange theory in that James and Lange believed that the generation of emotion was a virtually automatic response to physiological arousal, without the necessity of "higher order" cognitive processes intervening.

COGNITIVE-MOTIVATIONAL-RELATIONAL THEORY

Another important cognitive theory of emotion was produced by Richard Lazarus. Lazarus's theory evolved considerably during the 50 years he worked in the field of emotion and cognition, and it is known by several names, notably the **cognitive-motivational-relational theory** (Lazarus, 1991a, 1991b, 2000). However, the most important aspect of the theory is the notion that both an emotion and any related physiological changes occur *only* after a person interprets—or *appraises*—the meaning of the event. Unlike Schachter and Singer, to Lazarus, cognition always comes first and arousal and emotion second.

Returning to the supermarket for a moment, different people hold different opinions about spanking and its appropriateness. Some of us think it appropriate under all conditions of a parent's choosing, some think it appropriate only under certain conditions, and others believe it is never appropriate. Therefore, only those in the latter two groups should be expected to experience anger at the sight of a mother spanking her child. Moreover, the second group should only experience anger after appraising the specifics of the situation and concluding that the spanking is unjust. Therefore, even if the experience of anger appears instantaneous, cognitive appraisal of the situation must occur *prior* to arousal and emotion, according to Lazarus—albeit at lightning-fast speed and below the level of conscious awareness.

Some Emotional Experiences May Bypass Cognition

If cognitions cause emotions, as Lazarus, Schachter, and Singer argued, how is it that infants can be happy, sad, angry, surprised, fearful, and disgusted even though they have no language and relatively few well-developed cognitive concepts (Yirmiya, Erel, Shaked, & Solomonica-Levi, 1998)? And how is it that some nonhuman animals display the physiological arousal, behaviors, and facial expressions characteristic of human emotion (Baars, 2005; Panksepp, 2005a, 2005b)?

There is no doubt that emotion can emerge without *conscious* thought. For example, stimuli such as angry or happy faces flashed on a screen much too quickly for a person to become consciously aware of them can influence

Two-factor theory of emotion
▶ The theory proposed by Stanley Schachter and Jerome Singer which states that thoughts or perceptions of events directly trigger autonomic nervous system arousal—in agreement with the James-Lange theory. However, according to the two-factor theory, emotion will emerge only after a cognitive label is attached to the arousal to explain it.

Cognitive-motivational-relational theory of emotion
▶ The theory proposed by Richard Lazarus. This theory states that autonomic nervous system arousal occurs not directly, as stated in the James-Lange and two-factor theories, but only after the thought or event has been appraised so that the meaning of the event is interpreted by the person. In this theory, cognition always comes first.

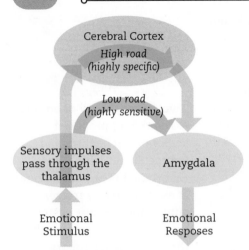

▲ **FIGURE 11.8** LeDoux's Dual Pathways to Fear. Joseph LeDoux hypothesized that there are two pathways to fear: a "high road" and a "low road." The initial fear response (low) travels directly from the sense organs (eyes, ears, etc.) to the thalamus and from there to the amygdala. This pathway is highly sensitive. A secondary response occurs as the sensory impulse is relayed from the thalamus to the cortex, where it is evaluated and appraised (the "high road"). If the stimulus is judged to be a genuinely fearful one, impulses are relayed to the amygdala and the body continues to respond in a fearful manner. Otherwise, the entire mechanism is shut down. This pathway is slower, but it is specific rather than sensitive.

Embodied emotion ▶
Embodied emotion theories assume that emotions are "captured" as body memories. Each time an emotion is experienced, the sights, sounds, physiological processes, and patterns of motor activity that occur are encoded in clusters of neurons assigned to the various sensory and motor modalities of the body. Over time, these experiences build a conception of the particular emotion in question, which a person may reactivate by thinking about or re-experiencing the emotion.

the person's mood and produce movement in the facial muscles associated with the particular emotion exhibited in the face flashed upon the screen (Dimberg, Thunberg, & Elmehed, 2000; Murphy, Monahan, & Zajonc, 1995). As explained earlier, however, cognitive theorists such as Lazarus (1991a, 1991b) have insisted that even in these cases, at least *some* form of cognitive appraisal must be occurring, even if it is below the level of awareness.

Yet substantial evidence from brain imaging studies shows that certain emotions, notably *fear*, may sometimes have direct pathways from perception to emotion that bypass the cortex—and therefore, cognition—entirely. This is a perspective that Robert Zajonc argued for over a quarter of a century (Zajonc, 1984). Evidence supporting his ideas comes most importantly from the work of neuroscientist Joseph LeDoux (1996, 2000). LeDoux demonstrated that there is a pathway of neural impulses from the thalamus, which receives and processes sensory signals, to the amygdala. The amygdala is activated during many emotions, but appears to be the most important brain region responsible for fear responses (Barot, Chung, Kim, & Bernstein, 2009). The amygdala in turn activates other brain structures which produce the physiological arousal associated with fear. This direct pathway to the amygdala accounts for the fact that we can respond instantly with fear to the appearance of potentially threatening visual or auditory stimuli. For example, a person coming quietly into a room and then speaking suddenly while you have been concentrating on a task might sound your fear alarm. ("Oh! You scared me!")

However, the direct pathway to fear, somewhat like most smoke alarms, is highly *sensitive* but not very *specific*. Highly sensitive mechanisms produce many false alarms, technically referred to as false positives (e.g., the person coming quietly into the room is just your little sister). On the other hand, highly *specific* mechanisms will only go off when they are supposed to, in the presence of the correct stimuli. But sometimes they may fail to go off at all if the stimulus isn't strong enough, creating false negatives. As you might see, the consequences of a fear mechanism not going off when it is supposed to are potentially much more severe (e.g., death) than such a mechanism firing numerous false alarms (false positives).

Yet, when a seeming threat occurs that turns out to be a false alarm, how do we recover our composure so quickly? ("Oh—it's just you. Can't you knock or walk a little louder when you come into the room?") According to LeDoux's findings, there are *two* pathways to fear (see Figure 11.8). The first is the rapid, direct pathway from the thalamus to the amygdala described previously, sometimes referred to as the "low road." However, signals are also traveling from the thalamus to the cerebral cortex, only more slowly. It is in the cortex that the threat is evaluated and appraised. This second pathway to fear—the "high road"—is highly *specific*, but not particularly sensitive. The results of the cortex's computations are then sent to the amygdala. If the threat is real, the amygdala continues to ring the alarm. If it is not, it shuts the fear response down.

Fear is an unusually powerful emotion. You can probably see why: Not responding to fear-inducing situations could easily result in death. Thus, we have evolved particularly sensitive mechanisms involving fear. This fact is understood well by advertisers, politicians, and others seeking to create persuasive messages. Those seeking to persuade use fear as a tool, particularly if the audience feels vulnerable to some threat (e.g., terrorism) and the message offers a coping strategy or hope for effective response to the threat (Crano & Prislin, 2006; Wood, 2000). Fear historically has been employed in the age-old practice of manipulating people into buying all kinds of useless products that allegedly protect them from a variety of ills, real and imagined, or supporting military actions, wrong-headed legislation, and all manner of social policies.

The tendency to be persuaded by fear may have its good side, however. It is now being used with some success by health psychologists and other professionals who wish to promote more constructive lifestyle choices like reducing alcohol consumption and smoking, and promoting safer driving practices (Das, de-Wit, & Stroebe, 2003).

Embodied Emotion: The Body Is the Mind

None of the theorists and researchers of emotion described earlier believe, as did the followers of René Descartes (see Chapter 1), that the mind is actually separate from the body. Nonetheless, they all describe the process of emotion metaphorically as including a "body" (physiological arousal, facial expression, posture, etc.) and a "mind" (cognitive appraisal, labeling, awareness of specific emotions, etc.; Barrett & Lindquist, 2008). More recently, a group of emotion researchers have suggested that when it comes to perceiving, recognizing, or thinking about emotion, to a large extent the body *is* the mind. The theories created by this group of researchers are loosely encompassed in the category of *embodied emotion* (Barrett & Lindquist, 2008; Halberstadt, Winkielman, Niedenthal, & Dalle, 2009; Niedenthal, 2007; Winkielman, Niedenthal, & Oberman, 2008).

What does the term **embodied emotion** actually mean? Embodied emotion theories generally share a number of assumptions (Barrett & Lindquist, 2008), but most central is this: *Emotions are "captured" as body memories.* Each time an emotion is experienced, the sights, sounds, physiological processes, and patterns of body movement that occur during the experience of the emotion are encoded in clusters of neurons assigned to each of these various modalities (sight, sound, physiological responses, etc.). Over time, these experiences form a conception of each particular emotion. A person returns to this conception each time he or she recognizes, recalls, or thinks about that emotion. In a sense, when thinking about or recognizing an emotion you are partially "reliving" or "reactivating" the original emotion as it was experienced in the various modalities of your body (Winkielman et al., 2008).

FACIAL AND POSTURAL FEEDBACK

From an embodied emotion perspective we ought to expect a very close correspondence between one's physiology and one's emotional life. Indeed, embodied emotion theorists have found a connection between assuming specific facial expressions or bodily postures and feeling specific emotions, a finding technically known as *facial* and *postural feedback.* As already discussed, there is a very strong *link* between each basic emotion and a specific facial expression. For example, when we feel happy or hear something funny, we do tend to smile. This fact led some researchers (e.g., Laird, 1974, 1984) to wonder what would happen if we forced ourselves to smile first? Might that change our emotional condition in the *direction* of happiness?

As depicted in Figure 11.9 and very briefly mentioned earlier, research over four decades in this **facial feedback hypothesis** has found that activating the muscles that form facial expressions associated with basic emotions can not

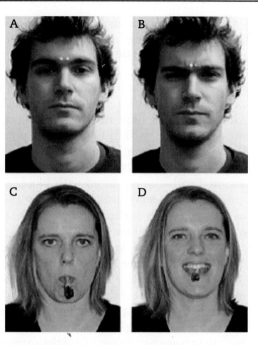
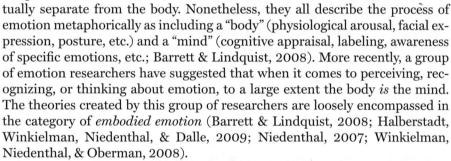

◀ FIGURE 11.9 Put on a Happy Face: The Facial Feedback Hypothesis. Researchers attached golf tees to the inside of participants' eyebrows (Photo A), and then asked the participants to bring the ends of the tees together (Photo B). This task was designed to force participants to contract their brow muscles in a manner similar to that which occurs naturally during negative emotions such as sadness. Those who furrowed their brow reported more sadness in response to disturbing photographs than those who did not engage in this exercise. In a separate study, researchers had one group of participants hold a pen between their lips, without touching their teeth to the pen, preventing the formation of a smile (Photo C). Another group held the pen between their teeth, facilitating a smile (Photo D). Those holding the pen between their teeth reported finding a series of cartoons funnier than did those holding the pen between their lips. (*Sources: Data from Larsen, Kasimatis, & Frey, 1992; Strack, Martin, & Stepper, 1988; figure reprinted from Niedenthal, 2007, p. 1002.*)

Facial feedback hypothesis
▶ The idea that the facial expression associated with a basic emotion increases the intensity of the experience of that emotion; and that purposely activating the muscles which form a facial expression of basic emotion may actually result in a person experiencing the emotion itself—or at least experiencing a mood change in a positive or negative direction (depending on the specific expression).

▲ **Stand Up Straight, Already!** Poor posture does more than detract from your attractiveness, interfere with proper breathing, and ultimately result in restricted movement in the head, shoulders, and neck: According to research in postural feedback, it may make you feel as unhappy as you look.

only increase the intensity of the corresponding emotion if one already feels it, but can sometimes actually *create* the experience of emotion or something close to it (Izard, 1990; McIntosh, 1996; Mori & Mori, 2009). While the effects of assuming a facial expression are not always specific to a particular basic emotion, at the very least they alter mood or emotional experience in a generally positive or negative direction, depending upon the expression. For example, smiling increases positive mood, particularly if the *orbicularis oculi* muscles are contracted. That's right—put on a happy face, and you'll feel better, just as your grandmother told you (Kleinke, Peterson, & Rutledge, 1998; Soussignon, 2002). In one study, simply having the muscles of the cheeks associated with smiling lifted with bandages increased happiness ratings in a group of volunteers (Mori & Mori, 2009). This works in the opposite direction as well—research participants who were instructed to assume a pained facial expression in response to burning heat sensations from a heat stimulator reported more pain than those instructed to assume a relaxed face (Salomons, Coan, Hunt, Backonja, & Davidson, 2008).

The body, as well as the face, offers feedback that may alter emotion. For example, research conducted during the 1990s showed that people who had been told to assume a slumped posture were more likely to report a depressed mood after receiving (bogus) information about their scores on achievement tests than were people receiving the same news in an upright posture (Stepper & Strack, 1993).

However, we should not exaggerate the effects of assuming a given facial expression or posture. Walking around with a broad grin on your face and your shoulders back is not likely to turn a miserable day into a sunny one. Emotion is a result of a great many factors in addition to facial expression and body posture (Duclos et al., 1989; McIntosh, 1996), and embodied emotion theorists do not rely upon facial and postural feedback as their only source of empirical support.

Which Theory of Emotion Is "Right"?

You may have become dizzy trying to disentangle the various claims of emotion theorists to come away with a take-home message about which theory is "correct." If you are looking for a take-home message, you are probably wasting your time. Each of the theories we have considered contributes a piece to the jigsaw puzzle of human emotion. Each theory looks at the problem from a slightly different perspective, stressing certain influences over others. But no single theory can unarguably be said to contribute the largest portion of the completed picture of emotion. Without doubt, physiology and cognition are both critical in the experience of emotion. In some cases, cognition may trump physiology, whereas in other cases the reverse may be true. In some cases, disentangling cognitive from physiological influences, determining which came first, or identifying the underlying neural events accompanying emotion may not be possible. Therefore, it is not necessary to become an adherent of one single theory, the way you ultimately must decide which candidate to vote for in an election. Instead it is probably best to focus on having a clear idea of the differences between these major theories of emotion.

IN SUMMARY

1. The James-Lange theory states that emotional stimuli trigger a physiological reaction. Only when awareness of this reaction reaches the cerebral cortex is emotion experienced. The Cannon-Bard theory states that once emotional stimuli are perceived, physiological responses and emotional experience occur simultaneously.

2. The Schachter and Singer two-factor theory states that that physiological arousal follows directly after perception of an emotional stimulus, but the process of cognitive labeling of the arousal intervenes prior to the experience of emotion. The Lazarus cognitive-motivational-relational theory states that no physiological arousal or emotional experience can occur unless cognitive appraisal and/or labeling has *already* occurred.

3. LeDoux demonstrated that some emotional experiences, notably fear, may entirely bypass the cerebral cortex and, therefore, cognition. This may occur if sensory signals pass through the thalamus and are routed directly to the amygdala before being processed by the cerebral cortex.

4. Embodied emotion theorists point to evidence collected by researchers in facial and postural feedback to support their contention that when an emotion is recognized, recalled, or thought about, the emotion is "reactivated" in neurons and physiological structures which participated in the original experiences of that specific emotion.

RETRIEVE!

1. Autonomic nervous system arousal is quite similar both in fear and anger—elevated heart rate and respiration, increased perspiration, increased blood pressure. Is this fact consistent with the James-Lange or Cannon-Bard theory?

a) James-Lange   **b)** Cannon-Bard

2. Explain the difference in the place held by cognition in the Schachter and Singer two-factor theory and Lazarus' cognitive-motivational-relational theory.

3. Joseph LeDoux proposed two "routes" by which fearful stimuli are processed by the human nervous system. One route, the "high road," passes from the thalamus to the cerebral cortex and from there to the amygdala. This route is said to be highly _____. The other route, which passes from the thalamus directly to the amygdala, is said to be highly _____.

a) specific/sensitive   **b)** sensitive/specific

4. Match the theory or theorists with the description/observation:

James-Lange theory	Emotions are captured as body memories.
Schachter-Singer two-factor theory	Some emotions (e.g., fear) have direct pathways from perception to emotion, bypassing the cortex.
Embodied emotion	When an emotional event is perceived, the autonomic nervous system and the cerebral cortex are stimulated by the thalamus at the same time.
Cannon-Bard theory	Emotion is only experienced following awareness of physiological responses to an event or thought.
Zajonc and LeDoux	Both emotion *and* associated physiological changes are only experienced after a person interprets the meaning of a thought or event.
Lazarus' cognitive-motivational-relational theory	Emotion is only experienced after a cognitive label is attached to physiological arousal in order to explain it.

How Do People Deal with Anger?

As we have already seen, negative emotions outnumber positive ones. An important aspect of human emotional life is coping on a day-to-day basis with these unpleasant feelings. Emotions such as *fear, anger, jealousy, envy, shame, guilt, disgust,* and *sadness* often present formidable challenges for human coping skills. We'll consider one of the most common, and without doubt the most dangerous, of the negative emotions: *anger.*

Anger Is Common, Varied, and Dangerous

Anger is an extremely common basic emotion that most people report experiencing from several times a week to several times a day (Averill, 1982). Most people know when they are angry, but pinning down a precise definition of a complex emotion like anger can be tricky. In the broadest sense, **anger** could be defined as a feeling of antagonism toward something or someone. Anger typically occurs as a reaction to an unpleasant event or idea—such as a belief that one has been harmed or threatened, or an injustice has occurred. However, anger may also exist as a character trait unrelated to any specific occurrence—a person's general tendency toward grumpiness, aggressiveness, and defensiveness.

The types of events eliciting anger—the "themes" or triggers—are exceptionally varied. Anger can be elicited by frustration when you are unable to realize a goal of some sort or are being interfered with in some way. Anger also results from being hurt by someone else; being insulted, denigrated, or rejected by someone important to you; or when experiencing disappointment, pain, or stress (Ekman, 2003a; Harmon-Jones & Harmon-Jones, 2007). Anger can range from vague annoyance to an all-consuming, fiery, homicidal rage. Although anger does not necessarily result in *aggression*—a deliberate effort to harm someone—it often does. Anger is therefore the most dangerous of all emotions. In fact, anger is defined in part as an emotion "linked associatively with an urge to injure some target" (Berkowitz & Harmon-Jones, 2004a, p. 108).

However, anger may sometimes be experienced as pleasurable (e.g., "righteous anger"), and some people are more prone toward enjoying anger than others (Harmon-Jones, cited by Ekman, 2003a, p. 125). Nonetheless, anger is generally extremely uncomfortable. In at least one world religion (Buddhism) it is considered one of the central causes of human suffering (Rahula, 1959), and it is also among the "seven deadly sins" of Christianity.

"Venting" Is Not an Effective Strategy for Dealing with Anger

"Venting to reduce anger is like using gasoline to put out a fire."

—Bushman (2002, p. 729)

Anger is difficult to avoid. Because each person's interests may not coincide with those of the next person, conflicts are bound to arise, and most people will feel unjustly treated on occasion. Anger and desire for revenge are typical human responses to such transgressions (McCullough, 2000; Pinker, 2011). The problem with anger, however, is that it often causes more suffering to the angry person than to the recipient of the anger. Although most of us usually do our best to control our anger when it arises and to look for ways to dissipate it, anger can lead to behavior that we later regret.

Anger ▶ A difficult-to-define basic emotion involving feelings of antagonism toward something or someone.

A popular view of anger depicts it as a kind of liquid substance that exists within a person's mind and body ("my anger"). When cooled, the substance is not noticeable and causes no problems. But when heated, it boils, turns to steam, and strains for release. Unless the anger is expressed, it will either create an explosion ("I'm about ready to explode"), or cause our "insides" to somehow fester ("His anger was eating him up inside"). According to this notion, you may be able to push anger around and situate it in various places in your mind, but you cannot get rid of it without expressing it.

The "liquid substance" idea applies to other emotions as well. "Express your feelings," we are urged, "don't keep them bottled up" (now the liquid is in a bottle!). As a general view of emotion this idea is known as the *hydraulic model of emotion*, because in a hydraulic system liquid circulates perpetually inside a machine or device to power it. The relief one may experience by expressing emotion is termed **catharsis**, which comes from the Greek word for "cleansing." As suggested earlier, anger is thought to demand catharsis or else bad things will happen. Anger catharsis is popularly termed *venting*. ("Go ahead, let it out—you need to vent.")

The hydraulic model of emotions was popularized in the work of Sigmund Freud, but it lost favor among scientific psychologists decades ago as a general explanation of emotions (Tavris, 1984, 1989). Nonetheless, the idea that catharsis is an effective tool to release anger lives on in psychology self-help books, advice columns, talk shows, movies, and television. Bushman (2002, p. 724) cites a good example: In the film *Analyze This*, a psychiatrist (played by Billy Crystal) tells an angry gangster (played by Robert De Niro), "You know what I do when I'm angry? I hit a pillow. Try that." Instead, the gangster pulls out a gun and fires several rounds into the pillow. Crystal: "Feel better?" De Niro: "Yeah, I do."

In fact, unless you are venting at the *specific person* who has angered you *and* you are convinced the person *will not retaliate*, any immediate feeling of relief is illusory, because venting at substitute targets such as pillows, walls, punching bags, or other people increases anger—it does not decrease it (Bandura, 1973; Bushman, 2002; Bushman, Baumeister, & Stack, 1999; Lohr, Olatunji, Baumeister, & Bushman, 2007). Venting is essentially a "rehearsal" of anger and aggression—it only serves to improve the "performance" by keeping angry feelings and thoughts alive. This is particularly true when you *ruminate* about the events that made you angry, focusing your thoughts on the offender and the offense as you vent (Rusting & Nolen-Hoeksema, 1998).

For example, aggression researcher Brad Bushman (2002) first angered a group of college students by providing false but stinging criticism of an essay they had written—criticism supposedly given by another participant in the study. One group of these students was encouraged to hit a punching bag while keeping a photo of the supposed offender in view and thinking about him or her. Another group was encouraged to think about becoming physically fit as they punched the bag. Yet another group did nothing at all. Those who were encouraged to ruminate about the offender while punching the bag became the angriest, most aggressive, and reported the most negative mood later on. Those who punched the bag but thought about becoming physically fit became less aggressive and angry than the first group. Those who did nothing at all became the least angry and aggressive of all groups.

What about "talking it out" with a friend—surely this is wise advice? Unfortunately, again, there is the problem of "rehearsing" one's anger. As a form of support, a friend may be inclined to justify your anger by agreeing with your assessment of the situation and who is to blame for it. Discussing your anger might lead to solutions, but it might also "freeze the anger in time" and make it an obsession (Tavris, 1984).

These findings do not imply that you ought to *ignore* your anger, particularly if it is ongoing. Ignoring problems does not make them go away. Depending on the specifics of the situation, confronting a person who has made you angry (in

▲ **The Angry Person May Suffer More Than the Target of Anger.** Although righteous anger may sometimes feel pleasurable (at least for a time), the angry person often suffers the most.

Catharsis ▶ From the Greek word for cleansing, catharsis refers to the relief one may experience by expressing emotion.

a relatively civil manner) can be extremely helpful, as can various other coping strategies including waiting the anger out ("counting to 10"), relaxation training, and even psychotherapy for more severe problems (Del Vecchio & O'Leary, 2004). Interestingly, one method that is highly effective (and free) is *forgiveness*, as described in the "Living Psychology" feature (e.g., Witvliet, Ludwig, & Vander Laan, 2001).

LIVING PSYCHOLOGY

To Forgive Is Human as Well as Divine

▲ **Shu—Forgiveness.** The Chinese character Shu means "forgiveness" and is composed of the symbols for woman, mouth, and heart. Forgiveness means many things to many people, but psychologists agree that forgiveness does *not* involve being a "doormat," giving up holding a person responsible for her or his actions, or remaining in destructive relationships. Forgiveness is not the same as forgetting or denying.

Forgiveness—which can occur through a conscious decision to forgive as well as the result of a generally forgiving disposition—is a cognitive, motivational, and emotional process that unfolds over time. As the person forgives, he or she willingly renounces the "right" to resentful, bitter, and hostile feelings and judgments toward the offending party, abandons grudges or plans for revenge, and may also intentionally foster compassion, generosity, and other positive emotions toward the offender (McCullough, Fincham & Tsang, 2003; Worthington, Witvliet, Pietrini, & Miller, 2007).

Forgiveness can have powerfully positive consequences for the forgiven, the forgiver, and for their relationship. It has been successfully used to improve adjustment to spinal cord injury among patients who are able to forgive those responsible for their injury; reduce levels of depression, anxiety, and posttraumatic stress; increase self-esteem and hope; increase overall well-being; reduce substance abuse; increase self-esteem among middle-school victims of bullying; decrease marital discord and disruption; and improve outcome in treatment of sexual and emotional abuse (Bono, McCullough, & Root, 2008; Fincham, Hall, & Beech, 2006; Flanagan, Vanden Hoek, Ranter, & Reich, 2012; Freedman & Enright, 1996; Lin, Mack, Enright, Krahn, & Baskin, 2004; Maltby, Macaskill, & Day, 2001; Orcutt, 2006; Reed & Enright, 2006; Witvliet, 2005; Witvliet & McCullough, 2007). Forgiveness has been shown to have beneficial effects on Americans following the September 11, 2001 attacks; Rwandans following the catastrophic Tutsi genocide; and among former child soldiers from the Congo and Uganda (Fehr, Gelfand, & Nag, 2010).

Research even suggests that forgiveness may improve physiological health, including beneficial effects on cardiovascular disease and hypertension (Lawler et al., 2003; Witvliet & McCullough, 2007; Worthington & Scherer, 2004). These effects may be specific to forgiveness, and not a result of the reduction in anger that typically accompanies forgiveness. Thus, the point of forgiveness is not to do someone else a favor. It is to promote *your own* well-being and, if appropriate, heal relationships that you consider important. When one forgives, one may be released from the prison of one's own anger and resentment. ■

IN SUMMARY

1. Anger is a feeling of antagonism toward someone or something. It is generally experienced in response to an event or idea, but it may also exist as a character trait. Anger is generally an unpleasant feeling, but it may sometimes be pleasurable.

2.	Anger often causes more suffering to the angry person than to its recipient. "Venting" anger appears to offer relief only when directed at the specific person who has angered you *and* you are convinced the person will not retaliate. Otherwise, venting increases anger. Although "talking it out" with a friend may sometimes be helpful, it may also serve as a "rehearsal" of the anger.
3.	One of the most promising methods for reducing anger is forgiveness, engaged in as a conscious decision unfolding over time.

RETRIEVE!

1.	True or false: Those who urge you not to keep your feelings "bottled up" are adhering to the hydraulic model of emotion.
2.	Punching pillows, walls, or punching bags when you are angry does not decrease anger, it simply "rehearses" it and often increases its longevity. However, "venting" may be of some help on occasion, but only if two conditions are met. What are these two conditions? **a)** You must vent at the specific person who has angered you, *and* you must be certain that the person will not retaliate against you. **b)** You are able to destroy something (e.g., break something), but the broken object cannot have value. **c)** You must vent at the specific person who has angered you, *and* you must then "make up" with the person. **d)** You must vent verbally, not physically, and afterward you must cease all attempts to vent.

Who Is Happy (and Why)?

Clearly, not all emotions are negative. As the movement toward positive psychology has gained momentum over the past 15 years, there has been an explosion of interest in the study of human strengths and positive emotions and attributes, including happiness, life satisfaction, and subjective well-being (Diener & Seligman, 2004; Diener, Ng, Harter, & Arora, 2010; Gable & Haidt, 2005; Lyubomirsky, Sheldon, & Schkade, 2005). A picture has begun to form of who among us is truly happy and what makes us happy, as well as what threatens happiness.

What is happiness? The larger meaning of this term has been debated by philosophers for thousands of years (Oishi, Diener, & Lucas, 2007) but there are two general senses in which *happiness* is used by psychologists. The first is to describe the basic emotion of enjoyment/happiness. Like other emotions, this form of happiness is intense, but fleeting. The other sense in which the term is used is to describe an overall subjective sense of well-being, contentment, fulfillment, and life satisfaction—the general feeling that things are going well. This is the sense in which the term is most often used by psychologists, and that's the way I will use the term in the discussion to follow.

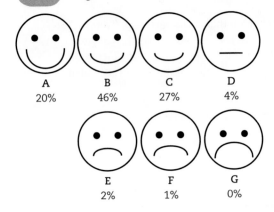

▲ FIGURE 11.10 Most People Are Reasonably Happy. In a 1976 survey of residents of Detroit, researchers asked their respondents to rate their general happiness and life satisfaction by choosing from seven simple face drawings ranging from a broad smile to a deep frown. As depicted here, 93% picked faces with a smile, and 66% picked one of the two happiest-looking faces. *(Source for figure: Myers, 2000; data from Andrews & Withey, 1976, pp. 207, 306.)*

Most People Are Reasonably Happy

Happiness and its long list of variants—enjoyment, contentment, satisfaction, gladness, fulfillment, well-being, and so forth—are important goals of most people's lives (Diener, Suh, Lucas, & Smith, 1999; King & Napa, 1998), and most of us appear to be reasonably happy when we consider our lives overall. Polls and psychology research studies consistently report that, when asked, most people around the world, regardless of race, sex, or form of government—unless they are living under conditions of extreme political suppression—report that they either are very happy and satisfied with their lives or reasonably so. Relatively few report being generally unhappy or unsatisfied (Biswas-Diener, Vittersø, & Diener, 2005; Diener, 2000; Inglehart, Basanez, Diez-Medrano, Halman, & Luijkx, 2004; see Figure 11.10). In a 2004 poll of a randomly selected sample of adult Americans conducted by a research company for *Time* magazine (Wallis, 2005), approximately 80% reported that they "generally wake up happy," feel happy "most of the time," and had thus far led either a good, very good, or "the best possible" life.[1]

These findings are not limited to Americans. David Myers and Ed Diener, among the founders of the modern positive psychology study of happiness, combined data from 916 previous surveys with samples totaling about 1,100,000 people from 45 industrialized nations (Myers & Diener, 1996). On a scale of "subjective well-being" ranging from 1 to 10, participants' average score was 6.75. Similar results were found for citizens of traditional societies (Biswas-Diener et al., 2005; Inglehart et al., 2004). In the Gallup World Poll, the first truly representative sample of the entire planet, most people reported experiencing more positive than negative feelings and generally believed that their psychological needs were met (Diener et al., 2010).

Findings that people are generally happy and satisfied with their lives occur regardless of how these variables are measured. Although most surveys simply ask people to rate how satisfied they are with their lives overall, Daniel Kahneman and his colleagues asked a sample of 909 women to fill out a highly detailed evaluation of *each* of the activities they engaged in the day before. These researchers gave participants a choice of adjectives to describe how they felt as they performed the activity—for example, *enjoying myself, happy, warm/friendly* or *frustrated/annoyed, depressed/blue, hassled/pushed around, angry/hostile.* Kahneman and his research team found that, while certain activities were rated more positively than others, participants rarely chose any negative adjectives to describe how they felt (Kahneman, Krueger, Schkade, Schwarz, & Stone, 2004).

Do these results surprise you? If so, you are not alone. Most people seem to believe that *they* may be generally happy, but *other people* are not. As an example, when a sample of people were asked to rank themselves in happiness as compared with famous people such as Oprah Winfrey, Bill Gates, and the Pope, almost 50% believed that they enjoyed greater happiness (Opinion Research Corporation, cited in Myers, 2000, p. 57).

When Money Buys Happiness

Most people believe that they would be happier if they had more money (Kahneman et al., 2004; Myers, 2000). However, one of the most interesting findings in research on happiness and well-being is that money does not *necessarily* buy happiness (Diener & Seligman, 2004). For example, Figure 11.11 shows that while the U. S. Gross National Product has increased dramatically

---

[1]*I have rounded off the figures to 80% because they differ very slightly for each of these questions, from 78% to 83%.*

Table 11.1 Life Satisfaction Compared among Various Groups

GROUP	RATING
Forbes magazine's "richest Americans"	5.8
Pennsylvania Amish	5.8
Inughuit Inuit people of Northern Greenland	5.8
Maasai of East Africa	5.7
Swedish representative (probability) sample	5.6
International college-student sample (47 nations, year 2000)	4.9
Illinois Amish	4.9
Calcutta slum dwellers	4.6
Fresno, California homeless	2.9
Calcutta pavement dwellers (homeless)	2.9

Note: Participants indicated their agreement with the statement "You are satisfied with your life" using a scale from 1 (complete disagreement) to 7 (complete agreement); 4 is neutral. *(Source: Diener & Seligman, 2004, p. 10.)*

▲ **FIGURE 11.11** Gross National Product Has Increased, but Life Satisfaction Has Remained the Same. *(Source: Diener & Seligman, 2004, p. 3.)*

since 1947, levels of life satisfaction have remained virtually the same. The same finding occurs when the income of U. S. citizens is examined—it has tripled in real (inflation-adjusted) dollars since the 1950s, but people are no happier for it (Myers, 2000).

In Table 11.1, a sample of *Forbes* magazine's "richest Americans" show levels of life satisfaction identical to the Pennsylvania Amish and the Inuit of Northern Greenland. The Maasai of Kenya and the entire Swedish nation are not far behind (Diener & Seligman, 2004).

High levels of happiness are possible even among nations whose inhabitants are quite poor. For example, as Figure 11.12 shows, Nigeria and El Salvador are among the very poorest nations, but also among the happiest; and the place whose citizens report the highest levels of happiness and life satisfaction, Puerto Rico, has a GNP (gross national product) of only approximately $10,000 per person.

However, it is also true that sometimes money *does* buy happiness . . . or at least comfort and life satisfaction (Diener et al., 2010). The relationship of money to happiness and life satisfaction is complicated. Returning to Figure 11.12, while many very poor nations report high levels of happiness and life satisfaction, *all* nations whose inhabitants report the *least* happiness are also among the poorest (GNPs below $5,000). Moreover, the majority of nations scoring in the higher "happiness" ranges have relatively high GNPs.

Figure 11.13 tells a somewhat similar story. Those individuals making over $90,000 or $100,000 per year report much greater overall happiness than those making very low five-figure incomes (under $20,000). However, the difference in reported happiness between those earning $100,000 and those earning $50,000 is practically nil. Thus, it seems that money *does* buy happiness to some degree, *but primarily for those who have relatively little money to begin with.*

WHAT SORT OF HAPPINESS DOES MONEY BUY?

The relation between money and happiness is clarified further by data from the recent Gallup World Poll (Diener et al., 2010). Positive psychologist Ed Diener and his colleagues discovered that income is related to happiness primarily in

▶ **FIGURE 11.12** International Comparison Chart of Happiness and Life Satisfaction. As part of the University of Michigan's World Values Survey, citizens from 81 nations were asked about their level of happiness and life satisfaction. Many countries (particularly in Latin America) with low per capita gross national products (GNPs) nonetheless report high levels of happiness and life satisfaction. On the other hand, *all* of the nations scoring in the "unhappy" range have per capita GNPs below $5,000—and the majority of nations scoring in the highest happiness ranges are relatively wealthy. *(Source: Inglehart et al., 2004.)*

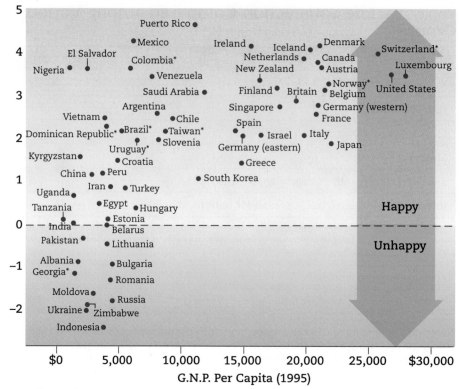

*Poll results for these countries were from 1995

Would you say you are happy . . .

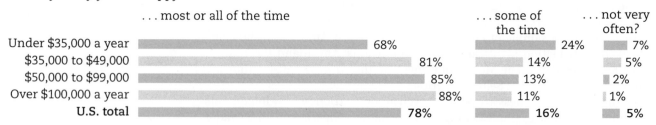

	Precentage indicating global happiness at family income of			
RESPONSE	Under $20,000	$20,000–$49,999	$50,000–$89,999	$90,000 and over
Not too happy	17.2	13.0	7.7	5.3
Pretty happy	60.5	56.8	50.3	51.8
Very happy	22.2	30.2	49.9	42.9

▲ **FIGURE 11.13** Comparison of Happiness Levels in the United States According to Income. In Graph A, taken from a 2005 *Time* magazine poll, there is little increase in overall happiness between Americans making over $35,000 per year and those making over $100,000 per year (although there is a slight increase). However, those earning *less* than $35,000 per year report markedly *reduced* levels of happiness. In Table B, taken from the NORC General Social Survey in 2004, the difference in reported happiness between those earning over $90,000 and those earning $50,000 is virtually nonexistent. However, those earning over $90,000 reported levels of happiness almost twice that of those earning less than $20,000. *(Sources: Graph A—*Time *magazine poll:* Time, *January 17, 2005, conducted Dec. 13–14, 2004, by telephone among 1,009 adult Americans; Table B—2004 NORC General Social Survey; figure adapted from Kahneman et al., 2006, p. 1909.)*

terms of satisfaction with one's standard of living, pleasure derived from the ownership of luxury conveniences, and overall life evaluation; but money is only weakly related to the experience of positive feelings (and lack of negative feelings), enjoyment of life, smiles, and laughter—the *emotional* side of happiness. Emotional happiness is much more strongly related to what Diener and colleagues refer to as *social psychological prosperity*—having the freedom to do as one wishes, learning, engaging in work that utilizes one's skills, being

Table 11.2 **Rankings of Selected Nations on Types of Prosperity**

This table ranks 18 nations from the World Gallop Poll on Gross Domestic Product (GDP, a measure of national income); social psychological prosperity; overall life evaluation; frequency of positive feelings; and frequency of negative feelings.

NATION	GDP/CAPITA	SOCIAL PSYCHOLOGICAL PROSPERITY	OVERALL LIFE EVALUATION	HIGH POSITIVE FEELINGS	LOW NEGATIVE FEELINGS
United States	1	19	16	26	49
Denmark	5	13	1	7	1
The Netherlands	7	36	4	3	26
Japan	14	50	24	44	6
Italy	18	33	20	67	63
Israel	20	56	11	61	64
New Zealand	22	12	9	1	21
South Korea	24	83	38	58	77
South Africa	35	42	53	29	44
Russia	36	72	56	79	42
Mexico	39	22	23	17	28
Costa Rica	41	6	18	4	38
Indonesia	59	63	57	24	43
India	61	85	46	63	22
Ghana	68	51	70	68	20
Nepal	76	88	69	50	10
Sierra Leone	87	80	87	87	86
Tanzania	89	58	86	52	32

Note: GDP = gross domestic product.

respected in the community, and having friends and family to count on in an emergency (see Table 11.2).

When Money Buys *Un*happiness

Can money ever buy *un*happiness? Movies and books are filled with wealthy characters who are miserable, but what does research say? People who strongly aspire to financial success beyond that necessary for a reasonably comfortable life frequently do experience *decreases* in their feelings of well-being, directly attributable to their focusing on material gain at the expense of performing work they consider meaningful or engaging in a satisfying family life and leisure activities (Kahneman et al., 2006; Kasser & Ryan, 1996; Nickerson, Schwarz, Diener, & Kahneman, 2003). Such income-focused individuals often judge their progress not by their actual wealth, but by their wealth as compared with others or as compared against some ideal standard (Boyce, Brown, & Moore, 2010; Frank, 1999). If you judge your financial status in a comparative way like this, you may be perpetually dissatisfied and unhappy (Johnson & Krueger, 2006).

**▲ What Happy People *Don't*
Do.** When John Robinson and
Steven Martin examined 34 years
of data collected from daily diary
studies, they found that those who
describe themselves as happy
engage in more social activities, religious observance, and newspaper
reading than those who describe
themselves as unhappy. On the
other hand, happy people watch
much less television than the unhappy (Robertson & Martin, 2008).

Finally, although earning large sums of money may not buy much emotional happiness, *spending* money might—*if you are spending it on others.*
In a series of longitudinal and experimental studies published in *Science,* the
premier American journal of scientific research, Elizabeth Dunn and her colleagues showed that higher levels of happiness and subjective well-being were
associated with larger percentages of a person's income spent on others as gifts
or contributions to charity (Dunn, Aknin, & Norton, 2008).

Happiness "Set Points" Are Not Set in Stone

If money does not always buy happiness—and chasing it can make a person
unhappy—what *does* increase feelings of emotional well-being? The factors
that determine a person's happiness begin with the person's "happiness set
point," a general level of subjective well-being to which we tend to return even
if we experience temporary periods of uncharacteristically higher or lower
levels.

Strong evidence suggests that people's typically chronic level of happiness
is to some degree a result of genetic inheritance (Lykken & Tellegen, 1996;
Lyubomirsky et al., 2005; Nes, Røysamb, Tambs, Harris, & Reichborn-
Kjennerud, 2006; Weiss, Bates, & Luciano, 2008). As discussed in Chapters 4
and 12, infant temperament and adult personality characteristics such as the
tendency to be cheerful and agreeable or to be pessimistic and moody have
genetic components and remain fairly constant throughout one's life. In the
same way, the tendency to report feeling happy and satisfied with life or unhappy and dissatisfied is also strongly influenced by genes and by the interaction of these genes with experiences in development (Weiss et al., 2008).
This happiness "set point"—the intrinsic level of happiness to which a person
repeatedly returns—also tends to remain relatively constant throughout life
(Lyubomirsky et al., 2005).

However, like baseline body weight as described in Chapter 10, one's happiness set point is not set in stone, and although people do *tend* to revert to
their set point following uncharacteristic changes in well-being—for example,
following divorce or the loss of a loved one—they are somewhat more likely to
experience lasting changes over time in happiness (or its opposite, depression
and anxiety) than in various other characteristics affected by genetics, such as
personality traits, blood pressure, and weight (Diener, Lucas & Scollon, 2006;
Fujita & Diener, 2005; Kendler et al., 2011; Lucas 2007).

What Makes People Happy

After examining the data on happiness, Sonja Lyubomirsky and her colleagues
estimated that about 50% of one's level of happiness is determined by happiness set point, 10% by one's life circumstances (e.g., income, environment,
social structure, and government), and 40% by one's "intentional activities"
(Lyubomirsky et al., 2005; Lyubomirsky & Layous, 2013). So what sort of "intentional activities" lead to happiness?

When researchers measure the quality of various aspects of people's lives
(friendships, income, work, love relationships, etc.) and compare these measurements against reported levels of happiness or life satisfaction, the most
important factors that emerge are *social* in nature. The same result is found if
people are prompted to look at their lives overall and list those factors which
they believe have contributed most importantly to their well-being. Research
repeatedly emphasizes the primacy of social relationships in the lives of happy
people (Diener et al., 2010; Diener & Seligman, 2002; Myers, 2000).

As suggested earlier, social factors associated with happiness include relationships with one's friends, children, romantic partners or spouses, and other
family; involvement with social networks; engaging in meaningful work; being a respected member of one's community; and contributions made to the

welfare of others. People who are very happy spend less time alone than people who are not (Diener & Seligman, 2002; Myers, 2000; Wallis, 2005). Although it is not clear if happier people have strong social relationships *because* they are happy, or if they are happy in part because of the relationships, it remains that strong social relationships are associated with happiness, and poor social relationships with unhappiness.

However, results may be different if one asks people *at the moment they are engaging in an activity* if they are feeling happy or enjoying themselves. For example, while a parent's relationship with his or her children may top the list of "happiness-inducing" factors, interacting with children definitely does *not* always afford parents the highest degrees of happiness and enjoyment *at the moment they are experiencing each interaction*. In the 2004 study by Daniel Kahneman and his colleagues described earlier, investigators measured women's levels of positive feeling at the time they engaged in specific activities. Taking care of their children was ranked very low—somewhere above housework and commuting, but lower than watching TV and eating. What did they give highest scores to? *Having sex* ("intimate relations")!

How can we account for this disparity in research findings? If you ask how a person is feeling about an activity at the moment, answers tend to describe levels of pleasure, enjoyment, and joy. However, pleasure, enjoyment, and joy describe happiness as a basic emotion—they describe states that are fleeting and are not necessarily identical to overall happiness, well-being, contentment, and life-satisfaction. As a parent, I can easily understand these women's responses. My kids can be a pain at any given moment, and caring for them can be tiring. However, the *intensity* of overall positive emotions I feel toward my children, and the strength of the beneficial effect they have on my life dwarf the daily hassles I also experience with them. As expressed by Ronald Inglehart and colleagues: ". . . one minute when your child comes running to greet you with a smile and a hug may be worth a hundred minutes of cleaning up after them" (Inglehart, Foa, Peterson, & Welzel, 2008, p. 279). As corny as that may sound to you, my own experience testifies that it is true—at least for some number of people.

◄ King of Happiness. Jigme Singye Wangchuck, king of the Himalayan nation of Bhutan from 1972 to 2006, startled much of the world by enacting a governmental policy stressing Gross National Happiness (GNH) over Gross National Product (GNP). GNH is not simply an idealistic notion. When Jigme Singye Wangchuck began his reign, Bhutan was severely impoverished and underdeveloped. The king was determined to institute policies that would allow for development, but would do so in a balanced manner that would bring environmental, cultural, educational, and spiritual development into harmony with economic development. The idea was to avoid the pitfall of blind pursuit of economic gain at the expense of other factors critical to life satisfaction (Exechieli, 2003). The government of Bhutan uses extensive diary surveys of the daily lives of citizens to measure growth in life satisfaction and subjective well-being of the Bhutanese people.

IN SUMMARY

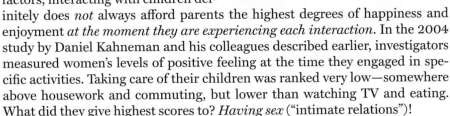

1. Happiness can be defined as an emotion (intense and fleeting) or a general level of subjective well-being and life satisfaction.

2. Most people describe themselves as generally happy with their lives, and most people believe they themselves are happier than others are.

3. Increased income results in increased happiness primarily if initial levels of income are quite low. Otherwise, income is not strongly related to levels of emotional happiness. However, citizens of nations with high GDPs are much more likely to express overall life satisfaction. Focusing one's life on making money can result in reduced happiness, particularly if one is comparing one's wealth with that of others or against an ideal standard.

4. Each person's general level of subjective well-being and life satisfaction is strongly influenced by a genetic "set point" to which each of us tends to return after uncharacteristic levels of increased or decreased happiness. However, these set points are not set in stone, and people are more likely to experience changes in happiness set point than in many other characteristics affected by genetics

5. Apart from genetics and life events beyond one's control, the factors which contribute the most to overall happiness, well-being, and life satisfaction are social in nature: friendships, love and parenting relationships, and contributions made to the welfare of others. However, such relationships do not always contribute the most to happiness as an intense and fleeting emotion.

RETRIEVE!

1. True or false: Since 1947, the U. S. gross national product (GNP) has increased dramatically. However, levels of life satisfaction have remained the same.

2. Research comparing per capita GNP of nations throughout the world with levels of life satisfaction tells a "story" similar to that told by research among Americans earning less than $35,000 and more than $100,000. What is this "story"?

3. True or false: The happiness set point tends to remain stable throughout one's lifetime, although change is possible.

4. Why might a person claim that raising children has brought him or her the greatest of happiness, and yet when asked about happiness at the moment of interaction with children report very low levels?

What Is Stress?

10:30 a.m.: Your cat wakes you up by planting himself on your chest, and you realize that your clock did not go off at 8:30 as it should have. Looking over at the clock through a hazy nest of warm blankets you realize that your first class is starting in 20 minutes. You leap out of bed, only to fall violently back as a result of a hammering headache—the remains of a night of partying at your best friend's birthday celebration. You decide to skip the class, roll over, and fall back to sleep.

11:00 a.m.: The phone rings and you decide to stumble over to answer it rather than having to listen to the robotic version of Beethoven's *Für Elise* that your roommate has programmed as the answering tone. On the other end of the phone is your best study buddy calling from the class on her cell phone, frantically asking why you are missing the midterm that had been rescheduled during the last class (the one you had to miss because of a work interview). Scrambling to find some clothes, you realize that you left your laundry in the washer when you stumbled into the house last night, and you are now forced to put on the clothes you wore the day before which do not smell all that pleasant.

11:15 a.m.: You virtually leap into your car. When you turn the ignition switch, the car is dead. You left the headlights on when you arrived home the night before.

Are you stressed yet?

Our emotional systems are intricately interwoven with processes of health and illness. In particular, *chronic stress* and the emotions connected with stress decrease our ability to fight disease; while healthful states are promoted when we discover ways to cope with and counter the effects of chronic stress. In the remainder of this chapter we shall consider mental and physical health problems connected with stress, mechanisms for coping with stress, and some behavioral tools for sustaining good health.

Stress Is a Response to Challenging or Threatening Events

Stress is of great interest to clinicians and researchers in **health psychology**, an interdisciplinary field that examines the ways that health and illness interact with psychology, biology, and society. Biologists often define *stress* as any event that threatens *homeostasis* of an organism—its ordinary physiological and neurobiological state at rest (Gunnar & Quevedo, 2007; Selye, 1956; Ulrich-Lai & Herman, 2009). Any adaptive neurobiological response that allows an organism to regain homeostasis in the face of changing circumstances is then termed a *stress response* (Cannon, 1929b; Holsboer & Ising, 2010; Segerstrom & Miller, 2004).

However, most psychologists define *stress* in a way that is closer to common understandings of the term: **Stress** is the psychological and physiological consequence of events that challenge a person's ability to *cope* and which threaten well-being or interfere with important goals (Lazarus & Folkman, 1984). Such life events are known as *stressors*, and they vary from the sorts of day-to-day hassles facing the hapless college student described earlier, to severe life crises such as the death of a loved one, the loss of a job, divorce, or life-threatening illness. Interestingly, even seemingly positive events such as a work promotion, marriage, graduation from college, or winning the lottery may sometimes cause stress if the event entails making a major life change (Holmes & Rahe, 1967; Hobson & Delunas, 2001).

Table 11.3 shows a list of 30 frequently occurring life events in order of their potential stressfulness as rated by a representative national sample of Americans during the 1990s (Hobson et al., 1998). The list, an abbreviated version of the Revised Social Readjustment Rating Scale (SRRS-R), paints a good portrait of the sorts of common events Americans rate as more stressful than others.

Are these events similarly stressful for non-Americans? The answer appears to be "yes," at least as far as college students are concerned. When Francis McAndrew and colleagues surveyed college and university students from Germany, India, South Africa (white and black students), and the United States, they found substantial agreement about the stressfulness of various life events (McAndrew, Akande, Turner, & Sharma, 1998).

Although the events listed in Table 11.3 are undoubtedly stressful for most people, it is important to realize that stress itself is *not* the event; it is a *response* to the event; it is a way of perceiving, experiencing, and interacting with an event (Lazarus, 1999). For example, a situation that is experienced by one person as a severe stressor—a jail sentence, divorce, or loss of a job—may be experienced by another person as a challenge and an opportunity for self-improvement and taking control of one's life. Such a person has developed a way of *coping* with specific types of potentially stressful events. Thus, potentially stressful events are always filtered through—and interpreted by—each person's unique psychology. Whether we experience a given event as profoundly stressful, mildly stressful, or not at all stressful often has more to do with what we bring to the event than the event itself (Beck, 1999; Lazarus, 1999; Seligman, 1990.) Knowledge of this fact is one of the keys to coping with stress, as explained later in the chapter.

Health psychology ▶ An interdisciplinary field which examines the ways that health and illness interact with psychology, biology, and society. Health psychologists work in clinical settings alongside medical doctors, or in academic settings teaching and conducting research.

Stress ▶ Biologists and psychologists define stress differently. Biologists usually define stress as any event that threatens homeostasis of an organism. Psychologists usually define stress as the psychological and physiological consequence of events which challenge a person's ability to cope and which threaten well-being or interfere with important goals. Each specific stressful event is termed a *stressor*.

Table 11.3 The 30 Most Stressful Life Events for Americans

1. Death of spouse/mate
2. Death of close family member
3. Major injury/illness to self
4. Detention in jail or other institution
5. Major injury/illness to close family member
6. Foreclosure on loan/mortgage
7. Divorce
8. Being a victim of crime
9. Being the victim of police brutality
10. Infidelity
11. Experiencing domestic violence/sexual abuse
12. Separation or reconciliation with spouse/mate
13. Being fired/laid-off/unemployed
14. Experiencing financial problems/difficulties
15. Death of close friend
16. Surviving a disaster
17. Becoming a single parent
18. Assuming responsibility for sick or elderly loved one
19. Loss of or major reduction in health insurance/benefits
20. Self/close family member being arrested for violating the law
21. Major disagreement over child support/custody/visitation
22. Experiencing/involvement in auto accident
23. Being disciplined at work/demoted
24. Dealing with unwanted pregnancy
25. Adult child moving in with parent/parent moving in with adult child
26. Child developing behavior or learning problem
27. Experiencing employment discrimination/sexual harassment
28. Attempting to modify addictive behavior of self
29. Discovering/attempting to modify addictive behavior of close family member
30. Employer reorganization/downsizing

(*Source: Abbreviated and adapted from Hobson et al., 1998, p. 7.*)

We Need Stress

Looking at the list in Table 11.3, we see a host of miseries few of us would voluntarily undergo. Although, as stated earlier, some positive events also produce stress, it is clearly negative events that are most likely to do so. When combined with various claims about the damaging effects of stress, this seems logically to lead to the conclusion that stress is *bad*.

In fact, stress, at least some degree of stress, is *not* a bad thing. Mild stress and the anxiety it produces can motivate us to accomplish goals and to protect ourselves and the people who are important to us. Moreover, although chronic, unremitting stress can be damaging to immune and nervous systems, as we shall see, relatively *brief* activation of the stress response strengthens immune systems and promotes various other adaptive responses (Cohen et al., 1998; Roozendaal, McEwan, & Chattarji, 2009; Segerstrom & Miller, 2004). Even when stress suppresses immune system functioning, this sometimes has a beneficial result, because too much immune system activity can be harmful to health if it occurs in the absence of serious infection (Segerstrom, 2007).

Thus, to some degree we need stress. It is when stress is *chronic and unrelenting* that it can lead to serious trouble. The problem is that stress-response mechanisms are primarily adaptive for *acute* stress—intense perhaps, but relatively short-lived. Resilience to chronic stress is a trickier proposition (Segerstrom & Miller, 2004).

However, while certain groups tend to experience more stress than others (for example, minority groups and the poor), and certain individuals are more likely than others to experience trauma in response to stress, stress is a universal experience of human beings. We are all stressed to one degree or another throughout our lives, and stressful events have been with us throughout our evolutionary history, yet we are not disabled by stress. Indeed, the most typical outcome for most people even after exposure to extreme stress—such as that experienced in warfare, under terrorist attacks, following the death of a loved one, or in cases of child abuse—is recovery and resilience, *not* trauma, disease, or dysfunction (Bonanno, 2005; Bonanno & Mancini, 2008; Bonanno, Westphal, & Mancini, 2011). Even survivors of experiences of inconceivable trauma and torment, such as Jews held in Nazi concentration camps during World War II, have in some cases displayed astonishing resilience (Barel, Van Ijzendoorn, Sagi-Schwartz, & Bakermans-Kranenburg, 2010).

The Stress Response Involves Activation and Adaptation

The first controlled observations of the way mammals respond to challenging or taxing events were made by Walter Cannon in 1915 (Cannon, 1929a). Cannon noted that under conditions of extreme environmental distress, such as cold or lack of oxygen, or attack by other animals, laboratory rodents experienced unusual activity in the sympathetic nervous and endocrine systems involving the release of hormones and redirection of energy stores. These processes biologically prepare the animal either to run from a problem or stay to fight or tough it out. Cannon coined the term **fight or flight** to describe these processes, because it appeared to him that the purpose of the stress response was to prepare the organism to struggle for survival, either by avoiding threat or facing it head-on.

But consider being stuck in freeway traffic during rush hour on a Friday afternoon. Your stress response kicks in, but what good would it be to try to fight or flee? You can't get anywhere. And allowing "road rage" to get the better of you could land you straight in the hospital or the local jail.

Here is a central part of the problem: *The short-term stress response takes away from long-term survival resources.* As Cannon noted, the sympathetic nervous system, which governs all functions vital to short-term crisis situations, is activated under stress. This activation suppresses many vital functions of the *parasympathetic* system, which governs the so-called vegetative functions—those crucial for keeping you alive in the long term, including digestion, sleep, and immune system functions. The reason that the stimulation of one system suppresses activity in the other is that the sympathetic and parasympathetic systems work as **opponent processes**. A rise in activity in one leads to a decrease of activity in the other.

Fight or flight ▶ Walter Cannon's term to describe the initial mammalian response to stress: activation of the sympathetic nervous system, suppression of the parasympathetic nervous system, and release of hormones adrenaline (epinephrine) and noradrenaline (norepinephrine) by the hypothalamic-pituitary-adrenocortical axis (HPA) of the endocrine system.

Opponent processes ▶ Any process which functions as the antagonist of another process. The autonomic nervous system consists of two opponent process subsystems: the sympathetic and parasympathetic nervous systems. If the sympathetic nervous system is activated, the parasympathetic system is suppressed. If the parasympathetic system is activated, the sympathetic system is suppressed.

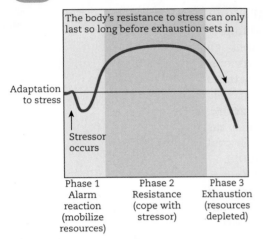

The body's resistance to stress can only last so long before exhaustion sets in

Adaptation to stress

Stressor occurs

Phase 1
Alarm
reaction
(mobilize
resources)

Phase 2
Resistance
(cope with
stressor)

Phase 3
Exhaustion
(resources
depleted)

▲ **FIGURE 11.14 The General Adaptation Syndrome (GAS).** Hans Selye was the first modern stress theorist. His GAS model shows how the initial response to threat (alarm phase) is adaptive, as is the resistance phase when the organism attempts to find ways to adapt and cope with the stressor. However, if stress continues and becomes chronic, the body's resources ultimately are depleted, and exhaustion sets in.

General Adaptation System (GAS) ▶ Hans Selye's model for mammalian response to chronic stress. GAS consists of three phases: Phase 1 (alarm), Phase 2 (resistance), and Phase 3 (exhaustion).

Tend and befriend ▶ Shelly Taylor's term which describes a response to stress that utilizes a strategy different from "fight or flight." In tend and befriend the adult affiliates with others and provides care to offspring. According to Taylor, women are far more likely than men to choose this alternate strategy for coping with stressful situations.

But while short-term suppression of parasympathetic activity may be beneficial in response to threat, what if the threat goes on for days, weeks, months, or longer? Suppression of sleep, digestion, and immune function for 10 minutes is one thing—for years running is quite another.

Hans Selye and the GAS Model

Hans Selye was an Austrian physician who emigrated to Canada in 1932 and coined the term *stress* as it is used currently (Selye, 1956). Drawing on Cannon's original observations of the stress response, he developed a model of effects of *chronic* stress activation known as the **General Adaptation Syndrome** or **GAS**.

As depicted in Figure 11.14, Selye's model first describes how the immediate reaction to a stressor prepares the organism to survive a threat by the intensely arousing action of mechanisms in the sympathetic nervous system and endocrine system, which allow stress-related hormones such as adrenaline and cortisol to be pumped into the blood. The outcome of the activation of these mechanisms is to make energy and strength readily available to an organism under threat ("fight or flight"), and to activate immune functions should they be needed. As these sympathetic nervous system functions are aroused, "nonemergency" activities of the parasympathetic nervous system, such as digestive activity and sleep, are suppressed. These initial stress responses constitute Phase 1 of the GAS model, the *alarm* phase, and they correspond to Cannon's "fight or flight."

In Phase 2, the individual *resists* the stressful condition for as long as possible by coping and adapting to the best of his or her ability (so the stage is called *resistance*). This phase is not as intense as Phase 1, but the body remains in its aroused state, and stress hormones continue to be pumped into the blood. But as the resistance phase continues, these hormones divert nutrients and oxygen that were originally bound for long-term maintenance of muscles and organs.

The combined effects the prolonged presence of these hormones leads to the third and final stage of the GAS, the aptly named *exhaustion* stage or Phase 3. The organism is literally "run down," and fatigue is inevitable. Vital regulation and rest functions have been compromised for so long that the body no longer has energy available to mobilize even for nonemergency activities.

You're stressed out!

Tend and Befriend: The Female Fight or Flight?

Do men and women respond to stress in the same way? Interestingly, the vast majority of research studies on the "fight or flight" response were conducted on males only—and male rodents to boot! Beginning with this observation, social psychologist Shelley Taylor and her associates advanced a potentially important new theory about *human* response to stress and threat (Taylor, 2002, 2006; Taylor et al., 2000).

Taylor does not deny that human beings experience the biological events in response to stress first described by Walter Cannon and Hans Selye, and she affirms that "fight or flight" accurately describes these events. However, in her view, this picture is incomplete. Under conditions of stress, human beings also experience a need to *affiliate*, as described in Chapter 10—to obtain support and comfort from others, and to provide support and comfort as well. Supportive social relationships have been shown to reduce stress, and Taylor suggests that the urge to tend to one's offspring and affiliate with other adults has been just as frequent a response to stress among humans over evolutionary times as fight or flight. She uses the phrase **tend and befriend** to describe the tendency to provide care and obtain support from others under conditions of stress.

However, recall from Chapter 10 that women's affiliation needs under conditions of stress are much stronger than men's. Taylor proposes that the tend-and-befriend response is therefore more common among women than men—although men also experience such responses under certain circumstances. To understand why this sex difference might exist, consider that in the environments of our ancestors, most women remained in a state of pregnancy or lactation (nursing) for a substantial portion of their lives (Symons, 1995). Because responses to threat are designed to increase the survival and reproductive success of any living organism, fighting or fleeing would not necessarily have been viable options for ancestral women under threat.

Unlike men, who would have endangered primarily their own lives when fighting, a woman choosing to fight would have endangered not only her own life but also the life of her unborn and nursing offspring—strongly reducing her reproductive success (Campbell, 2004). On the other hand, fleeing would not have been easy for a woman who was pregnant or nursing (or simply caretaking young children), and would likely have involved abandoning infants or children.

Instead, according to Taylor, women may have learned (a) to quiet, protect, and care for their children while blending into the environment (tending) and (b) to make effective use of the female social group for protection and other resources (befriending). These strategies for coping with threat then became part of women's psychology for dealing with stress in general, because the brain interprets all stresses similarly—whether they are actual physical threats or not.

▲ **Tend-and-Befriend During Wartime.** Under conditions of stress or threat, such as the military conflict in the Democratic Republic of the Congo, women may be more likely than men to offer care to children and seek support from others, particularly from other women.

OXYTOCIN: THE TEND-AND-BEFRIEND HORMONE

According to Taylor (2006), just as the hormones adrenaline and cortisol characterize the experience of fight-or-flight, the hormone oxytocin is the mechanism governing tend-and-befriend. As described in Chapter 2, oxytocin is associated with bonding between mothers and infants and also between adults of certain species, including humans (Bartels & Zeki, 2004; Carter, 2004; Gonzaga, Turner, Keltner, Campos, & Altemus, 2006). Oxytocin is also associated with reduction in the fight-or-flight response to stress—particularly in females—and in a reduction in stress responses generally. It is also associated with the tendency to affiliate (Taylor, 2006; Uvnas-Moberg, 1997). According to Taylor, under at least some conditions of stress, oxytocin is released, prompting desires to protect and care for one's children (tending) and/or affiliate with others (befriending).

Ethnic Minorities Experience Unique Stressors

Although all human beings experience stress, some people have a worse time of it than others. Research repeatedly shows that members of ethnic minorities and people living in poverty experience a greater number of stressful life events than others (Hatch & Dohrenwend, 2007). Although stressors associated with poverty may be easy to imagine and straightforward, members of ethnic minorities (and to some degree sexual and gender minorities) are subject to unique stressors not faced by members of majority groups, even the poor (Brondolo, Brady ver Halen, Pencille, Beatty, & Contrada, 2009; Okazaki, 2009).

Richard Contrada and his colleagues have divided these unique stressors into three categories (Contrada et al., 2000). The first is *ethnic discrimination*. For a minority group member in a society where inequality exists, the possibility of discrimination is always present, and by itself this represents pervasive ongoing stress requiring watchfulness and strategies for coping (Brondolo et al., 2009; C. T. Miller & Kaiser, 2001). For example, minority group members make ongoing decisions automatically as to whether or not some event or person's behavior represents discrimination or prejudice.

▲ **"Stop and Frisk" Is a Frequent Experience for Young Black Men.** Ethnic minorities may frequently experience stressors others rarely experience. In some urban areas, young African American men may be profiled for "stop and frisk" even if they have not behaved in a suspicious manner.

Own-group conformity pressure ▶ A stressful pressure to behave in a manner that a given ethnic group community believes is appropriate for one of its own.

Day-to-day discrimination is often subtle (e.g., having one's car stopped routinely by police officers primarily because one is young, male, and a person of color). As Contrada and his colleagues (2000) propose, members of minority ethnic groups are often torn between wanting to protect themselves from injustice and wanting very much to avoid perceiving discrimination where none exists—in other words, "false alarms" (Ruggiero & Taylor, 1997).

The second stressor is *stereotype threat*. Researchers have found that the standardized test performance of African Americans and women may decrease if they are exposed to information suggesting that members of their gender or ethnic group don't generally perform as well as others on such tests. Claude Steele calls this effect *stereotype threat* (Steele & Aronson, 2004). Stereotype threat may not only produce decreases in performance of tasks, but might actually affect the ability to learn new material in stereotype-related skills (Rydell, Rydell, & Boucher, 2010).

Own-group conformity pressure, the third unique stressor faced by minority groups, is just what it sounds like—a stressful pressure to behave in a manner that one's ethnic group community believes is appropriate for one of its own (Contrada et al., 2000; French & Chavez, 2010). For example, on some university campuses there is strong, unstated (or stated) pressure to maintain social contacts only within one's own ethnic group. For those individuals within an ethnic group who are interested in expanding their web of social contacts to include others, own-group conformity pressure can create day-to-day stress.

ETHNIC MINORITY MEMBERSHIP MAY ALSO PROTECT AGAINST STRESS

Ethnicity-related stressors seem likely to impact both physical and mental health of minority group members (Nazroo, 2003; Okazaki, 2009; Pascoe & Smart Richman, 2009; Utsey, Giesbrecht, Hook, & Stanard, 2008). But could ethnic minority membership also *protect* against stress and stress-related illness? Some research suggests that it might.

Epidemiological studies show that African Americans actually have lower rates of virtually all types of serious mental health problems than European Americans—and this includes lower rates of alcohol and drug abuse and antisocial personality disorder (Sue & Chu, 2003; Zhang & Snowden, 1999). Some studies have also found that Asian Americans respond less intensely than European Americans when they are exposed to psychological and physiological stressors in the laboratory (Shen, Stroud, & Niaura, 2004), and research has found that Mexican Americans who maintain ties to their culture also maintain higher levels of family support than non-Latino whites (Almeida, Molnar, Kawachi, & Subramanian, 2009). As Stanley Sue and June Chu (2003) suggest, many aspects of ethnic minority life may increase mental health—just as other aspects may decrease it.

IN SUMMARY

1.	Stress is usually defined as the psychological and physiological consequence of any event which challenges a person's ability to cope and which threatens well-being or interferes with important goals. Each specific stressful event is known as a stressor.
2.	The stress response is highly adaptive in the short term and serves important functions. The most common response to short-term stress—even severe stress—is resilience. However, chronic, unremitting stress can be damaging to brain and body.
3.	Fight or flight is the complex stress response first described by Walter Cannon and elaborated by Hans Selye in the general adaptation syndrome (GAS), which consists of three phases: Alarm, Resistance, and Exhaustion.

4.	According to Shelley Taylor, the tendency to care for infants and affiliate with others is a response to stress that is at least as common among women as fight or flight. The hormone oxytocin may trigger the desire to extend care and seek social support.
5.	Although ethnic minorities suffer unique stressors, aspects of ethnic minority life may also protect against stress. Unique stressors of minority groups include ethnic discrimination, stereotype threat, and own-group conformity pressure.

RETRIEVE!

1.	The activation of the sympathetic nervous system and endocrine system observed in rats under stress by Walter Cannon is called the _____ response.
2.	Short-term stress _____ immune systems, whereas long-term stress _____ immune systems. **a)** strengthens/damages **b)** damages/strengthens
3.	Name and describe the three phases of GAS. Which systems are affected during the alarm phase? Which hormones are released?
4.	According to Shelley Taylor, why have women evolved to use tend-and-befriend at least as often as fight-or-flight? Refer to living conditions of ancestral men and women, and probable sex differences in strategies for dealing with threatening situations.
5.	What is the term used to describe a situation where members of a minority group put pressure on an individual from their group not to behave in some particular way because "we don't do that"? **a)** stereotype threat **c)** reverse discrimination **b)** own-group conformity pressure **d)** ethnic extortion

Does Stress Cause Illness?

While it may seem like common sense that stress is more than uncomfortable and can cause more than psychological distress, does research support the idea that stress can make you physically sick? **Psychoneuroimmunology** is the study of the interaction between psychology, the nervous and endocrine systems, and immune systems. Scientists working in this field study the effects of stress and other psychological variables on the weakening of immune resistance and resultant illnesses. Let's examine some of their findings.

Psychoneuroimmunology
▶ The scientific study of the interaction of psychology, nervous and endocrine systems, and immune systems.

Stress Affects Immune Systems

Earlier I mentioned that chronic, unrelenting stress interferes with and suppresses immune functioning. Compromised immune functioning may then affect the aspects of the brain that regulate how we think and feel. Thus, there is a "feedback loop" between the brain and immune systems (Marland, Bachen, Cohen, Rabin, & Manuck, 2002; G. Miller, Chen, & Cole, 2009). Three areas of potential influence of stress-related immune suppression on disease have been of particular interest to psychoneuroimmunologists: the common cold, coronary heart disease (CHD), and depression.

▲ **Stress Enhances, Then Suppresses, Immune Functions.** Acute, short-term stress has been shown to enhance immune functioning. However, long-term, severe, chronic stress—such as that endured by soldiers deployed during wartime—suppresses the functioning of immune systems.

Coronary heart disease (CHD) ▶ The result of buildup of plaque along the walls of arteries, impairing their ability to supply oxygen and nutrients to muscles of the heart. Plaque consists largely of fatty acids, cholesterol, and calcium deposits.

STRESS INCREASES SUSCEPTIBILITY TO THE COMMON COLD

"Don't leave the house with your hair wet and without your scarf and hat—you'll catch a miserable cold!" How many of us endured such warnings as children? In fact, being cold does *not* increase your chances of catching a cold. The reason we get more colds in the winter is probably that we stay indoors more and are exposed to more viruses from other people. Viruses, not cold weather, cause colds. So go ahead—wash your hair and run outside in your underwear in 35-degree weather if it suits you (and the local ordinances allow it).

However, you can catch a cold from stress—as long as you are also exposed to the cold virus (and, I suppose, if you become *really cold* it could be stressful, so perhaps you'd better ignore what I said about going out in your underwear). Psychoneuroendocrinologist Sheldon Cohen has devoted many years to the study of the effects of stress on the common cold (Cohen, 1996; Cohen et al., 2008; Cohen, Janicki-Deverts, & Miller, 2007). The results? As depicted in Figure 11.15:

1. People who are under stress catch colds more often.

2. People exposed to cold viruses under quarantined laboratory conditions are more likely to catch a cold if they were under stress prior to being exposed to the viruses—and the higher the number and intensity of psychological stressors, the higher the risk of catching cold.

3. Positive emotional style—a general tendency to be happy, lively, and calm—protects against contracting the common cold, just as negative emotional style increases the chances of catching a cold.

STRESS IS ASSOCIATED WITH RISK OF HEART DISEASE

Coronary heart disease (**CHD**) involves the buildup of *plaque* (deposits of fatty acids, cholesterol, and calcium) along the walls of arteries, impairing their ability to supply oxygen and nutrients to muscles of the heart. Coronary heart disease is now the leading cause of death in the Western world, and if trends continue approximately 50% of adult men and 35% of adult women will develop CHD in their lifetimes (Rosamond et al., 2007). Although most of the risk factors for CHD are straightforward—smoking, high blood pressure, high cholesterol, family history of CHD, and diabetes—more than 60% of CHD patients have only one or none of these risk factors, leading investigators to look in other directions (Brydon, Magid, & Steptoe, 2006).

Powerful correlational evidence now links chronic stress and certain personality factors with coronary heart disease. For example, in a 9-year longitudinal study involving 12,000 healthy male volunteers, those facing chronic work and marital stressors were 30% more likely to die of coronary heart disease than those not facing such stressors. These results were found after controlling for factors such as smoking, alcohol, consumption, cholesterol levels, and diet (Matthews & Gump, 2002). In a study of 17,000 adults, those who had experienced a greater number of stressful experiences in childhood were three times more likely to die of CHD than those who reported few such experiences (study by Maxia Dong and colleagues, 2004, cited by G. E. Miller & Blackwell, 2006). The most common chronic stressors associated with heart disease risk are low socioeconomic status, work stress, low levels of social support, marital distress, and the strain of caring for children or for elderly or disabled relatives (Rozanski, Blumenthal, Davidson, Saab, & Kubzansky, 2005).

In addition to chronic stressors, certain personality attributes have been linked to the development of CHD or protection against it. You may have heard yourself or someone you know referred to as a "Type-A" person. The expression has become a synonym for an overly competitive, impatient, easily irritated, ambitious person who can never relax—a "workaholic." You probably also know the opposing personality type, too, the "Type B" person—the mellow

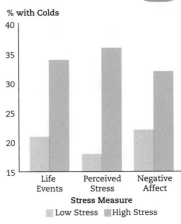

% with Colds

"No, Thursday's out. How about never—is never good for you?"

▲ **"Type-A" Personality Has Its Good as Well as Bad Side.** Type-A personality—the hard-driving, intense, impatient, easily angered, workaholic type—has been associated with risk for coronary heart disease. However, it is primarily the hostile/angry aspect of Type-A behavior that is associated with increased risk of disease. The other side of Type-A—experiencing a sense of control over one's life—has beneficial consequences.

▲ **FIGURE 11.15 Stress and the Common Cold.** As this graph shows, the likelihood of catching a cold is affected by stressful life events, perceptions that one is under stress, and a generally negative emotional style. *(Source: Cohen, 1996, p. 88)*

one who goes with the flow, never getting upset, not lazy, but never working *too* hard or worrying *too* much about anything.

The Type-A/Type-B model was developed by two cardiologists (heart specialists) who based their model on the results of the Western Collaborative Group Study, a 9-year study of more than 3,000 men in their late 30s (M. Friedman & Ulmer, 1984). Specifically, the **Type-A personality** has three characteristics:

1. An exaggerated sense of urgency about time, trying to accomplish as much as possible in the shortest period possible.
2. Intense ambition and competitiveness.
3. A tendency toward irritability, hostility, and anger.

However, as attractive as this two-personality-type model may be, subsequent research has shown that it is primarily the anger, hostility, and irritability component of Type A personality that is associated with heart disease, not ambition or a sense of urgency about time—and even anger and hostility only increase the risk of heart disease modestly (Eaker, Sullivan, Kelly-Hayes, D'Agostino, & Benjamin, 2004; Player, King, Mainous, & Geesey, 2007; Rutledge & Hogan 2002).

STRESS MAY TRIGGER DEPRESSION

Stress is associated with psychological disorders as well as disorders of the body such as colds and heart disease. Stress is most prominently associated with *depression* (Hammen, 2005). Depression (which I discuss in greater depth in Chapter 13) is a long-standing, debilitating condition characterized not only by sadness but also by loss of the ability to experience pleasure and by feelings of hopelessness, helplessness, and worthlessness. Depression is also frequently accompanied by extreme fatigue, sleep disturbances, and loss of appetite.

Type-A personality
▶ A personality type characterized (a) an exaggerated sense of urgency about time; (b) intense ambition and competitiveness; and (c) a tendency toward irritability, hostility, and a short anger fuse.

Stress and depression are powerfully linked. Although not every stressed person becomes depressed (what a calamity that would be!), 80% of cases of *major depression*—the most severe form of the condition—*are* immediately preceded by major stressful life events, and these life stressors are two-and-a-half times more likely to be found in the lives of depressed individuals than others (Hammen, 2005; Mazure, 1998).

By itself, this connection would not be convincing evidence that stress actually *causes* depression, however, because it is possible that a person with a tendency toward depression might actually create stressful events in his or her life—in other words, it would be possible for the illness to cause the stress rather than the other way around. For example, while misery may love company, as the saying goes, company definitely does not love misery (Coyne, 1976; Joiner, 1996). A depressed person is simply not pleasant to be around. Such people may find themselves isolated from others because of their depression. Social isolation can be highly stressful, even dangerous in that lack of social support is associated with increased risk of coronary heart disease and other sources of premature death (Lett et al., 2007; T. W. Smith & Ruiz, 2002; Uchino, Uno, & Holt-Lunstad, 1999).

Fortunately, a number of studies have been able to control for the possibility that depression causes stress rather than the other way around by focusing on stresses that occur due to "acts of God" such as the death of a spouse or exposure to natural disasters (Kessler, 1997). Thus, the idea that stress actually does lead to depression is supported by evidence.

AT THE FOREFRONT

Placebo: Treatment or Nontreatment?

One provocative area of research in psychoneuroimmunology is the study of the **placebo**. A placebo is any bogus procedure, or inactive (inert) substance—corn starch or milk sugar, for example—administered to a person who believes the procedure or substance is a genuine treatment. The idea behind this is that the patient's belief in the treatment may trigger actual psychological or biochemical processes which may have a beneficial effect (Price, Finniss, & Benedetti, 2008; Tilburt, Emanuel, Kaptchuk, Curlin, & Miller, 2008).

WHAT PLACEBOS CAN AND CANNOT DO

Are placebos powerful, low-cost treatments, as some enthusiastic promoters suggest (Wampold, Imel, & Minami, 2007; Wampold, Minami, Tierney, Baskin, & Bhati, 2005), or are they relatively useless nontreatments, as skeptics argue (Hróbjartsson & Gøtzsche, 2001, 2004, 2007)? If placebos are useless, doctors are not taking note: Approximately 50% of physicians surveyed by Jon Tilburt and his colleagues reported either that they did prescribe placebos as classically defined (inert substances such as sugar pills) or, more commonly, they prescribed substances that while not technically inert, had no known use for the ailment in question. These active substances were prescribed in the hopes that they would produce a beneficial placebo effect (Tilburt et al., 2008).

Although there is no evidence that placebos have the sort of pervasive, wondrous effects at no risk to the patient that some believe, there is good evidence that under specific circumstances, placebos can be beneficial—although their effects are usually moderate. There are some isolated exceptions, but most reliable evidence suggests that when placebos work at all, they tend to affect *symptoms* rather than *signs*. **Symptoms** are patient complaints. **Signs** are objective observations by doctors, test results, and

Placebo ▶ Any bogus procedure or inactive (inert) substance—cornstarch or milk sugar, for example—administered to a patient who believes the substance or procedure is a genuine treatment. Although placebos are sometimes given to patients whose symptoms have no organic cause—to satisfy the patient's desire to be "treated"—research has shown that placebos can sometimes trigger physiological events which actually reduce symptoms.

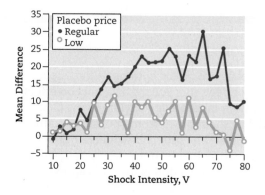

◀ **FIGURE 11.16 Always Buy the Name-Brand Placebo—Refuse All Generics!** As you can see from this figure, as the voltages of shocks administered to volunteers increased in intensity, higher levels of pain relief were experienced from the "expensive" placebo as compared with the "discount" version. *(Source: Waber et al., 2008, p. 1017.)*

so forth. In other words, placebos may make you *feel* better, but they don't necessarily make you *get* better (Evans, 2003, p. 33).

Although placebos can be used to treat certain psychological disorders as described in Chapter 14, and they may have effects on respiratory and cardiovascular functioning, the primary symptom treatable with placebos is pain (Buhle, Stevens, Friedman, & Wager, 2012; Price et al., 2008). Pain is by definition a symptom and not a sign, because it cannot be measured other than through a patient's own report. Even the most hardened placebo skeptics agree that placebos can treat pain, although they may question the size of placebo effects on pain (Hróbjartsson & Gøtzsche, 2001, 2004, 2007).

Of course, this does *not* mean that placebos are as useful as active pain-killers in treating pain. Active pain-killers, such as drugs derived from opium (morphine, percocet, dilaudid, etc.), are always more effective than placebos—usually at least twice as effective (Kirsch, 2002). However, placebos are considerably more effective in controlling pain than using no treatment at all, and they can increase the effectiveness of active pain killers.

Are some placebos "better" than others? Yes! Apparently, the more expensive the placebo, the better it works. Rebecca Waber and her colleagues subjected volunteer participants to varying levels of voltages of shocks, from slightly painful to extremely painful. Subjects' pain was treated with what they had been told was a "new opioid analgesic" with a very fast onset time. However, half the volunteers were told that the pills had a regular drugstore price of $2.50 per pill while the other half were told that the pills had been discounted to 10 cents per pill (Waber, Shiv, Carmon, & Ariely, 2008).

As depicted in Figure 11.16, as the voltage of shocks increased, the "expensive" placebo had substantially better pain reduction properties. In all, 85% of participants obtained some relief from the "expensive" placebo, whereas only 61% obtained relief from the discount pill.

Even more surprising are preliminary findings which raise the possibility that placebos may be effective even if patients are fully aware that they are not receiving a genuine treatment. Ted Kaptchuk and his research team randomly assigned one group of patients suffering from irritable bowel syndrome (which causes diarrhea and other digestive complaints) to a placebo condition where they were honestly told that they would be receiving "placebo pills made of an inert substance like sugar pills, that have been shown in clinical studies to produce significant improvement in IBS symptoms through mind-body self-healing processes." Another group was randomly assigned to receive no treatment. The placebo group—in spite of full knowledge that they had taken a placebo—showed substantial relief from symptoms and improvement in quality of life. No such effect was found for the no-treatment group (Kaptchuk et al., 2010).

Symptom ▶ In medical terminology, a symptom is a patient complaint of a problem. This is contrasted with a *sign*, which is an objective indication of the presence of disease that the physician can observe or measure by test.

Signs ▶ In medical terminology, a sign is an objective indication of the presence of disease that the physician can observe or measure by test (e.g., broken bone, fever, swelling, abnormal cardiogram, skin eruptions, etc.). This is contrasted with a *symptom*, which is a patient complaint ("I've been feeling dizzy and easily fatigued").

AT THE FOREFRONT: PLACEBO

CONTINUED

▲ **Voodoo—the Ultimate Nocebo.** Second- or third-century A.D. Egyptian voodoo doll.

Nocebo ▶ When a placebo creates an unwanted or adverse effect, primarily because the person believes the bogus treatment or substance to have harmful effects.

PLACEBO HAS AN EVIL TWIN: NOCEBO

All drugs have side effects, and placebos are no exceptions. When a placebo creates an unwanted or adverse effect, it is known as a **nocebo** effect (literally, *I will harm*). In his book on the placebo effect Dylan Evans (2003) uses the example of "voodoo death" as the most extreme possible example of nocebo. You have probably seen at least one movie in which a curse is placed upon a character, who subsequently meets an untimely end. Often this is played out in a voodoo scenario, where a doll is used to represent the unfortunate victim, and the doll endures all manner of indignities—from being stuck with pins to having its head cut off.

In numerous cultures around the world, sane and competent individuals have attested to the fact that people have been known to die after such a curse has been place upon them—provided that they were aware that the curse had been placed, and were themselves believers in the power of such curses. Given that these deaths *only* occur when the victim both believes in the curse and is also aware that one has been placed, there is a possibility that a nocebo effect is at work (Meador, 1992). Of course, other explanations are possible, such as that the victim radically altered his or her behavior in some harmful way upon hearing of the curse.

But more ordinary nocebo effects occur all the time, including headache, nausea, dizziness, numbness, allergic rashes, and difficulty breathing. Some of the side effects experienced when taking medication may be nocebo effects rather then responses to active ingredients in medication (Barsky, Saintfort, Rogers, & Borus, 2002). Recent research has shown that placebo and nocebo responses involve virtually opposite patterns of neurotransmitter activity in the brain. Placebo increases the activity of endorphins and dopamine, while nocebo decreases the activity of these neurotransmitter systems (Scott et al., 2008). ■

IN SUMMARY

1.	Psychoneuroimmunology is the study of the interaction between psychology, the nervous and endocrine systems, and immune systems.
2.	Stress can increase susceptibility to colds, and evidence also strongly suggests that stress and negative emotional style increase the risk of coronary heart disease (CHD). Stress may also trigger depression.
3.	Placebos have been shown to effectively treat pain under certain circumstances, although these effects are not at all as strong as those of actual pain-killing drugs. Nocebo effects include the experience of apparent side effects of medications that are not actually the result of the medications themselves.

RETRIEVE!

1.	True or false: Short-term stress strengthens immune systems.
2.	True or false: A positive emotional style actually protects against the common cold.

3. Which of the following is NOT one of the three defining characteristics of the Type-A personality?

a) urgency about time

b) lack of interest in others

c) intense ambition and competitiveness

d) irritability, hostility, and anger

4. True or false: Placebos primarily help a person to *feel* better rather than actually *get* better.

Coping: How Can Stress Be Managed?

This chapter has made it clear that chronic stress is unpleasant, destructive, and potentially dangerous. However, the good news is that stress can be managed, and it is often not too difficult to do. Managing stress is **coping**—the complex and highly variable processes by which we ensure that the demands of potentially stressful situations do not overwhelm our psychological or material resources. If we are successfully coping we are successfully *dealing* with a stressful situation (Folkman & Moskowitz, 2004; Taylor & Stanton, 2007).

Because stress is so pervasive in the modern world, and it seems to negatively affect so many psychological and biological systems, many claims are made about the effectiveness of various stress-reduction methods. Unfortunately, not all of these claims are grounded in evidence, and even when the effectiveness of techniques has been demonstrated, the *magnitude* of their effects—that is, how *much* stress they relieve—has sometimes been exaggerated (Taylor, 1999).

We will review coping methods for which at least some evidence of effectiveness exists in relieving chronic stress. However, not every method is appropriate for every situation or person. If you are experiencing stress, you should choose methods *that you can stick with* and that are a good fit with the origin of your stress.

Coping ▶ Any process by which an organism attempts to manage stress—to ensure that the demands of potentially stressful situations do not overwhelm psychological or material resources.

Optimism

Although certain types of events will cause stress to almost anyone, regardless of his or her psychology (e.g., hearing the screeching of a subway train or living with a chronic debilitating illness), many of the things that we find stressful are not necessarily intrinsically as stressful as we experience them to be. As mentioned earlier in the chapter, our cognitive responses to these events—the way we think about them—may exaggerate or even create their stressful character.

Consider the loss of a job. This can mean "the end of life on earth as we know it" or the beginning of an adventurous hunt for a more satisfying career. An unfair, overly critical professor can be a painful thorn in one's side (or elsewhere) or a challenge to be overcome. The glass is either half empty or half full, and to some degree you have a choice about how you see it.

Researchers have found that people with certain mental attributes may be protected against the effects of stress to some degree. One characteristic that will predict how people react to stress is **explanatory style**—how we explain

Explanatory style ▶ How people explain the good and bad events of their lives and make predictions about future events based upon these explanations. One way of categorizing explanatory styles is the dimension optimism vs. pessimism.

the good and bad events of our lives and make predictions about the future based on these explanations. One of the founders of the positive psychology movement, Martin Seligman (1990), made an important contribution to understanding the management of stress when he had the relatively simple insight that people can be divided into to two categories based on the way they explain bad events in their lives: *optimists* and *pessimists*. Optimism and pessimism are distinguished by differences in three dimensions of explanation of bad events: *internal/external*, *permanent/temporary*, and *catastrophic/ surmountable*.

Pessimists are people whose explanations for bad events involve perceptions of the events as *internal* ("It was my fault I got fired"), *permanent* ("I'll never be able to get as good a job again"), and *catastrophic* ("Without this job I can't pay for school—I'll have to drop out and my life will be ruined"). Research conducted over five decades suggests that people with pessimistic explanatory styles are more vulnerable than optimists to a host of stress-related diseases and a shortened life span (Giltay, Geleijnse, Zitman, Hoekstra, & Shouten, 2004; O'Donovan et al., 2009; Peterson, Seligman, & Vaillant, 1988).

On the other hand, optimists are people who see bad events as resulting from causes that are *external* ("My boss has a hard time dealing with assertive women"), *temporary* ("I shouldn't have too much trouble getting another job"), and *surmountable* ("Even if I don't get a job right away, I'll be eligible for financial aid"). Optimism protects the individual from the effects of stress.

Optimists live longer, happier, healthier lives (Kubzansky et al., 2002; Rasmussen, Scheier, & Greenhouse, 2009). Optimism also results in more time spent experiencing positive emotions, and researchers have found that psychological well-being is directly translated into eating well, sleeping well, exercising, and engaging in fewer self-destructive behaviors (e.g., cigarette smoking), and it has an entirely independent effect on mortality—that is, apart from its effect on diet, sleep, and unhealthy habits (Chida & Steptoe, 2008; Ong, 2010; Steptoe, Dockray, & Wardle, 2009; Steptoe, O'Donnell, Marmot, & Wardle, 2008).

What if you are a diehard pessimist and don't think you can do much about it? Preliminary evidence supports Martin Seligman's contention that optimism can be learned (Gillham, Reivich, Jaycox, & Seligman, 1995; Goldwurm, Bielli, Corsale, & Marchi, 2006). For example, 10- to 12-year old children considered at high risk for depression in adolescence as a result of mild current depression and disturbed family histories were taught optimism skills in a series of workshops. Over a period of 2 years it was found that the children trained in optimism had only half the rate of depressive symptoms as the group that had not experienced the training, and the benefits of the optimism training actually grew over time, during the stressful period of transition from middle to high school (Gillham et al., 1995).

Aerobic Exercise

Aerobic exercise ▶
Physical exercise involving large muscle groups which increases oxygen consumption and elevates heart rate.

There is no longer any doubt that **aerobic exercise**—any physical exercise involving large muscle groups which increases oxygen consumption and elevates heart rate—reduces vulnerability to some of the typical effects of chronic stress. Aerobic exercise can lift your mood and self-esteem; treat depression with effects equal to—and in some cases better than—antidepressant drugs; reduce anxiety; increase psychological resilience to stress; and protect against cardiovascular disease, type 2 diabetes, and hypertension (Field, 2009; Hamer, Taylor, & Steptoe, 2006; Spalding, Lyon, Steel, & Hatfield, 2004).

Aerobic exercise is also free. It needs no special equipment (although special equipment can be loads of fun), can be engaged in at any time, and generally has no negative side effects if it is done in moderation. Brisk walking, jogging, running, cycling, stair-climbing, rowing, dance, aerobic gym and martial arts workouts, swimming—all are forms of aerobic exercise.

◄ **Run for Pleasure and Fitness . . . Walk for Health.** Although high-intensity aerobic exercise, such as distance running and cycling, greatly increases fitness and may be highly pleasurable, it has not demonstrated superiority in terms of health benefits. A brisk 30-minute walk 5 days a week is all you need to reduce risk of heart disease, stroke, type 2 diabetes, depression, and hypertension.

Unfortunately, it can be difficult to motivate yourself to exercise regularly, even though it has many pleasurable aspects and positive health benefits. Only about 30% of people in Western nations exercise regularly, and about 50% of those who begin an exercise program quit within 3 to 6 months (Brawley & Rodgers, 1993; Salmon, 2001). So if you choose to use aerobic exercise to combat stress, you should formulate a program that is *realistic*.

The good news in this respect is that most research indicates that the sort of extreme cardiovascular workouts popular today—running, "spinning," aerobics classes, and other aerobic uses of gym equipment—are not necessary for stress reduction and other health benefits. Despite their pleasurable aspects and ability to increase *fitness* (aerobic capacity), extreme workouts don't seem to have much of a *health* advantage over a half hour of moderate exercise (such as brisk walking) engaged in at least 5 days a week (Slentz et al., 2007). Thus, you don't need to sweat buckets for an hour or two to improve your health or reduce stress.

Meditation

Relaxation is the antithesis of stress. People who are relaxed are by definition less stressed than those who are tense. They have lower heart rate, blood pressure, and rates of respiration. Many stress-reduction techniques are designed to promote what Herbert Benson (1983) initially termed the **relaxation response**—a self-induced alteration in consciousness that results in decreased physiological and psychological arousal, and increased attention to the moment.

The models for Benson's relaxation response were Buddhist and Hindu meditation techniques, although relaxation is not the ultimate goal of these techniques, as mentioned in Chapter 6. However, it was through studying what meditators actually *did* that Benson concluded that the relaxing effects of meditation could be detached from their spiritual roots and experienced by anyone.

Meditation has been shown to reduce stress, lower blood pressure, and increase positive mood; it may even reduce mortality from heart disease and other ailments (Anderson, Liu, & Kryscio, 2008; Barnes, Treiber, & Davis, 2001; Praissman, 2008; Speca, Carlson, Goodey, & Angen, 2000). In one

Relaxation response ▶ Herbert Benson's term to describe an alteration in consciousness that results in decreased physiological and psychological arousal and increased attention to the moment.

Mindfulness-based stress reduction (MBSR) ▶ A form of meditation training developed by Dr. Jon Kabat-Zinn at University of Massachusetts Medical School. MBSR is based upon Buddhist meditation and psychology, but it lacks the emphasis on insight. The key to MBSR is mindfulness—maintaining a concentrative, nonjudgmental attention to the present moment.

study, **mindfulness-based stress reduction (MBSR)**, a form of meditation training based on Buddhist meditation and psychology (but without the emphasis on insight) has been shown to activate parts of the brain associated with positive emotion and to strengthen immune response (Davidson et al., 2003; Witek-Janusek et al., 2010; see also Collins & Dunn, 2005).

LIVING PSYCHOLOGY

How to Meditate

As briefly mentioned in Chapter 6, the term *meditation* may sometimes refer to contemplation or focused prayer, as found in Western religious teachings. However, in the context of stress reduction techniques, the term usually applies to meditation techniques based upon Hindu or Buddhist practices. Although many such techniques exist, most are variations on one theme: concentration on a single "mental object," such as the breath or a special sound or word (mantra), and relaxed attention to the moment. Here is a step-by-step guide to learning to meditate.

First, find a relatively quiet, dimly lit room. Sit forward in a chair with your back comfortably straight but not stiff—in what Mark Williams and his colleagues call a "dignified" posture (Williams, Teasdale, Segal, & Kabat-Zinn, 2007). If you prefer to sit in one of several traditional cross-legged postures using a meditation cushion, do so—they are stable positions which encourage meditators to remain still. However, it is not necessary to sit in some special posture on the floor to meditate. Pick a posture that you can maintain for the entire period of meditation.

Now place your left upturned cupped hand over the right in your lap and close your eyes. Bring your attention to your breath—either to its point of entry and exit at the tip of your nostrils or to your lower abdomen below the navel which rises and falls as you breathe. Pick one of these points—the tip of the nostrils or the abdomen. This point will be your meditation "home base."

Take three deep breaths and then breathe naturally through the nose. Do not try to breathe deeply or control your breathing in any other special way. Just notice your breath as it comes in and goes out at the tip of the nostrils or at your abdomen, whichever you have chosen. Do not try to "empty your mind" (not possible) or do anything else with your mind at all. Just breathe naturally and focus your attention on your breathing.

You may (actually, you *will*) find your thoughts and attention straying. This is absolutely normal and does not mean that you are not meditating "correctly." It is not a cause for worry at all. Notice that your thoughts have strayed and then *gently* nudge your mind back to your breathing, without judging or criticizing yourself, whenever you find your mind straying. Even

▶ **You Don't Have to Sit Cross-Legged to Meditate.** Although traditional cross-legged and kneeling postures have certain unique benefits for meditators, the important thing is that you are comfortable. Most Western people have grown up sitting on chairs, not on the floor, and their muscles are not used to cross-legged postures. You can obtain full benefits of meditation while sitting with your back comfortably straight in a chair. Pictured at right is the proper position for your hands.

if your mind strays 100 or 1,000 times—just gently nudge it back to your breathing each time.

That's all there is to it. You may find yourself feeling bored, sleepy, emotionally elated or upset, or annoyed. All of this is natural. Just keep bringing your attention back to your breath and don't pass judgment on anything that happens or anything that you feel. You may begin to feel stiffness or pain. Usually, this will pass. Notice that you're feeling stiffness or pain, and then bring your attention back to your breath. If the pain becomes more than you can handle, and you really do need to shift position, then do so—but try to maintain your new position. Don't shift back and forth from one position to another.

Ideally you should meditate for 25 to 30 minutes at a time at least once a day, preferably twice—morning and afternoon or early evening. Keep a watch with you so that you can peek at the time when it feels as though your time might be up. You may find in the beginning that you can't do it for more than a few minutes at a time without feeling uncomfortable. Make a commitment to try it for at least 10 minutes at a time, and then over a period of weeks, slowly increase each session until you have reached 25 to 30 minutes. ■

Social Support

Social support is the perception or experience that one is loved, esteemed, and cared for by others; that one is part of a network of people who engage in mutual assistance and accept mutual obligations to one another (Wills, 1991). People with social support carry this knowledge around with them. They know that they can count on certain people in times of need. It makes intuitive sense that such people should be better able to cope with stress, and research demonstrates unequivocally that they can (Taylor et al., 2004; Taylor & Stanton, 2007).

Interestingly, the actual *use* of social support is not necessarily what provides health and stress-reduction benefits. In many cases it seems to be the simple *knowledge* that support is there if it were needed (Master et al., 2009). For example, women who gaze at a photograph of their romantic partner while enduring experimentally induced pain rate the experience as less unpleasant than women gazing at a photograph of a stranger, holding the hand of a stranger, or squeezing a rubber ball. But holding the hand of one's partner was not more effective than simply gazing at his photograph—in fact, it was slightly *less* effective (Master et al., 2009)!

Indeed, *un*utilized social support may sometimes be even more beneficial than utilized support, perhaps because support from overbearing or overly intrusive friends and relations may actually increase stress (Taylor et al., 2004). Utilizing social support opportunities appears to be particularly risky for members of collectivist cultures such as those in East Asia, where burdening others with one's problems can be highly stressful and seen as inappropriate (Taylor, Welch, Kim, & Sherman, 2007). Consistent with the notion that utilizing social support may not always be the key to its beneficial consequences, Stephanie Brown and her colleagues found that it may be better to give than to receive: In their sample of older married adults, it was the *providing* of social support—not the receiving of it—which increased longevity (Brown, Nesse, Vinokur, & Smith, 2003).

On the other hand, providing social support may also be quite stressful, because stress can be contagious—some people take on the stress of those whom they are trying to help (Belle, 1991). This is particularly problematic for women, because they so often assume the role of caretaker, and their network of social support is usually so much larger than men's—encompassing many more potentially stressed-out individuals.

Social support ▶ The perception or experience that one is loved, esteemed, and cared for by others, and is part of a network of people who engage in mutual assistance and accept mutual obligations to one another.

Religion and Spiritual Life

Increasingly substantial research demonstrates that those who attend communal religious services and meetings, or who describe themselves as turning to religion to help them cope in times of stress, tend to be healthier, happier, and to live longer than those who do not (Diener, Tay, & Myers, 2011; McCullough, Friedman, Enders, & Martin, 2009; Powell, Shahabi, & Thoresen, 2003; Schnall et al., 2008). Those attending religious services also appear to enjoy higher levels of self-esteem, particularly if their society values religion (Gebauer, Sedikides, & Neberich, 2012). The size of the differences between the religious and the nonreligious is usually only small to moderate on average, but when it comes to living longer, healthier, and happier lives, with higher levels of self-esteem, small to moderate differences are rather important to most of us.

Because these results could easily be misinterpreted, it should be pointed out that the studies from which these findings are drawn are correlational, and it may not be religion *per se* that is responsible for the beneficial outcomes. For example, it is possible that happier or healthier people are more attracted to religion in the first place. People who take their religion seriously also often make healthier lifestyle choices (e.g., avoiding abuse of drugs or alcohol). Participation in a religious congregation is also a form of social support, and it creates support networks. Religion and spirituality may impart meaning and purpose to a person's life, which may help protect against depression and other types of negative emotion (Diener et al., 2011). As we have already seen, negative emotion is known to increase the negative effects of chronic stress, including effects on immune systems (Levin, Chatters, & Taylor, 2005).

A recent analysis by Ed Diener and his colleagues of data collected from many hundreds of thousands of people from 154 nations around the world may go a long way to clarifying the relationship between religion and subjective feelings of well-being. Diener and his research team found that more religious people did tend to report somewhat higher levels of subjective well-being—but only if religious life was associated in the person's society with respect, social support, and a sense of meaning and purpose in life. If a person's culture did not provide these qualities to its more religious citizens, there was no association between religion and subjective well-being. This is somewhat in accord with findings that religious people experience higher levels of self-esteem, but only if their society values religion (Diener, Tay, & Myers, 2011).

What sorts of nations *do* provide greater respect, social support, and a sense of meaning and purpose to the more religious? In general, these are nations and states whose citizens confront conditions brought on by poverty, war, famine, and frequent natural disasters. Perhaps not surprisingly, these also tend to be the more religious of nations. In nations whose citizens are much less likely to face these sorts of difficult conditions (for example, most of Western Europe, North America, and highly developed Asian nations such as Japan), religion is not associated with increased subjective well-being. Indeed, even within a single nation, if conditions differ according to region, so can the association between religion and feelings of well-being. For example, as Table 11.4 shows, the more religious of the United States are also the states with highest levels of poverty. These states also tend toward greater association between religion and respect, social support, and a sense of meaning and purpose in life. As expected, religion is more likely to be associated with increased subjective feelings of well-being in these states.

Can religion cause *harmful* health outcomes, or *increase* stress? This is a question rarely asked amid the flurry of positive findings for the effects of religion. Pargament (1997) proposes that "negative" religious coping—beliefs

Table 11.4 **The United States According to Religiosity**

Religiosity of States: "Is Religion an Important Part of Your Daily Life?"

STATE	RELIGIOSITY	STATE	RELIGIOSITY
Mississippi	0.88	Florida	0.66
Alabama	0.85	Minnesota	0.65
Louisiana	0.82	Maryland	0.64
South Carolina	0.79	Illinois	0.64
Tennessee	0.79	Wisconsin	0.63
Arkansas	0.79	Montana	0.62
North Carolina	0.77	Idaho	0.62
Georgia	0.77	Wyoming	0.62
Kentucky	0.76	New Jersey	0.61
Oklahoma	0.75	Arizona	0.61
Texas	0.75	District of Columbia	0.59
West Virginia	0.72	Colorado	0.59
South Dakota	0.71	California	0.58
Utah	0.71	New York	0.57
Missouri	0.70	Nevada	0.55
Kansas	0.70	Alaska	0.55
Virginia	0.70	Connecticut	0.54
Indiana	0.69	Oregon	0.54
North Dakota	0.69	Washington	0.54
Nebraska	0.69	Hawaii	0.53
New Mexico	0.68	Rhode Island	0.52
Pennsylvania	0.67	Maine	0.51
Ohio	0.67	Massachusetts	0.50
Iowa	0.67	New Hampshire	0.48
Delaware	0.66	Vermont	0.44
Michigan	0.66		

(Source: Diener et al., 2011, p. 1282.)

that one is being punished or abandoned by God for a misdeed, or that an illness is a result of sin—can increase psychological problems associated with stress, such as depression and anxiety. Higher levels of religious involvement may also sometimes increase the effects of chronic family or economic stress (George & Larson, 2002). Finally, in their worldwide analysis, Ed Diener and his colleagues found that in societies with extremely low levels of religious observance and belief—for example, Sweden, where only about 16% of people profess any religious belief at all—being religious is actually associated with

Table 11.5 25 Most, 25 Least Religious among 154 Nations on Five Continents

Responses to the question "Is religion an important part of your daily life?" Figure is percentage answering "Yes."

25 Most Religious		25 Least Religious (least religious is last):	
COUNTRY	**RELIGIOSITY**	**COUNTRY**	**RELIGIOSITY**
Egypt	0.99	Uruguay	0.42
Bangladesh	0.99	Germany	0.41
Sri Lanka	0.99	Hungary	0.41
Somaliland	0.99	Lithuania	0.41
Saudi Arabia	0.98	Luxembourg	0.40
Indonesia	0.98	Belgium	0.39
Malawi	0.98	Iceland	0.39
Laos	0.98	Latvia	0.36
Mauritania	0.98	Vietnam	0.35
Niger	0.98	New Zealand	0.35
Senegal	0.98	Albania	0.35
Afghanistan	0.98	Bulgaria	0.35
Comoros	0.98	Cuba	0.35
Congo (Kinshasa)	0.98	Netherlands	0.33
Djibouti	0.98	Belarus	0.33
Pakistan	0.97	Australia	0.32
Nigeria	0.97	Russia	0.32
Tanzania	0.97	United Kingdom	0.30
Myanmar	0.97	Finland	0.28
Sierra Leone	0.97	France	0.27
Bahrain	0.97	Czech Republic	0.26
Guinea	0.97	Japan	0.26
Philippines	0.96	Hong Kong	0.23
Liberia	0.96	Norway	0.22
Sudan	0.96	Denmark	0.19
United Arab Emirates	0.96	Estonia	0.17
Jordan	0.95	Sweden	0.16

(Source: Diener et al., 2011, p. 1285)

◀ **Stress Reduction Mechanism?**

reduced subjective feelings of well-being. Thus, it seems that religion is associated with an increased sense of well-being only if a person's culture is supportive of religion. Table 11.5 lists the 25 most and 25 least religious societies around the world (Diener et al., 2011).

If All Else Fails, Get a Dog

No kidding. Karen Allen and her colleagues randomly assigned a group of highly stressed, hypertensive stockbrokers, who lived alone and did not own pets, to either adopt a pet or not adopt one. They found that when placed under stressful conditions in a laboratory setting, the blood pressure of the (randomly assigned) pet owners increased by less than half of what was measured in the non–pet owners (Allen, Shykoff, & Izzo, 2001). A number of other studies have linked pet ownership to lowered stress, cholesterol, and blood pressure; and to better recovery following heart attacks and stressful experiences of social rejection (Friedmann, Barker, & Allen, 2011; Headly & Grabka, 2011; McConnell, Brown, Shoda, Statyton, & Martin, 2011).

Why should owning pets have positive benefits for a person's health? One possibility is suggested by studies of women conducted by Karen Allen and her colleagues (Allen, Blascovich, & Mendes, 2002). These researchers found that women who were attempting a stressful mental task in the laboratory with their spouse or best friend present experienced very high rises in blood pressure as a result of the stress. However, women who had their pet in the room with them instead experienced only very slight rises in blood pressure under conditions of stress. Allen (2003) speculates that pets are a form of social support offering unconditional acceptance and positive regard. They are "people" who love you even if you can't do a task properly—in comparison to friends and spouses who may (rightly or wrongly) be perceived as judgmental.

Not all researchers accept findings of beneficial effects of pet ownership, and a substantial number of studies fail to find any effect (Herzog, 2011; Parslow, Jorm, Christensen, Rodgers, & Jacomb, 2005). Moreover, perhaps because many researchers in this field are pet owners themselves, potentially *negative* aspects of pet ownership (e.g., stressful effects of a pet's death) are investigated much less often (Allen, 2003). In fact, little attention was paid to a recent study of heart-attack victims which found that pet owners were more—not less—likely to die or suffer another attack within a year of the first (G. Parker et al., 2010)! Nonetheless, the bulk of the research does suggest at least a potentially beneficial role for our nonhuman animal comrades. As is so often said, however—more research is needed (Herzog, 2011)!

IN SUMMARY

1.	Some methods of coping with chronic stress that have demonstrated effectiveness include aerobic exercise, relaxation training and meditation, social support, optimism, religion and spiritual life, and pet ownership.
2.	The relaxation response is a self-induced alteration in consciousness that results in decreased physiological and psychological arousal, and increased relaxed attention to the moment. The relaxation response is one aspect of most forms of meditation, although relaxation is primarily a "side effect" of meditation and not its purpose.
3.	People whose lives include social support networks are better able to cope with stress. However, it is not necessary for a person actually to utilize his or her social support network for beneficial effects on stress to be felt, and sometimes utilization of social support can be counterproductive.
4.	Optimistic and pessimistic explanatory styles differ along three dimensions of explanation: internal/external, permanent/temporary, and catastrophic/surmountable. An optimistic explanatory style inoculates a person from the effects of stress.
5.	For reasons not completely understood, those with higher levels of religious involvement appear to experience fewer negative effects of stress than others. However, it is likely that most, but perhaps not all, of this is explainable by the indirect effects of religion, such as increased social support, superior health habits, increased sense of purpose, and positive emotion.
6.	Some research suggests that pet ownership may reduce stress.

RETRIEVE!

1.	What is the term psychologists use to describe a self-induced alteration in consciousness that results in decreased physiological and psychological arousal, and relaxed attention to the moment?
2.	What aspect of social support appears to be the most important in reducing stress?
3.	Distinguish the way optimistic and pessimistic explanatory styles fall along the three dimensions internal/external, permanent/temporary, and catastrophic/surmountable.
4.	Participation in communal religion and personal religious practice has been shown to reduce the negative effects of stress. What are at least two possible explanations for why this might be true, apart from a direct effect of religion on health and well-being?
5.	What is one explanation for beneficial effects of pet ownership on stress?

Looking Back

Chapter 11 in Review

WHAT IS EMOTION?

- Emotions are short-lived psychological states that include feeling, physiological changes, and behavioral responses. Moods are generally less intense and longer lasting. Affect is the "raw material" from which moods and emotions are created.
- Emotions help to guide rational choices and decisions, and without them we would likely not survive very long. "Emotional intelligence" is the ability to identify, manage, and express one's emotions constructively.

ARE SOME EMOTIONS "BASIC"?

- Most researchers agree that basic emotions exist. A basic emotion is innate, distinct, and primary—all other emotions are derived from the primary set of basic emotions. Fear, anger, sadness, enjoyment/happiness, disgust, contempt, and surprise are generally recognized as basic emotions. Paul Ekman's facial action coding system (FACS) catalogs the facial muscle configurations associated with each basic emotion. Basic emotions may blend or play off one another in sequence. Culture may affect emotion recognition and display rules.

HOW DO PSYCHOLOGISTS EXPLAIN EMOTION?

- The James-Lange theory viewed emotion as feeling—a physiological response to a situation that the mind later interprets as emotion. The Cannon-Bard theory proposed instead that emotion is simultaneously experienced by both the autonomic nervous system and the cerebral cortex. The Schachter-Singer two-factor theory argued that physiological arousal occurs first, but that the person experiences emotion only when a cognitive label is attached to the arousal. In his cognitive-motivational-relational theory, Richard Lazarus argues that *both* physiological arousal *and* emotion will only occur after a person appraises the meaning of a given event.

- Some emotions may bypass cognition entirely. Neuroscientist Joseph LeDoux has identified a pathway of neural impulses from the thalamus to the amygdala, the principal center of fear response. This is the pathway for instantaneous fear response without the intervention of cognitive activity. However, fear may also occur following cognitive appraisal.
- Embodied emotion theorists believe that emotions are "captured" as "body memories." When an emotion is experienced, sensory phenomena and physiological and motor patterns of activity are encoded in clusters of neurons. These experiences form a conception of each particular emotion, and a person returns to it each time he or she recognizes, recalls, or thinks about that emotion. Under such conditions, the relevant clusters of neurons are activated.

HOW DO PEOPLE DEAL WITH ANGER?

- Anger involves antagonism toward something or someone; it is common, has varied triggers, and can be dangerous. It generally occurs when a person feels unfairly treated or deliberately harmed, or if he or she is aware of such things happening to someone else. Anger is generally an unpleasant experience, but "righteous anger" can be experienced as pleasant.
- Catharsis does not relieve anger unless you are venting at the specific person who has angered you and you are convinced the person will not retaliate. Forgiveness is a cognitive, motivational, and emotional process that unfolds over time. Forgiveness has been shown to be an effective treatment for anger and may have numerous psychological, interpersonal, and health benefits.

WHO IS HAPPY (AND WHY)?

- Happiness can be defined as the relatively fleeting basic emotion happiness/enjoyment, or as an overall subjective sense of well-being. Most people throughout the world are reasonably happy in the sense of

subjective well-being. Money does not increase happiness unless the initial level of income is very low. There are "happiness set points" largely determined by genetics, but these set points can change as a result of circumstances. Levels of happiness are determined by happiness set point, life circumstances, and intentional activities, particularly social activities.

WHAT IS STRESS?

- Psychologists define stress as the psychological and physiological consequences of events that challenge a person's ability to cope and which threaten well-being or interfere with important goals. These life events are called stressors. Stress is more than an event—it is a way of responding to events.
- Stress can be positive if it is relatively mild and motivates people to accomplish goals or protect themselves against threats. Brief activation of a stress response strengthens immune systems; but chronic, unremitting stress is damaging. Walter Cannon described the biological processes triggered in response to extreme stress as the "fight or flight response." Hans Selye developed the General Activation Syndrome (GAS) model, which consists of the alarm phase, resistance, and exhaustion. Females are less likely to respond with fight or flight, and more likely to "tend and befriend."

DOES STRESS CAUSE ILLNESS?

- Psychoneuroimmunology has identified a feedback loop between the brain and immune systems. Chronic stress depresses immune systems, resulting in reduced ability to fight off disease, and development of unhealthful patterns of cognition and emotion. There is a link between chronic stress and upper-respiratory disease, chronic heart disease, and depression. However, the link between stress and depression may be mediated by genetics.
- A placebo is any inert substance or bogus treatment administered to a

Looking Back continued

person who believes the procedure or substance is genuine. When effective, placebos usually exert their effects on symptoms, such as pain, rather than signs. Nocebo is placebo's "evil twin."

- Ethnic minorities experience unique stressors: ethnic discrimination, stereotype threat, and own-group conformity pressure.

However, some ethnic minorities may also experience unique protection against stress.

COPING: HOW CAN STRESS BE MANAGED?

- Coping is the management of stress. Effective methods of coping include engaging in an ongoing program of moderate aerobic exercise;

meditation based upon Buddhist and Hindu techniques; increasing social support; promoting an optimistic outlook; practicing a religious or spiritual discipline; and pet ownership.

Key Terms

Aerobic exercise, 556
Affect, 514
Anger, 532
Basic emotion, 519
Cannon-Bard theory of emotion, 526
Catharsis, 533
Cognitive-motivational-relational theory of emotion, 527
Coping, 555
Coronary heart disease (CHD), 550
Display rules, 522
Duchenne smile, 520
Embodied emotion, 529

Emotion, 513
Emotional intelligence, 516
Explanatory style, 555
Facial action coding system, 520
Facial feedback hypothesis, 529
Fight or flight, 545
General Adaptation System (GAS), 546
Health psychology, 543
James-Lange theory of emotion, 525
Mindfulness-based stress reduction (MBSR), 558
Mood, 513

Nocebo, 554
Opponent processes, 545
Own-group conformity pressure, 548
Placebo, 552
Psychoneuroimmunology, 549
Relaxation response, 557
Signs, 553
Social support, 559
Stress, 543
Symptom, 553
Tend and befriend, 546
Two-factor theory of emotion, 527
Type-A personality, 551

Test Yourself

1. How do emotions differ from moods? What is affect? What are the two dimensions of affect?

2. Name the seven basic emotions described in this chapter.

3. Why would it have been unlikely that our ancestors could have survived without emotion, according to the chapter? How does the story of "Elliot" provide evidence for this idea?

4. What is the term Paul Ekman uses to describe his catalog of the muscular configurations involved in creating facial expressions of basic emotion?

5. Distinguish a false positive result from a false negative.

6. What are the four ways that display rules vary, as identified by Paul Ekman?

7. Distinguish the James-Lange theory of emotion from the Cannon-Bard theory. Distinguish the two-factor-theory from the cognitive-motivational-relational theory.

8. Provide evidence from comparisons of U.S. Gross National Product from 1947 to the present to support the idea that "money does not buy happiness." What are the two conditions under which research has shown that money *can* buy happiness?

9. How is it that a person may claim that being a parent has given them the greatest happiness of their lives, and yet if they are asked at any given moment if they are enjoying caring for their children, they may answer in the negative?

10. True or false: Regardless of an individual's personal characteristics and psychology, events such as losing a job or divorce will always be equally stressful.

11. Which bodily system is *de*-activated under stress?
    a) endocrine system
    b) sympathetic nervous system
    c) parasympathetic nervous system
    d) central nervous system

12. What happens during each of the phases of GAS?

13. Which hormone is associated with the tend-and-befriend response? Which sex is most likely to respond to stress with tend-and-befriend?

14. Short- and long-term stress have different effects on immune systems. What is this difference?

Test Yourself continued

15. Name at least three of the most common chronic stressors associated with developing coronary heart disease (CHD).

16. Which aspect of the "Type-A" personality is associated with increased risk of CHD?

17. Name the six strategies for coping with stress discussed in this chapter.

18. True or false: People who begin a program of aerobic exercise to combat stress generally stay with the program for at least 2 years.

19. True or false: Knowing that social support is available in times of stress is not enough to help a person cope—the person must actually *utilize* social support resources.

20. There are three dimensions of explanatory style: internal/external, permanent/temporary, and catastrophic/surmountable. How do optimistic and pessimistic styles fall along these dimensions?

21. What is meant by the statement: "Placebos primarily affect symptoms, not signs."

22. True or False: Owning a dog may help to reduce stress.

23. Although stress and depression are strongly linked in correlational studies, this does not prove that stress *causes* depression. What is one other possible explanation for this correlation?

12

Personality

Chapter Outline

FREEZE FRAME

Sometime during the 1960s, identical twin girls were born in New York City and immediately were surrendered for adoption. Believing that twins were generally too much for adoptive parents to handle, the adoption agency decided to place the girls in separate homes. Although they were placed with different families, the girls, who came to be known as Amy and Beth, did end up in environments that were similar in certain respects: Both were placed in Jewish homes in New York State; they both ended up with adoptive mothers who did not work but stayed at home to care for their new blonde, blue-grey-eyed infant daughters; and both girls acquired new brothers who were 7 years their senior.

As recounted by Lawrence Wright (1997), however, the similarities in the girls' rearing environments and early experiences ended there. Amy did not fare well. Her new family was lower middle-class, with parents who emphasized academic achievement, self-control, and tradition. However, the mother was an insecure, withdrawn woman who had few friends. She ultimately came to perceive of Amy as a problem of sorts—an outsider in the family who seemed to

be more trouble than she was worth. The father held similar views about his new daughter.

On the other hand, Beth's new family was sophisticated, spontaneous, and dynamic. They cared less for education and propriety than for material success and the "good things of life." The new mother was self-confident, cheerful, and energetic. Both she and her husband loved their new daughter and doted on her.

Amy's family functioned well but only as a unit of three (mother, father, and son). Amy stood on the outside looking in. But Beth's family was an inclusive circle, with Beth at the very center.

What kind of an effect do you imagine these vastly different family environments had on the personalities of the two girls as they grew up? Prevailing wisdom in psychology during most of the 20th century would predict serious problems for Amy, but relatively few for Beth. And, in fact, Amy did have serious problems. She was a difficult infant, fussy and demanding. As a growing child, she bit her nails, wet her bed, sucked her thumb while clinging tenaciously to her blanket, and was frightened of being left alone. She suffered from nightmares. By the age of 10, she had developed what Wright describes as an "artificial quality" that manifested itself in excessive fantasizing and pretend play, and frequent claims of (nonexistent) physical illness. She was socially withdrawn, like her adoptive mother, and she lacked the maturity expected in children of her age range. She was exactly what one might expect growing up in a home where she was something of an outcast.

But what of Beth? Did her emerging personality reflect the positive family environment she enjoyed, as Amy's appeared to reflect an unfortunate and unwelcoming environment? You might be surprised to learn that in most ways, Beth's personality was indistinguishable from Amy's. Beth wet her bed, bit her nails, sucked her thumb, carted her blanket around, and was afraid to be left alone. Like Amy, she experienced (or claimed) illnesses where none existed, became lost in pretend play, and if anything, exhibited a personality even more "artificial" than her twin's. Psychological testing revealed that Beth's sense of alienation from her "doting" mother was, in Wright's words, "eerily the same" as Amy's alienation from her rejecting mother.

How do we become the people we are? Or do we *become* at all? Perhaps we simply *are*. Amy and Beth shared 100% of their genes in common, yet each inhabited a strikingly different familial environment. Do the "eerie" similarities in these girls' personality profiles suggest that everything psychologists have taught us about the importance of rearing environment in personality development is wrong—little more than myth? Is personality merely a question of genetic endowment? If true, then what should we make of the fact that not everything about Amy's personality was identical to Beth's? There were uncountable differences between the two girls, and there is no way that one could have been mistaken for the other. The story of Beth and Amy once again demonstrates the importance both of nature and nurture.

In this chapter we will explore personality—the characteristics and behavior patterns that define us as individuals. What are we like? How did we get to be that way? Will we always stay much the same as we are now, or can we change? Do the situations in which we find ourselves determine our behavior, or is our behavior mostly determined by stable characteristics, either innate or acquired over time? Such questions strike to the core of each person's sense of himself or herself as an individual person.

What Is Personality?

"Ajani is a little slow, but she has a great personality."

"Max is a funny dude—he has a lot of personality."

Have you ever heard someone spoken of in these ways? The term *personality* is sometimes used to describe appealing or attractive aspects of the way a person behaves. In this casual use of the term, personality is something that some of us have a lot of and some of us lack. Another casual use suggests that a person might possess the great version of personality or the terrible version.

In psychological science, however, no one has any more personality than anyone else, and no one's personality is better than anyone else's. This is not because psychologists are fair-minded, politically correct folks who don't want to leave anyone out. It is because the term *personality* has a technical meaning quite different from the casual ones just described. Unfortunately, however— and you must be used to hearing this by now—personality psychologists are not in agreement as to the true nature of this technical definition. The lack of agreement as to what actually constitutes personality points once again to the difficulty facing psychological scientists. *Personality* is an abstract concept whose definition is not universally agreed upon, and yet psychologists wish to measure and study it as though it were a concrete reality acknowledged by all.

Like All Others, Some Others, and No Other

In spite of lack of agreement in the field of personality psychology, we can build a useful definition of personality based upon many of the points raised by researchers. Back in 1953, personality psychologists Henry Murray and Clyden Kluckhohn proposed a simple formula to explain exactly which aspects of the human being are encompassed in the term *personality*. According to Kluckhohn and Murray, each person is in certain respects (1) like all other persons; (2) like some other persons; and (3) like no other person. This idea is the starting point for a definition of personality.

1. *Each person is like* all *other persons*. Human beings have an evolved nature that sets them apart from other animals. Once again, there is not very much agreement as to what constitutes human nature in its specifics, but everyone would agree that there are some respects in which all humans differ from all corn flea beetles. In other words, human beings have psychological characteristics and behavioral tendencies that are typical of our species—that unite us, set us apart from individuals of other species, reflect our evolutionary history, and constitute our human nature. These *species-typical* human psychological mechanisms and behavioral tendencies form one aspect of personality. To some degree, then, each unique person reflects a variation on these basic human nature themes (Buss, 2009; McAdams & Olson, 2010; McAdams & Pals, 2006).

▲ **Personality Is Relatively Enduring.** Anyone can get mad. But if a person has a tendency to anger easily, to be belligerent and start fights unnecessarily, he or she may score high in the personality trait *hostility*.

Personality ▶ Personality is the set of common human psychological characteristics and unique patterns of traits and behavior possessed by each individual. These sets of traits and behavior patterns are organized, integrated, and relatively enduring.

2. *Each person is like* some *other persons.* In spite of our psychological unity as human beings, it is obvious that there are many aspects of experience and behavior in which we are *not* all alike. And yet, even given these *individual differences*, there may still be many people who are quite similar in certain respects. For example, most of us know a number of people—not just one—who are usually very outgoing, and a number of people who are usually shy. These relatively enduring attributes that are shared by many, but which also distinguish one individual from another, are known as *traits. Kind, hostile, intelligent, responsible, funny, childish . . .* all these are traits shared by more than one person in the world but not by everyone. Traits are a critically important component of personality.

3. *Each person is like* no *other person.* The idea of individual differences also extends to the unique *pattern* of traits and behaviors that make up a *specific* human being. Regardless of human nature and the commonality of traits, each person is also entirely unique in many respects. Two individuals may be outgoing to approximately the same degree—but each person will express this trait in somewhat different ways, at different times and places, dependent upon different sets of circumstances. Indeed, there may be certain circumstances in which the person behaves in a manner virtually opposite to that in which he or she behaves under other circumstances.

Moreover, each of us has a unique set of characteristic goals, beliefs, social roles, self-concepts, and plans for our lives, termed *characteristic adaptations* by psychologist Dan McAdams[1] (McAdams et al., 2004; McAdams & Olson, 2010; McAdams & Pals, 2006). These characteristic adaptations play out in *self-narratives*, the stories we tell ourselves about ourselves. They reflect the way we understand the events of our lives and our place in the world, giving meaning to our unique identities.

We now have the makings of a workable group of factors that help define personality. **Personality** consists of:

- Unique variations on the set of evolved mental and behavioral characteristics which all human beings share to some degree as a result of our common evolutionary history
- Traits
- Characteristic adaptations (goals, plans, beliefs, social roles, etc.)
- Self-narratives (Church, 2010; McAdams & Olson, 2010; Sheldon, 2004).

Personality Is Organized, Integrated, and Relatively Enduring

The species-typical mental and behavioral characteristics, traits, characteristic adaptations and self-narratives in the preceding list of factors that constitute personality need to be augmented with one important point: These qualities are *organized, integrated,* and *relatively enduring.* What does this mean? *Organized* means that a person's personality forms a coherent picture that might be described in words. However, in describing this coherent picture, you may need to do more than use trait terms ("She's a kind person"). You may also need to make reference to situational factors. A person may behave one way in one context, but another way in another context ("She's very kind with children, but cruel to her employees").

Integrated means that the various aspects of personality are related to—and work with—one another. People are not merely a random collection of traits, mental and behavioral tendencies, characteristic adaptations, and self-narratives that may be described by adjectives and references to situations. Aspects of personality form a *whole* person.

---

[1]*The term* adaptations *as used by McAdams is not the same as used by evolutionary biologists and psychologists.*

Relatively enduring means that personality is fairly constant over extended periods of time. Most people are not kind and outgoing 6 months out of the year, but hostile and shy the next 6. Although certain aspects of personality are subject to change, as we shall see, most aspects are remarkably stable.

Thus, our full, workable definition of personality might be stated in this way: *Personality consists of variations on common human mental and behavioral characteristics, traits, characteristic adaptations, and self-narratives. These factors are organized, integrated, and relatively enduring.*

IN SUMMARY

1.	Like many concepts in psychology, "personality" is an abstraction, and psychologists may differ in their ideas about how it ought to be defined.
2.	In spite of difficulties and disagreements in defining personality, for our purposes personality will be defined as variations on common human mental and behavioral characteristics, traits, characteristic adaptations, and self-narratives. These factors are organized, integrated, and relatively enduring.

RETRIEVE!

1.	What do personality psychologists mean when they say that each person is like all others, like some others, and like no other?
2.	Define the terms *organized*, *integrated*, and *relatively enduring* as applied to a definition of personality.

What Are the "Grand Theories" of Personality?

The field of personality psychology was once dominated by what are usually termed the **grand theories** (Cervone & Shoda, 1999). The word *grand* in this context does not necessarily mean "excellent"; it simply means "big." These were theories developed by pioneers of personality psychology who worked primarily during the first 60 or 70 years of the 20th century when *behaviorism, psychoanalysis,* and *humanistic psychology* were the dominant theories, as described in Chapter 1. These early personality psychologists wanted their theories to address large issues in the study of personality—in certain cases, they wanted their theories to explain virtually *everything there was to explain* about human personality. The "grand theorists" were usually well-read, sophisticated men and women, often steeped in philosophy as well as psychology. They each had numerous disciples, and they all were strongly influential. Although their theories are far less influential than they once were, they continue to have adherents, and certain of their insights have been incorporated into more modern theorizing about psychology. I'll begin with the work of the most influential psychologist in modern history, Sigmund Freud (1856–1939).

Grand theories ▶ The term given to describe theories of personality, primarily developed during the early to mid-20th century, whose creators wished to address all of the important areas of study of personality. The most prominent grand theories were those developed by psychoanalysts, behaviorists, and humanists.

Sigmund Freud and Psychoanalysis: The Life of the Unconscious Mind

The first of the grand theorists is surely the most "grand"—Sigmund Freud. As briefly discussed in Chapter 1, Freud's influence on Western culture has been massive, and this aspect of his influence shows no particular signs of abating, even as the presence of Freudian theory in the field of psychology has diminished quite substantially over the past several decades, having endured widespread—often quite severe—criticism (Crews, 2007).

What was Freud's theory? Freud developed his ideas over time. The Freud of 1905 is not the Freud of 1925, for example, and he used various terminologies quite differently from one period of his work to the next. Freud termed his work as a whole *psychoanalysis*, because it involved the analysis of conflicts which occurred within a person's own mind, or *psyche*—conflicts that were often played out below the person's level of awareness in that region of the mind Freud referred to as the unconscious.

Psychoanalysis includes a psychotherapeutic technique which I describe in Chapter 15; for now we are concerned with the theoretical aspect. Psychoanalytic theory is enormously complex—perhaps the most complex in the history of psychology. However, for our purposes, Freud's theory of personality may be divided into three central components:[2] a *structural model of the mind*, a theory of *psychosexual development*, and theories of *dynamic processes*.

STRUCTURAL MODEL OF THE MIND: ID, EGO, SUPEREGO

By the early 1920s, Freud (1923/1962) had come to believe that the mind consisted of a number of integrated processes or metaphorical "structures" that eventually were called *id* ("it"), *ego* ("I"), and *superego* ("over me"). The id, ego, and superego are not organic structures—that is, Freud didn't suggest that they resided in some particular area of the brain. Instead, they are metaphors for qualities possessed by the human mind, with unknown neural origins in the brain.

According to Freud, in the beginning of human life there is nothing but **id**, also termed the *primary process*. Ancient, mindless, irrational—id is the structure of the mind that cannot distinguish between reality and fantasy, lacks moral restraint or even a conception of right and wrong, and cares only for the satisfaction of its own cravings. Id functions primarily at the level of the unconscious mind and is driven by the **pleasure principle**: to seek pleasure and avoid pain. Id is expressed in dreams, in superstition, in uncontrolled aggressive or immoral behavior, and in satisfaction of basic drives such as sex, hunger, and thirst.

Just as id functions according to the pleasure principle, **ego**, the *secondary process*, functions according to the **reality principle**. Ego—partly conscious, partly unconscious—allows the person to survive, mediating between the demands of the real world and the blind strivings of the id. Unlike id, ego contains organizational and decision-making properties and, while it also seeks to obtain pleasure and avoid pain, it is primarily concerned with assuring the safety and functioning of the individual. It allows the individual to delay striving for pleasure if delaying gratification will ultimately be beneficial. If reality demands that wishes from the id not be expressed, the ego is instrumental in controlling or *repressing* these id instincts—that is, keeping them unconscious, under a metaphorical lock and key and away from the person's awareness.

▲ **Sigmund Freud (1856–1939).** Freud's influence on modern Western culture is incalculable, but his influence on psychology has waned.

Id ▶ That part of Freud's structural model which represents the irrational portion of the mind which lacks moral restraint or a conception of right and wrong, and cares only for satisfaction of its own cravings—seeking pleasure and avoiding pain (the *pleasure principle*). The id operates primarily at the level of the unconscious mind and can be expressed in dreams, uncontrolled behavior, and satisfaction of basic drives.

Pleasure principle ▶ According to Freud, the pleasure principle drives a person to seek pleasure and rewarding experiences, while avoiding pain and discomfort. It is the pleasure principle which drives the *id*.

---

[2]*A fourth component, metapsychology, is too complex to be considered here.*

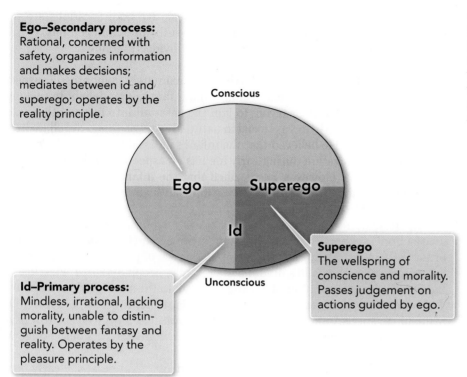

Ego–Secondary process:
Rational, concerned with safety, organizes information and makes decisions; mediates between id and superego; operates by the reality principle.

Conscious

Ego   Superego

Id

Unconscious

Id–Primary process:
Mindless, irrational, lacking morality, unable to distinguish between fantasy and reality. Operates by the pleasure principle.

Superego
The wellspring of conscience and morality. Passes judgement on actions guided by ego.

◀ **FIGURE 12.1 Freud's Structural Model of the Mind.** Although many attempts have been made to create diagrams based on Freud's structural model of the mind, none are fully accurate because Freud's descriptions of id, ego, and superego are not based on a map-like idea.

The ego thus serves both the demands of reality and the strivings of the id. But it has a third master as well: *Superego*. **Superego** represents the conscience and is the wellspring of human morality, according to Freudian theory. Superego watches the work of ego and passes judgment on it. It punishes the psyche with guilt or shame when it perceives that wrong has been done, and points the individual in the direction of ideal behavior. Figure 12.1 presents a diagram of Freud's structural model of the mind.

STAGES OF PSYCHOSEXUAL DEVELOPMENT

Freud proposed that human beings are born with a fund of energy which he termed **libido**, the life-force which is erotic in nature. Although libido has a sexual foundation, its effects are felt far beyond simple sexual experience. Consider a small child dropped off for the first time at a day-care center. She may cry or just sit in a corner, refusing to play or eat. In Freud's view, this in part because a portion of the child's flow of libidinal energy has become "attached" (a processes termed *cathexis*) to the child's mental image of her mother, who has metaphorically taken the energy away with her. Since one's supply of libido is limited, the loss of some of this energy may result in lessened vitality or will to participate in life. According to this idea, the little girl is crying because, in a real sense, a part of her was taken away when the mother departed.

Understanding libido is essential to understanding what Freud referred to as the **stages of psychosexual development**, summarized in Table 12.1. All human beings, according to Freud, experience an inevitable progression through developmental periods in childhood, each of which represents a stage in psychological growth related to sexual life. If the stages are not navigated properly, **neurosis** may result in adulthood—crippling emotional illness and distortion of personality.

During each psychosexual stage, the libidinal energy of the infant or toddler is focused on a different, specific part of his or her body that is particularly

Ego ▶ Ego, also termed *secondary process*, is the aspect of Freud's structural model which represents that part of the mind which operates according to the *reality principle*. Partly conscious, partly unconscious, the ego mediates between the demands of the real world, the blind strivings of the id, and the judgments of the superego.

Reality principle ▶ According to Freud, just as the pleasure principle drives the id, the ego is driven by the reality principle. The reality principle allows the person to delay gratification in the service of a later beneficial outcome, and is the principle by which the ego makes decisions bearing on the survival and functioning of the person.

Superego ▶ According to Freud's structural model, the superego represents the individual's conscience, and is the origin of human morality. The superego observes the work of the ego and passes judgment on it—punishing the psyche with guilt or shame for wrongdoing, and pointing in the direction of ideal behavior.

Libido ▶ Freud proposed that human beings are born with a limited fund of psychic "energy," or life force, which he termed *libido*. This life force has an erotic foundation, although its effects need not be explicitly sexual in nature nor bear only upon sexual life.

Stages of psychosexual development ▶ Freud believed that children pass through five developmental stages of psychosexual growth. For healthy personality to develop, the child must successfully complete the tasks and resolve the conflicts which typically occur at each stage. Fixation at any particular stage may result in adult neurosis or distortion of personality. The stages are termed *oral, anal, phallic (Oedipal), latency,* and *genital.*

Neurosis ▶ A general term describing adult emotional illness or distortion of personality, popularized in the writings of Freud and his followers. Until relatively recently, *neurosis* continued to be used as a "catch-all" for psychological disorder, but it was abandoned in favor of more specific diagnostic labels drawn from psychiatry.

sensitive to pleasurable stimulation. These sensitive body locations are referred to as **erogenous zones** (primarily the mouth, anus, and genitals).

The stages of psychosexual development are divided as follows.

Stage One: The Oral Stage (From birth to approximately 18 months.) I suspect that few parents watching their 7-month-old infant taking delight in sucking on the piano bench legs or trying to jam the cat's tail into her mouth would characterize these activities as sexual in nature. However, Freud did characterize them this way. He believed that the infant's incessant focus on the mouth as a mode of exploration during early life has an aspect of erotic gratification associated with it. However, he specified that the infant's oral eroticism is a *pregenital* sexuality, clearly devoid of the kinds of sexual emotions and meanings attributed to erotic behavior by adults.

If the developmental arc of the oral stage is somehow disturbed—if undersatisfaction or oversatisfaction of oral impulses occur (for example, too much or too little breastfeeding), or if there is some type of psychological trauma at this stage—then the child's libidinal energy may become *fixated.* Fixation in the Freudian sense is rather like being left back in the same grade at school—year, after year, after year, throughout all of one's life. It occurs when a child is unable to successfully resolve the conflicts typical at any given stage of psychosexual development. He or she then displays characteristics of the stage in adult personality.

For example, according to psychoanalytic theory, fixation at the early part of the oral stage may result in the person developing an *oral-incorporative personality* type. The oral-incorporative personality is highly dependent on others; he or she likes to eat, smoke, drink or use drugs; and tends to be a good listener—sometimes to the point of gullibility. Fixation at later portions of the oral stage may result in an *oral-sadistic* personality type. Such people are sarcastic, cynical, and use words in a "biting" manner. These ideas exemplify the importance of metaphor in Freud's work. Oral-sadistic personality types metaphorically "bite" other people, whereas oral-incorporative personalities metaphorically "take things in" (food, drink, other people's words).

Stage Two: The Anal Stage (Approximately 18 months through age 3.) As infants become toddlers and acquire more control over their world, according to Freud they enter the anal stage, characterized by the acquisition of new skills such as language and bowel control. If fixation occurs in the early portion of the anal stage, when the anus is the primary erogenous zone and the greatest pleasure is derived from expelling feces, the child may grow up with an *anal-expulsive* personality. Such people care little for rules, may be disorderly or sloppy in their personal habits, and are prone to highly emotional outbursts. However, they also tend toward generosity (symbolically giving away their beloved feces to others!).

In contrast, if fixation occurs at the later portion of the anal stage, when the greatest pleasure is being derived from retaining feces to master bowel control, the *anal-retentive* personality type may develop. Anal-retentive types are orderly, preoccupied with rules, stingy, and stubborn.

Stage Three: The Phallic (Oedipal) Stage (Approximately age 3 or 4 through age 5 or 6.) Freud termed this stage "phallic" because the boy child supposedly is preoccupied with his penis and the girl child with her *lack* of penis—a problem known as *penis envy.* It is during this critical phallic stage that the *Oedipus complex* arises and must be resolved for healthy personality development to occur. The **Oedipus complex** is Freud's term for his notion that children of this age experience a powerful desire to erotically possess the other-sex parent and "do away" with the same-sex parent, who is a rival of sorts.

How is this eerie melodrama resolved? In the case of the boy child, Freud proposed that because each boy experiences jealousy toward the father and a wish for his death (or removal from the scene by other means), he fears the father's rage and retaliation. Specifically, the boy fears that he might be castrated by his father (castration is the removal of the testicles or penis or both). Thus, in Freud's own words (Freud, 1925/1991) "In boys . . . the [Oedipus] complex is not simply repressed, it is literally smashed to pieces by the shock of threatened castration" (p. 341).

At this point, the intense erotic attachment to the mother is abandoned. For this abandonment to occur, however, the boy—no longer fighting the father—learns to internalize the image of the father by *identifying* with him. In this way he gets to possess the mother indirectly by, in effect, *becoming* his father. Most important, the father is a symbol of moral authority, and in identifying with his father and resolving the Oedipus complex the boy develops a superego.

The situation of the girl child is quite different, according to Freud, in his description of the *female Oedipus complex* (sometimes termed *Electra complex*). The girl's story begins similarly, with an erotic attachment to the mother who is her primary caretaker and therefore the primary love object. However, just as in some vague way the boy is supposed to become aware of the possibility of castration, in an equally vague manner Freud asserted that the girl comes to perceive her genitals as inferior to those of the male, whose penis she envies. (Freud apparently assumed that every 3-year-old girl had seen a penis.)

Because the poor little girl realizes that both she and her mother lack this important phallic attribute and the male authority which it symbolizes, she comes to devalue and reject the mother as a love object, transferring her erotic longings to her father, whom she hopes will supply her with the penis she lacks—or its substitute in the form of impregnation with a baby. (Again, Freud did not specify exactly how a 3-year-old girl was supposed to understand the nature of pregnancy or sexual intercourse.)

Unlike the boy child, the girl is not motivated to resolve her female Oedipal complex by fear of castration because, as far as she is concerned, she has already suffered castration! Therefore, her motivation to resolve the problem is much less powerful than the boy's. Instead, she realizes that female qualities

▲ **The Odd Couple: Anal Expulsive, Anal Retentive.** In the highly successful 1960s television program *The Odd Couple*, Jack Klugman portrayed a disorderly, sloppy, but relaxed and generous personality type, whereas Tony Randall portrayed a rule-bound, stingy, ultra-orderly type. These are stereotypical characterizations of the anal expulsive and anal retentive personality types.

Erogenous zone ▶ Any area of the body with particular sensitivity to pleasurable stimulation, generally associated with sexuality.

Oedipus complex ▶ Freud's belief that children in the phallic stage (age 3 or 4 through age 5 or 6) experience powerful erotic desires for the opposite-sex parent, while wishing to eliminate the same-sex parent who is perceived as a rival. According to Freud, the Oedipus complex arises and is resolved differently for boys and girls, with girls experiencing an incomplete resolution. According to Freud, a successful resolution of the Oedipus complex results in the development of an adequate superego.

Table 12.1 Freud's Stages of Psychosocial Development

STAGE	AGES	EROGENOUS ZONE	PERSONALITY TYPE IF FIXATED
Oral	Birth–18 months	Lips, tongue, gums	*Oral incorporative* (dependent; likes to eat, drink, and smoke; good listener but tends toward gullibility) *Oral sadistic* (sarcastic, cynical, "biting" with words)
Anal	18 months through age 3	Anus	*Anal expulsive* (generous, disregard for rules or order, may be sloppy and slovenly) *Anal retentive* (orderly, stingy, stubborn, preoccupied with rules)
Phallic (Oedipal)	Age 3 through 5 or 6	Genitals	Failure to resolve Oedipus complex results in various neuroses
Latency	Age 6 to puberty	Reduced interest in sex	Not applicable
Genital	Puberty	Genitals	Not applicable

possessed by her mother are appealing to her father, and this begins her identification with her same-sex parent. Eventually there is a lessening of erotic longing for her father as she learns that these desires are not going to be fulfilled.

Stage Four: Latency (Approximately age 6 until the onset of gonadarche at puberty.) During the latency stage, the child's sexual interests supposedly lessen in urgency as same-sex friendships assume a position of greater importance in the child's life.

Stage Five: Genital Stage (From gonadarche in early adolescence through adulthood.) In the genital stage, sex resumes its place of importance as libidinal energy is focused once again upon the genitals—this time as an expression of adult sexuality.

DYNAMIC PROCESSES

Dynamics as Freud used the term implies the idea of constant motion, energy, and conflict between component parts of the mind. His view of the mind is therefore a dynamic view because the id, ego, and superego are constantly interacting, in motion, and in conflict. Various mental processes are pressed into service by the mind in its efforts to navigate and resolve the conflicts with which it is continuously faced.

Dreams and Dream Work Among the most prominent of these dynamic processes are dreams. Freud believed that dreams are expressions of unconscious sexual or aggressive wishes and conflicts, expressed in symbolic form. Analysis of the *latent* (hidden) meanings of dreams is an important part of psychoanalysis as a therapy. Freudian dream interpretation is a process of interpretive virtuosity, where imagery and events with no apparent sexual or aggressive content whatever can be reinterpreted by the psychoanalyst—often in a most tortuous and seemingly unlikely fashion—as expressions of forbidden sexual or aggressive impulses.

Anna Freud's Ego Defense Mechanisms Other dynamic processes of the mind are **ego defense mechanisms**. These mechanisms are used by the ego to keep threatening or anxiety-provoking material from reaching awareness. Although Freud did discuss a few types of ego-defenses—primarily **repression**, where an unacceptable wish, thought, or memory is removed from conscious awareness—this idea was actually developed fully by his daughter, Anna Freud (1895–1982). Table 12.2 lists some of the most important of the ego defenses with a description of each.

FREUD UNDER SIEGE: WHY THE FUSS OVER PSYCHOANALYSIS?

No theory in the history of psychology has generated so much intense controversy as psychoanalysis. It is not easy to find someone in the field of psychology who is indifferent to it, or to Freud's theories in general. This is undoubtedly in keeping with the extent of their influence, the fact that they deal so directly with sexuality and aggression, love and hate, parent and child—and that they make so many claims that can only be described as "grand" if not grandiose. Indeed, despite Freud's pervasive influence, the man and his theories have been under siege in many quarters (Crews, 2007; Farrell, 1996). Critics charge that the theoretical map of the human mind devised by Freud is one of the least supported by conventional scientific evidence (Eysenck & Wilson, 1973; MacMillan, 1997; Popper, 1962; but see Westen, 1998, for a contrasting view). Thus, I have described it in detail, not because it is critical to an understanding of human psychology, but simply because it is critical to an understanding of one of the major influences on modern Western life and ideas.

Ego defense mechanisms ▶ A group of psychological mechanisms described in part by Sigmund Freud but primarily by his daughter, Anna Freud. The ego uses these mechanisms to keep threatening material from reaching awareness. The defense mechanisms include repression, denial, displacement, projection, reaction formation, sublimation, and undoing.

Repression ▶ An ego defense mechanism identified by Freud, where an unacceptable wish, thought, or impulse is removed from conscious awareness.

Table 12.2 Important Ego Defense Mechanisms as Described by Anna Freud (1936/1966)

DEFENSE MECHANISM	DESCRIPTION	EXAMPLE
1. Denial	When events or realities that are threatening to the ego are ignored.	Parents whose son has recently died refuse to change anything in his room, keeping it exactly as it was when their child was alive.
2. Displacement	When a sexual or aggressive impulse is redirected from the actual (threatening) target to another, less threatening target.	A man who works in his father's machine shop, and is bullied his father throughout the day, comes home and yells at his wife instead of expressing rage to the father. (The wife then yells at her kids instead of the husband, the kids kick the dog, the dog bites the cat. . . .)
3. Projection	When one's own unacceptable wishes or impulses are attributed to the person who was the object of the unacceptable wish or impulse.	A brother who is sexually attracted to his sister accuses her of making incestuous advances.
4. Reaction formation	When an unacceptable wish or impulse is transformed into an exaggerated version of its opposite.	A woman is kept a virtual prisoner in her own home because she must care for a tyrannical elderly mother. Instead of experiencing the anger she really feels toward the mother, the daughter dotes on her instead, repeatedly assuring the mother (and herself) of her undying daughterly love.
5. Repression	Removal from conscious awareness or memory of an unacceptable wish or impulse. Repression plays a role in most of the other defense mechanisms.	A highly moral woman experiences sexual attraction to a teenage boy while at a beach, and later cannot recall even having seen the boy.
6. Sublimation	When an unacceptable wish or impulse is "translated" into a socially acceptable behavior.	A man who experiences sadistic fantasies of torturing women becomes a magician performing "sawing the lady in half" and other tricks involving binding and committing fantasy atrocities on his female assistant.
7. Undoing	Unconscious "atoning" for an unacceptable thought or behavior through a second, acceptable, thought or behavior.	A child tortures a small animal in the woods. When she returns home she is particularly kind to her pet.

But how does psychoanalysis fare as a theory? Psychoanalysis is highly comprehensive, perhaps the most comprehensive theory in the history of psychology. There are few aspects of human life about which psychoanalysis has nothing to say. Moreover, psychoanalysis has generated some of the most novel assertions in the history of behavioral science (e.g., 3-year-old girls want to murder their mothers and appropriate their fathers' penises). Whereas some of these concepts—such as the Oedipus complex and penis envy—are counterintuitive to say the least, and may seem difficult to believe, some fit very well with ordinary experience and are clearly insightful—for example, the notion that a person may transfer his or her anger from an unacceptable target (e.g., his boss) to an "acceptable" one (his dog) without being aware of having done so.

However, psychoanalysis fails as a scientific theory in a great many respects. Often, it proposes convoluted, complex explanations where a simple, ordinary one will do. For example, Freud attributed an asthmatic attack in one of his female patients, known as Dora, to an (unsubstantiated) incident from Dora's childhood where, supposedly, she witnessed her parents having sex. Freud apparently didn't consider a more probable cause—that Dora simply had a case of asthma and sometimes had attacks. The same patient's cough

Parsimony ▶ In science, the term *parsimony* describes the principle that if there are more than one competing explanations for some phenomenon, each plausible, scientists like to choose the simpler of the explanations. This is because simpler explanations contain fewer assumptions that might be incorrect. The principle of parsimony is also known as Occam's Razor.

Falsification ▶ When a theory is shown through empirical evidence to be false.

was attributed to her desire to engage in oral sex with her father, rather than to a tickly throat—or, perhaps more likely (given that she was Freud's patient) to second-hand cigar smoke (Crews, 1995). When more than one plausible explanation exists for some phenomenon, scientists like to choose the simpler of the explanations. This is because simpler explanations contain fewer assumptions that might be incorrect—in a sense, they contain fewer "parts" that can "go wrong." This is known as the principle of **parsimony**, or *Occam's Razor*. Psychoanalysis consistently violates parsimony.

Furthermore, psychoanalysis is often unnecessarily laden with jargon that is mysterious even to professional psychologists. Psychoanalysis is also frequently contradictory and occasionally incoherent, making it difficult to establish consensus regarding any particular question. Because psychoanalytic principles and statements may be interpreted in so many ways, the theory is, for the most part, impossible to *disprove*. According to mainstream scientific philosophy, one criterion for a sound scientific theory is that it specifies the conditions under which it can be disproved, or falsified (Popper, 1962). Psychoanalysis rarely allows for **falsification**. There is sometimes an "Alice in Wonderland" quality to psychoanalysis, where things can mean anything that one wants them to mean. This can be frustrating to those trained in methods of psychological science.

Some scientists *have* tried to test certain of Freud's ideas, but results have not been very impressive. Although young children clearly do become possessive of their parents, no evidence has been found to substantiate the universal existence of an Oedipus complex as Freud described it. Similarly, evidence does not support Freud's structural model of the mind (id, ego, superego), his view of the purpose of dreams, and numerous other constructs of psychoanalysis. His notion that traumatic memories and fantasies about these memories are frequently "repressed" is contradicted by most current research in memory, which suggests that traumatic memories are in general recalled more often, more clearly, and more accurately than other types of memories (see Chapter 8).

Moreover, while Freud was generally correct in his claims that unconscious mental activity exists, he was not the first to recognize this truth, and current research (described throughout this book) clearly shows that mental processes that occur below the level of awareness are radically different from those envisioned by Freud. Moderate support does exist for some of Freud's ideas, however, such as the existence of personality types that Freud described using the terms "anal" and "oral" (Fisher & Greenberg, 1996). Substantial support also exists for more general observations initiated by Freud—for example, that early childhood experiences can affect the development of personality or that a person may feel contradictory emotions toward another person simultaneously, such as love and hate (Westen, 1998). Finally, as suggested earlier, empirical research has supported certain of the defense mechanisms identified by Freud and his daughter Anna and described in Table 12.2 (Baumeister, Dale, & Sommer, 1998).

The Neo-Freudians: Keeping the Baby, Throwing Out the Bathwater

Over the decades that followed the establishment of psychoanalysis as a discipline, numerous students of Freud, and their students in turn, broke with Freudian orthodoxy (sometimes breaking off friendships with Freud himself in the process) and created their own schools of thought with psychoanalysis as a base. Psychologists such as these are generally referred to as "neo-Freudians," but many reject the label, and it can be misleading to lump them together. They are often very far apart in their points of view, as depicted in Figure 12.2.

As with Freud's views, the work of the neo-Freudians, while massive in scope and frequently insightful, has been difficult to test. Nonetheless, these

Ego Psychologists: Anna Freud (l) and Erik Erikson (r). Ego psychologists accepted much of Freudian psychoanalysis, but emphasized the importance of ego functions over those of the id which preoccupied much of Freud's thinking.

  Object Relations Theorists: Melanie Klein (l) and D. W. Winnicott (r). Object relations theorists such as Klein and Winnicott stressed the importance in personality development of interrelationships between the infant/child and other people and objects in the child's world. By "interrelationships" object relations theorists include the child's own internalized mental representations of these relationships.

  Social-analytic Theorists: Left-to-Right: Karen Horney, Erich Fromm. Some groups of psychoanalysts working primarily in the United States believed that Freud placed insufficient importance on social and political factors. These theorists often held strong humanistic beliefs. Horney is credited with being the first theorist of women's psychology, and Fromm wished psychoanalysis to further the cause of social reform.

   Mavericks: Left-to-Right, Carl Jung, Alfred Adler, Jacques Lacan. Numerous psychoanalysts went on to form their own schools, sometimes associated with them alone. Jung is best noted for his emphasis on spirituality, myth, and universal symbols; Adler focused on the importance to healthy personality development of creating democratic structures within the family which stressed equality (including gender equality); Lacan, perhaps the most contemporary of the neo-Freudians, paradoxically asked psychoanalysts to return to Freud's original writings as a way of stressing the importance of language in subjective human experience.

◀ **FIGURE 12.2 The Neo-Freudians.** This chart summarizes the work of some of the more important of the neo-Freudians.

theorists have made their mark upon psychoanalysis as a theory and a practice. Indeed, it is currently far more likely to find psychoanalysts who adhere primarily to the ideas of one or more of the neo-Freudians than to the ideas of Freud himself. The neo-Freudians kept the "baby" of the essential insights of psychoanalysis—for example, that much behavior was motivated by unconscious forces and conflicts originating in childhood experiences—but threw out the "bathwater" of specific Freudian ideas and treatment techniques that had not stood the test of time.

The Behaviorists: Personality Is a Learning Experience

The essence of behaviorism is *learning*, a topic to which I have devoted an entire chapter (Chapter 7). Thus, we will consider behaviorist approaches to personality only very briefly here. Although the behaviorists were not primarily interested in personality development, as were the psychoanalysts, strict behaviorist theorists such as John B. Watson and B. F. Skinner had much to say about personality, treating it as they would any other psychological variable: by analyzing behavior according to principles of learning. Behaviors acquired through association between stimuli or experiences of reinforcement and punishment become both the definition and expression of each person's personality.

As a hypothetical example, consider a child whose mother is overly anxious about illness. At the slightest sign of a minor symptom in her son she grows concerned, paying the child an inordinate amount of attention he does not otherwise receive from her. She keeps him home from school at a mere sign of a sniffle, and on these occasions she caters to the boy's every whim. He gets to drink Coca-Cola (not otherwise allowed), watch television, and play video games to his heart's content, and enjoy having his mother read to him. In short, he receives a high degree of positive reinforcement for being sick. According to the behaviorist view, such treatment might be instrumental in

Self-concept ▶ The sum total of a person's evaluation of the nature and quality of his or her unique existence. Self-concept includes social, physiological, and psychological aspects.

Accurate empathy ▶ Carl Rogers' term to describe the quality of communication between two people where each person genuinely listens to the other's words, hears the words, perceives the intention accurately, and withholds judgment.

Congruence ▶ Carl Rogers' term to describe an environment of development where those surrounding the developing person are *genuine*—that is, truly being themselves and not presenting a self that reflects the values and wishes of others.

Unconditional positive regard ▶ Carl Rogers' term to describe relationships where the love and approval a person receives from important others is given freely and is not dependent upon conditions. For example, if a therapist treats a client with approval, respect, and high regard when the client behaves in a way the therapist thinks is constructive—but not if the client engages in self-destructive behavior—this is *conditional* rather than *unconditional* positive regard.

shaping an adult personality that includes excessive preoccupation with matters of health and disease, constant experience of symptoms (*hypochondria*), and generalized anxiety.

Experiences of reinforcement and punishment undoubtedly exert important effects on the developing personality. However, the behaviorists' insistence that principles of learning could explain virtually all aspects of personality—or at least those aspects of personality that could be studied scientifically—lost favor during the 1960s and 1970s. During these years, cognitive and evolutionary theories of psychology began to emerge along with an extremely popular new force in psychology—*humanistic psychology*.

The Humanists: Faith in Humankind

The founders of humanistic psychology had faith in human nature. They were unashamedly optimistic, and in this sense they are the "spiritual forefathers and foremothers" of the more recent movement in *positive psychology*, which focuses upon human strengths rather than human weaknesses, failings, and disorders (Seligman, Linley, & Joseph, 2004). According to humanists such as Carl Rogers and Abraham Maslow, human beings are reasoning creatures, born with free will and innate strivings for positive goals. The humanists believed that people face problems in a generally rational manner and try to make good decisions that will benefit themselves and others. This is in sharp contrast to Freudian psychoanalysts, who, with their melodramatic scenarios of good and evil fighting it out on the battlefield of the unconscious, held a distinctly pessimistic view of the human condition.

As briefly discussed in Chapter 1, Carl Rogers (1902–1987) is probably the person most often associated with personality from a humanistic psychology perspective. In certain respects Rogers, who began his career as a Divinity student, was carrying forward the optimistic conception of human nature popularized by the 19th-century Romantic philosopher Jean-Jacques Rousseau. Like Rousseau, Rogers believed that human beings are born basically good; he maintained that each of us is designed to develop into a competent, fulfilled, and compassionate human being—what he called a *fully functioning person*—unless we lack a growth-promoting environment. Such an environment is one that enables each individual to develop a healthy **self-concept**—an intrinsic evaluation of the quality of his or her unique existence in the world. Self-concept answers the questions, "Who and what am I really? How should my unique existence be evaluated?" For a person to develop a healthy self-concept, the environment must fulfill four interrelated conditions: *accurate empathy, congruence, unconditional positive regard*, and *positive self-regard*.

By **accurate empathy**, Rogers meant that those around a child during his or her formative years must truly listen and *hear* the child—withholding judgment and wishing only to communicate. **Congruence** implies that those around the growing person are *genuine*—they are truly being themselves and are not presenting a self which reflects others' values and wishes rather than their own.

Unconditional positive regard and **positive self-regard** are interdependent ideas. For a person to develop positive self-regard—feelings of self-esteem, self-worth, and being loved and accepted—he or she needs to be treated with *unconditional* positive regard by others. This means that the approval and love we receive from important people in our lives are freely and fully given, regardless of flaws in our own behavior or character. In unconditional positive regard, approval and acceptance are not based upon any conditions. As a counterexample, a young child may come to learn that she is loved and approved of *only* if she refrains from wetting her bed, spilling her food, getting poor grades at school, or some other transgression. Refraining from these behaviors then become the **conditions of worth**. Conditions of worth are conditions the child must fulfill to receive the acceptance and love

▲ **The Humanists.** (*left to right*) Carl Rogers (1902–1987), Abraham Maslow (1908–1970), and Rollo May (1909–1994) were the most prominent figures of the humanist movement in psychology of the 1960s and 1970s.

she needs—a situation opposite to that of unconditional positive regard, and therefore one that will not promote positive self-regard.

Rogers was adamant that growing up in a health-promoting environment was not only a question of having loving parents and a supportive family. To a large degree it necessitated being surrounded by a *culture* supportive of mental health. Rogers claimed that it was cultural influences that were the major factor in evil behavior by human beings (cited by May, 1982).

Rogers' psychotherapy techniques were firmly rooted in his view of personality and human nature in that he attempted to create a relationship between therapist and client based upon unconditional positive regard, empathy, and acceptance; allowing the client to receive what had been lacking in important early relationships.

In addition to Abraham Maslow (1908–1970), whose important work on human motivation is covered in Chapter 10, another humanist bears mentioning: Rollo May (1909–1994). May is particularly interesting because, while he is associated with the humanist movement, he had a view of human life in many ways radically different from that of other humanists. Rather than viewing human beings as essentially good—corrupted only by cultural forces and personal experiences in childhood—May saw human beings as an "organized bundle of potentialities," with as much capacity for evil as for good (1982, p. 11). According to May, if culture creates evil, it is human beings who create their own culture, and thus it is human beings who are responsible for evil. May (1969, 1981) evolved a version of *existentialist* philosophy that placed responsibility for facing the realities of life and death—and the anxieties these realities engender—squarely on the shoulders of the individual.

Positive self-regard ▶ Carl Rogers' term to describe feelings of self-worth and self-esteem, and being loved and accepted. According to Rogers, positive self-regard is dependent upon experiences of unconditional positive regard from others.

Conditions of worth ▶ According to Carl Rogers, conditions of worth are the conditions a person must fulfill to obtain love and approval from important people in his or her life. These conditions only exist within relationships which lack unconditional positive regard.

CRITICAL THINKING ABOUT PSYCHOLOGY

Humanists such as Carl Rogers stressed the importance of **self-esteem**— each person's cognitive and emotional assessment of his or her own self-worth. Self-esteem is of great interest to a lot of people. It is one of the most frequently studied concepts in psychology (Watson, Suls, & Haig, 2002), and interest in self-esteem doesn't end in the psychology lab. What

Self-Esteem: It Feels Good, but What Does It Actually Do?

CRITICAL THINKING ABOUT PSYCHOLOGY

CONTINUED

Self-esteem ▶ A person's cognitive and emotional assessment or evaluation of his or her self-worth. Self-esteem may be *global*—a person's assessment of overall self-worth—or *specific* to a given domain.

began as a psychological concept has become a household word. To some degree, this is understandable. Self-esteem *feels good*, and reduced self-esteem *feels bad*. People with high self-esteem tend to be happier, suffer less from depression, and are more likely to enjoy the good things that happen to them to the fullest and more likely to help others do the same (Baumeister, Campbell, Krueger, & Vohs, 2003; Krueger, Vohs, & Baumeister, 2008; Wood, Heimpel, & Michela, 2003). People will go to great lengths to maintain feelings of self-esteem (Pyszczynski, Greenberg, Solomon, Arndt, & Schimel, 2004; Sherman & Cohen, 2002).

Why exactly does self-esteem feel so good? Several theories have been proposed. Researchers adhering to a unique theory known as *terror management theory* (described in greater detail in Chapter 15) suggest that self-esteem acts as a psychological buffer against the pervasive general anxiety all human beings feel when faced with the knowledge of their own inevitable death (Greenberg, 2008; Pyszczynski et al., 2004; Schmeichel et al., 2009). According to terror management theory, because we understand how vulnerable we really are, feelings of security depend upon achieving a kind of symbolic immortality through valued roles, attributes, and accomplishments. Self-esteem imparts meaning to a life that could end at any time.

Another approach, known as *sociometer theory*, focuses on the possibility that one's level of self-esteem provides important feedback about social acceptance or rejection (Leary & Baumeister, 2000; Leary, 2004). In other words, self-esteem is a kind of social barometer. High self-esteem is a signal that you are likely to be socially accepted and unlikely to be rejected. Regardless of the true explanation for the importance of self-esteem to human beings, however, it is beyond doubt that most people are highly motivated to maintain self-esteem. But does self-esteem have the near-magical properties frequently attributed to it?

"DISAPPOINTING" FINDINGS

According to the pronouncements of various self-help books and experts voicing their opinions regularly on television talk shows, self-esteem can be credited with improving school performance, success in work, interpersonal relationships, and numerous other life endeavors. And the absence of self-esteem can be blamed for criminality, prejudice, teenage pregnancy, drug and alcohol abuse, and sexual excesses. Are these ideas well founded?

The short answer appears to be "No" to all of the above—or at least little evidence in favor of such beliefs has yet been found (Baumeister et al., 2003; Bushman et al., 2009; Crocker & Park, 2004; Krueger et al., 2008; Leary, 1999). This may come as a shock, contradicting much of what you may have heard. However, beginning with the "disappointing" findings of the California Task Force on Self-Esteem in 1989 (Mecca, Smelser, & Vasconcellos, 1989) and ending with the extensive review conducted in 2003 by the American Psychological Society Task Force on Self-Esteem headed by Roy Baumeister, it seems that many common beliefs about self-esteem are not supported by evidence (Baumeister et al., 2003).

For example, there is no evidence that high self-esteem improves school performance, although there is some evidence that doing well in school might increase self-esteem—but only mildly. Based on these findings, programs designed to improve children's school performance by raising their self-esteem are not likely to succeed. Indeed, evidence suggests that artificially boosted self-esteem might actually result in *decreased* school performance (Gailliot & Baumeister, 2007)! If you overestimate your abilities, you might underestimate the amount of work that needs to be done to complete schoolwork successfully.

Another area believed by many to be affected by self-esteem is interpersonal relations. But while it is often said that "loving oneself is a prerequisite for loving others," Baumeister and his research team report that high-self-esteem individuals do not necessarily have superior social skills and interpersonal skills, although they often *think* they do. Those with high self-esteem rate themselves as more popular and socially adept than those with low self-esteem, but when rated by others (peers, teachers, co-workers) or when other, more objective measures are used, the self-assessments of high-self-esteem people are not confirmed. In fact, in some cases, those with high self-esteem receive *lower* ratings than low-self-esteem people, with the added problem that when their pride is challenged they can become angrier than those with low self-esteem. As Baumeister and his colleagues put it, "[T]he superior social skills and interpersonal successes of people with high self-esteem exist mainly in their own minds." (2003, p. 20).

There are at least two areas, however, where at least some evidence does link low self-esteem with negative outcomes. The most straightforward of these is eating disorders. Low self-esteem *is* strongly related to the development of *bulimia nervosa* (Baumeister et al., 2003). The other area is less straightforward—aggression and delinquent "acting-out" behavior. Baumeister and his colleagues could find only a single methodologically sound

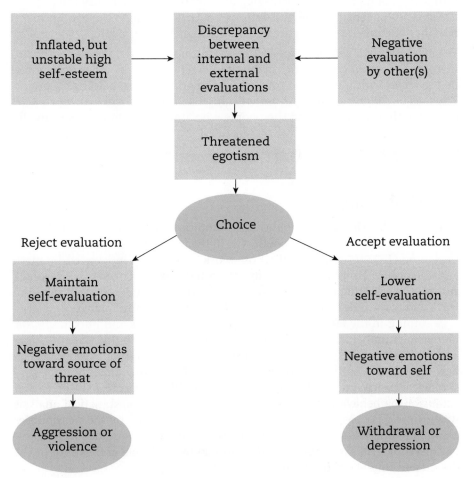

◄ **FIGURE 12.3 High Self-Esteem Can Lead to Aggression and Violence.** Roy Baumeister and his colleagues present a model of how threatened egotism in persons with narcissistic, unstable, or defensive self-esteem can lead to aggression and violence. When the person's inflated self-esteem conflicts with negative evaluations of others, the person must choose between accepting or rejecting those negative evaluations. If the evaluations are rejected, violence may ultimately result. If they are accepted, withdrawal or depression may result. *(Figure adapted from Baumeister et al., 1996, p. 12.)*

CRITICAL THINKING ABOUT PSYCHOLOGY

CONTINUED   study which suggested that low self-esteem might be associated with aggressive acting-out behavior, but subsequently Brad Bushman and his colleagues looked "longer and harder" at the research and conducted more of their own, and concluded that there is no link whatever between low self-esteem and aggression (Bushman et al., 2009; but see Webster, Kirkpatrick, Nezlek, Smith, & Paddock, 2007, for a different view).

Even more surprising is the fact that substantial evidence does point to *high* self-esteem as a frequent culprit in aggression (Baumeister, Bushman, & Campbell, 2000; Bushman et al., 2009)! High self-esteem results from many things, and one of these is *narcissism*—an inflated view of the self that can lead to aggressive retaliation when pride is threatened (Thomaes, Bushman, de Castro, Cohen, & Denissen, 2009). This type of self-esteem has been termed *defensive*, or *fragile high self-esteem* (Kernis, Lakey, & Heppner, 2008; Salmivalli, Kaukiainen, Kaistaniemi, & Lagerspetz, 1999). The combination of high self-esteem with narcissism is a dangerous combination.

Roy Baumeister and his colleagues label this the "dark side of self-esteem," and present a model to explain how high self-esteem can lead to aggression and violence (Baumesiter, Smart, & Boden, 1996). In the model, depicted in Figure 12.3, a person with inflated—but relatively unstable—high self-esteem confronts the discrepancy between his or her own highly positive self-evaluations and the negative evaluations of others—a condition that is threatening to the ego. At this point, the person is forced to choose between two alternatives: either accept the negative evaluations of others, which lowers self-esteem, brings on negative feelings about the self, and can lead to withdrawal or depression; or reject others' evaluations, maintain self-esteem, and experience negative feelings and hostility toward the sources of those whose evaluations are threatening to the ego. If this hostility becomes severe, aggression and violence may result.

Yet, realistic high self-esteem—self-esteem that is not defensive and does not result from an unrealistically inflated view of the self—does appear to be associated with increased prosocial behaviors, that is, helping others. Thus, as one study showed, those with high self-esteem are overrepresented both as bullies *and* as the people who stand up to bullies (Salmivalli et al., 1999). ■

Winds of Change

The "grand theories" of personality were ambitious, influential, frequently insightful, and sometimes even poetic—as in the cases of Freud and his student Carl Jung (1875–1961), both of whose work was heavily influenced by myth and metaphor. However, as already suggested, many of these theories lack substantial scientific evidence to support them, and many are constructed in ways that make it difficult or impossible to test them scientifically.

Beginning in the late 1950s and throughout the 1960s and into the 1970s, increasing numbers of psychologists grew dissatisfied with this state of affairs and disillusioned with the accepted psychological wisdom of their time. The new science of cognitive psychology was demonstrating that internal psychological processes could be studied scientifically, in contrast to the earlier claims of the behaviorists. With the advent of computers, statistical analysis was growing far easier and more sophisticated. Spurred by the possibilities computers offered, and due to the maturing of research methods in psychology, psychologists were also growing more knowledgeable and skillful in the design and conduct of research.

It had also become clear that psychoanalysis as a method of psychotherapy—a technique that could require over a thousand (very expensive) visits to an analyst's office stretched out over years—did not have a very impressive track record for treating serious emotional and psychiatric illnesses. Because the practice of psychotherapy was growing exponentially, psychologists, health insurance companies, and the general public were coming to demand more systematic and scientific ways of determining which therapeutic techniques were useful and cost-effective and which were not. The word of "the experts" was no longer sufficient.

In sum, although psychoanalysis, behaviorism, and humanism continued to exert influence in the world of personality psychology—and continue to do so at least to some degree to the present day—the era of domination of the field by these theories began to draw to a close during the 1970s, setting the stage for the advent of research-based theories of personality (Robins, Gosling, & Craik, 1999).

IN SUMMARY

1.	The psychoanalytic theory of Sigmund Freud may be divided into three central components: a structural model of the mind, a theory of development, and theories of dynamic processes. The structural model of the mind consists of id, ego, and superego. The theory of psychosexual development consists of five stages, each centered around a different erogenous zone and typical psychological conflicts. "Dynamic processes" refers primarily to dreams and their interpretation, and to ego defense mechanisms as defined by Freud and his daughter Anna.
2.	The neo-Freudians had widely varying points of view, but they are united in that they all have accepted at least a portion of psychoanalytic ideas.
3.	The behaviorists used learning theory to analyze personality. They believed that a person's character is a result of experiences of operant and classical conditioning.
4.	The humanists had faith in human nature and tended toward optimism about the human condition. They believed that human beings are reasoning creatures, born with free will and innate strivings for positive goals. Rollo May, also associated with the humanistic movement in psychology, created a theory of psychology based in existentialist philosophy. He believed that human beings have an innate capacity for evil, just as they do for good, but that they have the freedom to choose.
5.	People strive hard to maintain feelings of self-esteem. However, a person's overall level of self-esteem may not predict the types of consequences that many people believe that it does.
6.	The grand theories of personality were ambitious and often insightful, but they lost influence in contemporary psychology either because they were not testable by scientific methods or because they had been tested and found wanting.

RETRIEVE!

1.	When a person commits a spontaneous murder motivated by hatred, which component of the mind is at work, according to Freud? When the person experiences profound guilt and remorse following the act, which component is at work? As the person decides to enter a guilty plea, hoping for a reduced sentence, which component is at work?

2.	What are the characteristics of an oral incorporative personality? Oral sadistic? What are the characteristics of an anal retentive type? Anal expulsive?
3.	According to Freud, the boy's Oedipus complex is "shattered," but the girl's resolves slowly. What is Freud's explanation for this difference?
4.	Name and describe at least four of the ego defense mechanisms identified by Freud's daughter Anna.
5.	Name at least two objections to Freud's theories that have been voiced over the years.
6.	J. J. is a very hostile young man. He is quick to pick a fight, and he responds to insults with threats of physical violence or actual violence. Imagine a set of possible experiences in J. J.'s early life that a behaviorist might consider to have been the main factors responsible for these aspects of J. J.'s personality.
7.	What is the difference between unconditional positive regard and positive self-regard, according to Carl Rogers? What is accurate empathy?
8.	True or false: High self-esteem is associated with greater success at school, forming friendships, and the lower likelihood of drug abuse and aggression.

How Do Traits and Situations Affect Personality?

Traits ▶ Stable, enduring personality attributes and motives for behavior. Traits may generally be described using adjectives (e.g., extraverted, conscientious, cheerful, honest, compassionate). Traits are limited in number, and each person differs in the degree to which they display any particular trait.

States ▶ Emotions, moods, or other characteristics and attributes which are temporary in nature. States can be contrasted with traits, which are assumed to be enduring. For example, *anger* is a temporary state, whereas *short-tempered* is a relatively enduring trait.

In response to the focus of psychoanalysis on pathology and the unconscious, during the mid-1930s, a young psychologist named Gordon Allport devised a theory of personality based on the notion of **traits**—relatively stable personality characteristics, attributes, and motivations that can be commonly captured in adjectives such as *honest, cheerful, kind, short-tempered, conscientious,* and so forth. This initiated an important new movement toward a more scientific account of personality than that offered in earlier personality theories, including psychoanalysis.

Traits Describe—but Do Not Explain—Personality

To identify the number of possible personality traits in existence, Allport and a colleague extracted 17,953 adjectives from *Webster's New International Dictionary* that were in some way descriptive of personal attributes (Allport & Odbert, 1936). A portion of these words described personality characteristics, some of which were stable, and others usually temporary (e.g., *joyful, angry, embarrassed*). The stable characteristics, of which there were about 4,500, were referred to as traits by Allport, and the temporary characteristics—often related to moods or emotions—were termed **states**.

Allport's work initiated what came to be known as the **trait perspective**. Because traits *describe* a person's characteristic patterns of behavior, thought, emotion, and motivation without offering an *explanation* of the origins of these characteristics—as was the goal of earlier grand theories—the trait perspective was a significant change in focus for psychologists. Allport's trait theory was also the starting point for the first attempts to build truly empirical, research-based theories of personality.

▲ **Eysenck's Superordinate Traits Interact.** Top Left: Extraversion + Emotional Stability (carefree, outgoing, lively, optimistic); Top Right: Extraversion + Emotional instability (touchy, aggressive, excitable). Bottom Left: Introversion + Emotional Stability (calm, peaceful, controlled). Bottom Right: Introversion + Emotional Instability (worried, anxious, moody, pessimistic).

▲ In the 1994 film *The Mask*, actor Jim Carrey portrays a bank clerk who could be described by trait terms such as *shy, unassuming*, and *timid*... that is, until he finds a magic mask and puts it on. At this point he assumes a personality that could be described with trait terms such as *vulgar, extraverted*, and *manic*.

EYSENCK'S TWO-FACTOR MODEL OF PERSONALITY

Allport's work was popular because it made intuitive sense. The adjectives Allport and Odbert (1936) extracted from the dictionary were words that ordinary people use to describe their own characteristics and those of others. However, what makes intuitive sense is not necessarily true. German-born psychologist Hans Eysenck, who fled the Nazis in the 1930s and settled in Great Britain, also believed in the concept of traits. However, Eysenck was adamant that while intuitive sense was appealing, what truly mattered were facts—and only facts (Eysenck & Nias, 1982). It was Eysenck's work that brought personality from the era of the grand theories into the contemporary era of research-based personality theory.

In collaboration with his wife, Sybil, Eysenck created a new trait-based theory of personality within the framework of empirical research and revised it continuously over time as research results showed one or another aspect of the theory incorrect. According to Eysenck, Allport's 4,500 trait terms "boiled down" statistically to 2 basic *trait dimensions*—known as **superordinate traits**—with all other trait labels being redundant of these two "umbrella traits" and subsumed under them. A trait dimension is a trait label constructed of two opposing concepts or poles (e.g., *hostile-kind, dominant-submissive, shy-outgoing*), where any degree of the trait may exist between the poles (Eysenck & Eysenck, 1963).

Thus, his original model is known as the two-factor model. The superordinate trait dimensions are *extraversion–introversion* and *emotional instability-stability*. Introversion–extraversion means the degree to which a person is reserved, quiet, and thoughtful, versus assertive, outgoing, and sociable. By *emotional instability* (often termed *neuroticism*), Eysenck is referring to the degree to which a person has enduring tendencies toward various types of negative emotional states (e.g., anxiety, moodiness). Emotional stability indicates a very low level of such tendencies. Eysenck considered these superordinate dimensions to be primarily genetic in origin and grounded in neurophysiology.

As depicted in Figure 12.4, Eysenck was particularly interested in the way these two superordinate traits interacted with one another. For example, if

Trait perspective ▶ A branch of personality psychology which emphasizes description rather than explanation of people's characteristic patterns of behavior, thought, emotion, and motivation. Those working from the trait perspective adhere to the idea that human personality may be reduced to a limited number of traits and trait profiles.

Superordinate traits ▶ Hans Eysenck's term for the two basic trait dimensions within which all possible lower-order traits could be found. The superordinate trait dimensions are extraversion–introversion and emotional instability–emotional stability.

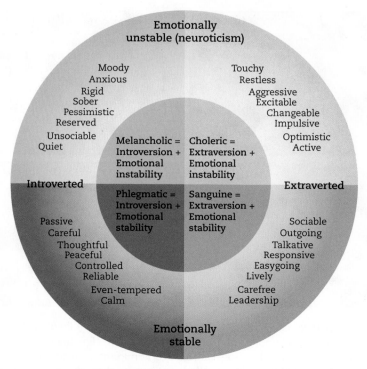

▲ **FIGURE 12.4 Hans Eysenck's Two-Factor Model of Personality.** Eysenck's original two-factor model demonstrates the way that different personality characteristics result from the interaction of the two dimensions *introversion–extraversion* and *emotional instability–emotional stability*. For example, as the trait adjectives close to the *introversion* pole move in the direction of the emotionally unstable pole, they assume increasingly undesirable aspects of introversion—for example, anxiety. The same is true in the case of extraversion: Emotionally unstable extraverts tend toward aggression and touchiness. The same holds true in reverse as the introversion or extraversion trait terms move in the direction of emotional stability. *(Diagram adapted from Eysenck, 1958.)*

you were high in both introversion *and* emotional instability, you would tend toward moodiness, anxiety, pessimism, and would be socially withdrawn. However, if you were high in introversion and *low* in emotional instability, you would express the more ideal form of introversion—calm and even-tempered, peaceful, thoughtful, and reliable.

As time went on, Hans and Sybil Eysenck modified this model substantially, incorporating a third dimension: *psychoticism*, or vulnerability to serious mental illness. However, this third dimension has remained somewhat controversial, and it is the original two-factor model that is probably more frequently referred to by those describing Eysenck's work.

THE "BIG FIVE": A FIVE-FACTOR MODEL

Although Eysenck's model was useful, some personality researchers suspected that it may have reduced personality from too many factors to too few. A group of psychologists, among them Robert McCrae and Paul Costa, conducted statistical research in nations throughout the world and found evidence to support a **five-factor model** of personality, often termed the "Big Five" (Goldberg, 1990; McCrae & Costa, 1996, 1997, 2013; McCrae, Terracciano et al., 2005; McCrae, 2009; Allik & McCrae, 2004). The Big Five is currently the most widely accepted trait model of personality (Funder, 2001; McCrae & Costa, 2013).

The five factors are labeled ***O**penness to experience*, ***C**onscientiousness*, ***E**xtraversion*, ***A**greeableness*, and ***N**euroticism*. (An easy way to remember them is the acronym OCEAN.) Table 12.3 describes the characteristics of high and low scorers for each of the five factors.

Five-factor model (the "Big Five") ▶ An empirical trait model of personality consisting of five trait dimensions or factors within which all other "lower-order" traits can be found. The five factors are openness to experience, conscientiousness, extraversion, agreeableness, and neuroticism. The "Big Five" is the most widely accepted trait model of personality.

Table 12.3 The Five-Factor Model of Personality (the "Big Five")

The five factors are summarized in the acronym OCEAN
Openness to Experience   **High scorers** are imaginative, curious, intellectual, creative, and artistic, and they dislike routine.   **Low scorers** are conventional and practical, they enjoy routine, are not oriented toward intellectual pursuits, and are "down-to-earth."
Conscientiousness   **High scorers** are careful, thorough, well-organized, and responsible.   **Low scorers** are careless, inefficient, disorganized, and irresponsible.
Extraversion   **High scorers** are sociable, energetic, assertive, and oriented toward others.   **Low scorers** are passive, reserved, quiet, and oriented toward self.
Agreeableness   **High scorers** are warm, kind, empathetic, compassionate, and trusting.   **Low scorers** are hostile, suspicious, unkind, and lacking in trust and compassion.
Neuroticism   **High scorers** are easily upset, anxious, emotional, and self-pitying, and they tend to worry.   **Low scorers** are even-tempered, comfortable with themselves, calm, and emotionally stable.

A. Mortality

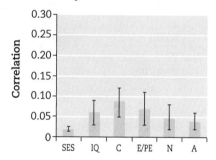

B. Divorce

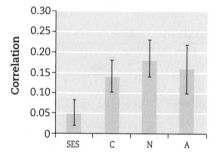

C. Occupational Outcomes

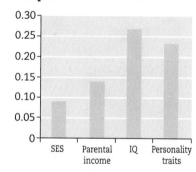

▲ **FIGURE 12.5 Traits Matter.** Brent Roberts and his colleagues found that, in the case of mortality (Graph A), the traits conscientiousness (high) and extraversion/positive emotion (high) were more predictive of greater longevity than either SES or IQ. In the case of divorce (Graph B), levels of conscientiousness, agreeableness, and neuroticism were all more predictive than SES variables such as education and income. (There was insufficient evidence about the effects of IQ to include it in the graph.) In the case of occupational attainment, only IQ was more predictive of level of occupational advancement than personality traits as a whole.

How convincing is the research in favor of the five-factor model? Very convincing. People's scores on personality inventories really do appear to cluster in a small number of factors, approximately five, although there is some difference of opinion about the exact number and how best to label them (Allik et al., 2010). Research in the Big Five has been conducted on five continents among members of at least 50 cultures, and the five factors have been shown to describe personality in all of these cultures (Allik & McCrae, 2004; Allik et al., 2010; McCrae, 2009; McCrae et al., 2005; Schmitt, Allik, McCrae, & Benet-Martínez, 2007).

Finally, longitudinal research has shown that the Big Five personality traits *matter*. They account for a portion of the differences between people in rates of divorce, educational and occupational success, and even longevity (Ozer & Benet-Martínez, 2006; Roberts et al., 2007). Using controlled longitudinal research, Brent Roberts and his colleagues assessed the importance of personality traits versus the importance of cognitive ability (e.g., IQ) and socioeconomic status (SES) in predicting three outcomes: divorce, occupational success, and age of death. Figure 12.5 presents their findings. As you can see, only in the case of occupational success did a non-personality factor (IQ) produce higher correlations with eventual outcome than one or more personality trait scores.

LIVING PSYCHOLOGY

What Is Your Big Five Score?

Assessing your Five Factor score is not a difficult matter, although for full accuracy you would need to use a more complex and up-to-date test than the informal version presented here—for example, the complete **Revised NEO Personality Inventory (NEO PI-R)**. Your score would also need to be interpreted according to professionally defined criteria. What follows is a very brief test adapted from one presented by Nathan Brody and Howard Ehrlichman (1998, pp. 28–30). You can take the complete, authorized Five Factor test online at http://www.personalitytest.net.

Revised NEO Personality Inventory (NEO PI-R) ▶ The most frequently used test of the five-factor model of personality ("Big Five")

BRODY & EHRLICHMAN'S SHORTENED BIG FIVE TEST

Indicate how true each of the following terms is in describing you:

1 = Not at all true of me; I am almost never this way

2 = Mostly not true of me; I am rarely this way

3 = Neither true nor untrue of me, or I can't decide

4 = Somewhat true of me; I am sometimes this way

5 = Very true of me; I am very often this way

1 ___ imaginative	6 ___ intelligent	11 ___ original	16 ___ insightful	21 ___ clever
2 ___ organized	7 ___ thorough	12 ___ efficient	17 ___ responsible	22 ___ practical
3 ___ talkative	8 ___ assertive	13 ___ active	18 ___ energetic	23 ___ outgoing
4 ___ sympathetic	9 ___ kind	14 ___ soft-hearted	19 ___ warm	24 ___ generous
5 ___ tense	10 ___ anxious	15 ___ nervous	20 ___ worrying	25 ___ self-pitying

SCORING THE BIG FIVE TEST

To determine your scores for Openness to Experience (O), Conscientiousness (C), Extraversion (E), Agreeableness (A), and Neuroticism (N), copy the numbers you entered for each item and add each line horizontally (e. g, add items 1 + 6 + 11 + 16 + 21 to get your score for O).

Item 1 ___	Item 6 ___	Item 11 ___	Item 16 ___	Item 21 ___	= Score for O ___
Item 2 ___	Item 7 ___	Item 12 ___	Item 17 ___	Item 22 ___	= Score for C ___
Item 3 ___	Item 8 ___	Item 13 ___	Item 18 ___	Item 23 ___	= Score for E ___
Item 4 ___	Item 9 ___	Item 14 ___	Item 19 ___	Item 24 ___	= Score for A ___
Item 5 ___	Item 10 ___	Item 15 ___	Item 20 ___	Item 25 ___	= Score for N ___

Now that you have your score, what do you do with it? For example, what if your score were 21 for O—does that mean you are high or low in *openness to experience*? You might compare your score for O against your score for N to determine which is higher, but how much would this actually tell you? The problem with a test like this is that there are no cutoff points by which the score may be interpreted. You must compare your score against *norms*—averages created by administering the test to large numbers of people similar to yourself and computing the mean (average) scores for each scale. These means become the cutoff points for "below average" and "above average" scores for each of the scales.

One potential problem with comparing your score against norms is that there is always the chance that the samples of people used to "norm" the test are not, in fact, similar to you. For example, in their presentation of their brief version of the Big Five test, Brody and Ehrlichman published norms derived from university psychology students at their respective schools. However, if you are a returning student (e.g., past the age of 50), are university students an appropriate group with which to compare yourself? What if Brody and Ehrlichman teach at small Midwestern schools (they don't, but what if?), and you go to NYU, UCLA, or San Francisco State University—or vice versa? These are important questions to consider. In any case, to satisfy your curiosity, here are the mean norms published by Brody and Ehrichman:

	O	C	E	A	N
Means for Women	19.4	20.2	19.0	22.2	18.5
Means for Men	20.3	18.8	18.0	18.8	16.3

One last point: I suspect that you were not surprised by your scores. People rarely are. On many levels, we know ourselves quite well, and tests such as the Big Five simply hold up a mirror—presenting us with an image we have little choice but to view every day. ■

Situations Can Powerfully Influence Behavior

In a sense, trait models of personality such as Allport's, Eysenck's and the Big Five literally define personality as "a set of scores along a set number of trait dimensions." If you feel that personality is more than a just a set of trait scores, there are many who would agree with you (Funder, 2001, 2009).

Think about yourself for a moment. What sorts of trait adjectives would others use to describe you? Generous? Sneaky? Tender-hearted? Mean? Honest? Now think back carefully over your life and try to remember specific occasions where you behaved quite differently—perhaps even opposite—to what the trait adjective would predict. If traits are stable and enduring, and "honesty" is one of your traits, for example, how is it then that you cheated on your algebra midterm in 8th grade and lied to your parents about where you were sleeping the night of the senior prom? Were you "not yourself" on those days?

In 1968, at the height of popularity of the trait theories of Allport, Eysenck, and others (but before the development of the Big Five), a little book was published that asked a very rude question: If traits are real, stable, and enduring, why is it that people's scores on inventories of personality traits *do not predict how they will actually behave on any given occasion?* The book was *Personality and Assessment*, and it was written by personality theorist Walter Mischel. Mischel pointed out that the correlations between people's trait scores on personality tests and their behavior in research studies of personality were very small. Someone who scored very high in extraversion on the Big Five test might, for example, behave in a very reserved fashion in a mock "party" set up by researchers to study social interaction.

Mischel argued that it was *situations*, not traits, which played the largest role in determining behavior. People behave differently depending upon the particular situation in which they find themselves. According to this idea, the very concepts "traits" and "personality" are not particularly meaningful when

Person-situation controversy
▶ A major debate within personality psychology beginning during the 1960s in the work of Walter Mischel. The debate contrasted the views of those who believed traits were of primary importance in determining behavior and those who believed that situations—not traits—determine behavior.

▲ **People Behave Differently in Different Situations.** On the top is a photo of Naima knitting in her great-grandmother's living room, under the woman's watchful eye. If you first met her in this setting, you would probably describe her as sedate, polite, thoughtful, and somewhat introverted. On the bottom is Naima in another setting entirely, playing Dracula's Daughter, far from her great-grandmother's domain. If you first met her in this setting, you would describe her as assertive, playful, and entirely irreverent.

it comes to behavior, and in fact may be little more than illusions. The **person-situation controversy** had erupted.

Mischel's critique was devastating, and it quite literally created havoc in the field. Research and publishing in personality psychology waned quite dramatically, and a number of major graduate programs in personality psychology closed down (Swann & Seyle, 2005). (Personal note: I received my Ph.D. in the personality area of the Department of Psychology at UCLA in the final year this major was being offered.)

Finally, in the late 1970s, personality psychologists struck back! A researcher named Seymour Epstein took aim at Mischel's work and fired an equally devastating critique right back at him. Epstein (1979) argued that the only reason behavior did not appear to correlate with traits in the research studies Mischel had examined was that these studies only looked at *a single slice of behavior*—the one instance of behavior (generally an artificial situation set up by researchers) that had been observed in the study itself.

Epstein proposed that traits did indeed predict behavior if behavior were examined on a number of occasions, not just one, and the results *aggregated*, or averaged. Epstein argued that traits were tendencies, and that people were not robots, behaving identically on every occasion according to their dispositions. Thus, one needed to take in the big picture and observe the person over time, because a trait would not necessarily be apparent on any given single occasion.

Who is right, Mischel or Epstein? Is it traits or situations that are the best predictors of behavior? As we shall now see, Mischel and Epstein were both right (Fleeson, 2004; Funder, 2009; Kammrath, Mendoza-Denton, & Mischel, 2005).

Traits and Situations Form Revealing Patterns

Mischel (1979) agreed that Epstein had made an important point. Single instances of behavior cannot be used to determine whether people do or do not behave consistently according to some trait measure. However, Mischel continued to insist that how one behaves in one type of situation may not reflect how one behaves in another type of situation. A person who is consistently "honest" in her aggregated dealings with her friends and family may be consistently "dishonest" when she takes tests or fills out tax forms. Therefore, according to Mischel, measures which focused on traits alone were still uninformative of personality.

Take, for example, two high school students, Meghan and Kara. On the Big Five test, each ends up with an identical score for *extraversion*. However, each student has certain idiosyncratic aspects to her extraverted personality. Meghan is very outgoing at home and with friends, but in the classroom she is shy and never raises her hand—even when she knows the answer. Also, when she gets within 20 feet of a boy she turns into the proverbial wallflower. Kara, on the other hand, is passive and obedient at home, relatively quiet around her friends, but shines in the classroom and is very outgoing in her interactions with boys.

If one were to give each student a *separate* extraversion score for each situation, it might look like this:

	Home	Classroom	Friends	Boys
High Extraversion	Meghan	Kara	Meghan	Kara
Low Extraversion	Kara	Meghan	Kara	Meghan

If you were to connect each student's scores for all four situations by drawing separate (diagonal) lines from column to column, two entirely opposite zig-zag patterns would emerge. And yet, each student has two high scores and two low scores, potentially averaging out to an identical numeric score for extraversion. If all we knew about Meghan and Kara was that they both had the same average extraversion score on a test such as the Big Five, we would conclude that they were very similar to each other in their behavior, but in fact they are quite dissimilar.

Does this mean that trait scores are worthless? Not at all. As two decades of research following Epstein's work has demonstrated, trait scores *do* reflect general tendencies, and if one looked at many more situations over time, it would undoubtedly turn out that both Meghan and Kara display more extraverted behavior than introverted (Funder, 2001). The point of this hypothetical example is that if you truly wish to understand Kara and Meghan as individuals, trait scores are not enough. You also need to understand their unique **trait-situation behavior profiles**—the patterns created by the intersection of their traits with the specific situations in which they find themselves (Cervone & Shoda, 1999; Furr, 2009; Mischel, Shoda, & Mendoza-Denton, 2002; Kammrath et al., 2005).

According to the trait-situation behavior profile[3] model developed by Walter Mischel and Yuichi Shoda, each person possesses stable *patterns* of interaction between traits and situations. These patterns are somewhat like "if . . . then . . . else" statements in computer programming language (Cervone & Shoda, 1999; Kammrath et al., 2005; Mischel et al., 2002). For example, as applied to Meghan: "*If* in the presence of boys or in the classroom, *then* look away and don't speak much . . . *else* (i.e., otherwise) talk nonstop, gesture animatedly, and don't forget to laugh a lot."

According to Mischel and Shoda, trait-situation behavior profiles are organized, integrated, and relatively enduring, fulfilling our definition of *personality*. Thus, both Epstein and Mischel were correct: Traits *and* situations are at the center of personality, and they both must be considered to understand how personality is expressed in behavior.

Trait-situation behavior profile ▶ The unique, stable behavior patterns created by the interaction of a person's traits with specific situations. Trait-situation behavior profiles are like "If . . . then . . . else" statements in computer language. For example, "*If* I am at school, *then* I will behave politely, honestly, and conscientiously . . . *else* (i.e., otherwise) I will do my best to avoid my responsibilities, cheat whenever possible, and use foul language." Trait-situation behavior profiles account for the fact that people may appear to display different traits depending upon the situation.

CRITICAL THINKING ABOUT PSYCHOLOGY

Astrology: Is Personality in the Stars?

According to Harris Poll survey research conducted in 2003, approximately 40% of young adult Americans believe in astrology; that is, they accept the notion that the positions of the stars and planets influence the course of a person's life on earth and his or her character traits (The Harris Poll, 2003). A separate study conducted in 2001 by the National Science Foundation reported that 28% of Americans believe that astrology is "scientific," whereas another 18% are "not sure," for a total of 46% who either believe that astrology is valid or are not sure (National Science Foundation, 2002).

The vast majority of scientists—if not all scientists—*are* sure. Astrology is a good example of a pseudoscience, as described in Chapter 1. For example, astrology is not self-correcting but changes only for arbitrary reasons (e.g., social fashion), if at all; it relies on testimonials, anecdotes, and bold statements; it uses jargon to obscure rather than clarify; it cannot produce scientific evidence to support its validity (indeed, virtually all such evidence denies its validity); it overinterprets coincidence; it uses "after the fact" (*post-hoc*) reasons to explain away its failures; and, perhaps most important, it simply doesn't do what it says it can do—that is, *it doesn't work*

---

[3]*Mischel and Shoda use the phrase* situation behavior profile *instead of* trait-situation behavior profile *as I have done here. I have changed the term in this way because I believe it is more descriptive of the concept. In any case, other names are used by other researchers to describe this idea—for example, Person X Situation profile.*

CRITICAL THINKING ABOUT PSYCHOLOGY

CONTINUED

(Kelly, 1997, 1998, Voas, 2007; see Dean, Mather, & Kelly, 1996, for reviews of evidence).

If you believe in astrology, or are on the fence, at least consider that tests of astrologers' ability to do what they say they can do, conducted with astrologers nominated by other astrologers as being the best, under conditions favorable to and accepted by the astrologers themselves, have repeatedly failed to provide evidence in support of astrology. In such tests, astrologers are typically given the dates and times of birth for a group of people and asked to construct their charts. They are then given personality profiles for each subject with no identifying information, and asked to match the personality profiles with the charts. Under such conditions, astrologers do no better than chance—that is, no better than if they had blindly drawn the answers from a hat. Astrologers fail to perform even when offered large cash prizes for successful performance (Dean, 1987; McGrew & McFall, 1990; Nanninga, 1996/1997).

In addition to such tests of professional astrologers, some tests have looked at ordinary people's ability to identify their own charts. For example, Dean (1987) offered people interpretations of their personality based on their own chart and other charts. When he asked them to pick out the interpretations that had been derived from their actual chart, they did no better than chance. One French psychologist offered readers of a Paris newspaper a free "full chart" personal horoscope. Ninety-four percent of those receiving the horoscope reported that the reading was accurate. However, in fact the horoscope given to each respondent was that of Marcel Petiot, who, in 1944, sadistically murdered 27 people in his home.

More recently, David Voas of the University of Manchester in Great Britain used British census data to look at 10 million marriages to test the most basic of astrological predictions—that certain sun signs would be attracted to certain other signs, and the personalities of people born under those signs would be compatible with each other. Voas found that no combination of sun signs was found among married couples more frequently than would be expected by chance (Voas, 2007).

What is truly interesting about all this is that intelligent people still believe in astrology, and those who do are generally not at all convinced by evidence or logic. In other words, astrology is a *data proof* topic. People will believe regardless of evidence that it cannot do what believers claim that it can.

Why is belief in astrology immune to evidence? This is a complex question. Attempts to explain important aspects of life in terms of the supernatural or paranormal are pervasive in all known human societies (Brown, 1991), suggesting that tendencies toward such beliefs may be part of human psychological nature. Human beings also have a tendency to mentally construct patterns from events that conceivably could be related, particularly if these events have an impact on important aspects of life. This pattern-finding skill—"putting two and two together"—likely evolved over evolutionary time because it aided in survival and reproduction. The problem is that we sometimes see patterns where none really exist, and "overinterpret" coincidence and chance occurrences (Dawes, 2001).

Finally, astrology, like many belief systems, may be helpful for some people in dealing with stressful life events, negative self-concepts, and general uncertainties about living (Glick, Gottesman, & Jolton, 1989). Attempts to understand oneself and the world are important components of human nature. Although astrological information is illusory, it may nonetheless help fulfill these basic human needs (Lilqvist & Lindeman, 1998). ■

IN SUMMARY

1. Traits are stable personality characteristics; states are usually temporary. The trait perspective focuses on description, rather than explanation of personality.

2. In the two-factor model of personality created by Hans and Sybil Eysenck, introversion–extraversion and emotional instability–stability are superordinate traits. All possible traits are in some way derived from these two dimensions.

3. The five-factor model ("Big Five") is the most widely accepted trait model of personality. The five factors are openness to experience, conscientiousness, extraversion, agreeableness, and neuroticism ("OCEAN"). The five-factor model has been shown to be reliable and valid cross-culturally. Levels of five-factor traits are associated with important life outcomes including divorce, educational and occupational attainment, and longevity.

4. Situations are often as important as traits in determining behavior, although traits still predict behavior with some accuracy if behaviors are aggregated (combined) rather than looked at individually. Trait-situation behavior profiles, which take both traits and situations into account, are more predictive of behavior than either situations or traits taken alone.

5. All evidence suggests that astrology is a pseudoscience with no validity. It has not been shown to predict the future, nor to identify a person's personality any better than chance.

RETRIEVE!

1. Jorge is very high in extraversion but very low in emotional instability. Using Eysenck's two-factor model, describe Jorge's personality in two or three adjectives. Jorge's sister Mariana is low in extraversion but high in emotional instability. Describe her personality in two or three adjectives.

2. Raven has always been interested in art and artists. Her teachers consider her imaginative, original, and insightful in her work. Unlike some of the other students in her class with artistic temperaments, she is also highly organized, efficient, and responsible. However, she tends to keep to herself, is somewhat shy, and avoids hanging out in groups of friends, preferring to be only with one other person at a time. Although she is hard to get to know due to the fact that she is reserved, those who do get to know her find her to be warm, sympathetic, and kind-hearted. She is rarely upset or anxious, and even though she has a disability due to a childhood accident, she is rarely self-pitying. Raven is (choose *high* or *low*): _____ in openness to experience; _____ in conscientiousness; _____ in extraversion; _____ in agreeableness; and _____ in neuroticism.

3. Why are trait scores not enough to account for someone's personality? Why are trait-situation behavior profiles important?

4. List at least three characteristics of astrology that qualify it as a pseudoscience. Describe at least one research study which demonstrates that astrology doesn't work.

How Do Genes, Environments, and Culture Influence Personality?

I began this chapter with the story of Amy and Beth, identical twins separated at birth and raised by different families. Although their family environments differed in so many respects, Amy and Beth shared many (relatively unusual) personality traits. As their story suggests, at least some portion of personality differences among people is due to differences in genetic inheritance, as you might expect having come this far in the book (McGuffin, Riley, & Plomin, 2001; Plomin & Caspi, 1999; Saudino, 2005; Weiss, Bates, & Luciano, 2008). In this section we will explore the interplay of genes, environments, and culture in the development of personality.

Genes Play an Important Role in Personality Development

The claim that genes play a role in personality was once highly controversial, but it has now entered the mainstream of personality and developmental psychology (Maccoby, 2002; Rutter, 2002).[4] When one thinks about it, there should be nothing controversial about such findings. At least some genetic influence on most traits is found for all known species of life (Lynch & Walsh, 1998).

However, certain personality traits are more or less heritable than others, and heritability estimates usually differ somewhat from one study to the next. Various methodological limitations in most research studies on this question virtually guarantee that the estimates will not be precise (Collins, Maccoby, Steinberg, Hetherington, & Bornstein, 2000). Nonetheless, findings of behavior genetics studies show a great deal of reliability in the general picture they draw. As Table 12.4 shows, studies conducted using the Big Five and Eysenck's two superordinate factors as indicators of personality show that approximately 50% on average of the differences among people in these traits are due to genetic factors (Bouchard, 2004). There are even substantial genetic influences on trait-situation behavior profiles (Borkenau, Riemann, Spinath, & Angleitner, 2006).

Nonshared Environments Are Equally Important

If approximately 50% of the differences among people in traits are due to genetic causes, this means that 50% are due to environmental causes. Given the fact that both genes and environments contribute to personality approximately equally (see Table 12.4), is it possible to determine which aspects of the environment are most important to the development of personality?

In Chapter 4 we saw that the environmental component of child temperament was contributed by the *nonshared* rather than the *shared* environment. The same appears to hold true for adolescent and adult personality. If you recall from Chapter 4, the unique experiences encountered by each developing child are known as the **nonshared environment** because these environmental factors are experienced only by the child in question and not by other children in the home. Environmental factors shared by all children living in a home—parent education, income, beliefs and attitudes, childrearing and

Nonshared environment ▶ The unique environmental factors and experiences encountered by each developing child but not encountered by other children in the home. For example, a childhood illness, a traumatic experience, a different set of friends, and so forth.

---

[4]*Still controversial, however, are claims about the heredity of behaviors that might result from personality variables: criminality, substance use, divorce, and so forth.*

discipline styles, and so forth—are termed the **shared environment**. Virtually all available behavior genetics research (summarized in Table 12.4) suggests that it is the child's unique experiences in the world, rather than the shared environment to which all children living in a home are exposed, that contributes virtually all of the environmental influence on adolescent and adult personality (Bouchard, 2004; Plomin, DeFries, Craig, & McGuffin, 2003; Saudino, 2005).

But if the nonshared environment is of primary importance, what *sorts* of nonshared experiences are most critical to personality development? This is a controversial question, but three possibilities have been suggested frequently: *Differing parental treatment of each child, peer influence,* and simple *chance*.

WHEN PARENTS TREAT EACH CHILD DIFFERENTLY

Research showing that the nonshared rather than the shared environment is most important in shaping personality has elicited one major objection: It implies that parenting has little or nothing to do with the way personality develops. However, one aspect of the nonshared environment that would accord a more important role to parenting in personality development is a situation where parents treat each of their children quite differently. When they do this, they are in a sense creating separate environments for each child (Vandell, 2000).

Consider a young woman we will call Kelly, whose life was consumed by her very promising career as a ballerina. Kelly's career was derailed when she

Shared environment ▶ Environmental factors and experiences shared by all children living in a home—for example, the parent's socioeconomic status, language and culture, beliefs and attitudes, and childrearing and discipline styles.

Table 12.4 **Genetic and Environmental Influences on Personality**

Heritability (h2) represents the average portion of differences among people in personality that can be explained by genetic inheritance. Environmental influence is the sum of shared and nonshared environmental influence in the development of personality differences. As you can see, no contribution of shared environment has been found in behavior genetic studies of the Big Five and Eysenck's two superordinate factors.

TRAIT	HERITABILITY (H2) (GENETIC INFLUENCE)	SHARED ENVIRONMENTAL INFLUENCE	NONSHARED ENVIRONMENTAL INFLUENCE
Big Five			
Extraversion	.54	None	.46
Agreeableness	.42	None	.58
Conscientiousness	.49	None	.51
Neuroticism	.48	None	.52
Openness to Experience	.57	None	.43
Eysenck's Two Superordinate Factors			
Extraversion–Introversion	.50	None	.50
Emotional Instability–Stability	.44	None	.56

(Source: Adapted from Bouchard, 2004, p. 150.)

▲ **Socialization and Status Systems Sometimes Conflict.** According to Judith Rich Harris' theory of personality development (Harris, 2006), motivations to conform and motivations to stand out or compete often conflict. Pictured here are (left) Chinese school children and (right) Deng Linlin, winner of the 2012 individual gold medal on balance beam.

accidentally became pregnant at age 22. She gave birth to a healthy baby boy, but resented her son for his part in altering the course of her ballet career. However, Kelly gradually came to accept and even enjoy her new life as a mother and part-time dance teacher. When her son was ready to start school, she had a second child; this time the pregnancy was planned, and Kelly had no reason to feel resentment toward the new baby. It was her first child, and only the first, who bore the brunt of Kelly's resentment during the child's formative years.

Differing treatment of children in a family might also result from divorce, sudden parental unemployment, and other changes in family circumstances. Such changes may occur at a critical period in the development of one sibling, but not another. It is important to remember, however, that if a parent treats one child differently to the other *due to differences in the child's genotypes* (i.e., child-to-parent effects as discussed in Chapter 4), this would be considered a genetic influence, not an environmental one. Thus, the possibility that differing treatment of each child contributes to personality would only hold in cases where the child's genotypes are not related to these differences in treatment.

PEER GROUPS

Judith Rich Harris (1998, 2006) has been the most vocal proponent of the idea that peer groups, not parents, are the primary socializers of children (see Chapter 9). According to Harris, it is mainly from peers that children learn the ways of their society and culture. Harris proposes that peers are not only primarily responsible for making us *similar* to one another, particularly to others of the same sex and age; but they also have an important role in making us *different* from one another—in shaping our personalities (Harris, 2006).

According to Harris, personality develops in large part according to the unique ways each child learns to resolve the conflict between the desire to "fit in" with peers and the desire to "stand out" from them. Harris refers to this as the conflict between the *socialization system*, which prompts the child to conform to the expectations of his or her peers; and the *status system*, which prompts the developing child to compete with others in order to establish his or her unique identity and contributions. Each child learns entirely different strategies for conforming and competing based upon prior experience, and Harris proposes that developing these strategies is the primary "engine" driving personality development.

For example, Keiko is an eighth-grader in a middle school that heavily emphasizes sports performance. Try as she may to conform to the expectations of the other students, however, Keiko is hopeless in sports. Instead, she devotes time to study and reading and attains status and admiration as a high-scoring student ("standing out") who is generous sharing her gifts by tutoring her fellow students ("fitting in").

CHANCE

Ten-year-old Gabriel is browsing in the children's room at the library, but his sister is sick at home. At the library Gabriel makes a new friend—a boy whose mother turns out to be a music teacher. Gabriel ends up taking music lessons from the mother, an event that has an impact on his personality by promoting concentration, discipline, admiration from peers and parents, and an artistic worldview. On the other hand, Gabriel's sister is never exposed to this influence. This scenario is an example of how simple *chance* is often at work as part of the nonshared environment.

It may be that no single chance event contributes very greatly to personality, but when many of them are taken together they represent a cumulative effect that would cause children in the same family to be substantially different in personality (Pinker, 2002; Turkheimer & Waldron, 2000). If so, it may turn out that identifying the important aspects of the nonshared environment is virtually impossible; it may be that no single variable is of very great importance in itself, and so none will stand out statistically in research (Plomin & Daniels, 1987, p. 8).

Culture May Influence Personality, but Not in Expected Ways

Are Americans rude, arrogant, and self-centered? Are Canadians friendly and hospitable, Latinos hot-tempered, Chinese and Japanese industrious, and Germans rule-bound? You probably have heard jokes which play on such **national character stereotypes**—shared ideas about the typical personality type for any given culture or nation.

It may surprise you to learn that such stereotypes are not only held by those outside the culture in question. That's right—research has shown that people in a given culture tend to agree with many of the stereotypes held about their own culture by outsiders. Anthony Terracciano and his colleagues asked almost 40,000 participants in 49 cultures around the world to describe the character of a typical member of their culture (Terracciano et al., 2005). These researchers found significant consensus among participants as to their national character, and in general, these perceptions were in accord with stereotypes held by outsiders. For example, Americans consider themselves somewhat rude and overly assertive, Canadians, friendly, Japanese and English introverted and reserved, Australians extraverted, and so forth.

However, *consensus* is not the same as *accuracy* (McCrae & Terracciano, 2006). Nevertheless, it is true that stereotypes often hold grains of truth. For example, throughout the world women are thought by most people to be generally warmer, more agreeable and friendly, more emotionally open than men, but also more anxious or moody. Men in turn are considered more assertive than women (Williams & Best, 1990). Research shows that these stereotypes are largely accurate throughout the world, although the size of the differences between men and women is not very large (Costa, Terracciano, & McCrae, 2001; Feingold, 1994; Lippa, 2010; Schmitt, Realo, Voracek, & Allik, 2008).

What of national character stereotypes? Americans may agree that they are disagreeable, and Canadians may agree that they are agreeable—but are they? Terracciano and his colleagues were able to test the accuracy of national character stereotypes as well as their consistency in people's perceptions. These researchers not only asked people to describe a typical member of their culture, they also administered the Revised NEO Personality Inventory (NEO-PI-R), the formal test of the Five Factor (Big Five), to their sample of 40,000. In other words, they actually *measured* the personalities of typical members of each culture. Did the measured personalities correspond to the national stereotypes? In a word: No. Indeed, many of the judgments of national character were virtually the opposite of what was found on the Big Five self-report tests and tests of others' personalities by objective observers.

National character stereotypes ▶ Shared ideas about the typical personality type for any given culture or nation. National character stereotypes have been shown to lack validity in spite of the fact that members of the culture in question frequently accept the stereotype.

A similar lack of connection between national stereotypes and actual personality profiles was found in a study of personality across 56 nations conducted by David Schmitt and his colleagues (Schmitt et al., 2007). As McCrae and Terracciano (2006, p. 160) flatly declare, "There does not appear to be even a kernel of truth in stereotypes of national character. . . . They are fictions." Although these "fictions" are often perpetuated in a light-hearted manner, as McCrae and Terracciano point out, history attests that such inaccurate stereotypes can have tragic consequences, fueling institutions such as slavery and acts of genocide and war.

IN SUMMARY

1. Genetic inheritance plays an important role in personality. Approximately 50% of differences among people in Big Five or two-factor superordinate traits are due to genetics, and 50% are due to the nonshared environment.

2. Three aspects of the nonshared environment are often suggested as being particularly important in personality development: differing treatment of children in the home by a parent; peer relationships; and chance.

3. Judith Rich Harris proposes that the primary "engine" driving personality is conflict between the socialization and status systems.

4. Cross-cultural research has shown that national character stereotypes are inaccurate.

RETRIEVE!

1. A parent's level of education, income, level of warmth and affection, and child-rearing techniques are all part of the _____ environment. A child's unique experiences in the world are part of the _____ environment.

2. According to Judith Rich Harris, how would conflict between status and socialization systems mold personality? Try to imagine a hypothetical scenario.

3. How might chance help to shape a child's personality? Imagine a hypothetical scenario.

Personality assessment
▶ The field of personality measurement. Personality is generally assessed using projective tests, which reflect personality as it is "projected" on to test materials by the test-taker, and objective tests, which use computer analysis to empirically measure personality characteristics.

How Is Personality Measured?

When a researcher attributes some portion of differences in a personality trait to heredity and some portion to environment, or proposes that a particular personality trait affects a person's chances of experiencing divorce, how does the researcher measure the personality trait in the first place?

The measurement of personality is known as **personality assessment**. When you took the brief Big Five test on page 592 or the approved, formal test

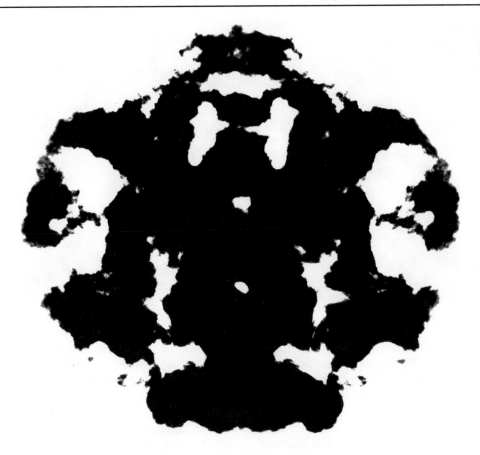

◄FIGURE 12.6 Typical Rorschach Image. The Rorschach test is a highly controversial projective test of personality or psychiatric illness.

at http://www.personalitytest.net, you were participating in personality assessment. Tests that measure some aspect of psychology are known as *assessment instruments*. There are two basic categories of personality assessment instruments: *projective tests* and *objective tests*.

Projective Tests Interpret Personality

Projective tests emerged during the mid-20th century primarily from psychoanalysis and related theories. They are termed "projective" because the person taking the test is said to unconsciously "project" his or her personality or psychiatric disorder into test items that might seem quite ambiguous—that is, on their face they may be interpreted in a great many ways.

For example, the **Rorschach test** (see Figure 12.6) presents a test-taker with a standard set of 10 cards, each containing symmetrical inkblots, five in color and five in black and white. (You can create a typical Rorschach-type image yourself by pouring a small blot of ink in the middle of a piece of paper and folding the paper in half.) The psychologist administering the test asks the test-taker to view the cards and describe what he or she sees in each blot and to identify the specific areas of the blot from which the image was seen. The test administrator writes down everything the test-taker says and then interprets it, based on a standardized scoring method (Exner, 2003). The researcher or clinician then arrives at judgments about the test-taker's personality or mental health.

You might wonder how such a process can lead to an understanding of personality and mental health problems. According to those who support the use of the Rorschach (and there are many fewer of these than there once were), the test is meant to be an adjunct to other forms of assessment and should not be used alone to diagnose mental illness or assess personality (Aronow, Reznikoff, & Moreland, 1995; Merlo & Barnett, 2001). However, proponents

Rorschach test ▶ A projective personality and mental health test originally devised by Hermann Rorschach in 1921. The test consists of a standard set of five color and five black-and-white symmetrical inkblots. The test-taker is then asked to describe what he or she sees in each blot and to identify the specific areas of the blot from which the image is constructed. The Rorschach is perhaps the most controversial of personality assessment instruments, with numerous critics claiming that the test lacks reliability and/or validity.

▶ **FIGURE 12.7** Thematic Apperception Test (TAT).

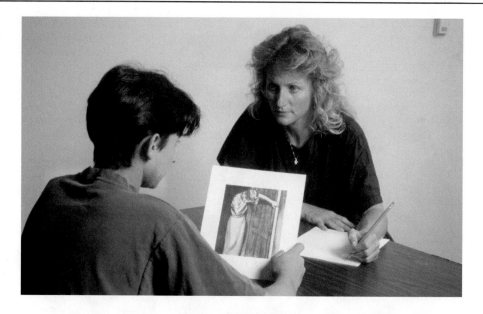

Validity ▶ The degree to which a test actually measures what it is intended to measure.

Reliability ▶ A reliable test is constructed so that if it is intended to measure something enduring about a person, the person will score much the same if taking the test on two or more separate occasions. A reliable test is also one which will report the same result regardless of who is doing the scoring—in other words, scoring is not subjective and will not differ from one rater to the next.

do insist that the test is an important measure of personality and mental health (Viglione & Taylor, 2003; Weiner, Spielberger, & Abeles, 2002).

On the other hand, the Rorschach has been sharply criticized—indeed, it is one of the most heavily criticized of all psychological tests currently in use. Critics charge, first, that the test lacks **validity**. A valid test is one that actually measures what it is supposed to measure. For example, if a test is supposed to measure *depression* but is actually measuring *neuroticism* or ordinary sadness, it is not a valid test of depression. Critics charge that the standards for scoring the Rorschach are not valid and may cause psychologically normal people to appear to have serious psychological disturbances (Garb, Wood, Lilienfeld, & Nezworski, 2005).

Second, critics claim that the test lacks *reliability*. The term **reliability** can be used in a number of different ways. In one sense, it means that if a test is intended to measure something enduring about a person, such as personality, the person ought to score much the same if taking the test on two separate occasions. Reliability also means that a person should get the same test result regardless of who is doing the scoring; scoring should not be subjective and should not differ from one rater to the next. By claiming that the Rorschach lacks reliability, critics are primarily suggesting that its scoring is overly subjective and that different raters will produce different interpretations of the same test results. These critics insist that use of the Rorschach—particularly as part of expert testimony in criminal court cases—should immediately be curtailed (Garb, 1999; Garb et al., 2005; Hunsley, Lee, & Wood, 2003).

Another projective test is the **Thematic Apperception Test** (TAT; Murray, 1943). In the TAT, 31 emotionally loaded, but ambiguous, drawings are shown and the test-taker is asked to tell the "story" of the drawing. According to proponents of the test, the test-taker, in creating the story, reveals important motives, drives, conflicts, emotions, and other psychological variables (see Figure 12.7).

For decades a serious drawback to the TAT has been that while some standards for scoring the test did exist, only a very tiny portion of psychologists actually used these standards. The vast majority relied instead on their own subjective impressions of the meanings of the test-takers "stories" and comments (Hunsley et al., 2003; Pinkerman, Haynes, & Keiser, 1993; Rossini & Moretti, 1997). Clearly, such a process cannot be said to be valid or reliable. However, in recent years the TAT has been revitalized, with a number of researchers devising workable scoring methods that have shown at least some validity and reliability (McClelland, 1999; Westen, 1991; Woike & McAdams,

2001). Whether these newer scoring schemes will be widely used is a separate question (Hunsley et al., 2003).

Objective Tests Are Constructed Empirically

Take a moment to respond to the following statements as either true or false about yourself: "At times I get strong cramps in my lower intestines." "I like rhyming poetry." "Sometimes there is a feeling like something is sitting on my head." "I used to like to touch my toes in gym class." "I would like to be a bill collector." "At times I feel like smashing someone's nose."

Do you think your answers would help to objectively measure important aspects of your personality and determine whether you suffer from mental health problems? These statements are adapted from items drawn from the **Minnesota Multiphasic Personality Inventory** (**MMPI**), the first, and probably still the most frequently used, objective test of personality (although a revised version called MMPI-2RF is now used). Tests such as the MMPI are referred to as "objective" because they are constructed empirically and scored by computer, so subjectivity does not enter into their interpretation.

For example, the empirical method used to create the MMPI is known as the *criterion-key method*. This technique is based on the fact that people who have certain traits or are experiencing certain states (e.g., shyness, depression, paranoia, or anxiety) tend to endorse certain statements as true about themselves while identifying other statements as false. The responses to these statements given by the test-taker can then be used to construct a person's trait or state profile (low in *depression*, high in *anxiety*, high in *paranoia*, moderate in *shyness*, etc.).

In the criterion-key method, the statements to which the test-taker responds (known as test items, or simply *items*) do not need to correspond at face value to any particular personality characteristic or mental state. For example, a valid scale for shyness created by the criterion-key method need not necessarily contain items such as "I feel embarrassed easily around others" or "I dislike being the center of attention." The only criterion for inclusion of an item is that, for whatever reason—known or unknown, understood or not understood—shy people have been found by empirical testing to endorse that item. Therefore, if depressives tended to endorse an item like "I enjoy wearing different colored socks, but only as long as one of them is not beige," such an item could appear on the Depression scale of an empirically valid criterion-keyed test of depression (although the likelihood of this particular item appearing is rather dim).

Although some of the items on the MMPI sound comical enough to have generated numerous parodies of the test, the MMPI-2 has repeatedly demonstrated validity in assessing personality traits associated with different types of mental health problems (Garb, Florio, & Grove, 1998). It has also demonstrated validity in assessing normal personality traits, but to a somewhat lesser degree. The test is used in a wide variety of psychiatric and nonpsychiatric settings to assess areas of personality vulnerability to psychological problems; for example, career counselors often use it, as do human resource offices in the context of the hiring of new employees.

The shortened Big Five test which you took earlier in the chapter is another example of an objective test created empirically, as is its parent, the Revised NEO Personality Inventory (NEO PI-R). However, unlike the MMPI-2RF, the NEO PI-R uses items with *face validity*. In contrast to the criterion-key method, face validity means that an item not only has been shown to be valid empirically, but it also makes intuitive sense considering what it is intended to measure. For example, a face-valid item to measure introversion might read, "I am uncomfortable in large gatherings and parties." Like the MMPI-2, the NEO PI-R is used in a wide variety of settings, but unlike the MMPI-2 it is primarily used to diagnose normal, rather than abnormal, personality traits.

Thematic Apperception Test (TAT) ▶ The TAT is a projective personality test first devised during the 1930s by Henry Murray and Christiana Morgan. In the TAT the test-taker is presented with 31 emotionally loaded but ambiguous drawings and asked to tell the "story" of the drawings. According to proponents of the test, in doing so the test-taker reveals important motives, drives, conflicts, and emotions.

Minnesota Multiphasic Personality Inventory (MMPI) ▶ The first and most frequently used objective test of personality. It has shown particular validity in distinguishing between abnormal personality traits indicating mental health problems, and, to a lesser extent, validity in distinguishing normal personality traits.

IN SUMMARY

1. In projective tests, test-takers are believed to "project" aspects of their personalities and mental health problems onto test items that are ambiguous and may be interpreted in different ways.

2. Two of the most frequently used projective tests are the Rorschach inkblot test and the Thematic Apperception Test (TAT). The Rorschach has been sharply criticized for problems with reliability and validity. The TAT traditionally has had problems with those administering the test failing to adhere to standardized scoring methods.

3. Objective tests rely on statistical methods to score personality tests by computer, avoiding problems of subjectivity. The Minnesota Multiphasic Personality Inventory (MMPI-2) was created using the criterion-key method. The Revised NEO Personality Inventory (NEO PI-R) was created using face validity.

RETRIEVE!

1. If a test instrument measures what it is intended to measure, it is said to be _____. If two different raters score the same person's test similarly—or if that person scores similarly when taking the test on two separate occasions—the test is said to be _____.

2. For many decades, there were serious problems with the way the TAT was scored. What were these problems?

3. How does the criterion-key method of personality test construction work? What is a face-valid item?

Does Personality Change over Time?

"For most of us, by age 30 the character has set like plaster and will never soften again."

—William James (1890/1981)

"It was a clarification that came to me while I was there on that walk. I was not the same person when I came back from the walk. I don't know if I'd call it a divine intervention, or a personal, powerful insight. I'm not sure what it was. I changed."

—Research participant in C'de Baca and Wilbourne (2004, p. 535)

"Am I always going to be this way?" Without doubt, every one of us has asked himself or herself this question at least once, on the heels of some characteristic but ill-advised (read: *stupid*) bit of behavior. There's good news for those who would like to change their behavior. Behavioral change is entirely possible. People alter seemingly intractable habits and behavior patterns every day.

▲ **How Much Do People Change?**
Abbie Hoffman (1936–1989) was a controversial political activist. As a young man, he was arrested dozens of times in the context of civil rights protests, protests against the war in Vietnam, and anticapitalist demonstrations. He was flamboyant, grandiose, reckless, and his protests were often tinged with humor. However, he was serious in intent. As he grew into his 50s while a fugitive from authorities, he became less flamboyant, less reckless, less grandiose, and less thrill-seeking— as would be predicted by research in the effects on personality of maturation. However, he remained serious in his commitment to social activism, repeatedly risking capture.

Cigarette smokers and heroin users quit. Obsessed, jilted lovers stop calling their exes and playing the Corrine Rae Bailey CD that always makes them cry. People unplug the TV and put it in the basement. People who characteristically fly into violent rages and get into fistfights learn to stop doing so (sometimes with the help of behavioral therapy, religion, or court sentencing).

Changing personality, however, is not the same as changing habits or behavior. Let us return to the first part of our definition of personality: *Personality consists of variations on common human mental and behavioral characteristics.* . . . "Common human mental and behavioral characteristics" cannot be done away with, unless one can find a way to change one's species. For example, if you are a human being, you will probably have a tendency to feel at least a bit of excitement and perhaps anxiety when you are about to jump out of an airplane for the first time. You will probably grieve more after the death of your own child than the death of another's child. You will care what others think of you, or at least what certain specific other people think. And so on.

There are a few respects, however, in which common human psychological characteristics actually *predict* moderate personality change. Human beings, on average, grow somewhat less emotional and less open to new experiences, but more cooperative, self-disciplined, and agreeable over time. These changes are captured in the term *maturity*, and they occur cross-culturally (Donnellan & Lucas, 2008; Helson, Jones, & Kwan, 2002; McAdams & Olson, 2010; Morizot & Le Blanc, 2003).

Beyond common human psychological characteristics, much of the remainder of personality consists of individual differences in traits and unique patterns of interactions between traits, situations, and behavior. Are these traits and trait-situation behavior patterns stable and consistent throughout the life span? Can we change them through willpower, therapy, religion, work, or personal relationships?

Traits Are Surprisingly—but Not Entirely—Stable

Most available evidence suggests one basic idea about personality traits: They are remarkably stable from childhood through adulthood, but they are not entirely stable. Personality traits do change to some degree over the life span, at least until middle age (Caspi, Roberts, & Shiner, 2005; Hampson & Goldberg, 2006; Helson et al., 2002; Roberts & DelVecchio, 2000). However, it is also true that these changes may be relatively limited after ages 30 to 50 (Ferguson, 2010; McCrae & Costa, 1994; Terracciano, Costa, & McCrae 2006).

▶ **FIGURE 12.8 Personality Traits Become More Stable over Time.** The average consistency of personality traits at various age ranges suggests that personality is at its most stable from age 50 through age 73. *(Source for graph: Roberts & DelVecchio, 2000, p. 15.)*

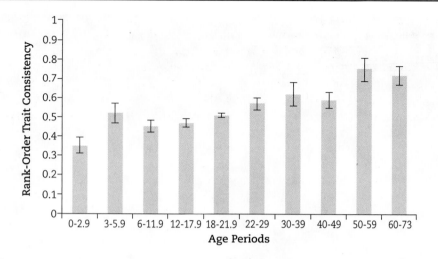

EVIDENCE OF TRAIT STABILITY

Let us look first at evidence of the stability of traits. It is sobering to consider that even infant and toddler temperament—active or passive, contented or "difficult," friendly or fearful—may predict adult personality to some degree, and can be seen as evidence of long-term stability of traits. Only measures of cognitive ability are more consistent over time than personality traits (Caspi et al., 2005, p. 466). For example, Sarah Hampson and Lewis Goldberg (2006) found remarkable continuities in traits between childhood and adulthood in their 40-year study of personality from elementary school through middle age. Similar results were found in a comprehensive meta-analysis of longitudinal research conducted prior to 2000 by Brent Roberts and Wendy DelVecchio (2000). As you can see in Figure 12.8, Roberts and DelVecchio found that personality is least stable prior to age 3 (when it is measured as *temperament*), and most stable past age 50. Although personality traits are subject to change to some degree throughout life, beginning in adulthood changes in traits are relatively minimal (Ferguson, 2010). As we grow older, we do become more "set in our ways."

Findings of moderate long-term stability of traits are not always popular (McCrae & Costa, 1994). Many people bristle at this idea, perhaps because they interpret such findings as affronts to the power of human beings to change. However, recall that a personality trait is not the same as a personal habit or behavior; the latter may always be amenable to change. Moreover, acceptance of one's own personality traits may represent a type of wisdom (McCrae & Costa, 1994). This idea was expressed eloquently by a person who experienced a profound self-acceptance in the context of a course in meditation:

> I'd been at this month-long meditation course, and the [teacher] said that we weren't becoming different people, that we were becoming the person that we always were. Right there, at that moment was when I began the serious thought, "I'm ready to accept that person—warts and all." A door opened and I walked through it and the door behind me closed and I never worried about opening that door again. It was just a total opening of myself. (Cited in C'de Baca & Wilbourne, 2004, p. 536.)

EVIDENCE OF CHANGE IN LEVELS OF TRAITS

The foregoing discussion has made it clear that personality traits are relatively stable over the life span. However, *relatively* stable implies that traits are not *entirely* stable. Indeed, personality traits are amenable to change, particularly in childhood, adolescence, and young adulthood (Caspi et al., 2005; Hampson & Goldberg, 2006; Lodi-Smith, Geise, Roberts, & Robins, 2009; Specht,

Egloff, & Schmukle, 2011). Moreover, as mentioned earlier, the process of maturation creates certain predictable changes as we grow older.

Most of the evidence of stability in traits comes from research looking at the *pattern* of traits (usually, the Big Five) in each participant in a longitudinal study from one time to the next. Does a person high in extraversion but low in conscientious at age 20 look much the same at age 30? Or have they now become low in extraversion and high in conscientiousness? This type of study is therefore looking at **rank-order stability**, because stability is measured by comparing the pattern of rank order of the traits (from low to high) in each person from one time to the next.

On the other hand, most of the evidence for trait change has come from studies which look at **mean-level stability** rather than rank-order stability. In this type of analysis, investigators do not measure change in rank order for each person's pattern of Big Five trait scores. Instead they compare the average score of the *entire group* of participants on each single trait separately, to see if change has occurred over time for that trait. Thus, if the average score of the group is higher on extraversion in 2004 than in 1994 or 1984, change in the personality trait "extraversion" has occurred, and this is evidence of *lack* of stability of that trait.

And, indeed, evidence of mean-level trait change is substantial (Helson et al., 2002; Helson & Soto, 2005). Interestingly, however, trait change occurs most frequently in young adulthood—not in adolescence, as would be expected based on common beliefs about adolescence as a time of rapid changes in self-concept and identity (Caspi et al., 2005). Another surprising finding from mean-level trait research is that individual traits can change well past the ages when the rank order of traits has become highly stable (in middle age). In a study spanning 40 years, Ravenna Helson and her colleagues found mean-level trait change at least for certain traits in groups of participants well into their 70s (Helson et al., 2002).

Other Aspects of Personality May Also Change

Recall that personality consists of more than traits. Interactions among traits, situations, environments, cognitions, emotions, and behavior can produce personal characteristics that are a part of our personality and that may change—sometimes quite dramatically—over time. For example, our goals, values, beliefs, social roles, and plans for our lives may change considerably. This aspect of personality has been termed **characteristic adaptations** by personality psychologist Dan McAdams (McAdams, 2004; McAdams & Olson, 2010).

However, changes in characteristic adaptations do not necessarily imply a change in traits. For example, at age 20, a person high in openness to experience on the Big Five might take up sky diving, whereas at age 80 the same person might decide to learn to cook food from a foreign culture. A person obsessively interested in political activism at age 22 might become obsessively interested in protecting the environment at age 52. Same tune, different lyrics.

There is one type of personality change that may be more fundamental than changes in characteristic adaptations. According to Dan McAdams, in addition to traits, trait-situation behavior profiles, and characteristic adaptations, there is yet a fourth level of personality: the *self-narrative*. **Self-narratives** are internal "life stories" that evolve over time—stories and myths that we tell to ourselves about ourselves and which reflect our understandings of our place in the world. Self-narratives are about the *meanings* we give to our personalities and to our very identities (McAdams, 2001; McAdams et al., 2004; McAdams & Olson, 2010; McAdams & Pals, 2006).

These stories come complete with settings, scenes, characters, plots, and themes. They are based on biographical events, but because we select which

Rank-order stability ▶ A measure of personality stability based upon the pattern of rank order of traits (from high to low) for each person in a sample from one measurement period to the next.

Mean-level stability ▶ A measure of personality stability based upon comparison of the mean score for each individual trait among a sample as a whole from one measurement period to the next.

Characteristic adaptations ▶ Dan Adams' term to describe aspects of personality such as goals, values, beliefs, social roles, and plans for the future. According to Adams, characteristic adaptations change substantially over the life span.

Self-narratives ▶ Internal "narratives of the self" which evolve through the life span. Self-narratives are stories and myths people tell themselves about events in their lives and personal characteristics which reflect their current understanding of their place in the world and the meaning of their life.

events to recall, how to recall them, and how to interpret our recollections, self-narratives are not the same as simple biography. As an example, the way a person views the "story" of his or her childhood may change dramatically during an episode of clinical major depression. It is the same childhood recalled, but events previously viewed in a positive light may now take on a mournful tone. The good times will be downplayed or forgotten altogether, and unpleasant events elevated in importance. Images that were once filled with color will now be seen in gray or in black and white. Meanings of events will be translated into the language of guilt, grief, and hopelessness.

According to McAdams (2001), the self-narrative is an aspect of personality that has assumed particular prominence in the modern industrial world. This is because issues of *identity* are not as clear-cut as they were in earlier centuries. Our self-narratives address problems of establishing and maintaining a self-concept in a world where our identities are not thrust upon us at birth and maintained throughout life, but where we are instead allowed a certain degree of choice in the matter. We can change careers repeatedly, move to new geographic locations if we choose, associate with different social groups and ethnicities, and learn a myriad of new skills. Our self-narratives help us adapt to these many types of identity change.

IN SUMMARY

1.	Rank-order trait stability is stability in the ordering of traits for each individual—an indication of which traits are high or low relative to the others in a single person from one time to the next. Mean-level trait stability refers to stability from one time to the next in the average level of each trait among a sample of people.
2.	Personality traits are surprisingly stable from childhood to adulthood, particularly if stability is measured through rank order of traits. However, trait change has also been noted, particularly if measured by mean levels of individual traits.
3.	Characteristic adaptations are a person's goals, values, beliefs, social roles, and plans. These aspects of personality may change substantially. Self-narratives are internal "narratives of the self" that evolve over time. They are also subject to substantial change.

RETRIEVE!

1.	In which ways should we expect people to change as they grow older?
2.	According to research in mean-level trait stability, at which point in life is the highest degree of trait change seen?
3.	Give an example of how changes in characteristic adaptations may not reflect changes in traits.
4.	Why has the self-narrative aspect of personality assumed particular importance in the modern world?

Looking Back

Chapter 12 in Review

WHAT IS PERSONALITY?

- Each person is like all other persons in some ways (human attributes), like just some other persons in certain ways (differences in traits), and like no other person in other ways (unique qualities). Personality is the set of common human psychological characteristics and unique patterns of traits and behavior possessed by each individual. These sets of traits and behavior patterns are organized, integrated, and relatively enduring.

WHAT ARE THE "GRAND THEORIES" OF PERSONALITY?

- The grand theories of personality include psychoanalysis, behaviorism, and humanism. Psychoanalysis is possibly the most complex theory in the history of psychology and also the most controversial. Three central components of the theory are the structural model of the mind, theory of psychosexual development, and theories of dynamic processes. The structural model of the mind includes id, ego, and superego. The five stages of psychosexual development are the oral, anal, phallic, latency, and genital. Freud believed that dreams contained hidden symbolic meanings that express forbidden sexual and aggressive wishes and impulses. Ego defenses, as detailed by Freud's daughter Anna, include repression, denial, displacement, projection, reaction formation, sublimation, and undoing. Neo-Freudians accept certain tenets of psychoanalysis, but have built their own theories based upon some of Freud's ideas.
- Behaviorist theories of personality assert that personality is learned behavior, and that one acquires personality traits through operant and classical conditioning.
- The founders of humanistic psychology were optimistic, believed in free will, and had faith in human nature—believing that people generally face problems in a rational manner. Humanistic psychologist Carl Rogers believed that each person needs a growth-promoting environment to grow into the fully functioning, competent, fulfilled human being he or she was designed to be. For a person to develop a healthy self-concept, four conditions are necessary: accurate empathy, congruence, unconditional positive regard, and positive self-regard. Rollo May incorporated existentialist philosophy into his psychology and saw human beings as an "organized bundle of potentialities" with as much capacity for evil as for good.
- Self-esteem is a person's cognitive and emotional assessment of his or her own self-worth. People with high self-esteem are happier, suffer less from depression, and are more likely to enjoy the good things that happen to them to the fullest and help others do the same. Two theories attempt to explain the importance of self-esteem: terror management theory, which suggests that self-esteem acts as a buffer against the anxiety we all feel when reminded of our own inevitable death; and sociometer theory, which focuses on the idea that a person's level of self-esteem gives important feedback about social acceptance or rejection. Contrary to popular belief, there is no evidence that self-esteem promotes better school performance, success on the job, or better interpersonal relationships; nor that low self-esteem causes criminality, prejudice, teenage pregnancy, drug or alcohol abuse, or sexual problems. Low self-esteem is strongly linked to eating disorders, however, and it may be linked to aggression or antisocial behavior in men.

HOW DO TRAITS AND SITUATIONS AFFECT PERSONALITY?

- Traits are relatively stable personality characteristics, attributes, and motivations. Gordon Allport identified 4,500 possible traits. Trait psychology emphasizes description of a person's characteristic patterns of behavior, thought, emotion, and motivation. Hans Eysenck created the two-factor model, which views personality as having a limited number of characteristics which interact within any individual and can be measured using psychological tests. Eysenck proposed two basic trait dimensions, extraversion–introversion and emotional instability–stability (neuroticism).
- Some psychologists, including Lewis Goldberg and Robert McRae, developed a five-factor model (the "Big Five") after conducting statistical research in nations throughout the world. The five factors are **O**penness to experience, **C**onscientiousness, **E**xtraversion, **A**greeableness, and **N**euroticism.
- Walter Mischel argued that situations, not traits, play the largest role in determining behavior. However, Seymour Epstein proposed that if a person were observed on a number of occasions and the person's behavior "aggregated" or averaged out, the effects of traits would be apparent. Later work by Mischel and Shoda suggested that people's behavior is best understood by looking at the patterns created by the intersection of people's traits with the various situations in which they find themselves—patterns known as trait-situation behavior profiles.

HOW DO GENES, ENVIRONMENTS, AND CULTURE INFLUENCE PERSONALITY?

- Genes play an important role in personality development. However, some personality traits are more heritable than others, and heritability estimates may vary from study to study. On average, approximately 50% of differences among people in Big Five or Eysenck's two-factor traits is due to genetic factors.
- Nonshared environments contribute the bulk of the environmental portion of influence on personality. The nonshared environment consists of each child's unique experiences in the world. Nonshared environmental experiences that are likely to have the greatest effects on personality include simple chance, peer influence, and the possibility of differing parental treatment of

Looking Back continued

each child. Judith Rich Harris is the most vocal proponent of the idea that peer groups, not parents, are the primary socializers of children and the strongest influences upon the development of personality.

- National character stereotypes are shared ideas about the typical personality type for a given culture or nation. Although many of these stereotypes are widely held, research using the Big Five to test personalities of representative members of various nations and cultures has shown that the stereotypes generally lack validity.

HOW IS PERSONALITY MEASURED?

- Personality assessment is the measurement of personality. Projective tests (e.g., Rorschach and TAT)

emerged primarily from psychoanalytic theory, and they are designed to allow a person to "project" his personality unconsciously onto ambiguous test items. Objective tests of personality (e.g., MMPI-2 and NEO PI-R) are constructed empirically and scored by computer.

DOES PERSONALITY CHANGE OVER TIME?

- Personality traits are relatively stable over time. Evidence of trait stability comes primarily from research in rank-order stability, which measures an individual's scoring on various traits over time. These studies show that temperament is stable to age 3, and personality is most stable past age 50. Evidence for changes over time in traits comes

from research using mean-level stability. In this type of analysis, researchers compare the average score of the entire group of participants on each single trait separately, to see if change has occurred over time for that trait.

- Other aspects of personality may undergo considerable change without necessarily signaling trait change. Characteristic adaptations include goals, values, beliefs, social roles, plans for the future, and self-narratives.

Key Terms

Accurate empathy, 582
Characteristic adaptations, 609
Conditions of worth, 582
Congruence, 582
Ego, 574
Ego defense mechanisms, 578
Erogenous zone, 576
Falsification, 580
Five-factor model, 590
Grand theories, 573
Id, 574
Libido, 575
Mean-level stability, 609
Minnesota Multiphasic Personality Inventory (MMPI), 605
National-character stereotypes, 601

Neurosis, 575
Nonshared environment, 598
Oedipus complex, 576
Parsimony, 580
Personality, 572
Personality assessment, 602
Person-situation controversy, 594
Pleasure principle, 574
Positive self-regard, 582
Rank-order stability, 609
Reality principle, 575
Reliability, 604
Repression, 578
Revised NEO Personality Inventory (NEO PI-R), 592
Rorschach test, 603

Self-concept, 582
Self-esteem, 584
Self-narratives, 599
Shared environment, 575
Stages of psychosexual development, 575
States, 588
Superego, 574
Superordinate traits, 589
Thematic Apperception Test (TAT), 604
Traits, 588
Trait perspective, 589
Trait-situation behavior profile, 595
Unconditional positive regard, 582
Validity, 604

Test Yourself

1. The sets of traits and behavior patterns which make up personality according to the definition used in the text are organized, _____, and relatively _____.

2. What are the three central components of Freud's theory of personality?

3. During which psychosexual stage does the superego form, according

to Freud? Which conflict must the child resolve for the superego to form properly?
a) oral stage/castration complex
b) phallic stage/castration complex
c) anal stage/Oedipus complex
d) phallic stage/Oedipus complex

4. Name and describe at least three of the ego-defense mechanisms identified by Anna Freud.

5. According to Carl Rogers, when a person truly listens and *hears* another—withholding judgment and wishing only to communicate—what quality is that person displaying?
a) unconditional positive regard
b) accurate empathy
c) conditions of worth
d) positive self-regard

Test Yourself continued

6. How do terror management theorists explain the importance of self-esteem? How do sociometer theorists explain the importance of self-esteem?

7. A relatively enduring personality characteristic or attribute that may be captured in adjectives is known as a _____. A temporary characteristic, mood, or emotion is known as a _____.

8. What are Eysenck's original two superordinate trait dimensions? Name the "Big Five" factors of the five-factor model.

9. A controversy emerged during the 1960s in the field of personality psychology because Walter Mischel showed that people's scores on measures of personality traits do not predict how they behave on any particular occasion. What is the name given to this controversy? What was the main criticism that Seymour Epstein made of Mischel's conclusions?

10. The unique patterns formed by the intersection of people's traits with the situations in which the find themselves are known as:
a) trait-situation behavior profiles
b) self-narratives
c) characteristic adaptations
d) trait-situation-behavior patterns

11. Aproximately ____% of the differences among people in Big Five personality traits are due to genetic inheritance.

12. Which aspects of the nonshared environment are most commonly proposed as constituting the environmental influence on personality differences among people?

13. Conflict between which two "systems" is responsible for much of the peer influence on personality development, according to Judith Rich Harris?

14. Which of the following are important objective tests of personality? (circle as many as apply)
a) NEO PI-R
b) Rorschach inkblot test
c) TAT
d) NET

15. What is the name of the method by which the MMPI-2 was constructed?

16. According to cross-cultural research, how accurate are national character stereotypes?
a) remarkably accurate
b) somewhat accurate
c) somewhat accurate, but only for East Asians and Westerners
d) not at all accurate

17. On average, human beings experience personality change simply due to the aging process. In which ways do people tend to change as a result of maturity?

18. When measures of _____ stability are used, very little change is shown in traits past middle age. However, when measures of _____ are used, trait change is seen well into the 70s.

Psychological
disorders

Chapter Outline

FREEZE FRAME

▲ "The Scream" (Skrik) by Edvard Munch, 1893.

Anu was the most amazing woman I had encountered in all of my (modestly eventful) 23 years. She was, first of all, brilliant—and I mean too brilliant to keep track of. Often I could not follow a great deal of what she said because it was couched in the language of physics—never my strong point—and she liked to draw connections between recent findings in experimental physics or mathematics and any number of seemingly unrelated events or phenomena. I remember her convincingly trying to argue that passion could be expressed in mathematical terms. (Well, it convinced me at the time, anyway.)

She was not only a fiery intellectual. She played the cello beautifully and was teaching herself flute and electric guitar. This was the late 1960s and, like many of our generation, she had a political agenda—but unlike many who were searching for answers, Anu knew exactly how to end the war in Vietnam, how to redistribute wealth in the United States so as to build an equitable democracy, and how to create racial justice. She was none too happy about the treatment of women in society either. She was as charming, admirable, and compelling as any 23-year-old could wish for.

However, over a period of time I noticed that spending time with her was growing more and more exhausting.

Yes, she was exuberant and exciting, but sometimes even I could see that she wasn't really making a lot of sense. She was just making too many connections that didn't really *connect*. I often felt overwhelmed by the speed and pressure of her speech; sometimes it was so intense that I had to fight the impulse to place my hands over my ears. Also, she didn't seem to sleep—ever. I felt confident that she was not a vampire, but when I would awaken after spending the night at her apartment, there she was, pounding away at her typewriter or playing scales on the cello, regardless of when I awoke—in the middle of the night, at dawn, or late in the morning.

I started to realize that something might be really wrong when one morning I awoke to find her sitting at the foot of the bed, grinning like a Cheshire cat. She told me she wanted to go out to eat. I asked where. She answered, "Paris," and dropped two round-trip plane tickets on the bed. "We leave in 5 hours." I knew she was saving up for graduate school, so I couldn't believe she would do something so foolish. Also, I didn't even own a valid passport! When I mentioned this unfortunate fact, her face fell. She grew confused, looked miserable, and I couldn't really follow what she was saying. I suddenly felt frightened for her, without really knowing why. I left her apartment that morning with a sense of foreboding and unreality.

I didn't hear from Anu for many weeks, and no one answered when I rang her doorbell. One day she called me—from the Women's House of Detention in Greenwich Village. It appears that she had spent all of her savings on clothes, stereo equipment, and woodblock prints by well-known Japanese artists, and then continued to live (in high style) by intentionally bouncing checks. When I came to bail her out, the woman I found at the House of Detention bore very little resemblance to the woman I knew. Anu could barely speak. Her beautiful strutting posture was gone, and now she shuffled as though she had had a stroke. As soon as I escorted her into a taxicab outside the House of Detention, she began weeping uncontrollably. I just couldn't believe what I was seeing. But then, I knew nothing about manic-depressive illness, currently termed *bipolar disorder*.

What are psychological disorders such as Anu experienced? Are they medical conditions, diseases in the same sense that multiple sclerosis, hepatitis, and cancer are diseases? Or are they "social constructions," ways in which each culture decides to explain unusual behavior and states of mind? In this chapter we will examine psychological disorders—those, like manic-depressive illness and *schizophrenia*, which people frequently refer to as "madness," and those that may be less severe in symptoms but are nonetheless equally debilitating.

What Is a Psychological Disorder?

How do psychiatrists and psychologists know when symptoms constitute a **psychological disorder** (mental illness), as opposed to being just unusual behavior—or even a person's completely reasonable behavior under unusual circumstances? Imagine a mother whose 7-year-old daughter is diagnosed with a rare, incurable blood disease. The mother finds herself overwhelmed with sadness, feelings of hopelessness and helplessness, and guilt about some of her past behavior toward her daughter. She cries for hours every day and has difficulty sleeping or eating. She is unable to work. Is this woman suffering from a mental disorder (*major depression*), or is she reacting understandably to the knowledge that her beloved child will soon die an excruciatingly painful death?

More abstract philosophical and moral questions might also be asked: Are people who commit cruel, violent acts and experience no remorse whatever suffering from a disorder (*antisocial personality disorder*), or are they just engaging in bad (or evil) behavior? Is a young man who devotes all the years of his youth to the care of his sick and aged parents at the expense of his own social life a morally righteous person, or is he suffering from *avoidant personality disorder with dependent features*?

It may surprise you to learn that psychologists have yet to agree on what does and does not constitute a psychological disorder (Frances & Widiger, 2012). Although most mental health professionals use the categories and diagnostic criteria of disorders created by the American Psychiatric Association and listed in their ***Diagnostic and Statistical Manual of Mental Disorders*** (**DSM**) (American Psychiatric Association, 2013), many apparently do so primarily because the DSM is the only widely accepted, coherent set of guidelines for making psychological diagnoses in the United States.[1] In other words, many in the mental health field do not necessarily agree with the diagnostic categories and criteria contained in the DSM (Horwitz & Wakefield, 2007, 2012; Houts, 2001; Krueger & Markon, 2006; Lilienfeld & Marino, 1999). Such psychotherapists and psychiatrists may use the manual only as one part of a larger process of arriving at a diagnosis, or use it merely as a means of obtaining reimbursement from health insurers who almost always require that a DSM diagnosis be given. Indeed, some mental health professionals believe that the entire enterprise of putting psychological symptoms into distinct categories as though they represented unique illnesses that one has or doesn't have is flawed and counterproductive (Hyman, 2010).

However, prior to the creation of the DSM, now in its fifth revised edition (American Psychiatric Association, 2013), different clinicians had their own ideas about what constituted mental illness. The same patient might be given an entirely different diagnosis or no diagnosis at all, depending on which clinician he or she happened to visit. So the DSM has created a degree of diagnostic order because it specifies precise criteria that must be met before any particular diagnosis of disorder can be given.

Yet, as stated, in spite of the widespread use of the DSM, there are actually a number of different ideas about what standards ought to be used when deciding whether a person has a psychological disorder. The DSM provides only one such idea. Each of these views makes an important contribution to understanding **abnormal psychology**—states of mind and behavior that deviate both from the statistical norm (the average) and from what the mental health field considers to be healthy psychological functioning. Let us now examine

Psychological disorder
▶ Psychological disorder is defined differently by different theorists and in different contexts. In its broadest sense, the definition is circular: any recognizable cluster of behaviors and states of mind that mental health professionals agree constitute mental illness and to which they attach a descriptive label.

***Diagnostic and Statistical Manual of Mental Disorders* (DSM)** ▶ The manual published by the American Psychiatric Association which classifies, describes, and presents diagnostic criteria for psychological disorders. The DSM is the standard for diagnosis among psychologists as well as psychiatrists, and presents the medical model of mental illness in the most coherent and consistent fashion yet devised.

Abnormal psychology ▶ The scientific study of states of mind and behavior which deviate both from the statistical norm (the average) and from what mental health professionals consider to be healthy psychological functioning.

---

[1]The International Classification of Diseases *is a second coherent system of classification, but it is used primarily in Europe and Great Britain.*

three of the more important ideas about psychological disorder: The *DSM view*, the *myth of mental illness view*, and the *harmful dysfunction* view.

The DSM View: Disorder = Dysfunction and Distress (or Impairment)

As stated, the DSM view of psychological disorder is the standard in the field of clinical psychology and psychiatry. It is relatively simple, but was arrived at over many years of refinement—and argument. In essence, according to the DSM, two primary conditions exist in any psychological disorder: (a) *psychological dysfunction*; and (b) *personal distress* or *impairment in functioning*. We will examine each of these factors separately.

PSYCHOLOGICAL DYSFUNCTION

According to the DSM view, **psychological dysfunction** is a breakdown in mental functioning—cognitive, emotional, or behavioral. However, the DSM recognizes that boundaries between the functional and dysfunctional may be impossible to determine with complete precision—these are *fuzzy boundaries*, as described in Chapter 9. Consider Supreme Court Justice Potter Stewart's famous definition of pornography: "I know it when I see it" (*Jacobellis v. Ohio*, 1964). What Justice Stewart meant was that, while he could not outline *exactly* where pornography begins and art or ordinary entertainment ends, by a certain point material takes on the obvious form of pornography and loses the qualities of art or ordinary entertainment.

In the same way, according to the DSM it is impossible to state exactly where functional ends and dysfunctional begins—yet the categories themselves are valid. At some point, a person's emotions, cognitions, or behavior are clearly dysfunctional. However, critics of the DSM point out that we are still left with the problem of who decides when a person is dysfunctional and when he or she is not. Who decides whether a person must feel depressed for 2 weeks to be dysfunctional, rather than 4 weeks or 4 days? Thus, the DSM view of psychological dysfunction to some degree must reflect social judgments or cultural values and cannot be said to be as objective as medical judgments of dysfunction in physical organs such as the heart or lungs (Wakefield, 1999, 2003).

PERSONAL DISTRESS OR IMPAIRMENT

In general, a person with a psychological disorder is extremely distressed or upset by it. However, this is not always the case. For example, a person with *antisocial personality disorder* may not be at all distressed by his or her condition. Antisocial personality disorder is a condition characterized by extremely selfish and often unlawful behavior; lying and other forms of deceit; lack of concern for the feelings, needs, or suffering of others; aggression or violence; recklessness and disregard for safety; and lack of remorse for all the foregoing. Thus, it is *the rest of us* who are generally upset by a person's antisocial personality disorder—not the "sufferer." The concept of **impairment in functioning** is offered in the DSM view to cover those situations where a person has symptoms of a disorder but does not experience personal distress. Impairment in functioning refers to problems experienced in important areas of life as a result of the psychological symptoms: problems in work, school, or personal relationships, for example; or trouble with the law.

However, people frequently become severely distressed when they are not disordered—think about the last time you fell in love with someone who rejected you. And, as critics point out, the DSM provides no objective standards for deciding when psychological symptoms have actually caused significant impairment in important areas of one's life. Who is to say? Thus, personal distress and/or impairment also pose logical problems as objective markers of psychological disorder.

▲ Gary Leon Ridgway—Sick, Evil, or Both? Gary Leon Ridgway, among the most prolific serial killers in modern history, murdered at least 50 women during a period of 2½ years. Serial killers are routinely said to suffer from *antisocial personality disorder* (formerly known as *psychopathy* or *sociopathy*)—a disorder characterized by persistent lying, violations of law and the rights of others, lack of empathy, aggressive or violent behavior, inability to tolerate boredom, recklessness, disregard for others' safety, and lack of remorse for wrongdoing. However, critics charge that applying this label to a person like Ridgway trivializes the enormity of his criminal behavior and implies a reduction in his moral responsibility for taking so many innocent lives.

Psychological dysfunction
▶ Any breakdown in mental functioning—cognitive, emotional, or behavioral. The boundaries between "functional" and "dysfunctional" are often fuzzy, however, and there is wide disagreement as to how to characterize these boundaries.

In sum: The DSM view is undoubtedly an advance in practicality and utility over previous diagnostic systems, but critics charge that it has problems of its own because, in spite of its claims to objectivity, criteria for disorder actually remain to some degree subjective and dependent upon social judgments and cultural values.

The Myth of Mental Illness View: Disorders Are Social Judgments, Not "Illnesses"

> *"If you talk to God, you are praying. If God talks to you, you have schizophrenia."*
>
> —Thomas Szasz

In 1961, psychiatrist Thomas Szasz surprised (and annoyed) his profession by proposing that diagnoses of "mental illness" were little more than social judgments about people's unusual behavior, made in the guise and language of medical science. According to this **myth of mental illness view**, mental "illnesses" do not exist in the sense that medical illnesses exist. This is because medical illnesses involve some sort of demonstrable, structural change and malfunction of a part of the body—broken bone, infected tissue, growth of a tumor, and so forth (termed *lesions* by Szasz). Apart from a very small number of conditions (which Szasz exempted from his critique), no one has yet been able to identify specific anatomical or biochemical "lesions" in the brain that are specific to particular psychological disorders and are always present when the illness is present. Szasz concluded that terms such as "psychological disorder" or "mental illness" were little more than metaphors to describe what amount to "problems in living." Indeed, for the half-century before his death in 2012, Szasz denounced the **medical model** of mental illness, which views psychological problems as similar to physical illnesses, claiming that the model was grossly misleading and damaging to the individual and society (Szasz, 2007).

However, Szasz's ideas are sometimes inaccurately portrayed. He did not propose that people don't "really" experience severe psychological distress, nor was he proposing that such people shouldn't be treated for their mental pain with psychotherapy or drugs. Szasz emphasized that people should have the right to be given any sort of treatment for their symptoms they deemed fit (including illegal or dangerous treatments). He was primarily concerned with the problem of individuals being committed to psychiatric institutions against their will, merely on the basis of a psychiatrist's diagnosis of mental illness—a legal procedure known as **involuntary commitment** or *civil commitment*. Szasz was also concerned about possible negative social and psychological consequences to a person of merely being labeled with a mental illness diagnosis (Szasz, 2007; e.g., Goffman, 1961; Jamison, 2006).

Szasz initially expressed his ideas during a time when involuntary commitments to mental institutions (his most important objection) were far more common than they are now. Indeed, since the development of psychiatric medications and the advent of *managed care*—which has transferred the managing of health care costs from the consumer to insurance companies and large organizations—the trend has been to do everything possible to keep patients *out* of mental institutions. This policy is known as **deinstitutionalization**. Deinstitutionalization is meant to serve the dual purpose of reducing costs and allowing patients to attempt to live productive lives.

Moreover, it is not true, as Szasz claimed, that all true illnesses involve "lesions" in tissue or organs. For example, hypertension is a *real* illness that involves no lesions. Numerous other examples may also be found (Wakefield, 1992).

Nonetheless, certain of Szasz's ideas are insightful. They emphasize the simple truth that beliefs about what does or does not constitute a psychological

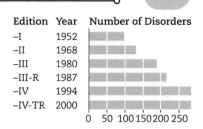

Edition	Year	Number of Disorders
–I	1952	
–II	1968	
–III	1980	
–III-R	1987	
–IV	1994	
–IV-TR	2000	

0 50 100 150 200 250

▲ **The DSM in Five Revisions.** The *Diagnostic and Statistical Manual of the American Psychiatric Association* is the standard reference work for diagnosing psychological disorders. With each revision, changes are made in conditions considered to be disorders and diagnostic criteria for these disorders. As you can see, the number of conditions considered to be "disorders" has increased significantly with each edition of the DSM up to and including the DSM-5 (not shown here). In addition, the criteria for diagnosing some disorders in the DSM have been relaxed in the new revision, increasing the number of people who potentially qualify for a diagnosis of mental illness. *(Source: American Psychiatric Association; figure from Carey, 2008.)*

Impairment in functioning
▶ The concept used for diagnosis in the DSM to cover situations where a person has symptoms of a disorder but does not experience personal distress.

Myth of mental illness view
▶ A view of psychological disorder pioneered by Thomas Szasz which proposes that "mental illness" is really a metaphor for problems in living and does not refer to actual illness or disease processes.

▶ **"Problems in Living"?** The patient depicted in this photo is suffering from catatonia, an extremely severe symptom of psychotic disorder characterized by a loss of ordinary forms of bodily movement. A person with this condition may remain frozen and immobile for many hours at a time or may be unable to contain movement—engaging in seemingly purposeless, excited, and repetitive movements to the point of literally dropping from exhaustion—or even losing his or her life. Most psychologists and psychiatrists would likely disagree with Thomas Szasz that such a condition is best described merely as a "problem in living."

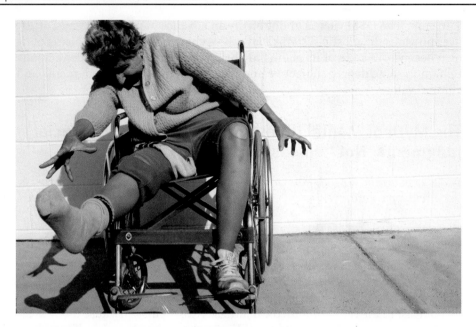

Medical model ▶ The general term used to describe views of psychological disorder which frame them in a medical context. Unlike the myth of mental illness view, medical models view psychological disorders as actual illnesses with specific causes and which necessitate treatment with psychotherapy, medication, or some other process.

Involuntary commitment (civil commitment) ▶ When a person is admitted to a psychiatric facility (mental hospital) against his or her will by order of the court. Proceedings to commit someone in this way may be brought by individuals or the state.

disorder inevitably contain strong elements of social judgment and are generally not as straightforward as judgments about physical disorders. Szasz also correctly observed that being labeled with a mental illness can sometimes have far-reaching negative consequences for a person. Despite widespread public education about mental health, psychiatric illnesses—unlike most physical illnesses—create a **stigma**, a sort of "mark" of shame or disgrace. A stigma due to mental illness can follow a person throughout his or her life (Goffman, 1961; Jamison, 2006).

The Harmful Dysfunction View: Fact *and* Social Judgment Define Disorder

The **harmful dysfunction view**, articulated by Jerome Wakefield (e.g., 2003, 2010; Horwitz & Wakefield, 2007, 2012), is an attempt to avoid some of the logical problems presented by the DSM and myth of mental illness views, while incorporating the strongest aspects of both of those approaches. Wakefield agrees with the myth of mental illness view that judgments of the *harmful* nature of certain behaviors or states of mind are always and forever social judgments involving cultural values. For example, it is a social and cultural judgment that there is harm in hearing voices that are not there, using illegal drugs in excess, weeping for no apparent reason and feeling worthless, or being terrified of flying in an airplane.

However, Wakefield also states that the *dysfunction* aspect of psychological disorder can be treated as a matter of objective fact and need not be subject to social judgment as is the case for the DSM view of dysfunction. What is the factual basis of "dysfunction," according to Wakefield? Dysfunction occurs when a psychological attribute or mechanism *fails to perform the function for which it was shaped through evolution by natural selection* (see Chapter 3).

One might well wonder how one is to know which functions a psychological attribute evolved to perform. Wakefield (2003) suggests that the function of a psychological attribute or mechanism—like the function of a physical organ, such as the heart—can be defined by looking at the effects of the mechanism and asking: Do these effects help explain why the mechanism or attribute came into being in the first place?

Consider *anxiety*, for example. The *effect* of anxiety is to make us tense and wary of dangerous or potentially harmful situations. Without anxiety we might decide to take a swim in water clearly marked "Warning—Shark

▲ **Harmful Dysfunction in Obsessive-Compulsive Disorder.** Obsessive-compulsive disorder (OCD) is an extremely severe disorder characterized by distressingly intrusive and anxiety-provoking thoughts, and compulsive behaviors designed to reduce the anxiety. One frequent "theme" of OCD is pollution by disease-causing germs, and OCD sufferers sometimes engage in crippling hand-washing rituals which prevent them from leaving the house or engaging in normal activities. They may scrub their skin raw from excessive washing. This behavior is *harmful* (a social judgment) but also demonstrates a *dysfunction* of psychological mechanisms regulating health and hygiene.

Infested!" or tell the highway patrol officer giving us a speeding ticket exactly what we thought of her (and her entire extended family). Human beings cannot survive without anxiety—it is a blessing.

However, what if we tremble with anxiety at the very thought of leaving our house to go to the movies with an attractive classmate, and cancel the date as a result? Our anxiety mechanism is no longer performing the function for which it came into being, protecting us from danger and harm. Anxiety clearly could not have evolved to prevent people from interacting socially (especially in a romantic context).

Although the harmful dysfunction view is a bold attempt to solve the problems of defining "psychological disorder," like the other views it has its weaknesses. For one thing, our state of knowledge about the functions of *psychological* mechanisms is still quite primitive compared to our understanding of the functions of *physiological* mechanisms such as the heart. We may believe that we understand the function of anxiety clearly, but what about the functions of premenstrual symptoms, jealousy, or aggressive acting out in childhood? There may be disagreements as to their function. Without knowing their function, how can we determine whether *premenstrual dysphoric disorder*, *delusions (jealous type)*, or childhood *conduct disorder*—all of which appear in the DSM-5—are valid disorders? Therefore, until our understanding of the functions of psychological mechanisms becomes more sophisticated and complete, the harmful dysfunction view, despite its promise, may not be very much more useful than the DSM view.

In short, each of the views of psychological disorder just discussed makes important contributions to our understanding of disorder, yet each has weaknesses and is incomplete. However, both harmful dysfunction and DSM

Deinstitutionalization ▶ A policy instituted in the United States and other industrialized nations during the 1960s which encouraged shorter hospital stays for those with mental illnesses and provided stricter criteria by which people with psychological disorders or developmental disabilities could be hospitalized in the first place.

Stigma ▶ A social "badge" or mark of shame or disgrace resulting from a person's behavior or membership in a disapproved or discriminated-against group. Social stigma traditionally has been a problem for those diagnosed with psychological disorders.

Harmful dysfunction view ▶ A view of psychological disorder pioneered by Jerome Wakefield. According to the harmful dysfunction view, disorder exists when symptoms cause harm according to subjective social or cultural judgments, *and* there is objective evidence of dysfunction. Dysfunction is said to exist only when a psychological characteristic or mechanism is not performing the function for which it evolved through natural selection.

views, when considered together, capture aspects of "common sense" ideas about mental illness typical of the general public (Haslam & Giosan, 2002). They also overwhelmingly capture perspectives of the majority of mental health professionals. Therefore, my treatment of psychological disorder for this chapter will draw primarily from these views.

What about "Insanity?"

Many of us grew up thinking that "sanity" and "insanity" defined whether a person was of sound mind or mentally ill. However, while people use these terms casually in reference to mental health, in fact they are not mental health terms. *Sane* and *insane* are primarily legal terms referring to criminal responsibility. A person who is *insane* does not understand the nature or consequences of his or her behavior or cannot tell right from wrong—therefore, he or she should not be held responsible for criminal behavior. Thus, occasionally (but far less frequently than the movies and television would have us believe) attorneys will use the **insanity defense** in an effort to demonstrate that while their clients committed crimes, the clients should not be held responsible. However, as shown in Table 13.1, the insanity defense is used exceptionally rarely—and it is even more rarely successful.

The Number of People with Disorders Is Not Known with Certainty

How many people suffer from psychological disorders? Although there are numerous estimates, at least in the United States these estimates are highly unlikely to be accurate. Conducting surveys to estimate the prevalence of psychological disorders is a tricky business. Designing a survey to avoid one potential problem—say, underestimation of those in need of mental health services—often results in another problem, for example, counting people as disordered who are merely responding in a normal fashion to distressing life events (Wakefield, Schmitz, First, & Horwitz, 2007). Push one bubble down, and another pops up. Surveys from the 1980s and 1990s suffered from the

Insanity defense ▶ A criminal defense strategy based upon the proposition that a defendant did commit a crime but should not be held responsible because he or she did not understand the nature or consequences of the crime or could not distinguish between right and wrong.

Table 13.1 Public Perceptions of the Insanity Defense versus Actual Use and Outcomes

	PUBLIC PERCEPTION	ACTUAL
A. Use of the insanity defense		
Percentage of felony indictments resulting in an insanity plea.	37%	0.9%
Percentage of insanity pleas resulting in acquittal.	44%	26%
B. Disposition of insanity acquittees		
Percentage of insanity acquittees sent to a mental hospital.	50.6%	84.7%
Percentage of insanity acquittees set free.	25.6%	15.3%
Conditional Release		11.6%
Outpatient		2.6%
Release		1.1%
C. Length of confinement of insanity acquittees (in months)		
All crimes	21.8	32.5
Murder		76.4

(Adapted from Silver et al., 1994, p. 67.)

tendency to identify many *false positives*—characterizing people as disordered whose complaints were relatively minor or whose symptoms may have been serious, but were understandable human responses to distressing life events. Such symptoms generally resolve on their own without treatment (Horwitz & Wakefield, 2006; Wakefield, Schmitz, First, & Horwitz, 2007). To correct the problem of false positives, some national surveys conducted during the early part of the 21st century contained detailed questions about severity of symptoms in an attempt to avoid painting a bleaker picture of the prevalence of mental illness among Americans than is realistic (Kessler, Chiu, Demler, & Walters, 2005). Although estimates from this research showed that only relatively small numbers of Americans suffered from severe symptoms of psychological disorder (see Table 13.2), the surveys did not solve one basic problem: Human beings may experience many types of symptoms—even severe symptoms—on a temporary basis as normal responses to stressful life events. If such a person were identified as "disordered" in a research study simply as a result of the severity of symptoms, it would still amount to a false positive (Horwitz & Wakefield, 2007; Parker, 2007; Wakefield, Schmitz, & Baer, 2010).

On the other hand, surveys such as these may also fail to identify cases of serious mental illness in need of treatment—that is, *false negatives*. This may occur because people can choose whether they wish to consent to be interviewed for surveys. It may be that some people with serious symptoms are among those refusing to participate (Kessler et al., 2005). Indeed, it is possible that many with the most severe symptoms would be among this group.

Bearing all of these problems in mind, I was at first frankly reluctant to offer statistical estimates of prevalence rates of the various disorders discussed in this chapter. I ultimately decided to include the estimates from the National Comorbidity Survey Replication (Kessler et al., 2005), as shown in Table 13.2, because they are likely the closest to reasonable "ballpark" figures available. But keep in mind that these figures are just that—ballpark figures that may not be as accurate as one might wish.

Table 13.2 One-Year U.S. Prevalence Estimates of Three Selected DSM Psychological Disorder Categories[1]

- The **1-year prevalence** figure describes the percentage of the population which could be diagnosed with any clinical disorder within a given year. The **severity** figures describe the percentage of people whose symptoms reach different levels of seriousness (*serious* or *mild to moderate*).

- The first severity figure given is the percentage of the population with that level of seriousness of disorder. For example, a total of 18.1% of Americans experience symptoms of one of the anxiety, obsessive-compulsive, and trauma-related disorders, but only 4.1% of Americans have serious symptoms.

- The second percentage figure (the one in parenthesis) is the percentage *of those with the disorder* who have a given level of symptom seriousness. Thus, of the 18.1% of the population with an anxiety disorder, 22.8% have serious symptoms, but 77.2% have only mild or moderate symptoms.

CATEGORY OF DISORDER	1-YEAR PREVALENCE	Severity	
		SERIOUS	MILD TO MODERATE
All Anxiety, Obsessive-Compulsive, and Trauma/Stress-Related Disorders	18.1	4.1 (22.8)	14.0 (77.2)
Depressive and Bipolar Disorders	9.5	4.3 (45.0)	6.17 (55.0)
All Substance Use and Addictive Disorders	3.8	1.1 (29.6)	2.7 (70.5)
TOTAL % OF POPULATION WITH ANY DISORDER	26.2	5.8 (22.3)	20.4 (77.7)

[1]Table uses DSM-5 category labels, but research was published using DSM-IV-TR category labels. (*Source: Kessler et al., 2005.*)

Table 13.3 **Eight Categories of DSM-5 Major Mental Disorders**

CATEGORY	EXAMPLES (SUBTYPES)	SYMPTOMS
Substance-Use and Addictive Disorders	Alcohol Use Disorder	Compulsive alcohol use; consistent impaired functioning at home, school or work as a consequence of alcohol use; craving for alcohol; apparent loss of control over use.
	Opioid Use Disorder	Compulsive use of prescription opioid drugs; craving for opioid drugs; consistent impaired functioning at home, school, or work as a consequence of use; apparent loss of control over use.
Schizophrenia and other psychotic disorders	Schizophrenia	Bizarre delusions or hallucinations, disorganized speech and thought; inappropriate emotional responses (including little or no emotional response); self-absorption; social dysfunction.
	Schizoaffective Disorder	Psychotic symptoms similar to those in schizophrenia alternating with mood disturbances including depression or mania.
Depressive and Bipolar Disorders	Major Depression	Sad or listless mood; change in sleep, weight or appetite patterns; feelings of worthlessness and guilt; difficulty experiencing pleasure; fatigue, hopelessness, thoughts of death and suicide.
	Bipolar Disorder	Swings between profound depression and highly energized mood (mania). Mania can take the form of extreme elation, creativity, and grandiosity or anger and irritability; mania and depression are sometimes experienced simultaneously (mixed state).
Anxiety Disorders	Generalized Anxiety Disorder	Chronic excessive worry and anxiety that is difficult to control, accompanied by factors such as restlessness or tension, fatigue, sleep disturbance, difficulty concentrating.
	Specific Phobia	Excessive fear and anxiety experienced in the presence of a specific object or situation (e.g., spiders, snakes, blood, heights, air travel); intentional avoidance of the feared object or situation.
Obsessive-Compulsive Disorders	Obsessive-Compulsive Disorder	Recurrent and persistent unwanted thoughts or mental images; combined with compulsive, repetitive, often ritualistic behaviors (e.g., hand-washing) that the person feels driven to perform and that take up a substantial amount of time and cause impairment or distress and dysfunction.
	Hoarding Disorder	Difficulty and distress in discarding or parting with possessions (regardless of their lack of value); strong urge to save items, resulting in filling up and cluttering living areas.
Feeding and Eating Disorders	Anorexia Nervosa	Refusal to maintain minimally normal body weight leading to abnormally low weigh; intense fear of gaining weight; disturbance in the perception of one's body weight or shape.
	Bulimia Nervosa	Recurrent episodes of binge eating accompanied by inappropriate behavior (e.g., use of laxatives or induced vomiting) designed to keep the eating from resulting in weight gain.
Wake-Sleep Disorders	Primary Insomnia	Chronic difficulty falling or staying asleep resulting in significant distress or impairment in important areas of life
	Narcolepsy	Chronic, irresistible attacks of sleep at inappropriate times (e.g., sitting at the dinner table, walking along the street).
Trauma and Stressor-Related Disorders	Post-Traumatic Stress Disorder	After experiencing or witnessing an event that involves actual or threatened death or serious injury, one re-experiences the event in memory, nightmares or flashbacks; avoids thoughts of the event or places associated with the event; may have sleep or concentration problems and other symptoms.

Major Mental Disorders and Personality Disorders

The DSM-5 categorizes each psychological disorder according to its quality, symptoms, course, severity, and other phenomena. The system is somewhat complicated and includes many scores of different diagnoses listed under various divisions and subdivisions, but for our purposes, we can first divide disorders into two general categories which, taken together, contain the conditions of greatest interest to most clinical and counseling psychologists: *major mental disorders* and *personality disorders*. In the remainder of the chapter, we will focus on disorders that fall within these two umbrella categories.

The category *major mental disorders* includes those conditions most likely to come to the attention of a psychiatrist or clinical psychologist, and they tend to result in the most severe distress and/or impairment—although this is by no means always the case. Major mental disorders are subdivided by general types of symptoms, for example, *anxiety disorders, obsessive-compulsive disorders, depressive disorders, feeding and eating disorders, substance use and addictive disorders*, and so forth. These subdivisions in turn all contain groups of specific disorders. For example, the *anxiety disorders* category includes generalized anxiety disorder, panic disorder, and specific phobia, among others. All of these disorders include anxiety as a principle symptom.

Table 13.3 lists eight subcategories of major mental disorders in the DSM-5, including representative examples of specific disorders from each category. I will discuss several of these major clinical disorders in the following sections, and will conclude the chapter with a discussion of personality disorders.

IN SUMMARY

1.	In the myth of mental illness view of psychological disorders, mental problems are not "illnesses" but rather problems in living to which medical labels have been affixed.
2.	The DSM view, the accepted view of the psychiatry and clinical psychology professions, uses the criteria of dysfunction and personal distress or impairment in functioning to diagnose disorders.
3.	The harmful dysfunction view incorporates evolutionary and social science insights. It proposes that judgments of harm always contain elements of social judgment and cultural values, but judgments of dysfunction can be based upon fact—whether a psychological attribute or mechanism is performing the function for which it was shaped through evolution by natural selection.
4.	*Insanity* is primarily a legal term, not a mental health term.
5.	Estimates of the prevalence of mental disorders are likely to be inaccurate.
6.	Disorders may be divided into two general categories: major mental disorders and personality disorders.
7.	The DSM-5 categorizes and subdivides disorders according to general types of symptoms, severity, course, and other phenomena.

RETRIEVE!

1. When Thomas Szasz advanced the view that mental illnesses were little more than problems in living to which medical labels had been attached, what was his primary concern?

a) misdiagnosis

b) involuntary commitment

c) deinstitutionalization

d) poor standards of care in mental hospitals

2. What are the two primary components of psychological disorder, according to the DSM-5?

3. According to the harmful dysfunction view, how should "dysfunction" be determined?

4. True or false: Almost one-quarter of all serious felony indictments in the United States result in an insanity plea.

5. Why does the chapter state that rates of psychological disorders are not known with certainty?

What Are Anxiety Disorders?

Anxiety ▶ An unpleasant feeling of apprehension and worry experienced in anticipation of some sort of threat. Anxiety includes cognitive, emotional, physiological, and behavioral components. Anxiety tends to be *future-oriented*, in that it typically is experienced in response to anticipation of a future threat, rather than in response to an immediate threat, which is the domain of *fear*.

Anxiety is an unpleasant feeling of tension, physiological arousal (e.g., increased heart rate), and apprehension or worry that greets us when we anticipate some sort of threat (Barlow, 2002a). Anxiety is *future-oriented* because an anxious person is apprehensive about something that may happen in the immediate or distant future. Anxiety is not the same as *fear*, which is a present-oriented emotion, and is evoked by threats that are *already* occurring (Barlow, Brown, & Craske, 1994). Fear generally elicits the fight-or-flight stress response as described in Chapter 11. Although fear is present in certain anxiety disorders (e.g., *panic disorder* and *phobia*), it is not characteristic of most anxiety disorders.

As mentioned earlier in the chapter, without anxiety, we'd be in *deep* trouble. Indeed, Issac Marks and Randolph Nesse (1994) hypothesize that the most severe and dangerous of all the anxiety disorders does not appear in the DSM and has yet to be described in the research literature. This is because the people who have it don't know they have it, feel just fine, and don't end up in psychiatrists' offices—they end up at the wrong end of other people's fists, at the bottom of cliffs, and in the morgue. Marks and Nesse term the condition *hypophobia*—too little anxiety!

Whether or not there actually turn out to be a group of people who ought to be more anxious, without doubt the most distressing and generally debilitating anxiety disorders (and the only ones recognized by the DSM) are those which result from inappropriately *heightened* anxiety. This sort of anxiety can be extremely intense, irrational, and uncontrollable. It disrupts many or all aspects of the sufferer's life (Beard, Weisberg, & Keller, 2010; Olatunji, Cisler, & Tolin, 2007). Severe anxiety not only disrupts a person's life, it may shorten it. A high level of anxiety is strongly associated with increased risk of death due to coronary heart disease (Hamer, Malloy, & Stamatakis, 2008; Shibeshi, Young-Xu, & Blatt, 2007). Depending on the particular condition, up to twice as many women as men suffer from anxiety disorders (Craske, 2003).

Anxiety disorders have a high likelihood of coexisting or overlapping with one another and with other types of disorders, a problem called **comorbidity** (see Figure 13.1). More than 50% of patients who receive a diagnosis of anxiety disorder are diagnosed with two or more such disorders (T. A. Brown, Campbell, Lehman, Grisham, &Mancill, 2001). Anxiety is also very closely linked with depression—at least 50% of those people diagnosed with an anxiety disorder are also diagnosed with depression, and for those with multiple anxiety disorders the figure for comorbid depression may be much higher (Miyazaki, Aihide, & Nomura, 2010; J. M. Murphy et al., 2004). Unfortunately, the greater the comorbidity in anxiety disorders, the lower the likelihood of recovery and greater the chance of relapse if recovery does occur (Bruce et al., 2005).

Generalized Anxiety Disorder Defines the Experience of Anxiety

"I'm constantly juggling images of doom—even in my sleep."

—Jen

Generalized anxiety disorder (GAD) can be thought of as the "basic" anxiety disorder, in a way defining the essential experience of anxiety (but see Horwitz & Wakefield, 2012 for a different view). People who suffer from generalized anxiety are driven by uncontrollable worry and apprehension about the future. They fret continuously about almost anything and everything. Unlike rational worrying, which can be useful (though unpleasant) as long as it leads to problem solving and as long as it can be turned off, the worrying of GAD patients is often irrational and leads them nowhere. It does not help them solve their problems, and they cannot stop the process no matter how much they would like to. GAD sufferers may experience irritability, difficulty concentrating, and muscle tension throughout the day, and sleep may also be disturbed. GAD grinds the person down. The condition usually becomes chronic, and many sufferers never experience full relief from their symptoms (van der Heiden, Methorst, Muris, & van der Molen, (2011).

Figure 13.2 describes the basic criteria used by DSM-5 to diagnose generalized anxiety disorder.

Phobias Are Irrational Fears

"Eventually I had to move back to the city. I know it sounds stupid but there was just too many spiders out there and I couldn't really handle it."

—LaShan

When you see someone with a bleeding cut, do you feel faint and want to flee the room? Have you avoided camping in the woods or even visiting the country because you are deathly afraid of snakes or spiders? Do you forgo visiting your grandparents because you are so terrified of flying? Fears such as these—irrational, powerful, highly specific, and disruptive—are known as **specific phobias**. Whereas *fear* is a normal response to realistic danger, *phobia* is an abnormal response to unrealistic perception of danger. Most people have a mild form of phobic response to one thing or another (for me it's rats and heights), but specific phobias severe enough to be diagnosed can sometimes cause serious problems. Phobias are the most common of the anxiety

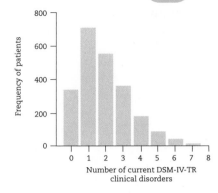

▲ **FIGURE 13.1 Most Psychiatric Patients Have More than One Disorder.** In a study of 2,300 psychiatric outpatients, Mark Zimmerman and his colleagues found that of those who still had a diagnosis of clinical disorder at the time of the study, 63% had at least two diagnoses, and 35% had three or more. Only 37% had a single diagnosis. (*Source: Zimmerman, McGlinchey, Chelminski, & Young, 2008, p. 2002.*)

Comorbidity ▶ The co-occurrence of more than one disorder either simultaneously or at different points in the life span.

Generalized anxiety disorder (GAD) ▶ GAD is characterized by ceaseless, pervasive, and uncontrollable worry and apprehension about the future. Worry in GAD is often irrational, and results in physical symptoms such as muscle tension as well as irritability, sleep difficulty, and difficulty concentrating.

Specific phobia ▶ A powerful but irrational fear of a specific object, animal, or situation. The most common phobias are often those for which evolutionary roots are suspected (e.g., fear of the dark or heights, fear of spiders or snakes, fear of the sight of blood, etc.)

▶ **FIGURE 13.2** Criteria for Diagnosing Generalized Anxiety Disorder (GAD).

Symptoms:
- Excessive, difficult to control anxiety and worry
- One or more of the following symptoms:
  1. Restlessness or feeling on edge
  2. Difficulty concentrating or mind going blank
  3. Irritability
  4. Muscle tension

disorders (Kessler et al., 2005), but they are frequently the least disabling because most of them are narrowly focused on specific objects and situations that generally can be avoided.

As mentioned briefly in Chapter 3, there are certain phobias that are typical in human beings, probably as a result of our human evolutionary history: fear of heights, small spaces, the dark; snakes, spiders, small rodents; and the sight of blood (Darwin, 1877; Nesse, 1990; LoBue & DeLoache, 2008; Öhman, Carlsson, Lundqvist, & Ingvar, 2007). Although these "evolutionary" phobias are the most common, the list of documented phobias is extraordinarily long and varied. Human beings are fabulously creative when it comes to being terrified. Consider: fear of flowers (*anthophobia*), fear of infinity (*apeirophobia*), fear of beautiful women (*caligynophobia*), fear of gravity (*barophobia*), fear of teenagers (*ephibephobia*) . . . the list of potential phobias is exceedingly long—about as long as the list of Greek nouns (Maser, 1985)! Such creatively named conditions may or may not describe actual phobias experienced by real people, as these sorts of phobias generally do not appear in the psychological literature. Still—they are fun to hypothesize.

SOCIAL PHOBIA: A DISORDER OF SHYNESS

Social phobia ▶ Irrational anxiety over social or performance situations where one is likely to be exposed to unfamiliar people and the prospect of embarrassment or humiliation exists. Social phobia is a controversial diagnosis, because social phobia is an extreme expression of the normal characteristic of shyness. Some theorists worry that people who are "painfully shy" are being labeled as "mentally disordered."

Another important type of phobia is **social phobia**, known in the DSM-5 as *social anxiety disorder*. In people with social phobia, the ordinary character trait of shyness reaches extreme dimensions and significantly impairs normal functioning. A person with social phobia is highly anxious about social or performance situations involving exposure to unfamiliar people. The fear of embarrassing or humiliating oneself is overwhelming, and may become so intense that it triggers a *panic attack* (see p. 629).

However, perhaps more than any other anxiety disorder, social phobia demonstrates that borders between ordinary human experience and psychological disorder can be fuzzy. For example, 20 years ago, social phobia was considered a rare condition; but according to current survey statistics, social phobia is the most common of all anxiety disorders, more common even than specific phobias (Craske & Waters, 2005; Ruscio et al., 2008). Are people getting radically shyer with each passing year? People have not changed; definitions of social phobia have changed so that they currently include large numbers of people who in previous years would not have received a diagnosis at all (Horwitz &

◄ **From Shyness to Social Phobia.** Shyness is a normal trait that may be expressed to varying degrees in infant temperament virtually from birth. Although the vast majority of shy infants do not develop social phobia as adults, persistent shyness in childhood does increase the risk of later diagnosis with social phobia (Chavira, Stein, & Malcarne, 2002).

Wakefield, 2012; Wakefield, Horwitz, & Schmitz, 2005). We will discuss this issue in detail later in the chapter.

Panic Disorder: Anxious about Fear

"I just can't go through that again."

—Jonathan

A **panic attack** is one of the most frightening experiences a person can undergo short of an actual catastrophe. The classic type of panic attack is entirely unexpected—it seems to arrive "out of the blue." I say "seems to arrive" because careful inquiry often determines that the attack actually had a specific trigger—for example, being in an anxiety-provoking situation or having recently experienced one (Kessler et al., 2006). Panic attacks may be as brief as a minute or last as long as an hour or even longer, although the average panic attack reaches a peak at about 10 minutes and then subsides.

The experience of a panic attack is one of overwhelming terror. You may feel unable to breathe and experience an intense need to flee. Perspiration may flow as your heart pounds in your ears, your chest tightens, and you feel that you are losing all control. Things often seem unreal during an attack, and sufferers may conclude that they are having a heart attack, dying, or losing their minds.

However, it would be wrong to confuse panic *attacks* with panic *disorder*. Large numbers of people who never develop a psychological disorder have had one or more panic attacks (Craske et al., 2010; Kessler et al., 2006). However, as much as the experience is unpleasant, they do not develop intense anxiety over the prospect of experiencing another one. This is the essence of **panic disorder**: The sufferer feels overwhelmingly *anxious* about the prospect of experiencing the *fear* engendered by a panic attack. Thus, those with panic disorder have had one or (usually more) panic attack and do everything they can to avoid another one (Barlow, 2002b; Craske et al., 2010).

For those who go on to develop panic disorder, a large number also develop **agoraphobia**—a fear of being in public places, crowds, or potentially unsafe situations from which escape would be difficult (e.g., riding in a car). Developing agoraphobia in panic disorder is understandable, because the sufferer feels a pressing need to be in a "safe" location should he or she have a panic attack (Barlow & Craske, 2007). Agoraphobia can become so severe that a person becomes virtually a prisoner in his or her house (although this is not a typical outcome of agoraphobia). Table 13.4 lists places commonly avoided by those with agoraphobia.

Panic attack ▶ A brief period—generally peaking at about 10 minutes—within which a person experiences overwhelming anxiety focused upon unexplainable, terrifying physical sensations. These sensations may include shortness of breath, tightness in the chest, a feeling of unreality, perspiration, pounding of the heart, and an overpowering urge to flee. Panic attacks are not uncommon in the population and do not necessarily signify psychological disorder.

Panic disorder ▶ An anxiety disorder characterized by intense anxiety over the prospect of experiencing a panic attack. Thus, people with panic disorder have experienced at least one such attack. Panic disorder may sometimes lead to *agoraphobia*, a fear of being in public places, crowds, or locations from which escape would be difficult.

Agoraphobia ▶ An anxiety disorder characterized by fear of finding oneself in a potentially unsafe location from which escape would be difficult. This commonly includes crowds, public places, movie theaters, cars, and so forth.

Table 13.4 Places Commonly Avoided by People with Agoraphobia

Driving or riding in cars
Flying
Crowds
Restaurants
Being far from home
Hairdressing salon or barbershop
Wide open spaces
Boats
Auditoriums
Escalators
Traveling by subway, bus, or taxi
Waiting in lines
Stores
Theaters
Being in an unfamiliar area
Taking long walks
Closed-in spaces (e.g., basements)
Being home alone
Elevators
Supermarkets

(Adapted from Barlow & Craske, 2007, pp. 5–6.)

Triple vulnerability theory
▶ An integrated model of anxiety disorders created by David Barlow. According to the triple vulnerability theory, anxiety disorders result from the interaction of three factors: generalized biological vulnerability, generalized psychological vulnerability, and specific psychological vulnerability.

Anxiety Results from Combinations of Causes

Although there are many theories of the origins of specific psychological disorders, there is one theme that unifies most current theories of mental illness—disorders usually result from combinations of causes, including biological, social-environmental, psychological, and life experience factors. Theories of mental illness that take several interacting categories of causes into consideration are known as *integrated* theories or models. The idea that psychological disorders have single causes, such as poor relationships with one's parents or an early traumatic experience, has been largely abandoned, at least by most scientific psychologists.

Take, for example, the **triple vulnerability theory** of anxiety disorders devised by David Barlow (Barlow, 2002a) and depicted in Figure 13.3. According to Barlow's integrated model, anxiety disorders result from the interaction of (a) *generalized biological vulnerability*, or any aspect of a person's genetic inheritance that predisposes him or her to be more sensitive to anxiety-provoking situations; (b) *generalized psychological vulnerability*, or general cognitive characteristics or beliefs that make a person vulnerable to anxiety—for example, believing that the world is an unpredictable and dangerous place over which one has little control; and (c) *specific psychological vulnerability*, highly specific beliefs learned over the course of one's life that are related to the symptoms of a *specific* anxiety disorder.

For example, some children are raised by parents who are highly concerned about how they are perceived by other people, and who may impart alarmist messages about the negative consequences of embarrassing or humiliating oneself in front of others. These children may carry such beliefs with them into adulthood. Consider what might happen if such a child also were to have inherited a generalized biological vulnerability and acquired a generalized psychological vulnerability toward anxiety. Under conditions of stress, the embarrassment/humiliation beliefs the child had adopted become *specific* psychological vulnerabilities. The end result of the interaction of all these vulnerabilities may be the blossoming of social phobia (social anxiety disorder).

Obsessive-Compulsive and Trauma-Related Disorders Are in Categories All Their Own

Prior to the publication of the DSM-5 (American Psychiatric Association, 2013), the major mental disorders known as obsessive-compulsive disorder (OCD) and post-traumatic stress disorder (PTSD) were included in the category of anxiety disorders. This made sense, given that anxiety is prominent in the development and expression of these conditions. However, because certain aspects of these disorders are unique—and because new conditions related to OCD and PTSD were "voted in" to the DSM-5 in 2013—OCD and PTSD now appear in categories distinct from the anxiety disorders: *obsessive-compulsive disorders* and *trauma-related disorders*. Nonetheless, they are likely still thought of as anxiety disorders by most mental health practitioners. For example, treatment for OCD, at least, is generally provided by clinics that specialize in the treatment of anxiety disorders.

Obsessive-Compulsive Disorder Can Dominate a Person's Life

"I'll just get a thought in my head, and I can't put it out. It's just there all the time. I think about it when I go to bed, I think about it when I get up . . ."

—Quoted in Barlow and Durand (2009, p. 160)

Have you ever left the house after turning off the lights and locking the doors, only to turn back once again "just to make sure" you got all the lights and all the locks? You may have chuckled at your "obsessiveness," but for some people, checking "just to make sure" is not a laughing matter. These are sufferers from **obsessive-compulsive disorder (OCD)**, a severe disorder characterized by persistent, intrusive, anxiety-provoking thoughts (*obsessions*), often combined with a strong urge (*compulsion*) to perform repetitive, ritualistic behaviors (e.g., "checking") or mental acts (e.g., mentally repeating words in a certain order) designed to relieve the anxiety provoked by the obsessive thoughts (Grabill et al., 2008; Steketee & Barlow, 2002).

Typically, the obsessions of a person diagnosed with OCD are irrational or even nonsensical. For example, some OCD sufferers feel that unless their hands or body are completely germ-free, mortal danger will result. In dread of contamination, the person may return over and over again to the washroom—sometimes for hours at a time—to wash their hands repeatedly, often specifying the exact number of times each hand or arm must be washed. After a time they may feel satisfied that they are clean, only to have to return again to the washroom within moments of leaving. Occasionally the washing ritual continues for so long that top layers of skin become painfully worn away. Although obsessions and compulsions generally coincide in OCD, some sufferers may experience obsessions without associated compulsions (Torres et al., 2006).

OCD is a very rare disorder, probably occurring in no more than 0.5% to 1% of the population each year (Kessler et al., 2005). However, it is a frequently crippling disorder, often requiring hospitalization and likely to include any number of anxiety or depressive disorders existing alongside the basic OCD symptoms (Torres et al., 2006). Some of the most common obsessions and compulsions of OCD sufferers are listed in Table 13.5.

OCD sufferers usually (but not always) understand at a basic level that their obsessions and compulsions are unreasonable (Catapano et al., 2010). However, understanding the irrationality of their symptoms does not appear to offer relief to those with OCD. They are imprisoned by their obsessions regardless.

Generalized Biological Vulnerability (e.g., high sensitivity to potentially threatening situations, easy triggering of "false alarms")

Generalized Psychological Vulnerability (e.g., beliefs that the world is a dangerous place, beliefs that one has little control over events)

Specific Psychological Vulnerability (Learned beliefs that one must never embarrass oneself in front of others.)

STRESS

SOCIAL ANXIETY DISORDER

▲ **FIGURE 13.3 Barlow's Triple Vulnerability Theory of Anxiety Applied to Social Phobia.** David Barlow's theory of the origin of anxiety disorders is an *integrated* model. It assumes that most anxiety disorders result from the interaction of generalized biological vulnerability (inherited), generalized psychological vulnerability (developed over time), and specific psychological vulnerability (learned).

Obsessive-compulsive disorder (OCD) ▶ A severe anxiety disorder characterized by persistent, intrusive, anxiety-provoking thoughts usually combined with strong but irrational urges to perform repetitive, ritualistic behaviors or mental acts designed to relieve the anxiety provoked by the intrusive thoughts.

Table 13.5 Common Obsessions and Compulsions of Sufferers from Obsessive-Compulsive Disorder (OCD)

According to Naureen Attiullah and her colleagues (2000), the obsessions of OCD sufferers often fall into one of the following categories.

OBSESSION CATEGORY	DESCRIPTION	RELATED COMPULSIONS
Contamination obsessions (the most common type)	Intense fear of dirt, germs, bodily wastes, or environmental hazards	Repetitive hand washing or house cleaning
Doubt obsessions	Anxiety that one will be responsible for a catastrophic event as a result of carelessness	"Checking" rituals—e.g., returning home again and again and again to make sure the doors are locked, windows closed, gas turned off, etc.
Symmetry obsessions	Feelings of extreme unease if things are not arranged "just so"	Repeating the arranging and rearranging of objects on a desk, clothes in closet, etc. until things are "perfect." May need to walk through arches (e.g., doorways) through the exact center or move in other sorts of symmetrical patterns

▶ **Hoarding Disorder—An Addition to DSM-5 Obsessive-Compulsive Disorders** Some people develop an intense preoccupation with hoarding objects—fearful that if they throw anything away, they may someday urgently need it. Objects hoarded may include those with no conceivable use, such as the case of one woman who included among her store of objects a 20-year collection of used sanitary napkins (Barlow & Durand, 2009). Hoarding disorder was recently voted into the DSM-5 as a recognized disorder in its own right.

Post-traumatic stress disorder (PTSD) ▶ A disorder triggered by an experience of extremely severe trauma which evokes horror, feelings of helpless, and fear for one's life or the lives of those for whom one cares. Symptoms may include re-experiencing the traumatic event in nightmares, flashbacks, or intrusive thoughts, negative changes in mood or cognition, and symptoms of physiological arousal and reactivity.

Resilience ▶ The ability to emerge relatively intact from unexpected adverse events or to recover fully from any temporary symptoms. Resilience is the most common human response to trauma.

Risk factor ▶ Any variable whose presence increases the probability that a person will be diagnosed with a particular disorder. Because risk factors are only correlated with a disorder, they cannot be said to be causes of the disorder. They simply help researchers predict who is more or less likely ultimately to develop a disorder.

Post-Traumatic Stress Disorder: A Rare Response to Trauma

"Basra is always with me. I never really made it all the way home."

—U. S. soldier, later diagnosed with post-traumatic
stress disorder following deployment in Iraq

Traumatic exposure to death, threats of death, or sexual violation may result in **post-traumatic stress disorder** (PTSD) in certain people. The traumatic trigger for PTSD may be experienced oneself or it may be witnessed as it occurs to another person. PTSD is a generally chronic disorder characterized by four basic symptoms:

- *Re-experiencing the traumatic event* in nightmares, daytime "flashbacks," or intrusive thoughts.
- *Negative changes in mood and cognition* that may include difficulty experiencing a full range of emotional responses, detachment from other people, loss of interest in activities, and problems recalling aspects of the traumatic event.
- *Changes in physiological arousal levels and reactivity* that may result in sleep problems, exaggerated startle response, bursts of anger or irritability, and reckless or self-destructive behavior.

Trauma and stressor-related disorders such as PTSD are virtually unique in the DSM in that their cause may be specified with certainty—a traumatic event. However, research has shown that in the United States, at least 60% of men and 50% of women may have been exposed to severely traumatic events, yet only a small minority of these—approximately 1.3% in any given year—develop serious symptoms of PTSD, while an additional 2.2% develop mild to moderate symptoms (Kessler et al., 2005; see also Perkonigg, Kessler, Storz, & Wittchen, 2000 for European statistics).

In fact, as briefly mentioned in Chapter 11, the most common reaction of adults exposed to potentially traumatizing events is **resilience**—the ability to emerge relatively intact from unexpected adverse events, or to recover in relatively short order from any temporary symptoms experienced (Bonanno, Brewin, Kaniasty, & La Greca, 2010; Bonanno, Westphal, & Mancini, 2011; Shalev, 2002). In a study of a randomly selected group of 2,752 New Yorkers in the 6 months following the September 11th attack, 65% had no signs of trauma, or at most one sign, and only 6% qualified for a diagnosis of chronic PTSD (Bonanno, Galea, Bucciarelli, & Vlahov, 2006). In a separate study of

28,692 New Yorkers who had been actively involved in the rescue and recovery effort at the World Trade Center, only 12.4% qualified for a PTSD diagnosis 2 to 3 years after the disaster (Perrin et al., 2007). Similar results were found in a separate study of 10,132 individuals who participated in the rescue, recovery, or clean-up at the World Trade Center (Stellman et al., 2008). Clearly, human beings have evolved to be able to be resilient in the face of trauma, which has seemingly been a pervasive part of human history. Moreover, even serious PTSD symptoms, such as those experienced by an unfortunate number of soldiers recently returned from the Iraq and Afghanistan wars, can be treated successfully if treatment is initiated early on and is focused specifically on trauma issues (Burki, 2010).

RISK FACTORS FOR PTSD

Why, then, do some people develop PTSD symptoms, but not others? Although this question cannot be answered with certainty, a number of **risk factors** for PTSD have been identified in research. A risk factor is any factor whose presence increases the probability that a person will be diagnosed with a particular disorder. However, because a risk factor is only *correlated* with a diagnosis, it cannot be said necessarily to be a *cause* of the disorder. Risk factors may indeed be part of the cause of a disorder, or they may be completely unrelated to the disorder—instead, related to a third variable that causes both the risk factor *and* the disorder simultaneously.

As an example, drinking is a traditional risk factor for lung cancer, but only because people who drink tend to smoke more than others and are more likely than nondrinkers to hang out in smoky bars and clubs (in the days when smoking was routinely permitted in bars and clubs!). In this case, smoking is responsible both for lung cancer and for the relationship of alcohol to lung cancer.

Table 13.6 lists risk factors for developing PTSD following a potentially traumatic event and factors predicting resilience. Resilience factors are those which push a potentially traumatic event in the direction of positive outcome; risk factors are those which predict trauma and disorder (Hoge, Austin, & Pollack, 2007).

▲ **Psychological Disorders after Hurricane Katrina.** The worst natural disaster in the United States in 75 years, Hurricane Katrina was associated with nearly 2,000 deaths. At least 500,000 other people were displaced or made homeless. When natural disasters result in continuing, ongoing stress, rates of symptoms of psychological disorder are greatly increased. Five to 7 months after the disaster, 16% of New Orleans residents sampled showed at least some signs of PTSD (Galea et al., 2007).

Table 13.6 **Trauma and Resilience following Potentially Traumatic Events**

RISK FACTORS	PREDICTORS OF RESILIENCE
Being female (women experience PTSD twice as often after similar potentially traumatic experience)	Being male
Rumination following trauma	Optimistic, accepting attitude, positive emotions
Trauma occurs in childhood	Being middle-aged or elderly
Lower levels of education and cognitive ability	Higher levels of education and cognitive ability
Low income/poverty	Income well above poverty
Lack of perceived social support	Perception of social and family support
History of family psychological disorder	No family history of psychological disorder
Presence of another psychological disorder (comorbidity)	No comorbid disorder, no substance abuse
Genetic vulnerabilities	Genetic protective factors
More severe trauma and subsequent stress or trauma	Sense of preparedness and control when meeting potentially traumatic event
Previous exposure to trauma or extreme stress	No previous exposure to trauma or extreme stress

(Sources: Bonanno et al., 2007; Bonanno, Westphal, & Mancini, 2011; Breslau, 2002; Etkin & Wager, 2007; Galea et al., 2007; Hoge, Austin, & Pollack, 2007; Perkonigg et al., 2000; McNally & Shin, 1995.)

LIVING PSYCHOLOGY

Beware of Psychology Students' Disease!

There is an oft-repeated saying: "A little knowledge is a dangerous thing." Medical students are famous for demonstrating the wisdom of this cliché by diagnosing themselves with all manner of horrid illnesses they have recently learned about, a tendency that is so common it has been given a clinical label: *medical students' disease* (Moss-Morris & Petrie, 2001).

Although I've been unable to locate any mention in the literature of a similar disease common to psychology students, I've seen it often enough to be able to claim at least anecdotal evidence for its existence. In fact, I saw it in my daughter Naima at age 9 as she was reading over my shoulder as I wrote about obsessive-compulsive disorder. "I think I have a mild form of that," she informed me. I asked why, and she answered, "Because I feel kind of uncomfortable if my shelf isn't organized neatly, and at night I sometimes get up to make sure the hamsters' cage door is really closed."

As you learn about psychological disorders it is important to bear in mind that most of them are expressions of ordinary human traits, but carried to extremes. Using obsessive-compulsive disorder as an example, Table 13.7 lists a number of occasional obsessions and intrusive thoughts reported by ordinary people with no diagnosis of psychological disorder.

If you have obsessive or intrusive thoughts of this kind, it may result from stress or may simply be a quirk of your personality or behavior with no particular explanation. In any case, given the rarity of obsessive-compulsive disorder, you should always assume that the disorder is *not* present unless pressing evidence suggests that it is (see discussion of base rates in Chapter 9). ∎

Table 13.7 Obsessions and Intrusive Thoughts Reported by Nonclinical Samples

Harming	Contamination or Disease
Impulse to jump out of high window	Thought of catching a disease from public pools or other public places
Idea of jumping in front of a car	
Impulse to push someone in front of train	Thoughts I may have caught a disease from touching toilet seat
Wishing a person would die	
While holding a baby, having a sudden urge to kick it	Idea that dirt is always on my hand
Thoughts of dropping a baby	
The thought that if I forget to say goodbye to someone, they might die	
Thought that thinking about horrible things happening to a child will cause it	
Inappropriate or Unacceptable Behavior	**Doubts About Safety, Memory, and So On**
Idea of swearing or yelling at my boss	Thought that I haven't locked the house up properly
Thought of doing something embarrassing in public, like forgetting to wear a top	Idea of leaving my curling iron on the carpet and forgetting to pull out the plug
Hoping someone doesn't succeed	Thought that I've left the heater and stove on
Thought of blurting out something in church	Idea that I've left the car unlocked when I know I've locked it
Thought of "unnatural" sexual acts	Idea that objects are not arranged perfectly

(*Source: Barlow & Durand, 2009, p. 162.*)

IN SUMMARY

1. The anxiety disorders discussed in the chapter include generalized anxiety disorder, specific phobia and social phobia, panic disorder. Obsessive-compulsive disorder (OCD) and post-traumatic stress disorder (PTSD) have traditionally been considered anxiety disorders, but the DSM now lists them in separate categories.

2. Many of the symptoms of anxiety disorders are common in somewhat milder form in people with no psychological disorder.

3. Theories of the causes of mental illness that take several interacting categories of causes into consideration—biology, society, behavior, and experience—are known as integrated theories or models. Barlow's triple vulnerability theory of anxiety disorders is one such integrated model.

RETRIEVE!

1. Anxiety is _____-oriented, whereas fear is _____-oriented.

2. List at least three common specific phobias. Why are these phobias so common?

3. A person who is afraid to be in public places, crowds, or potentially unsafe situations is suffering from _____. This condition often is associated with what other anxiety disorder?

4. What are the four primary symptoms of PTSD? List at least three risk factors for the disorder. List at least three factors predicting resilience.

5. Which of the following is NOT a common obsessive theme of obsessive-compulsive disorder (OCD)?

a) doubts about safety or memory

b) fear of making an irreversible mistake

c) contamination or disease

d) harming

6. Which of the following is NOT one of the "triple vulnerabilities" of the triple vulnerability model?

a) generalized biological vulnerability

b) specific biological vulnerability

c) generalized psychological vulnerability

d) specific psychological vulnerability

What Are Depressive and Bipolar Disorders?

"When I got into bed last night, the thought suddenly occurred to me that I did not deserve to sleep next to you. I didn't even deserve to sleep in our bed. I thought, I ought to go and sleep at the foot of the children's bed, like a dog. When I woke up this morning and was feeding the kids their breakfast, I thought, I don't even deserve to eat."

—From a note left to his wife by a patient suffering from major depressive disorder

Depression ▶ A mood state characterized by sadness, low energy, fatigue, regret or guilt, feelings of low self-worth, hopelessness, and helplessness.

Mania ▶ A highly energized mood state characterized by exaggerated feelings of elation, unrealistically high self-esteem, racing thoughts, reduced need for sleep, and ceaseless energy. Mania may sometimes by dysphoric—characterized by anger, agitation, and irritability rather than elation.

Mood is the quality of subjective emotional feeling that one is experiencing at any given time. Like emotions, moods can function properly, or they can dysfunction—sometimes causing extremely severe problems in living. There are two primary directions that mood can take when it is no longer functioning properly. The first is **depression**, a state characterized by exaggerated and prolonged feelings of sadness, hopelessness, grief, guilt, and low feelings of self-worth. The flip side is **mania**, characterized by ceaseless energy, exaggerated feelings of elation, unrealistically high self-esteem, and racing thoughts; or, alternately, by highly "energized" negative states including anger, anxiety, or extreme irritability. If a person is depressed but has never experienced mania, a *depressive disorder* may be diagnosed. A *bipolar disorder* diagnosis is reserved for those who have experienced both depression and mania. In this portion of the chapter I will describe the most characteristic forms of depressive and bipolar disorders.

Major Depressive Disorder: The Most Severe Form of Depression

Virtually every one of us has "felt depressed" at some time. For most people, these painful feelings are not extraordinarily intense, and they pass relatively quickly. However, normal sadness or depressed mood is to clinical depression as a street-corner game of one-on-one is to an NBA championship. Just as cigarette smoking negatively affects virtually all bodily organs, major depression affects all aspects of a person's life: mood, thoughts, bodily sensations and symptoms, and behavior.

Consider the note reprinted at the start of this section of the chapter. The author of the note, whose name is Rafael, had been suffering from *major depressive disorder* for over 8 months when he wrote it. By that time, his feelings of guilt, worthlessness, grief, and hopelessness were so entrenched that he could not see the absurdity of his statements. They were honest descriptions of his thoughts and emotions. Rafael's symptoms were manifested physically as well as emotionally. He had lost 9 pounds and had trouble sleeping more than a few hours per night, usually waking long before the sun had risen. A professional musician, he had lost interest in playing his instrument and could no longer work. Five months into the depression he had tried to stab himself to death and had been saved only by emergency surgery.

Major depressive disorder (major depression) is the most severe form of depression, and, with the exception of the phobias, is the most commonly diagnosed of all psychological disorders (Kessler, Chiu, Demler, & Walters, 2005),). However, of the 13 to 14 million Americans (approximately 6.7%) who qualify for a DSM diagnosis of major depression in any given year, approximately two-thirds experience only mild to moderate symptoms (Kessler et al., 2003; Kessler, Merikangas, & Wang, 2007).

As with anxiety disorders, many more women than men are diagnosed with major depression and, as depicted in Figure 13.4, increasing numbers of people seem to be experiencing depression over their lifetimes. A person born during the years 1925–1945 is much less likely to report ever having had symptoms of clinical depression than someone born during the years 1945–1965; and that person in turn is much less likely to report having ever had depressive symptoms than a person born during the years 1965–1985. Does this mean that depression really is becoming more common? Not necessarily. Older people may hold values that constrain them from acknowledging symptoms of depression, they may interpret symptoms differently, or they may be less likely to recall symptoms that may have occurred decades in the past (Giuffra & Risch, 1994; Kessler et al., 2003). Moveover, criteria for diagnosing depression may inadvertently include people responding in a normal fashion to abnormally stressful events (Horwitz & Wakefield, 2007). The question of increasing rates of depression is discussed in greater detail on pp. 650–651. Table 13.8 lists symptoms of major depression based upon the DSM-5 diagnostic criteria.

Major depression can have serious consequences. Depressive disorders are the leading cause of disability in the United States and among the leading causes of disability in every continent of the world other than Africa (where HIV/AIDS is the leading cause) (Üstün, Ayuso-Mateos, Chatterji, Mathers, & Murray, 2004). Although often considered only to affect mental health, depression has serious effects on physical health and is associated with numerous medical conditions. Indeed, as Figure 13.5 shows, depression is associated with a reduction in overall health to a greater extent than asthma, angina (a nonfatal heart condition), arthritis, and diabetes. When depression co-occurs with any of these conditions, the result is even more profound (Moussavi et al., 2007).

Although depression and anxiety are not the same, they do co-occur extremely frequently. However, while only approximately 50% of those with an anxiety disorder also suffer from depression, almost all patients with depression suffer from symptoms of anxiety—and the majority could likely be diagnosed with a DSM anxiety disorder (T. A. Brown et al., 2001). The frequent comorbidity of anxiety and depression shouldn't be surprising, because they share many (but not all) of the same symptoms. Table 13.9 lists symptoms of anxiety shared in depression.

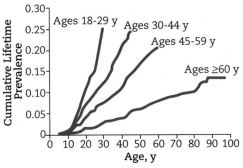

▲ **FIGURE 13.4 Is Depression Becoming More Common?** Researchers disagree as to whether the trend for younger cohorts to experience higher rates of depression is real or a result of differences between the young and old in memory for depressive episodes, willingness to report them, interpretation of symptoms, or changes in diagnostic criteria. (*Source: Kessler et al., 2003, p. 3099.*)

Table 13.8 **Symptoms of Major Depressive Disorder (based upon DSM-5 diagnostic criteria)**

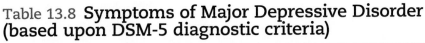

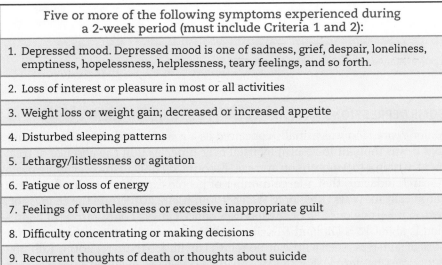

Five or more of the following symptoms experienced during a 2-week period (must include Criteria 1 and 2):
1. Depressed mood. Depressed mood is one of sadness, grief, despair, loneliness, emptiness, hopelessness, helplessness, teary feelings, and so forth.
2. Loss of interest or pleasure in most or all activities
3. Weight loss or weight gain; decreased or increased appetite
4. Disturbed sleeping patterns
5. Lethargy/listlessness or agitation
6. Fatigue or loss of energy
7. Feelings of worthlessness or excessive inappropriate guilt
8. Difficulty concentrating or making decisions
9. Recurrent thoughts of death or thoughts about suicide

▶ **FIGURE 13.5** Depression versus Other Serious Health Conditions. *(Source: Moussavi et al., 2007, p. 854.)*

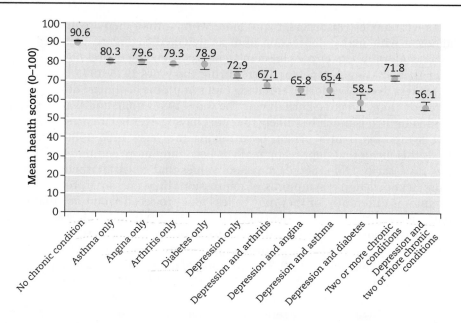

Table 13.9 **Symptoms of Anxiety and Depression: Distinct and Shared**

PURE ANXIETY	PURE DEPRESSION	SHARED IN ANXIETY AND DEPRESSION
Apprehension	Diminished interest in sex	Pessimism (expecting the worst)
Tension	Hopelessness	Worry
Trembling	Depressed mood	Poor concentration
Worry	Lack of pleasure	Irritability
Edginess	Loss of interest	Sleep problems
Nightmares	Thoughts of suicide	Crying
		Guilt
		Fatigue
		Poor memory
		Feelings of worthlessness
		Helplessness

(Source: Adapted from Zinbarg et al., 1994.)

SOME DEPRESSIONS ARE PARTICULARLY DIFFICULT TO TREAT

Major depression was initially conceived as a *time-limited* condition, meaning that it was thought to resolve by itself over time, even in the absence of treatment, within 4 to 9 months on average (Eaton et al., 1997). However, more recent research indicates that a large number of people experience major depression chronically for years (Kessler & Wang, 2009; Klein, 2010), and the chances of a person relapsing once he or she has experienced at least one episode of depression is about 75% (Boland & Keller, 2009). Even with treatment, as many as 50% of sufferers receive little or no relief (Huynh & McIntyre, 2008; Rubinow, 2006; see Chapter 14). For this reason, the DSM-5 has included a new category, *persistent depression*, to describe depression that is chronic. From a "big picture" perspective, then, major depression more often than not is a chronic condition whose symptoms may come and go over the years but do not permanently disappear (Kessler et al., 2003, 2007). The severity of symptoms also tends to worsen over time—that is, each episode may sensitize the individual to further, more severe subsequent episodes (Post, 1992).

How Depression Arises

As with most psychological disorders, causes of depression are not known with certainty. However, it is clear that depression is a destination to which many roads may lead (Cicchetti & Rogosch, 1996; Lau & Eley, 2010). Over the years researchers have mapped these roads to the best of their ability. As with anxiety disorders, most current models of how depression arises are *integrated*, encompassing biological, psychological, and social factors.

GENETIC VULNERABILITY AND STRESS

Depression runs in families, and studies in behavior genetics have determined that a large part of the story of depression is genetic vulnerability (Holmans 2007; Lau & Eley, 2010; Plomin & McGuffin, 2003; see Figure 13.6). Although there is no gene or set of genes that *cause* a person to suffer depression, genetic inheritance can *predispose* a person to become depressed *if* other conditions are also present (Caspi et al., 2003; Cervilla et al., 2007; Kendler, Hettema, Butera, Gardner, & Prescott, 2003). The idea that a genetic predisposition toward an illness can become activated under certain conditions, but not activated in the absence of these conditions, is known as the **diathesis stress model** (Monroe & Simons, 1991).

What are the conditions or experiences that can trigger depression in genetically vulnerable individuals? If you recall from Chapter 11, experiences of stress are strongly linked to the onset of depression, and certain types of stressors may be more likely than others to trigger depression. These tend to be experiences involving loss of important relationships, loss of status, and humiliation (Horwitz & Wakefield, 2007; Kendler et al., 2003). Romantic rejection often involves both loss of a relationship *and* humiliation, and this may be why depression frequently follows divorces and romantic breakups.

Recently, genetic research in depression has become more sophisticated as researchers have begun to focus on the interplay of genetics and environments (Lau & Eley, 2010). Specifically, researchers are asking two relatively new questions:

1. If depression results from a genetic vulnerability combined with certain life experiences or environments, why do certain people—but not others—tend to have these environmental experiences?

2. Why do certain people have these experiences but never become depressed?

The second question—why do certain people have negative or stressful experiences but never become depressed—refers to gene-environment interactions, as described in Chapter 3. Some research has implicated a region along the 5-HTT gene known as 5-HTTLPR in the relationship between stress and depression—that is, as an explanation for why stress triggers depression in some people but not others (Caspi et al., 2003; Wankurl, Wüst, & Otte, 2010). The 5-HTT gene comes in two forms or *alleles*: a short allele and a long allele. If the research turns out to be correct—and it has been challenged frequently—those people who inherit the short version will be more likely to respond to stress by becoming depressed.

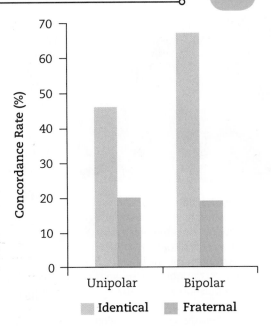

▲ **FIGURE 13.6 Heritability of Depressive and Bipolar Disorders.** If one identical (monozygotic) twin has been diagnosed with major depression, there is a 46% chance that the other twin, who shares 100% of genes in common with the first, will also be diagnosed (a rate known as *concordance*). For fraternal (dizygotic) twins, who share only 50% of genes in common, the concordance rate is only 20%. Heritability of bipolar disorders is even stronger. The concordance rate for identical twins is approximately 67%, while the rate for fraternal twins is only 19% (Gottesman, 1991). *(Source: Barlow & Durand, 2009, p. 481).*

Diathesis stress model ▶ A model of psychological disorder which proposes that mental illness is most likely to be found in a person who has both genetic vulnerability to the condition *and* exposure to life experiences which contribute to the onset of the illness.

▲ **Chemical Imbalance?** Drinking alcohol may help reduce social anxiety, but does this mean that social anxiety disorder is caused by a lack of alcohol in the blood? There is a flaw in the logic of assuming that depression is caused by an imbalance in neurotransmitters simply because drugs which alter neurotransmitter balances sometimes reduce depression (Moncrieff & Cohen, 2006).

The first question—Why do certain people tend to have the type of negative or stressful experiences that trigger depression?—refers to gene-environment correlation, also discussed in Chapter 3 (Kendler & Baker, 2007). Gene-environment correlations describe ways that a person's genetic makeup can help create his or her environment. For example, a person with a genetic predisposition to engage in stormy relationships—a predisposition often shared by the person's parents and siblings—may grow up in a stormy household and then be exposed to stormy relationships in adulthood. Stormy relationships are stressful, and therefore, the person's genetic makeup has helped to create a stressful environment.

IS DEPRESSION DUE TO A "CHEMICAL IMBALANCE"?

You may have heard that depression is due to a "chemical imbalance in the brain," referring in particular to low levels of the neurotransmitter serotonin. However, the idea that depression is caused by a neurotransmitter "imbalance" is at best greatly oversimplified and misleading (France, Lysaker, & Robinson, 2007; Hindmarch, 2001; Lacasse & Leo, 2005).

The first problem is that, while some depressed people do show unusual neurotransmitter balances, others (probably the majority) do not (France et al., 2007; Valenstein, 1998). Furthermore, when balances are unusual they are sometimes found in a direction opposite to the expected one—for example, more rather than less availability of the neurotransmitter (Barton et al., 2008).

More to the point, when healthy volunteers have their levels of serotonin or norepinephrine intentionally lowered in research studies (for example, through dietary restrictions or by other means), they do not become depressed. Similarly, when drugs which boost the availability of these neurotransmitters are administered to depressed patients, the drugs frequently do not work—or if they do, it often takes many weeks or even months for any therapeutic effect to be felt. In other words, alterations of neurotransmitter levels in themselves do not alter mood (Booij et al., 2002; Delgado, 2000; Hindmarch, 2001).

Interestingly, the strongest evidence in favor of the "chemical imbalance" theory is simultaneously the weakest. It has been assumed that neurotransmitter imbalances cause depression because antidepressant drugs alter neurotransmitter levels and sometimes also reduce symptoms of depression. However, just because drugs that increase levels of a neurotransmitter (sometimes) reduce symptoms of depression does not necessarily mean that depression is due to low levels of that neurotransmitter. Aspirin reduces symptoms of headache, but headache is not caused by low levels of aspirin in the blood. Plaster casts reduce symptoms of broken bones (indeed, they "cure" broken bones), but a broken foot is not caused by the absence of a plaster cast around the foot (Leo & Lacasse, 2008; France et al., 2007).

If the chemical imbalance theory is not accepted among scientists as the explanation for depression, why is it repeated so often in so many places? One likely reason is that pharmaceutical companies use the theory in their advertising because they (correctly) believe that people will assume that if a condition is caused by a "chemical imbalance," the best way to correct the condition is to use drugs that alter the balance of these chemicals (Barclay, 2005; Grow, Park, & Han, 2006; Leo & Lacasse, 2008). The chemical imbalance theory is also favored by mental health advocacy organizations (which, interestingly, are funded in large part by the pharmaceutical industry; Marshall & Aldhous, 2006). These organizations like the theory because they believe that it will help the public accept psychological disorders as legitimate illnesses and reduce the stigma of mental illness. Similarly, doctors often use it with depressed patients because they believe it will help them to accept that they have an illness (Deacon & Baird, 2009).

Yet it is important to maintain an attitude of skepticism toward claims that are not well supported—even if one believes that the claim may have a beneficial effect. Although there is little doubt that some sort of link exists between depression and serotonin as well as other neurotransmitters—for example, the 5-HTT gene implicated in the stress/depression link is a serotonin transporter gene—the specific nature of the relationship between depression and neurotransmitters is still far from clear and likely quite subtle in nature (Mukherjee, 2012). A simple neurotransmitter "imbalance" or deficiency cannot be said to lie at the heart of depression (Barton et al., 2008).

COGNITIVE VULNERABILITIES

The onset of depression has also been linked to *cognition*—how we think about ourselves, our lives, and our world (Gotlib & Joorman, 2010). Cognitive psychologists have shown that depressed people exhibit cognitive biases in virtually all aspects of cognition—memory, perception, attention, and interpretation of events. In other words, our own habitual patterns of thinking, processing information, and responding to various events in our lives can be important stressors in themselves. Two major theories have greatly expanded our understanding of these cognitive underpinnings of depression: Lyn Abramson and Lauren Alloy's *hopelessness theory* (Abramson, Alloy, & Metalsky, 1995) and Aaron Beck's theory of the *negative cognitive triad* (Beck, Rush, Shaw, & Emery, 1987).

Hopelessness Theory During the 1960s, psychologist Martin Seligman found that if rodents and dogs were given unpleasant but not dangerous electric shocks, they were able to continue to function as long as they were taught a way to escape from the shocks. Under these conditions, they continued to work to avoid the shocks, and continued to behave relatively normally. However, if these animals were given no way to avoid the shocks, they began to behave in a helpless manner and endured the shocks and did not even attempt to take advantage of avenues of escape that were subsequently offered. They had "given up" in a way that reminded Seligman and his colleagues of human depression. Seligman termed this response **learned helplessness** (Seligman, 1975). Seligman proposed that if human beings come to believe, for whatever reason, that they have no control over the negative events of their lives, they may experience learned helplessness and suffer depression.

Later, Lyn Abramson and Lauren Alloy refined Seligman's ideas to focus on the factor of *hopelessness* rather than helplessness (Abramson et al., 1995). According to this "revised" theory, generally known as **hopelessness theory**, learned helplessness is not enough to explain depression, because a sense of helplessness is equally present in anxiety. According to Abramson and Alloy, the factor that causes helplessness to lead to depression rather than anxiety is *hopelessness*—the idea that things can never get better.

How does hopelessness arise? Abramson and Alloy identified a negative cognitive style which creates vulnerability to the hopelessness of depression (Alloy et al., 2006). This cognitive style is similar to that described in the discussion of pessimism in Chapter 11. According to Abramson and Alloy, the cognitive style most likely to lead to depression has three characteristics:

- Negative events are attributed to *internal* causes and personal failings ("It's all my fault—I'm just stupid.").
- Causes of negative events are thought to be *stable* and *global*—that is, they are likely to endure, be repeated in the future, and apply not only to the matter at hand but to a great many other types of situations ("I'll probably fail the next test too. I guess I'm just not cut out for academic work.").
- Severe *negative consequences* are anticipated to follow from negative events ("I'll probably get kicked out of school altogether.").

The Negative Cognitive Triad These ideas are highly compatible, if not overlapping, with Aaron Beck's view of depression as resulting from a

Learned helplessness ▶ Martin Seligman's term to describe the passivity and resignation which an animal may experience after coming to believe that it is unable to control or halt an aversive event. Learned helplessness then interferes with the animal's ability to recognize when it is in fact able to halt or control the event. Seligman originally theorized that learned helpless lies at the root of depressive disorders.

Hopelessness theory ▶ A revision of learned helplessness theory created by Lyn Abramson and Lauren Alloy. Hopelessness theory proposes that a negative cognitive style leads to depression. This negative cognitive style includes three aspects: (a) attributing negative events to internal causes; (b) considering causes of negative events to be stable and global; and (c) anticipating severe negative consequences from negative events.

▶ **FIGURE 13.7** The Negative Cognitive Triad. According to cognitive therapy founder Aaron Beck, depression results from habitual patterns of irrational, erroneous negative thoughts about the self, the world, and the future (Beck et al., 1987).

The Self ("I'm just a loser")

The World ("It's dog eat dog everywhere I go")

Irrational Negative Beliefs ("Cognitive errors")

The Future ("Things are just going to get worse")

Negative cognitive triad ▶
Aaron Beck's term to describe a set of irrational, chronic, and erroneous beliefs about the self, the world, and the future.

negative cognitive triad depicted in Figure 13.7 (Beck et al., 1987). According to Beck, depression can result from irrational cognitive "errors"—chronic patterns of thinking that create vulnerability to depression and revolve around three aspects of existence (hence the term "triad"). The negative cognitive triad includes irrational beliefs about:

- *The self.* Erroneous beliefs about the self include feelings that one is worthless, a failure, a bad or evil person.
- *The world.* Erroneous beliefs about the world include ideas that the world is uniformly a joyless, cold, uncontrollable, and unforgiving place.
- *The future.* Erroneous beliefs about the future focus on predictions of hopelessness and doom.

According to Beck's cognitive model, thoughts such as these may actually precipitate the neurohormonal and other biological events that ultimately lead to major depression.

Negative cognitive style not only makes one vulnerable to depression, it also increases the chances of experiencing stressful and depressing events in much the same way that genetic makeup can help shape the environment in gene-environment correlations (Hammen, 1991; Safford, Alloy, Abramson, & Crossfield, 2007). Consider a very simple example—the stress of romantic disappointments. If "misery loves company but company does not love misery," a person who holds the kinds of beliefs described in the negative cognitive triad and hopelessness models is unlikely to have much success as a romantic partner. Even people who are very loving, compassionate, and supportive tend to grow tired of continual hopelessness and negativity in their interactions with their partner.

Women Have Much Higher Rates of Depression

One finding in the field of abnormal psychology that is as monotonous as it is puzzling is that rates of depression in women are almost always substantially higher than those for men. As depicted in Figure 13.8, around the world and throughout the life span, beginning in mid-adolescence, women are on average twice as likely as men to suffer from depression (Hyde, Mezulis, & Abramson, 2008). What is responsible for this lopsided ratio? Undoubtedly, the answer to this question involves a complex interaction of biological, emotional, and cognitive variables, as well as factors related to personal

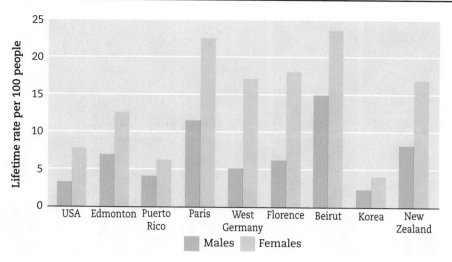

▲ **FIGURE 13.8** Sex Differences in Lifetime Rates of Depression. *(Source: Barlow & Durand, 2009, p. 236.)*

▲ **Is the Postmodern World Causing Depression?** Evolutionary theorists propose that rates of depression are rising because we are consistently exposed through the mass media to images of the "best and brightest"—individuals with whom we cannot hope to compete. This occurs in the context of an increasingly "anonymous" world, where traditional family and community ties are breaking down. These ties once served as buffers against the daily stress of competition and failure (Nesse & Williams, 1994).

experiences more common in the lives of girls and women than boys and men (Hyde et al., 2008).

However, some researchers suggest that cognitive factors may play a particularly strong role. For example, there is evidence that women are more susceptible than men to the kinds of negative cognitive styles described on pp. 641–642, and these negative cognitions—which result in feelings of hopelessness—may have a greater impact on depression in women than in men (Hankin & Abramson, 2002; Hyde et al., 2008). But negative cognitive styles resulting in hopelessness are not the only cognitive factor implicated in sex differences in depression. Susan Nolen-Hoeksema identified a related but separate problem known as *rumination*. **Rumination** is the tendency to focus inwardly and brood on the possible causes and consequences of negative emotions and events (Nolen-Hoeksema, Wisco, & Lyubomirsky, 2008; Nolen-Hoeksema, 2012). When feeling sad or otherwise distressed, many people believe that it is a good idea to "mull things over" so they may understand why they feel as they do and find solutions to their problems. However, research supports Nolen-Hoeksema's view that this sort of repetitive rumination over problems is counterproductive, as it perpetuates negative feelings rather than resolving them (Lyubomirsky & Tkach, 2003). Women tend to ruminate over past and future events and negative emotional states, whereas men are more likely to take actions to try to solve problems or try to forget them, for example, by drinking (Lewinsohn, Gotlib, Lewinsohn, Seeley, & Allen, 1998). Research shows that rumination may lead to the onset of depression—and if rumination is combined with negative cognitive style, it predicts a depression of longer duration (Nolen-Hoeksema et al., 2008).

Rumination ▶ Focusing inwardly and brooding on the possible causes and consequences of past or future negative emotions and events.

Bipolar Disorders Are a Spectrum, Not a Single Disorder

According to *Webster's Third New International Dictionary, exuberance* is the quality of "feeling joyously unrestrained and enthusiastic; excessively high-spirited, uninhibited, and full of life." Sound good? For the vast majority of the population it is. But for the 2% of the population diagnosed with bipolar disorders—such as my friend Anu, whose circumstances were described at the opening of this chapter—it can signal the disastrous onset of mania (Merikangas et al., 2007).

The traditional view of bipolar disorder (also known as *manic depressive illness*) is of a condition characterized by cycles of depression and mania that alternate over time, usually separated by several months. The manic phase

▲ **Is Depression a Female Problem?** Beginning in adolescence, women's rates of depression are about twice those of men. Beginning in adolescence women also encounter more stressful events, respond more negatively to these events, and are more likely to suffer from negative styles of cognition that increase the risk of depression.

▲ **FIGURE 13.9 Bipolar Disorders and Creativity.** Many scientists, writers, artists, musicians, actors, and performers are either known or strongly suspected to have had bipolar disorders. The association between bipolar disorders and creativity is well established, and some researchers hypothesize that similar constellations of genes predispose a person either toward creative work, bipolar disorders, or both—depending on life experience factors (Jamison, 1996a). Pictured here are (top row) Kurt Cobain, Sir Isaac Newton, Florence Nightingale, Mark Twain, Virginia Woolf; (bottom row) Thelonious Monk, Kurt Vonnegut, Winston Churchill, Nina Simone, and Jean-Claude Van Damme.

Hypomania ▶ A less extreme form of mania characterized by reduced need for sleep, increased sexuality and humor, feelings of mental clarity, enjoyment of life, self-esteem, charm, grandiosity, and increased ability to do productive work.

is usually described as beginning with an initially exuberant state known as **hypomania**, characterized by a reduced need for sleep along with increased sexuality, humor, feelings of mental "clarity" and enjoyment of life, self-esteem, charm, grandiosity, and ability to do productive work. Indeed, some of the greatest artists, writers, scientists, and political leaders in history have had manic depressive illness and have produced important works during hypomanic phases (Jamison, 1996a; see Figure 13.9). It can be exceedingly difficult to convince someone in this state that they have a psychological disorder.

Moreover, exuberant feelings such as these often spiral out of control, blossoming into full-blown mania. Severe mania is marked by unpleasantly high-pressured, often incoherent speech; racing thoughts and delusions of grandeur; bizarre behavior including nonsensical and frequently catastrophic decisions involving money and business, risky and self-destructive sexual behavior; and inability to sleep or experience any sort of calm. Interestingly, bipolar disorders are among the relatively few psychological disorders affecting men about as frequently as women (Diflorio & Jones, 2010).

MOST CASES DO NOT RESEMBLE THE "CLASSICAL" DESCRIPTION

Although many people with a bipolar disorder, including Anu, do experience these classical symptoms of mania followed by crushing experiences of depression, most cases probably do *not* resemble this picture (Sato, Bottlender, Sievers, & Möller, 2005). For example, many people with a bipolar disorder rarely if ever experience classical mania, but experience primarily depression with an occasional hypomanic episode (Post et al., 2003). (Indeed, depression dominates over mania as a rule in bipolar disorders.) More challenging still are the many cases characterized by *mixed states*—mania and depression experienced virtually simultaneously.

Even when mania is clearly present, it often does not involve the expected feelings of euphoria but instead irritability, intrusive racing thoughts, and agitation (Akiskal & Benazzi, 2003). This sort of manic experience is said to be *dysphoric* (unpleasant) rather than *euphoric* (exhilarating). Finally, some research suggests that a number of factors often seen as "side effects" of bipolar disorders, or "comorbid" symptoms, may actually turn out to be unrecognized aspects of the illness itself—for example, cognitive dysfunction, substance abuse, or eating disorder (Soreca, Frank, & Kupfer, 2009). In sum, there is a broad spectrum of bipolar disorders, symptoms may vary, and diagnosing these disorders can be tricky (see special issue of *Journal of Affective Disorders*, vol. 73, 2003).

Depressive and Bipolar Disorders Increase the Risk of Suicide

Psychological disorders are not only unpleasant to experience—they are dangerous as well because suicide is a serious risk for sufferers. Approximately 35,000 people commit suicide each year in the United States (about 800,000 throughout the world), and of these, 90% to 98% could probably be diagnosed with a psychological disorder (National Institutes of Mental Health, 2010; World Health Organization, 2011a, 2011b; Värnik, 2012). However, bear in mind that while almost all suicide victims could be diagnosed with a psychological disorder, the overwhelming majority of people with a psychological disorder never commit suicide (Cavanagh, Carson, Sharpe, & Lawrie, 2003; Conner, Duberstein, Conwell, Seidlitz, & Caine, 2001)! Moreover, it cannot be said that a person's disorder has *caused* his or her suicide. Suicide is a highly complex action that involves more than psychological disorder. It involves social, economic, environmental, and cultural factors, and it often occurs during the context of individual or family crisis.

As you might expect, the disorders with the highest mortality rates from suicide are the depressive and bipolar disorders. Suffering from major depression constitutes the single most important known risk factor for suicide apart from a previous suicide attempt (Schneider, Müller, & Philipp, 2001). Somewhere between 56% and 87% of those attempting suicide could be diagnosed with major depression (Rihmer, 2007). Whereas the general suicide risk for persons with depression is nowhere near as high as psychologists once believed, for certain individuals the risk is quite high. Rates of suicide are highest for those who have been hospitalized with extremely severe depression, who experienced their first depression episode at an earlier age, whose depressions are longer lasting, and who show little response to antidepressants (Perroud et al., 2010).

As Table 13.10 suggests, suicide is distressingly common around the world, causing more deaths annually than war or murder (World Health Organization, 2011a; 2011b). Moreover, taken as a whole, suicide has increased around the world over the past 50 years, particularly among men (see Figure 13.10).

Surprisingly, however, despite increases in rates of suicide around the world, the opposite seems to be the case in the United States: Suicide among adolescents in the United States did increase until the mid-1990s, but it has been decreasing dramatically ever since. Suicides among adults over the age of 45 also showed a steady and substantial decline since 1970, although there has been a slight increase in suicide rates in this age group among European Americans over the past several years (Hu, Wilcox, Wissow, & Baker, 2008; McKeown, Cuffe, & Schulz, 2006; see Figure 13.11).

Indeed, despite much publicity in recent years about suicide among young people, completed suicide and unsuccessful suicide attempts are both very rare among children and adolescents throughout the world (Gould, Greenberg, Velting, & Shaffer, 2003; Kochanek, Murphy, Anderson, & Scott, 2004; World Health Organization, 2013). While we routinely hear statistics stating that suicide is "the third leading cause of death among children and adolescents" it needs to be kept in mind that young people in this age group rarely die of *any* cause, so the statistic "third leading cause" actually refers to a relatively small number of deaths—264 children and adolescents between the ages of 5 and 14 (Kochanek et al., 2004). Regardless of the relatively small size of this number (in a nation of 62 million children and adolescents to the age of 14),

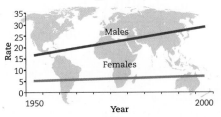

Evolution of Global Suicide Rates 1950-2000 (per 100,000)

▲ **FIGURE 13.10 Fifty-Year Evolution of Suicide Rates.** World suicide rates have increased substantially over the past 50 years, particularly among men. *(Source: World Health Organization 2002b.)*

Table 13.10 15 Nations with Highest Suicide Rates (based on reports to the World Health Organization as of 2011)

Suicide rate[1] per 100,000 Inhabitants

COUNTRY	YEAR REPORTED	MALES	FEMALES	TOTAL	NUMBER OF ACTUAL SUICIDES	MALE-FEMALE RATIO[2]
Lithuania	2009	61.3	10.4	34.1	1,138	5.9
South Korea	2009	39.9	22.1	31.0	15,413	1.8
Sri Lanka	1991	44.6	16.8	31.0	5,347	2.7
Russian Fed.	2006	53.9	9.5	30.1	42,855	5.7
Belarus	2007	48.7	8.8	27.4	2,663	5.5
Guyana	2006	39.0	13.4	26.4	202	2.9
Kazakhstan	2008	43.0	9.4	25.6	4,009	4.6
Hungary	2009	40.0	10.6	24.6	2,461	3.8
Japan	2009	36.2	13.2	24.4	30,707	2.7
Latvia	2009	40.0	8.2	22.0	516	4.9
Slovenia	2009	34.6	9.4	21.9	447	3.7
Ukraine	2009	37.8	7.0	21.2	9,716	5.4
Belgium	2005	28.8	10.3	19.4	2,028	2.8
Finland	2009	29.0	10.0	19.3	1,032	2.9
Serbia	2009	28.1	10.0	18.8	1,376	2.8

[1]Please understand that these figures are rates per 100,000. If a nation has a large population, the rate might be relatively low even though the total number of suicides is relatively high. Similarly, the rate might be high but the total low if the population is small.

[2] The rate is given as a figure for number of male suicides for every one female suicide. Example: In Lithuania in 2009 there were 5.9 male suicides for every 1 female suicide.

(Source: Värnick, 2012.)

each one of these deaths is a mournful tragedy. Losing a child to suicide is the worst experience most parents might endure. Added to the simple fact of the child's violent death may be a mix of feelings of guilt, shame, anger, and self-recrimination. Did I do enough to prevent this? Am I at fault? (Cantor, 1975.)

MEN ARE AT HIGHER RISK

Numerous factors affect the likelihood of a person attempting suicide apart from severity of illness, the most glaring of these being sex. With only a very few exceptions in certain parts of Asia, throughout the world men are vastly more likely than women to commit suicide. For example, men with major depression are anywhere from 4 to 25 times more likely than women with depression to die by suicide, depending upon the severity of the illness (Blair-West & Mellsop, 2001; Brådvik, Mattisson, Borgren, & Nettelbladt, 2008).

As Figure 13.12 shows, the suicide risk for women with moderate depression is quite low—approximately 0.5%, and for severe depression the rate is about 6%. For men however, the risk in moderate depression is about 6%, and for severe depression it increases to 25%! Overall, however (not focusing on suicide in major depression), in the United States men are 4.4 times more likely to commit suicide than women (Kochanek et al., 2004).

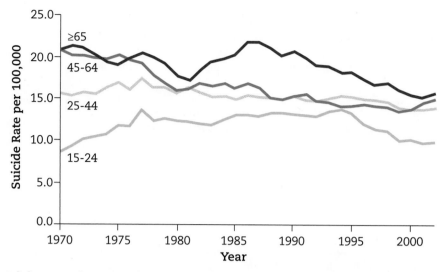

◀FIGURE 13.11 U.S. Suicide Rates **Are Decreasing.** *(Source: McKeown, Cuffe, & Shulz, 2006, p. 1745–1746.)*

Adolescents (age 15–24): Rates increased from 1970 to 1995 but have been decreasing substantially ever since. 1995 rate: 13.3 per 100,000. 2002 rate: 9.9 per 100,000

Young Adults (age 25–44): Rates have decreased slightly since 1970, from 15.4 per 100,000 to 14.0 per 100,000 in 2002.

Adults (age 45–64): Rates have decreased substantially since 1970, from 20.6 per 100,000 to 14.9 per 100,000 in 2002. However, there was a slight rise in suicides in this age bracket between 1999 and 2002, from 13.5 per 100,000 to 14.9 per 100,000.

Older Adults (over age 65): Rates have decreased substantially since 1970, from 20.8 per 100,000 to 15.6 per 100,000 in 2002.

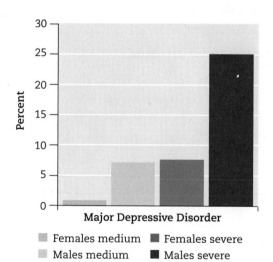

◀**FIGURE 13.12** **Suicide Risk According to Sex and Severity of Depression.** A longitudinal study lasting 50 years assessed the comparative lifetime risk for suicide in a sample of 3,563 Swedish participants. Of these, 503 were diagnosed with clinical depression. Less than 1% of the women died through suicide, regardless of severity of depression. Of the men, 19.6% with moderate depression, and 25% of the men with severe depression, died by suicide. *(Source: Brådvik et al., 2008.)*

IN SUMMARY

1. The most severe depressive disorder is major depressive disorder. Bipolar disorders cover a spectrum of symptoms but generally include major depression and hypomania or full mania. Symptoms of anxiety often overlap those of depression.

2. Contemporary models of the causes of depression are integrated models that include genetic, biochemical, and psychosocial components. However, depression is not caused by a "chemical imbalance."

3. Psychological factors in the onset of depression include cognitive vulnerabilities as described in hopelessness theory and the negative cognitive triad.

4. Women have much higher rates of depression (but not bipolar disorder) than men.

5. Depression greatly increases the risk of suicide. Suicide rates have increased globally over the past 50 years, but have decreased substantially in the United States. Men are at much higher risk than women.

RETRIEVE!

1. True or false: Most people who experience a single episode of major depression go on to experience more episodes in their lifetimes.

2. List at least four symptoms that depression and anxiety have in common.

3. Describe two problems with the "chemical imbalance" theory of depression.

4. Which of the following is NOT among the components of negative cognitive style as described in hopelessness theory?

a) negative events attributed to internal causes

b) negative events attributed to stable and global causes

c) negative events attributed to consequences of previous (bad) behavior

d) negative events thought to have severe negative consequences

5. The tendency to focus inwardly on possible causes and consequences of negative events and emotions is known as _____.

6. What is the term used to describe the highly pleasurable aspect of bipolar disorders characterized by reduced need for sleep, increased mental clarity, enjoyment of life, self-esteem, sexuality and humor, grandiosity, and creativity?

Are Depression and Anxiety Overdiagnosed?

As mentioned at the outset of the chapter, not everyone agrees with the DSM view of psychological disorder or supports the changes that have been made in diagnostic criteria in the various revisions of the DSM. In particular, a number of voices recently have been raised to argue that DSM diagnostic criteria—when combined with the increasing influence of the pharmaceutical industry on the psychiatric profession and mass media—are slowly "transforming" ordinary human experiences of sadness and anxiety into disorders. In other words, disorder is being diagnosed where no disorder exists (Horwitz & Wakefield, 2007, 2012; Wakefield et al., 2005). Critics such as Allan Horwitz and Jerome Wakefield worry that this *overdiagnosis* is in part responsible for apparent "epidemics" of certain mental disorders. Some in the medical profession see something similar at work in the world of medical illness (Kaplan, 2006; Welch, Schwartz, & Woloshin, 2011).

Clearly, any diagnosis can be wrong. Diagnosis can result in identifying a disorder where none exists (overdiagnosis, or a *false positive*), or failing to diagnose a true disorder (underdiagnosis, or a *false negative*). The problems with underdiagnosis are relatively straightforward: A person with a condition needing treatment fails to get the treatment he or she needs. The person suffers, the family may suffer, individuals who come in contact with the person may suffer, and society suffers. However, there are a number of less obvious potential harms in overdiagnosis as well:

1. *If a person is overdiagnosed, he or she may be taking unnecessary risks in being treated.* This is because, as discussed in the next chapter, *all* treatments have side effects. Although some of these side effects are extremely minimal and may be virtually undetectable, some can be quite dangerous—even life threatening. Therefore, with every treatment the question always must be asked: What are the potential benefits, and what are the potential risks? For genuinely serious conditions, one accepts greater risk (Welch et al., 2011).

2. *Mental illness often carries stigma.* Being diagnosed with a mental illness has consequences. If one is truly mentally ill, these consequences can be positive—a reduction in suffering as a result of treatment, for example, or a lessening of self-blame for one's condition. But if a person is not mentally ill yet receives a diagnosis, that person may find him or herself unnecessarily stigmatized—something that can affect one's self-image, relationships, even prospects for employment in certain careers. (Imagine running for president of the United States or applying to the Secret Service with a history of bipolar disorder or panic disorder!) Despite the best efforts of the mental health profession to educate the public, stigma is still frequently associated with mental illness.

3. *Overdiagnosis can result in unnecessary healthcare costs.* Treatment of psychological disorders costs money. The patient pays (at least in insurance premiums), insurance companies pay, and taxpayers pay.

4. *Overdiagnosis may foster a distorted view of human nature.* Overdiagnosis may tend to create a general impression that mental suffering, confusion, anxiety, sadness, and so forth are disorders in need of treatment, rather than—much more frequently—ordinary human experiences in response to difficult life circumstances or events.

These ideas are controversial, and some researchers propose that the harms of underdiagnosis are serious enough to risk the possibility of overdiagnosis (Campbell-Sills & Stein, 2005; Hickle, 2007). Yet, the arguments of critics of overdiagnosis—most prominently Allan Horwitz and Jerome Wakefield—are increasingly influential and deserve detailed treatment here. I will discuss Horwitz and Wakefield's arguments as applied to two disorders: major depression and social phobia (social anxiety disorder).

Social Phobia: When Is It Truly Dysfunctional?

At least some degree of wariness around strangers, fear of rejection and criticism, and fear of embarrassing or humiliating oneself in front of a group (and thus losing status) are part of human nature. These character traits—which can be loosely captured in the term *shyness*—may have evolved because they aided survival and reproductive success by preventing people from engaging in unwise behavior that might cause loss of status and social rejection. Another function of shyness may have been to discourage people from being too trusting of strangers who might have hostile intentions (Craske & Waters,

2005; Hofman & Barlow, 2002; Wakefield et al., 2005). But people differ in the degree to which they exhibit these traits, and some of us seem shy virtually from infancy as part of temperament (see Chapter 4, pp. 165–167). So, at what point does shyness represent a symptom of disorder rather than a normal personality trait at a more extreme level of expression?

Based on the harmful dysfunction perspective described earlier in the chapter, Horwitz and Wakefield propose that only if the normal human mechanism of shyness is *not functioning as it was intended to function* does a person have a disorder (Horwitz & Wakefield, 2012; Wakefield et al., 2005). If shyness evolved to cause us to be wary of strangers or avoid embarrassment or humiliation in front of a group, then extremely shy people cannot be said to be dysfunctional. This remains true even if they are distressed by their shyness or if it causes some measure of impairment given the demands of life in the modern world. After all, as Wakefield remarks, being short and unattractive may cause anxiety and distress and may even impair a person's ability to find work. But being short and unattractive does not constitute a disorder (Wakefield et al., 2005).

Who, then, *does* deserve a diagnosis of social phobia, according to Horwitz and Wakefield? These researchers propose that dysfunction of the shyness trait would be obvious and social phobia should be diagnosed if shyness is experienced even in situations where the possibility of embarrassment, humiliation, or rejection is truly unlikely. For example, what if a person experienced these emotions sitting in a darkened movie theater? This is a social situation, and the person is surrounded by individuals, yet, the person is in little or no danger of having negative social judgments applied from other theatergoers (unless he or she crunches popcorn too loudly during the movie, I suppose). The embarrassment and humiliation potential ought to be low to nonexistent in a darkened theater, so shyness is dysfunctional in this situation. Social phobia might also reasonably be diagnosed if a person's shyness is so extreme that he or she is unable to make a living or interact socially. In such cases, the shyness "mechanism" is interfering with fundamental activities related to survival and reproduction and is therefore dysfunctional by Horwitz and Wakefield's criteria.

On the other hand, disorder or not, social phobia can be paralyzing and it can substantially reduce a person's quality of life. Laura Campbell-Sills and Murray Stein (2005) acknowledge that social phobia may be overdiagnosed, but they argue that the label "disorder" is helpful for individuals suffering from extreme shyness because it tends to facilitate access to treatment. People with psychological disorders are not the only ones who seek and benefit from treatment—those with life problems that could include extreme shyness also use mental health services. However, insurance companies are far less likely to offer reimbursement unless a medical (DSM) diagnosis of disorder is given. This is a thorny issue that highlights the intersection of social, economic, and medical factors in the diagnosis and treatment of psychological problems.

When Ordinary Sadness Becomes Disorder

If you recall, rates of depression seem alarmingly high, and these rates have increased substantially over the past century (see Figure 13.4 on p. 637). There are a number of ways to interpret these statistics, however, and more than one interpretation may be true to some extent. For example, sufferers may have become much more willing to report and seek professional treatment for depression. This would increase the reported rates of depression. On the other hand, it may be that people truly *are* more depressed now than in generations past, a perspective often taken by many evolutionary psychologists (Nesse & Williams, 1994).

However, Horwitz and Wakefield are concerned that depression is being overdiagnosed as a result the way psychological disorders are characterized in the DSM—a problem made worse by the influence of the pharmaceutical industry in its aggressive marketing of antidepressant medications directly to consumers (Horwitz & Wakefield, 2007). The primary problem, according to Horwitz and Wakefield, is this: Feelings of profound sadness, guilt, low self-worth, fatigue, loss of pleasure, sleeplessness, and reduced appetite are ordinary human responses to severely stressful life events, such as the death of a loved one, life-threatening illness, loss of status or financial security, or the breakup of a marriage or other important relationship. Yet, the DSM does not take these sorts of contexts into account when applying a diagnosis of major depression.

Horwitz and Wakefield argue that this is a serious failing of the DSM given that there are important differences between depressive disorder and normal human responses to severely negative life events. What are these differences? First, the symptoms of actual depression are generally out of proportion to the severity of whatever events the person is coping with. In their book *The Loss of Sadness*, Horwitz and Wakefield describe many people whose depressions began at high points in their lives—for example, just at the time of winning a major literary award. In contrast, severe but ordinary symptoms of sadness are in proportion to serious negative events in a person's life.

The second quality which distinguishes ordinary sadness from depression is that ordinary sadness resolves over time, as a person's circumstances change or he or she recovers the strength to forge ahead with life. Depression, on the other hand, typically takes on a life of its own divorced from circumstances and contexts of a person's life; it does not necessarily respond to an improvement in objective life circumstances.

Again, not everyone is in agreement with this critique, and some argue that the increased rates of treatment for depressive symptoms since the 1980s have saved numerous lives, increased productivity and employability, improved access to health insurance for those in need, and decreased the stigma attached to mental illness (Hickle, 2007). According to this view, the benefits of increased diagnosis and treatment outweigh any potential harm of "mislabeling" ordinary sorrow.

IN SUMMARY

1. Some critics argue that DSM criteria when combined with the influence of the pharmaceutical industry are creating widespread overdiagnosis of psychological disorders.

2. Horwitz and Wakefield argue that even extreme shyness is an ordinary human trait. Only if shyness is not functioning as it was intended to function over evolutionary time should it be diagnosed as social phobia. Others argue that even if social phobia is overdiagnosed, those overdiagnosed may still receive benefit from treatment for extreme shyness.

3. Horwitz and Wakefield argue that symptoms of depression also may be ordinary human responses to highly stressful life events. There are qualities that distinguish these ordinary human responses from true depression.

RETRIEVE!

1. Describe a hypothetical situation where extreme shyness would qualify for a diagnosis of social phobia according to Horwitz and Wakefield's harmful dysfunction view.

2. Describe two qualities that differentiate symptoms of depression originating from true disorder from ordinary human responses to highly stressful life events.

What Is Schizophrenia?

Schizophrenia ▶
Schizophrenia is a group of related psychotic conditions characterized by severely distorted perception and experience of reality, disorganized thought and speech, and inappropriate emotions and emotional responses.

Psychotic disorder ▶ Any disorder that includes extremely severe distortion in thinking and perception, where a person's ability to grasp reality and respond rationally is badly impaired.

Positive symptoms ▶
Symptoms of schizophrenia which include the *addition* of something to a person's behavior which are not expected of a mentally healthy person. These are the more obvious symptoms of schizophrenia, such as delusions, hallucinations, and disorganized use of language.

Negative symptoms ▶ The less obvious symptoms of schizophrenia, which include the *absence* of characteristics which are expected of a mentally healthy person. Negative symptoms include flat affect, anhedonia, alogia, and avolition.

Schizophrenia is a group of related *psychotic* disorders characterized by severely distorted perception and experience of reality, disorganized thought and speech, and inappropriate emotions or emotional responses. Schizophrenia is the most common of the **psychotic disorders**—disorders characterized by severely impaired ability to grasp reality and respond rationally. It is psychotic disorders that are probably most commonly associated in the public mind with mental illness or "madness," even though these conditions actually characterize a tiny minority of people with psychological disorders, and an even smaller minority of the general population. No more than 1% of the population at most will suffer from schizophrenia during their lifetimes (Kessler, Birnbaum, et al., 2005; Pogue-Geile & Yokley, 2010).

In addition to being the most common psychotic disorder, schizophrenia is the most debilitating and potentially disabling (Walker, Kestler, Bollini, & Hochman, 2004). However, there are many misconceptions about schizophrenia. It is often confused with *dissociative identity disorder* or "split personality" (see "Critical Thinking about Psychology: *Sybil* and the Epidemic of Multiple Personalities" at the end of this chapter). The word *schizophrenia* loosely translates as "split mind," which is likely responsible for the confusion.

Because the behavior of those who suffer from schizophrenia is unusual and unpredictable, many people assume that people with schizophrenia are uniquely dangerous. These stereotypes may recently have grown more prevalent as a result of a number of seemingly senseless mass shootings in the United States by persons who were likely suffering from some sort of psychological disorder. However, violence among schizophrenics is extremely unusual. The vast majority are isolated, withdrawn, and pose no threat whatever (Elbogen & Johnson, 2009; National Institute of Mental Health, 2009). It is also sometimes thought that equal numbers of men and women are affected, but in fact, schizophrenia is one of the relatively few psychological disorders for which men are at substantially higher risk (Messias, Chen, & Eaton, 2007).

Aspects of schizophrenia are often present in childhood, although obvious signs are typically seen, and the illness diagnosed, in adolescence or early adulthood. Symptoms generally remain in some form on and off throughout the life span, although many people with schizophrenia recover enough to lead relatively normal lives at least for periods of time—sometimes substantial periods of time (Jobe & Harrow, 2005; Messias et al., 2007; Walker et al., 2004). However, the typical outcome for people diagnosed with schizophrenia is generally worse than that of the other disorders discussed in this chapter, and homelessness frequently goes hand in hand with schizophrenia. Suicide, while less common in schizophrenia than often supposed, does end the life of many (Jobe & Harrow, 2010; Palmer, Pankrantz, & Bostwick, 2005).

Symptoms May Be Positive and Negative

Symptoms experienced by those with schizophrenia are generally divided into two categories: *Positive symptoms* and *negative symptoms*. As they are used here, "positive" and "negative" do not mean "good" and "bad." **Positive symptoms** are those in which something is *added* to the person's behavior that should *not* be there, such as *hallucinations* and *delusions*. **Negative symptoms** are those suggesting that something which *should* be there is lacking. This usually refers to appropriate emotional responses, facial expressions, or the ability to speak normally.

POSITIVE SYMPTOMS

The most common positive symptoms of schizophrenia are *hallucinations* and *delusions*. Hallucinations are false sensory experiences, such as hearing voices or "seeing things" that aren't there. Delusions are incorrect and grossly distorted thoughts and beliefs, not widely shared by other members of one's culture. Following are some common delusions.

- *Delusions of persecution*—the idea that people are plotting to do one harm.
- *Delusions of grandeur*—the belief that one is a person of importance and accomplishment, such as a U.S. president or even a holy person such as Jesus Christ or Buddha.
- *Delusions of reference*—the tendency to interpret various public messages as though they were intended for one personally. For example, a simple headline in a newspaper may be thought to be a coded message from the CIA warning one personally of an imminent attack from space aliens or a terrorist group. A radio announcer's use of the word "you" to refer to all listeners may be interpreted as referring only to the schizophrenic personally.

Schizophrenics are not the only ones to experience delusions and hallucinations. These are common human experiences. For example, one often hears or sees things that are not there during the "twilight" period between sleep and wakefulness. But while a fleeting hallucination might occur and frighten you during a high fever or as you fall asleep, those suffering from schizophrenia often feel as though there is no escape from the voices in their heads, and they may build their entire lives around delusional ideas.

NEGATIVE SYMPTOMS

Negative symptoms are qualities that are "conspicuous by their absence." At least 25% of those with schizophrenia display negative symptoms (Malla et al., 2002). There are four basic types of negative symptoms:

- *Alogia* ("poverty of speech") refers to a difficulty in replying appropriately to questions. Schizophrenics with alogia may not reply to questions at all or may reply with only a single word or brief phrase, and often not logically responsive to the question.
- *Anhedonia* or difficulty experiencing pleasure in normal daily activities. Anhedonia is also frequently present in depression, and in fact there is significant overlap of negative symptoms in depression and schizophrenia (Walker et al., 2004).
- *Avolition* or difficulty making decisions or initiating or continuing activities. Avolition is similar to the more common word *apathy*.
- *Flat affect* or inappropriately emotionless expression even in the midst of highly emotional conversation or events. A person with flat affect may be seething or weeping inside, but you would not know it. Thus, flat affect does not mean that the person with schizophrenia is not experiencing emotion (Kring & Caponigro, 2010).

Although positive symptoms of schizophrenia such as hallucinations and delusions are certainly the most exotic aspects of the illness—and the ones most commonly thought of when the term *schizophrenia* is used—they are often of less critical importance in the lives of most schizophrenics than negative symptoms. For example, Roger Brown and Richard Herrnstein (cited by Carson, 1996, p. 1133) describe a meeting of Schizophrenics Anonymous which they attended:

> The members each seemed to come alone, trailing in and out of the night, with almost no group acknowledgement of the successive arrivals. . . . [The group's leader that night] began with

▲ Homelessness is a frequent outcome of schizophrenia.

▲ Many with schizophrenia manage to live highly exemplary lives in spite of their illness. Tom Harrell, diagnosed in 1967 with paranoid schizophrenia, is considered one of the finest jazz trumpeters of his generation and has released over 20 CDs as leader of his own group.

an optimistic testimony about how things were going with him, designed in part to buck up the others. Some of them also spoke hopefully; others were silent and stared at the floor throughout. I gradually felt hope draining out of the group as they began to talk of their inability to hold jobs, of living on welfare, of finding themselves overwhelmed by simple demands. Nothing bizarre was said or done; there was rather a pervasive sense of inadequacy, of lives in which each day was a dreadful trial. Doughnuts and coffee were served, and then each one, still alone, trailed off into the Cambridge night.

What I saw a little of at the meeting of Schizophrenics Anonymous is simply that there is something about schizophrenia that the antipsychotic drugs do not cure or even remit on a long-term basis.

The Search for Causes of Schizophrenia

The search for a direct cause of schizophrenia has been puzzling and frustrating. Although genetics appear to be a dominant cause (Pogue-Geile & Yokley, 2010), there is no one set of genes or obvious anatomical or neurochemical dysfunctions or "markers" that can reliably be associated with schizophrenia (Bray, 2008; Walker, Shapiro, Esterberg, & Trotman, 2010). Like mood and anxiety disorders, schizophrenia is almost certainly a result of a number of converging factors. We will examine three of them.

GENETICS

It is now beyond doubt that sets of genes are involved in causing a person to be vulnerable to developing schizophrenia. Numerous studies have demonstrated clearly that the closer the degree of genetic relatedness a person holds to a family member with schizophrenia, the greater is the risk of that person developing the illness himself or herself (Gottesman, 1991). Figure 13.13 dramatically demonstrates how the risk of being diagnosed with schizophrenia increases in an orderly, linear fashion according to the degree of genetic relatedness between relatives.

As shown in Figure 13.14, Irving Gottesman and Aksel Bertelsen (1989) compared rates of schizophrenia in the children of pairs of identical twins and fraternal twins where only one of each pair of twins had the illness. The researchers found, first, that children of pairs of identical (monozygotic) twins—where only one of the twins had schizophrenia—had a 17% risk of developing the disorder regardless of whether the twin with schizophrenia was the parent or aunt/uncle.

However, the story is very different for fraternal (dizygotic) twins. In this case, if the twin with schizophrenia was the parent, the child's risk of developing schizophrenia was, as before, 17%. However, if the twin with the illness was the aunt or uncle, the child's chance of developing schizophrenia was only 2%. Thus, certain genes predispose a person to schizophrenia—genes that may be carried by people who do not develop the illness themselves.

ENDOPHENOTYPES

While behavior genetics studies such as those just described have confirmed that a link exists between genetics and schizophrenia, recent studies in molecular genetics have attempted to identify possible candidate genes responsible for vulnerability to schizophrenia (Duan, Sanders, & Gejman, 2010). However, over the years many exciting findings of apparent links to specific genes in schizophrenia have proven to be false leads. Very recent studies that have only been made possible due to the mapping of the human genome have demonstrated why these false leads may be occurring—it may be the case that

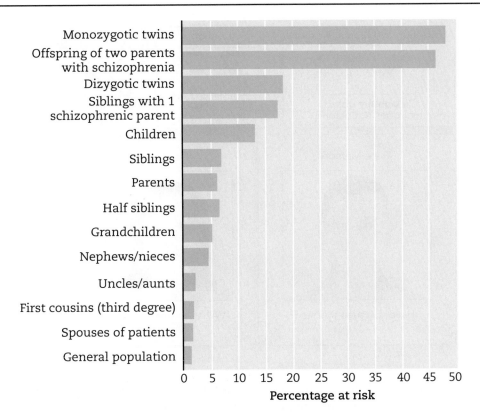

◀ **FIGURE 13.13** Risk of Developing Schizophrenia by Degree of Genetic Relatedness. *(Data from Gottesman, 1991; figure from Barlow & Durand, 2009, p. 481.)*

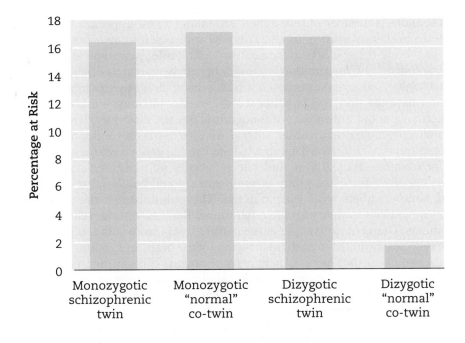

◀ **FIGURE 13.14** Risk of Developing Schizophrenia in the Children of Identical and Fraternal Twins When Only One Twin Has the Illness. *(Data from Gottesman, 1991; figure from Barlow & Durand, 2009, p. 482.)*

scores, hundreds, or even thousands of genes are potential contributors to the risk of schizophrenia, and that these genes are common variations, not rare sets of genes. While each genetic variant exerts only a small effect, combined together they confer a powerful vulnerability to developing schizophrenia (International Schizophrenia Consortium, 2009). Moreover, these genes likely interact in particular ways—turning each other on and off in the manner described in Chapter 3. Given the massively complex nature of schizophrenia, this complexity of genetic activity should not be unexpected. Indeed, very recent genome-wide analysis suggests the possibility that looking for specific

▶ FIGURE 13.15 Neurocognitive Testing for Endophenotypes in Schizophrenia. Raquel Gur and her colleagues administered a battery of neurocognitive tests such as those depicted here to a group of multigenerational families, each of which contained at least some members with schizophrenia. The object was to identify endophenotypes of schizophrenia—relatively straightforward characteristics with a genetic basis that are found in those with the disorder and also in close genetic relatives. *(Source: Braff et al., 2007, p. 706.)*

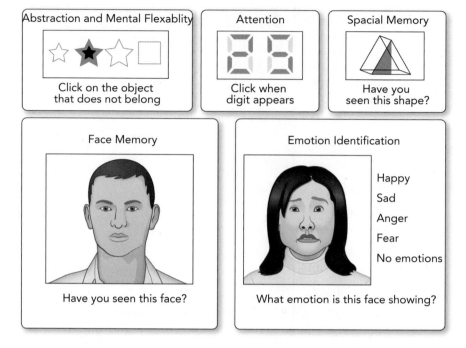

Abstraction and Mental Flexablity
Click on the object that does not belong

Attention
Click when digit appears

Spacial Memory
Have you seen this shape?

Face Memory
Have you seen this face?

Emotion Identification
Happy
Sad
Anger
Fear
No emotions
What emotion is this face showing?

Endophenotype ▶ A characteristic or symptom of a disorder that is present in people with that disorder and also is present to a greater degree than would be expected by chance in close genetic relatives of the person with the disorder. Endophenotypes are considered to reflect what is heritable about a given disorder but, unlike most disorders, are considered simple and straightforward enough to lend themselves to genetic analysis.

genes responsible for specific psychological disorders may be misguided for a simple reason: The same complex genetic interactions may be responsible for numerous psychological symptoms of disorder (Cross-Disorder Group of the Psychiatric Genomics Consortium, 2013).

Therefore, a number of researchers are taking a new approach to locating genetic markers of schizophrenia. This new approach is known as *endophenotyping* (Braff, Schork, & Gottesman, 2007). An **endophenotype** is any single characteristic or symptom that is present in people with a specific psychological disorder and is also present at a high rate in close genetic relatives who do not have the disorder. In other words, an endophenotype is part of what is heritable about a disorder—although it is not the disorder itself. Unlike a complex psychological disorder, such as schizophrenia, the endophenotype is simple and straightforward enough to lend itself to genetic analysis.

For example, Raquel Gur and her colleagues administered a battery of *neurocognitive* tests to a group of multigenerational families, each of which had some members with schizophrenia. They administered the same tests to a comparison sample of multigenerational families with no schizophrenic members (Gur et al., 2007). A neurocognitive test is any test that taps a cognitive skill closely linked to particular regions of the brain and assumed to have a genetic component. The tests included assessments of attention, verbal memory, memory for faces, spatial memory, ability to recognize emotion in facial expressions, and so forth—all skills that have been shown to be deficient in people with schizophrenia (Braff et al., 2007; see Figure 13.15)

As depicted in Figure 13.16, Gur and her colleagues found that people with schizophrenia did show deficits in these neurocognitive skills—but so did their relatives who did *not* have schizophrenia. On the other hand, these deficits were not seen in the comparison group of families with no schizophrenic members. This strongly suggests that these deficits are part of what is inherited in schizophrenia, qualifying them as endophenotypes. Because these characteristics are relatively straightforward, they will lend themselves to molecular genetic analysis in the future (Gur et al., 2007).

NEURODEVELOPMENTAL FACTORS

While behavior genetic, molecular genetic, and endophenotyping studies all establish the importance of genetics in the development of schizophrenia,

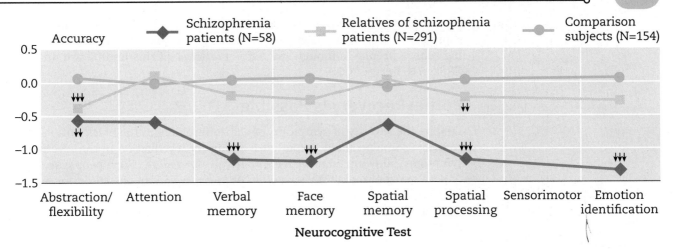

FIGURE 13.16 Neurocognitive Skills as Endophenotypes. The pattern of accuracy scoring for the battery of neurocognitive tests administered by Gur and her colleagues is quite similar for family members with schizophrenia and their genetic relatives. However, the pattern is quite different for families in the comparison group. *(Source: Gur et al., 2007, p. 816.)*

there is much more than genes to the story. One of the most promising attempts to explain nongenetic components of schizophrenia involves *neurodevelopmental* factors. A **neurodevelopmental** factor is one that affects the brain but which is not genetic in origin; instead, it is rooted in events that occur after the moment of conception. Originally this meant that the focus for researchers would be prenatal events—experiences of the fetus while in the womb. However, as the nature of early brain development became better understood, neurodevelopmental researchers in schizophrenia have expanded their work to include events in adolescence (Walker et al., 2010).

Scientists conducting research on neurodevelopmental factors in schizophrenia argue that while sets of genes might predispose a person to schizophrenia, without certain types of experiences occurring during early development—either prenatally, at birth, or during adolescence—schizophrenia will not develop. According to this hypothesis, prenatal, birth, or adolescent experiences can cause subtle forms of damage in the frontal and temporal lobes (forebrain) which result in disruption of brain development. However, this damage does not become apparent until late adolescence or early adulthood, when it shows up as symptoms of schizophrenia (Conklin & Iocono, 2002; Mjellem and Kringlen 2001).

Take the finding that many identical twin pairs are discordant for schizophrenia—one twin has the disorder, but the other does not. When twins are born, their deliveries are invariably high-risk, and it is not unusual for one or both infants to experience brief lack of oxygen or other distress during delivery (MacNeil & Cantor-Graae, 2000). According to the neurodevelopmental hypothesis, in such cases the more badly affected twin would be more likely to develop schizophrenia as a teen or young adult.

Schizophrenia has also been linked to a mother's exposure to influenza or rubella virus during the second trimester of pregnancy—a time critical for fetal brain growth and sorting of individual cortical neurons (A. S. Brown, 2006; A. S. Brown & Susser, 2002). Women who get the these illnesses during their second trimester of pregnancy are about twice as likely as others to give birth to a child who will eventually develop schizophrenia (A. S. Brown et al., 2000).

Some researchers point to the fact that there are no unambiguous descriptions of schizophrenia in medical or world literature prior to 1800. These researchers suggest the possibility that a specific virus came into existence at about that time (just as HIV apparently came into existence only during the latter half of the 20th century) and that this virus is responsible for a portion of cases of schizophrenia (Gottesman, 1991). Recent research has looked at the association between the human *herpes* virus and schizophrenia, but results have been conflicting (Brown, Schaefer, Quesenberry, Shen, & Susser, 2006; Shirts et al., 2007). A viral agent found in cat feces, *T. gondii*, has also

Neurodevelopmental ▶ Any factor which affects the brain but does not have a genetic origin. Neurodevelopmental events may occur prior to birth, at birth, of after birth.

been suggested as a culprit (watch out for that litter box!), and research does show that exposure to *T. gondii* moderately increases the risk of developing schizophrenia—although the *hows* and *whys* of this finding are unclear (Yolken & Torrey, 2008).

Partial Recovery Is Possible

Despite the severity of symptoms of schizophrenia and the bleak outlook for recovery, some people do experience a long-term reduction in the severity of symptoms, allowing them to live a relatively normal life. Such people are said to have schizophrenia that is *residual* or *in remission*. In one study, for example, 40% of patients with schizophrenia experienced such long-lasting (but not permanent) periods of recovery (Harrow, Grossman, Jobe, & Herbener, 2005).

IN SUMMARY

1.	Schizophrenia is a disabling psychological disorder which consists of both positive and negative symptoms. Positive symptoms are those in which something is added to the person's behavior that should not be there, such as hallucinations and delusions. Negative symptoms are those in which something that should be there is absent—for example, appropriate emotional responses.
2.	Like mood and anxiety disorders, schizophrenia is almost certainly a result of a number of converging factors. Genetics play a large role, but the "genes for schizophrenia" have not yet been identified, likely because many sets of common genes are potentially involved or because the same genetic interactions are responsible for many psychological disorders. A new strategy for investigating genetic links to schizophrenia is endophenotyping.
3.	Neurodevelopmental factors in schizophrenia may include prenatal exposure to virus or nutritional deficiency, birth complications, or developmental problems in adolescence.

RETRIEVE!

1.	List at least two positive and three negative symptoms of schizophrenia.
2.	Luann is the daughter of a pair of fraternal (dizygotic) twins. Luann's aunt has schizophrenia, but her mother does not. True or false: Luann has approximately a 17% chance of developing schizophrenia herself.
3.	A characteristic possessed by people with a psychological disorder and also present to a degree among the person's genetic relatives who do not have the disorder is known as a(n) _____.
4.	Women who get the flu during their second trimester of pregnancy are about twice as likely as others to give birth to a child who ultimately will develop schizophrenia. Maternal exposure to the flu is therefore known as a _____ factor in schizophrenia.

What Are Personality Disorders?

Earlier in this chapter I mentioned that, in addition to the major mental disorders, there is a second important category of disorder: personality disorders. **Personality disorders** are pervasive, chronic patterns of dysfunctional thinking, feeling, and relating to the world that generally begin in adolescence and last throughout a person's life According to the DSM-5, those with personality disorders suffer impairments in at least two of the following areas of personality functioning:

- *Identity*: A person's sense of being a unique individual with clear boundaries between his or her self and others, a stable sense of self-esteem, and ability to self-evaluate.
- *Self-direction:* The ability to pursue meaningful goals and reflect upon one's behavior.
- *Empathy*: Being able to understand and appreciate others' experiences and motivations and to tolerate differing perspectives.
- *Intimacy*: The ability to form close, long-lasting connections with others.

In spite of the potential seriousness of symptoms of personality disorders, they do not usually result in the same degree of distress or impairment and dysfunction caused by the major mental disorders. Thus, they are sometimes referred to as "madness without loss of reason." Nevertheless, in keeping with the fact that personality disorders are chronic and begin early in life, they are usually more difficult to treat than the major mental disorders.

Personality disorders ▶ Pervasive, chronic patterns of inner experience and behavior which generally begin in adolescence, are inflexible, and are expressed throughout many areas of a person's life. These patterns cause distress and/or impairment, but symptoms are generally not as severe as those of clinical disorders.

Table 13.11 **The 10 Personality Disorders of DSM-5**

PERSONALITY DISORDER	BRIEF DESCRIPTION
Antisocial personality disorder	Violation of the rights of others; lack of empathy; reckless and impulsive; callous; lack of remorse, deceitfulness, often criminal behavior, aggression and violence, substance abuse
Avoidant personality disorder	Feelings of inadequacy, low self-esteem, extreme sensitivity to criticism, restricts social activities, fear of being shamed
Borderline personality disorder	Rollercoaster emotions and relationships, unstable self-image, lack of control over impulses, fear of abandonment, tendency to self-harm, feelings of emptiness, neediness and mistrust
Dependent personality disorder	Needs to be taken care of, submissive, clinging behavior, needs constant reassurance, difficulty making independent decisions
Histrionic personality disorder	Excessive emotion, attention-seeking, seductiveness, suggestible and frequently changing opinions
Narcissistic personality disorder	Need for admiration, grandiosity, lack of empathy with others, beliefs that one is "special" and the rules do not apply, seemingly high self-esteem that is actually easily crushed.
Obsessive-compulsive personality disorder	Preoccupied with order, perfection, and control; lack of flexibility and openness to new experiences
Paranoid personality disorder	Distrust and suspiciousness of others, easily offended, hyper-vigilant (always on the lookout)
Schizoid personality disorder	Detachment from social relationships, emotion, and pleasure
Schizotypal personality disorder	Avoidance of social relationships; discomfort being around people; eccentric appearance and behavior

▲ **Personality Disorders: "Madness without Loss of Reason."** The 1999 film *Girl, Interrupted*, directed by James Mangold, dramatized the true story of Susanna Keysen, an adolescent girl who was hospitalized with a diagnosis of *borderline personality disorder*. Those diagnosed with BPD are frightened of abandonment, impulsive, unstable in their sense of self; tend to make suicidal threats or engage in self-mutilation; are plagued by feelings of emptiness; and involve themselves in stormy relationships where they may alternate between idealizing and severely devaluing their partner. Despite Keysen's hospitalization, most people with personality disorders are not impaired to the same degree as those with clinical disorders. Pictured here are Winona Ryder as Keysen and Angelina Jolie as a fellow patient.

There are 10 personality disorder diagnoses in the DSM-5, plus a category that could include any disorder with mixed or unique traits, known as *trait-specific* personality disorder. Table 13.11 describes the 10 basic disorders very briefly, and I will then describe three of them in greater detail. However, please remember that having some of the symptoms of any of the personality disorders—or even *all* of the symptoms of one or more of them—does *not* mean you have the disorder. In order for personality disorder to be diagnosed, these symptoms must seriously interfere with your ordinary life. In other words, personality disorders are extreme variations on normal human traits (Svrakic, Lecic-Tosevski, & Divac-Jovanovic, 2009).

One additional, perhaps more important, note of warning: Personality disorders are among the most controversial of DSM diagnoses (Widiger, 2011). One problem is that these disorders are almost always diagnosed by picking and choosing from the menu offered (e.g., "borderline personality disorder with features of avoidant and narcissistic personality disorders"). It is actually rare for a person to be diagnosed with only one personality disorder (Clarkin, 2008; Lenzenweger, Lane, Loranger, & Kessler, 2007).

Given that so many symptoms of personality disorder are routinely diagnosed at once, and the same symptoms may show up in several diagnoses, many theorists now believe that the separate categories of personality disorder created by the DSM do not accurately reflect the way these disorders exist in nature, or the way most people actually experience them (Clarkin, 2008; Krueger & Markon, 2006; Lenzenwager et al., 2007). These researchers propose that the symptoms making up personality disorders should be viewed primarily as *dimensions* rather than *categories* (Bernstein, Iscan, & Maser, 2007; Svrakic et al., 2009). As mentioned earlier, the DSM is a categorical diagnostic system by which an individual either has a given disorder or does not. However, it appears to be the case that personality disorders—perhaps more than other diagnoses—do not generally represent separate disorders that one "has" or "does not have." They may more realistically be seen as clusters of symptoms occurring to varying degrees in people with personality problems (Bernstein, Iscan, & Maser, 2007). Nevertheless, as imperfect as these diagnoses may be, they do describe something important—and given that all 10 diagnoses survived the publication of DSM-5, they are unlikely to disappear in the near future.

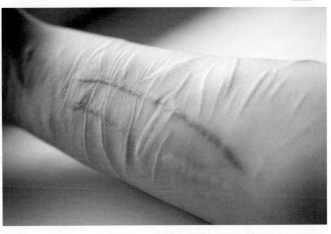

Paranoid Personality Disorder Fosters Mistrust

Although most of us know someone who we think of as "paranoid," **paranoid personality disorder** (**PPD**) goes beyond simple mistrust of others' motives or a tendency to feel under attack when criticized. As with other personality disorders, these tendencies must be so pervasive, severe, and enduring that they create serious problems for the person or those with whom he or she comes into contact. The stance of mistrust and suspicion of others' motives among those with PPD is maintained even in the face of strong evidence that suspicions are unfounded.

The person with PPD is preoccupied with threats—real or imagined—and does not take another person's seemingly harmless or even helpful behavior at face value. PPD sufferers strongly expect to be betrayed, humiliated, and taken advantage of (Bernstein & Useda, 2007), and often interpret criticism as an attack. They are argumentative, do not easily confide in others, and are ready to pounce on any remark that may be twisted to imply another person's hostile intent. People with PPD are firm believers in "Do unto them before they do unto you."

Borderline Personality Disorder Leads to a Stormy Life

Borderline personality disorder (**BPD**) is one of the most prevalent of the personality disorders, afflicting as many as 20% of those being treated in inpatient psychiatric hospital wards. People suffering from borderline personality disorder also frequently end up in emergency rooms or cared for by emergency medical personnel, because the large majority attempt to injure themselves in some way—with substantial numbers attempting or committing suicide (Bradley, Conklin, & Westen, 2007). However, borderline personality disorder is also a particularly controversial diagnosis. Beliefs about BPD among mental health professionals have changed substantially over the years and continue to be in flux. Indeed, the majority of personality disorder researchers—even those who might defend categorical diagnoses—believe that the diagnosis of BPD needs to be substantially revised if not abandoned (Bernstein, Iscan, & Maser, 2007).

Yet, without doubt the symptoms now collected in the BPD diagnosis are unfortunately common. Those currently diagnosed with BPD tend to be highly impulsive, moody, frightened of abandonment, unstable in their sense of self, and plagued by feelings of emptiness and/or worthlessness. They frequently involve themselves in stormy relationships where they may alternate between idealizing and severely devaluing their partner: "I can't live without you!" one day, "Get out of my sight!" the next—and vice versa. In addition, as mentioned earlier, they may engage in self-injury or mutilation, for example "cutting" their limbs with razor blades.

Borderline personality disorder often emerges in adolescence, but, while aspects of BPD can be lifelong, unlike many other personality disorders, symptoms of BPD may fade over time (Robinson, 2005; Zanarini, Frankenburg, Hennen, & Silk, 2004).

▲ **Borderline Personality Disorder May Leave Scars.** While the DSM-5 diagnosis of borderline personality disorder is highly controversial, the symptoms of BPD are all too real. Those diagnosed with borderline personality disorder frequently injure themselves, often through "cutting"—using a razor blade to make repeated cuts on the arms and legs, cuts which form scars over time.

Paranoid personality disorder (PPD) ▶ Paranoid personality disorder is characterized by mistrust and suspicion of others' motives. Those with PPD expect to be betrayed, humiliated, and taken advantage of. They are hostile and argumentative, and do not easily confide in others.

Borderline personality disorder (BPD) ▶ A controversial personality disorder diagnosis describing a person who is impulsive, moody, and frightened of abandonment. BPD sufferers have an unstable sense of self, and are plagued by feelings of emptiness and/ or worthlessness. Their relationships tend to be stormy, and they often engage in self-injuring behavior.

Obsessive-Compulsive Personality Disorder Wants Rules Obeyed

Obsessive-compulsive personality disorder (**OCPD**) is *not* the same thing as obsessive-compulsive disorder (OCD), an anxiety disorder described in detail on pages 630–631. It is true that the two conditions do share certain symptom traits, and some people suffering from OCPD may go on to develop OCD. The two disorders may also run in the same families. However, as a general rule, if OCPD occurs along with a major mental disorder, that disorder is *not* OCD—it is more commonly an eating disorder or depressive disorder (Fineberg, Sharma, Sivakumaran, Sahakian, & Chamberlain, 2007).

What are the symptoms of OCPD? In a general way, people with OCPD are preoccupied with orderliness, perfectionism, and remaining in control—while lacking flexibility and openness (Hummelen, Wilberg, Pedersen, & Karterud, 2008). Moreover, because of their obsession with orderliness, rules, perfection, and control, they tend to be inefficient (although ultraconscientious) workers. They are inefficient because they will place order and perfection above productivity ("I'm going do this the right way or not do it at all!").

OCPD sufferers make lists, obey rules, adhere rigidly to schedules, and believe that the devil is in the details. They often cannot finish tasks because their standards are set so high. They also have a hard time delegating tasks to others, because they fear the task will not be performed properly. When it comes to morality and ethics, they think in black and white terms. They are miserly when it comes to money, and many OCPD sufferers (like those with hoarding disorder, described on p. 632) have a hard time throwing out objects that are no longer useable, even if they are broken or worn out.

Obsessive-compulsive personality disorder (OCPD) ▶ A personality disorder characterized by preoccupation with orderliness, perfection, and control. Those with OCPD consequently lack flexibility and openness. Because they are obsessed with perfection, they are inefficient (although scrupulously conscientious), because they place order and perfection above productivity. They think in black-and-white terms when it comes to morality, are miserly with money, and find it difficult to delegate tasks to others.

CRITICAL THINKING ABOUT PSYCHOLOGY

Sybil and the Epidemic of Multiple Personalities

One of the most common images of mental illness is that of a person with "split personality" or "multiple personality disorder," referred to in the DSM-5 as **dissociative identity disorder (DID)**. DID is one of a group of **dissociative disorders**, a DSM category involving one of several types of breakdowns of memory, perception, awareness, or identity. Despite the "multiple personality" tag, DID is not related to personality disorders as described in this section. Although depictions of people with multiple personalities appear with astounding regularity on TV and movie screens, prior to the 1970s there were only 79 documented cases in all of the world literature in clinical psychology (Lilienfeld & Lynn, 2003). However, by 1986 the number had reached 6,000, and by one estimate, at the end of the 20th century the number had reached 40,000 (Marmer, 1998). The overwhelming majority of these reported cases were in the United States.

What happened? Did American clinicians alone suddenly become experts in recognizing a long-hidden mental disorder, or did something set off an epidemic?

The initial wave of reports occurred only after the publication in the United States of the best-selling book *Sybil*, written in 1973 by Flora Schreiber, and the broadcast of the 1976 television film based on the book, starring Sally Field (Kihlstrom, 2005). The book and film told the purportedly true story of a woman called Sybil who, after suffering severe abuse as a child, retreated into a large number of distinct and autonomous personalities, known as *alters*. According to the story, by creating a number of separate personalities, the woman *dissociated* herself from the abuse and in this way defused the trauma and reduced her extreme anxiety. This explanation of DID has come to be known as the *post-traumatic model* of DID (e.g., Gleaves, 1996).

Dissociative identity disorder (DID) ▶ A highly controversial DSM diagnosis characterized by the emergence of more than one autonomous "personality" within the same body. Formerly known as "multiple personality disorder."

Dissociative disorder ▶ A DSM category of disorder where there is one of several types of breakdowns of memory, perception, awareness, or identity.

▲ **Sally Field as "Sybil" and the Real Shirley Mason.** Pictured here are images of two of "Sybil's" alters as portrayed by Sally Field in the 1976 film *Sybil*. At right is the real Shirley Mason (1923–1998).

But the "Sybil" case, based on the life of a woman whose real name was Shirley Mason, has been "thoroughly discredited" (Kihlstrom, 2005, p. 243; Nathan, 2011; Paris, 2012). Many of the book's premises, including Mason's childhood abuse and her purported multiple personalities, were apparently fabricated by Mason's psychiatrist and the author of the book for the dual purposes of creating what they thought would be a good therapeutic environment for Mason (who was without doubt a deeply troubled individual) and selling a book about her therapy to a publisher (Borch-Jacobsen, 1997; Rieber, 2006).

Regardless of whether Shirley Mason did or did not have multiple personalities, dissociative identity disorder is perhaps the single most controversial diagnoses in the DSM. Although some psychologists and psychiatrists accept the diagnosis as legitimate (e.g., Dalenberg et al., 2007; Gleaves, 1996; Putnam & Lowenstein, 2000), approximately 86 % of Canadian and 75% of American psychiatrists believe that there is insufficient scientific evidence to support the validity of the concept. Consequently, research interest in DID has fallen off sharply following its peak at the height of the seeming epidemic (Lalonde, Hudson, Gigante, & Pope, 2001; Pope, Barry, Bodkin, & Hudson, 2006), and some researchers have simply termed it a "psychiatric fad" (Paris, 2012, p. 1078). Taken as a whole, the psychiatric profession is skeptical about DID—if not about its actual existence, at least about how frequently it is diagnosed (Piper & Merskey, 2004a, 2004b).

However, most commentators agree that most DID diagnoses do not result from deliberate fraud. One group of psychologists accepts that DID is in most cases a "real" condition in the sense that a number of people—mostly women in psychotherapy—are experiencing something extremely unusual and powerful. However, these theorists deny that the cause of DID is rooted in childhood trauma, as suggested by the post-traumatic theory. Instead, they propose that the disorder is in most cases a direct result of the mass media fascination with the condition, and of equal fascination on the part of psychotherapists who treat it. According to this idea, these therapists, using powerfully suggestive techniques, unwittingly lead their patients to create the illness during therapy. The term **iatrogenesis** is used in cases where a clinician unwittingly (or intentionally) creates symptoms of an illness instead of healing an illness (Barlow, 2010; Lilienfeld et al., 1999).

Several pieces indirect evidence support this view of DID:

- Therapeutic practices engaged in by proponents of DID include the use of highly powerful suggestion techniques such as hypnosis and

Iatrogenesis ▶ When a clinician unwittingly (or intentionally) creates symptoms of an illness in his or her capacity as a healthcare giver.

CRITICAL THINKING ABOUT PSYCHOLOGY

CONTINUED

guided imagery. If alters do not appear spontaneously, DID therapists may "call them out," or ask to speak to them ("Is it possible that there is another part of you with whom I haven't spoken?").

- Patients rarely show unambiguous symptoms of DID prior to going into therapy, and in general, the longer a patient remains in therapy, the more alters appear. This goes against the general therapeutic principle that the major features of an illness usually become better, not worse, the longer one is in treatment (Lilienfeld & Lynn, 2003).
- The vast majority of DID patients are diagnosed by a very small group of clinicians. In one study, over 90% of clinicians stated that they had never seen a single case of DID, while three psychiatrists reported having seen 20 patients each with DID (Modestin, cited in Lilienfeld & Lynn, 2003; see also Mai, 1995).

No one of these findings conclusively demonstrates that DID is created by media portrayals and deluded therapists. Even if many or even most cases are created in this fashion, there may well be a few that result from other causes, including traumatic childhood experiences; and some research does suggest that the picture may sometimes be more complicated than skeptics propose. For example, certain interesting physiological and cognitive differences have sometimes been noticed between alters (personalities) (Miller, Blackburn, Scholes, White, & Mamalis, 1991; Tsai, Condie, Wu, & Chang, 1999). Clearly, *something* interesting is going on, although it undoubtedly "goes on" far less frequently than most people suppose. ■

IN SUMMARY

1. Personality disorders are pervasive, chronic patterns of dysfunctional thinking and relating to the world which generally begin in adolescence and last throughout a person's life span. While these conditions may be serious, they do not usually result in the same degree of distress or impairment and dysfunction caused by the major mental disorders.

2. There are 10 basic personality disorders categorized in the DSM-5.

3. The chapter discusses symptoms of paranoid personality disorder, borderline personality disorder, and obsessive-compulsive personality disorder.

4. The classification system currently used to diagnose personality disorders is highly controversial, and many researchers believe that the category system for personality disorders does not reflect the way these disorders occur in nature or are experienced by sufferers.

5. Dissociative identity disorder (DID) is among the most controversial of all DSM diagnoses, and most psychiatrists do not believe there is enough evidence for its existence to justify its inclusion in the DSM.

RETRIEVE!

1. True or false: The large majority of researchers believe that personality disorders represent distinct disorders that should be placed within a categorical diagnostic system.

2. Match the personality disorder on the left with the numbers of all the appropriate symptoms listed on the right.

Paranoid personality disorder

Borderline personality disorder

Obsessive-compulsive disorder

1. Self-injury
2. Expects to be taken advantage of
3. Seeks perfection and control
4. Frightened of abandonment
5. Preoccupied with threats
6. Stormy relationships
7. Interprets criticism as an attack
8. Feelings of emptiness
9. Preoccupation with rules and order
10. Lacks flexibility and openness
11. Suspicious and mistrustful

3. Name two pieces of evidence that indirectly support the view that the "epidemic" of dissociative identity disorder was primarily created by psychotherapists and the media.

Looking Back

Chapter 13 in Review

WHAT IS A PSYCHOLOGICAL DISORDER?

- Psychologists have yet to agree on what does and does not constitute a psychological disorder. Most psychologists use the DSM for diagnosis, but they do not necessarily agree with the diagnostic categories and criteria in the DSM. There are three principal ideas about what constitutes psychological disorder: the DSM view, the myth of mental illness view, and harmful dysfunction view.
- The number of people with psychological disorders is not known with certainty. Surveys may identify people as "disordered" who are merely responding in a normal way to adverse events (false positives); or they may fail to identify people who are actually disordered for various reasons (false negatives). The term "insanity" is a legal term, not a medical or psychological term.
- The DSM-5 categorizes each psychological disorder according to its quality, symptoms, severity, course, and other phenomena. The two

DSM categories of greatest interest to most counseling and clinical psychologists are the major mental disorders and personality disorders. Comorbidity refers to a situation where a person has more than one diagnosis of psychological disorder at a time or over the lifetime.

WHAT ARE ANXIETY DISORDERS?

- Generalized anxiety disorder (GAD) defines the basic experience of anxiety: a feeling of tension, physiological arousal, and apprehension or worry about events that have not yet occurred.
- Phobias are powerful, disruptive, irrational fears. Specific phobias refer to a specific feared object, animal, or situation. Social phobia is a controversial diagnosis in which ordinary shyness is taken to a dysfunctional extreme.
- Panic disorder consists of powerful anxiety over the possibility of experiencing a panic attack.
- Anxiety disorders result from combinations of causes. The triple vulnerability theory of David Barlow

proposes that they result from the interaction of generalized biological vulnerability, generalized psychological vulnerability, and specific psychological vulnerability.
- Obsessive-compulsive disorder (OCD) is the most severe anxiety disorder, consisting of persistent, intrusive, anxiety-provoking thoughts (obsessions), often combined with a strong urge (compulsion) to perform repetitive, ritualistic behaviors or mental acts designed to relieve the anxiety provoked by the obsessive thoughts.
- Post-traumatic stress disorder (PTSD) is a rare response to trauma. PTSD may consist of experiences of "reliving" the traumatic event, negative changes in mood and cognition, and changes in physiological arousal levels and reactivity.

WHAT ARE DEPRESSIVE AND BIPOLAR DISORDERS?

- Depressive disorders are characterized by sadness, hopelessness, helplessness, grief, guilt, and low

Looking Back continued

feelings of self-worth; bipolar disorders are characterized by ceaseless energy, elation, unrealistically high self-esteem, racing thoughts, and/or explosive anger, anxiety, or extreme irritability.

- Major depressive disorder is the most commonly diagnosed psychological disorder. Virtually all patients with depression also suffer from anxiety. Many people suffer from chronic, persistent depression, and some are treatment-resistant.

- Genotypes, in combination with environmental factors, can predispose a person to become depressed. Depression is not due to a "chemical imbalance," although many sorts of biochemical changes may be associated with depression. Abramson and Alloy's hopelessness theory and Beck's theory of negative cognitive triad describe cognitive vulnerabilities that can trigger depression given conducive sets of circumstance. Women have much higher rates of depression and anxiety than men.

- Bipolar disorders are a spectrum of disorders, not a single disorder. The classical picture of manic depression as alternating cycles of depression and hypomania or mania is not typical. Depression dominates over mania in bipolar disorders.

- The vast majority of people who commit suicide could likely be diagnosed with a psychological disorder (e.g., depression), although the vast majority of those with psychological disorders never commit suicide. Rates of suicide have increased over the past 50 years, but decreased in the United States. The large majority of completed suicides are men.

ARE DEPRESSION AND ANXIETY OVERDIAGNOSED?

- Critics such as Allan Horwitz and Jerome Wakefield argue that anxiety and depressive disorders are being overdiagnosed as a result of peculiarities of DSM diagnostic criteria and the influence of the pharmaceutical industry. They suggest that ordinary human responses to extremely stressful life events are being mistaken for psychological disorder.

WHAT IS SCHIZOPHRENIA?

- Schizophrenia affects very few people, but it is the most common psychotic disorder (i.e., a disorder characterized by severely impaired ability to grasp reality and respond rationally). Its symptoms can be divided into two categories: positive symptoms (e.g., hallucinations and delusions) and negative symptoms

(e.g., lack of appropriate emotional responses, facial expressions, or normal speech). Schizophrenia has a strong genetic component, and neurodevelopmental factors may also play a role in its development.

WHAT ARE PERSONALITY DISORDERS?

- Personality disorders are pervasive, chronic patterns of dysfunctional thinking and relating to the world. The personality disorders tend to be relatively stable through the life span and thus are fairly resistant to treatment. However, compared with other psychological disorders, they result in a milder degree of impairment and dysfunction.

- Those with personality disorder suffer impairment in at least two of the following areas: identity, self-direction, empathy, and intimacy.

- There are 10 basic personality disorders according to the DSM-5.

- Dissociative identity disorder (DID or "multiple personality") is perhaps the most controversial diagnosis in the DSM. Some researchers suggest that the "epidemic" of DID over recent decades was created by the media and well-meaning but deluded psychotherapists. Most psychiatrists do not believe there is enough evidence to justify the inclusion of DID in the DSM.

Key Terms

Test Yourself

1. In the _____ view of psychological disorder, psychological disorders are metaphors for problems in living.
   a) myth of mental illness
   b) DSM
   c) harmful dysfunction

2. According to the DSM view, two primary conditions must be satisfied to diagnose any psychological disorder. What are they?

3. How is "dysfunction" defined in the harmful dysfunction view?

4. _____ are chronic, ongoing patterns of dysfunctional thinking and responding that are inflexible, generally begin in adolescence, and reveal themselves in many areas of a person's life.
   a) bipolar disorders
   b) anxiety disorders
   c) major mental disorders
   d) personality disorders

5. True or false: Post-traumatic stress disorder is a rare response to life-threatening trauma.

6. Chronic, unremitting, and irrational worry is characteristic of which disorder?
   a) phobia
   b) obsessive-compulsive disorder
   c) generalized anxiety disorder
   d) panic disorder

7. Those advocating the harmful dysfunction view believe that many people are being labeled with "social phobia" who do not deserve it. Which of the following circumstances would qualify a person for a diagnosis of social phobia according to harmful dysfunction theorists?
   a) A woman is too anxious to ask an attractive man out on a date.
   b) A man is so frightened of embarrassment that he cannot go for job interviews and remains unemployed.
   c) A student is too frightened to give the school valedictorian speech.
   d) A woman walks rather than riding a bus for fear of embarrassing herself while sitting next to a stranger.

8. True or false: A person who has had more than three panic attacks qualifies for a diagnosis of panic disorder.

9. Name at least two common "themes" of obsessions in obsessive-compulsive disorder, and at least one compulsion associated with each of the themes you choose.

10. Which of the following is NOT one of the three vulnerabilities of the triple vulnerability theory?
    a) generalized biological vulnerability
    b) specific biological vulnerability
    c) generalized psychological vulnerability
    d) specific psychological vulnerability

11. True or false: Almost all people with anxiety also suffer from depression.

12. One reason people believe that depression is more common now than in the past is that surveys report a higher lifetime prevalence rate for depression among those born in the later part of the 20th century as compared with those born earlier. However, these statistics do not necessarily demonstrate that depression is more common. Why?

13. True or false: Research has now determined that depression is caused by a chemical imbalance in the brain.

14. What are the three characteristics of the negative cognitive style identified by hoplessness theorists Abramson and Alloy? What is the negative cognitive triad, as identified by Aaron Beck?

15. True or False: Rumination is the tendency to dwell upon negative events of one's life.

16. Allan Horwitz and Jerome Wakefield are concerned that depression is being overdiagnosed. What are the two qualities which differentiate ordinary sadness in response to distressing life events from depressive disorder, according to these theorists?

17. A relatively mild form of mania that is highly pleasurable and may result in increased work productivity is _____.
    a) hedonic mania
    b) hypomania
    c) dysphoric mania
    d) euphoric mania

18. Some bipolar individuals experience symptoms of depression and mania virtually simultaneously. What is this condition called?
    a) rapid cycling
    b) dysphoria
    c) mixed-states
    d) dissociation

19. True or false: In almost every nation, men commit suicide in much higher numbers than women.

20. List at least two positive and three negative symptoms of schizophrenia.

21. A characteristic or symptom that is present in people with a specific disorder and is also present at a high rate in close genetic relatives who do *not* have the disorder is known as:
    a) a genotype
    b) a phenotype
    c) an endophenotype
    d) an endogenotype

22. People suffering from this personality disorder often tend to injure themselves intentionally. They are impulsive, moody, frightened of abandonment, and unstable in their sense of self. They are often involved in stormy relationships. What is the disorder?
    a) borderline personality disorder
    b) paranoid personality disorder
    c) histrionic personality disorder
    d) antisocial personality disorder

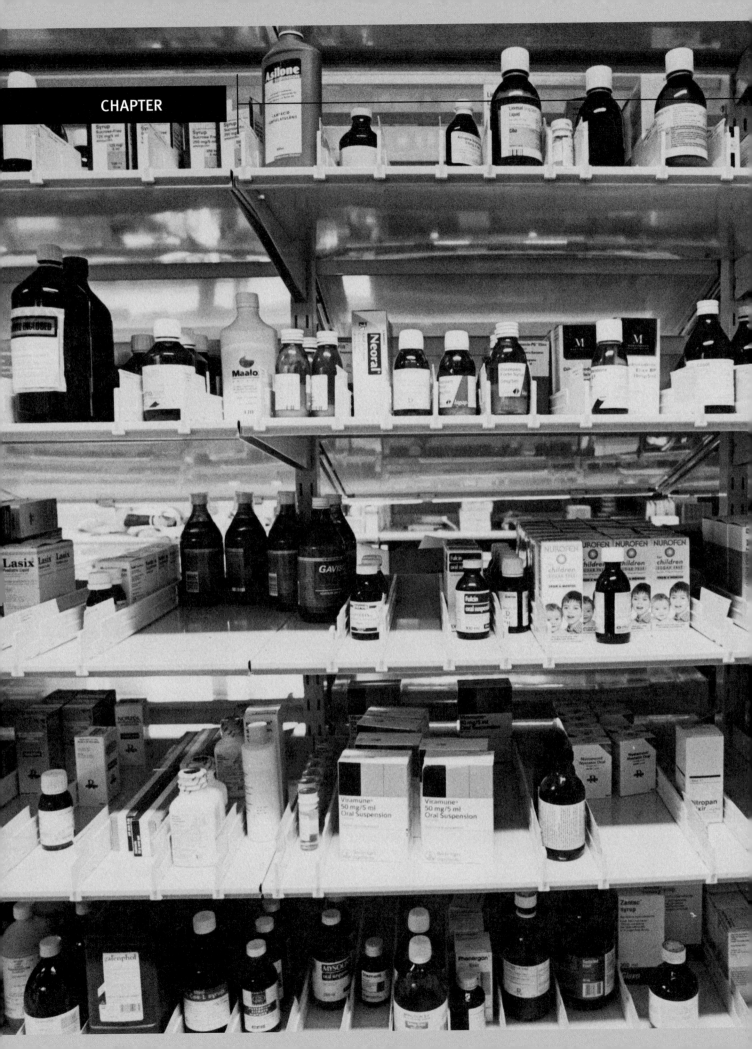

Treatment

Chapter Outline

FREEZE FRAME

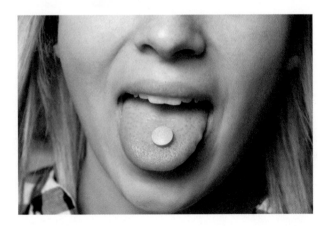

"You asked me to write about what it was like, so here goes. . . .

"Each morning I hoped I would not have to leave my bed, not that day, not ever. I would keep turning, finding a new position, pulling the covers around me and wishing I could sink deeper into the bed. When I just couldn't stand the bed any longer, I would watch television, which only made me feel worse. I'd stopped answering the phone or calling people I knew. I just didn't want to subject other people, even my friends, to my leprous condition. It was as though I were slowly pulling out all my connections to this life. I remember one morning I awoke from a nightmare shouting for help, but instead of being relieved that 'it was all just a dream,' I was actually bitterly disappointed to be back in the reality of my own life. (I think of that James Taylor song where he says, 'It breaks my heart to awaken.')

"Finally my mother called Omar to ask him what was going on with me. Then I had to endure daily visits from my mom during which she bitched and moaned at me non-stop to see a psychotherapist, which I eventually did just to get her off my back. The therapist did nothing for me whatsoever, on top of which I couldn't stand her. She asked me questions like, 'How are you feeling today?' How am I feeling? How the f— do you think I'm feeling?

"Actually, I take that back, Lucy (the therapist) did do something very important for me—she advised me to see a psychiatrist and try to get on antidepressants. I had never in my life thought of taking any kind of drug like that at all, but when I looked in the mirror and saw all the weight I had lost and how much sadness was in my face, I decided to try it.

"The picture above was taken by Omar just nine weeks later. I was back at school, making up as much of the work as I could (I'd had to drop a few classes, but that was no biggie because I was ahead of things anyway), I was eating again, had gone back to the gym, and started to write again. One morning I "suddenly noticed" that the season had changed—it was spring and I had basically just missed the entire winter! It was amazing.

"I thought the depression was done and over. But three months after that, the pills stopped working. It was as though the depression was a virus that had adapted to the presence of the drug and built up immunity to it. This time I became truly terrified because the hopelessness was so severe. Strangely enough, the psychiatrist suggested I go back into psychotherapy! But she told me to try CBT [cognitive-behavior therapy]. The CBT seemed to help in spite of all the idiotic homework I had to do for the therapist, because I started to feel better again within about another month or so, although I didn't feel as well as I had at the beginning of the antidepressant therapy. So then the CBT therapist suggested I stop taking the old antidepressant, which wasn't working anyway, and try a different one. So she sent me back to the psychiatrist! I was getting dizzy from all this.

"I'm not sure exactly when my depression finally lifted entirely, but I remember walking to school one day and thinking: 'Hey. I'm okay.' I'd like to say that it was as though it had never happened, but in some ways I think I've changed permanently—sort of how I imagine what might happen to a soldier who fights in a war for the first time. You don't go through something like that and stay the same. Anyway . . . that's it. I hope this is okay, and thanks for giving me the chance to write about it."

—Paloma, age 30

Drug company advertising and mental health clinic pamphlets often give the impression that treatment for psychological disorders is a straightforward matter, like taking an antibiotic for an ear infection. This is not always the case—and probably is not even usually the case. Many people search for painful months or even years to find a treatment that works, and large numbers receive little benefit from treatment (Goldberg, Privett, Ustun, Simon, & Linden, 1998; Rubinow, 2006; Westen & Morrison, 2001; Wisniewski et al., 2009). In addition, there is no treatment—pill or therapy—that is free of the potential for serious side effects (Kirsch, 2005; Lieberman, Stroup, McEvoy, Swartz, & Rosenheck, 2005; Lilienfeld, 2007).

Yet millions of people receive treatment for mental health problems every year, and many of these sufferers do find relief for their symptoms—sometimes dramatic relief. The treatments for psychological disorders can be classified into two general categories: psychological approaches, which include various kinds of individual and group psychotherapies and other services; and biological approaches, which include the use of drugs, electrical stimulation, and psychosurgery. In this chapter I will describe these treatments and some thorny issues surrounding their use.

What Is Psychotherapy?

When people think of treatments for psychological disorders, psychotherapy is often the first method that comes to mind. But is psychotherapy merely a matter of "talking it out" with another person? Is talking to a qualified psychotherapist very much different from talking one's problems over with a friend, family member, or religious advisor?

Psychotherapy Involves a Healing Personal Relationship

When a psychotherapist works with a client a unique, healing relationship is formed. Prior to the 20th century this type of relationship did not exist. Confidential discussions between individuals and respected relatives, friends, teachers, mentors, priests, rabbis, and ministers occurred in times of trouble and stress, but these relationships differed substantially from that of the modern psychotherapy relationship in at least five ways:

▲ **The Consulting Room.** The appearance of a psychotherapist's consulting room is often carefully constructed to create a particular type of environment conducive to therapeutic work.

- *In psychotherapy the focus is entirely on the client's needs and problems.* Efforts are made to ensure that the therapists' needs and problems do not enter into the relationship.
- *The therapist is paid a fee for his or her time and expertise.*
- *The psychotherapy relationship takes place in a structured setting.* Typically this setting is the therapists' consulting room, although therapy may also be conducted by telephone or even computer under certain circumstances (Andrews, Cuijpers, Craske, McEvoy, & Titov, 2010; Beckner, Vella, Howard, & Mohr, 2007). A key ethical principle is that therapists and clients rarely interact socially.
- *Each meeting between the therapist and the client is time-limited.* A typical session lasts 50 minutes and occurs once, twice, or sometimes three times weekly.
- *The psychotherapy relationship is expected to terminate.* The quality of most other personal relationships is judged by their longevity. Exactly the opposite is the case in psychotherapy: By most standards, a therapeutic relationship that lasts a lifetime would be judged a dismal failure.

People Enter Psychotherapy for Many Reasons

Treatment for psychological disorders is undoubtedly the most important function of **psychotherapy**, but it is not the only function. Although a DSM diagnosis (see Chapter 13) almost always must be given to a client for insurance reimbursement to take place, many people who enter psychotherapy do not have a psychological disorder. What, then, are they doing in therapy?

Some people enter therapy because they are suffering psychologically as a normal consequence of a distressing event, such as the death of a loved one or the breakup of an important relationship (Horwitz & Wakefield, 2007). People may also seek therapy when they are facing or contemplating a turning point in life—a career change, for example, or a divorce. They use therapy to sort out their thoughts and feelings about this impending change. Others have found themselves mired in self-defeating habits and patterns of relating to others, and are looking for help in making changes in their general approach to life. In these cases, people use therapy to better the quality of their lives or for self-improvement.

Psychotherapy ▶ A unique, modern, healing relationship involving a client and a paid therapist. The relationship is temporary and focused entirely on the needs and problems of the client. Each meeting of therapist and client is time-limited, confidential, and conducted in a structured setting.

There Are Different Styles of Psychotherapy

As you might expect given the many ideas about the causes of psychological disorders discussed in the previous chapter, there are many ideas about how best to administer psychotherapy. By the close of the 20th century, at least 400 different types of psychotherapy had been created.

In addition to reflecting different theoretical orientations and perspectives about the causes of psychological disorders and emotional distress, styles of therapy also reflect differences in philosophy about the therapist-client relationship. For example, *psychoanalysis* historically has characterized the analyst as a mentally sound "doctor" treating "patients" who are, at least in comparison, less than mentally sound. *Behavior therapists* see themselves as something closer to a teacher and the client as a student whose task it is to substitute adaptive patterns of behavior for maladaptive patterns. *Cognitive therapists* see the therapist-client relationship as that of two collaborators on relatively equal footing, using "hypothesis-testing" techniques to correct irrational or inaccurate beliefs that might be triggering the client's emotional pain or dysfunction.

Table 14.1 lists and briefly describes the styles of therapy we will explore.

Psychotherapists' Training Varies Widely

In the United States, Great Britain, and Canada, anyone—including a person who never graduated from high school—can call himself or herself a "psychotherapist," print up cards, open an office, and begin treating clients. No laws would be broken unless the person claims to have a license or an academic degree he or she does not actually possess. The term *psychotherapist* is thus *unprotected* by laws governing its use.[1] Indeed, therapy is practiced by a great many unlicensed paraprofessionals, some of whom have little or no specific knowledge of psychology or training in administering therapy other than that derived from attending workshops.

Paraprofessional ▶ A person who has obtained a nonprofessional level of education in a field such as education, law, or psychology, but who has obtained a job performing some of the duties ordinarily carried out by professionals.

Paraprofessional therapists may be religious or spiritual counselors, substance-abuse counselors, art and dance therapists, crisis intervention workers, suicide hotline operators, rape and child sexual abuse counselors, and so forth. While some paraprofessionals may have questionable skills, some perform therapy just as successfully as those with advanced degrees and licensing. In fact, paraprofessionals sometimes achieve results superior to those of highly trained therapists (Atkins & Christensen, 2001; Lambert, 2005).

More commonly, however, psychotherapists receive extensive training, and many (but not all) have advanced educational degrees in medicine, psychology, social work, education, or a similar field. The psychotherapy occupations requiring the most rigorous education in psychology are *clinical psychologist* and *counseling psychologist*, both of which require a Ph.D. or Psy.D.[2] in psychology as well as a certain number of hours performing psychotherapy under the supervision of an experienced therapist. Training in certain styles of clinical or counseling psychology may also require that the student experience at least some psychotherapy himself or herself. About half of all advanced degrees in psychology are awarded in clinical and counseling psychology (Mayne, Norcross, & Sayette, 2000).

How do the professions of clinical and counseling psychology differ? This is a controversial topic. However, the two undoubtedly have more similarities than differences (Cobb et al., 2004). Clinical and counseling psychologists perform much the same work, although counseling psychology graduate programs

---

[1] *Although the term* psychotherapist *is unprotected as of this writing, there are movements to change this, although they have not as yet been successful.*

[2] *A Psy.D. is a professional degree in psychology specifically designed for those entiring clinical fields. Training is similar to that given to Ph.D. students, although there generally is less emphasis on conducting and interpreting research.*

Table 14.1 Psychotherapies at a Glance

THERAPY	THEORETICAL PERSPECTIVE	FOUNDERS	KEY CONCEPTS
Psychoanalysis	Psychoanalysis	Sigmund Freud	Disorders caused by unresolved intrapsychic conflicts; long-term, intensive analysis; sometimes on a daily basis; analyst as interpreter and neutral observer; insight necessary for healing.
Psychodynamic Therapy	Psychodynamic	No founder	Disorders often (but not always) caused by unresolved intrapsychic conflicts; therapy usually, but not always, long-term; therapist free to conduct therapy as he or she sees fit; insight necessary for healing.
Behavior Therapy	Behaviorist	Joseph Wolpe	Disorders caused by learned, maladaptive behaviors; therapy systematic and short-term; therapist as teacher; client learns to substitute adaptive behaviors for maladaptive behaviors; insight unnecessary for healing.
Rational Emotive Behavior Therapy (REBT)	Cognitive	Albert Ellis	Disorders and psychological suffering caused by irrational and absolutist beliefs (the ABC model); therapy usually relatively short-term; therapist as blunt challenger of such beliefs; altering the beliefs alleviates the emotional suffering.
Cognitive and Cognitive-Behavior Therapy (CT/CBT)	Cognitive	Aaron Beck and others	Disorders and psychological suffering caused or worsened by distorted patterns of thinking biased against the self and resultant behaviors; Therapy designed to be short-term; therapist as "scientist-collaborator" with client, testing client's beliefs against evidence; changing the way one thinks changes how one feels.
Client-Centered Therapy	Humanistic	Carl Rogers	Disorders and psychological suffering caused by lack of unconditional positive regard, genuineness, and acceptance from others; therapy usually long term; therapist as an empathic, caring person, allowing the client to direct therapy and offering unconditional acceptance.
Family Therapy	Family Systems	Murray Bowen	The family is considered an organic unit or "system" wherein members interact dynamically. No one person is singled out for treatment—rather, the entire family is the "client."
Integrative Therapy	Multiple sources	No founder	Probably more common than any of the others; techniques tailored to individual client; "Use what works!" is key.

Table 14.2 The Theoretical Perspectives of Clinical and Counseling Psychologists

(Based on data collected among 1,379 randomly selected clinical and counseling psychologists by Bechtoldt, Norcross, Wyckoff, Pokrywa, & Campbell, 2001)

THEORETICAL PERSPECTIVE (N = 1,379)		%
Integrative/eclectic	400	29
Cognitive	358	26
Psychodynamic	163	12
Behaviorist	130	9
Humanistic	87	6
Family systems	52	4
Psychoanalytic	46	3
Other	143	10

are generally housed in departments of education rather than psychology departments.

Table 14.2 compares the proportions of clinical and counseling psychologists who adhere to each of the perspectives from which the various styles of psychotherapy listed in Table 14.1 evolved.

IN SUMMARY

1. Psychotherapy is a healing personal relationship created during the 20th century. Although it bears certain things in common with other types of confidential conversations in times of trouble, it is unique in a number of ways.

2. Advanced education is not necessary to practice psychotherapy, but most therapists have received extensive training of some sort, and many hold advanced graduate degrees. About half of advanced degrees are held by clinical and counseling psychologists.

3. Different styles of therapy have emerged from differing theories about the causes of psychological disorders and different philosophies about the appropriate relationship of therapist to client.

4. People enter therapy for many reasons, including issues not related to the treatment of psychological disorders—for example, crisis intervention, self-improvement, and betterment of the quality of life.

RETRIEVE!

1. List at least three ways in which the psychotherapy relationship differs from other relationships involving confidential healing conversation.

2. True or false: Unlicensed paraprofessionals may conduct therapy that is as effective as that conducted by therapists with extensive training and experience.

3. True or false: As a general rule, anyone can practice as a psychotherapist without a professional degree, as long as the person does not claim to have such a degree.

How Do Styles of Psychotherapy Differ?

As stated earlier, styles of therapy differ because psychologists differ in their beliefs about the causes of psychological distress and the sorts of client-therapist relationships that are most conducive to recovery. Although there are literally hundreds of therapy styles in existence, a few may be singled out as the most influential over the past half-century: *psychoanalysis, psychodynamic psychotherapy, behavior therapy, cognitive therapies,* and *integrative therapy.*

Psychoanalysis: Uncommon, but Influential

I should begin my discussion of common forms of psychotherapy with the one that is the least common, but in some ways most influential: psychoanalysis. As discussed in Chapters 1 and 12, the very first organized form of psychotherapy was psychoanalysis, created by Sigmund Freud (1856–1939) and Bertha Pappenheim (1859–1936), a patient of Freud's mentor Josef Breuer. Psychoanalysis is not only the first, but also by far the most expensive and time-intensive form of psychotherapy—requiring three to five visits per week for many years, sometimes more than a decade. That could add up to as much as $500,000 for the complete treatment!

Psychoanalysis is also the most controversial of all forms of legitimate psychotherapy. Indeed, Drew Westen (1998) observes that most current theorists and researchers in psychology probably consider the techniques of psychoanalysis ineffective and wasteful at best—although he adds that therapists themselves are often more generous in their evaluation of Freud as a theorist.

Psychoanalysis as practiced by Freud and his followers is usually referred to as *classical psychoanalysis*. It is based on Freud's notion that psychological problems are caused by intrapsychic conflict—tension within a person's own mind between mental forces that are at odds with one another. These conflicts are thought to be primarily *unconscious*—that is, the person is unaware of their existence. According to Freud, such conflicts typically involve "forbidden" sexual or aggressive desires and impulses often rooted in childhood experiences (see Chapter 12). It is the job of psychoanalysis to uncover such conflicts so that they can be realistically faced and resolved. Thus, the goal of classical psychoanalysis is insight, or accurate self-knowledge. To obtain insight, however, the patient must overcome his or her own *resistance* to this knowledge—a resistance based on fear and anxiety about facing unpleasant truths.

Techniques of classical psychoanalysis include *dream work*, where patients' dreams are interpreted by the analyst with assistance from the patients' own *free associations* to the dream material. In free association, the patient—typically lying in a relaxed position on a couch or seated in a comfortable armchair—relates to the analyst all thoughts and ideas that go through his or her mind when thinking about dream imagery or describing important events and relationships of his or her childhood. The purpose of free association is to allow unconscious material to be expressed without censorship from the patient's conscious mind.

The role of the psychoanalyst is that of a neutral observer and interpreter. He or she avoids eye contact while the patient is free associating, and may even remain out of sight, seated in a chair behind the patient. The reason for this emotionally cool approach is that the psychoanalyst wants *transference* to develop so that it may be analyzed. Transference refers to the psychoanalytic belief that patients in therapy may *transfer* their feelings about their spouse,

▲ The Analyst's Couch?
Traditionally, psychoanalysts allowed their patients to recline for greater relaxation and often seated themselves behind their patients to allow *transference* to develop. Modern psychoanalysts do not necessarily adhere to these practices.

Psychodynamic psychotherapy ▶ A general approach to psychotherapy based on principles originating in psychoanalysis. Psychodynamic theorists share psychoanalytic beliefs that unconscious emotional and motivational processes exert important effects on a person, that the origins of personality are in childhood, and that human beings create symbolic mental representations of the self and important personal relationships.

parent, or other important people in their lives (even themselves) onto the therapist. By analyzing this transference, the therapist hopes to encourage insight in the patient. This process must proceed unimpeded by the actual personality and other characteristics of the analyst. Thus, the analyst remains a blank figure, waiting to be "colored in" by the patient.

PSYCHOANALYSIS TODAY

Psychoanalysis was a highly influential movement in that it introduced the idea that simply talking to a trained mental health professional could provide substantial relief from symptoms of mental illness. However, as discussed in Chapter 12, Freud and the theory and therapy he created have been soundly criticized on numerous grounds (Crews, 1996; Macmillan, 1996). For these reasons—and undoubtedly also due to its cost and lengthy course—psychoanalysis is currently among the least frequently performed styles of therapy (see Table 14.2).

Nonetheless, psychoanalysis has evolved substantially since Freud's day, particularly in Europe, and few modern analysts consider themselves to be direct followers of Freud. Far more popular than classical Freudian analysis is analysis based on *object relations theory*. Object relations theorists do acknowledge a debt to Freud, and they continue to stress the importance of intrapsychic conflict, transference, and many other psychoanalytic concepts. However, they do not focus exclusively on sex and aggression as the basis for these conflicts, and they place much more importance than Freud did on the *quality* of a person's actual relationships with important others.

Psychodynamic Psychotherapy

Perhaps the most important development in psychoanalysis in the later 20th century was the "detaching" of Freud and the object relations theorists from their fairly rigid prescriptions for how to conduct therapy. The result is termed modern **psychodynamic psychotherapy** (Shedler, 2010; Westen, 1998). The term *psychodynamic* implies the idea of intrapsychic conflict. Thus, psychodynamic therapists accept many of the principles of psychoanalytic theory of the mind and behavior, but have discarded the technique of psychoanalysis itself as a form of therapy. Jonathon Shedler (2010) has compiled a list of features that differentiate the techniques of psychodynamic therapy from many other types of therapy. Among these features are:

- Focus on helping the client to express emotion
- Exploring situations where the client tries to avoid distressing thoughts or feelings in therapy
- Identifying recurring psychological themes in the client's inner world and life experiences
- Discussing past experiences—often long-past childhood experiences
- Focus on the client's relationships with other people
- Focus on the relationship between the client and therapist
- Exploring the client's fantasy life and dreams

Like psychoanalysis, psychodynamic therapy is generally expected to take time, often years. However, in keeping with the general movement toward devising briefer types of psychotherapeutic treatment, during the 1980s and 1990s short-term versions of psychodynamic theory were developed and are being used now with increasing frequency (Dewan, Weerasekera, & Stormon, 2009; Leichsenring, Rabung, & Leibing, 2004; Messer, 2001).

Behavior Therapy: Changing Maladaptive Behavior

Behavior therapy was created in direct opposition to psychoanalytic and psychodynamic therapy. It is based on the behaviorists' and social learning theorists' views that psychological disorders represent learned patterns of *maladaptive* (counterproductive) behaviors. According to behavior therapists, all the insight in the world is useless if it does not help to reshape behavior by substituting *adaptive* (productive, desired) behaviors and associations for those that are maladaptive. Although discussions of thoughts, feelings, and past events may enter into behavior therapy, its focus is on present, observable, changeable behavior. Above all, the behavior therapist is a *teacher*—taking an active role in therapy, helping the client to learn tested techniques to change learned patterns of unwanted behavior. Behavior therapies are often termed *behavior modification* because they use classical and operant conditioning techniques (see Chapter 7) to modify the client's unwanted behaviors.

The "mother" of behavior therapy was Mary Cover Jones (1896–1987), a student of John Watson, the founder of the behaviorist movement in psychology. Although Jones later rejected many of the behaviorists' views in favor of an approach that focused on the uniqueness of the individual (Rutherford, 2000), her successful attempt to "extinguish" (remove) the fear of furry animals in a 3-year old boy named Peter is the first recorded use of behavior therapy techniques (M. C. Jones, 1924a, 1924b). Jones accomplished this feat by bringing a rabbit increasingly close to Peter over time, but pairing each exposure with a piece of Peter's favorite candy. In this way she used classical conditioning to help Peter develop pleasurable associations with rabbits.

EXPOSURE THERAPIES

Jones' research was conducted during a time when psychoanalysis was in the spotlight, and not much attention was paid to her work until several decades later when the field of behavior therapy was officially named and founded by South African psychiatrist Joseph Wolpe (1915–1997). Deeply committed to the behaviorist approach, Wolpe created a number of techniques to treat anxiety, particularly phobia, through controlled *exposure* of the phobic person to the feared object or situation.

The best known of Wolpe's techniques elaborates on the procedure used by Jones to treat little Peter. Known as **systematic desensitization** (Wolpe, 1982), this technique exposes the client over time to increasingly intense and uncomfortable mental or visual images of the feared object or situation ("Imagine that you're walking past a room with a snake inside . . . now imagine that you're opening the door . . . now you're going inside the room. . . ."). These increasingly intense images are known as the *anxiety hierarchy*.

While navigating the anxiety hierarchy, the client simultaneously engages in relaxation exercises such as *progressive muscle relaxation*—systematically tightening and then relaxing the major muscle groups throughout the body. The idea behind this practice is that relaxation is incompatible with anxiety—the two cannot be present in a person at the same time. After learning to reduce anxiety in the face of the anxiety hierarchy during treatment sessions, the client is encouraged to try the technique in the actual phobic situation. Alternatively, if feasible, the entire process can be accomplished *in vivo*—that is, using the actual phobic object during the process of systematic desensitization.

Another technique similar to systematic desensitization is **flooding**. While systematic desensitization gently and systematically turns up the heat using an anxiety hierarchy, flooding takes a more brutal approach and essentially tosses the client in at the highest possible level of anxiety-provoking situation and holds him or her there—sometimes for hours at a time. For example, a person with a phobia of small animals might be required to sit with a lab rat on his lap for an hour or more. (Of course, no one is literally *required* to do this—flooding therapy is done strictly by mutual agreement.)

One basic assumption underlies both systematic desensitization and flooding: Phobias are maintained by avoidance of the feared object or situation,

Behavior therapy ▶ Techniques of therapy based on learning principles of behaviorism and social learning theory. The point of behavior therapy is to teach the client how to substitute adaptive patterns of behavior for maladaptive patterns. Behavior therapy techniques utilize classical and operant conditioning strategies (see Chapter 7).

Systematic desensitization ▶ A behavior therapy technique primarily used to treat phobias and certain other anxiety disorders. Systematic desensitization involves controlled, incremental exposure to phobic stimuli while simultaneously practicing relaxation techniques that are incompatible with anxiety.

Flooding ▶ An exposure therapy used to treat phobia and other anxiety disorders. Flooding involves non-incremental, total immersion in anxiety-producing phobic stimuli for a prolonged period.

▶ **Virtual Reality Exposure Therapy.**
Virtual reality technology makes
exposure therapy more feasible
for a wider variety of problems. It
appears to work at least as well as
exposure to the real thing—and
in some cases, better (Powers &
Emmelkamp, 2008).

Exposure therapy ▶ Any
technique of behavior therapy
based on the idea that only
through exposure to feared
stimuli can the anxiety
produced by that stimuli be
lessened. Although exposure
therapy technically refers to
any such technique, the term
is used most often to refer
to contemporary therapies
rather than earlier behavior
therapies such as systematic
desensitization.

Operant therapies ▶ A type
of behavior therapy based on
principles of learning that
relis on operant conditioning,
in which rewards or
punishments for a person's
spontaneous behaviors
are used to shape desired
behaviors.

**Contingency management
(CM)** ▶ A type of operant
treatment used in various
types of institutions (e.g.,
substance abuse rehab,
psychiatric wards, prisons).
In CM treatment a person
is rewarded with tangible,
desirable goods, prizes,
or privileges for engaging
in desirable behaviors
and avoiding undesirable
behaviors.

and the solution is to compel the phobic person to face his or her fears directly.
During exposure the person is also exposed to corrective *information* about
the feared object or situation (Foa & Kozak, 1986). For example, after hours
with a lab rat on his lap the sufferer can see clearly that the rat is harmless.

Although systematic desensitization and flooding are used with less frequency than in the past, they have formed the basis of contemporary **exposure
therapies**, all of which are based on Wolpe's original insight that exposing a
person to a feared stimulus under controlled conditions can reduce or eliminate the fear. Using streamlined techniques and new technologies such as virtual reality, clinicians have devised exposure treatments that accomplish in
a single day-long session what previously took weeks to accomplish through
systematic desensitization (Antony & Barlow, 2002; Sharp & Espie, 2004).

OPERANT THERAPIES

Exposure therapies are based on models taken from classical conditioning.
Through these therapies, the client learns to form new associations to feared
stimuli. **Operant therapies** are also based on principles of learning, but they
rely on operant conditioning, in which rewards or punishments for a person's spontaneous behaviors are used to shape desired behaviors (see Chapter
7). One such operant technique is known as **contingency management**
(Higgins, Silverman, & Washio, 2011). In contingency management, a person
is rewarded with tangible, desirable goods, prizes, or privileges for engaging in
desired behaviors and avoiding undesirable behaviors.

An early form of contingency management was the *token economy* (Kazdin,
2001). In a token economy, inmates of an institution—be it a school, mental hospital, or prison—earn chips or tokens for performing desired behaviors. The tokens may then be cashed in for snacks, books or other goods, TV
privileges, visitation rights, and so forth, depending on the particular type of
institution.

However, token economies are difficult to set up and maintain. For this reason, and also in keeping with the movement toward shortened hospital stays
for psychiatric patients, new methods using the basic ideas behind token
economies have been devised to treat outpatients, particularly those with substance abuse problems. These methods work by allotting prizes (or chances to
win prizes) to those who have remained abstinent from the abused substance
and have engaged in various productive behaviors, such as spending time with
their families (Higgins, Silverman, & Heil, 2007; Lewis & Petry, 2005). As

described in the "Freeze Frame" feature that opens Chapter 7, contingency management added to standard outpatient substance abuse treatments can often work where ordinary treatments standing alone have failed (Rash, Alessi, & Petry, 2008).

Cognitive Therapies: Changing Feelings by Changing Thoughts

During the mid-1950s an event occurred that was to have major repercussions for the field of psychotherapy in later decades: A maverick psychoanalyst named Albert Ellis (1913–2007) grew dissatisfied with the classical psychoanalysis he was practicing. He decided that remaining silent while seated on a chair behind a reclining, free-associating client on a near-daily basis was a waste of time. He tried switching to a form of psychodynamic therapy, but he didn't find that much better. In thinking about his own life, Ellis decided that it was the written works and ideas of the great philosophers of history and other authors that had helped him deal with his own problems—more successfully and easily than all the psychoanalysis he had experienced himself. He concluded that rational *thought* was the best possible cure for *emotional* distress. As Ellis later declared, "[W]hat we call emotion is nothing more than a certain kind—a biased, prejudiced kind—of thought, and that human beings can be taught to control their feelings by controlling their thoughts . . ." (Ellis, 1957, p. 344). Ellis's insight marked the birth of *cognitive therapies*—treatments based on the principle that changes in thoughts and actions can produce changes in feeling.

RATIONAL-EMOTIVE BEHAVIOR THERAPY (REBT)

Based on his insights, Ellis devised a new form of therapy that ultimately came to be called **rational-emotive behavior therapy** (**REBT**; Ellis, 2001). According to Ellis, people grow up with illogical, absolutist, and counterproductive ideas such as, "If I don't perform perfectly I'm a failure," "If I don't make a lot of money I'll be unhappy," "I can't make it on my own," and so forth.

Unlike most other forms of therapy, the REBT therapist can be highly confrontational and forceful. Ellis believed that his clients often needed the cold water of reality splashed in their faces. REBT therapists may bluntly dispute their clients' beliefs, as a parent might do for a confused child: "Where is it written that life is always fair? It usually isn't, so get over that idea as quickly as you can," is an example of therapeutic advice that might be conveyed during an REBT session.

COGNITIVE THERAPY (CT)

Although highly respected, REBT is quite unconventional in the world of established psychotherapy, and it did not initially have a very great impact beyond Ellis's circle of followers. However, during the 1960s, a psychiatrist named Aaron Beck, influenced by Ellis's work and also by scientific research and theories that link cognition and emotion, devised what he termed **cognitive therapy** (**CT**; Beck, 1991, 2005; Beck, Rush, Shaw, & Emery, 1979). Beck, like Ellis, had previously practiced psychoanalysis. He noticed that people with emotional disturbances tended to experience "automatic thoughts" that were highly unrealistic, self-defeating, and biased against themselves. For example, they may expand a single shortcoming into the categorical statement "I never do anything right." According to Beck, repeated "self-talk" of this sort and automatic, biased interpretations of events are frequently the cause of psychological disturbance—or if not always the direct cause, they represent serious roadblocks to recovery.

Where do these biased interpretations of events come from? According to Beck, a person may interpret events in a distorted way when he or she

Rational-emotive behavior therapy (REBT) ▶ A form of therapy devised by Albert Ellis and based on the idea that emotional distress is rooted in illogical, absolutist, and counterproductive ideas and beliefs. REBT is *directive*—the therapist's job is to forcefully dispute the client's illogical and unrealistic beliefs.

Cognitive therapy (CT) ▶ The therapy principally devised by Aaron Beck that suggests that when people possess underlying dysfunctional core beliefs about the self, the world, and the future, they respond to events with automatic thoughts that are self-defeating and biased against the self. These thoughts trigger negative emotional experiences and can lead to disorders such as depression and anxiety. Unlike REBT, with which it shares a cognitive approach, the cognitive therapist does not forcefully dispute the client's unrealistic beliefs but helps the client to test these beliefs in the manner of a scientist testing a hypothesis.

possesses dysfunctional, underlying core beliefs about the self, the world, and the future—the *negative cognitive triad* we described in Chapter 13. For example, one such dysfunctional belief might be, "If I can't succeed at something important, I'm a complete failure" (Beck, 2005).

Although Beck's basic idea is somewhat similar to Ellis's views, CT is quite different from REBT. Cognitive therapists are not confrontational, and they do not offer advice. Instead, they attempt to form a gentler "scientific collaboration" with their clients, whereby clients' distorted beliefs are "tested" against real-world evidence. A man may feel like a complete failure yet have a wife and children who are devoted to him, earn in excess of $200,000 a year, and be this year's Pulitzer Prize winner in literature. It would be one of the tasks of the cognitive therapist to help the client use these facts as evidence of areas of life in which the client is not at all a failure.

COGNITIVE BEHAVIOR THERAPY (CBT)

Cognitive behavior therapy (CBT) ▶ A development of behavior therapy that attempts to unite traditional behavior therapy with Beck's cognitive therapy. CBT is based on the idea that cognition, emotion, and behavior are linked in a circle of mutual influence and reinforcement. Although CBT is not identical to CT (cognitive therapy), the term *cognitive behavior therapy* is often used to refer to either therapy.

Although cognitive therapy was (and continues to be) enormously influential, after a time some behavior therapists and their allies in the cognitive camp came to the conclusion that the link between cognition and emotion is a complicated one that needs to include both cognition and *behavior* (Rachman, 2009). As depicted in Figure 14.1, thought, emotion, and behavior are linked in a circle of mutual influence and reinforcement (Hollon & Beck, 1994). This perspective led to the development of **cognitive behavior therapy** (**CBT**; Godfried, 2003; O'Donohue, Fisher, & Hayes, 2003).

To see how CBT works, consider Rodney, who has been earning a modest living as a writer for several years. As a result of genetic and life experience factors, Rodney has acquired dysfunctional ideas about himself ("I'm a fraud"), the world ("It's next to impossible to get ahead unless you have big-time connections"), and the future ("I'm going to end up penniless in the streets").

Now, what might happen if Rodney submits a short story on which he has pinned hopes of wider success to a magazine for which he has always wanted to write—but the story is rejected? Because Rodney thinks of himself, the world, and the future as he does, his reaction to the rejection is the following *thought*: "I knew this would happen; I'm just not good enough. I'm such a loser." These thoughts lead to the *feelings* of sadness, worthlessness, and hopelessness. The thought also leads to *behaviors*—in this case, Rodney doesn't revise the manuscript and resubmit it, and he stops work on the novel he is close to finishing ("My stuff is worthless anyway"). He begins to drink heavily. These behaviors further reinforce the thoughts of failure because they provide "evidence" of failure—after all, you can't have a successful writing career if you don't finish your work and submit it. Still more self-defeating behaviors, thoughts, and emotions follow as Rodney ends up in a deepening spiral of despair.

According to the cognitive behavior therapy framework, this cycle needs to be broken not only by disputing dysfunctional beliefs and interpretations, as in cognitive therapy, but also by substituting constructive behaviors for self-defeating ones.

CBT has become extremely popular as a therapy, perhaps eclipsing CT in number of practitioners. However, over the years the distinction between CT and CBT has been lost to some extent, because the term *cognitive behavior therapy* is often used regardless of which type of therapy is being discussed (Beck, 2005), and many people are confused about whether a difference actually exists.

MINDFULNESS-BASED COGNITIVE THERAPY (MBCT)

The newest form of cognitive therapy found to be useful in combating depression—particularly relapse in depression—is mindfulness-based cognitive therapy (MBCT; Segal et al., 2010; Segal, Williams & Teasdale, 2002). Mindfulness-based cognitive therapy is a relatively brief (8-week) program

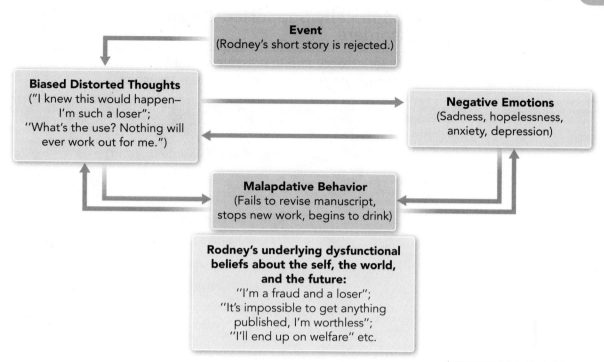

▲ **FIGURE 14.1** Cognitive-Behavioral View of the Origin of Psychological Symptoms. According to cognitive behavior therapists, cognition, emotion, and behavior mutually influence and reinforce one another. When a person has underlying negative beliefs about the self, the world, and the future (the negative cognitive triad), negative events can trigger cognitions that influence both emotion and behavior. Emotion and behavior in turn influence one another and also the probability of further negative cognitions.

that blends CBT with meditation techniques based on Buddhist practices. Randomized-controlled trials have shown MBCT to be at least as effective as other forms of cognitive therapy and antidepressant medication in treating and preventing relapse in major depression (Coelho, Canter, & Ernst, 2007; Kuyken et al., 2008; Segal et al., 2010).

CBT AND EMPIRICALLY SUPPORTED TREATMENTS

CBT is part of an influential movement to create therapies whose worth can be objectively evaluated in controlled research. This is done using a method similar to that used to evaluate drugs prior to their release on the market, the *randomized controlled trial* (RCT). In randomized controlled trials, researchers statistically compare the performance of the therapy or drug against a placebo and/or a "no-treatment" condition—a group of people who are on a waiting list and receive no treatment until after the study period is complete. Psychotherapies that demonstrate superiority over no treatment for a given disorder are known as **empirically supported treatments** (**ESTs**; Hollon, 2006; Siev, Huppert, & Chambless, 2009). As a result of the advent of managed care for psychological problems and controversy over the effectiveness of certain psychotherapies (e.g., psychoanalysis), psychologists wishing to be reimbursed by insurance companies for their services are increasingly compelled to demonstrate that their therapies work and are cost-effective. (See Table 14.3 for a partial list of ESTs for anxiety and depressive disorders.)

Because they are intended to be cost-effective, ESTs tend to be relatively brief—often lasting no more than 6 to 8 weeks. They use highly specific techniques that can be described in treatment manuals and taught relatively easily to any psychotherapist competent enough to participate in a research study of therapy outcomes. CBT lends itself particularly well to this model because it is based on clear principles and techniques; it does not necessarily rely on therapists' empathy, the "fit" between therapist and client, or other difficult-to-measure variables. (However, as we shall see later, such variables may be of more critical importance in the therapeutic process than some in the EST movement believe.)

Empirically supported treatment (EST) ▶ A psychotherapy EST is therapy that has demonstrated statistically significant superiority over no treatment (and in some cases also to a placebo therapy) in a series of randomized clinical trials. Psychotherapy ESTs are generally brief and consist of highly specific techniques that may be described in treatment manuals.

Table 14.3 A Partial List of Empirically Supported Treatments (ESTs) for Anxiety and Depressive Disorders

The following is a partial list of ESTs for anxiety and depressive disorders based on their popularity in graduate training programs and clinical internships

CLASS OF DISORDERS	DISORDER	TREATMENT
Anxiety	Generalized anxiety disorder	Cognitive behavior therapy (CBT)
	Panic attacks	Cognitive behavior therapy (CBT)
	Obsessive-compulsive disorder	Exposure therapies
	Specific phobia	Exposure therapies
	Agoraphobia	Exposure therapies
	Social phobia	Exposure therapies
Depressive	Major Depression	Behavior therapy
		Cognitive behavior therapy (CBT)
		Interpersonal therapy (IPT) (Note: IPT is a brief type of therapy for depression with roots in psychodynamic therapy)

(Adapted from data supplied in Woody et al., 2005.)

LIVING PSYCHOLOGY

Cognitive Therapy to Fight Depression

According to cognitive therapists, depression can be caused, and is always worsened, by unrealistic, biased, and counterproductive ways of thinking. Cognitive therapists have identified a number of specific patterns of distorted thinking in vulnerable individuals that can lead to depression. Here are a few of these patterns:

1. *Overgeneralization.* Taking a single negative event and concluding that all events in your life will be similar. For example, you get laid off and conclude that you'll always have a hard time holding a job.

2. *Disqualifying the positive.* Only negative experiences are meaningful— positive experiences "don't count" for one reason or another ("Yeah, everyone who's read my poetry loves it, but they're all people who know me—of course they're going to like it. Their praise doesn't count.")

3. *Catastrophizing* and *minimizing.* When negative events occur (you are turned down for a promotion at work or score poorly on an important test), life on earth as you know it is over. You'll end up homeless for sure. That's catastrophizing. When positive events occur (you win a prestigious scholarship to study at Berklee College of Music), "nothing much will probably come of it." That's minimizing.

4. *Mind-reading.* Assuming that you know people's thoughts and motivations without evidence. For example, if your girlfriend seems withdrawn and irritable one day, you conclude that she's getting tired of you. It doesn't occur to you that the real reason is that she only got 2 hours of sleep the night before and has to face a late shift at work.

5. *Magnifying.* Blowing things out of proportion. A small mistake becomes a tragic failure; a minor suggestion is interpreted as scathing criticism. Things are "overwhelming," "impossible," "huge." You "can't stand this anymore," you're "losing it," you're "going to fall apart" (McKay, Davis & Fanning, 2007).

6. *Filtering.* You only pay attention to, and recall, the negative, while letting the positive slip by. Consider a day when your professor sharply criticizes your work, you are hired for the job you've been hoping for, your romantic partner finally declares his or her love for you, and you win $100 in a football pool—yet you only think about your professor's criticism. It's been a "horrendous" day.

These patterns of distorted thought, as well as a number of others identified by cognitive therapists, are automatic habits. Many of us, even if we are not clinically depressed, may engage in them from time to time, but they are dysfunctional when they take over and become the dominant way in which a person thinks. To assess how prevalent someone's distorted thinking is, a cognitive-behavior therapist may ask the person to keep a "thought journal." This exercise not only shows the therapist how often the person engages in self-defeating thoughts, but can also help the person become aware of these habits and, over time, work on breaking them.

You can do this on your own. For example, make a five-column table, and try to keep track of what goes through your mind immediately before and during experiences of unpleasant emotions. The columns include the *situation*, your *feelings*, your *thoughts* directly before and during the unpleasant feelings, the type of cognitive *distortion* reflected in your thoughts, and *rational responses* to these cognitive distortions. Two hypothetical examples are reproduced here.

SITUATION	FEELINGS	THOUGHTS	DISTORTIONS	RATIONAL RESPONSE
Driving home, stuck on freeway	Hopelessness, depression, resentment	This is my whole life . . . stuck on freeways, stuck in classes, stuck at work . . . I can't stand this anymore.	Magnifying; filtering	This is not my whole life. Actually, the traffic's usually good at this time and I only have a semester to go. After that, no school and a new job. I can easily stand it for another six months.
Made dinner for my girlfriend, burned the curry and the dessert	Depression, anxiety, low self-worth	I never do anything right—she's going to think I'm a real loser . . . I am a real loser.	Fortune-telling; overgeneralization; emotional reasoning	This is ridiculous. I just burned one dinner. I'm actually good at a lot of things, and everyone messes up when they cook once in a while. How would I feel about her if she had burned a dinner? Would I think she was a "loser"? Why should I think that about me?

(Source: Table created by author based on ideas suggested in Burns, 1999, and McKay, Davis, & Fanning, 2007.)

The rational response in Column 5 is important. In a sense, cognitive therapy asks you to look at your own life from a scientific perspective, evaluating the evidence for your beliefs in a rational manner. Research has shown that *intentional* substitution of rational, positive habits of thought may have important beneficial effects even on extremely severe clinical depressions (Beck, 2005; Beck, Rush, Shaw, & Emery, 1987). ■

Integrative Therapy: Using What Works

As popular as psychodynamic, behavior, and cognitive therapies are, the majority of therapists do not adhere to a single theoretical orientation, but instead exercise the freedom to conduct therapy as they believe would be most

▲ **Client-Centered Therapy.** Although Carl Rogers' client-centered therapy is not as popular as it once was, it has had an enormous influence on the entire way in which the therapist-client relationship is conceived. It is no longer as easy as it once was to distinguish the client from the therapist in photographs!

Integrative therapy ▶ Any therapy that draws from more than one current of psychotherapeutic theory and technique.

Client-centered therapy ▶ The humanistic therapy founded during the late 1940s and 1950s by Carl Rogers. The goal of client-centered therapy is to promote personal growth in the client in a nondirective manner by treating the client with dignity, empathy, and unconditional positive regard.

Bibliotherapy ▶ The practice of using self-help books as adjuncts to psychotherapy or as therapeutic tools in the absence of psychotherapy.

helpful. This approach is known as **integrative therapy**, sometimes termed *eclectic therapy* (see Table 14.2). What is integrative/eclectic therapy? It is psychotherapy that draws from more than one current of psychotherapeutic theory and technique (Strieker & Gold, 2008). Integrative therapists may adhere generally to one established style of therapy but utilize techniques of other styles as they seem appropriate; or they may create their own form of therapy by integrating many strands of theory and technique from seemingly unrelated styles. Finally, they may attempt to distill from all forms of psychotherapy those factors held in common by all and which represent the essence of the healing relationship (Norcross, 2005). The philosophy of integrative therapy is simple: "Use what works!"

CLIENT-CENTERED THERAPY

In addition to techniques drawn from the therapies already described, many integrative therapists use techniques of **client-centered therapy**, the therapy founded during the late 1940s and 1950s by humanist psychologist Carl Rogers and described briefly in Chapters 1 and 13. Rogers believed that the client, not the therapist, is the expert in his or her own life—and that the client must therefore be allowed to control the direction of therapy according to his or her needs. Rogers stressed the importance of the therapist extending unconditional positive regard and acceptance to the client regardless of the client's behavior or personal characteristics. The client-centered therapist acts as a kind of mirror, allowing the client to clarify his or her own feelings, and helping the client to make choices congruent with his or her goals.

Although relatively few contemporary therapists adhere strictly to Rogerian therapy, his influence is enormous on therapy as a whole, beyond the world of integrative therapy. It is primarily due to Rogers that the "doctor-patient" relationship of psychoanalysis and early psychotherapy evolved into the modern "therapist-client" relationship—a relationship based on equality of status and shared goals.

Bibliotherapy: Reading Your Way to Relief?

In addition to entering psychotherapy with a professional psychotherapist, people suffering from psychological distress may also engage in various sorts of self-help programs and techniques. Self-help can occur every day outside of a formal setting, and therapeutic change can come from unexpected directions—while watching a movie, talking to a friend or family member, practicing a religion, or reading a book (Lampropoulos & Spengler, 2005). Indeed, *self-help books* are among the most lucrative wings of the publishing industry, and the very large majority of all psychotherapists prescribe these books to their patients as adjuncts to therapy—a practice known as **bibliotherapy** (Christensen & Jacobson, 1994; Norcross et al., 2000).

But do these books actually help? This is a complicated question for a number of reasons, not least of which is that the quality of self-help books varies enormously. Unlike scientific publications that must pass review by peers who examine the validity of the text, the only criterion necessary for the publication of a self-help book is that the publisher believes it will make money. There is no requirement that the book contains a single factual statement—although of course, that's always a plus!

A second problem is that, even if the book is solidly based in psychological science, without guidance from a therapist or knowledgeable mental health provider there is no guarantee that the reader will apply the book's techniques and suggestions effectively. Thus, there is a big difference between using these books with at least minimal guidance from a therapist (even if by telephone) and using them without any guidance at all—where their helpfulness appears to be more limited, particularly for those with serious psychological disorders (Rosen, Glasgow, & Moore, 2003).

◀**Therapy?** Self-help books have been shown to produce results comparable to those of psychotherapy for less serious mental health problems. When used in conjunction with therapy for more serious problems, they can lessen the amount of necessary contact time between client and therapist. However, the quality of these books varies widely, and self-help books can be harmful as well as helpful.

Additionally, some of the writers of these books promote ideas that are not only incorrect from the standpoint of psychological science, but are potentially harmful (Rosen et al., 2003; Wood, Perunovic, & Lee, 2009). Therapists have occasionally faced lawsuits for having prescribed books that harmed rather than helped (Slovenko, 1994). So "let the buyer beware": If you wish to use these books, make sure the ones you choose are written by authors who are fully qualified to write them and who buttress their ideas by citing credible published research.

Bearing all of these problems in mind, however, evidence does suggest that under favorable conditions, bibliotherapy can be quite useful—that is, when a science-based book is "prescribed" by a knowledgeable therapist and used with his or her guidance. Indeed, some research shows that the use of books such as David Burns's *Feeling Good*, which forms the basis for the material presented on fighting depression in the "Living Psychology" feature earlier in this chapter, can have positive benefits in treating depression. Such benefits have been found to be at least equal to those provided by antidepressant medication (Naylor et al., 2010).

IN SUMMARY

1.	Psychoanalysis was the first form of therapy and is the most expensive and lengthy. Important concepts in psychoanalysis include insight, transference, the unconscious, dream analysis, and free association. Psychodynamic therapy shares some ideas in common with psychoanalysis, principally the importance of intrapsychic conflict and insight, but it uses therapy techniques that are much more varied and flexible.
2.	Behavior therapists attempt to teach the client to substitute adaptive behaviors for maladaptive behaviors. Behavior therapy techniques include systematic desensitization, flooding, and contemporary exposure therapies; and operant therapies such as the token economy and contingency management interventions.
3.	Cognitive therapies are based on the idea that changing a person's thoughts can change the way he or she feels. Cognitive therapies include rational emotive behavior therapy (REBT), cognitive therapy (CT), and cognitive behavior therapy (CBT).
4.	Empirically supported treatments (ESTs) are those that have demonstrated superiority over no treatment in randomized controlled trials. ESTs are usually relatively brief and use highly specific techniques that can be described in treatment manuals.

5. Integrative, or eclectic, therapy draws from many currents of psychotherapeutic thought, sometimes including ideas and techniques drawn from the client-centered therapy of Carl Rogers.

6. Bibliotherapy may be therapeutic, but primarily when it is used under the guidance of a psychotherapist who has "prescribed" material that is science-based.

RETRIEVE!

1. The tension caused by mental forces that may be at odds with one another is known in psychoanalysis and psychodynamic therapy as _____.

a) transference   b) insight   c) intrapsychic conflict   d) interpsychic tension

2. Which of the following is NOT among the techniques of psychodynamic psychotherapies?

a) focus on helping the client to express emotion

b) exploring situations where the client tries to avoid distressing thoughts or feelings

c) discussing long-past childhood experiences

d) examining irrational and dysfunctional thinking

3. What is the behavior therapy technique pioneered by Joseph Wolpe? What is the name currently given to the group of therapies of which this technique is considered an early example?

4. According to cognitive therapists, cognitive errors and biased interpretations are in part the cause of depression. However, something must *underlie* these errors and biased interpretations for depression to develop. What is this *underlying* factor?

5. A therapist who draws from theory and technique of more than one style of therapy is practicing _____.

a) psychodynamic therapy   c) behavior therapy

b) integrative therapy   d) rational-emotive behavior therapy

6. Which of the following is NOT among the dysfunctional thinking habits identified by cognitive psychologists and discussed earlier?

a) disqualifying the positive   d) ruminating

b) minimizing and catastrophizing   e) filtering

c) mind-reading

What Are Group, Couple, and Family Therapies?

In general, psychotherapy involves a *dyadic relationship*—that is, a relationship between two people, in this case the therapist and the client. However, therapy sometimes involves more than two people. This typically occurs under one of three types of situations: *group therapy, family therapy,* and *couple therapy.*

Group Therapy Involves Three or More

In **group therapy**, a number of clients engage in therapy in inter-action with one or more therapists. The number of group members may be as few as three, but is typically in the range of five to ten, and sometimes more. As in individual therapy, the techniques and procedures of group therapy usually reflect the theoretical orienta-tion of the particular therapist(s) running the group (e.g., psycho-dynamic, behavior, cognitive; Brabender, 2002). Group therapy is conducted in a wide variety of settings—consulting rooms, offices, weekend retreats, hospitals, prisons, and so forth.

Why would a person enter therapy with a group, rather than as an individual? There are a number of reasons. Sometimes a therapist might consider social isolation to be a major part of a person's problem, or a person may be suffering from the perception that his or her problems are unique or a result of a personal moral failure. In such cases, exposure to others with men-tal health problems can help the person to become less isolated or to realize that others are faced with similar problems. Because group therapy partici-pants are often helped by the insights of others in the group, as well as those of the therapist, being of assistance to others in the group can itself be a thera-peutic experience. Group therapy may also allow the therapist to obtain direct knowledge of how a client actually relates to other people, rather than relying on the client's own statements.

▲ **Alcoholics Anonymous (AA).** In church basements, auditoriums, of-fice buildings, prisons, and school-rooms around the world, Alcoholics Anonymous members share their "experience, strength, and hope" to help one another recover from alcohol abuse problems. Alcoholics Anonymous (AA) is the first and best known of the modern self-help groups.

SELF-HELP SUPPORT GROUPS

Earlier we described self-help as administered through bibliotherapy. There is also a special type of therapeutic self-help that may be found in the **self-help support group**. However, these self-help groups do not constitute *psychotherapy* as we have defined it, and they appear to work in ways that differ in many respects from group therapy (Burlingame & Baldwin, 2011). This is because such groups are usually free of charge, may be ongoing in-definitely, and are constructed entirely of people suffering from a particular problem in common. Moreover, there is generally no mental health profes-sional running the group or acting as facilitator (although this may happen occasionally).

Self-help groups exist for sufferers of specific physical diseases, psychologi-cal disorders, drug and alcohol abuse, compulsive gambling, parenting prob-lems, former victims of child abuse, and so forth. In 1997, the number of people who had ever participated in self-help groups was estimated to be approxi-mately 25 million (8 to 10 million annually), and the number of such groups estimated at about 500,000 (Kessler, Mickelson, & Zhao, 1997). As with so many other aspects of life, the Internet has entered the self-help arena—many thousands of self-help groups are meeting through Internet forums and chat rooms (King & Moreggi, 2007). Self-help groups may also be centered around a given self-help book, series of books, or other output such as blog by an au-thority whose ideas group members respect.

How helpful are self-help groups in actuality? Available research (which is not extensive) supports the use of self-help groups and Internet self-help in achieving therapeutic outcomes, either as part of a larger treatment plan or standing alone. Because self-help groups are extremely cost-effective (you can't get much more cost-effective than free), they deserve far more attention than they have received from mental health researchers (Lampropoulos & Spengler, 2005).

Group therapy ▶ When groups of three or more people engage in therapy under the guidance of one or more therapists.

Self-help support group ▶ A therapeutic group based on mutual support that is generally not headed by a mental health professional (and is therefore not an example of psychotherapy). Also in contrast to psychotherapy, most self-help groups are free and ongoing indefinitely. They are generally organized around a particular issue—for example, substance abuse, cancer survival, child abuse, mental illness, and so forth.

Family Therapy: The Family as a System

One theoretical approach not yet discussed, but which is favored by a num-ber of therapists, is known as *family systems theory* (Bowen, 1978; Cox &

Family therapy ▶ A form of psychotherapy that involves an entire family (or other closely connected group) rather than a single individual. Family therapy emerged from family systems theory, which proposes that the problems of an individual in a family cannot be understood outside of the context of the family as an integrated, organic unit.

Family systems theory ▶ The view that the family is an integrated, organic unit that may be analyzed somewhat the way systems analysts view computer systems in organizations.

Payley, 2003; Hargrove, 2009). It is from this approach that **family therapy** emerged. In family therapy, no particular individual is singled out for treatment; rather, the whole family is treated.

In **family systems theory**, the family is considered an integrated, organic unit, or *system*, much as systems analysts view computer systems in organizations. According to this idea, each person plays a role (or several roles) and interacts dynamically with other members. The problems of one family member affect the behavior and emotional lives of the other family members in an interlocking and constantly evolving "living" pattern in which the family as a whole "is greater than the sum of its parts [its members]" (Cox & Paley, 2003, p. 193).

Consider a formerly obedient and studious teenage girl who has been found to be shoplifting, playing hooky from school, lying, having sex with unusual partners, and smoking marijuana late at night in her room (while wearing headphones perched over her purple-tinted hair). Her parents view her behavior as bizarre, and they decide to bring her for mental health treatment—thinking that if her problems are "fixed," the family can go back to a peaceful life. A *family systems* therapist, however, views the girl's behavior in the context of a family life which may itself be disordered. The family systems therapist is not so much interested in what is going on *inside* the girl as in understanding what is going on between the girl and the other family members.

For example, the parents may not have respected the daughter's *boundaries*, or efforts to establish her individual identity as she reached adolescence. Or they may have been overly invested in her accomplishments—pushing her too hard to succeed in an attempt to advance their own goals and agendas at their daughter's expense. Perhaps one of the parents has a drinking problem, or the parents are experiencing marital conflict to which the daughter is responding and, consequently, also contributing. The daughter's behavior may also be causing the parents to clamp down on their (entirely blameless) son's activities. This might cause resentment on his part and surreptitious acting out against his sister, which only serves to worsen her behavior. All of these dramas are played out in family therapy, where the entire family, sometimes including all the siblings and even grandparents, are the "client" in need of treatment.

Couple Therapy for Marital or Individual Distress

Couple therapy ▶ A form of psychotherapy involving a married, cohabitating, or dating couple. Couple therapy may be used to treat relationship distress or the mental health problems of one member of the couple.

A family may be considered a type of group, and so family therapy qualifies as a form of group therapy. However, a couple is a dyad, not a group, and so **couple therapy** is a unique form of psychotherapy involving a couple, be they married, dating seriously, or cohabiting (living together).

There are two general categories of reasons why a couple enters therapy together: (a) to treat *relationship distress*, the general name given for relationship problems encountered by couples; or (b) to address the mental health problems of a specific member of the couple (Snyder, Castellani, & Whisman, 2006). However, it is the issue of relationship distress that is usually associated with the term *couple therapy*. I will have more to say about couple therapy in the next portion of the chapter.

IN SUMMARY

1. Group therapy, family therapy, and couple therapy are all forms of therapy that involve more than two people in the therapeutic relationship.

2. Group therapy involves three or more people and at least one mental health professional. Self-help support groups are therapeutic endeavors involving groups, but they are technically not considered to be group therapy, and they generally (but not always) lack the participation of a mental health professional.

3. Family therapy emerged from family systems theory. Family systems theorists view the entire family as an integrated organic unit or system. In family therapy it is the entire family that is the "client" rather than a given individual.

4. People may enter couple therapy either to treat the mental health of one member of the couple, or to treat marital distress.

RETRIEVE!

1. Name three reasons why a person might participate in group therapy.

2. Why are self-help groups not considered to be "psychotherapy" even though they may be therapeutic?

3. True or false: A family systems psychotherapist consulted because of the troubling behavior of a single individual may insist on treating all members of the person's family, including parents, children, siblings, and even grandparents.

Does Psychotherapy Work?

I have described different styles of therapy, but I haven't said much about how well any or all of them actually work. After all, just because a treatment exists and may produce some sort of effect is no guarantee that it actually does what it is supposed to do.

In 1977, Mary Smith and Gene Glass produced the first meta-analysis of the research in outcomes of psychotherapy. Recall that a meta-analysis is a statistical procedure in which researchers combine data from a large number of studies to produce statistics that can summarize the studies' overall findings. Smith and Glass found unequivocally that those participants in psychotherapy outcome research who were actually given therapy did better than those in control groups who received no treatment (see Figure 14.2). Since the work of Smith and Glass, so many studies reporting similar results have been published that psychotherapy's superiority to no treatment is considered "proven" (demonstrated) and is not controversial (Grissom, 1996; Jacobson & Christensen, 1996; Wampold, 2001, 2007).

So, then, *psychotherapy works*—right? Unfortunately, the issue is more complicated than that. The answer to the question of whether or not psychotherapy works depends entirely on what is meant by "works."

What Does "Works" Mean? Efficacy and Effectiveness

Almost all of the research studies that have demonstrated the superiority of psychotherapy over no treatment are studies of *efficacy*. The term **efficacy** has a highly specific meaning in medicine and psychology. An efficacious therapy

Efficacy ▶ An efficacious treatment is one that has been shown to be superior to a placebo in randomized clinical trials (RCTs). Because it is difficult to construct a placebo psychotherapy, the term *efficacious* is often applied to therapies that have only shown themselves superior to no treatment.

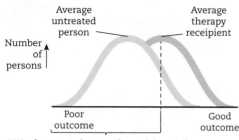

80% of untreated research participants have poorer outcomes than the average participant receiving therapy

▲ **FIGURE 14.2 Psychotherapy Is Superior to No Treatment.** Meta-analysis of almost 500 psychotherapy outcome studies showed that the average research participant who received therapy was better off than 80% of the participants who received no treatment. *(Adapted from Smith, Glass, & Miller, 1980.)*

Randomized Controlled Trial (RCT) ▶ A randomized controlled trial is a research study used to evaluate a therapy or treatment where the research participants are randomly assigned to receive either the treatment of interest, a competing treatment, no treatment, or—if possible—a placebo treatment.

Effective ▶ An effective treatment is one that has shown itself to have significant utility in the "real world" of practicing clinicians treating patients in clinics, hospitals, consulting rooms, and medical offices.

is one that has proven itself in randomized controlled trials to be superior to no treatment—that is, superior to the simple healing effects of the passage of time (Wampold, 2001).[3] A **randomized controlled trial (RCT)** is a research study used to evaluate a treatment where the research participants are randomly assigned to receive either the treatment of interest, no treatment, or—if possible—a placebo treatment. Some RCTs also include another group assigned to a competing treatment for comparison.

However, psychotherapy researchers take pains to differentiate the term *efficacy* from the term *effective*. An **effective** treatment is one that has utility in the real world of practicing psychotherapists treating distressed clients in hospitals and consulting rooms—situations which may differ in any number of ways from the world of laboratory research (Chambless & Hollon, 1998; Seligman, 1995; Wampold, 2007). Many clinicians consider it important to maintain the distinction between these terms because an "empirically supported" efficacious treatment—one that is statistically superior to no treatment (or a placebo) in research studies—may not be effective in the real world.

How might a treatment be shown to be efficacious yet not be effective? First, it may be that the type of treatment a volunteer for a psychotherapy study receives from those running the study is substantially better than the typical quality of treatment received by a client in an outpatient clinical setting.

Second, randomized controlled trial (RCT) study designs may not be as appropriate for testing psychotherapies as they are for testing drug or other biology-based treatments. For example, RCTs do not take into account the simple fact that some therapists are better than others and some therapy *relationships* are better than others. Indeed, some *clients* are better than others at bringing about their own healing during therapy (Norcross & Lambert, 2011). The success or lack of success of a particular treatment might be tied more to the quality of the therapist, the client, and the therapeutic relationship than to the specific treatment (Norcross & Wampold, 2011; Wampold, 2009).

Third, the type of people who volunteer for such studies may differ from those who typically seek therapy (Baker, McFall, & Shoham, 2008; Wampold, 2001, 2007; Westen Novotny, & Thompson-Brenner, 2004). Perhaps most important, however, a treatment might offer more improvement than no treatment at all—and thus qualify as *efficacious*—but may not actually alleviate the problem to a meaningful degree, and therefore be *ineffective* (Christensen & Heavey, 1999; Jacobson & Truax, 1991).

Considering all of this, if by "psychotherapy works" we mean that psychotherapy is efficacious, then *psychotherapy works*. The majority of people who participate in RCTs and who have psychological disorders or other types of serious psychological distress are better off after psychotherapy than they would have been if they had received no treatment at all. The efficacy of psychotherapy is at least as large in effect size as many medical treatments for physical illnesses, and far better than some of these treatments. Perhaps more to the point, therapy is as good—or better—than psychoactive medication (*pharmacotherapy*), at least for depression and anxiety (Hollon, Stewart, & Strunk, 2006).

However, if by "psychotherapy works" we mean that psychotherapy *heals* psychological disorders or lessens psychological distress to a meaningful degree in the world outside the laboratory, then the jury is still out to some degree. We do not know for certain whether or not psychotherapy is

---

[3]*In the world of medicine an efficacious treatment must also show itself superior to a placebo treatment. However, creating a placebo therapy is a far more difficult proposition than it may seem.*

effective in actual practice or that its effects are large enough to be considered meaningful.

COUPLE THERAPY AS A CASE IN POINT

To understand why "the jury is still out" on the effectiveness of psychotherapy, consider the case of couple therapy, which was described earlier. In virtually every research study that compares distressed couples receiving therapy with those who receive no treatment at all, the couples who experience couple therapy come out ahead in positive benefit (Jacobson & Addis, 1993; Snyder et al., 2006). This universal indication of positive benefit would seem to be extraordinarily good news. But, in fact, it is neither good news nor bad news. Basically, it is no news.

Let's say the average number of explosive fights in which a sample of distressed couples engage per week at the beginning of a study is 10, and the average rating they give of their feelings about one another and their relationship is a 2 on a scale from 1 (sucks) to 10 (rocks). Suppose that at the end of couple therapy treatment, the average number of explosive fights per week is 6 (a 40% drop) and the average rating of partner and relationship is 4 (a full two-point increase). In behavior science language—given enough couples participating in the study—the program participants undoubtedly would show "statistically significant" improvement when compared with those couples receiving no treatment. Furthermore, the strength of statistical improvement—the effect size—would likely be large. This is clear evidence of the efficacy of the therapeutic treatment.

On paper (especially *news*paper!) this study seems impressive, but in fact it is not. The problem is this: The goal of the couple therapy program is to reduce explosive fights to *zero* (or nearly so)—not to 6 a week! (Think of all those broken dishes and fists through walls.) The goal is also to increase the partners' ratings of one another to somewhere toward the "rocks" end of the rating scale and decidedly away from the "sucks" end. An average rating of 4 is still closer to the "sucks" than the "rocks" pole.

The results of our little study may have been *statistically significant*, but they lack the most important form of significance for a study such as this: **clinical significance** (Jacobson & Truax, 1991). Like the term *effectiveness*, "clinical significance" refers to effects that are important and meaningful in the real world. Because most distressed couples, if left to their own devices, do not improve (and may actually worsen), even minor and entirely unsatisfactory improvements in the relationships of couples who receive therapy might produce statistically significant results of substantial effect size when compared with untreated couples (Christensen & Heavey, 1999).

When looked at this way, studies of couple therapy tell a rather less optimistic story than the statistics at first appear to tell: According to more detailed analyses, only approximately 35% to 40% of couples receiving couple therapy actually move from the status of "distressed" couple to that of "nondistressed" couple. Moreover, even when couples are helped by couple therapy, results are not necessarily long-lasting. Although relationship improvements usually do tend to last at least 6 months, by 1 to 4 years following therapy, a substantial portion of "improved" couples—between 30% and 60%—go right back to the former distressed state, and frequently divorce (Christensen & Heavey, 1999; Snyder et al., 2006).

NEW EFFECTIVENESS STUDIES OF INDIVIDUAL PSYCHOTHERAPY

What about individual psychotherapy? It has been difficult to design psychotherapy outcome studies that approximate the way therapy is actually conducted in real-world settings. Studies that have attempted to do this have produced mixed results, likely due to methodological problems (Wampold, 2007). However, using a new research strategy for examining the actual

▲ **Couple Therapy.** Only a minority of couples receiving couple therapy in research studies move from the "distressed" to "nondistressed" status, and of those that do, a substantial number do not maintain the gains they achieved. Thus, the statistical superiority of couple therapy over no treatment is not always translated into clinical significance.

Clinical significance ▶
When a statistical effect in a treatment outcome study is large enough and meaningful enough to suggest that the treatment being tested would be effective in the world outside of the research study.

conduct of ordinary psychotherapy in community HMO (managed care) and university counseling center settings, at least two relatively recent studies showed that psychotherapy was effective—with effect sizes similar to those seen in efficacy studies of empirically supported treatments (Minami et al., 2008; Minami et al., 2009). However, to truly demonstrate the effectiveness of therapy, a great many such studies will need to be conducted under varied circumstances by independent research teams.

No One Style of Therapy Has Proved Superior Overall

Despite the large number of legitimate therapy styles available, most efficacy studies show that no one of these forms is superior to any other in general outcome (Benish, Imel, & Wampold, 2008; Lambert, 2005; Luborsky et al., 2002; Miller, Wampold, & Varhely, 2008; Spielmans, Pasek, & McFall, 2007; Wampold, 2007; Wampold et al., 2011). Of course, it is always possible that a given person is temperamentally better suited to one style or another, and a few types of therapy are narrowly focused and intended to apply only to certain conditions. For example, *exposure therapies* (described on pp. 677–678) are generally intended to to treat phobias or other fearful states, and *interpersonal therapy* (IPT) was designed as a short-term therapy for depression. However, no one therapy has a better *overall* track record. This equality of success rates among therapies has been referred to as the "**dodo bird verdict**," after the dodo's pronouncement at the end of a race in Lewis Carroll's *Alice in Wonderland:* "At last, everybody has won and all shall have prizes."

Not everyone agrees with this general finding (Lilienfeld, 2007; Olatunji & Hollon, 2010), and claims are often made that one or another form of therapy has proved superior for some particular condition. For example, *cognitive-behavior therapy* (CBT) is often claimed to be the best choice for treatment of depression and some anxiety disorders, while behavior therapy is sometimes said to be preferable for phobias, alcohol and drug abuse, and some childhood disorders.

However, evidence in support of these claims is not very strong (Benish et al., 2008; Miller et al., 2008; Parker, Roy, & Eyers, 2003; Wampold, Minami, Baskin, & Tierney, 2002). For example, CBT has been shown to be superior to other therapies of depression only when styles of therapy poorly suited to treating depression (e.g., *progressive muscle relaxation*) are included in the analysis. If only legitimate therapies appropriate for depression are considered, the statistical advantage for CBT disappears (Spielmans et al., 2007; Wampold et al., 2002; but see Olatunji & Hollon, 2010, for a different view).

Thus, most evidence supports the dodo bird verdict with one extremely important qualifier: The general equality of outcome for the various therapies extends *only* to those therapies that are based on legitimate psychological principles and intended to be used for the disorder in question (Benish et al., 2008; Dawes, 1996; Spielmans et al., 2007; Wampold, 2001, 2007). Innumerable forms of treatment exist that are based on pseudoscientific principles or untested ideas. Some of these treatments may lack value entirely or actually be very harmful (Barlow, 2010; Dimidjian & Hollon, 2010; Lilienfeld, 2007; Norcross, Koocher, & Garofalo, 2006; see pp. 694–695). Clearly, calling something "therapy" does not make it therapeutic.

Psychotherapy May Work for the "Wrong Reasons"

Despite the demonstrated efficacy (and possible effectiveness) of psychotherapy, not everyone benefits from it—even when compared with no treatment. But when psychotherapy does work, *why* does it work? Each type of therapy is based on (sometimes radically) different theories of the nature and origin of psychological disorders and distress. Yet, as we have already seen, with a few specific exceptions, all legitimate forms of psychotherapy work about equally

Dodo bird verdict ▶ A phrase used to sum up the "take-home message" of outcome research in psychotherapy: No legitimate form of therapy is superior to any other in general outcome. The phrase is borrowed from an incident in Lewis Carroll's *Alice in Wonderland*, wherein a dodo bird announces of a race, "At last, everybody has won and all shall have prizes." The dodo bird verdict applies only to legitimate forms of psychotherapy appropriate for a given condition.

well. This "dodo bird verdict" as regards therapy efficacy implies an important idea: *The explanation each therapy school gives for the effectiveness of its therapy may not be correct* (Benish et al., 2008; Blatt & Zuroff, 2005; Luborsky et al., 2002; Wampold, 2001, 2007).

Here is an example: Logically, if it were true that depression is caused by distorted and biased cognitions, as proposed by cognitive therapists, then it would be something of a mystery how therapies such as psychodynamic therapy—which do not address these cognitions—could possibly work. Yet, psychodynamic therapy can relieve depression (Leichsenring & Rabung, 2009; Shedler, 2010).

Consider another puzzle: Research has repeatedly demonstrated that the success of psychotherapy is not dependent on the level of degree training a therapist receives. Paraprofessional students and others with no postgraduate training in psychology at all, applying legitimate forms of psychotherapy, have success rates approximately equal to those obtained by Ph.D. therapists (Atkins & Christensen, 2001; Christensen & Jacobson, 1994; Michael, Huelsman, & Crowley, 2005). Moreover, the amount of experience a therapist possesses does not seem to give any particular advantage. Seasoned therapists with decades of experience do not have success rates higher than those who are brand new to the profession (Bickman, 1999; Christensen & Jacobson, 1994; Garske & Anderson, 2003; Strupp & Hadley, 1979; Vocisano et al., 2004).

But how is it possible that credentialed therapists with experience have success rates no better than graduate students with little or no experience? In most professions this would be a ridiculous suggestion. Andrew Christensen and Neil Jacobson (1994) consider the outcome of electricians or surgeons dispensing services without extensive training. In the first case, the outcome would be dead trainees, and in the second, dead patients.

How can we explain the dodo bird verdict and the lack of importance of experience and credentials for therapeutic success? One possible answer, first proposed by Saul Rosenzweig in 1936, has been elaborated on by countless theorists over the years (Ahn & Wampold, 2001; Frank & Frank, 1991; Wampold, 2001, 2007, 2010): Therapy may work not as a result of any specific "ingredients" of individual therapies, but as a result of factors that appear to be shared by *all* legitimate therapies—known as **common factors**.

A number of studies have used sophisticated designs to determine if, in fact, given therapies are efficacious for the reasons their practitioners claim. These studies, known as **dismantling studies**, compare results of a form of therapy against results of the same therapy *minus* those aspects thought by its proponents to be the "active ingredients"—the defining elements of the therapy that set it apart from other treatments. Logically, if there is no difference in results between the therapy containing its active ingredient and the same therapy without the active ingredient, some other force must be at work in causing improvement in the client.

For example, in the case of psychodynamic therapy, it is believed that intrapsychic conflict resulting from early childhood experiences is a primary cause of psychological distress in adulthood. Psychodynamic therapists believe that insight is necessary to resolve these conflicts and heal psychological pain. If a version of psychodynamic therapy were administered *minus* all discussion of early childhood, or minus the promotion of insight, it ought not to work—at least according to psychodynamic theorists. However, meta-analyses of dismantling studies have shown that there are *no significant differences* between the outcomes of therapies with or without their "active ingredients" (Ahn & Wampold, 2001; Spielmans et al., 2007).

WHAT ARE THE COMMON FACTORS?

If it is common factors, not active ingredients, that are responsible for therapeutic change—and not everyone agrees that this is true—what are the common factors? This question cannot be answered with certainty (Kazdin, 2005).

Common factors ▶ Hypothesized factors common to all legitimate forms of psychotherapy that are responsible for actual therapeutic effects.

Dismantling study ▶ A study that seeks to isolate the factors responsible for the efficacy of a form of therapy. The dismantling study compares outcome results of a form of therapy against that same therapy minus its "active ingredient" (e.g., cognitive therapy but without training to identify and correct irrational cognitions).

Therapeutic alliance ▶ A hypothesized common factor of psychotherapy that refers to the positive emotions between therapist and client, the therapist's empathy for the client, and both parties' joint commitment to therapeutic work.

Therapist allegiance ▶ The therapist's commitment to the specific type of therapy he or she has chosen to use.

Therapist competence ▶ The degree to which a therapist tends to produce good results regardless of client or therapy techniques.

However, according to Bruce Wampold (2001), a major proponent of the common factors approach, there are probably three principal factors: **therapeutic alliance, therapist allegiance,** and **therapist competence**.

1. *Therapeutic alliance.* The word *alliance* implies the idea of a connection or union toward a common goal. The therapeutic alliance is built on the positive emotions and affection between therapist and client, the therapist's empathy for the client, and both parties' joint commitment to accomplish the important work of healing.

2. *Therapist allegiance. Allegiance* refers to the therapist's intellectual commitment to the specific type of therapy he or she has chosen to practice. Therapists' belief in their therapy may be transmitted to clients in a convincing "story" about the causes of the client's distress and plan to alleviate it. This increases both parties' hope, confidence, and willingness to engage in effortful activity within therapy.

3. *Therapist competence.* Although some therapists and clients are better suited to one another than to others—and their better "fit" produces good results—it is also true that some therapists appear to produce generally more positive outcomes regardless of the identity of their clients or what type of therapy they are providing. They are simply better at what they do (Okiishi et al., 2006; Okiishi, Lambert, Nielsen, & Ogles, 2003).

The idea of common factors may go a long way toward explaining the dodo bird verdict and findings that therapist experience and credentials do not seem to make much of a difference in therapist effectiveness overall. All three common factors hypothesized as playing a major role in therapeutic success—therapeutic alliance, allegiance, and therapist competence—apply equally to all legitimate forms of therapy and can all be strong in the absence of advanced degree and years of experience.

Psychotherapy Can Also Cause Harm

It is no secret that psychotherapy is not always helpful. However, the fact that psychotherapy can sometimes be *harmful* is less often discussed and even more rarely researched (Dimidjian & Hollon, 2010; Lilienfeld, 2007; Nutt & Sharpe, 2008). If you recall from the previous chapter, when harm is caused by a clinician whose job it is to heal, it is known as *iatrogenic* harm. How might this occur in psychotherapy?

First, psychotherapy—like surgery or drug treatment—carries with it the potential for unintended side effects. Consider Haim, who worked in a career he hated for a boss who was a tyrant. As a result of therapy and the support of his therapist, he finally made the leap to quit his job and change careers. Unfortunately, Haim had three children to support, and his career aspirations did not work out as he (and his therapist) had expected. When Haim then desperately tried to find work in his old profession he was unable to do so. His family ended up on public assistance. If we accept the hypothesis that none of this would have happened had it not been for therapy, then Haim's current situation could be viewed as a kind of unintended side effect of therapy.

Second, psychotherapy can instill false beliefs in clients about the nature and causes of their problems. Logically, this *must* be happening all the time. This is because psychotherapies are usually built on specific theories about the nature and causes of psychological disorders. However, these theories often contradict one another radically and cannot all be true at the same time. Someone has to be getting it wrong!

Third, harm in therapy can also occur as the result of simple incompetence on the part of the therapist. Although a therapist may be incompetent regardless of his or her training, harm due to incompetence probably most often occurs in the context of **potentially harmful psychotherapies (PHPs;**

Potentially harmful psychotherapies (PHPs) ▶ Therapies that may result in iatrogenic (therapist-caused) harm to clients.

Table 14.4 A Provisional List of Potentially Harmful Therapies (PHPs)

POTENTIALLY HARMFUL THERAPIES	DESCRIPTION	POTENTIAL HARM
Critical incident stress debriefing	3–4 hour therapy session (or sessions) conducted among people exposed to an extreme, potentially traumatic experience. Conducted within 24–72 hours of the event.	Risk of increasing post-traumatic symptoms.
Scared Straight interventions for conduct problems	Intended to frighten adolescents away from a life of crime by exposing them to the harsh realities of prison life.	Risk of worsening of conduct problems.
Facilitated communication	Therapist "assists" child or communication-impaired client to communicate by holding the hand or arm as the child/client types on a keyboard. Therapists unknowingly are producing the communications themselves.	Risk of false accusations of child abuse against family members.
Attachment therapies (e.g., holding, rebirthing)	May include abusive treatment of child, humiliation, physical restraint in effort to release child's supposed rage or maladaptive functioning.	Risk of humiliation, serious physical injury, and death.
Recovered-memory therapy	Suggestive techniques including hypnosis, medication, guided imagery in effort to release "repressed" memories of childhood trauma.	Risk of producing false memories of trauma, false accusations of child abuse against family members, wrongful imprisonment, deterioration of family relationships.
Dissociative-identity disorder (DID)-oriented therapy	Use of suggestive interview methods and hypnosis in an effort to uncover hidden childhood traumas and contact client's "alters."	May induce dissociative identity disorder or induce client with DID to create additional "alters." (However, evidence is correlational.)
Grief counseling for normal bereavement	Counseling for those who have recently lost a loved one to death.	May increase depressive symptoms and grief.
Expressive-experiential therapies (e.g., Gestalt, encounter groups)	Encourages clients to experience powerful emotions and catharsis, often in confrontation with therapist or group.	For some people, may worsen painful emotions.
Boot-camp interventions for conduct disorder	Military-style "get tough" approach adolescent conduct problems.	Risk of worsening conduct problems; has resulted in death.
DARE programs (Drug Abuse Resistence Education)	Use of uniformed police officers to teach schoolchildren about risks of drugs and resistance to peer pressure regarding drug use.	May increase use of drugs, alcohol, and cigarettes.

(Source: Based on Lilienfeld, 2007.)

Lilienfeld, 2007; Norcross et al., 2006). Potentially harmful psychotherapies are untested or inadequately tested treatments, often based on pseudoscientific theories, which have been shown to cause harm under certain conditions. As detailed in Table 14.4, PHPs have created harms ranging from simple humiliation and the worsening of disorders to the destruction of entire families and even deaths of clients.

Culture Plays a Role in Psychotherapy

Most psychotherapies are administered under the assumption that, with minor adjustments, they may be applied to anyone, regardless of culture,

▲ **Recovered Memories?** In 1994, Katrina Fairlie was referred to a psychotherapist because it was concluded that the severe abdominal pains she was experiencing had no organic cause. The therapist used hypnosis and medication as part of an attempt to recover "repressed memories" of childhood abuse that he believed were at the root of her troubles. Eventually, Fairlie reported memories of her father raping her and beating a 6-year-old girl to death with an iron bar. In 1995 Fairlie determined that her memories were false and withdrew her allegations. Later, the police concurred that the case had no merit and dropped their investigation. In 2005, Fairlie sued the medical authorities responsible referring her for therapy and was awarded $40,000 in damages. Many thousands of similar cases occurred throughout the 1980s and 1990s, primarily in the United States and Great Britain. (*Source: Madeley, 2007.*)

ethnicity, gender, religion, or personal philosophy. To some degree this assumption equates psychotherapy with medical treatment—rather like administering an antibiotic to treat an infection. However, this assumption has been challenged frequently (Frank & Frank, 1991; Wampold, 2001, 2007; Westen et al., 2004).

One problem with viewing therapy as a "one-size-fits-all-more-or-less" medical treatment is the fact that individual differences in clients—for example, cultural differences—may strongly affect treatment (Dwairy, 1999; Tseng, 2004; Van Dyk & Nefale, 2005). Consider the following story related by Bruce Wampold (2001). A young Asian woman earning her Ph.D. in the United States entered therapy for depression. She had been married traditionally, by family arrangement rather than for love, and the expectations of her (highly traditional) husband conflicted in many respects with her desires for her education and professional career. Having been raised in the United States for a substantial number of her early years, the woman was acculturated to Western views of individual accomplishment and equality of the sexes. Her husband, on the other hand, expected her to be a traditional wife and put her homemaking duties ahead of her ambitions.

Although the woman had made a decision to divorce her husband as a result of this conflict, she was torn with contradictory feelings about her decision. Her American side favored commitment to her education and career goals, but she also felt that she belonged in the (collectivist) culture of her origin. She was deeply committed to her family and their world, where divorce would not only bring shame, but would also make it difficult for her sister to find a husband of means and prestige.

The therapist, an American cognitive-behavior therapy practitioner, focused exclusively on her "rights" to an egalitarian marriage, career goals, and personal happiness. He treated her ambivalent feelings about her impending divorce as obstacles to be overcome rather than core parts of her sense of self. He was unable, or unwilling, to view her cultural background as a legitimate psychological force that needed to be acknowledged and incorporated into her treatment. Eventually, she felt forced to terminate therapy.

As Wen-Shing Tseng (2004) suggests, every person is affected by his or her own culture. Tseng emphasizes the importance of acknowledging the impact of culture for all clients, including those from the majority culture in a multicultural setting.

Therapists Are People

Therapists are not special people; they are ordinary people who have been trained to provide a special service. Like all humans, they make mistakes, and can be misguided.

They also often find themselves patients of other therapists. In a national survey of practicing psychothrapists, Harrison Pope and Barbara Tabachnick (1994) found that 84% of those who participated in the survey had been in therapy. Approximately 61% had experienced clinical depression, 29% had contemplated suicide, and 4% had attempted suicide. Although the overwhelming majority of the sample found the experience of therapy helpful, a sizable minority—22%—also found it harmful.

Psychological Services beyond Psychotherapy

Before leaving the topic of psychological treatment of mental disorders, we should consider an important issue: Even if the quality of psychotherapy continues to improve—for example, as a result of research in empirically supported treatments (ESTs) or new ways to measure therapy effectiveness—psychotherapy as a practice is not enough to substantially reduce the rates and burden of mental illness in the United States. This is true for a number of reasons, as explored by Alfred Kazdin and Stacey Blase (2011). First, the number of qualified therapists is limited. Second, these therapists are centered primarily in a limited number of areas—large, affluent, urban centers. Third, the vast majority of therapists are English-speaking European Americans. Although this certainly does not disqualify them from treating people of color or those whose primary language is other than English, as we already have seen, culture can play a role in the delivery of effective therapy. Considering all of the this, as Kazdin and Blase conclude, it appears that appropriate psychology-based mental health treatment is unavailable to the vast majority of people in need of it.

According to Kazdin and Blase, it is important to think beyond psychotherapy as the primary mode of delivering psychological treatment for psychological disorders. They propose a "portfolio" model that includes emphasis on prevention and the use of technologies that are widely accessible to almost anyone. These technologies include the use of the Internet, telephone, television, and even smartphones. For example, in an application known as Mobile Therapy, texting has been used to convey feedback to and from anorexia nervosa patients following their release from inpatient treatment. These text messages provide the patients with cognitive therapy techniques to use in response to ongoing self-reports of mood changes throughout the day.

No one knows how useful these new technologies will turn out to be. However, it is clear that, at present, the need for psychological services has outstripped their supply.

IN SUMMARY

1. Meta-analyses consistently show that psychotherapy is efficacious. However, research studies have not yet established that psychotherapy is effective in the world outside the laboratory.

2. All legitimate therapies seem about equally efficacious, as long as the therapy is based upon legitimate psychological principles and is appropriate to the condition being treated. One explanation for this "dodo bird verdict" is that therapy works due to common factors, not specific ingredients.

3. The most important common factors are likely the therapeutic alliance, therapist allegiance, and therapist competence.

4. Psychotherapy can cause harm as well as healing. Therapies that have the potential to cause harm (iatrogenesis) are known as potentially harmful psychotherapies (PHPs).

5. Most people in need of psychological services do not have access to them.

RETRIEVE!

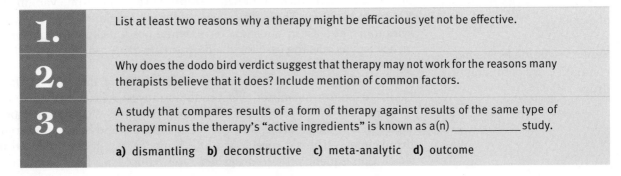

1. List at least two reasons why a therapy might be efficacious yet not be effective.

2. Why does the dodo bird verdict suggest that therapy may not work for the reasons many therapists believe that it does? Include mention of common factors.

3. A study that compares results of a form of therapy against results of the same type of therapy minus the therapy's "active ingredients" is known as a(n) _____ study.

a) dismantling **b)** deconstructive **c)** meta-analytic **d)** outcome

4.

Which of the following is NOT among the most frequently suggested of the common factors in therapeutic change?

a) therapeutic alliance

c) therapist competence

b) therapist allegiance

d) therapeutic techniques

5.

Explain the difference between clinical significance and statistical significance.

What Is Pharmacotherapy?

So far in this chapter we have examined psychological approaches to helping people cope with problems and treating psychological disorders. However, over the past several decades, a second major approach to treatment has come to rival psychological approaches in prominence—the use of psychoactive medications such as antidepressants and other techniques that act directly on the body. For the remaining portion of the chapter we shall consider the nature of these treatments.

Pharmacotherapy Uses Psychoactive Medications

Pharmacotherapy ▶ The use of drugs and other substances to treat psychological disorders or distress. Pharmacotherapy is based on psychopharmacology, the study of the effects of drugs and other substances on mood, emotion, and behavior.

Psychopharmacology is the study of how drugs and other substances affect emotion, mood, and behavior (Meyer & Quenzer, 2005). **Pharmacotherapy** is the use of drugs and other substances (e.g., nutritional supplements) to treat psychological disorders and distress. Although there are a great many such *psychoactive* drugs (drugs that affect the mind), they generally fall into one of four categories of use: those used primarily to treat depression, those used for bipolar disorder, those used for anxiety, and those for psychotic disorders such as schizophrenia.

It should be understood, however, that there is a good deal of *off-label prescribing* of these medications—prescribing a drug to treat some condition for which it was not initially intended, but for which it may have some utility (Haw & Stubbs, 2005). For example, certain antidepressant drugs are commonly used off-label for conditions as varied as anxiety, sexual dysfunction, substance abuse, eating disorders, sleep problems, and personality disorders; drugs to treat epilepsy are commonly used to treat bipolar disorders.

Anxiety Is Treated with Anxiolytics

Anxiolytic ▶ Any drug or other substance whose primary use is the treatment of anxiety.

Benzodiazepine ▶ The most common class of anxiolytic drugs.

Drugs that treat symptoms of anxiety are known as **anxiolytics**. With a few exceptions, anxiolytic drugs currently in use generally belong to a single class of medications known as **benzodiazepines** (e.g., Librium, Valium, Xanax, Klonopin, Atavan). These drugs are mildly sedating and may reduce anxiety symptoms, at least in the short term, while not knocking the person off his or her feet as was the case for the *barbiturate* drugs previously used to treat anxiety.

Benzodiazepines create anxiolytic effects in part through regulation of GABA, a neurotransmitter that produces muscle relaxation and sensations of calm as it binds to specialized neuron receptors (Roy-Byrne, 2005). At higher doses, benzodiazepines induce symptoms and sensations similar to drunkenness—slurred speech, giddiness, unsteady gait, and reduced inhibitions. Consequently, these drugs are often abused, and serious dependence and addiction can result (O'Brien, 2005). When dependence does result, even if it has occurred through legitimate, relatively low-dose use, it is important to withdraw from these drugs under medical supervision, because the withdrawal symptoms can be quite severe and include seizures.

Benzodiazepines have demonstrated their usefulness in anxiety disorders (Martin et al., 2007). However, their therapeutic effects tend to decrease over time, while unwanted side effects—including dependence, cognitive decline, and risk of accidents—increase (Barker, Greenwood, Jackson, & Crowe, 2004; Neutel, 2005). Thus, most authoritative sources suggest only short-term use lasting a few weeks or several months at most. Nonetheless, a substantial number of users take these drugs for many years or even decades.

Depression Is Treated with Antidepressants

Antidepressant drugs are now the most commonly prescribed of all drug types in the United States—more popular than drugs to lower blood pressure or cholesterol (Cohen, 2007). Their use has more than quadrupled in the past 20 years, particularly among those with less severe symptoms, who make up the majority of users (Mojtabai, 2008). As Figure 14.3 shows, currently, 6.1% of American men and 13.8% of women have been treated with antidepressants.

The growth in use of these medications is undoubtedly one of the most astonishing success stories in the history of pharmaceutical marketing (Kravitz et al., 2005).

There are four principal classes of antidepressant drugs: (1) *MAO inhibitors*, currently used very rarely in the United States, more commonly in Europe; (2) *tricyclic antidepressants*, among the first antidepressants developed; (3) *selective serotonin reuptake inhibitors* (SSRIs), probably the most commonly prescribed; and (4) so-called *third-generation antidepressants*—a catch-all category that includes antidepressants with unique chemical structures (*atypical antidepressants*) as well as the new serotonin/norepinephrine reuptake inhibitors (SNRIs).

SELECTIVE SEROTONIN REUPTAKE INHIBITORS (SSRIS)

Selective serotonin reuptake inhibitors (SSRIs), likely the most commonly prescribed antidepressants, selectively block the reuptake of the neurotransmitter serotonin, in contrast to the drugs like the early tricyclics, which act on several neurotransmitter systems at once. This selectivity was considered desirable at the time when the drugs were devised because it was believed that selecting only a single neurotransmitter system might reduce most of the side effects associated with the tricyclic drugs.

Do SSRIs have fewer troublesome side effects? In short, no. As Table 14.5 shows, they just have different *side effect profiles*, with some side effects being more common than with tricyclics, and others less common. The SSRIs are also often rumored to be faster acting and more effective than tricyclics. In fact, however, they are neither faster acting nor more effective (Anderson, 2001; Hansen, Gartlehner, Lohr, Gaynes, & Carey, 2005; Williams et al., 2000). Moreover, the dodo bird verdict applies to SSRI drugs as well as to therapy: No one of these drugs is more effective overall than any other (Hansen et al., 2005; Rush et al., 2006).

Nevertheless, SSRIs (including drugs with brand names such as Prozac, Paxil, Celexa, Lexepro, and Zoloft) have left the tricyclics in the dust in the frequency of their prescription (Pirraglia, Stafford, & Singer, 2003). Drug companies aggressively market SSRIs because these companies hold the patents to the newer SSRI drugs, whereas the older tricyclics have been produced generically for decades.

What industry marketing has not emphasized (and often fails to mention altogether) is that SSRIs can produce withdrawal symptoms on discontinuation

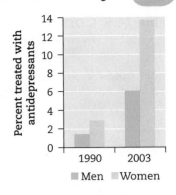

▲ FIGURE 14.3 The Rise in Antidepressant Use. The percentage of the population treated with antidepressants has more than quadrupled since the early 1990s. Antidepressants are now the most frequently prescribed drug in the United States—beating out drugs to reduce blood pressure and cholesterol (Cohen, 2007). As of 2002, in any given month 10.6% of women and 5.2% of men were using an antidepressant (National Center for Health Statistics, 2007), and numbers are likely to be higher currently. *(Source: Mojtabai, 2008.)*

Antidepressant ▶ Any drug or other substance whose primary purpose is the treatment of depression.

Selective serotonin reuptake inhibitors (SSRIs) ▶ A relatively recently developed type of antidepressant drug that blocks the reuptake of the neurotransmitter serotonin, while having relatively little effect on other neurotransmitters—in contrast to the tricyclics and MAO inhibitors.

Table 14.5 Comparison of SSRI/SNRI and Tricyclic Antidepressant Side Effects

CLASS OF ANTIDEPRESSANT	SIDE EFFECT
MORE COMMON IN SSRIs AND SNRIs (e.g., Paxil, Zoloft, Prozac, Cymbalta, Effexor, Lexepro, Celexa, Serzone)	Various sexual dysfunctions (may continue after discontinuation of drug) Headache Trembling Agitation Insomnia Nausea and vomiting Diarrhea Anxiety and nervousness
MORE COMMON IN TRICYCLICS (e.g., Elavil, Anafranil, Norpramin, Tofranil)	Dizziness Dry mouth Blurred vision Drowsiness Constipation and urinary difficulty Cardiovascular problems (sometimes serious) Weight gain

(Sources include British National Health Service [www.clinicalanswers.nhs.uk/resource/depress.gif] and emedexpert [www.emedexpert.com].)

SSRI discontinuation syndrome ▶ A drug withdrawal syndrome associated with the use of at least some of the SSRI and SNRI antidepressants. The syndrome may consist of flu-like symptoms, dizziness, weakness, nausea, fatigue, feelings of "unreality," loss of balance, light-headedness, "electric-shock" sensations, and other symptoms.

Third-generation antidepressants ▶ The most recent group of antidepressants to be developed, these drugs include serotonin-norepinephrine reuptake inhibitors (SNRIs) as well as drugs with unique ("atypical") chemical structures and physiological mechanisms.

(Haddad & Anderson, 2007; Hosenbocus & Chahal, 2011; Kotzalidis et al., 2007). Between 35% and 50% of people attempting to discontinue taking SSRIs experience unpleasant, flu-like symptoms including dizziness, weakness, nausea, fatigue, feelings of "unreality," loss of balance, light-headedness, and "electric-shock" sensations (Rosenbaum, Fava, Hoog, Ascroft, & Krebs, 1998). These symptoms may continue for weeks and are not the result of a "rebound" of depression. This **SSRI discontinuation syndrome** may cause some individuals to continue to take these medications long after they no longer need them.

THIRD-GENERATION ANTIDEPRESSANTS

Beginning in the late 1980s, a new group of antidepressants was developed that fall generally into the catch-all category **third-generation antidepressants.** The most frequently prescribed of these third-generation drugs are the *serotonin-norepinephrine reuptake inhibitors* or SNRIs (e.g., brand names Effexor, Cymbalta). The SNRI drugs are based on the idea that combining selectivity for the neurotransmitter norepinephrine as well as for serotonin might produce superior results to those produced by serotonin selectivity alone (Nelson, Mazure, Jatlow, Bowers, & Price, 2004). The SNRIs are *not* superior in efficacy to other antidepressants overall (Freemantle, Anderson, & Young, 2000), and they may also produce withdrawal symptoms on discontinuation. However, they may work better for certain people under specific circumstances (Anderson, 2001).

Bipolar Disorders Are Treated with Mood Stabilizers

As mentioned in Chapter 13, people suffering from bipolar disorders are far more frequently depressed than manic. However, they are not generally treated with antidepressants. These drugs do not seem to help very many people with bipolar depressions, and in some cases they may foster a chronically irritable and unhappy state (El-Mallakh & Karippot, 2005; Sachs et al., 2007). Therefore, antidepressants are used only with caution in the treatment of bipolar disorder.

Instead, there are three classes of drugs that are used to treat the disruptions of mood and cognition found in bipolar disorders: *lithium, anticonvulsants*, and second-generation *antipsychotics*. All of these drugs are intended to function as **mood stabilizers** when used with bipolar disorders because they are intended to treat both mania and depression simultaneously. Let's examine each category.

Lithium is unique among drugs used to treat psychiatric disorders because it is a naturally occurring body salt. No one knows why it works in controlling mania, and its pharmacological actions are somewhat mysterious. More than 50 years of research studies have established its efficacy in helping to control the manic phases of bipolar disorder—reducing the risk of manic episodes over the long term by about 40%—though it is less successful in controlling depressive symptoms (Geddes, Burgess, Hawton, Jamison, & Goodwin, 2004; Goodwin & Goldstein, 2003). However, while lithium provides at least some relief for 30% to 50% of patients taking the drug, this leaves 50% to 70% for whom lithium provides no relief. Moreover, the benefit received by many in the 30% to 50% group may only be partial. Lithium seems to work less often and less powerfully than once believed (Geddes et al., 2004), and it can have a number of serious side effects—including seizures or coma if the blood levels of the drug become too high.

Anticonvulsants (e.g., Tegretol, Depakote, Lamictal) were primarily designed to treat seizure disorders such as epilepsy. Like lithium, their biochemical action is not completely understood, and it is equally unclear why they should help to even out mood swings in bipolar patients. These drugs have the advantage of being much less toxic than lithium, and patients do not seem to resist taking them as much as they do lithium.

Second-generation antipsychotics (e.g., Seroquel, Abilify). The new "second-generation" antipsychotic medications, described in the following section on treatment of schizophrenia, have also come into use to treat bipolar disorder (McIntyre & Konarski, 2005). Claims have been made that they have shown efficacy similar to that of the anticonvulsants, but, like lithium (and the anticonvulsants), when they do work they are better at controlling mania than depression. This is unfortunate, given that those with bipolar disorders experience depression at least three times as frequently as mania, and depression tends to cause the worst problems for sufferers (Yatham, 2005). These drugs can also have extremely severe side effects, as discussed in the next section.

Schizophrenia Is Treated with Antipsychotics

Introduced during the 1950s, *first-generation antipsychotics*, with brand names such as Thorazine, Mellaril, and Haldol, altered the treatment of schizophrenia and other psychotic disorders by reducing the severity of positive symptoms. As discussed in Chapter 13, positive symptoms refer to those symptoms of psychosis that involve "something being there that should not be there"—for example, hallucinations, delusions, and general agitation. First-generation antipsychotics work primarily by restricting the availability of the neurotransmitter *dopamine* either by blocking dopamine receptors entirely or inhibiting the neurotransmitter's release.

However, the first-generation antipsychotics proved less useful than originally believed. Fewer than 50% of those taking them found substantial and/or lasting improvement (American Psychiatric Association, 2000; Meyer & Quenzer, 2005). These drugs also have very serious side effects. Patients frequently report feeling "drugged out," overly sedated, and unable to think or concentrate. More serious, however, the first generation drugs (particularly if used long-term) can cause *tardive dyskinesia*, a largely untreatable and irreversible neurological disorder. Tardive dyskinesia is characterized

Mood stabilizers ▶ A general term used to describe a number of classes of drugs used to treat bipolar disorders. These drugs include anticonvulsants, lithium, and second-generation antipsychotics.

by repetitive, involuntary movements such as grimacing, protrusion of the tongue, lip smacking or puckering, and rapid eye blinking. Involuntary and odd movements and twitching of the fingers, arms, legs, and torso may also occur. Tardive dyskinesia is uncomfortable to have and not pretty to watch, and its potentially irreversible nature makes it a particularly loathsome possibility to contemplate. Indeed, in many cases it is a much more serious problem than the one the patient began taking the antipsychotic drug to try to resolve.

Because of the seriousness of such side effects, and because medical researchers wished to create more effective drugs, a new generation of antipsychotics has been developed known as **second-generation antipsychotics** (e.g., Seroquel, Abilify). The new drugs are promoted by their manufacturers as having fewer serious side effects than the first-generation drugs, but as so often occurs with pharmaceutical industry claims, research doesn't support this idea. Second-generation antipsychotics substantially increase the risk not only of tardive dyskinesia, but also of diabetes, stroke, and heart disease. The overall tolerability of these drugs is no better than the first-generation antipsychotics. They are also about 10 times as expensive to use (Douglas & Smeeth, 2008; Kane, 2004; Rosenheck, Leslie, & Doshi, 2008).

If their side effects are just as severe overall, do they at least work better than the first-generation antipsychotics? Extensive, well-controlled comparison studies show that there are virtually no advantages to the newer drugs in efficacy (P. B. Jones et al., 2006; Ronsenheck et al., 2008; Sikich et al., 2008; Swartz et al., 2007). To underscore these findings, in one major study, approximately 75% of study participants who had been assigned to the newer drugs discontinued their use due to side effects and/or lack of effectiveness (Lieberman et al., 2005).

Second-generation antipsychotics ▶ Recently developed drugs designed to treat psychotic disorders such as schizophrenia, but also used as mood stabilizers in bipolar disorder.

IN SUMMARY

1.	Pharmacotherapy is the treatment of psychological symptoms with drugs or other substances.
2.	Anxiety is treated with anxiolytics, primarily benzodiazepine drugs. Azapirone drugs such as buspirone are also used, and may be preferable for long-term use.
3.	The principal classes of antidepressant drugs are MAO inhibitors; tricyclic antidepressants (TCAs); selective serotonin reuptake inhibitors (SSRIs); and the "third-generation antidepressants, including the serotonin/norepinephrine reuptake inhibitors (SNRIs).
4.	SSRIs and SNRIs were originally promoted as being more effective, faster acting, and causing fewer side effects than MAO inhibitors and tricyclic drugs. However, none of these claims is supported by research.
5.	Bipolar disorder is treated with mood stabilizers, including lithium, anticonvulsants, and atypical antipsychotics. These drugs are generally better at controlling mania than depression, although depression is much more typical of bipolar disorder than is mania.
6.	Schizophrenia is treated with first- and second-generation antipsychotics. Although the second-generation drugs are promoted as having fewer or more mild side effects and being more effective, as with the antidepressants, research has not borne out these claims.

RETRIEVE!

1.	True or false? Most medical authorities assert that benzodiazepines are safe and effective for long-term use.

2.	Name at least two side effects more common in SSRIs/SNRIs than in tricyclic antidepressants.
3.	Which of the following is NOT among the known side effects of antipsychotic drugs? **a)** tardive dyskinesia **b)** excessive sedation **c)** diabetes and stroke **d)** heart disease **e)** All of the preceding are potential side effects of antipsychotics.
4.	Which of the following drugs are derived from naturally occurring body salts? **a)** SSRIs **b)** MAO inhibitors **c)** lithium **d)** anticonvulsants
5.	True or false? The second-generation antipsychotic drugs are somewhat more effective, and have fewer side effects, than the first-generation drugs.

Does Pharmacotherapy Work?

We have already seen that evidence of the efficacy/effectiveness of pharmacotherapy is much less convincing than many claims made for the medications. However, the question of efficacy and effectiveness of pharmacotherapy needs to be examined perhaps with even greater care—and boldness—than we gave to the same issue as regards psychotherapy. For, although psychotherapy can be harmful as we have already discussed, it is not as potentially harmful as pharmacotherapy as a general rule. In other words, the side effects of drugs are usually more worrisome than those of legitimate forms of psychotherapy.

There is another, more important reason to be fearless in assessing pharmacotherapy: It supports many billions of dollars of profits annually for multinational pharmaceutical corporations. Without being overly cynical, it is a matter of common sense to refrain from relying on industry pronouncements and advertisements regarding their products, or taking scientific research at face value when much of it is funded by the very companies whose products are being tested.

Because the economic stakes are so high, it is not possible to discuss the effectiveness of pharmacotherapy without first addressing the influence of the pharmaceutical industry on scientific and popular beliefs about these drugs. This is a thorny issue that has become increasingly pressing as a result of surprising recent research findings and journalistic exposés.

Large Corporations Manage Information about Pharmacotherapy

"What is the purpose of publications? [The] purpose of data is to support, directly or indirectly, the marketing of our product."

—Sales document from Pfizer Corporation
(cited by Moffatt & Elliott, 2007. p. 18)

▲ **The Long Arm of the Pharmaceutical Industry.** Joseph Biderman (left) is a highly respected Harvard University psychiatrist—perhaps the most influential researcher in the world in the field of child psychiatry. He was particularly important in promoting the new diagnosis of "childhood bipolar disorder" and in advocating the treating of children with powerful antipsychotic medications. Dr. Biderman was found to have failed to disclose "consulting fees" earned from the pharmaceutical companies likely totaling over $2 million (Harris & Carey, 2008). Dr. Frederick K. Goodwin (right) is an extremely influential psychiatrist and host of the popular radio program *The Infinite Mind*. Dr. Goodwin has made major contributions to the study of bipolar disorders and has promoted the view that certain medications used to treat "childhood bipolar disorder" are "safe and effective" (Harris, 2008). It was later discovered that Dr. Goodwin had received substantial payments from the drug companies that manufacture the medications he promoted.

Ghostwriting ▶ The practice of having professional writers write up reports of studies in articles bearing the names of researchers who did not contribute to the writing of the article and may not have been involved in the design and conduct of the study.

"The whole entire paper from start to finish is an advertisement."

—Drummond Rennie, former editor of the *Journal of the American Medical Association*, referring to pharmaceutical industry-funded research articles (cited by Vedantam, 2006)

Corporations cannot be blamed for attempting to present their products in the best light possible. However, pharmaceutical corporate practices apparently exceed simple "best light possible" marketing strategies. Recent research has documented the ways in which pharmaceutical companies powerfully influence how (and how often) their drugs are prescribed, how research on drugs' efficacy is designed and conducted, how the data are analyzed and the articles written, which studies are published, and the conclusions drawn by the authors of research articles (Bekelman, Li, & Gross, 2003; Bero, Oostvogel, Bacchetti, & Lee, 2007; DeAngelis & Fontanarosa, 2008; Kravitz et al., 2005; Moffatt & Elliott, 2007; Sismondo, 2007, 2008a, 2008b). Increasingly numerous journalistic exposés support these research findings (Harris, 2008, 2009; Harris & Carey, 2008; Singer, 2009; Vedantam, 2006).

Consider a meta-analysis by Lisa Bero and her colleagues of pharmaceutical industry-funded studies in which the efficacy of one drug is compared against that of another. In this review, the researchers found that if one of the drugs was shown to be statistically superior to the other, the study was 20 times more likely to have been funded by the company producing the "winning" drug. Worse still, if the conclusions of the authors of the study as they discussed the statistical findings favored the drug, the study was about *35 times* more likely to have been funded by the manufacturer (Bero et al., 2007). Virtually every research analysis that has examined this question has produced the same result (Heres et al., 2006; Sismondo, 2008b).

There are a surprisingly large number of coordinated techniques used by pharmaceutical companies, often rather secretively, to manage the way information about their products reaches scientists and the general public, techniques when taken together are termed *ghostmanagement*. We'll look at just two specific categories of these techniques: *ghostwriting* and *publication bias*.

GHOSTWRITING

Ghostwriting is a common practice in the writing of medical articles. Often the purported authors of articles make very few or no contributions to the actual writing, and may have had little or nothing to do with the design and conduct of the study reported in the article. Nonetheless, their names appear as authors on an "honorary" basis for political reasons, to enhance the stature of the article, or because these researchers' schedules are too tight to allow them actually to do much more than review and/or edit articles printed under their names. Ghostwriting is no secret, and while it may seem strange to some, it does not necessarily compromise the quality of scientific evidence—in fact, people who are good at research are not necessarily good writers; therefore, ghostwriting theoretically can improve the finished product (Healy & Cattell, 2003; Jacobs et al., 2005).

However, if ghostwriters are hired by the very corporations whose products are being tested in the research study in question, problems of bias can and do arise in the final products (Singer, 2009). Consider the highly successful antidepressant Zoloft (sertaline). By means of lawsuit via the Freedom of Information Act, researchers David Healy and Dinah Cattell gained access to a document that demonstrated the extent to which articles on Zoloft had been ghostwritten by writers hired by the manufacturer, Pfizer (Healy & Cattell, 2003). Using this document, Healy and Cattell were able to compare the characteristics of ghostwritten articles of Pfizer-funded studies of Zoloft against studies neither ghostwritten nor funded by Pfizer.

Several things distinguished the Pfizer-sponsored articles from others. First, the Pfizer-sponsored articles contained approximately twice as many authors listed per article, were on average almost three times as long, had more prestigious and prolific researchers listed as authors, and were published in more prestigious journals. Thus, these articles have likely had more impact on the field of psychiatry and medical knowledge. They were also, virtually without exception, favorable to Zoloft—overstating its true efficacy and underreporting the drug's side effects. Making up somewhere between 18% and 40% of the initial scientific research on Zoloft, Pfizer-sponsored research articles have helped to shape the way medical professionals and the public currently view the drug (Sismondo, 2007).

PUBLICATION BIAS

Publication bias is the systematic exclusion of certain types of results from publication in favor of other types of results. There are several pharmaceutical company practices which result in publication bias, but the most prominent method is to submit for publication primarily those articles that report favorable results while relegating studies producing negative results to a dusty file drawer or encouraging journal editors to do so. As an example, Erick Turner and his colleagues (Turner, Matthews, Linardatos, Tell, & Rosenthal, 2008) used the Freedom of Information Act to obtain data on 74 trials of 12 antidepressants submitted to the FDA for approval during the years 1987 to 2004. As Figure 14.4 shows, only approximately 51% of these studies showed positive results for the drugs in question. However, all but one of these positive studies was published. On the other hand, only 3 of the 49% of studies showing negative results were published, and several studies whose results were deemed questionable by the FDA were published in a way that incorrectly suggested that the results had been positive. Thus, looking only at the data available to the public as well as scientists, it appears as though 94% of the studies showed positive results—not 51%, as was actually the case (see also Melander, Ahlqvist-Rastad, Meijer, & Beermann, 2003).

Ultimately, industry ghostwriting practices and publication bias should come as no surprise. Recent research has shown that approximately two-thirds of academic department chairs and other leaders in medical and psychiatric fields have financial ties to the pharmaceutical industry (Campbell et al., 2007), presenting numerous opportunities for conflicts of interest. Indeed, in 2009, the

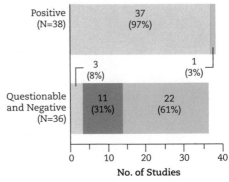

■ Published, agrees with FDA decision
■ Published, conflicts with FDA decision
■ Not published

▲ **FIGURE 14.4 Bias in Publication of Antidepressant Studies Reviewed by the FDA.** Of the 74 studies of 12 antidepressants evaluated by the FDA, 38 showed positive results for the drug in question and 33 showed negative (or questionable) results. However, of the 38 positive studies 37 were published, and only one remained unpublished. Of the 33 negative or questionable studies, only 3 were published in a way that correctly identified the results as negative. Another 11 of these studies were published in a way that incorrectly interpreted the results as positive (although the FDA had deemed the results negative or questionable). *(Adapted from Turner et al., 2008, p. 256.)*

Publication bias ▶ The systematic exclusion of certain types of results from publication in favor of other types of results. Publication bias can result from a number of different practices, including withholding certain types of results from submission to journals, editorial decisions on the part of journal editors, and submitting data from the same study multiple times to give the impression that more studies found a particular result than is actually the case.

federal government initiated a lawsuit against the makers of the popular anti-depressants Lexapro and Celexa for concealing evidence of the drugs' ineffec-tiveness, misrepresenting information about their safety, and paying kickbacks to physicians for prescribing the drugs (Harris, 2009).

Eliminating Publication Bias Reveals a Different Picture of Antidepressants

With a basic understanding of pharmaceutical company influence as a back-drop, let us now take another look at research on the efficacy and effectiveness of one type of psychiatric drug: antidepressants.

In 2002, in part due to revelations of pharmaceutical industry "ghost man-agement" of antidepressant research, Irving Kirsch and his colleagues used the Freedom of Information Act to obtain *all* clinical data submitted to the FDA from the major pharmaceutical companies seeking approval for the six most widely prescribed of the newer antidepressant drugs (Kirsch, Moore, Scoboria, & Nicholls, 2002). Kirsch and colleagues' meta-analysis of these data—published in an article with the provocative title, "The Emperor's New Drugs"—showed that when all research intentionally held back from publi-cation by the pharmaceutical industry was taken into account, between 80% and 90% of apparent effects of antidepressants were duplicated by placebos. This means that 80% to 90% of patients who appeared to improve after tak-ing antidepressants were actually improving as a result of placebo effects of the drugs, rather than any pharmacological action. Stated another way, an-tidepressants showed only a 10% to 20% statistical advantage over placebos (Kirsch, Moore, Scoboria, & Nicholls, 2002).

However, subsequent analyses by Kirsch's colleagues and by an indepen-dent research team showed that the small advantage of antidepressants over placebos applied only to patients with the most extremely severe depres-sions—patients who do not respond to placebos. Therefore, for those with mild, moderate, and even severe depressions—but not the very most severe—antidepressants apparently have *no* clinically significant (meaningful) advan-tage over placebos (Fournier et al., 2010; Huedo-Medina, Johnson, & Kirsch, 2012; Kirsch et al., 2008).

As dismal a picture of antidepressant *efficacy* as these figures paint, data on antidepressant *effectiveness* look equally grim. Researchers from the National Institutes of Mental Health followed approximately 4,000 patients at out-patient clinics at 40 treatment locations as part of the Sequenced Treatment Alternatives to Relieve Depression trials, or STAR*D (Rush et al., 2006). When researchers from this large-scale effectiveness study looked at data from a subset of the 4,000 patients—those most representative of the types of patients who generally seek treatment for depression in clinic settings—they found that only 24% of these patients received relief from their depression af-ter taking antidepressants (76% received no relief) (Wisniewski et al., 2009). Because this was an effectiveness study without placebo control groups, this 24% would have included both placebo responders and medication respond-ers. Therefore, there is no way to know with certainty how many patients in the group that experienced relief—if any—did so as a result of the pharmaco-logical action of the medication rather than its placebo effects.

WHAT DO THESE FINDINGS MEAN? SHOULD ANTIDEPRESSANTS BE PRESCRIBED?

Although Kirsch and colleagues' statistical findings, those of researchers who replicated them (e.g., Fournier et al., 2010) and the STAR*D data are not generally disputed, *the meaning*, or implications, of these findings is still a source of hot debate. In addition to various claims that methodological issues are at least partly responsible for the poor showing of antidepressant drugs

▲ **Alternative Treatments for Depression.** For most people, the common herb St. John's Wort and a program of regular physical exercise are each just as effective against depression as antidepressant drugs—and they have fewer negative side effects. However, St. John's Wort should be used only under the supervision of a mental health professional, because not all types and dosages of the herb are equally effective.

(Fountoulakis & Möller, 2011; Nelson, Thase, & Khan, 2008), several commentators have suggested that as long as antidepressants show *any* statistical superiority over placebos, they should continue to be prescribed.

For example, Walter Brown (2002) argues that antidepressants can function as placebos, exerting antidepressant effects in this manner. But they can also exert true effects for the very small group of extremely depressed individuals who do not respond to placebos. Because the prevalence of depression is so high, Brown argues, this "small group"—even if it only accounted for 10% of those with depression—might actually amount to a large number of people being helped by antidepressants.

Yet, as Kirsch and his colleagues point out in response to these arguments, anti-depressants often have very serious side effects, whereas the herb St. John's wort, with many fewer and less serious side effects, appears to work at least as well as antidepressants—if the correct type and dose is used (Linde, Berner, & Kriston, 2008; Szegedi, Kohnen, Dienel, & Kieser, 2005; Wheatley, 2006). For unknown reasons, physical exercise also seems to be about as effective as antidepressants in treating major depression, and its side effects are actually beneficial (i.e., an increase in the patient's physical fitness; Babyak et al., 2000; Lindwall, Rennemark, Halling, Berglund, et al., 2007; Trivedi, Greer, Grannemann, Chambliss et al., 2006).

Finally, although some individual studies show psychotherapy to be superior to antidepressants, and some show antidepressants to be superior to psychotherapy, systematic reviews show the two to be virtually identical in efficacy (DeRubeis et al., 2005; Hollon et al., 2005; Khan, Faucett, Lichtenberg, Kirsch, & Brown, 2012). Given the existence of alternative treatments such as psychotherapy, exercise, and St. John's wort, Kirsch and his colleagues argue that the continued use of antidepressant drugs should be questioned until research demonstrating clear and meaningful superiority over placebos is produced.

There are many who disagree with this recommendation—no doubt including patients who have watched their depressions vanish, or nearly vanish, during the course of antidepressant treatment—people such as Paloma, whose story was recounted at the opening of the chapter. These individuals might find it hard to swallow the notion that the risks of antidepressant use outweigh their benefits. Here we come up against one of those instances where conflict may exist between findings of research in psychology and psychiatry, and the day-to-day practice of psychologists and psychiatrists and the experiences of their clients and patients (Nelson et al., 2008). As suggested at the opening of Chapter 1 of this book, tension of this sort is far from rare.

IN SUMMARY

1.	The pharmaceutical industry influences how drugs are prescribed, how research on drugs' efficacy is designed and conducted, how the data are analyzed and the articles written, which studies are published, and the conclusions drawn by the authors of research articles. Two techniques of this "ghostmanagement" used by pharmaceutical corporations to exert this influence are ghostwriting and publication bias.
2.	Recent research has shown that antidepressants only hold a 10% to 20% advantage over placebos at best, and this slight numerical edge is accounted for by the lack of placebo response among a very small group of the most extremely severely depressed individuals. For the large majority of people currently using antidepressants, the drugs are indistinguishable from placebos.
3.	Some argue that even if antidepressants hold only a slight statistical edge over placebos they ought to be prescribed so that they may help the small group of severely depressed placebo nonresponders. Others counter that the potential negative side effects of antidepressants outweigh their usefulness.
4.	The herb St. John's wort, physical exercise, and psychotherapy all have efficacy equal to that of antidepressants with many fewer negative side effects.

RETRIEVE!

1.	Several research studies described in this portion of the chapter suggest that pharmaceutical corporations influence the content of medical research. Describe the findings of at least one of these studies.
2.	Why should ghostwriting and publication bias in the pharmaceutical field "come as no surprise"?
3.	The statistical edge of antidepressants over placebos in patients' ratings for depression equals approximately: **a)** 1%–5% **b)** 10%–20% **c)** 20%–25% **d)** 40%–50%

Electroconvulsive therapy (ECT) ▶ A treatment for psychological disorders (primarily treatment-resistant depression) that consists of passing a low-voltage electrical current through a person's brain for a brief moment, resulting in seizure and convulsion. ECT is usually conducted multiple times for any given case.

What Other Biological Treatments Are Available?

Although pharmaceutical remedies are the most frequently used biological treatments, there are alternative biologically based modes available for treating psychological disorders. As a general rule, however, these treatments—including *electroconvulsive therapy, electrical* and *magnetic brain stimulation*, and *psychosurgery*—are used when other methods have failed.

Electroconvulsive Treatment Is Controversial

Oh no! *Shock treatment!*

With the exception of *psychosurgery*, which consists of invasive surgical procedures on the brain (see p. 710), **electroconvulsive therapy (ECT)** is the most controversial of all treatments for psychological disorders. ECT is used principally in cases of severe depressions that have not responded to other treatments. The distaste many people have for the idea of ECT stems partly from the versions of the technique used during the early years of its development, which can be described as somewhat barbaric. Those procedures were quite painful and were often applied by force to unwilling patients. They sometimes resulted in severe physical injury (e.g., multiple bone fractures), cognitive damage, and death. There is a Frankenstein-esque quality to many people's images of ECT, and the name itself is enough for people to denounce the treatment—even if the same people accept the treatment when it is described to them using a different name (Andrade & Thyagarajan, 2007).

However, ECT techniques have changed quite dramatically over the past few decades, and today ECT is considered by most psychiatric organizations and clinicians to be generally safe (American Psychiatric Association Task Force, 2001; Fink & Taylor, 2007; Royal College of Psychiatrists, 1995). However, in 2011, the Food and Drug Administration agreed to review the treatment in regard to safety and other concerns (U. S. Food and Drug Administration, 2011) and, in truth, ECT is not entirely safe (Rose, Fleishmann, Wykes, Leese, & Bindman, 2003; Sackeim et al., 2007; Sterling, 2000). (But as we have already seen, neither is drug therapy or even psychotherapy!)

During ECT, the patient is first anesthetized (rendered unconscious) and given a muscle relaxant drug to prevent bone fractures during convulsions. The patient is then strapped to a table and a low-voltage electric shock is passed through the brain for a split second, causing the patient to experience an epilepsy-like seizure and subsequent convulsions. These convulsions last for a few minutes. The treatment is repeated each day for about 6 to 10 days on average.

As with psychopharmacology, but much more so, opinions are often extreme regarding ECT, and it is quite easy to find two highly competent clinicians or researchers who will disagree radically about how well ECT actually works and whether it is safe (Fink & Taylor, 2007; Sterling, 2000). It is understandable that contradictory opinions about ECT may exist among informed scientists. Despite the fact that ECT has been studied for over 50 years, the quality of the evidence is not very good relative to the quality of the outcome research in psychotherapy or even psychopharmacology (Rose et al., 2003; Sackeim et al., 2007; UK ECT Review Group, 2003).

However, the evidence, such as it is, suggests several conclusions. First, the dangers of ECT are often overstated by some patient support groups and mental health activists. For example, as of this writing there is no evidence that ECT causes structural brain damage (Lisanby, 2007), and ECT is not a sadistic practice as it is sometimes portrayed. In terms of mortality, it is one of the very safest procedures performed under general anesthesia, with accidental death being an exceptionally rare event (Greenberg & Kellner, 2005).

On the other hand, the dangers of ECT are also often *under*stated by psychiatrists and professional organizations. In particular, in addition to producing states of highly unpleasant confusion and disorientation, ECT does cause memory loss (often to a serious degree) in a substantial number of patients undergoing the treatment (Lisanby, 2007; Gregory-Roberts, Naismith, Cullen, & Hickie, 2010; Rose et al., 2003). Although clinicians often note some "transient" (temporary) memory impairment, it is usually glossed over and, in fact, ECT can cause long-term or even permanent memory loss (Gregory-Roberts et al., 2010; Lisanby, 2007; Sackeim et al., 2007).

What about the efficacy of ECT? According to the available evidence, ECT does seem to work at least as well or better than pharmacotherapy in the treatment of severe depression that has not responded to other treatment (Greenberg & Kellner, 2005; Pagnin, de Queiroz, Pini, & Cassano, 2004; UK ECT Review Group, 2003). However, like all treatments, ECT must be viewed from a cost-benefit perspective—is the benefit worth the risk? In the case of ECT, opinions are polarized.

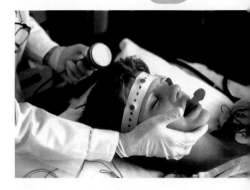

▲ **Electroconvulsive Therapy (ECT).** Although it is not as dangerous as many believe, ECT has more serious effects on memory than some defenders claim. Nevertheless, it is at least as effective in treating depression as pharmacotherapy.

Magnetic Brain Stimulation

Inducing seizures using electrical current was first introduced into psychiatry about 75 years ago, and ECT has become routine as a treatment for treatment-resistant depression. However, several new biological treatments that utilize various types of electrical and magnetic stimulation techniques are in development for treatment of this type of severe depression. **Repetitive transcranial magnetic stimulation (rTMS)** involves placing an electromagnetic coil on the scalp. The coil sends short electromagnetic pulses through the skull, gently stimulating the cerebral cortex. If you're wondering what this might feel like, it produces the sensation of someone gently knocking or tapping on your head. Some patients experience mild tension, headache, or other discomfort while undergoing rTMS. The most serious side effect is the possibility of seizure, but newer techniques have lowered this risk.

Does rTMS work? Evidence in favor of the technique began to trickle in after 2005, and in 2008 the FDA approved the technique for use in treating depression. However, this decision seemed to be based more on consideration of the safety of the technique than its effectiveness. Some research has shown significant antidepressant effects for rTMS, substantially greater than that produced by mock rTMS (placebo) (George et al., 2010; Stern, Tormos, Press, Pearlman, & Pascual-Leone, 2007), and a number of recent meta-analyses have come down in favor of the technique (Berlim, Van den Eynde, & Daskalakis, 2013; Slotema, Blom, Hoek, & Sommer, 2010), suggesting that it is probably about equal to ECT in efficacy.

Psychosurgery

As briefly described in Chapter 2, early techniques of psychosurgery were generally ineffective as well as extremely dangerous, resulting in brain damage, mental disability, personality change, and high rates of death. Claims have been made (some accurate, some exaggerated) that these procedures were sometimes used against people whose behavior was disapproved rather than people who truly needed help for psychological distress (Mashour, Walker, & Martuza, 2005; Ögren & Sandlund, 2007). Early psychosurgical techniques primarily involved *lobotomy* procedures, which consist of cutting connections to the prefrontal cortex (or damaging it in various ways). Most societies consider such techniques barbaric, and they are frequently outlawed.

However, modern techniques of psychosurgery have evolved, although they are fairly strictly controlled and conducted at few sites around the world. These techniques are generally used only as a last resort in severe cases of neurological as well as psychological disorders including Parkinson disease, anorexia nervosa, obsessive-compulsive disorder, and treatment-resistant depression. One such technique is known as **deep brain stimulation (DBS)**. In DBS, electrodes are implanted in various regions of the brain, and the electrodes are coupled to an external device that sends out stimulating electrical pulses (Mayberg et al., 2005). Although this procedure is promoted as being less potentially damaging than ordinary surgery, DBS is brain surgery, and brain surgery carries risks. Immediate risks of DBS include infection, epileptic seizures, hemorrhage, unwanted personality change, disturbances of speech and memory, dementia, psychiatric symptoms, and death—including death by suicide (Clausen, 2010). Long-term risks are unknown (Bejerot, 2003).

Closing Remarks: The Future of Treatment Is Integrative

Treatment for psychological disorders and distress is an enormously complex and extensive topic, and I hope that this chapter has reflected this scope and complexity. However, in separating treatments into categories either large

Repetitive transcranial magnetic stimulation (rTMS) ▶ A technique being developed for treatment of depression that consists of sending short electromagnetic pulses though the cerebral cortex by means of a coil placed on the scalp.

Deep brain stimulation (DBS) ▶ A relatively new technique of psychosurgery used to treat Parkinson disease and being tested for use in psychological disorders, particularly depression. In deep brain stimulation electrodes are implanted in various regions of the brain and coupled to an external device that sends out stimulating electrical pulses.

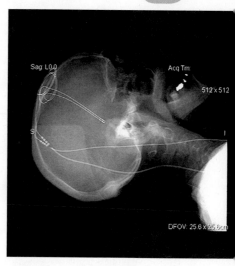

▲ **Deep Brain Stimulation.** In this modern psychosurgical technique, electrodes are implanted in regions of the brain where it is thought that neuronal signals are being blocked. The electrodes are coupled to a device that sends out electrical signals in an effort to stimulate the region artificially.

▲ **The "Ice Pick" or Transorbitol Lobotomy.** Invented by Walter Freeman (center), this psychosurgical procedure was performed on many thousands of Americans during the 1930s and 1940s. The technique involves hammering an ice pick through the back of the eye socket into the brain. It results in brain damage, mental disability, and personality change and has few if any known positive benefits. The ice pick lobotomy has been described as "recklessness bordering on lunacy."

(biological/psychological) or small (cognitive therapies / SSRI antidepressants / deep brain stimulation), there may be a natural tendency to assume that the various treatments compete with one another. For example, the question "which is better—medication or therapy?" is often asked, and to a certain extent there do remain clinicians who are strictly partisan to one or the other approach.

However, partisanship in treatment of psychological disorders is fading rapidly as it becomes increasingly apparent that psychological disorders are caused by the interaction of biological, psychological, and social variables. Consequently, increasing numbers of clinicians have realized that effective treatment must address the biological, psychological, and social lives of each individual. This model of treatment is known as the **integrative treatment model** (Barlow & Durand, 2005).

As an example, although it is true that there has been a very large increase in the number of people whose only treatment for anxiety or depression is the use of psychoactive medications, a large number of those using these medications are also undergoing psychotherapy. They may also have been prescribed an exercise regimen or meditation practice by their doctors, and they may have been advised to read books about depression (bibliotherapy). The client may also have joined a self-help group of people attempting to recover from depression. This is integrative treatment.

In looking back over this chapter, a picture of recovery from psychological disorders begins to form. Whereas there are a great many valuable treatments, the power of placebo in comparison with these treatments is surprisingly strong. Even when a treatment does work better than placebo, the client or patient is often a more important figure in his or her own recovery than depictions of treatment usually suggest (Khan et al., 2012). Psychotherapy is a good example of this idea. Therapy appears to work largely because of the unique

Integrative treatment model ▶ A model of treatment that reflects the reality that most current mental health treatment involves multiple modalities (e.g., psychotherapy plus medication plus bibliotherapy).

partnership between therapist and client. So while film and television depictions usually exalt the clinician or the treatment as the hero or heroine of the story of psychological disorders, it appears that the sufferer can often make the greatest contribution to his or her own recovery.

IN SUMMARY

1. Electroconvulsive therapy (ECT) is the most controversial of all nonsurgical treatments for psychological disorders. Used primarily in cases of extremely severe, treatment-resistant depression, ECT consists of passing a split-second, low-voltage electric shock through the brain. This triggers seizures and convulsions which last for several minutes.

2. Opinions are extreme regarding ECT, and evidence regarding its safety and efficacy, while extensive, is not of very good quality. The worst side effect of ECT is serious memory loss, which, while generally of short duration, can be permanent.

3. Repetitive transcranial magnetic stimulation (rTMS) involves the placing of an electromagnetic coil on the scalp which sends short pulses through the skull, stimulating the cerebral cortex. In deep brain stimulation (DBS), electrodes are surgically implanted in regions of the brain in which it is thought that neuronal signals are blocked. These treatments are all experimental.

4. The future of treatment for psychological disorders appears to involve integrated methods and significant input from the patient.

RETRIEVE!

1. What is one reason that the risk of memory loss in ECT has been underestimated by psychiatrists?

2. True or false: According to available evidence, ECT works at least as well or better than pharmacotherapy in the treatment of severe treatment-resistant depression.

3. _____ is a new biological treatment that involves placing an electromagnetic coil on the scalp and sending short electromagnetic pulses through the skull.

a) rTMS **b)** VNS **c)** DBS **d)** NBC

4. True or false? Most people are treated with more than one type of treatment concurrently (e.g., psychotherapy plus medication).

Looking Back

Chapter 14 in Review

WHAT IS PSYCHOTHERAPY?
- Psychotherapy is a unique, healing, personal relationship. Psychotherapists' training varies widely; the term *psychotherapist* is generally unregulated by laws. Although many therapists receive extensive training and have advanced degrees, in many cases paraprofessionals with little training perform therapy just as successfully. The psychotherapy occupations of clinical psychologist and counseling psychologist both require a Psy.D. or Ph.D. degree.
- People enter therapy for help with psychological disorders, but also to treat ordinary suffering arising

Looking Back continued

from a distressing event, or from conflicts and problems of ordinary life. There are many styles of psychotherapy, and no one style of legitimate psychotherapy has proved superior overall.

HOW DO STYLES OF PSYCHOTHERAPY DIFFER?

- Psychoanalysis, the first "talk therapy," is based on the notion that psychological problems are caused by unconscious, intrapsychic conflicts. The goal of psychoanalysis is insight. Neo-Freudian psychoanalysis is based on object relations theory and other theories. Pychodynamic therapy is based on theories of psychoanalysis, but its therapeutic techniques differ greatly from psychoanalysis.
- Behavior therapy is based on the behaviorist view that psychological disorders are learned patterns of maladaptive behaviors. Following in the footsteps of Mary Cover Jones, Joseph Wolpe created techniques to treat anxiety through controlled exposure to the feared object while the client simultaneously practices relaxation or engages in rational thoughts. Systematic desensitization is one such technique; flooding is another. Operant therapies are another approach of behavior therapy.
- Cognition-based therapies include rational-emotive behavior therapy, cognitive therapy, cognitive-behavior therapy, and mindfulness-based cognitive therapy (MBCT). Rational-emotive behavior therapy (REBT) is based on the idea that psychological disorders originate in a person's illogical, absolutist, and counterproductive ideas about living. Cognitive therapy (CT) somewhat similarly proposes that emotional problems are brought on by "automatic thoughts" that are highly unrealistic, self-defeating, and biased against the self. Cognitive behavior therapy (CBT) assumes a complex link between cognition and emotion that includes behavior. CBT therapists blend techniques of cognitive therapy and behavior therapy.

Mindfulness-based cognitive therapy (MBCT) is a brief therapy for depression that blends techniques of CBT with meditation techniques. Psychotherapies that demonstrate superiority over no treatment for a given disorder are known as empirically supported treatments (ESTs). They may or may not be effective in real-world settings.

- Integrative therapy (eclectic therapy) draws from more than one current of psychotherapeutic theory and technique. In addition to using techniques of many of the therapies already mentioned, integrative therapists are often influenced by client-centered therapy of humanistic psychologist Carl Rogers.

WHAT ARE GROUP, COUPLE, AND FAMILY THERAPIES?

- In group therapy, at least three clients engage in therapy with one or two therapists. Group therapy is less costly than individual therapy. Exposure to a number of others with similar problems may be helpful, as can offering help to others. Group therapy allows the therapist to observe how a client relates to other people. Self-help support groups, while potentially therapeutic, do not constitute psychotherapy.
- Family therapy is generally based on family systems theory, which does not single out a particular individual for treatment—the whole family is treated. The family is considered an integrated, organic unit or system. Couple therapy is a form of therapy involving married, dating, or cohabiting couples and a therapist.

DOES PSYCHOTHERAPY WORK?

- In 35 years of research, psychotherapy has been shown to be superior to no treatment, and it is at least as efficacious as medication for depression and anxiety. Dismantling studies suggest that psychotherapy may work not as a result of any specific "ingredients" of a given therapy style, but as a result of factors such as therapeutic alliance, therapist allegiance, and therapist competence.

- Calling something "therapy" does not make it therapeutic, and psychotherapy may sometimes cause harm. This is particularly true for the group of treatments known as potentially harmful psychotherapies (PHPs). Culture plays a role in psychotherapy, and "one size fits all" treatments may ignore important differences based on culture.

WHAT IS PHARMACOTHERAPY?

- Pharmacotherapy is the use of drugs or other substances to treat psychological distress. Although these drugs usually fall into one of four categories—anxiolytics, antidepressants, mood stabilizers, and antipsychotics—they are often prescribed "off-label" to treat conditions for which they were not intended.
- Anxiolytic drugs (e.g., benzodiazepines) are used to treat anxiety. Benzodiazepines produce their effects in part through GABA regulation. At high doses these drugs produce symptoms similar to drunkenness, and the drugs are frequently abused. The drugs were intended only for short-term use, but many people use them for years or decades.
- Antidepressants are the most commonly prescribed of all drug types in the United States, and their use has quadrupled in the past 20 years, particularly among those with less severe symptoms. There are four principal classes of antidepressants: MAO inhibitors, tricyclic drugs, selective serotonin reuptake inhibitors (SSRIs), and third-generation drugs including serotonin/norepinephrine reuptake inhibitors (SNRIs).
- Selective serotonin reuptake inhibitors (SSRIs) selectively act on serotonin systems rather than several neurotransmitter systems simultaneously. SSRIs do not have fewer side effects than TCAs (just different side effects) and are not faster acting, but they have "left TCAs in the dust" due to pharmaceutical industry marketing campaigns. SSRI drugs may produce serious withdrawal symptoms.

Looking Back continued

- The most frequently prescribed third-generation antidepressants are the serotonin-norepinephrine reuptake inhibitors (SNRIs), which are based on the idea that combining selectivity for the neurotransmitter norepinephrine as well as for serotonin might produce superior results to those produced by serotonin selectivity alone.

- Bipolar disorders are treated with mood stabilizers including lithium, anticonvulsant drugs such as Depakote, and second-generation antipsychotic drugs. Schizophrenia is treated with antipsychotic drugs. First-generation antipsychotics reduced the severity of positive symptoms. Second-generation antipsychotics have been promoted as more effective and safer than first-

generation drugs, but extensive research has demonstrated that these claims lack validity.

DOES PHARMACOTHERAPY WORK?

- The pharmaceutical industry powerfully influences public and medical professionals' beliefs about pharmacotherapy. Meta-analytic research using data bases that include studies held back from publication or FDA viewing shows that, with the exception of the most extremely severe depressions, antidepressants are no more efficacious than placebos, and effectiveness research has produced similarly disappointing findings. Nonetheless, some researchers suggest that these statistical findings underestimate the drugs' usefulness as placebos.

WHAT OTHER BIOLOGICAL TREATMENTS ARE AVAILABLE?

- Other biology-based treatments for psychological disorder includude electroconvulsive therapy (ECT), repetitive transcranial magnetic stimulation (rTMS), and psychosurgery. Early psychosurgery techniques of lobotomy were ineffective and dangerous, and they caused brain damage, mental disability, and personality change. One new technique known as deep brain stimulation is promoted as being less dangerous than ordinary psychosurgery with more manageable side effects.

- The future of treatment for psychological disorders is integrative—including biological, psychological, and social aspects.

Key Terms

Test Yourself

1. List three aspects of psychotherapy that distinguish it from other types of supportive relationships.

2. No legitimate style of psychotherapy has shown overall superiority to any other style. What is the name given to this idea?
   a) the blue-footed booby effect
   b) the swallow verdict
   c) the dodo bird verdict
   d) the duck decision

3. Tension within a person's own mind between mental forces that are at odds with one another is known as _____ conflict.
   a) intrapsychic
   b) interpsychic
   c) contrapsychic
   d) bipsychic

4. Maya is a therapist who believes that the origins of personality lie in early childhood experiences and that unconscious emotional and motivational processes exert important effects on a person's

Test Yourself continued

behavior. Maya is most likely to conduct which type of therapy?

a) behavior therapy

b) cognitive-behavior therapy

c) rational-emotive therapy

d) psychodynamic therapy

5. Damien has a terror of public speaking, yet his work necessitates that he do so frequently. His therapist guides him through a series of increasingly intense anxiety-provoking images related to public speaking (e.g., standing outside the auditorium, entering the auditorium, walking to the podium, and so forth) while guiding Damien in progressive muscle relaxation. What is the name of the therapeutic technique being used by Damien's therapist?

a) flooding

b) cognitive-behavior therapy

c) systematic desensitization

d) contingency management intervention

6. Which type of therapy is based on the ABC theory of emotional disturbance?

a) behavior therapy

b) cognitive therapy

c) cognitive-behavior therapy

d) rational-emotive therapy

7. Which type of therapy is based on the idea that irrational automatic thoughts that are biased against the self—when interacting with dysfunctional underlying core beliefs about the self, the world, and the future—can cause psychological disorders such as depression or anxiety?

a) behavior therapy

b) cognitive therapy

c) psychoanalysis

d) integrative therapy

8. A psychotherapy that has shown itself to be superior to no treatment in series of randomized controlled trials is known as a(n) _____.

a) empirically supported treatment

b) effective treatment

c) evidence-based treatment

d) clinically significant treatment

9. Therapy that draws from a number of different theoretical perspectives and techniques is termed _____.

a) interindividual therapy

b) interdependent

c) interactive therapy

d) integrative therapy

10. Give at least two reasons that self-help groups, while possibly therapeutic, do not constitute psychotherapy.

11. What are the two general categories of reasons why a couple might decide to enter couple therapy?

12. What is the difference between a therapy that is *effective* and a therapy that is *efficacious*?

13. In a controlled randomized trial, the outcome for a therapy for depression was measured by participants' depression ratings on a scale from (1) *not at all depressed* to (7) *severely depressed*. At the start of the study, participants had an average depression rating of 6.3. At the end of the study, they had an average depression rating of 5.0. This result was statistically significant with a moderately large effect size. However, critics pointed out that the trial was actually a failure. Why?

14. What are the three factors most frequently hypothesized to be the "common factors" in psychotherapeutic success?

15. What is the term used to describe the type of harm that may be caused by potentially harmful psychotherapies (PHPs)?

16. What is the term used to describe a drug used to treat anxiety? Depression? Bipolar disorder? Psychotic disorders?

17. True or false: The SSRI and SNRI (third-generation) antidepressants are more effective, faster acting, and have fewer side effects than the tricyclics drugs.

18. True or false: The second-generation antipsychotics are more effective and have fewer side effects than the first-generation drugs.

19. Name two categories of techniques used by pharmaceutical companies to manage the way information about their products reaches scientists and the general public.

20. Name two ways in pharmaceutical companies promote publication bias in a manner favorable to their products.

21. True or false: The large majority of people who use antidepressants belong to the group for whom these drugs do not differ in efficacy from placebos.

22. True or false: Current techniques of electroconvulsive therapy (ECT) frequently result in severe injury.

social
Psychology

Chapter Outline

Freeze Frame

Samuel Dryfus[1] was 56 when he was recruited by psychological researchers to administer the shocks. The year was 1961; the place, Yale University. Out of curiosity, Dryfus had responded to a newspaper ad offering $4.00 for one hour's participation in a "study of memory" to be conducted at Yale. In 1961, $4.00 was the equivalent of about $30.00 today, and Dryfus had not been doing all that well for the past year, so it seemed worthwhile.

When Dryfus arrived, a man with a white lab coat and an authoritative air told him that this was to be a study of the effects of punishment on learning. Using microphone communication, Dryfus, whose role was that of the "teacher," was to present a series of word pairs to another participant—the "learner"—who was strapped to a chair in another room and wired to electrodes. The learner, a jolly-looking man with a straw hat introduced as Mr. Wallace, was supposed to recall the second word of each pair after being prompted with the first word by Dryfus. If he answered incorrectly, Dryfus was to administer an electric shock. Each time Mr. Wallace answered incorrectly, Dryfus was to increase the voltage of the shock.

Dryfus found himself seated at a "shock generator" console with an array of switches marked with specific voltages: 15v, 30v, 45v, up through 100v, 150v, and ending at 450. Each number was also marked with a label beginning with *Mild Shock*, up through *Strong Shock, Very Strong Shock, Intense Shock, Extreme Intensity Shock*, and ending with *Danger— Severe Shock, XXX*. Dryfus hadn't exactly been prepared for something like this, and in fact he began to have serious misgivings when Mr. Wallace mentioned to the experimenter that he had a mild heart condition which he thought the experimenter ought to be aware of. But the experimenter kept authoritatively reassuring both participants that "nothing bad is going to happen here."

[1]*Not his actual name.*

Whether or not "something bad" did happen that day, and on the many other days of testing in what have come to be known as "the Milgram studies" (after their author, Stanley Milgram), is a matter of opinion. As Mr. Wallace made error after error, the voltage of the shocks given by Dryfus increased until Mr. Wallace could be heard screaming in pain and pleading to be allowed to leave. He reminded the experimenters that he had heart problems and insisted that he could not be held against his will. As the voltage increased, Dryfus began to express dismay to the experimenter, pleading that he did not want to hurt Mr. Wallace any longer. But the experimenter kept insisting that "no lasting tissue damage" would result from the shocks. He also declared that Dryfus must continue with the experiment; that he had "no other choice."

If you were in this situation, how do you think you would react? Would you continue to administer shocks? Most of us undoubtedly believe that we would not. When a group of psychiatrists was asked in advance how many of the research participants were likely to continue to administer shocks up through the "Danger Severe Shock XXX" level, they predicted that fewer than 1% would do so. But in fact, between 62% and 65% of all participants tested by Milgram obeyed the experimenter and administered shocks to the danger level, with 50% administering the very highest level of shocks—even when the "learner" fell silent after prolonged screaming at the highest voltages, apparently seriously injured to the point of unconsciousness or death (Milgram, 1963, 1974; Packer, 2008).

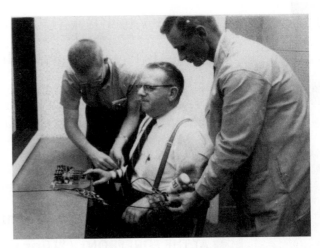

▲ The "Learner" Is Strapped Into the Chair and Wired to Electrodes.

These findings are surprising and dismaying—but if you recall from our brief discussion of these studies in Chapter 1, in fact no actual electric shocks were administered to the learner at all. The "learner" and the "experimenter" were both actors hired by Milgram, and the console, electrodes, and all the rest were entirely bogus. Nor was the study about the effects of punishment on learning. It was about obedience to authority. Milgram wanted to know under what circumstances seemingly ordinary people could be persuaded by authority figures to injure or even torture other human beings. Coming after revelations of the atrocities of Nazi Germany during World War II and Stalin's Soviet Union of the 1930s and 1940s, these questions seemed particularly important.

Important questions they may be, but not everyone was entirely pleased with Milgram for his efforts. Although Milgram and his study are now held in very high esteem by many, and his findings are among the most widely discussed in all of psychology (Blass, 1999, 2009; Burger, 2009), it may surprise you to learn that this research almost ruined Milgram's career—and, as we discussed in Chapter 1, it also helped to trigger major changes in ethical guidelines for psychologists.

We shall consider the implications of the Milgram studies in greater detail later in the chapter. However, the central point Milgram was trying to make was that *the situation in which a person may find himself or herself has a profound impact on how that person behaves.* Someone who has rarely committed even minor cruelty might be convinced to perpetrate cruel acts if the conditions are right.

Social psychology is the study of the influence of social situations on the individual—and the influence of the individual on social situations (Ruscher & Hammer, 2004). A situation like the Milgram studies might indeed cause an ordinarily easy-going sort of person to engage in surprisingly cruel behavior; on the other hand, a habitually disruptive or aggressive person might cause what would have been a placid group meeting to drift into a destructive free-for-all.

Social psychology is the lens through which psychologists view the social individual by himself or herself, as well as in pairs of two, in groups of 10, and in crowds of 20 and 20 million. These social interactions are the focus of this chapter. In the first section we will consider the social self on its own—the face each of us presents to himself or herself and to the world. Specifically, we will look at how individuals manage their own perceptions of themselves, guarding against negative self-judgments and attempting to maintain feelings of self-worth. In subsequent sections we shall look at the self as it relates to others in interpersonal interactions, the effects others have on us, and how conflict may arise between groups, sometimes leading to catastrophic aggression. We shall also explore those situations in which people may inexplicably sacrifice their time, efforts, and even risk their lives for others—seemingly with no expectation of personal benefit.

What Is Psychological Self-Defense?

If social psychology is in part the study of the influence of social situations on the individual, exactly who *is* the individual inside the social situation? In answering this question, social psychologists often focus on the idea of the **self**—each person's subjective awareness of, and ideas about, his or her own individual nature, characteristics, and very existence (Klein, 2012; Markus & Kitayama, 2010; Ruscher & Hammer, 2004). What sort of person am I? What do I believe? What are my strengths and weaknesses? What should others expect of me and what do I truly want for myself? To which groups do I belong? How do I compare with others, or with myself in former times? The self is a bridge between the social world and the inner world of each person (Leary, 2007).

Because the self is constantly making self-evaluations, it must be able to defend against its own negative judgments. Psychological tools by which the self engages in "self-defense" are amazingly diverse and numerous (Tesser, Crepaz, Collins, Cornell, & Beach, 2000). It seems that over and above our desire for accurate information about ourselves stands the desire to feel good about ourselves—to protect feelings of self-worth (Pyszczynski, Greenberg, Solomon, Arndt, et al., 2004; Sherman & Cohen, 2002; Taylor & Brown, 1988). I begin the chapter by discussing some of the more common "self-defense" techniques.

Social psychology ▶ The scientific study of the influence of social situations on individuals, and the influence of individuals on social situations. Social psychologists often focus on the idea of the self and study the social individual alone, in interpersonal situations, and in groups.

Self ▶ Each person's awareness of, and ideas about, his or her own individual nature, characteristics, and existence.

Cognitive Biases Are Potent Self-Defense Weapons

As described in Chapter 9, a cognitive bias is any systematic distortion in thinking, memory, and perception. A person experiencing cognitive bias will have a predictable tendency to arrive at certain conclusions over others, to see things one way rather than another, recall certain types of events but forget others, and so forth. Cognitive biases are powerful "self-defense" weapons. There are a number of specific cognitive biases identified by social psychologists, and we shall examine two: the *self-serving bias* and *positive illusions*.

THE SELF-SERVING BIAS

Suppose you are living with one other person either as roommates or as a couple. If you and your partner were asked what percentage of the housework and other domestic chores you each perform during the week, how do you think you would respond? If each partner's answer were an accurate estimate of his or her contribution, adding the figures together would logically obtain the sum of 100%. (Your dishwashing + partner's dishwashing = 100% of dishwashing.) But when people are actually asked such questions, their answers rarely total 100%. Why? Because each partner will *overestimate* the amount of time he or she spends performing these behaviors, resulting in a total estimate exceeding 100% (Ross & Sicoly, 1979). The same phenomenon occurs when members of a work group or a sports or debating team estimate the percentage they each contribute toward the overall group effort (Gilovich & Savitsky, 1999; Kruger & Gilovich, 1999).

As described in detail in Chapter 9, although human beings have the capacity for accurate perception and judgments of themselves and their world, they also appear to be prone to making certain types of systematic, pervasive errors of thinking and perceiving. One of these is known as the **self-serving bias**, a tendency to make various sorts of judgment errors—always in your own favor. The self-serving bias comes in three basic types:

1. *Overestimating your own contributions.* Thus, the "greater than 100%" effect just described.

2. *Overestimating your positive attributes relative to others—seeing yourself as "better than average."* As one commentator put it, "The one thing that unites all human beings, regardless of age, gender, religion, economic status or ethnic background, is that deep down inside we all believe that we are above average drivers" (Barry, cited by Myers, 2002, p. 95; Chambers & Widschitl, 2004; Leary, 2007). Obviously, not everyone can be above average, or "above average" would *be* average! People also tend to believe themselves to be smarter, more athletic, more attractive, more ethical, and less prejudiced than others. As David Myers (2002) observes, even psychologists—who know all about the self-serving bias—are victims of it to as great an extent as others. Nine out of ten professors believe themselves to be superior to their colleagues!

3. *Attributing your successes and good deeds to your own efforts or characteristics, and your bad deeds and failures to circumstances, bad luck, or other people.* When you do well on a test, or get a good mark on a paper, do you attribute it to simple dumb luck or to the professor's brilliant teaching talent and easy grading scheme—or do you take credit for your hard work and knowledge? If you're like most students, it will be the latter. But what if you get a lousy mark? Do you again take responsibility? Do you say things like, "I didn't study," "I suck in Chemistry," or "I'm not a very good student in general"? Such responses are less likely. Far more common are: "The professor can't teach," "The test was unfair," "The grading system is totally arbitrary," "I had the flu," and so forth. (Sound at all familiar?)

Self-serving bias ▶ The tendency to make systematic judgment errors in one's favor in any of three ways: overestimating one's contributions, overestimating one's positive attributes relative to others, and attributing successes and good deeds to one's own efforts but failures and bad deeds to circumstances, bad luck, or other people.

POSITIVE ILLUSIONS

Would you say that a large part of mental health is being able to perceive things as they actually are? This certainly has been an important part of most traditional definitions of mental health favored by psychologists and psychiatrists as well as movie makers, novelists, and the rest of the general public (Gana, Alaphilippe, & Bailly, 2004). A stereotype of a mentally ill person is someone who believes things that are patently false (e.g., "I am Jesus of Nazareth"), or hearing or seeing things that are not there (e.g., "hearing voices"). However, in 1988, social psychologists Shelley Taylor and Jonathon Brown surprised the world of social and clinical psychology by proposing that certain less extreme forms of inaccurate perception of reality—biases they termed *positive illusions*—may suggest the presence of mental *health* rather than mental illness.

Taylor and Brown termed these biases **positive illusions** because they are not only designed to present the self to itself in a positive (but unrealistic) way, but also because they appear to benefit the individual possessing them (Taylor & Brown, 1994; Taylor, Lerner, Sherman, Sage, & McDowell, 2003). Positive illusions are false beliefs with beneficial consequences (McKay & Dennett, 2009). According to Taylor and Brown, those with positive illusions experience more positive moods and feelings of well-being, are more motivated to achieve goals, persist in their efforts to a greater extent, are more effective, and are more successful generally.

Like the self-serving bias described earlier, positive illusions come in three types:

1. *Uncritically positive views of the self.* For example, Taylor and Brown cite extensive research that shows that people's ratings of their own personalities are more positive than the evaluations of unbiased raters who observe them interacting with others. Well-adjusted individuals also tend to recall their performance on various tasks as better than it actually was, and to think they have improved in abilities they value even when they actually have not improved at all.

2. *Illusions of Control.* Most people believe they have more control over events in their lives than is actually the case. In particular, people greatly underestimate the ever-present factor of *chance*, and will explain events in terms of their own skill that could not possibly be due to skill. For example, people often believe that they are more likely to win the lottery if they personally purchase the ticket (Wortman, 1975).

3. *Unrealistic optimism.* When researchers surveyed 137 couples applying for marriage licenses, and asked them to estimate the percentage of marriages that end in divorce, they correctly (for the late 1980s-early 1990s, at any rate) estimated that 50% of marriages failed. However, when they were asked to estimate the probability that *their own* marriage would fail, most of them answered *zero* percent (Baker & Emery, 1993). So where are all the divorcees?

These findings reflect yet another persistent positive illusion of human beings—the tendency to view the future with unrealistic optimism. As David Myers (2002) reports, students believe themselves to be more likely than their classmates to become prosperous homeowners, and less likely to be stricken by a heart attack, become alcoholic, or be fired from a job. Motorcyclists believe themselves less likely than other motorcyclists to be injured in an accident, smokers are confident they won't get cancer, heterosexual adolescents having unprotected sex are sure they won't get pregnant, and shoppers buy clothes that fit too snugly because they are certain to lose weight in the near future. Even earthquake victims believe they are less likely than others to die of natural disasters—after only a few weeks have passed since the disaster. All of these beliefs and behaviors (except the shopping, perhaps) have potentially serious health consequences, yet they appear to be more typical of

Positive illusions ▶
Systematic biases and illusions that not only are self-serving by presenting the self in a positive way, but also are associated with positive mental health and other consequences for the person possessing them. Positive illusions include uncritically positive views of the self, illusions of control, and unrealistic optimism.

▲ **Are You under Any Illusions about Your Romantic Partner? It Might Be Best to Keep Them.** Some theories propose that unrealistically idealizing your spouse or romantic partner is a recipe for disastrous disillusionment down the line. However, psychologists researching positive illusions have found that married couples and romantic partners who unrealistically idealize one another stay in love longer and have more satisfying relationships. Individuals in these relationships may even come to see themselves as their partners see them (P. J. E. Miller et al., 2006; Murray et al., 2011).

Social comparison theory
▶ A group of theories initially formulated by Leon Festinger that describe how and why people may compare themselves to others to rationally evaluate themselves or enhance their self-concepts and defend against negative self-judgments.

mentally healthy than slightly depressed or psychologically stressed individuals (Fischer, Greitemeyer, & Frey, 2007; Ruehlman, West, & Pasahow, 1985).

Indeed, the vast majority of the world's population, living in the vast majority of countries of the world, express optimism about their lives (Gallagher & Lopez, 2009). Given events on the world stage during the past century—as well as unfortunate events in the lives of so many individuals—it is at least reasonable to ask whether all this optimism is warranted. As described in Chapter 11, however, it does appear to foster good mental and physical health.

Positive illusions may benefit romantic and marital relations as well. In a 13-year longitudinal study of newlyweds, those couples who viewed each other in an unrealistically idealized light at the start of their marriage were *more* likely to remain loving and *less* likely to divorce over the 13-year period of the study (P. J. E. Miller, Niehuis, & Huston, 2006). Similar results were found by an independent group of researchers in a 3-year longitudinal study (Murray, Griffin, Derrick, Harris, & Aloni, 2011).

However, the idea that positive illusions are associated with mental health is not universally accepted (Colvin & Block, 1994). For example, some argue that unrealistic optimism can translate into artificially inflated self-esteem. People with unrealistic or unstable levels of self-esteem sometimes run into interpersonal problems; others may perceive them negatively because they tend to be overly defensive or even hostile when criticized (Baumeister, Campbell, Krueger, & Vohs, 2003; Kernis, Lakey, & Heppner, 2008). Thus, it may be that there is an optimal level, or margin, for positive illusions. If these illusions distort the truth to too great an extent, they may have unhappy consequences or may be associated with reduced mental health (Baumeister, 1989).

The Ups and Downs of Comparing Yourself to Others

Self-evaluation does not occur only through techniques of bias and positive illusion. People may also compare themselves to others for purposes of self-evaluation. Unfortunately, while these comparisons may enhance a person's self-esteem, they may also trash it unmercifully, depending on a number of factors. Theories exploring the ways in which people make social comparisons, their reasons for doing so, and the consequences of comparison judgments are known collectively as **social comparison theory**.

The originator of social comparison theory, social psychologist Leon Festinger (1954), initially believed that people generally make comparisons with other people who are similar to them. The purpose of these comparisons, according to Festinger, is the *self-evaluative* motive—you use them to rationally evaluate your own abilities and clarify your opinions and beliefs. When you compare your grades with those of others in your class, you may be motivated by self-evaluative concerns. The same motive may be at work when you compare your opinions against those of others in your group or nation published in public opinion polls.

However, there are two other reasons for making social comparisons: self-enhancement and self-defense. Researchers during the 1980s observed that people do not always compare themselves to similar others. Sometimes they choose to compare themselves to those who are *dissimilar*—specifically, *less* capable, *less* fortunate, *less* healthy, wealthy, or wise. The purpose of these kinds of comparisons is to boost one's own feelings of self-worth. Making a comparison with another person who is in a *downward* relation to you may lead to a sense of superiority, safety, competence, and well-being (Wills, 1981; Wood, Taylor, & Lichtman, 1985). According to this theory of downward comparison, comparing oneself to a person better off or more capable—that is, making an *upward* comparison—invariably makes a person feel inferior.

Although these ideas were insightful, newer research suggests that the story may be a little more complicated: Both upward and downward comparisons "have their ups and downs" (Suls, Martin, & Wheeler, 2002). For example, upward comparisons may not generate unhappiness and lowered self-esteem in all cases, as previously believed. People may sometimes compare themselves with those in a superior position to them to *boost* their self-esteem by putting themselves in the same category as those who are more competent or fortunate ("My voice is kind of like Beyoncé's"), or increase their motivation to achieve goals by using upward targets as models ("Damn, Beyoncé's good! I'm going to work at this until I can do it like she does!"; Johnson & Stapel, 2010). In the same way, a downward comparison may not always improve things. By bringing to mind those in an inferior relationship, a person may also be reminded that it is entirely possible for the same fate to befall him or her (Suls et al., 2002).

Cognitive Dissonance: When Attitudes and Behavior Clash

Sometimes the comparisons we make for self-evaluation are not between ourselves and other people, but between our attitudes and our behavior. For example, suppose you (quite rightly) believe that the odds in gambling are stacked outrageously in favor of the house, and you tend to disparage those who get sucked into gambling games—yet one day you find yourself on a plane bound for Las Vegas!

Social comparison theorist Leon Festinger (1957) proposed an enormously influential theory to highlight the sort of tension or anxiety people often feel when their freely chosen behavior contradicts their attitudes in some way. He called this uncomfortable state **cognitive dissonance** because a person's behavior and attitudes are not in harmony.

We know what behavior is, of course—but what is an attitude, and how does it differ from a belief? An attitude is an evaluative response to some person, idea, object, or event. It is a "feeling" experience, because it indicates like or dislike. A belief, in contrast, is a cognitive experience—it indicates what we *think* is true or untrue. Attitudes usually stem from beliefs. If we *believe* that racism is a destructive force in society, our *attitude* will tend to be antiracist. Attitudes are highly predictive of behavior most of the time, particularly attitudes that emerge from personal experience rather than from learned ideas or second-hand knowledge. For example, if you lost a family member in an automobile accident caused by a drunk driver, you might be especially likely to believe that no one should drive after drinking even a small amount of alcohol, and you might have a very positive attitude about "designated driver" programs.

Yet sometimes attitudes do not predict behavior, and when this happens, people may experience anxiety and tension. According to cognitive dissonance theory, for these uncomfortable feelings to resolve, something has to give: (a) the attitude has to change; (b) the behavior has to cease; or (c) beliefs about the discrepancy between them have to change.

Returning to your Vegas jaunt, you might: (a) refuse to gamble once you actually got there (behavior change); (b) "suddenly" realize that gambling also has an entertainment purpose, and decide that you are willing to pay for this entertainment by losing a certain amount of money at the gaming tables (attitude change); or (c) decide that it's okay to be a fool or hypocrite every once in a while, as long as you don't do it on a regular basis (change in beliefs about the discrepancy between attitude and behavior).

Although not all experiences of discrepancy between attitude and behavior result in attempts to resolve cognitive dissonance (Cooper & Fazio, 1984), the theory has continued to provide a rich source of hypotheses for social psychology research (Harmon-Jones & Harmon-Jones, 2007).

▲ **Cognitive Dissonance: When Your Behavior and Attitudes Are Out of Sync.** In 2008, Elliot Spitzer—who was elected Governor of New York on a platform which stressed a return to ethics in government—was found to have spent more than $80,000 over a period of several years on sex with high-priced call girls. The ensuing scandal led to his resignation. Although there is no way of knowing whether Spitzer was ever sincere in his interest in ethical reform in government, if he was, it is possible that he experienced cognitive dissonance resulting from his sexual activities while in office.

Cognitive dissonance ▶ Cognitive dissonance is the anxiety or tension that arises when people behave in ways that run contrary to their attitudes. People may resolve cognitive dissonance by changing their attitudes to bring them in line with their behavior; ceasing the behavior; or changing their beliefs about the discrepancy between their attitudes and behavior.

When Self-Defense Fails, the Self May Attempt to Change

Suppose that a person's self-evaluation produces an unpleasant result—regardless of his or her best use of bias, positive illusion, social comparison, and cognitive dissonance resolution to enhance self-esteem. For example, what if a person can simply no longer ignore real problems resulting from self-defeating behaviors such as overeating, binge drinking, or smoking? Or what if it should become undeniably clear that procrastination is causing problems on the job, or poor choices in romantic partners are repeatedly ending in disaster? If negative self-judgments continue over a prolonged period and attempts to maintain self-esteem and self-worth are unsuccessful, the self may engage in the difficult work of *self-change*. As we shall see, however, self-change can be challenging.

SELF-REGULATION AND SELF-CONTROL

If you've attempted to change something about yourself you don't like, and most people have by the time they are young adults, it will likely come as no surprise to you that an important factor in successful change is often *self-control*. **Self-control** involves resisting temptation or impulse; in a sense, it is laying aside a powerful, immediate desire, response, or goal in the service of more important, overriding long-term goals (McCullough & Willoughby, 2009). Self-control is a specific aspect of the more general concept *self-regulation*. **Self-regulation** includes all of the ways that the self monitors and exerts control over its responses so as to accomplish goals and live up to personal standards (Baumeister & Vohs, 2004; McCullough & Willoughby, 2009).[2] Saying "I'll pass, thanks" if you are trying to lose weight and you are offered a tasty desert is an example of self-control; deciding to apply to a particular graduate program and then following through with all the complicated, often annoying, steps to do so—some but not all of which may involve self-control—is self-regulation.

As you may have observed, people differ in a general way in their ability to be self-controlled—to exert "willpower." A person able to exert self-control when the dessert tray is passed around is also likely to be someone who is able to remain at home to practice her musical instrument when her friends have invited her out to a movie, hold her tongue when her tongue needs to be held, and resist the temptation to call Mr. or Ms. Wrong on the phone. In other words, self-control is a trait (Baumeister, Gailliot, DeWall, & Oaten, 2006).

And self-control is not merely associated with success at changing bad habits or resisting various sorts of temptations. As Steven Pinker observes, few other traits predict a healthy and happy life as well as self-control (Pinker, 2011). In a famous series of experiments, Walter Mischel and his colleagues gave preschool children a difficult choice: They could eat one marshmallow (or Oreo cookie or similar treat) now, or, if they could resist eating it for 15 minutes, they would be allowed to eat two. The children were left alone in a room with the selected treat sitting invitingly on a table, and their behavior was filmed (Mischel, Ebbesen, & Zeiss, 1972). Although a sizable number of children immediately accepted the "one treat now" option, the majority at least put up a struggle to resist. As described by journalist Jonah Leher (2009):

> Some cover their eyes with their hands or turn around so that they can't see the tray. Others start kicking the desk, or tug on their pigtails, or stroke the marshmallow as if it were a tiny stuffed animal. One child, a boy with neatly parted hair, looks carefully around the room to make sure that nobody can see

Self-control ▶ That aspect of self-regulation which involves suppressing a powerful immediate desire or goal in the service of a more important overriding long-term goal. Self-control typically involves resisting temptation.

Self-regulation ▶ All of the ways that the self monitors and exerts control over its responses so as to accomplish goals and live up to personal standards.

---

[2]*Some theorists use these terms more or less interchangeably to refer to self-control.*

him. Then he picks up an Oreo, delicately twists it apart, and licks off the white cream filling before returning the cookie to the tray, a satisfied look on his face.

▲ **Self-Control and Delayed Gratification.** Preschool children who were able to withstand the temptation to eat one marshmallow now, for the reward of eating two after 15 minutes of waiting, grew into children and adults with a very large number of life advantages, including higher levels of mental and physical health, academic success, and successful interpersonal relationships. *(Source for photo: Study reenactment, University of Rochester, 2012.)*

Although these studies provided interesting results at the time about individual differences in self-control, the real worth of these studies was not apparent for many years. Mischel and his colleagues were interested in what the ability to delay gratification in early childhood might predict about later life, and the researchers followed the original children for the next 40 years, checking in on them periodically. They found that those who were able to wait out the 15 minutes obtained higher SAT scores in high school and went on to higher academic achievements, had better emotional and cognitive functioning in adolescence, higher levels of self-esteem, less illicit drug use, and better stress-coping skills (Mischel et al., 2011). Similar long-term studies of self-control in childhood show that children who demonstrate willpower and the ability to delay gratification are less likely to be obese in later childhood, less likely to be bullies or display aggression, have lower levels of depression, higher GPAs, and less psychopathology in adulthood—including lower rates of alcoholism, and personality or eating disorders. Overall, these children also tend to grow up to be physically healthier and have better relationships with others (Kubzansky, Martin, & Buka, 2009; Seeyave et al., 2009; Tangney, Baumeister, & Boone, 2004).

Indeed, contrary to stereotypes of highly controlled individuals as being "uptight, repressed, neurotic, bottled up, wound up, obsessive-compulsive, or fixated at the anal stage of psychosexual development . . . the more self-control people have, the better their lives are. The people at the top of the scale [of self-control are] the mentally healthiest" (Pinker, 2011, p. 599; see Tangney et al, 2004). There seem to be few, if any, drawbacks to the ability to be self-controlled.

But if self-control—like intelligence—is associated with so many positive life outcomes, the question of whether this attribute can be taught or purposely acquired in childhood becomes an important question to ask. Roy Baumeister and his colleagues approached this question first by suggesting a model of self-control that likens it to a muscle (Baumeister et al., 2006; Baumeister, Vohs, & Tice, 2007; Muraven & Baumeister, 2000). Consider the metaphors we use to describe self-control: will*power*, *exercising* the will, *force* of will, *strength* of will. We *force* ourselves to say "no" to the chocolate mousse, and use *effort* to control our tempers (Pinker, 2011). According to Baumeister and colleagues' *strength model* of self-control, self-control exists in a limited quantity that differs among people, just as people differ in physical strength. Sustained efforts at self-control can exceed a person's capacity, and the "self-control muscle" may become fatigued—just as would happen to the upper body and arms after too many repetitions at the bench press. At that point, the ability to exert self-control will weaken, and further efforts may fail.

There is evidence now to support this idea (Baumeister et al., 2006; Gailliot et al., 2007; Hagger, Wood, Stiff, & Chatzisarantis, 2010; Muraven & Baumeister, 2000). Baumeister and his colleagues have demonstrated repeatedly that the strenuous exercise of self-control in one situation will cause a reduction in the ability to do so in a subsequent situation. For example, hungry participants forced to sit in a room where the smell of fresh-baked chocolate chip cookies hangs in the air—but who are required to refrain from sampling the cookies—expend much less time and effort attempting to solve difficult puzzles subsequently than participants who were allowed to eat the cookies (Baumeister, Bratslavsky, Muraven, & Dice, 1998). A large number of similar situations were concocted by these researchers, with alternative explanations cleverly controlled for.

Some biological evidence further supports the muscle metaphor of self-control. Just as blood glucose is depleted when a person engages in muscular

▲ The Dark Side of Hope?
Although people frequently succeed in their attempts to make self-improvement change—for example, losing weight—failure is more likely if a person has unrealistic or perfectionistic goals. This may lead to a demoralizing cycle of repeated attempts and repeated failures.

exercise, blood glucose also drops during tasks demanding the exercise of will—and people who experience this drop in blood glucose can revive their willpower for subsequent tasks by drinking sugar-sweetened liquid (Gailliot et al., 2007)!

Baumeister and colleagues reasoned that if the muscle metaphor really held, a person ought to be able to "exercise" the will systematically over time and build up self-control "muscle" through the strengthening of relevant neural connections, resulting in increases in the strength of willpower across the board. For example, adhering strictly to a diet ought to make it easier to maintain an aerobic exercise regimen or refrain from watching as much television. So research participants were asked to spend several weeks or months performing willpower exercises on a regular basis—for example, using their left hand (if they are right-handed) for tasks such as tooth brushing or operating a computer mouse, keeping detailed food diaries, holding to money management plans, avoiding cursing, and so forth. These participants were then given willpower-draining tasks similar to those used in the original experiments. Not only was the exercise group much less vulnerable to depletion of the will in the lab, but their newly built-up willpower was also evident in events of their daily lives. They smoked and drank less, were more responsible in their finances, improved their study habits, watched less television, and experienced other admirable changes.

SELF-CHANGE OFTEN DOES NOT HAPPEN AS PLANNED

Unfortunately, self-improvement change often doesn't happen as planned. Consider New Year's resolutions. More than 50% of American adults make such resolutions each year, most of the time vowing to change behaviors related to health such as eating, drinking, and smoking, but also behaviors related to interpersonal relationships and self-defeating habits (Norcross, Ratzin, & Payne, 1989). Unfortunately, people tend to make the same resolutions year after year—on average, for 5 to 10 years (Polivy & Herman, 2002)! Although people *do* successfully make these kinds of changes every day—we do stop smoking, stop drinking, lose weight, and start exercising—failure rates are still quite high (Prochaska, DiClemente, & Norcross, 1992; Li & Liu, 2004). Even when success seems to have been achieved, it is sometimes temporary, with one step forward and two steps back being a commonplace experience.

Although self-control no doubt plays its part in many of these failures, there are factors unrelated to self-control also at work. In a series of provocative articles, social psychologists Janet Polivy and Peter Herman propose that people attempting self-improvement often have unrealistic beliefs about the self-change process, and that it is the beliefs themselves that spell failure. These beliefs involve four aspects of the self-change process: the *speed* with which self-change will occur, the *ease* with which change can be accomplished, the *amount* of change that is likely (or even possible), and the *rewards* that lie at the end of the self-change process (Polivy & Herman 2000, 2002; Trottier, Polivy, & Herman, 2009). For example, dieters often expect to lose a *lot* of weight, relatively *quickly*, and relatively *easily*. But dieters don't just expect to lose weight. They often expect their entire bodies to be reshaped, their romantic lives to change, job opportunities to open up, and their total image to be converted (Brownell, cited by Polivy & Herman, 2002). Considering that failure is defined as not achieving one's goals, a great many attempts at self-improvement change are doomed to failure simply because the goals themselves are unrealistic. This may lead to a self-defeating cycle of repeated attempts and failures, a cycle Polivy and Herman term the **false hope syndrome** (see also Zilbergeld, 1983).

False hope syndrome ▶ A cycle of repeated failure in self-improvement attempts brought on by unrealistic ideas about the speed or ease with which self-change will occur, the amount of change that is likely or even possible, and the rewards that will accrue from self-improvement changes.

IN SUMMARY

1. Social psychology is the study of the ways that situations influence people's behavior and the way people's characteristics or behavior can influence the situations in which they find themselves. It is the study of the ways in which people interact.

2. People seek to maintain feelings of self-worth in the face of their own negative judgments of themselves. One method of "psychological self-defense" is the self-serving bias, which takes several forms but allows us to see ourselves as better than we actually are in various respects. Another is positive illusions—biases and mental illusions that are associated with better adjustment and mental health.

3. Social comparisons can be used to evaluate the self rationally or for purposes of self-enhancement and "self-defense." In making self-enhancement and self-defense comparisons, people usually compare themselves with those less competent or less fortunate, known as downward comparison.

4. When one's attitudes are not in accord with one's behavior, cognitive dissonance may arise. People may resolve cognitive dissonance by changing attitudes, behavior, or the way they think about the discrepancy between the two.

5. Self-control is a relatively stable trait that is associated with a great many positive benefits over the life span. Being self-controlled in one area predicts the ability to be self-controlled in other areas.

6. Although people can make self-improvement changes, they often have unrealistic beliefs about the speed, ease, and amount of change likely, and the potential rewards.

RETRIEVE!

1. "I only failed the driving test because the examiner had a hangover and was irritable. I could still smell the liquor on his breath." The person uttering this statement might be under the influence of:

  a) a positive illusion.   **c)** the self-serving bias.

  b) cognitive dissonance.   **d)** downward comparison.

2. "I'm a lot better than I used to be about studying. I think I've gotten more serious about school lately." The person making this statement may be accurate, or he or she might be experiencing which aspect of positive illusions?

  a) uncritically positive views of the self

  b) illusions of control

  c) unrealistic optimism

3. True or false: Research suggests that self-control may have properties similar to a muscle in that it can become fatigued and may also be able to be strengthened through exercise.

4. What is the name of the syndrome that often occurs under conditions where people hold unrealistic ideas about the speed, ease, amount, and rewards of self-change?

  a) false expectations syndrome   **c)** self-defeat syndrome

  b) false hope syndrome   **d)** repeated failure syndrome

How Do We Present Ourselves to Others?

When someone says, "I couldn't care less what other people think of me," you can be sure that this is not the whole story. Human beings do not only care about their own evaluations of themselves—they also care greatly what other people think of them, at least certain others (Leary, 2001; Sabini, Siepmann, & Stein, 2001b). Indeed, concerns about how others see us are among the most powerful of motives for social behavior. Saving face, avoiding embarrassment, and appearing to be a person with valuable qualities are important human goals, even if we do not always notice that they play a part in how we behave (Sabini et al., 2001a). Consequently, we pay attention to how other people react to us and often try to control the way we appear to others. We do this to advance our own interests (i.e., getting something we want) or just to make sure we are being "ourselves" or the selves we want to be.

Impression Management Involves Motivation and Construction

Impression management

▶ The process by which people attempt to monitor and control the impressions that others form of them. Impression management consists of two components: impression motivation and impression construction.

Monitoring and attempting to control how we appear to other people is known as *self-presentation* or **impression management** (Goffman, 1959; Leary, 1995; 2011; Sadler, Hunger, & Miller, 2010.) Some situations elicit a stronger drive to manage impressions than others. At one end of the continuum are situations where we are so deeply engrossed in what we're doing that we are oblivious to other people's responses or evaluations. In those situations we are entirely unmotivated to engage in impression management. For example, I might find myself shedding tears at the end of a particularly compelling film and not much care how silly I look. At the other end of the continuum are situations where it is virtually impossible *not* to think about what sort of impression one is making—say, on one's first day teaching in a lecture hall in front of 350 students. But more often than not, impression management activity occurs between these extremes and below the level of conscious awareness. No matter what activity we are engaged in, we are usually unconsciously (or barely consciously) scanning the social landscape for information about how we are coming off to other people.

Mark Leary and Robin Kowalski (1990) describe impression management as consisting of two processes: *impression motivation* and *impression construction*. Once we are motivated actually to manage our impression—to obtain a desired goal, increase self-esteem, or alter our public identity—we have to construct the impression we wish to make. This does not imply at all that we are constructing a false identity of some sort. People often attempt to create an impression that is consistent with the person they perceive themselves to be. Indeed, it sometimes takes special effort to make certain that people see "the real us" ("I know I hang out with the stoners sometimes, but I'm not really like them"; Jones & Pittman, 1982; Goffman, 1959).

The impression construction process is affected by a number of factors. One factor is self-concept—our total perception and evaluation of who we really are as individuals and social beings. We might want people to see "who we really are" or hide it. Considering that most people's self-concept also includes a general feeling that it is immoral to blatantly lie, the self-concept usually (but, of course, not always) limits the range of possible impressions a person is comfortable making.

A person's *desired* and *undesired identity images* are also factors affecting the impression construction process. How we present ourselves is determined

▲ **Fashion Is an Impression Management Tool.** Teenagers are noted for their use of fashion as a tool of impression construction. Fashion projects or hides aspects of one's self-concept and reflects people's desired and undesired identity images.

not only by the person we think we are, but also by the person we would like—or not like—to be. For example, we may behave as if we already possess attributes we not only would like to have but believe we ultimately will have. This lessens the feeling of dishonesty about such a presentation and, in fact, might actually increase the chances of our ultimately fulfilling such destinies. The expression *dress for success* conveys this idea.

Self-Presentation in Cyberspace

The Internet is enormously powerful, and it is transforming almost every aspect of our lives at a very rapid pace (Ito et al., 2008; Kraut, Brynin, & Kessler, 2006; V. Miller, 2010). Like it or not, a great deal—a *very* great deal—of self-presentation occurs over the Internet in computer-mediated communication (CMC). From Internet relay chat rooms, bulletin boards and forums, texting and instant messaging, e-mail, blogging, and peer-to-peer (P2P) programs, to *social networking* sites such as Facebook, Tumblr, and Twitter, we are presenting ourselves to one another all the time. What is unique about all of this self-presentation is that it we do it without sharing the same physical space, without seeing or hearing one another, and often without even learning each other's real name, age, or sex. With the advent of wireless technology, even developing and third-world areas that lag behind the West in the numbers of people "wired" are quickly catching up (Bargh & McKenna, 2004; Shyam & Bhoria, 2011).

Computer Dating

Online dating is one form of self-presentation using computer-mediated communication that has changed in only a few years from a marginalized activity about which "cool" people snickered to a mainstream format for meeting people and forming relationships (Finkel, Eastwick, Karney, Reis, & Sprecher, 2012). In a nationally representative sample interviewed in 2009, 22% of heterosexual couples reported that they had met over the Internet, with online dating accounting for the majority of these meetings (the rest occurred on social networking sites). However, having been introduced by mutual friends still accounted for more "how we met" stories than online dating and social networking (Finkel et al., 2012).

Behavioral scientists disagree about the social effects of the communication over the Internet (di Gennaro & Dutton, 2007). Some researchers look to the Internet and associated electronic media as an amazing opportunity to break down racism, national borders, and narrow divisions among people, while uniting people according to deeply held values and beliefs and increasing the breadth of social networks. Others see it as portending disastrous outcomes for interpersonal relationships—creating sterile, superficial forms of exchange that promote a lack of genuineness and the breakdown of communities and extended families. These researchers predict that an entire generation of lonely individuals will emerge as a result of widespread CMC.

▲ **You May Feel Bathed in a Spotlight, but Is Anyone Watching?** During embarrassing or prideful moments people often feel as though they were bathed in a spotlight, but quite often other people are too busy thinking about themselves and their own concerns to notice what is happening to others.

Although there is some evidence to support both views, in general, most evidence of CMC's negative effects was collected in the early years of online life, when relatively few people were wired (Kraut et al., 1998). Newer research suggests that the Internet is less destructive to personal relationships and is associated with more positive outcomes than naysayers expected (Stevens & Morris, 2007; Sum, Mathews, Hughes, & Campbell, 2008; Valkenburg & Peter, 2009a, 2009b; Finkel et al., 2012).

The reasons for the contradictory findings in research on the effects of CMC may have been clarified to some extent by researchers Patti Valkenburg and Jochen Peter (2009a, 2009b). When they looked at the effects of CMC on adolescents, they found that it can have positive effects primarily when it is used to sustain previously existing friendships rather than to create new cyber-relationships with unseen individuals. In the period of the 1990s, when most of the negative findings emerged from research, only a small percentage of people, even in the "developed" world, had daily access to CMC. Today, of course, it is a medium used by the overwhelming majority of adolescents and young adults in Western nations to maintain their existing friendships and family relationships.

According to Valkenburg and Peter (2009a, 2009b), CMC is most beneficial when it stimulates online *self-disclosure*. As discussed in Chapter 10, self-disclosure is an important component of *intimacy*—itself an important part of the experience of *belonging*. When online communication results in self-disclosure, the quality of participants' relationships is improved, leading to increased overall well-being. However, Valkenburg and Peter also note that the research suggests a sex difference in the experience of CMC among adolescents: It seems to benefit boys far more than girls. Because girls may be more adept at self-disclosure in general, they may not need the safe haven to experiment with self-disclosure which the Internet offers as much as adolescent boys do. Another interesting finding is that, contrary to popular belief, personality profiles placed in social networking websites such as Facebook are more likely to reflect an honest presentation of one's characteristics than an idealized or fantasized self (Back et al., 2010; Vazire & Gosling, 2004).

Our Ideas of How Others See Us Are Often Wildly Off Track

A 1999 social psychology article by Thomas Gilovich and Kenneth Savitsky opens by recalling a scene from the Steve Martin film *The Lonely Guy:*

> Steve Martin arrives at a restaurant and is asked by the maitre d', "How many in your party, sir?" When Martin replies that he is dining alone, the maitre d' raises his voice and asks with astonishment, "Alone?" The restaurant falls silent as everyone stares at Martin in disbelief. To make matters worse, a spotlight suddenly appears from nowhere and follows Martin as he is escorted to his seat. (Gilovich & Savitsky, 1999, p. 165)

The discomfort of fearing what people will think about us at some awkward moment is familiar to everyone. Perhaps we don't care what people will think if we are dining alone, but what if we were to write a very private e-mail and accidentally send it to a group of 13,000 people? What if we have just gotten a really terrible haircut—that no stylist can do anything to correct—right before an important meeting, party, or date? It may surprise you to learn that such awkwardness is noticed less often, and judged less harshly, than most of us think at such moments.

Research shows that the "spotlight" in which we feel bathed during embarrassing (or triumphant) moments is generally of our own making. In the words of Thomas Gilovich, people tend to believe that "the social spotlight shines more brightly on them than it actually does" (Gilovich & Savitsky, 1999, p. 166). Others simply are not watching. Why? *They are too busy worrying about their own spotlights to pay attention to ours.* Gilovich calls this self-centered judgment about the impression one is making on others the **spotlight effect**.

In one study, Gilovich and his colleagues had Cornell University undergraduate volunteers put on a T-shirt with a large picture of 1970s lounge-style singer Barry Manilow—not a person with the highest level of cultural currency on the Cornell campus at the end of the 20th century (Gilovich, Medvec, & Savitsky, 1999). Each of the T-shirt wearers then went into a separate room where other students, dressed normally, were engaged in filling out questionnaires (which were actually bogus). After remaining in the room for a while filling out the same questionnaire, and mentally squirming with embarrassment over his or her uncool attire, the Manilow T-shirt wearer was called out on a pretext. He or she was then asked to predict how many of the other students had noticed the T-shirt. Later, the students in the rooms were also asked to indicate if they had noticed the picture on the student's T-shirt.

The T-shirt wearers made predictions that were exactly twice as high as the number of people who had actually noticed the shirt. The experiment was repeated with other students, this time using a face with greater currency on campus at the time, such as Bob Marley or Martin Luther King, Jr. This time the T-shirt wearers predicted that *six* times as many people would notice the shirt as actually noticed it.

Not only is our presence in a room wearing embarrassing (or cool) garments not particularly noticed by strangers, but in a separate study, Gilovich and his colleagues showed that people who surreptitiously leave a room during an important meeting greatly overestimate the likelihood that they will be missed (Savitsky, Gilovich, Berger, & Medvec, 2003). Apparently, we are not as "conspicuous by our absence" as we think (p. 386)!

Finally, Savitsky, Epley, and Gilovich (2001) have shown that people forgive social blunders and embarrassing acts to a much greater extent than we assume. Because everyone has experienced such things, even when people do notice them, they apparently empathize more often than condemn (Epley, Savitsky, & Gilovich, 2002, p. 300).

Spotlight effect ▶ Thomas Gilovich's term to describe egocentric judgments of the impression one is making on others. According to Gilovich, people tend to believe that "the social spotlight shines more brightly on them than it actually does."

IN SUMMARY

1.	Attempting to control how we appear to others is known as self-presentation or impression management. Impression management consists of two processes: impression motivation and impression construction.
2.	Much self-presentation currently occurs over the Internet in computer-mediated communication (CMC). Most research suggests that CMC enhances communication and relationships, particularly if these relationships already exist, and if self-disclosure results from it.
3.	The spotlight effect is the self-centered tendency of people to believe that other people pay more attention to their negative or positive behaviors than is actually the case.

RETRIEVE!

1.	Name the two components of the impression *construction* process.

2. Identify at least two ways that computer-mediated communication might benefit social relationships, and two ways CMC might have a negative impact.

3. Taking a seat on the subway, Margo is certain that everyone notices the pimple that recently appeared on her nose. Margo may be making this assumption due to the

a) self-serving bias.   c) spotlight effect.

b) egocentric bias.   d) size of the pimple.

How Do We Explain Our Own and Others' Behavior?

Attribution ▶ The process of explaining behavior in terms of characteristics of the person, the situation, or an interaction between the two; or in terms of whether a behavior is intentional or unintentional.

Although evaluation of the self is often of paramount importance to a person, in navigating the social world, people also are concerned with *explaining* their own behavior and the behavior of other people. For example: As you walk down the street, you pass a man talking to himself audibly, uttering a string of angry curses. Do you wonder if he is merely having a bad day, or do you assume that he is mentally ill? **Attribution** is the process of explaining behavior—ours or someone else's—in terms of causes that refer to characteristics of the person (*dispositional cause*), the situation (*situational cause*), or an interaction between the two (Heider, 1958; Sabini et al., 2001a). Deciding that the man uttering the angry curses is mentally ill is emphasizing a dispositional cause for his behavior. Deciding that he is having a very bad day emphasizes situational causes. Another class of attributions categorize a person's actions as either *intentional* or *unintentional*, according to whether the person chose to engage in the behavior or if the behavior was in some way unintended or not under the person's control (Malle, Knobe, & Nelson, 2007).

When people are given enough time and motivation, they often make very accurate attributions about the causes of their own and others' behavior (E. E. Jones, 1990). However, time and motivation are often in short supply. The ability to make accurate snap judgments is therefore equally or more important, and although human beings are sometimes good at this, in certain ways we may be biased against accuracy. Most research in attribution theory has emphasized these biases, and findings in attribution theory are among the most widely known in all of social psychology. However, accepted notions of attribution theory recently have been challenged, as we shall see in our discussion of the two most famous attributional biases: the *fundamental attribution error* and the *actor-observer bias*.

The Fundamental Attribution Error: Mistaking the Situation for the Person

Fundamental Attribution Error (FAE) ▶ The tendency to attribute other people's behavior to those individuals' dispositions and other internal factors, while ignoring or underestimating the possibility that situation factors may have played an important or determining role.

It is very difficult to explain to very small children that actors portraying characters in films or on stage are not the characters they portray. The most difficult thing for children to grasp is that someone who behaves in a mean or scary way on film might actually be a loving and gentle person off-camera. It often takes several years for this realization to truly sink in. Children seem born making the **fundamental attribution error** (**FAE**), the tendency to attribute other people's behavior to their (internal) dispositions, while ignoring or underestimating the possibility that behavior may be influenced by situational (external) factors (L. Ross, 1977).

In 1967, Edward Jones and Victor Harris introduced the FAE (also termed the *correspondence bias*) in a classic study that has been repeated in different ways over the decades (Allison, Mackie, Muller, & Worth, 1993; Napolitan & Goethals, 1979). In the Jones and Harris research, undergraduate research participants were asked to read a speech supposedly written by a fellow student presenting a view either favoring or opposing a famous world leader of the day. One group was told that the student had chosen his or her position freely. Another group was told that the student had been specifically instructed which position to take. The participants were asked to assess the student's true attitude toward the world leader. Surprisingly, whether the student had supposedly been instructed to take a particular position made little difference in these assessments. If the speech was favorable, the participants assumed that the writer's attitude was favorable regardless of whether or not they were told that the writer had been required to take a particular position.

Why does the fundamental attribution error occur? In a 1995 article, Daniel Gilbert and Patrick Malone made an attempt at analyzing the FAE in depth. According to Gilbert and Malone, when an observation of behavior is made, information about possible situational influences is often invisible to the observer. All we see is a sunny, well-scrubbed, smiling restaurant server—we don't see the fact that he just got a letter of acceptance that morning from Stanford University graduate school. Thus we conclude that he is an energetic, fastidious, cheerful person by nature. Had we come in the day before we might very well have seen a sullen, unshaven person who hadn't taken a bath in 3 days.

If an immediate attribution is required, it is easier and makes sense to attribute people's behavior to internal, dispositional causes. Gilbert and Malone propose that this tendency evolved over evolutionary time because, although it may sometimes result in error, the advantages of being able to make rapid attributions outweigh the downside of sometimes being wrong.

HOW FUNDAMENTAL IS THE FUNDAMENTAL ATTRIBUTION ERROR?

For its first 30 years, the fundamental attribution error was a mainstay of social psychological research, and one of its most well-documented findings. However, since the mid-1990s, the FAE has fallen on hard times (Fein, 2001). As described in Chapter 3, its first major challenges came from cross-cultural researchers who found that the FAE was much weaker and sometimes nonexistent when tested among East Asians such as Chinese, Koreans, and Japanese—thus seeding doubt that the FAE was truly universal. If the FAE is not universal, the evolutionary explanation offered by Gilbert and Malone is thrown into doubt (Choi, Nisbett, & Norenzayan, 1999; Masuda & Kitayama, 2004; Miyamoto & Kitayama, 2002).

The next challenge came from a startling article written in 2001 by John Sabini and his colleagues (Sabini et al., 2001b). This article strongly argued that social psychologists working with the FAE have for several decades misunderstood the implications of their own research. Sabini and his colleagues set out to show that people do *not* have a general tendency to underestimate the importance of situational factors in explaining people's behavior. Indeed, Sabini and colleagues argue that although dispositions and situations exist, it is not logically possible to separate dispositional from situational causes of behavior.

Consider the "famous world leader" experiment just described, which involved the reading of essays purportedly in favor or against the leader. Research participants tended to attribute the position taken in an essay to the actual attitude held by the student who supposedly wrote the essay—even though the student writers reportedly had been told which position to take. Social psychologists have interpreted this as evidence that people ignore situational factors in explaining others' behavior (the writer was specifically told which position to take), relying instead on dispositional explanations (the writer really believed in his or her position).

However, Sabini and his colleagues point out that, rather than overestimating the importance of dispositional factors over situational factors, the participants may simply have been comparing the relative importance of *two dispositional factors*: the first being beliefs about the world leader, and the second being the simple desire to avoid embarrassment and save face. According to Sabini and colleagues, the desire to avoid embarrassment is a far more powerful *dispositional* motive among Americans than social psychologists generally suppose (R. S. Miller, 1995). People who write essays taking positions they were instructed to take (but in which they do not believe) may merely be attempting to avoid the embarrassment of confronting the experimenter because they are sensitive to embarrassment. This is a dispositional explanation, not a "situational" explanation. Thus, the participants in the world leader study may have concluded, perhaps erroneously, that beliefs about the world leader were a more important dispositional factor than the desire to avoid embarrassment (another dispositional factor).

The problem is that every "situational" cause must simultaneously imply the presence of a "dispositional" cause and vice versa. Indeed, "dispositions" and "situations" are so intricately interwoven that many psychologists believe it is useless to try to separate them (Funder, 2001; J. I. Krueger & Funder, 2004; Lewin, 1935; Sabini et al., 2001a, 2001b). Consider a normally law-abiding teenage boy who, for one reason or another, ends up hanging out with peers who like to drink, shoplift, and steal cars. The boy finds himself committing these very acts. Have situational factors—the presence of a charismatic peer leader, for example, or pressure to conform to group standards—overwhelmed the boy's dispositional factors of honesty and moral sense? It may be just as logical to say that *some* dispositional factors—the desire to be accepted by peers and avoid rejection—were stronger than *other* dispositional factors, including honesty and moral sense (Sabini et al., 2001a, 2001b).

It may also be very hard to determine where a "situation" ends and a "person" begins. Consider a large lecture hall class. Is this the same "situation" for the professor and the students? Is it the same situation for a student there to learn about globalization and world economy as for a student there to flirt with the woman with multiple braids who usually sits in the 12th row aisle seat (Sabini et al., 2001a)? To some extent, the situation is determined by the person and the person by the situation.

Most response to the article by Sabini and his colleagues has been favorable (Commentaries to Sabini et al., 2001a), although some commentators warn that in finding fault with previous interpretations, Sabini and his colleagues may have gone too far and thrown out the FAE baby with the FAE bathwater (Fein, 2001; L. Ross, 2001). But in 2010, Christopher Bauman and Linda Skitka took another approach and, instead of challenging the logic of the person/situation distinction in the FAE, pointed out that the vast majority of research studies on this cognitive bias were conducted on convenience samples of university students. They examined a nationally representative sample of American adults and found that only about half showed evidence of the FAE at all. Thus, the FAE—if we accept its logic—may only exist as an interesting bias in some individuals, such as college students.

The Actor-Observer Bias: Mistaking the Person for the Situation

The fundamental attribution error coin has a flip side known as the **actor-observer bias**. It gets its name from the idea that people hold a separate bias depending on whether they are the *actor* in a situation (biased toward situational explanations) or the *observer* (biased toward dispositional explanations, as in the FAE). Actor-observer bias occurs primarily when a person makes an attribution for his or her *own* behavior. Think about it: When another driver cuts in front of you on the freeway, he or she is a "drunken pig" or a "menace on

Actor-observer bias ▶ A systematic bias toward attributing your own behavior primarily to situational factors, but others' behavior to dispositional factors.

the road," but when you do the same thing to someone else, you're just late for a dermatologist appointment it took you a month and a half to get. According to social psychologists working with the actor-observer bias, in judging our own behavior we tend to be biased in favor of situational attributions because we are aware of the many ways that circumstances alter our behavior (E. E. Jones & Nisbett, 1971).

However, as with FAE, the actor-observer bias has been challenged in recent years (Malle, 2006; Malle et al., 2007). In an extensive meta-analysis of decades of research on the actor-observer bias, Bertram Malle has shown that this bias is found only inconsistently, and only when certain types of research methods are used—primarily those in which participants must choose between specific situational and dispositional explanations listed on questionnaires rather than being allowed to offer their own freely chosen explanations for their behavior. Moreover, when the actor-observer bias does appear in these limited circumstances, it generally does so only when people are making attributions for their own *negative* behaviors (recall the "menace on the road" example). Indeed, when we are attempting to explain our *positive* behaviors, we are all too willing to attribute them to our own marvelous dispositions as part of the self-serving bias described earlier.

IN SUMMARY

1.	Attribution is the process of explaining behavior in terms of causes that are either intentional or unintentional, dispositional or situational.
2.	The fundamental attribution error (FAE) is the tendency of people to attribute other people's behavior to dispositional causes, ignoring the possibility that situational factors are primarily responsible for the behavior. Recent research has questioned the universality and even the existence of the FAE.
3.	The actor-observer bias is the tendency to attribute one's own behavior to situational causes while attributing other people's behavior to dispositional causes.

RETRIEVE!

1.	How has cross-cultural research on the fundamental attribution error (FAE) thrown doubt on Gilbert and Malone's evolutionary explanation of the reason people make the FAE?
2.	How can the *situational* explanation "She likes him because he's handsome" be stated just as plausibly as a *dispositional* explanation?
3.	True or false: The actor-observer bias occurs primarily when people make attributions for their own positive behaviors.

Who Attracts Whom?

People often find themselves drawn to others—for friendship, romance, or sex—for reasons that may not be immediately apparent to either person. The study of **attraction** is an important part of social psychology. Why are we drawn to certain people but not to others?

Attraction ▶ Factors that draw a person toward another for friendship, sex, romance, or other sort of relationship.

Positive Assortment

Grandpa A swears that "opposites attract," while Grandpa B insists that "birds of a feather flock together." (The grandmas just grumble and walk away.) So who's right? Do we seek mates who are similar to ourselves? Or do we look for people whose attributes complement ours, or who are in some way *different*—perhaps for the excitement and stimulation to be found in novel things? The answer is, overwhelmingly, that we are far more likely to seek mates who are similar to ourselves. This mating tendency was originally known by social psychologists as the *matching phenomenon*, but recently psychologists increasingly are calling it by the name used by biologists—**positive assortment** (Bleske-Rechek, Remiker, & Baker, 2009).

Positive assortment has been documented for everything from intelligence to personality, attitudes and values, education, attractiveness, occupation, race, age, education, religion, political attitudes . . . even height, weight, pinkie finger length, and having freckles (Bleske et al., 2009; Gonzaga, Campos, & Bradbury, 2007; Hur, 2003; Mealey, 2000, p. 319; Luo & Klohnen, 2005)! Investigators have found not only that people tend to positively assort, but also that in general they are happier in such pairings, their relationships are more stable, there are fewer infidelities and divorces, and they even seem to raise more children to maturity than couples in "opposites attract" relationships (Bleske-Rechek et al., 2009; Botwin, Buss, & Shackelford, 1997; Gonzaga et al., 2007; Luo & Klohnen, 2005).

Positive assortment (matching phenomenon) ▶ The tendency to mate with a person who is similar to you in various characteristics. Positive assortment has been documented for attractiveness, height, weight, occupation, religion, age, race, education, political attitudes, and so forth.

The Mere Exposure Effect

Books and movies are filled with stories of people dead set on causing other people to fall in love with them. The objects of their affection are indifferent (or even hostile) . . . at first. The suitors figure out endless ways to insinuate their presence into the love of their life's life. Eventually, over time, their unrequited love is returned. One of the factors in causing the change of heart may be the **mere exposure effect** (Monahan, Murphy, & Zajonc, 2000; Zajonc, 1968, 2001). Researchers have found that people come to appreciate almost anything the more times they are exposed to it, be it letters, shapes, syllables, melodies, faces—or people. According to the founder of mere exposure theory, Robert Zajonc, it is part of our evolved psychology to be cautious around unfamiliar objects and people, and to be more open to familiar stimuli and individuals (Zajonc, 1968). This idea is consistent with findings of cross-cultural research in human universals (Brown, 1991).

But does increasing exposure actually work to increase attraction between people? Some research suggests that it does. Harry Reis and his colleagues conducted two studies to test this hypothesis (Reis, Maniaci, Eastwick, & Caprariello, 2011). In the first, the researchers randomly exposed groups of male-female pairs of college students who were unknown to one another to face one another and engage in a short conversations prompted by specific questions one of the participants was to ask the other. One randomly assigned group was only given two questions, resulting in a relatively short interaction. The other group was given six questions, resulting in a much longer interaction. Those participating in the longer interactions subsequently reported higher levels of attraction to each other.

In the second study, participants were paired anonymously with an online chat partner of the same sex whom they did not know. They were told to engage in 10- to 15-minute chats (with no restriction on content) at least once a day for either 1, 2, 4, 6, or 8 days, depending on their random assignment. As predicted, partners' liking for each other increased as a function of the number of days they engaged in the chat routines.

Mere exposure effect ▶ The human tendency to come to prefer people or things merely because they have become familiar. The founder of mere exposure theory, Robert Zajonc, hypothesizes that the mere exposure effect has evolved in human psychology because it would have enhanced our survival and reproductive success to be generally cautious around unfamiliar objects and people.

Beauty Is Not Entirely in the Eye of the Beholder

Is beauty only skin deep? Is it merely in eye of the beholder? Or, as French statesman and philosopher Michel de Montaigne maintained, is beauty a "powerful and advantageous quality" that "holds the first place in human relations"? The notion that beauty exists only in the eye of the beholder has a long philosophical history, and belief in this maxim is helped along by the idiosyncratic nature of ideals of beauty in certain cultures. For example, in some tribal societies, unusual scarring or distortion of the body (e.g., an elongated earlobe or lower lip) is considered beautiful. In our own society, bodily thinness in women is treasured more than in most places—although the degree to which men in Western societies *actually* prefer extremely slender women has been greatly exaggerated, with most men preferring women in the low-normal weight range (Singh & Young, 1995; Swami, Neto, Tovée, & Furnham, 2007; Swami & Tovée, 2007). Nonetheless, considering differences in ideas about attractive body weight, unusual standards for body scars or body distortion, and the variance in aesthetic tastes in music and art around the world—how can it *not* be true that beauty is in the eye of the beholder?

Although there is variance in aesthetic taste in music and art worldwide, this variance is not as great as many people think (Komar, Melamid, & Wypijewski, 1999; Voland & Grammer, 2003). Similarly, when it comes to human physical attractiveness, there is considerable agreement across cultures and ethnicities about what constitutes attractiveness; at a fundamental level, physical attractiveness is only partially in the eye of the beholder (Gallup & Frederick, 2010; Gangestad & Scheyd, 2005; D. Jones, 1996; Langlois et al., 2000; Singh, Dixson, Jessop, Morgan, & Dixson, 2009; Sugiyama, 2005). Cultural variance does exist for specific standards in bodily adornment, decoration, or weight, and a person's standards for what is attractive may even change to some degree as he or she moves from one culture to another (Tovée, Swami, Furnham, & Mangalparsad, 2006). However, there appear to be a number of underlying facial and bodily characteristics of attractiveness on which all cultures yet studied seem to agree. Let's now explore this phenomenon.

WHAT DETERMINES FACIAL ATTRACTIVENESS?

A person might be judged attractive in face but unattractive in body, or vice versa, but both men and women judge a person's overall attractiveness primarily by the person's facial features (Peters, Rhodes, & Simmons, 2007). Nevertheless, human faces are amazingly similar. Figure 15.1 is a photographic demonstration of a single female face evolving through a succession of very slight computer morphings to appear to depict three individuals of differing racial/ethnic ancestries. The changes necessary to indicate different racial/ethnic groups are very slight, underscoring the universality of human facial features and attractiveness.

Sensitivity to attractive faces emerges very early in human beings; even newborn infants prefer attractive to unattractive faces by spending more time looking at them when given a choice (Hoss & Langlois, 2003; Van Duuren, Kendell-Scott, & Stark, 2003). Indeed, infants even prefer attractive *cat* faces to unattractive ones (Quinn, Kelly, Lee, Pascalis, & Slater, 2008)!

What are the specific qualities that are considered universally attractive in men's and women's faces? There are four general cues to facial attractiveness in both sexes: *age, symmetry, averageness,* and *exaggerated femininity and masculinity.*

Age Age is the most obvious quality that affects facial attractiveness: younger faces are considered more attractive than older ones (Furnham, Mistry, & McClelland, 2004). Although attractiveness decreases in men's faces as they age, women are perceived to lose facial attractiveness with age much more

▲ **Attractive?** Although women often believe that men prefer extremely thin female bodies, studies repeatedly show that men prefer normal body weight, if slightly on the low–normal side. Most men (and women) find emaciation in women—such as depicted in this photo—quite unappealing. On the other hand, despite wide variation around the world in what is considered attractive body weight for women, waists that are slender when compared with the hips have always been considered attractive, throughout history and regardless of culture (Singh, 2006).

▶ **FIGURE 15.1** *(Source: Karl Grammer. Used with permission.)*

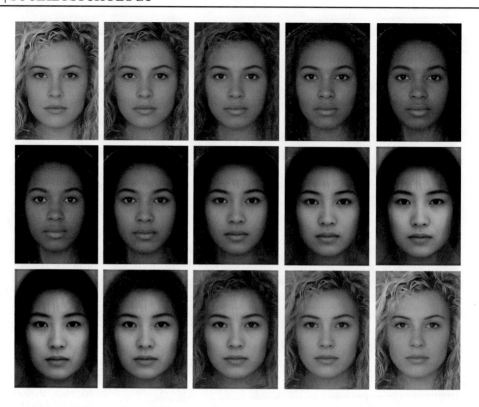

▲ **FIGURE 15.2 More Symmetrical, More Attractive.** Large numbers of experiments using computer morphing technology have shown that increasing the symmetry of a face increases its attractiveness. Left to right: normal symmetry, high symmetry (Rhodes 2006).

rapidly. Both male and female research participants agree—as do centuries of world literature and drama as well as the cash receipts of advertisers, film makers, and pornographers—that women's facial attractiveness peaks in late adolescence and young adulthood, and begins to decline soon after (Buss, 1994/2003).

Both the power of age as a factor in beauty—and its fragility—was famously put by 1970s supermodel Lauren Hutton, who recalls, "[At age 18] I awoke to the realization that if you're a young, blue ribbon egg-bearer [i.e., gorgeous, fertile female], there's *nothing* you can't get away with. Nobody who hasn't been there has *any* idea, and even those who have won't really understand until after the stampede has passed because there's so much dust in the air" (cited by Symons, 1996).

Symmetry The human face and body, like many structures in nature, is constructed to be generally symmetrical. In other words, each side of the face or body is (more or less) the mirror image of the other side. However, there are always slight fluctuations in size and shape—your right eyebrow may be very slightly higher than your left, for example, or one earlobe very slightly longer. Nature does not endow any of us with perfectly symmetrical anatomical structures. Yet some of us are lucky enough to have, well, more *symmetrical* symmetry. As depicted in Figure 15.2, increasing the symmetry of a face using computer morphing technology increases the attractiveness of the face.

Some researchers have proposed that symmetrical features serve as a kind of "honest advertisement" of the health of one's genes and immune system (Fink, Neave, Manning, & Grammer, 2006; Rhodes et al., 2007; Thornhill & Gangestad, 2006). Why would this be the case? Because it takes a strong immune system to maintain symmetry during the process of growth all the way from conception to adulthood (Thornhill & Gangestad, 2006). As we develop, our bodies (and, more important, our faces) contend with unnumerable potential challenges in the form of genetic mutations, parasites, infection, nutritional deficiencies, and so forth, all of which can cause minor fluctuations in symmetry (Polak, 2003).

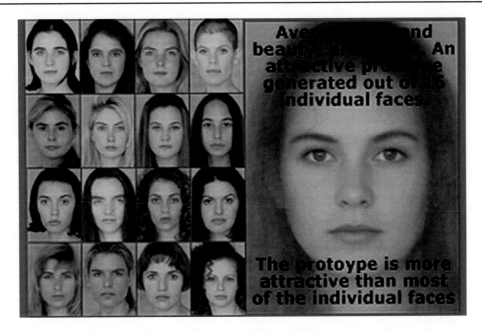

Average and beauty An attractive prototype generated out of 16 individual faces

The protoype is more attractive than most of the individual faces

◄FIGURE 15.3 More Average, More Attractive. When a single face is created by averaging many faces together, the composite is generally considered more attractive than most of the individual faces. In this image, 16 women's faces were averaged to form the composite image at the right, that was judged more attractive than almost all of the individual faces. (Source: Karl Grammer. Used with permission.)

Averageness Although you might think that the most attractive faces are the ones that are anything but average; in fact, the quality of averageness has an even stronger effect on judgments of attractiveness than does symmetry (Gangestad & Scheyd, 2005; Rhodes, 2006). As depicted in Figure 15.3, when a single composite photograph is created on a computer by averaging the information from a group of photographs of faces—in a sense, superimposing the faces on one another—the composite face is rated as more attractive than almost any of the individual faces (Grammer & Thornhill, 1994; Langlois & Roggman, 1990). In this sense the term *average* does not mean "ordinary"; rather, it means including within it many kinds of genetic contributions.

Why should a face that reflects many kinds of genetic contributions be attractive? Evolutionary psychologists propose that the more numerous the genetic contributions, the stronger is the person's immune system and ability to withstand disease. Like symmetry, averageness may be an "honest advertisement" of genetic health that may be passed on to offspring (Rhodes, 2006).

Exaggerated Masculinity and Femininity Beginning in adolescence, men's and women's faces develop differently and typically show different characteristics, primarily as a result of differences between men and women in the average ratio of testosterone to estrogen (Swaddle & Reierson, 2002; Thornhill & Gangestad, 2006). As depicted in Figure 15.4, "masculine" faces tend toward narrower and smaller eyes (relative to face size), longer and more pronounced chins, more developed brows and cheekbones, and thinner lips. "Feminine" faces tend to have larger eyes (relative to face size), less developed brows, the appearance of high cheekbones, shorter and less pronounced chins that appear more fragile or graceful, and fuller lips. These sex differences are referred to as *sexual dimorphism* in the structure and appearance of faces.

Sexual dimorphism strongly influences the attractiveness of faces, but it plays out quite differently depending on whether men's or women's faces are being rated for attractiveness—and whether men or women are doing the rating. In the case of women's attractiveness, both men and women agree overwhelmingly that attractive female faces are highly "feminized" faces (Gangestad & Scheyd, 2005; Law-Smith et al., 2006; Rhodes, 2006). An "averaged" composite female face whose features have been further feminized is rated more attractive than a simple averaged composite female face.

When it comes to men's faces, the relationship between attractiveness and women's preferences for "masculinity" is far more complex. Women's ratings

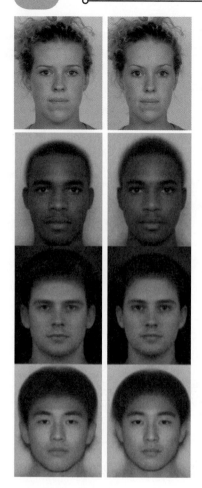

▲ **Beauty Is Only Partially in the Eye of the Beholder.** Collages of photos of women from different societies are regularly reproduced to demonstrate wide disparities in what is considered beautiful around the world. However, while collages such as this one do depict variance in the type of ornamentation and body alteration (e.g., stretched earlobes) considered attractive from culture to culture, these faces all display the basic standard of a "feminized" female face found attractive in all cultures yet studied. (Top left to bottom right: Young women of Surma of Ethiopia, Afar of Djibouti, Afghanistan, China, Greece, Mejecodoteri of Venezuela.)

▲ **FIGURE 15.4 More "Feminized," More Attractive; More "Masculinized" … It Depends.** Both men and women agree that a more "feminized" female face (top right) is more attractive than a less feminized face (top left). However, women's preferences may shift according to a number of factors, perhaps most importantly the phase of their reproductive cycle and their age. Women who do not use hormonal contraceptives (e.g., "the pill") find more masculinized faces (such as the three at bottom left) more appealing during the time of peak fertility. At other times, less masculinized features are preferred, such as those at bottom right. *(Sources: Welling, Jones, & DeBruine, 2008, p. 164; Penton-Voak, et al., 2004, p. 362.)*

of attractiveness of men's faces are highly dependent on *context*, and there is no consistent overall preference. For example, women's ratings respond to various cultural factors and also to whether the face is being rated as a potential short-term partner (preference for highly masculine features) or a long-term partner (preference for less masculine features; Penton-Voak, Jacobson, & Trivers, 2004).

Women's preferences for highly masculine or less masculine faces may also depend on the women's reproductive status. Women who use hormonal contraception such as birth control pills show no consistent preference; but women who do not use hormonal birth control show a consistent preference for highly masculine faces during the time of peak fertility when pregnancy is most likely. At other times, more "feminine" male faces may be preferred (Johnston, Hagel, Franklin, Fink, & Grammer, 2001: Little, Jones, & DeBruine, 2008). Moreover, women around the ages of the gonadarche of puberty—when reproductive potential is low—are much more likely to prefer less masculinized male faces (think of all those devoted Justin Bieber fans!). Postmenopausal women are also more likely to prefer less masculinized faces (Little, et al., 2010).

Why should women's preferences for masculinized faces be highest when they are in fertile phases of their menstrual cycle and when they are of child-bearing age? Evolutionary psychologists speculate that strongly masculinized faces are an "honest advertisement" of the immune status of the man in question. This is because masculinization in facial features is an indication of higher levels of testosterone, and testosterone tends to compromise the immune system. Thus, any male who can "afford" high levels of testosterone is a man with a potent immune system—an immune system that can be passed on to potential offspring, increasing the reproductive success of the mother and her children. At the time of peak fertility, when pregnancy is most possible, women may shift their preferences in facial features to those which promise to increase the reproductive success of potential offspring (Little et al., 2008). However, this is only a hypothesis—and it remains a controversial one.

IN SUMMARY

1. People tend to be drawn to others with whom they share characteristics, a tendency known as positive assortment or the matching phenomenon.

2. The mere exposure effect demonstrates that people come to prefer things or people with which they are more familiar.

3. People emphasize the face in judgments of attractiveness. The four most important factors in cross-cultural judgments of attractiveness are age, symmetry, averageness, and exaggerated masculinity/femininity (sexual dimorphism).

4. Judgments of male facial attractiveness are more complex than judgments of the facial attractiveness of females. Women's ratings of male facial attractiveness may change according to context and the woman's reproductive status.

RETRIEVE!

1. True or false: American men prefer women who are well below normal weight (extremely thin) over women of normal weight.

2. True or false: Newborn infants prefer to gaze at attractive versus unattractive faces.

3. How do researchers explain people's preference for symmetrical faces? For average faces?

4. Describe at least two characteristics of highly "masculine" and two characteristics of highly "feminine" faces.

How Do Other People Affect Our Opinions and Behavior?

In the first four sections of this chapter, we discussed the social self in interaction and interrelationship with other selves. For the remainder of the chapter we shall consider the social self in groups. People often find themselves behaving differently when in groups than when alone or when interacting with just one or two others. In groups, people may extend help where normally they would withhold it or ignore pleas for help where ordinarily they would give assistance without hesitation. They may make decisions that go against their ordinary inclinations merely because other people are doing it. They may lie or tell the truth uncharacteristically, obey authorities who order them to harm others, or refuse to betray their principles on pain of death or disgrace. They may leap in front of speeding trains to save complete strangers, or they may torture innocent civilians to death, smiling all the way. They may surrender their own lives for their children, for strangers, for nations, for gods, or for ideas. The study of group behavior is one of the finest accomplishments of social psychology.

People Conform for Many Reasons

Take a look at the lines depicted in Figure 15.5. As you can see, on the right of the figure is a series of three lines to compare in length to the line on the left, the standard line.

▶ **FIGURE 15.5**

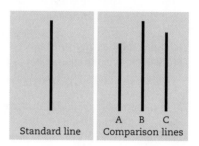

Standard line   A B C
Comparison lines

Which of the three lines on the right is approximately the same length as that standard line? If you chose B, you'd be (more or less obviously) correct. But what do you think it would take to get you to answer "A"? Five shooters of tequila and misplacement of your contact lenses? In fact, all that has been necessary for thousands of intelligent, sober college students to answer "A" is the mere fact that *all the other people around them* answer "A." They have been willing to lie about their beliefs, even when those beliefs are obviously correct, simply to avoid embarrassment and loss of face (Sabini et al., 2001a).

How do we know this? In 1951, social psychologist Solomon Asch conducted a classic experiment in group **conformity**—the tendency of people to bring their behavior and/or attitudes in line with group norms and pressures. In this experiment, the procedure is to have several college students sit around a table, all of whom are confederates (accomplices) of the experimenter except one. The stated task is to judge which of the lines on one side of a card was identical in length to the line on the other side (see also Asch, 1956).

The first few rounds go as expected, with everyone guessing correctly. However, on the next round, all of the confederates answer incorrectly—and clearly so. When it comes time for the actual participant to answer, what does he or she do? There's some squinting and hesitation, but eventually the participant agrees with the group that "A" was identical in length to the standard line (the clearly incorrect answer). In Asch's work, fully one-third of participants went along with the group.

Under what sorts of circumstances will people blindly follow group direction? In the mid-20th century, Morton Deutsch and Harold Gerard (1955) identified two types of motivation and influence to conform: *informational* and *normative*. Informational motivations and influences are not based on the fear of looking foolish or wanting to be liked, but rather on a rational desire to seek realistic information about some situation from the group and adjust behavior accordingly. As an example, suppose you were sitting in a movie theater enjoying a movie along with 100 or more other people. If you were to smell smoke, observe the rest of the audience heading for an exit, and decide to follow along after them, you would be experiencing the informational motivation to conform. On the other hand, normative motivations and influences reflect the desire to obtain approval from the group or avoid embarrassment— as in the case of participants in the Asch experiment who conformed to an obviously incorrect group opinion. Although these normative and informational

Conformity ▶ The tendency of people to bring their behavior, attitudes, and/ or beliefs in line with group norms and pressures. The motivation to conform may be informational, based on a rational desire to seek realistic information of some situation from a group; or the motivation may be normative, based on a person's desire to obtain approval from the group or avoid embarrassment.

influences and motivations to conform are distinct, they often overlap (David & Turner, 2001).

Normative influence to conform is particularly powerful. It does not merely cause people to say things they know are false. It can cause people to use drugs, refuse to offer aid to strangers in need, or commit cruel acts in times of war. It also often goes undetected by the person being influenced (Nolan, Schultz, Cialdini, Goldstein, & Griskevicius, 2008). Jessica Nolan and her colleagues conducted two studies which demonstrated that people are often unaware of normative influences in their lives. In their first study, Nolan and colleagues surveyed a randomly selected group of Californians about their energy conservation activities and reasons for conserving energy. The most important reasons given by survey respondents for their own motivations to conserve energy were to "benefit society" and "protect the environment." The least important reason given was "because other people are doing it."

However, Nolan also asked respondents whether they agreed with various statements about saving energy: Does it benefit society? Does it protect the environment? Are other Californians doing it? and so forth. These answers were then correlated with the survey respondents' *actual* self-reported conservation efforts (e.g., turning off electric lights in the home when not in use, conservative use of air conditioners). The best predictor of a person's actual self-reported conservation efforts was how strongly he or she believed that other people were doing it! As Table 15.1 shows, the correlation between "other people doing it" and energy conservation behavior was twice as strong as that for the next strongest pairing ("benefit to society").

In the second of their two studies, Nolan and her colleagues went beyond correlations and used an experimental design to test the importance of unconscious normative influence. They randomly divided a sample of California households into four groups and used different sorts of appeals to each group to conserve energy, conveyed in flyers attached to their doors. In three of the groups they used appeals such as saving money, benefiting society, and protecting the environment. For the fourth group, they simply conveyed the information that the majority of the respondent's neighbors were conserving energy. (A fifth, the control group, received neutral information about how to conserve energy.) Can you guess which of the groups actually conserved the most energy in the study follow-up period? As Table 15.2 shows, those who received the "your neighbors are all doing it" flyer consumed the least energy in the short term and long term.

Table 15.1 Mean Explanations for Energy Conservation and Correlation between Beliefs about Energy Conservation and Self-Reported Conservation Behavior

	Naïve Explanations for Energy Conservation		Correlation Between Broad Beliefs About Conservation and Self-Reported Behavior	
	M	**SD**	**R**	**SE**
Environmental protection	3.41_a	.75	$.06_a$	.04
Benefit to society	3.17_b	.77	$.23_b$	.04
Saving money	3.07_c	.76	$.03_a$	.04
Other people are doing it	2.93_d	.83	$.45_c$	.04

(Source: Nolan et al., 2008.)

Table 15.2 Short-Term and Long-Term Energy Consumption According to Specific Energy Conservation Appeal

| | Energy Consumption in Average Daily Kilowatt Hours (kWh) | | | |
| | Short Term | | Long Term | |
CONDITION	M	SE	M	SE
Environmental protection	14.12	.39	16.89	.81
Social responsibility	14.18	.41	17.52	.85
Self-interest	14.01	.40	17.45	.82
Social norm	12.97	.44	16.10	.93
Information control	14.42	.45	17.36	.94

(Source: Nolan et al., 2008.)

Groupthink Is Dangerous

Groupthink ▶ A way of thinking and behaving in groups whereby decisions are made not as a result of rational considerations and weighing of evidence, but as a result of group members not wanting to adversely affect group morale, make waves, or appear disloyal to leaders. The frequent end result of groupthink is the adoption of highly flawed plans and policies.

A particularly dangerous type of conformity behavior is known as **groupthink** (Janis, 1989, 2007). Psychologist Irving Janis originally borrowed this term from the George Orwell novel *1984* to describe situations where counterproductive or even disastrous and tragic group decisions are made not from rational considerations but as a result of group members not wanting to adversely affect group morale, make waves, or appear disloyal to the group leader.

The term *groupthink* was first applied in social psychology to the grossly flawed plan authorized by President John F. Kennedy and the CIA in 1961 to destroy Fidel Castro's newly formed communist government by invading Cuba at the Bay of Pigs with a ragtag army of Cuban exiles. Because of the influence of groupthink, the possible consequences of this invasion were not carefully considered. Those who had previously fulfilled the important role of "devil's advocate" in Kennedy's cabinet—challenging assumptions to determine their soundness or considering how a plan might fail as well as how it might succeed—were silenced by unspoken pressure to support the president and maintain morale. The result was catastrophe for all involved—the invaders were easily defeated, hundreds of people lost their lives, and the reputation of the United States suffered.

Groupthink can be discerned lurking behind numerous other historical decisions that have led to fiascoes. The Bush administration's 2003 decision to invade Iraq may be seen as an example of groupthink in a couple of ways. First, decision makers apparently grossly overestimated the probability that former Iraqi dictator Saddam Hussein was hiding arsenals of "weapons of mass destruction." Second, they mistakenly anticipated that U.S. forces would be greeted with open arms by most Iraqi citizens on the ground (Mackenzie, 2006; Rodrigues, Assmar, & Jablonski, 2005). Instead, no such weapons were found, and most Iraqis resented the presence of U.S. troops.

Groupthink breeds and is fed by overconfidence, and effective leaders recognize the dangers of such unrealistic group decision making. Following the Bay of Pigs, President Kennedy instituted a series of "checks and balances" to insure that decision making would be more productive in the future. Based on these policies, Janis (1989) proposed a number of safeguards against groupthink, including the use of impartial, outside advisors; leaders refraining from taking a strong stand on a given issue at the outset of discussions; and the assigning to certain individuals the role of "devil's advocate" to identify potential problems with a given proposal. Table 15.3 summarizes six common symptoms of groupthink.

Bystander Apathy, Tragedy, and Public Outrage

Shortly after 3:00 in the morning on March 13, 1964, a murder occurred in the Kew Gardens neighborhood of Queens in New York City that has horrified and fascinated psychologists, criminologists, and ordinary people ever since. Twenty-eight-year-old Catherine "Kitty" Genovese, returning home from her job as manager of Ev's Eleventh Hour Bar, was attacked on the sidewalk in front of a two-story Tudor-style building and across the street from a ten-story apartment building. A man named Winston Moseley stabbed Kitty twice in the back and then jumped into his car and backed away from the scene. Kitty got up and tried to make her way around to the rear of the two-story building to reach her own home but was unable to make it. She collapsed in the small hallway of the building. At that point, Moseley got out of his car, found Kitty, stabbed her again multiple times, sexually assaulted her, and fled. Kitty died in the ambulance on her way to the hospital.

As it stands, it is a gruesome and tragic story of the violent end of a young life. But there are details of this crime that have given it a kind of ghastly immortality. The following is taken from the initial account in the *New York Times* on March 27, 1964:

> For more than half an hour thirty-eight respectable, law-abiding citizens in Queens watched a killer stalk and stab a woman in three separate attacks in Kew Gardens. Twice the sound of their voices and the sudden glow of their bedroom lights interrupted him and frightened him off. Each time he returned, sought her out and stabbed her again. Not one person telephoned the police during the assault; one witness called after the woman was dead. (Gansberg, 1964)

The *Times* account suggested that Kitty had screamed for a full half-hour, "Oh my God, he stabbed me! Please help me! I'm dying, I'm dying!" Yet not one of the 38 supposed witnesses to this horror so much as lifted a finger— not to go to her aid, not even to phone the police. They simply watched the crime with dispassion. The news reportage of this crime not only led to major changes in the way crimes are reported to the police (including the

▲ **Kitty Genovese.** The killing of Kitty Genovese in Queens, New York, in 1964 initiated the study of the conditions under which bystanders will respond to pleas for help from strangers. However, for decades Genovese's killing was mythologized: Beliefs that 38 neighbors stood by and refused to offer help as she was killed are entirely inaccurate.

Table 15.3 Six Symptoms of Groupthink

SYMPTOM	DESCRIPTION
Collective rationalization	Everyone in the group shares the same faulty explanations for why a particular strategy or tactic is necessary, or why an apparent "red flag" warning of weakness in a plan should be ignored.
Pressure to conform	There is spoken or unspoken pressure among members to agree to a particular plan—often the plan supported by the leader.
Illusion of invulnerability	The possibility that a plan may fail is not considered.
Illusion of moral correctness	The group never questions the rightness of its actions (e.g., "God is on our side").
Bias toward outgroup members	Those on the outside of the group who disagree or who may be outright enemies are underestimated in strength or intelligence, considered weak, "evil," or otherwise inferior.
Illusion of unanimous consensus	Because of pressure to conform, there may appear to be unanimous consensus at meetings—while individual members may still harbor many private doubts and disagreements.

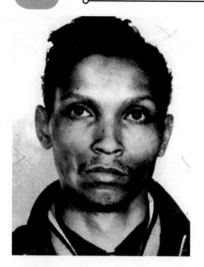

▲ Winston Mosely, Kitty Genovese's Killer.

Bystander effect ▶ The tendency for a person to be less likely to intervene and offer help to a stranger in an emergency situation when there are other people there who might reasonably be thought able to help. The more people present, the less likely the bystander is to offer aid.

institution of the 911 call), but also opened up an entire area of social psychology dealing with the conditions under which people will administer or withhold aid to strangers in need. It also helped to establish a view of modern urban life as peopled by uncaring and apathetic citizens (Manning, Levine, & Collins, 2007).

MASS SUSCEPTIBILITY TO DUBIOUS NEWS REPORTING

Before discussing the findings of social psychologists on what has come to be called the **bystander effect**—the tendency of people to be less likely to help strangers in need if there are other people present at the scene—it needs to be said that another important aspect of social psychology is reflected in the story of Kitty Genovese: the willingness of people to believe news accounts that violate commonsense ideas of what is likely and what is not. Although the sexual assault and murder of Kitty Genovese is all too true, the story of her betrayal by 38 of her neighbors is greatly exaggerated (Manning et al., 2007; Rasenberger, 2004). Some of the facts of this case remain in dispute, but recent research has offered the following correctives to the mythology that surrounds this crime:

- It is untrue that no one phoned the police. The police were called immediately following the first attack on Kitty Genovese (although this call did not result in immediate dispatch of police to the scene).
- Only three eyewitnesses were known to have actually seen Kitty attacked—not 38 (and these three *do* bear responsibility for their inaction). An unknown number of people—probably many *more* than 38—did hear Kitty scream during the initial attack, however, and they have been the subject of intense criticism for their failure to investigate (Skoller, 2008).
- The three actual eyewitnesses saw Kitty get up and walk away and not return. One testified that he thought Kitty was drunk. Another thought Kitty had been struck, not stabbed. Many of those who only heard something assumed that it was a lovers' quarrel or drunken altercation (the attack took place near a neighborhood bar). No one saw the sexual assault or the completion of the murder.
- No one watched anything for anywhere near as long as half an hour. The first attack lasted only a few moments. The second attack lasted at least several minutes, but only one neighbor could even have been in a position to see any of it.
- Only one witness was reported to have heard Kitty cry that she had been stabbed.
- Kitty was still alive when the police arrived.
- The purported inaction of Kitty Genovese's neighbors has been used for decades as an example of the unwillingness of members of *groups* to act at the scene of emergencies. However, it is doubtful that the residents of Kew Gardens, living in their separate apartments and not interacting with one another, could be said in any legitimate sense to constitute a group (Manning, Levine, & Collins, 2008).

THE BYSTANDER EFFECT

Regardless of the degree of mythology surrounding this case, it is undeniably true that an unknown number of people chose not to help Kitty Genovese when they clearly understood (or should have understood) that she was under some sort of attack—even if the specific nature of the attack and its severity were not entirely clear. Ironically, however exaggerated, accounts of the Genovese murder prompted important research to be conducted on the conditions under which people will withhold aid to others.

What are these conditions? The initial work was done by John Darley and Bibb Latané (1968). Instead of representing "big-city apathy" as it had been characterized, however, Darley and Latané demonstrated that the *presence of others* at a scene allows each individual to diffuse responsibility with the rationale that "someone else is bound to take care of it." The more people are present at a scene, the less likely any specific person is to offer aid.

Although Darley and Latané's early work was insightful, it was not until 2011 that researchers took a more comprehensive and systematic look at the bystander effect (Fischer et al., 2011). Integrating 50 years of research in a meta-analysis, Peter Fischer and his colleagues made a more precise identification of when strangers will or will not intervene on behalf of those in need, and the results of this analysis were in some ways surprising.

Fischer and colleagues first affirmed the general rule that the presence of groups of bystanders in critical situations does reduce the likelihood of any single individual offering aid. However, surprisingly, the more dangerous the circumstance and the more clear-cut the physical danger, the *more* likely—not less likely—bystanders are to offer aid. This is probably true in part because a group of people may support one another physically, so each individual feels less fearful of intervening. Think for a moment: Attempting to disarm a violent offender with five other people supporting you may seem a lot less daunting than attempting the task alone. In part it may also be true because in truly dangerous situations the need for aid to be offered is usually completely unambiguous (unlike the Genovese case), and it may be harder to rationalize failing to act ("Oh, it's probably just a lover's quarrel."). Finally, and perhaps not surprisingly, the presence of males among a group of bystanders increases the likelihood of help being offered in times of physical danger, and if the bystanders are known to one another and not strangers, the chances of aid being offered are increased still more.

Deindividuation in Groups: Human Beings at Their Worst

The bystander effect is fed by people's tendency to feel more anonymous and less accountable for their behavior in groups. This feeling sometimes results in **deindividuation**—a lessening of self-awareness or identity when in a group, leading to reduced concern with how your behavior will be evaluated by others. Under such conditions a person might behave in ways he or she normally would not. Deindividuation can have disastrous consequences if it occurs in interaction with a social role that puts one in a position of power over other individuals—for example, the role of prison guard.

Consider the Stanford prison experiment, conducted (but never completed) by Philip Zimbardo at Stanford University in California (Zimbardo, 1973). Zimbardo and his colleagues wished to examine changes in individual behavior that might accompany changes in social roles—the various roles one is expected to play in the course of one's life such as mother, doctor, soldier, student, and so forth. They created a role-play situation in which undergraduate students were randomly assigned to be "prisoners" or "guards" in a highly realistic prison situation that even included being "arrested" by actual police and "booked" prior to imprisonment.

The experiment was supposed to run for 2 weeks, but by the end of only 6 days it had to be closed down. Why? The majority of the students had taken on attributes of their roles to such a degree that their behavior became virtually indistinguishable from that of actual prisoners and guards under deindividuating conditions. The guards became increasingly sadistic, treating the prisoners with cruelty that would not be allowed with animals. The prisoners, for their part, had become so traumatized that their behavior was servile; they thought only of escape and experienced genuine hatred for the guards.

It should be emphasized that the guards had been randomly assigned to their position, and were no different psychologically from the group that had been randomly assigned to be prisoners. According to Zimbardo, the Stanford experiment demonstrated that such situations often emerge, not because of "a

Deindividuation ▶ A lessening of self-awareness or identity within a group, leading to increased feelings of anonymity and reduced concern for how one's behavior will be evaluated by others in the group.

▲ **Wesley Autry, the Hero of Harlem.**

Altruism ▶ The offering of assistance to others without the expectation of immediate reward.

few bad apples" but because "the barrel itself is rotten" (CNN Access, 2004; Zimbardo, 2007).

According to other researchers, however, the situation appears to be somewhat more complex than Zimbardo allows (Carnahan & McFarland, 2007; Mastronianni, 2007). For example, although the Stanford students were randomly assigned to be prisoners and guards, all the participants had knowingly volunteered for an experiment in prison life. Thomas Carnahan and Sam McFarland (2007) have shown that students willing to volunteer for a study of prison life such as the Zimbardo study may be more psychologically predisposed than ordinary students toward personality traits associated with aggressiveness, authoritarianism, narcissism (inflated ideas of the self), and dominance; they may also be lower on positive traits such as altruism and empathy. It may be that factors of the prison situation interacted with the personality factors of the volunteers to create the abuses that arose during Zimbardo's study.

Altruism: Human Beings at Their Best

If a man fell onto the subway tracks in front of your eyes, would you jump onto the tracks to help him? What if a train were hurtling into the station? Shortly after noon on January 2, 2007, a 50-year-old construction worker named Wesley Autrey was standing on the platform of the 137th Street–City College subway station in Manhattan, taking his two daughters, Syshe, 4, and Shuqui, 6, home before heading to work. Suddenly, a young man in the station collapsed in convulsive seizure. The man attempted to rise, stumbled to the platform edge, and fell to the tracks between the two rails. Just then the headlights of a train appeared around the bend as it made for the station. Autrey leapt to the tracks and lay atop the fallen man, covering him with his own body as the train, unable to stop, ran over the two—missing Autrey's head and body by inches. Hearing the screams of onlookers, Autry shouted. "I've got two daughters up there. Let them know their father's O.K." Later, Autrey—who refused medical help because he claimed that nothing was wrong—told a reporter, "I don't feel like I did something spectacular; I just saw someone who needed help. I did what I felt was right" (Buckley, 2007). Unlike Autrey, the rest of the world thought Autrey *did* perform something spectacular. Among other honors, he was a guest at President Bush's 2008 State of the Union address and was showered with gifts and offers of employment. He ended up as one of *TIME Magazine*'s 100 most influential people in the world in 2007.

When hearing stories of bystanders failing to help, sadistic aggression in role-play situations, and selfishness winning out over helpfulness, many shrug and pass it off to "human nature." But stories such as Wesley Autrey's show another side to human nature that is equally prevalent. **Altruism**—the offering of assistance to others without the expectation of immediate reward—is all around us. Consider the heroism of ordinary office workers who helped their colleagues escape from the burning World Trade Center buildings on September 11, 2001. Or the selflessness of aging Japanese retirees who volunteered for cleanup jobs at the Fukushima Daichi nuclear reactor after it was damaged by the 2011 earthquake and tsunami. These older workers were willing to perform tasks requiring exposure to unsafe levels of radiation, sparing younger workers who had much more to lose (or, at least, many more years of life to lose) should they develop radiation sickness, cancer, or other ill effects. As thousands of similar but less publicized deeds around the world attest daily, human nature is as altruistic as it is selfish, and as cooperative as it is aggressive.

Indeed, altruism is "in our genes," literally. Like *prosocial* emotions such as empathy and compassion, the capacity for altruism has evolved to be part of human psychology (de Waal, 2008; Dugatkin, 1997, 2006; Goetz, Keltner, & Simon-Thomas, 2010; Piliavin & Charng, 1990; Trivers, 1971, 2002). Behavior genetics studies have shown that differences among people in their tendencies toward altruism are in part genetic in origin (Rushton, 2004), and recent research has observed a sense of fairness and willingness to share emerging in some infants as young as 15 months (Schmidt & Sommerville, 2011).

Altruism is part of a larger group of behaviors termed *prosocial* because they may promote the well-being of society as a whole. However, from a psychological perspective, altruism presents a "problem." Although we know that people *do* perform clearly altruistic acts, it is not always apparent *why* they do so. Why should people like Wesley Autrey offer help to complete strangers at the risk of their own safety or that of their loved ones? Why should a person contribute money to a charitable cause when that money could be used instead for his or her own family's benefit?

TWO TYPES OF CAUSES OF ALTRUISM: PROXIMATE AND ULTIMATE

In our discussion of sex differences in *aggression* in Chapter 10, we identified two kinds or classes of explanations for behaviors that interest psychologists. The first type of explanation focuses on explaining the immediate, direct causes of an act. Immediate, direct causes are known as **proximate causes**. Proximate causes of animal behavior (including human behavior) include not only motivations, but also physiological, biochemical, and neural processes as well as learning. Usually, when we ask, "Why did he/she do that?" we are referring to proximate causes, and most branches of psychology (evolutionary psychology being an exception) focus on proximate explanations for behavior. In the case of altruistic acts, psychologists interested in proximate causes are usually interested in the *motivations* for the acts (Batson et al., 1999; de Waal, 2008). For example, what motivated Wesley Autrey to risk his own life to save the life of a stranger? What was he thinking and feeling?

The second type of cause for a behavior, known as an **ultimate cause**, explains why some type of behavior—altruism, for example—exists in the first place. In other words, ultimate explanations show how the *effects* of some behavior would have benefited the survival and reproduction of human beings over evolutionary time and therefore evolved through natural selection (Alcock, 2009; Dugatkin, 1997, 2006; Scott-Phillips, Dickens, & West, 2011; Trivers, 1971, 2002). When we ask why people are altruistic, we may be interested in proximate explanations, ultimate explanations, or both.

As an example, consider honeybees, which commit altruistic acts when they sting intruders, sacrificing their lives to protect the hive. Is their motivation one of kindness and compassion toward their fellow bees and a sense of cooperative civic spirit? Probably not. It is far more likely that the motivation—a proximate cause of their altruistic act—is one of aggression, to injure the intruder. However, the ultimate cause of their behavior throughout the evolutionary history of honeybees has been one of altruism—personal sacrifice that benefits others without expectation of immediate reward (de Waal, 2008, p. 280).

PROXIMATE EXPLANATIONS OF ALTRUISM: EMPATHY, MIRROR NEURONS, AND EGOISM

Some researchers suggest that the important human quality of *empathy* is the proximate explanation for many or even most altruistic acts (Batson, 2010; Batson et al., 1999; de Waal, 2008). **Empathy** is the ability to take another person's perspective, to *feel* how that person feels, understand *why* the person feels as he or she does, and often (but not always) come to share the feeling at least to some degree (Decety, Michalska, & Akitsuki, 2008; de Waal, 2008; Jackson, Meltzoff, & Decety, 2005).

In an interesting neuroscientific look at brain mechanisms involved in empathy, Phillip Jackson and his colleagues showed participants photographs of hands and feet in situations where they were about to be painfully cut by knives or garden shears, jammed in doors, or other predicaments we would rather not think about (Jackson et al., 2005). As shown in Figure 15.6, these

Proximate causes ▶ Proximate causes are the immediate causes of behavior—*how* something occurs. Proximate causes of behavior include motivations; physiological, biochemical, and neural processes; and learning. Most psychologists focus on proximate explanations of behavior.

Ultimate causes ▶ Ultimate causes of behavior are forces that shaped the capacity or tendency for the behavior in human beings over evolutionary time—*why*, rather than *how*, a behavior occurs. Unlike most other psychologists, evolutionary psychologists focus primarily on ultimate explanations of behavior.

Empathy ▶ The ability to take another person's perspective, understand why the person feels as he or she does, and perhaps also come to share that feeling to some degree (although this is not a necessary component of empathy).

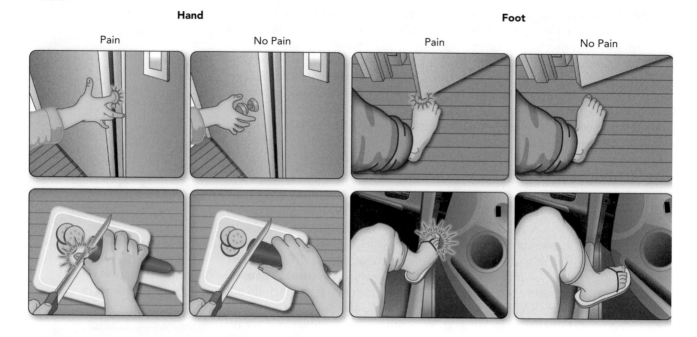

Hand   **Foot**

Pain   No Pain   Pain   No Pain

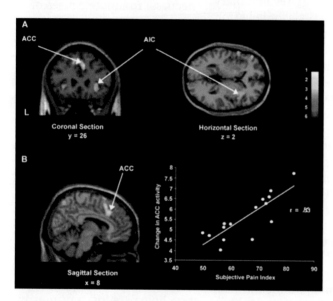

▲ **FIGURE 15.6 Sharing the Pain of Others: The Neuroscience of Empathy.** When research participants were exposed to images of impending pain and injury, specific areas of the anterior cingulated cortex (ACC) and anterior insulate cortex (AIC) were activated that were not activated when viewing virtually identical images without the implication of impending pain and injury. The areas of the ACC and AIC are indicated in these images from different perspective views of the brain. The scatterplot graph shows the strong correlation between the activation of the ACC and AIC and participants reports of their own sensitivity to pain. *(Source: Jackson et al., 2005, pp. 773, 775.)*

photos were contrasted with photos where the hands and feet were in no danger.

Jackson and his colleagues found that areas of the brain normally activated when one experiences pain were also activated simply by viewing *someone else* about to experience pain (Decety et al., 2008). The more pain-sensitive the participants reported that they generally were, the more activation was seen in these brain areas. Jackson and colleagues' findings reflect the workings of mirror neurons, which we have described in Chapter 7. Mirror neurons are specific neurons in the brain which fire when an individual engages in a behavior or experiences an emotion, and also fire when the individual observes someone else engaging in the same behavior or experiencing the same emotion. Mirror neurons are an important component of proximate explanations for empathy and altruism because they offer a neural mechanism by which a connection is established between one individual and another (Decety & Jackson, 2006; Iacoboni, 2009).

Of course, many apparently altruistic acts can also be motivated by the desire to be thanked, to "look good" in front of others, to increase one's own self-esteem, or even to "expand the boundaries of the self" by including another individual within those boundaries (Cialdini, Brown, Lewis, Luce, & Neuberg, 1997). Such motivations are termed *egoistic*, or self-interested. However, researchers have been able to demonstrate experimentally that egoism is not an adequate explanation for many altruistic acts. Empathy, in contrast, does seem to be at least a major motivating force (de Waal, 2008), if not the whole story (Pinker, 2011).

ULTIMATE EXPLANATIONS: INCLUSIVE FITNESS AND RECIPROCAL ALTRUISM

If empathy is the primary proximate explanation for altruism, where does empathy come from? It is a maxim of evolutionary biology that individuals rarely act directly against their own genetic interests—that is, in a way that would

◄ **Does Empathy Exist in Nonhuman Animals?** At least two aspects of empathy—the ability to take the perspective of another individual and understand why another individual is distressed—have been shown to occur in nonhuman animals, notably in apes. Here a young chimpanzee consoles a screaming male who has been defeated in a fight. *(Source: de Waal, 2008, p. 284.)*

▲ **Worker Bees: What's In It for Them?** Worker honey bees basically live their lives—and sacrifice their lives altruistically—in service to the queen. How could such a thing have evolved? William Hamilton's theory of inclusive fitness explains the worker bees' altruism. In honeybee colonies, the degree of genetic relatedness between the bees is exceptionally high. In sacrificing their lives to the queen, worker bees are ensuring that their own genetic line will continue.

compromise their reproductive success (Dawkins, 1976; Dugatkin, 2006; Trivers, 2002). If organisms acted repeatedly against their genetic interests, they would be "out-competed" by individuals who always acted in favor of their genetic interests. Over evolutionary time, the genetic line of those acting against their interests would die out, and so would the tendency to behave in this way! Therefore, according to the logic of evolutionary theory, empathy and altruism *must* have functioned over evolutionary time in some way to increase our ancestors' success in surviving and reproducing. Two well-tested evolutionary theories explain how this might happen.

Theory of Inclusive Fitness In 1964, a young British biologist named William Hamilton solved a puzzle that evolutionists had been struggling with for many decades: Why do some animals give their lives so that others in their group may live? Certain animals risk their lives to warn the group of approaching danger. Others live only to serve their queen, never reproducing and even sacrificing their lives for their own bodies to be used as food. How could such characteristics survive?

Hamilton (1964) solved this problem by demonstrating mathematically that the important thing in natural selection is not physical survival or even physical reproduction—it is *gene* survival and *gene* reproduction. The resulting theory is called the **theory of inclusive fitness** because, in contrast to an exclusive focus on the survival and reproduction of an individual, it states that an organism is reproductively fit to the extent that it passes on its genetic line to new generations. For example, your genetic line survives not only in your children, but also (to a lesser but still important extent) in your siblings, cousins, nieces, and nephews. Each child shares approximately 50% of his or her genes in common with each parent and approximately the same in common with each sibling, but approximately the same frequency of gene survival would occur in two of the parent's grandchildren (25% in each), two nieces or nephews (25% in each), or four cousins (12.5% in each).

To understand the reasoning behind Hamilton's theory, it is helpful to realize that because bodies are temporary (they always die), natural selection cannot operate to make its small incremental changes over time on individuals. It can only do so on genes, which, barring mutation, are potentially immortal. Therefore, if you were to race into a burning building to save your children, grandchildren, and a few nieces or nephews—all of whom are genetic kin—even if you were to die, by saving them you would be contributing massively to your own genetic survival. This altruistic act would ultimately serve your own genetic self-interest. However, the *motivation*—the emotions you are feeling at the time—are likely to be entirely empathetic and not at all egoistic.

Consider the story of Karen Svaerd, a Swedish tourist who ran *directly into* the oncoming tsunami wave in Southeast Asia on December 26, 2004,

Theory of inclusive fitness
► William Hamilton's mathematics-based evolutionary theory of altruism directed toward kin. The theory stresses the fact that natural selection operates on genes, not on individuals and their bodies. Altruistic acts directed toward genetic kin may increase a person's own evolutionary "fitness" if the act increases the kin's survival or reproductive success. This may happen even if the individual sacrifices his or her life during the altruistic act, depending on the number of kin helped by the act or the closeness of the genetic link to the kin (e.g., sacrificing your life so that one of your children or 10 first-cousins may live increases your fitness more than sacrificing your life for one grandchild or 10 second-cousins).

▶ **Reciprocal Altruism.** Robert Trivers' theory of reciprocal altruism states that altruistic acts, and the emotions which accompany them, should be expected when there is a reasonable expectation that the favor may be returned in the future and the costs of engaging in the act are lower than the potential benefit. (Left) Macaque monkeys groom one another, a relatively low-cost act with strong positive benefits when one is groomed in return. (Right) Reciprocal altruism occurs on the playground as children take turns pushing one another on the swing.

to rescue her three children, as all other people were frantically running in the opposite direction (the entire family survived, by the way). You can be sure that at that moment she was *not* thinking about the survival of her genes through her offspring, but only of her desperate love and concern for her children. Thus, empathy as an emotion may have evolved to help motivate organisms to engage in actions that assist genetic survival, even if it might mean putting their own physical survival at risk.

Theory of Reciprocal Altruism But what of people like Wesley Autrey? Why is altruism also frequently directed toward complete strangers who are not our kin? In 1971, Robert Trivers, whose theory of parental investment and sexual selection is discussed in Chapter 3, devised an ultimate explanation for altruism directed toward non-kin known as the **theory of reciprocal altruism**. The basic idea is that psychological attributes that motivate altruism, such as empathy, will evolve under conditions where altruism is expected to be reciprocated at some point in the future—either to oneself or one's kin. Recall that, according to evolutionary theory, human psychology was shaped under conditions of life in very small bands of hunters and gatherers, where many were genetically related and all knew one another. Acts of altruism were probably expected to be returned. If you have a poor week of fishing, I will share my catch with you and your family; when I have a poor week, the favor will likely be returned. Each person gains more than his or her costs (Cosmides & Tooby, 1992). Under such conditions, empathy and the altruism it can inspire may have had highly positive genetic payoffs—increasing, rather than decreasing, reproductive success and survival. Human beings have evolved to be altruistic, loving, and cooperative—just as we have also evolved to be selfish and aggressive when conditions seem to demand it.

Theory of reciprocal altruism
▶ Robert Trivers' evolutionary theory of altruism directed toward non-kin. The theory proposes that psychological attributes that motivate altruism toward non-kin, such as empathy, will only evolve under conditions where there is some expectation that altruistic acts will be reciprocated in the future—either to oneself or one's kin.

IN SUMMARY

1. Conformity may be influenced and motivated by informational or normative concerns. Normative influences are particularly powerful, and often occur unnoticed by the person conforming.

2. Groupthink is a particularly dangerous type of conformity behavior that occurs because members do not want to make waves, affect group morale, or appear disloyal. Groupthink results in counterproductive (or disastrous) group decisions.

3.	The rape and murder of Kitty Genovese precipitated research in the bystander effect. However, the popular conception of the crime against Genovese—that focuses on 38 apathetic bystanders standing by and not intervening—is exaggerated. Bystanders are most likely to offer aid when the situation involves unambiguous physical danger, if males are present, and if the bystanders are known to one another.
4.	Deindividuation is a lessening of self-awareness and reduced concern about how your behavior may be evaluated by others in the group. It may occur when people feel anonymous and less accountable for their actions in groups.
5.	Altruism and prosocial behavior are as much a part of human nature as is selfishness and cruelty. Proximate explanations of altruism include empathy, egoism, and mirror neurons. Ultimate explanations include William Hamilton's theory of inclusive fitness and Robert Trivers' theory of reciprocal altruism.

RETRIEVE!

1.	Distinguish informational from normative influences and motivations in conformity behavior. Give one hypothetical example of each.
2.	On January 28, 1986, the Space Shuttle *Challenger* exploded shortly after liftoff, killing its seven crew members. Prior to the disaster, a series of problems had postponed the launch date, and NASA scientists and engineers were eager to begin the mission. The day before the launch, an engineer brought up concerns about the structural integrity of the *Challenger*. However, the group making decisions about the mission ignored the engineer's warning. They felt that "all was well" and did not want to examine their decision carefully. Some who had concerns were afraid to voice them to avoid lowering morale or compromising the image of NASA. Which social behavioral phenomenon was most clearly responsible for the Space Shuttle *Challenger* disaster? **a)** deindividuation **b)** informational influences **c)** groupthink **d)** bystander effect
3.	Why have some researchers proposed that the events during the Stanford prison experiment cannot completely be explained by the characteristics of the mock-prison situation?
4.	Which theory would explain a well-known biologist's joking remark, "I wouldn't race into a burning building to save my brother, but I might do it to save three cousins and a niece." Why does this theory explain the joke?

How Does Intergroup Conflict Lead to Aggression?

"Kill the Pig! Cut his throat! Kill the pig! Bash him in!"

—William Golding, from *Lord of the Flies*, Chapter 7

If you read William Golding's *Lord of the Flies* in high school, you may recall its grim vision of human nature as linked inescapably to murderous and barbarous aggression and conflict between groups. Much of the history of the world since the dawn of civilization would seem to bear out this pessimistic

Intergroup conflict ▶
Nonharmonious relations
between groups.

Genocide ▶ A deliberate
and systematic attempt to
destroy or exterminate an
entire people based on their
nationality, religion, racial
group, or ethnicity.

Stereotyping ▶ Attributing
clusters of traits to specific
categories of individuals
or objects. These clusters
of traits create an image or
conception of the "typical"
member of the category or
its stereotype. Stereotypes of
social groups often contain
a degree of accuracy but are
also frequently misapplied.
Stereotypes are misapplied
when one assumes that
any given individual from a
group is likely to display the
average characteristics of the
group, or when inaccurate
information about the group's
average characteristics is
used to construct the group
stereotype in the first place.

view. What causes the seemingly never-ending pattern of prejudice, conflict, aggression, and violence between groups? This is the question addressed by much research and theory in social psychology. Indeed, **intergroup conflict**—the social psychological term to describe nonharmonious relations among groups—has been called "the problem of the century" by Susan Fiske (2004) because it has been the root cause of many millions of deaths and unimaginable human suffering resulting from aggression and violence.

In Chapter 10 we examined *aggression* as a human motivation. If you recall, aggression is a general term used when an individual or group carries out an action intended to harm another individual or group. Aggression does not always result in violence, but it is always intended to harm, and it is always experienced as harmful in some way by its recipient. A person's aggressive behavior may be triggered by the interaction of any number of factors involving the person himself or herself as well as characteristics of the situation.

However, it is in the context of intergroup conflict that aggression can reach the heights of violent expression in war and **genocide**—the deliberate attempt to exterminate an entire people. We shall now examine psychological factors that often lead to aggression in the context of intergroup conflict: stereotyping, prejudice, ingroup bias, obedience to authority, and realistic group conflict.

Stereotyping Can Lead to Prejudice

One hears quite a lot about *stereotypes* as though they were inherently inaccurate, irrational, or even evil. However, **stereotyping**—attributing clusters of traits to specific categories of individuals and objects—is an intrinsic property of the human mind without which we might have difficulty functioning properly or even surviving. Just imagine trying to navigate the enormous complexity of life without lumping things together that share common characteristics—we would be "flabbergasted by every new thing we encounter" (Pinker, 2002, p. 203). To some degree we *must* assume that certain things are true about objects and individuals based on the category to which they belong (Fiske & Neuberg, 1990). If you are at war, and you see a person wearing a uniform of the opposing army, you do not need to ask if he intends to shoot at you. That's stereotyping.

Although stereotyping is a wonderful ability for which we all ought to be grateful, it can backfire and cause serious problems to the individual and society when stereotypes are applied inappropriately to social groups and individuals from those groups. To understand why stereotyping backfires, we need to first affirm that many social stereotypes are fairly accurate in the sense that they actually do describe certain characteristics of the average member of a group (Clabaugh & Morling, 2004; Diekman, Eagly, & Kulesa, 2002; Jussim, Cain, Crawford, Harber, & Cohen, 2009). For example, people are generally quite accurate in their stereotypes of sex differences in personality traits, behaviors, and interests, based on analyses of actual average differences between men and women (Hall & Carter, 1999; Lippa, 2010; Schmitt, Realo, Voracek, & Allik, 2008; Valla & Ceci, 2011).

However, just because stereotypes often hold a degree of accuracy regarding the *average* characteristics of groups, applying stereotypes *to individuals* from a group is dangerous, because individuals very often do *not* conform to the average at all. Moreover, the information we receive about the characteristics of social groups, and from which we form our stereotypes, is sometimes grossly exaggerated. For example, consider Victorian-era stereotypes of women as being too "hormonally driven" to succeed in professions such as medicine or law. Currently, a large proportion of lawyers and doctors in the United States are female—indeed, women dominate some fields of medicine, and if current rates of women's entry into medical school continue, women will soon dominate *most* nonsurgical fields of medicine (BBC, 2009; McInstry, 2008). Thus, although many women do experience discomfort and other symptoms coinciding with changes in the reproductive cycle, these changes clearly have no impact on their ability to succeed as doctors and lawyers or to function at high-level jobs.

Worse still, sometimes the information we receive is "managed" by governments or other special interests and is not merely exaggerated, but is mostly or entirely inaccurate. Consider the information that American citizens received about Africans by the slave-owning class in the 1700s and 1800s, or that Germans received about its Jewish citizens from Hitler's propaganda machine in the 1930s and 1940s. The inappropriate application of stereotypes to individuals has a name: **prejudice**, the tendency to "prejudge" an individual based on beliefs about, or feelings toward, the group to which the person belongs.

Although prejudice consists of cognitive, emotional, and behavioral aspects, stereotyping primarily represents cognitive aspects of prejudice. Stereotypes are "cool" forms of bias, that may not have immediately obvious symptoms or consequences and may be hidden; cool forms of bias may be compared with emotional, "hot" forms that we associate with the most destructive consequences of prejudice, including genocidal violence (Cuddy, Fiske, & Glick, 2007; Fiske, 2004). As Figure 15.7 depicts, prejudice is related to *racism*—an institutionalized form of prejudice—but the terms may also be interpreted differently.

GROUP STEREOTYPES HAVE CHANGED

Although stereotypes can be quite powerful, they are not all-powerful. Some evidence suggests that stereotypes are primarily applied to individuals when no specific information about that person is available. Once information about a person becomes available that contradicts stereotypes, the stereotype is often (but not always) abandoned (Madon et al., 1998). It is also interesting to note that in the decades since World War II, stereotypes about groups such as Asians, Jews, and African Americans have become *more* widespread, not *less*, in the sense that Americans are in greater agreement regarding the stereotypical characteristics of these and other ethnic groups. However, the *content* of the stereotypes has changed—it has become far more favorable. In other words, more stereotyping is occurring, but the characteristics attributed to groups are more flattering than in the past (Madon et al., 2001).

Amy Cuddy and Susan Fiske and their colleagues have created a model of newer forms of *moderate bias*—bias that is not exceedingly strong—in which positive and negative stereotyping may coexist. For example, some groups, such as the intellectually disabled or the elderly, are often considered incompetent and generally useless, but at the same time expected to be sweet and warm. Other groups, such as rich people, Jews, and Asians—are thought to be highly competent and intelligent, but suspected also of being in some way sneaky, threatening, or cold (Cuddy et al., 2007; Fiske, Cuddy, Glick, & Xu, 2002).

According to Fiske and Cuddy and their colleagues, stereotyping can be captured on two dimensions, *competence* and *warmth*. This allows that a group can be ranked as high on one dimension but low on the other. Apparently positive stereotypes—for example, that a group is very intelligent or wealthy—may mask negative bias if that group is simultaneously seen to lack warmth. The positive stereotype of intelligence or wealth is thus tinged with envy and resentment. Similarly, high rankings on warmth can elicit pity rather than admiration if there is a simultaneous low ranking on competence.

Figure 15.8 "maps" the ways in which moderate attitudes of bias are expressed by Americans toward selected groups, all of which are stereotyped both in negative and/or positive ways. These attitudes cluster according to the relative ratings of warmth and competence given each group by representative samples of Americans (Cuddy et al., 2007).

Ingroup Bias May Also Lead to Prejudice

Another human tendency that we would do well to control in the modern world, but that may have had survival value for our evolutionary ancestors,

▲ **FIGURE 15.7 Racism Is Structural; Prejudice Is Personal.** Although the terms *racism* and *prejudice* can be used interchangeably, some theorists stress the importance of defining these terms differently. From this perspective, *racism* exists when the social institutions are structured so that certain racial or ethnic groups are systematically disadvantaged, oppressed, or violated (e.g., Feagin, 2006). Thus, racism exists not only in people's minds, but also in law, policy, religion, mass media, education, and so forth. *Racism* is largely responsible for past concentrations of African Americans in menial jobs. However, the white man receiving a shoe shine from this young African American—although he might benefit from racism in various ways—may or may not be personally *prejudiced* against black people.

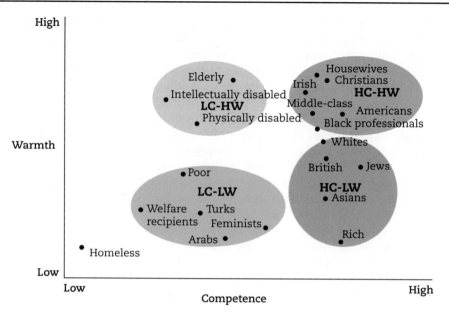

LC-HW = low competence, high warmth (such groups are pitied)
LC-LW = low competence, low warmth (such groups are treated with contempt)
HC-LW = high competence, low warmth (such groups are envied)
HC-HW = high competence, high warmth (such groups are admired)

▲ **FIGURE 15.8 Positive and Negative Stereotypes of Groups in the United States.** The "bias map" depicted here graphs the ways in which various groups are stereotyped by Americans in positive and negative ways. Emotions of envy, pity, contempt, or admiration are associated with these stereotypes, depending on where the group falls on the dimensions of competence and warmth. For example, Jews are rated the most competent, but they are also rated low in warmth, so the emotion associated with these stereotypes is envy. The homeless are rated lowest in both competence and warmth, so they are viewed with contempt. The elderly, the intellectually disabled, and physically disabled are given high ratings for warmth, but low ratings for competence, so they are viewed with pity. Only groups rated high in warmth *and* competence—for example, housewives and Christians—are admired without ambivalence. *(Source: Cuddy et al., 2007, p. 638.)*

Ingroup bias ▶ The tendency of human beings to favor and extend loyalty to members of their own group. Ingroup members are generally trusted more than outgroup members, and ingroup bias sometimes (but not always) leads to prejudice or even hatred toward members of outgroups. Ingroup bias tends to be automatic, and it is triggered as soon as group identity is created.

is **ingroup bias**. Ingroup bias is the tendency to favor and extend loyalty to members of one's own group (the *ingroup*) over others, termed the *outgroup*. Ingroup bias exists universally in all societies yet studied, and has been shown in part to have a genetic basis (Bernhard, Fischbacher, & Fehr, 2006; Brewer, 2007; Lewis & Bates, 2010; Sumner, 1906/1959). We are more approving and forgiving of members of our ingroup, and we donate more of our time and resources to them. We trust them more, support them in their endeavors, and will sometimes even give up our lives for them. We cheer on *our* sports team, *our* school, *our* nation, *our* ethnicity, *our* fashion style, *our* musicians.

The tendency toward ingroup bias is so strong that researchers can create artificial groups by randomly assigning people to two categories by tossing a coin ("Okay, you'll be in the Reds and you'll be in the Blues"), and people will immediately show allegiance to their temporary ingroup by allocating members greater cash rewards in games constructed by the researchers (e.g., Tajfel & Turner, 1979). Thus, ingroup bias is not only pervasive throughout the world; it also seems to appear spontaneously as soon as a group identity is created, even a relatively arbitrary group identity (Brewer, 2007). Moreover, researchers have found that different brain regions are activated when participants view faces of members of ingroups to which they have been arbitrarily assigned as opposed to equally arbitrarily assigned outgroup members (Van Bavel, Packer, & Cunningham, 2008). However, although this sort of allegiance can spontaneously appear to ingroups created from random characteristics, it also needs to be said that specific types of categories—for example, race, religion, or nationality—are much more likely to result in ingroup bias or show bias in a more virulent form (Lewis & Bates, 2010).

Ingroup bias would not be so bad if it consisted only of favoritism and loyalty toward one's ingroup. Unfortunately, it often (but not always) also leads to prejudice against outgroups. People may be more suspicious of members of the outgroup, consider them more potentially dangerous, disparage them in relation to members of one's ingroup, and view them as "all alike"—in contrast to members of one's ingroup, who are perceived as varied in their characteristics (Ostrom & Sedikides, 1992; Quillian & Pager, 2001). Unfortunately, "all alike" often refers to negative characteristics rather than positive attributes.

"Sorry, we're all cat people. The dog people are in that boat over there."

▲ **Ingroup Bias.** Ingroup bias is a universal tendency to favor members of one's own group over others. Ingroup bias does not always lead to negative attitudes toward outgroups, but it often does.

One of the most famous demonstrations of automatic ingroup bias and prejudice against outgroups was conducted during the mid-1950s by Muzafer and Carolyn Sherif and their colleagues at a summer camp in Robbers Cave State Park in Oklahoma (Sherif, 1966). In the Robbers Cave experiment, the campers (all 11-year-old boys) were randomly assigned to two groups and allowed to give names to their groups ("Eagles" and "Rattlers"). At first the groups were kept entirely separate—indeed, neither group knew of the other's existence. After the members of each group had spent some time creating ingroup relationships and spontaneously developing hierarchies, the groups were introduced to one another and taken through a series of competitive games. During this time they developed extremely intense group rivalries that went over the line of competitive spirit and into the realm of abusive mischief (destruction of property, cruel taunting, fighting, etc.).

However, Sherif and his colleagues were interested in seeing if these negative manifestations of ingroup bias could be reduced by setting up situations in which the two groups had to cooperate. At first, they simply brought the groups together for friendly activities—Fourth of July celebration, the showing of a film, and so forth. Such activities did little to reduce the group rivalries. Only when the groups had to cooperate to achieve *important* common goals—such as discovering the reason for the failure of the camp's water supply to deliver water—was rivalry was reduced substantially. The groups eventually ended up in a friendly relationship.

DEHUMANIZATION OF THE OUTGROUP

Ingroup bias may have consequences that go beyond simple prejudice and institutional racism (see Figure 15.7). Consider some of the more severe expressions of human aggression often termed *evil* in a moral or religious context: genocide, torture, rape, wars of aggression, and the slaughter of innocents. Some of this behavior can seem not merely horrifying but literally incomprehensible (Pinker, 2011). How can human beings treat one another in this manner?

One part of the puzzle may include *dehumanization* of the outgroup. Dehumanization has no accepted definition in psychological science, but it may be useful in helping to understand extreme violence and aggression against outgroups. It refers to one human being viewing another as less than human in some way—as a beast or animal. African Americans were legally considered less than human (legally two-thirds of a human being, to be exact) throughout much of early American history, and this view was used to justify their enslavement. Hitler portrayed the Jewish people as less than human to justify genocide against them.

How does dehumanization occur? This is no doubt a complex process that includes socioeconomic as well as psychological variables. However, one factor that appears to be present frequently when dehumanization occurs is the emotion of *disgust* at the outgroup. In Chapter 11 we briefly mentioned disgust as one of the basic human emotions. Disgust likely evolved to help protect human beings from disease-causing organisms present in feces, rotting food, and other such organic products that universally evoke disgust (Oaten, Stevenson, & Case, 2009; Rozin, Haidt, & McCauley, 1999, 2009).

However, according to psychologist Paul Rozin, disgust has evolved in human culture over the centuries to include objects that threaten not the health of the body but the *purity of the soul.* We are therefore disgusted at things that remind us of our animal nature and the fragility of our mortality—festering wounds, amputations, and so forth. Because humans often view other animals as lower forms of life bereft of souls, being reminded of our animal nature may cause us to feel debased, dirty, or polluted. This serves as a threat to the purity of our souls (Rozin et al., 1999, 2009).

According to Rozin and his colleagues, disgust has strayed even farther from its origins to include moral and social disgust. Depending on the culture or the individual, acts such as abuse of the helpless (children, elderly, animals), murder, rape, genocide, mutilation of corpses, corporate greed, and the notion of human cloning may be considered just as disgusting as rotting meat. Such acts violate the spiritual integrity of the human being, rather than the bodily integrity—they are harmful to the soul. We respond to them with revulsion, just as we do to bodily wounds and deformities.

The connection between morality and disgust has been demonstrated empirically. Researchers have shown that people are more likely to be charitable in a clean-scented room than in a neutral- or unpleasant-smelling one, are more likely to make harsh moral judgments when exposed to foul odors, and are more likely to express moral disgust after drinking a noxious liquid (Eskine, Kacinik, & Prinz, 2011; Liljinquist, Zhong, & Galinsky, 2010; Schnall, Haidt, Haidt, Clore, & Jordan, 2008).

In general, this expansion of disgust into the moral arena may serve an important socialization function, helping to enforce standards of morality. However, disgust for despised outgroups and individuals has been used as a weapon throughout history, when people assign to despised groups the characteristics associated with ordinarily disgusting objects—for example, filth, odor, sliminess, and decay (Nussbaum, 2001). The characterization of certain groups as disgusting is one step toward their dehumanization and the legitimizing of genocide (Bloom, 2004).

But why describe a despised group as disgusting rather than merely dangerous? According to Bloom (2004), it is because disgust originated as a response to bodies, not souls—it is fundamentally a bodily emotion. If a person is characterized as a body only, without a soul, that person lacks moral worth; we are not obligated to extend empathy and compassion to that person. Throughout history, many despots, propagandists, and warmongers have understood that disgust can be used to get people to commit horrendous atrocities by "robbing" the victims of their souls in the minds of the perpetrators.

INGROUP BIAS BEGINS EARLY

Most people assume that ingroup biases and prejudice against outgroups are learned in childhood from adults. But how true is this? Racial and ethnic ingroup bias and prejudice against people of other races has been documented in children as young as age 4 (Bar-Haim, Ziv, Lamy, & Hodes, 2006). And researchers such as David Kelly and Yair Bar-Haim have found that infants as young as 3 months already show a preference for gazing at faces of members of their own racial/ethnic group, and are better able to recognize same-race faces (Bar-Haim et al., 2006; Kelly et al., 2007).

However, *newborn* infants show no preference whatever for same-race faces, and if the infant is continually exposed to people of different racial/ethnic groups during the first months of life, preference and better recognition for same-race faces never develops at all (Bar-Haim et al., 2006; Kelly et al., 2005). This finding may have important implications because, under certain circumstances, adult racial prejudice can be diminished or eliminated through contact with members of racial/ethnic outgroups. We will explore these circumstances later in the chapter.

Prejudice Can Be Subtle and Unconscious

Most research and ordinary experience—including the election of Barack Obama as U.S. president—shows that the kind of blatant forms of prejudice against groups such as women, Jews, gays and lesbians, African Americans, Latinos, and Asians has receded in intensity in the United States over the past half-century (Schuman, Steeh, Bobo, & Kyrsan, 1997; Sniderman & Carmines, 1997). And, as we have seen, stereotypes about previously stigmatized groups have become more favorable. However, blatant prejudice often has been replaced by more subtle, and sometimes entirely unintended and unconscious, forms of moderate bias (Fiske, 2004; Nosek, Greenwald, & Banajji, 2007).

For example, even people who do not consider themselves prejudiced, and who do not endorse stereotypically negative ideas about a group, may display automatic, unconscious bias known as **implicit prejudice** (Greenwald & Nosek, 2001; Greenwald, Oaks, & Hoffman, 2003). Studies using the *implicit association test* (IAT) show that some people have greater difficulty rapidly associating positive words and concepts with images flashed briefly on a screen of people from specific racial/ethnic groups, genders, and ages—while negative words and concepts are more easily associated with these images (Greenwald & Nosek, 2001; Nosek et al., 2007). For example, in one version of the test, the participant is faced with a computer screen and two buttons, one marked "White or pleasant" and the other marked "Black or unpleasant." A series of images are flashed on the screen of faces of African Americans, European Americans, pleasant words, and unpleasant words. If the image is of either an unpleasant word or an African American face, the participant presses the button "Black or unpleasant." If the image is of a pleasant word or a European American face, the other button is pressed. The time it takes for the person to make a judgment and press a button is recorded. The task is then reversed, with the buttons marked "White or unpleasant" and "Black or pleasant." Again, the length of time it takes for participants to make their judgments is recorded. If, on average, it takes longer to press the "Black or pleasant," than the "White or pleasant" button—and a shorter time to press the "Black or unpleasant" than the "White or unpleasant" button—the participant is presumed to be biased against African Americans.

Although implicit psychology—mental activity that occurs below a person's level of awareness—is certainly a reality, and results of research using the IAT are interesting and provocative, critics have challenged the validity of tests such as the IAT and their applicability to real-world situations (Arkes & Tetlock, 2004; Gawronski, 2009; Gawronski, LeBel, & Peters, 2007). Some claims for the applicability and accuracy of the IAT are exaggerated, and it has been shown experimentally that a person can fake responses on the IAT, at least to some degree, and remain undetected (Fiedler & Bluemke, 2005; Gawronski, 2009).

It may seem difficult to prevent implicit prejudice since people are, by definition, not conscious of it. But when individuals have been made aware of it and are highly motivated to rid themselves of it, they are able to do so, at least to an extent (Maddux, Barden, Brewer, & Petty, 2005; Peruche & Plant, 2006). Implicit bias can also be reduced in people who have been exposed to various social influences, such as the presence of an admired member of the outgroup (Lowery, Hardin, & Sinclair, 2001). Thus, generally low levels of conscious prejudice and high motivation to remain unprejudiced may have profoundly positive effects on unconscious, implicit bias as well (Fiske, 2004).

Implicit prejudice ▶
Automatic, unconscious bias against a group. Implicit prejudice tends to be subtle and often exists even in people who do not consider themselves prejudiced.

Prejudice in the Face of Terror and Death

Human beings are unique among animals in their ability to be self-reflective and think symbolically. Among other things, this ability allows us to be aware of the awesome grandeur of being alive. Unfortunately, it also allows us to experience terror and dread in the knowledge that our lives will one day come to an end. According to terror management theory, which was briefly described in Chapter 12, this *existential dilemma*—a problem rooted in the basic facts of human existence—has implications for understanding prejudice and intergroup conflict and violence. **Terror management theory** (**TMT**) proposes that much human behavior is motivated by a need to "manage" or reduce the terror that results from awareness of our eventual death. According to TMT, human beings accomplish terror management in two ways: (a) by strengthening beliefs in their worldview and cultural values, and (b) by increasing feelings of self-esteem. Thus, increasing beliefs that one is a "valuable member of a meaningful universe" is the human way of transcending and defeating death by elevating oneself above simple existence through one's personal accomplishments and adherence to a coherent worldview (Burke, Martens, & Faucher, 2010; Greenberg, 2008; Pyszczynski et al., 2004; Solomon, Greenberg, & Pyszczynski, 2000, p. 201).

However, a problem arises when we encounter people with cultural values different from our own. According to terror management theory, the mere existence of different worldviews and cultural values constitutes a challenge to the absolute validity of our own—and hence, a challenge to the management of terror. To regain self-esteem and reassert belief in one's cultural values, people often resort to putting others down (ingroup bias and prejudice), attempting to force others to change (the missionary strategy), or wiping them out entirely through war and genocide—the "ultimate solution" to terror management (Hayes, Schimel, & Williams, 2008).

Obedience to Authority

When Nazi war criminal Adolf Eichmann was tried for his crimes before an Israeli court in 1961 he insisted in his defense—as had numerous Nazis before him during the Nuremberg tribunals of the late 1940s—that he was "only following orders." According to him, although he knowingly deported many millions of Jews to death camps, he was not responsible for their deaths. If anyone was responsible, it was the higher-ups who gave Eichmann his orders. As described in the "Freeze Frame" feature that began this chapter, the specter of evil perpetrated in the name of obedience to authority motivated Stanley Milgram to conduct his studies of obedience to authority (Milgram, 1963, 1974).

If you recall from Chapter 1, Milgram found that a dismaying percentage of individuals—up to 65% in some of the studies—were willing to administer what they believed to be highly dangerous levels of shocks to an innocent person when instructed to do so by a person in authority as part of a supposed experiment in the psychology of learning. The participants were willing to administer these shocks in spite of their own stated moral discomfort—a discomfort communicated in clear expressions of distress.

WHAT DO THE MILGRAM FINDINGS MEAN?

Much can be—and has been—said and argued about the Milgram studies. The ethics of the studies and the reasons for the high rates of obedience Milgram found have been debated for more than 50 years. However, we should now confront the question of how much of the violence and aggression in intergroup conflict is attributable to obedience to authority. Can ordinary people be made to commit atrocities merely because they are instructed to do so by persons in positions of authority? This certainly has been the lesson most commentators have drawn from the Milgram studies (Blass, 1999). Milgram himself suggested that if death camps like those seen in Nazi Germany were set up in the United

▲ **Genocide: The Ultimate Solution in Terror Management?** In 1994, between 500,000 and 1 million Rwandan Tutsi were slaughtered by extremist elements from the Hutu majority. According to terror management theory, war and genocide—apart from their economic and political aspects—are extreme "solutions" to the psychological problem of terror in the face of one's own inevitable death.

Terror management theory (TMT) ▶ An existential psychological theory that proposes that much human behavior is motivated by a need to manage or reduce the terror.

States, "one would be able to find sufficient personnel for those camps in any medium-sized American town" (cited by Blass, 1999, pp. 955–956).

However, some critics have argued that participants in Milgram's study, rather than blindly following the orders of someone *in* authority (the experimenter), may simply have trusted that the experimenter, in the original studies purportedly a Yale University professor, was *an* authority—in other words, an *expert*.[3] The Milgram participants may have believed his claims that the "learner" would not be seriously harmed (Mixon, 1976; Morelli, 1983).

Perhaps more important, although it is tempting to draw parallels between the behavior of the participants in Milgram's studies and that of wartime criminals and perpetrators of genocide, to some degree these parallels rely primarily on the drama inherent in the Milgram studies and less on an accurate reading of history (Darley, 1995, Mastroianni, 2002; Waller, 2007). Specifically, James Waller (2007, pp. 111–112) points out four primary ways in which the conditions of the Milgram studies do not correspond to the actualities of mass killing and genocide:

1. The participants in the Milgram studies were assured by a strict but nonetheless apparently benevolent expert that no real harm would befall the "learner." The reverse is generally the case in genocide and mass killing. Perpetrators are well aware that they are destroying human life at the behest of a person bent on torturing, maiming, and killing.

2. Milgram found that if participants were given an excuse to avoid obeying the experimenter (e.g., if the experimenter left the room), they would generally avoid administering shocks. Thus, Milgram's participants apparently did not want to cause pain to the "learner." Unfortunately, this cannot be said for those who perpetrate genocide and mass killing. For example, while certain individuals carrying out orders to kill and torture Jews during the Nazi holocaust did avoid doing so when the opportunity presented itself, a shocking number enthusiastically committed these atrocities even when conditions would have allowed disobedience to occur. Indeed, for certain of the so-called "Jew hunts" that occurred late in the war, "there were so many volunteers that some of them had to be turned away" (Browning, cited by Mastroianni, 2002, p. 167; Goldenhagen, 1996).

3. Milgram's participants demonstrated serious mental conflict sometimes approaching real anguish when delivering the shocks. This contrasts with the outright sadism and enjoyment of killing and torturing that are often (but, of course, not always) demonstrated by perpetrators of genocide and wartime atrocities.

4. The Milgram studies lasted approximately 1 hour, whereas acts of genocide and wartime atrocity occur time and again, sometimes lasting over a period of years. Thus, Milgram's participants had little time to reflect on their situation, whereas those perpetrating genocide and atrocity often have months or years.

To some degree, Milgram was aware of the limits of comparing his findings with conditions of actual genocide. He raised the question, "Is the obedience observed in the laboratory comparable to that seen in Nazi Germany?" and answered, "Is a match flame comparable to the Chicago fire of 1898?" (Milgram, 1974, p. 175).[4] Nonetheless, in spite of their limitations, the Milgram studies have shown clearly that individuals are willing to inflict severe, potentially dangerous pain on complete strangers at the request of an expert or authority figure (Waller, 2007).

---

[3]*In the days of the Milgram studies, a university professor—particularly at a school such as Yale University—was likely to be accorded a degree of unquestioned respect greater than that which exists today.*
[4]*Mastroianni (2002) corrects Milgram's date—the fire was in 1871.*

AT THE FOREFRONT

"Ultimate" Aggression: What Motivates a Suicide Terrorist?

Suicide terrorism is the act of intentionally taking one's own life in order to commit violence against public (usually civilian) targets. Although these sorts of attacks have existed throughout recorded history (Atran, 2003; Sprinzak, 2000), there has been an extraordinary increase in suicide terrorism since the 1990s, and some terrorist organizations have come to rely on these actions to achieve their objectives (Pape, 2005). In a sense, suicide terrorism is a kind of "ultimate" aggressive act because the intention is to harm not only others, but oneself as well. Because suicide terrorists are highly motivated to die, not to survive, their motivations remain a puzzle to most people.

Common stereotypes of suicide bombers paint a portrait of psychologically disturbed and cowardly individuals. They are usually described as fanatics who emerge in ignorance from cultures of poverty and desperation. However, suicide terrorists are at least as likely—and often *more* likely—to come from educated and economically secure segments of the populations of the countries of their origin. Most are neither ignorant nor impoverished (A. B. Krueger & Maleckova, 2003). Furthermore, there is no evidence to suggest that suicide terrorists are suffering from psychological disorder (Atran, 2003). They do not exhibit socially dysfunctional behavior, such as chronic unemployment or social isolation, nor do they display suicidal tendencies. They do not appear to suffer from depression, hopelessness, or an attitude that they have nothing to lose (Atran, 2003; Hassan, 2001; Townsend, 2007). And, contrary to public perceptions, they are not necessarily motivated by religious fanaticism (Capell & Sahliyeh, 2007; Kassim, 2008). Even among Islamic groups, about one-third of attacks are carried out by secular Islamists (Pape, 2005).

In all, apart from tending to be young, unattached, and generally male, suicide terrorists seem largely indistinguishable from others in their general demographic group. While it may appear to many that "a person has to be crazy" to do something like blow himself or herself up to kill other people, this may not strictly be the case. How, then, does an "ordinary," educated young person with social opportunities for personal advancement come to be motivated to take his or her own life while committing political mass murder?

Interestingly, given the lack of common psychological factors among suicide terrorists, attempts to answer this question purely from a psychological perspective—for example, by trying to formulate psychological profiles of a typical suicide bomber—seem likely to fail (Grimland, Apter, & Kerkhof, 2006; Kruglanski, Chen, Deschesne, Fishman, & Orehek, 2009). Numerous theorists working in the field of suicide terrorism suggest instead that suicide terrorism needs to be understood from a broad perspective that includes political as well as psychological, social, religious, experiential, and ideological factors (Atran, 2003; M. Bloom, 2005; Hassan, 2001; Pape, 2005; Schumm et al., 2006; Sprinzak, 2000).

For example, many of these researchers emphasize the need to understand nationalistic responses to foreign occupation, and to examine the organizations that recruit and sponsor suicide terrorism—with particular focus on the leaders of these organizations, who themselves would never consider committing suicide for their cause. Small groups of recruits address one another as "brother" and are strongly encouraged to think of one another as family. Eventually, "family commitment" becomes so strong that the recruit is willing to make a (videotaped) contract to die. As Scott Atran reports, recruits believe that by sacrificing themselves they will help secure the future of their spiritual "family" as well as advance the interests of their own genetic families. This idea is stated explicitly in terrorist propaganda: "Each [martyr] has a special place—among them are brothers, just as there are sons and those even more dear" (Atran, 2003, p. 1537).

These sorts of tactics as used on recruits are enormously powerful. According to Atran's evolutionary perspective, they may trigger evolved psychological mechanisms designed to "override" rational considerations of self-interest or even survival. This may be possible because throughout evolutionary history, under certain circumstances some individuals' own reproductive success—the survival of their DNA—may have been enhanced through the sacrifice of their lives if such sacrifice greatly benefited the survival of their genetic kin.

However, the power of charismatic leaders and rigid organizational control seems inadequate to explain suicide terrorism in all its complexity (Kruglanski et al., 2009). Arie Kruglanski and his colleagues take a different approach and propose that all the "dots" of the suicide terrorism puzzle—ideological causes, religious feeling, experiences of trauma and humiliation at the hands of occupational forces, rigid organizational structure headed by charismatic leaders—can be "connected" with the psychological notion of *significance quest* as the underlying motive for suicide terrorism. According to this idea, all human beings strive to live a life that goes beyond gratification of the self; a life that has personal significance and meaning and that allows each individual to avoid "the nightmare of ending up as 'a speck of insignificant dust in an uncaring universe'" (Kruglanski et al., 2009, p. 335). Under certain circumstances, this *quest for significance* motivates individuals to perform "supreme" acts of "goodness" from the perspective of their society—in this case, the "brotherhood" of terrorists or occupied peoples under severe threat (Kruglanski et al., 2009, p. 335).

For suicide terrorists, their acts place them in the group of the "exalted elite" of immortal martyrs. There is an almost god-like status connected to the supreme status of suicide bomber among groups that recruit such individuals. This contrasts sharply with what may have otherwise been lives of disappointment and insignificance, regardless of income or education (p. 335). Thus, according to Kruglanski and his colleagues, the paradox of suicidal terrorism is "the willingness to die in an act . . . motivated by the desire to live forever" (Kruglanski et al., 2009, p. 336) ■

▲ **Understanding Suicide Bombing.** An Afghan family walks together as British soldiers and the Afghan National Police secure the site of a suicide bomb blast. The attack, which killed seven and wounded more than 50, took place on a major road leading out of Kabul 2 days ahead of Afghanistan's presidential elections in 2009. Most experts in suicide terrorism agree that suicide bombing cannot be understood simply in psychological terms but must also include political and social factors.

Intergroup Contact: Reducing Prejudice in Jittery Times

Researchers have struggled for decades with the important problem of reducing prejudice. Indeed, few topics have generated as much research and writing as the topic of prejudice (Paluck & Green, 2009). As this book attests, the field of psychology—unlike "hard" sciences such as chemistry and physics—is characterized by ideas that sometimes become obsolete before the ink is dry. However, in 1954, Gordon Allport created a theory of how prejudice can be diminished that has stood the test of time. A half-century later, only minor alterations have been made to his basic idea (Pettigrew, 1998; Pettigrew & Tropp, 2006). According to Allport's **intergroup contact theory**, prejudice is diminished when positive, constructive contact occurs between members of different groups. What are the contexts under which constructive contact is experienced? Allport hypothesized four features of constructive intergroup contact:

1. *Equal status.* There should be equal status between the two groups in the setting in which contact occurs. For example, prejudice was not typically reduced from contacts between European Americans and African

Intergroup contact theory
▶ Gordon Allport's theory describing the ways in which constructive group contact can diminish prejudice.

Americans under conditions of slavery or workplaces where blacks carried out menial tasks while whites were managers and owners.

2. *Common goals.* Contact should also occur under conditions characterized by common goals between groups. Modern, integrated sports teams are a prime example of intergroup settings characterized by common goals.

3. *Intergroup cooperation.* These common goals must be attained through intergroup cooperation. In the Robbers Cave experiment, Sherif (1966) demonstrated that children who had been manipulated into thinking of one another as belonging either to the ingroup or to the outgroup—and who reacted in a hostile manner to members of the outgroup—could learn to consider outgroup members favorably under conditions of cooperation to achieve common goals.

4. *Formalized social support.* Intergroup contact should occur under conditions supported by law or custom, or be otherwise socially formalized. Thus, contact occurring between prison cellmates cooperating for the common goal of escape is not necessarily likely to lead to reduced prejudice.

Although the four contexts leading to reduced prejudice through contact are important, it is not always necessary to have them all. There are numerous conditions under which intergroup contact leads to reduced prejudice and ingroup bias even when one or more of these criteria is not met (Pettigrew & Tropp, 2006). One of these is the existence of genuine *friendship*—characterized by close social contact, intimacy, and positive emotions. Moreover, when two people of the same sex (but different ethnicity) interact, there is a tendency for the outcome to be better than in the other-sex interactions (Toosi, Babbitt, Ambady, & Sommers, 2011).

One interesting test of the contact hypothesis was carried out among college dormitory roommates. Noting that rooming together as college freshmen fulfilled all four of the conditions Allport identified, researches randomly assigned college freshmen to share a room with a roommate of their own or another race (Shook & Fazio, 2009). What were the results? In fact the researchers did find that, in the interracial roommate pairs, negative racial attitudes and anxiety existed but decreased over time as the roommates came to know one another. On the other hand, the participants deemed these interracial roommate friendships less satisfying than those they experienced in same-race pairings.

In any case, evidence collected over the past 40 years paints a generally positive picture of changes in the way different ethnic groups relate to one another in the United States. As contact between individuals of different groups increases—and it has—the outcomes of these interactions have become generally more positive (Toosi et al., 2011). Intergroup contact is not a quick fix to prejudice. Undoubtedly, numerous factors continue to stand in the way of full intergroup acceptance. Nonetheless, the news from the social and behavioral sciences seems better than one might have expected.

Lessons of Abu Ghraib

It would be a serious error to "over-psychologize" intergroup conflict, focusing too much on prejudices and biases, be they rational or irrational, and ignoring the fact that intergroup conflict and aggression often occur as a result of real group conflicts of interest based in socioeconomic or political realities. The sociopolitical histories and situations of groups in conflict need to be evaluated alongside cognitive and emotional aspects of prejudice (Okami, 1992). The principal theory of intergroup conflict which stresses the idea that conflict may have origins in socioeconomic realities is known as *realistic group conflict theory* (Campbell, 1965; J. W. Jackson, 1993; King, Knight, & Hebl, 2010; Sherif & Sherif, 1966).

This leads us full circle, back to the case of the abuses of Iraqi prisoners by U.S. forces at Abu Ghraib prison described in the "Freeze Frame" feature at the beginning of Chapter 1 of this book. At that time we asked, "How did this happen?" The social psychological principles we have examined in the preceding pages may shed some light. Susan Fiske, Lasana Harris, and Amy Cuddy (2004) claim that ordinary social processes—not extraordinary individual evil—created Abu Ghraib (see also Zimbardo, 2007). What are these processes?

▲ **The Prison at Abu Ghraib, Renamed the Central Baghdad Detention Facility.** After the prisoner abuse scandal, the U.S. Army assigned brigades to clean and renovate the infamous prison.

- The soldiers guarding the prisoners had experienced extreme provocation, taunting, and harassment by the citizens they believed they had been sent to "liberate." They saw comrades dying daily and unpredictably (*realistic group conflict*, pp. 764–765).
- The guards encountered the prisoners in their "role" as enemies. This strongly activated *ingroup bias* (pp. 755–759), and the clash of values in a wartime context increased the need for *terror management* (p. 760). All of this resulted in a "hot" form of prejudice (p. 755), including feelings of disgust toward the outgroup, promoting views of the prisoners as less than human, and increasing aggressive feelings and behavior.
- Given an environment supporting aggression and prisoners deemed less than human, *deindividuation* within the *social role* of guard (pp. 747–748), and *conformity* to one's peers through normative influence (pp. 742–744) increased the likelihood of the abusive events at Abu Ghraib.
- The Milgram studies described at the opening of the chapter and on pp. 760–761 show that *obedience to authority* is also part of the social psychology calculus of Abu Ghraib.

However, while the factors cited by Fiske, Harris, and Cuddy are likely critical to an understanding of the events at Abu Ghraib, they are unlikely to explain these events in full. Recall that recent research has suggested that students who volunteer for experiments such as the Stanford prison experiment differ from others in being more aggressive, authoritarian, narcissistic, and dominant. Could it be that at least some of the guards at Abu Ghraib were different from ordinary soldiers—that "bad apples" were present—even if the barrel itself was also rotten?

As Thomas Carnahan and Sam McFarland (2007) point out, the Abu Ghraib guards most heavily involved with abuse of prisoners had volunteered for their duties, some of them having cited prior experience in the corrections industry to bolster their application. As it turns out, at least one of these soldiers already had a record of abusiveness and had been fired from a job in corrections as a result. One of the women pictured in the photographs of the abuse spent "many of her nights" at the prison block in spite of not being assigned there and having already been disciplined for not being where she was supposed to be at those times (Zernike, cited by Carnahan & McFarland, 2007, p. 612). Thus, a complete account of the events at Abu Ghraib may need to include the person in the situation.

Considering this interplay of person and situation and the tendency of various theorists to stress one or the other in trying to explain human mental life and behavior, we can look back over all the material discussed in this book and see a pattern: Human life is enormously complex; so much so that single variables on their own seldom explain very much. Yet psychologists are often preoccupied with examining single variables. This is the way of science. Large portraits are painted in small segments. Only rarely are grand discoveries made by single individuals. It is only when all of the work of the hard-working scientists engaged in psychological science is considered together that pictures of real human beings begin to form.

IN SUMMARY

1. Stereotyping is an important aspect of human cognition, and some group stereotypes hold a degree of accuracy. However, stereotypes are also frequently inappropriately applied to groups or individuals from groups.

2. Ingroup bias is the tendency to favor and show loyalty to one's group over others. Ingroup bias appears to be triggered automatically, as soon as a group identity is created. People who do not consider themselves prejudiced may display subtle forms of bias known as implicit prejudice.

3. Terror management theory proposes that prejudice is one way that people manage the existential problem created by their awareness of the inevitability of their own death.

4. Many parallels have been drawn over the years between the Milgram obedience studies and the fact that seemingly ordinary people may commit monstrous acts during war or genocidal conflict when ordered to do so. However, these parallels sometimes ignore the many ways the conditions of obedience to authority in the Milgram studies differ dramatically from those in war or genocide.

5. Social psychological principles focusing on the effect of situations on the individual go a long way toward explaining the events of Abu Ghraib, but it is likely that personal characteristics need to be included for a more complete account.

RETRIEVE!

1. True or false: In the model of stereotyping proposed by Susan Fiske and Amy Cuddy, the two dimensions along which people stereotype groups of others are warmth and competence.

2. True or false: Newborn infants show a preference for own-race faces and better recognize faces of members of their own racial group.

3. Some critics have suggested that the behavior of Milgram's research participants may not have been due to their blindly obeying an authority figure. What is at least one other explanation for their behavior? Name at least two ways that the conditions of the Milgram studies differed from that of real-life mass-killing in wartime or genocide.

4. Why would encountering a person with different cultural values threaten a person's management of terror in the face of ultimate certain death?

5. What are the four factors Gordon Allport identified that promote a reduction of prejudice due to intergroup contact?

Looking Back

Chapter 15 in Review

WHAT IS PSYCHOLOGICAL SELF-DEFENSE?

- Social psychology is the study of the influence of social situations on the individual and vice versa. Social psychologists examine the individual alone, in dyads, small and large groups, and entire societies.

- The self-serving bias is the tendency to make judgment errors in your own favor: overestimating your own contributions and attributes, crediting success to your own efforts or qualities, and blaming bad deeds and failures on circumstances. Positive illusions present the self to itself in a positive but

Looking Back continued

unrealistic way and also have positive consequences.

- Social comparison theory explores the ways that people compare themselves to others. People often make comparisons only with people similar to them, and primarily for self-evaluative purposes. However, people may also compare themselves to *dis*similar others—particularly downward comparisons—to self-enhance.
- Cognitive dissonance is an anxious or tense state brought about when people realize that their behavior contradicts their firmly held attitudes. In order for this tension to resolve, either the attitude has to change, the behavior has to cease, or beliefs about the discrepancy have to change.
- If negative self-judgments continue over a prolonged period, the self may engage in the difficult work of change. By the time most people reach adulthood, they have made an attempt to change something about themselves. However, many of these attempts fail. In the false hope syndrome, a person repeatedly attempts to accomplish goals that are unrealistic or even impossible.

HOW DO WE PRESENT OURSELVES TO OTHERS?

- Unconsciously monitoring and attempting to control how we appear to other people is known as impression management. The spotlight effect is an egocentric judgment in which people believe that other people are paying more attention to them than is the case. Much self-presentation occurs through computer-mediated communication (CMC). Most research supports the view that CMC has generally (but not exclusively) positive benefits, particularly if it stimulates online self-disclosure—an important component of intimacy.

HOW DO WE EXPLAIN OUR OWN AND OTHERS' BEHAVIOR?

- Attribution theory explores the process by which people explain their or others' behavior in terms of causes that refer to characteristics of the person (*dispositional cause*),

the situation (*situational cause*), or an interaction between the two; and which also may refer to whether the behavior is intentional or unintentional. The fundamental attribution error (FAE) is the tendency to attribute others' behavior to their (internal) dispositions, while ignoring the possibility that situational (external) factors may have played an important role.

- The actor-observer bias occurs primarily when one makes situational explanations for one's own (generally negative) behavior instead of considering dispositional factors. Social psychologists suggest that this occurs because we are aware of the many ways circumstances will alter our behavior, and often not as aware that this may also be true of others.

WHO ATTRACTS WHOM?

- The tendency to become attracted to others who are similar to oneself is known by biologists as positive assortment and by social psychologists as the matching phenomenon. People are highly likely to positively assort when they mate, and positively assorted pairings are happier, more stable, have fewer infidelities and divorces, and result in more children raised to maturity. The mere exposure effect is the tendency to appreciate something more, merely as a result of being repeatedly exposed to it.
- Beauty is not entirely in the eye of the beholder. Although there are cultural differences in preferred clothing or adornments, facial scarring or distortion, and body weight (but not shape), there are universal standards for specific facial features and body shape. General cues to male and female facial attractiveness include age, symmetry, averageness, and exaggerated femininity and masculinity.

HOW DO OTHER PEOPLE AFFECT OUR OPINIONS AND BEHAVIOR?

- Conformity may be motivated by informational or normative concerns, or by the desire to maintain self-concept by protecting feelings of self-esteem. Informational

motivations are based on a rational desire to seek realistic information about a situation. Normative motives reflect the desire to obtain approval from the group. Groupthink is a particularly dangerous type of conformity behavior that is sometimes partly responsible for disastrous governmental decisions.

- The bystander effect is the tendency of people to be less likely to help strangers in need if other people are present at the scene. Research into the bystander effect was stimulated by the Kitty Genovese sexual assault and murder case.
- Deindividuation is a lessening of self-awareness or identity when in a group, leading to reduced concern with how your behavior will be evaluated by others. Research on deindividuation was initiated following surprising results of Zimbardo's prison experiment.
- Altruism is the offering of assistance to others without the expectation of immediate reward. It is part of a larger group of behaviors termed *prosocial*, because they may promote the well-being of society. There are two classes of explanations for altruism: proximate causes and ultimate causes. Proximate explanations include empathy, activity of mirror neurons, and egoism. Ultimate explanations include the theories of inclusive fitness and reciprocal altruism.

HOW DOES INTERGROUP CONFLICT LEAD TO AGGRESSION?

- Stereotyping is an intrinsic property of the human mind, but it can lead to prejudice. Since the early 20th century, group stereotypes have become more widespread but less negative. Stereotyping exists along two dimensions: competence and warmth.
- Ingroup bias, the tendency to favor one's own group over others, frequently also involves prejudice against or dehumanization of members of the outgroup. One factor that is present frequently when dehumanization occurs is the emotion of disgust.
- Implicit prejudice is prejudice that is automatic and unconscious.

Looking Back continued

Terror management theory (TMT) proposes that much human behavior is motivated by a need to "manage" or reduce the terror that results from our awareness that one day we will die. When we encounter people with different cultural values, our management of terror may be challenged. To regain self-esteem and reassert belief in one's cultural values, people resort to putting others down, attempting to force others to change, or wiping them out entirely through war and genocide.

- In the Milgram studies of obedience to authority, a dismaying percentage of individuals were willing to administer supposedly highly dangerous levels of shocks to an innocent person when instructed to do so by a person in authority as part of a purported experiment in the psychology of learning. These studies have been argued about for a half-century. Today, social psychologists continue to look for methods of reducing prejudice and preventing incidents like the demeaning of prisoners in Iraq's Abu Ghraib prison.

Key Terms

Actor-observer bias, 734
Altruism, 748
Attraction, 735
Attribution, 732
Bystander effect, 746
Cognitive dissonance, 723
Conformity, 742
Deindividuation, 747
Empathy, 749
False hope syndrome, 726
Fundamental Attribution Error (FAE), 732
Genocide, 754

Groupthink, 744
Implicit prejudice, 759
Impression management, 728
Ingroup bias, 756
Intergroup conflict, 754
Intergroup contact theory, 763
Mere exposure effect, 736
Positive assortment, 736
Positive illusions, 721
Prejudice, 755
Proximate causes, 749
Self, 719
Self-control, 724

Self-regulation, 724
Self-serving bias, 720
Social comparison theory, 722
Social psychology, 719
Spotlight effect, 731
Stereotyping, 754
Suicide terrorism, 762
Terror management theory (TMT), 760
Theory of inclusive fitness, 751
Theory of reciprocal altruism, 752
Ultimate causes, 749

Test Yourself

1. Quite a number of social psychological effects and biases were described in this chapter. Match each of the following with its description. (Important note: The list does NOT include *every* type

Fundamental attribution error	The tendency to make judgment errors in your own favor. Comes in three types.
Deindividuation	Uncritically positive views of the self, illusions of control, and unrealistic optimism
Self-serving bias	An uncomfortable tension a person may feel if their freely chosen behavior contradicts their attitude
Mere exposure effect	A person may egocentrically overestimate the degree to which he or she is the focus of other people's attention.
Positive illusions	"Mistaking the situation for the person"
Groupthink	"Mistaking the person for the situation"
Spotlight effect	Being attracted to someone similar to yourself
Positive assortment	Finding something attractive or appealing simply because you have been exposed to it previously
Actor-observer bias	Counterproductive group decisions are made because group members are afraid to appear disloyal to the leader or do not want to adversely affect group morale.
Cognitive dissonance	A lessening of self-awareness or identity when in a group, leading to reduced concern for how your behavior will be evaluated by others

Test Yourself continued

2. Which of the following is NOT a component of the self-serving bias?
   a) overestimating one's contributions
   b) overestimating one's positive attributes
   c) overestimating one's chances of success
   d) attributing successes to one's own efforts or characteristics, and failures to bad luck or other people

3. Name the three categories of positive illusions.

4. What are the two basic categories of motives for making social comparisons?

5. When a person's behavior conflicts with his or her attitudes, anxiety or tension may arise. What is the name that social psychologists give to this condition?
   a) spotlight effect
   b) low-balling
   c) cognitive dissonance
   d) deindividuation

6. What is the difference between an attitude and a belief?

7. Which of the following is NOT among the sorts of unrealistic beliefs about self-improvement change that may lead to the false-hope syndrome?
   a) change will be fast
   b) change will be permanent
   c) change will be easy
   d) the amount of change will be great
   e) the rewards of change will be enormous

8. What are the two processes of impression management?

9. True or false: Most research suggests that relationships created on the Internet are superficial, promote a lack of genuineness, and increase rather than decrease feelings of loneliness.

10. True or false: Research shows that people are much more likely to forgive embarrassing social blunders than the person making the blunder generally supposes.

11. The tendency to attribute other people's behavior to their dispositions while underestimating the possibility that situational factors

played an important role is known as the _____.
   a) actor-observer bias
   b) spotlight effect
   c) fundamental attribution error
   d) mere exposure effect

12. True or False: Critics of the actor-observer bias claim that the bias only appears when a person makes an attribution for his or her own negative behaviors.

13. What is the term used to describe the fact that people come to appreciate almost anything the more times they are exposed to it?

14. What is the social psychological term for what biologists call positive assortment? What is the phenomenon that these terms describe?

15. Which of the following is NOT one of the factors that determine the attractiveness of women's faces cross-culturally?
   a) averageness
   b) shape of features (eyes, nose, mouth)
   c) symmetry
   d) exaggerated femininity

16. Which of the following is NOT among the motivators of conformity behavior as identified by social psychologists?
   a) informational motives
   b) motives to maintain self-concept
   c) normative motives
   d) motives to advance status

17. Which of the following is NOT among the conditions that must be present for a bystander to offer help to a stranger in need?
   a) The event must be interpreted as an emergency.
   b) The stranger must not be from an outgroup.
   c) The bystander must believe that he or she ought to take responsibility.
   d) The bystander actually makes a decision to act.

18. A lessening of a person's self-awareness or identity with a group, leading to reduced concern with how his or her behavior will be evaluated by the group, is known as _____.
   a) groupthink
   b) deindividuation
   c) dehumanization
   d) reverse spotlight effect

19. True or false: In the Stanley Milgram studies of obedience, only a relatively small minority obeyed the "professor" by administering apparently dangerous and painful voltages of electric shock.

20. Which of the following is NOT one of the ways in which the Milgram studies differ in their conditions from actual cases of obedience to authority in mass-killing and genocide?
   a) The participants in the Milgram studies who obeyed were generally those who had histories of aggressive or hostile behavior. In actual war and genocide, ordinary people with no such histories may become involved.
   b) Participants in the Milgram study often displayed anguish, and if given an excuse—e.g., if the "professor" left the room—participants in the Milgram studies often refrained from obeying. Perpetrators of genocide often commit their acts enthusiastically.
   c) Participants in the Milgram study had reason to believe that the "learner" would not be seriously harmed. Perpetrators of genocide know that their victims will be tortured and killed.
   d) The Milgram studies lasted about 1 hour, whereas acts of genocide and wartime atrocity continue often over very long periods of time, sometimes lasting years.

21. What are at least two proximate explanations for human altruism?

22. According to Trivers' theory of reciprocal altruism, what are the conditions that must be present for altruistic motivations toward non-kin to evolve?

23. According to Hamilton's theory of inclusive fitness, why is a person likely to feel more protective and altruistic toward a parent, child, or sibling than a grandparent, uncle, aunt, or cousin?

24. What is the basic premise of terror management theory?

25. What are the four conditions under which intergroup contact is constructive and leads to reduced prejudice, according to Gordon Allport's intergoup contact theory?

Glossary

Abnormal psychology The scientific study of states of mind and behavior which deviate both from the statistical norm (the average) and from what mental health professionals consider to be healthy psychological functioning.

Absentmindedness Lapses of attention that result in a failure to recall information. Absentmindedness can result from a failure to encode properly or lapse of attention/preoccupation at the moment of retrieval.

Absolute threshold The minimum intensity necessary for a stimulus to be detected by the appropriate sense organ at least 50% of the time.

Academic psychology Basic research and teaching for the purpose of advancing knowledge in psychology.

Accommodation Piaget's term for the process whereby a person alters his or her schema to incorporate new information or experiences.

Achievement motivation An aspect of competence motivation which describes the motivation to attain and to accomplish. A person generally measures his or her attainments and accomplishments in relation to those of others, so the achievement motivation involves comparing oneself to others.

Acoustic encoding Memory encoding according to the sound of the stimulus being encoded.

Acquisition In classical conditioning, acquisition is the process of acquiring a conditioned response.

Action potential The electrical impulse that conveys information from one neuron to another, or from the neuron to bodily muscles and glands.

Active gene-environment correlation A correlation between environment and genotype that results from active choices made by an organism.

Actor-observer bias A systematic bias toward attributing your own behavior primarily to situational factors, but others' behavior to dispositional factors.

Adaptations Characteristics of organisms that have evolved over evolutionary time because they confer reproductive or survival advantages. Adaptations arise as a result of small, incremental changes in the genome of organisms over many generations, and they represent solutions to specific challenges and pressures faced recurrently by the organism.

Addiction A term frequently used to describe drug dependence. Originally, the term included withdrawal, tolerance, and craving as necessary components, but currently, addiction has no precise definition.

Adolescence Literally, "becoming adult." Adolescence includes cultural as well as biological dimensions. Adolescence begins at age 10, according to the World Health Organization, but the termination of adolescence is highly dependent on sociocultural factors.

Adrenarche The maturation of the adrenal glands at about age 10.

Aerobic exercise Physical exercise involving large muscle groups which increases oxygen consumption and elevates heart rate.

Affect A general feeling state which provides the "raw material" from which emotions and moods are created. Affect differs along two dimensions: valence (positive-negative) and activation or arousal (high-low).

Affordances A quality of any object (such as a toy) that allows for specific types of experiences.

Agonist Any substance that mimics the action of a neurotransmitter and binds to the neurotransmitter receptor.

Agoraphobia An anxiety disorder characterized by fear of finding oneself in a potentially unsafe location from which escape would be difficult. This commonly includes crowds, public places, movie theaters, cars, and so forth.

Algorithms A step-by-step set of computational instructions to correctly solve a specific type of problem. Algorithms have a specified beginning and ending and can be applied identically to any problem of the type they were designed to solve.

Alkaloids Any compound with drug-like effects found naturally in a plant.

Allele One of two or more forms a particular gene might take. "Genetic differences" among people occur because people inherit unique collections of alleles.

Alpha waves The brain waves that predominate in relaxed, wakeful states while eyes are closed, and in sleep onset.

Altered state of consciousness A temporary but radical change in the overall pattern of a person's normal subjective experience.

Altruism The offering of assistance to others without the expectation of immediate reward.

Alzheimer's disease A neurodegenerative disease characterized by increasingly severe memory loss, confusion, difficulty speaking or comprehending speech, and difficulty with self-care. Alzheimer's disease is the most common type of dementia.

Ambivalence When a person experiences conflicting emotions or motivations—being "of two minds" about something.

American Psychological Association An association founded in 1892 by G. Stanley Hall and others to advance the interests of psychology as a profession and science.

Amphetamines A family of stimulant drugs that exert their effects primarily by increasing levels of norepinephrine, serotonin, and dopamine in the brain.

Amplitude The intensity of a sound or light output source expressed in the height of light or sound waves.

Anal intercourse Insertion of a man's penis in his partner's anus.

Anger A difficult-to-define basic emotion involving feelings of antagonism toward something or someone.

Anorexia nervosa An eating disorder usually characterized by a refusal to maintain normal body weight for one's age and height; intense fear of gaining weight or becoming fat; and a disturbed perception of one's body weight or shape, exaggerated emphasis on body weight or shape when making self-evaluations, or a denial of the seriousness of one's current low body weight. Sometimes one or more of these symptoms is not present, however.

Antagonist Any substance that blocks the receptors of a particular neurotransmitter, decreasing the availability and effects of the neurotransmitter.

Antidepressant Any drug or other substance whose primary purpose is the treatment of depression.

Anxiety An unpleasant feeling of apprehension and worry experienced in anticipation of some sort of threat. Anxiety includes cognitive, emotional, physiological, and behavioral components. Anxiety tends to be *future-oriented*, in that it typically is experienced in response to anticipation of a future threat, rather than in response to an immediate threat, which is the domain of *fear*.

Anxiolytic Any drug or other substance whose primary use is the treatment of anxiety.

Apex dreaming The most intense, bizarre, nonrational, and hallucinatory dreaming.

Appetite A desire to eat. Unlike hunger, which always results from a need for energy or overall nutrition, appetite can result from any number of causes including, but not limited to, hunger. Appetite is highly influenced or even controlled by psychological, social-environmental, or cultural factors.

Applied psychology Use of psychological principles and methods to address the problems of the individual, society, or industry.

Approach-avoidance The distinction between motivations to seek positive experiences and motivations to avoid negative experiences.

Artificial intelligence (AI) Computers or other machines that display intelligent behavior or mimic human thought. The term is also used to refer to the branch of computer science that studies the design of intelligent agents and creates AI computers and machines.

Assimilation Piaget's term to describe the process whereby a person processes a new experience by fitting it into a preexisting schema.

Associative learning Changes in an organism's knowledge or behavior that result from the association of two or more events or stimuli, or of a stimulus and a response. The most common forms of associative learning are classical conditioning, operant conditioning, and vicarious conditioning (observational learning).

Astrology The belief that the position of the stars and planets can affect people's life events or personalities.

Attachment According to attachment theorists, attachment is the special intimate bond that develops between infant and caregiver, generally the mother, beginning when the infant is about 6 months old.

Attraction Factors that draw a person toward another for friendship, sex, romance, or other sort of relationship.

Attribution The process of explaining behavior in terms of characteristics of the person, the situation, or an interaction between the two; or in terms of whether a behavior is intentional or unintentional.

Audition The sense of hearing.

Auditory cortex Portion of the temporal lobe that interprets transduced auditory signals.

Auditory nerve A nerve that conducts transduced auditory signals to the thalamus, to be then relayed to the auditory cortex.

Auditory receptors Hair cells of the inner ear that receive auditory signals.

Authoritarian parents Characterized by imposition of strict rules (the rationales for which are left unexplained to children), expectation of obedience, and severe punishment.

Authoritative parents Characterized by clear rules, fair enforcement, a warm environment, and the use of reason rather than force.

Autonomic nervous system A part of the peripheral nervous system. The autonomic nervous system consists of sympathetic and parasympathetic subsystems that regulate involuntary activities of muscles, glands, and organs.

Availability heuristic A heuristic that biases people toward using mental information that is more easily "accessible" or mentally available. The availability heuristic is used when coming to a judgment about how often something occurs or how likely it is to occur in the future.

Axon A narrow extension in many neurons that transmits electrical neural impulses from cell body to terminal.

Base rate The basic probability of something occurring in a population, expressed as a percentage. Can also be understood as an indication of how prevalent something is in a population.

Baseline body weight Sometimes referred to as weight set point, the baseline body weight is the fairly consistent body weight achieved over time by maintaining an energy balance.

Basic emotion Universal, innate, distinct emotions from which a vast number of other emotions may be derived. Characteristic facial expressions and/or body language are generally associated with basic emotions. Psychologists are not in agreement as to the number of basic emotions, which specific emotions are basic, or even if the concept itself is valid.

Basilar membrane A collection of stiff fibers housed within the cochlear of the inner ear. The basilar membrane contains the hair cells that act as auditory receptors.

Behavior genetics The study of the influence of genes and environments on individual differences in behavior. Behavior geneticists measure the differences in some trait among a sample of people and attempt to quantify the portion of these differences that is due to genes and the portion that is due to environment.

Behavior therapy Techniques of therapy based on learning principles of behaviorism and social learning theory. The point

of behavior therapy is to teach the client how to substitute adaptive patterns of behavior for maladaptive patterns. Behavior therapy techniques utilize classical and operant conditioning strategies (see Chapter 7).

Behavioral neuroscience Branch of neuroscience that studies the neural basis of behavior. Behavioral neuroscientists study the entire nervous system, not just the brain, and they may use non-human as well as human animals for study.

Behaviorism The early movement in psychology founded by John B. Watson, who held that only behavior—not internal mental states—could be studied scientifically. Behaviorists believed that behavior was shaped primarily or entirely by experience.

Belief persistence Once a belief is formed and confirmed, it can be highly resistant to change, even when disconfirming evidence is inescapable.

Benzodiazepine The most common class of anxiolytic drugs.

Beta waves The brain waves that predominate in waking states and are present in REM.

Bias A systematic distortion in perception, cognition, or memory as a result of some aspect of one's current psychology.

Biased sample A sample that is not truly representative of the population from which it was drawn.

Bibliotherapy The practice of using self-help books as adjuncts to psychotherapy or as therapeutic tools in the absence of psychotherapy.

Binocular cues Cues to depth perception that necessitate both eyes—specifically retinal disparity and convergence.

Bisexual (bi) The term used to describe a sexual orientation marked by varying degrees of attraction to both sexes.

Blind In an experiment, when the research participants are unaware of which level of the independent variable they have received and/or are unaware of the nature of the researcher's hypothesis.

Blind spot An area formed by the optic disc that contains neither rods nor cones.

Blocking When a memory has been encoded properly and primed by a retrieval cue yet cannot be retrieved.

Borderline personality disorder (BPD) A controversial Cluster B personality disorder diagnosis describing a person who is impulsive, moody, and frightened of abandonment. BPD sufferers have an unstable sense of self, and are plagued by feelings of emptiness and/or worthlessness. Their relationships tend to be stormy, and they often engage in self-injuring behavior.

Brain waves Characteristic electrical brain activity of various frequencies termed alpha, beta, theta, and delta.

Brightness constancy The facet of perceptual constancy that allows us to perceive an object as the same brightness regardless of the available illumination.

British empiricism A 17th-century philosophical movement which held that the mind had no innate content—personal experience was responsible for the development of all thoughts, beliefs, and knowledge.

Bulimia nervosa An eating disorder usually characterized by recurrent episodes of binge-eating, where there is a sense of lack of control over the quantity of food eaten; behavior designed to compensate for binging, such as purging (forced vomiting), abuse of laxatives, excessive exercise, or fasting; and self-evaluation that is unduly influenced by body shape and weight concerns.

Bystander effect The tendency for a person to be less likely to intervene and offer help to a stranger in an emergency situation when there are other people there who might reasonably be thought able to help. The more people present, the less likely the bystander is to offer aid.

Caffeine A stimulant alkaloid of coffee, tea, chocolate, and certain other plants.

Cannabis Cannabis sativa is the plant from which marijuana, hashish, and THC are derived.

Cannon-Bard theory of emotion The theory proposed by Walter Cannon and Phillip Bard which states that during the perception of an event, sensory impulses are first relayed to the thalamus. From there the impulses are relayed to the autonomic nervous system and the cerebral cortex at about the same time, rather than to the autonomic nervous system first and secondly to the cerebral cortex, as proposed in the James-Lange theory.

Case study A descriptive research method in which the researcher gathers detailed, qualitative information about a single individual.

Catharsis From the Greek word for cleansing, catharsis refers to the relief one may experience by expressing emotion.

Causal effect When a change in one variable causes a change in another.

Cell body (soma) The bulb-like end of the neuron containing the cell nucleus. Energy for the neuron is generated here, and waste is eliminated.

Central nervous system (CNS) The brain and spinal cord. Organizes and interprets the information received from peripheral nervous system (PNS) and sends commands back to the PNS to take actions or make adjustments to bodily functions.

Central pattern generators Circuits of neurons that generate routine, rhythmic movements and are controlled entirely by the spine with no input from the brain.

Cerebellum ("little brain) The second largest structure in the central nervous system, located in the hindbrain. The cerebellum coordinates sensory inputs and affects balance by assisting visual-spatial perception. It is also involved at least to some degree in attention, learning and memory, and appropriate expression of emotion.

Cerebral cortex The outer layers of the hemispheres of the forebrain. Interprets raw sensory information, initiates voluntary movement, and is home to higher cognitive processes.

Cerebral hemispheres The forebrain is divided nearly symmetrically into left and right hemispheres connected by the bundle of axons known as the corpus collosum. The structures of each hemisphere correspond almost exactly to those in the opposite hemisphere, although there are also subtle, but important, differences left and right.

Change blindness The inability to detect changes in a scene following a brief distraction.

Characteristic adaptations Dan Adams' term to describe aspects of personality such as goals, values, beliefs, social roles, and plans for the future. According to Adams, characteristic adaptations change substantially over the life span.

Childhood amnesia The term used to describe the fact that adults do not have accurate, coherent memory for events of early childhood. Theorists currently propose that coherent memories are not retained for events prior to the fourth birthday.

Child-to-parent effects When the behavior of a child alters the way the parent behaves toward the child—including the parent's overall parenting style (e.g., authoritative, authoritarian, or permissive).

Chromosomes Rod-like bodies, present in every human cell, made up of proteins and strands of DNA.

Chunk Individual items that are grouped together in memory because they are meaningfully associated with one another (but only weakly related or unrelated to items in other chunks).

Circadian pacemaker The "master control" for a person's various circadian cycles, consisting of a group of neurons forming the suprachiasmatic nuclei of the hypothalamus.

Circadian rhythm Any biochemical, physiological, or behavioral cycle that adheres to a near-24-hour schedule.

Clairvoyance The ability to predict the future or have knowledge of events that have transpired outside of one's own experience.

Classical conditioning (Pavlovian conditioning) A type of associative learning discovered by Ivan Pavlov. Classical conditioning occurs when an innate (or otherwise reflexive) response known as the unconditioned response (UCR) is triggered by a neutral stimulus as a result of repeated pairings of the neutral stimulus with an unconditioned stimulus (UCS). The UCS is a stimulus that would naturally trigger the reflexive response without a conditioning procedure.

Client-centered therapy The humanistic therapy founded during the late 1940s and 1950s by Carl Rogers. The goal of client-centered therapy is to promote personal growth in the client in a nondirective manner by treating the client with dignity, empathy, and unconditional positive regard.

Clinical significance When a statistical effect in a treatment outcome study is large enough and meaningful enough to suggest that the treatment being tested would be effective in the world outside of the research study.

Clitoral hood A stretch of protective tissue surrounding the clitoris.

Closure A Gestalt law of perceptual grouping that states that if there is a gap in the image of a familiar object, people will mentally fill in the missing elements.

Cocaine An alkaloid of the coca plant in concentrated form.

Cochlea A pea-sized, tube-like structure of the inner ear filled with fluid and curled into the shape of a snail. The cochlea is the central component of the inner ear.

Cognition Human mental processes concerned with information and knowledge. Cognition includes thinking, memory, language, intelligence, and perception of the world through the senses.

Cognitive behavior therapy (CBT) A development of behavior therapy that attempts to unite traditional behavior therapy with Beck's cognitive therapy. CBT is based on the idea that cognition, emotion, and behavior are linked in a circle of mutual influence and reinforcement. Although CBT is not identical to CT (cognitive therapy), the term *cognitive behavior therapy* is often used to refer to either therapy.

Cognitive behaviorism The psychological school founded by Edward Tolman. Cognitive behaviorists agree with radical behaviorists that behavior is lawful and can be analyzed using concepts of reinforcement and punishment, but they disagree that this analysis must necessarily exclude cognition. Cognitive behaviorists pioneered the concepts of cognitive maps and latent learning.

Cognitive bias Any tendency toward systematic violation of principles of rational decision-making, judgment, or memory.

Cognitive developmental theory of moral reasoning Lawrence Kohlberg's three-level, six-stage theory of moral reasoning.

Cognitive dissonance Cognitive dissonance is the anxiety or tension that arises when people behave in ways that run contrary to their attitudes. People may resolve cognitive dissonance by changing their attitudes to bring them in line with their behavior; ceasing the behavior; or changing their beliefs about the discrepancy between their attitudes and behavior.

Cognitive map A mental representation of the structure, location, or attributes of some phenomenon.

Cognitive neuroscience Branch of neuroscience that focuses on the human brain to reveal the neural basis of cognition and emotion.

Cognitive science Branches of science that study mental activities and attributes involved in collecting, processing, storing, retrieving, and manipulating information. Cognitive scientists may come from disciplines as varied as psychology, linguistics, philosophy, neuroscience, and computer science.

Cognitive therapy (CT) The therapy principally devised by Aaron Beck that suggests that when people possess underlying dysfunctional core beliefs about the self, the world, and the future, they respond to events with automatic thoughts that are self-defeating and biased against the self. These thoughts trigger negative emotional experiences and can lead to disorders such as depression and anxiety. Unlike REBT, with which it shares a cognitive approach, the cognitive therapist does not forcefully dispute the client's unrealistic beliefs but helps the client to test these beliefs in the manner of a scientist testing a hypothesis.

Cognitive-motivational-relational theory of emotion The theory proposed by Richard Lazarus. This theory states that autonomic nervous system arousal occurs not directly, as stated in the James-Lange and two-factor theories, but only after the thought or event has been appraised so that the meaning of the event is interpreted by the person. In this theory, cognition always comes first.

Cohabiting Living together in a romantic relationship without formal marriage.

Color constancy The facet of perceptual constancy that allows us to perceive an object as the same color regardless of the amount or type of illumination.

Common factors Hypothesized factors common to all legitimate forms of psychotherapy that are responsible for actual therapeutic effects.

Comorbidity The co-occurrence of more than one disorder either simultaneously or at different points in the life span.

Competence motivation The need to be effective in one's life—to be able to perform some action or task successfully.

Computational theory of mind (CTM) The notion that the mind functions as an information processor in a manner loosely analogous to a computer.

Conception The fusion of the nuclei of a sperm and ovum. Also termed *fertilization*.

Concepts Mental categories into which we can place people, places, things, events, or ideas that share common characteristics. In creating concepts, the similarities between phenomena placed in the mental category are emphasized, and the differences are ignored.

Concrete operations stage Piaget's developmental stage lasting from approximately age 7 to 11 or 12, and characterized by mastery of tasks involving the application of logic.

Conditioned response (CR) In classical conditioning, the term conditioned response (CR) is used to describe the innate unconditioned response (UCR) after it been has come to be elicited by the a neutral stimulus.

Conditioned stimulus (CS) In classical conditioning, the CS is the originally neutral stimulus that comes to elicit the innate, unconditioned response (UCR) after conditioning.

Conditions (of an experiment) Groups to which participants may be assigned in an experiment. In an experiment with only one independent variable, each level of the independent variable is also known as a condition of the experiment.

Conditions of worth According to Carl Rogers, conditions of worth are the conditions a person must fulfill to obtain love and approval from important people in his or her life. These conditions only exist within relationships which lack unconditional positive regard.

Cones Photoreceptors specialized for day vision, color vision, and capturing fine detail.

Confirmation bias The tendency to pay more attention and accord more weight to evidence that confirms what we already believe—or even to seek such evidence out—while ignoring evidence that would disconfirm our beliefs.

Conformity The tendency of people to bring their behavior, attitudes, and/or beliefs in line with group norms and pressures. The motivation to conform may be informational, based on a rational desire to seek realistic information of some situation from a group; or the motivation may be normative, based on a person's desire to obtain approval from the group or avoid embarrassment.

Confounding variable In an experiment, any variable that exerts a measurable effect on the dependent variable without the knowledge of the experimenter. Technically, this means that a confounding variable is one whose values change systematically along with changes in the values of the independent variable.

Congenital adrenal hyperplasia (CAH) A congenital hormonal

disorder resulting in a greater (or sometimes lesser) production of sex steroids by the adrenal glands. Researchers have been particularly interested in CAH girls who have experienced unusual prenatal levels of exposure to androgens such as testosterone.

Congenital malformation (birth defect) Any physical abnormality or defect present at birth. Congenital malformations may result from genetic causes or prenatal events, including exposure to radiation, drugs and alcohol, or maternal illness.

Congruence Carl Rogers' term to describe an environment of development where those surrounding the developing person are *genuine*—that is, truly being themselves and not presenting a self that reflects the values and wishes of others.

Connectionism The belief that the mind is constructed of complex networks of interconnected units similar to the neural networks of the brain. Connectionism is a domain-general theory of how the mind works, in contrast to domain-specific or modular theories.

Consciousness studies The study of consciousness—a field created by psychologists, philosophers, and neuroscientists.

Consciousness No definition of consciousness has been agreed upon, but John Searle's "commonsense" definition includes three components: qualitativeness, subjectivity, and unity.

Conservation The child's understanding that an object may retain its identity even if its appearance has changed.

Consistency bias The tendency to recall one's past attitudes, feelings, and beliefs in a way that brings them in line with one's *current* attitudes, feelings, and beliefs.

Constructivism The stage theory of child development devised by Jean Piaget. Constructivism holds that each child actively constructs an understanding of the world based on experience and his or her stage of psychological and biological maturation.

Context-dependent memory When retrieval of a memory is enhanced in contexts that were similar to the one that existed when the memory was encoded.

Contingency management (CM) A type of operant treatment used in various types of institutions (e.g., substance abuse rehab, psychiatric wards, prisons). In CM treatment a person is rewarded with tangible, desirable goods, prizes, or privileges for engaging in desirable behaviors and avoiding undesirable behaviors.

Continuous reinforcement When a behavior is reinforced every time it occurs.

Control group Those participants in an experiment who do not receive the level of the independent variable that is of primary interest to the researchers, but are used instead for comparison purposes.

Control In an experiment, making certain that nothing else changes along with changes in the independent variable. More generally, the term control may encompass any technique used to avoid the influence of confounding variables.

Conventional morality According to Lawrence Kohlberg, moral judgment of school-age children and young adolescents, based on respect for law, social norms, and rules set by authorities.

Convergence A binocular cue to depth perception based on the fact that ocular muscles rotate eyes inward when viewing close objects.

Coping Any process by which an organism attempts to manage stress—to ensure that the demands of potentially stressful situations do not overwhelm psychological or material resources.

Cornea Transparent membrane comprised of nerve fibers that covers the eye.

Coronary heart disease (CHD) The result of buildup of plaque along the walls of arteries, impairing their ability to supply oxygen and nutrients to muscles of the heart. Plaque consists largely of fatty acids, cholesterol, and calcium deposits.

Corpus callosum Bundle of axons (white matter) that connects the right and left cerebral hemispheres.

Correlate Any factor or variable that co-occurs with some other variable.

Correlation coefficient A statistic which quantifies the strength and direction of correlation (association) between two variables. The correlation coefficient ranges from -1.0 (a perfect negative correlation) to +1.0 (a perfect positive correlation). A correlation coefficient near 0 indicates no association between the variables in question.

Correlation When a change in one variable can predict change in another variable because the variables are associated in some way. However, the association between the variables may not be causal in nature.

Correlational research A method of study in which the researcher measures two or more variables as they already exist to see if there is an association (correlation) between them.

Couple therapy A form of psychotherapy involving a married, cohabitating, or dating couple. Couple therapy may be used to treat relationship distress or the mental health problems of one member of the couple.

Crack A solid form of cocaine somewhat similar to freebase, "cooked" from cocaine, water, and baking soda or lye. Street crack often contains other chemical components.

Cranial nerves Nerves originating in the brain stem.

Craving Overpowering feelings of "wanting" and depending upon a drug.

Critical period (sensitive period) A stage in development when the brain displays increased sensitivity to certain types of stimuli and will develop in specific ways if these stimuli are encountered. Certain skills (e.g., normal vision or language development) may need to be developed during critical periods to develop normally, and social deprivation during critical periods in infancy and toddlerhood results in various types of cognitive impairment.

Critical thinking A series of interrelated cognitive skills designed to help one see things as they actually are, free from bias and error.

Crystallized intelligence (Gc) Cattell and Horn's term used to refer to skills or knowledge one acquires as a result of exposure to education and culture—what one has learned.

Cultural psychology The comparative study of psychology as it exists in different cultures.

Culture of modernization A term sometimes used to describe the vast transformations being experienced by developing nations in response to globalization. These transformations occur in economy, social structure, food abundance and variety, technology, birth and death rates, relations between the sexes, urbanization, and so forth.

Culture The total pattern of behavior exhibited by citizens of any given society, and the total products of a given society.

Data Literally, "pieces of information." Singular: datum.

Debriefing When the purpose of a study, its procedures, and its potential value, are explained to a participant after his or her participation is complete. Debriefing is particularly important in studies which have involved some measure of deception.

Deep brain stimulation (DBS) A relatively new technique of psychosurgery used to treat Parkinson's disease and being tested for use in psychological disorders, particularly depression. In deep brain stimulation electrodes are implanted in various regions of the brain and coupled to an external device that sends out stimulating electrical pulses

Deindividuation A lessening of self-awareness or identity within a group, leading to increased feelings of anonymity and reduced concern for how one's behavior will be evaluated by others in the group.

Deinstitutionalization A policy instituted in the United States and other industrialized nations during the 1960s which encouraged shorter hospital stays for those with mental illnesses and provided stricter criteria by which people with psychological disorders or developmental disabilities could be hospitalized in the first place.

Delta waves The slow brain waves that predominate at Stage 4 sleep.

Dementia (senility) Age-related severe memory loss, confusion, problems with speech and comprehending others, and difficulty with self-care.

Dendrites The branch-like projections of neurons that receive electrochemical stimulation from other neurons.

Dependent variable (DV) The variable being measured in an experiment to determine if the manipulation of the independent variable has had any effect.

Depolarization A disruption of the resting potential balance between negatively- and positively-charged ions within and outside of the neuron. Depolarization begins the process of the firing of an action potential.

Depressants (hypnotics) Drugs that depress the central nervous system (but are not narcotics).

Depression A mood state characterized by sadness, low energy, fatigue, regret or guilt, feelings of low self-worth, hopelessness, and helplessness.

Depth perception The visual perceptual mechanism that allows for the judgment of distance of objects and creates a "3-D" image even though retinal images are "2-D."

Descriptive statistics Basic statistics which provide descriptions of a set of data (e.g., percentage, mean, median, mode)

Descriptive study A study that characterizes a sample in relation to variables of interest to the researcher. Descriptive studies answer questions of who, what, when, and how, but cannot determine if one variable influences another. The category "descriptive research" includes surveys, case studies, and naturalistic observations.

Developmental psychology The scientific study of changes and continuities in human psychology over time.

Developmental stages The idea that human beings pass through periods of development with distinct boundaries, and that reflect qualitatively different types of cognitive activity.

Diagnostic and Statistical Manual of Mental Disorders (DSM) The manual published by the American Psychiatric Association which classifies, describes, and presents diagnostic criteria for psychological disorders. The DSM is the standard for diagnosis among psychologists as well as psychiatrists, and presents the medical model of mental illness in the most coherent and consistent fashion yet devised.

Directionality In correlational research, even if two variables are related causally, it may not be clear which variable caused the other to change.

Discrimination In classical conditioning, when one neutral stimulus produces a conditioned response, but another, similar neutral stimulus does not.

Dismantling study   A study that seeks to isolate the factors responsible for the efficacy of a form of therapy. The dismantling study compares outcome results of a form of therapy against that same therapy minus its "active ingredient" (e.g., cognitive therapy but without training to identify and correct irrational cognitions).

Displacement   The quality of language that allows one to converse about things that do not exist, exist in other places, or are abstractions.

Display rules   Implicit cultural standards and expectations which regulate the way emotion is displayed.

Dissociative disorder   A DSM category of disorder where there is one of several types of breakdowns of memory, perception, awareness, or identity.

Dissociative identity disorder (DID)   A highly controversial DSM-IV-TR diagnosis characterized by the emergence of more than one autonomous "personality" within the same body. Formerly known as "multiple personality disorder."

Dizygotic (fraternal) twins   Twins who emerge from two ova (eggs) and share only 50% of their genes in common, on average.

DNA (deoxyribonucleic acid)   A complex molecule with a characteristic spiraling shape. DNA contains the genetic instructions for heredity in all living organisms.

Dodo bird verdict   A phrase used to sum up the "take-home message" of outcome research in psychotherapy: No legitimate form of therapy is superior to any other in general outcome. The phrase is borrowed from an incident in Lewis Carroll's *Alice in Wonderland*, wherein a dodo bird announces of a race, "At last, everybody has won and all shall have prizes." The dodo bird verdict applies only to legitimate forms of psychotherapy appropriate for a given condition.

Double-blind   In an experiment, when both those running the experiment and the research participants are unaware of which level of the independent variable each participant is receiving and/or are unaware of the nature of the researchers' hypothesis.

Drive theory   A theory initially proposed by Clark Hull in 1943 which proposed that behavior is motivated primarily by the desire to reduce unpleasant conditions of arousal which have resulted from basic physiological needs.

Drive   The desire to reduce unpleasant arousal states resulting from basic psychological needs.

Dualism   The view that the mind and matter (including the body) belong in separate categories and are constructed of different material.

Duchenne smile   A smile of genuine enjoyment or pleasure, characterized by contraction of the orbicularis oculi muscle surrounding the eye. This muscle is extremely difficult to contract at will.

Ear canal   An outer ear structure that funnels sound to the eardrum.

Early adulthood   A newly coined term for the developmental stage between adolescence and adulthood.

Eating disorder   Any of a number of complex conditions involving unhealthful patterns of eating or not eating. The most commonly diagnosed of medically recognized eating disorders are *bulimia nervosa* and *anorexia nervosa*. However, *binge-eating disorder*, which has not yet been accepted by the medical profession (but is likely to be in the future), is more common than anorexia and bulimia combined.

Ecstasy (MDMA)   A psychedelic drug derived from amphetamines.

Effect size   An inferential statistic that estimates the magnitude of the relationship between variables.

Effective   An effective treatment is one that has shown itself to have significant utility in the "real world" of practicing clinicians treating patients in clinics, hospitals, consulting rooms, and medical offices.

Efficacy   An efficacious treatment is one that has been shown to be superior to a placebo in randomized clinical trials (RCTs). Because it is difficult to construct a placebo psychotherapy, the term *efficacious* is often applied to therapies that have only shown themselves superior to no treatment.

Effortful control   The dimension of temperament that describes the extent to which an infant or child is able to focus or shift attention, inhibit inappropriate behavior, and plan actions constructively. Similar to executive functions in adults.

Ego defense mechanisms   A group of psychological mechanisms described in part by Sigmund Freud but primarily by his daughter, Anna Freud. The ego uses these mechanisms to keep threatening material from reaching awareness. The defense mechanisms include repression, denial, displacement, projection, reaction formation, sublimation, and undoing.

Ego   Ego, also termed *secondary process*, is the aspect of Freud's structural model which represents that part of the mind which operates according to the *reality principle*. Partly conscious, partly unconscious, the ego mediates between the demands of the real world, the blind strivings of the id, and the judgments of the superego.

Egocentric bias   The tendency to recall past events in a way that enhances one's current view of oneself.

Egocentric   When a person lacks the ability to see things from the perspective of another person.

Elaborative rehearsal   Mentally encoding information into long-term memory in a way that is personally meaningful and associates the new information with information that already exists in long-term memory.

Electroconvulsive therapy (ECT)   A treatment for psychological disorders (primarily treatment-resistant depression) that consists of passing a low-voltage electrical current through a person's brain for a brief moment, resulting in seizure and convulsion. ECT is usually conducted multiple times for any given case.

Electroencephalograph (EEG)   The instrument that measures electrical activity produced by the brain in waves of current termed brain waves.

Electromagnetic radiation   Energy that travels around the world in waves of variable intensity (amplitude) that are separated by varying lengths known as wavelengths.

Embodied emotion   Embodied emotion theories assume that emotions are "captured" as body memories. Each time an emotion is experienced, the sights, sounds, physiological processes, and patterns of motor activity that occur are encoded in clusters of neurons assigned to the various sensory and motor modalities of the body. Over time, these experiences build a conception of the particular emotion in question, which a person may reactivate by thinking about or re-experiencing the emotion.

Embryo   The developing human organism at approximately 2 weeks following fertilization, after rapid cell division in the zygote has taken place.

Emotion   A psychological state consisting of subjective experience or feeling, physiological changes, and behavioral responses. Emotions tend to be intense, attributable to a potentially identifiable cause, and relatively short-lived.

Emotional intelligence   The ability to identify, manage, and express one's emotions constructively and to empathize with the emotions of others.

Empathy   The ability to take another person's perspective, understand why the person feels as he or she does, and perhaps also come to share that feeling to some degree (although this is not a necessary component of empathy).

Empirical   The idea that knowledge should be obtained through personal experience.

Empirically supported treatment (EST)   A psychotherapy EST is therapy that has demonstrated statistically significant superiority over no treatment (and in some cases also over a placebo therapy) in a series of randomized clinical trials. Psychotherapy ESTs are generally brief and consist of highly specific techniques that may be described in treatment manuals.

Empiricism The philosophical tradition that emphasizes the importance of experience in acquiring knowledge. In the "nature-nurture" debate in psychology, empiricism is contrasted with nativism, the belief that at least some aspects of human psychology are innate.

Encoding The memory process of "translating" sensory impressions into meaningful perceptions that may then be stored as memory.

Endocrine system The system of glands and the hormones they produce.

Endometrium The lining of the uterus.

Endophenotype A characteristic or symptom of a disorder that is present in people with that disorder and also is present to a greater degree than would be expected by chance in close genetic relatives of the person with the disorder. Endophenotypes are considered to reflect what is heritable about a given disorder but, unlike most disorders, are considered simple and straightforward enough to lend themselves to genetic analysis.

Endorphin A neurotransmitter that binds to the same receptor sites as opioid drugs and is associated with relief from pain.

Energy balance Energy balance is maintained by taking in only as many calories as are expended overall in activity and the maintenance of bodily functions.

Environmental mismatch When a psychological adaptation is expressed in an environment different from the one in which it evolved and to which it is not suited.

Episodic memory Memories acquired through personal experience. Episodic memories are one subtype of explicit (declarative) memory.

Equipotentiality An early neuroscientific theory proposing that all parts of the cortex contributed equally to all aspects of mind.

Erogenous zone Any area of the body with particular sensitivity to pleasurable stimulation, generally associated with sexuality.

Ethanol The ingestible form of alcohol contained in alcoholic beverages.

Ethics A set of orderly rules for correct behavior, particularly within some specific discipline or workplace.

Evolutionary psychology A multidisciplinary approach to psychology based on evolutionary principles, especially Darwin's theory of natural selection.

Executive functions Those cognitive functions involved in managing attention, planning constructive action, inhibiting inappropriate action, and remaining flexible in responding to situations.

Experimental group Those participants in an experiment who receive the level of the independent variable whose effects on a dependent variable are of primary interest to the researchers.

Experimenter effect Any confounding variable introduced by the experimenter's behavior.

Explanatory style How people explain the good and bad events of their lives and make predictions about future events based upon these explanations. One way of categorizing explanatory styles is the dimension of optimism vs. pessimism.

Explicit knowledge Factual knowledge that can be articulated and transmitted to others. Explicit knowledge is "knowing that," as compared with procedural knowledge, which is "knowing how."

Explicit memory (declarative memory) Conscious memories for personal experiences (episodic memory) or facts about the world (semantic memory).

Exposure therapy Any technique of behavior therapy based on the idea that only through exposure to feared stimuli can the anxiety produced by that stimuli be lessened. Although exposure therapy technically refers to any such technique, the term is used most often to refer to contemporary therapies rather than earlier behavior therapies such as systematic desensitization.

External validity The degree to which research results may generalize to the world outside the laboratory.

Extinction When a learned behavior ceases to be performed. In classical conditioning, extinction will occur when the conditioned stimulus occurs repeatedly without being paired with the unconditioned stimulus.

Extrasensory perception (ESP) Acquiring information by means other than the senses (e.g., telepathy, clairvoyance).

Extraversion In temperament theory, the dimension of temperament that describes the degree to which an infant or child lacks shyness, is highly active, anticipates pleasurable activities, laughs and smiles frequently, and desires closeness with others.

Extrinsic motivation A category of motivation which compels a person to engage in a behavior for an external reward that the behavior might bring.

Facial action coding system Paul Ekman's coding scheme of the facial muscle configurations which create expressions of basic emotion.

Facial feedback hypothesis The idea that the facial expression associated with a basic emotion increases the intensity of the experience of that emotion; and that purposely activating the muscles which form a facial expression of basic emotion may actually result in a person experiencing the emotion itself—or at least experiencing a mood change in a positive or

negative direction (depending on the specific expression).

False hope syndrome A cycle of repeated failure in self-improvement attempts brought on by unrealistic ideas about the speed or ease with which self-change will occur, the amount of change that is likely or even possible, and the rewards that will accrue from self-improvement changes.

False memory Memory of an event that did not actually occur. In some cases, blatantly inaccurate recollection of details of an event that did occur may also be considered a false memory.

Falsification When a theory is shown through empirical evidence to be false.

Family systems theory The view that the family is an integrated, organic unit that may be analyzed somewhat the way systems analysts view computer systems in organizations.

Family therapy A form of psychotherapy that involves an entire family (or other closely connected group) rather than a single individual. Family therapy emerged from family systems theory, which proposes that the problems of an individual in a family cannot be understood outside of the context of the family as an integrated, organic unit.

Fertilization The fusion of the nuclei of a sperm and ovum. Also termed *conception.*

Fetal alcohol syndrome (FAS) A congenital disorder resulting from prenatal maternal alcohol use.

Fetus The developing human organism after the embryonic stage has passed, at about 8 to 9 weeks after fertilization.

Fight or flight Walter Cannon's term to describe the initial mammalian response to stress: activation of the sympathetic nervous system, suppression of the parasympathetic nervous system, and release of hormones adrenaline (epinephrine) and noradrenaline (norepinephrine) by the hypothalamic-pituitary-adrenocortical axis (HPA) of the endocrine system.

Figure Gestalt psychology term for that aspect of a visual image upon which a person focuses, while relegating other aspects of the image to the background (ground).

First pain Initial sharp sensations at the moment of a painful stimulus.

Five-factor model (the "Big Five") An empirical trait model of personality consisting of five trait dimensions or factors within which all other "lower-order" traits can be found. The five factors are openness to experience, conscientiousness, extraversion, agreeableness, and neuroticism. The "Big Five" is the most widely accepted trait model of personality.

Fixation Being "stuck" in a specific way of mentally representing a problem. Fixation may occur when one applies previously successful problem-solving strategies to new problems that may or may not best be solved with these strategies.

Fixed-interval (FI) schedule A partial reinforcement schedule that provides reinforcement for the first operant behavior after a specific interval of time has passed.

Fixed-ratio (FR) schedule A partial reinforcement schedule that provides reinforcement after a specific number of operant behavioral responses.

Flavor During chewing, molecules are released and travel up behind the roof of the mouth where they are sensed by the olfactory epithelium as retronasal olfactory sensations. When combined with *taste*, these sensations create flavor.

Flooding An exposure therapy used to treat phobia and other anxiety disorders. Flooding involves non-incremental, total immersion in anxiety-producing phobic stimuli for a prolonged period.

Flow Mihaly Csikszentmihalyi's term to describe experiences when one is fully immersed in what one is doing—where there is a timeless, effortless focus on an activity from which one is not easily distracted. During flow a person may lose track of time and experience little fatigue.

Fluid intelligence (*Gf*) Cattell and Horn's term used to refer to largely innate analytic skills and abstract reasoning ability.

Forebrain The large, upper geographic area of the brain controlling the "higher" brain functions. Consists of two cerebral hemispheres, each of which contains a limbic system, cerebral cortex, and thalamus.

Forgetting curve The discovery made by Hermann Ebbinghaus that forgetting follows a pattern according to the passage of time, with most memory loss occurring rapidly, and the pace then slowing.

Formal operations stage Piaget's developmental stage beginning at age 11 or 12, and characterized by the ability to apply systematic logic to abstract concepts and to think hypothetically and skeptically.

Fovea A small region near the center of the retina that contains the greatest concentration of cones and thus provides the clearest images and sharpest focus.

Freebase A method of using cocaine where the active ingredient of cocaine is isolated and smoked. Unlike cocaine in powder form (cocaine hydrochloride), it is not soluble in water and cannot be snorted or administered through injection.

Frequency (of sound waves) The number of sound waves per second, expressed as hertz units.

Functional magnetic resonance imaging (fMRI) The use of MRI whereby continuous images of the brain are generated while a research participant engages in specific tasks.

Functionalism The psychological school championed by William James which held that the mind could only be understood by referring to the purposes for which it was shaped through evolution.

Functionalist perspective Those taking the functionalist perspective on learning believe that learning mechanisms such as classical conditioning evolved because they fulfill functions—in this case, preparing the organism for what is to come. Theorists taking this perspective believe that learning mechanisms evolved because they increased the survival and reproductive success of organisms that possessed them.

Fundamental Attribution Error (FAE) The tendency to attribute other people's behavior to those individuals' dispositions and other internal factors, while ignoring or underestimating the possibility that situation factors may have played an important or determining role.

Fuzzy boundaries When it is not precisely clear where a concept begins and ends, or what does or does not belong in the concept.

g See General intelligence

Gambler's fallacy A misperception of randomness that causes a person to believe that the likelihood of a random event is affected by events that precede it. For example, people often incorrectly assume that the likelihood of tails occurring in a fair coin toss will increase according to the number of times heads has come up in succession.

Gate control theory A theory of pain perception that emphasizes the activity not only of pain signals from the injury site but also of pain blocking signals originating in the brain or elsewhere in the body.

Gender identity Each person's subjective perception of the sex to which he or she belongs and/or with which he or she identifies. Gender identity develops in early childhood as a consequence of genetic, hormonal, and social factors.

Gender roles Social beliefs about what constitute appropriate behaviors for males and females—what activities they should engage in, jobs they should perform, clothing they should wear, and so forth.

Gender schema theory A cognitive theory of gender development which describes the way each child forms a mental template about gender which changes over time as a result of social experiences.

Gender stereotypes Social beliefs about how a "typical" man or woman behaves. Gender stereotypes could include a person's interests, capabilities, appearance, tendencies, and so forth.

Gender The term originally applied to human beings during the 1960s as part of *gender identity* and later broadened to refer to all aspects of maleness and femaleness that were assumed to be primarily psychological or social in nature, rather than biological.

Gene The unit of heredity in living organisms. Genes are constructed of strands of DNA and grouped together along each chromosome.

Gene-environment correlation. When a person's environment is correlated with his or her genotype. Example: When a musically gifted child (genotype) lives in a home where music is played frequently and where musical instruments are available.

Gene-environment interaction When an experience affects people differently as a result of the differences in their genotypes.

General adaptation system (GAS) Hans Selye's model for mammalian response to chronic stress. GAS consists of three phases: Phase 1 (alarm), Phase 2 (resistance), and Phase 3 (exhaustion).

General aggression model (GAM) Craig Anderson and Brad Bushman's theory of aggression which holds that whether aggression does or does not occur in any interaction is dependent upon a complex interaction between four factors: personal characteristics; characteristics of the situation; emotions, thoughts, and biological arousal levels; and decision-making processes.

General intelligence (*g*) A way of referring to a person's underlying general capacity to process complex information—to perform well on a variety of mental tasks. General intelligence, or *g*, was initially hypothesized by Charles Spearman.

Generalization In classical conditioning, when an animal displays a conditioned response (CR) to a neutral stimulus that is similar, but not identical, to the conditioned stimulus (CS).

Generalized anxiety disorder (GAD) GAD is characterized by ceaseless, pervasive, and uncontrollable worry and apprehension about the future. Worry in GAD is often irrational, and results in physical symptoms such as fatigue and tension as well as irritability, sleep difficulty, and difficulty concentrating.

Generativity vs. stagnation Erik Erikson's view of the characteristic conflict of middle-adulthood between productivity and concern for future generations on one hand, and living a self-centered existence on the other.

Generativity The quality of language that allows a speaker to use a relatively small number of words and grammatical structures to compose a theoretically infinite number of sentences and new ideas.

Genitals Male and female sexual organs. Although sexual organs may serve reproductive functions, they serve functions related to sexual behavior and elimination of urine as well. The male sexual organ is the penis; the female sexual organs are the vulva (including the clitoris) and the vagina.

Genocide A deliberate and systematic attempt to destroy or exterminate an entire people based on their nationality, religion, racial group, or ethnicity.

Genotype The unique collection of alleles that contribute to (or entirely determine) specific traits in living organisms.

Gestalt school An early school of psychology that emphasized the mechanisms by which human beings create perceptions of meaningful "wholes" from inherently fragmented and meaningless sensory signals.

Gestalt German for "whole form" or "shape."

GHB (Gamma-hydroxybutyrate) A CNS depressant drug initially marketed as a food supplement for bodybuilders.

Ghostwriting The practice of having professional writers write up reports of studies in articles bearing the names of researchers who did not contribute to the writing of the article and may not have been involved in the design and conduct of the study.

Gland A bodily organ that synthesizes and/or releases hormones.

Glia Cell type that builds the myelin sheath that surrounds the axon of some neurons, and helps to develop and maintain neuron synapses.

Goal-setting theory An important theory of work motivation devised by Edwin Locke and Gary Latham. According to goal-setting theory, work motivation and performance are enhanced when *specific* and *difficult* (but not impossible) goals are set. Setting specific and difficult goals directs attention toward appropriate activities to reach goals, increases effort to achieve goals, and increases persistence in working toward goals.

Gonadarche The maturation of the sexual organs during puberty.

Gonads Reproductive organs which produce reproductive cells, or *gametes*. The male gonad is the testes; the female gonad is the ovaries.

Good continuation A Gestalt law of perceptual grouping that states that any visual elements which suggest a continued line will be grouped together.

Good subject tendency The general desire of research participants to please the experimenter or give the experimenter what he or she "wants."

Grand theories The term given to describe theories of personality, primarily developed during the early to mid-20th century, whose creators wished to address all of the important areas of study of personality. The most prominent grand theories were those developed by psychoanalysts, behaviorists, and humanists.

Gray matter Cell bodies, unmyelinated axons, dendrites, and glia.

Ground Gestalt psychology term for those aspects of a visual image relegated to the background.

Group therapy When groups of three or more people engage in therapy under the guidance of one or more therapists.

Groupthink A way of thinking and behaving in groups whereby decisions are made not as a result of rational considerations and weighing of evidence, but as a result of group members not wanting to adversely affect group morale, make waves, or appear disloyal to leaders. The frequent end result of groupthink is the adoption of highly flawed plans and policies.

Gustation Sense of taste.

Habituation A simple type of nonassociative learning that occurs when a stimulus comes to elicit decreasing response from an organism as a result of the organism's repeated exposure to the stimulus over time. "I got used to it" expresses the idea of habituation.

Hard problem The term given to the question of how the human brain is able to produce consciousness.

Harmful dysfunction view A view of psychological disorder pioneered by Jerome Wakefield. According to the harmful dysfunction view, disorder exists when symptoms cause harm according to subjective social or cultural judgments, *and* there is objective evidence of dysfunction. Dysfunction is said to exist only when a psychological characteristic or mechanism is not performing the function for which it evolved through natural selection.

Hashish A pasty or gummy concentrated form of cannabis, generally stronger in its effects than marijuana.

Health psychology An interdisciplinary field which examines the ways that health and illness interact with psychology, biology, and society. Health psychologists work in clinical settings alongside medical doctors, or in academic settings teaching and conducting research.

Hemispheric specialization The unique specializations of the two hemispheres of the cerebral cortex.

Heredity The transfer of genetic characteristics from parent to offspring.

Heritability A statistic that estimates the extent of genetic influence in the differences among a sample of people on a particular trait.

Heroin A powerful, semi-synthetic opioid narcotic derived from morphine.

Heterosexual (straight) The term used to describe a primary sexual preference for members of the other sex.

Heuristics Mental problem-solving short-cuts or "rules of thumb." Heuristics are very fast and often accurate, but they are not always accurate, and relying upon them can result in numerous erroneous assumptions.

Hindbrain A lower geographic area of the brain containing the cerebellum, medulla, pons, and reticular formation.

Homeostasis Literally meaning "to stay the same," the term *homeostasis* is used to describe a steady, regulated state where various physiological processes (e.g., water intake, blood sugar, body temperature) are maintained at appropriate levels.

Homosexual (gay or lesbian) The term used to describe a primary sexual preference for members of one's own sex.

Hooking up A sexualized encounter between two strangers or brief acquaintances that may or may not include sexual intercourse. Hookups usually occur on only one occasion.

Hopelessness theory A revision of learned helplessness theory created by Lyn Abramson and Lauren Alloy. Hopelessness theory proposes that a negative cognitive style leads to depression. This negative cognitive style includes three aspects: (a) attributing negative events to internal causes; (b) considering causes of negative events to be stable and global; and (c) anticipating severe negative consequences from negative events.

Hormone A chemical synthesized and/or released by a gland.

Hostile aggression A type of aggression where the ultimate purpose is harming the victim. Hostile aggression is generally accompanied by emotion, such as anger, and is often (but not always) impulsive. This is in contrast to *instrumental aggression*, where the aggressor has an ultimate purpose other than harming the victim.

Human aggression The general term used when a person carries out an act intended to harm another in some way. However, for an act to constitute aggression, the aggressor must believe that the act is harmful, and the target of aggression must be motivated to avoid the behavior.

Human genome The entire set of hereditary "instructions," encoded in DNA, for creating a human organism. The human genome exists within every cell of every human body.

Human sexual response The process by which a person becomes sexually aroused, experiences orgasm (or not, as the case may be), and returns to a pre-aroused state.

Human sexual response cycle Models of human sexual response. The first such model was created by William Masters and Virginia Johnson in 1966.

Human sexuality An umbrella label describing human sex, gender, and sexual behavior.

Human universal A human trait, custom, or sociocultural practice that exists in every known society.

Humanistic psychology The movement in psychology founded during the 1950s primarily by Carl Rodgers and Abraham Maslow as a reaction against psychoanalysis and behaviorism. Humanistic psychology held that human behavior was not determined by unconscious drives or by learning, but that people had free will to choose. The humanists emphasized the intrinsic worth and dignity of the human being.

Hunger A primarily homeostatic drive state turned on and off by physiological changes in the body and intended to satisfy needs for immediate energy and/or overall nutrition. Hunger naturally leads to eating.

Hypnagogia A dream-like state at sleep onset during which a person may or may not be aware that he or she is experiencing hallucinations or delusions.

Hypnosis An interaction between "hypnotist" and "subject" involving suggestions for "imaginative experiences."

Hypomania A less extreme form of mania characterized by reduced need for sleep, increased sexuality and humor, feelings of mental clarity, enjoyment of life, self-esteem, charm, grandiosity, and increased ability to do productive work.

Hypothesis A specific, testable prediction about what will happen given certain circumstances. Hypotheses are often drawn from theories, which are sets of interconnected ideas and statements used to explain facts.

Iatrogenesis When a clinician unwittingly (or intentionally) creates symptoms of an illness in his or her capacity as a healthcare giver.

Id That part of Freud's structural model which represents the irrational portion of the mind which lacks moral restraint or a conception of right and wrong, and cares only for satisfaction of its own cravings—seeking pleasure and avoiding pain (the *pleasure principle*). The id operates primarily at the level of the unconscious mind and can be expressed in dreams, uncontrolled behavior, and satisfaction of basic drives.

Identity vs. role confusion Erik Erikson's view of the characteristic conflict of adolescence between an integrated sense of personal identity and confusion between possible "selves" and roles.

Identity A sense of oneself as a unique being different from others; an understanding of one's place in the world.

Impairment in functioning The concept used for diagnosis in the DSM to cover situations where a person has symptoms of a disorder but does not experience personal distress.

Impasse When a person has made repeated unsuccessful attempts to solve a problem yet possesses the mental ability to solve the problem.

Implicit memory A memory that affects how we behave without our conscious awareness of the memory itself.

Implicit prejudice Automatic, unconscious bias against a group. Implicit prejudice tends to be subtle and often exists even in people who do not consider themselves prejudiced.

Impression management The process by which people attempt to monitor and control the impressions that others form of them. Impression management consists of two components: impression motivation and impression construction.

Imprinting Learning that occurs rapidly during a critical period and which the animal is biologically prepared to acquire.

Inattentional blindness The inability to see highly visible objects at which one is looking directly when attention is drawn elsewhere.

Incentives Any rewarding condition that provides a motive for some behavior.

Independent variable (IV) The variable being manipulated in an experiment to determine possible effects on a dependent variable (DV). The independent variable is "free" to take on any values the investigator decides to give it. These values are known as levels of the independent variable.

Industrial and organizational psychology (I/O psychology) The study of psychology in the context of work.

Infancy The developmental stage beginning at birth to about age 1.

Inferential statistics Statistics which help determine the probability that research results reflect actual relationships among variables, or which quantify the magnitude of this relationship.

Informed consent When those participating in a research study have a thorough understanding of the study's potential risks and benefits. Informed consent is a cornerstone of the ethical conduct of research involving human beings.

Ingroup bias The tendency of human beings to favor and extend loyalty to members of their own group. Ingroup members are generally trusted more than outgroup members, and ingroup bias sometimes (but not always) leads to prejudice or even hatred toward members of outgroups. Ingroup bias tends to be automatic, and it is triggered as soon as group identity is created.

Insanity defense A criminal defense strategy based upon the proposition that a defendant did commit a crime but should not be held responsible because he or she did not understand the nature or consequences of the crime or could not distinguish between right and wrong.

Insight *Insight* is the term used to describe a situation where the solution to a problem appears suddenly "as if from nowhere" after an impasse had been reached and it seemed that the problem was not solvable.

Insomnia A chronic difficulty falling asleep, staying asleep, and/or being unable to obtain restful sleep.

Instinct An innate, automatic behavior tendency that will occur reliably in all normally developed members of a species in response to a releasing stimulus, or cue, from the environment. Because of past difficulties in identifying instincts, more often than not the term *fixed-action pattern* is used instead of the term *instinct*.

Instinctive drift When an instinctive pattern of behavior interferes with the operant conditioning of a behavior.

Institutional Review Board (IRB) An institutional ethics body that must approve and monitor research studies involving human and animal participants.

Instrumental aggression A type of aggression which has an ultimate purpose other than causing harm to the victim. Ultimate aggression is often (but not always) planned, and is not necessarily accompanied by an emotion such as anger, although it may be. Instrumental aggression is in contrast to *hostile aggression*, where the ultimate purpose is harming the victim.

Integrative therapy Any therapy that draws from more than one current of psychotherapeutic theory and technique.

Integrative treatment model A model of treatment that reflects the reality that most current mental health treatment involves multiple modalities (e.g., psychotherapy plus medication plus bibliotherapy).

Interference theory The notion, subscribed to by most memory researchers, that problems in retrieving memories results from the interference of one memory with another. There are two types of interference: *proactive* and *retroactive*.

Intergroup conflict Nonharmonious relations between groups.

Intergroup contact theory Gordon Allport's theory describing the ways in which constructive group contact can diminish prejudice.

Internal language faculty The notion, initially proposed by Noam Chomsky and originally termed the *language acquisition device* (LAD), that human beings possess innate, specialized cognitive structures dedicated to acquiring and using language.

Internal working model Attachment theorists' notion that the quality of a child's understanding of his or her place in the world, and his or her expectations about the behavior of others, reflect the quality of attachment relations in infancy.

Interneuron Communicates only with adjacent neurons.

Intersex Unusual genetic, anatomical, or neurohormonal conditions which render it difficult to classify an infant as strictly male or female.

Intimacy vs. isolation Erik Erikson's view of the characteristic conflict of early adulthood between social isolation and the formation of a genuinely intimate bond with another person.

Intimacy Interpersonal relationships, or moments within relationships, characterized by warmth, closeness, and mutual support and communication. Intimacy is frequently present in relationships of belonging, and some researchers characterize intimacy as a need and motivator in itself.

Intrinsic motivation A category of motivation which compels a person to engage in a behavior because the behavior is rewarding for its own sake, rather than providing some sort of additional external incentive or reward.

Intuition Literally, "knowledge from within." Obtaining knowledge or understanding without conscious effort or rational thought and often without conscious awareness. Intuition is immediate and unexpected. Although intuition may contain nonempirical aspects, it is an empirical way of knowing because its development depends upon a lifetime of personal experiences.

Involuntary commitment (civil commitment) When a person is admitted to a psychiatric facility (mental hospital) against his or her will by order of the court. Proceedings to commit someone in this way may be brought by individuals or the state.

Ion An atomic particle that carries primarily a positive or negative electrical charge.

IQ (Intelligence Quotient) A statistical measure of performance on intelligence tests based upon comparisons of a person's score with the average scores of others of his or her age. IQ was originally conceived as a measure of children's performance. When tests began to be administered to adults, new computational formulas had to be devised.

Iris A muscular structure of the eye around the pupil that expands and contracts to regulate the amount of light entering the eye.

James-Lange theory of emotion The theory proposed by Carl Lange and William James which states that thoughts or the perception of events trigger directly autonomic nervous system changes; awareness of these changes reaches the cerebral cortex; and only then is there an experience of emotion.

Jet lag Symptoms caused by travel across multiple time zones by moving west-to-east or from east-to-west.

Just noticeable difference (JND) The smallest difference between two stimuli that can be detected by the appropriate sense organ at least 50% of the time.

Latent learning Learning that occurs without obvious reinforcement, and that is not apparent in behavior.

Law of effect Edward Thorndike's discovery that behaviors which lead to a satisfying state of affairs are "stamped in," while behaviors that lead to an unsatisfying or annoying state of affairs are "stamped out." The law of effect formed the basis for B. F. Skinner's discoveries of operant conditioning principles.

Learned helplessness Martin Seligman's term to describe the passivity and resignation which an animal may experience after coming to believe that it is unable to control or halt an aversive event. Learned helplessness then interferes with the animal's ability to recognize when it is in fact able to halt or control the event. Seligman originally theorized that learned helpless lies at the root of depressive disorders.

Learning A fundamental way that organisms change. Learning is difficult to define precisely, but it involves relatively enduring change in knowledge and/or behavior resulting from specific experiences.

Lens A transparent structure of the eye that flattens or thickens to help focus light upon the retina.

Level of analysis The particular aspect or level of a problem to which a theory is addressed.

Levels of processing framework The model of memory originated by Fergis Craik and Robert Lockhart which denies the existence of distinct memory stages or stores. Instead, it proposes that the more deeply an item is processed, the more likely it is to be recalled.

Levels of the independent variable The values assigned by the experimenter to the independent variable.

Libido Freud proposed that human beings are born with a limited fund of psychic "energy," or life force, which he termed *libido*. This life force has an erotic foundation, although its effects need not be explicitly sexual in nature nor bear only upon sexual life.

Lifespan perspective The prevailing perspective in developmental psychology that emphasizes the importance of studying human development throughout life, rather than focusing exclusively on infancy and childhood, as has often been the case (particularly in the United States).

Limbic system A group of large structures and smaller nuclei that regulate mood, emotion, memory, and basic drives. Includes at least the hypothalamus, hippocampus, amygdala, basal ganglia, and nucleus accumbens.

Linguistic relativity hypothesis The modified "weak form" of the Sapir-Whorf hypothesis (linguistic determinism). Linguistic relativity theory proposes that the way we construct reality is affected, but not necessarily determined, by our language.

Lobes of the cerebral cortex Four large divisions of the cerebral cortex into which specific brain structures are grouped. The lobes are named for the skull bones beneath which they lie: occipital, parietal, temporal, and frontal.

Loneliness An overwhelmingly unpleasant feeling which results when there is a discrepancy between one's perceptions of the interpersonal relationships one has and the relationships one wishes to have. Loneliness does not arise from any particular situation, and one may be alone and never feel lonely. Loneliness results from a person's interpretation of the *meaning* of being alone or isolated from specific others.

Long-term mating A committed, ongoing sexual relationship (e.g., marriage).

Long-term memory (LTM) The deepest level of encoding of information—a theoretically limited memory store that contains memories for facts, autobiographical events, and learned skills. LTM is a component of the modal model of memory.

LSD (lysergic acid diethylamide25) A powerful psychedelic drug.

Lucid dream A type of apex dream where the dreamer becomes aware that he or she is dreaming.

Magnetic resonance imaging (MRI) Brain imaging technique that uses radio waves and protons within a magnetic field to produce detailed images of the brain or other neural tissue.

Magnetoencephalography (MEG) A brain imaging technology by which recordings are made of magnetic fields generated by neural activity.

Maintenance rehearsal Actively repeating or thinking about information so that it remains in short-term memory.

Mania A highly energized mood state characterized by exaggerated feelings of elation, unrealistically high self-esteem, racing thoughts, reduced need for sleep, and ceaseless energy. Mania may sometimes by dysphoric—characterized by anger, agitation, and irritability rather than elation.

Manipulation of the independent variable When the experimenter makes a purposeful change in the independent variable (IV) to measure any resultant change in the dependent variable (DV).

Marijuana (cannabis) A mild psychedelic drug derived from the leaves of cannabis sativa, a flowering plant originally indigenous to Asia.

Masturbation Pleasuring oneself through manipulation of one's own genitals.

Mean A descriptive statistic measuring the numerical average in a set of data.

Mean-level stability A measure of personality stability based upon comparison of the mean score for each individual trait among a sample as a whole from one measurement period to the next.

Mechanoreceptors Sensory receptors embedded in the skin that play a role in tactition.

Median A descriptive statistic which reports the score above and below which 50% of the sample has scored—that is, the "middle" score.

Medical model The general term used to describe views of psychological disorder which frame them in a medical context. Unlike the myth-of-mental-illness view, medical models view psychological disorders as actual illnesses with specific causes and which necessitate treatment with psychotherapy, medication, or some other process.

Meditation The term has many definitions, but Eastern meditation generally involves at minimum the qualities of relaxed attention and not-thinking.

Melatonin A hormone of the pineal gland, stimulated by darkness and inhibited by light, which is associated with the onset of sleep.

Memory span The amount of information that can be held in a memory store at any one time. The capacity of short-term memory averages four to five items or chunks of information.

Memory From the cognitive perspective, memory involves the encoding, storage, and retrieval of information. Neuroscientists are more likely to define memory as learning-induced changes in the activity of neurons.

Menopause The cessation of a woman's menstrual cycles—the culminating event of the climacteric.

Mental images A type of thought composed of representations in picture form.

Mere exposure effect The human tendency to come to prefer people or things merely because they have become familiar. The founder of mere exposure theory, Robert Zajonc, hypothesizes that the mere exposure effect has evolved in human psychology because it would have enhanced our survival and reproductive success to be generally cautious around unfamiliar objects and people.

Meta-analysis A research study that uses rigorous statistics to summarize data reported in a collection of studies that examine a particular hypothesis or research question. It is a "study of studies."

Metabolic rate The speed with which food is transformed into energy.

Microsleeps Barely perceptible and involuntary periods of sleep lasting between 3 and 15 seconds.

Midbrain A small, lower geographic area of the brain containing the inferior and superior colliculi among other structures.

Mindfulness-based stress reduction (MBSR) A form of meditation training developed by Dr. Jon Kabat-Zinn at University of Massachusetts Medical School. MBSR is based upon Buddhist meditation and psychology, but it lacks the emphasis on insight. The key to MBSR is mindfulness—maintaining a concentrative, nonjudgmental attention to the present moment.

Minnesota Multiphasic Personality Inventory (MMPI) The first and most frequently used objective test of personality. It has shown particular validity in distinguishing between abnormal personality traits indicating mental health problems, and, to a lesser extent, validity in distinguishing normal personality traits.

Mirror neurons A neuron that fires both when an animal performs an action and when the animal observes another performing the same action. Mirror neurons are associated with imitation of others' behavior, and comprehension of others' thoughts, intentions, and emotions.

Misattribution When a memory is attributed to a source other than its actual origin.

Misinformation effect When a person exposed to incorrect information about an event they have experienced later recall the event in a distorted manner by incorporating the false information.

Modal model of memory The traditional model of memory initially devised by Richard Atkinson and Richard Shiffrin. The modal model views memory as consisting of three stages or stores: sensory memory, short-term memory (STM), and long-term memory (LTM).

Mode A descriptive statistic representing the most frequently occurring score in a set of data.

Modeling Learning through imitation of the behaviors of individuals whom one admires.

Modular model A model of the mind that sees the mind as a large collection of components (modules), each of which provides solutions only to specific types of problems.

Molecular genetics Molecular geneticists attempt to identify specific genes responsible for differences among people in particular traits.

Monocular cues Cues to depth perception that can operate even when only one eye is available. Specifically: relative size, texture gradient, linear perspective, interposition, atmospheric influence, and position on the horizon.

Monozygotic (identical) twins Twins who emerge from a single ovum (egg) and share 100% of their genes in common.

Mood stabilizers A general term used to describe a number of classes of drugs used to treat bipolar disorders. These drugs include anticonvulsants, lithium, and second-generation antipsychotics.

Mood A feeling state that is typically less intense than an emotion, but which may last for a much longer time. Moods may or may not be attributable to specific causes.

Morality This term is defined differently in different contexts, but generally describes personal or social beliefs, feelings, and behavior regarding what is right or wrong.

Morphine An alkaloid of opium used as a potent pain killer.

Motivation Mental states which cause people to engage in behavior directed toward achieving some goal or satisfying a need or desire (purposive behavior). Motivations initiate actions, direct them toward the desired goal, and help the person sustain the necessary effort to attain the goal.

Motor neuron A neuron primarily responsible for communication to the muscles and organs.

Müller-Lyer illusion A visual illusion where two lines of identical length appear to be of unequal length.

Myelin sheath Fatty substance surrounding the axon of some neurons. Myelin increases the speed of neuronal transmission.

Myth of mental illness view A view of psychological disorder pioneered by Thomas Szasz which proposes that "mental illness" is really a metaphor for problems in living and does not refer to actual illness or disease processes.

Narcolepsy Chronic disruption of the sleep homeostat and sleep cycle. Those suffering from narcolepsy may feel the irresistible urge to sleep at any time, generally falling directly into REM sleep.

Narcotics Although this term is often used casually to refer to illicit drugs in general, technically it refers only to those derived from opium (opioid drugs).

National character stereotypes Shared ideas about the typical personality type for any given culture or nation. National character stereotypes have been shown to lack validity in spite of the fact that members of the culture in question frequently accept the stereotype.

Nativism The view that at least some human abilities and tendencies are innate. Often contrasted with empiricism in "nature-nurture" debates.

Natural concept Concepts that are easy for people to learn because they exist as part of the natural or social world.

Natural experiment A situation that occurs naturally, but that creates conditions for drawing conclusions about cause and effect.

Naturalistic observation A descriptive research method used to systematically observe "real life" behavior in a naturalistic setting.

Nature-nurture debate A long-standing debate over whether innate biology or environmental experience is the most critical factor in the development of human behavioral characteristics.

Need to affiliate The need to mingle with other people in the same space. Affiliation does not necessarily imply that strong relationships are formed (although they may be), only that one is near other people.

Need to belong An innate need hypothesized by Roy Baumeister and Mark Leary. According to Baumeister and Leary, for belonging needs to be met, a person must experience frequent, primarily positive interactions with at least a few other people. These interactions must take place in the context of stable, enduring relationships where there is concern for one another's welfare.

Need An internal state of tension that motivates a person to perform some action.

Negative cognitive triad Aaron Beck's term to describe a set of irrational, chronic, and erroneous beliefs about the self, the world, and the future.

Negative correlation When an increase in one variable is associated (correlated) with a decrease in another variable.

Negative emotionality The dimension of temperament that describes the degree to which an infant or child is easily frustrated, fearful, uncomfortable, sad, or difficult to soothe.

Negative punishment When the consequence of a behavior is the removal of something reinforcing, generally something rewarding.

Negative reinforcement When a behavior is reinforced through the removal of something that decreases the likelihood of the behavior. Generally it is something aversive or unpleasant that is removed in negative reinforcement.

Negative symptoms The less obvious symptoms of schizophrenia, which include the *absence* of characteristics that are expected of a mentally healthy person. Negative symptoms include flat affect, anhedonia, alogia, and avolition.

Nerve An enclosed bundle of axons forming a communication channel within the peripheral nervous system (outside of the brain or spine).

Neurodevelopmental Any factor which affects the brain but does not have a genetic origin. Neurodevelopmental events may occur prior to birth, at birth, or after birth.

Neuron The cell type that transmits information throughout the nervous system.

Neuroscience The multidisciplinary study of the nervous system.

Neurosis A general term describing adult emotional illness or distortion of personality, popularized in the writings of Freud and his followers. Until relatively recently, *neurosis* continued to be used as a "catch-all" for psychological disorder, but it was abandoned in favor of more specific diagnostic labels drawn from psychiatry.

Neurotransmitter Chemical substances that carry neural signals from one neuron to another across a neuronal synapse.

Neutral stimulus A stimulus that has no natural relationship to an innate response it nonetheless eventually comes to elicit through classical conditioning. For example, a tone has no natural relationship to the human eye-blink response, but a person can be conditioned to blink when hearing a tone if the tone has been repeatedly paired with puffs of air blown at the eye.

Night terrors A parasomnia consisting of episodes during which the sleeper may suddenly sit up in bed screaming in fear, flail, or run as though pursued by a terrifying attacker. Night terrors are not caused by nightmares.

Nocebo When a placebo creates an unwanted or adverse effect, primarily because the person believes the bogus treatment or substance to have harmful effects.

Nociception The component of the sense of touch that registers pain.

Node of Ranvier The gap between myelin sheaths of axon segments

Noise In signal detection theory, noise acknowledges that detection of sensory stimuli may be affected by the occurrence of other, competing stimuli, or by varying psychological states of the perceiver.

Nonmedical use of drugs The use of psychoactive drugs for "recreational" purposes.

Non-rapid-eye-movement (NREM) Sleep Stages 2–4, characterized by cognitive activity, ordinary dreaming, and reduced brain and nervous system activity relative to REM.

Nonshared environment The unique environmental factors and experiences encountered by each developing child but not encountered by other children in the home. For example, a childhood illness, a traumatic experience, a different set of friends, and so forth.

Normal distribution A bell-shaped pattern of scores reflecting predictable individual differences in scoring on standardized tests.

Nurture assumption The term used by Judith Rich Harris to refer to widespread beliefs that parents are the primary socializers of children and that the behavior of parents has a profound impact on the personalities and behavior of their children as adolescents and adults.

Obese Refers to a pathological level of fatness. Obesity is not the same as *overweight*, a lesser degree of heaviness that may or may not cause health problems. Obesity and overweight are defined in practice somewhat differently in different contexts.

Object permanence The child's understanding that objects continue to exist even if they are no longer in view.

Observational learning Learning through the observation of others. Mechanisms of observational learning include modeling and vicarious reinforcement.

Obsessive-compulsive disorder (OCD) A severe anxiety disorder characterized by persistent, intrusive, anxiety-provoking thoughts usually combined with strong but irrational urges to perform repetitive, ritualistic behaviors or mental acts designed to relieve the anxiety provoked by the intrusive thoughts.

Obsessive-compulsive personality disorder (OCPD) A Cluster C personality disorder characterized by preoccupation with orderliness, perfection, and control. Those with OCPD consequently lack flexibility and openness. Because they are obsessed with perfection, they are inefficient (although scrupulously conscientious), because they place order and perfection above productivity. They think in black-and-white terms when it comes to morality, are miserly with money, and find it difficult to delegate tasks to others.

Obstructive sleep apnea (OSA) A sleep disorder caused by narrowing at various sites along the upper airway leading to repeated nightly episodes of inability to breathe.

Occipital lobe Cerebral cortex lobe containing the primary visual cortex (VI) and visual association areas.

Oedipus complex Freud's belief that children in the phallic stage (age 3 or 4 through age 5 or 6) experience powerful erotic desires for the opposite-sex parent, while wishing to eliminate the same-sex parent who is perceived as a rival. According to Freud, the Oedipus complex arises and is resolved differently for boys and girls, with girls experiencing an incomplete resolution. According to Freud, a successful resolution of the Oedipus complex results in the development of an adequate superego.

Olfaction Sense of smell.

Olfactory bulb A tiny extension of the olfactory cortex that interprets olfactory signals as smell.

Olfactory epithelium A patch of mucous membrane inside the nasal cavity containing olfactory sensory neurons.

Olfactory receptors Sensory receptors of the olfactory sensory neurons that receive olfactory signals.

Operant behavior Any behavior of an organism that produces a consequence that is either reinforcing or punishing. In radical behaviorist experimental research, the operant behavior is the behavior the experimenter is attempting to shape or condition.

Operant chamber ("Skinner box") The apparatus B. F. Skinner designed to study operant learning in rats. The operant chamber includes a container of food pellets in a container mounted to the outside of the cage, designed so that the pellets will be delivered to the rat when the rat presses down on a lever near its food tray. The cage is placed within a soundproof, temperature controlled, ventilated chamber.

Operant conditioning (operant learning, instrumental learning) A form of conditioning in which the consequences of a behavior affect the probability that the behavior will be repeated in the future.

Operant therapies A type of behavior therapy based on principles of learning that relies on operant conditioning, in which rewards or punishments for a person's spontaneous behaviors are used to shape desired behaviors.

Operational definition A precise definition of a variable in terms that can be utilized for a research study.

Opioids Any drug derived from opium.

Opium The dried nectar of the common popaver somniferum (poppy) flower containing a number of alkaloids including morphine.

Opponent Process Theory The theory of color vision that proposes that because certain wavelengths of light cannot be combined in an additive process, colors are created in color vision by mixing in three opposing pairs: blue vs. yellow, red vs. green, and black vs. white.

Opponent processes Any process which functions as the antagonist of another process. The autonomic nervous system consists of two opponent process subsystems: the sympathetic and parasympathetic nervous systems. If the sympathetic nervous system is activated, the parasympathetic system is suppressed. If the parasympathetic system is activated, the sympathetic system is suppressed.

Optic disc The area where the optic nerve leaves the retina.

Optic nerve The nerve that carries neural signals from the back of the retina to the central nervous system.

Optimal arousal theory A theory proposed in reaction to problems with drive theory, optimal arousal theory states that people seek to maintain an optimal level of arousal. This could mean reducing levels of arousal from unpleasantly high levels, as described in drive theory, but it could also mean *increasing* levels

of arousal from unpleasantly low levels, as in states of boredom or excessive rest.

Oral-genital sex Stimulating a partner's genitals with the lips or tongue. Stimulation of the penis in this way is known as *fellatio*. Stimulation of the vulva in this way is known as *cunnilingus*. Common slang for oral genital sex includes *blow job*, *going down*, *giving head*, and *blowing*.

Ordinary dreaming Dreams depicting relatively realistic activities and recognizable characters.

Orgasm The psychological and physiological "climax" of sexual activity as described in the sexual response cycle. Orgasm is characterized by intense physical pleasure and euphoria, muscle contraction and spasm, and sharply increased heart rate and respiration. Orgasm in men is followed by a refractory (rest) period, but women may experience additional successive serial orgasms.

Orgasmic platform A tube-like tightening of the outer third of the vagina during the plateau phase of the sexual response cycle.

Ossicles Three tiny bones of the middle ear that amplify sound. The bones are called the hammer, anvil, and stirrup.

Outer ear Outer structure of the ear, consisting primarily of the pinna and ear canal.

Ovaries The female gonad.

Overdose Taking a lethal or nonlethal but toxic dose of a drug.

Ovum The female reproductive cell following initial cell division at the point of fertilization.

Own-group conformity pressure A stressful pressure to behave in a manner that a given ethnic group community believes is appropriate for one of its own.

Panic attack A brief period—generally peaking at about 10 minutes—within which a person experiences overwhelming anxiety focused upon unexplainable, terrifying physical sensations. These sensations may include shortness of breath, tightness in the chest, a feeling of unreality, perspiration, pounding of the heart, and an overpowering urge to flee. Panic attacks are not uncommon in the population and do not necessarily signify psychological disorder.

Panic disorder An anxiety disorder characterized by intense anxiety over the prospect of experiencing a panic attack. Thus, people with panic disorder have experienced at least one such attack. Panic disorder may sometimes lead to *agorabphobia*, a fear of being in public places, crowds, or locations from which escape would be difficult.

Paranoid personality disorder (PPD) Paranoid personality disorder is a Cluster A personality disorder characterized by mistrust and suspicion of others' motives. Those with PPD expect to be

betrayed, humiliated, and taken advantage of. They are hostile and argumentative, and do not easily confide in others.

Paranormal Events that defy ordinary explanation.

Paraprofessional A person who has obtained a nonprofessional level of education in a field such as education, law, or psychology, but who has obtained a job performing some of the duties ordinarily carried out by professionals.

Parapsychology A branch of psychology that studies paranormal abilities, primarily extrasensory perception and telekinesis.

Parasomnias A group of sleep disorders characterized by unusual or bizarre physical behaviors, perceptions, dreams, or emotions during sleep.

Parasympathetic nervous system Division of the autonomic nervous system that returns the body to resting state following arousal and maintains that resting state.

Parietal lobe Lobe of the cerebral cortex containing the somatosensory cortex and somatosensory association areas.

Parsimony In science, the term *parsimony* describes the principle that if there are more than one competing explanations for some phenomenon, each plausible, scientists like to choose the simpler of the explanations. This is because simpler explanations contain fewer assumptions that might be incorrect. The principle of parsimony is also known as Occam's Razor.

Partial reinforcement effect The name given to research findings which show that conditioned behaviors are more enduring and difficult to extinguish when they are reinforced periodically rather than continuously.

Partial reinforcement When a behavior is reinforced periodically rather than continuously. Partial reinforcement can be determined by the passage of time (an interval schedule) or the number of times an organism performs a behavior (a ratio schedule).

Participant effect Any confounding variable introduced by the participant's behavior Demand characteristics: Any action or attitude on the part of the experimenter that cues the research participants as to what sort of behavior the experimenter would prefer to see.

Participant observational study A naturalistic descriptive study where the researcher not only observes, but also participates in what he or she is observing.

Patriarchy Any social organization where the large majority of the uppermost positions in political and social hierarchies are occupied by men.

Penile erection Engorgement of the spongy columns of the penis with blood during sexual excitement.

Perceived self-efficacy Albert Bandura's term to describe one's core beliefs about ability to produce change or accomplish a specific task through one's own effort. Although some people may be higher than others in perceived self-efficacy across many domains, perceived self-efficacy is not a trait in which a person can be globally high or low. It always refers to specific tasks, and a person high in perceived self-efficacy on one task can be quite low on another.

Perception Organization and interpretation of sensory signals by the brain.

Perceptual constancy The ability to perceive an object as itself regardless of changes in angle of viewing, distance, or illumination.

Perceptual set The expectations, biases, and preconceptions that we bring to a given perception.

Peripheral nervous system Cranial and spinal nerves that allow communication to take place between the brain and body. Consists of two divisions: somatic nervous system and autonomic nervous system.

Permissive parents Characterized by highly accepting and warm relations between parent and child, but little in the way of setting boundaries, limits, or rules.

Persistence When an unpleasant memory intrudes upon a person's thoughts against his or her will.

Personality assessment The field of personality measurement. Personality is generally assessed using projective tests, which reflect personality as it is "projected" onto test materials by the test-taker, and objective tests, which use computer analysis to empirically measure personality characteristics.

Personality disorders Pervasive, chronic patterns of inner experience and behavior which generally begin in adolescence, are inflexible, and are expressed throughout many areas of a person's life. These patterns cause distress and/or impairment, but symptoms are generally not as severe as those of clinical disorders.

Personality Personality is the set of common human psychological characteristics and unique patterns of traits and behavior possessed by each individual. These sets of traits and behavior patterns are organized, integrated, and relatively enduring.

Person-situation controversy A major debate within personality psychology beginning during the 1960s in the work of Walter Mischel. The debate contrasted the views of those who believed traits were of primary importance in determining behavior and those who believed that situations—not traits—determine behavior.

Peyote A psychedelic cactus.

Pharmacotherapy The use of drugs and other substances to treat psychological disorders or distress. Pharmacotherapy is based on psychopharmacology, the study of the effects of drugs and other substances on mood, emotion, and behavior.

Phenotype Any potentially observable trait or characteristic of a living organism. Phenotypes may be physiological, biochemical, anatomical, behavioral, or mental.

Photoreceptors Neurons dedicated to capturing light in order to initiate transduction.

Phrenology Pseudoscientific theory that proposed that personality characteristics could be determined by skilled examinations of bumps on the top of the skull.

Pineal gland Gland situated in the brain that releases the hormone melatonin, important in regulating the sleep/wake cycle.

Pinna The visible structure of the outer ear that collects sounds and orients us to the placement of their source.

Pitch Highness or lowness of a sound.

Pituitary gland Gland situated in the brain that secretes a variety of hormones and triggers other glands to secrete their hormones. Helps regulate blood pressure; body growth; aspects of pregnancy, childbirth and lactation; and the functioning of sex and reproductive organs.

Placebo Any bogus procedure or inactive (inert) substance—cornstarch or milk sugar, for example—administered to a patient who believes the substance or procedure is a genuine treatment. Although placebos are sometimes given to patients whose symptoms have no organic cause—to satisfy the patient's desire to be "treated"—research has shown that placebos can sometimes trigger physiological events which actually reduce symptoms.

Placenta The flat organ connected to the uterus on one side and to the embryo on the other. The developing fetus receives nutrition and oxygen from the mother through the placenta, and this organ also provides protection for the fetus from attack by the mother's own immune defenses.

Plasticity The brain's ability to change in response to learning, practice, and sensory input; and the ability of specialized regions of the brain to adapt if necessary to perform tasks for which they are not ordinarily used.

Plateau The second stage of the sexual response cycle representing peak excitement levels. Although Masters and Johnson applied this stage both to men and women, evidence suggests that only women experience plateau—marked by the retraction of the clitoris beneath the clitoral hood and the formation of the orgasmic platform.

Pleasure principle According to Freud, the pleasure principle drives a person to seek pleasure and rewarding experiences, while avoiding pain and discomfort. It is the pleasure principle which drives the *id*.

Polarization The resting potential balance between primarily negatively-charged ions within a neuron and positively charged ions without.

Population The larger group of interest to a researcher, from which he or she will draw a smaller sample for the purposes of conducting a research study.

Positive assortment (matching phenomenon) The tendency to mate with a person who is similar to you in various characteristics. Positive assortment has been documented for attractiveness, height, weight, occupation, religion, age, race, education, political attitudes, and so forth.

Positive correlation When an increase in one variable is associated (correlated) with an increase in another variable.

Positive illusions Systematic biases and illusions that not only are self-serving by presenting the self in a positive way, but also are associated with positive mental health and other consequences for the person possessing them. Positive illusions include uncritically positive views of the self, illusions of control, and unrealistic optimism.

Positive punishment When the consequence of a behavior is the addition or presentation of something that decreases the likelihood that the behavior will be repeated. Generally it is something unpleasant or aversive that is added or presented.

Positive reinforcement When a behavior is reinforced through the addition or presentation of something that increases the likelihood that the behavior will be repeated. Generally it is something pleasant or rewarding that is added or presented.

Positive self-regard Carl Rogers' term to describe feelings of self-worth and self-esteem, and being loved and accepted. According to Rogers, positive self-regard is dependent upon experiences of unconditional positive regard from others.

Positive symptoms Symptoms of schizophrenia which include the *addition* of something to a person's behavior which are not expected of a mentally healthy person. These are the more obvious symptoms of schizophrenia, such as delusions, hallucinations, and disorganized use of language.

Postconventional morality According to Lawrence Kohlberg, moral judgment based on abstract principles and personal beliefs.

Post-synaptic neuron The "receiving" neuron in neuronal communication.

Post-traumatic stress disorder (PTSD) An anxiety disorder triggered by an experience of extremely severe trauma which evokes horror, feelings of helpless, and fear for one's life or the lives of those for whom one cares. Symptoms may include re-experiencing the traumatic event in nightmares or flashbacks, numbing, and symptoms of physiological arousal resulting in sleep problems, bursts of anger, or an exaggerated startle response.

Potentially harmful psychotherapies (PHPs) Therapies that may result in iatrogenic (therapist-caused) harm to clients.

Practical intelligence A concept hypothesized by Robert J. Sternberg to describe the ability to come up with efficient solutions to everyday problems.

Preconventional morality According to Lawrence Kohlberg, moral judgment based on the prospect of reward or punishment.

Preoperational stage Piaget's developmental stage lasting from approximately age 2 to 7, and characterized by development of the symbolic capacity of the child's mind.

Pre-synaptic neuron The "sending" neuron in neuronal communication.

Primary reinforcer Any consequence of behavior that is intrinsically reinforcing to virtually any member of the species being conditioned. Primary reinforcers are intrinsically reinforcing because they are essential for the survival or reproduction of the organism (examples: food, water, sex, air, shelter, etc.).

Primary sex characteristics Development in the reproductive and sexual organs.

Proactive interference When an old memory interferes with the retrieval of a new memory.

Probability sampling Any sampling procedure in which the probability of an individual being selected for the sample is known in advance and selection is on a generally random basis (e.g., simple random sampling).

Problem An obstacle that stands in the way of achieving some goal.

Procedural knowledge Knowledge that is applied to the performance of a task. Procedural knowledge reflects skills and abilities—"knowing how" as compared with "knowing that" (explicit knowledge).

Procedural memory Implicit memory for skills involving motor coordination.

Prototype An example of a concept or category that is thought to be particularly typical or representative.

Proximate causes Proximate causes are the immediate causes of behavior—how something occurs. Proximate causes of behavior include motivations; physiological, biochemical, and neural processes; and learning. Most psychologists

focus on proximate explanations of behavior.

Proximity A Gestalt law of perceptual grouping that states that people tend to group figures together that are near one another.

Pseudoscience Non-science performed for non-scientific goals but with the surface appearance of science.

Psi The parapsychology term for paranormal abilities such as extrasensory perception and telekinesis.

Psychedelic mushrooms A general term used for various psychedelic fungi.

Psychedelics Drugs that substantially alter one's perception of reality.

Psychiatry A branch of medicine concerned with diagnosing and treating mental health problems.

Psychoactive drug Any substance with properties that affect mental life or consciousness in some way.

Psychoanalysis A theory and psychotherapeutic technique founded by Sigmund Freud and based upon the notion that human beings are driven by unconscious conflicts and desires originating primarily in experiences of early childhood.

Psychodynamic psychotherapy A general approach to psychotherapy based on principles originating in psychoanalysis. Psychodynamic theorists share psychoanalytic beliefs that unconscious emotional and motivational processes exert important effects on a person, that the origins of personality are in childhood, and that human beings create symbolic mental representations of the self and important personal relationships.

Psychological adaptation A mental characteristic that evolved through natural selection to provide solutions to specific types of problems encountered over evolutionary time by our human ancestors.

Psychological disorder Psychological disorder is defined differently by different theorists and in different contexts. In its broadest sense, the definition is circular: any recognizable cluster of behaviors and states of mind that mental health professionals agree constitute mental illness and to which they attach a descriptive label.

Psychological dysfunction Any breakdown in mental functioning—cognitive, emotional, or behavioral. The boundaries between "functional" and "dysfunctional" are often fuzzy, however, and there is wide disagreement as to how to characterize these boundaries.

Psychological science The modern scientific study of psychology, originating in the late 19th century.

Psychology The scientific study of mind and behavior.

Psychometric Objective measurement of a psychological attribute (such as

intelligence or personality) using standardized tests.

Psychoneuroimmunology The scientific study of the interaction of psychology, nervous and endocrine systems, and immune systems.

Psychophysicists Scientists who study sensation and perception.

Psychosocial stages Erik Erikson's notion that there are eight developmental stages from infancy to old age, during which each person experiences a characteristic conflict that must be resolved.

Psychotherapy A unique, modern, healing relationship involving a client and a paid therapist. The relationship is temporary and focused entirely on the needs and problems of the client. Each meeting of therapist and client is time-limited, confidential, and conducted in a structured setting.

Psychotic disorder Any disorder that includes extremely severe distortion in thinking and perception, where a person's ability to grasp reality and respond rationally is badly impaired.

Publication bias The systematic exclusion of certain types of results from publication in favor of other types of results. Publication bias can result from a number of different practices, including withholding certain types of results from submission to journals, editorial decisions on the part of journal editors, and submitting data from the same study multiple times to give the impression that more studies found a particular result than is actually the case.

Punishment When the consequence of a behavior decreases the likelihood that it will continue or be repeated in the future.

Pupil A small opening in the iris of the eye.

Qualitative research Any research study (generally descriptive research) that collects extremely detailed information which conveys the quality of the research participant's experience. Qualitative data are very rich but do not easily lend themselves to quantitative (statistical) analysis.

Qualitativeness The feature of consciousness which suggests that something is conscious only if it "feels like something" to be that thing.

Quantitative performance Performance on tasks necessitating mathematics skills.

Quantitative research Any research study that collects data in a form that may be analyzed statistically. Typically, quantitative research is conducted using larger samples than is possible in qualitative research projects.

Radical behaviorism B. F. Skinner's version of behaviorism, also referred to as experimental analysis of behavior. Radical behaviorists propose that all behavior is lawful—and any given behavior can be analyzed empirically by examining the reinforcements and punishments which follow the behavior. The term "radical" has been applied to this school of psychology because radical behaviorists believe that psychology can only be a science of behavior and never a science of "mind."

Random assignment to conditions When each participant has an equal chance of being assigned to any of the conditions of the experiment (i.e., any of the levels of the independent variable).

Randomized Controlled Trial (RCT) A randomized controlled trial is a research study used to evaluate a therapy or treatment where the research participants are randomly assigned to receive either the treatment of interest, a competing treatment, no treatment, or—if possible—a placebo treatment.

Rank-order stability A measure of personality stability based upon the pattern of rank-order of traits (from high to low) for each person in a sample from one measurement period to the next.

Rapid-eye-movement (REM) The fifth stage of sleep characterized by high levels of brain and nervous system activity and intensely vivid, hallucinatory dreaming.

Rational-emotive behavior therapy (REBT) A form of therapy devised by Albert Ellis and based on the idea that emotional distress is rooted in illogical, absolutist, and counterproductive ideas and beliefs (the ABC theory of emotional disturbance). REBT is *directive*—the therapist's job is to forcefully dispute the client's illogical and unrealistic beliefs.

Rationalism The philosophical movement founded by René Descartes which held that beliefs should be formed through the use of reason, rather than relying upon personal experience or the pronouncements of authorities.

Reactive gene-environment correlation When an organisms' genotype evokes responses in others, creating an environment that shares characteristics with that genotype.

Reality principle According to Freud, just as the pleasure principle drives the id, the ego is driven by the reality principle. The reality principle allows the person to delay gratification in the service of a later beneficial outcome, and is the principle by which the ego makes decisions bearing on the survival and functioning of the person.

Recursion The quality of language that allows any sentence to be extended indefinitely by embedding clauses or phrases within it or following it.

Red-green color deficiency When M- and L-cones (see Trichromatic theory of color) are equally sensitive to red and green, making differentiation of these colors impossible.

Reflex An innate, involuntary neuromuscular response to stimuli.

Reformulated frustration-aggression hypothesis Leonard Berkowitz's revision of an earlier theory which stated that all aggression is in response to the frustration of a goal. According to the reformulated theory, frustration is only one of many types of unpleasant events that could lead to aggression. The theory holds that aggression occurs when an unpleasant event (e.g., provocation by another person, extreme noise) may trigger feelings, images, and memories associated with the physiological changes that ordinarily accompany threat and danger.

Refractory period The postorgasm period for men, during which a man is unable to achieve an erection. The refractory period may last from minutes to days, depending upon the man's age, health, how often he has been engaging in sex, and the degree to which he is attracted to his partner.

Reinforcement When the consequence of a behavior increases the likelihood that the behavior will continue or be repeated in the future.

Relaxation response Herbert Benson's term to describe an alteration in consciousness that results in decreased physiological and psychological arousal and increased attention to the moment.

Reliability A reliable test is constructed so that if it is intended to measure something enduring about a person, the person will score much the same if taking the test on two or more separate occasions. A reliable test is also one which will report the same result regardless of who is doing the scoring—in other words, scoring is not subjective and will not differ from one rater to the next.

REM-sleep behavior disorder A parasomnia where the sleeper is missing the muscle paralysis component of REM sleep and "acts out" confrontational and violent dreams.

Renewal In classical conditioning, renewal is a resurgence of an extinguished behavior if the animal is placed in a different context from the one in which extinction originally occurred and the original conditioned stimulus (CS) is once again presented.

Repetition priming When performance on a task improves as a result of previous implicit exposure.

Repetitive transcranial magnetic stimulation (rTMS) A technique being developed for treatment of depression that consists of sending short electromagnetic pulses though the cerebral cortex by means of a coil placed on the scalp.

Replication When a research study is repeated by other researchers working independently. Replications may be exact, following the procedures of the original study to the letter, or they may

be conceptual—repeating the essence of the study but using somewhat different procedures, variables, or operational definitions.

Representativeness heuristic When people are confronted with an example of a person or thing that they do not know how to categorize or explain, they may compare the new person or thing with *prototypes* of various categories until a "match" is found.

Repression An ego defense mechanism identified by Freud, where an unacceptable wish, thought, or impulse is removed from conscious awareness.

Research methods This term is used differently in different contexts, but it is used here to refer to general strategies that may be used for conducting research. There are three basic categories of research method: sescriptive, experimental, and correlational.

Resilience The ability to emerge relatively intact from unexpected adverse events or to recover fully from any temporary symptoms. Resilience is the most common human response to trauma.

Resolution The stage of the sexual response cycle where a person returns to a nonaroused state.

Response bias In signal detection theory, response bias refers to the fact that a person may be biased in favor of, or against, the detection of a stimulus.

Resting potential The "default" resting setting of a neuron—the setting that would be maintained if no action potentials were fired.

Retina A light-sensitive membrane spread out across most of the inner surface of the rear of the eye. It is upon the retina that images are formed.

Retinal disparity A binocular cue to depth perception based on the fact that each eye takes in a slightly different, but overlapping, view.

Retrieval cue Any hint or association that helps one retrieve a long-term memory.

Retrieval Recognizing or recalling something from long-term memory.

Retroactive interference When a new memory interferes with the retrieval of an old memory.

Re-uptake When the pre-synaptic neuron reabsorbs some of the neurotransmitter molecules it has released, following binding of the neurotransmitter to receptor sites in the post-synaptic neuron.

Revised NEO Personality Inventory (NEO PI-R) The most frequently used test of the five-factor model of personality ("Big Five").

Rich false memory A vivid false memory replete with rich detail and emotional content.

Risk factor Any variable whose presence increases the probability that a person will be diagnosed with a particular disorder.

Because risk factors are only correlated with a disorder, they cannot be said to be causes of the disorder. They simply help researchers predict who is more or less likely ultimately to develop a disorder.

RNA (ribonucleic acid) A chemical compound found in each cell nucleus and cytoplasm. RNA carries out the job of constructing protein from "instructions" contained in genes.

Rods Photoreceptors specialized to allow night vision and vision in low light.

Rohypnol (flunitrazapam) A highly potent benzodiazepine drug often used to treat severe insomnia (street name: "roofies").

Rorschach test A projective personality and mental health test originally devised by Hermann Rorschach in 1921. The test consists of a standard set of five color and five black-and-white symmetrical inkblots. The test-taker is then asked to describe what he or she sees in each blot and to identify the specific areas of the blot from which the image is constructed. The Rorschach is perhaps the most controversial of personality assessment instruments, with numerous critics claiming that the test lacks reliability and/or validity.

Rumination Focusing inwardly and brooding on the possible causes and consequences of past or future negative emotions and events.

Sadism-masochism (SM) A global term that includes sexual interest in providing or experiencing pain, domination, humiliation, and/or bondage.

Safety ratio A statistic expressing the potential toxicity of a drug in terms of the dose one would need to take to cause death.

Sample A relatively small group of individuals selected to represent a larger group—the population from which the sample is drawn.

Sapir-Whorf hypothesis (linguistic determinism) The notion that the way we construe reality is determined by the way our particular language is constructed.

Schemas A mental structure or cognitive model that represents some aspect of the world and how it works.

Schizophrenia Schizophrenia is a group of related psychotic conditions characterized by severely distorted perception and experience of reality, disorganized thought and speech, and inappropriate emotions and emotional responses.

Science A unique, systematic, self-correcting empirical method of obtaining knowledge about the natural world. Science incorporates empirical observation and logical inference and is characterized by specific goals and methods. Science is skeptical in outlook.

Scientific method A classical sequence of five steps involved in the acquisition of scientific knowledge. In fact, science

is often accomplished with variations on this sequence, and as such the scientific method should more accurately be termed scientific methods.

Second pain The generally longer lasting, less localized, and more unpleasant pain sensations, conducted along the slower C-fibers.

Secondary oocyte The mature, unfertilized, female reproductive cell.

Secondary reinforcer A reinforcer that has become associated through conditioning with one or more primary reinforcers (examples: money and status).

Secondary sex characteristics Development in anatomy and physiology which occur during puberty but are not directly related to the genitals or gonads. For example, growth of pubic and underarm hair, changes in height, breast development, changes in body shape, development of chest hair, changes in vocal pitch, and so forth.

Second-generation antipsychotics Recently developed drugs designed to treat psychotic disorders such as schizophrenia, but also used as mood stabilizers in bipolar disorder.

Second-order conditioning A form of classical conditioning in which an organism is first conditioned to a neutral stimulus; and then that stimulus is used to condition the organism to a new neutral stimulus. For example, a dog conditioned to salivate upon hearing a tone by pairing the tone with food, may then be conditioned to associate the tone with a new neutral stimulus—a bell. The dog will then salivate upon hearing the bell, even if the bell was never actually paired with the unconditioned stimulus of food.

Selective serotonin reuptake inhibitors (SSRIs) A relatively recently developed type of antidepressant drug that blocks the reuptake of the neurotransmitter serotonin, while having relatively little effect on other neurotransmitters—in contrast to the tricyclics and MAO inhibitors.

Self Each person's awareness of, and ideas about, his or her own individual nature, characteristics, and existence.

Self-concept The sum total of a person's evaluation of the nature and quality of his or her unique existence. Self-concept includes social, physiological, and psychological aspects.

Accurate empathy Carl Rogers' term to describe the quality of communication between two people where each person genuinely listens to the other's words, hears the words, perceives the intention accurately, and withholds judgment.

Self-control That aspect of self-regulation which involves suppressing a powerful immediate response or goal in the service of a more important overriding long-term goal. Self-control typically involves resisting temptation.

Self-esteem A person's cognitive and emotional assessment or evaluation of his or her self-worth. Self-esteem may be *global*—a person's assessment of overall self-worth—or *specific* to a given domain.

Self-help support group A therapeutic group based on mutual support that is generally not headed by a mental health professional (and is therefore not an example of psychotherapy). Also in contrast to psychotherapy, most self-help groups are free and ongoing indefinitely. They are generally organized around a particular issue—for example, substance abuse, cancer survival, child abuse, mental illness, and so forth.

Self-narratives Internal "narratives of the self" which evolve through the life span. Self-narratives are stories and myths people tell themselves about events in their lives and personal characteristics which reflect their current understanding of their place in the world and the meaning of their life.

Self-regulation All of the ways that the self monitors and exerts control over its responses so as to accomplish goals and live up to personal standards.

Self-serving bias The tendency to make systematic judgment errors in one's favor in any of three ways: overestimating one's contributions, overestimating one's positive attributes relative to others, and attributing successes and good deeds to one's own efforts but failures and bad deeds to circumstances, bad luck, or other people.

Semantic encoding Memory encoding according to the meaning of the stimulus.

Semantic memory Memory for facts one has learned, as opposed to personal experiences. Semantic memory is one type of explicit (declarative) memory.

Sensation The receiving of raw physical or chemical energy through the sense organs.

Sensitization A simple type of nonassociative learning that occurs when a stimulus comes to elicit increased response from an organism as a result of the organism's repeated exposure to the stimulus over time.

Sensorimotor stage Piaget's developmental stage lasting from birth to approximately age 2, and characterized by unthinking responses to internal and external stimuli and events.

Sensory adaptation The tendency for one's sensitivity to stimuli to be lessened over time during continuous exposure.

Sensory memory The memory stage that very briefly stores large amounts of fleeting sensory impressions. Sensory memory is comprised of iconic store (visual) and echoic store (auditory).

Sensory neuron A neuron that transmits sensory information to the brain.

Serial orgasms Repeated orgasms in women after returning directly to the plateau phase, with no intervening resolution phase (often called *multiple orgasms*).

Sex differences in cognition A field of research focused primarily upon possible sex differences in verbal, visual-spatial, and quantitative (mathematics) ability, motivation, and/or performance.

Sex play Sexual behavior of children that is primarily exploratory or playful in nature. Children throughout the world engage in sex play, and such play appears to be generally harmless unless it is accompanied by guilt or aggression.

Sex reassignment surgery A surgical procedure sometimes chosen by transsexuals where artificial genitals of the sex with which the transsexual identifies are formed from his or her own genital tissue as well as inorganic (plastic) material.

Sex-typed play and toy preferences Preferences for toys and play styles associated with either boys or girls. Sex-typed play and toy preferences emerge at early ages.

Sexual aggression Sexual acts committed on another person without that person's consent. Sexual aggression includes rape, sexual assault, and sexual abuse.

Sexual fantasy Sexual activity in thought or mental images and reveries of a sexual nature.

Sexual intercourse The term generally reserved to describe insertion of a man's penis in a woman's vagina.

Sexual orientation A complex term that is defined differently by different people. The *three-factor* model takes into account (a) the sex of the people with whom one most desires to have sex; (b) the sex of the people with whom one actually has sex; and (c) the label one chooses to apply to one's sexual identity (gay, straight, or bisexual). The *desire-driven* model defines sexual orientation as "an enduring erotic desire for members either of one's own sex, the other sex, or both—regardless of the actual sex of the persons with whom one engages in sex and regardless of the label one used to apply to oneself." The *continuum* model suggests that categories like *gay*, *straight*, and *bisexual* cannot adequately capture sexual orientation at all—proposing instead that people can vary greatly in the extent to which they experience same-sex and other-sex desires and behaviors.

Shape constancy The facet of perceptual constancy that allows us to perceive an object as the same shape regardless of the angle from which we view it.

Shaping by successive approximation (shaping for short) Successive reinforcement of those operant behaviors that come increasingly closer to the behavior one ultimately wishes to reinforce.

Shared environment Environmental factors and experiences shared by all children living in a home—for example, the parent's socioeconomic status, language and culture, beliefs and attitudes, and childrearing and discipline styles.

Short-term mating Sexual behavior that is casual in nature and not part of a committed relationship.

Short-term memory (STM) Short-term memory is a memory store used for attending to information in the short term. Short-term memory is limited in the length of time the memory can remain active—no longer than about 20 seconds. It is also limited in the amount of information that can be stored. No more than about four to five items or chunks of information. STM is one component of the modal model of memory.

Signal detection theory A theory that attempts to explain how stimuli are detected by factoring in the variables of human judgment and bias.

Signs In medical terminology, a sign is an objective indication of the presence of disease that the physician can observe or measure by test (e.g., broken bone, fever, swelling, abnormal cardiogram, skin eruptions, etc.). This is contrasted with a *symptom*, which is a patient complaint ("I've been feeling dizzy and easily fatigued").

Similarity A Gestalt law of perceptual grouping which states that people tend to group figures together if they are similar to one another.

Size constancy The facet of perceptual constancy that allows us to perceive an object as the same size regardless of the size of its image on our retina.

Skepticism A philosophical approach or point of view based upon the scientific method which proposes that compelling evidence of a claim should be presented before one comes to believe in the claim.

Sleep cycle The repeating pattern of Stages 2–5 sleep that recurs four to six times throughout the night following sleep onset (Sleep Stage 1).

Sleep debt When the sleep homeostat creates the urge to make up for lost sleep by sleeping longer or more frequently than usual.

Sleep homeostasis A balance between sleep and waking, governed by the sleep homeostat.

Sleep homeostat Coordinated biochemical, neural, and psychological functions that "keep track" of the amount of sleep a person has had relative to the number of hours of waking.

Sleep mentation Any and all mental activity occurring during sleep, including "sleep thinking" and various levels of dreaming.

Sleep stages The five stages of sleep, including a period of sleep onset, three periods of NREM, and one of REM sleep. Each stage is associated with characteristic brain wave activity, and the stages are played out during the night in repeating pattern (the sleep cycle).

Sleep thinking (cognitive activity) Rational, directed thought occurring during NREM sleep.

Sleepwalking A *parasomnia* characterized by wandering, often aimlessly, during late-REM sleep.

Social comparison theory A group of theories initially formulated by Leon Festinger that describe how and why people may compare themselves to others to rationally evaluate themselves or enhance their self-concepts and defend against negative self-judgments.

Social intuitionism Positive psychologist Jonathan Haidt's theory of moral judgment. The theory proposes that moral judgments are more often than not the result of intuition and emotion rather than reasoning. Reasoning tends to occur after the fact to explain to oneself or others why one has arrived at a particular moral judgment.

Social motivation The innate human motivation to interact with other humans.

Social phobia Irrational anxiety over social or performance situations where one is likely to be exposed to unfamiliar people and the prospect of embarrassment or humiliation exists. Social phobia is a controversial diagnosis, because social phobia is an extreme expression of the normal characteristic of shyness. Some theorists worry that people who are "painfully shy" are being labeled as "mentally disordered."

Social psychology The scientific study of the influence of social situations on individuals, and the influence of individuals on social situations. Social psychologists often focus on the idea of the self and study the social individual alone, in interpersonal situations, and in groups.

Social role theory A theory that proposes that people behave in highly variable ways according to differences in the type of social organization in which they live.

Social support The perception or experience that one is loved, esteemed, and cared for by others, and is part of a network of people who engage in mutual assistance and accept mutual obligations to one another.

Society An enduring and cooperating group whose members have developed institutions and organized patterns of interaction.

Sociocognitive theory of hypnosis A theory that explains hypnotic effects in terms other than "altered states"—generally emphasizing the subject's social role in the hypnotic interaction.

Sociocultural perspective A general approach to psychology that focuses on the ways society and culture mold and influence behavior.

Somatic nervous system The nerves that regulate voluntary actions and convey sensory information to the brain.

Somatosensory area Area of the cortex where tactile sensations are perceived.

Specific phobia A powerful but irrational fear of a specific object, animal, or situation. The most common phobias are often those for which the evolutionary roots are suspected (e.g., fear of the dark or heights, fear of spiders or snakes, fear of the sight of blood).

Sperm The male reproductive cell.

Spinal cord Thin, tubular bundle of nerve tracts contained in the vertebrae of the spinal column.

Spinal reflexes Automatic motor actions in response to stimulation. Spinal reflexes bypass the brain entirely.

Split-brain surgery (callosotomy) A surgical procedure used to treat epilepsy, where the corpus callosum is severed or partially severed.

Spontaneous recovery When an extinguished behavior reemerges (but in a somewhat weaker form) after the organism has rested from exposure to the classically conditioned stimulus. Spontaneous recovery differs from renewal, where an extinguished behavior reemerges specifically because the organism is placed in a context different from the one in which extinction occurred.

Spotlight effect Thomas Gilovich's term to describe egocentric judgments of the impression one is making on others. According to Gilovich, people tend to believe that "the social spotlight shines more brightly on them than it actually does."

SSRI discontinuation syndrome A drug withdrawal syndrome associated with the use of at least some of the SSRI and SNRI antidepressants. The syndrome may consist of flu-like symptoms, dizziness, weakness, nausea, fatigue, feelings of "unreality," loss of balance, lightheadedness, "electric-shock" sensations, and other symptoms.

Stages of psychosexual development Freud believed that children pass through five developmental stages of psychosexual growth. For healthy personality to develop, the child must successfully complete the tasks and resolve the conflicts which typically occur at each stage. Fixation at any particular stage may result in adult neurosis or distortion of personality. The stages are termed *oral, anal, phallic (Oedipal), latency,* and *genital.*

Stanford-Binet Intelligence Scale The first version of the IQ test created by Alfred Binet. The purpose of the test was to predict academic performance so that children of deficient ability could be identified and placed in special remedial programs. The test has been revised four times over its 100-year history.

State-dependent memory When retrieval of a memory is enhanced by internal states such as mood or drug effects that were present when the memory was encoded.

States Emotions, moods, or other characteristics and attributes which are temporary in nature. States can be contrasted with traits, which are assumed to be enduring. For example, *anger* is a temporary state, whereas *short-tempered* is a relatively enduring trait.

Statistical literacy A term used by Gerd Gigerenzer and his colleagues to describe a basic arithmetic understanding of the nature of statistical claims, particularly those used in health sciences.

Statistical significance An inferential statistical procedure that allows one to determine the probability that one's research results reflect actual relationships among variables and are not due to chance factors.

Stereotype threat Reduced task or test performance when negative stereotypes about the sex or minority group to which a person belongs are activated in his or her own mind.

Stereotyping Attributing clusters of traits to specific categories of individuals or objects. These clusters of traits create an image or conception of the "typical" member of the category or its stereotype. Stereotypes of social groups often contain a degree of accuracy but are also frequently misapplied. Stereotypes are misapplied when one assumes that any given individual from a group is likely to display the average characteristics of the group, or when inaccurate information about the group's average characteristics is used to construct the group stereotype in the first place.

Stigma A social "badge" or mark of shame or disgrace resulting from a person's behavior or membership in a disapproved or discriminated-against group. Social stigma traditionally has been a problem for those diagnosed with psychological disorders.

Stimulants Drugs that increase alertness and energy.

Storage The memory process whereby meaningful perceptions are retained as memory.

Strengths Martin Seligman describes strengths as those enduring qualities which result from a person having consistently made constructive life choices in specific areas. Strengths are the choices one makes which lead to the development of universally valued virtues such as wisdom, courage, humanity, and justice.

According to Seligman there are 24 principal human strengths.

Stress Biologists and psychologists define stress differently. Biologists usually define stress as any event that threatens homeostasis of an organism. Psychologists usually define stress as the psychological and physiological consequence of events which challenge a person's ability to cope and which threaten well-being or interfere with important goals. Each specific stressful event is termed a *stressor.*

Structuralism A defunct psychological school founded by Edward Titchener, a student of Wilhelm Wundt. Structuralists believed that experience could be broken down into separate sensory components or "structures." The structuralists used introspection as a tool to investigate the structures of experience.

Subjectivity In consciousness studies this word means that consciousness can only be experienced by an individual being and cannot exist independently.

Subliminal perception When a stimulus is perceived unconsciously (implicitly), either when it is below the absolute threshold or is presented too briefly to reach conscious awareness.

Subtractive color mixture When new colors are formed by mixing pigmented substances such as paints.

Suggestibility A type of misattribution where a memory originates in suggestions made to a person by someone else.

Superego According to Freud's structural model, the superego represents the individual's conscience, and is the origin of human morality. The superego observes the work of the ego and passes judgment on it—punishing the psyche with guilt or shame for wrongdoing, and pointing in the direction of ideal behavior.

Superordinate traits Hans Eysenck's term for the two basic trait dimensions within which all possible lower-order traits could be found. The superordinate trait dimensions are extraversion/introversion and emotional instability/emotional stability.

Suprachiasmatic nuclei (SCN) A group of neurons of the hypothalamus that constitute the circadian pacemaker.

Survey A descriptive research method used to obtain self-report data about people's experiences, attitudes, or feelings.

Survival reflex An innate, involuntary neuromuscular response that serves a functional purpose and likely evolved because it assisted the organism in survival or reproduction.

Sympathetic nervous system Division of the autonomic nervous system that mobilizes the body for arousal, particularly in response to a threat of some sort, but also in response to certain other conditions.

Symptom In medical terminology, a symptom is a patient complaint of a problem. This is contrasted with a *sign*, which is an objective indication of the presence of disease that the physician can observe or measure by test.

Synapse   The juncture of the pre-synaptic and post-synaptic neuron.

Synaptic gap   The miniscule space over which neurons pass their neurotransmitters, from the terminal of the presynaptic neuron to the dendrites of the post-synaptic neuron.

Synaptic pruning   A neurological process that "weeds out" the number of seldom-used brain neurons to allow those that are being used frequently to be maintained efficiently. Synaptic pruning begins in infancy and continues through adolescence.

Synaptic receptors   Openings that are embedded in the dendrites of neurons to which neurotransmitters bind during the process of neuronal communication.

Systematic desensitization   A behavior therapy technique primarily used to treat phobias and certain other anxiety disorders. Systematic desensitization involves controlled, incremental exposure to phobic stimuli while simultaneously practicing relaxation techniques that are incompatible with anxiety.

Tactition   The touch component of the sense of touch.

Taste buds   Clusters of cells covering areas of the tongue and (to a lesser extent) the roof of the mouth which house taste receptors.

Taste receptors   Receptors contained in taste buds, each specialized to sense certain kinds of molecules associated with various tastes.

Taste   Gustatory sensations received by the tongue. They are limited to sweet, salty, sour, and bitter, and possibly also umami and fatty.

Telepathy   Thought transference.

Temperament   Each infant's relatively consistent behavioral characteristics, characterized by Mary Rothbart within three dimensions: effortful control, negative emotionality, and extraversion. Temperament emerges as a result of genetic and other biological factors as well as environmental factors, but most theorists stress the importance of biology.

Temporal lobe   Lobe of the cerebral cortex containing the auditory cortex, auditory association areas, and Wernicke's area.

Tend and befriend   Shelly Taylor's term which describes a response to stress that utilizes a strategy different from "fight or flight." In tend and befriend, the adult affiliates with others and provides care to offspring. According to Taylor, women are far more likely than men to choose this alternate strategy for coping with stressful situations.

Teratogen   Any harmful substance, bacteria, or virus that can be transferred through the placenta to a developing mammalian organism.

Terminal   The small bulb-like structure at the end of neuron axons that contains the vesicles from which neurotransmitters are released.

Terror management theory (TMT)   An existential psychological theory that proposes that much human behavior is motivated by a need to manage or reduce the terror.

Testes   The male gonad.

Thalamus   A lower forebrain structure that conveys sensory information to the cerebral cortex and receives instructions from the cortex regarding the regulation of sensory and emotional signals.

THC   The active ingredient in cannabis, often taken in pill form.

Thematic Apperception Test (TAT)   The TAT is a projective personality test first devised during the 1930s by Henry Murray and Christiana Morgan. In the TAT the test-taker is presented with 31 emotionally loaded but ambiguous drawings and asked to tell the "story" of the drawings. According to proponents of the test, in doing so the test-taker reveals important motives, drives, conflicts, and emotions.

Theorem of the indifference of the indicator   Charles Spearman's idea that you can take a person's score on any test of mental ability and use it in a general way to predict his or her score on a test of any other mental ability.

Theory of inclusive fitness   William Hamilton's mathematics-based evolutionary theory of altruism directed toward kin. The theory stresses the fact that natural selection operates on genes, not on individuals and their bodies. Altruistic acts directed toward genetic kin may increase a person's own evolutionary "fitness" if the act increases the kin's survival or reproductive success. This may happen even if the individual sacrifices his or her life during the altruistic act, depending on the number of kin helped by the act or the closeness of the genetic link to the kin (e.g., sacrificing your life so that one of your children or 10 first-cousins may live increases your fitness more than sacrificing your life for one grandchild or 10 second-cousins).

Theory of mind   The ability to understand that other people have mental states that are different from one's own. Theory of mind usually emerges in a child between ages 3 and 5.

Theory of natural selection   Charles Darwin's theory of how the most important types of evolutionary events occur.

Theory of parental investment and sexual selection   Robert Trivers' theory which explains various sex differences as resulting from unequal minimal levels of parental investment in reproduction between males and females.

Theory of reciprocal altruism   Robert Trivers' evolutionary theory of altruism directed toward nonkin. The theory proposes that psychological attributes that motivate altruism toward nonkin, such as empathy, will only evolve under conditions where there is some expectation that altruistic acts will be reciprocated in the future—either to oneself or one's kin.

Theory   A set of interconnected ideas and statements used to explain facts.

Therapeutic alliance   A hypothesized common factor of psychotherapy that refers to the positive emotions between therapist and client, the therapist's empathy for the client, and both parties' joint commitment to therapeutic work.

Therapist allegiance   The therapist's commitment to the specific type of therapy he or she has chosen to use.

Therapist competence   The degree to which a therapist tends to produce good results regardless of client or therapy techniques.

Thermoception   The component of the sense of touch that registers temperature.

Thermoreceptors   Sensory receptors embedded in the skin that register temperature.

Theta waves   The brain waves that predominate at Stage 2 and Stage 3 sleep.

Third variable problem   In a correlational study, when a variable the researcher had not considered is responsible for observed effects in both of the variables of interest. The third variable problem is also referred to as an illusory correlation.

Third-generation antidepressants   The most recent group of antidepressants to be developed, these drugs include serotonin-norepinephrine reuptake inhibitors (SNRIs) as well as drugs with unique ("atypical") chemical structures and physiological mechanisms.

Thought   The active process of mentally manipulating information in order to solve problems, make decisions, increase knowledge, or fantasize. Thought consists of mental images and concepts.

Three-strata theory   An empirically based theory of intelligence devised by John B. Carroll that blends the idea of *g* with Horn and Cattell's Gf-Gc theory and the idea that intelligence includes multiple cognitive abilities.

Tip-of-the-tongue phenomenon (TOT)   A type of *blocking* where there is a powerful sensation that a word or name is remembered but somehow is out of reach.

Tolerance   A progressive need for more and more of a drug to achieve the same effect.

Total sleep deprivation   Going entirely without sleep for 24 hours or more.

Touch   The principal sense that obtains sensory information from the skin. It is comprised of three "subsenses" tactition, thermoception, and nociception.

Tract A bundle of axons (usually enclosed in a myelin sheath) that forms a communication channel within the central nervous system (brain or spine).

Trait perspective A branch of personality psychology which emphasizes description rather than explanation of people's characteristic patterns of behavior, thought, emotion, and motivation. Those working from the trait perspective adhere to the idea that human personality may be reduced to a limited number of traits and trait profiles.

Traits Stable, enduring personality attributes and motives for behavior. Traits may generally be described using adjectives (e.g., extraverted, conscientious, cheerful, honest, compassionate). Traits are limited in number, and each person differs in the degree to which they display any particular trait.

Traits Relatively stable, enduring personal characteristics, attributes, and motives for behavior.

Trait-situation behavior profile The unique, stable behavior patterns created by the interaction of a person's traits with specific situations. Trait-situation behavior profiles are like "If . . . then . . . else" statements in computer language. For example, "*If* I am at school, *then* I will behave politely, honestly, and conscientiously . . . *else* (i.e., otherwise) I will do my best to avoid my responsibilities, cheat whenever possible, and use foul language." Trait-situation behavior profiles account for the fact that people may appear to display different traits depending upon the situation.

Transduction The conversion of raw physical or chemical energy into sensory signals.

Transgender An umbrella term of identity referring to any and all situations where a person is unhappy in the gender to which he or she was assigned at birth.

Transience The "fading" of memories from long-term memory. Transience describes what most people mean when they say "forgetting."

Transsexual A person who identifies with the sex other than the one to which he or she was assigned at birth and takes at least some steps to present himself or herself as a person of that other sex.

Trial and error The most basic problem-solving strategy, where potential solutions are eliminated one at a time.

Triarchic theory of successful intelligence Robert J. Sternberg's theory that intelligence consists of three distinct types: analytic intelligence, creative intelligence, and practical intelligence.

Trichromatic theory of color The theory that describes how all colors are created through the additive mixture of blue, green, and red. Trichromacy results because S-, M-, and L-cones in the retina are particularly sensitive to short, medium, or long wavelengths—which correspond to the perception of blue, green, and red.

Triple vulnerability theory An integrated model of anxiety disorders created by David Barlow. According to the triple vulnerability theory, anxiety disorders result from the interaction of three factors: generalized biological vulnerability, generalized psychological vulnerability, and specific psychological vulnerability.

True experiment A research study where the experimenter satisfies all criteria necessary for causality to be inferred in the research results. These criteria usually include random assignment to conditions, manipulation of variables, use of control conditions, and control over confounding variables.

Two-factor theory of emotion The theory proposed by Stanley Schachter and Jerome Singer which states that thoughts or perceptions of events directly trigger autonomic nervous system arousal—in agreement with the James-Lange theory. However, according to the two-factor theory, emotion will emerge only after a cognitive label is attached to the arousal to explain it.

Tympanic membrane (eardrum) Membrane stretched across the end of the ear canal which vibrates in response to sound waves and marks the border between the outer and middle ear.

Type-A personality A personality type characterized by (a) an exaggerated sense of urgency about time, (b) intense ambition and competitiveness, and (c) a tendency toward irritability, hostility, and a short anger fuse.

Ultimate causes Ultimate causes of behavior are forces that shaped the capacity or tendency for the behavior in human beings over evolutionary time—why, rather than how, a behavior occurs. Unlike most other psychologists, evolutionary psychologists focus primarily on ultimate explanations of behavior.

Umbilical cord The tissue that delivers oxygen and nutrients to the embryo/fetus through the placenta and absorbs waste products. It is the eventual source of the infant's navel.

Unconditional positive regard Carl Rogers' term to describe relationships where the love and approval a person receives from important others is given freely and is not dependent upon conditions. For example, if a therapist treats a client with approval, respect, and high regard when the client behaves in a way the therapist thinks is constructive—but not if the client engages in self-destructive behavior—this is *conditional* rather than *unconditional* positive regard.

Unconditioned Response (UCR) In classical conditioning, the UCR is the innate or otherwise reflexive response triggered without conditioning by an unconditioned stimulus (UCS).

Unconditioned stimulus (UCS) In classical conditioning, the UCS is the stimulus that naturally triggers the innate (or otherwise reflexive) response, known as the unconditioned response (UCR).

Unity In consciousness studies, the idea that consciousness is always a single, unified experience.

Universal grammar The concept originated by Noam Chomsky to describe a basic internal structure or set of intrinsic rules that languages share in common.

Uterus The female womb.

Vaginal lubrication Slippery, clear, and fragrant fluid secreted on the walls of the vagina during sexual excitement.

Validity The degree to which a test actually measures what it is intended to measure.

Variable Any factor whose magnitude or category can vary.

Variable-interval (VI) schedule A partial reinforcement schedule that provides reinforcement at unpredictable time intervals.

Variable-ratio (VR) schedule A partial reinforcement schedule that provides reinforcement after an unpredictable number of behavioral responses.

Verbal performance Performance on tasks necessitating skill in all areas of language use and memory. May include knowledge of vocabulary, grammar, and spelling; reading comprehension; verbal reasoning; and speed of processing of language-related tasks.

Vicarious conditioning Learning through observing the rewarding or punishing consequences of other people's behavior.

Vipassana Traditional Buddhist "insight" meditation that uses either concentrative or open meditation as a starting point only. The object of Vipassana is to see into the "true nature of things" according to the Buddhist worldview.

Visual cortex The area of the brain that interprets visual neural signals.

Visual encoding Memory encoding according to the visual appearance of the stimulus.

Visual-spatial performance Performance on tasks necessitating skills in mentally "working with" visual and spatial imagery and information.

Vitreous humor A gel-like substance through which light must pass before arriving at the retina. The vitreous humor fills 80% of the volume of the eye.

Vomeronasal organ (VNO) A small area inside the nasal cavities of mammals that receives pheromonal signals. Not likely to be the source of pheromonal communication in humans.

Wavelength A measure of the lengths between electromagnetic waves.

Weber's law A mathematical expression of the idea that for any given stimulus, the just noticeable difference (JND) is always proportionate to the level of the standard stimulus.

Wechsler Adult Intelligence Scale (WAIS®-III) A standardized test of intelligence designed by David G. Wechsler. This was the first test to extend the IQ to include testing of adults.

Wechsler Intelligence Scale for Children (WISC®-IV) A standardized test of intelligence for children devised by David G. Wechsler.

White matter Axons with myelin sheaths.

Withdrawal Unpleasant physiological (and psychological) symptoms experienced when the body is deprived of a drug to which it has become adapted.

Wording effects Potential biases caused by the way survey questions, or questionnaires used in other types of research, are worded.

Work motivation Mental forces which determine the form, direction, intensity, and persistence of each person's work-related activities.

Working memory Working memory is defined in different ways by different theorists, and is often used synonymously for (or in place of) short-term memory. As used here, the term describes "what happens" in short-term memory when information is manipulated or processed "online."

Zen A small Buddhist sect emphasizing the use of concentrative and/or open meditation alone to achieve enlightenment. Zen is a Chinese development based upon Chinese Taoism and Mahayana Buddhism.

Zygote The fused nuclei of a sperm and ovum.

References

CHAPTER 1

Ambady, N. (2010). The perils of pondering. Intuition and thin slice judgments. *Psychological Inquiry, 21,* 271–278.

Ambady, N., & Rosenthal, R. (1993). Half a minute. Predicting teacher evaluations from thin slices of nonverbal behavior and physical attractiveness. *Journal of Personality and Social Psychology, 64,* 431–441.

American Psychological Association Research Office. (2003). *Where are new psychologists going? Employment, debt, and salary data.* Washington, DC. American Psychological Association.

Anderson, C. A., & Murphy, C. R. (2003). Violent video games and aggressive behavior in young women. *Aggressive Behavior, 29,* 423–429.

Archer, J. (2004). Sex differences in aggression in real-world settings. A meta-analytic review. *Review of General Psychology, 8(4),* 291–322.

Baker, T. B., McFall, R. M., & Shoham, V. (2008). Current status and future prospects of clinical psychology. Toward a scientifically principled approach to mental and behavioral health care. *Psychological Science in the Public Interest, 9,* 68–103.

Bandura, A. (2001). Social cognitive theory. An agentic perspective. *Annual Review of Psychology, 52,* 1–26.

Barkow, J. H. (2006). *Missing the revolution. Darwinism for social scientists.* Oxford, UK. Oxford University Press.

Baumrind, D. (1964). Some thought on ethics of research. After reading Milgram's "Behavioral study of obedience." *American Psychologist, 19,* 421–423.

Beck, A. T. (2005). The current state of cognitive therapy. *Archives of General Psychiatry, 62,* 953–959.

Beck, A. T., Rush, A. J., Shaw, B. F., & Emery, G. (1979). *Cognitive therapy for depression.* New York. Guilford Press.

Braun, J., Kahn, R. S., Froehlich, T., Auinger, P., & Langphear, B. P. (2006). Exposures to environmental toxicants and attention deficit hyperactivity disorder in U.S. children. *Environmental Health Perspectives.* Retrieved from http://www.ehponline .org/members/2006/9478/9478.pdf on October 8, 2006.

Britt, R. R. (2005). The odds of dying. *Live Science.* Retrieved from http://www .livescience.com/3780-odds-dying.html on May 26.

Buss, D. M. (Ed.) (2005). *The handbook of evolutionary psychology.* Hoboken, NJ. John Wiley & Sons.

Buss, D. M. (2009). The great struggles of life. Darwin and the emergence of evolutionary psychology. *American Psychologist, 64,* 140–148.

Cacioppo, J. T. (2004). Common sense, intuition, and theory in personality and social psychology. *Personality and Social Psychology Review, 8,* 114–122.

Calhoon, H. M., McKeigue, P. M., & Davey Smith, G. (2003). Problems of reporting genetic associations with complex outcomes. *Lancet, 361,* 865–872.

Cautin, R. L. (2009a). The founding of the Association for Psychological Science. Part 1. Dialectical tensions within organized psychology. *Perspectives on Psychological Science, 4,* 211–223.

Cautin, R. L. (2009b). The founding of the Association for Psychological Science. Part 2. The tipping point and early years. *Perspectives on Psychological Science, 4,* 224–235.

Cavalieri, P. (2004). *Animal question. Why nonhuman animals deserve human rights.* New York. Oxford University Press.

Cavalieri, P. (2006). The animal debate. A reexamination. In P. Singer (Ed.), *In defense of animals. The second wave* (pp. 54–68). Malden, MA. Blackwell Publishing

Chomsky, N. (1975). *Reflections on language.* New York. Harcourt Brace Jovanovich.

Christakis, D.A., Zimmerman, F.J., DiGiuseppe, D.L., & McCarty, C.A. (2004). Early television exposure and subsequent attentional problems in children. *Pediatrics, 113,* 708–713.

Coelho, H. F., Canter, P. H., & Ernst, E. (2007). Mindfulness-based cognitive therapy. Evaluating current evidence and informing future research. *Journal of Consulting Clinical Psychology, 75,* 1000–1005.

Cohen, P. (2007, November 25). Freud is widely taught at universities except in the psychology department. *New York Times.* Retrieved on November 25, 2007 from www.nytimes.com.

Correll, J., Park, B., Judd, C. M., & Wittenbrink, B. (2002). The police officer's dilemma. Using ethnicity to disambiguate potentially threatening individuals. *Journal of Personality & Social Psychology, 83,* 1314–1329.

Cosmides, L., & Tooby, J. (2005). Neurocognitive adaptations designed for social exchange. In D. M. Buss (Ed.), *The handbook of evolutionary psychology* (pp. 584–627). Hoboken, NJ. John Wiley & Sons.

Cosmides, L., & Tooby, J. (2008). Beyond intuition and instinct blindness. Toward an evolutionarily rigorous cognitive science. In J. E. Adler & J. L. Rips (Eds.), *Reasoning. Studies of human inference and its foundations* (pp. 843–865). New York. Cambridge University Press.

Crews, F. (2007). *Follies of the wise. Dissenting essays.* Emeryville, CA. Shoemaker & Hoard.

Dawes, R. M. (1994). *House of cards.* New York. The Free Press.

Dawes, R. M., Faust, D., & Meehl, P. E. (1989). Clinical vs. actuarial judgment. *Science, 243,* 1668–1674.

Diener, E. (2009). Positive psychology. Past, present and future. In J. S. Lopez & C. R. Snyder (Eds.), *Oxford handbook of positive psychology* (2nd ed., pp. 7–11). New York. Oxford University Press.

Ekman, P., Davidson, R. J., Ricard, M., & Wallace, B. A. (2005). Buddhist and psychological perspectives on emotions and well-being. *Psychological Science, 14,* 59–63.

Epstein, S. (2010). Demystifying intuition. What it is, what it does, and how it does it. *Psychological Inquiry, 21,* 295–312.

Evans, G. W., & Kantrowitz, E. (2002). Socioeconomic status and health. The potential role of environmental risk exposure. *Annual Review of Public Health, 23,* 303–331.

Faraone, S. V. (2004). Genetics of adult attention-deficit/hyperactivity disorder. *Psychiatric Clinics of North America, 27,* 303–321.

Faust, D. (2007). Decision research can increase the accuracy of clinical judgment and thereby improve patient care. In S. O. Lilienfeld & W. T. O'Donohue (Eds.), *The great ideas of clinical science. 17 principles that every mental health professional should understand* (pp. 49–76).

Ferguson, C. J., & Heene, M. (2012). A vast graveyard of undead theories. Publication bias and psychological science's aversion to the null. *Perspectives on Psychological Science, 7,* 555–561.

Fodor, J. A. (1983). *The modularity of mind. An essay on faculty psychology.* Cambridge, MA. MIT Press.

Gable, S. L., & Haidt, J. (2005). What (and why) is positive psychology? *Review of General Psychology, 9*, 103–110.

Garb, H. N. (2005). Clinical judgment and decision making. *Annual Review of Clinical Psychology, 55*, 3.1–3.23.

Gazzaniga, M. S. (2005). Forty-five years of split-brain research and still going strong. *Nature Reviews Neuroscience, 6*, 653–659.

Gazzaniga, M. S. (2010). Neuroscience and the correct level of explanation for understanding mind. An extraterrestrial roams through some neuroscience laboratories and concludes earthlings are not grasping how best to understand the mind-brain interface. *Trends in Cognitive Sciences, 14*, 291–292.

Gigerenzer, G., Gaissmaier, W., Kurz-Mileke, E., Schwartz, L. M., & Woloshin, S. (2008). Helping doctors and patients make sense of health statistics. *Psychological Science in the Public Interest, 8*, 53–96.

Giner-Sorolla, R. (2012). Science or art? How aesthetic standards grease the way through the publication bottleneck but undermine science. *Perspectives on Psychological Science, 7*, 562–572.

Gourevitch, P., & Morris, E. (2008, March 24). Exposure. The woman behind the camera at Abu Ghraib. *The New Yorker.* Retrieved from www.thenewyorker.com on June 8, 2008.

Hagen, M. A. (2003). Faith in the model and resistance to research. *Clinical Psychology. Science & Practice, 10*, 344–348.

Hall, M. (2005, January 15). Mat man meets tsunami heroes. *The Guernsey Press and Star.* Retrieved from www.thisisguernsey.com/news on January 21, 2005.

Halpern, D. F. (2003) *Thought and knowledge. An introduction to critical thinking.* Mahwah, NJ. Erlbaum.

Halpern, D. F. (2007a). The nature and nurture of critical thinking. In R. J. Sternberg, H. Roediger, & D. F. Halpern (Eds.), *Critical thinking in psychology* (pp. 1–14). New York. Cambridge University Press.

Halpern, D. F. (2007b). *Critical Thinking in Psychology.* New York. Cambridge University Press.

Hepper, P. G. (1991). An examination of fetal learning before and after birth. *Irish Journal of Psychology, 12*, 95–107.

Hersh, S. M. (2004, May 10). Torture at Abu Ghraib. *The New Yorker.* Retrieved from http://www.newyorker.com/archive/2004/05/10/040510fa_fact?currentPage=1 on May 25, 2011.

Hertwig, R., & Gigerenzer, G. (1999). The "conjunction fallacy" revisited. How intelligent inferences look like reasoning errors. *Journal of Behavioral Decision Making, 12*, 275–305.

Hodgkinson, G. P., Langan-Fox, J., & Sadler-Smith, E. (2008). Intuition. A fundamental bridging construct in the behavioral sciences. *British Journal of Psychology, 99*, 1–27.

Hunt, Morton (1993). *The story of psychology.* New York. Doubleday.

Ioannidis, J. P. A. (2005). Why most published research findings are false. *PLoS Medicine, 2.* Retrieved from http://medicine.plosjournals.org/archive on March 14, 2007.

James, W. (1890/1981). *Principles of psychology* (Vols. 1 and 2). Cambridge, MA. Harvard University Press.

Jaynes, J. (1976). *The origin of consciousness in the breakdown of the bicameral mind.* Boston. Houghton Mifflin.

Kisilevsky, B. S., Hains, S. M., Lee, K., Xie, X., Huang, H., et al. (2003). Effects of experience on fetal voice recognition. *Psychological Science, 14*, 220–224.

Kotler, J. A., Wright, J. C., & Huston, A. C. (2001). Television use in families with children. In J. Bryant & J. A. Bryant (Eds.), *Television and the American family* (2nd ed., pp. 33–48). Mahwah, NJ. Lawrence Erlbaum Associates.

Kuyken, W., Watkins, E., Holden, E., White, K., Taylor, R. S., et al. (2010). How does mindfulness-based cognitive therapy work? *Behaviour Research and Therapy, 48*, 1105–1112.

Landau, J. D., Druen, P. B., & Arcuri, J. A. (2002) Methods for helping students to avoid plagiarism. *Teaching of Psychology, 29*, 112–115.

Landau, J. D. (2002). Teaching tips. Understanding and preventing plagiarism. *Teaching Psychology.* Association for Psychological Science. Retrieved from http://www.psychologicalscience.org/teaching/tips/tips_0403.cfm on May 26, 2011

Lilienfeld, S. O., Lynn, S. J., & Lohr, J. M. (2003b). Science and pseudoscience in clinical psychology. Initial thoughts, reflections, and considerations. In S. O. Lilienfeld, S. J Lynn, & J. M. Lohr (Eds.), *Science and pseudoscience in clinical psychology* (pp. 1–14). New York. Guilford.

Lilienfeld, S. O., Lynn, S. J., & Lohr, J. M. (Eds.) (2003a). *Science and pseudoscience in clinical psychology.* New York. Guilford.

Matsumoto, D., & Hee Yoo, S. (2006). Toward a new generation of cross-cultural research. *Perspectives on Psychological Science, 1*, 234–250.

Matsumoto, D., Yoo, S. H., & Nakagawa, S. (2008). Culture, emotion regulation, and adjustment. *Journal of Personality and Social Psychology, 94*, 925–937.

McBurney D. H. (2000). *Research Methods* (5th ed.). Belmont, CA. Wadsworth.

McCabe, D. L., Treviño, L. K., & Butterfield, K. D. (2001). Cheating in academic institutions. A decade of research. *Ethics & Behavior, 11*, 219–232.

Milgram, S. (1963). Behavioral study of obedience. *Journal of Abnormal and Social Psychology, 67*, 371–378.

Milgram, S. (1974). *Obedience to authority. An experimental view.* New York. Harper-Collins.

Miller, N. E. (1985). The value of behavioral research on animals. *American Psychologist, 40*, 423–440.

Miller, C. J., Marks, D. M., Miller, S. R., Berwid, O. G., Kera, E. C., et al. (2007). Television viewing and risk for attention problems in preschool children. *Journal of Pediatric Psychology, 32*, 448–452.

Mitchell, G. (2012). Revisiting truth or triviality. The external validity of research in the psychological laboratory. *Perspectives on Psychological Science, 7*, 109–117.

Miyamoto, Y., Nisbett, R. E., & Masuda, T. (2006). Culture and the physical environment. Holistic versus analytic perceptual affordances. *Psychological Science, 17*, 113–119.

Moonesinghe, R., Khoury, M. J., Cecile, A., & Janssens, J. W. (2007). Most published research findings are false—but a little replication goes a long way. *PLoS Medicine, 4.* Retrieved from http://medicine.plosjournals.org on March 14, 2007.

Moore, M. M. (1995). Courtship signaling and adolescents. "Girls just wanna have fun"? *Journal of Sex Research, 32*, 319–328.

Moore, M. M. (2002). Courtship communication and perception. *Perceptual and Motor Skills, 94(1)*, 97–105.

Morelli, M. (1983). Milgram's dilemma of obedience. *Metaphilosophy, 14*, 183–189.

Morris, E. (2008, May 19). The most curious thing. *New York Times.* Retrieved from www.nytimes.com on June 12, 2008.

Morrison, A.R. (2001). Personal reflections on the "animal-rights" phenomenon. *Perspectives in Biology and Medicine, 44*, 62–75.

Myers, D. G. (2002). *Intuition. Its powers and perils.* New Haven, CT. Yale University Press.

Myers, D. G. (2007). The powers and perils of intuition. Understanding the nature of our gut instincts. *Scientific American Mind,* June/July, 24–31.

Myers, D. G. (2010). Intuitions's powers and perils. *Psychological Inquiry, 21*, 371–377.

New heroes, new hope. (2005, January 6). *People.* Retrieved from www.people.com on August 1, 2009.

Nichols, A. L., & Maner, J. K. (2008). The good subject effect: Investigating participant demand characteristics. *Journal of General Psychology, 135*, 151–165.

Nieh, H. (Ed. and Co-trans.). (1981). *Literature of the hundred flowers. Vol 1. Criticism and polemics.* New York. Columbia University Press.

Nisbett, R. E., & Miyamoto, Y. (2005). The influence of culture. Holistic versus analytic perception. *Trends in Cognitive Science, 9*, 467–473.

Orne, M. T. (1962). On the social psychology of the psychological experiment. With particular reference to demand characteristics and their implications. *American Psychologist, 17*, 776–783

Pashler, H., & Wagenmakers, E-J. (2012). Editors' introduction to the special section on replicaability in psychological science. A crisis of confidence?

Perspectives on Psychological Science, 7, 528–530.

Paul, E. F., & Paul, J. (2001). *Why animal experimentation matters. The use of animals in medical research.* New Brunswick, NJ. Social Philosophy and Policy Foundation.

Pelham, B. W., & Blanton, H. (2003). *Conducting research in psychology. Measuring the weight of smoke.* Belmont, CA. Thomson/Wadsworth.

Pinker, S., & Jackendoff, R. (2005). The faculty of language. What's special about it? *Cognition, 95,* 201–236.

Pinker, S. (1997). *How the mind works.* New York. Norton.

Pinker, S. (2002). *The blank slate. The modern denial of human nature.* New York. Viking.

Plomin, R., DeFries, J. C., Craig, I. W., & McGuffin, P. (Eds.) (2003). *Behavioral genetics in the postgenomic era.* Washington, DC. American Psychological Association.

Popper, K. (1959). *The logic of scientific discovery.* New York. Basic Books.

Rahula, W. (1959). *What the Buddha taught.* New York. Grove Press.

Robins, R. W., Gosling, S. D., & Craik, K. H. (1999). An empirical analysis of trends in psychology. *American Psychologist, 54,* 117–128.

Robinson, P. (1989). *Aristotle's psychology.* New York. Columbia University Press.

Ruscio, J. (2006). *Critical thinking in psychology. Separating sense from nonsense* (2nd ed.). Monterey Park, CA. Wadsworth.

Sadler-Smith, E. (2008). *Inside intuition.* Abington, UK. Routledge.

Sagan, C. (1995). *The demon-haunted world. Science as a candle in the dark.* New York. Random House.

Sarnoff, S. K. (2001). *Sanctified snake oil. The effect of junk science on public policy.* Westport, CT. Praeger Publishers.

Seligman, M. E. P., Steen, T. A., Park, N., & Peterson, C. (2005). Positive psychology progress. Empirical validation of interventions. *American Psychologist, 60,* 410–421.

Shea, C. (2011, November 17). Fraud scandal fuels debate over practices of social psychology. *The Chronicle of Higher Education.* Retrieved from www.chronicle.com on November 17, 2011.

Shermer, M. (1997). *Why people believe weird things. Pseudoscience, superstition, and other confusions of our time.* New York. W. H. Freeman.

Simmons, J. P., Nelson, L. D., & Simonsohn, U. (2011). False-positive psychology. Undisclosed flexibility in data collection and analysis allows presenting anything as significant. *Psychological Science, 22,* 1359–1366.

Starbuck, E. D. (1943). A student's impressions of James in the middle '90's [sic] [Note to students. middle 1890s]. *Psychological Review, 50,* 128–131. Retrieved from www.library.upenn.edu on January 25, 2013.

Steele, C. M., & Aronson, J. A. (2004). Stereotype threat does not live by

Steele and Aronson alone. *American Psychologist, 59,* 47–48.

Swets, J. A., Dawes, R. M., & Monahan, J. (2000). Psychological science can improve diagnostic decisions. *Psychological Science in the Public Interest, 1(1),* 1–26.

Tavris, C. (1992). *The mismeasure of women.* New York. Touchstone.

Tooby, J., & Cosmides, L. (1992). The psychological foundations of culture. In J. H. Barkow, L. Cosmides, & J. Tooby (Eds.), *The adapted mind. Evolutionary psychology and the generation of culture* (pp. 19–136). New York. Oxford University Press.

Tversky, A., & Kahneman, D. (2005). *Judgment under uncertainty. Heuristics and biases.* North Hampton, MA. Edward Elgar Publishing.

Westen, D. (1998). The scientific legacy of Sigmund Freud. Toward a psychodynamically informed psychological science. *Psychological Bulletin, 124,* 333–371.

Westen, D. (2005). Implications of research in cognitive neuroscience for psychodynamic psychotherapy. In G. O. Gabbard, J. S. Beck, & J. Holmes (Eds.), *Oxford textbook of psychotherapy* (pp. 443–448). New York. Oxford University Press.

Williams, W., & Ceci, S. J. (1998). *Escaping the advice trap.* Kansas City, MO. Andrews McMeel Publishing.

Willis, J., & Todorov, J. (2006). First impressions. Making up your mind after a 100-ms exposure to a face. *Psychological Science, 17,* 592–598.

Yeo, S. (2007). First-year university science and engineering students' understanding of plagiarism. *Higher Education Research and Development, 26,* 199–216.

CHAPTER 2

Adamec, R. E., Burton, P., Shallow, T., & Budgell, J. (1999). NMDA receptors mediate lasting increases in anxiety-like behaviour produced by the stress of predator exposure—implications for anxiety associated with post-traumatic stress disorder. *Physiology and Behavior, 65,* 723–737.

Adolphs, R., Tranel, D., & Buchanan, T. W. (2005). Amygdala damage impairs emotional memory for gist but not details of complex stimuli. *Nature Neuroscience, 8,* 512–518.

Adolphs, R., Tranel, D., & Damasio, A. R. (1998). The human amygdale in social judgment. *Nature, 393,* 470–474.

Andersen, P., Morris, R. G. M., Amaral, D. G., Bliss, T. V. P., & O'Keefe, J. (2007). *The hippocampus book.* London. Oxford University Press.

Anderson, B. J. (2011). Plasticity of gray matter volume. The cellular and synaptic plasticity that underlies volumetric change. *Developmental Psychobiology, 53,* 456–465.

Angulo, M. C., Kozlov, A. S., Charpak, S., & Audinat, E. (2004). Gultamate released from glial cells synchronizes neuronal activity in the hippoxampus. *The Journal of Neuroscience, 24,* 6920–6927.

Aron, A., Fisher, H., Mashek, D. J., Strong, G., Haifang, L., & Brown, L. L. (2005). Reward, motivation, and emotion systems associated with early stage intense romantic love. *Journal of Neurophysiology, 94,* 327–337.

Ashton, H., & Hassan, Z. (2006). Best evidence topic report. Intranasal naloxone in suspected opioid overdose. *Emergency Medicine Journal, 23,* 221–223.

Barrière, G., Leblond, H., Provencher, J., & Rossignol, S. (2008). Prominent role of the spinal central pattern generator in the recovery of locomotion after partial spinal cord injuries. *Journal of Neuroscience, 28,* 3976–3987.

Bartels, A., & Zeki, S. (2004). The neural correlates of maternal and romantic love. *NeuroImage, 12,* 1155–1166.

Bartz, J. A., Zaki, J., Bolger, N., Hollander, E., Ludwig, N. N., et al. (2010). Oxytocin selectively improves empathic understanding. *Psychological Science, 21,* 1426–1428.

Baxter, M. G. and Murray, E. A. (2002). The amygdala and reward. *Nature Reviews Neuroscience, 3,* 563–573.

Beeman, M. J., & Chiarello, C. (1998). Complementary right- and left-hemisphere language comprehension. *Current Directions in Psychological Science, 7,* 2–8.

Bell, E. C., Willson, M. C., Wilman, A. H., Dave, S., & Silverstone, P. H. (2006). Males and females differ in brain activation during cognitive tasks. *Neuroimage, 30,* 529–538.

Blanchard, D. C., & Blanchard, R. J. (1972). Innate and conditioned reactions to threat in rats with amygdaloid lesions. *Journal of Comparative and Physiological Psychology, 81,* 281–290.

Blanke, O., Landis, T., Mermoud, C., Spinelli, L., & Safran, A. B. (2003). Direction-selective motion blindness after unilateral posterior brain damage. *European Journal of Neuroscience, 18,* 709–722.

Bloom (2004). *Descartes' baby.* New York. Basic Books.

Blumstein, S. E., & Amso, D. (2013). Dynamic functional organization of language. Insights from functional neuroimaging. *Perspectives on Psychological Science, 8,* 44–48.

Bower, J. M., & Parsons, L. (2003). Rethinking the lesser brain. *Scientific American, 289,* 50–57.

Brass, M., & Haggard, P. (2007). To do or not to do. The neural signature of self-control. *The Journal of Neuroscience, 27,* 9141–9145.

Brizendine, L. (2006). *The female brain.* New York. Morgan Road Books.

Buckner, R. L. (2010). The role of the hippocampus in prediction and imagination. *Annual Review of Psychology, 61,* 27–48.

Busigny, T., Joubert, S., Flician, O., Ceccaldi, M., & Rossion, B. (2010). Holistic perception of the individual face is specific and necessary. Evidence from a study of acquired prosopagnosia. *Neuropsychologia, 48,* 4057–4092.

Cabeza, R., & Moscovitch, M. (2013). Memory systems, processing modes, and components. Functional Neuroimaging evidence. *Perspectives on Psychological Science, 8,* 49–55.

Cahill, L. (2006). Why sex matters for neuroscience. *Nature Reviews Neuroscience, 7,* 477–484.

Cannon, W.B. (1929) Organization for physiological homeostasis. *Physiological Reviews, 9,* 399–431.

Carreiras, M., Lopez, J., Rivero, F., & Corina, D. (2005). Linguistic perception. Neural processing of a whistled language. *Nature, 433,* 31–32.

Carter, C. S. (2004). Oxytocin and the prarie vole. A love story. In J. T. Cacioppo & G. G. Berntson (Eds.), *Essays in social neuroscience* (pp. 53–63). Cambridge, MA. MIT Press.

Chapman, L. A., Wade, S. L., Walz, N. C., Taylor, H. G., Stancin, T., et al. (2010). Clinically significant behavior problems during the initial18 months following early childhood traumatic brain injury. *Rehabilitation Psychology, 55,* 48–57.

Clements, A. M., Rimrodt, S. L., Abel, J. R., Blankner, J. G., Mostofsky, S. H., et al.. (2006). Sex differences in cerebral laterality of language and visuaspatial processing. *Brain and Language, 98,* 150–158.

Coleman, M. R., Rodd, J. M., Davis, M. H., Johnsrude, I. S., Menon, D. K., et al. (2007). Do vegetative patients retain aspects of language comprehension? Evidence from fMRI. *Brain, 130,* 2494–2507.

Coltheart, M. (2006). What has functional neuroimaging told us about the mind (so far)? *Cortex. A Journal Devoted to the Study of the Nervous System and Behavior, 42,* 323–331.

Coltheart, M. (2013). How can functional neuroimaging inform cognitive theories? *Perspectives on Psychological Science, 8,* 98–103.

Corballis, P. M., Funnell, M. G., & Gazzaniga, M. S. (2002). Hemispheric asymmetries for simple visual judgments in the split brain. *Neuropsychologia, 40,* 401–410.

Cosgrove, K. P., Mazure, C. M., & Staley, J. K. (2007). Evolving knowledge of sex differences in brain structure, function, and chemistry. *Biological Psychiatry, 62,* 847–855.

Coulthard, E., Parton, A., & Husain, M. (2007). The modular architecture of the neglect syndrome. Implications for action control in visual neglect. *Neuropsychologia, 45,* 1982–1984.

Dennett, D. C. *Consciousness explained.* (1991). Boston. Little, Brown and Company.

DeWall, C. N., MacDonald, G., Webster, G. D., Masten, C. L., Baumeister, R. F., et al. (2010). Acetaminophen reduces social pain. Behavioral and neural evidence. *Psychological Science, OnlineFirst.* Retrieved from pss.sagepub.com on June 30, 2010.

Diamond, L. M (2004). Emerging perspectives on distinctions between romantic love and sexual desire. *Current Directions in Psychological Science, 13,* 116–119.

Domes, G., Heinrichs, M., Michel, A., Berger, C., & Herpertz, S. C. (2007). Oxytocin improves "mind-reading" in humans. *Biological Psychiatry, 61,* 731–733.

Eagly, A. H. (1995). The science and politics of comparing women and men. *American Psychologist, 50,* 145–158.

Eagly, A. H., Mladinic, A., & Otto, S. (1991). Are women evaluated more favorably than men? An analysis of attitudes, beliefs, and emotions. *Psychology of Women Quarterly, 15,* 203–216.

Eisenberger, N. I., Lieberman, M. D., & Williams, K. D. (2003). Does rejection hurt? An fMRI study of social exclusion. *Science, 302,* 290–292.

Elston, G. N. (2003). Cortex, cognition and the cell. New insights into the pyramidal neuron and prefrontal function. *Cerebral Cortex, 13,* 1124–1138.

Feinstein, J. S., Adolphs, R., Damasio, A., & Tranel, D. (2011). The human amygdala and the induction and experience of fear. *Current Biology, 21,* 34–38.

Feldman, R., Weller, A., Zagoory-Sharon, O., & Levine, A. (2007). Evidence for a neuroendocrinological foundation of human affiliation. Plasma oxytocin levels across pregnancy and the postpartum period predict mother–infant bonding. *Psychological Science, 18,* 965–970.

Field, E. F., & Pellis, S. M. (2008). The brain as the engine of sex differences in the organization of movement in rats. *Archives of Sexual Behavior, 37,* 30–42.

Fine, C. (2010). From scanner to sound bite. Issues in interpreting and reporting sex differences in the brain. *Current Directions in Psychological Science, 22,* 417–428.

Finger, S. (1994) History of Neuropsychology. In D. Zaidel (Ed.), *Neuropsychology* (pp. 1–28). San Diego, CA. Academic Press.

Forster, B., & Corballis, M. C. (2000). Interhemispheric transfer of colour and shape information in the presence and absence of the corpus callosum. *Neuropsychologia, 38(1),* 32–45.

Gaser, C., & Schlaug, G. (2003). Brain structures differ between musicians and non-musicians. *The Journal of Neuroscience, 23,* 9240–9245.

Gazzaniga, M. S. (2010). Neuroscience and the correct level of explanation for understanding mind. An extraterrestrial roams through some neuroscience laboratories and concludes earthlings are not grasping how best to understand the mind-brain interface. *Trends in Cognitive Sciences, 14,* 291–292.

Gazzaniga, M. S., Bizzi, E., Chalupa, L. M., Grafton, S. T., Heatherton, T., et al. (Eds.) (2009). *The cognitive neurosciences* (4th ed.). Cambridge, MA. MIT Press.

Gazzaniga, M. S., Ivry, R. B., & Mangun, G. R. (2002). *Cognitive neuroscience. The biology of the mind* (2nd ed.). New York. Norton.

Gazzaniga, M. S., Ivry, R. B., & Mangun, G. R. (2008). *Cognitive neuroscience. The biology of the mind* (3rd ed.). New York. Norton.

Gazzaniga, M. S., & Smylie, C. S. (1984). Dissociation of language and cognition. A psychological profile of two disconnected right hemispheres. *Brain 107,* 145–153.

Geary, D. C. (2007). An evolutionary perspective on sex differences in mathematics and the sciences. In S. J. Ceci & W. Williams (Eds.), *Are sex differences in cognition responsible for the underrepresntation of women in scientific careers?* (pp. 173–188). Washington, DC. American Psychological Association.

Glickstein, M. (2003). The cerebellum and its disorders. *New England Journal of Medicine, 348,* 180–181.

Goldstein, J. M., Seidman, L. J., Horton, N. J., Makris, N., Kennedy, D. N., et al. (2001). Normal sexual dimorphism of the adult brain assessed by *in vivo* magnetic resonance imaging. *Cerebral Cortex, 11,* 490–497.

Gonzaga, G. C., Turner, R. A., Keltner, D., Campos, B., & Altemus, M. (2006). Romantic love and sexual desire in close relationships. *Emotion, 6,* 163–179.

Grabowski, T. J., Damasio, H., Eichorn, G. R., & Tranel, D. (2003). Effects of gender on blood flow correlates of naming concrete entities. *Neuroimage, 20,* 940–954.

Graziano, M. S. A., Taylor, C. S. R., & Moore, T. (2002). Complex movements evoked by microstimulation of precentral cortex. *Neuron, 34,* 841–851.

Guillery, R. W., Feig, S. L., & Lozsádi, D. A. (1998). Paying attention to the thalamic reticular nucleus. *Trends in Neurosciences, 21,* 28–32.

Habel, U., Windischberger, C., Derntl, B., Robinson, S., & Kryspin-Exner, I. (2007). Amygdala activation and facial expressions. Explicit emotion discrimination versus implicit emotion processing. *Neuropsychologia, 45,* 2369–2377.

Halpern, D. F., Benbow, C. P., Geary, D. C., Gur, R. C., Hyde, J. S., & Gersbacher, M. A. (2007). The science of sex differences in science and methematics. *Psychological Science in the Public Interest, 8,* 1–51.

Hamann, S. (2009). The human amygdale and memory. In P. J. Whalen, & E. A. Phelps (Eds.), *The human amygdale* (pp. 177–203). New York. Guilford Press.

Handlin, L., Hydbring-Sandberg, E., Nilsson, A., Eidebäck, M., Jansson, A., et al. (2011). Short-term interaction between dogs and their owners. Effects on oxytocin, cortisol, insulin, and heart rate—An exploratory study. *Anthrozoös, 24,* 301–315.

Hannan, C. K. (2006). Neuroscience and the impact of brain plasticity on Braille reading. *Journal of Visual Impairment & Blindness, 100,* 397–413.

Hardman, J. G., Limbird, L. E., & Gilman, A. G. (2001). *The pharmacological basis of therapeutics* (10th ed.).

Harris, S. (2012). *Free Will*. New York. Free Press.

Hassabis, D., Kumaran, D., Vann, S., & McGuire, E. A. (2007). Patients with hippocampal amnesia cannot imagine new experiences. *PNAS, 104,* 1726–1731.

Hawley, C. A., Ward, A. B., Magnay, A. R., & Long, J. (2004). Outcome following childhood head injury. A population study. *The Journal of Neurology, Neurosurgery, and Psychiatry, 75,* 737–742.

Haynes, J. D. (2011). Decoding and predicting intentions. *Annals of the New York Academy of Sciences, 1224,* 9–21.

Herculano-Houzel, S., & Lent, R. (2005). Isotropic fractionator. A simple, rapid method for the quantification of total cell and neuron numbers in the brain. *The Journal of Neuroscience, 25,* 2518–2521.

Hiller, J. (2005). Gender differences in sexual motivation. *Journal of Men's Health and Gender, 2,* 339–345.

Hochberg, L. R. (2008). Turning thought into action. *New England Journal of Medicine, 359,* 1175–1177.

Hochberg, L. R., Serruya, M. D., Friehs, G. M., Mukand, J. A., Saleh, M., et al. (2006). Neuronal ensemble control of prosthetic devices by a human with tetraplegia. *Nature, 442, 164*–171.

Hofer, A., Siedentopf, C. M., Ischebeck, A., Rettenbacher, M. A., Verius, M., et al. (2007). Sex differences in brain activation patterns during processing of positively and negatively valenced emotional words. *Psychological Medicine, 37,* 109–119.

Hounsfield, G. N. (1973). Computerised transverse axial scanning (tomography). Part 1. Description of system. *British Journal of Radiology, 46,* 1016–1022.

Hubel, D. H., & Wiesel, T. N. (1970). The period of susceptibility to the physiological effects of unilateral eye-closure in kittens. *Journal of Physiology, 206,* 419–436.

Husain, M., & Rorden, C. (2003). Non-spatially lateralized mechanisms in hemispatial neglect. *Nature Reviews. Neuroscience, 4,* 26–36.

Huxley, A. F. (1959) Ion movements during nerve activity. *Annals of New York Academy of Sciences, 81,* 221–246.

Hyde, K. L., Lerch, J., Norton, A., Forgeard, M., Winner, E., et al. (2009). Musical training shapes structural brain development. *The Journal of Neuroscience, 29,* 2019–2025.

Kalin, N. H., Shelton, S. E., Davidson, R. J., & Kelley, A. E. (2001). The primate amygdala mediates acute fear but not the behavioral and physiological components of anxious temperament. *Journal of Neuroscience, 21,* 2067–2074.

Kast, B. (2001). Decisions, decisions . . . *Nature, 411,* 126–128.

Kentros, C. (2006). Hippocampal place cells. The "where" of episodic memory. *Hippocampus, 16,* 743–754.

Kerr, D., Kelly, A-M., Dietze, P., Damien, J., & Barger, B. (2009). Randomized controlled trial comparing the effectiveness and safety of intranasal and intramuscular naloxone for the treatment of suspected heroin overdose. *Addiction, 104,* 2067–2074.

Kim, J-N., & Shadlen, M. N. (1999). Neural correlates of a decision in the dorsolateral prefrontal cortex of the macaque. *Nature Neuroscience 2,* 176–185.

Kimura, D. (2004). Human sex differences in cognition. Fact, not predicament. *Sexualities, evolution, and gender, 6,* 45–53.

Kolata, G (2003). *Ultimate fitness. The quest for truth about exercise and health.* New York. Farrar, Straus, & Giroux.

Komura, Y., Tamura, R., Uwano, T., Nishiko, H., Kaga, K., et al.. (2001). Retrospective and prospective coding for predicted reward in the sensory thalamus. *Nature, 412,* 546–549.

Koob, G. F., & Le Moal, M. (2008). Addiction and the brain antireward system. *Annual Review of Psychology, 59,* 29–53.

Kosfeld, M., Heinrichs, M., Zak, P. J., Fischbacher, U., Fehr, E., et al. (2005). Oxytocin increases trust in humans. *Nature, 435,* 673–676.

Kuyken, W., Watkins, E., Holden, E., White, K., Taylor, R. S., et al. (2006). How does mindfulness-based cognitive therapy work? *Behaviour Research and Therapy, 48,* 1105–1112.

Lamb, T., & Yang, J. E. (2000). Could different directions of infant stepping be controlled by the same locomotor central pattern generator? *Journal of Neurophysiology, 83,* 2814–2824.

Larsen, C. C., Bonde, L. L., Bogdanovic, N., Laursen, H., Graem, N., et al. (2006). Total number of cells in the human newborn telencephalic wall. *Neuroscience, 139,* 999–1003.

LeDoux, J. E. (2000). Emotion circuits in the brain. *Annual Review of Neuroscience, 23,* 155–184.

LeDoux, J. E. (2007). The amygdale. *Current Biology, 17,* R868–874.

Lenroot, R. K., & Giedd, J. N. (2010). Sex differences in the adolescent brain. *Brain and Cognition, 72,* 46–55.

Libet, B. (1985). Unconscious cerebral initiative and the role of conscious in voluntary action. *Behavioral and Brain Science, 8,* 529–566.

Lieberman, M. D. (2000). Intuition. A social cognitive neuroscience approach. *Psychological Bulletin, 126,* 109–137.

Liechti, M. E., & Vollenweider, F. X. (2000). Acute psychological and physiological effects of MDMA ("ecstasy") after haloperidol pretreatment in healthy humans. *European Neuropsychopharmacology, 10,* 289–295.

Lindenfors, P., Nunn, C. L., & Barton, R. A. (2007). Primate brain architecture and selection in relation to sex. *BMC Biology, 5.* Retrieved from http://www.biomedcentral.com/content/pdf/1741-7007-5-20.pdf on May 11, 2007.

Machado, C. J., Kazama, A. M., & Bachevalier, J. (2009). Impact of amygdala, orbital frontal, or hippocampal lesions on threat avoidance and emotional reactivity in nonhuman primates. *Emotion, 9,* 147–163.

Macmillan, M. (2000). Restoring Phineas Gage. A 150th retrospective. *Journal of the History of the Neurosciences, 9(1),* 42–62.

Macmillan, M., & Lena, M. L. (2010). Rehabilitating Phineas Gage. *Neuropsychological Rehabilitation, 20,* 641–658.

MacNeilage, P. F., Rogers, L. J., & Vallortigara, G. (2009, July). Origins of the left and right brain. *Scientific American,* 60–67.

Maguire, E. A., Vargha-Khadem, F., & Hassabis, D. (2010). Imagining fictitious and future experiences. *Neuropsychologia, 48,* 3187–3192.

Marder, E., & Bucher, D. (2001). Central pattern generators and the control of rhythmic movements. *Current Biology, 11,* R986–R996.

Mashour, G. A., Walker, E. E., & Martuza, R. L. (2005). Psychosurgery. Past, present, and future. *Brain Research Reviews, 48,* 409–419.

Mattson, J., & Simon, M. (1996). *The pioneers of NMR and magnetic resonance in medicine.* Ramat Gan, Israel. Bar-Ilan University Press.

Max, J. E., Levin, H. S., Landis, J., Schachar, R., Saunders, A., et al. (2005). Predictors of personality change due to traumatic brain injury in children and adolescents in the first six months after injury. *Adolescent Psychiatry, 44,* 435–442.

Max, J. E., Levin, H. S., Schachar, R. J., Landis, J., Saunders, A. E., et al. (2006). Predictors of personality change due to traumatic brain injury in children and adolescents six to twenty-four months after injury. *The Journal of Neuropsychiatry and Clinical Neurosciences, 18,* 21–32.

Melzer, P., & Ebner, F. (2008). Braille, plasticity, and the mind. In J. J. Rieser, D. H. Ashmead, F. E. Ebner, & A. L. Corn (Eds.), *Blindness and plasticity in navigation and object perception* (pp. 85–112). New York. Psychology Press.

Menon, V. & Levitin, D. J. (2005). The rewards of music listening. Response and physiological connectivity of themesolimbic system. *NeuroImage, 28,* 175–184.

Mestel, R. (2012, June 19). Florida spear gun accident. Stories of brain injury survivors. *Los Angeles Times.* Retrieved on July 6, 2012 from www.latimes.com.

Mikolajczak, M., Gross, J. J., Lane, A., Corneille, O., de Timary, P., et al. (2010). Oxytocin makes people trusting, not gullible. *Psychological Science, 21,* 1072–1074.

Miller, E. K., & Cohen, J. D. (2001). An integrative theory of prefrontal cortex function. *Annual Review of Neuroscience, 24,* 167–102.

Miller, G. A. (2010). Mistreating psychology in the decades of the brain.

Perspectives in Psychological Science, 5, 716–743.

Miller, S. C., Kennedy, C., DeVoe, D., Hickey, M., Nelson, T., et al. (2009). Examination of changes in oxytocin levels in men and women before and after interaction with a bonded dog. *Anthrozoös, 22,* 31–42.

Milner, B. (1988). Description of amnesia patient H. M. In F. E. Bloom, A. Lazerson, & L. Hofstadter (Eds.), *Brain, Mind, and Behavior.* New York. W. H. Freeman.

Mitelman, S. A., Brickman, A. M., Shihabuddin, L., Newmark, R., Chu, K. W., et al. (2005). Correlations between MRI-assessed volumes of the thalamus and cortical Brodmann's areas in schizophrenia. *Schizophrenia Research, 75,* 265–281.

Mitelman, S. A., Byne, W., Kemether, E. M., Hazlett, E. A., Buchsbam, M., et al. (2005). Metabolic disconnection between the mediodorsal nucleus of the thalamus and cortical Brodmann's areas of the left hemisphere in schizophrenia. *The American Journal of Psychiatry, 162,* 1733–1735.

Miyamoto, Y., Nisbett, R. E., & Yasuda, T. (2006). Culture and the environment. *Psychological Science, 17,* 113–119.

Moor, B. G., Crone, E. A., & van der Molen, M. W. (2010). The heartbrake of social rejection. Heart rate deceleration in response to unexpected peer rejection. *Psychological Science, 21,* 1326–1333.

Moruzzi, G., & Magoun, H. (1949). Brain stem reticular formation and activation of the EEG. Electroencephalography and Clinical Neurophysiology, *1,* 455–473.

Murray E. A. (2007) The amygdala, reward and emotion. *Trends in Cognitive Sciences, 11,* 489–497.

Nagasawa, M., Kikusui, T., Onaka, T., & Ohta, M. (2009). Dog's gaze at its owner increases owner's urinary oxytocin during social interaction. *Hormones and Behavior, 55,* 434–441.

Narumoto, J., Okada, T., Sadato, N., Fukui, K., & Yonekura, Y. (2001). Attention to emotion modulates fMRI activity in human right superior temporal sulcus. *Cognitive Brain Research, 12,* 225–231.

Naughton, M., Mulrooney, J. B., & Leonard, B. E. (2000). A review of the role of serotonin receptors in psychiatric disorders. *Human Psychopharmacology. Clinical and Experimental, 15,* 397–415.

Nishimaru H., Restrepo C. E., Ryge, J., Yanagawa, Y., & Kiehn, O. (2005) Mammalian motor neurons corelease glutamate and acetylcholine at central synapses. *Proceedings of the National Academy of Sciences, 102,* 5245–5249.

Ohnishi, T., Matsuda, H., Asada, T., Aruga, M., Hirakata, M., et al. (2001). Functional anatomy of musical perception in musicians. *Cerebral Cortex, 11,* 754–760.

Ordway, G.A., Schwartz, M., & Frazer A. (2007). *Brain Norepinephrine. Neurobiology and Therapeutics.* New York. Cambridge University Press, 2007.

Owen, A. M., Coleman, M. R., Boly, M., Davis, M. H., Laureys, S., et al. (2006). Detecting awareness in the vegetative state. *Science, 313,* 1402.

Owen, A. M., Coleman, M. R., Boly, M., Davis, M. H., Laureys, S., et al. (2007). Using functional magnetic resonance imaging to detect covert awareness in the vegetative state. *Archives of Neurology, 64,* 1098–1102.

Pack, A. K., & Pawson, L. J. (2010). Neuroglial modulation in peripheral sensory systems. *The Neuroscientist, 16,* 342–348.

Page, M. P. A. (2006). What can't functional neuroimaging tell the cognitive psychologist? *Cortex. A Journal Devoted to the Study of the Nervous System and Behavior, 42,* 428–443.

Pantev, C., Ross, B., Fujioka, T., Trainor, L. J., Schulte, M., et al. (2003). Music and learning-induced cortical plasticity. *Annals of the New York Academy of Sciences, 999,* 438–450.

Penfield, W., & Perot, P. (1963). The brain's record of auditory and visual experience. *Brain, 86,* 595–696.

Pert, C. B., & Snyder, S. H. (1973). The opiate receptor. Demonstration in nervous tissue. *Science, 179,* 1011–1014.

Pfrieger, F. W. (2002). Role of glia in synapse development. *Current Opinion in Neurobiology, 12,* 486–490.

Phelps, E. A. (2006). Emotion and cognition. Insights from the study of the human amygdala. *Annual Review of Psychology, 57,* 27–53.

Pinker, S. (2002). *The blank slate.* New York. Viking.

Puldrack, R. A. (2010). Mapping mental function to brain structure. How can cognitive neuroimaging succeed? *Perspectives on Psychological Science, 5,* 753–761.

Pyka, M., Busse, C., Seidenbecher, C., Gundelfinger, E. D., & Faissner, A. (2011). Astrocytes are crucial for survival and maturation of embryonic hippocampal neurons in neuron-glia cell-insert coculture assay. *Synapse, 65,* 41–53.

Ramnani, N., & Owen, A. M. (2004). The anterior prefrontal cortex. What can functional imaging tell us about function? *Nature Reviews. Neuroscience, 5,* 184–194.

Rauch, S. L., Shin, L. M., & Wright, C. L. (2003) Neuroimaging studies of amygdala function in anxiety disorders. *Annals of the New York Academy of Sciences, 985,* 389–410.

Rejection really does hurt. (2003, October 18). *New Scientist.* Retrieved from www.newscientist.com on November 14, 2004.

Ridley, M. (2003). *The Red Queen. sex and the evolution of human nature.* New York. Harper.

Rothman, R. B., & Baumann, M. H. (2006). Balance between dopamine and serotonin release modulates behavioral effects of amphetamine-type drugs. *Annals of the New York Academy of Sciences, 1074,* 245–260.

Ryle, G. (1949). *The concept of mind.* Chicago. The University of Chicago Press.

Sacks, O. (1985). *The man who mistook his wife for a hat.* London, UK. Duckworth.

Salamone, J. D. (2002). Functional significance of nucleus accumbens dopamine. Behavior, pharmacology and neurochemistry. *Behavioral Brain Research, 137(1),* 1.

Salamone, J. D., & Correa, M. (2002). Motivational views of reinforcement. Implications for understanding the behavioral functions of nucleus accumbens dopamine. *Behavioral Brain Research, 137(1),* 3–25.

Salamone, J. D., Correa, M., Farrar, A., & Mingote, S. M. (2007). Effort-related functions of nucleus accumbens dopamine and associated forebrain circuits. *Psychopharmacology, 19,* 461–482.

Sapolsky, R. M. (1996). Why stress is bad for your brain. *Science, 273(5276),* 749–750.

Satpute, A. B., & Lieberman, M. D. (2006). Integrating automatic and controlled processes into neurocognitive models of social cognition. *Brain Research, 1079(1),* 86–97.

Schad, A., Schindler, K., Schelter, B., Maiwald, T., Brandt, A., et al. (2008). Application of a multivariate seizure detection and prediction method to non-invasive intracranial long-term EEG recordings. *Clinical Neurophysiology, 119,* 197–211.

Schmahmann, J. D. (2004). Disorders of the cerebellum. Ataxia, dysmetria of thought, and the cerebellar cognitive affective syndrome. *Journal of Neuropsychiatry and Clinical Neuroscience, 16,* 367–378.

Scoville, W., & Milner, B. (1957). Loss of recent memory after bilateral hippocampal lesions. *Journal of Neurology, Neurosurgery, and Psychiatry, 20,* 11–21.

Shermer, M. (2008). Why you should be skeptical of brain scans. *Scientific American Mind, October/November,* 67–71.

Sidtis J. J., Volpe B. T., Holtzman, J. D., Wilson, D. H., & Gazzaniga, M. S. (1981). Cognitive interaction after staged callosal section. Evidence for transfer of semantic activation. *Science, 212,* 344–346.

Sperry, R. (1974). Lateral specialization in the surgically separated hemispheres. In F. Schmitt & F. Worden (Eds.), *The neurosciences. Third study program* (pp. 5–19). Cambridge, MA. MIT Press.

Sperry, R. (1982). Some effects of disconnecting the cerebral hemispheres. *Science, 217,* 1223–1226.

Stein, M. B., Simmons, A. N., Feinstein, J. S., & Paulus, M. P. (2007). Increased amygdala and insula activation during emotion processing in anxiety-prone subjects. *American Journal of Psychiatry, 164,* 318–327.

Sterpenich, V., D'Argembeau, A., Desseilles, M., Balteau, E., Albouy, G., et al. (2006). The locus ceruleus is involved in the successful retrieval of emotional memories in humans. *Journal of Neuroscience, 26,* 7416–7423.

Strick, P. L., Dum, R. P., & Fiez, J. A. (2009). Cerebellum and nonmotor function. *Annual Review of Neuroscience, 32,* 413–434.

Svenningsson, P., Chergui, K. Rachleff, I. Flajolet, M., Zhang, X., et al. (2006). Alterations in 5-HT receptor by p11 in depression-like states. *Science, 311,* 77–80.

Swaab, D. F., Chung, W. C. J., Kruijver, F. P. M., Hofman, M. A., & Ishunina, T. A. (2001). Structural and functional sex differences in the human hypothalamus. *Hormones and Behavior, 40,* 93–98.

Taylor, S. E., Saphire-Bernstein, S., & Seeman, T. E. (2010). Are plasma oxytocin in women and plasma vasopressin in men biomarkers of distressed pair-bond relationships? *Psychological Science, 21,* 3–7.

Theoret, H., Merabet, L., & Pascual-Leone, A. (2004). Behavioral and neuroplastic changes in the blind. Evidence for functionally relevant cross-modal interactions. *Journal of Physiology, Paris, 98,* 221–233.

Thompson, R. F. (2005). In search of memory traces. *Annual Review of Psychology, 56,* 1–23.

Tobler, P. N., Fiorello, C. D., & Schultz, W. (2005). Adaptive coding of reward value by dopamine neurons. *Science, 307,* 1642–1645.

Tortora, G. J., & Derrickson, B. (2006). *Principles of anatomy and physiology* (12th ed.). New York. John Wiley and sons.

Trachtenberg, J. T., Chen, B. E., Knott, G. W., Feng, G., Sanes, J. R., et al. (2002). Long-term *in vivo* imaging of experience-dependent synaptic plasticity in adult cortex. *Nature, 420,* 788–794.

Turner, R. A., Altemus, M., Yip, D. N., Kupferman, E., Fletcher, D., et al. (2002). Effects of positive and negative emotion on oxytocin, prolactin and ACTH in women. *Stress, 5,* 269–276.

Ullian, E. M., Sapperstein, S. K., Christopherson, K. S., & Barres, B. A. (2001). Control of synapse number by glia. *Science, 291,* 657–660.

Uttal, W. R. (2001). *The new phrenology. The limits of localizing cognitive processes in the brain.* Cambridge, MA. MIT Press.

Valtin, H. (2002). "Drink at least eight glasses of water a day." Really? Is there scientific evidence for "8×8"? *American Journal of Physiology, 283,* R993–1004.

Vargha-Khadem, F., Gadian, D. G., Watkins, K. E., Connelly, A., Van Paesschen, W., et al. (1997). Differential effects of early hippocampal pathology on episodic and semantic memory. *Science, 277,* 376–380.

Vul, E., Harris, C., Winkielman, P., & Pashler, H. (2009). Puzzlingly high correlations in fMRI studies of emotion, personality, and social cognition. *Perspectives on Psychological Science, 4,* 274–290.

Weisberg, L. A., Garcia, C., & Strub, R. (1996). *Essentials of clinical neurology* (3rd ed.). St. Louis, MO. Mosby.

Whalen, P. J., Davis, C. F., Oler, J. A., Kim, H., Kim, M., et al. (2009). Human amygdale responses to facial expressions of emotion. In P. Whalen & E. A. Phelps (Eds.), *The human amygdale* (pp. 265–288). New York. Guilford Press.

Youngson, R. M., & Schott, I. (1998). *Medical blunders.* New York. New York University Press.

CHAPTER 3

Allman, W. F. (1995). *Stone Age present. How evolution has shaped modern life—from sex, violence and language, to emotions, morals, and communities.* New York. Touchstone.

Archer, J. (2009). Does sexual selection explain human sex differences in aggression? *Behavioral and Brain Sciences, 32,* 249–311.

Adams, G., & Plaut, V. C. (2003). The cultural grounding of personal relationship. Friendship in North American and West African worlds. *Personal Relationships, 10,* 333–347.

Allport, G. W. (1955). *Becoming.* New Haven, CT. Yale University Press.

Apatow, J., Robertson, S., & Townsend, C. (Producers), & Apatow, J. (Director). (2005). *The 40-Year-Old Virgin* [motion picture]. United States. Universal Studios.

Archer, J. (2004). Sex differences in aggression in real-world settings. A meta-analytic review. *Review of General Psychology, 8,* 291–232.

Archer, J. (2009). Does sexual selection explain human sex differences in aggression? *Behavioral and Brain Sciences, 32,* 249–311.

Arnett, J. (2008). The neglected 95%. Why American psychology needs to become less American. *American Psychologist, 63,* 602–614.

Aubrey, J. S. (2004). Sex and punishment. An examination of sexual consequences and the sexual double standard in teen programming. *Sex Roles, 50,* 505–514.

Barkow, J. H. (1989). *Darwin, sex, and status. Biosocial approaches to mind and culture.* Toronto, Canada. University of Toronto Press.

Barkow, J. H. (2006). *Missing the revolution. Darwinism for social scientists.* Oxford, UK. Oxford University Press.

Barrett, H. C. (2005). Adaptations to predators and prey. In D. M. Buss (Ed.), *The handbook of evolutionary psychology* (pp. 200–223). Hoboken, NJ. John Wiley & Sons.

Bateman, A. J. (1948). Intrasexual selection. *Drosophila. Heredity, 2,* 349–368.

Baumeister, R. F., & Leary, M. R. (1995). The need to belong. Desire for interpersonal attachments as a fundamental human motivation. *Psychological Bulletin, 117,* 497–529.

Baumeister, R. F., & Tice, D. M. (2001). *The social dimension of sex.* Boston, MA. Allyn & Bacon.

Beer, J. M., Arnold, R. D., & Loehlin, J. C. (1998). Genetic and environmental influences on MMPI factor scales. Joint model fitting to twin and adoption data. *Journal of Personality and Social Psychology, 74,* 818–827.

Berglund, A., & Rosenqvist, G. (2003). Sex role reversal in pipefish. *Advances in the Study of Behavior, 32,* 131–167.

Bouchard, T. K., Jr. (1996a). Behavior genetic studies of intelligence, yesterday, and today. The long journey from plausibility to proof. *Journal of Biosocial Science, 28,* 527–555.

Bouchard, T. J., Jr. (1996b). IQ similarity in twins reared apart. Findings and responses to critics. In R. Sternberg & C. Grigorenko (Eds.), *Intelligence. Heredity and environment* (pp. 126–160). New York. Cambridge University Press.

Bouchard, T. J. (2004). Genetic influence on human psychological traits. *Current Directions in Psychological Science, 13,* 148–151.

Bouchard, T. J., Jr., Lykken, D. T., McGue, M., Segal, N. L., & Tellegen, A. (1990). Sources of human psychological differences. The Minnesota study of twins reared apart. *Science, 250,* 223–228.

Bouchard, T. J. Jr., Segal, N. L., Tellegen, A., McGue, M., Keyes, M., et al. (2004). Genetic influences on social attitudes. Another challenge to psychology from behavior genetics. In L. F. DiLalla (Ed.), *Behavior genetics principles. Perspectives in development, personality, and psychopathology. Decade of behavior* (pp. 89–104). Washington, DC. American Psychological Association.

Brouwers, S. A., van Hemert, D. A., Breugelmans, S. M., & van de Vijver, F. J. R. (2004). A historical analysis of empirical studies published in Journal of Cross-Cultural Psychology 1970–2004. *Journal of Cross-Cultural Psychology, 35,* 251–262.

Brown, D. E. (1991). *Human universals.* New York. McGraw-Hill.

Buss, D. M. (1989). Sex differences in human mate preferences. Evolutionary hypotheses testing in 37 cultures. *Behavioral and Brain Sciences, 12,* 1–49.

Buss, D. M. (1994). *The evolution of desire.* New York. Basic Books.

Buss, D. M. (Ed.) (2005). *The handbook of evolutionary psychology.* Hoboken, NJ. John Wiley & Sons.

Buss, D. M. (2009a). The great struggles of life. Darwin and the emergence of evolutionary psychology. *American Psychologist, 64,* 140–148.

Buss, D. M. (2009b). How can evolutionary psychology successfully explain personality and individual differences. *Perspectives on Psychological Science, 4,* 359–366.

Champagne, F. A., & Mashoodh, R. (2009). Genes in context. Gene-environment interplay and the origins of individual differences in behavior. *Current Directions in Psychological Science, 18,* 127–131.

Chiappe, D., & MacDonald, K. (2005). The evolution of domain-general mechanisms in intelligence and learning. *The Journal of General Psychology, 132(10)*, 5–40.

Choi, I., Dalal, R., Kim-Prieto, C., & Park, H. (2003). Culture and judgment of causal relevance. *Journal of Personality and Social Psychology, 84*, 46–59.

Choi, I., & Nisbett, R. E. (1998). Situational salience and cultural differences in the correspondence bias and the actor-observer bias. *Personality and Social Psychology Bulletin, 24*, 949–960.

Clark, R. D. (1990). The impact of AIDS on gender differences in willingness to engage in casual sex. *Journal of Applied Social Psychology, 20 (Part 2)*, 771–782.

Clark, R. D., & Hatfield, E. (1989). Gender differences in receptivity to sexual offers. *Journal of Psychology and Human Sexuality, 2*, 39–55.

Cosmides, L., & Tooby, J. (1987). From evolution to behavior. Evolutionary psychology as the missing link. In J. Dupre (Ed.), *The latest on the best. Essays on evolution and optimality* (pp. 277–306). Cambridge, MA. MIT Press.

Cosmides, L., & Tooby, J. (2000). Evolutionary psychology and the emotions. In M. Lewis & J. M. Haviland-Jones (Eds.), *Handbook of emotions* (2nd ed., pp. 91–115). New York. Guilford Press.

Cosmides, L., & Tooby, J. (2008). Beyond intuition and instinct blindness. Toward an evolutionarily rigorous cognitive science. In J. E. Adler & J. L. Rips (Eds.), *Reasoning. Studies of human inference and its foundations* (pp. 843–865). New York. Cambridge University Press.

Darwin, C. (1859/2003). *On the origin of species*. Edited by Joseph Carroll. Ontario, Canada. Broadview Texts.

Darwin, C. (1871/1874). *The descent of man and selection in relation to sex* (2nd ed.). London. John Murray. Retrieved from http://darwin-online.org.uk/converted/pdf/1874_Descent_F944.pdf on January 28, 2013.

Dawkins, R.. (1989). *The selfish gene* (Rev. ed.). New York. Oxford University Press.

DeCasper, A. J., & Spence, M. J. (1986). Prenatal maternal speech influences newborns' perception of speech sounds. *Infant Behavior and Development, 9*, 133–150.

Deepest Desires (2002). In Natasha Bondy (Dir.) *Human instinct* (television documentary series). Great Britain. BBC/The Learning Channel.

Dick, D. M. (2011). Gene-environment interaction in psychological traits and disorder. *Annual Review of Psychology, 7*, 383–409.

Dollard, J., & Miller, N. (1941). *Social learning and imitation*. New Haven. Yale University Press.

Eagly, A. H. (1995). The science and politics of comparing women and men. *American Psychologist, 50*, 145–158.

Eagly, A. H., & Wood, W. (1999). The origins of sex differences in human behavior. Evolved dispositions versus social roles. *American Psychologist, 54*, 408–423.

Fieder, M., & Huber, S. (2007). Parental age difference and offspring count in humans. *Biology Letters*. Retrieved from www.journals.royalsoc.ac.uk on September 3, 2007.

Field, T. M., Woodson, R., Greenberg, R., & Cohen, D. (1982). Discrimination and imitation of facial expressions by neonates. *Science, 218*, 179–181.

Fisher, R. A. (1925). *Statistical methods for research workers*. Edinburgh, UK. Oliver and Boyd.

Fox, N. A., Hane, A. A., & Pine, D. S. (2007). Plasticity for affective neurocircuitry. How the environment affects gene expression. *Current Directions in Psychological Science, 16*, 1–5.

Gallop Poll (February 11, 2009). On Darwin's birthday, only 4 in 10 believe in evolution. Retrieved from http://www.gallup.com/poll on March 4, 2011.

Gangestad, S. W., & Simpson, J. A. (2000). The evolution of human mating. Trade-offs and strategic pluralism. *Behavioral and Brain Sciences, 23*, 573–644.

Ge, X., Donnellan, M. B., & Harper, L. (2003). Are we finally ready to move beyond "nature vs. nurture"? In A. C. Crouter & A. Booth (Eds.), *Children's influence on family dynamics* (pp. 37–48). Hillsdale, NJ. Lawrence Erlbaum Associates.

Geary, D. C. (2010). *Male, female. The evolution of human sex differences* (2nd ed.). Washington, DC. American Psychological Association.

Gelfand, M. J., & Diener, E. (2010). Culture and psychological science. Introduction to the special section. *Perspectives on Psychological Science, 5*, 390.

Ghera, M. M., Hane, A. A., Malesa, E. M., & Fox, N. A. (2006). The role of infant soothability in the relation between infant negativity and maternal sensitivity. *Infant Behavior and Development, 29*, 289–293.

Gilbert, D. T., & Malone, P. S. (1995). The correspondence bias. *Psychological Bulletin, 117*, 21–38.

Goldberg, S. (1993). *Why men rule. A theory of male dominance*. Chicago. Open Court.

Gould, S. J. (1981, May). Evolution as fact and theory. *Discover*, May, 34–37.

Gould, S. J. (1997, June 12). Darwinian fundamentalism. *The New York Review of Books, KLIV(10)*, 24–27.

Haidt, J. (2007). The new synthesis in moral psychology. *Science, 316*, 998–1002.

Harden, K. P., Hill, J. E., Turkheimer, E., & Emery, R. E. (2008). Gene-environment correlation and interaction in peer effects on adolescent alcohol and tobacco use. *Behavior Genetics, 38*, 339–347.

Haworth, C. M. A., Wright, M. J., Luciano, M., Martin, N. G., de Geus, E. J. C., et al. (2010). The heritability of general cognitive ability increases linearly from childhood to young adulthood. *Molecular Psychiatry, 15*, 1112–1120.

Haworth, C. M. A., & Plomin, R. (2010). Quantitative genetics in the era of molecular genetics. *Journal of the American Academy of Child & Adolescent Psychiatry, 49*, 783–793.

Heine, S. J. (2005). Constructing good selves in Japan and North America. In R. M. Sorrentino, D. Cohen, J. M. Olson, & M. P. Zanna (Eds.), *Culture and social behavior. The tenth Ontario Symposium* (pp. 115–143). Hillsdale, NJ. Lawrence Erlbaum Associates.

Heine, S. J., & Norenzayan, A. (2006). Toward a psychological science for a cultural species. *Perspectives on Psychological Science, 1*, 251–269.

Henrich, J., Heine, S. J., & Norenzayan, A. (2010). The weirdest people in the world? *Behavioral and Brain Sciences, 33*, 61–83.

Hofstede, G. H. (2001). *Culture's consequences. Comparing values, behaviors, institutions and organizations across nations* (2nd ed.). Thousand Oaks, CA. Sage Publications.

Hofstede, G. H., & McCrae, R. R. (2004). Personality and culture revisited. Linking traits and dimensions of culture. *Cross-Cultural Research, 38*, 52–88.

Horwitz, A. V., Videon, R. M., Schmitz, M. F., & Davis, D. (2003). Rethinking twins and environments. Possible social sources for assumed genetic influences in twin research. *Journal of Health and Social Behavior, 44*, 111–129.

Hubel, D. H., & Wiesel, T. N. (1970). The period of susceptibility to the physiological effects of eye closure in kittens. *Journal of Physiology, 206*, 419–436.

Human Genome Project Information (2008, September 19). How many genes are in the human genome? Retrieved from http://www.ornl.gov/sci/techresources/Human_Genome/faq/genenumber.shtml on January 28, 2013.

Huxley, R. R. (2000). Nausea and vomiting in early pregnancy. Its role in placental development. *Obstetrics and Gynecology, 95*, 779–782.

Hyde, J. S. (2006). The gender similarities hypothesis. *American Psychologist, 60*, 581–592.

Johnson, W., Turkheimer, E., Gottesman, I. I., & Buchard, J. Jr. (2009). Beyond heritability. Twin studies in behavioral research. *Current Directions in Psychological Science, 18*, 217–220.

Kenrick, D. T., & Li, N. (2000). The Darwin is in the details. *American Psychologist, 55*, 1060–1061.

Kenrick, D. T., Li, N. P., & Butner, J. (2003). Dynamical evolutionary psychology. Individual decision-rules and emergent social norms. *Psychological Review, 110(1)*, 3–28.

Kisilevsky, B. S., Hains, S. M., Lee, K., Xie, X., Huang, H., et al. (2003). Effects of experience on fetal voice recognition. *Psychological Science, 14*, 220–224.

Kisilevsky, B. S., Hains, S. M., Brown, C. A., Lee, C. T., Cowperthwaite, B., et al. (2009). Fetal sensitivity to properties of maternal speech and language. *Infant Behavior & Development, 32*, 59–71.

Krueger, R. F., & Johnson, W. (2008). Behavioral genetics and personality. In L. A. Pervin, O. P. John, & R. W. Robins (Eds.), *Handbook of personality. Theory and research* (3rd ed., pp. 287–310). New York. Guilford.

Krueger, R. F., South, S., Johnson, W., & Iacono, W. (2008). The heritability of personality is not always 50%. Gene-environment interactions and correlations between personality and parenting. *Journal of Personality, 76,* 1485–1521.

Krützen, M., Mann, J., Heithaus, M. R., Connor, R. C., Bejder, L, et al. (2005). Cultural transmission of tool use in bottlenose dolphins. *Proceedings of the National Academy of Sciences, 102,* 8939–8943.

Lake, R. I., Eaves, L. J., Maes, H. H., Heath, A. C., & Martin, N. G. (2000). Further evidence against the environmental transmission of individual differences in neuroticism from a collaborative study of 45,850 twins and relatives on two continents. *Behavior Genetics, 30,* 223–233.

Larsen, E. J., & Witham, L. (1998). Leading scientists still reject God. *Nature, 394,* p. 313.

Leary, M. R., & Cox, C. B. (2008). Belongingness motivation. A mainspring of social action. In J. Y. Shah, & W. L. Gardner (Eds.), *Handbook of motivation science* (pp. 27–40). New York. Guilford Press.

Lenski, R. E. (2000, September). *Evolution. Fact and theory.* American Institute of Biological Sciences. Retrieved from http://www.actionbio science.org/evolution/lenski.html on March 4, 2010.

Leonardo, E. D., & Hen, R. (2006). Genetics of affective and anxiety disorders. *Annual Review of Psychology, 57,* 117–137.

Lewontin, R. C. (1981). Evolution/creation debate. A time for truth. *Bioscience 31,* 559.

Lieberman, D., Pillsworth, E. G., & Haselton, M. G. (2011). Kin affiliation across the ovulatory cycle. Females avoid fathers when fertile. *Psychological Science, 22,* 13–18.

Lippa, R. A. (2007). The preferred traits of mates in a cross-national study of heterosexual and homosexual men and women. An examination of biological and cultural influences. *Archives of Sexual Behavior, 36,* 193–208.

Lippa, R. A. (2009). Sex differences in sex drive, sociosexuality, and height across 53 nations. Testing evolutionary and social structural theories. *Archives of Sexual Behavior, 38,* 631–651.

LoBue, V., & deLoache, J. S. (2008). Detecting the snake in the grass. Attention to fear-relevant stimuli by adults and young children. *Psychological Science, 19,* 284–289.

Loehlin, J. C., Horn, J. M., & Willerman, L. (1990). Heredity, environment, and personality change. Evidence from the Texas Adoption Project. *Journal of Personality, 58(1),* 221–243.

Maccoby, E. E. (2002). Parenting effects. Issues and controversies. In J. G. Borkowski, S. L. Ramey, & M. Bristol-Power (Eds.), *Parenting and the child's world* (pp. 35–46). Mahwah, NJ. Lawrence Erlbaum Associates.

Machery, E., & Cohen, K. (2011). An evidence-based study of the evolutionary behavioral sciences. *British Journal of the Philosophy of Science, 63,* 177–226.

Maner, J. K., & Kenrick, D. T. (2010). Evolutionary social psychology. In R. F. Baumeister & E. J. Finkel (Eds.), *Advanced social psychology. The state of the science* (pp. 613–653). New York. Oxford University Press.

Markus, H. R., & Kitayama, S. (1998). The cultural psychology of personality. *Journal of Cross-Cultural Psychology, 29,* 63–87.

Markus, H. R., Uchida, Y., Omoregie, H., Townsend, S. S. M., & Kitayama, S. (2006). Going for the gold. Models of agency in Japanese and American contexts. *Psychological Science, 17,* 103–112.

Marshall-Pescini, S., & Whiten, A. (2008). Chimpanzees (pan troglodytes) and the question of cumulative culture. An experimental approach. *Animal Cognition, 11,* 449–456.

Mathes, E. W., King, C. A., Miller, J. K., & Reed R. M. (2002). An evolutionary perspective on the interaction of age and sex differences in short-term sexual strategies. *Psychological Reports, 90,* 949–956.

Matsumoto, D., & Hee Yoo, S. (2006). Toward a new generation of cross-cultural research. *Perspectives on Psychological Science, 1,* 234–250.

Maurer, D., Mondloch, C. J., & Lewis, T. L. (2007). Sleeper effects. *Developmental Science, 10(1),* 40–47.

McGue, M., Bouchard, T. J., Jr., Iacono, W. G., & Lykken, D. T. (1993). In R. Plomin & G. E. McClearn (Eds.), *Nature, nurture, and psychology* (pp. 59–76). Washington, DC. American Psychological Association.

McGuffin, P., Riley, B., & Plomin, R. (2001). Toward behavioral genomics. *Science, 291,* 1232–1249.

Meltzoff, A. N., & Moore, M. K. (1983). Newborn infants imitate adult facial gestures. *Child Development, 54,* 702–709.

Meltzoff, A. N., & Moore, M. K. (1989). Imitation in newborn infants. Exploring the range of gestures imitated and the underlying mechanisms. *Developmental Psychology, 25,* 954–962.

Miller, J. D., Scott, E. C., & Okamoto, S. (2006). Public acceptance of evolution. *Science, 313,* 765–766.

Nesse, R. M. (2005). Maladaptation and natural selection. *Quarterly Review of Biology, 80,* 62–70.

Nishida, T., Matsusaka, T., & McGrew, W. C. (2009). Emergence, propagation or disappearance of novel behavioral patterns in the habituated chimpanzees of Mahale. A review. *Primates, 50,* 23–36.

Nisbett, R. E., & Miyamoto, Y. (2005). The influence of culture. Holistic versus analytic perception. *Trends in Cognitive Science, 9,* 467–473.

Norenzayan, A., & Heine, S. J. (2005). Psychological universals. What are they and how can we know? *Psychological Bulletin, 131,* 763–784.

Obama, B. (1995/2007). *Dreams from my father.* New York. Crown.

O'Connor, T. B., Deater-Deckard, K., Fulker, D., Rutter, M., & Plomin, R. (1998). Genotype-environment correlations in late childhood and early adolescence. Antisocial behavioral problems and coercive parenting. *Developmental Psychology, 34,* 970–981.

Öhman, A., & Mineka, S. (2003). The malicious serpent. Snakes as a prototypical stimulus for an evolved module of fear. *Current Directions in Psychological Science, 12,* 5–9.

Okami, P., & Shackelford, T. (2001). Human sex differences in sexual psychology and behavior. *Annual Review of Sex Research, 12,* 186–241.

Oliver, M. B., & Hyde, J. S. (1993) Gender differences in sexuality. A meta-analysis. *Psychological Bulletin, 114,* 29–51.

Olson, J. M., Vernon, P. A., Harris, J. A., & Jang, K. L. (2001). The heritability of attitudes. A study of twins. *Journal of Personality and Social Psychology, 80,* 845–860.

Öngel, Ü., & Smith, P. B. (1994). Who are we and where are we going? JCCP approaches its 100th issue. *Journal of Cross-Cultural Studies, 25,* 25–53.

Panksepp, J., & Panksep, J. B. (2000). The seven sins of evolutionary psychology. *Evolution and Cognition, 6,* 108–131.

Peplau, L. A. (2003). Human sexuality. How do men and women differ? *Current Directions in Psychological Science, 12,* 189–192.

Pepper, G. V., & Craig Roberts, S. (2006). Rates of nausea and vomiting in pregnancy and dietary characteristics across populations. *Proceedings of the Royal Society/Series B, 273,* 2675–2679.

Petersen, J. L., & Hyde, J. S. (2010). A meta-analytic review of research on gender differences in sexuality. *Psychological Bulletin, 136,* 21–38.

Petrill, S. A., Lipton, P. A., Hewitt, J. K., Plomin, R., Cherny, S. S., et al. (2004). Genetic and environmental contributions to general cognitive ability through the first 16 years of life. *Developmental Psychology, 40,* 805–812.

Pinker, S. (2002). *The blank slate. The modern denial of human nature.* New York. Viking.

Plomin, R., Corley, R., Caspi, A., Fulker, D. W., & DeFries, J. (1998). Adoption results for self-reported personality. Evidence for nonadditive genetic effects? *Journal of Personality and Social Psychology, 75,* 211–218.

Plomin, R., DeFries, J. C., & Loehlin, J. C. (1977). Genotype-environment interaction and correlation in the analysis of human behavior. *Psychological Bulletin, 84*, 309–322.

Plomin, R., DeFries, J. C., McClearn, G. E., & McGuffin, P. (2008). *Behavioral genetics* (5th ed.). New York. Worth.

Plomin, R., & Spinath, F. M. (2004). Intelligence. Genetics, genes, and genomics. *Journal of Personality and Social Psychology, 86*, 112–129.

Profet, M. (1992). Pregnancy sickness as adaptation. A deterrent to maternal ingestion of teratogens. In J. H. Barkow, L. Cosmides, & J. Tooby (Eds.), *The adapted mind. Evolutionary psychology and the generation of culture* (pp. 327–366). New York, NY. Oxford University Press.

Ptashne, M., & Gann, A. (2002). *Genes and signals.* Woodbury, NY. Cold Spring Harbor Laboratory Press.

Quinones-Vidal, E., Lopez-Garcia, J. J., Penaranda-Ortega, M., & Tortosa-Gil, F. (2004). The nature of social and personality psychology as reflected in JPSP, 1965–2000. *Journal of Personality and Social Psychology, 86*, 435–462.

Rendell, L., & Whitehead, H. (2001). Culture in whales and dolphins. *Behavioral and Brain Sciences, 24*, 309–382.

Ridley, M. (2003). *The red queen. Sex and the evolution of human nature.* New York. Penguin.

Rietveld, M. J., Hudziak, J. J., Bartels. M., Van Beijsterveldt, C. E. M., & Boomsma, D. I. (2004). Heritability of attention problems in children. I. cross-sectional results from a study of twins, age 3–12 years. *Journal of Child Psychology and Psychiatry, 45*, 577–588.

Rose, H., & Rose, S. (2000). *Alas, poor Darwin. Arguments against evolutionary psychology.* London. Jonathan Cape.

Ross, L. (1977) The intuitive psychologist and his short-comings. Distortions in the attribution process. In L. Berkowitz (Ed.), *Advances in experimental social psychology* (Vol. 10, pp. 173–220). San Diego, CA. Academic Press.

Rozin, P. (1976). Psychological and cultural determinants of food choice. In T. Silverstone (Ed.), *Appetite and food intake* (pp. 286–312). Berlin. Dahlem Konferenzen.

Rutter, M. (2007). Gene-environment interdependence. *Developmental Science, 10(1)*, 12–18.

Rutter, M., O'Connor, T. G., and the English and Romanian Adoptees (ERA) Study Team. (2004). Are there biological programming effects for psychological development? Findings from a study of Romanian adoptees. *Developmental Psychology, 40*, 81–94.

Sargeant, B. L., & Mann, J. (2009). From social learning to culture. Intrapopulation variation in bottlenose dolphins. In K. N. Laland & G. Bennett (Eds.), *The question of animal culture* (pp. 152–173). Cambridge, MA. Harvard University Press.

Saudino, K. J. (2005). Behavioral genetics and child temperament.

Developmental and Behavioral Pediatrics, 26, 214–223.

Schacter, D. L. (2001). *The seven sins of memory.* New York. Houghton Mifflin.

Schmitt, D. P. (2003). Universal sex differences in the desire for sexual variety. Tests from 52 nations, 6 continents, and 13 islands. *Journal of Personality and Social Psychology, 85(1)*, 85–104.

Schmitt, D. P. (2005). Sociosexuality from Argentina to Zimbabwe. A 48-Nation study of sex, culture, and strategies of human mating. *Behavioral and Brain Sciences, 28*, 247–311.

Schmitt, D. P., Jonason, P. K., Byerley, G. J., Flores, S. D., Illbeck, B. E., et al. (2012). A reexamination of sex differences in sexuality. New studies reveal old truths. *Current Direction in Psychological Science, 21*, 135–139.

Schmitt, D. P., & Pilcher, J. J. (2004). Evaluating evidence of psychological adaptation. How do we know one when we see one? *Psychological Science, 15*, 643–649.

Sedikides, C., Gaertner, L., & Toguchi, Y. (2003). Pancultural self-enhancement. *Journal of Personality and Social Psychology, 84*, 60–70.

Sedikides, C., & Gregg, A. P. (2008). Self-enhancement. Food for thought. *Perspectives on Psychological Science, 3*, 102–116.

Segal, N. L. (2010). Twins. The finest natural experiment. *Personality and Individual Differences, 49*, 317–323.

Segerstråle, U. (2000). *Defenders of the truth. The battle for science in the sociobiology debate and beyond.* New York. Oxford University Press.

Sengupta, S. (2003, September 26). Facing death for adultery, Nigerian woman is acquitted. *New York Times.* Retrieved from http://www.nytimes.com/2003/09/26/world/facing-death-for-adultery-nigerian-woman-is-acquitted.html?ref=aminalawal on October 12, 2004.

Skuse, D. H., Mandy, W. P., Scourfield, J. (2005). Measuring autistic traits. heritability, reliability, and validity of the social and communication disorders checklist. *British Journal of Psychiatry, 187*, 568–572.

Sprecher, S., McKinney, K., & Orbuch, T. (1987). Has the double standard disappeared? An experimental test. *Social Psychology Quarterly, 50*, 24–31.

Symons, D. (1979). *The evolution of human sexuality.* New York. Oxford University Press.

Symons, D. (1995). Beauty is in the adaptations of the beholder. The evolutionary psychology of human female sexual attractiveness. In P. R. Abramson & S. D. Pinkerton (Eds.), *Sexual nature, sexual culture* (pp. 80–120). Chicago. University of Chicago Press.

Taylor, S. E. (2006). Tend and befriend. Biobehavioral bases of affiliation under stress. *Current Directions in Psychological Science, 15*, 273–277.

Taylor, S. E., & Brown, J. D. (1994). "Illusion" of mental health does not

explain positive illusions. *American Psychologist, 49*, 972–973.

Tomasello, M., & Herrmann, E. (2010). Ape and human cognition. What's the difference? *Current Directions in Psychological Science, 19*, 3–8.

Tooby, J., & Cosmides, L. (1992). The psychological foundations of culture. In J. H. Barkow, L. Cosmides, & J. Tooby (Eds.), *The adapted mind. Evolutionary psychology and the generation of culture* (pp. 19–136). New York. Oxford University Press.

Trivers, R. L. (1972). Parental investment and sexual selection. In B. Campbell (Ed.), *Sexual selection and the descent of man, 1871–1971* (pp. 136–179). Chicago. Aldine.

Tucker-Drob, E. M., Rhemtulla, M., Harden, K. P., Turkheimer, E., & Fask, D. (2011). Emergence of a gene × socioeconomic status interaction on infant mental ability between 10 months and 2 years. *Psychological Science, 22*, 125–133.

Turkheimer, E., Haley, A., Waldron, M., D'Onofrio, B., & Gottesman, I. I. (2003). Socioeconomic status modifies heritability of IQ in young children. *Psychological Science, 14*, 623–628.

van den Berghe, P. L. (2009). Sexual selection and social roles. Two models or one? *Behavioral and Brain Sciences, 32*, 291–292.

von Hippel, W., & Trivers, R. (2011). The evolution and psychology of self-deception. *Behavioral and Brain Sciences, 34*, 1–56.

Wadden, T. A., Brownell, K. D., & Foster, G. D. (2002). Obesity. Responding to the global epidemic. *Journal of Consulting and Clinical Psychology, 70*, 510–525.

Wadsworth, S. J., Corley, R. P., Hewitt, J. K., Plomin, R., & DeFries, J. C. (2002). Parent-offspring resemblance for reading performance at 7, 12, and 16 years of age in the Colorado Adoption Project. *Journal of Child Psychology & Psychiatry, 43*, 769–774.

Whiten, A., Goodall, J., McGrew, W. C., Nishida, T., Reynolds, V., et al. (1999). Cultures in chimpanzees. *Nature, 299*, 682–685.

Whiten, A., Horner, V., & de Waal, F. B. M. (2005). Conformity to cultural norms of tool use in chimpanzees. *Nature, 437*, 737–740.

Whiten, A., Spiteri, A., Horner, V., Bonnie, C. E., Lambeth, S. P., et al. (2007). Transmission of multiple traditions within and between chimpanzee groups. *Current Biology, 17*, 1–6.

Williams, G. C. (1966). *Adaptation and natural selection. A critique of some current evolutionary thought.* Princeton, NJ. Princeton University Press.

Witham, L. (1997, April 11). Many scientists see God's hand in evolution. *The Washington Times*, p. A8. Retrieved from http://www.ncseweb.org on October 15, 2008. For greater detail see. http://www.ncseweb.org/resources/rncse_content/vol24/9863_polling_the_creationismevolut_12_30_1899.asp

Wood, W., & Eagly, A. H. (2002). A cross-cultural analysis of the behavior of women and men. Implications for the origins of sex differences. *Psychological Bulletin, 128,* 699–727.

Wood, W., & Eagly, A. H. (2007). Social structural origins of sex differences in human mating. In S. W. Gangestad, & J. A. Simpson (Eds.), *The evolution of mind. Fundamental questions and controversies* (pp. 383–390). New York. Guilford Press.

Wright, L. (1997). *Twins. And what they tell us about who we are.* New York. Wiley & Sons.

CHAPTER 4

Adams, R., & Laursen, B. (2001). The organization and dynamics of adolescent conflict with parents and friends. *Journal of Marriage and the Family, 63,* 97–110.

Ainsworth, M. D. S., Blehar, M., Waters, E., & Wall, S. (1978). *Patterns of attachment.* Hillsdale, NJ. Lawrence Erlbaum Associates.

Andersson, B-E. (1992). Effects of day care on cognitive and socioemotional competence of thirteen-year-old Swedish schoolchildren. *Child Development, 63(1),* 20–36.

Arnett, J. (1992). Reckless behavior in adolescence. A developmental perspective. *Developmental Review, 12,* 339–373.

Arnett, J. (2010). Oh, grow up! Generational grumbling and the new life stage of emerging adulthood—commentary on Trzesniewski & Donnellan (2010). *Perspectives on Psychological Science, 5,* 89–92.

Arnold, M. L. (2000). Stage, sequence, and sequels. Changing conceptions of morality, post-Kohlberg. *Educational Psychology Review, 12,* 365–383.

Avis, N. E., Stellato R., Crawford S., Bromberger, J., Ganz, P., et al. (2001). Is there a menopausal syndrome? Menopause status and symptoms across ethnic groups. *Social Science and Medicine, 52,* 345–356.

Baillargeon, R.. (2002). The acquisition of physical knowledge in infancy. A summary in eight lessons. In U. Goswami (Ed.), *Blackwell handbook of child cognitive development* (pp. 47–83). Oxford, UK. Blackwell.

Baillargeon, R., Spelke, E. S., & Wasserman, S. (1985). Object permanence in five-month-old infants. *Cognition, 20,* 191–208.

Balsam, K. F., Beauchaine, T. P., Rothblum, E. D., & Solomon, S. E. (2008). Three-year follow-up of same-sex couples who had civil unions in Vermont, same-sex couples not in civil unions, and heterosexual married couples. *Developmental Psychology, 44,* 102–116.

Baltes, P. B. (1987). Theoretical propositions of life-span developmental psychology. On the dynamics between growth and decline. *Developmental Psychology, 23,* 611–626.

Baltes, P. B., Lindenberger, U., & Staudinger, U. M. (2006). Life span theory in developmental psychology. In R. M. Lerner & W. Damon (Eds.), *Handbook of child psychology* (6th ed., Vol 1). *Theoretical models of human development* (pp. 569–664). Hoboken, NJ. John Wiley & Sons.

Baltes, P. B., Staudinger, U. M., & Lindenberger, U. (1999). Lifespan psychology. Theory and application to intellectual functioning. *Annual Review of Psychology, 50,* 471–507.

Barkow, J. H., Cosmides, L., & Tooby, J. (Eds.). (1992). *The adapted mind.* New York. Oxford University Press.

Baron-Cohen, S., Leslie, A. M., & Firth, U. (1985). Does the autistic child have a "theory of mind"? *Cognition, 21,* 37–46.

Baumrind, D. (1967). Child care practices anteceding three patterns of preschool behavior. *Genetic Psychology Monographs, 75,* 43–88.

Baumrind, D. (1987). A developmental perspective on adolescent risk taking in contemporary America. In C.E. Irwin, Jr. (Ed.), *Adolescent social behavior and health* (pp. 93–125). San Francisco, CA. Jossey-Bass.

Baumrind, D. (1996). The discipline controversy revisited. *Family Relations, 45,* 405–414.

Belsky, J. (2001). Developmental risks (still) associated with early child care. *Journal of Child Psychology and Psychiatry, 42,* 845–859.

Belsky, J. (2009). Classroom composition, childcare history, and social development. Are childcare effects disappearing or spreading? *Social Development, 18,* 230–238.

Berger, A. S. (1993). *Dying and death in law and medicine. A forensic primer for health and legal professionals.* Westport, CT. Praeger.

Berger, A., Tzur, G., & Posner, M. I. (2006). Infant brains detect arithmetic errors. *Proceedings of the National Academy of Sciences. Psychology, 103,* 12649–12653.

Blanchflower, D. G., & Oswald, A. J. (2008). Is well-being U-shaped over the life cycle? *Social Science and Medicine, 66,* 1733–1749.

Bloom, P. (2004). *Descartes' baby. How the science of child development explains what makes us human.* New York. Basic Books.

Bloom, P. (2010, May 3). The moral life of babies. *New York Times.* Retrieved from http://www.nytimes.com/2010/05/09/magazine/09babies-t.html?pagewanted=all on June 2, 2010.

Bowlby, J. (1988). *A secure base. Parent-child attachment and healthy human development.* New York. Basic Books.

Brown, B. B., & Klute, C. (2006). Friendships, cliques, and crowds. In G. R. Adams & M. D. Berzonsky (Eds.), *Blackwell handbook of adolescence* (pp. 330–348). Oxford, UK. Blackwell Publishing.

Brown, D. E. (1991). *Human universals.* New York. McGraw-Hill.

Brownlee, S. (2005, August 1). Inside the teen brain. Mysteries of the teen years. *U.S. News & World Report.* Retrieved from http://www.usnews.com/usnews/culture/articles/990809/archive_001644.htm on January 30, 2013.

Buss, A. H., & Plomin, R. (1984). *Temperament. Early developing personality traits.* Hillsdale, NJ. Lawrence Erlbaum Associates.

Buss, D. M. (Ed.) (2005). *The handbook of evolutionary psychology.* Hoboken, NJ. John Wiley.

Cacabelos, R., Fernandez-Novoa, L., Lombardi, V., Kubota, Y., & Takeda, M. (2005). Molecular genetics of Alzheimer's disease and aging. *Methods and Findings of Experimental Clinical Pharmacology, 27(Suppl. A),* 1–573.

Callaghan, T., Rochat, P., Lillard, A., Claux, M. L., Odden, H., et al. (2005). Synchrony in the onset of mental-state reasoning. Evidence from five cultures. *Psychological Science, 16,* 378–384.

Caspi, A. (2000). The child is father of the man. Personality continuities from childhood to adulthood. *Journal of Personality and Social Psychology, 78,* 158–172.

CBS News. (February 11, 2009). Whiz kid, 13, to graduate college. Retrieved from http://www.cbsnews.com/stories/2003/04/21/tech/main550399.shtml on September 2, 2011.

Chassin, L., Hussong, A., Barrera, M., Jr., Molina, B., Trim, R., et al. (2004). Adolescent substance use. In R. Lerner & L. Steinberg (Eds.), *Handbook of adolescent psychology* (2nd ed., pp. 665–696). New York. John Wiley.

Christiansen, S. L., & Palkovitz, R. (1998). Exploring Erikson's psychosocial theory of development. Generativity and its relationship to parental identity, intimacy, and involvement with others. *Journal of Men's Studies, 7,* 133–156.

Cohen, L. B., & Marks, K. S. (2002). How infants process addition and subtraction events. *Developmental Science. 5,* 186–201.

Coles, C. D. (1993). Saying "goodbye" to the "crack baby." *Neurotoxicology and Teratology, 15,* 290–292.

Collins, W. A., & Laursen, B. (2004). Parent-adolescent relationships and influences. In R. M. Lerner & L. Sternberg (Eds.), *Handbook of adolescent psychology* (2nd ed., pp. 331–361). Hoboken, NJ. John Wiley & Sons.

Collins, W. A., Maccoby, E. E., Steinberg, L., Hetherington, M. E., & Bornstein, M. H. (2000). The case for nature and nurture. *American Psychologist, 55,* 218–232.

Collins, W. A., Welsh, D. P., & Furman, W. (2009). Adolescent romantic relationships. *Annual Review of Psychology, 60,* 631–652.

Cray, L., Woods, N. F., & Mitchell, E. S. (2010). *Menopause. The Journal of The North American Menopause Society, 17,* 972–977.

Cregger, M. E., & Rogers, W. A. (1998). Memory for activities for young,

young-old, and old adults. *Experimental Aging Research, 24,* 195–201.

Crouter, A. C., & Booth, A. (Eds.) (2006). *Romance and sex in adolescence and emerging adulthood. Risks and opportunities.* Mahwah, NJ. Lawrence Erlbaum Associates.

Cubed, M. (2002). *The national economic impacts of the child care sector.* National Child Care Association. Retrieved from www.nccanet.org on April 3, 2006.

Dahl, R. E., & Spear, L. P. (Eds.). (2004). *Adolescent brain development. Vulnerabilities and opportunities.* New York. New York Academy of Sciences.

Dawson, T. L. (2002). New tools, new insights. Kohlberg's moral judgment stages revisited. *International Journal of Behavioral Development, 26,* 154–166.

Day, N. L., & Richardson, G. A. (1993). Cocaine use and crack babies. Science, the media, and miscommunication. *Neurotoxicology and Teratology, 15,* 293–294.

DeCasper, A. J., & Spence, M. J. (1986). Prenatal maternal speech influences newborns' perception of speech sounds. *Infant Behavior and Development, 9,* 133–150.

Decety, J., Michalska, K., & Akitsuki, Y. (2008). Who caused the pain? An fMRI investigation of empathy and intentionality in children. *Neuropsychologia, 46,* 2607–2614.

DiFranza, J. R., Aligne, C. A., & Weitzman, M. (2004). Prenatal and postnatal environmental tobacco smoke exposure and children's health. *Pediatrics, 113 (4, Suppl.),* 1007–1015.

Doss, B. D., Rhoades, G. K., Stanley, S. M., & Markman, H. M. (2009). The effect of the transition to parenthood on relationship quality. An 8-year prospective study. *Journal of Personality and Social Psychology, 96,* 601–619.

Duffy, R. D., & Sedlacek, W. E. (2007). The work values of first year college students. Exploring group differences. *The Career Development Quarterly, 55,* 359–364.

Dunn, J., & Plomin, R. (1990). *Separate lives. Why siblings are so different.* New York. Basic Books.

Dye, J. L. (2008). *Fertility of American Women. 2006.* Washington, DC. U. S. Census Bureau. Retrieved from www.census.gov on November 22, 2008.

Dykas, M. J., & Cassidy, J. (2011). Attachment and the processing of social information across the life span. Theory and evidence. *Psychological Bulletin, 137,* 19–46.

Else-Quest, N., Hyde, J., Goldsmith, H., & Van Hulle, C. (2006). Gender differences in temperament. A meta-analysis. *Psychological Bulletin, 132,* 33–72.

Ennis, R. H. (1975). Children's ability to handle Piaget's propositional logic. A conceptual critique. *Review of Educational Research, 45,* 1–41.

Erikson, E. H. (1963). *Childhood and society* (2nd ed.). New York Norton.

Erikson, E. H. (1968). *Identity. Youth and crisis.* New York. Norton.

Erikson, E. H. (1982). *The life cycle completed. A review.* New York. Norton.

Espy, A., Fang, H., Johnson, C., Wiebe, S. A., Stopp, C., et al. (2011). Prenatal tobacco exposure. Developmental outcomes in the neonatal period. *Developmental Psychology, 47,* 153–169.

Evenson, R. J., & Simon, R. W. (2005). Clarifying the relationship between parenthood and depression. *Journal of Health and Social Behavior, 46,* 341–358.

Eyler, F. D., Behnke, M., Garvan, C. W., Woods, N. S., Wobie, K., et al. (2001). Newborn evaluations of toxicity and withdrawal related to prenatal cocaine exposure. *Neurotoxicology and Teratology, 23,* 399–411.

Fernald, A. (2004). Auditory development in infancy. In G. Beemner & A. Fogel (Eds.), *Blackwell handbook of infant development* (pp. 35–70). Malden, MA. Blackwell Publishing.

Ferri, C. P., Prince, M., Brayne, C., Brodaty, H., Fratiglioni, L., et al. (2005). Global prevalence of dementia. A Delphi consensus study. *Lancet, 366,* 2112–2117.

Finke, J. (2003). The traditional music and cultures of Kenya. Retrieved from http://www.bluegecko.org/kenya/ on June 2, 2007.

Fischer, K. W., & Bidell, T. R. (1998). Dynamic development of psychological structures in action and thought. In R. M. Lemer (Ed.), *Handbook of child psychology. Vol 1. Theoretical models of human development* (5th ed., pp. 467–561). Hoboken, NJ. John Wiley & Sons.

Fisher, L., Ames, E. W., Chisholm, K., & Savoie, L. (1997). Problems reported by parents of Romanian orphans adopted to British Columbia. *International Journal of Behavioral Development, 20(1),* 67–82.

Flavell, J. H. (1996). Piaget's legacy. *Psychological Science, 7,* 200–203.

Flavell, J. H., Miller, P. H., & Miller, S. A. (1993). *Cognitive development.* Englewood Cliffs, NJ. Prentice-Hall.

Flieller, A. (1999). Comparison of the development of formal thought in adolescent cohorts aged 10 to 15 years (1967–1996 and 1972–1993). *Developmental Psychology, 35,* 1048–1058.

Floyd, R. L., O'Connor, M. J., Sokol, R. J., Bertrand, J., & Cordero, J. F. (2005). Recognition and prevention of fetal alcohol syndrome. *Obstetrics and Gynecology, 106,* 1059–1064.

Frank, D. A., Augustyn, M., Knight, W., Pell, T., & Zuckerman, B. (2001). Growth, development, and behavior in early childhood following prenatal cocaine exposure. A systematic review. *JAMA, 285,* 1613–1625.

Frank, D. A., Rose-Jacobs, R., Beeghly, M., Wilbur, M., Bellinger, D., et al. (2005). Level of prenatal cocaine exposure and 48-month IQ. Importance of preschool enrichment. *Neurotoxicology and Teratology, 27(1),* 15–28.

Frayser, S. (1985). *Varieties of sexual experience.* New Haven, CT. HRAF.

Furman, W., & Buhrmester, D. (1992). Age and sex in perceptions of networks of personal relationships. *Child Development, 63,* 103–115.

Furstenberg, F. F., Jr., Kennedy, S., McLoyd, V. C., Rumbaut, R. G., & Settersten, R. A., Jr. (2004). Growing up is harder to do. *Contexts, 3,* 33–41.

Gardner, M., & Steinberg, L. (2005). Peer influence on risk taking, risk preference, and risky decision making in adolescence and adulthood. An experimental study. *Developmental Psychology, 41,* 625–635.

Gelman, R. (1972). The nature and development of early number concepts. In H. W. Reese (Ed.), *Advances in child development and behavior* (pp. 115–167). New York. Academic Press.

Giedd, J. N. (2004). Structural magnetic resonance imaging of the adolescent brain. *Annals of the New York Academy of Sciences, 1021,* 77–85.

Giedd, J. N. (2008). The teen brain. Insights from neuroimaging. *Journal of Adolescent Health, 42,* 335–343.

Gilovich, T., Griffin, D., & Kahneman, D. (2002). *Heuristics and biases. The psychology of intuitive judgment.* New York. Cambridge University Press.

Gogtay, N., Giedd, J. N., Lusk, L., Hayashi, K. M., Greenstein, D., et al. (2004). Dynamic mapping of human cortical development during childhood through early adulthood. *Proceedings of the National Academy of Sciences, USA, 101,* 8174–8179.

Graham, J. E., Christian, L. M., & Kiecolt-Glaser, J. K. (2006). Marriage, health, and immune function. In S. R. Beach, M. Z. Wamboldt, N. J. Kaslow, R. E. Heyman, et al. (Eds.), *Relational processes and DSM-V. Neuroscience, assessment, prevention, and treatment* (pp. 61–76). Washington, DC. American Psychiatric Association.

Graham, J., Nosek, B. A., Haidt, J., Iyer, R., Koleva, S., et al. (2011). Mapping the moral domain. *Journal of Personality and Social Psychology, 101,* 366–385.

Greider, K. (1995, July/August). Crackpot ideas. *Mother Jones.* Retrieved from http://www.come-over.to/FAS/crackbaby.htm on January 28, 2006.

Habek, D., Habek, J. C., Ivanisevic, M., & Djelmis, J. (2002). Fetal tobacco syndrome and perinatal outcome. *Fetal Diagnosis and Therapy, 17,* 367–371.

Haidt, J. (2001). The emotional dog and its rational tail. A social intuitionist approach to moral judgment. *Psychological Review, 108,* 814–834.

Haidt, J. (2007). The new synthesis in moral psychology. *Science, 316,* 998–1002.

Haidt, J. (2008). Morality. *Perspectives in Psychological Science, 3,* 65–72.

Haidt, J., & Bjorklund, F. (2008). Social intuitionists answer six questions about morality. In W. Sinnott-Armstrong (Ed.), *Moral psychology. Vol. 2. The cognitive science of morality* (pp. 181–217). Cambridge, MA. MIT Press.

Haidt, J., & Graham, J. (2007). When morality opposes justice. Conservatives have moral intuitions that liberals may not recognize. *Social Justice Research, 20*. Retrieved from http://faculty.virginia.edu/haidtlab/articles/ on November 21, 2008.

Haidt, J., & Kesebir, S. (2010). Morality. In S. T. Fiske, D. T. Gilbert, & G. Lindzey (Eds.), *The handbook of social psychology* (5th ed., pp. 797–832). Hoboken, NJ. John Wiley & Sons.

Hanington, L., Ramchandani, P., & Stein, A. (2010). Parental depression and child temperament. Assessing child to parent effects in a longitudinal population study. *Infant Behavior and Development, 33,* 88–95.

Harris, J. R. (1995). Where is the children's environment? A group socialization theory of development. *Psychological Review, 102,* 458–489.

Harris, J. R. (1998). *The nurture assumption.* New York. The Free Press.

Harris, J. R. (2006). *No two alike. Human nature and human individuality.* New York. Norton.

Harris, J. R. (2009). Attachment theory underestimates the child. *Behavioral and Brain Sciences, 32,* 30.

Harris Poll. (2008). *Widely held attitudes to different generations.* Retrieved on May 15, 2010 from http://www.harrisinteractive.com/NEWS/allnewsbydate.asp?NewsID=1328.

Hauser, M., Cushman, F., Young, L., Jin, K-X., & Mikhail J. (2007). A dissociation between moral judgments and justifications. *Mind and Language, 22,* 1–21.

Hawkins, D. N., & Booth, A. (2005). Unhappily ever after. Effects of long-term, low-quality marriages on well-being. *Social Forces, 84(1),* 452–471.

Henry, D. B., Schoeny, M. E., Deptula, D. P., & Slavick, J. T. (2007). Peer selection and socialization effects on adolescent intercourse without a condom and attitudes about the costs of sex. *Child Development, 78,* 825–838.

Herdt, G., & McClintock, M. K. (2000). The magical age of 10. *Archives of Sexual Behavior, 29,* 587–606.

Hertzog, C., Kramer, A. F., Wilson, R. S., & Lindenberger, U. (2009). Enrichment effects on adult cognitive development. *Psychological Sciences in the Public Interest, 9,* 1–65.

Hespos, S., Ferry, A. L., & Rips, L. J. (2009). Five-month-old infants have different expectations for solids and liquids. *Psychological Science, 20,* 603–611.

Holt-Lunstad, J., Birmingham, W., & Jones, B. Q. (2008). Is there something unique about marriage? The relative impact of marital status, relationship quality, and network social support on ambulatory blood pressure and mental health. *Annals of Behavioral Medicine, 35,* 239–244.

Hubel D. H., & Wiesel, T. N. (1970). The period of susceptibility to the physiological effects of unilateral eye closure in kittens. *Journal of Physiology, 206,* 419–436.

Ikonomidou, C., Bittigau, P., Ishimaru, M. J., Wozniak, D. F., Koch, C., et al.. (2000). Ethanol-induced apoptotic neurodegeneration and fetal alcohol syndrome. *Science, 287,* 1056–1060.

Jackson, P. L., Rainville, P., & Decety, J. (2006). Empathy examined through the neural mechanisms involved in imagining how I feel versus how you feel pain. An event-related fMRI study. *Neuropsychologia, 44,* 752–761.

Johnson, S. C., Dweck, C. S., & Chen, F. S. (2007). Evidence for infants' internal working models of attachment. *Psychological Science, 18,* 501–502.

Jones, T. (2002, January 13). Bringing up genius. *The Washington Post,* W7.

Kagan, J. (1994). *Galen's prophecy. Temperament in human nature.* New York. Basic Books.

Kagan, J. (2003). Biology, context and developmental inquiry. *Annual Review of Psychology, 54,* 1–23.

Kaplan, R. M., & Kronick, R. G. (2006). Marital status and longevity in the United States population. *Journal of Epidemiology and Community Health, 60,* 760–765.

Kastenbaum, R. (2000). *The psychology of death* (3rd ed.). New York. Springer.

Kendler, K. S. (1996). Parenting. A genetic-epidemiologic perspective. *American Journal of Psychiatry, 153,* 11–20.

Kerr, M., & Stattin, H. (2003). Parenting adolescents. Action orreaction? In A. C. Crouter & A. Booth (Eds.), *Children's influence on family dynamics* (pp. 121–151). Mahwah, NJ. Erlbaum.

Kiecolt-Glaser JK, Newton TL (2001). Marriage and health. His and hers. *Psychological Bulletin* 127:472–503.

Kisilevsky, B. S., Hains, S. M., Lee, K., Xie, X., Huang, H., et al. (2003). Effects of experience on fetal voice recognition. *Psychological Science, 14,* 220–224.

Kisilevsky, B. S., Hains, S. M., Brown, C. A., Lee, C. T., Cowperthwaite, B., et al. (2009). Fetal sensitivity to properties of maternal speech and language. *Infant Behavior & Development, 32,* 59–71.

Klaczynski, P. A. (2001). Analytic and heuristic processing influences on adolescent reasoning and decision making. *Child Development, 72,* 844–861.

Klaczynski, P. A., & Narasimham, G. (1998). Development of scientific reasoning biases. Cognitive versus egoprotective explanations. *Developmental Psychology, 34,* 175–187.

Klimstra, T. A., Hale, W. W., III, Raaijmakers, Q. A. W., Branje, S. J. T., & Meeus, W. H. J. (2009). Maturation of personality in adolescence. *Journal of Personality and Social Psychology, 96,* 679–689.

Koball, H. L., Moiduddin, E., Henderson, J., Goesling, B., & Besculides, M. (2010). What do we know about the link between marriage and health? *Journal of Family Issues, 31,* 1019–1040.

Kohlberg, L. (1963). The development of children's orientations toward a moral

order. Sequence in the development of moral thought. *Vita Humana, 6,* 11–33.

Krebs, D. (2005). The evolution of morality. In D. M. Buss (Ed.), *The handbook of evolutionary psychology* (pp. 747–771). Hoboken, NJ. John Wiley & Sons.

Krebs, D. L., & Denton, K. (2005). Toward a more pragmatic approach to morality. A critical evaluation of Kohlberg's model. *Psychological Review, 112,* 629–649.

Kreppner, J. M., Rutter, M., Beckett, C., Castle, J., Colvert, E., et al. (2007). Normality and impairment following profound early institutional deprivation. A longitudinal follow-up into early adolescence. *Developmental Psychology, 43,* 931–946.

Kübler-Ross, E. (1969). *On death and dying.* New York. Macmillan.

Kuhn, D. (2006). Do cognitive changes accompany developments in the adolescent brain? *Perspectives in Psychological Science, 1(1),* 59–67.

Lachman, M. E. (Ed.). (2001). *Handbook of midlife development.* New York. Wiley.

Lachman, M. E. (2004). Development in midlife. *Annual Review of Psychology, 55,* 305–331.

Larson, R., & Verma, S. (1999). How children and adolescents spend time across cultural settings of the world. Work, play and developmental opportunities. *Psychological Bulletin, 125,* 701–736.

Larson, R. W., Moneta, G., Richards, M. H., & Wilson, S. (2002). Continuity, stability, and change in daily emotional experience across adolescence. *Child Development, 73,* 1151–1165.

Law, K. L., Stroud, L. R., LaGasse, L. L., Niarura, R., Liu, J., et al. (2003). Smoking during pregnancy and newborn neurobehavior. *Pediatrics, 111,* 1318–1323.

Lawford, H., Pratt, M. W., Hunsberger, B., & Pancer, M. S. (2005). Adolescent generativity. A longitudinal study of two possible contexts for learning concern for future generations. *Journal of Research on Adolescence, 15,* 261–273.

Lemery, K. S., Goldsmith, H. H., Klinnert, M. D., & Mrazek, D. A. (1999). Developmental models of infant and childhood temperament. *Developmental Psychology, 35,* 189–204.

Leslie, A. M. (2000). "Theory of mind" as a mechanism of selective attention. In M. Gazzaniga (Ed.), *The new cognitive neurosciences* (2nd ed., pp. 135–1248). Cambridge, MA. MIT Press.

Levinson, D. J. (1986). A conception of adult development. *American Psychologist, 41(1),* 3–13.

Levy, B. (2009). Stereotype embodiment. A psychosocial approach to aging. *Current Directions in Psychological Science, 18,* 332–336.

Lorenz, K. (1937). The companion in the bird's world. *Auk, 54,* 245–273.

Lourenço, O., & Machado, A. (1996). In defense of Piaget's theory. A reply to 10 common criticisms. *Psychological Review, 103(1),* 143–164.

Low, G., & Molzahn, A. E. (2007). Predictors of quality of life in old age.

A cross-validation study. *Research in Nursing & Health, 30,* 14–150.

Lumeng, J. C., Cabral, H. J., Gannon, K., Heeren, T., & Frank, D. A. (2007). Pre-natal exposures to cocaine and alcohol and physical growth patterns to age 8 years. *Neurotoxicology & Teratology, 29,* 446–457.

Luna, B., Garver, K., Urban, T., Lazar, N., & Sweeney, J. (2004). Maturation of cognitive processes from late childhood to adulthood. *Child Development, 75,* 1357–1372.

Lyubomirsky, S., & Boehm, J. K. (2010). Human motives, happiness, and the puzzle of parenthood. Commentary on Kenrick et al. (2010). *Perspectives on Psychological Science, 5,* 327–334.

Maccari, S., Piazza, P. V., Kabbaj, M., Barbazanges, A., Simon, H., et al. (1995). Adoption reverses the long-term impairment in glucocorticoid feedback induced by prenatal stress. *Journal of Neuroscience, 15,* 110–116.

Maccoby, E. E. (2002). Parenting effects. Issues and controversies. In J. G. Borkowski, S. L. Ramey, & M. Bristol-Power (Eds.), *Parenting and the child's world. Influences on academic, intellectual, and social-emotional development* (pp. 35–46). Mahwah, NJ. Lawrence Erlbaum Associates.

Maccoby, E. E., & Martin, J. A. (1983). Socialization in the context of the family. Parent-child interaction. In E. M. Hetherington (Vol. Ed.) & P. H. Mussen (Editor-in-Chief), *Handbook of child psychology. Vol. 4. Socialization, personality and social development* (4th ed., pp. 1–101). New York. Wiley.

Maciejewski, P. K., Zhang, B., Block, S. D., & Prigerson, H. G. (2007). An empirical examination of the stage theory of grief. *Journal of the American Medical Association, 297,* 716–723.

Mahoney, J. L., Stattin, H., & Lord, H. (2004). Unstructured youth recreation centre participation and antisocial behaviour development. Selection influences and the moderating role of antisocial peers. *International Journal of Behavioural Development, 28,* 553–560.

Mallozzi, V. M. (2005, April 14). One millionaire's strange cry. Tickets, Please! *New York Times.* Retrieved from www.nytimes.com on April 25, 2006.

Markham, J. A., Morris, J. R., & Juraska, J. M. (2007). Neuron number decreases in the rat ventral, but not dorsal, medial prefrontal cortex between adolescence and adulthood. *Neuroscience, 144,* 961–968.

Mastroeni, D., Grover, A., Delvaux, E., Whiteside, C., Coleman, P. D., et al. (2011). Epigenetic mechanisms in Alzheimer's disease. *Neurobiology of Aging, 32,* 1161–1180.

Matusov, E., & Hayes, R. (2000). Sociocultural critique of Piaget and Vygotsky. *New Ideas in Psychology, 18,* 215–239.

Maurer, D., Mondloch, C. J., & Lewis, T. L. (2007). Sleeper effects. *Developmental Science, 10(1),* 40–47.

Maxwell, K. A. (2002). Friends. The role of peer influence across adolescent risk behaviors. *Journal of Youth and Adolescence, 31,* 267–277.

Mayes, L. C., Granger, R. H., Bornstein, M. H., & Zuckerman, B. (1992). The problem of prenatal cocaine exposure. A rush to judgment. *JAMA, 267,* 406–408.

McAdams, D. P. (2001). Generativity in midlife. In M. E. Lachman (Ed.), *Handbook of midlife development* (pp. 395–443). New York. Wiley.

McAdams, D. P., & Logan, R. L. (2004). What is *generativity*? In E. de St. Aubin, D. P. McAdams, & T. Kim (Eds.), *The generative society. Caring for future generations* (pp. 15–31). Washington, DC. American Psychological Society.

McClintock, M. K., & Herdt, G. (1996). Rethinking puberty. The development of sexual attraction. *Current Directions in Psychological Science, 5,* 178–182.

McCrae, R. R., Costa, P. T., Jr., Ostendorf, F., Angleitner, A., Hrebickova, M., & Avia, M. D., et al. (2000). Nature over nurture. Temperament, personality, and life span development. *Journal of Personality and Social Psychology, 78,* 173–186.

McGeown, K. (2005). Life in Ceausescu's Institutions. *BBC News.* Retrieved from http://news.bbc.co.uk on September 8, 2006.

Meredith, P., & Noller, P. (2003). Attachment and infant difficultness in postnatal depression. *Journal of Family Issues, 24,* 668–686.

Messinger, D. S., Bauer, C. R., Das, A., Seifer, R., Lester, B. M., et al. (2004). The maternal lifestyle study. Cognitive motor, and behavioral outcomes of cocaine-exposed and opiate-exposed infants through three years of age. *Journal of Pediatrics, 113,* 1677–1685.

Mikhail, J. (2007). Universal moral grammar. Theory, evidence, and the future. *Trends in Cognitive Sciences, 11,* 143–152.

Mizuno, K., Mizuno, N., Shinohara, T., & Noda, M. (2004). Mother-infant skin-to-skin contact after delivery results in early recognition of own mother's milk odour. *Acta Paediatrica, 93,* 1640–1645.

Moffitt, T. (1993). Adolescence-limited and life-course-persistent antisocial behavior. A developmental taxonomy. *Psychological Review, 100,* 674–701.

Monahan, K. C., Steinberg, L., & Cauffman, E. (2009). Affiliation with antisocial peers, susceptibility to peer influence and antisocial behavior during the transition to adulthood. *Developmental Psychology, 45,* 1520–1530.

Moon, C., Lagercrantz, H., & Kuhl, P. (2013). Language experienced *in utero* affects vowel perception after birth. a two-country study. *Acta Paediatrica, 102,* 156–160.

Morra, S., Gobbo, C., Marini, Z., & Sheese, R. (Eds.). (2008). *Cognitive development.*

Neo-Piagetian perspectives. New York. Taylor & Francis/Lawrence Earlbaum Associates.

Mortimer, J. T. (2003). *Working and growing up.* Cambridge, MA. Harvard University Press.

Murray, S. A., Grant, E., Grant., A., & Kendall, M. (2003). Dying from cancer in developed and developing countries. Lessons from two qualitative interview studies of patients and their careers. *British Medical Journal, 326,* 368–372.

National Institute on Aging. (2006). Alzheimer's disease fact sheet. Retrieved from http://www.nia.nih.gov/Alzheimers/Publications/adfact.htm on May 3, 2006.

Neimark, E. D. (1975). Longitudinal development of formal operations thought. *Genetic Psychology Monographs, 91,* 171–225.

Nelson, C. A. (1999). Neural plasticity and human development. *Current Directions in Psychological Science, 8,* 42–45.

Nelson, K. S., Kushlev, K., English, T., Dunn, E. W., & Lyubomirsky, S. (2013). In defense of parenthood. Children are associated with more joy than misery. *Psychological Science, 24,* 3–10.

Neuspiel, D. R. (1993). Cocaine and the fetus. Mythology of severe risk. *Neurotoxicology and Teratology, 15,* 305–306.

New York Times. (2009, May 17). A new trend in motherhood. Retrieved from www.nytimes.com on June 13, 2009.

Newcombe, N. S. (2002). The nativist-empiricist controversy in the context of recent research on spatial and quantitative development. *Psychological Science, 13,* 395–401.

NICHD Early Child Care Research Network. (2001). Child-care and family predictors of preschool attachment and stability from infancy. *Developmental Psychology, 37,* 847–862.

NICHD Early Child Care Research Network. (2003). Does amount of time spent in child care predict socioemotional adjustment during the transition to kindergarten? *Child Development, 74,* 976–1005.

NICHD Early Child Care Research Network. (2006). Child-care effect sizes for the NICHD study of early child care and youth development. *American Psychologist, 61,* 99–116.

NICHD Early Child Care Research Network. (2010). Testing a series of causal propositions relating time in child care to children's externalizing behavior. *Developmental Psychology, 46,* 1–17.

Nilsson, L. (1993). *A child is born.* New York. DTP/Seymour Lawrence.

Nishitani, S., Miyamura, T., Tagawa, M., Sumi, M., Takase, R., et al. (2009). The calming effect of a maternal breast milk odor on the human newborn infant. *Neuroscience Research, 63,* 66–71.

Nomaguchi, K. M., & Milkie, M. A. (2003). Costs and rewards of children. The effects of becoming a parent on adults' lives. *Journal of Marriage and Family, 65*, 356–374.

O'Connor, T. G., Deater-Deckard, K., Fulker, D. W., Rutter, M., & Plomin, R. (1998). Genotype-environment correlations in late childhood and early adolescence. Antisocial behavioral problems and coercive parenting. *Developmental Psychology, 34*, 970–981.

O'Connor, T. G., Hawkins, N., Dunn, J., Thorpe K., Golding, J., et al. (1998). Family type and depression in pregnancy. Factors mediating risk in a community sample. *Journal of Marriage and the Family, 60*, 757–770.

Okie, S. (2009, January 26). The epidemic that wasn't. *New York Times*. Retrieved from www.nytimes.com on January 26, 2009.

Padilla-Walker, L. M., & Bean, R. A. (2009). Negative and positive peer influence. Relations to positive and negative behaviors for African American, European American, and Hispanic adolescents. *Journal of Adolescence, 32*, 323–337.

Palmert, M. R., Hayden, D. L., Mansfield, M. J., Crigler, J. F., Jr., Crowley, W. F., Jr., et al.(2001). The longitudinal study of adrenal maturation during gonadal suppression. Evidence that adrenarche is a gradual process. *Journal of Clinical Endocrinology and Metabology, 86*, 4536–4542.

Pascalis, O., & Kelly, D. J. (2009). The origins of face processing in humans. Phylogeny and ontogeny. *Perspectives on Psychological Science, 4*, 200–209.

Pascalis, O., de Schonen, S., Morton, J., Duruelle, C., & Grenet, F. (1995). Mother's face recognition in neonates. A replication and an extension. *Infant Behavior and Development, 18*, 79–85.

Piaget, J. (1952). *The origins of intelligence in children*. New York. International Universities.

Piaget, J. (1954). *The construction of reality in the child*. New York. Basic Books.

Pinker, S. (2008, January 13). The moral instinct. New York Times. Retrieved from http://www.nytimes.com/2008/01/13/magazine/13Psychology-t.html?pagewanted=all&_r=0 on Janurary 17, 2008.

Plassman, B. L., Langa, K. M., Fisher, G. G., Heeringa, S. G., Weir, D. R, et al. (2007). Prevalence of dementia in the United States. The aging, demographics, and memory study. *Neuroepidemiology, 29*, 125–132.

Plomin, R., DeFries, J. C., Craig, I. W., & McGuffin, P. (Eds.) (2003). *Behavioral genetics in the postgenomic era*. Washington, DC. American Psychological Association.

Pokoradi, A., Iversen, L., & Hannaford, P. C. (2011). Factors associated with age of onset and type of menopause in a cohort of UK women. *American Journal of Obstetrics & Gynecology, 205*, e1-13. Retrieved from www.AJOG.org on September 5.

Posner, M. I., Rothbart, M. K., & Sheese, B. E. (2007). Attention genes. *Developmental Science, 10(1)*, 24–29.

Premack, D., & Woodruff, G. (1978). Does the chimpanzee have a theory of mind? *Behavioral and Brain Sciences, 1*, 512–526.

Public Agenda. (2000). Child care. Red flags. Retrieved from www.publicagenda.com on April 4, 2006.

Reebye, P. N., Ross, S. E., & Jamieson, K. (1999). A literature review of child-parent/caregiver attachment theory and cross-cultural practices influencing attachment. Retrieved from www.attachmentacrosscultures.org on April 10, 2006.

Remer, T., Boye, K. R., Hartmann, M. F., & Wudy, S. A. (2005). Urinary markers of adrenarche. Reference values in healthy subjects, aged 3–18 years. *Journal of Clinical Endocrinology and Metabolism. Clinical and Experimental, 90*, 2015–2021.

Roberts, S. (2006, October 15). To be married is to be outnumbered. *New York Times*. Retrieved from www.nytimes.com on May 30, 2007.

Rose, J. S., Chassin, L., Presson, C. C., & Sherman, S. J. (1999). Peer influences on adolescent cigarette smoking. A prospective sibling analysis. *Merrill-Palmer Quarterly, 45(1)*, 62–84.

Rose, S. A., & Feldman, J. F. (1995). Prediction of IQ and specific cognitive abilities at 11 years from infancy measures. *Developmental Psychology, 31*, 685–696.

Rose-Jacobs, R., Cabral, H., Posner, M. A., Epstein, J., & Frank, D. A. (2002). Do "we just know"? Masked assessors' ability to accurately identify children with prenatal cocaine exposure. *Developmental and Behavioral Pediatrics, 23*, 340–346.

Rose, T. L., & Fischer, K. W. (2009). Dynamic development. A neo-Piagetian approach. In U. Müller, J. I. Carpendale, & L. Smith (Eds.), *The Cambridge companion to Piaget* (pp. 400–421). New York. Cambridge University Press.

Ross, C. E., & Mirowsky, J. (2008). Age and the balance of emotions. *Social Science & Medicine*, 2391–2400.

Rothbart, M. K. (2007). Temperament, development, and personality. *Current Directions in Psychological Science, 16*, 207–212.

Rothbart, M. K., Sheese, B. E., & Conradt, E. D. (2009). Childhood temperament. In P. J. Corr & G. Matthews (Eds.), *The Cambridge handbook of personality psychology* (pp. 177–190). New York. Cambridge University Press.

Rothbart, M. K., & Bates, J. E. (2006). Temperament. In W. Damon, R. Lerner, & N. Eisenberg (Eds.), *Handbook of child psychology. Vol 3. Social, emotional, and personality development* (6th ed., pp. 99–166). New York. Wiley.

Rothbart, M. K., Ahadi, S. A., Hershey, K. L., & Fisher, P. (2001). *Child Development, 72*, 1394–1408.

Ruthsatz, J., & Detterman, D. K. (2003). An extraordinary memory. The case study of a musical prodigy. *Intelligence, 31*, 509–518.

Rutter, M., O'Connor, T. G., and the English and Romanian Adoptees (ERA) Study Team. (2004). Are there biological programming effects for psychological development? Findings from a study of Romanian adoptees. *Developmental Psychology, 40(1)*, 81–94.

Sadler, T. W. (2004). *Langman's medical embryology* (9th ed.). Philadelphia. Lippincott, Williams, & Wilkins.

Sai, F. Z. (2005). The role of the mother's voice in developing mother's face preference. Evidence for intermodal perception at birth. *Infant and Child Development, 14(1)*, 29–50.

Salmon, D. P., & Bondi, M. W. (2009). Neuropsychological assessment of dementia. *Annual Review of Psychology, 60*, 257–282.

Salthouse, T. A., (2004). Localizing age-related individual differences in a hierarchical structure. *Intelligence, 32*, 541–561.

Salthouse, T. A. (2006). Mental exercise and mental aging. Evaluating the validity of the "use it or lose it" hypothesis. *Perspectives on Psychological Science*, 68–87.

Salthouse, T.A. (2011). Effects of age on time-dependent cognitive change. *Psychological Science, 22*, 682–688.

Saudino, K. J. (2005). Behavioral genetics and child temperament. *Journal of Developmental & Behavioral Pediatrics, 26*, 214–223.

Sbarra, D. A., & Nietert, P. J. (2009). Divorce and death. Forty years of the Charleston Heart Study. *Psychological Science, 20*, 107–113.

Schlegel, A., & Barry, H. (1991). *Adolescence. An anthropological inquiry*. New York. Free Press.

Schweinart, L. J., Motie, J., Xiang, Z., Barnett, W. S., Belfield, C. R., et al. (2004). *Lifetime effects. The High/Scope Perry preschool study through age 40*. Monographs of the High/Scope Educational Research Foundation, 14. Ypsilanti, MI. High/Scope Press.

Shurkin, J. N. (2009, November/December). Decoding dementia. *Scientific American Mind*, 56–63.

Shuwairi, S. M., Albert, M. K., & Johnson, S. P. (2007). Discrimination of possible and impossible objects in infancy. *Psychological Science, 18*, 303–307.

Shweder, R. A., Mahapatra, M., & Miller, J. G. (1990). Culture and moral development. In J. W. Stigler, R. A. Sweder, & G. Herdt (Eds.), *Cultural psychology. Essays on comparative human development* (pp. 130–204). Cambridge, MA. Cambridge University Press.

Shweder, R. A., Much, N. C., Mahapatra, M., & Park, L. (1997). The "big three" of morality (autonomy, community, divinity) and the "big three" explanations of suffering. In A. Brandt & P. Rozin (Eds.),

Morality and health (pp. 119–169). New York. Routledge.

Siegler, R. S., & Ellis, S. (1996). Piaget on childhood. *Psychological Science, 7,* 211–215.

Sigelman, C. K., & Rider, E. A. (2006). *Life-span human development.* Belmont, CA. Thomson/Wadsworth.

Silverman, D. K., (2011). A clinical case of an avoidant attachment. *Psychoanalytic Psychology, 28,* 293–310.

Simpson, J. A. (1987). The dissolution of romantic relationships. Factors involved in relationship stability and emotional distress. *Journal of Personality and Social Psychology, 53,* 683–692.

Simpson, J. A. Collins, W. A., Tran, S., & Haydon, K. C. (2007). Attachment and the experience and expression of emotions in romantic relationships. A developmental perspective. *Journal of Personality and Social Psychology, 92,* 355–367.

Simpson, J. A., Rholes, W. S., & Winterheld, H. A. (2010). Attachment working models twist memories of relationship events. *Psychological Science, 21,* 252–259.

Slutske, W. S., Moffitt, T. E., Poulton, R., & Caspi, A. (2012). Undercontrolled temperament at age 3 predicts disordered gambling at age 32. A longitudinal study of a complete birth cohort. *Psychological Science, 23,* 510–516.

Smeeding, T., & Phillips, K. R. (2002). Cross-national differences in employment and economic sufficiency. *Annals of the American Academy of Political and Social Science, 580,* 103–133.

Smetana, J. G., Campione-Barr, N., & Metzger, A. (2006). Adolescent development in interpersonal and societal contexts. *Annual Review of Psychology, 57,* 255–284.

Smetana, J. G., Schlagman, N., & Adams, P. W. (1993). Preschool children's judgments about hypothetical and actual transgressions. *Child Development, 64,* 202–214.

Snarey, J. R. (1985). Cross-cultural universality of social-moral development. A critical review of Kohlbergian research. *Psychological Bulletin, 97,* 202–232.

Spear, L. P. (2000a). The adolescent brain and age-related behavioral manifestations. *Neuroscience and Biobehavioral Reviews, 24,* 417–463.

Spear, L.P. (2000b). Neurobehavioral changes in adolescence. *Current Directions in Psychological Science, 8,* 168–172.

Spelke, E. S. (1998). Nativism, empiricism, and the origins of knowledge. *Infant Behavior & Development, 21,* 181–200.

Spelke, E. S., Phillips, A., & Woodward, A. L. (1995). Infants' knowledge of object motion and human action. In D. Sperber, D. Premack, & A. J. Premack (Eds.), *Causal cognition. A multidisciplinary debate* (pp. 44–78). New York. Clarendon Press/Oxford University Press.

Staff, J., & Mortimer, J. T. (2007). Educational and work strategies from adolescence to early adulthood.

Consequences for educational attainment. *Social Forces, 85,* 1169–1194.

Steinberg, L. (2007). Risk taking in adolescence. New perspectives from brain and behavioral science. *Current Directions in Psychological Science, 16,* 55–59.

Steinberg, L., & Morris, A. S. (2001). Adolescent development. *Annual Review of Psychology, 52,* 83–110.

Stone, A. A., Schwartz, J. E., Broderick, J. E., & Deaton, A. (2010). A snapshot of the age distribution of psychological well-being in the United States. *Proceedings of the National Academy of Sciences.* Pre-publication version retrieved from www.pnas.org on June 2, 2010.

Storandt, M. (2008). Cognitive deficits in the early stages of Alzheimer's disease. *Current Directions in Psychological Science, 17,* 198–202.

Stutzer, A., & Frey, B. S. (2006). Does marriage make people happy, or do happy people get married? *The Journal of Socio-Economics, 35,* 326–347.

Subotnik, R. F., Olszewski-Kubilius, P., & Worrell, F. C. (2011). Rethinking giftedness and gifted education. A proposed direction forward based on psychological science. *Psychological Science in the Public Interest, 12,* 3–54.

Subramanian, S. V., Kim, F., & Kawachi, I. (2005). Covariation in the socioeconomic determinants of self-rated health and happiness. A multivariate multilevel analysis of individuals and communities in the USA. *Journal of Community Health, 59,* 664–669.

Taylor, P, (Ed.). (2010). *The decline of marriage and rise of new families.* Pew Research Center. Retrieved from http://pewsocialtrends.org/files/2010/11/pew-social-trends-2010-families.pdf on March 7, 2011

Taylor, M., Hulette, A. C., & Dishion, T. J. (2010). Longitudinal outcomes of young high-risk adolescents with imaginary companions. *Developmental Psychology, 46,* 1632–1636.

Thiessen, V., & Looker, D. E. (1999). Diverse directions. Young adults' multiple transitions. In W. R. Heinz (Ed.), *From education to work. Cross-national perspectives* (pp. 46–64). New York. Cambridge University Press.

Thompson, R. A., & Raikes, H. A. (2003). Toward the next quarter-century. Conceptual and methodological challenges for attachment theory. *Development and Psychopathology, 15,* 691–718.

Thorton, A., & Young-DeMarco, L. (2001). Four decades of trends in attitudes toward family issues in the United States. The 1960s through the 1990s. *Journal of Marriage and Family, 63,* 1009–1037.

Trionfi, G., & Reese, E. (2009). A good story. Children with imaginary companions create richer narratives. *Child Development, 80,* 1301–1313.

Trzesniewski, K. H., & Donnellan, M. B. (2010). Rethinking "Generation Me". A study of cohort effects from 1976–2006.

Perspectives in Psychological Science, 5, 58–75.

Turiel, E., Killen, M., & Helwig, C. C. (1987). Morality. Its structure, function, and vagaries. In J. Kagan & S. Lamb (Eds.), *The emergence of morality in young children* (pp. 155–243). Chicago. University of Chicago Press.

Twenge, J. M., & Campbell, W. K. (2010). Birth cohort differences in the monitoring the future dataset and elsewhere. Further evidence for Generation Me—commentary on Trzesniewski & Donnellan (2010). *Perspectives in Psychological Science, 5,* 81–88.

Twenge, J. M., & Campbell, K. W., & Freeman, E. C. (2012). Generational differences in young adults' life goals, concern for others, and civic orientation, 1966–2009. *Journal of Personality and Social Psychology, 102,* 1045–1062.

U.S. Bureau of the Census. (2010a, November 10). U.S. Census Bureau reports men and women wait longer to marry. Retrieved from http://www.census.gov/newsroom/releases/archives/families_households/cb10-174.html on September 2, 2011.

U.S. Bureau of the Census. (2010b). Families and living arrangements. Retrieved from http://www.census.gov/population/www/socdemo/hh-fam/cps2010.html on September 2, 2011

U.S. National Center for Health Statistics. (1995). Advance report of final divorce statistics, 1989 and 1990. *Monthly Vital Statistics Report, 43,* 1–31.

U.S. National Center for Health Statistics. (2006). Births, marriages, divorces, and deaths. *National Vital Statistics Reports, 54,* 1–6.

U.S. National Center for Health Statistics. (2010). Births marriages, divorces, and deaths. Provisional data for 2009. *National Vital Statistics Reports, 58.* Retrieved from http://www.cdc.gov/nchs on March 8, 2011.

Uller, C., Carey, S., Huntley-Fenner, G., & Klatt, L. (1999). What representations might underlie infant numerical knowledge? *Cognitive Development, 14,* 1–36.

Umberson, D. (1992). Gender, marital status and the social control of health behavior. *Social Science & Medicine, 34,* 907–917.

United Nations Statistics (2000). World marriage patterns 2000. Department of Economic and Social Affairs, Population Division. Retrieved from http://www.un.org/esa/population/publications on May 14, 2006.

Vaillant, G. (2002). *Aging well. Surprising guideposts to a happier life from the landmark Harvard Study of Adult Development.* Boston. Little, Brown and Company.

Vaillant, G. E. (1977). *Adaptation to life.* Boston. Little, Brown.

Van Berkum, J. J. A., Holleman, B., Nieuwland, M., Otten, M., & Murre, J. (2009). Right or wrong? The brain's fast response to morally objectionable statements. *Psychological Science, 20,* 1092–1099.

Vygotsky, L. S. (1929). The problem of the cultural development of the child. *Journal of Genetc Psychology, 36,* 415–32. Retrieved from http://www.marxists.org/archive/vygotsky/works/1929/cultural_development.htm on January 29, 2014.

Walls, R. T. (2000). Vocational cognition. Accuracy of 3rd-, 6th-, 9th-, and 12th-grade students. *Journal of Vocational Behavior, 56,* 137–144.

Wang, S-H, Baillargeon, R., & Brueckner, L. (2004). Young infants' reasoning about hidden objects. Evidence from violation-of-expectation tasks with test trials only. *Cognition, 93,* 167–198.

Webb, S. J., Monk, C. S., & Nelson, C. A. (2001). Mechanisms of postnatal neurobiological development. Implications for human development. *Developmental Neuropsychology, 19,* 147–171.

Weisfeld, G. E. (1999). *Evolutionary principles of human adolescence.* New York. Basic Books.

Wellman, H. M., Cross, D., & Watson, J. (2001). Meta-analysis of theory-of-mind development. The truth about false belief. *Child Development, 72,* 655–684.

The Williams Institute. (2010). Census snapshot. 1010. Retrieved from http://services.law.ucla.edu/williamsinstitute/home.html on September 3, 2010.

Willis, S. L., & Schaie, K. W. (1999). Intellectual functioning in midlife. In S. L. Willis, & J. D. Reid (Eds.), *Life in the middle. Psychological and social development in middle age* (pp. 233–247). San Diego. Academic Publishers.

Wilson, E. O. (1975). *Sociobiology, the new synthesis.* Cambridge, MA. Harvard University Press.

Wimmer, H., & Perner, J. (1983). Beliefs about beliefs. Representation and the containing function of wrong beliefs in young children's understanding of deception. *Cognition, 13,* 103–128.

Winner, E. (1996). *Gifted children.* New York. Basic Books.

Woo, H., & Raley, K. (2005). A small extension to "Costs and Rewards of Children. The effects of Becoming a Parent on Adults' Lives." *Journal of Marriage and Family, 67,* 216–221.

Wynn, K. (1992). Addition and subtraction by human infants. *Nature, 358,* 749–750.

Yang, Y. (2008a). Long and happy living. Trends and patterns of happy life expectancy in the U.S., 1970–2000. *Social Science Research 37,* 1235–1252.

Yang, Y. (2008b). Social inequalities in happiness in the United States, 1972 to 2004. An age-period-cohort analysis. *American Sociological Review, 73,* 204–226.

CHAPTER 5

Abramov, I., & Gordon, J. (1994). Color appearance. On seeing red—or yellow, or green, or blue. *Annual Review of Psychology, 45,* 451–485.

Ackerman, J. M., Nocera, C. C., & Bargh, J. A. (2010). Incidental haptic sensations influence social judgments and decision. *Science, 328,* 1712–1715.

Alcock, J. E. (2003). Give the null hypothesis a chance. Reasons to remain doubtful about the existence of psi. *Journal of Consciousness Studies, 10*(6–7), 29–50.

Alva, N. (2007). Inattentional blindness, change blindness, and consciousness. In M. Velmans & S. Schneider (Eds.) *The Blackwell companion to consciousness* (pp. 504–511). Malden, MA. Blackwell.

Amedi, A., Merebet, L. B., Camproden, J., Bermphol, F., Fox, S., et al. (2008). Neural and behavioral correlates of drawing in an early blind painter: a case study. *Brain Research, 1242,* 252–262.

Auer, E. T., Jr., Bernstein, L. E., Sungkarat, W., & Singh, M. (2007). Vibrotactile activation of the auditory cortices in deaf versus hearing adults. *Neuroreport, 18,* 645–648.

Auty, S., & Lewis, C. (2004). Exploring children's choice. The reminder effect of product placement. *Psychology & Marketing, 21,* 697–713.

Bahrami, B., Lavie, N., & Rees, G. (2007). Attentional load modulates responses of human primary visual cortex to invisible stimuli. *Current Biology, 20,* 509–513.

Bavelier, D., Dye, M. W. G., & Hauser, P. C. (2006). Do deaf individuals see better? *Trends in Cognitive Sciences, 10,* 512–518.

Bem, D. J. (2011). Feeling the future. Experimental evidence for anomalous retroactive influences on cognition and affect. *Journal of Personality and Social Psychology, 100,* 407–425.

Blackmore, S. (2004). *Consciousness. An introduction.* New York. Oxford University Press.

Blackmore, S. J. (1990, September 22). The lure of the paranormal. *New Scientist,* 62–65.

Boduroglu, A., Shah, P., & Nisbett, R. E. (2009). Cultural differences in allocation of attention in visual information processing. *Journal of Cross-Cultural Psychology, 40*(3), 349–360.

Bothmer, E. von. (2006). What the nose doesn't know. *Scientific American, 17,* 62–27.

Broyles, S. J. (2006). Paranoia over subliminal advertising. What's the big uproar this time? *Journal of Consumer Marketing, 23,* 312–313.

Burns, J. E. (2003). What is beyond the edge of the known world? *Journal of Consciousness Studies, 10*(6–7), 7–28.

Bushnell, I. W. R. (2001). Mother's face recognition in newborn infants. Leaning and memory. *Infant and Child Development, 10*(1–2), 67–74.

Cahill, L. (2006). Why sex matters for neuroscience. *Nature Reviews Neuroscience, 7,* 477–484.

Chabris, C., & Simons, D. (2010). *The invisible gorilla.* New York. Crown.

Chang, S., Newell, J., & Salmon, C. T. (2009). Product placement in entertainment media. Proposing business process models. *International Journal of Advertising, 28,* 783–806.

Chua, H. F., Boland, J. E., & Nisbett, R. E. (2005). Cultural variation in eye movements during scene perception. *Proceedings of the National Academy of Sciences, 102,* 12629–12633.

Coan, J. A., Schaefer, H. S., & Davidson, R. J. (2006). Lending a hand. Social regulation of the neural response to threat. *Psychological Science, 17,* 1032–1039.

Cooper, S. A., Joshi, A. C., Seenan, P. J., Hadley, D. M., Muir, K. W., et al. (2012). Akinetopsia. acute presentation and evidence for persisting defect in motion vision. *Journal of Neurology, Neurosurgery, and Psychiatry, 83,* 229–230.

Craig, J. C., & Rollman, G. B. (1999). Somesthesis. *Annual Review of Psychology, 50,* 305–331.

du Feu, M., & Fergusson, K. (2003). Sensory impairment and mental health. *Advances in Psychiatric Treatment, 9,* 95–103.

Eagle, M. N. (1959). The effects of subliminal stimuli of aggressive content upon conscious cognition. *Journal of Personality, 23,* 578–600.

Edwards, R. R., Campbell, C., Jamison, R. N., & Wiech, K. (2009). The neurobiological underpinnings of coping with pain. *Current Directions in Psychological Science, 18,* 237–241.

Field, T. M. (2001). *Touch.* Cambridge, MA. MIT Press

Froufe, M., & Schwartz, C. (2001). Subliminal messages for increasing self-esteem. *The Spanish Journal of Psychology, 4,* 19–25.

Gatchel, R. J., Peng, Y. B., Peters, M. L., Fuchs, P. N., & Turk, D. C. (2007). The biopsychosocial approach to chronic pain. Scientific advances and future directions. *Psychological Bulletin, 133,* 581–624.

Gibson, E. J., & Walk, R. D. (1960). The "visual cliff." *Scientific American, 202,* 67–71.

Glicksohn, J. (1990). Belief in the paranormal and subjective paranormal experience. *Personality and Individual Differences, 11,* 675–683.

Goh, J. O., & Park, D. C. (2009). Culture sculpts the perceptual brain. *Progress in Brain Research, 178,* 95–111.

Goh J.O., Tan, J.C, Park, D.C. (2009). Culture Modulates Eye-Movements to Visual Novelty. *PLoS One, 4,* e8238. Retrieved from http://www.plosone.org/article/info%3Adoi%2F10.1371%2Fjournal.pone.0008238 on January 31, 2013

Goldstein, E. B. (2010). *Sensation and perception* (8th ed.). Belmont, CA. Wadsworth/Cengage.

Greenwald, A. G., Spangenberg, E. R., Pratkanis, A. R., & Eskenazi, J. (1991). Double-blind tests of subliminal self-help audiotapes. *Psychological Science, 2,* 119–122.

Gregory, R. L. (1973). A discussion of G. H. Fisher's "Towards a new explanation for the geometrical illusions. apparent depth or contour proximity?" and the inappropriate constancy scaling theory. *British Journal of Psychology 64*, 623–626.

Gregory, R. L. (1997). *Eye and brain. The psychology of seeing* (5th ed.). Princeton, NJ. Princeton University Press.

Grosser, B. I., Monti-Bloch, L., Jennings-White, C., & Berliner, D. L. (2000). Behavioral and electrophysiological effects of androstadienone, a human pheromone. *Psychoneuroendocrinology, 25*, 289–299.

Halsey, R., & Chapanis, A. (1951) On the number of absolutely identifiable spectral hues. *Journal of the Optical Society of America, 41*, 1057–1058.

Harlow, H. F. (1958). The nature of love. *American Psychologist, 13*, 573–685.

Harlow, H, F., & Zimmerman, R. R. (1959). Affectional responses in the infant monkey. *Science, 130*, 421–432.

Hertenstein, M. J. (2002). Touch. Its communicative functions in infancy. *Human Development, 45*, 70–94.

Hertenstein, M. J., Keltner, D., App, B., Bulleit, B. A., & Jaskolka, A. R. (2006). Touch communicates distinct emotions. *Emotion, 6*, 528–533.

Horton, J. X., & Trobe, J. D. (1999). Akinetopsia from nefazodone toxicity. *American Journal of Opthalmology, 128*, 530–531.

Hubel, D. H. (1995). *Eye, brain, and vision.* New York. Scientific American Library.

Hunsley, J., Lee, C. M., & Wood, J. M. (2003). Controversial and questionable assessment techniques. In S. O. Lilienfeld, S. J. Lynn, & J. M. Lohr (Eds.), *Science and pseudoscience in clinical psychology* (pp. 39–76). New York. The Guilford Press.

Hyman, R. (1989). *The elusive quarry. A scientific appraisal of psychical research.* New York. Prometheus Books.

Jacob, S. Kinnunen, J. S., Metz, J., Cooper, M., & McClintock, M. K. (2001). Sustained human chemosignal unconsciously alters brain function. *Neuroreport, 12*, 2391–2394.

Jeffers, S. (2003). Physics and claims for anomalous effects related to consciousness. *Journal of Consciousness Studies, 10*(6–7), 135–152.

Johnston, R. E. (1998). Pheromones, the vomeronasal system, and communication. From hormonal responses to individual recognition. *Annals of the New York Academy of Sciences, 855*, 333–348.

Jones, G. (2005). Echolocation. *Current Biology, 15*, R484–R488.

Judd, D., & Kelly, K. (1939). Method of designating colors. *Journal of Research of the National Bureau of Standards, 23*, 355.

Kaiser, P., & Boynton, R. (1996) *Color vision.* Washington, DC. Optical Society of America.

Kanwisher, N. (2006). What's in a face? *Science, 311*, 617–618.

Kanwisher, N., & Yovel, G. (2006). The fusiform face area. A cortical region specialized for the perception of faces. *Philosophical Transactions of the Royal Society B, 361*, 2109–2128.

Keefe, F. J., & France, C. R. (1999). Pain. Biopsychosocial mechanisms and management. *Current Directions in Psychological Science, 8*, 137–141.

Kennedy, J. E. (2001). Why is psi so elusive? A review and proposed model. *Journal of Consciousness Studies, 65*, 219–246.

Kennedy, J. M., & Juricevic, I. (2006). Foreshortening, convergence, and drawings of a blind adult. *Perception, 35*, 847–851.

Kleinschmidt, A., & Cohen, L. (2006). The neural bases of prospagnosia and pure alexia. Recent insights from functional neuroimaging. *Current Opinion in Neurology, 19*, 386–391.

Kohl, J. V., Atzmuller, M., Fink, B., & Grammer, K. (2007). Human pheromones. Integrating neuroendocrinology and ethology. *Activitas Nervosa Superior, 49*, 123–135.

Laugerette, F., Passilly-Degrace, P., Patris, B., Niot, I., Febbraio, M., et al. (2005). CD36 involvement in orosensory detection of dietary lipids, spontaneous fat preference, and digestive secretions. *The Journal of Clinical Investigation, 115*, 3177–3184.

Levi, D. M., Klein, S., A., & Aitsebaomo, A. P. (1985). Vernier acuity, crowding, and cortical magnification. *Vision Research, 25*, 963–977.

Liberles, S. D., & Buck, L. B. (2006). A second class of chemosensory receptors in the olfactory epithelium. *Nature, 442*, 645–650.

Liu, J., Harris, A., & Kanwisher, N. (2010). Perception of face parts and face configurations. An fMRI study. *Journal of Cognitive Neuroscience, 22*, 203–211.

Macchi Cassia, V., Turati, C., & Simion, F. (2004). Can a nonspecific bias toward top-heavy patterns explain newborns' face preference? *Psychological Science, 15*, 379–383.

Mack, A. (2003). Inattentional blindness. Looking without seeing. *Current Directions in Psychological Science, 12*, 180–184.

Macmillan, N. A., & Creelman, C. D. (2005). *Detection theory. A user's guide* (2nd ed.). Mahwah, NJ. Lawrence Erlbaum Associates.

Marwick, B. (1978). The Soal-Goldney experiments with Basil Shackleton. New evidence of data manipulation. *Proceedings of the Society for Psychical Research, 56*, 250–281.

Masuda, T., & Nisbett, R. E. (2001). Attending holistically versus analytically. Comparing the context sensitivity of Japanese and Americans. *Journal of Personality and Social Psychology, 81*, 922–934.

Matthes, J, Schemer, C., & Wirth, W. (2007). More than meets the eye. Investigating the hidden impact of brand placements in television magazines. *International Journal of Advertising, 26*, 477–503.

Maurer, D., Mondloch, C. J., & Lewis, T. L. (2007). Sleeper effects. *Developmental Science, 10*(1), 40–47.

McClintock, M. K. (2000). Human pheromones. primers, releasers, signalers, or modulators? In K. Wallen & J. E. Schneider (Eds.), *Reproduction in context* (pp. 355–420). Cambridge, MA. MIT Press.

Medeiros, J. A. (2006). *Cone shape and color vision. Unification of structure and perception.* Blountsville, AL. Fifth Estate.

Melzack, R., & Casey, K. L. (1968). Sensory, motivational, and central control determinants of pain. A new conceptual model. In D. R. Kenshalo (Ed.), *The skin senses* (pp. 423–443). Springfield, IL. Charles C. Thomas.

Melzack, R., & Wall, P. D. (1965). Pain mechanisms. A new theory. *Science, 150*, 971–979.

Melzack, R., & Wall, P. D. (1983). *The challenge of pain.* New York. Basic Books

Miller, S. L., & Maner, J. L. (2010). Scent of a woman. Men's testosterone responses to olfactory ovulation cues. *Psychological Science, 21*, 276–283.

Mizushige, T., Inoue, K., & Fushiki, T. (2007). Why is fat so tasty? Chemical reception of fatty acid on the tongue. *Journal of Nutritional Science and Vitaminology (Tokyo), 53*, 1–4.

Monohan, J. L., Murphy, S. T., & Zajonc, R. B. (2000). Subliminal mere exposure. Specific, general, and diffuse effects. *Psychological Science, 11*, 462–466.

Moore, D. W. (2005, June 16). Three in four Americans believe in paranormal. *Gallup News Service.* Retrieved from http://home.sandiego.edu/~baber/logic/gallup.html on March 3, 2006.

Moore, T. E. (1995). Subliminal self-help auditory tapes. An empirical test of perceptual consequences. *Canadian Journal of Behavioural Science, 27*(1), 9–20.

Moscovitch, M., Winocur, G., & Behrmann, M. (1997). What is special about face recognition? Nineteen experiments on a person with visual object agnosia and dyslexia but normal face recognition. *Journal of Cognitive Neuroscience, 9*, 555–604.

Most, S. B., Scholl, B. J., Clifford, E. R., & Simons, D. J. (2005). What you see is what you set. Sustained inattentional blindness and the capture of awareness. *Psychological Review, 112*, 217–242.

Motluk, A. (2005, January 29). Senses special. The art of seeing without sight. *New Scientist.* Retrieved from www.newscientist.com on January 1, 2006.

Moulson, M. C., Westerlund, A., Fox, N. A., Zeanah, C. H., & Nelson, C. A. (2009). The effects of early experience on face recognition. An event-related potential study of institutionalized children in Romania. *Child Development, 80*, 1039–1056.

Mueller, K. L., Hoon, M. A., Erlenbach, I., Chandrashekar, J., Zuker, C. S., et al. (2005). The receptors and coding logic for bitter taste. *Nature, 434*, 225–229.

Murphy, S. T., Monahan, J. L., & Zajonc, R. B. (1995). Additivity of nonconscious affect. Combined effects of priming and exposure. *Journal of Personality and Social Psychology, 69*, 589–602.

Nagasako, E. M., Oaklander, A. L., & Dworkin, R. H. (2003). Congenital insensitivity to pain. An update. *Pain, 101*, 213–219.

Nawrot, M. (2003). Disorders of motion and depth. *Neurologic Clinics, 21*, 609–629.

Nelson, C. A. (2001). The development and neural bases of face recognition. *Infant and Child Development, 10*, 3–18.

Nisbett, R. E. & Miyamoto, Y. (2005). The influence of culture. Holistic versus analytic perception. *Trends in Cognitive Science, 9*, 467–473.

Norenzayan, A., & Nisbett, R. E. (2000). Culture and causal cognition. *Current Directions in Psychological Science, 9*, 132–135.

Palmer, R. K. (2007). The pharmacology and signaling of bitter, sweet, and umami taste. *Molecular Intervention, 7*, 87–98.

Palmer, S. E. (2002). Perceptual grouping. It's later than you think. *Current Directions in Psychological Science, 11*, 101–106.

Park, D. C., & Huang, C-M. (2010). Culture wires the brain. A cognitive neuroscience perspective. *Perspectives on Psychological Science, 5*, 391–400.

Pascalis, O., & Kelly, D, J. (2009). The origins of face processing in humans. Phylogeny and Ontogeny. *Perspectives on Psychological Science, 4*, 200–209.

Pedersen, D. M., & Wheeler, J. (1983). The Müller-Lyer illusion among Navajos. *Journal of Social Psychology, 121(1)*, 3–6.

Pelphrey, K. A., & Morris, J. P. (2006). Brain mechanisms for interpreting the actions of others from biological motion cues. *Current Directions in Psychological Science, 15*, 136–140.

Ploner, M., Gross, J., Timmermann, L., & Schnitzler, A. (2002). Cortical representation of first and second pain sensation in humans. *PNAS, 99*, 12444–12448.

Pratkanis, A. R. (1992, Spring). The cargo-cult science of subliminal persuasion. *Skeptical Inquirer*. Retrieved from www.csicop.org on September 4, 2006.

Pratkanis, A. R., Eskenazi, J., & Greenwald, A. G. (1994). What you expect is what you believe (but not necessarily what you get). A test of the effectiveness of subliminal self-help audiotapes. *Basic & Applied Social Psychology, 15*, 251–276.

Quinn, P. C., Bhatt, R. S., Brush, D., Grimes, A., & Sharpnack, H. (2002). Development of form similarity as a Gestalt grouping principle in infancy. *Psychological Science, 13*, 320–341.

Ramachandran, V. S. (1992). Filling in gaps in perception. Part 1. *Current Directions in Psychological Science, 1*, 199–205.

Rogers, S. (1992–1993). How a publicity blitz created the myth of subliminal advertising. *Public Relations Quarterly, 37*, 12–17.

Rolls, E. T. (2006). Brain mechanisms underlying flavour and appetite. *Philosophical Transactions of the Royal Society of London, Series B. Biological Sciences, 361*, 1123–1136.

Rubin, N. (2001). Figure and ground in the brain. *Nature Neuroscience, 4*, 857–858.

Russell, T. G., Rowe, W., & Smouse, A.D. (1991). Subliminal self-help tapes and academic achievement. An evaluation. *Journal of Counseling and Development, 69*, 359–362.

Ruys, K. I., & Stapel, D. A. (2008). How to heat up from the cold. Examining the preconditions for (unconscious) mood effects. *Journal of Personality and Social Psychology, 94*, 777–791.

Savic, I., Berglund, H., & Lindström, P. (2005). Brain response to putative pheromones in homosexual men. *Proceedings of the National Academy of Sciences. USA, 102*, 7356–7361.

Savic, I., Berglund, H., Gulyas, B., & Roland, P. (2001). Smelling of odorous sex hormone-like compounds causes sex-differentiated hypothalamic activations in humans. *Neuron, 31*, 661–668.

Sedgwick, H. (2001). Visual space perception. In E. B. Goldstein (Ed.), *Blackwell handbook of perception* (pp. 128–167). Oxford, UK. Blackwell.

Segall, M. H., Campbell, D. T., & Herskovits, M. J. (1966). *The influence of culture on visual perception.* Indianapolis, IN. Bobbs-Merrill.

Simons, D. J., & Chabris, C. F. (1999). Gorillas in our midst. Sustained inattentional blindness for dynamic events. *Perception, 28*, 1059–1074.

Simons, D. J., & Levin, D. T. (1998). Failure to detect changes to people in a real-world interaction. *Psychonomic Bulletin & Review, 5*, 644–649.

Slaughter, V., Stone, V. E., & Reed, C. (2004). Perception of faces and bodies. Similar or different? *Current Directions in Psychological Science, 13*, 219–223.

Smith, K. H., & Rogers, M. (1994). Effectiveness of subliminal messages in television commercials. Two experiments. *Journal of Applied Psychology, 79*, 866–874.

Sobel, N., & Brown, W. M. (2001). The scented brain. Pheromonal responses in humans. *Neuron, 31*, 512–514.

Sufka, K. J., & Price, D. D. (2002). Gate control theory reconsidered. *Brain and Mind, 3*, 277–290.

Symons, D. (1993). The stuff that dreams aren't made of. Why wake-state and dream-state experiences differ. *Cognition, 47*, 181–217.

Taylor, C. R. (2009). Product placement. A hot topic gets hotter. *International Journal of Advertising, 28*, 753–756.

Torralba, A., & Olivia, A. (2003). Statistics of natural image categories. *Network. Computation in Neural Systems, 14*, 391–412.

Trappey, C. (1996). A meta-analysis of consumer choice and subliminal advertising. *Psychology and Marketing, 13*, 517–530.

Tsao, D. Y., Freiwald, W. A., Tootell, R. B. H., & Livingstone, M. S. (2006). A cortical region consisting entirely of face-selective cells. *Science, 311*, 670–674.

Turati, C., Bulf, H., & Simion, F. (2008). Newborns' face recognition over changes in viewpoint. *Cognition, 106*, 1300–1321.

Turati, C., Valenza, E., Leo, I., & Simion, F. (2005). Three-month-olds' visual preference for faces and its underlying visual processing mechanisms. *Journal of Experimental Child Psychology, 90*, 255–273.

Vargas, P. T. (2008). Implicit consumer cognition. In P. C. Haugtvedt, P. M. Herr, & F. R. Kardes (Eds.), *Handbook of consumer psychology* (pp. 477–504). New York. Taylor & Francis Group/Lawrence Erlbaum Associates.

Varnum, M. E. W., Grossmann,. I, Kitayama, S., & Nisbett, R. E. (2010). The origin of cultural differences in cognition. The social orientation hypothesis. *Current Directions in Psychological Science, 19*, 9–13.

Varvoglis, M. (1997). What is PSI? What isn't? Retrieved from http://www.parapsych.org/what_is_psi_varvoglis.htm on September 12, 2006.

Wada, Y., & Yamamoto, T. (2001). Selective impairment of facial recognition due to a haematoma restricted to the right fusiform and lateral occipital region. *Journal of Neurology and Neurosurgery in Psychiatry, 71*, 254–257.

Wagenmakers, E-J., Wetzels, R., Bordsboom, D., & van der Maas, H. (2011). Why psychologists must change the way they analyze their data. The case of psi. Comment on Bem. *Journal of Personality and Social Psychology, 100*, 426–432.

Wertheimer, M. (1950). Laws of organization in perceptual forms. In W. D. Ellis (Ed.), *A sourcebook of Gestalt psychology* (pp. 71–81). New York. Humanities Press. (Original work published 1923).

Winman, A. (2004). Do perfume additives termed human pheromones warrant being termed pheromones? *Physiology & Behavior, 82*, 697–701.

Wolfe, J. M., Kluender, K. R., Levi, D. M., Bartoshuk, L. M., Herz, R. S., et al. (2009). *Sensation and perception* (2nd ed.). Sunderland, MA. Sinauer.

Wyart, C., Webster, W. W., Chen, J. H., Wilson, S. R., McClary, A., et al. (2007). Smelling a single component of male sweat alters levels of cortisol in women. *The Journal of Neuroscience, 27*, 1261–1265.

Wysocki, C. J., & Preti, G. (2004). Facts, fallacies, fears, and frustrations with human pheromones. *The Anatomical Record, 218A*, 1201–1211.

Yaksh, T. L. (1999). Regulation of spinal nociceptive processing. Where we went when we wandered onto the path marked by the gate. *Pain 6, (Suppl.)*, S149–S152.

Zeki, S. (1991). Cerebral akinetopsia (visual motion blindness). A review. *Brain, 114 (Part 2)*, 811–824.

Zhao, G. Q., Zhang, Y., Hoon, M., Chandrashekar, J., Erlenbach, I., et al. (2003). The receptors for mammalian sweet and umami taste. *Cell, 115,* 255–266.

CHAPTER 6

Achermann, P. (2004). The two-process model of sleep regulation revisited. *Aviation, Space, and Environmental Medicine, 75(Suppl. 1),* A37–A43.

Acker, C. J. (2002). *Creating the American junkie. Addiction research in the classic era of narcotic control.* Baltimore, MD. Johns Hopkins University Press.

Aloia, M. S., Arnedt, J. T., Davis, J. D., Riggs, R. L., & Byrd, D. (2004). Neuropsychological sequelae of obstructive sleep apnea-hypopnea syndrome. A critical review. *Journal of the International Neuropsychological Society, 10,* 772–785.

American Psychiatric Association (2000) *Diagnostic and Statistical Manual of Mental Disorders, Text Revision—DSM IV-TR.* Washington, DC. American Psychiatric Association.

American Psychological Association (2005). New definition. Hypnosis. Retrieved from www.apa.org/divisions/div30/define_hypnosis.htm.

Amsterdam, J. D., Li, Y., Soeller, I., Rockwell, K., Mao, J. J., & Shults, J. (2009). A randomized, double-blind, placebo-controlled trial of oral matricaria recutita (chamomile) extract therapy for generalized anxiety disorder. *Journal of Clinical Psychopharmacology, 29,* 378–382.

Anthony, J. C., Warner, L. A., & Kessler, R. C. (1994). Comparative epidemiology of dependence on tobacco, alcohol, controlled substances, and inhalants. Basic findings from the National Comorbidity Survey. *Experimental and Clinical Psychopharmacology, 2,* 244–268.

Austin, J. H. (1998). *Zen and the brain. Toward an understanding of meditation and consciousness.* Cambridge, MA. MIT Press.

Bagai, K. (2010). Obstructive sleep apnea, stroke, and cardiovascular diseases. *Neurologist, 16,* 329–339.

Baggott, M., Jerome, L., & Stuart, R. (2001/2005). 3, 4-methylenedioxymethamphetamine (MDMA). A review of the English-language scientific and medical literature (2005 update). Multidisciplinary Association for Psychedelic Studies. Retrieved from http://www.maps.org/research/mdma/protocol/litreview.html on January 27, 2006.

Bambico, F. R., Nguyen, N-T., Katz, N., & Gobbi, G. (2010). Chronic exposure to cannabinoids during adolescence but not during adulthood impairs emotional behaviour and monoaminergic neurotransmission. *Neurobiology of Disease, 37,* 641–655.

Barber, T. X. (1979). Suggested "hypnotic" behavior. The trances paradigm versus an alternative paradigm. In E. Fromm & R. E. Shor (Eds.), *Hypnosis. Developments in research and new perspectives* (pp. 217–271). Chicago. Aldine.

Barber, T. X., & Calverley, D. S. (1965). Empirical evidence for a theory of "hypnotic" behaviour. Effects on suggestibility of five variables typically included in hypnotic induction procedures. *Journal of Consulting Psychology, 29,* 98–107.

Bartels, A., & Zeki, S. (1998). The theory of multistage integration in the visual brain. *Proceedings of the Royal Society B, 265,* 2327–2332.

Baumann, M., Clark, R., Budzynski, A., Partilla, J., Blough, B., et al. (2005). N-substituted piperazines abused by humans mimic the molecular mechanism of 3, 4-methlenedioxymethamphetamine (MDMA or "Ecstasy)." *Neuropsychopharmacology, 39,* 550–560.

Becker, P. M. (2006). Insomnia. Prevalence, impact, pathogenesis, differential diagnosis, and evaluation. *Psychiatric Clinics of North America, 29,* 855–870.

Berman, S., O'Neill, J., Fears, S., Bartzokis, G., & London, E. D. (2008). Abuses of amphetamines and structural abnormalities in brain. *Addiction Reviews, 1141,* 195–220.

Blackmore, S. (2004). *Consciousness. An introduction.* New York. Oxford University Press.

Blackmore, S. (2005). *Consciousness. A very short introduction.* New York. Oxford University Press.

Blavivas, A. J., Patel, R., Hom, D., Antigua, K., & Ashtyani, H. (2007). Quantifying microsleep to help assess subjective sleepiness. *Sleep Medicine, 8,* 156–159.

Bonnie, R. J., & Whitebread, C. H. (1999). *The marijuana conviction. A history of marijuana prohibition in the United States.* New York. Lindesmith Center.

Booth, M. (1999). *Opium. A history.* New York. St. Martin's Griffin.

Bootzin, R. R., & Epstein, D. R. (2011). Understanding and treating insomnia. *Annual Review of Clinical Psychology, 7,* 435–458.

Brådvik, L., Hulenvik, P., Frank, A., Medvedeo, A., & Berglund, M. (2007). Self-reported and observed heroin overdoses in Malmoe. *Journal of Substance Use, 12,* 119–126.

Brecher, E. M. (1972). The "heroin overdose" mystery and other occupational hazards of addiction. In E. M. Brecher and the Editors of Consumer Reports Magazine, *The Consumers Union report on licit and illicit drugs.* Retrieved http://www.druglibrary.org/schaffer/Library/studies/cu/cu12.htm on November 12, 2008.

Brown, D. (1991). *Human universals.* Boston, MA. McGraw-Hill.

Brown, J. B. (2007/2008, December/January). Psychedelic healing? *Scientific American Mind,* 67–71.

Brügger-Anderson, T., Pönitz, V., Snapinn, S., Dickstein, K; for the OPTIMAAL study group. (2008). Moderate alcohol consumption is associated with reduced long-term cardiovascular risk in patients following a complicated acute myocardial infarction. *International Journal of Cardiology.* Advance publication retrieved from http://www.sciencedirect.comon November 13, 2008.

Budney, A. J., & Wiley, J. (2001). Can marijuana use lead to marijuana dependence? In M. E. Carroll & B. J. Overmier (Eds.), *Animal research and human health. Advancing human welfare through behavioral science* (pp. 115–126). Washington, DC. American Psychological Association.

Bulkeley, K., & Kahan, T. L. (2008). The impact of September 11 on dreaming. *Conciousness and Cognition, 17,* 1248–1256.

Burroughs, W. S. (1959). *Naked lunch.* New York. Grove Press.

Buysse, D. J., Grunstein, R., Horne, J., & Lavie, P. (2010). Can improvement in sleep positively impact on health? *Sleep Medicine Reviews, 14,* 405–410.

Buysse, D. J., Germain, A., & Moul, D. E. (2005). Diagnosis, epidemiology, and consequences of insomnia. *Primary Psychiatry, 12,* 37–44.

Carey, T. J., Moul, D. E., Pilkonis, P., Germain, A., & Buysse, D. J. (2005). Focusing on the experience of insomnia. *Behavioral and Sleep Medicine, 3,* 73–86.

Cartwright, R. (1996). Dreams and adaptation to divorce. In D. Barrtett (Ed.), *Trauma and dreams* (pp. 178–185). Cambridge, MA. Harvard University Press.

Cartwright, R. (2005). Dreaming as a mood regulation system. In. M. Kryger, T. Roth, & W. Dement (Eds.), *Principles and practice of sleep medicine* (4th ed., pp. 565–572). Philadelphia. W. B. Saunders.

Cartwright, R., Agargun, M. Y., Kirkby, J., & Friedman, J. K. (2006). Relation of dreams to waking concerns. *Psychiatry Research, 141,* 261–270.

Centers for Disease Control. (1998, May 22). *Morbidity and Mortality Weekly Report, 47.* Retrieved from http://www.cdc.gov/mmwr/PDF/wk/mm4719.pdf on March 16, 2011.

Centers for Disease Control. (2005a). Annual smoking-attributable mortality, years of potential life lost, and productivity losses—United States, 1997–2001. *Morbidity and Mortality Weekly Report, 54,* 625–628.

Centers for Disease Control. (2005b). Cigarette smoking among adults. United States, 2003. *Morbidity and Mortality Weekly Report, 54,* 509–513.

Centers for Disease Control. (2012, January). Binge drinking. Nationwide problem, local solutions. *CDC Vital Signs.* Retrieved from http://www.cdc.gov/VitalSigns/pdf/2012-01-vitalsigns.pdf on January 22, 2012.

Chalmers, D. J. (1995). Facing up to the problem of consciousness. *Journal of Consciousness Studies, 3,* 200–219.

Chang, L., Alicata, D., Ernst, T., & Volkow, N. (2007). Structural and metabolic brain changes in the striatum associated with methamphetamine abuse. *Addiction, 102(Suppl. 1),* 16–32.

Chassin, L., Presson, C., Rose, J., Sherman, S., & Prost, J. (2002). Parental smoking cessation and adolescent smoking. *Journal of Pediatric Psychology, 27,* 485–496.

Cheyne, J. A. (2005). Sleep paralysis episode frequency and number, types, and structure of associated hallucinations. *Journal of Sleep Research, 14,* 319–324.

Cirelli, C., & Tononi, G. (2008). Is sleep essential? *PLoS Biology, 6,* 1605–1611. Retrieved from www.plosbiology.org on October 27, 2008.

Cohen, P. J. (2009). Medical marijuana. The conflict between scientific evidence and political ideology, part. Part one of two. *Journal of Pain and Palliative Care Pharmacotherapy, 23,* 4–25.

Cole, J., Sumnall, H., & Grob, C. (2002a). Sorted. Ecstasy. *The Psychologist, 15,* 464–467.

Cole, J., Sumnall, H., & Grob, C. (2002b). Where are the casualties? *The Psychologist, 15,* 474.

Coles, C. D. (1993). Saying "goodbye" to the "crack baby." *Neurotoxicology and Teratology, 15,* 290–292.

Compton, W. M., Thomas, Y. F., Stinson, F. S., & Grant, B. F. (2007). Prevalence, correlates, disability, and comorbidity of DSM-IV drug abuse and dependence in the United States. *Archives of General Psychiatry, 64,* 566–576.

Conroy, R. T., & Mills, J. N. (1970). *Human circadian rhythms.* London. Churchill.

Coren, S. (1998). Sleep deprivation, psychosis and mental efficiency. *Psychiatric Times, 15.* Retrieved from http://www.psychiatrictimes.com/p980301b.html on January 7, 2006

Coren, S. (2009). Sleep health and its assessment and management in physical therapy practice. The evidence. *Physiotherapy Theory and Practice, 25,* 442–452.

Costello, D. M., Dierker, L. C., Jones, B. L., & Rose, J. S. (2008). Trajectories of smoking from adolescence to early adulthood and their psychosocial risk factors. *Health Psychology, 27,* 811–818.

Courtney, K. E., & Polich, J. (2009). Binge drinking in young adults. Data, definitions, and determinants. *Psychological Bulletin, 135,* 142–156.

Crick, F., & Koch, C. (2007). A neurobiological framework for consciousness. In M. Velmans & S. Schneider (Eds.), *The Blackwell companion to consciousness* (pp. 567–579). Malden, MA. Blackwell Publishing.

Curry, S. J., Mermelstein, R. J., & Sporer, A. K. (2009). Therapy for specific problems. Youth tobacco cessation. *Annual Review of Psychology, 60,* 229–255.

Dagan, Y., & Doljansky, J. T. (2006). Cognitive performance during sustained wakefulness. A low dose of caffeine is equally effective as modafinil in alleviating the nocturnal cognitive decline. *Chronobiology International, 23,* 973–983.

D'Agostino, A., & Limosani, I. (2010). Hypnagogic hallucinations and sleep paralysis. In M. Goswami, S. R. Pandi-Perumal, & M. J. Thorpy (Eds.),

Narcolepsy. A clinical guide (pp. 87–97). Totowa, NJ. Humana Press.

Dal Cin, S., Gibson, B., Zanna, M. P., Shumate, R., & Fong, G. T. (2007). Smoking in movies, implicit associations of smoking with the self, and intentions to smoke. *Psychological Science, 18,* 559–563.

Damasio, A. (2010). *The self comes to mind. Constructing the conscious brain.* New York. Pantheon/Random House.

Darke, S., & Zador, D. (1996). Fatal heroin "overdose". A review. *Addiction, 91,* 1765–1772.

Darke, S., & Zador, D. (2000). Heroin-related deaths in New South Wales, Australia, 1992–1996. *Drug and Alcohol Dependence, 60,* 141–150.

Davidson, R. J., Kabat-Zinn, J., Schumacher, J., Rosenkranz, M., Muller, D., et al. (2003). Alterations in brain and immune function produced by mindfulness meditation. *Psychosomatic Medicine, 65,* 564–570.

Davis, R., Rizwani, W., Banerjee, S., Kovacs, M., Haura, E., Coppola, D., et al. (2009). Nicotine promotes tumor growth and metastasis in mouse models of lung cancer. *PLoS One, 4.* e7524. Retrieved from www.plosone.org on February 8, 2013.

Degenhardt, L., Hall, W., & Lynskey, M. (2001). The relationship between cannabis use, depression and anxiety among Australian adults. Findings from the national survey of mental health and well-being. *Social Psychiatry and Psychiatric Epidemiology, 36,* 219–227.

Dement, W. C., & Kleitman, N. (1957). The relation of eye movements during sleep to dream activity. An objective method for the study of dreaming. *Journal of Experimental Psychology, 53,* 339–346.

Dietz, P., Jolley, D., Fry, C., & Bammer, G. (2005). Transient changes in behaviour lead to heroin overdose. Results from a case-crossover study of non-fatal overdose. *Addiction, 100,* 636–642.

Dijk, D-J., & Archer, S. N. (2009). Circadian and homeostatic regulation of human sleep and cognitive performance and its modulation by PERIOD 3. *Sleep Medicine Clinics, 4,* 111–125.

Doghramji, P. P. (2004). Recognizing sleep disorders in a primary care setting. *Journal of Clinical Psychiatry, 65 (Suppl. 16),* 23–26.

Domhoff, G. W. (1996). *Finding meaning in dreams. A quantitative approach.* New York. Plenum Press.

Domhoff, G. W. (2003). *The scientific study of dreams. Neural networks, cognitive development, and content analysis.* Washington, DC. American Psychological Association.

Domhoff, G. W. (2010). Dream content is continuous with waking thought, based on preoccupations, concerns, and interests. *Journal of Clinical Sleep Medicine, 5,* 203–215.

Dorus, E., Dorus, W., & Rechtschaffen, A. (1971). The incidence of novelty in dreams. *Archives of General Psychiatry, 25,* 364–368.

Drug Abuse Warning Network (DAWN). (2003a). *Area profiles of drug-related mortality.* U. S. Department of Health and Human Services. Retrieved from http://dawninfo.samhsa.gov/files/ME_report_2003_Front.pdf on January 31, 2006.

Drug Abuse Warning Network (DAWN). (2003b). *Interim national estimates of drug-related emergency department visits.* U. S. Department of Health and Human Services. Retrieved from http://dawninfo.samhsa.gov/files/DAWN_ED_Interim2003.pdf on January 31, 2006.

Drug Abuse Warning Network (DAWN). (August, 2003c). Marijuana-related emergency department visits by youth. *The DAWN Report.* Retrieved from http://dawninfo.samhsa.gov/old_dawn/pubs_94_02/shortreports/files/DAWN_marijuana_tdr.pdf on March 15, 2011.

Drug Abuse Warning Network (DAWN). (2004). *National estimates of drug-related emergency department visits.* Rockville, MD. Substance Abuse and Mental Health Services Administration. Retrieved from https://dawninfo.samhsa.gov/files/DAWN2k4ED.htm on November 11, 2006.

Drug Abuse Warning Network (DAWN). (2006). Emergency department visits involving dextromethorphan. *The New Dawn Report.* Retrieved from https://dawninfo.samhsa.gov/files/TNDR10DXM.htm on November 22, 2006.

Drug Abuse Warning Network (DAWN). (2010). *Drug Abuse Warning Network, 2007. National Estimates of Drug-Related Emergency Department Visits.* Rockville, MD. Substance Abuse and Mental Health Services Administration.

Durand, M. V. (2006). Night terrors. In J. E. Fisher, & W. T. O'Donohue (Eds.), *Practitioner's guide to evidence-based psychotherapy* (pp. 654–659). New York. Springer.

Duster, T. (1972). *The legislation of morality. Law, drugs, and moral judgment.* New York. Free Press.

Ellenbogen, J. M., Hu, P. T., Payne, J. D., Titone, D., & Walker, M. P. (2007). Human relational memory requires time and sleep. *Proceedings of the National Academy of Sciences, 104,* 7723–7728.

ElSohly, M. A. (2001). Drug-facilitated sexual assault. *Southern Medical Journal, 94,* 655–656.

Espie, C. A. (2002). Insomnia. Conceptual issues in the development persistence, and treatment of sleep disorder in adults. *Annual Review of Psychology, 53,* 215–243.

European Monitoring Centre for Drugs and Drug Addiction. (2003). *Report on the risk assessment of PMMA in the framework of the joint action on new synthetic drugs.* Lisbon, Portugal. Retrieved from www.emcdda.europa.eu/ on February 3, 2006.

Ezzati, M., & Lopez, A. D., (2003). Estimates of global mortality attributable to smoking in 2000. *Lancet, 362,* 847–852.

Farthing, G. W. (1992). *The psychology of consciousness.* Englewood Cliffs, NJ. Prentice Hall.

Ferreira, M. P., & Willoughby, D. (2008). Alcohol consumption. The good, the bad, and the indifferent. *Applied Physiology, Nutrition, and Metabolism, 33,* 12–20.

Ferrie, J. E., Shipley, M. J., Cappuccio, F. P., Brunner, E., Miller, M. A., et al. (2007). A prospective study of change in sleep duration. Associations with mortality in the Whitehall II cohort. *Sleep. Journal of Sleep and Sleep Disorders Research, 30,* 1659–1666.

Fisher, S., & Greenberg, R. (1996). *Freud scientifically appraised.* New York. John Wiley.

Fisk, J. E., & Montgomery, C. (2008). Real-world memory and executive processes in cannabis users and non-users. *Journal of Psychopharmacology, 22,* 727–736.

Fosse, R., Stickgold, R., & Hobson, J. A. (2004). Thinking and hallucinating. Reciprocal changes in sleep. *Psychophysiology, 41,* 298–305.

Foulkes, D. (1962). Dream reports from different stages of sleep. *Journal of Abnormal and Social Psychology, 65,* 14–25.

Fox, A. (2011). The origins of drunkenness. In A. Fox, & M. MacAvoy (Eds.), *Expressions of drunkenness (four hundred rabbits)* (pp. 53–119). New York. Routledge/Taylor & Francis Group.

Fox, A., & MacAvoy, M. (Eds). (2011). *Expressions of drunkenness (four hundred rabbits).* New York. Routledge/Taylor & Francis Group.

Freedman, N. D., Park, Y., Abnet, C. C., Hollenbeck, A. R., & Sinha, R. (2012). Association of coffee drinking with total and cause-specific mortality. *New England Journal of Medicine, 366,* 1891–1904.

Friedan, T. R., & Blakeman, D. E. (2005). The dirty dozen. 12 myths that undermine tobacco control. *American Journal of Public Health, 95,* 1500–1506.

Gable, R. S. (2004a). Acute toxic effects of club drugs. *Journal of Psychoactive Drugs, 36(1),* 303–313.

Gable, R. S. (2004b). Comparison of acute lethal toxicity of commonly abused psychoactive substances. *Addiction, 99,* 686–696.

Gable, R. S. (2006). Acute toxicity of drugs versus regulatory status. In J. M. Fish (Ed.), *Drugs and society. U. S. Public Policy* (pp. 149–162). Lanham, MD. Rowman & Littlefield.

Gais, S., Lucas, B., & Bom, J. (2006). Sleep after learning aids memory recall. *Learning & Memory, 13,* 259–262.

Gallop Poll. (July 30, 2010). U. S. drinking rate edges up slightly to 25-year high. Retrieved from www.gallup.com on March 16, 2011.

Gami, A. S., Howard, D. E., Olson, E. J., & Somers, V. K. (2005). Day-night pattern of sudden death in obstructive sleep apnea. *New England Journal of Medicine, 352,* 1206–1214.

Gandhi, B., & Oakley, D. A. (2005). Does "hypnosis" by any other name smell as sweet? The efficacy of "hypnotic" inductions depends on the label "hypnosis." *Consciousness and Cognition, 14,* 304–315.

Gilestro, G. F., Tononi, G., & Cirelli, C. (2009). Widespread changes in synaptic markers as a function of sleep and wakefulness in *drosphila. Science, 324,* 109–112.

Gilpin, E. A., White, M. M., Messer, K., & Pierce, J. P. (2007). Receptivity to tobacco advertising and promotions among young adolescents as a predictor of established smoking in young adulthood. *American Journal of Public Health, 97,* 1489–1495.

Gorman, D. M., & Derzon, J. H. (2002). Behavioral traits and marijuana use and abuse. A meta-analysis of longitudinal studies. *Addictive Behaviors, 27,* 193–206.

Gottlieb, D. J., Punjabi, N. M., Newman, A. B., Resnick, H. E., et al.. (2005). Association of sleep time with diabetes mellitus and impaired glucose tolerance. *Archives of Internal Medicine, 165,* 863–868.

Gould, K. S., Hirvonen, K., Koefoed, V. F., Røed, B. K., Sallinen, M., et al. (2009). Effects of 60 hours of total sleep deprivation on two methods of high-speed ship navigation. *Ergonomics, 52,* 1469–1486.

Gouzoulis-Mayfrank, E., & Daumann, J. (2006). Neurotoxicity of methylenedioxyamphetamines (MDMA; ecstasy) in humans. How strong is the evidence for persistent brain damage? *Addiction, 101,* 348–361.

Grant, I., Gonzalez, R., Carey, C. L., Natarajan, L., & Wolfson, T. (2003). Non-acute (residual) neurocognitive effects of cannabis use. A meta-analytic study. *Journal of the International Neuropsychological Society, 9,* 679–689.

Griffiths, R. R., Richards, W. A., Johnson, M., McCann, U., & Jesse, U. (2008). Mystical-type experiences occasioned by psilocybin mediate the attribution of personal meaning and spiritual significance 14 months later. *Journal of Psychopharmacology, 22,* 621–632.

Griffiths, R. R., Richards, W. A., McCann, U. D., & Jesse, R. (2006). Psilocybin can occasion mystical-type experiences having substantial and sustained personal meaning and spiritual significance. *Psychopharmacology, 187,* 268–283.

Grinspoon, L., & Bakalar, J. B. (1995). Marihuana as medicine. A plea for reconsideration. *JAMA, 273,* 1875–1876.

Gunaratana, H. (1991). *Mindfulness in plain English.* Boston. Wisdom Publications.

Gupta, B. D., Jani, C. B., & Shah, P. H. (2001). Fatal "bhang" poisoning. *Medicine, Science, and Law, 41,* 349–352.

Hall, C. S., & Van de Castle, R. (1966). *The content analysis of dreams.* New York. Appleton-Century-Crofts.

Hallmayer, J., Faraco, J., Lin, L., Hesselson, S., Winkelmann, J., et al. (2009). Narcolepsy is strongly associated with the T-cell receptor alpha locus. *Nature Genetics, 41,* 708–711.

Harrison, Y., & Horne, J. A. (2000). The impact of sleep deprivation on decision making. A review. *Journal of Experimental Psychology. Applied, 6,* 236–249.

Hartmann, E. (2000). The waking-to-dreaming continuum and the effects of emotion. *Behavioral and Brain Sciences, 23,* 947–950.

Harvey, A. G. (2008). Insomnia, psychiatric disorders, and the transdiagnostic perspective. *Current Directions in Psychological Science, 17,* 299–303.

Hashibe, M., Morgenstern, H., Cui, Y., Tashkin, D. P., Zhang, Z-F., et al. (2006). Marijuana use and the risk of lung and upper aerodigestive tract cancers. Results of a population-based case-control study. *Cancer Epidemiological Biomarkers Preview, 15.* Retrieved from http://cebp .aacrjournals.org/content/15/10/1829 .long on June 24, 2010.

Heath, D. B. (1995). An anthropological view of alcohol and culture in international perspective. In D. B. Heath (Ed.), *International handbook on alcohol and culture* (pp. 328–347). Westport, CT. Greenwood Press.

Heatherton, T. E., & Sargent, J. D. (2009). Does watching smoking in movies promote teenage smoking? *Current Directions in Psychological Science, 18,* 63–67.

Hedges, D. W., Woon, F. L., & Hoopes, S. P. (2009). Caffeine-induced psychosis. *CNS Spectrums, 14,* 127–129.

Heishman, S. J., Kozlowski, L. T., & Henningfield, J. E. (1997). Nicotine addiction. Implications for public health policy. *Journal of Social Issues, 53,* 13–33.

Henry, J. A., Oldfield, W. L. G., & Kon, O. M. (2003). Comparing cannabis with tobacco. *British Medical Journal, 326,* 942–943.

Herxheimer, A., & Waterhouse, J. (2003). The prevention and treatment of jet lag. *British Medical Journal, 326,* 296–297.

Hicks, R. A., Fernandez, C., & Pellegrini, R. J. (2001). The changing sleep habits of university students. An update. *Perceptual and Motor Skills, 93,* 648.

Hilgard, E. R. (1986). *Divided consciousness. Multiple controls in human thought and action.* New York. Wiley.

Hobson, J. A. (2002). *Dreaming. An introduction to the science of sleep.* New York. Oxford University Press.

Hobson, J. A., Pace-Schott, E. F., & Stickgold, R. (2000). Dreaming and the brain. Toward a cognitive neuroscience of conscious states. *Behavioral and Brain Sciences, 23,* 793–1121.

Hoffman, A. (1970). The discovery of LSD and subsequent investigations of naturally occurring hallucinogens. In F. J. Ayd, Jr., & B. Blackwell (Eds.), *Discoveries in biological psychiatry* (pp.

91–106). New York. J. B. Lippincott. Excerpt retrieved from http://www.psychedelic-library.org/hofmann.htm on September 9, 2006.

Hu, P., Stylos-Allan, M., & Walker, M. P. (2006). Sleep facilitates consolidation of emotional declarative memory. *Psychological Science, 17,* 891–898.

Hulme, O., Friston, K. F., & Zeki, S. (2009). Neural correlates of stimulus reportability. *Journal of Cognitive Neuroscience, 21,* 1602–1610.

Infante, M., & Benca, R. (2005). Treatment of insomnia. *Primary Psychiatry, 12,* 47–56.

Iranzo, A., Santamaria, J., & Tolosa, E. (2009). The clinical and pathophysiological relevance of REM sleep behavior disorder in neurodegenerative diseases. *Sleep Medicine Review, 13,* 385–401.

Iverson, L. (2003). Comparing cannabis with tobacco. Arithmetic does not add up. *British Medical Journal, 327,* 165.

Johanson, C., Roehrs, T., Schuh, K. & Warbasse, L. (1999). The effects of cocaine on mood and sleep in cocaine dependent males. *Experimental and Clinical Psychopharmacology, 7,* 1–9.

Johnston, L. D., O'Malley, P. M., Bachman, J. G., & Schulenberg, J. E. (2012). *Monitoring the future national results on adolescent drug use. Overview of key findings, 2011.* Ann Arbor. Institute for Social Research, The University of Michigan. Retrieved from www.monitoringthefuture.org on February 3, 2012.

Juliano, L. M., & Griffiths, R. R. (2004). A critical review of caffeine withdrawal. Empirical validation of symptoms and signs, incidence, severity, and associated features. *Psychopharmacology, 176(1),* 1–29.

Kakigi, R., Nakata, H., Inui, K., Hiroe, N., Nagata, O., et al. (2005). Intracerebral pain processing in a yoga master who claims not to feel pain during meditation. *European Journal of Pain, 9,* 581–589.

Karch, W., Stephens, B. C., & Nazareno, G. V. (2001). GHB. Club drug or confusing artifact? *American Journal of Forensic Medicine and Pathology, 22,* 266–269.

Kihlstrom, J. F. (1998). Dissociations and dissociation theory in hypnosis. Comment on Kirsch and Lynn (1998). *Psychological Bulletin, 123,* 186–191.

Kihlstrom, J. F. (2005). Is hypnosis an altered state of consciousness or *what?* Comment. *Contermporary Hypnosis, 22,* 34–38.

Kihlstrom, J. F. (2008). The domain of hypnosis, revisited. In M. R. Nash & A. J. Barnier (Eds.), *The Oxford handbook of hypnosis. Theory, research, and practice* (pp. 21–52). New York. Oxford University Press.

Killgore, W. D., Killgore, D. B., Day, L. M., Li, C., Kamimori, G. H., et al. (2007). The effects of 53 hours sleep deprivation on moral judgment. *Sleep, 30,* 345–352.

King, L. A., & Corkery, J. M. (2010). An index of fatal toxicity for drugs of misuse. *Human Psychopharmacology, 25,* 162–166.

Kirsch, I. (2005). Empirical resolution of the altered state debate. *Contemporary Hypnosis, 22,* 18–23.

Kirsch, I., & Lynn, S. J. (1995). The altered state of hypnosis. Changes in the theoretical landscape. *American Psychologist, 50,* 846–858.

Kirsch, I., Mazzoni, G., & Montgomery, G. H. (2007). Remembrance of hypnosis past. *American Journal of Clinical Hypnosis, 49,* 171–178.

Kubik, A., Zatloukal, P., Dolezal, J., Syllabova, L., Kara, J., et al. (2008). A case-control study of lifestyle and lung cancer associations by histological types. *Neoplasma, 55,* 192–199.

Kugelberb, F. C., Holmgren, A., Eklund, A., & Jones, A. W. (2010). Forensic toxicology findings in deaths involving gamma-hydroxybutyrate. *International Journal of Legal Medicine, 124,* 1–6.

Kyle, S. D., Espie, C. A., & Morgan, K. (2010). ". . . Not just a minor thing, it is something major, which stops you from functioning daily." Quality of life and daytime functioning in insomnia. *Behavioral Sleep Medicine, 8,* 123–140.

LaBerge, S., DeGracia, D. J., Kunzendorf, R. G., & Wallace, B. (2000). Varieties of lucid dreaming experience. In, S. LaBerge, D. J. DeGracia, R. G. Kunzendorf, & B. Wallace (Eds.), *Individual differences in conscious experience* (pp. 269–307). Amsterdam. John Benjamins.

Lauderdale, D. S., Knutson, K. L., Yan, L. L., Rathouz, P. J., Hulley, S. B., et al. (2006). Objectively measured sleep characteristics among early-middle-aged adults. *American Journal of Epidemiology, 164(1),* 5–16.

Lavie, P. (2001). Sleep-wake as a biological rhythm. *Annual Review of Psychology, 52,* 277–303.

Lazar, S. W., Kerr, C. E., Wasserman, R. H., Gray, J. R., Greve, D. N., et al. (2005). Meditation experience is associated with increased cortical thickness. *Neuroreport, 28,* 1893–1897.

Lee, W. M. (2004). Acetaminophen and the U. S. Acute Liver Failure Study Group. Lowering the risks of hepatic failure. *Hapatology, 41,* 6–9.

Leproult, R., & Van Cauter, E. (2010). Role of sleep and sleep loss in hormonal release and metabolism. *Endocrine Development, 17,* 11–21.

Lim, J., & Dinges, D. F. (2010). A meta-analysis of the impact of short-term sleep deprivation on cognitive variables. *Psychological Bulletin, 136,* 375–389.

Luders, E., Toga, A. W., Lepore, N., & Gaser, C. (2009). The underlying anatomical correlates of long-term meditation. *NeuroImage, 45,* 672–678.

Lynn, S. J., & Kirsch, I. (2006). *Essentials of clinical hypnosis. An evidence-based approach.* Washington, DC. American Psychological Association.

Lynn, S. J., Lock, T., Loftus, E. F., Krackow, E., & Lilienfeld, S. O. (2003). The remembrance of things past. Problematic memory recovery techniques in psychotherapy. In S. O Lilienfeld, S. J. Lynn, & J. M. Lohr (Eds.), *Science and pseudoscience in clinical psychology* (pp. 205–293). New York. The Guilford Press.

Lynn, S. J., Vanderhoff, H., Shindler, K., & Stafford, J. (2002). Defining hypnosis as a trance vs. cooperation. Hypnotic inductions, suggestibility, and performance standards. *American Journal of Clinical Hypnosis, 44,* 231–240.

MacAndrew, C., & Edgerton, R. B. (1969). *Drunken comportment. A social explanation.* Chicago. Aldine.

Macleod, J., Oakes, R., Copello, A., Crome, I., Egger, M., et al. (2004). Psychological and social sequelae of cannabis and other illicit drug use by young people; A systematic review of longitudinal general population studies. *The Lancet, 363,* 1579–1588.

Males, M. (1996). *The scapegoat generation.* Monroe, ME. Common Courage Press.

Manber, R. (2000). Night terrors. In A. E. Kazdin (Ed.), *Encyclopedia of psychology* (Vol. 5, pp. 444–446). Washington, DC. American Psychological Association.

Manna, A., Raffone, A., Perrucci, M. G., Nardo, D., Ferretti, A., Tartaro, A., et al. (2010). Neural correlates of focused attention and cognitive monitoring in meditation. *Brain Research Bulletin, 82,* 46–56.

Marano, H. E. (2003, November/December). Sleep or suffer. *Psychology today.* Retrieved from http://www.psychologytoday.com on January 15, 2006.

Marchalant, Y., Brothers, H. M., & Wenk, G. L. (2008). Inflammation and aging. Can endocannabinoids help? *Biomedicine and Pharmacotherapy, 62,* 212–217.

Marin, J. M. Carrizo, S. J., Vicente, E., & Agusti, A. G. (2005). Long-term cardiovascular outcomes in men with obstructive sleep apnoea-hypopnea with or without treatment with continuous positive airway pressure. An observational study. *Lancet, 365,* 1046–1053.

Mazzoni, G., Heap, M., & Scoboria, A. (2010). Hypnosis and memory. Theory, laboratory research, and applications. In S. J. Lynn, J. W. Rhue, & I. Kirsch (Eds.), *Handbook of clinical hypnosis* (2nd ed., pp. 709–741). Washington, DC. American Psychological Association.

McCarley, R. W. (2007). Neurobiology of REM and NREM sleep. *Sleep Medicine, 8,* 302–330.

McCook, A. (2005). Renewed faith in ecstasy. *The Scientist, 19.* Retrieved from http://www.the-scientist.com/2005/2/28/13/1/ on January 30, 2006.

Merskey, H. (2004). Opium. The best remedy. *Pain Research and Management, 9,* 12.

Mokdad, A. H., Marks, J. S., Stroup, D. F., & Gerberding, J. L. (2004). Actual causes of death in the United States, 2000. *JAMA, 291,* 1238–1244.

Morgan, M. J. (2000). Ecstasy (MDMA). A review of its possible persistent psychological effects. *Psychopharmacology, 152,* 230–248.

Morgan, M. J. (2002). Throwing out the baby with the bathwater? *The Psychologist, 15,* 468–469.

Morton, J. (2005). Ecstasy. Pharmacology and neurotoxicity. *Current Opinion in Pharmacology, 5(1),* 79–86.

Mullins, M. E. (1999). Laboratory confirmation of flunitrazepam in alleged cases of date rape. *Emergency Medicine, 6,* 966–968.

Nagel, T. (1974). What is it like to be a bat? *Philosophical Review, 83,* 435–450.

National Sleep Foundation. (2005). *2005 Sleep in America Poll.* Retrieved from www.sleepfoundation.org on January 9, 2006.

National Sleep Foundation. (2010). *2010 Sleep in America Poll.* Retrieved from www.sleepfoundation.org on March 15, 2011.

National Sleep Foundation. (2011). *2011 Sleep in America Poll.* Retrieved from www.sleepfoundation.org on March 15, 2011.

Neame, A. (2003, November). Beyond "drink spiking". Drug and alcohol-facilitated sexual assault. *Briefing. Australian Center for the Study of Sexual Assault, 2.* Retrieved from http://www.aifs .gov.au/acssa/pubs/briefing/b2.html on February 3, 2006.

Neubert, D. (1999). Risk assessment and preventative hazard minimization. In H. Marquardt, S. G. Schafer, R. McClellan, & F. Welsch (Eds.), *Toxicology* (pp. 1153–1186). San Diego, CA. Academic Press.

Nickles, C., Brecht, D. Klinger, E., & Bursell, A. (1998). The effects of current concern- and nonconcern-related waking suggestions and nocturnal dream content. *Journal of Personality and Social Psychology, 75,* 242–255.

Nielsen, T. A. (2000). A review of mentation in REM and NREM sleep. "Covert" REM sleep as a possible reconciliation of two opposing models. *Behavioral and Brain Sciences, 23,* 793–1121.

Nielsen, T. A., Zadra, A. L., Simard, V., Saucier, S. & Stenstrom, P. (2003). The typical dreams of Canadian university students. *Dreaming, 13,* 211–235.

NORML. (2013). States that have decriminalized. Retrieved from http://norml.org on February 11, 2013.

Nutt, D., King, L. A., Saulsbury, W., & Blakemore, C. (2007). Development of a rational scale to assess the harm of drugs of potential misuse. *Lancet, 369,* 1047–1053.

Oexman, R. D., T. L., Knotts, & Koch, J. (2002). Working while the world sleeps. A consideration of sleep and shift work design. *Employee Responsibilities & Rights Journal, 14,* 145–157.

Ogilvie, R. D. (2001). The process of falling asleep. *Physiological Review, 5,* 247–270.

Ohayon, M. M., Priest, R. G., Caulet, M., & Guilleminault, C. (1996). Hypnagogic and hypnopompic hallucinations. Pathological phenomena? *The British Journal of Psychiatry, 169,* 459–467.

Ohayon, M. M. (2002). Epidemiology of insomnia. What we know and what we still need to learn. *Sleep Medicine Review, 6,* 97–111.

Oudiette, D., Leu, S., Pottier, M., Buzare, M-A, Brion, A., et al. (2009). Dreamlike mentations during sleepwalking and sleep terrors in adults. *Sleep. Journal of Sleep and Sleep Disorders Research, 32,* 1621–1627.

Pack, A. I. (2006). Advances in sleep-disordered breathing. *American Journal of Respiratory and Critical Care Medicine, 173,* 7–15.

Parrot, A. (2002). Very real, very damaging. *The Psychologist, 15,* 472–473.

Parrott, A. C. (1999). Does cigarette smoking *cause* stress? *American Psychologist, 54,* 817–820.

Patterson, D. R. (2004). Treating pain with hypnosis. *Current Directions in Psychological Science, 13,* 252–260.

Payne, J. D., Stickgold, R., Swanberg, K., & Kensinger, E. A. (2008). Sleep preferentially enhances memory for emotional components of scenes. *Psychological Science, 19,* 781–788.

Peele, S., & Grant, M. (Eds.). (1999). *Alcohol and pleasure.* Philadelphia. Brunner/Mazel.

Perron, B. E., Bohnert, A. S. B., Monsell, S. E., Vaughn, M. G., Epperson, M., & Howard, M. O. (2011). Patterns and correlates of drug-related ED visits. Results from a national survey. *American Journal of Emergency Medicine, 29,* 704–710.

Pierce, J. P. (2007). Tobacco industry marketing, population-based tobacco control, and smoking behavior. *American Journal of Preventative Medicine, 33(Suppl. 6),* 327–334.

Pletcher, M. J., Vittinghoff, E., Kalhan, R., Ruchman, J., Safford, M., et al. (2011). Association between marijuana exposure and pulmonary function over 20 years. *JAMA, 307,* 173–181.

Rácsmany, M., Conway, M. A., & Demeter, G. (2010). Consolidation of episodic memories during sleep. Long-term effects of retrieval practice. *Psychological Science, 21,* 80–85.

Ram, S., Seirawan, H., Kumar S. K., Clark, G. T. (2010). Prevalence and impact of sleep disorders and sleep habits in the United States. *Sleep and Breathing, 14,* 63–70.

Randall, S., Roehrs, T. A., & Roth, T. (2008). Over-the-counter sleep aid medications and incominia. *Primary Psychiatry, 15,* 52–58.

Rasch, B., & Born, J. (2008). Reactivation and consolidation of memory during sleep. *Current Directions in Psychological Science, 17,* 188–192.

Rechtschaffen, A. (1998). Current perspectives on the function of sleep. *Perspectives in Biology and Medicine, 41,* 359–390.

Reissig, C. J., Strain, E. C., & Griffiths, R. R. (2009). Caffeinated energy drinks—A growing problem. *Drug and Alcohol Dependence, 99,* 1–10. Retrieved from www.elsevier.com on October 27, 2008.

Reneman, L. (2003). Designer drugs. How dangerous are they? *Journal of Neural Transmission, 66 (Suppl.),* 61–83.

Richert, A. C., & Baran, A. S. (2003). A review of common sleep disorders. *CNS Spectrums, 8,* 102–109.

Riggs, A. T., Dysken, M., Kim, S. W., & Opsahl, J. M. (1991). A review of disorders of water homeostatis in psychiatric patients. *Psychosomatics, 32,* 133–146.

Room, R. (2001). Intoxication and bad behaviour. Understanding cultural differences in the link. *Social Science & Medicine, 53,* 189–198.

Rosenbaum, M. (2002). Ecstasy. America's new *Reefer Madness. Journal of Psychoactive Drugs, 34(1),* 1–9.

Roset, P. N., Farre, M., de la Torre, R., Mas, M., Menoyo, E., et al. (2001). Modulation of rate of onset and intensity of drug effects reduces abuse potential in healthy males. *Drug and Alcohol Dependence, 64,* 285–298.

Russo, M. B., Kendall, A. P., Johnson, D. E., Sing, H. C., Thorne, D. R., et al. (2005). Visual perception, psychomotor performance, and complex motor performance during an overnight air refueling simulated flight. *Aviation, Space, and Environmental Medicine, 76(Suppl. 1),* C92–C103.

Sargent, J. D., Stoolmiller, M., Worth, K. A., Dal Cin, S., Wills, T. A., et al. (2007). Exposure to smoking depictions in movies. Its association with established adolescent smoking. *Archives of Pediatric and Adolescent Medicine, 161,* 849–856.

Saxvig, I. W., Lundervold, A. L., Gronli, J., Ursin, R., Bjorvatn, B., et al. (2008). The effect of a REM sleep deprivation procedure on different aspects of memory function in humans. *Psychophysiology, 45,* 309–317.

Schenck, C. H., & Mahowald, M. W. (2005). Rapid eye movement and non-REM parasomnias. *Primary Psychiatry, 12,* 67–74.

Schenck, C. H., & Mahowald, M. W. (2010). Therapeutics for parasomnias in adults. *Sleep Medicine Clinics, 5,* 689–700.

Schenkein, J., & Montagna, P. (2006). Self-management of fatal familial insomnia. Part I. What is FFI? *Medscape General Medicine, 8.* Retrieved from www.pubmedcentral.nih.gov on October 27, 2008.

Science Daily (2009, December 20). Cannabis damages young brains more than originally thought, study finds. Retrieved from http://www.sciencedaily. com/releases/2009/12/091217115834. htm on January 14, 2009.

Scott-Ham, M., & Burton, F. C. (2005). Toxicological findings in cases of alleged drug-facilitated sexual assault in the United Kingdom over a 3-year period. *Journal of Clinical Forensic Medicine, 12,* 175–186.

Searle, J. R. (1997). *The mystery of consciousness.* New York. New York Review of Books.

Searle, J. R. (2000). Consciousness. *Annual Review of Neuroscience, 23,* 557–578.

Schep, L. J., Slaughter, R. J., Vale, J. A., Beasley, M. G., & Gee, P. (2011). The clinical toxicology of the designer "part pills" benzylpiperazine and trifluoromethylphenylpiperazine. *Clinical Toxicology, 49,* 131–141.

Sheehan, P. W., & Perry, C. W. (1976). *Methodologies of hypnosis.* Hillsdale, NJ. Lawrence Erlbaum Associates.

Shepherd, G. M. (1988). *Neurobiology* (2nd ed.). New York. Oxford University Press.

Sidney, S. (2003). Comparing cannabis with tobacco—again. *British Medical Journal, 327,* 635–636.

Siegel, R. (2005). *Intoxication. The universal drive for mind-altering substances.* Rochester, VT. Park Street Press.

Singh, G. (2000). Gazstrointestinal complications of prescription and over-the-counter nonsteroidal anti-inflammatory drugs. A view from the ARAMIS database. *American Journal of Therapeutics, 7,* 115–121.

Slaughter, L. (2000). Involvement of drugs in sexual assault. *Journal of Reproductive Medicine, 45,* 425–430.

Sleep. Spring cleaning for the brain? (2009, April 11). *Science Daily.* Retrieved from www.sciencedaily.com on May 19, 2009.

Social Issues Research Centre (SIRC). (2006). Culture, chemistry, and consequences. Retrieved from http://www.sirc.org/publik/drinking4.html on December 4, 2006.

Solms, M. (2000). Dreaming and REM sleep are controlled by different brain mechanisms. *Behavioral and Brain Sciences, 23,* 793–1121.

Spanos, N. P. (1991). A sociocognitive approach to hypnosis. In S. J. Lynn & J. W. Rhue (Eds.), *Theories of hypnosis. Current models and perspectives* (pp. 324–363). New York. Guilford Press.

Spanos, N. P. (1996). Hypnosis. Mythology versus reality. In *Multiple identities and false memories. A sociocognitive perspective* (pp. 17–28). Washington, DC. American Psychological Association.

Spanos, N. P., & Chaves, J. F. (1989). *Hypnosis. The cognitive-behavioral perspective.* Buffalo, NY. Prometheus.

Spiegel, K., Leproult, R., & Van Cauter, E. (1999). Impact of sleep debt on metabolic and endocrine function. *The Lancet, 354,* 1435–1439.

Spiegel, D. (1994). Hynosis. In R. E. Hales, S. C. Yudofshy, & J. A. Talbott (Eds.), *The American Psychiatric Press textbook of psychiatry* (2nd ed., pp. 1115–1142). Washington, DC. American Psychiatric Association.

Spiegel, D. (2010). Hypnosis in the treatment of posttraumatic stress disorders.

In S. J. Lynn, J. W. Rhue, & I. Kirsch (Eds.), *Handbook of clinical hypnosis* (2nd ed., pp. 415–432). Washington, DC. American Psychological Association.

Squier, L. H., & Domhoff, G. W. (1998). The presentation of dreaming and dreams in introductory psychology textbooks. A critical examination with suggestions for textbook authors and course instructors. *Dreaming, 8,* 149–168.

Szelenberger, W., Niemcewicz, S., & Dabrowska, A. J. (2005). Sleepwalking and night terrors. Psychopathological and psychophysiological correlates. *International Review of Psychiatry, 17,* 263–270.

Takeuchi, T., Miyasita, A., Inugami, M., & Yamamoto, Y. (2001). Intrinsic dreams are not produced without REM sleep mechanisms. Evidence through elicitation of sleep onset REM periods. *Journal of Sleep Research, 10,* 43–52.

Tan, W. C., Lo, C., Jong, A., Xing, L., Fitzgerald, M. J., et al. (2009). Marijuana and chronic obstructive lung disease. A population-based study. *CMAJ, 180,* 814–820.

Tanner-Smith, E. E. (2006). Pharmacological content of tablets sold as "ecstasy." Results from an online testing service. *Drug and Alcohol Dependence, 83,* 247–254.

Tarone, R. E., Blot, W. J., & McLaughlin, J. K. (2004). Nonselective nonaspirin nonsteroidal anti-inflammatory drugs and gastrointestinal bleeding. Relative and absolute risk estimates from recent epidemiologic studies. *American Journal of Therapy, 11,* 17–25.

Tart, C. T. (1972). States of consciousness and state-specific sciences. *Science, 176,* 1203–1210.

U. S. National Commission on Marihuana and Drug Abuse. (1972). *Marihuana. A signal of misunderstanding.* Retrieved from http://www.druglibrary.org/schaffer/Library/studies/nc/ncmenu.htm on February 4, 2006.

United Nations Office on Drugs and Crime. (2004). *United Nations world drug report, 2004.* Retrieved from http://www.unodc.org/unodc/world_drug_report.html on April 14, 2006.

United Nations Office on Drugs and Crime. (2010). *United Nations world drug report, 2010. Executive Summary.* Retrieved from http://www.unodc.org/unodc/en/data-and-analysis/WDR-2010.html on March 12, 2010.

Valli, K., Revonsuo, A., Palkas, O., Ismail, K. H., Ali, K. J., et al. (2005). The threat simulation theory of the evolutionary function of dreaming. Evidence from the dreams of traumatized children. *Consciousness and Cognition, 14,* 188–218.

Valli, K., Strandholm, T., Sillanmaiki, L., & Revonsuo, A. (2008). Dreams are more negative than real life. Implications for the function of dreaming. *Cognition and Emotion, 22,* 833–861.

van Duinen, H., Lorist, M. M., & Zijdewind, I. (2005). The effect of

caffeine on cognitive task performance and motor fatigue. *Psychopharmacology, 180,* 539–547.

Vineis, P., Alavanja, M., Buffler, P., Fontham, E., Franceschi, S., et al. (2004). Tobacco and cancer. Recent epidemiological evidence. *Journal of the National Cancer Institute, 96,* 99–106.

Vogel, G. W. (2000). Critique of current dream theories. *Behavioral and Brain Sciences, 23,* 1014–1016.

Voss, U., Holzmann, R., Tuin, I., & Hobson, A. J. (2009). Lucid dreaming. A state of consciousness with features of both waking and non-lucid dreaming. *Sleep. Journal of Sleep and Sleep Disorders Research, 32,* 1191–1200.

Vyazovskiy V. V., Cirelli, C., Pfister-Genskow, M., Faraguna, U., & Tononi, G. (2008). Molecular and electrophysiological evidence for net synaptic potentiation in wake and depression in sleep. *Nature Neuroscience, 11,* 200–208.

Wagner, F. A., & Anthony, J. C. (2002). From first drug use to drug dependence; developmental periods of risk for dependence upon marijuana, cocaine, and alcohol. *Neuropsychopharmacology, 26,* 479–488.

Wagstaff, G. (1994). Hypnosis. In A. M. Colman (Ed.), *Companion encyclopedia of psychology* (Vol. 2, pp. 991–1006). London. Routledge.

Wagstaff, G. F. (1999). Hypnosis and forensic psychology. In I. Kirsch, A. Capafons, & E. Cardeña-Buelna (Eds.). *Clinical hypnosis and self-regulation. Cognitive-behavioral perspectives* (pp. 277–308). Washington, DC. American Psychological Association.

Wagstaff, G. F., David, D., Kirsch, I., & Lynn, S. J. (2010). The cognitive-behavioral model of hypnotherapy. In S. J. Lynn, J. W. Rhue, & I. Kirsch (Eds.), *Handbook of clinical hypnosis* (2nd ed., pp. 179–208). Washington, DC. American Psychological Association.

Walker, M. P., & Stickgold, R. (2006). Sleep, memory, and plasticity. *Annual Review of Psychology, 57,* 139–166.

Walton, S. (2002). *Out of it. A cultural history of intoxication.* New York. Harmony.

Warner-Smith, M., Darke, S, Lynskey, M., & Hall, W. (2001). Heroin overdose. Causes and consequences. *Addiction, 96,* 1113–1125.

Watson C. P., Watt-Watson J. H., & Chipman, M. L. (2004). Chronic non-cancer pain and the long term utility of opioids. *Pain Research & Management, 9,* 19–24.

Weaver, D. R. (1998). The suprachiasmatic nucleus. A 25-year retrospective. *Journal of Biological Rhythms, 13,* 100–112.

Webb, W. B., & Agnew, H. W. (1975). Are we chronically sleep deprived? *Bulletin of the Psychochronic Society, 6,* 47–48.

Weddington,W., Brown, B., Haertzen, C., Cone, E., Dax, E., et al. (1990). Changes in mood, craving, and sleep during short-term abstinence reported by male cocaine addicts. a controlled, residential study. *Archives of General Psychiatry, 47,* 861–868.

Wilkins, M. R., and the Working Party on Cannabis and Cannabis-Based Medicines. (2006). Cannabis and cannabis-based medicines. Potential benefits and risks to health. *Clinical Medicine, 6,* 16–18.

Williams, M. J., Sutherland, W. H., Whelan, A. P., McCormick, M. P., & de Jong, S. A.et al. (2004). Acute effect of drinking red and white wines on circulating levels of inflammation-sensitive molecules in coronary artery disease. *Metabolism, 53,* 318–323.

Williams, M., Teasdale, J., Segal, Z., & Kabat-Zinn, J. (2007). *The mindful way through depression.* New York. Guilford Press.

Wolfe, M. M., Lichtenstein, D. R., & Singh, G. (1999). Gastrointestinal toxicity of nonsteroidal anti-inflammatory drugs. *New England Journal of Medicine, 341,* 1888–1899.

Wood, D. M., Stribley, V., Dargan, P. I., Davies, S., Holt, D. W., et al. (in press). Variability in the 3, 4-methylenedioxymethamphetamine content of "ecstasy" tablets in the U.K. *Emergency Medical Journal, 28,* 764–765.

World Health Organization (2003). *WHO world health report.* Retrieved from http://www.who.int/whr/2003/en/whr03_en.pdf on April 21, 2008.

World Health Organization (2004). Public health problems caused by harmful use of alcohol. Retrieved from http://www.who.int/gb/ebwha/pdf_files on February 1, 2006.

World Health Organization (2005). Why is tobacco a public health priority? Retrieved from http://www.who.int/tobacco/en/ on February 3, 2006.

World Health Organization (2008). *WHO report on the global tobacco epidemic, 2008. The MPOWER package.* Retrieved from http://www.who.int/tobacco/mpower/mpower_report_forward_summary_2008.pdf on March 12, 2010.

Wright, K. P., Jr., Gronfier, C., Duffy, J. F., & Czeisler, C. A. (2005). Intrinsic period and light intensity determine the phase relationship between melatonin and sleep in humans. *Journal of Biological Rhythms, 20,* 168–177.

Yang, C-M, Han, H-Y, Yang, M-H, Su, W-C., & Lane, T. (2010). What subjective experiences determine the perception of falling asleep during sleep onset period? *Consciousness and Cognition, 19,* 1084–1092.

Zeki, S. (2007). A theory of microconsciousness. In M. Velmans, & S. Scheider (Eds.), *The Blackwell companion to consciousness* (pp. 580–588). Malden, MA. Blackwell Publishing.

Zepelin, H., Siegel, J. M., & Tobler, I. (2005). Mammalian sleep. In M. H. Kryger, T. Roth, & W. C. Dement (Eds.), *Principles and practice of sleep medicine* (pp. 91–100). Philadelphia. Elsevier/Saunders.

Zuberi, S. M. (2010). Narcolepsy in childhood. *Journal of Pediatric Neurology, 8,* 79–80.

CHAPTER 7

American Academy of Pediatrics. (2001). Media violence. *Pediatrics, 108,* 1222–1226.

Anderson, C. A., & Bushman, B. J. (2002). Human aggression. *Annual Review of Psychology, 53,* 27–51.

Anderson, C. A., Berkowitz, L., Donnerstein, E., Huesmann, L. R., Johnson, J. D., et al. (2003). The influence of media violence on youth. *Psychological Science in the Public Interest, 4,* 81–110.

Anderson, C. A., Shibuya, A., Ihori, N., Swing, E. L., Bushman, B.J., et al. (2010). Violent video game effects on aggression, empathy, and prosocial behavior in Eastern and Western countries. A meta-analytic review. *Psychological Bulletin, 136,* 151–173.

Anrep, G. V. (1920). Pitch discrimination in the dog. *Journal of Physiology 53,* 367–385.

Azrin, N. H., Holz, W. C., & Hake, D. F. (1963). Fixed-ratio punishment. *Journal of the Experimental Analysis of Behavior, 6,* 141–148.

Bandura, A. (1965). Influence of models' reinforcement contingencies on the acquisition of imitative behaviors. *Journal of Personality and Social Psychology, 1,* 589–595.

Bandura, A. (1977). *Social learning theory.* Englewood Cliffs, NJ. Prentice-Hall.

Bandura, A. (1986). *Social foundations of thought and action. A social cognitive theory.* Englewood Cliffs, NJ. Prentice-Hall.

Bandura, A., Ross, D., & Ross, S. A. (1961). Transmission of aggressions through imitation of aggressive models. *Journal of Abnormal and Social Psychology, 63,* 575–582.

Bandura, A., Ross, D., & Ross, S. A. (1963). Imitation of film-mediated aggressive models. *Journal of Abnormal and Social Psychology, 66,* 3–11.

Bennett, R. J. (1998). Taking the sting out of the whip. Reactions to consistent punishment for unethical behavior. *Journal of Experimental Psychology. Applied, 4,* 248–262.

Bloom, P. (2004). *Descaretes' baby.* New York. Basic Books.

Boe, E. E., & Church, R. M. (1967). Permanent effects of punishment during extinction. *Journal of Comparative and Physiological Psychology, 63,* 486–492.

Bolles, R. C. (1970). Species-specific defense reactions and avoidance learning. *Psychological Review, 77,* 32–48.

Bouton, M. E. (1991). Context and retrieval in extinction and in other examples of interference in simple associative learning. In L. Dachowski & F. Flaherty (Eds.), *Current topics in animal learning. Brain, emotion, and cognition* (pp. 25–53). Hillsdale, NJ. Lawrence Erlbaum Associates.

Bouton, M. E., & King, D. A. (1983). Contextual control of the extinction of conditioned fear. Tests for the associative value of the context. *Journal of Experimental Psychology. Animal Behavior Processes, 9,* 248–265.

Breland, K., & Breland, M. (1961). The misbehavior of organisms. *American Psychologist, 16,* 681–684.

Browne, K. D., & Hamilton-Giachritsis, C. (2005). The influence of violent media on children and adolescents. A public-health perspective. *The Lancet, 365,* 702–710.

Bushman, B. J., & Anderson, C. A. (2001). Media violence and the American Public. Scientific facts versus media misinformation. *American Psychologist, 477–489.*

Cataneo, L., & Rozzolatti, G. (2009). The mirror neuron system. *Archives of Neurology, 66,* 557–560.

Chan, W. Y. M., Leung, H. T., Westbrook, R. F., & McNally, G. P. (2010). Effects of recent exposure to a conditioned stimulus on extinction of Pavlovian conditioning. *Learning & Memory, 17,* 512–521.

Childress, A. R., Mozley, P. D., McElgin, W., Fitzgerald, J., Reivich, M., et al. (1999). Limbic activation during cue-induced cocaine craving. *American Journal of Psychiatry, 156*(1), 11–18.

Christensen, A., & Jacobson, N. S. (2000). *Reconcilable differences.* New York. Guilford.

Congressional Public Health Summit. (July 26, 2000). Joint statement on the impact of entertainment violence on children. Retrieved from http://www.aap.org/advocacy/releases/jstmtevc.htm on October 14, 2005.

Cornwell, D., & Hobbs, S. (1976, March 18). The strange saga of Little Albert. *New Society,* 602–604.

Dahl, G., & DellaVigna, S. (2008, January). Does movie violence increase violent crime? Presented at the annual meeting of the American Economic Association, New Orleans, LA. Pre-publication version retrieved from http://www.aeaweb.org/an nual_mtg_papers/2008/2008_124.pdf on November 14, 2008.

Dobbs, D. (2006). A revealing reflection. *Scientific American Mind, 17,* 22–27.

Domjan, M. (2002). *Principles of learning and behavior* (5th ed.). Belmont, CA. Wadsworth.

Domjan, M. (2005). Pavlovian conditioning. A functional perspective. *Annual Review of Psychology, 56,* 179–206.

Domjan, M., Cusato, B., & Krause, M. (2004). Learning with arbitrary versus ecological conditioned stimuli. Evidence from sexual conditioning. *Psychonomic Bulletin & Review, 11,* 232–246.

Ferguson, C. J. (2010). Media violence effects and violent crime. Good science or moral panic? In C. J. Ferguson (Ed.), *Violent crime. Clinical and social implications* (pp. 37–56). Thousand Oaks, CA. Sage Publications.

Ferguson, C. J., & Kilburn, J. (2010). Much ado about nothing. The misestimation and overinterpretation of violent video game effects in Eastern and Western countries. Comment on Anderson et al. (2010). *Psychological Bulletin, 136*, 174–178.

Ferguson, C. J., Rueda, S. M., Cruz, A. M., Ferguson, D. E., Fritz, S., et al. (2008). Violent video games and aggression. Causal relationship or byproduct of family violence and intrinsic violence motivation? *Criminal Justice and Behavior, 35*, 311–332.

Ferguson, C. J., San Miguel, C., & Hartley, R. D. (2009). A multivariate analysis of youth violence and aggression. The influence of family, peers, depression, and media violence. *The Journal of Pediatrics, 155*, 904–908.

Ferrari, P. F., Rozzi, S., & Fogassi, L. (2005). Mirror neurons responding to observation of actions made with tools in monkey ventral premotor cortex. *Journal of Cognitive Neuroscience, 17*, 212–226.

Ferrari, P. F., Visalberghi, E., Paukner, A., Fogassi, L., Ruggiero, A., et al. (2006). Neonatal imitation in rhesus macaques. *PLoS Biology, 9*. Retrieved from www.plosbiology.org on September 11, 2006.

Field, T. M., Woodson, R. W., Greenberg, R., & Cohen, C. (1982). Discrimination and imitation of facial expressions by neonates. *Science, 218*, 179–181.

Fogassi, L., Ferrari, P. F., Gesierich, B., Rozzi, S., Cherisi, F., et al. (2005). Parietal lobe. From action organization to intention understanding. *Science, 308*, 662–667.

Foree, D. D., & LoLordo, V. M. (1973). Attention in the pigeon. Differential effects of food-getting versus shock-avoidance procedures. *Journal of Comparative and Physiological Psychology, 85*, 551–558.

Freedman, J. L. (2002). *Media violence and its effects on aggression.* Toronto. University of Toronto Press.

Frieman, J. (2002). *Learning and adaptive behavior.* Belmont, CA. Wadsworth.

Gallese, V. (2005). "Being like me." Self-other identity, mirror neurons, and empathy. In S. Hurley & N. Chater (Eds.), *Perspectives on imitation. From neuroscience to social science. Vol 1. Mechanisms of imitation and imitation in animals* (pp. 101–118). Cambridge, MA. MIT Press.

Gallese, V., Gernsbacher, M. A., Heyes, C., Hickok, G., & Iacoboni, M. (2011). Mirror neuron forum. *Perspectives on Psychological Science, 6*, 369–407.

Gallistel, C. R. (2000) The replacement of general-purpose learning models with adaptively specialized learning modules. In M. S. Gazzaniga (Ed.), *The new cognitive neurosciences* (pp. 1179–1191). Cambridge, MA. MIT Press.

Garcia, J. (1981). Tilting at the paper mills of Academe. *American Psychologist, 36*, 149–158.

Garcia, J., Brett, L. P., & Rusiniak, K. W. (1989). Limits of Darwinian conditioning. In S. B. Klein & R. R. Mowrer (Eds.), *Contemporary learning theories. Instrumental conditioning theory and the impact of biological constraints on learning* (pp. 181–203). Hillsdale, NJ. Lawrence Erlbaum Associates.

Garcia, J., & Koelling, R. A. (1966) Relation of cue to consequence in avoidance learning. *Psychonomic Science, 4*, 123–124.

Gershoff, E. T. (2002). Corporal punishment by parents and associated child behaviors and experiences. A meta-analytic and theoretical review. *Psychological Bulletin, 4*, 539–579.

Harris, B. (1979). Whatever happened to Little Albert? *American Psychologist, 34*, 151–160.

Harris, B. (2011). Letting go of Little Albert. Disciplinary memory, history, and the uses of myth. *Journal of the History of the Behavioral Sciences, 47*, 1–17.

Harris, J. R. (1998). *The nurture assumption.* New York. The Free Press.

Harris, J. R. (2006). *No two alike. Human nature and human individuality.* New York. Norton.

Hiby, E. F., Rooney, N. J., & Bradshaw, J. W. S. (2004). Dog training methods. Their use, effectiveness, and interaction with behaviour and welfare. *Animal Welfare, 13*, 63–69.

Higgins, S. T., Silverman, K., & Heil, S. H. (Eds.). (2007). *Contingency management in substance abuse treatment.* New York. Guilford.

Hollis, K. L. (1997). Contemporary research on Pavolovian conditioning. A "new" functional analysis. *American Psychologist, 52*, 956–965.

Hollis, K. L., Pharr, V. L., Dumas, M. J., Britton, G. B., & Field, J. (1997). Classical conditioning provides paternity advantage for territorial male blue gouramis (*Trichogsater trichopterus*). *Journal of Comparative Psychology, 111*, 219–225.

Huesmann, L. R. (2007). The impact of electronic media violence. Scientific theory and research. *Journal of Adolescent Health, 41(Suppl.)*, S6–S13.

Huesmann, L. R., & Taylor, L. D. (2006). The role of media violence in violent behavior. *Annual Review of Public Health, 27*, 393–415.

Iascoboni, M. (2009). Imitation, empathy, and motor neurons. *Annual Review of Psychology, 60*, 653–670.

Iacoboni, M., Molnar-Szakacs, I., Gallese, V., Buccino, G., Mazziotta, J. C., et al. (2005). Grasping the intentions of others with one's own mirror neuron system. *PLoS Biology, 3*. Retrieved from www.plos.org on May 1, 2007.

Ji, R.-R., Kohno, T., Moore, K. A., & Woolf, C. J. (2003). Central sensitization and LTP. Do pain and memory share similar mechanisms? *Trends in Neurosciences, 26*, 696–705.

Josephson, W. L. (1987). Television violence and children aggression. Testing the priming, social script, and disinhibition predictions. *Journal of Personality and Social Psychology, 53*, 882–890.

Kandel, E. (2000). Cellular mechanisms of learning and the biological basis of individuality. In E. Kandel, J. H. Schwartz, & T. M. Jessell (Eds.), *Principles of neural sciences* (pp. 1247–1257). New York. McGraw-Hill.

Kellog, S. H., Burns, M., Coleman, P., Stitzer, M., Wale, J. B., et al. (2005). Something of value. The introduction of contingency management interventions into the New York City Health and Hospital Addiction Treatment Service. *Journal of Substance Abuse Treatment, 28(1)*, 57–65.

Klein, E. D., & Zentall, T. R. (2003). Imitation and affordance learning by pigeons (*Columba livia*). *Journal of Comparative Psychology, 117*, 414–419.

Knight, D. C., Cheng, D. T., Smith, C. N., Stein, E. A., & Helmstetter, F. J. (2004). Neural substrates mediating human delay and trace conditioning. *The Journal of Neuroscience, 24*, 1187–1195.

Kohler, E., Keysers, C., Umiltà, M. A., Fogassi, L., Gallese, V., et al. (2002). Hearing sounds, understanding actions. Action representation in mirror neurons. *Science, 297*, 846–848.

Kuroshima, H., Kuwahata, H., & Fujita, K. (2008). Learning from others' mistakes in capuchin monkeys (*cebus paella*). *Animal Cognition, 11*, 599–609.

Lieberman, D. A. (2000). *Learning. Behavior and cognition* (3rd ed). Belmont, CA. Wadsworth.

LoBue, V., & deLoache, J. S. (2008). Detecting the snake in the grass. Attention to fear-relevant stimuli by adults and young children. *Psychological Science, 19*, 284–289.

Logue, A. W. (1998). Evolutionary theory and the psychology of eating. Retrieved from http://darwin.baruch.cuny.edu/faculty/LogueA.html on May 15, 2006.

Lorenz, K. (1937). The companion in the bird's world. *Auk, 54*, 245–273.

Matson, J. L., & Taras, M. E. (1989). A 20 year review of punishment and alternative methods to treat problem behaviors in developmentally delayed persons. *Research in Developmental Disabilities, 10*, 85–104.

Matthews, R. N., Domjan, M., Ramsey, M., & Crews, D. (2007). Learning effects on sperm competition and reproductive fitness. *Psychological Science, 18*, 758–762.

Meltzoff, A. N., & Moore, M. K. (1983). Newborn Infants Imitate Adult Facial Gestures. *Child Development, 54*, 702–709.

Miller, N. E., & Dollard, J. (1941). *Social learning and imitation.* New Haven. Yale University Press.

Morimoto, K., Fahnestock, M., & Racine, R. J. (2004). Kindling and status epilepticus models of epilepsy. Rewiring the brain. *Progress in Neurobiology, 73*, 1–60.

Öhman, A., & Mineka, S. (2003). The malicious serpent. Snakes as a prototypical stimulus for an evolved module of fear. *Current Directions in Psychological Science, 12,* 2–9.

Öhman, A., Carlsson, K., Lundqvist, D., & Ingvar, M. (2007). On the unconscious subcortical origin of human fear. *Physiology & Behavior, 92,* 180–185.

Olson, C. K. (2004). Media violence research and youth violence data. Why do they conflict? *Academic Psychiatry, 28,* 144–150.

Pappini, M. R. (2002). Pattern and process in the evolution of learning. *Psychological Review, 109,* 186–201.

Paul, D. B., & Blumenthal, A. L. (1989). On the trail of Little Albert. *The Psychological Record, 29,* 547–553.

Pavlov, I. (1927). *Conditioned reflexes* (G.V. Anrep, Trans.). London. Oxford University Press.

Pinker, S. (2011). *The better angels of our nature. Why violence has declined.* New York. Viking.

Post, R. M. (1992). Transduction of psychosocial stress into the neurobiology of recurrent affective disorder. *American Journal of Psychiatry, 149,* 999–1010.

Premack, D. (1971). Catching up with common sense, or two sides of a generalization. Reinforcement and punishment. In R. Glaser (Ed.), *The nature of reinforcement.* New York. Academic.

Rash, C. J., Alessi, S. M., & Petri, N. (2008). Contingency management is efficacious for cocaine abusers with prior treatment attempts. *Experimental and Clinical Psychopharmacology, 16,* 547–554.

Reich, D. A., Green, M. C., Brock, T. C., & Tetlock, P. E. (2007). Biases in research evaluation. Inflated assessment, oversight, or error-type weighting? *Journal of Experimental Social Psychology, 43,* 633–640.

Rescorla, R. A. (1968). Probability of shock in the presence and absence of CS in fear conditioning. *Journal of Comparative and Physiological Psychology, 66(1),* 1–5.

Rescorla, R. A., & Heth, C. D. (1975). Reinstatement of fear to an extinguished conditioned stimulus. *Journal of Experimental Psychology. Animal Behavior Processes, 1(1),* 88–96.

Rizzolatti, G., Fadiga, L., Fogassi, L., & Gallese, V. (2002). From mirror neurons to imitation. Facts and speculations. In A. N. Meltzoff & W. Prinz (Eds.), *The imitative mind. Development, evolution, and brain bases* (pp. 247–266). New York. Cambridge University Press.

Rizzolatti, G., Fadiga, L., Gallese, V., & Fogassi, L. (1996). Premotor cortex and the recognition of motor actions. *Cognitive Brain Research, 3,* 131–141.

Rizzolatti, G., Fogassi, L., & Gallese, V. (2006, November). Mirrors in the mind. *Scientific American,* 54–61.

Rizzolatti, G., & Fabbri-Destro, M. (2010). Mirror neurons. From discovery to autism. *Experimental Brain Research, 200,* 223–237.

Samelson, F. (1980). L. B. Watson's Little Albert, Cyril Burt's twins and the need for a critical science. *American Psychologist, 35,* 619–625.

Savage, J. (2004). Does viewing violent media really cause criminal violence? A methodological review. *Aggression and Violent Behavior, 10,* 99–128.

Savage, J., & Yancey, C. (2008). The effects of media violence exposure on criminal aggression. A meta-analysis. *Criminal Justice and Behavior, 35,* 1123–1136.

Schmitt, D. P., & Pilcher, J. J. (2004). Evaluating evidence of psychological adaptation. How do we know one when we see one? *Psychological Science, 15,* 643–649.

Seligman, M. E. P. (1970). On the generality of the laws of learning. *Psychological Review, 77,* 406–418.

Shettleworth, S. (1975). Reinforcement and the organization of behavior in golden hamsters. Hunger, environment, and food reinforcement. *Journal of Experimental Psychology. Animal Behavior Processes, 1,* 56–87.

Signorielli, N., Gerbner, G., & Morgan, M. (1995). Violence on television. The cultural indicators project. *Journal of Broadcasting and Electronic Media, 39,* 278–283.

Skinner, B. F. (1938). *The behavior of organisms. An experimental analysis.* New York. Appleton-Century-Crofts.

Skinner, B. F. (1956). A case history in scientific method. *American Psychologist, 11,* 221–233.

Skinner-Buzan, D. (2004, March 12). I was not a lab rat. *The Guardian.* Retrieved from http://www.guardian.co.uk/education/2004/mar/12/highereducation.uk on May 31, 2009.

Slater, L. (2004). *Opening Skinner's box.* New York. Norton.

Thorndike, E. L. (1898). Animal intelligence. An experimental study of the associative process in animals. *Psychological Review Monograph Supplement, 2,* 1–8.

Tolman, E. C. (1948). Cognitive maps in rats and men. *Psychological Review, 55,* 198–208.

Tolman, E. C., & Honzik, C. H. (1930). Introduction and removal of reward and maze performance in rats. *Publications in Psychology, 4,* 257–275.

Tooby, J., & Cosmides, L. (2005). Conceptual foundations of evolutionary psychology. In D. M. Buss (Ed.), *The handbook of evolutionary psychology* (pp. 5–67). Hoboken, NJ. John Wiley & Son.

Vicente, K. J. (2000). Is science an evolutionary process? Evidence from miscitations of the scientific literature. *Perspectives on Science, 8(1),* 53–69.

Watson, J. B., & Rayner, R. (1920). Conditioned emotional reactions. *Journal of Experimental Psychology, 3,* 1–14.

Wilson, T. D., DePaulo, B. M., Mook, D. G., & Klaaren, K. J. (1993). Scientists' evaluations of research. the biasing eVects of the importance of the topic. *Psychological Science, 4,* 322–325.

Wicker, B., Keysers, C., Plailly, J., Royet, J-P., Gallese, V., & Rizzolatti, G. (2003). Both of us disgusted in *my* instula. The common neural basis of seeing and feeling disgust. *Neuron, 40,* 655–664.

Wilson, T. D., DePaulo, B. M., Mook, D. G., & Klaaren, K. J. (1993). Scientists' evaluations of research. the biasing effects of the importance of the topic. *Psychological Science, 4(5),* 322–325.

Wilson S. M., Saygin A. P., Sereno M. I., & Iacoboni M. (2004). Listening to speech activates motor areas involved in speech production. *Nature Neuroscience, 7,* 701–2.

CHAPTER 8

Alexander, K. W., Quas, J. A., Goodman, G. S., Ghetti, S., Edelstein, R. S., et al. (2005). Traumatic impact predicts long-term memory for documented child sexual abuse. *Psychological Science, 16(1),* 33–40.

Anderson, M. C. (2003). Rethinking interference theory. Executive control and the mechanisms of forgetting. *Journal of Memory and Language, 49,* 415–445.

Atkinson, R. C., & Shiffrin, R. M. (1968). Human memory. A proposed system and its control processes. In K. W. Spence & J. T. Spence (Eds.), *The psychology of learning and motivation* (Vol. 2, pp. 89–195). New York. Academic Press.

Ayers, M. S., & Reder, L. M. (1998). A theoretical review of the misinformation effect. Predictions from an activation-based memory model. *Psychonomic Bulletin & Review, 5(1),* 1–21.

Baddeley, A. D. (1997). *Human memory. Theory and practice* (rev. ed.). East Sussex, UK. Psychology Press.

Baddeley, A. D. (2007). *Working memory, thought, and action.* New York. Oxford University Press.

Baddeley, A. D. (2012). Working memory. Theories, models, and controversies. *Annual Review of Psychology, 63,* 1–29.

Baddeley, A. D., Eysenck, M. W., & Anderson, M. C. (2009). *Memory.* New York. Psychology Press.

Bahrick, H. P. (2000). Long-term maintenance of knowledge. In E. Tulving & F. I. M. Craik (Eds.), *The Oxford handbook of memory* (pp. 347–362). New York. Oxford University Press.

Bahrick, H. P. (2005). The long-term neglect of long-term memory. Reasons and remedies. In A. F. Healy (Ed.), *Experimental cognitive psychology and its applications. Decade of behavior* (pp. 89–100). Washington, DC. American Psychological Association.

Bateman, R. L., III. (2002). *No Gun Ri. A military history of the Korean War incident.* Mechanicsburg, PA. Stackpole Books.

Beggs, J. M., Brown, T. H., Byrne, J. H., Crow, T., LeDoux, J. E., et al. (1999). Learning and memory. Basic mechanisms. In M. J. Zigmond, F. E. Bloom,

S. C. Landis, J. L. Roberts, & L. R. Squire (Eds.), *Fundamentals of neuroscience* (pp. 1411–1454). San Diego, CA. Academic Press.

Bernstein, D. M., & Loftus, E. F. (2009). How to tell if a particular memory is true or false. *Perspectives on Psychological Science, 4,* 370–374.

Bowers, J. S., Mattys, S. L., & Gage, S. H. (2009). Preserved implicit knowledge of a forgotten childhood language. *Psychological Science, 20,* 1064–1069.

Brenneis, C. B. (2000). Evaluating the evidence. Can we find authenticated recovered memory? *Journal of the American Psychoanalytic Association, 17(1),* 61–77.

Brewer, N., & Wells, G. L. (2006). The confidence-accuracy relationship in eyewitness identification. Effects of lineup instructions, foil similarity and target-absent base rates. *Journal of Experimental Psychology. Applied, 12,* 11–30.

Brewer, N., & Wells, G. L. (2011). Eyewitness identification. *Current Directions in Psychological Science, 20,* 24–27.

Brigham, J. C., Bennett, B. L., Meissner, C. A., & Mitchell, T. L. (2007). The influence of race on eyewitness memory. In R. C. L. Lindsay, D. F. Ross, J. D. Read, & M. P. Read (Eds.), *The handbook of eyewitness psychology. Vol. 2. Memory for people* (pp. 257–281). Mahwah, NJ. Lawrence Erlbaum Associates.

Brown, A. S. (1991). A review of the tip-of-the-tongue experience. *Psychological Bulletin, 109,* 204–223.

Brown, R., & Kulik, J. (1977). Flashbulb memories. *Cognition, 5,* 73–99.

Brown, R., & McNeil, D. (1966). The "tip of the tongue" phenomenon. *Journal of Verbal Learning and Verbal Behavior, 5,* 325–337.

Bruce, D., Wilcox-O'Hearn, L. A., Robinson, J. A., Phillips-Grant, K., Francis, L., et al. (2005). Fragment memories mark the end of childhood amnesia. *Memory and Cognition, 33,* 567–576.

Bruck, M., & Ceci, S. J. (1997). The suggestibility of small children. *Current Directions in Psychological Science, 6,* 75–79.

Bruck, M., & Ceci, S. J. (1999). The suggestibility of children's memory. *Annual Review of Psychology, 50,* 419–439.

Bruck, M., Ceci, S. J., Francoeur, E., & Renick, A. (1995). Anatomically detailed dolls do not facilitate preschoolers' reports of a pediatric examination involving genital touching. *Journal of Experimental Psychology. Applied, 1,* 95–109.

Cameron, J. J., Wilson, A. E., & Ross, M. (2004). Autobiographical memory and self-assessment. In D. R. Beike, J. M. Lambinen, & D. A. Behrend (Eds.), *The self and memory. Studies in self and identity* (pp. 207–226). New York. Psychology Press.

Cassel, W., Roebers, C., & Bjorklund, D. (1996). Developmental patterns of eyewitness responses to repeated and increasingly suggestive questions. *Journal of Experimental Child Psychology, 61,* 116–133.

Cave, C. B., & Squire, L. R. (1992). Intact verbal and nonverbal short-term memory following damage to the human hippocampus. *Hippocampus, 2,* 151–163.

Ceci, S. J., & Bruck, M. (1995). *Jeopardy in the courtroom. A scientific analysis of children's testimony.* Washington, DC. American Psychological Association.

Ceci, S. J., Loftus, E. W., Leichtman, M., & Bruck, M. (1994). The possible role of source misattributions in the creation of false beliefs among preschoolers. *International Journal of Clinical and Experimental Hypnosis, 42,* 304–320.

Cepeda, N. J., Vul, E., Rohrer, D., Wixted, J. T., & Pashler, H. (2008). Spacing effects in learning. A temporal ridgeline of optimal retention. *Psychological Science, 19,* 1095–1102.

Choi, H., & Smith, S. M. (2005). Incubation and the resolution of tip-of-the-tongue states. *Journal of General Psychology, 132,* 365–376.

Clark, R. E., & Squire, L. R. (1998). Classical conditioning and brain systems. The role of awareness. *Science, 280,* 77–81.

Cohen, G. (1990). Recognition and retrieval of proper names. Age differences in the fan effect. *European Journal of Cognitive Psychology, 2,* 193–204.

Cowan, N. (2001). The magical number 4 in short-term memory. A reconsideration of mental storage capacity. *Behavioral and Brain Sciences, 24,* 87–185.

Cowan, N. (2005). *Working memory capacity.* Hove, UK. Psychology Press.

Cowan, N. (2010). The magical mystery four. How is working memory capacity limited, and why? *Current Directions in Psychological Science, 19,* 51–57.

Craik, F. I. M. (2002). Levels of processing. Past, present . . . and future? *Memory, 10,* 305–318.

Craik, F. I. M., & Brown, S. C. (2000). Memory. Coding processes. In A. E. Kazdin (Ed.), *Encyclopedia of psychology* (Vol. 5, pp. 162–166). Washington, DC. American Psychological Association.

Craik, F. I. M., & Lockhart, R. S. (1972). Levels of processing. A framework for memory research. *Journal of Verbal Learning and Verbal Behavior, 11,* 671–684.

Craik, F. I. M., & Lockhart, R. S. (2009). Levels of processing and Zinchenko's approach to memory research. *Cultural-Historical Psychology, 2,* 14–18.

Cross, E. M., & Burke, D. M. (2004). Do alternative names block young and older adults' retrieval of proper names? *Brain and Language, 89,* 174–181.

Crowder, R. G. (1993). Short-term memory. Where do we stand? *Memory and Cognition, 21,* 142–145.

Darwin, C. J., Turvey, M. T., & Crowder, R. G. (1972). An auditory analogue of the Sperling partial report procedure. Evidence for brief auditory storage. *Cognitive Psychology, 3,* 255–267.

Davis, N., Gross, J., & Hayne, H. (2008). Defining the boundary of childhood amnesia. *Memory, 16,* 465–474.

Devilbiss, D. M., & Berridge, C. W. (2008). Cognition-enhancing doses of methylphenidate preferentially increase prefrontal cortex neuronal responsiveness. *Biological Psychiatry, 64,* 626–635.

Dunlosky, J., Rawson, K. A., Marsh, E. J., Nathan, M. J., & Washington, D. T. (2013). Improving students' learning with effective learning techniques. Promising directions from cognitive and educational psychology. *Psychological Science in the Public Interest, 14,* 1–58.

Ebbinghaus, D. L. (1964). *Memory. A contribution to experimental psychology.* New York. Dover. (Original work published 1885).

Eich, E. (1989). Theoretical issues in state dependent memory. In H. L. Roediger & F. I. M. Craik (Eds.), *Varieties of memory and consciousness. Essays in honor of Endel Tulving* (pp. 331–354). Hillsdale, NJ. Erlbaum.

Eligion, J. (2009, February 7). New efforts focus on exonerating prisoners in cases without DNA evidence. *New York Times.* Retrieved from http://www.nytimes.com/2009/02/08/nyregion/08exonerate.html?pagewanted=all&_r=0 on June 24, 2010.

Fleishman, D. A., Wilson, R. S., Gabrieli, J. D. E., Bienias, J. L., & Bennett, D. A. (2004). A longitudinal study of implicit and explicit memory in old persons. *Psychology and Aging, 19,* 617–625.

Freedman, M. L., & Martin, R. C. (2001). Dissociable components of short-term memory and their relation to long-term learning. *Cognitive Neuropsychology, 18,* 193–226.

Frenda, S. J., Nichols, R. M., & Loftus, E. F. (2011). Current issues and advances in misinformation research. *Current Directions in Psychological Science, 20,* 20–23.

Frick, A., & Johnston, D. (2005). Plasticity of dendritic excitability. *Journal of Neurobiology, 65,* 100–115.

Gardiner, J. M., Brandt, K. R., Baddeley, A. D., Vargha-Khadem, F., & Mishkin, M. (2008). Charting the acquisition of semantic knowledge in a case of developmental amnesia. *Neuropsychologia, 46,* 2865–2868.

Gelbard-Sagiv, H., Mukamel, R., Harel, M., Malach, R., & Fried, I. (2008). Internally generated reactivation of single neurons in human hippocampus during free recall. *Science, 322,* 96–101.

Geraerts, E., Arnold, M. M., Lindsay, D. S., Merckelbach, H., Jelicic, M., et al. (2006). Forgetting of prior remembering in persons reporting recovered memories of childhood sexual abuse. *Psychological Science, 17,* 1002–1008.

Geraerts, E., Bernstein, D. M., Merekelbach, H., Linders, C., Raymaerkers, L., et al. (2008). Lasting false beliefs and their behavioral consequences. *Psychological Science, 19,* 749–753.

Geraerts, E., Lindsay, D. S., Merckelbach, H., Jelicic, M., Raymaekers, L., et al. (2009). Cognitive mechanisms underlying recovered-memory experiences of childhood sexual abuse. *Psychological Science, 20,* 91–98.

Geraerts, E., Schooler, J., Merckelbach, H., Jelicic, M. J., Hauer, B. J. A., & Ambadar, Z. (2007). The reality of recovered memories. Corroborating continuous and discontinuous memories of childhood sexual abuse. *Psychological Science, 18,* 564–568.

Glanzer, M., & Cunitz, A. R. (1966). Two storage mechanisms in free recall. *Journal of Verbal Learning and Verbal Behavior, 5,* 351–360.

Gobet, F. (2005). Chunking models of expertise. Implications for education. *Applied Cognitive Psychology, 19,* 183–204.

Gobet, F., Land, P. C. R., Croker, S., Cheng, P. C.-H., Jones, G., et al. (2001). Chunking mechanisms in human learning. *Trends in Cognitive Science, 5,* 236–243.

Godden, D. R., & Baddeley, A. D. (1975). Context-dependent memory in two natural environments. On land and underwater. *British Journal of Psychology, 66,* 325–331.

Goetz, M. C., Goetz, P. W., & Robinson, M. D. (2007). What's the use of being happy? Mood states, useful objects, and repetition priming effects. *Emotion, 7,* 675–679.

Goff, L. M., & Roediger, H. L. (1998). Imagination inflation for action events. Repeated imaginings leads to illusory recollections. *Memory and Cognition, 26(1),* 20–33.

Goldstein, A. G., Chance, J. E., & Schneller, G. R. (1989). Frequency of eyewitness identification in criminal cases. A survey of prosecutors. *Bulletin of the Psychonomic Society, 27,* 71–74.

Goldstein, E. B. (2005). *Cognitive psychology. Connecting mind, research, and everyday experience.* Belmont, CA. Wadsworth/Thomson Learning.

Grant, A. (2006). Johnston gears up to launch center for learning and memory. Institute for Cellular and Molecular Biology. Retrieved from http://www.icmb.utexas.edu/Profile/Profile_Daniel_johnston.asp on May 15, 2007.

Greenberg, M. S., Westcott, D. R., & Bailey, S. E. (1998). When believing is seeing. The effect of scripts on eyewitness memory. *Law and Human Behavior, 22,* 685–694.

Gross, S. R. (2008). Convicting the innocent. *Annual Review of Law and Social Science, 4,* 173–192.

Gurung, R. A. R. (2005). How do students really study (and does it matter)? *Teaching of Psychology, 4,* 239–241.

Hadwin, A. F., & Winne, P. H. (1996). Study strategies have meager support. A review with recommendations for implementation. *Journal of Higher Education, 67,* 692–715.

Hadwin, A. F., Winne, P. H., Stockley, D. B., Nesbit, J. C., Woszczyna, C., et al. (2001). Context moderates students' self-reports about how they study. *Journal of Educational Psychology, 93,* 477–487.

Heaps, C. M., & Nash, M. (2001). Comparing recollective experience in true and false autobiographical memories. *Journal of Experimental Psychology. Learning, Memory, and Cognition, 27,* 920–930.

Herrmann, D., Raybeck, D., & Gruneberg, M. (2002). *Improving memory and study skills. Advances in theory and practice.* Seattle, WA. Hogrefe & Huber Publishers.

Hirst, W., Phelps, E. A., Buckner, R. L., Budson, A. E., Cuc, A., et al. (2009). Long-term memory for the terrorist attack of September 11. Flashbulb memories, event memories, and factors that influence their retention. *Journal of Experimental Psychology, 138*(2), 161–176.

Hyman, I. E., Jr., Husband, T. H., & Billings, F. J. (1995). False memories of childhood experiences. *Applied Cognitive Psychology, 9,* 181–197.

James, L. E. (2006). Specific effects of aging on proper name retrieval. Now you see them, now you don't. *The Journals of Gerontology, Series B. Psychological Sciences and Social Sciences, 61B,* P180–P183.

Jonides, J., Lewis, R. L., Nee, D. E., Lustig, C. A., Berman, M. G., et al. (2008). The mind and brain of short-term memory. *Annual Review of Psychology, 59,* 193–224.

Kelemen, W. L., & Creeley, C. E. (2003). State-dependent memory effects using caffeine and placebo do not extend to metamemory. *Journal of General Psychology, 130(1),* 70–86.

Kleider, H. M., Pezdek, K., Goldinger, S. D., & Kirk, A. (2008). Schema-driven source misattribution errors. Remembering the expected from a witnessed event. *Applied Cognitive Psychology, 22,* 1–20.

Knowlton, B. J., Mangels, J. A., & Squire, L. R. (1996). A neostriatal habit learning system in humans. *Science, 273,* 1399–1402.

Koppenaal, L., & Glanzer, M. (1990). An examination of the continuous distractor task and the "long-term recency effect." *Memory and Cognition, 18,* 183–195.

Koriat, A., Goldsmith, M., & Pansky, A. (2000). Toward a psychology of memory accuracy. *Annual Review of Psychology, 51,* 481–537.

Kuhl, B. A., Dudukovic, N. M., Kahn, I., & Wagner, A. D. (2007). Decreased demands on cognitive control reveal the neural processing benefits of forgetting. *Nature Neuroscience, 10,* 908–914.

Lampinen, J. M., Faries, J. M., Neuschatz, J. S., & Toglia, M. P. (2000). Recollections of things schematic. The influence of scripts on recollective experience. *Applied Cognitive Psychology, 14,* 543–554.

Levinson, A. (1999). Tatiana Cooley wins title, but she still sweats the small stuff. *SouthCoast Today.* Retrieved from http://www.s-t.com/daily/02-99/02-24-99/b04li047.htm on June 4, 2006.

Lindsay, D. S., Hagen, L., Read, J. D., Wade, K. A., & Garry, M. (2004). True photographs and false memories. *Psychological Science, 15,* 149–154.

Loftus, E. F. (1996). *Eyewitness testimony.* Cambridge, MA. Harvard University Press. (Original work published 1979.)

Loftus E. F. (1997). Memories for a past that never was. *Current Directions in Psychological Science, 6,* 60–65.

Loftus, E. F. (2003). Make-believe memories. *American Psychologist, 58,* 867–873.

Loftus, E. F. (2005). Planting misinformation in the human mind. A 30-year investigation of the malleability of memory. *Learning and Memory, 12,* 361–366.

Loftus, E. F. (2007). Memory distortions. Problems solved and unsolved. In M. Garry & H. Hayne (Eds.), *Do justice and let the sky fall. Elizabeth Loftus and her contributions to science, law, and academic freedom* (pp. 1–14). Mahwah, NJ. Lawrence Erlbaum Associates.

Loftus, E. F., & Bernstein, D. M. (2005). Rich false memories. The royal road to success. In A. F. Healy (Ed.), *Experimental cognitive psychology and its applications* (pp. 101–113). Washington, DC. American Psychological Association.

Loftus, E. F., Donders, K., Hoffman, H. G., & Schooler, J. W. (1989). Creating new memories that are quickly accessed and confidently held. *Memory and Cognition, 17,* 607–616.

Loftus, E. F., & Hoffman, H. G. (1989). Misinformation and memory. The creation of memory. *Journal of Experimental Psychology. General, 118,* 100–104.

Loftus, E. F., & Ketcham, K. (1994). *The myth of repressed memory. False memories and allegations of sexual abuse.* New York. St. Martin's Press.

Loftus, E. F., & Pickrell, J. E. (1995). The formation of false memories. *Psychiatric Annals, 25,* 720–725.

Lynn, S. J., & Payne, D. G. (1997). Memory as the theater of the past. The psychology of false memories. *Current Directions in Psychological Science, 6,* 55.

Lynn, S. J., Locke, T., Loftus, E. F., Krackow, E., & Lilienfeld, S. O. (2003). The remembrance of things past. Problematic memory recovery techniques in psychotherapy. In S. O. Lilienfeld, S. J. Lynn, & J. M. Lohr (Eds.), *Science and pseudoscience in clinical psychology* (pp. 205–239). New York. The Guilford Press.

Madrigal, A. (2008, April 24). Wired.com readers' brain-enhancing drug regimens. *Wired.* Retrieved from www.wired.com/print/medtech/drugs/news/2008/04/smart_drugs on June 10, 2009.

Maher, B. (2008, April 9). Poll results. Look who's doping. *Nature, 452,* 674–675.

Marcus, G. (2008). *Kluge. The haphazard construction of the human mind.* New York. Houghton Mifflin Company.

McHugh, P. (2008). *Try to remember. Psychiatry's clash over meaning, memory, and mind.* New York. Dana Publications.

McNally, R. J. (2003). *Remembering trauma.* Cambridge, MA. Harvard University Press.

McNally, R. J., & Geraerts, E. (2009). A new solution to the recovered memory debate. *Perspectives on Psychological Science, 4,* 126–134.

Mehlman, M. J. (2004). Cognition-enhancing drugs. *The Milbank Quarterly, 82,* 483–506.

Mitchell, D. B. (2006). Nonconscious priming after 17 years. Invulnerable implicit memory? *Psychological Science, 17,* 925–929.

Moss, M. (2000, May 31). The story behind a soldier's story. *New York Times.* Retrieved from http://partners.nytimes.com/library/national/053100korea-massacre-ap.html on May 12, 2006.

Murdoch, B. B., Jr. (1962). The serial position effect in free recall. *Journal of Experimental Psychology, 64,* 482–488.

Nathan, D., & Snedeker, M. (1995). *Satan's silence. Ritual abuse and the making of a modern American witch hunt.* New York. Basic Books.

Neath, I. (1993). Distinctiveness and serial position effects in recognition. *Memory & Cognition, 21,* 689–698.

Nee, D. E., Berman, M. G., Moore, K. S., & Jonides, J. (2008). Neuroscientific evidence about the distinction between short- and long-term memory. *Current Directions in Psychological Science, 17,* 102–106.

Nichols, E. A., Kao, Y-C., Verfaellie, M., & Gabrieli, J. D. E. (2006). Working memory and long-term memory for faces. Evidence from fMRI and global amnesia for involvement of the medial temporal lobes. *Hippocampus, 16,* 604–616.

Offer, D., Kaiz, M., Howard, K. I., & Bennett, E. S. (2000). The altering of reported experiences. *Journal of the Academy of Child & Adolescent Psychiatry, 39,* 735–742.

Ofshe, R., & Watters, E. (1994). *Making monsters. False memories, psychotherapy, and sexual hysteria.* New York. Charles Scribners' Sons.

Perfect, T. J., & Harris, L. J. (2003). Adult age differences in unconscious transference. Source confusion or identity blending? *Memory & Cognition, 31,* 570–580.

Perkins, K. K., & Wieman, C. E. (2005). The surprising impact of seat location on student performance. *The Physics Teacher, 43,* 30–33.

Peterson, L. R., & Peterson, M. J. (1959). Short-term retention of individual verbal items. *Journal of Experimental Psychology, 58,* 193–198.

Pezdek, K., Whetstone, T., Reynolds, K., Askari, N., & Dougherty, T. (1989). Memory for real-world scenes. The role of consistency with schema expectation. *Journal of Experimental Psychology. Learning Memory and Cognition, 15,* 587–595.

Porter, S., & Peace K. A. (2007). The scars of memory. A prospective, longitudinal investigation of the consistency of traumatic and positive emotional memories in adulthood. *Psychological Science, 18,* 435–441.

Rabinowitz, D. (2003). *No crueller tyrannies. Accusation, false witness, and other terrors of our times.* New York. Free Press.

Richardson, J. T., Best, J., & Bromley, D. G. (Eds.). (1991). *The Satanism scare.* New York. Aldine de Gruyter.

Roedigger, H. L., Agarwal, P. K., McDaniel, M. A., & McDermott, K. B. (2011). Enhanced learning in the classroom. Long-term improvements from quizzing. *Journal of Experimental Psychology. Applied, 17,* 382–395.

Roediger, H. L., III., & Gallo, D. A. (2001). Levels of processing. Some unanswered questions. In M. Naveh-Benjamin, M. Moscovitch, & H. L. Roediger III (Eds.), *Perspectives on human memory and cognitive aging. Essays in honour of Fergus Craik* (pp. 28–47). New York. Psychology Press.

Rofé, Y. (2008). Does repression exist? Memory, pathogenic, unconscious and clinical experience. *Review of General Psychology, 12,* 63–85.

Rohrer, D., & Pashler, H. (2007). Increasing retention without increasing study time. *Current Directions in Psychological Science, 16,* 183–186.

Ross, M., & Wilson, A. E. (2003). Autobiographical memory and conceptions of self. Getting better all the time. *Current Directions in Psychological Science, 12,* 66–69.

Schacter, D. L. (1994). Priming and multiple memory systems. Perceptual mechanisms of implicit memory. In D. L. Schacter & E. Tulving (Eds.), *Memory systems* (pp. 233–268). Cambridge, MIT Press.

Schacter, D. L. (1996). Searching for memory. The brain, the mind, and the past. *New York. Plenum Press.*

Schacter, D. L. (2001). *The seven sins of memory.* Boston, MA. Houghton Mifflin Company.

Schacter, D. L. (2004). When memory sins. (2004). In J. T. Cacioppo & G. G. Berntson (Eds.), *Essays in social neuroscience* (pp. 93–105). Cambridge, MA. MIT Press.

Schacter, D.L., Chiao, J.Y., & Mitchell, J.P. (2003). The seven sins of memory. Implications for self. *Annals of the New York Academy of Sciences,* 226–239.

Schank, R. C., & Abelson, R. (1977). *Scripts, plans, goals, and understanding.* Hillsdale, NJ. Lawrence Erlbaum Associates.

Scharfe, E., & Bartholomew, K. (1998). Do you remember? Recollections of adult attachment patterns. *Personal Relationships, 5,* 219–234.

Scheck, B., Neufeld, P., & Dwyer, J. (2000). *Actual innocence. Five days to execution and other dispatches from the wrongly convicted.* New York. Doubleday.

Schelach, L., & Nachson, I. (2001). Memory of Auschwitz survivors. *Applied Cognitive Psychology, 15,* 119–132.

Schooler, J. W., Bendiksen, M., & Ambadar, Z. (1997). Taking the middle line. Can we accommodate both fabricated and recovered memories of sexual abuse? In M. A. Conway (Ed.), *Recovered memories and false memories* (pp. 251–292). Oxford, UK. Oxford University Press.

Schwartz, B. L. (2002). *Tip-of-the-tongue states. Phenomenology, mechanism, and lexical retrieval.* Mahwah, NJ. Lawrence Erlbaum Associates.

Schwartz, B. L. (2010). The effects of emotion on tip-of-the-tongue states. *Psychonomic Bulletin & Review, 17,* 82–87.

Schwartz, B. L., & Frazier, L. D. (2005). Tip-of-the-tongue states and aging. Contrasting psycholinguistic and metacognitive perspectives. *Journal of General Psychology, 132,* 377–391.

Schwarz, A. (2012, June 10). The risky rise of the good-grade pill. *New York Times.* Retrieved from http://www.nytimes.com/2012/06/10/education/seeking-academic-edge-teenagers-abuse-stimulants.html?pagewanted=all&_r=0 on June 12, 2012.

Sederberg, P. B., Schulze-Bonhage, A., Madsen, J. R., Bromfield, E. B., Litt, B., et al. (2007). Gamma oscillations distinguish true from false memories. *Psychological Science, 18,* 927–932.

Smith, E. M., & Farah, M. J. (2011). Are prescription stimulants "smart pills"? The epidemiology and cognitive neuroscience of prescription stimulant use by normal healthy individuals. *Psychological Bulletin, 137,* 717–741.

Sperling, G. (1960). The information available in brief visual presentations. *Psychological Monographs. General and Applied, 74,* 1–29.

Squire, L. R., & Zola-Morgan, S. (1998). Episodic memory, semantic memory, and amnesia. *Hippocampus, 8,* 205–211.

Talmi, D., Grady, C. L., Goshen-Gottstein, Y., & Moscovitch, M. (2005). Neuroimaging the serial position curve. A test of single-store versus dual-store models. *Psychological Science, 16,* 716–723.

Taylor, S. E. (1989). *Positive illusions.* New York. Basic Books.

The Innocence Project (2010). Facts on post-conviction DNA exonerations. Retrieved from http://www.innocenceproject.org/Content/Facts_on_PostConviction_DNA_Exonerations.php on February 14, 2013.

Thompson, C. P., Skowronski, J. J., Larsen, S. F., & Betz, A. (1996). *Autobiographical memory. Remembering what and remembering when.* Hillsdale, NJ. Lawrence Erlbaum Associates.

Thompson, R. F. (2005). In search of memory traces. *Annual Review of Psychology, 56,* 1–23.

Tulving, E. (1972). Episodic and semantic memory. In E. Tulving & W. Donaldson

(Eds.), *Organization of memory* (pp. 381–403). New York. Academic Press.

Tulving, E. (2002). Episodic memory. From mind to brain. *Annual Review of Psychology, 53,* 1–25.

Tulving, E., & Craik, F. I. M. (Eds.). (2000). *The Oxford handbook of memory.* New York. Oxford University Press.

van Giezen, A. E., Arensman, E., Spinhoven, P., & Wolters, G. (2005). Consistency of memory for emotionally arousing events. A review of prospective and experimental studies. *Clinical Psychology Review, 25,* 935–953.

Vargha-Khadem, F., Gadian, D. G., Watkins, K. E., Connelly, A., Van Paesschen, W., et al. (1997). Differential effects of early hippocampal pathology on episodic and semantic memory. *Science, 277,* 376–380.

Watkins, M. J. (2002). Limits and province of levels of processing. Considerations of a construct. *Memory, 10,* 339–343.

Wells, G. L., & Bradfield, A. L. (1998). "Good, you identified the suspect". Feedback to eyewitnesses distorts their reports of the witnessing experience. *Journal of Applied Psychology, 83,* 360–376.

Wells, G. L., Malpass, R. S., Lindsay, R. C. L., Fisher, R. P., Turtle, J. W., et al. (2000). From the lab to the police station. A successful application of eyewitness research. *American Psychologist, 55,* 581–598.

Wilson, A. E., & Ross, M. (2001). From chump to champ. People's appraisals of their earlier and current selves. *Journal of Personality and Social Psychology, 80,* 572–584.

Wilson, A. E., & Ross, M. (2003). The identity function of autobiographical memory. Time is on our side. *Memory, 11,* 137–149.

Wixted, J. T. (2004). The psychology and neuroscience of forgetting. *Annual Review of Psychology, 55,* 235–269.

Woman in custody after forgetting baby. (2005, March 12). KATV. Retrieved from http://www.katv.com/news/stories/0305/213321.html on May 4, 2005.

Wright, D. B., Boyd, C. E., & Tredoux, C. G. (2001). A field study of own-race bias, in South Africa and England. *Psychology, Public Policy, and Law, 7,* 119–133.

Zhang, G., & Simon, H. A. (1985). STM capacity for Chinese words and idioms. Chunking and acoustical loop hypotheses. *Memory and Cognition, 13,* 193–201.

CHAPTER 9

Ableson, R. P. (1995). *Statistics as principled argument.* Hillsdale, NJ. Lawrence Erlbaum Associates.

American Psychiatric Association (2013). *Diagnostic and statistical manual of the American Psychiatric Association,* 5th edition. Washington, DC. American Psychiatric Association.

American Trucking Associations (2013). Professional truck drivers. Retrieved from http://www.truck line.com/About/Industry/Pages/ ProfessionalTruckDrivers.aspx on February 15, 2013.

Anderson, C. A. (2008). Belief perseverance. In R. Baumeister & K. D. Vohs (Eds.), *Encyclopedia of social psychology* (pp. 109–110). Thousand Oaks, CA. Sage Publications.

Anderson, S. R. (2004). *How many languages are there in the world?* Washington, DC. The Linguistic Society of America. Retrieved from http://www.lsadc.org/pdf_files/howmany.pdf on November 24, 2005.

Anderson, S. R., & Lightfoot, D. W. (1999). The human language faculty as an organ. *Annual Review of Physiology, 62,* 697–722.

Aslin, R. N. (2007). What's in a look? *Developmental Science, 10,* 48–53.

Barner, D., Li, P., & Snedeker, J. (2010). Words as windows to thought. The case of object representation. *Current Directions in Psychological Science, 19,* 195–200.

Batty, G. D., Wennerstad, K. M., Davey Smith, G., Gunnell, D., Deary, I. J., et al. (2009). IQ in late adolescence/early adulthood and mortality by middle age. Cohort study of one million Swedish men. *Epidemiology, 20,* 100–109.

Berry, C. M., & Sackett, P. R. (2009). Individual differences in course choice result in underestimation of the validity of college admissions systems. *Psychological Science, 20,* 822–830.

Best, J. (1990). *Threatened children. Rhetoric and concern about child-victims.* Chicago, IL. University of Chicago Press.

Borkenau, P., Mauer, N., Riemann, R., Spinath, F. M., & Angleitner, A. (2004). Think slices of behavior as cues of personality and intelligence. *Journal of Personality and Social Psychology, 86,* 599–614.

Bornstein, M. H., Hahn, C.-S., Bell, C., Haynes, O. M., Slater, A., Golding, J., et al. (2006). Stability in cognition across early childhood. A developmental cascade. *Psychological Science, 17,* 151–158.

Boroditsky, L. (2009). How does language shape the way we think? In M. Brockman (Ed.), *What's next. Dispatches on the future of science.* New York. Random House.

Brody, N. (2003a). Construct validation of the Sternberg triarchic abilities test. Comment and reanalysis. *Intelligence, 31,* 319–329.

Brody, N. (2003b). What Sternberg should have concluded. *Intelligence, 31,* 339–342.

Burnham, C. A., & Davis, K. G. (1969). The nine-dot problem. Beyond perceptual organization. *Psychonomic Science, 17,* 321–323.

Caprara, G. V., Vecchione, M., Alessandri, G., Gerbino, M., & Barbaranelli, C. (2011). The contribution of personality traits and self-efficacy beliefs to academic achievement. A longitudinal study. *British Journal of Educational Psychology, 81,* 78–96.

Carraher, T. N., Carraher, D. W., & Schliemann, A. D. (1985). Mathematics in the streets and in schools. *British Journal of Developmental Psychology, 3(1),* 21–29.

Carroll, J. B. (1993). *Human cognitive abilities. A survey of factor-analytic studies.* New York. Cambridge University Press.

Carroll, J. B. (1997). Psychometrics, intelligence, and public perception. *Intelligence, 24(1),* 25–52.

Ceci, S. J., & Williams, W. M. (1997). Schooling, intelligence, and income. *American Psychologist, 52,* 1051–1058.

Chabris, C., & Simons, D. (2010). *The invisible gorilla.* New York. Crown.

Chabris, C. F., Weinberger, A., Fontaine, M, & Simons, D. J. (2011). You do not talk about Fight Club if you do not notice Fight Club. Inattentional blindness for a simulated real-world assault. *i-Perception, 2,* 150–153.

Chandler, R. (1992). *Farewell, My Lovely.* New York. Vintage. (Original work published 1940.)

Chomsky, N. (1965). *Aspects of the theory of syntax.* Cambridge, MA. MIT Press.

Chomsky, N. (1972). *Language and mind* (enlarged ed.). New York. Harcourt Brace Jovanovich.

Chomsky, N. (1975). *Reflections on language.* New York. Harcourt Brace Jovanovich.

Chomsky, N. (1980). Rules and representations. *Behavioral and Brain Sciences, 3,* 1–61.

Cooper, E. F. (2005). *Missing and exploited children. Overview and policy concerns.* Congressional Research Service, Library of Congress. Retrieved from http://www.usembassy.it/pdf/other/RL31655.pdf on November 5, 2005.

Csikszentmihályi, M. (1990). The domain of creativity. In M. A. Runco & R. S. Albert (Eds.), *Theories of creativity* (pp. 190–212). Thousand Oaks, CA. Sage Publications.

Davies, I. R. L., Sowden, P. T., Jerrett, D. T., Jerrett, T., & Corbett, G. G. (1998). A cross-cultural study of English and Setswanta speakers on a colour triads task. A test of the Sapir-Whorf hypothesis. *British Journal of Psychology, 89,* 1–15.

Davies, M. F. (1997). Belief persistence after evidential discrediting. The impact of generated versus provided explanations on the likelihood of discredited outcomes. *Journal of Experimental Social Psychology, 33,* 561–578.

Davis, O. S. P., Haworth, C. M. A., & Plomin, R. (2009). Dramatic increase in heritability of cognitive development from early to middle childhood. An 8-year longitudinal study of 8,700 pairs of twins. *Psychological Science, 20,* 1301–1308.

Deary, I. J. (2012). Intelligence. *Annual Review of Psychology, 63,* 453–482.

Deary, I. J., Batty, D. G., Pattie, A., & Gale, C. R. (2008). More intelligent more dependable children live longer. A 55-year longitudinal study of a representative sample of the Scottish Nation. *Psychological Science,* *19,* 831–837.

Deary, I. J., Penke, L., & Johnson, W. (2010). The neuroscience of human intelligence differences. *Nature Reviews Neuroscience, 11,* 201–211.

Deary, I. J., Strand, S., Smith, P., & Fernandes, C. (2007). Intelligence and educational achievement. *Intelligence, 35,* 13–21.

Deary, I.J., Weiss, A., & Batty, G. D. (2010). Intelligence, personality, and health outcomes. *Psychological Science in the Public Interest, 11,* 53–79.

Deary, I. J., Whiteman, M. C., Whalley, L. J., Fox, H. C., & Starr, J. M. (2004). The impact of childhood intelligence on later life. Following up the Scottish mental surveys of 1932 and 1947. *Journal of Personality and Social Psychology, 86*(1), 130–147.

Duckworth, A. L., & Seligman, M. E. P. (2005). Self-discipline outdoes IQ in predicting academic performance of adolescents. *Psychological Science, 16,* 939–944.

Elman, J. L. (2001). Connectionism and language acquisition. In M. Tomasello & E. Bates (Eds.), *Language development. The essential readings* (pp. 295–306). Malden, MA. Blackwell Publishing.

Elman, J. L. (2005). Connectionist models of cognitive development. Where next? *Trends in Cognitive Sciences, 9,* 112–117.

Enard, W., Przeworski, M., Fisher, S. E., Lai, C. S., Wiebe, V., et al. (2002). Molecular evolution of *FOXP,* a gene involved in speech and language. *Nature, 418,* 869–872.

Esch, H. E., Zhang, S., Srinivasan, M. V., & Tautz, J. (2001). Honeybee dances communicate distances measured by optic flow. *Nature, 411,* 581–583.

Evans, C. S., & Evans, L. (1999). Chicken food calls are functionally referential. *Animal Behaviour, 58,* 307–319.

Evans, N., & Levinson, S. C. (2009). The myth of language universals. Language diversity and its importance for cognitive science. *Behavioral and Brain Sciences, 32,* 429–492.

Fergusson, D. M., Horwood, J. L., & Ridder, E. M. (2005). Show me the child at seven II. Childhood intelligence and later outcomes in adolescence and young adulthood. *Journal of Child Psychology and Psychiatry, 46,* 850–858.

Fodor, J. A. (1968). *Psychological explanation. An introduction to the philosophy of psychology.* New York. Random House.

Fodor, J. A. (1983). *The modularity of mind. An essay on faculty psychology.* Cambridge, MA. MIT Press.

Ganis, G., Thompson, W. L., & Kosslyn, S. M. (2004). Brain areas underlying visual mental imagery and visual perception. An fMRI study. *Cognitive Brain Research, 20,* 226–241.

Gardner, H. (1983). *Frames of mind. The theory of multiple intelligences.* New York. Basic Books.

Gardner, H. (2006). *Multiple intelligences. New Horizons* (rev. ed.). New York. Basic Books.

Gardner, H. (2008). *A multiplicity of intelligences.* In P. Mariën & J. Abutalebi (Eds.), *Neuropsychological research. A review* (pp. 17–23). New York. Psychology Press.

Gigerenzer, G., Gaissmaier, W., Kurz-Mileke, E., Schwartz, L. M., & Woloshin, S. (2008). Helping doctors and patients make sense of health statistics. *Psychological Science in the Public Interest, 8,* 53–96.

Gilovich, T., Griffin, D., & Kahneman, D. (2002). *Heuristics and biases. The psychology of intuitive judgment.* New York. Cambridge University Press.

Gilovich, T., Vallone, R., & Tversky, A. (1985). The hot hand in basketball. On the misperception of random sequences. *Cognitive Psychology, 17,* 295–314.

Gottfredson, L. S. (1997). Mainstream science on intelligence. An editorial with 52 signatories, history, and bibliography. *Intelligence, 24,* 13–23.

Gottfredson, L. S. (2003). Dissecting practical intelligence theory. Its claims and evidence. *Intelligence, 31,* 343–397.

Gottfredson, L. S., & Deary, I. J. (2004). Intelligence predicts health and longevity, but why? *Current Directions in Psychological Science, 13*(1), 1–4.

Greven, C. U., Harlaar, N., Kovas, Y., Chamorro-Premuzic, T., & Plomin, R. (2009). More than just IQ. School achievement is predicted by self-perceived abilities—but for genetic rather than environmental reasons. *Psychological Science, 20,* 753–762.

Grigorenko, E. L., Sternberg, R. J., & Strauss, S. (2006). Practical intelligence and elementary school teacher effectiveness in the United States and Israel. Measuring the predictive power of tacit knowledge. *Thinking Skills and Creativity, 1,* 14–33.

Grimshaw, G. M., Adelstein, A., Bryden, M., & MacKinnon, G. E. (1998). First-language acquisition in adolescence. Evidence for a critical period for verbal language development. *Brain and Language, 63,* 237–255.

Hauser, M. D., Chomsky, N., & Fitch, W. T. (2002). The faculty of language. What is it, who has it, and how did it evolve? *Science, 298,* 1569–1579.

Haworth, C. M. A., Wright, M. J., Luciano, M., Martin, N. G., de Geus, E. J. C., et al. (2010). The heritability of general cognitive ability increases linearly from childhood to young adulthood. *Molecular Psychiatry, 15,* 1112–1120.

Hennessey, B. A., & Amabile, T. M. (2010). Creativity. *Annual Review of Psychology, 61,* 569–598.

Hespos, S. J., & Spelke, E. S. (2004). Conceptual precursors to language. *Nature, 430,* 453–456.

Hoekstra, R. A., Bartels, M., & Boomsma, D. I. (2007). Longitudinal genetic study of verbal and nonverbal IQ from early childhood to young adulthood. *Learning and Individual Differences, 17,* 97–114.

Horn, J. L. (1991). Measurement of intellectual capabilities. A review of theory. In K. S. McGrew, J. K. Werder, & R. W. Woodcock (Eds.), *WJ-R technical manual.* Allen, TX. DLM.

Horn, J. L., & Cattell, R. B. (1966). Refinement and test of the theory of fluid and crystallized general intelligence. *Journal of Educational Psychology, 57,* 253–270.

Jackendoff, R. (1994). *Patterns in the mind. Language and human nature.* New York. Basic Books.

Jensen, A. R. (1998). *The g factor.* Westport, CT. Praeger.

Johnson, W., & Bouchard, T. J., Jr. (2005). The structure of human intelligence. It is verbal, perceptual, and image rotation (VPR), not fluid and crystallized. *Intelligence, 33,* 393–416.

Johnson, W., Bouchard, T. J., Jr., Krueger, R. F., McGue, M., & Gottesman, I. I. (2004). Just one *g.* Consistent results from three test batteries. *Intelligence, 32*(1), 95–107.

Johnson, W., McGue, M., & Iacono, W. G. (2006). Genetic and environmental influences on academic achievement. *Developmental Psychology, 42,* 514–532.

Johnson, W., te Nijenhuis, J., & Bouchard, T. J., Jr. (2008). Still just 1 *g.* Consistent results from five test batteries. *Intelligence, 36,* 81–95.

Jones, G. (2003). Testing two cognitive theories of insight. *Journal of Experimental Psychology. Learning, Memory, and Cognition, 29,* 1017–1027.

Jung-Beeman, M., Bowden, E. M., Haberman, J., Frymiare, J. L., Arambel-Liu, S., et al. (2004). Neural activity when people solve verbal problems with insight. *PLoS Biology, 2.* Retrieved from http://biology.plosjournals.org on November 17, 2005

Kahneman, D. (2011). *Thinking, fast and slow.* New York. Farrar, Straus, & Giroux.

Kaplan, C. A., & Simon, H. A. (1990). In search of insight. *Cognitive Psychology, 22,* 374–419.

Knoblich, G., Ohlsson, S., Haider, H., & Rhenius, D. (1999). Constraint relaxation and chunk decomposition in insight problem solving. *Journal of Experimental Psychology. Learning, Memory, and Cognition, 25,* 1534–1555.

Kosslyn, S. M., Thompson, W. L., & Ganis, G. (2006). *The case for mental imagery.* New York. Oxford University Press.

Kounious, J., & Beeman, M. (2009). The *Aha!* Moment. The cognitive neuroscience of insight. *Current Directions in Psychological Science, 18,* 210–216.

Kounios, J., Frymiare, J. L., Bowden, E. M., Fleck, J. I., Subramaniam, K., et al. (2006). The prepared mind. Brain activity prior to problem presentation predicts subsequent solution by sudden insight. *Psychological Science, 17,* 882–890.

Kuncel, N. R., & Hezlett, S. A. (2010). Fact and fiction in cognitive ability testing for admissions and hiring decisions. *Current*

Directions in Psychological Science, 19, 339–345.

Leon, D. A., Lawlor, D. A., Clark, H., Batty, G. D., & Macintyre, S. (2009). The association of childhood intelligence with mortality in adolescence to middle age. Findings from the Aberdeen 1950s cohort study. *Intelligence, 37,* 520–528.

Lichtenstein, S., Slovic, P., Fischhoff, B., Layman, M., & Combs, B. (1978). Judged frequency of lethal events. *Journal of Experimental Psychology, 4,* 551–578.

Lidz, J., Gleitman, H., & Gleitman, L. (2003). Understanding how input matters. Verb learning and the footprint of universal grammar. *Cognition, 87,* 151–178.

Lilienfeld, S. O., Ammirati, R., & Landfield, K. (2009). Giving debiasing away. Can psychological research on correcting cognitive errors promote human welfare? *Perspectives on Psychological Science, 4,* 390–398.

Liszkowski, U., Schaëfer, M., Carpenter, M., & Tomasello, M. (2009). Prelinguistic infants, but not chimpanzees, communicate about absent entities. *Psychological Science, 20,* 654–660.

Liu, J., Harris, A., & Kanwisher, N. (2010). Perception of face parts and face configurations. An fMRI study. *Journal of Cognitive Neuroscience, 21,* 203–211.

Lubinski, D. (2004). Introduction to the special section on cognitive abilities. 100 years after Spearman's (1904) "'General intelligence,' objectively determined and measured." *Journal of Personality and Social Psychology, 86(1),* 96–111.

Lubinski, D., Webb, R. M., Morelock, M. J., & Benbow, C. P. (2001). Top 1 in 10,000. A 10-year follow-up of the profoundly gifted. *Journal of Applied Psychology, 86,* 718–729.

Lyons, M. J., York, T. P., Franz, C. E., Grant, M. D., Eaves, L. J., et al. (2009). Genes determine stability and the environment determines change in cognitive ability during 35 years of adulthood.

Malotki, E. (1983). *Hopi time. A linguistic analysis of temporal concept in the Hopi language.* Berlin. Mouton de Gruyter.

Marcus, G. F., Fernandes, K. J., & Johnson, S. P. (2007). Infant rule learning facilitated by speech. *Psychological Science, 18,* 387–391.

Martin, L. T., & Kubzansky, L. D. (2005). Childhood cognitive performance and risk of mortality. A prospective cohort study of gifted individuals. *American Journal of Epidemiology, 162,* 887–890.

McArdle, J. J., Ferrer-Caja, E., Hamagami, F., & Woodcock, R. W. (2002). Comparative longitudinal structural analyses of the growth and decline of multiple intellectual abilities over the life span. *Developmental Psychology, 38(1),* 115–142.

McClelland, J. L., Botvinick, M. M., Noelle, D. C., Plaut, D. C., Rogers, T. T., et al. (2010). Letting structure emerge. Connectionist and dynamical systems approaches to cognition. *Trends in Cognitive Sciences, 14,* 348–356.

McGue, M., Bouchard Jr., T. J., Iacono, W. G., & Lykken, D. T. (1993). Behavioral genetics of cognitive ability. A lifespan perspective. In R. Plomin & G. E. McClearn (Eds.), *Nature, nurture, and psychology* (pp. 59–76). Washington, DC. American Psychological Association.

McKone, E., Kanwisher, N., & Duchaine, B. C. (2006). Can generic expertise explain processing for faces? *Trends in Cognitive Sciences, 11(1),* 8–15.

McWhorter, J. (1998). *Word on the street. Debunking the myth of a "pure" standard English.* New York. Basic Books.

McWhorter, J. (2003). *Doing our own thing. The degradation of language and music and why we should, like, care.* New York. Gotham Books.

Meehl, P. (1990). Appraising and amending theories. *Psychological Inquiry, 1,* 108–141.

Meehl, P. E., & Rosen, A. (1955). Antecedent probability in the efficiency of psychometric signs, or cutting scores. *Psychological Bulletin, 52,* 194–216.

Mumford, M. D., & Gustafson, S. B. (1988). Creativity syndrome. Integration, application, and innovation. *Psychological Bulletin, 103,* 27–43.

Myers, D. G. (2002). *Intuition.* New Haven, CT. Yale University Press.

Neisser, U., Boodoo, G., Bouchard, T. J., Jr., Boykin, A. W., Brody, N., Ceci, S. J., et al. (1996). Intelligence. Knowns and unknowns. *American Psychologist, 51,* 77–101.

Newport, E. L. (2002). Critical periods in language development. In L. Nadel (Ed.), *Encyclopedia of cognitive science* (pp. 737–740). London. Macmillan.

Newstead, S. E. (2000). Are there two different types of thinking? *Behavioral and Brain Science, 23,* 600–601.

Nickerson, R. S. (1998). Confirmation bias. A ubiquitous phenomenon in many guises. *Review of General Psychology, 2,* 175–220.

Nisbett, R. E., & Ross, L. (1980). *Human inference. Strategies and shortcomings of social judgment.* Englewood Cliffs, NJ. Prentice-Hall.

Nowak, M. A., Komarova, N. L., & Niyogi, P. (2001). Evolution of universal grammar. *Science, 291,* 114–118.

Nowak, M. A., Plotkin, J. B., & Jansen, V. A. A. (2000). The evolution of syntactic communication. *Nature, 404,* 495–498.

O'Craven, K. M., & Kanwisher, N. (2000). Mental imagery of faces and places activates corresponding stimulus-specific brain regions. *Journal of Cognitive Neuroscience, 12,* 1013–1023.

Ochs, E., & Schieffelin, B. B. (1984). Language acquisition and socialization. Three developmental stories. In R. Shweder & R. LeVine (Eds.), *Culture theory. Essays on mind, self, and emotion* (pp. 276–320). New York. Cambridge University Press.

Ostler, N. (2005). *Empires of the word.* New York. HarperCollins.

Paulus, P. P., & Nijstad, B. A. (Eds.). (2003). *Group creativity.* New York. Oxford University Press.

Petrill, S. A., Lipton, P. A., Hewitt, J. K., Plomin, R., Cherny, S. S., et al. (2004). Genetic and environmental contributions to general cognitive ability through the first 16 years of life. *Developmental Psychology, 40,* 805–812.

Pilling. M., & Davies, I. R. L. (2004). Linguistic relativism and colour cognition. *British Journal of Psychology, 95,* 429–455.

Pinker, S. (1994). *The language instinct.* New York. William Morrow & Co.

Pinker, S. (1997). *How the mind works.* New York. Norton.

Pinker, S. (2002). *The blank slate.* New York. Viking.

Pinker, S. (2004). Clarifying the logical problem of language acquisition. *Journal of Child Language, 31,* 949–953.

Pinker, S., & Jackendoff, R. (2005). The faculty of language. What's special about it? *Cognition, 95,* 201–236.

Pinker, S., & Jackendoff, R. (2009). The reality of a universal language faculty. *Behavioral and Brain Sciences, 32,* 465–466.

Plomin, R., Fulker, D. W., Corley, R., & DeFries, J. C. (1997). Nature, nurture, and cognitive development from 1 to 16 years. *Psychological Science, 8,* 442–447.

Plomin, R., & Petrill, S. A. (1997). Genetics and intelligence. What's new? *Intelligence, 24(1),* 53–77.

Plomin, R., & Spinath, F. M. (2004). Intelligence. Genetics, genes, and genomics. *Journal of Personality and Social Psychology, 86(1),* 112–129.

Pollick, A. S., & de Waal, F. B. M. (2007). Ape gestures and language evolution. *PNAS, 104,* 8184–8189.

Povinelli, D. J., & Bering, J. M. (2002). The mentality of apes revisited. *Current Directions in Psychological Science, 11,* 115–119.

Pullum, G. K. (1991). *The great Eskimo vocabulary hoax and other irreverent essays on the study of language.* Chicago, IL. University of Chicago Press.

Reynolds, D. J,. Jr., & Gifford, R. (2001). The sounds and sights of intelligence. A lens model channel analysis. *Personality and Social Psychology Bulletin, 27,* 187–200.

Roberson, D., Davies, I., & Davidoff, J. (2002). Color categories are not universal. Replications and new evidence. In B. Saunders & J. van Brakel (Eds.), *Theories, technologies, instrumentalities of color. Anthropological and historiographic perspectives* (pp. 25–35). Lanham, MD. University Press of America.

Rosch-Heider, E. (1972). Universals in color naming and memory. *Journal of Experimental Psychology, 93(1),* 10–20.

Runco, M. A. (2004). Creativity. *Annual Review of Psychology, 55,* 657–687.

Savage-Rumbaugh, E. S., Shanker, S. G., & Taylor, T. J. (1998). *Apes, language, and the human mind*. New York. Oxford University Press.

Schmitt, F. L., & Hunter, J. (2004). General mental ability in the world of work. Occupational attainment and job performance. *Journal of Personality and Social Psychology, 86*, 162–173.

Scullin, M. H., Peters, E., Williams, W. M., & Ceci, S. J. (2000). The role of IQ and education in predicting later labor market outcomes. Implications for affirmative action. *Psychology, Policy, and Law, 48*, 943–956.

Seyfarth, R. M., & Cheney, D. L. (2003). Signalers and receivers in animal communication. *Annual Review of Psychology, 54*, 145–173.

Shanker, S. G., Savage-Rumbaugh, E. S., & Taylor, T. J. (1999). Kanzi. A new beginning. *Animal Learning & Behavior, 27(1)*, 24–25.

Siegfried, T. (2010, March 27). Odds are it's wrong. *Science News, 177*. Retrieved from http://www.sciencenews.org/view/feature/id/57091 on May 9, 2010.

Silver, N. (2009, December 27). The odds of airborne terror. Retrieved from http://www.fivethirtyeight.com/2009/12/odds-of-airborne-terror.html on May 28, 2011.

Simons, D., & Chabris, C. (1999). Gorillas in our midst. sustained inattentional blindness for dynamic events. *Perception, 28*, 1059–1074.

Smith, S. M. (2003). The constraining effects of initial ideas. In P. Paulus & B. Nijstad (Eds.), *Group creativity. Innovation through collaboration* (pp. 15–31). Oxford, UK. Oxford University Press.

Spearman, C. (1904). "General intelligence," objectively determined and measured. *American Journal of Psychology, 13*, 201–293.

Spearman, C. E. (1927). *The abilities of man. Their nature and measurement.* New York. Macmillan.

Stanovich, K. E., & West, R. F. (2000). Individual differences in reasoning. Implications for the rationality debate? *Behavioral and Brain Sciences, 23*, 645–726.

Sternberg, R. J. (2000). The holey grail of general intelligence. *Science, 289*, 399–401.

Sternberg, R. J. (2003a). Issues in the theory and measurement of successful intelligence. A reply to Brody. *Intelligence, 31*, 331–337.

Sternberg, R. J. (2003b). Our research program validating the triarchic theory of successful intelligence. Reply to Gottfredson. *Intelligence, 31*, 399–413.

Sternberg, R. J. (2003c). *Wisdom, intelligence, and creativity synthesized.* New York. Cambridge University Press.

Sternberg, R. J. (2005). The triarchic theory of successful intelligence. In D. P. Flanagan & P. L. Harrison (Eds.), *Contemporary intellectual assessment. Theories, tests, and issues* (pp. 103–119). New York. Guilford Press.

Sternberg, R. J., & Davidson, J. E. (Eds.). (1995). *The nature of insight.* Cambridge, MA. MIT Press.

Sternberg, R. J., & Wagner, R. K. (1993). The *g*-ocentric view of intelligence and job performance is wrong. *Current Directions in Psychological Science, 2(1)*, 1–5.

Stickgold, R., & Walker, M. (2004). To sleep, perchance to gain creative insight? *Trends in Cognitive Sciences, 8*, 191–192.

Storm, B. C., & Angello, G. (2010). Overcoming fixation. Creative problem solving and retrieval-induced forgetting. *Psychological Science, 21*, 1263–1265.

Terrace, H. (1987). *Nim.* New York. Columbia University Press.

Thomas, M. (2004). *Universal grammar in second language acquisition. A history.* London. Routledge.

Thurstone, L. (1938). Primary mental abilities. *Psychometric Monographs (No.1).*

Thurstone, L. L., & Thurstone, T. G. (1941). Factorial studies of intelligence. *Psychometric Monographs (No. 2).*

Tooby, J., & Cosmides, L. (2005). Conceptual foundations of evolutionary psychology. In D. Buss (Ed.), *The handbook of evolutionary psychology* (pp. 5–67). Hoboken, NJ. John Wiley & Sons.

Topolinski, S., & Reber, R. (2010). Gaining insight into the "Aha" experience. *Current Directions in Psychological Science, 19*, 402–405.

Tse, C.-S., & Altarriba, J. (2008). Evidence against linguistic relativity in Chinese and English. A case of spatial and temporal metaphors. *Journal of Cognition and Culture, 8*, 335–357.

Turkheimer, E., Haley, A., Waldron, M., D'Onofrio, B., & Gottesman, I. I. (2003). Socioeconomic status modifies heritability of IQ in young children. *Psychological Science, 14*, 623–628.

Tversky, A., & Kahneman, D. (1973). Availability. A heuristic for judging frequency and probability. *Cognitive Psychology, 5*, 207–232.

Tversky, A., & Kahneman, D. (1974). Judgment under uncertainty. Heuristics and biases. *Science, 185*, 1124–1131.

Tversky, A., & Kahneman, D. (2005) Judgment under uncertainty. Heuristics and biases. In A. Tversky & D. Kahneman (Eds.), *Negotiation, decision making, and conflict management* (Vols. 1–3, pp. 251–258). Northampton, MA. Edward Elgar Publishing.

van der Lelly, H. K., Rosen, S., & McClelland, A. (1998). *Current Biology, 8*, 1253–1258.

Vargha-Khadem, F; Gadian, D. G., Copp, A., & Mishkin, M. (2005). *FOXP2* and the neuroanatomy of speech and language. *Nature Reviews Neuroscience, 6*, 131–138.

Verney, S. P., Granholm, E., Marshall, S. P., Malcame, V. L., & Saccuzo, D. P. (2005). Culture fair cognitive ability assessment. Information processing and psychophysiological approaches. *Assessment, 12*, 303–319.

von Frisch, K. (1967). *A biologist remembers.* Oxford, UK. Pergamon Press.

Vouloumanos, A., & Werker, J. F. (2007). Listening to language at birth. Evidence for a bias for speech in neonates. *Developmental Science, 10*, 159–164.

Westermann, G., Ruh, N., & Plunkett, K. (2009). Connectionist approaches to language learning. *Linguistics, 47*, 413–452.

Winne, P. H., & Nebit, J. C. (2010). The psychology of academic achievement. *Annual Review of Psychology, 61*, 653–678.

Wynne, C. D. L. (2004). *Do animals think?* Princeton, NJ. Princeton University Press.

Xu, Y., Liu, J., & Kanwisher, N. (2005). The M170 is selective for faces, not for expertise. *Neuropsychologia, 43*, 588–597.

Zuberbüler, K. (2003). Referential signaling in non-human primates. Cognitive precursors and limitations for the evolution of language. *Advances in the Study of Behavior, 33*, 265–3307.

CHAPTER 10

Alcock, J. (2001). *The triumph of sociobiology.* New York. Oxford University Press.

Alcock, J. (2009). *Animal behavior.* Sunderland, MA. Sinauer.

Alegria, M., Woo, M., Cao, Z., Torres, M., Meng, X.-L., et al. (2007). Prevalence and correlates of eating disorders in Latinos in the United States. *International Journal of Eating Disorders, 40(Suppl.)*, S15–S21.

American Psychiatric Association. (2013). Highlights of changes from DSM-IV-TR to DSM-5. Retrieved from www.psychiatry.org on February 26, 2013.

Anderson, C. A., & Bushman, B. J. (2002). Human aggression. *Annual Review of Psychology, 53*, 27–51.

Anderson-Fye, E. P., & Becker, A. E. (2003). Cross-cultural aspects of eating disorders. In J. K. Thompson (Ed.), *Handbook of eating disorders and obesity* (pp. 565–589). Hoboken, NJ. John Wiley.

Archer, J. (2004). Sex differences in aggression in real-world settings. A meta-analytic review. *Review of General Psychology, 8*, 291–232.

Archer, J. (2006). Testosterone and human aggression. An evaluation of the challenge hypothesis. *Neuroscience and Biobehavioral Reviews, 30*, 319–345.

Archer, J. (2009). Does sexual selection explain human sex differences in aggression? *Behavioral and Brain Sciences, 32*, 249–311.

Bandura, A. (1983). Psychological mechanisms of aggression. In R. G. Geen & E. Donnerstein (Eds.), *Aggression. Theories, research, and implications for policy* (pp. 11–40). New York. Academic Press.

Bandura, A. (2000). Self-efficacy. The foundation of agency. In W. J. Perrig & A. Grob (Eds.), *Control of human behavior, mental processes and consciousness* (pp. 17–33). Mahwah, NJ. Lawrence Erlbaum Associates.

Bandura, A. (2002). Social cognitive theory in cultural context. *Applied Psychology. An International Review, 51,* 269–290.

Bandura, A. (2007). Much ado over a faulty conception of perceived self-efficacy grounded in faulty experimentation. *Journal of Social and Clinical Psychology, 26,* 641–658.

Barkow, J. H. (2006). *Missing the revolution. Darwinism for social scientists.* Oxford, UK. Oxford University Press.

Barkow, J. H., Cosmides, L., & Tooby, J. (Eds.). (1992). *The adapted mind. Evolutionary psychology and the generation of culture.* New York. Oxford University Press.

Bateup, H.S., Booth, A., Shirtcliff, E., & Granger, D. A. (2002). Testosterone, cortisol and women's competition. *Evolution and Human Behavior, 23,* 181–192.

Baumeister, R. F. (1997). *Evil. Inside human violence and cruelty.* New York. W.H. Freeman.

Baumeister, R. F., & Dhavale, D. (2001). Two sides of romantic rejection. In M. R. Leary (Ed.), *Interpersonal rejection* (pp. 55–71). New York. Oxford University Press.

Baumeister, R. F., & Leary, M. R. (1995). The need to belong. Desire for interpersonal attachments as a fundamental human motivation. *Psychological Bulletin, 117,* 497–529.

Belcher, A. J., Laurenceau, J-P., Siegel, S. D., Graber, E. C., Cohen, L. H., & Dasch, K. B. (2011). Daily support in couples coping with early stage breast cancer. Maintaining intimacy during adversity. *Health Psychology, 30,* 665–673.

Bemporad, J. R. (1996). Self-starvation through the ages. Reflections on the prehistory of anorexia nervosa. *International Journal of Eating Disorders, 19,* 217–237.

Berkowitz, L. (1989). Frustration-aggression hypothesis. Examination and reformulation. *Psychological Bulletin, 106,* 59–73.

Berkowitz, L. (1993). Pain and aggression. Some findings and implications. *Motivation and Emotion, 17,* 277–293.

Bernhardt, P. C., Dabbs, J. M., Fielden, J. A., & Lutter, C. D. (1998). Testosterone changes during vicarious experiences of winning and losing among fans at sporting events. *Physiology and Behavior, 65,* 59–62.

Bettencourt, A. A., & Kernahan, C. (1997). A meta-analysis of aggression in the presence of violent cues. Effects of gender differences and aversive provocations. *Aggressive Behavior, 23,* 447–456.

Bhattacharya, R., Unadkat, A., & Connan, F. (2010). Cultural perspectives on eating disorders. In R. Bhattacharya, S. Cross, & D. Bhugra (Eds.), *Clinical topics in cultural psychiatry* (pp. 232–243). London, UK. Royal College of Psychiatrists.

Book, A. S., Starzyk, K. B., & Quinsey, V. L. (2001). The relationship between testosterone and aggression. A meta-analysis. *Aggression and Violent Behavior. A Review Journal, 6,* 579–599.

Brown, D. E. (1991). *Human universals.* Boston. McGraw-Hill.

Brown, L. V. (Ed.). (2007). *Psychology of motivation.* Hauppauge, NY. Nova Science.

Brownell, K. D., & Rodin, J. (1994). The dieting maelstrom. Is it possible and advisable to lose weight? *American Psychologist, 49,* 781–791.

Bulik, C. M. (2005). Exploring the gene-environment nexus in eating disorders. *Journal of Psychiatry and Neuroscience, 30,* 335–339.

Bulik, C. M., Thornton, L. M., Root, T. L., Pisetsky, E. M., Lichtenstein, P., & Pedersen, N. L. (2010). Understanding the relation between anoirexia nervosa and bulimia nervoist in a Swedish national twin sample. *Biological Psychiatry, 67,* 71–77.

Bushman, B. J., & Anderson, C. A. (2001a). Is it time to pull the plug on the hostile versus instrumental aggression dichotomy? *Psychological Review, 108,* 273–279.

Bushman, B. J., & Anderson, C. A. (2001b). Media violence and the American Public. Scientific facts versus media misinformation. *American Psychologist, 56,* 477–489.

Bushman, B. M., & Anderson, C. A. (2002). Violent video games and hostile expectations. A test of the General Aggression Model. *Personality and Social Psychology Bulletin, 28,* 1679–1686.

Buss, D. M. (Ed.). (2005). *Handbook of evolutionary psychology.* Hoboken, NJ. John Wiley & Sons.

Cacioppo, J. T., Hawkley, L. C., & Berntson, G. G. (2003). The anatomy of loneliness. *Current Directions in Psychological Science, 12,* 71–74.

Campfield, L. A., Smith, F. J., Rosenbaum, M., & Hirsch, J. (1996). Human eating. evidence for a physiological basis using a modified paradigm. *Neuroscience and Biobehavioral Review, 20,* 133–137.

Card, N. A., Stucky, B. D., Sawalani, G. M., & Little, T. D. (2008). Direct and indirect aggression during childhood and adolescence. A meta-analytic review of gender differences, intercorrelations, and relations to maladjustment. *Child Development, 79,* 1185–1229.

Caspit, J. T., Harrington, H., Moffitt, T. E., Milne, B. J., & Poulton, R. (2006). Socially isolated children 20 years later. Risk of cardiovascular disease. *Archives of Pediatric and Adolescent Medicine, 160,* 805–811.

Cassin, S. E., & von Ranson, K. M. (2005). Personality and eating disorders. A decade in review. *Clinical Psychology Review, 25,* 895–916.

Chang, W., Wong, W., & Teo, G. (2000). The socially oriented and individually oriented achievement motivation of Singaporean and Chinese students. *Journal of Psychology in Chinese Studies, 1,* 39–63.

A class of one. (1997). Transcript of *NewsHour with Jim Lehrer.* Retrieved from http://www.pbs.org/news hour/bb/race_relations/jan-june97/bridges_2-18.html on January 2, 2008.

Coles, R., & Ford, G. (1995). *The story of Ruby Bridges.* New York. Scholastic Press.

Collins, N. L., & Miller, L. C. (1994). Self-disclosure and liking. A meta-analytic review. *Psychological Bulletin, 82,* 407–475.

Covington, M. V. (2000). Intrinsic versus extrinsic motivation in schools. A reconciliation. *Current Directions in Psychological Science, 9(1),* 22–25.

Critser, G. (2003). *Fat land. How Americans became the fattest people in the world.* Boston, MA. Houghton Mifflin Company.

Csikszentmihalyi, M., Abuhamdeh, S., & Nakamura J. (2005). Flow. In A. J. Elliot & C. S. Dweck (Eds.), *Handbook of competence and motivation* (pp. 598–698). New York. Guilford Publications.

Dabbs, J. M. (2000). *Heroes, rogues, and lovers. Testosterone and behavior.* New York. McGraw Hill.

Daly, M., & Wilson, M. (1988). *Homicide.* New York. Aldine de Gruyter.

Deci, E. L. (1975). *Intrinsic motivation.* New York. Plenum.

Deci, E. L., & Ryan, R. M. (2000). The "what" and "why" of goal pursuits. Human needs and the self-determination of behavior. *Psychological Inquiry, 11,* 227–268.

DeWall, C. N., & Anderson, C. A. (2011). The general aggression model. In P. R. Shaver & M. Mikulincer (Eds.), *Human aggression and violence. Causes, manifestations, and consequences* (pp. 15–33). Washington, DC. American Psychological Association.

DeWall, C. N., MacDonald, G., Webster, G. D., Masten, C. L., Baumeister, R. F., et al. (2010). Acetaminophen reduces social pain. Behavioral and neural evidence. *Psychological Science, OnlineFirst.* Retrieved from http://pss.sagepub.com on June 30, 2010.

Dickens, C. (1838). *The adventures of Oliver Twist. A parish boy's progress.* London. Richard Bentley.

Diener, E. (2000). Subjective well-being. The science of happiness and a proposal for a national index. *American Psychologist, 55,* 34–43.

Diener, E., & Seligman, M. E. P. (2002). Very happy people. *Psychological Science, 13,* 81–84.

Diliberti, N., Bordi, P. L., Conklin, M. T., Roe, L. S., & Rolls, B. J. (2004). Increased portion size leads to increased energy intake in a restaurant meal. *Obesity Review, 12,* 562–568.

Dollard, J., Doob, L., Miller, N., Mowrer, O., & Sears, R. (1939). *Frustration and aggression.* New Haven, CT. Yale University Press.

Dovidio, J. F., & Gaertner, S. L. (1996). Affirmative action, unintentional racial biases, and intergroup relations. *Journal of Social Issues, 52*(4), 51–75.

Eagly, A. H., & Wood, W. (2009). Sexual selection does not provide an adequate theory of sex differences in aggression. *Behavioral and Brain Sciences, 32,* 276–277.

Eisenberger, N. I., (2012). Broken hearts and broken bones. A neural perspective on the similarities between social and physical pain. *Current Directions in Psychological Science, 21,* 42–47.

Elder, G. H., & Clipp, E. C. (1988). Wartime losses and social bonding. Influence across 40 years in men's lives. *Psychiatry, 51,* 177–198.

Elliot, A. J., & Church, M. A. (1997). A hierarchal model of approach and avoidance achievement motivation. *Journal of Personality and Social Psychology, 72,* 218–232.

Elliot, A. J., & Dweck, C. S. (2005). Competence and motivation. Competence as the core of achievement motivation. In A. Elliot & C. Dweck (Eds.), *Handbook of competence and motivation* (pp. 3–12). New York. Guilford Publications.

Festinger, L., Schacter, S., & Back, K. (1950). *Social pressures in informal groups. A study of human factors in housing.* Palo Alto, CA. Stanford University Press.

Finkelstein, E. A., Fiebelkorn, I. C., & Wang, G. (2003). National medical spending attributable to overweight and obesity. how much, and who's paying. *Health Affairs, 3,* 219–226.

Finkelstein, E. A., & Zuckerman, L. (2008). *The fattening of America. How the economy makes us fat, if it matters, and what to do about it.* Hoboken, NJ. John Wiley & Sons.

Fiske, S. T., & Yamamoto, M. (2005). Coping with rejection. Core social motives across cultures. In K. D. Williams, J. P. Forgas, & W. von Hippel (Eds.), *The social outcast. Ostracism, social exclusion, rejection, and bullying* (pp. 185–198). New York. Psychology Press.

Forgas, J. P., Williams, K. D., & Laham, S. M. (Eds.). (2005). *Social motivation. Conscious and unconscious processes.* New York. Cambridge University Press.

Gailliot, M. T., & Baumeister, R. F. (2007). Self-esteem, belongingness, and worldview validation. Does belongingness exert a unique influence upon self-esteem? *Journal of Research in Personality, 41,* 327–345.

Gardner, W. L., Pickett, C. L., & Brewer, M. B. (2000). Social exclusion and selective memory. How the need to belong influences memory of social events. *Personality & Social Psychology Bulletin, 26,* 486–496.

Grabe, S., Ward, L. M., & Hyde, J. S. (2008). The role of the media in body image concerns among women. A meta-analysis of experimental and correlational studies. *Psychological Bulletin, 134,* 460–476.

Gump, B. B., & Kulik, J. A. (1997). Stress, affiliation, and emotional contagion.

Journal of Personality and Social Psychology, 72, 305–319.

Hagerty, M. R. (1999). Testing Maslow's hierarchy of needs. National quality-of-life across time. *Social Indicators Research, 46,* 249–271.

Haller, M., & Hadler, M. (2006). How social relations and structures can produce happiness and unhappiness. A comparative analysis. *Social Indicators Research, 75,* 196–216.

Harlow, H. F. (1953). Learning by Rhesus monkeys on the basis of manipulation-exploration motives. *Science, 117,* 466–467.

Harlow, H. F., Harlow, M. K., & Meyer, D. R. (1950). Learning motivated by a manipulative drive. *Journal of Experimental Psychology, 40,* 228–234.

Harris, J. A. (1999). Review and methodological considerations in research on testosterone and aggression. *Aggression and Violent Behavior, 4,* 273–291.

Havel, P. J. (2001). Peripheral signals conveying metabolic information to the brain. Short-term and long-term regulation of food intake and energy homeostasis. *Experimental Biology and Medicine, 226,* 963–997.

Hawkley, L. C., & Cacioppo, J. T. (2007). Aging and loneliness. Downhill quickly? *Current Directions in Psychological Science, 16,* 187–191.

Hawkley, L. C., & Cacioppo, J. T. (2010). Loneliness matters. A theoretical and empirical review of consequences and mechanisms. *Annals of Behavioral Medicine, 40,* 218–227.

Hazan, C., & Shaver, P. R. (1994). Attachment as an organizational framework for research on close relationships. *Psychological Inquiry, 5,* 1–22.

Hebb, D. O. (1955). Drives and the C. N. S. (central nervous system). *Psychological Review, 62,* 243–254.

Heine, S. J., Kitayama, S., Lehman, D. R., Takata, T., Ide, E., et al. (2001). Divergent consequences of success and failure in Japan and North America. An investigation of self-improving motivations and malleable selves. *Journal of Personality and Social Psychology, 81,* 599–615.

Heinrich, L. M., & Gullone, E. (2006). The clinical significance of loneliness. A literature review. *Clinical Psychology Review, 26,* 695–718.

Hoek, H. W., & van Hoeken, D. (2003). Review of the prevalence and incidence of eating disorders. *International Journal of Eating Disorders, 34,* 383–396.

House, J. S., Landis, K. R., & Umberson, D. (1988). Social relationships and health. *Science, 241,* 540–545.

Hudson, J. I., Hiripi, E., Pope, H. G., Jr., & Kessler, R. C. (2007). The prevalence and correlates of eating disorders in the National Comorbidity Survey Replication. *Biological Psychiatry, 61,* 348–358.

Hull, C. L. (1943). *Principles of behavior.* New Haven, CT. Yale University Press.

Jacobi, C., Hayward, C., de Zwaan, M., Kraemer, H. C., & Agras, S. (2004). Coming to terms with risk factors for eating disorders. Application of risk terminology and suggestions for a general taxonomy. *Psychological Bulletin, 130,* 19–65.

James, W. (1981). *The principles of psychology* (Vol. 2). Cambridge, MA. Harvard University Press. (Original work published 1890.)

Kanfer, R. (1990). Motivation theory and industrial and organizational psychology. In M. D. Dunnette & L. M Hough (Eds.), *Handbook of industrial and organizational psychology Vol. 1* (2nd ed., pp. 75–170). Palo Alto, CA. Consulting Psychologists Press.

Katzman, M. A., Hermans, K. M. E., van Hoeken, D., & Hoek, H. W. (2004). "Not your typical island woman". Anorexia nervosa is reported only in subcultures in Curaçao. *Culture, Medicine, and Psychiatry, 28,* 463–492.

Keel, P. K., Brown, T. A., Holland, L. A., & Bodell, L. P. (2012). Empirical classification of eating disorders. *Annual Review of Clinical Psychology, 8,* 381–404.

Keesey, R. E., & Hirvonen, M. D. (1997). Body weight set-points. Determination and adjustment. *Journal of Nutrition, 127,* 1875S–1883S.

Kenrick, D. T., Griskevicius, V., Neuberg, S. L., & Schaller, M. (2010). Renovating the pyramid of needs. Contemporary extensions built upon ancient foundations. *Pespectives on Psychological Science, 5,* 292–314.

Kenrick, D. T., Neuberg, S. L., Griskevicius, V., Becker, D. V., & Schaller, M. (2010). Goal-driven cognition and functional behavior. The fundamental-motives framework. *Current Directions in Psychological Science, 19,* 63–67.

Keys, A. Brozek, J., Henschel, A., Mickelsen, O., & Taylor, H. L. (1950). *The biology of starvation.* Minneapolis. University of Minnesota Press.

Khatwani, K. (2003). *Theories of love and loss. A new conception of mourning* (Abstract only). Berkeley, CA. The Wright Institute. Retrieved from Dissertation Abstracts International. Section B. Sciences and Engineering, 64 (3-B).

Kissileff, H. R., Pi-Sunyer, F. X., Thornton, J., & Smith, G. P. (1981). C-terminal octapeptide of cholecystokinin decreases food intake in man. *American Journal of Clinical Nutrition, 34,* 154–160.

Kluger, A. N., & Tikochinsky, J. (2001). The error of accepting the "theoretical" null hypothesis. The rise, fall, and resurrection of commonsense hypotheses in psychology. *Psychological Bulletin, 127,* 408–421.

Klump, K. L., Burt, A. S., McGue, M., & Iacono, W. G. (2007). Changes in genetic and environmental influences on disordered eating across adolescence. A longitudinal twin study. *Archives of General Psychiatry, 64,* 1409–1415.

Korman, A. K. (1974). *The psychology of motivation*. Englewood Cliffs, NJ. Prentice-Hall.

Latham, G. P., & Pinder, C. C. (2005). Work motivation theory and research at the dawn of the twenty-first century. *Annual Review of Psychology, 56*, 485–516.

Latham, G. P., Stajkovic, A. D., & Locke, E. A. (2010). The relevance and viability of subconscious goals in the workplace. *Journal of Management, 36*, 234–255.

Laurenceau, J.-P., Feldman Barrett, L., & Pietromonaco, P. R. (1998). Intimacy as an interpersonal process. The importance of self-disclosure, partner disclosure, and perceived partner responsiveness in interpersonal exchanges. *Journal of Personality and Social Psychology, 74*, 1238–1251.

Laurenceau, J.-P., & Kleinman, B. (2006). Intimacy in personal relationships. In A. L. Bangelisti & D. Perlman (Eds.), *The Cambridge handbook of personal relationships* (pp. 637–653). New York. Cambridge University Press.

Leary, M. R., & Cox, C. B. (2008). Belongingness motivation. A mainspring of social action. In J. Y. Shah, & W. L. Gardner (Eds.), *Handbook of motivation science* (pp. 27–40). New York. Guilford Press.

Lee, S. (1995). Self starvation in context. Towards a culturally sensitive understanding of anorexia nervosa. *Social Science Medicine, 41*, 25–36.

Lee, S. (2001). Fat phobia in anorexia nervosa. Whose obsession is it? In M. Nasser, M. A. Katzman, & R. A. Gordon (Eds.), *Eating disorders and cultures in transition.* (pp. 40–54). New York. Taylor and Francis.

Lepper, M. P., Greene, D., & Nisbett, R. E. (1973). Undermining children's intrinsic interest with extrinsic reward. A test of the "overjustification" hypothesis. *Journal of Personality and Social Psychology, 28*, 129–137.

Littlewood, R. (1995). Psychopathology and personal agency. Modernity, culture change and eating disorders in South Asian societies. *British Journal of Medical Psychology, 68*, 45–63.

Littlewood, R. 2004. Commentary. globalization, culture, body image, and eating disorders. *Culture, Medicine and Psychiatry, 28*, 597–602.

Livshits, G., Kato, B. S., Wilson, S. G., & Spector, T. D. (2007). Linkage of genes to total lean body mass in normal women. *Journal of Clinical Endocrinology and Metabolism, 92*, 3171–3176.

Locke, E. A., & Latham, G. P. (2002). Building a practically useful theory of goal-setting and task motivation. *American Psychologist, 57*, 705–717.

Locke, E. A., & Latham, G. P. (2006). New directions in goal-setting theory. *Current Directions in Psychological Science, 15*, 265–268.

Lucas, R. E., Clark, A. E., Georgellis, Y., & Diener, E. (2004). Unemployment alters the set point for life satisfaction. *Psychological Science, 15*, 8–13.

Lustig, R. (2006a). The "skinny" on childhood obesity. How our Western environment starves kids' brains. *Pediatric Annals, 36*, 176.

Lustig, R. (2006b). Childhood obesity. Behavioral aberration or biochemical drive? Reinterpreting the First Law of Thermodynamics. *Nature. Clinical Practice Endocrinology & Metabolism, 2*, 447–458.

Marinak, B. A., & Gambrell, L. B. (2008). Intrinsic motivation and rewards. What sustains young children's engagement with text? *Literacy Research and Instruction, 47*, 9–26.

Markus, H. R., & Kitayama, S. (1998). The cultural psychology of personality. *Journal of Cross-Cultural Psychology, 29*, 63–87.

Maslow, A. H. (1970). *Motivation and personality* (2nd ed.). New York. Harper & Row.

Mazure, A., & Booth, A. (1998). Testosterone and dominance in men. *Behavioral and Brain Sciences, 21*, 353–363.

McAdams, D. P. (1989). *Intimacy. The need to be close.* New York. Doubleday.

McAdams, D. P. (1992). The intimacy motive. In C. P. Smith, J. W. Atkinson, & D. C. McClelland (Eds.), *Motivation and personality. Handbook of thematic content analysis* (pp. 224–228). New York. Cambridge University Press.

McAdams, D. P., & Vaillant, G. E. (1982). Intimacy motivation and psychosocial adjustment. A longitudinal study. *Journal of Personality Assessment, 46*, 586–593.

McClelland, D. C., Atkinson, J. W., Clark, R. A., & Lowell, E. L. (1953). *The achievement motive.* New York. Appleton-Century-Crofts.

McClelland, D. C., & Koestner, R. (1992). The achievement motive. In D. C. McClelland, & R. Koestner (Eds.), *Motivation and personality. Handbook of thematic content analysis* (pp. 143–152). New York. Cambridge University Press.

McDougall, W. (2005). *An introduction to social psychology.* Brockton, MA. Adamant Media Corporation. (Original work published 1912).

McWhirter, B. T. (1990). Loneliness. A review of current literature, with implications for counseling and research. *Journal of Counseling & Development, 68*, 417–422.

Melanson, K. J. (2004). Food intake regulation in body weight management. A primer. *Nutrition Today, 39*, 203–213.

Melanson, K. J., Westerp-Plantenga, M. S., Campfield, L. A., Saris, W. H. M. (1999). Blood glucose and meal patterns in time-blinded males, after aspartame, carbohydrate, and fat consumption, in relation to sweetness perception. *British Journal of Nutrition, 82*, 437–446.

Mitchell, T. R., & Daniels, D. (2003). Motivation. In W. C. Borman, D. R. Ilgen, & R. J. Klimoski (Eds.), *Handbook of psychology. Vol. 12. Industrial organizational psychology* (pp. 225–254). New York. Wiley.

Moore, T. E., & Pepler, D. J. (2006). Wounding words. Maternal verbal aggression and children's adjustment. *Journal of Family Violence, 21*, 89–93.

Murray, H. A. (1938). *Explorations in personality.* Oxford, UK. Oxford University Press.

Mutch, D. M., & Clément, K. (2006). Unraveling the genetics of human obesity. *PLoS Genetics, 2*, 1956–1963.

Nakamura, J., & Csikszentmihalyi, M. (2009). Flow theory and research. In S. J. Lopez & C. R. Snyder (Eds.), *Oxford handbook of positive psychology* (2nd ed., pp. 195–206). New York. Oxford University Press.

Nassar, M., Katzman, M. A., & Gordon, R. A. (Eds.). (2001). *Eating disorders and cultures in transition.* London. Brunner-Routledge.

Nicdao, E. G., Hong, S., & Takeuchi, D. T. (2007). Prevalence and correlates of eating disorders among Asian Americans. Results from the National Latino and Asian American study. *International Journal of Eating Disorders, 40(Suppl.)*, S22–S26.

Niemiec, C. P., Ryan, R. M., & Deci, E. L. (2009). The path taken. Consequences of attaining intrinsic and extrinsic aspirations in post-college life. *Journal of Research in Personality, 43*, 291–306.

O'Connor, D. B., Archer, J., & Wu, F. C. W. (2004). Effects of testosterone on mood, aggression and sexual behavior in young men. A double-blind, placebo-controlled, cross-over study. *Journal of Clinical Endocrinology and Metabolism, 89*, 2837–2845.

Oishi, S., Diener, E. F., Lucas, R. E., & Suh, E. M. (1999). Cross-cultural variations in predictors of life satisfaction. Perspectives from needs and values. *Personality and Social Psychology Bulletin, 25*, 980–990.

Peterson, C., & Seligman, M. E. P. (2004). *Character strengths and virtues. A handbook and classification.* Washington, DC. American Psychological Association.

Pettigrew, T. F. (1998). Intergroup contact theory. *Annual Review of Psychology, 49*, 65–85.

Pike, K. M., & Borovoy, A. (2004). The rise of eating disorders in Japan. Issues of culture and limitations of the model of "Westernization." *Culture, Medicine, and Psychiatry, 28*, 493–531.

Pinder, C. C. (1998). *Work motivation in organizational behavior.* Upper Saddle River, NJ. Prentice Hall.

Pinel, J. P. J., Assanand, S., & Lehman, D. R. (2000). Hunger, eating, and ill health. *American Psychologist, 55*, 1105–1116.

Pinker, S. (2011). *The better angels of our nature. Why violence has declined.* New York. Viking.

Polivy, J., & Herman, C. P. (2002). Causes of eating disorders. *Annual Review of Psychology, 53*, 187–213.

Quinn, P. C., & Slater, A. (2003). Face perception at birth and beyond. In O. Pascalis & A. Slater (Eds.), *The development of face processing in infancy and early childhood. Current perspectives* (pp. 3–12). Huntington, NY. Nova Science.

Rath, T. (2007). *StrengthsFinder 2.0. A new and upgraded edition of the online test from Gallup's Now, Discover Your Strengths.* New York. Gallup Press.

Roberts, M. E., Tchanturia, L., & Treasure, J. L. (2010). Exploring the neurocognitive signature of poor set-shifting in anorexia and bulimia nervosa. *Journal of Psychiatric Research, 44,* 964–970.

Rolls, B. J. (2003). The supersizing of America. Portion size and the obesity epidemic. *Nutrition Today, 38,* 42–53.

Ronen, S. (1994). An underlying structure of motivational need taxonomies. A cross-cultural confirmation. In H. C. Triandis, M. D. Dunnette, & L. M. Hough (Eds.), *Handbook of industrial and organizational psychology* (2nd ed., pp. 241–269). Palo Alto, CA. Consulting Psychologists Press.

Rotter, J. B. (1966). Generalized expectancies of internal versus external control of reinforcements. *Psychological Monographs, 80* (1, Whole No. 609).

Russell, G. F. M. (1995). Anorexia nervosa through time. In G. Szmulker, C. Dare, & J. Treasure (Eds.), *Handbook of eating disorders. Theory, treatment and research* (pp. 5–17). London. Wiley.

Ryan, R. M., & Deci, E. L. (2000). Intrinsic and extrinsic motivations. Classic definitions and new directions. *Contemporary Educational Psychology, 25,* 54–67.

Sai, F. Z. (2005). The role of the mother's voice in developing mother's face preference. Evidence for intermodal perception at birth. *Infant and Child Development, 14,* 29–50.

Sapolsky, R. M. (1997). *The trouble with testosterone. And other essays on the biology of the human predicament.* New York. Touchstone/Simon & Schuster.

Schachter, S. (1959). *The psychology of affiliation.* Stanford, CA. Stanford University Press.

Schaller, M., Neuberg, S. L., Griskevicius, V., & Kenrick, D. T. (2010). Pyramid power. A reply to commentaries. *Perspectives on Psychological Science, 5,* 335–337.

Schultheiss, O. C., Wirth, M. M., Torges, C. M., Pang, J. S, Villacorta, M. A., & Welsh, K. M. (2005). Effects of implicit power motivation on men's and women's implicit learning and testosterone changes after social victory or defeat. *Journal of Personality and Social Psychology, 88,* 174–188.

Schunk, D. H. (1996). Goal and self-evaluative influences during children's cognitive skill learning. *American Educational Research Journal, 33,* 359–382.

Schwartz, J., & Byrd-Bredbenner, C. (2006). Portion distortion. Typical portion sizes selected by young adults. *Journal of the American Dietary Association, 106,* 1412–1418.

Scott-Phillips, T. C., Dickins, T. E., & West, S. A. (2011). Evolutionary theory and the ultimate-proximate distinction in the human behavioral sciences. *Perspectives on Psychological Science, 6,* 38–47.

Seeman, T. (2001). How do others get under our skin? Social relationships and health. In C. D. Ryff & B. H. Singer (Eds.), *Emotion, social relationships, and health. Series in affective science* (pp. 189–210). London. Oxford University Press.

Seligman, M. E. P. (2002). *Authentic happiness. Using the new positive psychology to realize your potential for lasting fulfillment.* New York. Free Press.

Sherif, M., Harvey, O. J., White, J., Hood, W. R., & Sherif, C. (1961). Intergroup conflict and cooperation. The Robbers Cave Experiment. Middletown, CT. Wesleyan University Press. (Original work published 1954).

Shiovitz-Ezra, S., & Ayalon, L. (2010). Situational versus chronic loneliness as risk factors for all-cause mortality. *International Psychogeriatrics, 22,* 455–462.

Skinner, B. F. (1965). *Science and human behavior.* New York. The Free Press.

Stanton, S. J., Beehner, J. C., Saini, E. K., Kuhn, C. M., & LaBar, K. S. (2009). Dominance, politics, and physiology. Voters' testosterone changes on the night of the 2008 United States presidential election. *PLoS One, 4.* Retrieved from www.plosone.org on October 28, 2009.

Storey, A. E., Walsh, C. J., Quinton, R. L, & Wynne-Edwards, K. E. (2000). Hormonal correlates of paternal responsiveness in new and expectant fathers. *Evolution and Human Behavior, 21,* 79–95.

Striegel-Moore, R. H., & Bulik, C. M. (2007). Risk factors for eating disorders. *American Psychologist, 62,* 181–198.

Tajfel, H., & Billig, M. (1974). Familiarity and categorization in intergroup behavior. *Journal of Experimental Social Psychology, 10,* 159–170.

Tavris, C., & Aronson, E. (2007). *Mistakes were made (but not by me). How we justify foolish beliefs, bad decisions, and hurtful acts.* Orlando, FL. Harcourt.

Taylor, J. Y., Caldwell, C. H., Baser, R. E. Faison, N., & Jackson, J. S. (2007). Prevalence of eating disorders among Blacks in the national survey of American life. *International Journal of Eating Disorders, 40(Suppl.),* S10–S14.

Taylor, S. E. (2006). Tend and befriend. Biobehavioral bases of affiliation under stress. *Current Directions in Psychological Science, 15,* 273–277.

Taylor, S. E., Klein, L. C., Lewis, B. P., Gruenewald, T. L., Gurung, R. A. R., et al. (2000). Biobehavioral responses to stress in females. Tend-and-befriend, not fight-or-flight. *Psychological Bulletin, 107,* 411–429.

Taylor, S. E., Sherman, D. K., Kim, H. S., Jarcho, J., Takagi, K., et al. (2004). Culture and social support. Who seeks it and why? *Journal of Personality and Social Psychology, 87,* 354–362.

Tett, R. P., & Burnett, D. D. (2003). A personality trait-based interactionist model of job performance. *Journal of Applied Psychology, 88,* 500–517.

Thornton, L. M., Mazzeo, S. E., & Bulik, C. M. (2011). The heritability of eating disorders. Methods and current findings. In R. A. H. Adan & W. H. Kaye (Eds.), *Behavioral neurobiology of eating disorders. Current topics in behavioral neurosciences* (pp. 141–156). New York. Springer-Verlag.

Tinbergen, N. (1974). *Animal behavior.* Boston. Little Brown & Co.

Tolman, E. C. (1923). The nature of instinct. *Psychological Bulletin, 20,* 200–218.

Tooby, J., & Cosmides, L. (1992). The psychological foundations of culture. In J. H. Barkow, L. Cosmides, & J. Tooby (Eds.), *The adapted mind. Evolutionary psychology and the generation of culture* (pp. 19–136). New York. Oxford University Press.

Tremblay, A., Boule, N., Doucet, E., & Woods, S. C. (2005). Is the insulin resistance syndrome the price to be paid to achieve body weight stability? *International Journal of Obesity, 29,* 1295–1298.

Trivers, R. (2010). Deceipt and self-deception. In P. Kappeler, & J. Silk (Eds.), *Mind the gap. Tracing the origins of human universals* (pp. 373–393). Berlin. Springer-Verlag.

Trivers R (2011) *The Folly of Fools. The Logic of Deceit and Self-Deception in Human Life.* New York. Basic Books

Uchino, B. N., Uno, D., & Holt-Lunstad, J. (1999). Social support, physiological processes and health. *Current Directions in Psychological Science, 8,* 145–148.

Valdesolo, P., & DeSteno, D. (2008). The duality of virtue. Deconstructing the moral hypocrite. *Journal of Experimental Social Psychology, 44,* 1334–1338.

van Bokhoven, I; van Goozen, S. H. M., van Engeland, H., Schaal, B., Arseneault, L., et al. (2006). Salivary testosterone and aggression, delinquency, and social dominance in a population-based longitudinal study of adolescent males. *Hormones and Behavior, 50,* 118–125.

Wadden, T. A., Brownell, K. D., & Foster, G. D. (2002). Obesity. Responding to the global epidemic. *Journal of Consulting and Clinical Psychology, 70,* 510–525.

Wahba, M. A., & Bridwell, L. G. (1976). Maslow reconsidered. A review of research on the need hierarchy theory. *Organizational Behavior and Human Performance, 15,* 212–240.

Wakeling, A. (1996). Epidemiology of anorexia nervosa. *Psychiatry Research, 62,* 3–9.

Walls, R. T. (2000). Vocational cognition. Accuracy of 3rd-, 6th-, 9th-, and 12th-grade students. *Journal of Vocational Behavior, 56,* 137–144.

Wang, Y., & Beydoun, M. A. (2007). The obesity epidemic in the United States—Gender, age, socioeconomic, racial/ethnic, and geographic characteristics. A systematic review and meta-regression analysis. *Epidemiologic Reviews, 29,* 6–28.

Weiner, B. (1989). *Human motivation.* Mahwah, NJ. Lawrence Erlbaum Associates.

White, R. W. (1959). Motivation reconsidered. The concept of competence. *Psychological Review, 66,* 297–333.

Wilder, D. A., & Thompson, J. E. (1980). Intergroup contact with independent manipulations of in-group and out-group interaction. *Journal of Personality and Social Psychology, 38,* 589–603.

Willer, C. J., Speliotes, E. K., Loos, R. J. F., Li S., Lindgren, C. M., et al. (2008). Six new loci associated with body mass index highlight a neuronal influence on body weight regulation. *Nature Genetics.* Advance online publication retrieved from http://www.nature.com/ng on December 17, 2008.

Williams, K. D. (2001). *Ostracism. The power of silence.* New York. Guilford Press.

Williams, K. D., Cheung, C. K. T., & Choi, W. (2000). CyberOstracism. Effects of being ignored over the internet. *Journal of Personality and Social Psychology, 79,* 748–762.

Williamson, D. A., Gleaves, D. H., & Stewart, T. M. (2005). Categorical versus dimensional models of eating disorders. An examination of the evidence. *International Journal of Eating Disorders, 37,* 1–10.

Witt, L. A., & Ferris, G. R. (2003). Social skill as moderator of the conscientiousness-performance relationship. Convergent results across four studies. *Journal of Applied Psychology, 88,* 809–821.

Witt, L. A., Burke, L. A., Barrick, M. R., & Mount, M. K. (2002). The interactive effects of conscientiousness and agreeableness on job performance. *Journal of Applied Psychology, 87,* 164–169.

Woike, B. A., & McAdams, D. P. (2001). A response to Lilienfeld, Woods, & Garb. TAT-based personality measures have considerable validity. *American Psychological Society Observer, 14.* Retrieved from http://www.psychologicalscience.org/observer/0501/pspicomment.html on November 5, 2005.

Wonderlich, S. A., Joiner, T. E., Keel, P. K., & Williamson, D. A. (2007). Eating disorders diagnoses. Empirical approaches to classification. *American Psychologist, 62,* 167–180.

Wood, W., & Eagly, A. H. (2002). A cross-cultural analysis of the behavior of women and men. Implications for the origins of sex differences. *Psychological Bulletin, 128,* 699–727.

Woods, S. C., Chavez, M., Park, C. R., Riedy, C., Kaiyala, K., & Richardson, R. D., et al. (1995). The evaluation of insulin as a metabolic signal controlling behavior via the brain. *Neuroscience and Biobehavioral Reviews, 20* 139–144.

World Health Organization. (2008). *Global database on body mass index.* Retrieved from http://www.who.int/bmi/index.jsp on April 19, 2008.

Zadro, L., Williams, K. D., & Richardson, R. (2004). How low can you go? Ostracism by a computer is sufficient to lower self-reported levels of belonging, control, self-esteem, and meaningful existence. *Journal of Experimental Social Psychology, 40,* 560–567.

CHAPTER 11

Allen, K. (2003). Are pets a healthy pleasure? The influence of pets on blood pressure. *Current Directions in Psychological Science, 12,* 236–239.

Allen, K., Blascovich, K., & Mendes, W. B. (2002). Cardiovascular reactivity and the presence of pets, friends, and spouses. The truth about cats and dogs. *Psychosomatic Medicine, 64,* 727–739.

Allen, K., Shykoff, B. E., & Izzo, J. L. (2001). Pet ownership, but not ACE inhibitor therapy blunts home blood pressure responses to mental stress. *Hypertension, 38,* 815–820.

Almeida, J., Molnar, B. E., Kawachi, I., & Subramanian, S. V. (2009). Ethnicity and nativity status as determinants of perceived social support. Testing the concept of familism. *Social Science & Medicine, 68,* 1852–1858.

Anderson, J. W., Liu, C., & Kryscio, R. J. (2008). Blood pressure response to Transcendental Meditation. A meta-analysis. *American Journal of Hypertension, 21,* 310–316.

Andrews, F. M., & Withey, S. B. (1976). *Well-being. Americans' perceptions of life quality.* New York. Plenum Press.

Averill, J. R. (1982). *Anger and aggression. An essay on emotion.* New York. Springer-Verlag.

Baars, B. J. (2005). Subjective experience is probably not limited to humans. The evidence from neurobiology and behavior. *Consciousness and Cognition. An International Journal, 14(1),* 7–21.

Bandura, A. (1973). *Aggression. A social learning theory analysis.* Englewood Cliffs, NJ. Prentice Hall.

Barel, E., Van Ijzendoorn, M. H., Sagi-Schwartz, A., & Bakermans-Kranenburg, M. (2010). Surviving the holocaust. A meta-analysis of the long-term sequelae of a genocide. *Psychological Bulletin, 136,* 677–698.

Barnes, V. A., Treiber, F. A., & Davis, H. (2001). Impact of Transcendental Meditation on cardiovascular function during acute stress in adolescents with high normal blood pressure. *Journal of Psychosomatic Research, 51,* 597–605.

Barot, S. K., Chung, A., Kim, J. J., & Bernstein, I. L. (2009). Functional imaging of stimulus convergence in amygdalar neurons during Pavlovian fear conditioning. *PLos One, 4(7).* Retrieved from www.plosone.org on October 10, 2009.

Barrett, L. F. (2006). Are emotions natural kinds? *Perspectives on Psychological Science, 1,* 28–58.

Barrett, L. F., Gross, J., Christensen, T. C., & Benvenuto, M. (2001). Knowing what you're feeling and knowing what to do about it. Mapping the relation between emotion differentiation and emotion regulation. *Cognition and Emotion, 15,* 713–724.

Barrett, L. F., & Lindquist, K. (2008). The embodiment of emotion. In G. R. Semin & E. R. Smith (Eds.), *Embodied grounding. Social cognitive, affective, and neuroscientific approaches.* New York. Cambridge University Press.

Barrett, L. F., Mesquita, B., Ochsner, K. N., & Gross, J. J. (2007). The experience of emotion. *Annual Review of Psychology, 58,* 373–403.

Barsky, A. J., Saintfort, R., Rogers, M. P., & Borus, J. F. (2002). Nonspecific medication side effects and the nocebo phenomenon. *JAMA, 287,* 622–627.

Bartels, A., & Zeki, S. (2004). The neural correlates of maternal and romantic love. *Neuroimage, 21,* 1155–1166.

Baumeister, R. F., Bratslavsky, E., Finkenauer, C., & Vohs, K. D. (2001). Bad is stronger than good. *Review of General Psychology, 5,* 323–370.

Baumeister, R. F., Vohs, K. D., DeWall, C. N., & Zhang, L. (2007). How emotion shapes behavior. Feedback, anticipation, and reflection, rather than direct causation. *Personality and Social Psychology Review, 11,* 167–203.

Bechara, A., Damasio, H., Tranel, D., & Damasio, A. R. (1997). Deciding advantageously before knowing the advantageous strategy. *Science, 275,* 1293–1295.

Beck, A. T. (1999). *Prisoners of hate. The cognitive basis of anger, hostility, and violence.* New York. Harper-Collins.

Belle, D. (1991). Gender differences in the social moderators of stress. In A. Monat & R. S. Lazarus (Eds.), *Stress and coping. An anthology* (3rd ed., pp. 258–274). New York. Columbia University Press.

Benson, H. (1983). The relaxation response. Its subjective and objective historical precedents and physiology. *Trends in Neurosciences, 6,* 281–284.

Berkowitz, L., & Harmon-Jones, E. (2004a). Toward an understanding of the determinants of anger. *Emotion, 4,* 107–130.

Biswas-Diener, R., Vittersø, J., & Diener, E. (2005). Most people are pretty happy, but there is cultural variation. The Inughuit, the Amish, and the Maasai. *Journal of Happiness Studies, 6,* 205–226.

Bonanno, G. A. (2005). Resilience in the face of potential trauma. *Current Directions in Psychological Science, 14,* 135–138.

Bonanno, G. A., & Mancini, A. D. (2008). The human capacity to thrive in the face of potential trauma. *Pediatrics, 121,* 369–375.

Bonanno, G. A., Westphal, M., & Mancini, A. D. (2011). Resilience to loss and potential trauma. *Annual Review of Clinical Psychology, 7,* 511–535.

Bond, C. F., Jr., & DePaulo, B. M. (2006). Accuracy of deception judgments. *Personality and Social Psychology Review, 10,* 214–234.

Bond, C. F., Jr., & DePaulo, B. M. (2008). Individual differences in judging deception. Accuracy and bias. *Psychological Bulletin, 134*, 477–492.

Bono, G., McCullough, M. E., & Root, L. M. (2008). Forgiveness, feeling connected to others, and well-being. Two longitudinal studies. *Personality and Social Psychology Bulletin*, 182–195.

Boyce, C. J., Brown, D. A., & Moore, S. C. (2010). Money and happiness. Rank of income, not income, affects life satisfaction. *Psychological Science, 21*, 471–475.

Brawley, L. R., & Rodgers, W. M. (1993). Social-psychological aspects of fitness promotion. In P. Seraganian (Ed.), *Exercise psychology. The influence of physical exercise on psychological processes* (pp. 254–298). New York. Wiley.

Brondolo, E., Brady ver Halen, N., Pencille, M., Beatty, D., & Contrada, R. J. (2009). Coping with racism. A selective review of the literature and a theoretical and methodological critique. *Journal of Behavioral Medicine, 32*, 64–88.

Brown, S. L., Nesse, R. M., Vinokur, A. D., & Smith, D. M. (2003). *Psychological Science, 14*, 320–327.

Brydon, L., Magid, K., & Steptoe, A. (2006). Platelets, coronary heart disease, and stress. *Brain, Behavior, & Immunity, 20*, 113–119.

Buhle, J. T., Stevens, B. L., Friedman, J. J., & Wager, T. D. (2012). Distraction and placebo. Two separate routes to pain control. *Psychological Science, 23*, 246–253.

Bushman, B. J. (2002). Does venting anger feed or extinguish the flame? Catharsis, rumination, distraction, anger, and aggressive responding. *Personality and Social Psychology Bulletin, 28*, 724–731.

Bushman, B. J., Baumeister, R. F., & Stack, A. D. (1999). Catharsis, aggression, and persuasive influence. Self-fulfilling or self-defeating prophecies. *Journal of Personality and Social Psychology, 76*, 367–376.

Calder, A. J., Lawrence, A. D., & Young, A. W. (2001). Neuropsychology of fear and loathing. *Nature Reviews. Neuroscience, 2*, 352–363.

Campbell, A. (2004). Female competition. Causes, constraints, content, and contexts. *Journal of Sex Research, 41(1)*, 16–26.

Cannon, W. B. (1929a). *Bodily changes in pain, hunger, fear and rage. An account of recent researches into the functions of emotional excitement.* New York. D. Appleton.

Cannon, W. B. (1929b). Organization for physiological homeostasis. *Physiological Reviews, 9*, 399–431.

Carter, C. S. (2004). Oxytocin and the prairie vole. A love story. In J. T. Cacioppo & G. G. Berntson (Eds.), *Essays in social neuroscience* (pp. 53–63). Cambridge, MA. MIT Press.

Chida, Y., & Steptoe, A. (2008). Positive psychological well-being and mortality. A quantitative review of prospective observational studies. *Psychosomatic Medicine, 70*, 741–756.

Cohen, S. (1996). Psychological stress, immunity and upper respiratory infections. *Current Directions in Psychological Science, 5*, 86–90.

Cohen, S., Alper, C. M., Doyle, W. J., Adler, N., Treanor, J. J., & Turner, R. B. (2008). Objective and subjective socioeconomic status and susceptibility to the common cold. *Health Psychology, 27*, 268–274.

Cohen, S., Frank, E., Doyle, W. J., Skoner, D. P., Rabin, B. S., & Swaltney, J. M., Jr. (1998). Types of stressors that increase susceptibility to the common cold in healthy adults. *Health Psychology 17*, 214–223.

Cohen, S., Janicki-Deverts, D., & Miller, G. E. (2007). Psychological stress and disease. *Journal of the American Medical Association, 298*, 1685–1687.

Collins, M. P., & Dunn, L. F. (2005). The effects of meditation and visual imagery on an immune system disorder. Dermatomyositis. *Journal of Alternative and Complementary Medicine, 11*, 275–284.

Contrada, R. J., Ashmore, R. D., Gary, M. L., Coups, E., Egeth, J. D., et al. (2000). Ethnicity-related sources of stress and their effects on well-being. *Current Directions in Psychological Science, 9*, 136–139.

Costa, P. T., Jr., Terracciano, A., & McCrae, R. R. (2001). Gender differences in personality traits across cultures. Robust and surprising findings. *Journal of Personality and Social Psychology, 81*, 322–331.

Coyne, J. C. (1976). Depression and the response of others. *Journal of Abnormal Psychology, 85*, 186–193.

Crano, W. D., & Prislin, R. (2006). Attitudes and persuasion. *Annual Review of Psychology, 57*, 345–374.

Damasio, A. R. (1994). *Descartes' error. Emotion, reason and the human brain.* New York. Grosset/Putnam.

Das, E. H. H., deWit, J. B. F., & Stroebe, W. (2003). Fear appeals motivate acceptance of action recommendations. Evidence for a positive bias in the processing of persuasive messages. *Personality and Social Psychology Bulletin, 29*, 650–664.

Davidson, R. J., Kabat-Zinn, J., Schumacher, J., Rosenkranz, M., Muller, D., et al. (2003). Alterations in brain and immune function produced by mindfulness meditation. *Psychosomatic Medicine, 65*, 564–570.

Dawkins, R. (1976). *The selfish gene.* London. Oxford University Press.

Del Vecchio, T., & O'Leary, K. D. (2004). Effectiveness of anger treatments for specific anger problems. A meta-analytic review. *Clinical Psychology Review, 24(1)*, 15–34.

DePaulo, B. M. (2004). The many faces of lies. In A. G. Miller (Ed.), *The social psychology of good and evil* (pp. 303–326). New York. Guilford Press.

DePaulo, B. M., & Kashy, D. A. (1998). Everyday lies in close and casual relationships. *Journal of Personality and Social Psychology, 74*, 63–79.

DePaulo, B. M., Kashy, D. A., Kirkendol, S. E., Wyer, M. M., & Epstein, J. A. (1996). Lying in everyday life. *Journal of Personality and Social Psychology, 70*, 979–995.

DePaulo, B. M., Lindsay, J. L., Malone, B. E., Muhlenbruck, L., Charlton, K., et al. (2003). Cues to deception. *Psychological Bulletin, 129*, 74–118.

Diener, E. (2000). Subjective well-being. The science of happiness and a proposal for a national index. *American Psychologist, 55(1)*, 34–43.

Diener, E., Lucas, R. E., & Scollon, C. N. (2006). Beyond the hedonic treadmill. Revising the adaptation theory of well-being. *American Psychologist, 61*, 305–314.

Diener, E., Ng, W., Harter, J., & Arora, R. (2010). Wealth and happiness across the world. Material prosperity predicts life evaluation, whereas psychosocial prosperity predicts positive feeling. *Journal of Personality and Social Psychology, 99*, 52–61.

Diener, E., & Seligman, M. E. P. (2002). Very happy people. *Psychological Science, 13*, 81–84.

Diener, E., & Seligman, M. E. P. (2004). Beyond money. Toward and economy of well-being. *Psychological Science in the Public Interest, 5(1)*, 1–31.

Diener, E., Suh, E., Lucas, R. E., & Smith, H. L. (1999). Subjective well-being. Three decades of progress. *Psychological Bulletin, 125*, 276–302.

Diener, E., Tay, L., & Myers, D. G. (2011). The religion paradox. If religion makes people happy, why are so many dropping out? *Journal of Personality and Social Psychology, 101*, 1278–1290.

Dimberg, U., Thunberg, M., & Elmehed, K. (2000). Unconscious facial reactions to emotional facial expressions. *Psychological Science, 11(1)*, 86–89.

Duclos, S. E., Laird, J. D., Schneider, E., Sexter, M., Stern, L., et al. (1989). Emotion-specific effects of facial expressions and postures on emotional experience. *Journal of Personality and Social Psychology, 57*, 100–108.

Dunn, E. V., Aknin, L. B., & Norton, M. I. (2008). Spending money on others promotes happiness. *Science, 319*, 1687–1688.

Eaker, E. D., Sullivan, L. M., Kelly-Hayes, M., D'Agostino, R. B., Sr., & Benjamin, E. J. (2004). Anger and hostility predict the development of atrial fibrillation in men in the Framingham Offspring Study. *Circulation, 109*, 1267–1271.

Ekman, P. (1972). Universals and cultural differences in facial expressions of emotion. In J. Cole (Ed.), *Nebraska symposium on motivation 1971* (Vol. 19, pp. 207–283). Lincoln, NE. University of Nebraska Press.

Ekman, P. (1994). Strong evidence for universals in facial expressions. A reply to

Russell's mistaken critique. *Psychological Bulletin, 115,* 268–287.

Ekman, P. (2003). *Emotions revealed.* New York. Times Books.

Ekman, P., & Cordaro, D. (2011). What is meant by calling emotions basic. *Emotion Review, 3,* 364–370.

Ekman, P., & Friesen, W. V. (1975). *Unmasking the face.* Englewood Cliffs, NJ. Prentice-Hall.

Ekman, P., & Friesen, W. V. (1978). *Facial action coding system. A technique for measurement of facial movement.* Palo Alto, CA. Consulting Psychologists Press.

Ekman, P., & Rosenberg, E. L. (Eds.). (2005). *What the face reveals. Basic and applied studies of spontaneous expression using the facial action coding system.* New York. Oxford University Press.

Elfenbein, H. A., & Ambady, N. (2002). On the universality and cultural specificity of emotion recognition. A meta-analysis. *Psychological Bulletin, 128,* 203–235.

Elfenbein, H. A., & Ambady, N. (2003). Universals and cultural differences in recognizing emotions. *Current Directions in Psychological Science, 12,* 159–164.

Evans, D. (2001). *Emotion. The science of sentiment.* New York. Oxford University Press.

Evans, D. (2003). *Placebo. The belief effect.* London. Harper Collins.

Exechieli, E. (2003). Beyond sustainable development. Education for gross national happiness in Bhutan. (Master's thesis). Retrieved on September 14, 2009, from http://www.stanford.edu/dept/SUSE/ICE/monograph

Fehr, R., Glefand, M. J., & Nag, M. (2010). The road to forgiveness. A meta-analytic synthesis of its situational and dispositional correlates. *Psychological Bulletin, 136,* 894–914.

Feldman, L. A. (1995). Valence focus and arousal focus. Individual differences in the structure of affective experience. *Journal of Personality and Social Psychology, 69(1),* 153–166.

Field, T. (2009). Exercise. In T. Field (Ed.), *Complementary and alternative therapies research* (pp. 73–79). Washington, DC. American Psychological Association.

Fincham, F. D., Hall, J., & Beech, S. R. H. (2006). Forgiveness in marriage. Current status and future directions. *Family Relations, 55,* 415–427.

Flanagan, K. S., Vanden Hoek, K. K., Ranter, J. M., & Reich, H. A. (2012). The potential of forgiveness as a response for coping with negative peer experiences. *Journal of Adolescence, 35,* 1215–1223.

Folkman, S., & Moskowitz, J. T. (2004). Coping. Pitfalls and promise. *Annual Review of Psychology, 55,* 745–774.

Frank, R. (1999). *Luxury fever.* Princeton, NJ. Princeton University Press.

Freedman, S., & Enright, R. D. (1996). Forgiveness as an intervention goal with incest survivors. *Journal of Consulting and Clinical Psychology, 64,* 938–992.

French, S. E., & Chavez, N. R. (2010). The relationship of ethnicity-related stressors and Latino ethnic identity and well-being. *Hispanic Journal of Behavioral Sciences, 32,* 410–428.

Friedman, H. S., & Miller-Herringer, T. (1991). Nonverbal display of emotion in public and in private. Self-monitoring, personality, and expressive cues. *Journal of Personality and Social Psychology, 61,* 766–775.

Friedman, M., & Ulmer, D. (1984). *Treating type-A behavior—and your heart.* New York. Knopf.

Friedmann, E., Barker, S., & Allen, K. (2011). Physiological correlates and possible health care savings of pet ownership. In P. McCardles, S. McCune, J. A. Griffin, & Maholmes, V. (Eds.), *How animals affect us* (pp. 163–182). Washington, DC. American Psychological Association.

Fujita, F., & Diener, E. (2005). Life satisfaction set point. Stability and change. *Journal of Personality and Social Psychology, 88(1),* 158–164.

Gable, S. L., & Haidt, J. (2005). What (and why) is positive psychology? *Review of General Psychology, 9,* 103–110.

Gebauer, J. E., Sedikides, C., & Neberich, W. (2012). Religiosity, social self-esteem, and psychological adjustment. On the cross-cultural specificity of the psychological benefits of religiosity. *Psychological Science, 23,* 158–160.

George, L. K., & Larson, D. B. (2002). Explaining the relationships between religious involvement and health. *Psychological Inquiry, 13,* 190–200.

Gillham, J. Reivich, K., Jaycox, L., & Seligman, M. E. P. (1995). Prevention of depressive symptoms in schoolchildren. Two-year follow-up. *Psychological Science, 6,* 343–351.

Giltay, E. J., Geleijnse, J. M., Zitman, F. G., Hoekstra, T., & Shouten, E. (2004). Dispositional optimism and all-cause and cardiovascular mortality in a prospective cohort of elderly Dutch men and women. *Archives of General Psychiatry, 61(11),* 1126–1135.

Goldwurm, G. F., Bielli, D., Corsale, B., & Marchi, S. (2006). Optimism training. Methodology and results. *Homeostasis in Health and Disease, 44,* 27–33.

Goleman, D. (1995). *Emotional intelligence.* New York. Bantam Books.

Gonzaga, G. C., Turner, R. A., Keltner, D., Campos, B., & Altemus, M. (2006). Romantic love and sexual desire in close relationships. *Emotion, 6,* 163–179.

Gunnar, M., & Quevedo, K. (2007). The neurobiology of stress and development. *Annual Review of Psychology, 58,* 145–173.

Halberstadt, J., Winkielman, P, Niedenthal, P. M., & Dalle, N. (2009). Emotional conception. How embodied emotion concepts guide perception and facial action. *Psychological Science, 20,* 1254–1261.

Hamer, M., Taylor, A., & Steptoe, A. (2006). The effect of acute aerobic exercise on stress related blood pressure responses. A systematic review and meta-analysis. *Biological Psychology, 71,* 183–190.

Hammen, C. (2005). Stress and depression. *Annual Review of Clinical Psychology, 55,* 11.1–11.27.

Hancock, J. T., Thom-Santelli, J., & Ritchie, T. (2004). Deception and design. The impact of communication technology on lying behavior. *CHI Letters, 6,* 129–134.

Harmon-Jones, E. A., & Harmon-Jones, C. (2007). Anger. Causes and components. In T. A. Cavell & K. T. Malcolm (Eds.), *Anger, aggression and interventions for interpersonal violence* (pp. 99–117). Mahwah, NJ. Lawrence Erlbaum Associates.

Hartwig, M., & Bond, C. F., Jr. (2011). Why do lie-catchers fail? A lens model meta-analysis of human lie judgments. *Psychological Bulletin, 137,* 643–659.

Hatch, S. L., & Dohrenwend, B. P. (2007). Distribution of traumatic and other stressful life events by race/ethnicity, gender, SES and age. A review of the research. *American Journal of Community Psychology, 40,* 313–332.

Headley, B., & Grabka, M. (2011). Health correlates and possible health care savings of pet ownership. Results from national surveys. In P. McCardles, S. McCune, J. A. Griffin, & V. Maholmes (Eds.), *How animals affect us* (pp. 153–162). Washington, D.C.. American Psychological Association.

Herzog, H. (2011). The impact of pets on human health and psychological well-being. Fact, fiction, or hypothesis? *Current Directions in Psychological Science, 20,* 236–239.

Hobson, C. J., & Delunas, L. (2001). National norms and life-event frequencies for the Revised Social Readjustment Rating Scale. *International Journal of Stress Management, 8,* 299–314.

Hobson, C. J., Kamen, J., Szostek, J., Nethercut, C. M., Tiedmann, J. W., et al. (1998). Stressful life events. A revision and update of the Social Readjustment Scale. *International Journal of Stress Management, 5(1),* 1–23.

Holmes, T. H., & Rahe, R. H. (1967). The Social Readjustment Rating Scale. *Journal of Psychosomatic Research, 11,* 213–218.

Holsboer, F., & Ising, M. (2010). Stress hormone regulation. Biological role and translation into therapy. *Annual Review of Psychology, 61,* 81–109.

Horwitz, A. V., & Wakefield, J. C. (2007). *The loss of sadness. How psychiatry transformed normal sorrow into depressive disorder.* New York. Oxford University Press.

Hróbjartsson, A., & Gøtzsche, P. C. (2001). Is the placebo powerless?—An analysis of clinical trials comparing placebo with no treatment. *The New England Journal of Medicine, 21,* 1594–1602.

Hróbjartsson, A., & Gøtzsche, P. C. (2004). Is the placebo powerless? Update of a systematic review with 52 new randomized trials comparing placebo with no treatment. *Journal of Internal Medicine, 256,* 91–100.

Hróbjartsson, A., & Gøtzsche, P. C. (2007). Powerful spin on conclusion in Wampold and colleagues're-analysis of placebo vs. no-treatment trials despite similar results as in original review. *Journal of Clinical Psychology, 63,* 373–377.

Hupka, R. B., Lenton, A. P., & Hutchison, K. A. (1999). Universal development of emotion categories in natural language. *Journal of Personality and Social Psychology, 77,* 247–278.

Inglehart, R., Basanez, M., Diez-Medrano, J., Halman, L., & Luijkx, R. (2004). *Human beliefs and values. A cross-cultural sourcebook based on the 1999-2002 values surveys.* Mexico City, Mexico. Siglo XXI.

Inglehart, R., Foa, R. Peterson, C., & Welzel, C. (2008). Development, freedom, and rising happiness. A global perspective (1981-2007). *Perspectives on Psychological Science, 3,* 264–285.

Izard, C. E. (1990). Facial expressions and the regulation of emotion. *Journal of Personality and Social Psychology, 58,* 487–498.

Izard, C. E. (2007). Basic emotions, natural kinds, emotion schemas, and a new paradigm. *Perspectives in Psychological Science, 2,* 260–280.

Izard, C. E. (2009). Emotion theory and research. Highlights, unanswered questions, and emerging issues. *Annual Review of Psychology, 60,* 1–25.

Izard, C. E. (2011). Forms and functions of emotion. Matters of emotion-cognition interactions. *Emotion Review, 3,* 371–378.

James, W. (1981). *The principles of psychology* (Vol. 2). Cambridge, MA. Harvard University Press. (Original work published 1890.)

Johnson, W., & Krueger, R. F. (2006). How money buys happiness. Genetic and environmental processes linking finances and life satisfaction. *Journal of Personality and Social Psychology, 90,* 680–691.

Joiner, T. E., Jr. (1996). Depression and rejection. *Communication Research, 23,* 451–471.

Kahneman, D., Krueger, A. B., Schkade, D., Schwarz, N., & Stone, A. A. (2004). Would you be happier if you were richer? A focusing illusion. *Science, 312,* 1908–1910.

Kaptchuk, T. J., Friedlander, E., Kelley, J. M., Sanchez, M. N., Kokkotou, E., et al. (2010). Placebos without deception. A randomized controlled trial in irritable bowel syndrome. *PLoS One, 5,* e15591. Retrieved from www.plosone.org on October 26, 2011.

Kasser, T., & Ryan, R. (1996). Further examining the American dream. Differential correlates of intrinsic and extrinsic goals. *Personality and Social Psychology Bulletin, 22,* 280–287.

Kendler, K. S., Eaves, L. J., Loken, E. K., Pedersen, N. L., Middeldorp, C. M., et al. (2011). The impact of environmental experiences on symptoms of anxiety and depression across the life span. *Psychological Science, 22,* 1343–1352.

Kessler, R. C. (1997). The effects of stressful life events on depression. *Annual Review of Psychology, 48,* 191–214.

King. L. A., & Napa, C. K. (1998). What makes a life good? *Journal of Personality and Social Psychology, 75,* 156–165.

Kirsch, I. (2002). Yes, there *is* a placebo effect, but is there a powerful antidepressant drug effect? *Prevention & Treatment, 5.* Retrieved from http://journals.apa.org/prevention/volume5 on January 7, 2005.

Kleinke, C. L., Peterson, T. R., & Rutledge, T. R. (1998). Effects of self-generated facial expressions on mood. *Journal of Personality and Social Psychology, 74,* 272–279.

Kubzansky, L. D., Wright, R. J., Cohen, S., Weiss, S., Rosner, B., et al. (2002). Breathing easy. A prospective study of optimism and pulmonary function in the normative aging study. *Annals of Behavioral Medicine, 24,* 345–353.

Laird, J. D. (1974). Self-attribution of emotion. The effects of expressive behavior on the quality of emotional experience. *Journal of Personality and Social Psychology, 29,* 475–486.

Laird, J. D. (1984). The real role of facial response in the experience of emotion. A reply to Tourangeau and Ellsworth, et al. *Journal of Personality and Social Psychology, 47,* 909–917.

Larsen, R., Kasimatis, M., & Frey, K. (1992). Facilitating the furrowed brow. An unobtrusive test of the facial feedback hypothesis applied to unpleasant affect. *Cognition and Emotion, 6,* 321–338.

Lawler, K. A., Younger, J. Y., Piferi, R. A., Billington, E., Jobe, R., Edmondson, K., Jones, W. H. (2003). A change of heart. Cardiovascular correlates of forgiveness in response to interpersonal conflict. *Journal of Behavioral Medicine 26,* 373–393.

Lazarus, R. S. (1991a). Progress on a *cognitive-motivational-relational theory of emotion. American Psychologist, 46,* 819–834.

Lazarus, R. S. (1991b). *Emotion and adaptation.* New York. Oxford University Press.

Lazarus, R. S. (1999). *Stress and emotion. A new synthesis.* New York. Springer.

Lazarus, R. S. (2000). Cognitive-motivational-relational theory of emotion. In Y. Hanin (Ed.), *Emotions in sport* (pp. 39–63). Champaign, IL. Human Kinetics.

Lazarus, R. S., & Folkman, S. (1984). *Stress, appraisal, and coping.* New York. Springer.

LeDoux, J. E. (1996). *The emotional brain. The mysterious underpinnings of emotional life.* New York. Simon & Schuster.

LeDoux, J. E. (2000). Emotion circuits in the brain. *Annual Review of Neuroscience, 23,* 155–184.

Lett, H. S., Blumenthal, J. A., Babyak, M. A., Catellier, D. J., Carney, R. M., et al. (2007). Social support and prognosis in patients at increased psychosocial risk recovering from myocardial infarction. *Health Psychology, 26,* 418–427.

Levay, S., & Valente, S. M. (2002). *Human sexuality.* Sunderland, MA. Sinauer.

Levenson, R. (2011). Basic emotion questions. *Emotion Review, 3,* 379–386.

Levin, J., Chatters, L. M., & Taylor, R. J. (2005). Religion, health and medicine in African Americans. Implications for physicians. *Journal of the National Medical Association, 97,* 237–249.

Lin, W.-F., Mack, D., Enright, R. D., Krahn, D., & Baskin, T. W. (2004). Effects of forgiveness therapy on anger, mood, and vulnerability to substance use among inpatient substance-dependent clients. *Journal of Consulting and Clinical Psychology, 72,* 1114–1121.

Locke, E. A. (2005). Why emotional intelligence is an invalid concept. *Journal of Organizational Behavior, 26,* 425–431.

Loewenstein, G. F., Weber, E. U., Hsee, C. K., & Welch, N. (2001). Risks as feelings. *Psychological Bulletin, 127,* 267–286.

Lohr, J. M., Olatunji, B. O., Baumeister, R. F., & Bushman, B. J. (2007). The psychology of anger venting and empirically supported alternatives that do no harm. *The Scientific Review of Mental Health Practice, 5,* 53–64.

Lucas, R. E. (2007). Adaptation and the set-point model of subjective well-being. *Current Directions in Psychological Science, 16,* 75–79.

Lykken, D., & Tellegen, A. (1996). Happiness is a stochastic phenomenon. *Psychological Science, 7,* 186–189.

Lyubomirsky, S., & Boehm, J. K. (2010). Human motives, happiness, and the puzzle of parenthood. Commentary on Kenrick et al. (2010). *Perspectives on Psychological Science, 5,* 327–334.

Lyubomirsky, S., & Layous, K. (2013). How do simple positive activities increase well-being? *Current Directions in Psychological Science, 22,* 57–62.

Lyubomirsky, S., Sheldon, K. M., & Schkade, D. (2005). Pursuing happiness. The architecture of sustainable change. *Review of General Psychology, 9,* 11–113.

Maltby, J., Macaskill, A., & Day, L. (2001). Failure to forgive self and others. A replication and extension of the relationship between forgiveness, personality, social desirability, and general health. *Personality & Individual Differences, 30,* 881–885.

Marland, A. L., Bachen, E. A., Cohen, S., Rabin, B., & Manuck, S. B.(2002). Stress, immune reactivity, and susceptibility to infections. *Physiology and Behavior, 77,* 711–716.

Master, S. L., Eisenberger, N. I., Taylor, S. E., Naliboff, B. D., Shirinyan, D., et al. (2009). A picture's worth. Partner photographs reduce experimentally induced pain. *Psychological Science, 20,* 1316–1318.

Matsumoto, D., Consolacion, T., Yamada, H., Suzuki, R., Franklin, B., et al. (2002). American-Japanese cultural differences in judgments of emotional expressions of different intensities. *Cognition and Emotion, 16,* 721–747.

Matsumoto, D., & Ekman, P. (2004). The relationship among expressions, labels and descriptions of contempt. *Journal of Personality and Social Psychology, 87,* 529–540.

Matsumoto, D., Willingham, B., & Olide, A. (2009). Sequential dynamics of culturally moderated facial expressions of emotion. *Psychological Science, 20,* 1269–1275.

Matthews, K. A., & Gump, B. B. (2002). Chronic work stress and marital dissolution increase risk of posttrial mortality in men from the Multiple Risk Factor Intervention Trial. *Archives of Internal Medicine, 162,* 309–315.

Mayer, J. D., Salovey, P., & Caruso, D. R. (2004). Emotional intelligence. Theory, findings, and implications. *Psychological Inquiry, 15,* 197–215.

Mazure, C. M. (1998). Life stressors as risk factors in depression. *Clinical Psychology. Science and Practice, 5,* 291–313.

McAndrew, F. T., Akande, A., Turner, S., & Sharma, Y. (1998). A cross-cultural ranking of stressful life events in Germany, India, South Africa, and the United States. *Journal of Cross-Cultural Psychology, 29,* 717–727.

McConnell, A. R., Brown, C. M., Shoda, T. M., Statyton, L. E., & Martin, C. E. (2011). Friends with benefits. On the positive consequences of pet ownership. *Journal of Personality and Social Psychology, 101,* 1239–1252.

McCullough, M. E. (2000). Forgiveness as human strength. Theory, measurement, and links to well-being. *Journal of Social & Clinical Psychology, 19(1),* 43–55.

McCullough, M. E., Fincham, F. D., & Tsang, J. A. (2003). Forgiveness, forbearance, and time. The temporal unfolding of transgression-related interpersonal motivations. *Journal of Personality and Social Psychology, 84,* 540–557.

McCullough, M. E., Friedman, H. S., Enders, C. K., & Martin, L. R. (2009). Does devoutness delay death? Psychological investment in religion and its association with longevity in the Terman sample. *Journal of Personality and Social Psychology, 97,* 866–882.

McIntosh, D. N. (1996). Facial feedback hypotheses. Evidence, implications, and directions. *Motivation and Emotion. Special Issue, Part I, 20,* 121–147.

Meador, C. K. (1992). Hex death. Voodoo magic or persuasion? *Southern Medical Journal, 85,* 244–247.

Miller, C. T., & Kaiser, C. R. (2001). A theoretical perspective on coping with stigma. *Journal of Social Issues, 57(1),* 73–112.

Miller, G., Chen, E., & Cole, S. W. (2009). Health psychology. Developing biologically plausible models linking the social world and physical health. *Annual Review of Psychology, 60,* 501–524.

Miller, G. E., & Blackwell, E. (2006). Turning up the heat. Inflammation as a mechanism linking chronic stress, depression, and heart disease. *Current Directions in Psychological Science, 15,* 269–272.

Morris, W. N. (1999). The mood system. In D. Kahneman, E. Diender, & N. Schwartz (Eds.), *Well-being. The foundations of hedonic psychology* (pp. 169–189). New York. Russell Sage Foundation.

Mori, K., & Mori, H. (2009). Another test of the passive facial feedback hypothesis. When your face smiles, you feel happy. *Perceptual and Motor Skills, 109,* 76–78.

Murphy, S. T., Monahan, J. L., & Zajonc, R. B. (1995). Additivity of nonconscious affect. Combined effects of priming and exposure. *Journal of Personality and Social Psychology, 69,* 589–602.

Myers, D. G. (2000). The funds, friends, and faith of happy people. *American Psychologist, 55,* 56–67.

Myers, D. G., & Diener, E. (1996, May). The pursuit of happiness. *Scientific American, 274,* 54–56.

Naqvi, N. H., Rudrauf, D., Damasio, H., & Bechara, A. (2007). Damage to the insula disrupts addiction to cigarette smoking. *Science, 315,* 531–534.

Nazroo, J. Y. (2003). The structuring of ethnic inequalities in health. Economic position, racial discrimination, and racism. *American Journal of Public Health, 93,* 277–284.

Nes, R. B., Røysamb, E., Tambs, K., Harris, J. R., & Reichborn-Kjennerud, T. (2006). Subjective well-being. Genetic and environmental contributions to stability and change. *Psychological Medicine, 65,* 449–475.

Nesse, R. M. (1990). Evolutionary explanations of emotions. *Human Nature, 1,* 261–289.

Nesse, R. M. (1991). What good is feeling bad? The evolutionary benefits of psychic pain. *The Sciences,* November/December, 30–37.

Nesse, R. M., & Williams, G. C. (1994). *Why we get sick. The new science of Darwinian medicine.* New York. Times Books.

Neta, M., & Whalen, P. J. (2010). The primacy of negative interpretations when resolving the valence of ambiguous facial expressions. *Psychological Science OnLine First.* Retrieved from pss.sage.com on June 30, 2010.

Nickerson, C., Schwarz, N., Diener, E., & Kahneman, D. (2003). Zeroing in on the dark side of the American dream. A closer look at the negative consequences of the goal for financial success. *Psychological Science, 14,* 531–536.

Niedenthal, P. M. (2007). Embodying emotion. *Science, 316,* 1002–1005.

O'Donovan, A., Link, J., Dhabhar, F. S., Wolkowitz, O., Tillie, J. M., et al. (2009). Pessimism correlates with leukocyte telomere shortness and elevated interleukin-6 in post-menopausal women. *Brain, Behavior, and Immunity, 23,* 446–449.

Oishi, S., Diener, E., & Lucas, R. E. (2007). The optimum level of well-being. Can people be too happy? *Perspectives in Psychological Science, 2,* 346–360.

Okazaki, S. (2009). Impact of racism on ethnic minority mental health. *Perspectives on Psychological Science, 4,* 103–107.

Ong, A. D. (2010). Pathways linking positive emotion and health in later life. *Current Directions in Psychological Science, 19,* 358–362.

Orcutt, H. K. (2006). The prospective relationship of interpersonal forgiveness and psychological distress symptoms among college women. *Journal of Counseling Psychology, 53,* 350–361.

Panksepp, J. (2005a). Affective consciousness. Core emotional feelings in animals and humans. *Consciousness and Cognition. An International Journal, 14(1),* 30–80.

Panksepp, J. (2005b). Beyond a joke. From animal laughter to human joy? *Science, 308,* 62–63.

Panksepp, J. (2007a). Criteria for basic emotions. Is DISGUST a primary "emotion"? *Cognition and Emotion, 21,* 1819–1828.

Panksepp, J. (2007b). Neurologizing the psychology of affects. How appraisal-based constructivism and basic emotion theory can coexist. *Perspectives on Psychological Science, 2,* 281–296.

Pargament, K. I. (1997). *The psychology of religion and coping.* New York. Guilford.

Parker, G., Gayed, A., Owen, C., Hyett, M., Hilton, T., et al. (2010). Survival following an acute coronary syndrome. A pet theory put to the test. *Acta Psychiatrica Scandinavica, 121,* 65–70.

Parslow, R. A., Jorm, A. F., Christensen, H., Rodgers, B., & Jacomb, P. (2005). Pet ownership and health in older adults. Findings from a survey of 2,551 community-based Australians aged 60–64. *Gerontology, 51(1),* 40–47.

Pascoe, E. A., & Smart Richman, L. (2009). Perceived discrimination and health. A meta-analytic review. *Psychological Bulletin, 135,* 531–554.

Peterson, C., Seligman, M. E., & Vaillant, G. E. (1988). Pessimistic explanatory style is a risk factor for physical illness. A thirty-five year longitudinal study. *Journal of Personality and Social Psychology, 55(1),* 23–37.

Pinker, S. (2011). *The better angels of our nature. Why violence has declined.* New York. Viking.

Player, M. S., King, D. E., Mainous, A. G., III, & Geesey, M. E. (2007). Psychosocial factors and progression from prehypertension to hypertension or coronary heart disease. *Annals of Family Medicine, 5,* 403–411.

Plutchik, R. (1980). A general psychoevolutionary theory of emotion. In R. Plutchik & H. Kellerman (Eds.), *Emotion. Theory, research, and experience. Vol. 1. Theories of emotion* (pp. 3–33). New York. Academic Press.

Plutchik, R. (2003). *Emotions and life. Perspectives from psychology, biology, and evolution.* Washington, DC. American Psychological Association.

Powell, L. H., Shahabi, L., & Thoresen, C. E. (2003). Religion and spirituality. Linkages to physical health. *American Psychologist, 58*, 36–52.

Praissman, S. (2008). Mindfulness-based stress reduction. A literature review and clinician's guide. *Journal of the American Academy of Nurse Practice, 20*, 212–216.

Price, D. D., Finniss, D. G., & Benedetti, F. (2008). A comprehensive review of the placebo effect. Recent advances and current thought. *Annual Review of Psychology, 59*, 565–590.

Prinz, J. (2004). Which emotions are basic? In D. Evans & P. Cruse (Eds.), *Emotion, evolution, and rationality* (pp. 1–19). London. Oxford University Press

Rahula, W. (1959). *What the Buddha taught.* New York. Grove Press.

Rasmussen, H. N., Scheier, M. F., & Greenhouse, J. B. (2009). Optimism and physical health. A meta-analytic review. *Annals of Behavior Medicine, 37,* 239–256.

Reed, G. L., & Enright, R. D. (2006). The effects of forgiveness therapy on depression, anxiety, and posttraumatic stress for women after spousal emotional abuse. *Journal of Consulting and Clinical Psychology, 74,* 920–929.

Robertson, J. P., & Martin, S. (2008). What do happy people do? *Social Indicators Research, 89,* 565–571.

Roozendaal, B., McEwan, B. S., & Chattarji, S. (2009). Stress, memory, and the amygdala. *Nature Reviews. Neuroscience, 10,* 423–433.

Rosamond, W., Flegal, K., Friday, G., Furie, K., Go, A., et al. (2007). Heart disease and stroke statistics—2007 update. A report from the American Heart Association Statistics Committee and Stroke Statistics Subcommittee. *Circulation, 115,* e69–e171.

Rozanski, A., Blumenthal, J. A., Davidson, K. W., Saab, P. G., & Kubzansky, L. (2005). The epidemiology, pathophysiology and management of psychosocial risk factors in cardiac practice. *Journal of the American College of Cardiology, 45,* 637–651.

Ruggiero, K. M., & Taylor, D. M. (1997). Why minority group members perceive or do not perceive the discrimination that confronts them. The role of self-esteem and perceived control. *Journal of Personality and Social Psychology, 72,* 373–389.

Russell, J. A. (2003). Core affect and the psychological construction of emotion. *Psychological Review, 110,* 145–172.

Rusting, C. L., & Nolen-Hoeksema, S. (1998). Regulating responses to anger. Effects of rumination and distraction on angry mood. *Journal of Personality and Social Psychology, 74,* 790–803.

Rutledge, T., & Hogan, B.E. (2002). A quantitative review of prospective evidence linking psychological factors with hypertension development. *Psychosomatic Medicine, 64,* 758–766.

Rydell, R. J., Rydell, M. T., & Boucher, K. L. (2010). The effect of negative performance stereotypes on learning. *Journal of Personality and Social Psychology, 99,* 883–896.

Salmon, P. (2001). Effects of physical exercise on anxiety, depression, and sensitivity to stress. A unifying theory. *Clinical Psychology Review 21,* 33–61.

Salomons, T. V., Coan, J. A., Hunt, S. M., Backonja, M.-M., & Davidson, R. J. (2008). Voluntary facial displays of pain increase suffering in response to nociceptive stimulation. *The Journal of Pain, 9,* 443–448.

Schachter, S., & Singer, J. E. (1962). Cognitive, social, and physiological determinants of emotional state. *Psychological Review, 69,* 379–399.

Schnall, E., Wassertheil-Smoller, S., Swencionis, C., Zemon, V., Tinker, L., et al. (2008). The relationship between religion and cardiovascular outcomes and all-cause mortality in the women's health initiative observational study. *Psychology & Health.* Advance online publication retrieved from http://pdfserve.informa world.com on December 17, 2008.

Schrauf, R. W., & Sanchez, J. (2004). The preponderance of negative emotion words in the emotion lexicon. Cross-generational and cross-linguistic study. *Journal of Multilingual and Multicultural Development, 25,* 266–284.

Schulte, M. J., Ree, M. J., & Carretta, T. R. (2004). Emotional intelligence. Not much more than g and personality. *Personality and Individual Differences, 37(5),* 1059–1068.

Schyns, P. G., Petro, L. G., & Smith, M. L. (2009). Transmission of facial expressions of emotion co-evolved with their efficient decoding in the brain. Behavioral and brain evidence. *PLoS One, 4.* Retrieved from www.plosone.org on June 15, 2009.

Scott, D. J., Stohler, C. S., Egnatuk, C. M., Wang, H., Koeppe, R. A., et al. (2008). Placebo and nocebo effects are defined by opposite opioid and dopaminergic responses. *Archives of General Psychiatry, 65,* 220–231.

Segerstrom, S. C. (2007). Stress, energy, and immunity. *Current Directions in Psychological Science, 16,* 326–441.

Segerstrom, S. C., & Miller, G. E. (2004). Psychological stress and the human immune system. A meta-analysis of 30 years of inquiry. *Psychological Bulletin, 130,* 601–630.

Seligman, M. E. P. (1990). *Learned optimism. How to change your mind and your life.* New York. Free Press.

Selye, H. (1956). *The stress of life.* New York. McGraw Hill.

Serota, K. B., Levine, T. R., & Boster, F. J. (2010). The prevalence of lying in America. Three studies of self-reported lies. *Human Communication Research, 36,* 2–25.

Shen, B-J., Stroud, L. R., & Niaura, R. (2004). Ethnic differences in cardiovascular responses to laboratory stress. A comparison between Asian and White Americans. *International Journal of Behavioral Medicine, 11,* 181–186.

Slentz, C. A., Houmard, J. A., Johnson, J. L., Bateman, L. A., Tanner, C. J., et al. (2007). Inactivity, exercise training and detraining, and plasma lipoproteins. STRRIDE. A randomized, controlled study of exercise intensity and amount. *Journal of Applied Physiology, 103,* 432–442.

Smith, M. L., Cottrell, G. W., Gosselin, F., & Schyns, P. G. (2005). Transmitting and decoding facial expressions. *Psychological Science, 16,* 184–189.

Smith, T. W., & Ruiz, J. M. (2002). Psychosocial influences on the development and course of coronary heart disease. Current status and implications for research and practice. *Journal of Consulting and Clinical Psychology, 70,* 548–568.

Soussignan, R. (2002). Duchenne smile, emotional experience and autonomic reactivity. A test of the facial feedback hypothesis. *Emotion, 2,* 52–74.

Spalding, T. W., Lyon, L. A., Steel, D. H., & Hatfield, B. D. (2004). Aerobic exercise training and cardiovascular reactivity to psychological stress in sedentary young normotensive men and women. *Psychophysiology, 41,* 552–562.

Speca, M., Carlson, L. E., Goodey, E., & Angen, M. (2000). A randomized, waitlist controlled clinical trial. The effect of a mindfulness meditation-based stress reduction program on mood and symptoms of stress in cancer outpatients. *Psychosomatic Medicine, 62,* 613–622.

Steele, C. M., & Aronson, J. A. (2004). Stereotype threat does not live by Steele and Aronson alone. *American Psychologist, 59(1),* 47–48.

Stepper, S., & Strack, F. (1993). Proprioceptive determinants of emotional and nonemotional feelings. *Journal of Personality and Social Psychology, 64,* 211–220.

Steptoe, A., Dockray, S., & Wardle, J. (2009). Positive affect and psychobiological processes relevant to health. *Journal of Personality, 77,* 1747–1775.

Steptoe, A., O'Donnell, K., Marmot, M., & Wardle, J. (2008). Positive affect, psychological well-being, and good sleep. *Journal of Psychosomatic Research, 64,* 409–415.

Strack, F., Martin, L. L., & Stepper, S. (1988). Inhibiting and facilitating conditions of the human smile. A non-obtrusive test of the facial feedback hypothesis. *Journal of Personality and Social Psychology, 54,* 768–777.

Sue, S., & Chu, J. Y. (2003). The mental health of ethnic minority groups. Challenges posed by the Supplement to the Surgeon General's Report on Mental Health. *Culture, Medicine, and Psychiatry, 27,* 447–465.

Symons, D. (1995). Beauty is in the adaptations of the beholder. The evolutionary psychology of human female sexual attractiveness. In P. R. Abramson & S. D. Pinkerton (Eds.), *Sexual nature, sexual culture* (pp. 80–117). Chicago. University of Chicago Press.

Tavris, C. (1984). On the wisdom of counting to ten. Personal and social dangers of anger expression. *Review of Personality & Social Psychology, 5*, 170–191.

Tavris, C. (1989). *Anger. The misunderstood emotion.* New York. Touchstone.

Taylor, S. E. (1999). *Health psychology* (4th ed.). Boston. McGraw-Hill.

Taylor, S. E. (2002). *The tending instinct. How nurturing is essential to who we are and how we live.* New York. Holt.

Taylor, S. E. (2006). Tend and befriend. Biobehavioral bases of affiliation under stress. *Current Directions in Psychological Science, 15*, 273–277.

Taylor, S. E., Klein, L. C., Lewis, B. P., Gruenewald, T. L., Gurung, R. A. R., et al. (2000). Biobehavioral responses to stress in females. Tend-and-befriend, not fight-or-flight. *Psychological Bulletin, 107*, 411–429.

Taylor, S. E., Sherman, D. K., Kim, H. S., Jarcho, J., Takagi, K., et al. (2004). Culture and social support. Who seeks it and why? *Journal of Personality and Social Psychology, 87*, 354–362.

Taylor, S. E., & Stanton, A. L. (2007). Coping resources, coping processes, and mental health. *Annual Review of Clinical Psychology, 3*, 377–401.

Taylor, S. E., Welch, W. T., Kim, H. S., & Sherman, D. K. (2007). Cultural differences in the impact of social support on psychological and biological stress responses. *Psychological Science, 18*, 831–837.

Tilburt, J. C., Emanuel, E. J., Kaptchuk, T. J., Curlin, F. A., & Miller, F. G. (2008). Prescribing "placebo treatments." Results of national survey of US internists and rheumatologists. *BMJ, 337.* Retrieved from www.bmj.com on December 17, 2008.

Toronchuk, J. A., & Ellis, G. F. R. (2007). Disgust. Sensory affect or primary emotional system? *Cognition and Emotion, 21*, 1799–1818.

Trivers, R. (2010). Deceipt and self-deception. In P. Kappeler & J. Silk (Eds.), *Mind the gap. Tracing the origins of human universals* (pp. 373–393). Berlin. Springer-Verlag.

Tsai, J. L. (2007). Ideal affect. Cultural causes and behavioral consequences. *Perspectives on Psychological Science, 2*, 242–259.

Tsai, J. L., Knutson, B. K., & Fung, H. H. (2006). Cultural variation in affect valuation. *Journal of Personality and Social Psychology, 90*, 288–307.

Tsai, J. L., Louie, J., Chen, E., & Uchida, Y. (2007). Learning what feelings to desire. Socialization of ideal affect through children's storybooks. *Personality and Social Psychology Bulletin, 33*, 17–30.

Uchino, B. N., Uno, D., & Holt-Lunstad, J. (1999). Social support, physiological processes and health. *Current Directions in Psychological Science, 8*, 145–148.

Ulrich-Lai, Y. M., & Herman, J. P. (2009). Neural regulation of endocrine and autonomic stress responses. *Nature Reviews. Neuroscience, 10*, 397–409.

Utsey, S., Giesbrecht, N., Hook, J., & Stanard, P. M. (2008). Cultural, sociofamilial, and psychological resources that inhibit psychological distress in African Americans exposed to stressful life events and race-related stress. *Journal of Counseling Psychology, 55*, 49–62.

Uvnas-Moberg, K. (1997). Oxytocin linked antistress effects—The relaxation and growth response. *Acta Psychologica Scandanavica, 640(Suppl.)*, 38–42.

von Hippel, W., & Trivers, R. (2011). The evolution and psychology of self-deception. *Behavioral and Brain Sciences, 34*, 1–56.

Vrij, A. (2008). *Detecting lies and deceit. Pitfalls and opportunities* (2nd ed.). Chichester, England. John Wiley & Sons.

Vrij, A., Granhag, P. A., Mann, S., & Leal, S. (2011). Outsmarting the liars. Toward a cognitive lie detection approach. *Current Directions in Psychological Science, 20*, 28–32.

Vrij, A., Mann, S., Robbins, E., & Robinson, M. (2006). Police officers ability to detect deception in high stakes situations and in repeated lie detection tests. *Applied Cognitive Psychology, 20*, 741–755.

Waber, R. L., Shiv, B., Carmon, Z., & Ariely, D. (2008). Commercial features of placebo and therapeutic efficacy. *JAMA, 299*, 1016–1017.

Wallis, C. (2005, January 09). The new science of happiness. *Time*, A2–A68.

Wampold, B. E., Imel, Z. E., & Minami, T. (2007). The placebo effect. "Relatively large" and "robust" enough to survive another assault. *Journal of Clinical Psychology, 63*, 401–403.

Wampold, B. E., Minami, T., Tierney, S. C., Baskin, T. W., & Bhati, K. S. (2005). The placebo is powerful. Estimating placebo effects in medicine and psychotherapy from randomized clinical trials. *Journal of Clinical Psychology, 63*, 835–854.

Weiss, A., Bates, T. C., & Luciano, M. (2008). Happiness is a personal(ity) thing. The genetics of personality and well-being in a representative sample. *Psychological Science, 19*, 205–210.

Williams, M., Teasdale, J., Segal, Z., & Kabat-Zinn, J. (2007). *The mindful way through depression.* New York. Guilford Press.

Wills, T. A. (1991). Social support and interpersonal relationships. In M. S. Clark (Ed.), *Prosocial behavior* (pp. 265–289). Newbury Park, CA. Sage.

Winkielman, P., Niedenthal, P. M., & Oberman, L. (2008). The embodied emotional mind. In G. R. Semin & E. R. Smith (Eds.), *Embodied grounding. Social cognitive, affective, and neuroscientific approaches* (pp. 263–288). New York. Cambridge University Press.

Witek-Janusek, L., Albuquerque, K., Chroniak, K. R., Chroniak, C., Durazo-Arvisu. R., et al. (2010). Effect of mindfulness-based stress reduction on immune function, quality of life, and coping in women newly diagnosed with early stage breast cancer. *Brain, Behavior, and Immunity, 22*, 969–981.

Witvliet, C. V. O. (2005). Unforgiveness, forgiveness, and justice. Scientific findings on feelings and physiology. In E. L. Worthington, Jr. (Ed.), *Handbook of forgiveness* (pp. 305–319). New York. Routledge.

Witvliet, C. V. O., & McCullough, M. E. (2007). Forgiveness and health. A review and theoretical exploration of emotion pathways. In S. G. Post (Ed.), *Altruism and health. Perspectives from empirical research* (pp. 259–276). Oxford, UK. Oxford University Press.

Witvliet, C. v., Ludwig, T. E., & Vander Laan, K. L. (2001). Granting forgiveness or harboring grudges. Implications for emotion, physiology, and health. *Psychological Science, 12(2)*, 117–123.

Wood, W. (2000). Attitude change. Persuasion and social influence. *Annual Review of Psychology, 51*, 539–570.

Worthingon, E. L., Jr., Witvliet, C. V. O., Pietrini, P., & Miller, A. J. (2007). Forgiveness, health, and well-being. A review of evidence for emotional versus decisional forgiveness, dispositional forgivingness, and reduced unforgiveness. *Journal of Behavioral Medicine, 30*, 291–302.

Worthington, E. L., Jr., & Scherer, M. (2004). Forgiveness is an emotion-focused coping strategy that can reduce health risks and promote health resilience. Theory, review, & hypotheses. *Psychology & Health, 19*, 385–405.

Yirmiya, N., Erel, O., Shaked, M., & Solomonica-Levi, D. (1998). Meta-analyses comparing theory of mind abilities of individuals with autism, individuals with mental retardation, and normally developing individuals. *Psychological Bulletin, 124*, 283–307.

Yuki, M., Maddux, W. W., & Masuda, T. (2007). Are the windows to the soul the same in the East and West? Cultural differences in using the eyes and mouth as cues to recognize emotions in Japan and the United States. *Journal of Experimental Social Psychology, 43*, 303–311.

Zajonc, R. B. (1984). On the primacy of affect. *American Psychologist, 39*, 117–123.

Zhang, A. Y., & Snowden, L. R. (1999). Ethnic characteristics of mental disorders in five U.S. communities. *Cultural Diversity and Ethnic Minority Psychology, 5*, 134–146.

CHAPTER 12

Allik, J., & McCrae, R. R. (2004). Toward a geography of personality traits. Patterns of profiles across 36 cultures. *Journal of Cross-Cultural Psychology, 35*, 13–28.

Allik, J., Realo, A., Mõttus, R., Borkenau, P., Kuppens, P., et al. (2010). How people see others is different from how people see themselves. A replicable pattern across cultures. *Journal of Personality and Social Psychology, 99*, 870–882.

Allport, G. W., & Odbert, H. S. (1936). Trait names. A psycholexical study. *Psychological Monographs, 47(1, Whole No. 211)*.

Aronow, E., Reznikoff, M., & Moreland, K. (1995). The Rorschach. Projective technique or psychometric test? *Journal of Personality Assessment, 64*, 213–228.

Baumeister, R. F., Bushman, B. J., & Campbell, W. K. (2000). Self-esteem, narcissism, and aggression. Does violence result from low-self-esteem or from threatened egotism? *Current Directions in Psychological Science, 9*, 26–29.

Baumeister, R. F., Campbell, J. D., Krueger, J. L., & Vohs, K. D. (2003). Does high self-esteem cause better performance, interpersonal success, happiness, or healthier lifestyles? *Psychological Science in the Public Interest, 4(1)*, 1–44.

Baumeister, R. F., Dale, K., & Sommer, K. L. (1998). Freudian defense mechanisms and empirical findings in modern social psychology. Reaction formation, projection, displacement, undoing, isolation, sublimation, and denial. *Journal of Personality, 66*, 1081–1124.

Baumeister, R. F., Smart, L., & Boden, J. M. (1996). Relation of threatened egotism to violence and aggression. The dark side of high self-esteem. *Psychological Review, 103*, 5–33.

Borkenau, P., Riemann, R., Spinath, F. M., & Angleitner, A. (2006). Genetic and environmental influences on Person X Situation profiles. *Journal of Personality, 74*, 1451–1479.

Bouchard, T. J. (2004). Genetic influence on human psychological traits. *Current Directions in Psychological Science, 13*, 148–151.

Brody, N., & Ehrlichman, H. (1998). *Personality psychology. Science of individuality*. Englewood Cliffs, NJ. Prentice-Hall.

Brown, D. E. (1991). *Human universals*. New York. McGraw-Hill.

Bushman, B. J., Baumeister, R. F., Thomaes, S., Ryu, E., Begeer, S., & West, S. G. (2009). Looking again, and harder, for a link between low self-esteem and aggression. *Journal of Personality, 77*, 427–446.

Buss, D. M. (2009). How can evolutionary psychology successfully explain personality and individual differences? *Perspectives on Psychological Science, 4*, 359–366.

C'de Baca, J., & Wilbourne, P. (2004). Quantum change. Ten years later. *Journal of Clinical Psychology, 60*, 531–541.

Caspi, A., Roberts, B. W., & Shiner, R. L. (2005). Personality development. Stability and change. *Annual Review of Psychology, 56*, 453–484.

Cervone, D., & Shoda, Y. (1999). Beyond traits in the study of personality coherence. *Current Directions in Psychological Science, 8(1)*, 27–32.

Church, T. A. (2010). Current perspectives in the study of personality across

cultures. *Perspectives on Psychological Science, 5*, 441–449.

Collins, W. A., Maccoby, E. E., Steinberg, L., Hetherington, E. M., & Bornstein, M. H. (2000). Contemporary research on parenting. The case for nature and nurture. *American Psychologist, 55*, 218–232.

Costa, P. T., Jr., Terracciano, A., & McCrae, R. R. (2001). Gender differences in personality traits across cultures. Robust and surprising findings. *Journal of Personality and Social Psychology, 81*, 322–331.

Crews, F. C. (1995). *Memory wars. Freud's legacy in dispute*. New York. New York Review of Books.

Crews, F. C. (2007). *Follies of the wise. Dissenting essays*. Emeryville, CA. Shoemaker & Hoard.

Crocker, J., & Park, L. E. (2004). The costly pursuit of self-esteem. *Psychological Bulletin, 130*, 392–414.

Dawes, R. M. (2001) *Everyday irrationality. How pseudoscientists, lunatics, and the rest of us fail to think rationally*. Boulder, CO. Westview Press.

Dean, G. (1987). Does astrology need to be true? Part 2. *Skeptical Inquirer, 11*, 257–273.

Dean, G., Mather, A., & Kelly, I. W. (Eds.). (1996). Astrology. In *The encyclopedia of the paranormal* (pp. 47–99). Amherst, NY. Prometheus Books.

Donnellan, M. B., & Lucas, R. E. (2008). Age differences in the Big Five across the life span. Evidence from two national samples. *Psychology of Aging, 23*, 558–566.

Epstein, S. (1979). The stability of behavior. I. On predicting most of the people much of the time. *Journal of Personality and Social Psychology, 37*, 1097–1126.

Exner, J. E. (2003). *The Rorschach. A comprehensive system. Vol. 1. Basic foundations and principles of interpretation* (4th ed.). Hoboken, NJ. Wiley.

Eysenck, H. J. (1958). A short questionnaire for the measurement of two dimensions of personality. *Journal of Applied Psychology, 42*, 14–17.

Eysenck, H. J., & Nias, D. K. B. (1982). *Astrology. Science or superstition?* London. Penguin Books.

Eysenck, H. J., & Wilson, G. D. (1973). *The experimental study of Freudian theories*. London. Methuen.

Eysenck, S. B. G., & Eysenck, H. J. (1963). The validity of questionnaire and rating assessments of extraversion and neuroticism, and their factorial stability. *British Journal of Psychology, 54*, 51–62.

Farrell, J. (1996). *Freud's paranoid quest*. New York. New York University Press.

Feingold, A. (1994). Gender differences in personality. A meta-analysis. *Psychological Bulletin, 116*, 429–456.

Ferguson, C. J. (2010). A meta-analysis of normal and disordered personality across the life span. *Journal of Personality and Social Psychology, 98*, 659–667.

Fisher, S., & Greenberg, R. (1996). *Freud Scientifically Appraised*. New York. John Wiley & Sons.

Fleeson, W. (2004). Moving personality beyond the person-situation debate. The challenge and the opportunity of within-person variability. *Current Directions in Psychological Science, 13*, 83–87.

Freud, A. (1966). *The ego and machanisms of defense*. New York. International Universities Press. (Original work published 1936).

Freud, S. (1962). *The ego and the id*. New York. Norton. (Original work published 1923).

Freud, S. (1991). Some psychical consequences of the anatomical differences between the sexes. In A. Richards (ed.) *Penguin Freud Library, Vol. 7. On sexuality* (pp. 323–343). Harmondsworth, UK. Penguin.

Funder, D. C. (2001). Personality. *Annual Review of Psychology, 52*, 197–221.

Funder, D. C. (2009). Persons, behaviors, and situations. An agenda for personality psychology in the postwar era. *Journal of Research in Personality, 43*, 120–126.

Furr, R. M. (2009). Profile analysis in person-situation integration. *Journal of Research in Personality, 43*, 196–207.

Gailliot, M. T., & Baumeister, R. F. (2007). Self-esteem, belongingness, and worldview validation. Does belongingness exert a unique influence upon self-esteem? *Journal of Research in Personality, 41*, 327–345.

Garb, H. N. (1999). Call for a moratorium on the use of the Rorschach inkblot test in clinical and forensic settings. *Assessment, 6*, 313–317.

Garb, H. N., Florio, C. M., & Grove, W. M. (1998). The validity of the Rorschach and the Minnesota Multiphasic Personality Inventory. Results from meta-analyses. *Psychological Science, 9*, 402–404.

Garb, H. N., Wood, J. M., Lilinfeld, S. O., & Nezworski, M. T. (2005). Roots of the Rorschach controversy. *Clinical Psychology Review, 25*, 97–118.

Glick, P., Gottesman, D., & Jolton, J. (1989). The fault is not in the stars. Susceptibility of skeptics and believers in astrology to the Barnum effect. *Personality and Social Psychology Bulletin, 15*, 572–583.

Goldberg, L. R. (1990) An alternative description of personality. The big five factor structure. *Journal of Personality and Social Psychology, 59*, 1216–1229.

Greenberg, J. (2008). Understanding the vital human quest for self-esteem. *Perspectives on Psychological Science, 3*, 48–55.

Hampson, S. E., & Goldberg, L. R. (2006). A first large cohort study of personality trait stability over the 40 years between elementary school and midlife. *Journal of Personality and Social Psychology, 91*, 763–770.

Harris, J. R. (1998). *The nurture assumption. Why children turn out the way they do*. New York. Free Press.

Harris, J. R. (2006). *No two alike. Human nature and human individuality.* New York. Norton.

The Harris Poll. (2003, February 26). The religious and other beliefs of Americans. Poll #11. Retrieved on November 20, 2007 from http://www.harrisinteractive.com/harris_poll/index.asp?PID=359.

Helson, R., C., Jones, C., & Kwan, V. (2002). Personality change over 40 years of adulthood. Hierarchical linear modeling analyses of two longitudinal samples. *Journal of Personality and Social Psychology, 83(3)*, 752–766.

Helson, R. C., & Soto, C. J. (2005). Up and down in middle age. Monotonic and non-monotonic changes in roles, status, and personality. *Journal of Personality and Social Psychology, 89*, 194–204.

Hunsley, J., Lee, C. M., & Wood, J. M. (2003). Controversial and questionable assessment techniques. In S. O. Lilienfeld, S. J. Lynn, & J. M. Lohr (Eds.), *Science and pseudoscience in clinical psychology* (pp. 39–76). New York. Guilford Press.

James, W. (1981). *The principles of psychology* (Vol. 2). Cambridge, MA. Harvard University Press. (Original work published 1890.)

Kammrath, L. K., Menoza-Denton, R., & Mischel, W. (2005). Incorporating *If . . . then . . .* personality signatures in person perception. Beyond the person-situation dichotomy. *Journal of Personality and Social Psychology, 88*, 605–618.

Kelly, I. W. (1997). Modern astrology. A critique. *Psychological Reports, 81*, 1035–1066.

Kelly, I. W. (1998).Why astrology doesn't work. *Psychological Reports, 82*, 527–546.

Kerrnis, M. H., Lakey, C. E., & Heppner, W. L. (2008). Secure versus fragile high self-esteem as a predictor of verbal defensiveness. Converging findings across three different markers. *Journal of Personality, 76*, 477–512.

Krueger, J. I., Vohs, K. D., & Baumeister, R. F. (2008). Is the allure of self-esteem a mirage after all? *American Psychologist, 63*, 64–65.

Leary, M. R. (1999). The social and psychological importance of self-esteem. In R. M. Kowalski & M. R. Leary (Eds.), *The social psychology of emotional and behavioral problems. Interfaces of social and clinical psychology* (pp. 197–221). Washington, DC. American Psychological Association.

Leary, M. R. (2004). The function of self-esteem in terror management theory and sociometer theory. Comment on Pyszczynski et al. (2004). *Psychological Bulletin, 130*, 478–482.

Leary, M. R., & Baumeister, R. F. (2000). The nature and function of self-esteem. Sociometer theory. In M. P. Zanna (Ed.), *Advances in experimental social psychology* (Vol. 32, pp. 1–62). New York. Academic Press.

Lillqvist, O., & Lindeman, M. (1998). Belief in astrology as a strategy for self-verification and coping with negative life-events. *European Psychologist, 3,* 202–208.

Lippa, R. A. (2010). Gender differences in personality and interests. When, where, and why? *Social and Personality Psychology Compass, 4,* 1098–1010.

Lodi-Smith, J., Geise, A. C., Roberts, B. W., & Robins, R. W. (2009). Narrating personality change. *Journal of Personality and Social Psychology, 96*, 679–689.

Lynch, M., & Walsh, B. (1998). *Genetics and analysis of quantitative traits.* Sunderland, MA. Sinauer Associates.

Maccoby, E. E. (2002). Gender and group process. A developmental perspective. *Current Directions in Psychological Science, 11*, 54–58.

MacMillan, M. (1997). *Freud evaluated. The completed arc.* Cambridge, MA. MIT Press.

Matsumoto, D. (1999). Culture and self. An empirical assessment of Markus and Kitayama's theory of independent and interdependent self-construal. *Asian Journal of Social Psychology, 2*, 289–310.

May R. (1969). *Love and will.* New York. W. W. Norton.

May, R. (1981). *Freedom and destiny.* New York. W. W. Norton.

May, R. (1982). The problem of evil. An open letter to Carl Rogers. *Journal of Humanistic Psychology, 22(3)*, 10–21.

McAdams, D. P. (2001). The psychology of life stories. *Review of General Psychology, 5,* 100–122.

McAdams, D. P. (2004). Generativity and the narrative ecology of family life. In M. W. Pratt & B. H. Friese (Eds.), *Family stories and the life course. Across time and generations* (pp. 235–257). Mahwah, NJ. Lawrence Erlbaum Associates.

McAdams, D. P., Anyidoho, N. A., Brown, C., Yi, T. H., Kaplan, B., et al. (2004). Traits and stories. Links between dispositional and narrative features of personality. *Journal of Personality, 72*, 761–784.

McAdams, D. P., & Olson, B. D. (2010). Personality development. Continuity and change over the life course. *Annual Review of Psychology, 61*, 517–542.

McAdams, D. P., & Pals, J. L. (2006). A new big five. Fundamental principles for an integrative science of personality. *American Psychologist, 61*, 204–217.

McClelland, D. C. (1999). How the test lives on. Extensions of the Thematic Apperception Test approach. In L. Gieser & M. I. Stein (Eds.), *Evocative images. The Thematic Apperception Test and the art of projection* (pp. 163–175). Washington, DC. American Psychological Association.

McCrae, R. R (2009). The five-factor model of personality. Consensus and controversy. In P. J. Corr & G. Mattews (Eds.), *The Cambridge handbook of personality psychology* (pp. 148–161). New York. Cambridge University Press.

McCrae, R. R., & Costa, P. T. (1994). The stability of personality. Observations and evaluation. *Current Directions in Psychological Science, 3*, 173–175.

McCrae, R. R., & Costa, P. T., Jr. (1996). Toward a new generation of personality theories. Theoretical contexts for the five-factor model. In J. S. Wiggins (Ed.), *The five-factor model of personality. Theoretical perspectives* (pp. 51–87). New York. Guilford Press.

McCrae, R. R., & Costa, P. (1997). Personality trait structures as a human universal. *American Psychologist, 52*, 509–516.

McCrae, R. R., & Costa, P. (2013). Introduction to the empirical and theoretical status of the five-factor model of personality traits. In R. R. McCrae, and P. T. Coasta (Eds.), *Personality disorders and the five-factor model of personality* (3rd ed.). Washington, DC. American Psychological Association.

McCrae, R. R., & Terracciano, A. (2006). National character and personality. *Current Directions in Psychological Science, 15*, 156–161.

McCrae, R. R., Terracciano, A., and 78 members of the Personality Profiles of Culture Project. (2005). Universal features of personality traits from the observer's perspective. *Journal of Personality and Social Psychology, 88*, 547–561.

McGrew, J. H., & McFall, R. M. (1990), A scientific inquiry into the validity of astrology. *Journal of Scientific Exploration, 4,* 75–84. Further details appear in *Correlation* (1992), *11*, 2–10.

McGuffin, P., Riley, B., & Plomin, R. (2001). Genomics and behavior. Toward behavioral genomics. *Science, 291*, 1232–1249.

Mecca, A. M., Smelser, N. J., & Vasconcellos, J. (Eds.). (1989). *The social importance of self-esteem.* Berkeley, CA. University of California Press.

Merlo, L., & Barnett, D. (2001). All about inkblots. *Scientific American, 285*, 13.

Mischel, W. (1968). *Personality and assessment.* New York. Wiley.

Mischel, W. (1979). On the interface of cognition and personality. Beyond the person-situation debate. *American Psychologist, 34(9)*, 740–754.

Mischel, W., Shoda, Y., & Mendoza-Denton, R. (2002). Situation-behavior profiles as a locus of consistency in personality. *Current Directions in Psychological Science, 11*, 50–54.

Morizot, J., & Le Blanc, M. (2003). Searching for a developmental typology of personality and its relations to antisocial behaviour. A longitudinal study of an adjudicated men sample. *Criminal Behaviour and Mental Health, 13(4)*, 241–277.

Murray, H. A. (1943). *Thematic Apperception Test manual.* Cambridge, MA. Harvard University Press.

Murray, H. A., & Kluckhohn, C. (1953). *Personality in nature, society, and culture.* New York. Alfred Knopf.

Nanninga, R. (1996/1997). The astrotest. A tough match for astrologers. *Correlation, 15*, 14–20.

National Science Foundation. (2002) Science and technology. Public attitudes and public understanding. Indicators 2002. Retrieved on November 20, 2007 from http://www.nsf.gov/statistics/seind02/c7/c7h.htm.

Ozer, D. J., & Benet-Martínez, V. (2006). Personality and the prediction of consequential outcomes. *Annual Review of Psychology, 57*, 401–421.

Pinker, S. (2002). *The blank slate. The modern denial of human nature.* New York. Viking.

Pinkerman, J. E., Haynes, J. P., & Keiser, T. (1993). Characteristics of psychological practice in juvenile court clinics. *American Journal of Forensic Psychology, 11(2)*, 3–12.

Plomin, R., & Caspi, A. (1999). Behavioral genetics and personality. In L. A. Pervin & O. P. John (Eds.), *Handbook of personality. Theory and research* (pp. 251–276). New York. Guilford Press.

Plomin, R., & Daniels, D. (1987). Why are children in the same family so different from each other? *Behavioral and Brain Sciences, 10*, 1–16.

Plomin, R., DeFries, J. C., Craig, I. W., & McGuffin, P. (Eds.). (2003). *Behavioral genetics in the postgenomic era.* Washington, DC. American Psychological Association.

Popper, K. R. (1962). *Conjectures and refutations. The growth of scientific knowledge* (5th ed.) New York. Routledge.

Pyszczynski, T., Greenberg, J., Solomon, S., Arndt, J., & Schimel, J. (2004). Why do people need self-esteem? A theoretical and empirical review. *Psychological Bulletin, 130*, 435–468.

Roberts, B. W., & DelVecchio, W. F. (2000). The rank-order consistency of personality traits from childhood to old age. A quantitative review of longitudinal studies. *Psychological Bulletin, 126*, 3–25.

Roberts, B. W., Kuncel, N. R., Shiner, R., Caspi, A., & Goldberg, L. R. (2007). The power of personality. The comparative validity of personality traits, socioeconomic status, and cognitive ability for predicting important life outcomes. *Perspectives in Psychological Science, 2*, 313–345.

Robins, R. W., Gosling, S. D., & Craik, K. H. (1999). An empirical analysis of trends in psychology. *American Psychologist, 54*, 117–128.

Rossini, E. D., & Moretti, R. J. (1997). Thematic Apperception Test (TAT) interpretation. Practice recommendations from a survey of clinical psychology doctoral programs accredited by the American Psychological Association. *Professional Psychology. Research and Practice, 28*, 393–398.

Rutter, M. (2002). Nature, nurture, and development. From evangelism through science toward policy and practice. *Child Development, 73*, 1–21.

Salmivalli, C., Kaukiainen, A., Kaistaniemi, L., & Lagerspetz, K. M. J. (1999). Self-evaluated self-esteem, peer-evaluated self-esteem, & defensive egotism as predictors of adolescents' participation in bullying situations.

Personality and Social Psychology Bulletin, 25, 1268–1278.

Saudino, K. J. (2005). Behavioral genetics and child temperament. *Journal of Developmental & Behavioral Pediatrics, 26*, 214–223.

Schmeichel, B. J., Gailliot, M. T., Filardo, E.-A., McGregor, I., Gitter, S., et al. (2009). Terror management theory and self-esteem revisited. The roles of implicit and explicit self-esteem in mortality salience effects. *Journal of Personality and Social Psychology, 95*, 1077–1087.

Schmitt, D. P., Allik, J., McCrae, R. R., & Benet-Martínez, V. (2007). The geographic distribution of Big Five personality traits. Patterns and profiles of human self-description across 56 nations. *Journal of Cross-Cultural Psychology, 38*, 173–212.

Schmitt, D. P., Realo, A., Voracek, M., & Allik, J. (2008). Why can't a man be more like a woman. Sex differences in big five personality traits across 55 cultures. *Journal of Personality and Social Psychology, 94*, 168–182.

Seligman, M. P., Linley, P. A., & Joseph, S. (Eds.). (2004). *Positive psychology in practice.* Hoboken, NJ. John Wiley & Sons.

Sheldon, K. M. (2004). *Optimal human being. An integrated multi-level perspective.* Mahwah, NJ. Lawrence Erlbaum Associates.

Sherman, D. K., & Cohen, G. L. (2002). Accepting threatening information. Self-affirmation and the reduction of defensive biases. *Current Directions in Psychological Science, 11*, 119–123.

Specht, J., Egloff, B., & Schmukle, S. (2011). Stability and change of personality across the life course. The impact of age and major life events on mean-level and rank-order stability of the Big Five. *Journal of Personality and Social Psychology, 101*, 862–882.

Swann, W. B., Jr., & Seyle, C. (2005). Personality psychology's comeback and its emerging symbiosis with social psychology. *Personality and Social Psychology Bulletin, 31*, 155–165.

Terracciano, A., Abdel-Khalak, A. M., Ádám, N., Adamovová, L., Ahn, C.-k., et al. (2005). National character does not reflect mean personality trait levels in 49 cultures. *Science, 310*, 96–100.

Terracciano, A., Costa, P. T., & McCrae, R. R. (2006). Personality plasticity after age 30. *Personality and Social Psychology Bulletin, 32*, 999–1009.

Thomaes, S., Bushman, B. J., de Castro, B. O., Cohen, G. L., & Denissen, J. J. A. (2009). Reducing narcissistic aggression by buttressing self-esteem. *Psychological Science, 20*, 1536–1542.

Turkheimer, E., & Waldron, M. (2000). Nonshared environment. A theoretical, methodological, and quantitative review. *Psychological Bulletin, 126*, 78–108.

Vandell, D. L. (2000). Parents, peer groups, and other socializing influences. *Developmental Psychology, 36*, 699–710.

Viglione, D. J., & Taylor, N. (2003). Empirical support for interrater reliability of Rorschach comprehensive system coding. *Journal of Clinical Psychology, 59*, 111–121.

Voas, D. (2007). Ten million marriages. An astrological detective story. *Skeptical Inquirer, 32*, 53–55.

Watson, D., Suls, J., & Haig, J. (2002). Global self-esteem in relation to structural models of personality and affectivity. *Journal of Personality and Social Psychology, 83*, 185–197.

Webster, G. D., Kirkpatrick, L. S., Nezlek, J. B., Smith, C. V., & Paddock, E. L. (2007). Different slopes for different folks. Self-esteem instability and gender as moderators of the relationship between self-esteem and attitudinal aggression. *Self and Identity, 6*, 74–94.

Weiner, I. B., Spielberger, C. D., & Abeles, N. (2002). Scientific psychology and the Rorschach inkblot method. *The Clinical Psychologist, 55*, 7–12.

Weiss, A., Bates, T. C., & Luciano, M. (2008). Happiness is a personal(ity) thing. The genetics of personality and well-being in a representative sample. *Psychological Science, 19*, 205–210.

Westen, D. (1991). Clinical assessment of object relations using the TAT. *Journal of Personality Assessment, 56*, 56–74.

Westen, D. (1998). The scientific legacy of Sigmund Freud. Toward a psychodynamically informed psychological science. *Psychological Bulletin, 124*, 333–371.

Williams, J. E., & Best, D. L. (1990). *Sex and psyche. Gender and self viewed cross-culturally.* Newbury Park, CA. Sage Publications.

Woike, B. A., & McAdams, D. P. (2001, May/June). A response to Lilienfeld, Woods, and Garb. TAT-based personality measures have considerable validity. *American Psychological Society Observer, 14(5)*. Retrieved from www.psychologicalscience.org on November 29, 2007.

Wood, J. V., Heimpel, S. A., & Michela, J. L. (2003). Savoring versus dampening. Self-esteem differences in regulating positive affect. *Journal of Personality and Social Psychology, 85*, 566–580.

Wright, L. (1997). *Twins. And what they tell us about who we are.* New York. John Wiley & Sons.

CHAPTER 13

Abramson, L. Y., Alloy, L. B., & Metalsky, J. I. (1995). Hopelessness depression. In J. N. Buchanan & M. E. P. Seligman (Eds.), *Explanatory style* (pp. 113–134). Hillsdale, NJ. Lawrence Erlbaum Associates.

Akiskal, H. S., & Benazzi, F. (2003). Family history validation of the bipolar nature of depressive mixed states. *Journal of Affective Disorders. Special Issue. Validating the Bipolar Spectrum, 73(1–2)*, 113–122.

Alloy, L. B., Abramson, L. Y., Whitehouse, W. G., Hogan, M. E., Panzarella, C., et al. (2006). Prospective incidence of first onsets and recurrences of depression in individuals at high and low cognitive risk for depression. *Journal of Abnormal Psychology, 115,* 145–156.

American Psychiatric Association. (2013). *Diagnostic and statistical manual of mental disorders* (5th ed.). Washington, DC. American Psychiatric Association.

Angst, J. & Sellaro, R. (2000). Historical perspectives and natural history of bipolar disorder. *Biological Psychiatry, 48,* 445–57.

Attiullah, N., Eisen, J., & Rasmussen, S. A. (2000). Clinical features of obsessive-compulsive disorder. *Psychiatric Clinics of North America, 23,* 469–491.

Barclay, L. (2005, November). Advertisements for SSRIs may be misleading. *Medscape Medical News.* Retrieved from www.medscape.com/viewarticle/516262 on May 18, 2008.

Barlow, D. H. (Ed.). (2002a). *Anxiety and its disorders. The nature and treatment of anxiety and panic* (2nd ed.). New York. Guilford Press.

Barlow, D. H. (2002b). The phenomenon of panic. In D. H. Barlow (Ed.), *Anxiety and its disorders. The nature and treatment of anxiety and panic* (2nd ed.). New York. Guilford Press.

Barlow, D. H. (2010). Negative effects from psychological treatments. A perspective. *American Psychologist, 65,* 13–20.

Barlow, D. H., Brown, T. A., & Craske, M. G. (1994). Definitions of panic attacks and panic disorder in DSM-IV. Implications for research. *Journal of Abnormal Psychology, 103,* 553–554.

Barlow, D. H., & Craske, M. G. (2007). *Mastery of your anxiety and panic* (4th ed.). Albany, NY. Oxford University Press.

Barlow, D. H., & Durand, V. M. (2009). *Abnormal psychology. An integrative approach* (5th ed.). Belmont, CA. Wadsworth/Cengage.

Barton, D. A., Esler, M. D., Dawwod, T., Lambert, E. A., Haikerwal, D., et al. (2008). Elevated brain serotonin turnover in patients with depression. *Archives of General Psychiatry, 65,* 38–46.

Beard, C., Weisberg, R. B., & Keller, M. (2010). Health-related quality of life across the anxiety disorders. Findings from a sample of primary care patients. *Journal of Anxiety Disorders, 24,* 559–564.

Beck, A. T., Rush, A. J., Shaw, B. F., & Emery, G. (1987). *Cognitive therapy of depression.* New York. The Guilford Press.

Bernstein, D. P., Iscan, C., & Maser, J. (2007). Opinions of personality disorder experts regarding the DSM-IV personality disorders classification system. *Journal of Personality Disorders, 21,* 536–551.

Bernstein, D. P., & Useda, J. D. (2007). Paranoid personality disorder. In W. T. O'Donohue, K. A. Fowler, & S. O. Lilienfeld (Eds.), *Personality disorders. Toward the DSM-V* (pp. 41–63). Thousand Oaks, CA. Sage Publications

Blair-West G., & Mellsop G. (2001). Major depression. Does a gender-based

down-rating of suicide risk challenge its diagnostic validity? *Australian and New Zealand Journal of Psychiatry, 35,* 322–328.

Boland, R. J., & Keller, M. B. (2009). Course and outcome of depression. In I. H. Gotlib & C. L. Hammen (Eds.), *Handbook of depression* (2nd ed., pp. 23–43). New York. Guilford.

Bonanno, G. A., Brewin, C. R., Kaniasty, K., & La Greca, A. M. (2010). Weighing the costs of disaster. Consequences, risks, and resilience in individuals, families, and communities. *Psychological Science in the Public Interest, 11,* 1–49.

Bonanno, G. A., Galea, S., Bucciarelli, A., & Vlahov, D. (2006). Psychological resilience after disaster. New York City in the aftermath of the September 11th terrorist attack. *Psychological Science, 17,* 181–186.

Bonanno, G. A., Westphal, M., & Mancini, A. D. (2011). Resilience to loss and potential trauma. *Annual Review of Clinical Psychology, 7,* 511–535.

Booij, A. J. W., Van der Does, C., Benkelfat, J. D., Bremner, P. J., et al. (2002). Predictors of mood response to acute tryptophan depletion. A reanalysis. *Neuropsychopharmacology, 27,* 852–861.

Borch-Jacobsen, M. (1997). Sybil. The making of a disease. An interview with Dr. Herbert Spiegel. *New York Review of Books, 44,* 60–64.

Bradley, R., Conklin, C. Z., & Westen, D. (2007). Borderline personality disorder. In W. T. O'Donohue, K. A. Fowler, & S. O. Lilienfeld (Eds.), *Personality disorders. Toward the DSM-V* (pp. 167–201). Thousand Oaks, CA. Sage Publications.

Brådvik, L., Mattisson, C., Bogren, M., & Nettelbladt, P (2008). Long-term suicide risk of depression in the Lundby cohort 1947–1997. Severity and gender. *Acta Psychiatrica Scandinavia, 117,* 185–191.

Braff, D., Schork, N. J., & Gottesman, I. I. (2007). Endophenotyping schizophrenia. *American Journal of Psychiatry, 164,* 705–707.

Bray, N. J. (2008). Gene expression in the etiology of schizophrenia. *Schizophrenia Bulletin, 34,* 412–418.

Brown, A. S. (2006). Prenatal infection as a risk factor for schizophrenia. *Schizophrenia Bulletin, 32,* 200–202.

Brown, A. S., Schaefer, C. A., Quesenberry, C. P., Jr., Shen, L., & Susser, E. S. (2006). No evidence of relation between maternal exposure to herpes simplex virus type 2 and risk of schizophrenia? *American Journal of Psychiatry, 163,* 2178–2180.

Brown, A. S., Schaefer, C. A., Wyatt, R. J., Goetz, R., Begg, M. D., et al. (2000). Maternal exposure to respiratory infections and adult schizophrenia spectrum disorders. A prospective birth cohort study. *Schizophrenia Bulletin, 26,* 287–295.

Brown, A. S., & Susser, E. S. (2002). In utero infections and adult schizophrenia. *Mental Retardation and Developmental Disabilities Research Reviews, 8,* 51–57.

Brown, T. A., Campbell, L. A., Lehman, C. L., Grisham, J. R., & Mancill, R. B.

(2001). Current and lifetime comorbidity of the DSM-IV anxiety and mood disorders in a large clinical sample. *Journal of Abnormal Psychology, 110,* 585–599.

Bruce, S. E., Yonkers, K. A., Otto, M. W., Eisen, J. L., Weisberg, R. B., et al. (2005). Influence of psychiatric comorbidity on recovery and recurrence in generalized anxiety disorder, social phobia, and panic disorder. A 12-year prospective study. *American Journal of Psychiatry, 162,* 1179–1187.

Burki, T. (2010). Healing the mental scars of combat. *The Lancet, 376,* 1727–1728.

Campbell-Sills, L., & Stein, M. B. (2005). Justifying the diagnostic status of social phobia. A reply to Wakefield, Horwitz, and Schmitz. *Canadian Journal of Psychiatry, 50,* 320–323.

Cantor, P. (1975). The effects of youthful suicide on the family. *Psychiatric Opinion, 12,* 6–11.

Carey, B. (2008, December 18), Psychiatrists revising the book of human troubles. *New York Times,* p. A1.

Carson, R. C. (1996). Aristotle, Galileo, and the *DSM* taxonomy. The case of schizophrenia. *Journal of Consulting and Clinical Psychology, 64,* 1133–1139.

Caspi, A., Sugden, K., Moffitt, T. E., Taylor, A., Craig, I. W., et al. (2003). Influence of life stress on depression. Moderation by a polymorphism in the 5-HTT gene. *Science, 301,* 386–389.

Catapano, F., Perris, F., Fabrazzo, M., Cliffi, V., Giacco, D., DeSantis, V., et al. (2010). Obsessive-compulsive disorder with poor insight. A three-year prospective study. *Progress in Neuro-Psychopharmacology and Biological Psychiatry, 34,* 323–330.

Cavanagh, J. T. O., Carson, A. J., Sharpe, M., & Lawrie, S. M. (2003). Psychological autopsy studies of suicide. A systematic review. *Psychological Medicine, 33,* 395–405.

Cervilla, J. A., Molina, E., Rivera, M., Torres-González, F., Bellón, J. A., et al. (2007). The risk for depression conferred by stressful life events is modified by variation at the serotonin transporter 5HTTLPR genotype. Evidence from the Spanish PREDICT-Gene cohort. *Molecular Psychiatry, 12,* 748–755.

Chavira, D. A., Stein, M. B., & Malcarne, V. L. (2002). Scrutinizing the relationship between shyness and social phobia. *Journal of Anxiety Disorders, 16,* 595–598.

Cicchetti, D., & Rogosch, F. A. (1996). Equifinality and multifinality in developmental psychopathology. *Development and Psychopathology, 8,* 597–600.

Clarkin, J. F. (2008). Clinical approaches to Axis II cormorbidity. Commentary. *Journal of Clinical Psychology. In Session, 64,* 222–230.

Conklin, H. M., & Iacono, W. G. (2002). Schizophrenia. A neurodevelopmental perspective. *Current Directions in Psychological Science, 11*(1), 33–37.

Conner, K. R., Duberstein, P. R., Conwell, Y., Seidlitz, L., & Caine, E. D. (2001). Psychological vulnerability to completed suicide. A review of empirical studies. *Suicide & Life-Threatening Behavior, 31,* 367–385.

Craske, M. G. (2003). *Origins of phobias and anxiety disorders. Why more women than men?* Oxford, UK. Elsevier.

Craske, M. G., Kircanski, K., Epstein, A., Wittchen, H,-U., Pine, D. S., et al. (2010). Panic disorder. A review of DSM-IV panic disorder and proposals for DSM-V. *Depression and Anxiety, 27,* 93–112.

Craske, M. G., & Waters, A. M. (2005). Panic disorder, phobias, and generalized anxiety disorder. *Annual Review of Clinical Psychology, 1,* 197–225.

Cross-Disorder Group of the Psychiatric Genomics Consortium (2013). Identification of risk loci with shared effects on five major psychiatric disorders. A genome-wide analysis. *The Lancet.* Retrieved from http://proxy.library .upenn.edu:2135/science/article/pii/ S0140673612621291 on March 17, 2013.

Dalenberg, C., Loewenstein, R., Spiegel, D., Brewin, C., Lanius, R., et al. (2007). Scientific study of the dissociative disorders. *Psychotherapy and Psychosomatics, 76,* 400–401.

Darwin, C. (1877). A biographical sketch of an infant. *Mind, 2,* 285–294.

Deacon, B. J., & Baird, G. L. (2009). The chemical imbalance explanation of depression. Reducing blame at what cost? *Journal of Social and Clinical Psychology, 28,* 415–435.

Delgado, P. L. (2000). Depression. The case for a monoamine deficiency. *Journal of Clinical Psychiatry, 61(Suppl. 6),* 7–10.

Diflorio, A., & Jones, I. (2010). Is sex important? Gender differences in bipolar disorder. *International Review of Psychiatry, 22,* 437–452.

Duan, J., Sanders, A. R., & Gejman, P. V. (2010). Genome-wide approaches to schizophrenia. *Brain Research Bulletin, 83,* 93–102.

Eaton, W. W., Anthony, J. C., Gallo, J., Cai, G., Tien, A., et al. (1997). Natural history of diagnostic interview schedule/DSM-IV major depression. The Baltimore Epidemiologic Catchment Area follow-up. *Archives of General Psychiatry, 54,* 993–999.

Eich, E., Macaulay, D., Loewenstein, R. J., & Dihle, P. H. (1997). Memory, amnesia, and dissociative identity disorder. *Psychological Science, 8,* 157–173.

Eisen, J. L., & Rasmussen, S. A. (1993). Obsessive compulsive disorder with psychotic features. *Journal of Clinical Psychiatry, 54,* 373–379.

Elbogen, E. B., & Johnson, S. C. (2009). The intricate link between violence and mental disorder. Results from the National Epidemiologic Survey on Alcohol and Related Conditions. *Archives of General Psychiatry, 66,* 152–161.

Fineberg, N. A., Sharma, P., Sivakumaran, T., Sahakian, B., & Chamberlain, S. (2007). Does obsessive-compulsive personality disorder belong within the obsessive-compulsive spectrum? *CNS Spectrums, 12,* 467–475, 477–482.

France, C. M., Lysaker, P. H., & Robinson, R. P. (2007). The "chemical imbalance" explanation for depression. Origins, lay endorsement, and clinical implications. *Professional Psychology. Research and Practice, 38,* 411–420.

Francis, A. J., & Widiger, T. (2012). Psychiatric diagnosis. Lessons from the DSM-IV past and cautions for the DSM-5 future. *Annual Review of Clinical Psychology, 8,* 109–130.

Galea, S., Brewin, C. R., Gruber, M., Jones, R. T., King, D. W., et al. (2007). Exposure to hurricane-related stressors and mental illness after Hurricane Katrina. *Archives of General Psychiatry, 64,* 1427–1434.

Garlipp, P. (2008). Koro—A culture-bound phenomenon. Intracultural psychiatric implications. *German Journal of Psychiatry.* Retrieved from http:// www.gjpsy.uni-goettingen.de/ on May 17, 2008.

Garlow, S. J., Purselle, D., & Heninger, M. (2005). Ethnic differences in patterns of suicide across the life cycle. *American Journal of Psychiatry, 162,* 319–323.

Giuffra, L. A., & Risch, N. (1994). Diminished recall and the cohort effect of major depression. A simulation study. *Psychological Medicine, 24,* 375–383.

Gleaves, D. H. (1996). The sociocognitive model of dissociative identity disorder. A reexamination of the evidence. *Psychological Bulletin, 120,* 42–59.

Goffman, E. (1961). *Asylums.* Garden City, NY. Doubleday.

Goldberg, J., E., Harrow, M., & Grossman, L. S. (1995). Course and outcome in bipolar affective disorder. A longitudinal follow-up study. *American Journal of Psychiatry, 152,* 379–384.

Gotlib, I. H., & Joorman, J. (2010). Cognition and depression. Current status and future directions. *Annual Review of Clinical Psychology, 6,* 285–312.

Gottesman, I. I. (1991). *Schizophrenia genesis. The origins of madness.* New York. W. H. Freeman.

Gottesman, I. I., & Bertelsen, A. (1989). Confirming unexpressed genotypes for schizophrenia. Risks in the offspring of Fischer's Danish identical and fraternal discordant twins. *Archives of General Psychiatry, 46,* 867–872.

Gould, M. S., Greenberg, M. P. H., Velting, D. M., & Shaffer, D. (2003). Youth suicide risk and preventive interventions. A review of the past 10 years. *Journal of the American Academy of Child and Adolescent Psychiatry, 42,* 386–405.

Grabill, K., Merlo, L., Duke, D., Harford, K.-L., Keeley, M. L., et al. (2008). Assessment of obsessive-compulsive disorder. A review. *Journal of Anxiety Disorders, 22,* 1–17.

Grow, J. M., Park, J. S., & Han, Z. (2006). "Your life is waiting!" Symbolic meanings in direct-to-consumer antidepressant advertising. *Journal of Communication Inquiry, 30,* 163–188.

Gur, R. E., Nimgaonkar, V. L., Almasy, L., Calkins, M. E., Ragland, J. D., et al. (2007). Neurocognitive endophenotypes in a multiplex multigenerational family study of schizophrenia. *American Journal of Psychiatry, 164,* 813–819.

Hamer, M., Molloy, G. J., & Stamatakis, E. (2008). Psychological distress as a risk factor for cardiovascular events. *Journal of the American College of Cardiology, 52,* 2156–2162.

Hammen, C. (1991). Generation of stress in the course of unipolar depression. *Journal of Abnormal Psychology, 100,* 555–561.

Hankin, B. L., & Abramson, L. (2002). Measuring cognitive vulnerability to depression in adolescence. Reliabiity, validity, and gender differences. *Journal of Clinical Child and Adolescent Psychology, 31,* 491–504.

Harrow, M., Grossman, L.S., Jobe, T. H., & Herbener, E.S. (2005). Do patients with schizophrenia ever show periods of recovery? A 15-year multi-follow-up study. *Schizophrenia Bulletin, 31,* 723–734.

Haslam, N., & Giosan, C. (2002). The lay concept of "mental disorder" among American undergraduates. *Journal of Clinical Psychology, 58,* 479–485.

Henninger, P. (1992). Conditional handedness. Handedness changes in multiple personality disordered subject reflect shift in hemispheric dominance. *Consciousness and Cognition, 1,* 265–287.

Hickle, I. (2007). Is depression overdiagnosed? No. *British Medical Journal, 335,* 329.

Hindmarch, I. (2001). Expanding the horizons of depression. Beyond the monoamine hypothesis. *Human Psychopharmacology. Clinical and Experimental, 16,* 203–218.

Hofman, S. G., & Barlow, D. H. (2002). Social phobia (social anxiety disorder). In D. H. Barlow (Ed.), *Anxiety and its disorders. The nature and treatment of anxiety and panic* (2nd ed.). New York. Guilford Press.

Hoge, E. A., Austin, E. D., & Pollack, M. H. (2007). Resilience. Research evidence and conceptual considerations for post-traumatic stress disorder. *Depression and Anxiety, 24,* 139–152.

Holmans, P., Weissman, M. M., Zubenko, G. S., Scheftner, W. A., Crowe. R. R., et al. (2007). Genetics of recurrent early-onset major depression. Final genome scan report. *American Journal of Psychiatry, 164,* 248–258.

Horwitz, A. V., & Wakefield, J. C. (2006). The epidemic in mental illness. Clinical fact or survey artifact? *Contexts, 5,* 19–23.

Horwitz, A. V., & Wakefield, J. C. (2007). *The loss of sadness. How psychiatry transformed normal sorrow into depressive disorder.* New York. Oxford University Press.

Horwitz, A. V., & Wakefield, J. C. (2012). *All we have to fear. Psychiatry's transformation of natural anxieties into mental disorders.* New York. Oxford University Press.

Houts, A. C. (2001). The diagnostic and statistical manual's new white coat and circularity of plausible dysfunctions. Response to Wakefield, Part 1. *Behaviour Research and Therapy, 39,* 315–345.

Hu, G., Wilcox, H., Wissow, L. S., & Baker, S. P. (2008). Mid-life suicide. *American Journal of Preventative Medicine, 35,* 589–93.

Hughes, C. C. (1998). The glossary of "culture-bound syndromes" in DSM-IV. A critique. *Transcultural Psychiatry, 35,* 413–421.

Hummelen, B., Wilberg, T., Pedersen, G., & Karterud, S. (2007). The quality of the DSM-IV obsessive-compulsive personality disorder construct as a prototype category. *Journal of Nervous and Mental Disease, 196,* 446–455.

Huynh, N. N., & McIntyre, R. S. (2008). What are the implications of the STAR*D trial for primary care? A review and synthesis. *The Primary Care Companion to the Journal of Clinical Psychiatry, 10,* 91–96.

Hyde, J. S., Mezulis, A. H., & Abramson, L. Y. (2008). The ABCs of depression. Integrating affective, biological and cognitive models to explain the emergence of the gender difference in depression. *Psychological Review, 115,* 291–313.

International Schizophrenia Consortium. Purcell, S. M., Wray, N. R., Stone, J. L., Visscher, P. M., O'Donovan. M. C., et al. (2009). Common polygenic variation contributes to risk of schizophrenia and bipolar disorder. *Nature, 460,* 748–752.

Jacobellis v. Ohio, 378 U.S. 184 (1964).

Jamison, K. R. (1996a). *Touched with fire. Manic depressive illness and the artistic temperament.* New York. Free Press.

Jamison, K. R. (1996b). *An unquiet mind.* New York. Alfred A. Knopf.

Jamison, K. R. (2006). The many stigmas of mental illness. *The Lancet, 367,* 533–534.

Jobe, T. H., & Harrow, M. (2005). Long-term outcome of patients with schizophrenia. A review. *Canadian Journal of Psychiatry, 50,* 892–900.

Jobe, T. H., & Harrow, M. (2010). Schizophrenia course, long-term outcome, recovery, and prognosis. *Current Directions in Psychological Science, 19,* 220–225.

Kaplan, R. M. (2006). Overdiagnosis and pseudodisease. Too much of a "good thing?" In F. Porzsolt & R. M. Kaplan (Eds.), *Optimizing health. Improving the value of healthcare* (pp. 87–91). New York. Springer.

Kendler, K. S., & Baker, J. H. (2007). Genetic influences on measures of the environment. A systematic review. *Psychological Medicine, 37,* 615–626.

Kendler, K. S., Hettema, J. M., Butera, M. A., Gardner, C. O., & Prescott, C. A. (2003). Life event dimensions of loss, humiliation, entrapment, and danger in the prediction of onsets of major depression and generalized anxiety. *Archives of General Psychiatry, 60,* 789–796.

Kessel, N. (1965). Self-poisoning, Part I. *British Medical Journal, 2,* 1265–1270.

Kessler, R. C., Berglund, P., Demler, O., Jin, R., Koretz, D., et al. (2003). The epidemiology of major depressive disorder. Results from the National Comorbidity Survey Replication (NCS-R). *JAMA, 289,* 3095–3105.

Kessler, R. C., Birnbaum, H., Demler, O., Falloon, I. R., Gagnon, E., et al. (2005). The prevalence and correlates of non-affective psychosis in the National Comorbidity Survey Replication. *Biological Psychiatry, 58,* 668–676.

Kessler, R. C., Chiu, W. T., Demler, O., & Walters, E. E. (2005). Prevalence, severity, and comorbidity of 12-month DSM-IV disorders in the National Comorbidity Survey Replication. *Archives of General Psychiatry, 62,* 617–709.

Kessler, R. C., Chiu, W. T., Jin, R., Ruscio, A. M., Shear, K., et al. (2006). The epidemiology of panic attacks, panic disorder, and agoraphobia in the National Comorbidity Survey Replication. *Archives of General Psychiatry, 63,* 415–424.

Kessler, R. C., Merikangas, K. R., & Wang, P. S. (2007). Prevalence, comorbidity, and service utilization for mood disorders in the United States at the beginning of the 21st century. *Annual Review of Clinical Psychology, 3,* 137–158.

Kessler, R. C., & Wang, P. S. (2009). The epidemiology of depression. In I. G. Gotlib & C. L. Hammen (Eds.), *Handbook of depression* (2nd ed., pp. 5–22). New York. Guilford

Kihlstrom, J. F. (2005). Dissociative disorders. *Annual Review of Clinical Psychology, 1,* 227–253.

Klein, D. N. (2010). Chronic depression. Diagnosis and classification. *Current Directions in Psychological Science, 19,* 96–100.

Kochanek, K. D., Murphy S. L., Anderson, R. N., & Scott, C. (2004). *Deaths. Final data for 2002 National Vital Statistics Reports, 53*(5), DHHS Publication No. (PHS) 2005–1120. Hyattsville, MD. National Center for Health Statistics. Retrieved from http://www.cdc.gov/nchs/data/nvsr/nvsr53/nvsr53_05.pdf on May 22, 2008.

Kring, A. M., & Caponigro, J. M. (2010). Emotion in schizophrenia. Where feeling meets thinking. *Current Directions in Psychological Science, 19,* 255–259.

Krueger, R. F., & Markon, K. E. (2006). Understanding psychopathology. Melding behavior genetics, personality, and quantitative psychology to develop an empirically based model. *Current Directions in Psychological Science, 15,* 113–117.

Lacasse, J. R., & Leo, J. (2005). Serotonin and depression. A disconnect between the advertisements and the scientific literature. *PLoS Medicine, 2,* 1211–1216.

Lalonde, J. K., Hudson, J. I., Gigante, R. A., & Pope, H. G., Jr. (2001). Canadian and American psychiatrists' attitudes toward dissociative disorders diagnoses. *Canadian Journal of Psychiatry, 46,* 407–412.

Lau, J. Y. F., & Eley, T. C. (2010). The genetics of mood disorders. *Annual Review of Clinical Psychology, 6,* 313–337.

Lenzenweger, M. F., Lane, M. C., Loranger, A. W., & Kessler, R. C. (2007). DSM-IV personality disorders in the National Comorbidity Survey Replication. *Biological Psychiatry, 62,* 553–564.

Leo, J., & Lacasse, J. R. (2008). The media and the chemical imbalance theory of depression. *Society, 45,* 35–45.

Lewinsohn, P. M., Gotlib, I. H., Lewinsohn, M., Seeley, J. R., & Allen, N. B. (1998). Gender differences in anxiety disorders and anxiety symptoms in adolescents. *Journal of Abnormal Psychology, 107,* 109–117.

Lilienfeld, S. O., & Lynn, S. J. (2003). Dissociative identity disorder. Multiple personalities, multiple controversies. In S. O. Lilienfeld, S. J. Lynn, & J. M. Lohr (Eds.), *Science and pseudoscience in clinical psychology* (pp. 109–142). New York. Guilford.

Lilienfeld, S. O., Lynn, S. J., Kirsch, I., Chaves, J. F., Sarbin, T. R., et al. (1999). Dissociative identity disorder and the sociocognitive model. Recalling the lessons of the past. *Psychological Bulletin, 125,* 507–523.

Lilienfeld, S. O., & Marino, L. (1999). Essentialism revisited. Evolutionary theory and the concept of mental disorder. *Journal of Abnormal Psychology, 108,* 400–411.

LoBue, V., & DeLoache, J. S. (2008). Detecting the snake in the grass. Attention to fear-relevant stimuli by adults and young children. *Psychological Science, 19,* 284–289.

Lynn, S. J., Lilienfeld, S. O., Merckelbach, H., Giesbrecht, T., & van der Kloet, D. (2012). Dissociation and dissociative disorders. Challenging conventional wisdom. *Current Directions in Psychological Science, 21,* 48–53.

Lyubomirsky, S., & Tkach, C. (2003). The consequences of dysphoric rumination. In C. Papageorgiou & A. Wells (Eds.), *Rumination. Nature, theory and treatment of negative thinking in depression* (pp. 21–41). Chichester, England. John Wiley & Sons.

MacNeil, T. F., & Cantor-Graae, E. (2000). Minor physical abnormalities and obstetric complications in schizophrenia. Australian and New Zealand Journal of Psychiatry, 34, S65.

Mai, F. M. (1995). Psychiatrists' attitudes to multiple personality disorder. A questionnaire study. *Canadian Journal of Psychiatry, 40,* 154–157.

Malla, A. K., Takhar, J. J., Norman, R. M., Manchanda, R., Cortese, L., et al. (2002). Negative symptoms in first episode non-affective psychosis. *Acta Psychiatrica Scandinavia, 105,* 431–439.

Marks, I. M., & Nesse, R. M. (1994). Fear and fitness. An evolutionary analysis of anxiety disorders. *Ethology and Sociobiology, 15,* 247–261.

Marmer, S. S. (1998, December). Should dissociative identity disorder be considered a bona fide diagnosis? *Clinical Psychiatry News.*

Marshall, J., & Aldhous, P. (2006, October 28). Patient groups special. Swallowing the best advice? *New Scientist,* 18–22.

Maser, J. D. (1985). List of phobias. In A. H. Tuma & J. D. Maser (Eds.), *Anxiety and the anxiety disorders.* Hillsdale, NJ. Lawrence Erlbaum Associates.

McKeown, R. E., Cuffe, S. P., & Schulz, R. M. (2006). U.S. suicide rates by age group 1970–2002. An examination of recent trends. *American Journal of Public Health, 96,* 1744–1751.

Merikangas, K. R., Akiskal, H. S., Angst, J., Greenberg, P. E., Hirschfeld, R. M. A., et al. (2007). Lifetime and 12-month prevalence of bipolar spectrum disorders in the National Comorbidity Survey Replication. *Archives of General Psychiatry, 64,* 543–552.

Messias, E. L., Chen, C.-Y., & Eaton, W. W. (2007). Epidemiology of schizophrenia. Review of findings and myths. *Psychiatric Clinics of North America, 30,* 323–338.

Miller, S. D., Blackburn, T., Scholes, G., White, G. L., & Mamalis, N. (1991). Optical differences in multiple personality disorder. A second look. *Journal of Nervous and Mental Disease, 179,* 132–135.

Miyazaki, M., Aihide, Y., & Nomura, S. (2010). Diagnosis of multiple anxiety disorders predicts the concurrent comorbidity of major depressive disorder. *Comprehensive Psychiatry, 51,* 15–18.

Mjellem, N., & Kringlen, E. (2001) Schizophrenia, a review, with emphasis on the neurodevelopmental hypothesis. *Nordic Journal of Psychiatry, 55,* 301–309.

Moncrieff, J., & Cohen, D. (2006). Do Antidepressant cure or create abnormal brain states? *PLoS Medicine, 3,* 0961–0965. Retrieved from www.plos.org on July 12, 2007.

Monroe, S. M., & Simons, A. D. (1991). Diathesis stress theories in the context of life stress research. Implications for depressive disorders. *Psychological Bulletin, 110,* 406–425.

Moss-Morris, R., & Petrie, K. J. (2001). Redefining medical students' disease to reduce morbidity. *Medical Education, 35,* 724–728.

Moussavi, S., Chatterji, S., Verdes, E., Tandon, A., Patel, V., et al. (2007). Depression, chronic diseases, and decrements in health. Results from the World Health Surveys. *The Lancet, 370,* 851–858.

Mukherjee, S. (2012, April 19). Post-Prozac nation. The science and history of treating depression. *New York Times.* Retrieved from http://www.nytimes.com/2012/04/22/magazine/the-science-and-history-of-treating-depression.html?pagewanted=all&_r=0 on April 19, 2012.

Murphy, G. E. (1998). Why women are less likely than men to commit suicide. *Comprehensive Psychiatry, 39,* 165–175.

Murphy, J. M., Horton, N. J., Laird, N. M., Monson, R. R., Sobol, A. M., et al. (2004). Anxiety and depression. A 40-year perspective on relationships regarding prevalence, distribution, and comorbidity. *Acta Psychiatrica Scandinavica, 109,* 355–375.

National Institutes of Mental Health, (2009). Schizophrenia. Retrieved from http://www.nimh.nih.gov/health/publications/schizophrenia/schizophrenia-booket-2009.pdf on March 12, 2013.

National Institutes of Mental Health. (2010). Suicide in the U. S.. Statistics and Prevention. Retrieved from http://www.nimh.nih.gov/health/publications/suicide-in-the-us-statistics-and-prevention/index.shtml on March 11, 2013.

Nathan, D. (2011). *Sybil exposed.* New York. Free Press.

Nesse, R. M. (1990). Evolutionary explanations of emotions. *Human Nature, 1,* 261–289.

Nesse, R. M., & Williams, G. C. (1994). *Why we get sick. The new science of Darwinian medicine.* New York. Times Books.

Nolen-Hoeksema, S. (2001). Gender differences in depression. *Current Directions in Psychological Science, 10,* 173–176.

Nolen-Hoeksema, S. (2012). Emotion regulation and psychopathology. The role of gender. *Annual Review of Clinical Psychology, 8,* 61–87.

Nolen-Hoeksema, S., Wisco, B. E., & Lyubomirsky, S. (2008). Rethinking rumination. *Perspectives on Psychological Science, 3,* 400–424.

Öhman, A., Carlsson, K., Lundqvist, D., & Ingvar, M. (2007). On the unconscious subcortical origin of human fear. *Physiology & Behavior, 92,* 180–185.

Olatunji, J., Cisler, J., & Tolin, D. F. (2007). Quality of life in the anxiety disorders. A meta-analytic review. *Clinical Psychology Review, 27,* 572–582.

Olson, L. M., & Wahab, S. (2006). American Indians and suicide. A neglected area of research. *Trauma, Violence, and Abuse, 7,* 19–33.

Palmer, B. A., Pankratz, S., & Bostwick, J. M. (2005). The lifetime risk of suicide in schizophrenia. A reexamination. *Archives of General Psychiatry, 62,* 247–253.

Paris, J. (2012). The rise and fall of dissociative identity disorder. *The Journal of Nervous and Mental Disease, 200,* 1076–1079.

Parker, G. (2007). Is depression overdiagnosed? Yes. *British Medical Journal, 335,* 328–329.

Perkonigg, A., Kessler, R. C., Storz, S., & Wittchen, H.-U. (2000). Traumatic events and post-traumatic stress disorder in the community. Prevalence, risk factors and comorbidity. *Acta Psychiatrica Scandinavica, 101,* 46–59.

Perrin, M. A., DiGrande, L., Wheeler, K., Thorpe, L., Farfel, M., et al. (2007). Differences in PTSD prevalence and risk factors among World Trade Center rescue and recovery workers. *American Journal of Psychiatry, 164,* 1385–1394.

Perroud, N., Uher, R., Hauser, J., Rietschel, M., Henigsberg, N., et al. (2010). History of suicide attempts among patients with depression in the GENDEP project. *Journal of Affective Disorders, 123,* 131–137.

Piper, A., & Merskey, H. (2004a). The persistence of folly. A critical examination of dissociative identity disorder. Part I. The excesses of an improbable concept. *Canadian Journal of Psychiatry, 49,* 592–600.

Piper, A., & Merskey, H. (2004b). The persistence of folly. A critical examination of dissociative identity disorder. Part II. The defence and decline of multiple personality or dissociative identity disorder. *Canadian Journal of Psychiatry, 49,* 678–683.

Plomin, R., & McGuffin, P. (2003). Psychopathology in the postgenomic era. *Annual Review of Psychology, 54,* 205–228.

Pogue-Geile, M. F., & Yokley, J. L. (2010). Current research on the genetic contributors to schizophrenia. *Current Directions in Schizophrenia, 19,* 214–219.

Pope, H. G., Jr., Barry, S., Bodkin, A., & Hudson, J. (2006). Tracking scientific interest in the dissociative disorders. A study of scientific publication output 1984–2003. *Psychotherapy and Psychosomatics, 75,* 19–24.

Pope, H. G., Jr., Oliva, P. S., Hudson, J. I., Bodkin, J. A., & Gruber, A. J. (1999). Attitudes toward DSM-IV dissociative disorders diagnoses among board-certified American Psychiatrists. *American Journal of Psychiatry, 156,* 321–323.

Post, R. M. (1992). Transduction of psychosocial stress into the neurobiology of recurrent affective disorder. *American Journal of Psychiatry, 149,* 999–1010.

Post, R. M., Leverich, G. S., Altshuler, L. L., Frye, M. A., Suppes, T. M., et al. (2003). An overview of recent findings of the Stanley Foundation Bipolar Network (Part I). *Bipolar Disorders, 5,* 310–319.

Putnam, F. W., & Lowenstein, R. J. (2000). Dissociative identity disorder. In B. J. Sadock & V. A. Sadock (Eds.), *Kaplan and Sadock's comprehensive textbook psychiatry* (7th ed., Vol. 1, pp. 1552–1564).

Rieber, R. W. (1999). Hypnosis, false memory, and multiple personality. A trinity of affinity. *History of Psychiatry, 10(1),* 3–11.

Rieber, R. W. (2006). *The bifurcation of the self. The history and theory of dissociation and its disorders.* New York. Springer.

Rihmer, Z. (2007). Suicide risk in mood disorders. *Current Opinion in Psychiatry, 20,* 17–22.

Robinson, D. J. (2005). *Disordered personalities* (3rd ed.). Port Huron, MI. Rapid Psychler Press.

Rubinow, D. R. (2006). Treatment strategies after SSRI failure—Good news and bad news. *New England Journal of Medicine, 354,* 1305–1307.

Ruscio, A. M., Brown, T. A., Chiu, W. T., Sareen, J., Stein, M. B., et al. (2008). Social fears and social phobia in the United States from the National Comorbidity Survey Replication. *Psychological Medicine, 38,* 15–28.

Safford, S. M., Alloy, L. B., Abramson, L. Y., & Crossfield, A. G. (2007). Negative cognitive style as a predictor of negative life events in depression-prone individuals. A test of the stress generation hypothesis. *Journal of Affective Disorders, 99,* 147–154.

Salander Renberg, E. E. (1999). Parasuicide in a northern Swedish county 1989–1995 and its relation to suicide. *Archives of Suicide Research, 5,* 97–112.

Sato, T., Bottlender, R., Sievers, M., & Möller, H.-J. (2005). Evidence of depressive mixed states. *American Journal of Psychiatry, 162(1),* 193–194.

Schneider, B., Müller, J. M., & Philipp, M. (2001). Mortality in affective disorders. *Journal of Affective Disorders, 65,* 263–274.

Schreiber, F. (1973). *Sybil.* New York. Warner Books.

Scott, W. J. (1990). PTSD in DSM-III. A case in the politics of diagnosis and disease. *Social Problems, 37,* 294–310.

Seligman, M. E. P. (1975). *Helplessness. On depression, development and death.* San Francisco. W. H. Freeman.

Shalev, A. Y. (2002). Acute stress reactions in adults. *Biological Psychiatry, 51,* 532–543.

Shibeshi, W. A., Young-Xu, Y., & Blatt, C. M. (2007). Anxiety worsens prognosis in patients with coronary heart disease. *Journal of the American College of Cardiology, 20,* 2021–2027.

Shirts, B. H., Kim, J. J., Reich, S., Dickerson, F. B., Yolken, R. H., et al. (2007). Polymorphisms in MICB are associated with human herpes virus seropositivity and schizophrenia risk. *Schizophrenia Research, 94,* 342–353.

Soreca, I., Frank, E., & Kupfer, D. J. (2009). The phenomenology of bipolar disorder. What drives the high rate of medical burden and determines long-term prognosis? *Depression and Anxiety, 26,* 73–82.

Steketee, G., & Barlow, D. H. (2002). Obsessive-compulsive disorder. In D. H. Barlow, *Anxiety and its disorders. The nature and treatment of anxiety and panic* (2nd ed.). New York. Guilford.

Stellman, J. M., Smith, R. P., Katz, C. L., Sharma, V., Charney, D. S., et al. (2008). Enduring mental health morbidity and social function impairment in World Trade Center rescue, recovery, and cleanup workers. The psychological dimension of an environmental health disaster. *Environmental Health Perspectives, 116,* 1248–1253.

Stengel, E. (1952). Enquiries into attempted suicide. *Procedures of the Royal Society of Medicine, 45,* 613–620.

Sumathipala, A., Siribaddana, S. H., & Bhugra, D. (2004). Culture-bound syndromes. The story of dhat syndrome. *British Journal of Psychiatry, 184,* 200–209.

Svrakic, D. M., Lecic-Tosevski, D., & Divac-Jovanovic, M. (2009). DSM axis II. Personality disorders or adaptation disorders? *Current Opinion in Psychiatry, 22,* 111–117.

Szasz, T. (1961). The myth of mental illness. *American Psychologist, 15,* 113–118. New York. Harper & Row.

Szasz, T. S. (2007). The medicalization of everyday life. Syracuse, NY. University of Syracuse Press.

Torres, A. R., Prince, M. J., Bebbington, P. E., Bhugra, D., Brugha, T. S., et al. (2006). Obsessive-compulsive disorder. Prevalence, comorbidity, impact, and help-seeking in the British National Psychiatric Morbidity Survey of 2000. *American Journal of Psychiatry, 163,* 1978–1985.

Tsai, G. E., Condie, D., Wu, M.-T, & Chang, I.-W. (1999). Functional magnetic resonance imaging of personality switches in a woman with dissociative identity disorder. *Harvard Review of Psychiatry, 7,* 119–122.

Üstün, T. B., Ayuso-Mateos, J. L., Chatterji, S., Mathers, C., & Murray, C. J. L. (2004). Global burden of depressive disorders in the year 2000. *British Journal of Psychiatry, 184,* 286–392.

Valenstein, E. S. (1998). *Blaming the brain.* New York. Free Press.

van der Heiden, C., Methorst, G., Muris, P., & van der Molen, H. T. (2011). Generalized Anxiety Disorder. Clinical presentation, diagnostic features, and guidelines for clinical practice. *Journal of Clinical Psychology, 67,* 58–73.

Värnick, P. (2012). Suicide in the world. *International Journal of Environmental Research and Public Health, 9,* 760–771.

Vichi M, Masocco M, Pompili M, Lester D, Tatarelli, R., & Vanacore, N. (2010). Suicide mortality in Italy from 1980 to 2002. *Psychiatry Research 175(1-2):*89–97.

Wakefield, J. C. (1992). The concept of mental disorder. On the boundary between biological facts and social values. *American Psychologist, 47,* 373–388.

Wakefield, J. C. (1999). Evolutionary versus prototype analyses of the concept of disorder. *Journal of Abnormal Psychology, 108,* 374–399.

Wakefield, J. C. (2003). Dysfunction as a factual component of disorder. Reply to Houts, Part 2. *Behaviour Research and Therapy, 41,* 969–990.

Wakefield, J. C. (2010). Taking disorder seriously. A critique of psychiatric criteria for mental disorders from the harmful-dysfunction perspective. In T. Millon, R. F. Krueger, & E. Simonsen (Eds.), *Contemporary directions in psychopathology. Scientific foundations of the DSM-V and ICD-11* (pp. 275–300). New York. Guilford Press.

Wakefield, J. C., Schmitz, M. F., & Baer, J. C. (2010). Does the DSM-IV clinical significance criterion for major depression reduce false positives? Evidence from the National Comorbidity Survey Replication. *American Journal of Psychiatry, 167,* 298–304.

Wakefield, J. C., Horwitz, A. V., & Schmitz, M. F. (2005). Are we overpathologizing the socially anxious? Social phobia from a harmful dysfunction perspective. *Canadian Journal of Psychiatry, 50,* 317–319.

Wakefield, J. C., Schmitz, M. F., First, M. B., & Horwitz, A. V. (2007). Extending the bereavement exclusion for major depression to other losses. Evidence from the National Comorbidity Survey. *Archives of General Psychiatry, 64,* 433–440.

Walker, E., Kestler, L., Bollini, A., & Hochman, K. M. (2004). Schizophrenia. Etiology and course. *Annual Review of Psychology, 55,* 401–430.

Walker, E., Shapiro, D., Esterberg, M., & Trotman, H. (2010). Neurodevelopment and schizophrenia. Broadening the focus. *Current Directions in Psychological Science, 19,* 204–208.

Wankurl, M., Wüst, S., & Otte, C. (2010). Current developments and controversies. Does the serotonin transporter gene-linked polymorphic region (5-HTTLPR) modulate the association between stress and depression? *Current Opinion in Psychiatry, 23,* 582–587.

Welch, H. G., Schwartz, L. M., & Wologhin, S. (2011). *Overdiagnosed. Making people sick in the pursuit of health.* Boston, MA. Beacon Press.

Widiger, T. A. (2011). A shaky future for personality disorders. *Personality Disorders. Theory, Research, and Treatment, 2,* 54–67.

World Health Organization. (2011a). Suicide prevention (SUPRE). Retrieved from http://www.who.int/mental_health/prevention/suicide/suicideprevent/en/ on March 11, 2013.

World Health Organization. (2011b). Suicide rates per 100,000 by country, year and sex (Table). Retrieved from http://www.who.int/mental_health/prevention/suicide_rates/en/index.html on March 11, 2013.

World Health Organization (2013). Distribution of suicide rates (per 100,000) by gender and age, 2000. Retrieved from http://www.who.int/mental_health/prevention/suicide/suicide_rates_chart/en/index.html on March 16, 2013.

Yolken, R. H., & Torrey, E. F. (2008). Are some cases of psychosis caused by microbial agents? A review of the evidence. *Molecular Psychiatry, 13,* 470–479.

Zanarini, M. C., Frankenburg, F. R., Hennen, J., & Silk, J. R. (2004). Mental health service utilization by borderline personality disorder patients and Axis II comparison subjects followed prospectively for 6 years. *Journal of Clinical Psychiatry, 65,* 28–36.

Zimmerman, M., McGlinchey, J. B., Chelminski, I., & Young, D. (2008). Diagnostic co-morbidity in 2300 psychiatric out-patients presenting for treatment evaluation with a semi-structured diagnostic interview. *Psychological Medicine, 38*, 199–210.

Zinbarg, R. E., Barlow, D. H., Liebowitz, M., Street, L., Broadhead, E., et al. (1994). The DSM-IV field trial for mixed anxiety-depression. *American Journal of Psychiatry, 151*, 1153–1162.

CHAPTER 14

Ahn, H., & Wampold, B. E. (2001). Where oh where are the specific ingredients? A meta-analysis of component studies in counseling and psychotherapy. *Journal of Counseling Psychology, 48*, 251–257.

American Psychiatric Association. (2000). *Practice guidelines for the treatment of psychiatric disorders. Compendium 2000.* Washington DC. American Psychiatric Association.

American Psychiatric Association Task Force. (2001). *Practice of electroconvulsive therapy. Recommendations for treatment, training, and privileging* (2nd ed.). Washington, DC. American Psychiatric Press.

Anderson, I. M. (2001). Meta-analytical studies on new antidepressants. *British Medical Bulletin, 57*, 161–178.

Andrade, C., & Thyagarajan, S. (2007). The influence of name on the acceptability of ECT. The importance of political correctness. *Journal of ECT, 23*, 75–77.

Andrews, G., Cuijpers, P., Craske, M. G., McEvoy, P., & Titov, N. (2010). Computer therapy for the anxiety and depressive disorders is effective, acceptable, and practical health care. A meta-analysis. *PLoS One, 5*, e13196. Retrieved from http://www.plosone.org/article/info%3Adoi%2F10.1371%2Fjournal.pone.0013196 on April 4, 2011.

Antony, M. M., & Barlow, D. H. (2002). Specific phobias. In D. H. Barlow (Ed.), *Anxiety and its disorders. The nature and treatment of anxiety and panic* (2nd ed.; pp. 380–418). New York. Guilford Press.

Atkins, D. C., & Christensen, A. (2001). Is professional training worth the bother? The impact of psychotherapy training on client outcome. *Australian Psychologist, 36*, 122–130.

Babyak, M., Blumenthal, J. A., Herman, S., Khatri, P., Doraiswamy, M., et al. (2000). Exercise treatment for major depression. Maintenance of therapeutic benefit at 10 months. *Psychosomatic Medicine, 62*, 633–638.

Baker, T. M., McFall, R. M., & Shoham, V. (2008). Current status and future prospects of clinical psychology. *Psychological Science in the Public Interest, 9*, 67–103.

Barker, M. J., Greenwood, K. M., Jackson, M., & Crowe, S. F. (2004). Cognitive effects of long-term benzodiazepine use. A meta-analysis. *CNS Drugs, 18*, 37–48.

Barlow, D. H. (2010). Negative effects from psychological treatment. A perspective. *American Psychologist, 65*, 13–20.

Barlow, D. H., & Durand, M. V. (2005). *Abnormal psychology* (4th ed.). Belmont, CA. Thomson/Wadsworth.

Bechtoldt, H., Norcross, J. C., Wyckoff, L. A., Pokrywa, M. L., & Campbell, L. F. (2001). Theoretical orientations and employment settings of clinical and counseling psychologists. A comparative study. *The Clinical Psychologist, 54(1)*, 3–6.

Beck, A. T. (1991). Cognitive therapy. A 30-year retrospective. *American Psychologist, 46*, 368–375.

Beck, A. T. (2005). The current state of cognitive therapy. *Archives of General Psychiatry, 62*, 953–959.

Beck, A. T., Rush, A. J., Shaw, B. F., & Emery, G. (1979). *Cognitive therapy of depression.* New York. The Guilford Press.

Beckner, V., Vella, L., Howard, I., & Mohr, D. C. (2007). Alliance in two telephone-administered treatments. Relationship with depression and health outcomes. *Journal of Consulting and Clinical Psychology, 75*, 508–512.

Bejerot, S. (2003). Psychosurgery for obsessive-compulsive disorder—Concerns remain. *Acta Psychiatrica Scandanavia, 107*, 241–243.

Bekelman, J., Li, Y., & Gross, C. (2003). Scope and impact of financial conflicts of interest in biomedical research. A systematic review. *JAMA, 289*, 454–465.

Benish, S. G., Imel, Z. E., & Wampold, B. E. (2008). Relative efficacy of bona fide psychotherapies for treating posttraumatic stress disorder. A meta-analysis of direct comparisons. *Clinical Psychology Review, 28*, 746–758.

Berlim, M. T., Van den Eynde, F., & Daskalakis, Z. J. (2013). Clinically meaningful efficacy and acceptability of low-frequency repetitive transcranial magnetic stimulation (rTMS) for treating primary major depression. A meta-analysis of randomized, double-blind and sham-controlled trials. *Neuropsychopharmacology, 38*, 543–551.

Bero, L., Oostvogel, F., Bacchetti, P., & Lee, K. (2007). Factors associated with findings of published trials of drug-drug comparisons. Why some statins appear more efficacious than others. *PLoS Medicine, 4.* Retrieved from http://www.plosmedicine.org/article/info:doi/10.1371/journal.pmed.0040184 on June 7, 2008.

Beutler, L. E. (2002). The dodo bird is extinct. *Clinical Psychology. Science and Practice, 9*, 30–34.

Bickman, L. (1999). Practice makes perfect and other myths about mental health services. *American Psychologist, 54*, 965–978.

Blatt, S. J., & Zuroff, D. C. (2005). Empirical evaluation of the assumptions in identifying evidence based treatments in mental health. *Clinical Psychology Review, 25*, 459–486.

Bowen, M. (1978). *Family therapy in clinical practice.* Northvale, NJ. Jason Aronson, Inc.

Brabender, V. (2002). *Introduction to group therapy.* New York. Wiley.

Brown, W. A. (2002). Are antidepressants as ineffective as they look? *Prevention and Treatment, 5.* Retrieved from http://journals.apa.org/prevention/volume5/pre0050026c.html on August 8, 2005.

Burlingame, G. M., & Baldwin, S. (2011). Group therapy. In J. C. Norcross, G. R. Vandenbos, & D. K. Freedheim (Eds.), *History of psychotherapy. Continuity and change* (2nd ed., pp. 505–515). Washington, DC. American Psychological Association.

Burns, D. (1999). *Feeling good* (rev. ed.). New York. Avon Books.

Campbell, E. G., Weissman, J. S., Shringhaus, S., Rao, S. R., Moy, B., et al. (2007). Institutional academic-industry relationships. *JAMA, 298*, 1779–1786.

Chambless, D. L., & Hollon, S. D. (1998). Defining empirically supported therapies. *Journal of Counseling and Clinical Psychology, 66*, 7–18.

Christensen, A. & Heavey, C. L. (1999). Interventions for couples. *Annual Review of Psychology, 50*, 165–190.

Christensen, A., & Jacobson, N. S. (1994). Who (or what) can do psychotherapy. The status and challenge of nonprofessional therapies. *Psychological Science, 5*, 9–13.

Christianson, S. A. (Ed.). (1992). *The handbook of emotion and memory. Research and theory.* Hillsdale, NJ. Lawrence Erlbaum Associates.

Clausen, J. (2010). Ethical brain stimulation. Neuroethics of deep brain stimulation in research and clinical practice. *European Journal of Neuroscience, 32*, 1152–1162.

Cobb, H. C., Reeve, R. E., Shealy, C. N., Norcross, J. C., Schare, M. L., et al. (2004). Overlap among clinical, counseling, and school psychology. Implications for the profession and combined-integrated training. *Journal of Clinical Psychology, 60*, 939–955.

Coelho, H. F., Canter, P. H., & Ernst, E. (2007). Mindfulness-based cognitive therapy. Evaluating current evidence and informing future research. *Journal of Consulting and Clinical Psychology, 75*, 1000–1005.

Cohen, E. (2007, July 9). CDC. Antidepressants most prescribed drugs in the U. S. *CNN.com/health.* Retrieved from http://www.cnn.com/2007/HEALTH/07/09/antidepressants/index.html on June 5, 2008.

Cox, M. J., & Paley, B. (2003). Understanding families as systems. *Current Directions in Psychological Science, 15*, 193–196.

Crews, F. (1996). The verdict on Freud. *Psychological Science, 7*, 63–67.

Dawes, R. M. (1996). *House of cards. Psychology and psychotherapy built on myth.* New York. Free Press.

DeAngelis, C. D., & Fontanarosa, P. B. (2008). The adverse effects of industry influence. *JAMA, 299,* 1833–1835.

DeRubeis, R. J., Hollon, S. D., Amsterdam, J. D., Shelton, R. C., Young, P. R., et al. (2005). Cognitive therapy vs. medications in the treatment of moderate to severe depression. *Archives of General Psychiatry, 62,* 409–416.

Dewan, M., Weerasekera, P., & Stormon, L. (2009). Techniques of brief psychodynamic psychotherapy. In G. O. Gabbard (Ed.), *Textbook of psychotherapeutic treatments* (pp. 69–96). Arlington, VA. American Psychiatric Publishing.

Dimidjian, S., & Hollon, S. D. (2010). How would we know if psychotherapy were harmful? *American Psychologist, 65,* 21–33.

Douglas, I. J., & Smeeth, L. (2008). Exposure to antipsychotics and risk of stroke. Self controlled case series study. *BMJ, 337.* Retrieved from http://www.bmj.com/content/337/bmj.a1227 on December 22, 2008.

Dwairy, M. (1999). Toward psycho-cultural approach in middle-eastern societies. *Clinical Psychology Review, 19,* 909–915.

Ellis, A. (1957). Outcome of employing three techniques of psychotherapy. *Journal of Consulting and Clinical Psychology, 13,* 344–350.

Ellis, A. (2001). *Overcoming destructive beliefs, feelings, and behaviors. New directions for rational-emotive behavior therapy.* New York. Prometheus.

El-Mallakh, R. S., & Karippot, A. (2005). Antidepressant-associated chronic irritable dysphoria (acid) in bipolar disorder. A case series. *Journal of Affective Disorders Special Issue. Bipolar Depression. Focus on Phenomenology, 84(2-3),* 267–272.

Federal Drug Administration. (2011). Executive summary prepared for the January 27–28, 2011 meeting of the Neurological Devices Panel to discuss the classification of electroconvulsive therapy devices (ECT). Retrieved from www.fda.gov on April 6, 2011.

Fink, M., & Taylor, M. A. (2007). Electroconvulsive therapy. Evidence and challenges. *JAMA, 298,* 330–332.

Foa, E. B., & Kozak, M. J. (1986). Emotional processing of fear. Exposure to corrective information. *Psychological Bulletin, 99,* 20–35.

Fountoulakis K. N., & Möller H. J. (2011). Efficacy of antidepressants. A re-analysis and re-interpretation of the Kirsch data. *International Journal of Neuropsychopharmacology, 14,* 405–412.

Fournier, J. C., DeRubeis, R. J., Hollon, D. D., Dimidjian, S., Amsterdam, J. D., et al. (2010). Antidepressant drug effects and depression severity. A patient level meta-analysis. *JAMA, 303,* 47–53.

Frank, J. D., & Frank, J. B. (1991). *Persuasion and healing. A comparative study of psychotherapy* (3rd ed.). Baltimore. Johns Hopkins University Press.

Freemantle, N., Anderson, I. M., & Young, P. (2000). Predictive value of pharmacological activity for the relative efficacy of antidepressant drugs. Meta-regression analysis. *British Journal of Psychiatry, 177,* 292–302.

Garske, J. P., & Anderson, T. (2003). Toward a science of psychotherapy research. Present status and evaluation. In S. O. Lilienfeld, S. J. Lynn, & J. M. Lohr (Eds.), *Science and pseudoscience in clinical psychology* (pp. 145–175). New York. The Guilford Press.

Geddes, J. R., Burgess, S., Hawton, K., Jamison, K., & Goodwin, G. M. (2004). Long-term lithium therapy for bipolar disorder. Systematic review and meta-analysis of randomized controlled trials. *American Journal of Psychiatry, 161,* 217–222.

George, M. S., Lisanby, S. H., Avery, D., McDonald, W. M., Durkalski, V., et al. (2010). Daily left prefrontal transcranial magnetic stimulation therapy for major depressive disorder. A sham-controlled randomized trial. *Archives of General Psychiatry, 67,* 507–516.

Gibbons, R. D., Hendricks, C., Hur, K., Marcus, S. M., Bhaumik, D. K., & Mann, J. J. (2007). Relationship between antidepressants and suicide attempts. An analysis of the Veterans Health Administration data sets. *American Journal of Psychiatry, 164,* 1044–1049.

Godfried, M. R. (2003). Cognitive-behavior therapy. Reflections on the evolution of a therapeutic orientation. *Cognitive Therapy and Research, 27,* 53–69.

Goldberg, D., Privett, M., Ustun, B., Simon, G., & Linden, M. (1998). The effects of detection and treatment on the outcome of major depression in primary care. A naturalistic study in 15 cities. *British Journal of General Practice, 48,* 1840–1844.

Goodwin, F. K., & Goldstein, M. A. (2003). Optimizing lithium treatment in bipolar disorder. A review of the literature and clinical recommendations. *Journal of Psychiatric Practice, 9,* 333–343.

Greenberg, R. M., & Kellner, C. H. (2005). Electroconvulsive therapy. A selected review. *American Journal of Psychiatry, 13,* 268–281.

Gregory-Roberts, E. M., Naismith, S. L., Cullen, K. M., & Hickie, I. B. (2010). Electroconvulsive therapy-induced persistent retrograde amnesia. Could it be minimized by ketamine or other pharmacological approaches? *Journal of Affective Disorders, 126(1-2),* 39–45.

Grissom, R. J. (1996). The magical number .7 plus or minus .2. Meta-meta-analysis of the probability of superior outcome in comparisons involving therapy, placebo, and control. *Journal of Consulting and Clinical Psychology, 64,* 973–982.

Haddad, P., & Anderson, I. (2007). Recognizing and managing antidepressant discontinuation syndromes. *Advances in Psychiatric Treatment, 13,* 447–457.

Hansen, R. A., Gartlehner, G., Lohr, K. N., Gaynes, B. N., & Carey, T. S. (2005). Efficacy and safety of second-generation antidepressants in the treatment of major depressive disorder. *Annals of Internal Medicine, 143,* 415–426.

Hargrove, D. S. (2009). Psychotherapy based on Bowen family systems theory. In J. H. Bray & M. Stanton (Eds.), *The Wiley-Blackwell handbook of family psychology* (pp. 286–299). Malden, MA. Wiley-Blackwell.

Harris, G. (2008, November 22). Drugmakers paid radio host $1.3 million for lectures. *New York Times.* Retrieved from http://query.nytimes.com/gst/full page.html?res=9806EEDC153DF931A15752C1A96E9C8B63 on May 2, 2009.

Harris, G. (2009, September 1). Document details plan to promote costly drug. *New York Times.* Retrieved from http://www.nytimes.com/2009/09/02/business/02drug.html on June 30, 2010.

Harris, G., & Carey, B. (2008, June 8). Researchers fail to reveal full drug pay. *New York Times.* Retrieved from http://www.nytimes.com/2008/06/08/us/08conflict.html?pagewanted=all&_r=0 on June 8, 2008.

Haw, C., & Stubbs, J. (2005). A survey of the off-label use of mood stabilizers in a large psychiatric hospital. *Journal of Psychopharmacology, 19(4),* 402–407.

Healy, D., & Cattell, D. (2003). Interface between authorship, industry, and science in the domain of therapeutics. *British Journal of Psychiatry, 183,* 22–27.

Heres, S., Davis, J., Maino, K., Jetzinger, E., Kissling, W., et al. (2006). Why olanzapne beats risperidone, risperidone beats quetiapine, and quetiapine beats olanzapine. An exploratory analysis of head-to-head comparison studies of second-generation antipsychotics. *American Journal of Psychiatry, 163,* 1645.

Higgins, S. T., Silverman, K., & Heil, S. H. (Eds.). (2007). *Contingency management in substance abuse treatment.* New York. Guilford.

Higgins, S. T., Silverman, K., & Washio, Y. (2011). Contingency management. In M. Galanter & H. D. Kleber (Eds.), *Psychotherapy for the treatment of substance abuse* (pp. 193–218). Arlington, VA. American Psychiatric Publishing.

Hollon, S. D. (2006). Randomized clinical trials. In J. C. Norcross, L. E. Beutler, & R. F. Levant (Eds.), *Evidence-based practices in mental health. Debate and dialogue on the fundamental questions* (pp. 96–105). Washington, DC. American Psychological Association.

Hollon, S. D., & Beck, A. T. (1994). Cognitive and cognitive-behavioral therapies. In A. E. Bergin & S. L. Garfield (Eds.), *Handbook of psychotherapy and behavior change* (4th ed.; pp. 428–466). New York. Wiley.

Hollon, S. D., Jarrett, R. B., Nierenberg, A. A., Thase, M. E., Trivedi, M., & Rush, A. J. (2005). Psychotherapy and medication in the treatment of adult and geriatric depression. Which monotherapy or combined treatment? *Journal of Clinical Psychiatry, 66,* 455–468.

Hollon, S. D., Stewart, M. O., & Strunk, D. (2006). Enduring effects for cognitive behavior therapy in the treatment of depression and anxiety. *Annual Review of Psychology, 57*, 285–315.

Horwitz, A. V., & Wakefield, J. C. (2007). *The loss of sadness. How psychiatry transformed normal sadness into depressive disorder.* New York. Oxford University Press.

Hosenbocus, S., & Chahal, R. (2011). SSRIs and SNRIs. A review of the discontinuation syndrome in children and adolescents. *Journal of the Canadian Academy of Child and Adolescent Psychiatry, 20*, 60–67.

Huedo-Medina, T. B., Johnson, B. T., & Kirsch, I. (2012). Kirsch et al.' s (2008) calculatins are correct. Reconsidering Fountoulakis & Möller's re-analysis of the Kirsch data. *International Journal of Neuropsychopharmacology, 15*, 1193–1198.

Jacobs, A., Carpenter, J., Donnelly, J., Klapproth, J. F., Gertel, A., et al. (2005). The involvement of professional medical writers in medical publications. Results of a Delphi study. *Current Medical Research and Opinion, 21*, 311–316.

Jacobson, N. S., & Addis, M. E. (1993). Couples therapy. What do we know and where are we going? *Journal of Consulting and Clinical Psychology, 61*, 85–93.

Jacobson, N. S., & Christensen, A. (1996b). Studying the effectiveness of psychotherapy. How well can clinical trials do the job? *American Psychologist, 51*, 1031–1039.

Jacobson, N. S., & Truax, P. (1991). Clinical significance. A statistical approach to defining meaningful change in psychotherapy research. *Journal of Consulting and Clinical Psychology, 59(1)*, 12–19.

Jones, M. C. (1924a). A laboratory study of fear. The case of Peter. *Pedagogical Seminary, 31*, 308–315.

Jones, M. C. (1924b). The elimination of children's fears. *Journal of Experimental Psychology, 7*, 382–390.

Jones, P. B., Barnes, T. R., Davies, L., Dunn, G., Lloyd, H., et al. (2006). Randomized controlled trial of the effect on quality of life of second- vs. first-generation antipsychotic drugs in schizophrenia. Cost Utility of the Latest Antipsychotic Drugs in Schizophrenia Study (CUtLASS 1). *Archives of General Psychiatry, 63*, 1079–1087.

Kane, J. M. (2004). Tardive dyskinesia rates with atypical antipsychotics in adults. Prevalence and incidence. *Journal of Clinical Psychiatry, 65(Suppl. 9)*, 16–20.

Kazdin, A. E. (2001). *Behavior modification in applied settings* (6th ed.). Belmont, CA. Wadsworth.

Kazdin, A. E. (2005). Treatment outcomes, common factors, and continued neglect of mechanisms of change. *Clinical Psychology. Science and Practice, 12*, 184–188.

Kazdin, A. E., & Blase, S. L. (2011). Rebooting psychotherapy research and practice to reduce the burden of mental illness. *Perspectives on Psychological Science, 6*, 21–37.

Kessler, R. C., Mickelson, K. D., & Zhao, S. (1997). Patterns and correlates of self-help group membership in the United States. *Social Policy, 27*, 27–46.

Khan, A., Faucett, J., Lichtenberg, P., Kirsch, L., & Brown, W. A. (2012). A systematic review of comparative efficacy of treatments and controls for depression. *PLoS ONE, 7*, e41778. Retrieved from www.plosone.org on March 10, 2013.

King, S. A., & Moreggi, D. (2007). Internet self-help and support groups. The pros and cons of text-based mutual aid. In J. Gackenbach (Ed.), *Psychology and the Internet. Intrapersonal, interpersonal, and transpersonal implications* (2nd ed., pp. 221–244). San Diego, CA. Academic Press.

Kirsch, I. (2005). Medication and suggestion in the treatment of depression. *Contemporary Hypnosis, 22*, 59–66.

Kirsch, I., Deacon, B. J., Huedo-Medina, T. B., Scoboria, A., Moore, T. J., et al. (2008). Initial severity and antidepressant benefits. A meta-analysis of data submitted to the Food and Drug Administration. *PLoS Medicine, 5, 0260–0268.* Retrieved from http://www.plosmedicine.org/article/info:doi/10.1371/journal.pmed.0050045 on March 2, 2008.

Kirsch, I., Moore, T. J., Scoboria, A., & Nicholls, S. (2002). The emperor's new drugs. An analysis of antidepressant medication data submitted to the U.S. Food and Drug Administration. *Prevention & Treatment, 5.* Retrieved from http://journals.apa.org/prevention/volume5/toc-jul15-02.htm on July 5, 2005.

Kotzalidis, G. D., Patrizi, B., Caltagirone, S. S., Koukopoulos, A., Savoja, V., et al. (2007). The adult SSRI/SNRI withdrawal syndrome. A clinically heterogeneous entity. *Clinical Neuropsychiatry. Journal of Treatment Evaluation, 4*, 1–75.

Kravitz, R. L., Epstein, R. M., Feldman, M. D., Franz, C. E., Azari, F., et al. (2005). Influence of patients' requests for direct-to-consumer advertised antidepressants. A randomized controlled trial. *JAMA, 293*, 1995–2002.

Kuyken, W., Byford, S., Taylor, R. S., Watkins, E., Holden, E., White, K., et al. (2008). Mindfulness-based cognitive therapy to prevent relapse in recurrent depression. *Journal of Consulting and Clinical Psychology, 76*, 966–978.

Lambert, M. J. (2005). Early response in psychotherapy. Further evidence for the importance of common factors rather than "placebo effects." *Journal of Clinical Psychology, 61*, 855–869.

Lampropoulos, G. K., & Spengler, P. M. (2005). Helping and change without traditional therapy. Commonalities and opportunities. *Counselling Psychology Quarterly, 18*, 47–59.

Leichsenring, F., & Rabung, S. (2009). Analyzing effectivenss of long-term psychodynamic psychotherapy. In reply. *Journal of the American Medical Association, 301*, 932–933.

Leichsenring, F., Rabung, S., & Leibing, E. (2004). The efficacy of short-term psychodynamic psychotherapy in specific psychiatric disorders. A meta-analysis. *Archives of General Psychiatry 61*, 1208–1216.

Lewis, M. W., & Petry, N. M. (2005). Contingency management treatments that reinforce completion of goal-related activities. Participation in family activities and its association with outcomes. *Drug and Alcohol Dependence, 79*, 267–271.

Lieberman, J.A., Stroup, T. S., McEvoy, J. P., Swartz, M.S., & Rosenheck, R. A. (2005). Effectiveness of antipsychotic drugs in patients with chronic schizophrenia. *New England Journal of Medicine, 353*, 1209–1223.

Lilienfeld, S. O. (2007). Psychological treatments that cause harm. *Current Perspectives in Psychological Science, 2*, 53–70.

Linde, K., Berner, M. M., & Kriston, L. (2008). St. John's Wort for major depression. *Cochrane Database Systematic Review.* Retrieved from http://proxy.library.upenn.edu:2170/doi/10.1002/14651858.CD000448.pub3/full on July 14, 2010.

Lindwall, M., Rennemark, M., Halling, A., Berglund, J., & Hassmén, P. (2006). Depression and Exercise in Elderly Men and Women. Findings From the Swedish National Study on Aging and Care. *Journal of Aging and Physical Activity, 15*, 41–55.

Lisanby, S. H. (2007). Electroconvulsive therapy for depression. *New England Journal of Medicine, 257*, 1939–1945.

Luborsky, L., Rosenthal, R., Diguer, L., Andrusyna, T. P., Berman, J. S., et al. (2002). The dodo bird verdict is alive and well—Mostly. *Clinical Psychology. Science and Practice, 9(1)*, 2–12.

MacKillop, J., Lisman, S. A., Weinstein, A., & Rosenbaum, D. (2003). Controversial treatments for alcoholism. In S. O. Lilienfeld, S. J. Lynn, & J. W. Lohr (Eds.), *Science and pseudoscience in clinical psychology* (pp. 273–306). New York. Guilford.

Macmillan, M. (1996). *Freud evaluated. The completed arc.* Cambridge, MA. MIT Press.

Madeley, G. (2007, October 19). £20,000 payout for woman who falsely accused her father of rape after 'recovered memory' therapy. *Daily Mail.* Retrieved from www.dailymail.co.uk on June 4, 2008.

Martin, J. L. R., Sainz-Pardo, M., Furukawa, T. A., Martín-Sánchez, E., Seoane, T., et al. (2007). Benzodiazepines in generalized anxiety disorder. Heterogeneity of outcomes based on a systematic review and meta-analysis of clinical trials. *Journal of Psychopharmacology, 21*, 774–782.

Mashour, G. A., Walker, E. E., & Martuza, R. L. (2005). Psychosurgery. Past, present, and future. *Brain Research Reviews, 48*, 409–419.

Mayberg, H. S., Lozano, A. M., Voon, V., McNeely, H. E., Seminowicz, D., et al. (2005). Deep brain stimulation for treatment-resistant depression. *Neuron, 45,* 651–660.

Mayne, T. J., Norcross, J. C., & Sayette, M. A. (2000). *Insider's guide to graduate programs in clinical and counseling psychology* (2000–2001 ed.). New York. Guilford.

McIntyre, R. S., & Konarski, J. Z. (2005). Tolerability profiles of atypical antipsychotics in the treatment of bipolar disorder. *Journal of Clinical Psychiatry, 66(Suppl. 3),* 28–36.

McKay, M., Davis, M., & Fanning, P. (2007). *Thoughts and feelings. Taking control of your moods and your life* (3rd ed.). Oakland, CA. New Harbinger.

Melander, H., Ahlqvist-Rastad, J., Meijer, G., & Beermann, B. (2003). Evidence b(i)ased medicine—Selective reporting from studies sponsored by pharmaceutical industry. Review of studies in new drug applications. *British Medical Journal, 326,* 1171–1173.

Messer, S. B. (2001). What makes brief psychodynamic therapy time efficient. *Clinical Psychology. Science and Practice, 8,* 5–22.

Meyer, J. S., & Quenzer, L. F. (2005). *Psychopharmacology. Drugs, the brain, and behavior.* Sunderland, MA. Sinauer Associates.

Michael, K. D., Huelsman, T. J., & Crowley, S. L. (2005). Interventions for child and adolescent depression. Do professional therapists produce better results? *Journal of Child and Family Studies, 14,* 223–236.

Miller, S., Wampold, B., & Varhely, K. (2008). Direct comparisons of treatment modalities for youth disorders. A meta-analysis. *Psychotherapy Research, 18,* 5–14.

Minami, T., Davies, D. R., Tierney, S. C., Bettmann, J. E., McAward, S. M., et al. (2009). Preliminary evidence on the effectiveness of psychological treatments delivered at a university counseling center. *Journal of Counseling Psychology, 56,* 309–320.

Minami, T., Wampold, B. E., Serlin, R. C., Hamilton, E. G., Brown, G. S., et al. (2008). Benchmarking the effectiveness of psychotherapy treatment of adult depression in a managed care environment. A preliminary study. *Journal of Consulting and Clinical Psychology, 76,* 116–124.

Moffatt, B., & Elliott, C. (2007). Ghostmarketing. Pharmaceutical companies and ghostwritten journal articles. *Perspectives in Biology and Medicine, 50,* 18–31.

Mojtabai, R. (2008). Increase in antidepressant medication in the US adult population between 1990 and 2003. *Psychotherapy and Psychosomatics, 77,* 83–92.

National Center for Health Statistics. (2007). *Health, United States, 2007. With chartbook on trends in the health of Americans.* Hyattsville, MD. Centers for Disease Control. Retrieved from http://www.cdc.gov/nchs/data/hus/hus07.pdf on June 6, 2008.

Naylor, E. V., Anonuccio, D. O., Litt, M., Johnson, G. E., Spogen, D. R., et al. (2010). Bibliotherapy as a treatment for depression in primary care. *Journal of Clinical Psychology in Medical Settings, 17,* 258–271.

Nelson, J. C., Mazure, C. M., Jatlow, P. I., Bowers, M. B. J., & Price, L. H. (2004). Combining norepinephrine and serotonin reuptake inhibition mechanisms for treatment of depression. A double-blind, randomized study. *Biological Psychiatry, 55(3),* 296–300.

Nelson, J. C., Thase, M. E., & Khan, A. (2008). Are antidepressants effective? What's a clinician to think? *Journal of Clinical Psychiatry, 69,* 1014–1015.

Neutel, X. L. (2005). The epidemiology of long-term benzodiazepine use. *International Review of Psychiatry, 17,* 189–197.

Norcross, J. C. (2005). A primer on psychotherapy integration. In J. C. Norcross & M. R. Goldfried (Eds.), *Handbook of psychotherapy integration* (2nd ed., pp. 84–102). New York. Oxford University Press.

Norcross, J. C., Koocher, G. P., & Garofalo, A. (2006). Discredited psychological treatments and tests. A Delphi poll. *Professional Psychology. Research and Practice, 37,* 512–522.

Norcross, J. C., & Lambert, M. J. (2011). Psychotherapy relationships that work II. *Psychotherapy, 48,* 4–8.

Norcross, J. C., Santrock, J., Campbell, L., Smith, T., Sommer, R., et al. (2000). *Authoritative guide to self-help resources in mental health.* New York. Guilford Press.

Norcross, J. C., & Wampold, B. E. (2011). Evidence-based therapy relationships. Research conclusions and clinical practices. *Psychotherapy, 48,* 98–102.

Nutt, D. J., & Sharpe, M. (2008). Uncritical positive regard? Issues in the efficacy and safety of psychotherapy. *Journal of Psychopharmacology, 22,* 3–6.

O'Brien, C. P. (2005). Benzodiazepine use, abuse, and dependence. *Journal of Clinical Psychology, 66(Suppl. 2),* 28–33.

O'Donohue, W., Fisher, J. E., & Hayes, S. C. (Eds.). (2003). *Cognitive-behavior therapy. Applying empirically supported techniques in your practice.* New York. Wiley.

Ögren, K., & Sandlund, M. (2007). Lobotomy at a state mental hospital in Sweden. A survey of patients operated on during the period 1947–1958. *Nordic Journal of Psychiatry, 61,* 355–362.

Okiishi, J., Lambert, M. J., Eggett, D., Nielsen, S. L., Dayton, D. D., et al. (2006). An analysis of therapist treatment effects. Toward providing feedback to individual therapists on their clients' psychotherapy outcome. *Journal of Clinical Psychology, 62,* 1157–1172.

Okiishi, J., Lambert, M. J., Nielsen, S. L., & Ogles, B. M. (2003). Waiting for supershrink. An empirical analysis of therapist effects. *Clinical Psychology & Psychotherapy, 10,* 361–373.

Olatunji, B. O., & Hollon, S. D. (2010). Preface. The current status of cognitive behavioral therapy for psychiatric disorders. *Psychiatric Clinics of North America, 33,* xiii–xix.

Pagnin, D., de Queiroz, V., Pini, S., & Cassano, G. B. (2004). Efficacy of ECT in depression. A meta-analytic review. *Journal of ECT, 20,* 155–162.

Parker, G., Roy, K., & Eyers, K. (2003). Cognitive behavior therapy for depression? Choose horses for courses. *American Journal of Psychiatry, 160,* 825–834.

Pirraglia, P. A., Stafford, R. S., & Singer, D. E. (2003). Trends in prescribing of selective serotonin reuptake inhibitors and other newer antidepressant agents in adult primary care. *Primary Care Companion of Journal of Clinical Psychiatry, 5,* 153–157.

Pope, K. S., & Tabachnick, B. G. (1994). Therapists as patients. A national survey of psychologists' experiences, problems, and beliefs. *Professional Psychology. Research and Practice, 25,* 247–258.

Powers, M. B., & Emmelkamp, P. M. G. (2008). Virtual reality exposure therapy for anxiety. A meta-analysis. *Journal of Anxiety Disorders, 22,* 561–569.

Rachman, S. (2009). Psychological treatment of anxiety. The evolution of behavior therapy. *Annual Review of Clinical Psychology, 5,* 97–119.

Rash, C. J., Alessi, S. M., & Petry, N. (2008). Contingency management is efficacious for cocaine abusers with prior treatment attempts. *Experimental and Clinical Psychopharmacology, 16,* 547–554.

Rose, D., Fleischmann, P., Wykes, T., Leese, M., & Bindman, J. (2003). Patients' perspectives on electroconvulsive therapy. Systematic review. *British Medical Journal, 326,* 1363–1372.

Rosen, G. M., Glasgow, R. E., & Moore, T. E. (2003). Self-help therapy. The science and business of giving psychology away. In S. O. Lilienfeld, S. J. Lynn, & J. M. Lohr (Eds.), *Science and pseudoscience in clinical psychology* (pp. 399–424). New York. Guilford.

Rosenbaum, J. F., Fava, M., Hoog, S. L., Ashcroft, R. C., & Krebs, W. B. (1998). Selective serotonin inhibitor discontinuation syndrome. A randomized clinical trial. *Biological Psychiatry, 44,* 77–87.

Rosenheck, R. A., Leslie, D. L., & Doshi, J. A. (2008). Second-generation antipsychotics. Cost-effectiveness, policy options, and political decision making. *Psychiatric Services, 59,* 515–520.

Rosenzweig, S. (1936). Some implicit common factors in diverse methods of psychotherapy. "At last the dodo said, 'Everybody has won and all must have prizes.'" *American Journal of Orthopsychology, 49,* 298–304.

Royal College of Psychiatrists. (1995). *Fact sheet on ECT.* London. RCP.

Roy-Byrne, P. R. (2005). The GABA-Benzodiazepine receptor complex.

Structure, function, and role in anxiety. *Journal of Clinical Psychiatry, 66*(Suppl. 2), 14–20.

Rubinow, D. R. (2006). Treatment strategies after SSRI failure—Good news and bad news. *New England Journal of Medicine, 354,* 1305–1307.

Rush, A. J., Trivedi, M. H., Wisniewski, S. R., Stewart, J. W., Nierenberg, A. A., et al. (2006). Bubropion-SR, sertraline, or venlafaxine-XR after failure of SSRIs for depression. *New England Journal of Medicine, 354,* 1231–1242.

Rutherford, A. (2000). Mary Cover Jones (1896–1987). Retrieved from http://www.psych.yorku.ca/femhop/Cover%20Jones.htm on July 14, 2005. (Originally published in *The Feminist Psychologist,* Vol. 27, Summer 2000.)

Sachs, G. S., Nierenberg, A. A., Calabrese, M. D., Marangell, M. D., Wisniewski, S. R., et al. (2007). Effectiveness of adjunctive antidepressant treatment for bipolar depression. *New England Journal of Medicine, 356,* 1711–1722.

Sackeim, H. A., Prudic, J., Fuller, R., Keilp, J., Lavori, P. W., & Olfson, M. (2007). The cognitive effects of electroconvulsive therapy in community settings. *Neuropsychopharmacology, 32,* 244–254.

Segal, Z. V., Bieling, P., Young, T., MacQueen, G., Cooke, M., et al., (2010). Antidepressant monotherapy vs. sequential pharmacotherapy and mindfulness-based cognitive therapy, or placebo, for relapse prophylaxis in recurrent depression. *Archives of General Psychiatry, 67,* 1256–1264.

Segal, Z. V., Williams, J. M. G., & Teasdale, J. (2002). *Mindfulness-based cognitive therapy for depression. A new approach to preventing relapse.* New York. Guilford.

Seligman, M. E. P. (1995). The effectiveness of psychotherapy. The *Consumers Reports* Study. *American Psychologist, 50,* 965–974.

Sharp, J., & Espie, C. A. (2004). Brief exposure therapy for the relief of post-traumatic stress disorder. A single case experimental design. *Behavioural and Cognitive Psychotherapy, 32,* 365–369.

Shedler, J. (2010). The efficacy of psychodynamic psychotherapy. *American Psychologist, 65,* 98–109.

Siev, J., Huppert, J. D., & Chambless, D. L. (2009). The dodo bird, treatment technique, and disseminating empirically supported treatments. *The Behavior Therapist, 32,* 69, 71–76.

Sikich, L., Frazier, J. A., McClellan, J., Findling, R. L., Vitiello, B., et al. (2008). Double-blind comparison of first- and second-generation antipsychotics in early-onset schizophrenia and schizoaffective disorder. Findings from the Treatment of Early-Onset Schizophrenia Spectrum Disorders (TEOSS) study. *American Journal of Psychiatry, 165,* 1420–1431.

Singer, N. (2009, August 4). Medical papers by ghostwriters pushed therapy. *New York Times.* Retrieved from http://www.nytimes.com/2009/08/05/health/research/05ghost.html?pagewanted=all&_r=0 on June 30, 2010.

Sismondo, S. (2007). Ghostmanagement. How much of the medical literature is shaped behind the scenes by the pharmaceutical industry? *PLoS Medicine, 4,* 1429–1433. Retrieved from http://www.plosmedicine.org/article/info:doi/10.1371/journal.pmed.0040286 on June 8, 2008.

Sismondo, S. (2008a). How pharmaceutical industry funding affects trial outcomes. Causal structures and responses. *Social Science & Medicine, 66,* 1909–1914.

Sismondo, S. (2008b). Pharmaceutical company funding and its consequences. A qualitative systematic review. *Contemporary Clinical Trials, 29,* 109–113.

Slotema, C. W., Blom, J. D., Hoek, HY. W., & Sommer, I. E. (2010). *Journal of Clinical Psychiatry, 71,* 873–884.

Slovenko, R. (1994). Blaming a book. *Journal of Psychiatry and Law, 22,* 437–451.

Smith, M. L., & Glass, G. V. (1977). Meta-analysis of psychotherapy outcome studies. *American Psychologist, 32,* 752–760.

Smith, M. L., Glass, G. V., & Miller, T. I. (1980). *The benefits of psychotherapy.* Baltimore. Johns Hopkins University Press.

Snyder, D. K., Castellani, A. M., & Whisman, M. A. (2006). Current status and future directions in couple therapy. *Annual Review of Psychology, 57,* 317–344.

Spielmans, G. I., Pasek, L. F., & McFall, J. P. (2007). What are the active ingredients in cognitive and behavioral psychotherapy for anxious and depressed children? A meta-analytic review. *Clinical Psychology Review, 27,* 642–654.

Sterling, P. (2000). *Nature, 403,* 242.

Stern, W. M., Tormos, J. M., Press, D. Z., Pearlman, C., & Pascual-Leone, A. (2007). Antidepressant effects of high and low frequency repetitive transcranial magnetic stimulation to the dorsolateral prefrontal cortex. A double-blind, randomized, placebo-controlled trial. *Journal of Neuropsychiatry and Clinical Neuroscience, 19,* 179–186.

Strieker, G., & Gold, J. (2008). Integrative therapy. In J. L. Lebow (Ed.), *Twenty-first century psychotherapies. Contemporary approaches to theory and practice* (pp. 389–423). Hoboken, NJ. John Wiley & Sons.

Strupp, H. H., & Hadley, S. W. (1979). Specific vs. nonspecific factors in psychotherapy. A controlled study of outcome. *Archives of General Psychiatry, 36,* 1125–1136.

Swartz, M. S., Perkins, D. O., Stroup, T. S., Davis, S. M., Capuano, G., et al. (2007). Effects of antipsychotic medications on psychosocial functioning in patients with chronic schizophrenia. Findings from the NIMH CATIE study. *American Journal of Psychiatry, 164,* 428–436.

Szegedi, A., Kohnen, R., Dienel, M., & Kieser, M. (2005). Acute treatment of moderate to severe depression with hypericum extract WS 5570 (St. John's wort). Randomized controlled double blind non-inferiority trial versus paroxetine. *British Medical Journal, 330,* 503–507.

Trivedi, M. H., Greer, T. L., Grannemann, B. D., Chambliss, H. O., & Jordan, A. N. (2006). Exercise as an augmentation strategy for treatment of major depression. *Journal of Psychiatric Practice, 12,* 205–213.

Tseng, W.-S. (2004). Culture and psychotherapy. Asian perspectives. *Journal of Mental Health, 13,* 151–161.

Turner, E. H., Matthews, A. M., Linardatos, E., Tell, R. A., & Rosenthal, R. (2008). Selective publication of antidepressant trials and its influence on apparent efficacy. *New England Journal of Medicine, 358,* 252–260.

U.S. Food and Drug Administration. (2004). FDA Public Health Advisory, October 15, 2004. Retrieved from http://www.fda.gov/safety/medwatch/safetyinformation/safetyalertsforhumanmedicalproducts/ucm155488.htm on July 30, 2005.

UK ECT Review Group. (2003). Efficacy and safety of electroconvulsive therapy in depressive disorders. A systematic review and meta-analysis. *The Lancet, 361,* 799–808.

Van Dyk, G. A. J., & Nefale, M. C. (2005). The split-ego experience of Africans. Ubuntu therapy as a healing alternative. *Journal of Psychotherapy Integration, 15*(1), 48–66.

Vedantam, S. (2006, April 12). Comparison of schizophrenia drugs often favors firm funding study. *Washington Post.* Retrieved from http://www.washingtonpost.com/wp-dyn/content/article/2006/04/11/AR2006041101478.html on June 8. 2008.

Vocisano, C., Klein, D. N., Arnow, B., Rivera, C., Blalock, J. A., et al. (2004). *Psychotherapy. Theory, Research, Practice, Training, 41,* 255–265.

Wampold, B. E. (2001). *The great psychotherapy debate. Models, methods, and findings.* Mahwah, NJ. Lawrence Erlbaum Associates.

Wampold, B. E. (2007). Psychotherapy. The humanistic (and effective) treatment. *American Psychologist, 62,* 857–873.

Wampold, B. E. (2009). Clinical trials for the treatment of mental disorders. Two major flaws that limit interpretability. *The Canadian Journal of Psychiatry, 54,* 639–641.

Wampold, B. E. (2010). The research evidence for common factors models. A historically situated perspective. In B. L. Duncan, S. D. Miller, B. E. Wampold, & M. A. Hubble (Eds.), *The heart and soul of change. Delivering what works in therapy* (2nd ed., pp. 49–81). Washington DC. American Psychological Association.

Wampold, B. E., Budge, S. L., Laska, K. M., De Re, A. C., Baardseth, T. P., Flückinger, C., et al. (2011). Evidence-based treatments for depression and anxiety versus treatments-as-usual. A meta-analysis of direct comparisons. *Clinical Psychology Review, 31*, 1304–1312.

Wampold, B. E., Minami, T., Baskin, T. W., & Tierney, S. C. (2002). Meta-(re)analysis of the effects of cognitive therapy versus "other therapies" for depression. *Journal of Affective Disorders, 68*, 159–165.

Westen, D. (1998). The scientific legacy of Sigmund Freud. Toward a psychodynamically informed psychological science. *Psychological Bulletin, 124*, 333–371.

Westen, D., & Morrison, K. (2001). A multidimensional meta-analysis of treatments for depression, panic, and Generalized Anxiety Disorder. An empirical examination of the status of empirically supported therapies. *Journal of Consulting and Clinical Psychology, 69*, 875–899.

Westen, D., Novotny, C. M., & Thompson-Brenner, H. (2004). The empirical status of empirically supported psychotherapies. Assumptions, findings, and reporting in controlled clinical trials. *Psychological Bulletin, 130*, 631–663.

Wheatley, D. (2006). St. John's Wort in depression. The patient's dilemma. *Primary Care & Community Psychiatry, 11*, 137–142.

Williams J. W., Jr., Mulrow, C. D., Ciquette, E., Noel, P. H., Aquilar, C., et al. (2000). A systematic review of newer pharmacotherapies for depression in adults. Evidence report summary. *Annals of Internal Medicine, 132*, 743–756.

Wisniewski, S. R., Rush, A. J., Nierenberg, A. A., Gaynes, B. N., Warden, D., et al. (2009). Can Phase III trial results of antidepressant medications be generalized to clinical practice? A STAR*D report. *American Journal of Psychiatry, 166*, 599–607.

Wolpe, J. (1982). *The practice of behavior therapy* (3rd ed.). New York. Pergamon Press.

Wood, J. V., Perunovic, W. Q. E, & Lee, J. W. (2009). Positive self-statements. Power for some, peril for others. *Psychological Science, 20*, 860–866.

Yatham, L. (2005). Atypical antipsychotics for bipolar disorder. *Psychiatric Clinics of North America, 28*, 325–347.

CHAPTER 15

Alcock, J. (2009). *Animal behavior.* Sunderland, MA. Sinauer.

Allison, S. T., Mackie, D. M., Muller, M. M., & Worth L. T. (1993). Sequential correspondence biases and perceptions of change. The Castro studies revisited. *Personality & Social Psychology Bulletin, 19*, 151–157.

Allport, G. (1954). *The nature of prejudice.* Reading, MA. Addison-Wesley.

Arkes, H. R., & Tetlock, P. E. (2004). Attributions of implicit prejudice, or "would Jesse Jackson 'fail' the Implicit Association Test"? *Psychological Inquiry, 15*, 257–278.

Asch, S. E. (1956). Studies of independence and conformity. A minority of one against a unanimous majority. *Psychological Monographs, 70*, No. 416.

Atran, S. (2003). Genesis of suicide terrorism. *Science, 299*, 1534–1539.

Back, M. D., Stopfer, J. M., Vazire, S., Gaddis, S., Schmukle, S. C., et al. (2010). Facebook profiles reflect actual personality, not self-idealization. *Psychological Science, 21*, 372–374.

Baker, L. A., & Emery, R. E. (1993). When every relationship is above average. Perceptions and expectations of divorce at the time of marriage. *Law and Human Behavior, 17*, 439–450.

Bargh, J. A., & McKenna, K. Y. A. (2004). The Internet and social life. *Annual Review of Psychology, 55*, 573–590.

Bar-Haim, Y., Ziv, T., Lamy, D., & Hodes, R. M. (2006). Nature and nurture in own-race face processing. *Psychological Science, 17*, 159–163.

Batson, C. D. (2010). Empathy-induced altruistic motivation. In M. Mikulincer, & P. R. Shaver (Eds.), *Prosocial motives, emotions, and behavior. The better angels of our nature* (pp. 15–34). Washington, DC. American Psychological Association.

Batson, C. D., Ahmad, N., Yin, J., Bedell, S. J., Johnson. J. W., et al. (1999). Two threats to the common good. Self-interested egoism and empathy-induced altruism. *Personality and Social Psychology Bulletin, 25*(1), 3–16.

Bauman, C. W., & Skitka, L. J. (2010). Making attributions for behaviors. The prevalence of correspondence bias in the general population. *Basic and Applied Social Psychology, 32*, 269–277.

Baumeister, R. F. (1989). The optimal margin of illusion. *Journal of Social and Clinical Psychology, 8*, 176–189.

Baumeister, R. F., Bratslavsky, E., Muraven, M., & Tice, D. M. (1998). Ego depletion. Is the active self a limited resource? *Journal of Personality & Social Psychology, 24*, 1252–1265.

Baumeister, R. F., & Bushman, B. J. (2008). *Social psychology and human nature.* Belmont, CA. Thomson/Wadsworth.

Baumeister, R. F., Campbell, J. D., Krueger, J. I., & Vohs, K. D. (2003). Does high self-esteem cause better performance, interpersonal success, happiness, or healthier lifestyles? *Psychological Science in the Public Interest, 4*, 1–44.

Baumeister, R. F., Gailliot, M., DeWall, C. N., & Oaten, M. (2006). Self-regulation and personality. How interventions increase regulatory success, and how depletion moderates the effects of traits on behavior. *Journal of Personality, 74*, 1773–1801.

Baumeister, R. F., & Vohs, K. D. (2004). Self-regulation. In C. Peterson & M. E. P. Seligman (Eds.), *Character strengths and virtues. A handbook and classification* (pp. 499–516). Washington, DC/New York. American Psychological Association/Oxford University Press.

Baumeister, R. F., Vohs, K. D., & Tice, D. M. (2007). The strength model of self-control. *Current Directions in Psychological Science, 16*, 351–355.

BBC News. (2009, June 2). *Female medics to outnumber male.* Retrieved on March 18, 2013 from http://news.bbc.co.uk/2/hi/health/8077083.stm.

Bernhard, H., Fischbacher, U., & Fehr, E. (2006). Parochial altruism in humans. *Nature, 442*, 912–915.

Blass, T. (1999). The Milgram paradigm after 35 years. Some things we now know about obedience. *Journal of Applied Social Psychology, 29*, 955–978.

Blass, T. (2009). *The man who shocked the world. The life and legacy of Stanley Milgram.* New York. Basic Books.

Bleske-Rechek, A., Remiker, M. W., & Baker, J. P. (2009). Similar from the start. Assortment in young adult dating couples and its link to relationship stability over time. *Individual Differences Research, 7*, 142–158.

Bloom, M. (2005). *Dying to kill. The allure of suicide terrorism.* New York. Columbia University Press.

Bloom, P. (2004). *Descartes' baby. How the science of child development explains what makes us human.* New York. Basic Books.

Botwin, M., Buss, D. M., & Shackelford, T. K. (1997). Personality and mate preferences. Five factors in mate selection and marital satisfaction. *Journal of Personality, 65*, 107–136.

Brewer, M. B. (2007). The importance of being *We*. Human nature and intergroup relations. *American Psychologist, 62*, 728–738.

Brown, D. E. (1991). *Human universals.* New York. McGraw-Hill.

Buckley, C. (2007, January 3). Man is rescued by stranger on subway tracks. *New York Times.* Retrieved from http://www.nytimes.com/2007/01/03/nyregion/03life.html on January 6, 2007.

Burger, J. M. (2009). Replicating Milgram. Would people still obey? *American Psychologist, 64*, 1–11.

Burke, B. L., Martens, A., & Faucher, E. H. (2010). Two decades of terror management theory. A meta-analysis of mortality salience research. *Personality and Social Psychology Review, 14*, 155–195.

Buss, D. (2003). *The evolution of desire.* New York. Basic Books. (Original work published 1994).

Campbell, D. T. (1965). Ethnocentric and other altruistic motives. In D. Levine (Ed.), *Nebraska symposium on motivation* (Vol. 13). Lincoln, NE. University of Nebraska Press.

Capell, M. B., & Sahliyeh, S. (2007). Suicide terrorism. Is religion the critical factor? *Security Journal, 20*, 267–283.

Carnahan, T., & McFarland, S. (2007). Revisiting the Stanford Prison Experiment. Could participant self-selection have led to the cruelty?

Personality and Social Psychology Bulletin, 33, 603–614.

Chambers, J. R., & Widschitl, P. D. (2004). Biases in social comparative judgments. The role of nonmotivated factors in above-average and comparative-optimism effects. *Psychological Bulletin, 130,* 813–838.

Choi, I., Nisbett, R. E., & Norenzayan, A. (1999). Causal attribution across cultures. Variation and universality. *Psychological Bulletin, 125,* 47–63.

Cialdini, R. B., Brown, S. L., Lewis, B. P., Luce, C., & Neuberg, S. L. (1997). Reinterpreting the empathy-altruism relationship. When one into one equals oneness. *Journal of Personality and Social Psychology, 73,* 481–494.

Clabaugh, A., & Morling, B. (2004). Stereotype accuracy of ballet and modern dancers. *Journal of Social Psychology, 144,* 31–48.

CNN Access. (2004, May 21). Researcher. It's not bad apples, it's the barrel. Retrieved from http://www.cnn .com/2004/US/05/21/zimbardo.access/ on May 30, 2004.

Colvin, C.R., & Block, J. (1994). Do positive illusions foster mental health? An examination of the Taylor and Brown formulation. *Psychological Bulletin 116,* 3–20.

Commentaries to Sabini et al., 2001a. (2001). *Psychological Inquiry, 12,* 16–40.

Cooper, J., & Fazio, R. H. (1984). A new look at dissonance theory. In L. Berkowitz (Ed.), *Advances in experimental social psychology* (Vol. 17, pp. 229–267). New York. Academic Press.

Cosmides, L., & Tooby, J. (1992). Cognitive adaptations for social exchange. In J. Barkow, L. Cosmides, & J. Tooby (Eds.), *The adapted mind* (pp. 163–228). New York. Oxford University Press.

Cuddy, A. J. C., Fiske, S., & Glick, P. (2007). The BIAS map. Behaviors from intergroup affect and stereotypes. *Journal of Personality and Social Psychology, 92,* 631–648.

Darley, J. M. (1995). Constructive and destructive obedience. A taxonomy of principal-agent relationships. *Journal of Social Issues, 51,* 125–154.

Darley, J. M., & Latané, B. (1968). Bystander intervention in emergencies. Diffusion of responsibility. *Journal of Personality and Social Psychology, 8,* 377–383.

David, B., & Turner, J. C. (2001). Majority and minority influence. A single process self-categorization analysis. In C. K. W. De Dreu & N. K. De Vries (Eds.), *Group consensus and minority influence. Implications for innovation* (pp. 92–121). Malden, MA. Blackwell.

Dawkins, R. (1976). *The selfish gene.* Oxford, UK. Oxford University Press.

Decety, J., & Jackson, P. L. (2006). A social-neuroscience perspective on empathy. *Current Directions in Psychological Science, 15,* 54–58.

Decety, J., Michalska, J. L., & Akitsuki, Y. (2008). What caused the pain? An fMRI investigation of empathy and intentionality in children. *Neuropsychologia, 46,* 2607–2614.

Deutsch, M., & Gerard, H. B. (1955). A study of normative and informational social influences upon individual judgment. *Journal of Abnormal and Social Psychology, 51,* 629–636.

de Waal, F. B. M. (2008). Putting the altruism back into altruism. The evolution of empathy. *Annual Review of Psychology, 59,* 279–300.

Diekman, A. B., Eagly, A. H., & Kulesa, P. (2002). Accuracy and bias in stereotypes about the social and political attitudes of women and men. *Journal of Experimental and Social Psychology, 38,* 268–282.

Di Gennaro, C., & Dutton, W. H. (2007). Reconfiguring friendships. Social relationships and the Internet. *Information, Communication & Society, 10,* 591–618.

Dugatkin, L. A. (1997). *Cooperation among animals. An evolutionary perspective.* New York. Oxford University Press.

Dugatkin, L. A. (2006). *The altruism equation. Seven scientists search for the origins of goodness.* Princeton, NJ. Princeton University Press.

Epley, N., Savitsky, K., & Gilovich, T. (2002). Empathy neglect. Reconciling the spotlight effect and the correspondence bias. *Journal of Personality and Social Psychology, 83,* 300–312.

Eskine, K. J., Kacinik, N. A., & Prinz, J. J. (2011). A bad taste in the mouth. Gustatory disgust influences moral judgment. *Psychological Science, 22,* 295–299.

Feagin, J. R. (2006). *Systemic racism. A theory of oppression.* New York. Routledge.

Fein, S. (2001). Beyond the fundamental attribution era? *Psychological Inquiry, 12,* 16–46.

Festinger, L. (1954). A theory of social comparison processes. *Human Relations, 7,* 117–140.

Festinger, L. (1957). *A theory of cognitive dissonance.* Stanford, CA. Stanford University Press.

Fiedler, K., & Bluemke, M. (2005). Faking the IAT. Aided and unaided response control on the implicit association tests. *Basic and Applied Social Psychology, 27,* 307–316.

Fink, B., Neave, N., Manning, J., & Grammer, K. (2006). Facial symmetry and judgements of attractiveness, health and personality. *Personality and Individual Differences, 41,* 491–499.

Finkel, E. J., Eastwick, P. W., Karney, B. R., Reis, H. T., & Sprecher, S. (2012). Online dating. A critical analysis from the perspective of psychological science. *Psychological Science in the Public Interest, 13,* 3–66.

Fischer, P., Greitemeyer, T., & Frey, D. (2007). Ego depletion and positive illusions. Does the construction of positivity require regulatory resources? *Personality and Social Psychology Bulletin, 33,* 1306–1321.

Fischer, P., Krueger, J. I., Greitmeyer, T., Vogrincic, C., Kastenmüller, A., et al. (2011). The bystander effect. A meta-analytic review on bystander intervention in dangerous and non-dangerous emergencies. *Psychological Bulletin, 137,* 517–537.

Fiske, S. (2004). What we know now about bias and intergroup conflict, the problem of the century. In J. B. Ruscher & E. Y. Hammer (Eds.), *Current directions in social psychology* (pp. 124–131). Upper Saddle River, NJ. Pearson.

Fiske, S. T., Cuddy, A. J., Glick, P., & Xu, J. (2002). A model of (often mixed) stereotype content. Competence and warmth respectively follow from perceived status and competition. *Journal of Personality and Social Psychology, 49,* 65–85.

Fiske, S. T., Harris, L., & Cuddy, A. J. C. (2004). Why ordinary people torture enemy prisoners. *Science, 306,* 1482–1483.

Fiske, S. T., & Neuberg, S. L. (1990). A continuum model of impression formation from category-based to individuating processes. Influences of information and motivation on attention and interpretation. In M. P. Zanna (Ed.), *Advances in experimental social psychology* (Vol. 3, pp. 1–74). San Diego, CA. Academic Press.

Funder, D. C. (2001). The really, really fundamental attribution error. *Psychological Inquiry, 12,* 21–23.

Furnham, A., Mistry, D., & McClelland, A. (2004). The influence of age of the face and the waist to hip ratio on judgments of female attractiveness and traits. *Personality and Individual Differences, 36,* 1171–1185.

Gailliot, M. T., Baumeister, R. F., Schmeichel, B. J., DeWall, C. N., Maner, J. K., et al. (2007). Self-control relies on glucose as a limited energy source. Willpower is more than a metaphor. *Journal of Personality and Social Psychology, 92,* 325–336.

Gallagher, M. W., & Lopez, S. J. (2009, May). Optimism is universal? Exploring demographic predictors of optimism in a representative sample of the world. Poster presented at the 21st annual convention of the Association for Psychological Science, San Francisco, CA.

Gallup, G. G., Jr., & Frederick, D. A. (2010). The science of sex appeal. An evolutionary perspective. *Review of General Psychology, 14,* 240–250.

Gana, K., Alaphilippe, D., & Bailly, N. (2004). Positive illusions and mental and physical health in later life. *Aging and Mental Health, 8,* 58–64.

Gangestad, S. W., & Scheyd, G. J. (2005). The evolution of human physical attractiveness. *Annual Review of Anthropology, 34,* 523–548.

Gansberg, M. (1964, March 27). 37 who saw murder didn't call the police. *New York Times.* Retrieved from http://select .nytimes.com/gst/abstract.html?res=F1 0B16FB3A5C147A93C5AB1788D85F40 8685F9 on March 17, 2013.

Gawronski, B. (2009). Ten frequently asked questions about implicit measures and their frequently supposed, but not entirely correct answers. *Canadian Psychology, 50,* 141–150.

Gawronski, B., LeBel, E. P., & Peters, K. R. (2007). What do implicit measures tell us? *Perspectives on Psychological Science, 2,* 181–193.

Gilbert, D. T., & Malone, P. S. (1995). The correspondence bias. *Psychological Bulletin, 117,* 21–38.

Gilovich, T., Medvec, V. H., & Savitsky, K. (1999). The spotlight effect in social judgment. An egocentric bias in estimates of the salience of one's own actions and appearance. *Journal of Personality and Social Psychology, 78,* 211–222.

Gilovich, T., & Savitsky, K. (1999). The spotlight effect and the illusion of transparency. Egocentric assessments of how we are seen by others. *Current Directions in Psychological Science, 8,* 165–168.

Goetz, J. L., Keltner, D., & Simon-Thomas, E. (2010). Compassion. An evolutionary analysis and empirical review. *Psychological Bulletin, 136,* 351–374.

Goffman, E. (1959). *The presentation of self in everyday life.* Garden City, NY. Doubleday Anchor.

Goldenhagen, D. (1996). *Hitler's willing executioners. Ordinary Germans and holocaust.* New York. Knopf.

Gonzaga, G. C., Campos, B., & Bradbury, T. (2007). Similarity, convergence, and relationship satisfaction in dating and married couples. *Journal of Personality and Social Psychology, 93,* 34–48.

Grammer, K., & Thornhill, R. (1994). Human facial attractiveness and sexual selection. The role of averageness and symmetry. *Journal of Comparative Psychology, 108,* 233–242.

Greenberg, J. (2008). Understanding the vital human quest for self-esteem. *Perspectives on Psychological Science, 3,* 48–55.

Greeenwald, A. G., & Nosek, B. A. (2001). Health of the implicit association test at age 3. *Zeitschrift für Experimentelle Psychologie, 48,* 85–93.

Greenwald, A. G., Oakes, M. A., Hoffman, H. G. (2003). Targets of discrimination. Effects of race on responses to weapons holders. *Journal of Experimental Social Psychology, 39,* 399–405.

Grimland, M., Apter, A., & Kerkhof, A. (2006). The phenomenon of suicide bombing. A review of psychological and nonpsychological factors. *Crisis, 27,* 107–118.

Hall, J. A., & Carter, J. D. (1999). Gender-stereotype accuracy as an individual difference. *Journal of Personality and Social Psychology, 77,* 350–359.

Hamilton, W. D. (1964). The genetical evolution of social behavior. *Journal of Theoretical Biology, 7,* 1–52.

Harmon-Jones, E., & Harmon-Jones, C. (2007). Cognitive dissonance theory after 50 years of development. *Zeitschrift für Sozialpsychologie, 38,* 7–16.

Harris, L. T., & Fiske, S. T. (2007). Social groups that elicit disgust are differentially processed in mPFC. *Social Cognitive and Affective Neuroscience, 2,* 45–51.

Hassan, N. (2001, November 9). An arsenal of believers. Talking to the "human bombs." *The New Yorker,* November 19. Retrieved from http://www.newyorker.com/fact/content/?011119fa_FACT1 on September 27, 2005.

Hayes, J., Schimel, J., & Williams, T. J. (2008). Fighting death with death. The buffering effects of learning that worldview violators have died. *Psychological Science, 19,* 501–507.

Hagger, M. S., Wood, C., Stiff, C., & Chatzisarantis, N. L. D. (2010). Ego depletion and the strength model of self-control. A meta-analysis. *Psychological Bulletin, 136,* 495–525.

Heider, F. (1958). *The psychology of interpersonal relations.* New York. Wiley.

Hoss, R. A., & Langlois, J. H. (2003). Infants prefer attractive faces. In O. Pascalis, & A. M. Slater (Eds.), *The development of face processing in infancy and early childhood. Current perspectives* (pp. 27–38). Hauppauge, NY. Nova Science Publishers.

Hur, Y. (2003). Assortative mating for personality traits, educational level, religious affiliation, height, weight, and body mass index in parents of a Korean twin sample. *Twin Research, 6,* 467–470.

Iacoboni, M. (2009). Imitation, empathy, and mirror neurons. *Annual Review of Psychology, 60,* 653–670.

Ito, M., Horst, H., Bittanti, M., Boyd, D., Herr-Stephenson, B., et al. (2008). *Living and learning with new media. Summary of findings from the Digital Youth Project.* The MacArthur Foundation. Retrieved from http://digitalyouth.ischool.berkeley.edu/files/report/digitalyouth-WhitePaper.pdf on December 14, 2008.

Jackson, J. W. (1993). Realistic group conflict theory. A review and evaluation of the theoretical and empirical literature. *Psychological Record, 43,* 395–413.

Jackson, P. L., Meltzoff, A. N., & Decety, J. (2005). How do we perceive the pain of others? A window into the neural processes involved in empathy. *NeuroImage, 24,* 771–779.

Janis, I. L. (1989). *Crucial decisions. Leadership in policy-making and crisis management.* New York. Free Press.

Janis, I. L. (2007). Groupthink. In R. P. Vecchio (Ed.), *Leadership. Understanding the dynamics of power and influence in organizations* (pp. 163–176). Notre Dame, IN. University of Notre Dame Press.

Johnson, C. S., & Stapel, D. A. (2010). Harnessing social comparisons. When and how upward comparisons influence goal pursuit. *Basic and Applied Social Psychology, 32,* 234–242.

Johnston, V. S., Hagel, R., Franklin, M., Fink, B., & Grammer, K. (2001). Male facial attractiveness. Evidence for hormone-mediated adaptive design. *Evolution and Human Behavior, 22,* 251–267.

Jones, D. (1996). *Physical attractiveness and the theory of sexual selection.* Ann Arbor, MI. Museum of Anthropology, University of Michigan.

Jones, E. E. (1990). *Interpersonal perception.* New York. W. H. Freeman.

Jones, E. E., & Harris, V. A. (1967). The attribution of attitudes. *Journal of Experimental Social Psychology, 3(1),* 1–24.

Jones, E. E., & Nisbett, R. E. (1971). *The actor and the observer. Divergent perceptions of the causes of behavior.* New York. Basic Books.

Jones, E. E., & Pittman, T. S. (1982). Toward a general theory of strategic self-presentation. In J. Suls (Ed.), *Psychological perspectives on the self* (Vol. 1, pp. 231–262). Hillsdale, NJ. Lawrence Erlbaum Associates.

Jussim, L., Cain, T. R., Crawford, J. T., Harber, K., & Cohen, F. (2009). The unbearable accuracy of stereotypes. In T. D. Nelson (Ed.), *Handbook of prejudice, stereotyping, and discrimination* (pp. 199–227). New York. Psychology Press.

Kassim, S. H. (2008). The role of religion in the generation of suicide bombers. *Brief Treatment and Crisis Intervention, 8,* 204–208.

Kelly, D. J., Quinn, P. C., Slater, A. M., Lee, K., Ge, L., et al. (2007). The other-race effect develops during infancy. Evidence of perceptual narrowing. *Psychological Science, 18,* 1084–1089.

Kelly, D. J., Quinn, P. C., Slater, A. M., Lee, K., Gibson, A., et al. (2005). Three-month-olds, but not newborns, prefer own-race faces. *Developmental Science, 8,* F31–F36.

Kerrnis, M. H., Lakey, C. E., & Heppner, W. L. (2008). Secure versus fragile high self-esteem as a predictor of verbal defensiveness. Converging findings across three different markers. *Journal of Personality, 76,* 477–512.

King, E. B., Knight, J. L., & Hebl, M. R. (2010). The influence of economic conditions on aspects of stigmatization. *Journal of Social Issues, 66,* 446–460.

Klein, S. B. (2012). The self and science. Is it time for a new approach to the study of human experience? *Current Directions in Psychological Science, 21,* 253–257.

Komar, V., Melamid, A., & Wypijewski, J. (1999). *Painting by numbers. Komar and Melamid's scientific guide to art.* Berkeley, CA. University of California Press.

Kraut, R., Brynin, M., & Kessler, S. (Eds). (2006). *Computers, phones, and the Internet. Domesticating information technology.* New York. Oxford University Press.

Kraut, R., Patterson, M., Lundmark, V., Kiesler, S., Mukopadhyay, T., et al. (1998). Internet paradox. A social technology that reduces social involvement and psychological well-being? *American Psychologist, 53,* 1017–1031.

Krueger, A. B., & Maleckova, J. (2003). Education, poverty and terrorism. Is there a causal connection? *Journal of Economic Perspectives, 17,* 119–144.

Krueger, J. I., & Funder, D. C. (2004). Towards a balanced social psychology. Causes, consequences and cures for the problem-seeking approach to social behavior and cognition. *Behavioral and Brain Sciences, 27,* 313–376.

Kruger, J., & Gilovich, T. (1999). "Naïve cynicism" in everyday theories of responsibility assessment. On biased assumptions of bias. *Journal of Personality and Social Psychology, 76,* 743–753.

Kruglanski, A. W., Chen, X., Deschesne, M., Fishman, S., & Orehek, E. (2009). Fully committed. Suicide bombers' motivation and the quest for personal significance. *Political Psychology, 30,* 331–357.

Kubzansky, L. D., Martin, L. T., & Buka, S. L. (2009). Early manifestations of personality and adult health. A life course perspective. *Health Psychology, 28,* 364–372.

Langlois, J., Kalakanis, L., Rubenstein, A. J., Larson, A., Hallam, M., & Smoot, M. (2000). Maxims or myths of beauty? A meta-analytic and theoretical review. *Psychological Bulletin, 126,* 390–423.

Langlois, J. H., & Roggman, L. A. (1990). Attractive faces are only average. *Psychological Science, 1,* 115–121.

Law-Smith, M. J., Perrett, D. I., Jones, B. C., Cornwell, R. E., Moore, F. R., et al. (2006). Facial appearance is a cue to oestrogen levels in women. *Proceedings of the Royal Society B. Biological Sciences, 273,* 135–140.

Leary, M. R. (1995). *Self-presentation. Impression management and interpersonal behavior.* Boulder, CO. Westview Press.

Leary, M. R. (2001). Living in the minds of others without knowing it. *Psychological Inquiry, 12,* 28–29.

Leary, M. R. (2007). Motivational and emotional aspects of the self. *Annual Review of Psychology, 58,* 317–344.

Leary, M. R. (2011). Does impression management have an image problem? In M. R. Leary (Ed.), *50 prominent social psychologists describe their most unloved work* (pp. 96–100). New York. Oxford University Press.

Leary, M. R., & Kowalski, R. M. (1990). Impression management. A literature review and two-component model. *Psychological Bulletin, 107*(1), 34–47.

Leher, J. (2009, May 18). Don't! The secret of self-control. *The New Yorker.* Retrieved from http://www.newyorker.com/reporting/2009/05/18/090518fa_fact_lehrer on May 29, 2012.

Lewin, K. (1935). *Dynamic theory of personality.* New York. McGraw-Hill.

Lewis, G. J., & Bates, T. C. (2010). Genetic evidence for multiple biological mechanisms underlying in-group favoritism. *Psychological Science, 21,* 1623–1628.

Li, X., & Liu, M. (2004). A review of the self-change attempt. *Psychological Science (China), 27,* 104–106.

Liljinquist, K., Zhong, C.-B., & Galinsky, A. D. (2010). The smell of virtue. Clean scents promote reciprocity and charity. *Psychological Science, 21,* 381–383.

Lippa, R. A. (2010). Gender differences in personality and interests. When, where, and why? *Social and Personality Psychology Compass, 4,* 1098–1110.

Little, A. C., Jones, B. C., & DeBruine, L. M. (2008). Preferences for variation in masculinity in real male faces change across the menstrual cycle. Women prefer more masculine faces when they are more fertile. *Personality and Individual Difference, 45,* 478–482.

Little, A. C., Saxton, T. K., Roberts, S. C., Jones, B. C., DeBruine, L. M., et al. (2010). Women's preferences for masculinity in male faces are highest during reproductive age range and lower around puberty and post-menopause. *Psychoneuroendocrinology, 35,* 912–920.

Lowery, B. S., Hardin, C. D., & Sinclair, S. (2001). Social influence on automatic racial prejudice. *Journal of Personality and Social Psychology, 81,* 842–855.

Luo, S., & Klohnen, E. C. (2005). Assortive mating and marital quality in newlyweds. A couple centered approach. *Journal of Personality and Social Psychology, 88,* 304–326.

Mackenzie, D. L. (2006) (Abstract only). *Group hope. An antecedent of groupthink?* Dissertation Abstracts International. Section B. The Sciences and Engineering Vol. 66(10-B).

Maddux, W. W., Barden, J., Brewer, M. B., & Petty, R. E. (2005). Saying no to negativity. The effects of context and motivation to control prejudice on automatic evaluative responses. *Journal of Experimental Social Psychology, 41*(1), 19–35.

Madon, S., Guyll, M., Aboufadel, K., Montiel, E., Smith, A., et al. (2001). Ethnic and national stereotypes. The Princeton Trilogy revisited and revised. *Personality & Social Psychology Bulletin, 27,* 996–1010.

Madon, S., Jussim, L., Keiper, S., Eccles, J., Smith, A., et al. (1998). The accuracy and power of sex, social class, and ethnic stereotypes. A naturalistic study in person perception. *Personality and Social Psychology Bulletin, 24,* 1304–1318.

Malle, B. F. (2006). The actor-observer asymmetry. A (surprising) meta-analysis. *Psychological Bulletin, 132,* 895–919.

Malle, B. F., Knobe, J. M., & Nelson, S. E. (2007). Actor-observer asymmetries in explanations of behavior. New answers to an old question. *Journal of Personality and Social Psychology, 93,* 491–514.

Manning, R., Levine, M., & Collins, A. (2007). The Kitty Genovese murder and the social psychology of helping. The parable of the 38 witnesses. *American Psychologist, 62,* 555–562.

Manning, R., Levine, M., & Collins, A. (2008). The legacy of the 38 witnesses and the importance of getting

history right. *American Psychologist, 63,* 562–563.

Markus, H. R., & Kitayama, S. (2010). Cultures and selves. A cycle of mutual constitution. *Perspectives on Psychological Science, 5,* 420–430.

Mastroianni, G. R. (2002). Milgram and the holocaust. A reexamination. *Journal of Theoretical and Philosophical Psychology, 22,* 158–173.

Mastroianni, G. R. (2007). Zimbardo's apple. *Analyses of Social Issues and Public Policy, 7,* 251–254.

Masuda, T., & Kitayama, S. (2004). Perceiver-induced constraint and attitude attribution in Japan and the US. A case for the cultural dependence of the correspondence bias. *Journal of Experimental Social Psychology, 40,* 409–416.

McCullough, M. E., & Willoughby, B. L. B. (2009). Religion, self-regulation, and self-control. Associations, explanations, and implications. *Psychological Bulletin, 135,* 69–93.

McInstry, B. (2008). Are there too many female medical graduates? *British Medical Journal, 336,* 748–749.

McKay, R. T., & Dennett, D. C. (2009). The evolution of misbelief. *Behavioral and Brain Sciences, 32,* 493–461.

Mealey, L. (2000). *Sex differences. Developmental and evolutionary strategies.* San Diego, CA. Academic Press.

Milgram, S. (1963). Behavioral study of obedience. *Journal of Abnormal and Social Psychology, 67,* 371–378.

Milgram, S. (1974). *Obedience to authority. An experimental view.* New York. Harper-Collins.

Miller, P. J. E., Niehuis, S., & Huston, T. L. (2006). Positive illusions in marriage. A 13-year longitudinal study. *Personality and Social Psychology Bulletin, 12,* 1579–1594.

Miller, R. S. (1995). On the nature of embarrassability. Shyness, social evaluation, and social skill. *Journal of Personality, 63,* 315–339.

Miller, V. (2010). The Internet and everyday life. In Y. Jewkes & M. Yar (Eds.), *Handbook of Internet crime* (pp. 67–87). Devon, UK. Willan Publishing.

Mischel, W., Ayduk, O., Berman, M. G., Casey, B. M., Gotlib, I. H., et al. (2011). "Willpower" over the life span. Decomposing self-regulation. *Social Cognitive and Affective Neuroscience (SCAN), 6,* 252–256.

Mischel, W., Ebbesen, E. B., & Zeiss, A. R. (1972). Cognitive and attentional mechanisms in delay of gratification. *Journal of Personality and Social Psychology, 21,* 204–218.

Miyamoto, Y., & Kitayama, S. (2002). Cultural variation in correspondence bias. The critical role of attitude diagnosticity of socially constrained behavior. *Journal of Personality and Social Psychology, 83,* 1239–1248.

Mixon, D. (1976). Studying feignable behavior. *Representative Research in Social Psychology, 7,* 89–104.

Monahan, J. L., Murphy, S. T., & Zajonc, R. B. (2000). Subliminal mere exposure. Specific, general, and diffuse effects. *Psychological Science, 11*, 462–466.

Morelli, M. F. (1983). Milgram's dilemma of obedience. *Metaphilosophy, 14*, 183–189.

Muraven, M., & Baumeister, R. F. (2000). Self-regulation and depletion of limited resources. Does self-control resemble a muscle? *Psychological Bulletin, 126*, 237–259.

Murray, S. L., Griffin, D. W., Derrick, J. L., Harris, B., & Aloni, M. (2011). Tempting fate or inviting happiness? Unrealistic idealization prevents the decline of marital happiness. *Psychological Science, 22*, 619–626.

Myers, D. G. (2002). *Intuition.* New Haven, CT. Yale University Press.

Napolitan, D. A., & Goethals, G. R. (1979). The attribution of friendliness. *Journal of Experimental Social Psychology, 15*, 105–113.

Nolan, J. M., Schultz, P. W., Cialdini, R. B., Goldstein, N. J., & Griskevicius, V. (2008). Normative social influence is underdetected. *Personality and Social Psychology Bulletin, 34*, 913–923.

Norcross, J. C., Ratzin, A. C., & Payne, D. (1989). Ringing in the New Year. The change processes and reported outcomes of resolutions. *Addictive Behaviors, 14*, 205–212.

Nosek, B. A., Greenwald, A. G., & Banajji, M. R. (2007). The Implicit Association Test at age 7. Methodological and conceptual review. In J. A. Bargh (Ed.), *Social psychology and the unconscious. The automaticity of higher mental processes. Frontiers of social psychology* (pp. 265–292). New York. Psychology Press.

Nussbaum, M. C. (2001). *Upheavals of thought. The intelligence of emotions.* New York. Cambridge University Press.

Oaten, M., Stevenson, R. J., & Case, T. I. (2009). Disgust as a disease-avoidance mechanism. *Psychological Bulletin, 135*, 303–321.

Okami, P. (1992). Intolerable grievances patiently endured. Referent cognitions and group conflict as mediators of anti-Jewish sentiment among African-Americans. *Political Psychology, 13*, 727–753.

Ostrom, T. M., & Sedikides, C. (1992). Out-group homogeneity effects in natural and minimal groups. *Psychological Bulletin, 112*, 536–552.

Packer, D. J. (2008). Identifying systematic disobedience in Milgram's obedience experiments. A meta-analytic review. *Perspectives on Psychological Science, 3*, 301–304.

Paluck, E. L., & Green, D. P. (2009). Prejudice reduction. What works? A review and assessment of research and practice. *Annual Review of Psychology, 60*, 339–367.

Pape, R. A. (2005). *Dying to win. The strategic logic of suicide terrorism.* New York. Random House.

Penton-Voak, I. S., Jacobson, A., & Trivers, R. (2004). Populational differences in attractiveness judgements of male and female faces. Comparing British and Jamaican samples. *Evolution and Human Behavior, 25*, 355–377.

Peruche, B. M., & Plant, E.A. (2006). The implications of police officer attitudes towards criminal suspects. *Basic and Applied Social Psychology. 28*, 193–199.

Peters, M., Rhodes, G., & Simmons, L. W. (2007). Contributions of the face and body to overall attractiveness. *Animal Behaviour, 73*, 937–942.

Pettigrew, T. F. (1998). Intergroup contact theory. *Annual Review of Psychology, 49*, 65–85.

Pettigrew, T. F., & Tropp, L. R. (2006). A meta-analytic test of intergroup contact theory. *Journal of Personality and Social Psychology, 90*, 751–783.

Piliavin, J. A., & Charng, H.-W. (1990). Altruism. A review of recent theory and research. *Annual Review of Sociology, 16*, 27–65.

Pinker, S. (2002). *The blank slate.* New York. Viking.

Pinker, S. (2011). *The better angels of our nature. Why violence has declined.* New York. Viking.

Polak, M. (2003). *Developmental instability. Causes and consequences.* New York. Oxford University Press.

Polivy, J., & Herman, C. P. (2000). The false-hope syndrome. Unfulfilled expectations of self-change. *Current Directions in Psychological Science, 9*, 128–131.

Polivy, J., & Herman, C. P. (2002). If at first you don't succeed. False hopes of self-change. *American Psychologist, 57*, 677–689.

Prochaska, J. O., DiClemente, C. C., & Norcross, J. C. (1992). In search of how people change. Applications to addictive behaviors. *American Psychologist, 47*, 1102–1114.

Pyszczynski, T., Greenberg, J., Solomon, S., Arndt, J., & Schimel, J. (2004). Why do people need self-esteem? A theoretical and empirical review. *Psychological Bulletin, 130*, 435–468.

Quillian, L., & Pager, D. (2001). Black neighbors, higher crime? The role of racial stereotypes in evaluations of neighborhood crime. *American Journal of Sociology, 107*, 717–767.

Quinn, P. C., Kelly, D. J., Lee, K., Pascalis, O., & Slater, A. M. (2008). Preference for attractive faces in infants extends beyond conspecifics. *Developmental Science, 11*, 76–83.

Rasenberger, J. (2004, February 8). Kitty, 40 years later. *New York Times.* Retrieved from http://www.nytimes.com/2004/02/08/nyregion/kitty-40-years-later.html?pagewanted=all&src=pmon March 19, 2013.

Reis, H. T., Maniaci, M. R., Eastwick, P. W., & Caprariello, P. A. (2011). Familiarity does indeed promote attraction in live interaction. *Journal of Personality and Social Psychology, 101*, 557–570.

Rhodes, G. (2006). The evolutionary psychology of facial beauty. *Annual Review of Psychology, 57*, 199–226.

Rhodes, G., Yoshikawa, S., Palermo, R., Simmons, L. W., Peters, M., et al. (2007). Perceived health contributes to the attractiveness of facial symmetry, averageness, and sexual dimorphism. *Perception, 36*, 1244–1252.

Rodrigues, A., Assmar, E. M. L., & Jablonski, B. (2005). (English abstract only). La psicología y la invasion de Irak (Psychology and the invasion of Iraq). *Revista de Psicología Social, 20*, 387–398.

Ross, L. (1977) The intuitive psychologist and his short-comings. Distortions in the attribution process. In L. Berkowitz (Ed.), *Advances in experimental social psychology* (Vol. 10, pp. 173–220). San Diego, CA. Academic Press.

Ross, L. (2001). Getting down to fundamentals. Lay dispositionism and the attributions of psychologists. *Psychological Inquiry, 12*, 37–40.

Ross, M., & Sicoly, F. (1979). Egocentric biases in availability and attribution. *Journal of Personality and Social Psychology, 37*, 322–336.

Rozin, P., Haidt, J., & McCauley, C. R. (1999). Disgust. The body and soul emotion. In T. Dalgleish & M. J. Power (Eds.), *Handbook of cognition and emotion* (pp. 429–445). New York. Wiley.

Rozin, P., Haidt, J., & McCauley, C. R. (2009). Disgust. The body and soul emotion in the 21st century. In B. O. Olatunji, & D. McKay (Eds.), *Disgust and its disorders. Theory, assessment, and treatment implications* (pp. 9–29). Washington, DC. American Psychological Association.

Ruehlman, L. S., West, S. G., & Pasahow, R. J. (1985). Depression and evaluative schemata. *Journal of Personality, 53*, 46–92.

Ruscher, J. B., & Hammer, E. Y. (2004). The person in the situation. Self-protection, self-evaluation, and self-change. In J. B. Ruscher & E. Y. Hammer (Eds.), *Current directions in social psychology* (pp. 1–2). Upper Saddle-River, NJ. Pearson/Prentice Hall.

Rushton, P. J. (2004). Genetic and environmental contributions to pro-social attitudes. A twin study of social responsibility. *Proceedings of the Royal Society of London, 271*, 2583–2585.

Sabini, J., Siepmann, M., & Stein, J. (2001a). The really fundamental attribution error in social psychology research. *Psychological Inquiry, 12*, 1–15.

Sabini, J., Siepmann, M., & Stein, J. (2001b). Author's response to commentaries. *Psychological Inquiry, 12*, 41–48.

Sadler, M. E., Hunger, J. M., & Miller, C. J. (2010). Personality and impression management. Mapping the Multidimensional Personality Questionnaire onto 12 self-presentation tactics. *Personality and Individual Differences, 48*, 623–628.

Savitsky, K. Epley, N., & Gilovich, T. (2001). Is it as bad as we think? Overestimating the impact of our failures, shortcomings, and mishaps. *Journal of Personality and Social Psychology, 81,* 44–56.

Savitsky, K., Gilovich, T., Berger, G., & Medvec, V. H. (2003). Is our absence as conspicuous as we think? Overestimating the salience and impact of one's absence from a group. *Journal of Experimental Social Psychology, 39,* 386–392.

Schmidt, M. F. H., & Somerville, J. A. (2011). Fairness expectations and altruistic sharing in 15-month-old human infants. *PLoS One, 6,* e23223. Retrieved from http://www.plosone.org/article/info%3Adoi%2F10.1371%2Fjournal.pone.0023223 on October 15, 2011.

Schmitt, D. P., Realo, A., Voracek, M., & Allik, J. (2008). Why can't a man be more like a woman? Sex differences in big five personality traits across 55 cultures. *Journal of Personality and Social Psychology, 94,* 168–182.

Schnall, S. Haidt, J., Clore, G., & Jordan, A. (2008). Disgust as embodied moral judgment. *Personality and Social Psychology Bulletin, 34,* 1096–1109.

Schuman, H., Steeh, C., Bobo, L., & Kyrsan, M. (1997). *Racial attitudes in America. Trends and interpretations.* Cambridge, MA. Harvard University Press.

Schumm, W., R., Anderson, C. V., Brinneman, A. S. Magsanoc-Deoki, M. E., Pakhalchuk, A., et al. (2006). Re-analysis of Sageman's (2004) and Pape's (2005) data predicting Al'Quaeda membership and suicide terrorism. *Psychological Reports, 98,* 915–917.

Scott-Phillips, T. C., Dickens, T. E., & West, S. A. (2011). Evolutionary theory and the ultimate-proximate distinction in the human behavioral sciences. *Perspectives on Psychological Science, 6,* 38–47.

Seeyave, D. M., Coleman, S., Appugliese, D., Corwyn, R. F., Bradley, R. H., et al. (2009). Ability to delay gratification at age 4 years and risk of overweight at age 11 years. *Archives of Pediatric and Adolescent Medicine, 163.* Retrieved from http://archpedi.jamanetwork.com/article.aspx?articleid=381236 on May 20, 2012.

Sherif, M. (1966). *In common predicament. Social psychology of intergroup conflict.* Boston, MA. Houghton Mifflin.

Sherif, M., & Sherif, C. W. (1966). The rise of attitudes toward ingroup and outgroup. Experimental verification. In M. Sherif & C. W. Sherif (Eds.), *Groups in harmony and tension. An integration of studies of intergroup relations.* New York. Octagon Books.

Sherman, D. K., & Cohen, G. L. (2002). Accepting threatening information. Self-affirmation and the reduction of defensive biases. *Current Directions in Psychological Science, 11,* 119–123.

Shook, N. J., & Fazio, R. H. (2009). Interracial roommate relationships. An experimental field test of the contact hypothesis. *Psychological Science, 19,* 717–723.

Shyam, R., & Bhoria, A. (2011). Information technology (Internet). Effects on social participation and well-being of users. *Journal of the Indian Academy of Applied Psychology, 37,* 157–162.

Singh, D. (2006). Universal allure of the hourglass figure. An evolutionary theory of female physical attractiveness. *Clinics of Plastic Surgery, 33,* 359–370.

Singh, D., Dixson, B. J., Jessop, T. S., Morgan, B., & Dixson, A. F. (2009). Cross-cultural consensus for waist-hip ratio and women's attractiveness. *Evolution and Human Behavior, 31,* 176–181.

Singh, D., & Young, R. K. (1995). Body weight, waist-to-hip ratio, breasts, and hips. Role in judgments of female attractiveness and desirability for relationships. *Ethology and Sociobiology, 16,* 483–507.

Skoller, C. E. (2008). *Twisted confessions.* Austin, TX. Bridgeway Books.

Sniderman, P. M., & Carmines, E. G. (1997). Reaching beyond race. *Political Science & Politics, 30,* 466–471.

Solomon, S., Greenberg, J., & Pyszczynski, T. (2000). Pride and prejudice. Fear of death and social behavior. *Current Directions in Psychological Science, 9,* 200–204.

Sprinzak, E. (2000, September/October). Rational fanatics. *Foreign Policy,* 66–73.

Stevens, S. B., & Morris, T. L. (2007). College dating and social anxiety. Using the Internet as a means of connecting to others. *CyberPsychology & Behavior, 10,* 680–688.

Sugiyama, L. S. (2005). Physical attractiveness in adaptationist perspective. In D. M. Buss (Ed.), *Handbook of evolutionary psychology* (pp. 292–343). Hoboken, NJ. John Wiley & Sons, Inc.

Suls, J., Martin, R., & Wheeler, L. (2002). Social comparison. Why, with whom, and with what effect? *Current Directions in Psychological Science, 11,* 159–163.

Sum, S., Mathews, M. R., Hughes, I., & Campbell, A. (2008). Internet use and loneliness in older adults. *CyberPsychology & Behavior, 11,* 208–211.

Sumner, W. G. (1959). *Folkways. A study of the sociological importance of usages, manners, customs, mores, and morals.* New York. Blaisdell. (Original work published 1906.)

Symons, D. (1996). Forward. In D. Jones (Ed.), *Physical attractiveness and the theory of sexual selection.* Ann Arbor, MI. University of Michigan Museum of Anthropology.

Swaddle, J. P., & Reierson, G. W. (2002). Testosterone increases perceived dominance but not attractiveness of human males. *Proceedings of the Royal Society of London, Series B, 269,* 2285–2289.

Swami, V., Neto, F., Tovée, M. J., & Furnham, A. (2007). Preferences for female body weight and shape in three European countries. *European Psychologist, 12,* 220–228.

Swami, V., & Tovée, M. J. (2007). Relative contribution of profile body shape and weight to judgements of women's physical attractiveness in Britain and Malaysia. *Body Image, 4,* 391–396.

Symons, D. (1995). Beauty is in the adaptations of the beholder. The evolutionary psychology of human female sexual attractiveness. In P. R. Abramson & S. D. Pinkerton (Eds.), *Sexual nature, sexual culture* (pp. 80–118). Chicago. University of Chicago Press.

Tajfel, H., & Turner, J. C. (1979). An integrative theory of intergroup conflict. In W. G. Austin & S. Worchel (Eds.), *The social psychology of intergroup relations* (pp. 33–47). Monterey, CA. Brooks/Cole.

Tangney, J. P., Baumeister, R. F., & Boone, A. L. (2004). High self-control predicts good adjustment, less pathology, better grades, and interpersonal success. *Journal of Personality, 72,* 271–324.

Taylor, S. E., & Brown, J. D. (1988). Illusion and well-being. A social psychological perspective on mental health. *Psychological Bulletin, 103,* 193–210.

Taylor, S. E., & Brown, J. D. (1994). Positive illusions revisited. Separating fact from fiction. *Psychological Bulletin, 116,* 21–27.

Taylor, S. E., Lerner, J. S., Sherman, D. K., Sage, R. M., & McDowell, N. K. (2003). Are self-enhancing cognitions associated with healthy or unhealthy biological profiles? *Journal of Personality and Social Psychology, 85,* 605–615.

Tesser, A., Crepaz, N., Collins, J., Cornell, D., & Beach, S. (2000). Confluence of self-esteem regulation mechanisms. On integrating the self-zoo. *Personality and Social Psychology Bulletin, 26,* 1476–1489.

Thornhill, R., & Gangestad, S. (2006). Facial sexual dimorphism, developmental stability, and susceptibility to disease in men and women. *Evolution and Human Behavior, 27,* 131–144.

Toosi, N. R., Babbitt, L. G., Ambady, N., & Sommers, S. R. (2011). Dyadic interracial interactions. A meta-analysis. *Psychological Bulletin, 138,* 1–27.

Tovée, M. J., Swami, V., Furnham, A., & Mangalparsad, R. (2006). Changing perceptions of attractiveness as observers are exposed to a different culture. *Evolution and Human Behavior, 27,* 443–456.

Townsend, E. (2007). Suicide terrorists. Are they suicidal? *Suicide and Life-Threatening Behavior, 37,* 35–49.

Trivers, R. (1971). The evolution of reciprocal altruism. *Quarterly Review of Biology, 46,* 35–57.

Trivers, R. (2002). *Natural selection and social theory.* Oxford, UK. Oxford University Press.

Trottier, K., Polivy, J., & Herman, C. P. (2009). Effects of resolving to change one's own behavior. Expectations vs. experience. *Behavior Therapy, 40,* 164–170.

Valkenburg, P. M., & Peter, J. (2009a). The effects of instant messaging on the quality of adolescents' existing friendships. A longitudinal study. *Journal of Communication, 59,* 79–97.

Valkenburg, P. M., & Peter, J. (2009b). Social consequences of the Internet for adolescents. *Current Directions in Psychological Science, 18,* 1–5.

Valla, J. M., & Ceci, S. J. (2011). Can sex differences in science be tied to the long reach of prenatal hormones? Brain organization theory, digit ratio (2D/4D), and sex differences in preferences and cognition. *Perspectives on Psychological Science, 6,* 134–146.

Van Bavel, J. J., Packer, D. J., & Cunningham, W. A. (2008). The neural substrates of in-group bias. *Psychological Science, 19,* 1131–1139.

Van Duuren, M., Kendell-Scott, L., & Stark, N. (2003). Early aesthetic choices. Infant preference for attractive premature infant faces. *International Journal of Behavioral Development, 27,* 212–219.

Vazire, S., & Gosling, S. D. (2004). E-perceptions. Personality impressions based on personal websites. *Journal of Personality and Social Psychology, 87,* 123–132.

Voland, E., & Grammer, K. (Eds.). (2003). *Evolutionary aesthetics.* New York. Springer.

Waller, J. (2007). *Becoming evil. How ordinary people commit genocide and mass killing* (2nd ed.). New York. Oxford University Press.

Wills, T. A. (1981). Downward comparison principles in social psychology. *Psychological Bulletin, 90,* 245–271.

Wood, J. V., Taylor, S. E., & Lichtman, R. (1985). Social comparison in adjustment to breast cancer. *Journal of Personality and Social Psychology, 49,* 1169–1183.

Wortman, C. B. (1975). Some determinants of perceived control. *Journal of Personality and Social Psychology, 31,* 282–294.

Zajonc, R. B. (1968). Attitudinal effects of mere exposure. *Journal of Personality and Social Psychology Monograph, 9 (Part 2),* 1–27.

Zajonc, R. B. (2001). Mere exposure. A gateway to the subliminal. *Current Directions in Psychological Science, 10,* 224–228.

Zilbergeld, B. (1983). *The shrinking of America. Myths of psychological change.* Boston. Little Brown & Company.

Zimbardo, P. G. (1973). On the ethics of intervention in human psychological research. With special reference to the Stanford prison experiment. *Cognition, 2,* 243–256.

Zimbardo, P. G. (2007). *The Lucifer effect.* New York. Random House

CHAPTER 16 (bonus chapter)

Abma, J. C., Martinez, G. M., Mosher, W. D., & Dawson, B. S. (2004). Teenagers in the United States. Sexual activity, contraceptive use, and childbearing, 2002. *Vital Health Statistics 23.* Washington, DC. National Center for Health Statistics.

Abramson, P. R. (1992). Adios. A farewell address. *Journal of Sex Research, 29,* 449–450.

Alexander, G. M., & Hines, M. (2002). Sex differences in response to children's toys in nonhuman primates (*Cercopithecus aethiops sabaeus*). *Evolution and Human Behavior, 23,* 467–479.

Alexander, G. M., Wilcox, R., & Woods, R. (2009). Sex differences in infants' visual interest in toys. *Archives of Sexual Behavior, 38,* 427–433.

Allen, L. S. & Gorski, R. A. (1992). Sexual orientation and the size of the anterior commissure in the human brain. *Proceedings of the National Academy of Sciences of the United States of America, 89,* 7199–7202.

Aron, A., Fisher, H., Mashek, D. J., Strong, G., Li, H., & Brown, L. L. (2005). Reward, motivation, and emotion systems associated with early stage romantic love. *Journal of Neurophysiology, 94(1),* 327–337.

Auyeung, B., Baron-Cohen, S., Ashwin, E., Knickmeyer, R., Taylor, K., et al. (2009). Fetal testosterone predicts sexually differentiated childhood behavior in girls and boys. *Psychological Science.* Retrieved online in advance of print from http://www3.interscience.wiley.com on January 27, 2009.

Bae, Y., Choy, S., Geddes, C., Sable, J., & Snyder, T. (2000). Trends in educational equity of girls and women. *Education Statistics Quarterly, 2,* 115–120.

Bailey, J. M., Dunne, M. P., & Martin, N. G. (2000). Genetic and environmental influences on sexual orientation and its correlates in an Australian twin sample. *Journal of Personality and Social Psychology, 78,* 524–536.

Banerjee, R., & Lintern, V. (2000). Boys will be boys. The effect of social evaluation concerns on gender-typing. *Social Development, 9(3),* 397–408.

Barnett, S. M. (2007). Complex questions rarely have simple answers. *Psychological Science in the Public Interest, 8(1),* i–ii.

Bartels, A., & Zeki, S. (2000). The neural basis of romantic love. *NeuroReport, 11,* 3829–3834.

Bartels, A., & Zeki, S. (2004). The neural correlates of maternal and romantic love. *NeuroImage, 21,* 1155–1166.

Beck, D. M. (2010). The appeal of the brain in the popular press. *Perspectives on Psychological Science, 5,* 762–766.

Bem, S. L. (1974). The measurement of psychological androgyny. *Journal of Consulting and Clinical Psychology, 42,* 151–162.

Benbow, C. P., Lubinski, D., Shea, D. L., & Eftekhari-Sanjani, H. (2000). Sex differences in mathematical reasoning ability. Their status 20 years later. *Psychological Science, 11,* 474–480.

Benenson, J. F., Liroff, E. R., Pascal, S. J., & Cioppa, G. D. (1997). Propulsion. A behavioural expression of masculinity. *British Journal of Developmental Psychology, 15(1),* 37–50.

Berenbaum, S. A., & Hines, M. (1992). Early androgens are related to childhood sex-typed toy preferences. *Psychological Science, 3,* 203–206.

Berscheid, E. (2010). Love in the fourth dimension. *Annual Review of Psychology, 61,* 1–25.

Best, D. L. (2004). Gender roles in childhood and adolescence. In U. P. Gielen and

J. Roopnarine (Eds.), *Childhood and adolescence. Cross-cultural perspectives and applications. Advances in applied developmental psychology* (pp. 199–228). Westport, CT. Praeger Publishers.

Bigler, R. S. (1997). Conceptual and methodological issues in the measurement of children's sex typing. *Psychology of Women Quarterly, 21,* 53–69.

Blanchard, R. (2008). Review and theory of handedness, birth order, and homosexuality in men. *Laterality. Asymmetries of body, brain and cognition, 13,* 51–70.

Blanchard, R., Cantor, J. M., Bogaert, A. F., Breedlove, S, M., & Ellis, L. (2006). Interaction of fraternal birth order and handedness in the development of male homosexuality. *Hormones and Behavior, 49,* 405–414.

Bogaert, A. F. (2006). Biological versus non-biological older brothers and men's sexual orientation. *Proceedings of the National Academy of Sciences, 103,* 10771–10774.

Bussey, K., & Bandura, A. (1999). Social cognitive theory of gender development and differentiation. *Psychological Review, 106,* 676–713.

Byers, E. S., Henderson, J., & Hobson, K. M. (2009). University students' definitions of sexual abstinence and having sex. *Archives of Sexual Behavior, 38,* 665–674.

Byne, W., Tobet, S., Mattiace, L. A., Lasco, M. S., Kemether, E., Edgar, M. A., et al. (2001). The interstitial nuclei of the human anterior hypothalamus. An investigation of variation with sex, sexual orientation, and HIV status. *Hormones and Behavior, 40,* 86–92.

Cadinu, M., Maass, A., Rosabianca, A., & Kiesner, J. (2005). Why do women underperform under stereotype threat? Evidence for the role of negative thinking. *Psychological Science, 16,* 572–578.

Cameron, P., & Biber, H. (1973). Sexual thought throughout the lifespan. *Gerontologist, 13,* 144–147.

Campbell, A., Shirley, L., Heywood, C., & Crook, C. (2000). Infants' visual preference for sex-congruent babies, children, toys and activities. A longitudinal study. *British Journal of Developmental Psychology, 18(4),* 479–498.

Camperio-Ciani, A., Corna, F., & Capiluppi, C. (2004). Evidence for maternally inherited factors favouring male homosexuality and promoting female fecundity. *Proceedings of the Royal Society (England), 271,* 2217–2221.

Capaldi, D. M. (1996). The reliability of retrospective report for timing first sexual intercourse for adolescent males. *Journal of Adolescent Research, 11,* 375–387.

Caplan, J. B., & Caplan, P. J. (2005). The perseverative search for sex differences in mathematics ability. In A. M. Gallagher & J. C. Kaufman (Eds.), *Gender differences in mathematics* (pp. 25–47). Cambridge, UK. Cambridge University Press.

Casey, M. B., Nuttall, R. L., Pezaris, E., & Benbow, C. P. (1995). The influence of spatial ability on gender differences in mathematics college entrance test scores across diverse samples. *Developmental Psychology, 31,* 697–705.

Ceci, S. J., & Williams, W. M. (2010). Sex differences in math-intensive fields.

Current Directions in Psychological Science, 19, 275–279.

Ceci, S. J., Williams, W. M., & Barnett, S. M. (2009). Women's underrepresentation in science. Sociocultural and biological considerations. *Psychological Bulletin, 135,* 218–261.

Cecil, H., Bogart, L. M., Wagstaff, D. A., Pinkerton, S. D., & Abramson, P. R. (2002). Classifying a person as a sex partner. The impact of contextual factors. *Psychology and Health. An International Journal, 17,* 221–234.

Chabris, C. F., & Glickman, M. E. (2006). Sex differences in intellectual performance. Analysis of a large cohort of competitive chess players. *Psychological Science, 17,* 1040–1046.

Chivers, M. L., & Bailey, M. (2005). A sex difference in features that elicit genital response. *Biological Psychology, 70,* 115–120.

Chivers, M. L., Rieger, G., Latty, E., & Bailey, J. M. (2004). A sex difference in the specificity of sexual arousal. *Psychological Science, 15,* 736–744.

Chivers, M. L., Seto, M. C., Lalumière, M. L., Laan, E., & Grimbos, T. (2010). Agreement of self-reported and genital measures of sexual arousal in men and women. A meta-analysis. *Archives of Sexual Behavior, 39,* 5–56.

Cohen, L. (1995). The pleasures of castration. In P. R. Abramson & S. D. Pinkerton (Eds.), *Sexual nature, sexual culture* (pp. 276–304). Chicago. University of Chicago Press.

Cohen-Kettenis, P. T. (2005). Gender change in 46,XY persons with 5α-reductase-2 Deficiency and 17/β-Hydroxysteroid Dehydrogenase-3 Deficiency. *Archives of Sexual Behavior, 34,* 399–410.

Colapinto, J. (2000). *As nature made him. The boy who was raised as a girl.* New York. Harper Collins.

Coles, R., & Stokes, G. (1985). *Sex and the American teenager.* New York. Harper-Collins.

Collaer, M. L., & Hines, M. (1995). Human behavioral sex differences. A role for gonadal hormones during early development? *Psychological Bulletin, 118(1),* 55–107.

Collins, W. A., Welsh, D. P., & Furman, W. (2009). Adolescent romantic relationships. *Annual Review of Psychology, 60,* 631–652.

Crouter, A. C., & Booth, A. (Eds.). (2006). *Romance and sex in adolescence and emerging adulthood. Risks and opportunities.* Mahwah, NJ. Lawrence Erlbaum Associates.

Cullen, M. J., Hardison, C. M., & Sackett, P. R. (2004). Using SAT-grade and ability-job performance relationships to test predictions derived from stereotype threat theory. *Journal of Applied Psychology, 89,* 220–230.

Dar-Nimrod, I., & Heine, S. J. (2006). Exposure to scientific theories affects women's math performance. *Science, 314,* 435.

Davies, A. P. C., & Shackelford, T. K. (2006). An evolutionary perspective on gender similarities and differences. *American Psychologist, 61,* 640–641.

Dawood, K., Bailey, M. J., & Martin, N. G. (2009). Genetic and environmental influences on sexual orientation. In Y.-K. Kim (Ed.), *Handbook of behavior genetics* (pp.

269–279). New York. Springer Science Media.

de Graaf, H., & Rademakers, J. (2006). Sexual development of prepubertal children. *Journal of Psychology & Human Sexuality, 18,* 1–21.

Diamond, L. M. (2000a). Sexual identity, attractions, and behavior among young sexual-minority women over a two-year period. *Developmental Psychology, 36,* 241–250.

Diamond, L. M. (2000b). Explaining diversity in the development of same-sex sexuality among young women. *Journal of Social Issues, 56,* 297–313.

Diamond, L. M. (2003). What does sexual orientation orient? A biobehavioral model distinguishing romantic love and sexual desire. *Psychological Review, 110(1),* 173–192.

Diamond, L. M. (2004). Emerging perspectives on distinctions between romantic love and sexual desire. *Current Directions in Psychological Science, 13(3),* 116–119.

Diamond, L. M. (2005). A new view of lesbian subtypes. Stable versus fluid identity trajectories over an 8-year period. *Psychology of Women Quarterly, 29,* 119–128.

Diamond, L. M. (2008). *Sexual fluidity. Understanding women's love and desire.* Cambridge, MA. Harvard University Press.

Diamond, M., & Sigmundson, K. H. (1999). Sex reassignment at birth. In S. J. Ceci & W. M. Williams (Eds.), *The nature-nurture debate. The essential readings. Essential readings in developmental psychology* (pp. 55–75). Malden, MA. Blackwell Publishing.

Doherty, R. W., Hatfield, E., Thompson, K., & Choo, P. (1994). Cultural and ethnic influences on love and attachment. *Personal Relationships, 1,* 391–398.

Dunne, M. P., Bailey, J. M., Kirk, K. M., & Martin, N. G. (2000). The subtlety of sex-atypicality. *Archives of Sexual Behavior, 29,* 549–565.

Eals, M., & Silverman, I. (1994). The hunter-gatherer theory of spatial sex differences. Proximate factors mediating the female advantage in recall of object arrays. *Ethology and Sociobiology, 15,* 95–105.

Eaton, D. K., Kann, L., Kinchen, S., Ross, J., Hawkins, J., et al. (2006). Youth risk behavior surveillance. United States, 2005. *MMWR Surveillance Summaries, 55,* 1–108.

Ellis, B. J., & Symons, D. (1990). Sex differences in sexual fantasy. An evolutionary psychological approach. *Journal of Sex Research, 27,* 527–555.

Elwin, V. (1968). *The kingdom of the young.* Bombay. Oxford University Press.

Emanuele, E., Politi, P., Bianchi, M., Minoretti, P., Bertona, M., et al. (2006). Raised plasma nerve growth factor levels associated with early-stage romantic love. *Psychoneuroendocrinology, 31,* 288–294.

Endleman, R. (1989). *Love and sex in twelve cultures.* New York. Psyche Press.

Eshbaugh, E. M., & Gute, G. (2008). Hook-ups and sexual regret among college women. *The Journal of Social Psychology, 148,* 77–89.

Fausto-Sterling, A. (2000). *Sexing the body.* New York. Basic Books.

Feng, J., Spence, I., & Pratt, J. (2007). Playing an action video game reduces gender

differences in spatial cognition. *Psychological Science, 18,* 850–855.

Finer, L. B. (2007). Trends in premarital sex in the United States, 1954–2003. *Public Health Reports, 122,* 73–122.

Fisher, H. (2004). *Why we love. The nature and chemistry of romantic love.* New York. Henry Holt & Company.

Fiske, S. T., & Neuberg, S. L. (1990). A continuum model of impression formation from category-based to individuating processes. Influences of information and motivation on attention and interpretation. In M. P. Zanna (Ed.), *Advances in experimental social psychology* (Vol. 3, pp. 1–74). San Diego, CA. Academic Press.

Ford, C. S., & Beach, F. A. (1951). *Patterns of sexual behavior.* New York. Harper and Paul B. Hoeber.

Frayser, S. G. (1994). Defining normal childhood sexuality. An anthropological approach. *Annual Review of Sex Research, 5,* 173–217.

Freeman, C. E. (2005). *Trends in educational equity for girls and women. 2004.* (NCES 2005–016). Washington, DC. U.S. Government Printing Office.

Freund, K. (1974). Male homosexuality. An analysis of the pattern. In J. L. A. Loraine (Ed.), *Understanding homosexuality. Its biological and psychological bases.* New York. Elsevier.

Friedrich, W. N., Whiteside, S. P., & Talley, N. J. (2004). Noncoercive sexual contact with similarly aged individuals. What is the impact? *Journal of Interpersonal Violence, 19,* 1075–1084.

Galea, L. A. M., & Kimura, D. (1993). Sex differences in route learning. *Personality and Individual Differences, 14,* 53–65.

Gallagher, A., Levin, J., & Cahalan, C. (2002). GRE Research. Cognitive patterns of gender differences in mathematics admissions test. *ETS Report 02–19.* Princeton, NJ. Educational Testing Service.

Geary, D. C. (2010). *Male, female* (2nd ed.). Washington, DC. American Psychological Association.

Gonzaga, G. C., Turner, R. A., Keltner, D., Campos, B., & Altemus, M. (2006). Romantic love and sexual desire in close relationships. *Emotion, 6,* 163–179.

Graham, C. A. (2010). The DSM criteria for female orgasmic disorder. *Archives of Sexual Behavior, 39,* 256–270.

Greenberg, A. S., & Bailey, J. M. (1994). The irrelevance of the medical model of mental illness to law and ethics. *International Journal of Law and Psychiatry, 17,* 153–173.

Gregor, T. (1995). Sexuality and the experience of love. In P. R. Abramson & S. D. Pinkerton (Eds.), *Sexual nature, sexual culture* (pp. 330–350). Chicago. University of Chicago Press.

Halpern, D. F. (2004). A cognitive-process taxonomy for sex differences in cognitive abilities. *Current Directions in Psychological Science, 13,* 135–139.

Halpern, D. F., Benbow, C. P., Geary, D. C., Gur, R. C., Hyde, J. S., & Gersbacher, M. A. (2007). The science of sex differences in science and mathematics. *Psychological Science in the Public Interest, 8(1),* 1–51.

Halpern, D. F., Benbow, C. P., Geary, D. C., Gur, R. C., Hyde, J. S., & Gersbacher, M. A. (2007/2008, December/January). Sex, math, and scientific achievement. Why do men dominate the fields of science, engineering, and mathematics? *Scientific American Mind*, 45–49.

Hassett, J. M., Siebert, E. R., & Wallen, K. (2008). Sex differences in rhesus monkey toy preferences parallel those of children. *Hormones and Behavior, 54,* 359–364.

Hatfield, E., & Rapson, R. L. (2005). *Love and sex. Cross-cultural perspectives.* Lanham, MD. University Press of America.

Haugaard, J. J., & Tilly, C. (1988). Characteristics predicting children's responses to sexual encounters with other children. *Child Abuse & Neglect, 12,* 209–218.

Hazan, C., & Zeifman, D. (1999). Pair-bonds as attachments. Evaluating the evidence. In J. Cassidy & P. R. Shaver (Eds.), *Handbook of attachment theory and research* (pp. 336–354). New York. Guilford.

Hedges, L. V., & Nowell, A. (1995). Sex differences in mental scores, variability, and numbers of high-scoring individuals. *Science, 269,* 41–45.

Hendrick, C., & Hendrick, S. (2006). Styles of romantic love. In R. J. Sternberg & K. Weis (Eds.), *The new psychology of romantic love* (pp. 149–170). New Haven, CT. Yale University Press.

Herlitz, A, & Rehnman, J. (2008). Sex differences in episodic memory. *Current Directions in Psychological Science, 17,* 52–56.

Herman, R. A., & Wallen, K. (2007). Cognitive performance in rhesus monkeys varies by sex and prenatal androgen exposure. *Hormones and Behavior, 51,* 496–507.

Hines, M. (2004). *Brain gender.* New York. Oxford University Press.

Hines, M. (2006). Prenatal testosterone and gender-related behaviour. *European Journal of Endocrinology, 155(S1),* 115–121.

Hines, M. (2008). Monkeys, girls, boys and toys. A confirmation letter regarding "Sex differences in toy preferences. Striking parallels between monkeys and humans." *Hormones and Behavior, 54,* 478–479.

Hotchkiss, A. K., Ostby, J. S., Vandenbergh, J. G., & Gray, L. E. (2003). An environmental antiandrodgen, vinclozolin, alters the organization of play behavior. *Physiology and Behavior, 79,* 151–156.

Hsu, B., Kessler, C., Knapke, K., Diefenbach, P., & Elias, J. P. (1994). Gender differences in sexual fantasy and behavior in a college population. A ten-year replication. *Journal of Sex and Marital Therapy, 20,* 103–118

Hughes, M., Morrison, K., & Asada, K. J. K. (2005). What's love got to do with it? Exploring the impact of maintenance rules, love attitudes, and network support on friends with benefits relationships. *Western Journal of Communication, 69,* 49–66.

Hyde, J. S. (2005). The gender similarities hypothesis. *American Psychologist, 60,* 581–592.

Israel, G. E., & Tarver, D. E. (2001). *Transgender care. Recommended guidelines, practical information and personal accounts.* Philadelphia, PA. Temple University Press.

Jadva, V., Hines, M., & Golombok, S. (2010). Infants' preferences for toys, colors, and shapes. Sex differences and similarities. *Archives of Sexual Behavior, 39,* 1261–1273.

Jankowiak, W. R., & Fisher, E. F. (1992). A cross-cultural perspective on romantic love. *Ethnology, 31,* 149–155.

Jordahl, T., & Lohman, B. J. (2009). A bioecological analysis of risk and protective factors associated with early sexual intercourse of young adolescents. *Child Youth Services Review, 31,* 12–82.

Kendler, K. S., Thornton, L. M., Gilman, S. E., & Kessler, R. C. (2000). Sexual orientation in a U.S. national sample of twin and nontwin sibling pairs. *The American Journal of Psychiatry, 157,* 1843–1846.

Kimura, D. (1992). Sex differences in the brain. *Scientific American, 267,* 118–125.

Kinsey, A. C., Pomeroy, W. B., & Martin, C. E. (1948). *Sexual behavior in the human male.* Philadelphia, PA. Saunders.

Kinsey, A. C., Pomeroy, W. B., Martin C. E., & Gebhard, P. H. (1953). *Sexual behavior in the human female.* Philadelphia, PA. Saunders.

Knickmeyer, R. C., Wheelwright, S., Taylor, K., Raggatt, P., Hackett, G., et al. (2005). Gender-typed play and amniotic testosterone. *Developmental Psychology, 41,* 517–528.

Lamb, S., & Coakley, M. (1993). Normal childhood sexual play and games. Differentiating play from abuse. *Child Abuse and Neglect, 17,* 515–526.

Langfeldt, T. (1990). Early childhood and juvenile sexuality, development and problems. In M. E. Perry (Ed.), *Handbook of sexology. Vol. 7. Childhood and adolescent sexology* (pp. 179–200). New York. Elsevier Science.

Langström, N., Rahman, Q., Carlström, E., & Lichtenstein, P. (2008). Genetic and environmental effects on same-sex sexual behavior. A population study of twins in Sweden. *Archives of Sexual Behavior.* Advance of publication version retrieved from www.springerlink.com on December 12, 2008.

Larsson, I., Svedin, C.-G., & Friedrich, W. N. (2000). Differences and similarities in sexual behaviour among preschoolers in Sweden and USA. *Nordic Journal of Psychiatry, 54,* 251–257.

Laumann, E. O., Gagnon, J. H., Michael, R. T., & Michaels, S. (1994). *The social organization of sexuality.* Chicago, IL. The University of Chicago.

Laumann, E. O., Nicolosi, A., Glasser, D. B., Paik, A., Gingell, C., et al. (2005). Sexual problems among women and men aged 40–80 years. Prevalence and correlates identified in the Global Study of Sexual Attitudes and Behaviors. *International Journal of Impotence Research, 17,* 38–57.

Lee, J. A. (1976). *The colors of love. An exploration of the ways of loving* (rev. ed.). Ontario, Canada. New Press.

Leitenberg, H., & Henning, K. (1995). Sexual fantasy. *Psychological Bulletin, 117,* 469–496.

LeVay, S. (1991). A difference in hypothalamic structure between heterosexual and homosexual men. *Science, 253,* 1034–1037.

LeVay, S. (1996). *Queer science. The use and abuse of research into homosexuality.* Cambridge, MA. MIT Press.

Levay, S., & Valente, S. M. (2003). *Human sexuality.* Sunderland, MA. Sinauer.

Levine, T. R., Sato, S., Hashimoto, T., Verma, J. (1995). Love and marriage in eleven cultures. *Journal of Cross-Cultural Psychology, 26,* 554–557.

Lewin, C., Wolgers, G., & Herlitz, A. (2001). Sex differences favoring women in verbal, but not in visuospatial episodic memory. *Neuropsychology, 15,* 165–173.

Lieberman, D., & Hatfield, E. (2006). Passionate love. Cross-cultural and evolutionary perspectives. In R. J. Sternberg & K. Weis (Eds.), *The new psychology of romantic love* (pp. 274–297). New Haven, CT. Yale University Press.

Lindberg, S. M., Hyde, J. S., Linn, M. C., & Petersen, J. L. (2010). New trends in gender and mathematics performance. A meta-analysis. *Psychological Bulletin, 136,* 1123–1135.

Lippa, R. A. (2006). Is high sex drive associated with increased sexual attraction to both sexes? It depends on whether you are male or female. *Psychological Science, 17(1),* 46–52.

Lippa, R. A. (2007). The relation between sex drive and sexual attraction to men and women. A cross-national study of heterosexual, bisexual, and homosexual men and women. *Archives of Sexual Behavior, 36,* 209–222.

Lytton, H., & Romney, D. M. (1991). Parents' differential socialization of boys and girls. A meta-analysis. *Psychological Bulletin, 109,* 267–296.

Macrae, C. N., Milne, A. B., & Bodenhausen, G. V. (1994). Stereotypes as energy-saving devices. A peek inside the cognitive toolbox. *Journal of Personality and Social Psychology, 66,* 37–47.

Marazziti, D., Akiskal, H. S., Rossi, A., & Cassano, G. B. (1999). Alteration of the platelet serotonin transporter in romantic love. *Psychological Medicine, 29,* 741–745.

Marazziti, D., & Canale, D. (2004). Hormonal changes when falling in love. *Psychoneuroendocrinology, 29,* 931–936.

Martin, C. L., & Ruble, D. N. (2004). Children's search for gender cues. Cognitive perspectives on gender development. *Current Directions in Psychological Science, 13,* 67–70.

Martin, C. L., & Ruble, D. N. (2009). Patterns of gender development. *Annual Review of Psychology, 61,* 353–381.

Martin, C. L., Ruble, D. N., & Szkrybalo, J. (2002). Cognitive theories of early gender development. *Psychological Bulletin, 128,* 903–933.

Masters, W. H., & Johnson, V. (1966). *Human sexual response.* Boston. Little, Brown.

Masters, W. H., Johnson, V., & Kolodny, R. C. (1982). *Human sexuality.* Boston, MA. Little, Brown.

Mealey, L. (2000). *Sex differences. Developmental and evolutionary strategies.* San Diego, CA. Academic Press.

Meston, C. N., Levin, R. J., Sipski, M. L., Hull, E. M., & Heiman, J. R. (2004). Women's orgasm. *Annual Review of Sex Research, 15,* 173–257.

Meyer-Bahlburg, H. F. L. (2005). Gender identity outcome in female-raised 46,XY persons with penile agenesis, cloacal exstrophy of the bladder, or penile ablation. *Archives of Sexual Behavior, 34,* 423–438.

Meyer-Bahlburg, H. F. L. (2010). From mental disorder to iatrogenic hypogonadism. Dilemmas in conceptualizing gender identity variants as psychiatric conditions. *Archives of Sexual Behavior, 39,* 461–476.

Meyer-Bahlburg, H. F. L., Dolezal, C., Baker, S. W., Carlson, A. D., Obeid, J. S., et al. (2004). Prenatal androgenization affects gender-related behavior but not gender identity in 5–12-year-old girls with congenital adrenal hyperplasia. *Archives of Sexual Behavior, 33,* 97–104.

Miller, G. F. (1999). Sexual selection for cultural displays. In R. Dunbar, C. Knight, & C. Power (Eds.), *The evolution of culture* (pp. 71–91). Edinburgh, UK. Edinburgh University Press.

Moore, K. A., Driscoll, A. K., & Lindberg, L. D. (1998). *A statistical portrait of adolescent sex, contraception, and childbearing.* Washington, DC. The National Campaign to Prevent Teen Pregnancy.

Moore, D. S., & Johnson, S. P. (2008). Mental rotation in human infants. A sex difference. *Psychological Science, 19,* 1063–1066.

Mustanski, B. S., Bailey, J. M., & Kaspar, S. (2002). Dermatoglyphics, handedness, sex, and sexual orientation. *Archives of Sexual Behavior, 31,* 113–122.

National Research Council. (2010). *Gender differences at critical transitions in the careers of science, engineering, and mathematics faculty* Washington, DC. National Academies Press.

Newton, N., & Newton, M. (1967). Psychologic aspects of lactation. *New England Journal of Medicine, 272,* 1179–1196.

Nördenstrom, A., Servin, A., Bohlin, G., Larsson, A., & Wedell, A. (2002). Sex-typed toy play behavior correlates with the degree of prenatal androgen exposure assessed by *CYP21* genotype in girls with congenital adrenal hyperplasia. *Journal of Clinical Endocrinology and Metabolism, 87,* 5119–5124.

Offer, D., Kaiz, M., Howard, K. I., & Bennett, E. S. (2000). The altering of reported experiences. *Journal of the Academy of Child & Adolescent Psychiatry, 39,* 735–742.

Okami, P., & Shackelford, T. K. (2001). Human sex differences in sexual psychology and behavior. *Annual Review of Sex Research, 12,* 186–241.

Okami, P., Olmstead, R., & Abramson, P. R. (1997). Sexual experiences in early childhood. 18-year longitudinal data from the UCLA Family Lifestyles Project. *The Journal of Sex Research, 34,* 339–347.

Okazaki, S. (2002). Influences of culture on Asian Americans' sexuality. *Journal of Sex Research, 39,* 34–41.

Owen, J. J., Rhoades, G. K., Stanley, S. M., & Fincham, F. D. (2010). "Hooking up" among college students. Demographic and psychosocial correlates. *Archives of Sexual Behavior, 39,* 653–663.

Paoli, T., Palagi, E., Tacconi, G., & Tarli, S. B. (2006). Perineal swelling, intermenstrual cycle, and female sexual behavior in bonobos (*Pan paniscus*). *American Journal of Primatology, 68,* 333–347.

Pasterski, V. L., Geffner, M. E., Brain, C., Hindmarsh, P., & Brook, C. (2005). Prenatal hormones and postnatal socialization by parents as determinants of male-typical toy play in girls with congenital adrenal hyperplasia. *Child Development, 76(1),* 264–278.

Paul, E. L., McManus, B., & Hayes, A. (2000). "Hookups". Characteristics and correlates of college students' spontaneous and anonymous sexual experiences. *Journal of Sex Research, 37,* 76–88.

Pellegrini, A. D., & Smith, P. K. (1998). Physical activity play. The nature and function of a neglected aspect of play. *Child Development, 69,* 577–598.

Pinker, S. (2002). *The blank slate.* New York. Viking.

Quinn, D. M., & Spencer, S. J. (2001). The interference of stereotype threat with women's generation of mathematical problem-solving strategies. *Journal of Social Issues, 57(1),* 55–72.

Quinn, P. C., & Liben, L. S. (2008). A sex difference in mental rotation in young infants. *Psychological Science, 19,* 1067–1072.

Rahman, Q. (2005a). Fluctuating asymmetry, second to fourth finger length ratios and human sexual orientation. *Psychoneuroendocrinology, 30,* 382–391.

Rahman, Q. (2005b). The neurodevelopment of human sexual orientation. *Neuroscience and Biobehavioral Reviews, 29,* 1057–1066.

Reiber, C., & Garcia, J. R. (2010). Hooking up. Gender differences, evolution, and pluralistic ignorance. *Evolutionary Psychology, 8,* 390–404.

Reis, H. T., & Aron, A. (2008). Love. What is it, why does it matter, and how does it operate? *Perspectives on Psychological Science, 3,* 80–86.

Renk, K., Donnelly, R., McKinney, C., & Agliata, A. K. (2006). The development of gender identity. Timetables and influences. In Kam-Shing (Ed.), *Psychology of gender identity. An international perspective* (pp. 49–68). Hauppauge, NY. Nova Science Publishers.

Reynolds, M. A., Herbenick, D. L., & Bancroft, J. H. (2003). The nature of childhood sexual experiences. Two studies 50 years apart. In J. Bancroft (Ed.), *Sexual development in childhood* (pp. 134–155). Bloomington, IN. Indiana University Press.

Robinson, N. M., Abbott, R. D., Berninger, V. W., & Busse, J. (1996). The structure of abilities in math-precocious young children. Gender similarities and differences. *Journal of Educational Psychology, 88,* 341–352.

Robinson, P. (1989). *The modernization of sex.* Ithaca, NY. Cornell University Press. (Original work published 1979.)

Rothbaum, F., & Tsang, B. Y. (1998). Lovesongs in the U.S. and China. The nature of romantic love. *Journal of Cross-Cultural Psychology, 29,* 306–319.

Ruble, D. N., Taylor, L. J., Cyphers, L., Greulich, F. K., Lurye, L. E., et al. (2009). The role of gender constancy in early gender development. *Child Development, 78,* 1121–1136.

Ruscher, J. B., & Hammer, E. Y. (2004). The person in the situation. Self-protection,

self-evaluation, and self-change. In J. B. Ruscher, & E. Y. Hammer (Eds.), *Current directions in social psychology* (pp. 1–2). Upper Saddle River, NJ. Pearson/Prentice Hall.

Salonia, A., Giraldi, A., Chiverrs, M. L., Georgiadis, J. R., Levin, R., et al. (2010). Physiology of women's sexual function. Basic knowledge and new findings. *Journal of Sexual Medicine, 7,* 2637–2660.

Savic, I., & Lindström, P. (2008). PET and MRI show differences in cerebral asymmetry and functional connectivity between homosexual and heterosexual subjects. *Proceedings of the National Academy of Sciences, 105,* 9403–9408.

Savin-Williams, R. C. (2006). Who's gay? Does it matter? *Current Directions in Psychological Science, 15(1),* 40–44.

Savin-Williams, R. C. (2008). Then and now. Recruitment, definition, diversity, and positive attributes of same-sex populations. *Developmental Psychology, 44,* 135–138.

Savin-Williams, R. C., & Ream, G. L. (2007). Prevalence and stability of sexual orientation components during adolescence and young adulthood. *Archives of Sexual Behavior, 36,* 385–394.

Sax, L. (2002). How common is intersex? A reply to Anne Fausto-Sterling. *The Journal of Sex Research, 39,* 174–178.

Schmader, T. (2010). Stereotype threat deconstructed. *Current Directions in Psychological Science, 19,* 14–18.

Schurke, B. (2000). Young children's curiosity about other people's genitals. *Journal of Psychology & Human Sexuality, 12(1–2),* 27–48.

Severin, L., & Wyer, M. (2000). The science and politics of the search for sex differences. Editorial. *National Women's Studies Association Journal, 12,* vii.

Shaver, P. R., Morgan, H. J., & Wu, S. (1996). Is love a "basic" emotion? *Personal Relationships, 3,* 81–96.

Shaver, P. R., Wu, S., & Schwartz, J. C. (1992). Cross-cultural similarities and differences in emotion and its representation. A prototype approach. In M. S. Clark (Ed.), *Review of personality and social psychology* (Vol 13, pp. 175–212). Newbury Park, CA. Sage Publications.

Sinno, S. M., & Killen, M. (2009). Moms at work and dads at home. Children's evaluations of parental roles. *Applied Developmental Science, 13,* 16–29.

Smith, T. W. (2006). *American sexual behavior. Trends, socio-demographic differences, and risk behavior.* General Social Survey Topical Report No. 15, National Opinion Research Center, Version 6.0. Retrieved from www.norc.org on October 27, 2007.

So, W. W., Wong, F. Y., & DeLeon, J. (2005). Sex, HIV risks, and substance use among Asian American college students. *AIDS Education and Prevention, 17,* 457–468.

Sommer, V., & Vassey, P. L. (Eds.). (2006). *Homosexual behaviour in animals. An evolutionary perspective.* Cambridge, UK. Cambridge University Press.

Sprecher, S., Aron, A., Hatfield, E., Cortese, A., Potapova, E., & Leviskaya, A. (1994). Love. American style, Russian style, and Japanese style. *Personal Relationships, 1,* 349–369.

Steele, C. M., & Aronson, J. (1995). Stereotype threat and the intellectual test performance of African Americans. *Journal of Personality and Social Psychology, 69,* 797–811.

Stein, S. B. (1983). *Girls and boys. The limits of nonsexist childrearing.* New York. Charles Scribner's Sons.

Steinberg, L., & Morris, A. S. (2001). Adolescent development. *Annual Review of Psychology, 52,* 83–110.

Strand, S., Deary, I. J., & Smith, P. (2006). Sex differences in cognitive ability test scores. A UK national picture. *British Journal of Educational Psychology, 76,* 463–480.

Stricker, L. J., & Ward, W. C. (2004). Stereotype threat, inquiring about test takers' ethnicity and gender, and standardized test performance. *Journal of Applied Social Psychology, 34,* 665–693.

Su, R., Rounds, J., & Armstrong, P. I. (2009). Men and things, women and people. A meta-analysis of sex differences in interests. *Psychological Bulletin, 135,* 859–884.

Suschinsky, K. D., Lalumière, M. L., & Chivers, M. L. (2009). Sex differences in patterns of genital sexual arousal. Measurement artifacts or true phenomena? *Archives of Sexual Behavior, 38,* 559–573.

Sytsma, S. E. (2007). *Ethics and intersex.* Dordrecht, Netherlands. Springer.

Thompson, E. M., & Morgan, E. M. (2008). "Mostly straight" young women. Variations in sexual identity development. *Developmental Psychology, 44,* 15–21.

Thompson, S. (1990). Putting a big thing into a little hole. Teenage girls' accounts of sexual initiation. *The Journal of Sex Research, 27,* 341–362.

Thompson, S. (1995). *Going all the way. Teenage girls' tales of sex, romance & pregnancy.* New York. Hill and Wang.

Townsend, J. M., & Wasserman, T. H. (2011). Sexual hookups among college students. Sex differences in emotional reactions. *Archives of Sexual Behavior, 40,* 1173–1181.

Traeen, B., Stigum, H., & Sørensen, D. (2002). Sexual diversity in urban Norwegians. *The Journal of Sex Research, 39,* 249–259.

Unger, R. K. (1979). Toward a redefinition of sex and gender. *American Psychologist, 34,* 1085–1094.

Valla, J. M., & Ceci, S. J. (2011). Can sex differences in science be tied to the long reach of prenatal hormones? Brain organization theory, digit ratio (2D/4D), and sex differences in preferences and cognition. *Perspectives on Psychological Science, 6,* 134–146.

Vizcarral, M. B., Balladares, E., Candia, C., Lepe, M., & Saldivia, C. (2004). Sexual behavior during childhood, as reported later, during high school years. *Psicothema, 16(1),* 58–63.

Wai, J., Cacchio, M., Putallaz, M., & Makel, M. C. (2010). Sex differences in the right tail of cognitive abilities. A 30-year examination. *Intelligence, 38,* 412–423.

Wallen, K. (1996). Nature needs nurture. The influence of hormonal and social influences on the development of behavioral sex differences in rhesus monkeys. *Hormones and Behavior, 30,* 364–378.

Wallen, K. (2001). Sex and context. Hormones and primate sexual motivation. *Hormones and Behavior, 40,* 339–357.

Wallen, K. (2011). Female sexual arousal. Genital anatomy and orgasm in intercourse. *Hormones and Behavior, 59,* 780–792.

Wei, W., Lu, H., Zhao, H., Chen, C., Dong, Q, et al. (2012). Gender differences in children's arithmetic performance are accounted for by gender differences in language abilities. *Psychological Science.* Pre-publication version

retrieved from http://pss.sagepub.com/content/early/2012/02/17/0956797611427168 on March 4, 2012.

Weisner, T. S., & Wilson-Mitchell, J. E. (1990). Nonconventional family life-styles and sex typing in six-year-olds. *Child Development, 61,* 1915–1933.

West Virginia OMCFH (Office of Maternal Child and Family Health). (2007). *Adolescent health profile.* Retrieved from www.wvdhhr.org on October 27, 2007.

Witelson, S. F., Kigar, D. L., Scambougeras, A., Kideckel, D. M., Buck, B., et al. (2008). Corpus callosum anatomy in right-handed homosexual and heterosexual men. *Archives of Sexual Behavior, 37,* 857–863.

Wright, D., Parkes, A., Strange, V., Allen, E., Bonell, C., et al. (2008). The quality of young people's heterosexual relationships. A longitudinal analysis of characteristics shaping subjective experience. *Perspectives on Sexual and Reproductive Health, 40,* 226–237.

Wudy, S., Dorr, H. G., Solleder, C., Djalali, M., & Homoki, J. (1999). Profiling steroid hormones in amniotic fluid of midpregnancy by routine stable isotope dilution/gas chromoatography-mass spectrometry. Reference values and concentrations in fetuses at risk for 21-hydroxylase deficiency. *Journal of Clinical Endocrinology and Metabolism, 84,* 2724–2728.

Zosuls, K. M., Ruble, D. M., Tamis-LeMonda, C. S., Shrout, P. E., Bornstein, M. H., et al. (2009). The acquisition of gender labels in infancy. Implications for sex-typed play. *Developmental Psychology, 45,* 688–701.

Credits

the pain? An fMRI investigation of empathy and intentionality in children, 2611, Copyright (2008), with permission from Elsevier .

p. 195: (Top) Tom Kelley Archive/Getty Images

p. 195: (Bottom) dlewis33/iStock

p. 198: © David Howells/Corbis

p. 202: jarenwicklund/iStock

p. 205: © Lucian Coman/Shutterstock

p. 207: Associated Press/Spencer Green

p. 208: © pryzmat/Shutterstock

CHAPTER 5

p. 214: Tim Bieber/Getty Images

p. 216: (Top) Esref Armegan/Joan Eroncel

p. 216: (Bottom Left) Esref Armegan/Joan Eroncel

p. 216: (Bottom Right) Esref Armegan/Joan Eroncel

p. 221: NBCU Photo Bank/Getty Images

p. 222: Time & Life Pictures/Getty Images

p. 226: Omikron/Photo Researchers, Inc

p. 231: (Figure 5.13 1) LehaKoK/Shutterstock

p. 231: (Figure 5.13 2) LeftHannamariah/Shutterstock

p. 231: (Figure 5.13 3) Monkey Business Images/Shutterstock

p. 231: (Figure 5.13 4) GWImages/Shutterstock

p. 231: (Figure 5.13 5) ChristineGonsalves/Shutterstock

p. 231: (Figure 5.13 6) Pinosub/Shutterstock

p. 231: (Figure 5.13 7) Vasily Smirnov/Shutterstock.com

p. 231: (Figure 5.14 A) Larry St. Pierre/Shutterstock

p. 231: (Figure 5.14 B) llaszlo/Shutterstock

p. 231: (Figure 5.14 C) Ferenc Szelepcsenyi/Shutterstock

p. 232: (Figure 5.16 1)Tatjana Romanova/Shutterstock

p. 232: (Figure 5.16 2) Carleton Chinner/Shutterstock

p. 232: (Figure 5.16 3) Kjersti Joergensen/Shutterstock

p. 232: (Figure 5.16 4) Roby1960/Shutterstock

p. 234: Professors Pietro M. Motta & Alberto Caggiati/Photo Researchers, Inc

p. 238: sagas an/Shutterstock

p. 242: Photo Researchers, Inc.

p. 243: Blend Images/Shutterstock

p. 247: (Both images) Used with Permission from Aude Oliva

p. 248: Maureen Light Photography/Getty Images

p. 249: (B) W.E. Hill , 1923 "My Wife and My Mother-In-Law"

p. 251: Science Source/Photo Researchers, Inc

p. 252: (Figure 5.33 Left) Richard T. Nowitz/Photo Researchers, Inc

p. 252: (Figure 5.33 Right) Richard T. Nowitz/Photo Researchers, Inc

p. 252: (Top) kojihirano/Shutterstock

p. 252: (Bottom) Stocktrek Images/Getty Images

p. 253: (Figure 5.35) deimagine/iStock

p. 253: (Figure 5.37) defpicture/Shutterstock

p. 253: (Figure 5.38) Larry Landolfi/Photo Researchers, Inc

p. 253: (Figure 5.39) Jerry Schad/Photo Researchers, Inc

p. 254: (Figure 5.40) © GEORG HOCHMUTH/epa/Corbis

p. 254: (Figure 5.41) Wendy Kaveney Photography/Shutterstock

p. 254: (Figure 5.42) photo5963/Shutterstock

p. 259: Figure provided by Daniel Simons, www.theinvisiblegorilla.com

p. 260: Figure provided by Daniel Simons, www.theinvisiblegorilla.com

p. 261: Kovalchuk Oleksandr/Shutterstock

p. 262: (Figure 5.50 Top) Ewa Studio/Shutterstock

p. 262: (Figure 5.50 Bottom) neelsky/Shutterstock

p. 262: GeorgeBurba/iStock

CHAPTER 6

p. 268: Lisa Larsen/Time Life Pictures/Getty Images

p. 270: © Institute of Illegal Images

p. 273: Luca Tettoni/Corbis

p. 282: Goethe Museum, Frankfurt, Germany/Peter Willi/The Bridgeman Art Library

p. 284: (Bottom Left) urosr/Shutterstock

p. 284: (Top Right) Dario Diament/Shutterstock

p. 284: (Top Left) Anastasios71/Shutterstock

p. 284: (Bottom Right) EpicStockMedia/Shutterstock

p. 287: Arieliona/Shutterstock

p. 294: Alex Linghorn/Getty Images

p. 297: dwphotos/Shutterstock

p. 298: (Top) NLM/Science Source/Photo Researchers, Inc

p. 298: (Bottom) © Bettmann/CORBIS

p. 304: (Left) liubomir/Shutterstock

p. 304: (Right) Andrew Koturanov/Shutterstock

p. 305: (Left) Javier Tuana/Shutterstock

p. 305: (Center) Oleg Golovnvev/Shutterstock

p. 305: (Right) Kevin L. Chesson/Shutterstock

p. 310: Lost in Translation/NBC Universal

p. 311: (Left) jwblinn/Shutterstock

p. 311: (Center) Tim UR/Shutterstock

p. 311: (Right) Vadim Kolobanov/Shutterstock

p. 312: (Top Left) Associated Press/Michael S. Yamashita

p. 312: (Top Right) Stringer/Getty Images

p. 312: (Bottom) Meth Project Foundation

p. 313: William Casey/Shutterstock

p. 315: (Left) Charlie Edward/Shutterstock

p. 315: (Right) Yellowj/Shutterstock

p. 320: (1) Paula Bronstein/Getty Images

p. 320: (2) addimage/Shutterstock

p. 320: (3) Heike Rau/Shutterstock

p. 320: (4) Christopher Elwell/Shutterstock

CHAPTER 7:

p. 326: Myles McGuinness/Getty Images

p. 328: Kzenon/Shutterstock

p. 329: Walter Iooss Jr./Getty Images

p. 333: Norbert Wu/Minden Pictures/Corbis

p. 335: Associated Press/Kiichiro Sato

p. 338: (Figure 7.4) Reprinted with permission from the *American Journal of Psychiatry*, (Copyright 1999). Psychiatric Association.

p. 338: (Left) Jeff Grabert/Shutterstock

p. 338: (Center) Art_man/Shutterstock

p. 338: (Right) Dan Snyder/Shutterstock

p. 339: Little Albert Experiments, Archives of the History of American Psychology/ The Center for the History of Psychology, The University of Akron

p. 347: Robert Mearns Yerkes Papers (MS 569), Manuscripts and Archives, Yale University Library.

p. 349: Time & Life Pictures/Getty Images

p. 351: Ben Hider/Getty Images

p. 352: Shots Studio/Shutterstock

p. 355: Jonathan Kirn/Getty Images

p. 357: (Right) Ivan Kuzmin/Shutterstock

p. 357: (Left) Israel Hervas Bengochea/Shutterstock

p. 358: Gemenacom/Shutterstock

p. 359: Albert Bandura

p. 360: Ferrari et al

p. 361: (Right) Reprinted from *Neuron*, Vol. 40, Wicker, B., et al, The common neural basis of seeing and feeling disgust, 655-664, Copyright (2003), with permission from Elsevier

p. 361: (Left) Reprinted from *Trends in Cognitive Sciences*, Vol. 8, Rizzolatti et al., A Unifying View of the Basis of Social Cognition, 396-403, (2004), with permission from Elsevier.

p. 364: (Left) Associated Press/DC Comics, Jerry Robinson

p. 364: (Right) Images consisting of '*Crime Does Not Pay* vol. 33 cover' Copyright © 1944, William M. Gains, Agent, Inc., reprinted with permission. All rights reserved.

CHAPTER 8

p. 370: Ellen Denuto/Getty Images

p. 372: Ho/Associated Press

p. 377: (Figure 8.3) Belinda Images/SuperStock

p. 377: (Right) Zurijeta/Shutterstock

p. 384: (Top Left) Oleg Golovnev/Shutterstock

p. 384: (Top Center) David Rydevik

p. 384: (Top Right) Kevin Higley/Associated Press

p. 384: (Bottom Left) Associated Press

p. 384: (Bottom Right) Chao Soi Cheong/Associated Press

p. 390: Talmi, Deborah, et al., *Psychological Science* (Vol. 16, Issue 9)

pp. 716-723, copyright © 2005 by (Association for Psychological Science)

Reprinted by Permission of SAGE Publications.

p. 391: Yulia Popkova/Getty Images

p. 395: The Innocence Project

p. 397: Mike Derer/Associated Press

p. 401: Associated Press

CHAPTER 9

p. 414: Antonio Mo/Getty Images

p. 416: Bruce Yuanyue Bi/Getty Images

p. 418: Nancy Kanwisher

p. 419: (Top Left) Morgan Lane Photography/Shutterstock

p. 419: (Top Center) monticello/Shutterstock

p. 419: (Top Right) Kongsak/Shutterstock

p. 419: (Bottom) Jenn Huls/Shutterstock

p. 427: Mike Liu /Shuttestock

p. 431: (Left) © BBC/Corbis

p. 431: (Right) CBS Photo Archive/Getty Images

p. 433: nicoolay/iStock

p. 434: David Sacks/Getty Images

p. 436: Aubord Duloc/Shutterstock

p. 442: Thorsten Milse/Getty Images

p. 444: Ron Cohn/Gorilla Foundation/koko.org

p. 445: kowit sitthi /Shutterstock

p. 446: (Left) HO/Reuters/Corbis

p. 446: (Center) Susan Kuklin/Getty Images

p. 446: (Right) Great Ape Trust/dapd

p. 447: Rahmo/Shutterstock

p. 451: Denis Kuvaev/Shutterstock

p. 452: Davidson Institute/THINK Summer Institute

p. 453: (Left) Time & Life Pictures/Getty Images

p. 453: (Center) Time & Life Pictures/Getty Images

p. 453: (Right) Hulton Archive/Getty Images

CHAPTER 10

p. 464: Charles Hewitt/Getty Images

p. 466: (Left) Norman Rockwell Museum Collections/Provided Courtesy of the Norman Rockwell Family Agency

p. 466: (Right) Associated Press

p. 468: © Emily Flake, used with permission

p. 469: Bijlsma & Ruiter/Foto Natura/Minden Pictures/Corbis

p. 470: Clive Chilvers/Shutterstock

p. 472: (Left) Harlowe Primate Laboratory/University of Wisconsin

p. 472: (Right) Ami Parikh/Shutterstock

p. 474: Malcolm Browne/Associated Press

p. 481: Yevgen Kotyukh/Shutterstock

p. 483: Ariel Skelley/Getty Images

p. 485: Peter Dazeley/Getty Images

p. 492: (Left) arindambanerjee/Shutterstock

p. 492: (Right) Bird in Paradise/Shutterstock

p. 494: (Left) Anneka/Shutterstock

p. 494: (Right) Konstantin Sutyagin/Shutterstock

p. 496: John Moore/Getty Images

p. 498: Photodisc/Getty Images

p. 500: (A) v.s.anandhakrishna/Shutterstock

p. 500: (B) auremar/Shutterstock

p. 500: (C) Andrey Yurlov/Shutterstock

p. 500: (D) marcello farina/Shutterstock

p. 501: Associated Press/Peter Morrison

p. 505: (Left) Joe McNally/Getty Images

p. 505: (Right) AFP/Getty Images

CHAPTER 11

p. 510: pio3/Shutterstock

p. 512: Gregory James Van Raalte/Shutterstock

p. 514: (Bottom Left) abd/Shutterstock

p. 514: (Top Left) andrea michele piacquadio/Shutterstock

p. 514: (Top Right) Michael Poehlman/Getty Images

p. 514: (Bottom Right) Justin Guariglia/Getty Images

p. 515: David Matsumoto/Humintell

p. 519: Aspen Photo/Shutterstock

p. 520: (A) Nature Reviews Neuroscience 2001

p. 520: (B) Smith, Marie, et al., *Psychological Science* (Vol. 16, Issue 3) pp. 184-189, copyright © 2005 by (Association for Psychological Science) Reprinted by Permission of SAGE Publications.

p. 521: Paul Ekman, Ph.D./Paul Ekman Group, LLC

p. 522: Reprinted from *Journal of Experimental Social Psychology*, Vol. 43 Yuki, M, et al., Are the windows to the soul the same in the East and West? Cultural differences in using the eyes and mouth as cues to recognize emotions in Japan and the United States, 303-311, Copyright (2007), with permission from Society of Experimental Social Psychology.

p. 529: Halberstadt, Jamin, et al., *Psychological Science* (Vol. 20, Issue 10) pp. 1254-1261, copyright © 2009 by (Association for Psychological Science) Reprinted by Permission of SAGE Publications.

p. 530: Image Source/Getty Images

p. 533: Martin Novak/Shutterstock

p. 540: prodakszyn/Shutterstock

p. 541: AFP/Getty Images

P. 547: Rex Features via AP Images

p. 548: track5/iStock

p. 550: Graeme Robertson/Getty Images

p. 551: Robert Mankoff/The New Yorker Collection/www.cartoonbank.com

p. 554: © RMN-Grand Palais/Art Resource, NY

p. 557: (Left) pkchai/Shutterstock

p. 557: (Right) oliveromg/Shutterstock

p. 558: (Left) Image Source/Getty Images

p. 558: (Right) John Freeman/Getty Images

p. 563: jadimages/Shutterstock

CHAPTER 12:

p.568: bobbieo/Getty Images

p. 570: (Top) golf9c9333/Getty Images

p. 570: (Bottom) Sam Bassett/Getty Images

p. 572: STEEX/iStock

p. 574: Keystone/Getty Images

p. 577: © Handout/Reuters/Corbis

p. 581: (Row One Left) Hulton Archive/Getty Images

p. 581: (Row One Right)Time & Life Pictures/Getty Images

p. 581: (Row Two Left) Gamma-Keystone via Getty Images

p. 581: (Row Two Right) Barbara Young/Getty Images

p. 581: (Row Thee Left) SCIENCE SOURCE/ Getty Images

p. 581: (Row Three Right) Getty Images

p. 581: (Row Four Top Left) © Bettmann/CORBIS

p. 581: (Row Four Top Right) Universal History Archive/UIG

p. 581: (Row Four Bottom Left) Gamma-Rapho via Getty Images

p. 583: (Left) Michael Rougier, Time & Life Pictures/Getty Images

p. 583: (Center) © Ann Kaplan/CORBIS

p. 583: (Right) Hulton Archive/Getty Images

p. 589: (Margin) Licensed By: Warner Bros. Entertainment Inc. All Rights Reserved.

p. 589: (Top Left) Stone/Getty Images

p. 589: (Top Right) Vetta/Getty

p. 589: (Bottom Left) Kzenon/Shutterstock

p. 589: (Bottom Right) cloki/Shutterstock

p. 594: (Both images) Courtesy of Paul Okami

p. 600: (Both images) AFP/Getty Images

p. 603: Kheng Guan Toh /Shutterstock

p. 604: Lewis J. Merrim/Photo Researchers, Inc

p. 607: (Right) © Bettmann/CORBIS

p. 608: (Left) New York Daily News Archive/Getty Images

CHAPTER 13

p. 614: Aaron M. Cohen/Corbis

p. 616: Mario Tama/Getty Images

p. 618: Elaine Thompson/Pool/epa/Corbis

p. 620: Grunnitus Studio/Getty Images

p. 621: mast3r/Shutterstock

p. 628: Yuri Arcurs /Shutterstock

p. 629: Aletia/Shutterstock

p. 632: Sandy Huffaker/Corbis

p. 633: U.S. Coast Guard/Corbis

p. 640: Yuri Arcurs/Shutterstock

p. 642: (Top Left) YanLev/Shutterstock

p. 642: (Top Right) Johan Swanepoel/Shutterstock

p. 642: (Bottom Right) Cora Reed/Shutterstock

p. 643: Andrey Bayda/Shutterstock

p. 644: (Figure 13.9 Top Row 1) Redferns/Getty Images

p. 644: (Figure 13.9 Top Row 2) Georgios Kollidas/Shutterstock

p. 644: (Figure 13.9 Top Row 3) Hulton Archive/Getty Images

p. 644: (Figure 13.9 Top Row 4) Library of Congress

p. 644: (Figure 13.9 Top Row 5) George Charles Beresford/Public Domain Image

p. 644: (Figure 13.9 Bottom Row 1) AFP/Getty Images

p. 644: (Figure 13.9 Bottom Row 2) Wire Image/Getty Images

p. 644: (Figure 13.9 Bottom Row 3) Associated Press

p. 644: (Figure 13.9 Bottom Row 4) Redferns/Getty Images

p. 644: (Figure 13.9 Bottom Row 5) NBCU Photo Bank/Getty Images

p. 644: (Margin) luxorphoto/Shutterstock

p. 653: EML/Shutterstock

p. 654: Bob Willoughby/Redferns

p. 660: Bureau L.A. Collection/Sygma/Corbis

p. 661: Olga Sapegina/Shutterstock

p. 663: (Left and Center) NBC/Getty Images

p. 663: (Right) Associated Press

CHAPTER 14

p. 668: © ER Productions/Corbis

p. 670: Matthew Benoit/Shutterstock

p. 671: Adam Friedberg/Getty Images

p. 676: Images consisting of cover of *Psychoanalysis*, vol. 1, Copyright © (1955), William M. Gains, Agent, Inc., reprinted with permission. All rights reserved.

p. 678: Pasquale Sorrentino/Photo Researchers, Inc

p. 684: Adam Gregor/Shutterstock

p. 685: Associated Press/Mike Appleton

p. 687: John Van Hasselt/Corbis

p. 691: David Buffington/Getty Images

p. 696: Perthsire Picture Agency

p. 704: (Left) Used with permission, Joseph Biderman

p. 704: (Right) The New York Times/Redux Pictures

p. 707: (Left) LianeM/Shutterstock

p. 707: (Right) stefanolunardi/Shutterstock

p. 709: Will McIntyre/Getty Images

p. 711: (Left) © Bettmann/CORBIS

p. 711: (Right) Neil Borden/Getty Images

CHAPTER 15

p. 716: Georg Szabo/STOCK4B/Getty Images

p. 718: (Both images) From the film *Obedience* © 1968 by Stanley Milgram, copyright renewed 1993 by Alexandra Milgram and distributed by Alexander Street Press

p. 722: EugeneF/Shutterstock

p. 723: AFP/Getty Images

p. 725: J. Adam Fenster/University of Rochester

p. 726: Vadym Drobot/Shutterstock

p. 729: (Left) Cora Reed/Shutterstock

p. 729: (Right) Jon E Oringer/Shutterstock

p. 729: (Margin) www.cartoonstock.com

p. 730: Sparkling Moments Photography/Shutterstock

p. 737: Associated Press/Diane Bondareff

p. 738: (Margin) Image Courtesy of Gillian Rhodes

p. 738: (Top) Karl Grammer

p. 739: Karl Grammer

p. 740: (Figure 15.4 Top) Reprinted from *Personality and Individual Differences*, Vol. 44, Lisa L.M. Welling, et al., Sex drive is positively associated with women's preferences for sexual dimorphism in men's and women's faces, 161-170, Copyright (2008), with permission from Elsevier.

p. 740: (Figure 15.4 Margin Bottom) Reprinted from *Evolution and Human Behavior*, Vol. 25, I.S. Penton-Voak, et al., Populational differences in attractiveness judgements of male and female faces: Comparing British and Jamaican samples, 355-370, Copyright (2004), with permission from Elsevier.

p. 740: (Top Row Left) Ed Norton/Getty Images

p. 740: (Top Row Center) Sean Caffrey/Getty Images

p. 740: (Top Row Right) Lawren/Getty Images

p. 740: (Bottom Row Left) Gavin Hellier/Getty Images

p. 740: (Bottom Row Center) Steve Prezant/Corbis

p. 740: (Bottom Row Right) Javier Larrea/Getty Images

p. 745: New York Daily News Archive/Getty Images

p. 746: New York Police Department

p. 748: TIna Fienberg/The New York Times/Redux Pictures

p. 750: Reprinted from *NeuroImage*, Vol. 24, Jackson, P. L., et al., How do we perceive the pain of others? A window into the neural processes involved in empathy, 771-779, Copyright (2005), with permission from Elsevier.

p. 751: (Left) Photograph by Frans de Waal

p. 751: (Right) LilKar/Shutterstock

p. 752: (Left) Vishnevskiy Vasily/Shutterstock

p. 752: (Right) Jane September/Shutterstock

p. 755: AFP/Getty Images

p. 757: Donald Reilly/The New Yorker Collection/www.cartoonbank.com

p. 760: Associated Press/Brennan Linsley

p. 763: EdStock/iStock

p. 765: EdStock/iStock

CHAPTER 16 (bonus chapter)

p. 770: Paul Schutzer/Getty Images

p. 772: © Reuters/Corbis

p. 778: maiteali/iStock

p. 779: (Left) leisadavis/iStock

p. 779: (Right) Photo courtesy of Natia Chakvetadze

p. 780: (Left) REUTERS/Eliana Aponte

p. 780: (Right) Jiri Miklo/Shutterstock

p. 783: (Top Row 1) Howard Sayer/Shutterstock.com

p. 783: (Top Row 2) Arvind Balaraman/Shutterstock.com

p. 783: (Top Row 3 and 4) Alexander & Hines 2002

p. 784: (Top) © Ingrid Balabanova/Shutterstock.com

p. 784: (Bottom) © Samuel Borges/Shutterstock.com

p. 785: LifesizeImages/iStock

p. 787: lev radin/Shutterstock.com

p. 791: saswell/Shutterstock

p. 793: Albany Pictures/iStock

p. 794: Hasan Shaheed/Shutterstock

p. 797: Yuri Arcurs/Shutterstock

p. 798: fStop/Getty Images

p. 803: Alexander Shadrin/Shutterstock

p. 806: © MANDY GODBEHEAR/Shutterstick

p. 809: bogdan ionescu/Shutterstock.com

p. 811: Taxi/Getty Images

p. 813: AP Image/Dennis Farrell

p. 816: The Elephant Sanctuary

p. 820: (Both images) Reprinted from *NeuroImage*, Vol. 21, Bartels, A., & Zeki, The neural correlates of maternal and romantic love, 1155-1166., Copyright (2004), with permission from Elsevier.

Art development by Dragonfly Media Group:

Craig Durant and Mike Demaray

Illustrations by Dragonfly Media Group:

Craig Durant

Mike Demaray

Rob Duckwall

Helen Wortham

Rob Fedirko

Jarrett Jones

Name Index

Subject Index